THE NEW SMITH'S
BIBLE DICTIONARY

THE NEW SMITH'S
BIBLE DICTIONARY

By William Smith

COMPLETELY REVISED BY

REUEL G. LEMMONS

EDITOR, *Firm Foundation*, CHURCH OF CHRIST

IN ASSOCIATION WITH

VIRTUS GIDEON, PH.D.

SOUTHWESTERN BAPTIST THEOLOGICAL SEMINARY

ROBERT F. GRIBBLE, B.D., D.D.

AUSTIN PRESBYTERIAN THEOLOGICAL SEMINARY

J. W. ROBERTS, PH.D.

ABILENE CHRISTIAN COLLEGE, CHURCH OF CHRIST

A DOUBLEDAY-GALILEE BOOK

DOUBLEDAY & COMPANY, INC., GARDEN CITY, NEW YORK.

The New Smith's Bible Dictionary was originally published in hardcover by Doubleday & Company, Inc., in 1966.

Preface

Monumental among religious works of all time is the dictionary compiled by Dr. William Smith. Almost every other Bible Dictionary borrows heavily from it. It has been standard in the field as the King James Version of the Bible has been standard among versions.

Dr. Smith's great work appeared first in the latter part of the nineteenth century, in a four-volume set, which was later abridged by the author into a single volume.

Numerous adaptations and revisions have appeared since 1900, each of which incorporated certain information not available to Dr. Smith. The last such revision, however, is more than twenty-five years old.

An immense amount of information is available today that was not available even twenty-five years ago. Archeological discoveries, linguistic advances, better and more accurate scientific methods of dating, refined textual criticism, and new light from such sources as the Dead Sea Scrolls make it necessary to revise all older works and bring them up to date.

In this work the *Smith's Bible Dictionary* has been completely rewritten. Every article has received close examination by a competent scholar, and every variance with presently known facts has been corrected. Practically every article has been updated in some manner. Yet enough of Dr. Smith's work has been retained to preserve the high quality and standard of the original.

Mechanical improvements will make the use of this dictionary more practical. Pronunciation of proper names, in accord with the best available authorities, is added. Corrections in dates from Ussher's chronology are included where information is conclusive.

This dictionary limits itself to known facts and is devoid of speculative theories. Written for the average man, it will be a valuable aid in obtaining in condensed form the information sought in a Bible dictionary.

REUEL G. LEMMONS

REVISION WRITERS

HAROLD BAKER, PH.D., Louisiana State University
JAMES D. BALES, PH.D., University of California
BATSELL BARRETT BAXTER, PH.D., University of Southern California
RALPH D. BUCY, TH.M., Austin Presbyterian Theological Seminary
HARRY BUTLER, PH.D., Vanderbilt University
J. E. CHOATE, PH.D., Vanderbilt University
PAUL M. COOPER, M.TH., Harding College Graduate School of Religion
MACK WAYNE CRAIG, PH.D., Peabody Institute
MELVIN CURRY, M.A., Winona Lake Theological Seminary
FRED DANS, PH.D., University of Southern California (candidate)
DOUGLAS DEAN, PH.D., University of Alabama
CARROLL B. ELLIS, PH.D., Louisiana State University
B. DON FINTO, M.A., Harding College
LLOYD FRASHIER, PH.D., University of California
DEAN D. FREETLEY, ED.D., University of Illinois
DON GARDNER, M.A., Hardin-Simmons University
VIRTUS GIDEON, PH.D., Southwestern Baptist Theological Seminary
EDWIN S. GLEAVES, JR., PH.D., Emory University
JOHN CLIETT GOODPASTURE, B.D., Vanderbilt University
ROBERT F. GRIBBLE, B.D., D.D., Austin Presbyterian Theological Seminary
HOMER HAILEY, M.A., Southern Methodist University
CLINTON HAMILTON, PH.D., Florida State University
CONRAD HAYES, B.D., Southern Methodist University
ROBERT HELSTEN, M.A., Harding College
JAMES HODGES, PH.D., University of Chicago
ROBERT E. HOOPER, PH.D., Peabody Institute
ARLIE J. HOOVER, PH.D., University of Texas
GEORGE F. HOWARD, PH.D., Hebrew Union College
JIM HOWARD, M.TH., Harding College Graduate School of Religion
FERRELL JENKINS, M.A., Harding College Graduate School of Religion
WYATT JONES, ED.D., University of Alabama
MRS. HARRY O. KICKMAN, M.A., Southwestern Baptist Theological Seminary
WARREN D. KILDAY, PH.D., Washington State University
MORRIS P. LANDISS, PH.D., Vanderbilt University
REUEL G. LEMMONS, B.A., Abilene Christian College
JACK P. LEWIS, PH.D., Harvard; PH.D., Hebrew Union College

Revision Writers

NEIL LIGHTFOOT, PH.D., Duke University

DON McGAUGHEY, PH.D., Boston University

JOHN McRAY, M.A., Harding Graduate School of Religion

CARL MITCHELL, PH.D., University of Southern California

NICHIO NAGAI, D.H.L., University of Judaism

WILLIS C. OWENS, PH.D., Michigan State University

FRANK PACK, PH.D., University of Southern California

FINLEY C. PATTON, TH.M., Austin Presbyterian Theological Seminary

JAMES E. PRIEST, M.S., Abilene Christian College

NEALE PRYOR, M.TH., Harding College Graduate School of Religion

GARY RAYBURN, M.TH., Harding College Graduate School of Religion

J. W. ROBERTS, PH.D., University of Texas

R. L. ROBERTS, JR., M.A., Abilene Christian College; M.L.S., North Texas State University

J. P. SANDERS, PH.D., University of Southern California

JOE E. SANDERS, PH.D., Boston University

JACK SCOTT, B.D., Yale University

JOHN R. SHELL, TH.M., Austin Presbyterian Theological Seminary

JAMES SMYTHE, PH.D., University of Illinois

J. RIDLEY STROUP, PH.D., Peabody Institute

J. D. THOMAS, PH.D., University of Chicago

WILLIAM H. TIEMAN, TH.M., Austin Presbyterian Theological Seminary

T. B. UNDERWOOD, M.TH., Harding College Graduate School of Religion

HOWARD A. WHITE, PH.D., Tulane University

THOMAS C. WHITFIELD, PH.D., Peabody Institute

HERMAN WILSON, PH.D., University of Southern California

WILLIAM WOODSON, M.TH., Harding College Graduate School of Religion

M. NORVEL YOUNG, PH.D., Peabody Institute

JAMES K. ZINK, PH.D., Duke University

ABBREVIATIONS

I. BOOKS OF THE BIBLE

Gen.	Genesis
Ex.	Exodus
Lev.	Leviticus
Num.	Numbers
Deut.	Deuteronomy
Josh.	Joshua
Judg.	Judges
Ruth	Ruth
1 Sam.	1 Samuel
2 Sam.	2 Samuel
1 K.	1 Kings
2 K.	2 Kings
1 Chr.	1 Chronicles
2 Chr.	2 Chronicles
Ezra	Ezra
Neh.	Nehemiah
Est.	Esther
Job	Job
Ps.	Psalms
Prov.	Proverbs
Eccl.	Ecclesiastes
Song of S.	Song of Solomon
Isa.	Isaiah
Jer.	Jeremiah
Lam.	Lamentations
Ezek.	Ezekiel
Dan.	Daniel
Hos.	Hosea
Joel	Joel
Amos	Amos
Obad.	Obadiah
Jon.	Jonah
Mic.	Micah
Nah.	Nahum
Hab.	Habakkuk
Zeph.	Zephaniah
Hag.	Haggai
Zech.	Zechariah
Mal.	Malachi

Mt.	Matthew
Mk.	Mark
Lk.	Luke
Jn.	John
Acts	Acts
Rom.	Romans
1 Cor.	1 Corinthians
2 Cor.	2 Corinthians
Gal.	Galatians
Eph.	Ephesians
Phil.	Philippians
Col.	Colossians
1 Thess.	1 Thessalonians
2 Thess.	2 Thessalonians
1 Tim.	1 Timothy
2 Tim.	2 Timothy
Tit.	Titus
Philemon	Philemon
Heb.	Hebrews
James	James
1 Pet.	1 Peter
2 Pet.	2 Peter
1 Jn.	1 John
2 Jn.	2 John
3 Jn.	3 John
Jude	Jude
Rev.	Revelation

APOCRYPHAL BOOKS

Ecclus.	Ecclesiasticus
1 Esd.	1 Esdras
Enoch	Enoch
1–4 Macc.	1–4 Maccabees
Tobit	Tobit

II. VERSIONS

ASV The American Standard Edition of the Revised Version (RV), 1901
AV The Authorized Version, 1611, or
KJV The King James Version, 1611
NEB The New English Bible (New Testament, 1961)
RSV The Revised Standard Version, 1946, 1953
RV See ASV

III. OTHER BOOKS AND MATTERS

Ant. Josephus *Jewish Antiquities*
Apol. Justin Martyr *Apology*
CIG A. Boeckh, *Corpus Inscriptionum Graecarum*, Berlin, 1828–77
IDB *The Interpreter's Dictionary of the Bible*, Abingdon, 1962
JBL *Journal of Biblical Literature*, 1881–
Nat. Hist. Pliny *Natural History*
TD *Theological Dictionary of the New Testament*, tr. by G. W. Bromiley of Kittel's *Theologisches Wörterbuch*, Eerdmans, 1964–

IV. OTHER ABBREVIATIONS

A.D. Year of the Lord, after Christ
Aram. Aramaic

art. article
b. born
B.C. Before Christ
ca. about
cf. compare
ch(s). chapter(s)
Codex Designation for various Bible manuscripts: B (Vaticanus), Aleph (Sinaiticus), D (Bezae)
d. died
e.g. for example
etc. and so forth
f(f). following
  e.g., 5 f. = verse 5 following
  5 ff. = verses 5 and following
fl. flourished
Gr. Greek
Heb. Hebrew
Lat. Latin
i.e. that is
LXX Septuagint (OT translated into Greek)
M. Mishnah
mg. margin
MS(S) Manuscript(s)
MT Massoretic Text, the traditional Hebrew text of the OT
NT New Testament
OT Old Testament
Talmud Traditional Jewish work of the law of Moses including the Mishnah (text) and Gemara (commentary)
vs(s). verse(s)
Vulg. Vulgate, the Latin Bible

Sign = equals or the same as

GUIDE TO PRONUNCIATION

ā as in gāte   ĕ as in pĕt   ô as in lôrd

â as in vacâtion   ĕ as in silĕnt   ŏ as in pŏt

â as in fâre   ē as in watēr   ŏ as in cŏnfess

ă as in ădd   ī as in whīte   ōō as in sōōn

ă as in infănt   ĭ as in wĭll   ū as in ūse

ä as in fäther   ĭ as in glorĭfy   û as in ûnite

á as in ásk   î as in marîne   û as in bûrn

à as in testàment   ō as in ōak   ŭ as in hŭb

ē as in ēve   ô as in ôbey   ŭ as in cautioŭs

ê as in dêpend

THE NEW SMITH'S
BIBLE DICTIONARY

A

Aaron (âr'ŏn) elder brother of Moses and the first Jewish high priest. He was the son of Amram and Jochebed, and brother of Miriam (Num. 26:59). He was a Levite (Ex. 4:14) and "could speak well." Thus his first office was to be the "prophet," or spokesman of his brother who was "slow of speech" (Ex. 4:16). He was not only the organ of communication with Israel and Pharaoh (Ex. 4:30, 7:2), but also the instrument of working most of the miracles of the Exodus (Ex. 7:19 ff.). He is mentioned with Hur as staying up the weary hands of Moses when they were lifted up for the victory of Israel in the battle with Amalek (Ex. 17:9 f.). At Sinai when Moses as mediator entered the presence of God, Aaron was left to guide the people. He caused the people to make an image of Jehovah, in the well-known form of Egyptian idolatry (Apis or Mnevis) (Ex. 32:5). After Moses expressed his wrath for the deed, he prayed for the people and gained forgiveness for them and for Aaron (Ex. 32:19–34; Deut. 9:20). Shortly after he was consecrated to the new office of the high priest (Ex. 29; Lev. 8). In the story the delegated character of the Aaronic priesthood is clearly seen by the fact that in its inauguration the priestly office is borne by Moses as God's truer representative (see Heb. 7). The consecration is carried out by a threefold sacrifice: a sin offering, a burnt offering, and a meat offering. From this time on the history of Aaron is almost entirely that of the priesthood. He had a part with Miriam in the murmuring against Moses (Num. 12). On all other occasions he is spoken of as acting with Moses in the guidance of the people. He shared Moses' sin at Meribah as well as its punishment (Num. 20:10–12).

Aaron's death took place on Mount Hor, after the transference of his robes and office to Eleazar, who alone with Moses was present at his death and performed his burial (Num. 20:28). Hor is still called the "Mountain of Aaron." His wife was Elisheba (Ex. 6:23). His two sons, Eleazar and Ithamar, survived him. The high priesthood descended to the former and to his descendants until the time of Eli, who was of Ithamar (see Josephus *Ant.* V.xi.5, VIII.i.3). It continued in his line until Solomon, who took it from Abiathar and restored it to Zadok of the house of Eleazar (see 1 Sam. 2:30).

ab see **months**

ab *father* an element in the composition of many proper names. See **abba**

Abaddon (à-băd'ŭn) Heb. for destruction = Gr. Apollyon (Rev. 9:11; cf. Job 28:22).

Abagtha (à-băg'thà) a eunuch in the Persian court (Est. 1:10).

Abana (à'băn-à) a "river of Damascus" (2 K. 5:12), now called Barada. It rises in mountains east of the city and is lost in a marsh twenty-three miles from it.

Abarim (ăb'à-rĭm) mountains east of Jordan in Moab facing Jericho, 4000 feet above the Dead Sea (Deut. 32:49). From one peak, Mount Nebo, Moses viewed Palestine.

abba (ăb'à) emphatic form of **ab**, equivalent to "my" or "our father," found in Hebrew and rabbinic texts. Probably a familiar colloquial term such as would be used in family circles. It occurs many times in the LXX (Isa. 63:16); and in the NT three times with Greek word of same meaning (Mk. 14:36; Rom. 8:15; Gal. 4:6).

Abda (ăb'dà) 1. One of Solomon's foremen (1 K. 4:6).

2. Son of Shammua (Neh. 11:17), also called Obadiah (1 Chr. 9:16).

Abdeel (ăb'dē-ĕl) father of Shelemiah (Jer. 36:26).

Abdi (ăb'dī) 1. An ancestor of Ethan, one of David's temple singers (1 Chr. 6:44).

2. Father of Kish in the reign of Hezekiah (2 Chr. 29:12).

3. A man who had married a foreign wife (Ezra 10:26).

Abdiel (ăb'dĭ-ĕl) son of Guni and father of Ahi, a Gadite (1 Chr. 5:15).

Abdon (ăb'dŏn) 1. One of Israel's judges (Judg. 12:13, 15).

2. Son of Shashak (1 Chr. 8:23).

3. Firstborn son of Jehiel, son of Gibeon (1 Chr. 8:30, 9:36).

4. Son of Micah (2 Chr. 34:20), also called Achbor (2 K. 22:12).

5. A Levitical city in Asher (Josh. 21:30).

Abednego (à-bĕd'nē-gō) the Babylonian name of Azariah, one of three friends of Daniel (Dan. 3).

Abel (ā'bĕl) second son of Adam. His offering
God accepted rather than that of his brother
Cain, who then murdered him (Gen. 4:1–6).
Jesus spoke of Abel as the first martyr (Mt.
23:35). He was righteous in contrast to Cain
(1 Jn. 3:12) and heads the list of OT heroes
(Heb. 11:4).

abel- (ā'bĕl) a combining form used in several
Hebrew place names, probably meaning a
"meadow." See below.

Abel-beth-maacah (ā'bĕl-bĕth-mā'à-kà) 1. Important town near Dan in far northern Palestine (2 Sam. 20:15) taken by Ben-hadad king
of Syria (1 K. 15:20) and Tiglath-pileser III
king of Assyria (2 K. 15:29). Alternate name
Abel-maim (2 Chr. 16:4). See also 2 Sam.
20:14.

2. **Abel-keramim** "Watercourse (KJV plain)
of the vineyards" (Judg. 11:33), far point of
Jephthah's campaign against the Ammonites.

3. **Abel-meholah** a place in the East Jordan
valley (1 K. 4:12). The routed Midianites fled
here from Gideon (Judg. 7:22). Also home of
Elisha (1 K. 19:16 ff.).

4. **Abel-mizraim** the floor of Atad, east of
the Jordan where Jacob was mourned (Gen.
50:11).

5. **Abel-shittim** place in the plains of Moab,
in the Jordan valley, where Israel last rested
before crossing the Jordan (Num. 33:49).

Abez (ā'bĕz) a town in Issachar (Josh. 19:20).

Abi (ā'bī) short form of Abijah (2 Chr. 29:1),
mother of King Hezekiah (2 K. 18:2).

Abia or **Abiah** (à-bī'à) alternate forms of Abijah.

Abi-albon see **Abiel**

Abiasaph (à-bī'à-săf) (Ex. 6:24) also written
Ebiasaph (1 Chr. 6:23, 9:19). One of families
into which the Korahites, doorkeepers at the
temple, were divided. Samuel and Elkanah were
descended from them (1 Chr. 6:33 ff.).

Abiathar (à-bī'à-thàr) high priest and chief
counselor under David (1 Chr. 27:34). He was
fourth in descent from Eli of the line of Ithamar, the younger son of Aaron. The only son
of Ahimelech to escape the slaughter of his
father's house by Saul at the instigation of
Doeg the Edomite (1 Sam. 22), when he became high priest he fled to David bringing the
ephod. He thus was able to inquire often of the
Lord for the king (1 Sam. 23:9, 30:7; 2 Sam.
2:1, 5:19). Abiathar remained a firm friend to
David all his life (see 2 Sam. 2:1–3; 1 Chr.
15:11). Even in Absalom's rebellion he was
faithful (2 Sam. 15:24). Later he supported
Adonijah as successor to King David instead of
Solomon, for which he was banished to Anathoth, his native town, being spared only because of his service to David. The king put
Zadok into the high priesthood in his stead
(1 K. 2:27, 35). In the NT Mk. 2:26 erroneously gives Abiathar for Ahimelech, probably a clerical error which has been perpetuated. Some MSS omit "when Abiathar was
high priest."

Abib (ā'bīb) name of first Hebrew month, later
called Nisan. See **months**

Abidah or **Abida** (à-bī'dà) a son of Midian
(Gen. 25:4).

Abidan (à-bī'dăn) a chief of the tribe of Benjamin (Num. 1:11, 2:22). He helped in the
census.

Abiel (ā'bī-ĕl) 1. The grandfather of Kish
through Ner (1 Chr. 8:33, 9:39) and great-
grandfather of Saul and of Abner (1 Sam.
14:51). According to Hebrew custom Ner is
omitted from the line in 1 Sam. 9:1.

2. An Arbathite who was one of David's
mighty men (1 Chr. 11:32), given in 2 Sam.
23:31 as Abi-albon.

Abiezer (ā'bī-ē'zêr) 1. Eldest son of Gilead,
whose family were leaders in the tribe of Manasseh (Josh. 17:2; 1 Chr. 7:18; Num. 26:30
—Jeezer being a contracted form of the name).
He was the ancestor of Gideon.

2. Also one of David's mighty men (2 Sam.
23:27).

Abigail (ăb'ī-gāl) 1. Wife of Nabal, of
Mount Carmel. When David's messengers were
slighted by Nabal, she appeased David. When
Nabal died, David made her his wife (1 Sam.
25:14 ff.).

2. A sister of David, married to Jether the
Ishmaelite, mother of Amasa (1 Chr. 2:17).

Abihail (ăb'ī-hāl) 1. Father of Zuriel, a Levite of Moses' time (Num. 3:35).

2. Wife of Abishur (1 Chr. 2:29).

3. Son of Huri of Gad (1 Chr. 5:14).

4. Wife of Rehoboam, descendant of Eliab,
brother of David (2 Chr. 11:18).

5. Father of Esther (Est. 2:15).

Abihu (à-bī'hū) second son (Num. 3:2) of
Aaron by Elisheba (Ex. 6:23). One of those
accompanying Moses atop Sinai (Ex. 24:1).
Killed with Nadab for offering strange fire (Lev.
10:1).

Abihud (à-bī'hŭd) grandson of Benjamin (1
Chr. 8:3).

Abijah (à-bī'jà) also called **Abijam** 1. The
son and successor of Rehoboam in Judah for
three years. The first book of Kings (14:31–
15:8) relates that he was not righteous and
that he made war on Jeroboam of Israel. The
account of this war is much expanded in 2 Chr.
13. He was succeeded by Asa.

2. Second son of Samuel, called Abiah in

some versions. With older brother was made judge in Beer-sheba (1 Sam. 8:2). Their sin led to the demand for a king.

3. A son of Jeroboam I king of Israel (1 K. 14:1–18). He died in childhood, after Jeroboam's wife had been sent in disguise to seek help from the prophet Abijah.

4. A descendant of Eleazar for whom the eighth of the twenty-four courses of the priests was named (1 Chr. 24:10). John the Baptist's father was of this course (Lk. 1:5).

5. A priest during Nehemiah's time (Neh. 10:7).

6. The mother of Hezekiah (2 Chr. 29:1) also called Abi (2 K. 18:2).

7. A priest who returned with Zerubbabel from Babylon (Neh. 12:4).

8. The wife of Hezron, Judah's grandson (1 Chr. 2:24).

9. Son of Becher and grandson of Benjamin (1 Chr. 7:8).

Abilene (ăb'ĭ-lē-nĭ) a district (tetrarchy) (Lk. 3:1) of which the capital was Abila, a city on the eastern slope of the Anti-libanian Mount. It is a region fertilized by the river Barada (Biblical Abana). The city is eighteen miles from Damascus and thirty-eight from Baalbek. It was assigned to Herod the Great. After 4 B.C., it was attached to Syria and ruled by the tetrarch Lysanias. Later it was ruled by Agrippa I, then by governors, and finally by Agrippa II.

Abimael (à-bĭm'à-ĕl) a descendant of Joktan (Gen. 10:28; 1 Chr. 1:22).

Abimelech (à-bĭm'ĕ-lĕk) a name meaning "The father is king" borne by several Philistine kings, probably a title.

1. A Philistine king of Gerar (Gen. 20–21), who sent for and took Sarah, Abraham's wife, into his harem.

2. Another king of Gerar in the time of Isaac, who dealt similarly with Rebekah, Isaac's wife (Gen. 26:1).

3. Son of the judge Gideon by his Shechemite concubine (Judg. 8:31), who murdered all but one of his seventy brothers after his father's death. Jotham, the young brother who had concealed himself, persuaded the Shechemites to elect him king. To belittle Abimelech Jotham told his fable of the trees (Judg. 9:7–21). Abimelech after a reign of three years was struck by a stone thrown by a woman and slain by his guard.

4. Son of Abiathar, the high priest in the time of David (1 Chr. 18:16), also called Ahimelech (2 Sam. 8:17).

Abinadab (à-bĭn'à-dăb) 1. A Levite of Kirjath-jearim who kept the ark for twenty years (1 Sam. 7:1 f.).

2. Second son of Jesse, war companion of Saul (1 Sam. 16:8, 17:13).

3. A son of Saul, slain at Gilboa (1 Sam. 31:2).

4. Father of one of the chief officers of Solomon (1 K. 4:11).

Abinoam (à-bĭn'ō-ăm) father of Barak (Judg. 4:6).

Abiram (à-bī'răm) 1. A Reubenite who engaged with others in a conspiracy against Moses and Aaron (Num. 16).

2. Eldest son of Hiel, who fulfilled the curse of Joshua (Josh. 6:26) that he would die when the foundations of Jericho were laid (1 K. 16:34).

Abishag (ăb'ĭ-shăg) a Shunammite who comforted David in his old age (1 K. 1:2 ff.). See also 1 K. 2:13.

Abishai (à-bĭsh'ī) a son of David's sister Zeruiah and brother of Joab and Asahel (1 Chr. 2:16). He became a devoted follower of David, being with him in the night expedition to the camp of Saul, where he would have avenged David by stabbing the sleeping Saul had it not been for David. He was associated with Joab in the unfortunate killing of Abner (2 Sam. 3:30). He aided David in many exploits, for example, in the war against Hanun (2 Sam. 11:20). His last act of service was the rescue of the valley of Salt (1 Chr. 18:12), in the rebellion of Absalom (2 Sam. 16:9, 19:21, 18:2 ff.), in the rebellion of Sheba (2 Sam. 20:6, 10). Once he fought single-handed against three hundred (2 Sam. 23:18; 1 Chr. 11:20). His last act of service was the rescue of David from the gigantic Philistine Ishbi-benob (2 Sam. 21:17). The end of the checkered life of this noble servant of the king is not recorded.

Abishalom (à-bĭsh'à-lŏm) a form of the name of Absalom (see 1 K. 15:2, 10; 2 Chr. 11:20 f.; 2 Sam. 14:27 LXX).

Abishua (à-bĭsh'ū-à) 1. Son of Bela, the first-born of Benjamin (1 Chr. 8:4).

2. Son of Phinehas, in the genealogy of the high priest (1 Chr. 6:4 ff.; Ezra 7:4 f.).

Abishur (à-bī'shêr) a Judahite (1 Chr. 2:28 f.).

Abital (à-bī'tăl) one of David's wives (2 Sam. 3:4).

Abitub (à-bī'tŭb) son of Shaharaim by Hushim (1 Chr. 8:11).

Abiud (à-bī'ŭd) descendant of Zerubbabel in the genealogy of Jesus Christ (Mt. 1:13).

ablutions ceremonial or religious washings (see Mk. 7:4; Heb. 6:2, 9:10). See also **purification**

Abner (ăb'nêr) commander in chief of Saul's army (1 Sam. 14:50). He was a son of Ner, who was the brother of Kish (1 Chr. 9:36), the father of Saul. Abner, therefore, was Saul's cousin. It was he who led David before Saul after the death of Goliath (1 Sam. 17:57) and afterwards accompanied Saul when he sought David's life at Hachilah (26:3 ff.). After the death of Saul he rose to importance as the mainstay of his family. When David was made king of Judah at Hebron, Abner proclaimed the weak Ish-bosheth, Saul's son, king of Israel at Mahanaim beyond Jordan. War ensued and a "sore battle" was fought by armies led by Abner and Joab at Gibeon (2 Sam. 2:17), at which Ish-bosheth was defeated. Abner soon opened negotiations with David and was favorably received and worked for David's cause until he was treacherously murdered by Joab and Abishai. The deed caused David great sorrow—he followed Abner's bier and spoke a simple dirge over the slain (2 Sam. 3:33 f.).

Abraham (ā′brà-hăm) or **Abram** (ā′brăm) son of Terah and founder of the Hebrew nation. His family, descended from Shem, settled in Ur of the Chaldees. Terah was an idolater who served "other gods" (Josh. 24:2). Abraham's brothers were Nahor and Haran; his half sister Sarai became his wife. Haran died in Ur, and after this Abram took his father Terah, Haran's son Lot, and went forth to Haran in Northern Syria (Gen. 11:27–31), prompted (according to Stephen in Acts 7:2–4) by a call from God. At the death of Terah Abram, then seventy-five years old, at the direction of God (Gen. 12:5), came (along with Lot) to Shechem where he received the promise that his heirs would inherit this land (12:6–7). From there he was successively near Bethel (12:8), in Egypt due to a famine, where he passed off Sarai as his sister (12:10–20); again at Bethel (13:3), whence Lot separated from him; and at Hebron (13:18). Next he united with local chiefs to rescue Lot, who had been captured by an invading king in a battle at Dan in Northern Palestine (14:12). On his return he was met and blessed by Melchizedek, a priest-king of Salem, to whom Abram gave a tithe of the spoils.

At Hebron the promise that his descendants would become a mighty nation and possess the land was repeated with the assurance that not a house slave should be his heir but that he should yet have a son. It was at this point that Abram's faith at such a promise is said to have been reckoned to him for righteousness (Gen. 15:6), a statement which in the NT is interpreted as implying his justification or forgiveness on account of his faith. Here too occurred the "cutting of the covenant" by which God pledged the fulfillment of the promise and

Abram faithfulness to God. At Sarai's suggestion he took Hagar, Sarai's Egyptian maid, as wife, by whom Ishmael was born (Gen. 16). But thirteen years later he was told that not Ishmael but a son of Sarai should be the heir (Gen. 17). Circumcision was appointed to him as a sign of the covenant, following which his name was changed from Abram to Abraham and Sarai's to Sarah. Abraham now played the part of intercessor in delivering Lot and his two daughters from the destruction of Sodom (chs. 18–19). Abraham removed to the Negeb or South Country and lived among the Philistines at Gerar, where the incident of passing off Sarah as his sister was repeated (ch. 20). Finally at the age of 100 Abraham became the father of Isaac, following which Hagar and Ishmael were driven out (21:1–21). God then put Abraham's faith to the ultimate test by asking for the sacrifice of Isaac, the child of the promise. Abraham proceeded to carry out the instruction, being stopped by the angel of the Lord in the act of taking Isaac's life in sacrifice, "accounting that God was able to raise him from the dead" (Heb. 11:19); following this the spiritual blessing was repeated (Gen. 22). This certainly is the high mark in his obedience to God. Abraham returned to Hebron, where Sarah died (Gen. 23:2). He sent a servant to secure a wife for Isaac from the family of Nahor (Gen. 24). Later Abraham took Keturah as wife by whom he had six sons, the ancestors of the nomadic tribes south and east of Palestine. He lived to see his grandsons Jacob and Esau grow to be young men (Gen. 25:26). When he died at the age of 175 years, he was "gathered to his people" and laid beside Sarah in the tomb of Machpelah (Gen. 25:7–10).

In the NT there is frequent reference to Abraham as the father of the Jewish nation and also as the father of those who, like him, believe God and trust him that their faith may be reckoned as righteousness (Rom. 4:11; Gal. 3:7).

Absalom (ăb′sà-lŏm) the third son of David by Maachah (2 Sam. 3:3), most noted for his alienation of the people from his father the king and leading a revolt against him (2 Sam. 15–17). He is hardly mentioned until after David's great sin and then seems to be the fulfillment of the promise that evil should be raised against him from his own house. The first outbreak of violence was the violation of Absalom's sister Tamar by her half brother Amnon, which Absalom avenged two years later (13:22–32). After an exile of three years Absalom was recalled to Jerusalem through an artifice of Joab (14:1=24, 28–33). Following this, he repaid his father by "stealing the heart" of Israel (15:6) and finally led an outbreak against David from Hebron (15:7–14), forcing him to flee from Jerusalem (15:13–18). Absalom took over his father's harem, but delayed crushing David's forces until the king was able to gather an army of loyal supporters. In the battle at Gilead (18:1–8) Absalom was defeated and fled; but, as he rode, his hair was caught in the branches of a tree, and he was killed by Joab (18:9–17). David's grief at the loss even of such a son has become classic (18:31–33).

abyss in classical Greek the "bottomless" depths of the ocean or earth; in the LXX it translates Heb. *tehom*, referring to the waters of chaos (Gen. 1:2) and to the abode of the dead (Ps. 71:20). In the NT it is translated "deep" in some versions (Lk. 8:31), or "bottomless pit" (Rom. 10:7). It usually here refers to the abode of the dead (Rom. 10:7) or the realm of spirits (Rev. 9:1 ff., 11:7, 17:8, 20:1–3).

acacia a tree or its wood. Translated in KJV as **shittim wood.**

Accad (ăk'ăd) a city of Shinar—with Babel, Erech, and Calneh—mentioned as the beginning of Nimrod's kingdom (Gen. 10:10). Its position is quite uncertain, but it is thought to be represented by Agade in the district of the same name in Northern Babylonia, captured by Sargon I in 2447 B.C.

Accho (ăk'ō) the most important town on the seacoast of Syria, about thirty miles south of Tyre and lying on the bay north of Mount Carmel. The river Belus flows into the sea near the city, which is located on a small fertile plain about six miles wide. Accho fell to the lot of Asher, but it was never wrested from its original inhabitants (Judg. 1:31). In NT times it was called Ptolemais after the Egyptian kings who had held it. The only notice of it in the NT is in connection with Paul's passage from Tyre to Caesarea (Acts 21:7). It is now called Acca or Saint Jean d'Acre.

Aceldama (à-kĕl'dà-mà) "the field of blood," the name given by the Jews of Jerusalem to a "field" near Jerusalem purchased by Judas with the money which he received for betraying Christ, and so called from his violent death therein (Acts 1:18). The variant account (Mt. 27:3–10) may be regarded as the fuller story in which the priests bought it for him as a burying place for poor people after he had returned the money. Some think the term means "field of sleep," but the other title is preferable. The place is traditionally shown at

a vault on the hill which lies just south of the Hinnom valley.

Achaia (á-kā'yà) signifies in the NT a Roman province which included the whole of Ancient Greece south of Macedonia (including the Peloponnesus). Achaia and Macedonia are frequently used to mean all Greece (Acts 18:12, 19:21; Rom. 15:26, 16:5; 1 Cor. 16:15; 2 Cor. 1:1, 9:2, 11:10; 1 Thess. 1:7 f.). The name originally referred to a tiny slip of country on the northern coast of the Peloponnesus, whence, through the confederation of its towns to resist Macedonia, the name came to be applied to a wider territory until it was adopted by the Romans to name the province created at the conquest of the country in 146 B.C. At various times it was either an imperial or a senatorial province. Claudius had restored it to the Senate, and it was ruled by Gallio, called the "proconsul," when Paul was brought before his seat (KJV, "deputy").

Achaicus (à-kā'ĭ-kŭs) the name of a Christian mentioned only in 1 Cor. 16:17 and in late MSS in the subscription (vs. 25).

Achan (ā'kăn) an Israelite of Judah who secreted a portion of the spoil from the destruction of the city of Jericho and hid it in his tent, causing the defeat of Israel in the subsequent battle of Ai (Josh. 7). Achan was identified by lot and both he and his family were stoned. From similarity in names the valley where his death occurred received the name Achor "trouble" (Josh. 7:25–26).

Achar-Achan (1 Chr. 2:7)

Achaz (ā'kăz) NT (KJV) form of Ahaz king of Judah (Mt. 1:9).

Achbor (ăk'bôr) 1. Father of Baal-hanan king of Edom (Gen. 36:38 f.).

2. Son of Michaiah, a contemporary of Josiah (2 K. 22:12, 14; Jer. 26:22); also called Abdon (2 Chr. 34:20).

Achim (ā'kĭm) son of Sadoc and father of Eliud in our Lord's genealogy (Mt. 1:14).

Achish (ā'kĭsh) a Philistine king of Gath (called Abimelech in title to Ps. 34), with whom David twice found refuge as he fled from Saul. Once he escaped by feigning madness (1 Sam. 21:10 ff.). Again he fled there with 600 men and stayed a year and four months. See also 1 K. 2:40.

Achor (ā'kôr) [trouble] valley named for being the place where Achan was stoned (Josh. 7:24, 26).

Achsah (ăk'săh) the daughter of Caleb, who was promised to whoever should take Debir. Othniel, her father's younger brother, thus received her hand for taking the city. At her request the father added a gift of springs as a

Achshaph

dowry (Josh. 15:15–19; cf. Judg. 1:11–15, and 1 Chr. 2:49).

Achshaph (ák'shăf) a city in the territory of Asher (Josh. 19:25), originally the seat of a Canaanite king (11:1, 12:20). It is known from contemporary records (e.g., Tell el-Amarna Letters, fourteenth century B.C.). Probably modern Tell Kisan, six miles southeast of Acco.

Achzib (ăk'zĭb) 1. A city of Judah in the Shephelah (Josh. 15:44), near Mareshah, perhaps same as Chezib (Gen. 38:5).

2. A town in Asher (NT Galilee) from which the Canaanites were not expelled (Josh. 19:29). Later called Ecdippa. Now ez-Zib, nine miles north of Acre.

Acts of Apostles fifth book in the English NT, a second of two treatises by the author of the third gospel, traditionally known as Luke (see art. on **Luke**). 1. TITLE. Codex Sinaiticus (Aleph) reads simply *praxeis* ("Acts," "Deeds," or "Transactions"). Others have "of *the* apostles," etc. The book has only a sample of apostolic labors (mostly of Peter and Paul), and so "Acts of Apostles" seems most accurate. "Acts of the Holy Spirit" has been suggested as an appropriate title.

2. AUTHOR. No long discussion is possible. The author of Luke-Acts is nowhere identified. The first direct assertion comes from the period A.D. 160–200. The conclusion is a deduction from the instances where the author used an autobiographical source with the pronouns "we" and "us" (16:10–17, 20:5–16, 21:1–28:16) compared with the data listing Paul's companions. One who fits the circumstances is "Luke the Beloved Physician" (Col. 4:14; cf. 2 Tim. 4:10–11; Philemon 24). Modern scholarship has sought to establish Luke's authorship from the medical terminology used in the books. This argument (corrected by Henry J. Cadbury from its original form in W. K. Hobart) still has some value.

3. CONTENTS AND ARRANGEMENT. Luke begins the story where he had left off in the gospel (Acts 1:1), retelling the story of the ascension and the promises of Jesus to send the Holy Spirit and to return (1:8–11). The former promise was fulfilled a few days later on Pentecost with the Spirit coming upon the waiting disciples (2:1 ff.). Events of this day are taken as the "beginning" (11:15; cf. Lk. 24:47). Hence, Pentecost may be called "the birthday of the church." Luke details (according to the pattern of Acts 1:8) the events of the growing church, from its "continuing steadfastly" (2:42) to its new achievements (5:14, 6:7), its development of new leaders and

spokesmen (6:1–6, 8 ff.), and its problems (6:1 ff.), to its dispersion and mission preaching (8:26 ff.) following the death of Stephen (8:1). Here follows the climactic event of the conversion of Saul of Tarsus (9:1–22; cf. 22:3–29, 26:1–32) at about the time that the church was fixing itself on soil outside Palestine (9:31–43, 11:19–26) and reaching out for its first Gentile convert Cornelius (10:1–11:18). Notice of a famine and local persecution by Herod Agrippa I is given (11:27–12:25), following which Saul and Barnabas are located at Antioch in Syria (12:25; cf. 11:25–26). At this point the narrative breaks sharply, henceforth devoting its attention largely to Saul-Paul and his labors. Chapters 13–14 relate a long journey taken by Paul and Barnabas to Cyprus and to the interior of Asia Minor, which resulted in the conversion of large numbers of Gentiles. This posed the problem on their return to Antioch of the relation of the Gospel to Jews and Greeks, a matter settled by a trip to Jerusalem (ch. 15). Then we have a second journey (15:36–18:22) taking Paul through Asia Minor, then to Macedonia (Philippi, Thessalonica, Berea, Athens, and Corinth); then a third tour (18:23–21:17) is made, on which Paul stays three years at Ephesus and makes another trip through Greece before going to Jerusalem. The last section relates Paul's arrest in Jerusalem (21:17 ff.), his trial (ch. 23), his hearing and imprisonment at Caesarea under Felix (ch. 24), his appeal to Rome (chs. 25–26), his voyage and shipwreck (27:1–28:16), and his residence at Rome for two years (28:30). Here the story ends abruptly. Some think Luke intended a third volume.

4. THEMES AND PURPOSE. The author by his choice of events, his repetitions, etc., emphasizes several things. One is the leading and direction of the Holy Spirit (2:17, 16:6–10); others include the joy and fellowship of the early church, the arrangement (somewhat schematic) of the parallel careers of Peter and Paul, the missionary speeches and methods of the early preachers (Acts 2, 10, 13, 17), and especially the development of Gentile Christianity set over against the rebellion and hostility of the Jews (9:23, 13:45, 14:19, 17:5, 18:12, 20:3, 23:12 ff., 24:1, 25:7, 26:21). Many students have concluded that, apart from the general purpose of showing the development of the early church, the author intended the letter as an apologetic for the legality of Christianity by showing to the Roman authorities that at every step the Gospel had received recognition and proceeded in orderly fashion and that Jewish opposition was biased.

6

5. PLACE AND TIME. As to the time and place of writing we are left to gather the answer from the book itself. It seems most probable that the place was Rome, and the time near the end of Paul's two years there.

6. INTERPRETATION. Ancient commentators somewhat neglected Acts. In the beginnings of critical examination its genuineness was denied by F. C. Baur, who considered it a second-century treatise of early Catholic Christianity, glossing over what was reconstructed as prime factors in the origins of the church: a Paul-Peter opposition. The great work of Wm. Ramsay (e.g., *St. Paul the Traveller and Roman Citizen*, 1896) did much to restore confidence in Acts as a truly historical work. This work has culminated in Henry J. Cadbury's *The Place of Acts in History* (1954), which gives the mature judgment of a great scholar and student that Acts should be taken seriously as history. In view of this it is surprising to see the trend in the works of M. Dibelius and E. Haenchen (commentary on Acts in the H. A. W. Meyer's series) in which Luke is seen as dealing high-handedly with his sources and even introducing fictional accounts for his purpose. Against this method it would seem that Acts has vindicated itself and deserves a place as chief witness to the word of God in the early church and the methods and practices of the church in the age of inspiration.

Adah (ā'dà) 1. One of Lamech's wives and mother of Jabal and Jubal (Gen. 4:19).

2. One of the three wives of Esau, a Hittitess. She was the mother of Esau's firstborn son, Eliphaz (see Gen. 36). Also called Bashemath (Gen. 26:34).

Adaiah (à-dā'yà) 1. Maternal grandfather of King Josiah, from Boscath (2 K. 22:1).

2. A Levite and ancestor of Asaph, also called **Iddo** (1 Chr. 6:21, 41).

3. Son of Shimhi, a Benjaminite, also called Shema (1 Chr. 8:13, 21).

4. A priest, son of Jehoram (1 Chr. 9:12; Neh. 11:12).

5. An ancestor of Maaseiah, a captain who supported Jehoiada (2 Chr. 23:1).

6. A descendant of Bani who had married a foreign wife after the exile (Ezra 10:29).

7. The descendant of another Bani, who had also taken a foreign wife (Ezra 10:39).

8. A man of Judah, of the line of Pharez (Neh. 11:5).

Adalia (àd-à-lī'à) son of Haman (Est. 9:8).

Adam (ăd'ăm) the name of the first man, probably derived from "(the red) earth." It is a generic term applied to both Adam and Eve (Gen. 5:2) and is used frequently for "man" or "mankind." All men are sons of Adam or "man" (Deut. 32:8). The story of Adam's creation is told in two accounts—the repetition is probably stylistic, suiting the purpose of the author, and does not necessarily imply different "sources"—in Gen. 1:26-30 and 2. His disobedience and punishment—the fall—in ch. 3, his death and descendants in ch. 5. The Genesis account of creation and the fall provides the basis of all Biblical anthropology (doctrine of man). He is God's creation, made in God's image (Gen. 1:27), receiving a divine spirit which returns to God at death (Eccl. 12:7). As a result of the fall man is destined to death (Rom. 5:12-21). Man's fall has certainly placed him in the posture of sinfulness, and the Scriptures teach the complete universality of sin (Rom. 3:23) and thus, without redemption by Christ, the certainty of eternal condemnation. But the dogma of Adamic sin or total depravity, extending to the inheriting of the guilt of Adam's sin even by infants who are not responsible, is not to be attributed to the Scriptures. Christ, who became man, is called the Second Adam or the Antitype of the First (Rom. 5:14; 1 Cor. 15:45 ff.).

Adam (ăd'ăm) city on the Jordan "beside Zarethan" (Josh. 3:16), where the river stood and rose in a heap while the people crossed. Not definitely located.

Adamah (ăd'à-mà) a "fenced city" of Naphtali, between Chinnereth and Ramah (Josh. 19:36) and probably northwest of the Sea of Galilee.

adamant (ăd'à-mănt) translation of Heb. *shamir* (Ezek. 3:9 and Zech. 7:12). In Jeremiah 17:1 the translation is "diamond"; in other passages "briers" (Isa. 5:6). The Hebrews did not know our diamond. The stone (always used metaphorically in the Bible to compare the "hardness" of something) is usually thought to be emery or some form of corundum. Our English word "adamant" comes from this source.

Adami (ăd'à-mī) a place on the border of Naphtali (Josh. 19:33) joined with **Nekeb.**

Adar (ā'dàr) a place on the south edge of Judah (Josh. 15:3) called **Hazar-addar** in parallel list.

Adar see **months**

Adbeel (ăd'bē-ĕl) a son of Ishmael (Gen. 25:13; 1 Chr. 1:29).

Addan (ăd'ăn) a place in Babylonia whence some of the captivity who could not show their pedigree as Israelites returned with Zerubbabel to Judaea (Ezra 2:59). In the parallel lists (Neh. 7:61) the name is spelled Addon.

Addar (ăd'àr) son of Bela (1 Chr. 8:3), also called **Ard** (Num. 26:40).

adder a word used for any poisonous snake and applied in this general sense (thus also asp) by the translators. The translators generally also have used it interchangeably with cockatrice (Isa. 11:8). "Adder" is used to translate four different Hebrew words. The Jews seem to have been acquainted with some five or six species of poisonous serpents. Paul (Rom. 3:13) quotes the LXX of Ps. 140:3, "adder's poison is under their lips." The poison of venomous serpents is often employed by the sacred writers in a figurative sense to express the evil tempers of ungodly men.

Addi (ăd'ī) a son of Cosam in our Lord's genealogy (Lk. 3:28).

Addon see Addan

Ader (ā'dẽr) more correctly Eder, a Benjaminite, son of Beriah of Aijalon (1 Chr. 8:15).

Adiel (ā'dĭ-ĕl) 1. A prince of Simeon from Shimei (1 Chr. 4:36) who took part in the raid made by his tribe upon the Hamite shepherds of Gedor in time of Hezekiah.

2. A priest, ancestor of Maasiai (1 Chr. 9:12).

3. An ancestor of Azmaveth, David's treasurer (1 Chr. 27:25).

Adin (ā'dĭn) the ancestor of a family who returned with Zerubbabel (Ezra 2:15) and with Ezra (8:6) from Babylon. They joined in a covenant to separate themselves from the heathen (Neh. 10:16).

Adina (ăd'ĭ-nà) a Reubenite chief, one of David's captains beyond the Jordan (1 Chr. 11:42).

Adino (ăd'ĭ-nō) called the Eznite (2 Sam. 23:8). See Jashobeam

Adithaim (ăd-ĭ-thā'ĭm) a town of Judah in the Shephelah or low country (Josh. 15:36).

adjure to command or charge solemnly under oath or as if under an oath or a curse. The Hebrew word so translated sometimes means to cause someone to take an oath (1 K. 8:31) and again to charge or warn someone as if under a curse (1 Sam. 14:24). In Mt. 26:63 Jesus is charged by the high priest to testify under oath. Otherwise the meaning in Mk. 5:7 (a demoniac), Acts 19:13 (exorcists), and 1 Thess. 5:27 (Paul) is that of a most solemn charge as if the one addressed would be under a curse or oath if the thing is not done.

Adlai (ăd'lā or ăd'lī) ancestor of Shaphat, the overseer of David's herds (1 Chr. 27:29).

Admah (ăd'mà) one of the "cities of the plain" with its own king, coupled with Zeboiim (Gen. 10:19).

Admatha (ăd'má-thà) one of the seven princes of Persia (Est. 1:14) who helped banish Vashti.

Adna (ăd'nà) 1. Son of Pahath-moab, a priest who returned with Ezra and married a foreigner (Ezra 10:30).

2. A priest who returned from the Exile with Zerubbabel (Neh. 12:15).

Adnah (ăd'nà) 1. A Manassite deserter from Saul to David with a thousand of his tribe, who fought with David against the Amalekites (1 Chr. 12:20).

2. A captain of 300,000 men of Judah (2 Chr. 17:14).

Adoni-bezek (à-dō'nĭ-bē'zĕk) [lord of Bezek] king of Bezek of the Canaanites, vanquished by the tribe of Judah (Judg. 1:3–7), who cut off his thumbs and great toes, and brought him to Jerusalem where he died.

Adonijah (ăd'ō-nī'jà) 1. The fourth son of David by Haggith (2 Sam. 3:4). After the death of his three brothers, Amnon, Chileab, and Absalom, he put forward his pretension to the crown. But David had promised Bath-sheba that Solomon would become king (1 K. 1:30). Adonijah's cause was espoused by Abiathar and Joab. He acquired a large following (1 K. 1:9, 25), which prompted David to have Solomon brought in a procession to Gihon, near Jerusalem, where he was anointed and proclaimed king. This stroke alarmed Adonijah, who fled to the sanctuary and was pardoned by Solomon on condition that he "show himself a worthy man" (1 K. 1:52). After David's death, Solomon seems to have regarded his plea to marry Abishag, David's wife of his old age, as a fresh attempt to claim the throne, and he was executed (1 K. 2:19–25).

2. A Levite in the reign of Jehoshaphat (2 Chr. 17:8).

3. Neh. 10:16, see Adonikam.

Adonikam (ăd'ō-nī'kăm) ancestor of a group, part of whom (666 in number) returned from Babylon with Zerubbabel (Ezra 2:13; Neh. 7:18) and part with Ezra (Ezra 8:13). In the list of those who sealed Ezra's covenant the name is given as Adonijah (Neh. 10:16).

Adoniram (ăd'ō-nī'răm) chief receiver of the tribute under David (2 Sam. 20:24). Under Solomon he was chief of slave labor and sent to Lebanon for materials for building (1 K. 5:13 f.). He was stoned to death on a mission for Rehoboam to collect tribute from the rebellious Israelites (1 K. 12:28; 2 Chr. 10:18). The name is contracted to Adoram (2 Sam. 20:24) and to Hadoram (2 Chr. 10:18).

Adoni-zedek (à-dō'nī-zē'dĕk) [lord of Justice] the Amorite king of Jerusalem who organized a league with four other kings against Joshua and besieged Gibeon; they were defeated by Joshua and captured after taking refuge in a cave. They were slain and their bodies were hung on trees before being buried secretly (Josh. 10:1–27).

adoption the custom of taking children of other parents as one's own; so Pharaoh's daughter adopted Moses (Ex. 2:10). Such selection implies a decided preference and love on the part of the adopted parent, and thus adoption is used by Paul as a fit term to describe the process of conversion (Rom. 8:15, 23; Gal. 4:5; Eph. 1:5). Such adoption expresses the redeeming act of God in Christ as well as the relation of trust and affection, "because ye are sons, God hath sent forth the Spirit of his Son into your hearts, crying, Abba, Father" (Gal. 4:6). In Rom. 8:23 Paul uses the term of the future consummation of the privileges of sonship.

Adoraim (ăd'ō-rā'ĭm) a city built by Rehoboam (2 Chr. 11:9), now generally identified with Dura, about five miles west-southwest of Hebron. Same as Adora (1 Macc. 13:20).

adoration the acts or postures by which the Hebrews expressed reverence, submission, or worship. The earliest form seems to have been kissing the hand to the object of reverence (Job 31:26 f., here to the sun or moon; Hos. 13:2, to an idol). So Ps. 2:12 "kiss the Son" = "adore" or "worship." At other times the posture was by prostration (Gen. 17:3; Ps. 95:6). The act does not, however, always imply the paying of divine honors, since it was also used to receive visitors (Gen. 18:2), recognizing a superior (2 Sam. 14:4), or showing respect to an equal (1 K. 2:19). There were many variations such as multiplying the number of bowings (Gen. 33:3), laying hold of knees or feet, and kissing the ground (Mic. 7:17). The same customs prevailed in the time of Jesus and Peter (Acts 10:25). "Do honor" is often a proper rendering, though in some instances "worship" is obviously intended.

Adrammelech (ăd-răm'ĕ-lĕk) 1. [*Adar*, or possibly *the Lord*, is king]. The name given in 2 K. 17:31 to a god worshiped in Samaria by Israelites and Assyrian colonists from Sepharvaim. The adoration consisted (as in that to Molech) of burning children.

2. Son of the Assyrian king Sennacherib, who with his brother murdered his father about 660 B.C. in the temple at Nineveh after the failure of an Assyrian attack on Jerusalem (2 K. 19:37; 2 Chr. 32:21; Isa. 37:38).

Adramyttium (ăd'rá-mĭt'ĭ-ŭm) a seaport in the province of Asia of the district of Mysia. It was on a ship of this city that Paul sailed from Caesarea (Acts 27:2–6) on the voyage to Rome.

Adria (ā'drĭ-à) the sea west and north of the island of Crete and extending between Italy and Greece, the Adriatic Sea. The name was derived, according to ancient authors, from Atria, a city at the mouth of the Po river. Paul's ship on the way to Rome (Acts 27:27) was "driven to and fro in the Adria." Contemporary travelers (such as Josephus, who also suffered shipwreck in this sea—*Life* xv) attest to the danger to ships within it.

Adriel (ā'drĭ-ĕl) a son of Barzillai the Meholathite, to whom Saul gave his daughter Merab, although he had previously promised her to David (1 Sam. 18:19). His five sons David delivered to the Gibeonites (2 Sam. 21:8) in satisfaction for the endeavors of Saul to extirpate them, although the Israelites had originally made a league with them (Josh. 9:15). The spelling "Michal" (2 Sam. 21) may be due to an early scribal error.

Adullam (à-dŭl'ăm) a city of Judah in the lowland of the Shephelah (Josh. 15:35). It was an ancient city (Gen. 38:1, 12, 20), the seat of a Canaanite king smitten by Joshua (Josh. 12:15). In a cave of the area David found a place of refuge which he made his headquarters and where he was joined by his family (1 Sam. 22:1 f.; 2 Sam. 23:13; 1 Chr. 11:15). It was fortified by Rehoboam before Shishak's invasion in the tenth century B.C. (2 Chr. 11:7). It was reoccupied by the Jews after the Exile (Neh. 11:30) and was still a city in the time of the Maccabees (2 Macc. 12:38).

Adullamite (à-dŭl'ăm-īt) a native of Adullam (Gen. 38:1).

adultery sexual intercourse between a person and the husband or wife of another person. In the OT, circumstances (toleration of polygamy) rendered it practically impossible to make an offense between a man and another woman not his wife adultery. So the parties were always a married woman and a man not her husband. Jesus extended the term to apply to a divorced woman who remarries (Mk. 10:12). **Fornication** is the wider term and includes adultery. At an early date the sanctity of marriage is evidenced by the attitude of Pharaoh and Abimelech (Gen. 12, 20), who recoil from taking the wife of another.

Adultery was forbidden by Moses (Ex. 20:14; Deut. 5:18). The term was extended to cover the action of a free betrothed woman (Deut. 22:22–24). The guilty parties were to be put to death (Lev. 18:20, 20:20), probably by stoning (there is earlier mention of fire, Gen. 38:24). A bondwoman so offending was to be scourged and the man was to make a trespass offering (Lev. 19:20–22). In cases where no witnesses were found, the woman might be required to submit to the ordeal of drinking the waters of jealousy (Num. 5:11-19) to establish whether or not she was guilty. Later Jewish sentiment relaxed its severity, and divorce (as in the case of Joseph in the NT, Mt. 1:19) became the more common action of the offended husband.

The OT contains many condemnations of adultery and of those guilty (Job 31:11; Prov. 6:26 ff.; Ps. 50:18; Ezek. 16:32; Mal. 3:5). The wiles of the adulteress are described in Prov. 7:6-27.

In the NT the Greek word is *moicheuo* and its forms. Jesus taught that the lustful look made one guilty of the sin (Mt. 5:28) or that it came from the heart (Mt. 15:19; Mk. 7:21). He further made remarriage of a divorced man or woman adultery (Mt. 5:31 f., 19:3-9; Mk. 10:2-12; Lk. 16:18), though he made an exception where the wronged party was innocent (Mt. 5:32, 19:9). In this high view of the marriage relationship Jesus harks back to the original intention of God for marriage as a lifelong monogamous union. Such must be the view of the institution among his disciples. Later NT passages strongly condemn the sin (Rom. 13:9; 1 Cor. 6:9; Gal. 5:19; Heb. 13:4).

In both the Old and New Testaments adultery is used figuratively to describe unfaithfulness to God, especially worship of idols (Jer. 3:8 f.; Ezek. 23:37; Isa. 57:3; Hos. 2:4). Hosea's personal matrimonial troubles were used to develop an allegory of the Lord's love for unfaithful Israel. The NT continued this figure (Mt. 12:39, 16:4; James 4:4). John 8:2-11 is evidently not genuine in its present place in John, though it may have originally occurred in another context: e.g., Lk. 21:38, as in one group of MSS (Family 13).

Adummim (à-dŭm'ĭm) [red rocks, in the phrase "the pass or ascent of Adummim," thus something like "red rocks pass"] a pass leading up from the river Jordan to the hill country. It is described as "over against Gilgal" and "on the south side of the torrent" (Josh. 15:7, 18:17). It was one of the landmarks of the boundary of Benjamin. It is pointed out, not improbably, as the scene of the attack on the man in the parable of the Good Samaritan.

Advent a term used of the coming or the second coming of Christ.

adversary literally an opponent, the meaning of the Hebrew word Satan.

advocate frequent translation of the Gr. *parakletos* > whence Paraclete, rendered elsewhere by Comforter or Counselor. Used of Jesus in 1 John 2:1 and by him to refer to the Holy Spirit in the phrase "another Comforter" (Jn. 14:16). As our representative Christ makes intercession for man. The Holy Spirit thus performs the same service for the saints as the Spirit of the living Christ.

Aegypt see **Egypt**

Aeneas (ē-nē'ăs) a paralytic at Lydda, healed by Peter (Acts 9:33 f.).

Aenon (ē'nŏn) a place "near to Salim," at which John baptized (Jn. 3:23) while Jesus was teaching in Judea. The word in Aramaic means "springs" and the writer adds that the reason for John's preaching there was that there was "much water" there. The exact site of Salim and Aenon are unknown. A place in Perea beyond the Jordan has been accepted by some (IDB), it being located by them on the Wadi Kharrar, near Jericho by the ford of the Jordan across from Jericho. Other places claimed for it are: six miles south of Scythopolis in the Jordan valley (West); and near Nablus, east of Mount Gerizim. Others have argued for a secluded valley five miles northeast of Jerusalem at the entrance of Wadi Farah into Wadi Fowar, immediately above Jericho.

aeon (ē'ŏn) transliteration of the Gr. *aion*, variously translated as "world," "age"; and in the phrase "unto the ages of the ages" it has the meaning of "forever."

Agabus (ăg'à-bŭs) a Christian prophet in the apostolic age. He predicted (Acts 11:28) that a famine would take place in the reign of Claudius "through the whole world." Later (21:10) he foretold Paul's capture and deliverance to the Gentiles. There is some question about the time and extent of the famine. As Greek and Roman writers used "the world" of their world, so a Jewish writer could use it naturally of the Jewish world or Palestine. There was a famine in Palestine during Claudius' reign, between A.D. 44-47 (during governorships of Cuspius Fadus and Tiberius Alexander). If the "world" in a wider sense is meant, then the meaning is probably that there would be widespread local famines, not a universal one. In view of Antioch's local action, the former view is the more probable.

Agag (ā'găg) either two individual kings of Amalek, or perhaps the title of the kings of this country. Balaam predicted that a king of Jacob would surpass Agag (Num. 24:7). The other is the king spared by Saul in disobedience to God's command through Samuel. This action led to the rebuke and rejection of Saul. Agag was executed by the prophet (1 Sam. 15).

Agagite (ā'gà-gīt) a name applied to Haman, either because he was considered an enemy like king Agag, or through belief that he was descended from him (Est. 3:1, 10, 8:3, 5, 9:24).

agape (äg-ä'pā) the transliteration of the Greek word for "love," now frequently used in ethics to designate the "new commandment" of Jesus for his followers (Jn. 13:34; 1 Jn. 2:8 ff.; Mt. 5:44–46; Rom. 12:17–21).

agape (ăg'à-pĭ) the name used to designate the "love feasts" or meals provided for mutual fellowship and for charity for the poor, and for widows and orphans. That the early church practiced the custom is evident from Acts 2:42–46, 6:1–2 at Jerusalem, Acts 20:11 at Troas, and 1 Cor. 11:20 ff. at Corinth. At Corinth Paul rebuked the confusing of the love feast and the Lord's Supper and told those who could not wait for their brethren to eat before coming together, but it is a mistake to understand that Paul abolished these common meals. They were still being held in the time of Jude (vs. 12; cf. variant in 2 Pet. 2:13), who speaks of the false teachers as "hidden rocks at the love feasts as they banquet with you." Passages in the Didache (chs. 9–10), Ignatius (Smyrnaeans 8:2), Pliny's letter (X.97), Clement of Alexandria (*The Instructor* II.1 ff.), and Hippolytus (*Apostolic Constitutions* 26:5) give details of its observance in the second century. In early American rural church life "basket dinners," somewhat comparable, were well-known.

Agar see **Hagar**

agate a rock mentioned in several versions: of a stone in the high priest's breastplate (Ex. 28:19, 39:12), and (from a different Heb. word) of an ornamental stone and medium of exchange (Isa. 54:12; Ezek. 27:16). The true agate is a silicious stone of the quartz family, generally found in rounded nodules.

age, old besides the general respect of old age which early civilizations were wont to pay to age with its concomitant of wisdom, Israel was taught that it was a reward for piety (Ex. 20:12; Ps. 34:12 ff.). Thus in private life elders were honored for knowledge (Job 15:10); the young rose up before them (Lev. 19:32); they were allowed to speak first (Job 32:4); their grey hairs were considered a crown of glory (Prov. 16:31, 20:29). Attaining age was a blessing (Job 5:26) indicating peace (Zech. 8:4). In public life elders were usually chosen to places of responsibility (1 K. 12:8). So also in the church old age is to be respected (1 Tim. 5:1), and bishops are also elders (1 Pet. 5:1–4, and especially vs. 5).

Agee (ā'gē) a Hararite, father of Shammah, of the three mightiest men of David (2 Sam. 23:11).

agony a word meaning "suffering," derived from the Greek word for "contest." It is used often to designate the suffering of Jesus in the Garden and on the cross.

Agora (ăg'ô-rà) the Greek word (from the word meaning to lead together) for market or assembly in a Greek city, such as Athens or Corinth (Acts 17:17 ff.).

Agrapha (ăg'rà-fà) a word used by modern scholars to designate sayings accredited to Jesus but not contained in the four gospels. These Agrapha are found both in Acts (20:35) and in the epistles (1 Cor. 11:24 f.), in the margin of some MSS (as in Codex Bezae [Lk. 6:5]), in citations of early Christian authors, and heretical writers (such as the Gospel of Thomas). A few of these extrabiblical sayings may be genuine, though there is no way to establish this and they are of little value to us because of their fragmentary character and doubt as to genuineness.

agriculture the art of cultivating the soil, producing crops, and raising livestock. The word does not occur in the Scriptures (for which "husbandry" is used), but under it we may sum up the practices of Biblical lands and times. Though agricultural items are mentioned in the early Genesis stories (Gen. 4:2 ff., 9:20), they are little involved in the patriarchal stories (except for the cattle and herds) since the Hebrews then were nomadic. The invading tribes, however, found Palestine a rich land (Deut. 8:8), and agriculture became the basis of the Mosaic commonwealth with laws designed to keep the allotted land in the family. Especially rich sections were Haran (Perea) and Gaza, and such plains sections as Esdraelon. Israel learned cultivation of grapevines, figs, and olive trees from the Canaanites. Principal crops were wheat, rye, flax, cummin, fitches (RV, spelt), beans, lentils, and millet (cf. Ezek. 4:9). Rainfall was abundant compared to Egypt (Deut. 8:7, 11:8–12) but came mainly in autumn and winter (rarely after March). It was more marked at the beginning (the "early") and end (the "latter" rain). In the drier sections water was caught in terraces and stored in cisterns for irrigation. Plowing was usually with oxen (1 K. 19:19). Harvest of grain was by sickle or by pulling, and the grain was tied into sheaves, which were then carted (Amos 2:13) to threshing floors (2 Sam. 24:16, 18), where the grain was trampled out by oxen (Deut. 25:4), winnowed with fans or shovels (Isa. 30:24), and finally sifted through sieves (Amos 9:9). Besides grain probably the cultivation of vineyards is most frequently mentioned in Scripture. Grapes were gathered and crushed in an "upper" vat opening through a tunnel dug into the rock into a lower vat, where the juice was collected (see **wine**). The Scriptures abound with references to farm life, practices, and rights. Biblical metaphors or similes are often drawn from this way of life.

Agrippa (à-grĭp'à) names of two local rulers in the NT. See **Herod**

Agur (ā'gûr) the designation given to the source of the collection of sayings in Prov. 30. The point has been variously interpreted. Some make the name personal and make him the son of Jakeh, son of Queen of Massa (the Hebrew) or from Massa, a country to the east of Palestine, or an allegorical name for Solomon. The Vulg. renders *congregantis* and the LXX by the word meaning "be afraid."

Ahab (ā'hăb) 1. Son of King Omri, seventh king of the Divided Kingdom of Israel. He reigned twenty-two years in Samaria (1 K. 16:29). Though a fairly strong king keeping Moab under tribute (2 K. 3:4), several times carrying on war with Syria and Assyria, and building many cities, he was personally dominated by a wicked wife, Jezebel, daughter of Ethbaal, king of Sidon (1 K. 16:31) and priest of Astarte. Jezebel was fanatically devoted to the gods of Tyre. Ahab built a house for Baal in Samaria and made an Asherah (1 K. 16:32–33). The main narratives centering around Ahab concern the opposition to this idolatry carried on by the great prophet Elijah (1 K. 17–22). The story reaches a climax in the shameful steal of Naboth's vineyard and his murder (2 K. 9:26). Ahab was slain (as had been predicted by the prophet Micaiah) though disguised so as to appear inconspicuous in a battle with Aram. When he was brought to Samaria to be buried, the dogs licked up his blood in the very field which he had stolen from Naboth (1 K. 21:19; 2 K. 9:26). "There was none like unto Ahab, who sold himself to work wickedness in the sight of the Lord, whom Jezebel his wife stirred up" (1 K. 21:25).

2. A lying prophet, who deceived the captive Israelites in Babylon and was burnt to death by Nebuchadnezzar (Jer. 29:21).

Aharah (á-hâr'àh) third son of Benjamin (1 Chr. 8:1).

Aharhel (á-hâr'hĕl) an obscure name in the genealogy of Judah (1 Chr. 4:8).

Ahasai (à-hā'sī) a priest (Neh. 11:13).

Ahasbai (à-hăs'bī) father of Eliphelet, one of David's thirty-seven captains (2 Sam. 23:34).

Ahasuerus (á-hăz'û-ē'rŭs) [= Persian *Khshayarshā* = Gr. *Xerxes*] 1. The father of Darius the Mede (Dan. 9:1). Also known as Cyaxares, conqueror of Nineveh.

2. The Persian king who ruled in Susa (Est. 1:1). This king divorced his wife, Vashti, and married the Jewess Esther, cousin and ward of Mordecai. Most likely this king is to be identified with Xerxes, who reigned from 486 to 465 B.C. The Ahasuerus of Ezra 4:6, mentioned between Cyrus and Artaxerxes, is probably the same ruler, though he is sometimes taken to be Cambyses, Cyrus' son.

Ahava (à-hā'vá) an unidentified location in Babylon where Ezra collected the second expedition to return to Jerusalem. Both a place and a river are involved (Ezra 8:15, 21).

Ahaz (ā'hăz) eleventh king of Judah, son of Jotham. The date of his reign is now placed about 735–715 B.C.

Ahaziah (ā'há-zī'á) 1. Son of Ahab and Jezebel, the eighth king of Israel, who ruled only two years. He like his mother was an idolater and was rebuked for this by the prophet Elijah. The most important event of his reign was the rebellion of Moab which had previously been tributary to Israel (2 K. 1:1, 3:4–5). Ahaziah injured himself in a fall at the palace and died according to the word of Elijah (2 K. 1:2–17).

2. Fifth king of Judah, son of Jehoram and Athaliah, daughter of Ahab (called Azariah in 2 Chr. 22:6, Jehoahaz in 2 Chr. 21:17). He was an idolater, an ally of his uncle Jehoram, king of Israel. After being defeated by Hazael king of Syria, Ahaziah and Jehoram were killed by Jehu, who led a revolt in Israel. Ahaziah died at Megiddo (2 K. 9:27).

Ahban (á'băn) man of Judah, son of Abishur by Abigail (1 Chr. 2:29).

Aher (ā'hêr) ancestor of Hushim (or the Hushim) in an obscure passage (1 Chr. 7:12). Some consider it not a proper name and render it literally "another." It is not improbable that Aher and **Ahiram** as given in Num. 26:38 are the same.

Ahi (ā'hī) probably an abbreviated form of **Ahijah.** It occurs twice (1 Chr. 5:15, 7:34), but its place in the text is uncertain; the Vulg. and LXX do not consider it a proper name.

Ahiah or **Ahijah** (à-hī'à or à-hī'jà) a frequent name in the OT. 1. Son of Ahitub, brother of Ichabod, grandson of Phinehas, and greatgrandson of Eli, "the Lord's priest in Shiloh, wearing an ephod" (1 Sam. 14:3, 18). Saul made use of the ark through him to inquire of God's will. His name is not listed among the high priests (1 Chr. 6:50–53; Ezra 7:2–5), leading to the supposition that he may be the same as **Ahimelech** of 1 Sam. 21–22, also the son of **Ahitub.**

2. One of Solomon's princes (1 K. 4:3).

3. A prophet of Shiloh (1 K. 11:29, 14:2)

in the days of Solomon and Jeroboam. We have two remarkable predictions of his: one (1 K. 11:31 ff.) announcing the rending of the twelve tribes and the other (1 K. 14:6–16) the death of Abijah with the destruction of Jeroboam (cf. 2 Chr. 9:29).

4. Father of Baasha king of Israel (1 K. 15:27, 33).

5. Son of Jerahmeel (1 Chr. 2:25).

6. Son of Bela (1 Chr. 8:7).

7. One of David's mighty men (1 Chr. 11:36).

8. A Levite treasurer in David's reign (1 Chr. 26:20).

9. One of the "heads of the people" joining in the covenant with Nehemiah (Neh. 10:26).

Ahiam (ă-hī′ăm) one of David's mighty men (2 Sam. 23:33; 1 Chr. 11:35).

Ahian (à-hī′ăn) a Manassite, of the family of Shemidah (1 Chr. 7:19) in KJV.

Ahiezer (ā-hī-ē′zêr) 1. A chieftain of the tribe of Dan (Num. 1:12, 2:25, 7:66).

2. A chief of the archers in the time of David, a Benjaminite (1 Chr. 12:3).

Ahihud (à-hī′hŭd) 1. The son of Shelomi, prince of tribe Asher (Num. 34:27).

2. A chief of Benjamin (1 Chr. 8:7).

Ahijah see **Ahiah**

Ahikam (à-hī′kăm) son of Shaphan the scribe, an officer in the courts of Josiah and Jehoiakim, sent by Hilkiah to consult Huldah (2 K. 22:12–14). He was a protector of Jeremiah (Jer. 26:24). Father of Gedaliah later governor of Judah (Jer. 39:14, 40:5).

Ahilud (à-hī′lŭd) 1. Father of Jehoshaphat, chronicler in days of David and Solomon (2 Sam. 8:16; 1 K. 4:3; 1 Chr. 18:15).

2. One of Solomon's officers (1 K. 4:12).

Ahimaaz (ā-hĭm′à-ăz) 1. Father of Saul's wife, Ahinoam (1 Sam. 14:50).

2. Swift-footed son of Zadok, high priest during David's reign (2 Sam. 15:36, 18:19).

Ahiman (à-hī′măn) 1. One of the three giant Anakim seen by Caleb and the spies (Num. 13:22, 33). The whole race were later cut off by Joshua (Josh. 11:21) and the brothers slain (Judg. 1:10).

2. A gatekeeper of the Levites (1 Chr. 9:17).

Ahimelech (à-hĭm′ē-lĕk) the high priest at Nob in days of Saul (1 Sam. 22:1 f.) who gave David the showbread and the sword of Goliath, for which he was later killed by Saul along with eighty-five others. On his further identity, see **Abiathar** and **Ahiah.**

Ahimoth (à-hī′mŏth) a Levite of David's time (1 Chr. 6:25), appearing as Mahath in vs. 35 and Lk. 3:26).

Ahinadab (à-hĭn′à-dăb) one of Solomon's commissaries (1 K. 4:14).

Ahinoam (à-hĭn′ō-ăm) 1. Wife of Saul (1 Sam. 14:50).

2. A Jezreelite wife of David (1 Sam. 25:43), mother of his eldest son Amnon (2 Sam. 3:2). She and Abigail lived with David at the court of Achish (1 Sam. 27:3), was captured by the Amalekites at Ziklag (30:5) but rescued by David. She lived with the king at Hebron (2 Sam. 2:2).

Ahio (à-hī′ō) 1. Son of Abinadab who accompanied the ark when it was brought out of his father's house (2 Sam. 6:3 f.).

2. A Benjaminite son of Beriah who expelled the Gathites (1 Chr. 8:14).

3. The father or founder of Gibeon, a Benjaminite (1 Chr. 8:31).

Ahira (à-hī′rà) chief of the tribe of Naphtali (Num. 1:15, 2:29, 7:78, 83, 10:27).

Ahiram (à-hī′răm) a son of Benjamin (Num. 26:38). He probably appears in Gen. 46:21 in the shortened form Ehi, and in 1 Chr. 8:1 f. as Aharah, since both are referred to as the "third son."

Ahisamach (à-hĭs′à-măk) a Danite architect of the tabernacle (Ex. 31:6, 35:34, 38:23).

Ahishahar (à-hĭsh′à-hàr) a grandson of Benjamin (1 Chr. 7:10).

Ahishar (à-hī′shàr) Solomon's controller (1 K. 4:6).

Ahithophel (à-hĭth′ō-fĕl) [brother of foolishness] David's counselor much esteemed for his wisdom (2 Sam. 16:23), but who became a leader in the rebellion of Absalom. He was the grandfather of Bath-sheba (cf. 2 Sam. 11:3 with 23:34). When he joined Absalom's revolt, David prayed that his wisdom might be turned to foolishness (2 Sam. 15:31). David's grief at his treachery is thought to have found expression in the Messianic Psalms (Ps. 41:9, 55:12–14). It was at his advice that Absalom took over David's harem (2 Sam. 16:21). After having been foiled by Hushai, he despaired of success and returned home to "put his household in order and hanged himself" (17:1–23).

Ahitub (à-hī′tŭb) 1. Father of Ahimelech, son of Phinehas, an elder brother of Ichabod of the house of Eli (1 Sam. 14:3, 22:9, 11). There is no record that he served as high priest.

2. Father or grandfather of Zadok the high priest (1 Chr. 6:7 f.; 2 Sam. 8:17; Ezra 7:2) of the house of Eleazar. He was himself probably high priest (1 Chr. 9:11; Neh. 11:11).

3. Another Ahitub is introduced in 1 Chr. 6:11 f., but the passage is probably spurious.

Ahlab (à′lăb) a city of Asher near site of Tyre

from which the Canaanites were not expelled (Judg. 1:31).

Ahlai (ă′lī) 1. The father of Zabad, one of David's mighty men (1 Chr. 11:41).

2. A daughter of Sheshan given to her father's Egyptian slave Jarha and mother of Attai (1 Chr. 2:31 ff.).

Ahoah (à-hō′à) son of Bela and grandson of Benjamin (1 Chr. 8:4), also called Ahiah (1 Chr. 8:7), from which the family name Ahohite comes (2 Sam. 23:9, 28).

Aholah (à-hō′lä) see **Oholah** in some versions. A harlot used by Ezekiel as the symbol of Samaria compared with her sister **Aholibah,** who represents Jerusalem (Ezek. 23:4–5, 9–10, 36, 44).

Aholiab (à-hō′lĭ-ăb) a skillful embroiderer and weaver, a Danite, appointed by Moses with Bezaleel to erect the tabernacle (Ex. 35:30–35).

Aholibah (à-hō′lĭ-bà) see **Oholibah** in some versions. A harlot used to represent Jerusalem (Ezek. 23). See **Aholah**

Aholibamah (à-hŏl′ĭ-bā′mà) one of the three wives of Esau, a daughter of Anah and a descendant of Seir the Horite (Gen. 36:2, 25). In Gen. 26:34 she is also called Judith, probably a personal name, with the other name being her married name taken from the district in Edom. So Aholibamah occurs in the concluding list of the geographical-genealogical table (Gen. 36:40–43). Her three sons became the heads of tribes occupying Mount Seir; the nation was traditionally opposed to Israel (Num. 20:14 ff.). They were the forebears of the NT Idumaeans.

Ahumai (à-hŭ′mī) a Judahite, head of a Zorathite family (1 Chr. 4:2).

Ahuzam (à-hŭ′zăm) properly Ahuzzam, son of Ashur by Naarah, founder of Tekoa (1 Chr. 4:6).

Ahuzzath (à-hŭz′ăth) friend of Philistine king Abimelech who visited Isaac (Gen. 26:26).

Ai (ā′ī or ī) [the ruin] later forms Aiath and Aija (Neh. 11:31). 1. A royal city (cf. Josh. 8:23, 29, 10:1) of Canaan east of Bethel (Josh. 12:9) and beside Bethaven (7:2, 8:9) near which Abraham camped (Gen. 12:8, 13:3). It was the second city across the Jordan taken by Israel, and it was "utterly destroyed," though after an unsuccessful attempt marred by the sin of Achan (Josh. 7–12). A new town seems to have been established nearby as it is mentioned under form Aiath (Isa. 10:28) and men from Ai are mentioned in the return from exile (Ezra 2:28; Neh. 7:32).

Modern archaeologists had fixed on et-Tell two miles east-southeast of Bethel (modern Beitin) as the site of Ai. Evidence shows that the site was destroyed about 2000 B.C. and was not occupied during the time of the Israelite conquest. This has been taken as indicating that the Joshua stories are conflations of historical incidents of different times referred to Joshua. But at the end of the 1965 season the archaeological team investigating the site announced that it was being abandoned as the site of ancient Ai. The site is thus still uncertain.

2. A city near Heshbon in Ammon (Jer. 49:13).

Aiah (ā′yà) a descendant of Seir and ancestor of a wife of Esau (1 Chr. 1:40), also called Ajah (Gen. 36:24).

Aiath (ā′yăth) variant of **Ai** (Isa. 10:28).

Aija (ā-ī′jà) another form of name **Ai** (Neh. 11:31).

Aijalon or **Ajalon** (ā′jà-lŏn or ăj′à-lŏn) [a place of deer] 1. A place some fourteen miles west of Jerusalem below Beth-horon in an important pass into the hills of Judah. It is most familiar from its connection with Joshua's defeat of the five Canaanite kings where the sun stood still (Josh. 10:12). It was a Levitical city (Josh. 21:24), allotted but not possessed by Dan (Josh. 19:42; Judg. 1:35). For later references, see 2 Chr. 11:10, 28:18.

2. Burial place in Zebulun of the judge Elon (Judg. 12:12).

Ain (ā′ĭn) [an eye, also a spring, occurring most often in combination with other words forming the names of definite localities, as in En-gedi, En-gannim, etc.] it occurs alone: 1. A landmark on the eastern boundary of Palestine (Num. 34:11) of uncertain location.

2. One of the southernmost cities of Judah (Josh. 15:32), allotted to Simeon (Josh. 19:7) and given to the priests (Josh. 21:16).

Ajah see **Aiah**

Ajalon see **Aijalon**

Akan (ā′kăn) a chieftain of the Horites, descendant of Seir (Gen. 36:27), called **Jakan-jaakin** (1 Chr. 1:42).

Akkub (ăk′ŭb) 1. A descendant of Zerubbabel (1 Chr. 3:24).

2. A doorkeeper at the temple, whose descendants returned from Babylon (1 Chr. 9:17; Ezra 2:42).

3. One of the Nethinim returning with Zerubbabel (Ezra 2:45).

4. A Levite who assisted Ezra in expounding the Law (Neh. 8:7).

alabaster a stone from Egypt (calcium carbonate) or native Palestine (gypsum or calcium sulphate) used for making flasks, cruses, or jars (AV, boxes) for keeping perfumes. "Unguents," says Pliny, "keep best in alabaster vases" (XIII.4). The stone is of a creamy color and often veined. Such was used by Mary at Bethany at the house of Simon the leper (Mt. 26:7; Mk. 14:3) and the woman at the house of the Pharisee (Lk. 7:37).

Alameth see **Alemeth**

Alammelech (à-lăm'ĕ-lĕk) [king's oak] a place in Asher (Josh. 19:26).

alamoth (ăl'à-mŏth) a musical term of uncertain meaning, thought by some to be an instrument, by others a melody, or perhaps a women's choir, the word being derived from "like a flute" or "high-pitched as a woman."

Alemeth (ăl'ē-mĕth) 1. A Benjaminite descended from Jonathan (1 Chr. 8:36).

2. A city of the priests in Benjamin (1 Chr. 6:60–H 6:45). Seemingly the same as **Almon** (Josh. 21:18).

Alexander (III) the Great (ăl'ĕg-zăn'dêr) king of Macedon and the son of Philip II and Olympias. He was born at Pella in 356 B.C., and ascended the throne at the death of his father in 336. Having put down the hostility against him, two years later he crossed the Hellespont with the mission of civilizing the world. The great victories at Granicus and Issus (333) decided the fate of Asia and the East. In succession he conquered Tyre, Gaza, Egypt (where he founded Alexandria, 331). Darius king of Persia was defeated at Gaugamela the same year. In 327, after consolidating his conquests, he crossed the Indus and penetrated to the Hydaspes before he was forced by the discontent of his army to return west. He reached Susa in 325 and Babylon the next year, where he made his capital and where he died the following year. His empire was divided among four generals.

Alexander is not mentioned by name in the Bible but was described prophetically in Daniel. He is the great he-goat with the horn between his eyes which came against the ram and defeated him. He became great until the horn was broken and four notable ones came from it (Dan. 8:5–8—see also Dan. 8:18–22 where the ram is interpreted as Media and Persia, and the goat as the king of Greece). Josephus (*Ant.* XI.viii.1) followed by the Talmud (*Yoma* 69a) relates that Alexander dealt kindly with the Jews and was royally received by them at his invasion, relating that he had seen the God of the Jews in a dream. He is said to have worshiped at the temple before proceeding to Egypt.

Alexander powerfully affected the history of God's people. He settled Greeks in Palestine; Hellenized many Jews, and settled many others in foreign lands. In Alexandria, which he built

in Egypt, the Jewish Scriptures were translated into Greek (the Septuagint, usually abbreviated LXX).

Alexander in the NT: 1. Son of Simon the Cyrenian who bore Jesus' cross (Mk. 15:21).

2. One of the kindred of Annas the high priest (Acts 4:6) apparently in some high office.

3. A Jew at Ephesus put forward by his countrymen during the tumult raised by Demetrius the silversmith (Acts 19:33).

4. An Ephesian Christian who with Hymenaeus had made shipwreck of his faith (1 Tim. 1:20).

5. Alexander the coppersmith, mentioned as having done much evil to Paul; Timothy was to beware of him (could be same as 4).

Alexandrians the Jewish colonists of Alexandria who were admitted to citizenship and had a synagogue at Jerusalem (Acts 6:9).

algum (ăl'gŭm) (2 Chr. 2:8, 9:10 f.) or **almug** (1 K. 10:11 f.) a valuable wood used by Solomon in his temple and house and for making musical instruments. It came from Lebanon or from Ophir. Its exact identification is uncertain.

Aliah see **Alvah**

Alian see **Alvan**

allegory a figure of speech in which one thing is said or set forth in the form or image of another. Generally the first representation is consistent, but is also capable of admitting a moral or spiritual interpretation over and above its literal sense. It was used extensively in the OT (Isa. 5:1–7; Ps. 80), but very sparingly in the NT (e.g., Jn. 15:1–8). Aside from its conscious use by an original author, allegory had become a method of interpreting the OT narratives (by Aristobulus and Philo) in imitation of the Greek allegorizing of Homer. Philo insisted that the Law was historically true and to be observed literally. But he also insisted that there was a deeper and more spiritual meaning hidden behind the words of the OT narratives. Paul uses the story of Sarah and Hagar (Gal. 4:22–26) to draw out the superiority of the Christian privileges over the Jewish as by analogy. The usage means more than deducing spiritual truths from historical narratives. It is explained by F. Büchsel (TD) that the verb in Gal. 4:24 ["contain an allegory"] can mean: (1) "to explain or denote allegorically," or (2) "to speak allegorically." It is clear that Paul does not treat the narrative as an allegory in itself, as our AV would lead us to suppose, but draws from it a deeper sense than is conveyed by the immediate representation.

alleluia (ăl-lĕ-lŭ'yà) form of the transliterated

Hebrew word **hallelujah** [praise ye Jehovah] (Rev. 19:1). It occurs in the margin (of the LXX) in the same form (e.g., Ps. 105, 106). See **hallelujah**

alliances contracts or agreements between individuals or more especially treaties pledging mutual aid among nations. (For other aspects, see **covenant** and **testament**.) Alliances with Canaanites were forbidden to Israel (Deut. 7:2). Solomon made treaties for commercial purposes with Hiram king of Tyre (1 K. 5:2–12, 9:27) and Pharaoh king of Egypt (1 K. 10:28 f.). The period of Israel's Divided Kingdom was characterized by alliances of various kings with nations around them for defense against a threatening enemy. Thus when war broke out between Amaziah and Jeroboam II, a coalition was formed—Rezin king of Syria and Pekah on one side, and Ahaz and Tiglath-pileser king of Assyria on the other (2 K. 16:5–9). The result was the strengthening of Assyrian power. Judah and Israel were attacked separately and sought aid from Egypt, who was interested in maintaining Palestine as a barrier against Assyria. (See also 2 K. 17:4, 19:9, 36; Isa. 30:2.) Such alliances were deplored by the prophets as reliance upon human strength rather than divine aid. The party and individual alliances were made with a ceremony of religious rites: a victim was slain and divided into parts between which the parties passed (Gen. 15:10). This custom survived even to Jeremiah's time (Jer. 34:18–20). Generally speaking such contracts were accompanied by oaths (Josh. 9:15; Gen. 26:28; 1 Sam. 20:17), a feast (Ex. 24:11), a ritual of salting the sacrifices (Lev. 2:13; Num. 18:19; 2 Chr. 13:5), the marking of the agreement by a stone of memorial (Gen. 31:52), and the sending of presents (1 K. 15:18; Isa. 30:6). Fidelity to such agreements was a conspicuous feature of Israel's history even when not entered under open conditions (Josh. 9:18), with breaches considered very serious (2 Sam. 21:1; Ezek. 17:16). Due to the sacrifice of the victim for ratification the Hebrew term for making a covenant was "cutting" a covenant.

Allom see **Ami** and **Amon**

Allon (ăl'ŏn) 1. A Simeonite prince in the time of Hezekiah (1 Chr. 4:37).

2. A large strong tree (probably an oak) found combined in two place names: (a) Allon (or Elon) of the cities of Naphtali (Josh. 19:33). (b) Allon-bachuth [oak of weeping] where Deborah, Rebekah's nurse, was buried (Gen. 35:8).

Almodad (ăl-mō'dăd) son of **Joktan** (Gen. 10:26; 1 Chr. 1:20) and progenitor of an Arab tribe.

Almon (ăl'mŏn) or **Alemeth** a city with "suburbs" given to the priests (Josh. 21:18).

almond, almond tree a name of the flowering nutbearing tree, common in the Near East. There are two names in Hebrew: *luz* in Gen. 30:37 (where KJV wrongly translates **hazel**), and elsewhere *shaqedh* (Gen. 43:11; Num. 17:8; Jer. 1:11). The latter term, which may apply either to the tree or its fruit (from a word meaning "to awake"), was probably applied because the tree blooms early with the blossoms appearing before the leaves, and thus it was considered a harbinger of spring. (It has been known to bloom as early as January 9 in Palestine.) A twig can be made to blossom prematurely when budded branches are put in water. Aaron's rod of an almond tree miraculously bore fruit overnight. The tree was chosen to adorn the golden lampstand of the tabernacle (Ex. 25:33–36).

Almon-diblathaim (ăl'mŏn-dĭb'là-thā'ĭm) a Moabite city, one of the Israelites' last stations before crossing the Jordan (Num. 33:46 f.).

alms [Gr. *eleemosune*, pity, relief for the poor > Lat. *eleemosyna* > Anglo-Saxon *ael-maesse*, almsgiving] the practice of remembering the poor is deeply engrained in the OT, though the original has no single word for the practice. The duty of almsgiving, especially in kind, consisted mostly in leaving portions of the field, vineyard, or olive orchard unharvested for the poor (Lev. 19:9–10, 23:22; Deut. 15:11, 24:19, 26:2–13; Ruth 2:2) and in the tithe of the third year for "the Levite, the stranger, the fatherless, and the widow" (Deut. 14:28). The Bible often pronounces blessings upon such sharing (Job 31:17; Prov. 10:2, 11:4; Est. 9:22; Ps. 112:9; Acts 9:36, the case of Dorcas; and Acts 10:2, of Cornelius). In NT times there were thirteen receptacles in the temple for voluntary offerings (Mk. 12:41), one of which was for the education of poor children. Before the captivity there is no mention of begging, though it is mentioned in later times (Mt. 20:30; Mk. 10:46; Acts 3:2). Almsgiving played an important part in Jewish faith; the Talmud went so far as to interpret "righteousness" (in Gen. 18:19; Ps. 17:15) as almsgiving. Jesus (Mt. 6:2) denounced the ostentation which some Pharisees had allowed their liberality to the poor to become. (For the concern of the early church, see Mt. 6:1–4; Lk. 14:13; Acts 11:30, 20:35; Rom. 15:25–27; 1 Cor. 16:1–4; Gal. 2:10; 1 Tim. 5:10.)

almug see **algum**

aloes or **lign aloes** the name of a costly and

sweet-smelling substance used for perfume, evidently extracted from a tree (Ps. 45:8; Prov. 7:17; Song of S. 4:14; Jn. 19:39). Numbers 24:6 (AV, lign aloes) uses the term poetically of a tree by a brook.

The tree from which aloes was extracted was probably either the eaglewood or the white sandalwood (see **algum**) tree. The true aloe was a succulent plant, much like the American century plant; this was the source of a bitter medicine used in embalming, and perhaps Jn. 19:39 is to be referred to it.

Aloth (ā'lŏth) a place or district which with Asher was the ninth jurisdictional territory of Solomon (1 K. 4:16; AV form of **Bealoth**).

Alpha (ăl'fà) the first letter of the Greek alphabet, as Omega is the last. Used of Christ as the beginning of all things: "I am Alpha and Omega, the beginning and the end, the first and the last" (Rev. 1:8, 11, 21:6, 22:13; cf. Isa. 41:4). Both Greeks and Hebrews employed letters of the alphabet as numerals.

alphabet see **writing**

Alpheus (ăl-fē'ŭs) 1. The father of the apostle James the Less (Mt. 10:3; Mk. 3:18; Lk. 6:15; Acts 1:13), probably named to provide distinction from James son of Zebedee.

2. The father of Levi (Mk. 2:14).

altar a raised structure or location on which sacrifices of animals or incense were burned in worship, though some early Hebrew altars were erected as memorials in places hallowed, for example, by God's appearance (Gen. 12:7, 13:18, 26:25, 35:1), or as a witness (Ex. 17:15–16; Josh. 22:10–29). 1. The first altar recorded in the Bible is that built by Noah when he left the ark (Gen. 8:20). The frequent early mention indicates that there was early revelation to God's people of this as a chosen way of approach to him. Excavations at Megiddo, Beth-shan, Lachish, Hazar, and Zorah have revealed constructed altars in use in Canaanite cities from as early as 3000 B.C. and show that such structures played an important part in pagan religions also. Materials for altars might be earth or unhewn stones (Ex. 20:24, 25). This applies to the part on which the victim was laid, as casings of shittim wood overlaid with brass were built for the altar of burnt offerings.

Altars were frequently built on elevations or "high places," especially in idolatrous worship. These the Israelites were to destroy (Deut. 12:2), and the law of Moses provided that no altars were to be built except those first in the tabernacle and later in the temple (Lev. 17:8, 9; Deut. 12:13). These prohibitions were not strictly observed by pious worshipers (Judg.

6:24; 1 Sam. 7:9 f.; 2 Sam. 24:25; 1 K. 3:4). The sanctity attached to the altars made them a place of refuge or asylum (Ex. 21:14; 1 K. 1:50).

2. Two altars were to be built for the tabernacle: the altar of burnt offering (simply called the altar) and the altar of incense. (a) The first is described in Ex. 27:1–8 and 38:1–8. For details of dedication and offerings, see Ps. 118:27 (victim tied to its horns); Ex. 29:12; Lev. 4:7 ff., (the sprinkling of blood on the horns); Ex. 20:26 (no steps); Ex. 40:29 (its location at east door of tabernacle); Ex. 27:3; 1 Sam. 2:13 f.; Lev. 16:12; Num. 16:6 f. (its utensils all made of brass). Solomon's altar in the temple was built on the same pattern but larger. For details, see 2 Chr. 4:1, 7:7; 1 K. 8:64. On the altar a perpetual fire was to be kept burning (Lev. 6:12 f.). For the history of the altar from Solomon, see 2 Chr. 15:8, 29:18, 33:16; 2 K. 16:14. In the rebuilding of the temple the altar was built first (Ezra 3:2) and, according to Josephus, on the exact spot where Solomon's had stood.

(b) The altar of incense, also called the *golden* altar (Ex. 39:38; Num. 4:11), was placed before the veil of the tabernacle (Ex. 30:1–8) on which morning and evening sacrifices of incense were offered. See 1 K. 7:48, and 1 Chr. 28:18 for its description in Solomon's temple. Though places of prayer and communion are often called "altars," there is no mention of such in the NT. The altar is spiritualized to mean Jesus Christ's sacrifice for us and the privilege Christians have of worshiping in his name (Heb. 13:10). The altar of incense is the only altar which appears in the heavenly temple (Rev. 8:3–4), being symbolic of the prayers of disciples.

Al-Taschith (ăl-tăs'chĭth) a term found in introductory verse to Psalms 57–59, 75, and in Moses' prayer (Deut. 9:26), and meaning literally "Destroy not." Its significance is uncertain, conjecturally the beginning of a song or poem to the tune of which the Psalms were to be sung.

Alush (ā'lŭsh) the last station of the Israelites before Rephidim on the way to Sinai (Num. 33:13 f.).

Alvah (ăl'và) or **Aliah** (1 Chr. 1:51) a duke of Edom (Gen. 36:40).

Alvan (ăl'văn) a Horite, also written Alian (1 Chr. 1:40).

Amad (ā'măd) an unknown place in Asher (Josh. 19:26).

Amal (ā'măl) an Asherite (1 Chr. 7:35).

Amalek (ăm'à-lĕk) son of Eliphaz by his concubine Timnah, grandson of Esau and chieftain of Edom (Gen. 36:12).

Amalekites (ăm-ă-lĕk-īts') an ancient nomadic tribe occupying the Negeb and the peninsula of Sinai toward Egypt (Num. 13:29; 1 Sam. 15:7, 27:8). In Gen. 14:7 they are represented as existing in the days of Chedorlaomer's invasion in Abraham's time. This is, of course, in seeming contradiction to their being the offspring of Amalek from Esau (Gen. 36:15–16). This is explained as a prolepsis meaning that Chedorlaomer smote the land later occupied by Amalek; or following Arabian historians, others think the ancient Amalekites once occupied the shores of the Persian Gulf and were pressed westward by the growth of Assyria, and that later there was a mixture of these Eastern nomads with Amalek's descendants. After Gen. 14:7, the OT mentions their cowardly attack on Israel at Rephidim for which their destruction was decreed by the Lord (Ex. 17:8 ff.), their joining the Canaanites in repulsing Israel at Hormah (Num. 14:45), their joining in oppressions of Israel in the days of the Judges (Judg. 3:13, 6:3, 33), their defeat by Saul when he spared Agag (1 Sam. 15:8 ff.), and Amalekite's killing of Saul (2 Sam. 1:8 ff.), David's conquests of them (1 Sam. 30:18; 2 Sam. 8:12; 1 Chr. 18:11), and their final extermination by the Simeonites in Hezekiah's time (1 Chr. 4:43). No archaeological remains have so far been identified.

Amam (ā'măm) an unidentified town in South Judah (Josh. 15:26).

Amana (à-mā'nà) a mountain peak in the Anti-Lebanon range (Song of S. 4:8).

Amariah (ăm'à-rī'àh) 1. A high priest, ancestor of Ezra (1 Chr. 6:7, 52).

2. High priest in the reign of Jehoshaphat (2 Chr. 19:11).

3. Head of the Kohathites in the time of David (1 Chr. 23:19, 24:23).

4. Head of one of the courses of priests (2 Chr. 31:15; Neh. 10:3).

5. A Banite who had intermarried (Ezra 10:42).

6. Returned exile priest (Neh. 10:3, etc.).

7. Descendant of Pharez son of Judah (Neh. 11:4 = **Imri** in 1 Chr. 9:4).

8. Ancestor of Zephaniah (Zeph. 1:1).

Amarna, Tell el- (à-màr'nà, tĕll-ĕl) a mound in Egypt where a series of clay tablets were found in 1887 containing correspondence between the pharaohs of Egypt and local rulers of Palestine. They date from the fourteenth century B.C. and throw much light on conditions in Egypt and Palestine at that time.

Amasa (ă-mā'sà) 1. Son of Abigail, David's

sister (2 Sam. 17:25). He joined Absalom's rebellion and was appointed commander in chief of his forces. He was defeated by Joab (2 Sam. 18:6–7), was forgiven by David (19:13), and murdered by Joab (20:10).

2. A prince of Ephraim in reign of Ahaz (2 Chr. 28:12).

Amashai (à-măsh'ī) a priest of Nehemiah's time (Neh. 11:13).

Amasiah (ăm-à-sī'àh) a captain in the time of Jehoshaphat (2 Chr. 17:16).

Amath see **Hamath**

Amaziah (ăm'à-zī'à) 1. The son of Joash and eighth king of Judah in David's line (1 Chr. 3:12). He seems to have reigned as coregent with Joash his father, who was slain by conspirators (2 Chr. 24:25). He punished his father's murderers, sparing their children (2 K. 14:6; cf. Deut. 24:16). His rival king in Israel was Jehoash (2 K. 13:10, 14:1). The accounts of his reigns occur mostly in 2 K. 14 and 2 Chr. 25. The highlights were: (a) his use of Israelite mercenaries in assembling his army (2 Chr. 25:5–13), (b) his defeat of the inhabitants of Sela (Petra) connected with idolatrous worship of Edomite gods (2 K. 14:3–7; 2 Chr. 25:14), and (c) his challenge of Jehoash king of Israel, to battle at Beth-shemesh at which Amaziah was captured and returned as a captive to Jerusalem (2 Chr. 25:17–24). Amaziah was the victim of a conspiracy fifteen years after his father's death; he fled to Lachish, where he was killed (2 Chr. 25:27).

2. A Simeonite (1 Chr. 4:34).

3. A Levite (1 Chr. 6:45).

4. Priest who opposed Amos at Bethel (Amos 7:10, 12, 14).

ambassador a messenger sent usually for negotiation. In the OT it represents several words, most frequently *mal'ākh* and *tsīr*. Examples are seen in regard to Edom, Moab, and the Amorites (Num. 20:14, 21:21; Judg. 11:17–19), the Gibeonites (Josh. 9:4), and in Israel's intercourse with foreign monarchs (2 K. 18:17 f.), and for many purposes (2 K. 14:8, 16:7, 18:14; 2 Chr. 32:31). The Greek word is derived from the concept of age. In the NT the verb is found (2 Cor. 5:20; Eph. 6:20) as well as the noun (Lk. 14:32, 19:14). Sometimes little distinction is made between this idea and "angel." Basically they are the same.

amber a description of color of divine glory in visions of Ezek. 1:4, 27, 8:2. The word usually denotes a yellow fossil resin, but it has been thought that here it represents a metal. The LXX and Vulg. render it by *electron*, a compound of silver and gold.

Amen (ā'mĕn) [from Heb. *āmēn* > Gr.

amēn] the Hebrew root form means "the firm," and metaphorically "faithful"; hence the natural meaning of God as "the God of Amen" (Isa. 65:16; cf. Rev. 3:14 of Christ, "the Amen"). It was used in strong statements fixing as it were the stamp of truth on the assertion and making it binding as an oath (cf. Num. 5:22 and the "Amen" of the people at the reading of the blessings and curses in Deut. 27:15–26). The seriousness given a statement (virtually an oath) is shown by 1 K. 1:36, Jesus' use in Jn. 3:3, 5, and by its use as a proper response to an oath administered (Neh. 5:13; 1 Chr. 16:36; Jer. 11:5 mg.). It was the customary response to prayers in the synagogue and private devotions (though tradition says that it was not used in the temple), and this was continued in the churches in public worship (1 Cor. 14:16). Doxologies and praise passages (Rom. 9:5, 11:36, 15:33, 16:27; 2 Cor. 13:14), and the end of some books (Rom., 1 Cor., and Gal.) have it. The repetition of the word was for emphasis (Neh. 8:6; Rev. 5:14). The literal meaning is seen from the LXX translation by an optative of wish "may it become or happen," just the opposite of Paul's "God forbid."

amethyst a precious stone, third in the third row of the high priest's breastplate (Ex. 28:19, 39:12). It also occurs among the stones of the foundation of the Heavenly Jerusalem (Rev. 21:20). It is a deep-purple form of quartz. Curiously the stone was once thought to be an antidote for drunkenness, whence its name.

Ami (ā′mī) a servant of Solomon (Ezra 2:57).

Aminadab see **Amminadab**

Amittai (à-mĭt′ī) father of Jonah (2 K. 14:25; Jon. 1:1).

Ammah (ām′à) a hill on road to wilderness of Gibeon (2 Sam. 2:24).

Ammi (ăm′ī) [My people] a figurative name to be given to Israel in contrast with **Lo-ammi** [Not my people] (Hos. 1:9, 2:1).

Ammiel (ăm′ĭ-ĕl) 1. A spy from tribe of Dan (Num. 13:12).

2. Father of Machir (2 Sam. 9:4 f., 17:27).

3. Father of Bath-sheba, also called Eliam (1 Chr. 3:5; 2 Sam. 11:3).

4. A temple doorkeeper (1 Chr. 26:5).

Ammihud (ă-mī′hŭd) 1. An Ephraimite chieftain during the Exodus and an ancestor of Joshua (Num. 1:10, 2:18, 10:22; 1 Chr. 7:26).

2. A prince of the tribe of Simeon (Num. 34:20).

3. A prince of the tribe of Naphtali (Num. 34:28).

4. The father of Talmai king of Geshur (2 Sam. 13:37).

5. Descendant of Pharez (1 Chr. 9:4).

Amminadab (ă-mĭn′à-dăb) 1. A fourth generation descendant of Judah and an ancestor of Jesus Christ (Mt. 1:4; Lk. 3:33). A prince in Israel (Num. 1:7, 2:3; Ruth 4:19 f.; 1 Chr. 2:10).

2. A chief of sons of Uzziel of the Kohathites (Ex. 6:18) who were commissioned to bring the ark to Jerusalem (1 Chr. 15:10–12).

3. A name given, probably by a clerical error to Izhar (1 Chr. 6:22).

amminadib an uncertain translation in the AV of Song of S. 6:12. Instead of a personal name the ASV reads "my princely people."

Ammishaddai (ăm-ĭ-shăd′ī) a prince of the tribe of Dan at the Exodus (Num. 1:12, 2:25, 10:25).

Ammizabad (à-mĭz′à-băd) son of Benaiah who commanded the third division of David's army (2 Sam. 23:20–23; 1 Chr. 11:22–25, 27:6).

Ammon or **Ben-ammon** (ăm′ŏn) son of Lot by his youngest daughter (Gen. 19:38), the father of the Ammonites.

Ammonites (ăm′ŏn-īts) a people descended from Ben-ammi or Ammon, the son of Lot by his younger daughter and brother of Moab (Gen. 19:38; Ps. 83:6–8). Thus Moab and Ammon were related and the relation continued (Judg. 10:6; 2 Chr. 20:1; Zeph. 2:8). Since they were related by ancestry to Israel, the Israelites were forbidden to force their way through their land by battle (Deut. 2:19; cf. 23:4). The early land of the Ammonites came from their displacing the Zamzummin (Rephaim) near the Jabbok (Num. 21:24; Deut. 2:37, 3:16). Their land lay around their capital city of Rabbath-ammon (modern Ammon in Transjordan). They tried to reclaim this territory from Israel, claiming it belonged to them (Judg. 10:8, 11:13). The people were a fierce marauding type (1 Sam. 11:2; Amos 1:13) with a high degree of crafty cruelty (Jer. 41:6–7). They made occasional foray into Palestine (Judg. 3:13) and joined Moab in the Balaam affair (Deut. 23:4; Neh. 13:1). There was constant conflict between them (2 Sam. 10:4, 12:9; 1 Chr. 19:4, 20; 2 Chr. 20:1–25, 27:5; Jer. 49:1–6; Amos 1:13; Zeph. 2:8–9). The god of the Ammonites was **Molech,** generally named in the OT under the altered form of Milcom or Malcham.

Ammonitess woman of Ammonite race, e.g., **Naamah** (1 K. 14:21, 31) and **Shimeah** (2 Chr. 24:26; cf. 1 K. 11:1; and Neh. 13:23).

Amnon (ăm′nŏn) 1. Son of David who dishonored his half sister Tamar and was killed by Absalom (2 Sam. 13:1–29).

2. Son of Shimon (1 Chr. 4:20).

Amok (ā'mŏk) a priest who returned with Zerubbabel (Neh. 12:7, 20).

Amon (ăm'ŏn) 1. King of Judah, son and successor of Manasseh. He ruled two years (ca. 642–40), devoting himself to false gods, and was killed by a conspiracy, the perpetrators of which were in turn put to death (2 K. 21:19–23; 2 Chr. 33:21). He was succeeded by his son Josiah.

2. Prince or governor of Samaria in reign of Ahab (1 K. 22:26; 2 Chr. 18:25).

3. A descendant of Solomon's servant, who returned from the Exile, also called Ami (Neh. 7:59; Ezra 2:57).

Amon an Egyptian deity, Amon-Ra, whose chief seat of worship was No, Amon, or Thebes (Jer. 46:25; Ezek. 30:14–16; Nah. 3:8).

Amorite (ăm'ō-rīt) [mountain dwellers] one of the chief nations possessing Canaan before the Conquest. The Amorite was a descendant of Canaan, grandson of Noah (Gen. 10:16). The earliest Biblical location of the Amorites was the wilderness region west of the Dead Sea at En-gedi (Gen. 14:7, **Hazezon-tamar**), from where they stretched west to Hebron (Gen. 14:13; cf. 13:18). They were reported by Joshua's spies as living "in the mountains" (Num. 13:29; see also Josh. 5:1, 10:6, 11:3; Deut. 1:7, 20, 44). At the entrance into Western Palestine, Israel encountered them again in the region south of the Jabbok, from which they had driven Moab (Num. 21:13, 16). Sihon, their king, refused Israel passage and was defeated and his territory taken (Num. 21:21; Deut. 2:26, 32–33). Strictly speaking the "land of the Amorite" was that between the Jabbok and the Arnon, but it was said to include all Gilead and Bashan (Deut. 3:10), and extended to Hermon (3:8, 4:48). Those living west of the Jordan contended with Joshua in the Conquest (Josh. 10:5, 11:3); after this they are not mentioned except as early inhabitants. Modern archaeology has identified them with the Amurru with their capital at Mari (modern Tell Hariri) in Syria where the Euphrates bends toward the east. Later they invaded Babylonia, where they were in control until Hammurabi conquered them. Excavations at Mari have been productive of information concerning them. Their language was closely related to the Canaanite.

Amos (ā'mŏs) [burden bearer] 1. A prophet of the OT whose book is third in the OT canon, but who was the first of the writing prophets. He was a native of Tekoa in Judah

(six miles south of Bethlehem), originally a shepherd and dresser of sycamore trees who was called to the office of prophet though not trained in the prophetic office (1:1, 7:14, 15). He journeyed to the Northern Kingdom to prophesy briefly "in the days of Uzziah king of Judah, and of Jeroboam, son of Joash king of Israel" (1:1). Jeroboam had raised Israel to the height of military power and prosperity, restoring Israel's border from Hamath to the Sea of Arabah (2 K. 14:23–27). With such conquests completed, Israel became proud (Amos 6:13). But there existed great unrighteousness, oppression of the poor (8:4), idleness, luxury, and extravagance (3:15); idolatry (7:13, cf. 3:15; and in Judah see 4:4, 5:5, 8:14, 5:14, 21–23; cf. 2 K. 17:33). The true worship of the Lord was found burdensome (8:5). These conditions were rebuked by the prophet, which led to his expulsion from Israel and return to his native town. The book is divided into four parts: 1:1–2:3—Denunciation of the nations bordering Judah and Israel; 2:4–3:15—The state of these kingdoms especially Israel, exposing their sense of false security; 4:1–9:10—Amos' reception at Bethel. Here occur five oracles which describe the Lord's forbearance and justice, but which also foretell the punishment of Israel; 9:11–15—An epilogue in which the hope of messianic fulfillment and divine forgiveness are promised. The book is characterized by numerous rural and agricultural allusions (1:3, 2:13, 3:4 f.; 4:2, 6:12).

2. Son of Naum in ancestry of Jesus Christ (Lk. 3:25).

Amoz (ā'mŏz) the father of Isaiah (e.g., Isa. 1:1; 2 K. 19:2, 20).

Amphipolis (ăm-fĭp'ō-lĭs) a city, the capital of the first district of Macedonia, through which Paul and Silas passed (Acts 17:1). It was some thirty miles southwest of Philippi on the Via Egnatia, and on the river Strymon about three miles from the sea. It was an Athenian colony.

Amplias (ăm'plĭ-ăs) or **Ampliatus** (ăm'plĭ-ā'tŭs) a Christian at Rome (Rom. 16:8).

Amram (ăm'răm) 1. A Levite of the family of the Kohathites and father of Moses, Aaron, and Miriam (Ex. 6:18, 20; Num. 3:19; 1 Chr. 6:2 f., 18). He is called a "son" of Kohath, evidently in the sense of descendant, as the tribe numbered 8600 in the second generation (Num. 3:28).

2. Son of Dishon, descendant of Seir (1 Chr. 1:41), also "Hamran" or "Hemdan" (Gen. 36:26).

3. Son of Bani who married a foreign wife (Ezra 10:34).

Amramites descendants of **Amram** (1 Chr. 26:23).

Amraphel (ăm′ra-fĕl) a cohort of Chedorlaomer, who joined in a successful campaign against Sodom and Gomorrah and the cities of the plain (Gen. 14).

amulet an ornament, gem, or scroll pierced and worn about the neck, generally inscribed with holy words or characters and worn to ward off evils such as disease or snake bites. The English word does not occur in the KJV, but is to be understood in passages like Judg. 8:24; and Isa. 3:20.

Amzi (ăm′zī) 1. A Levite ancestor of Ethan, a singer (1 Chr. 6:46).

2. An ancestor of Adaiah who served in the temple (Neh. 11:12).

Anab (ā′năb) a town of Judah (Josh. 15:50) once belonging to the Anakim (Josh. 11:21). It is now probably a village of the same name fifteen miles southwest of Hebron.

Anah (ā′nà) son of Zibeon the Horite (Gen. 36:20), a prince and the father of Aholibamah, a wife of Esau (Gen. 36:2, 14, 25). Possibly the same as the Anah who found the "hot springs" (not "mules" as in the KJV) (Gen. 36:24).

Anaharath (à-nā′ha-răth) a place in Issachar, named with Shihon and Rabbith (Josh. 19:19).

Anaiah (à-nī′àh) 1. One of the men who stood on Ezra's right hand as he read the Law to Israel (Neh. 8:4).

2. One of "the heads of the people" (could be the same) who signed the covenant with Nehemiah (Neh. 10:22).

Anakim or **Anak** (ăn′à-kĭm or ā′năk) [long necked] the sons or children of Anak (Num. 13:33), who was the son of Arba (Josh. 15:13, 21:11). Arba himself is described as "a great one among the Anakim" (Josh. 14:15) showing that "Anak" was probably a racial rather than individual name. There seem to have been three divisions: Sheshai, Ahiman, and Talmai (Num. 13:22). Their home was Hebron (Num. 13:22; Josh. 15:13). Their giant appearance struck Israel with terror (Num. 13:22, 28; Deut. 9:2), who recalling the giants of the days of the flood compared them with the Nephidim (Num. 13:33; cf. Gen. 6:4). Joshua dispossessed them except for a remnant who took refuge in Philistia (Josh. 11:21–22).

Anamim (ăn′à-mĭm) a people or tribe descended from Mizraim (Gen. 10:13; 1 Chr. 1:11). Nothing further is known of them.

Anammelech (à-năm′ĕ-lĕk) one of the idols worshiped by colonists from Sepharvaim (possibly Sabraim in Syria) at Samaria after 721

B.C. As in Molech's rites children were burnt in his honor (2 K. 17:31).

Anan (ā′năn) a signer of the covenant with Nehemiah (Neh. 10:26).

Anani (à-nā′nī) a descendant of Zerubbabel in David's line (1 Chr. 3:24).

Ananiah (ăn′à-nī′àh) 1. An ancestor of Azariah, who assisted Nehemiah in rebuilding the wall (Neh. 3:23).

2. A place in which the Benjaminites lived after the Exile (Neh. 11:32), thought to be NT Bethany, two miles from Jerusalem.

Ananias (ăn′à-nī′ăs) 1. A high priest in Acts 23:2–5, and 24:1, before whom Paul was tried. His father was Nebedeus; he served A.D. 48–58. In 52 he was accused and then acquitted for conduct in an affair between the Jews and the Samaritans (Josephus *Ant.* XX.vi.2 f.). He was murdered by the sicarii at the beginning of the Jewish War (A.D. 66–70).

2. A disciple at Jerusalem in the early church, husband of Sapphira (Acts 5:1–5). The two conspired to lie about the price of a plot of land, pretending to give it all. Peter denounced the act as lying to the Holy Spirit and both were killed by divine wrath.

3. A Jewish disciple at Damascus (Acts 9:10–17), a devout man, of good report, who was ordered by the Lord in a vision to go to the penitent Saul of Tarsus. Though reluctant, he went and restored Saul's sight by the laying on of hands and commanded him to "arise and be baptized and wash away thy sins, calling on the name of the Lord" (Acts 22:16).

Anath (ā′năth) father of Shamgar (Judg. 3:31).

anathema a Greek word spelled either *anathema* or *anathēma* [from a root meaning "to set up" = "to set or hang up in a temple what has been devoted to a god"], which is used in the LXX to translate the Heb. *herem*, which means something "consecrated" or "devoted" to God. Some things so devoted belonged to the priest; some animals had to be slain (Lev. 27:28 f.). Such vows were made concerning Canaanite cities (Num. 21:2; Josh. 6:17) or individuals (Judg. 11:31; 1 Sam. 14:24), and the vow could not be breached (Josh. 7:25). Things so cursed were considered depraved and to be destroyed (Deut. 7:26, 13:15–16). In later times the term moves toward the idea of separated by "excommunication," but whether Paul's usage has that meaning or that of dislike or condemnation is disputed (Rom. 9:3; 1 Cor. 12:3, 16:22; Gal. 1:9). In heaven there will be no anathema (Zech. 14:11; Rev. 22:3).

Anathoth (ăn′à-thŏth) 1. Son of Becher, a Benjaminite (1 Chr. 7:8).

2. A signer of the covenant with Nehemiah (Neh. 10:19), or more likely a name standing for the men of Anathoth (Neh. 7:27).

Anathoth a priests' city in Benjamin (Josh. 21:18; 1 Chr. 6:60). Hither Solomon banished Abiathar (1 K. 2:26). It was the birthplace of Jeremiah (Jer. 1:1, 11:21), and it was mentioned in many connections (e.g., 2 Sam. 23:27; 1 Chr. 11:28, 12:3, 27:12). Its inhabitants returned from the Exile with Zerubbabel (Ezra 2:23; Neh. 7:27). The site was two or three miles north of Jerusalem.

anchor see **ship**

Ancient of Days phrase used in Dan. 7:9 of the one to whom the "one like unto the Son of man" came on the clouds. The expression is an Aramaism meaning "Aged One" and most likely refers to God (cf. Job 36:26).

Andrew (ăn'drōō) one of Christ's apostles (Jn. 1:40; Mt. 4:18). He was of Beth-saida, a brother of Simon and like his brother a fisherman. He had been a disciple of John the Baptist; but, when he saw John point to Jesus as the Lamb of God, he immediately followed him and brought Simon to him (Jn. 1:25–42). After this original call the disciples seemed to have returned to their vocation until later called more permanently by the Master (Mt. 4:18 f.). They were then among those appointed to the Twelve (Mt. 10:2; Mk. 3:18; Lk. 6:14; Acts 1:13). He is mentioned only a few times during the personal ministry, once in connection with the feeding of the 5000 (Jn. 6:6–9), the request of the Greeks to see Jesus (Jn. 12:22), and the questions about the destruction of the temple (Mk. 13:3). After Jesus' death he is not referred to again. Eusebius says he preached in Scythia, others in Achaia, where he is said to have been crucified.

Andronicus (ăn-drō'nĭ-kŭs) a Christian at Rome who, along with Junias, was saluted by Paul as kinsman and fellow captive, and as one "of note among the apostles" (Rom. 16:7) and Christians ("in Christ") before him. The term "apostle" here is used as elsewhere probably of the apostles (missionaries) of the churches (2 Cor. 8:19, 23; Phil. 2:25).

Anem (ā'nĕm) a city of Issachar (1 Chr. 6:73).

Aner (ā'nêr) 1. A Kohathite city of Manasseh west of the Jordan (1 Chr. 6:70).

2. An Amorite chief who aided Abraham in pursuit of the four kings (Gen. 14:13, 24).

Anethothite an inhabitant of **Anathoth.**

angel [Gr. *aggelos*, messenger, one sent] a race of spiritual beings, in nature exalted above man but infinitely removed from God whose creatures and servants they are. 1. SCRIPTURAL USE OF THE WORD. First the OT contains many references to the "Angel of God" or "Angel of the Lord," by which is certainly meant a manifestation of God himself, accepting worship due God (Gen. 16:7, 13, 31:11–13). In contrast to this angels are created (Ps. 148:2–5; Col. 1:16) spirits (Heb. 1:14) who, as servants of God, reject divine worship (Rev. 19:10, 22:9). Besides this higher application of the word we find the term used of any "messenger" of God, such as prophets (Isa. 42:19; Hag. 1:13; Mal. 3:1) or priests (Mal. 2:7). Sometimes the angel of a thing, especially of a natural phenomenon, seems to mean the thing itself, as the angel of the sea or fire (Rev. 16:5).

2. NATURE OF ANGELS. Of this little is said apart from their office. They are created like man and thus personal beings but are not sexual and reproductive (Lk. 20:34–36 "neither marry—are like angels"). They are spirits but are never said to be incorporeal. From the fact that man is to be like angels in the resurrection, and from the statements that his body is to be made—like Christ's (Phil. 3:21)—from the glorious nature of Christ's transfigured (Mt. 17) or resurrection body (Rev. 1:14–16) which can be compared to that of angels (Dan. 10:6), from angel's appearances in bodily form like man (Gen. 18–19; Lk. 24:4; Acts 1:10), and from the fact that both are often given identical titles (Job 1:6; Dan. 3:25, 28; and Ps. 8:5, 97:7), it has been concluded that men and angels differ only in degree and not in kind. For references to their more perfect nature, see Mt. 18:10; 1 Jn. 3:2; Gen. 1:31; Jude 6, though they too are limited (Job 4:18; Mt. 24:36; 2 Pet. 1:12). Some angels have rebelled against God and were cast down (Mt. 25:41; 2 Pet. 2:4; Jude 6).

3. OFFICE OF ANGELS. Angels in heaven are presented only in the attitude of service and adoration of God (1 K. 22:19; Isa. 6:1–3; Dan. 7:10; Rev. 6:11 ff.). Their ministry toward man is summarized in Heb. 1:14: "Are they not ministering spirits, sent forth to minister for them who shall be heirs of salvation?" They are often pictured as helping, keeping, and delivering the servants of God (e.g., Gen. 19:11; Ps. 91:11; Dan. 3:28; Acts 5:19). They guide the natural operations of the world and execute God's judgment (2 K. 19:35; Acts 12:23; Heb. 11:29), interpret dreams (Dan. 7:16, 10:7; Zech. 1:9), and guide the affairs of nations (e.g., Dan. 4:13, 23, 10:10, 13, 20, 21). Their appearances in connection with the birth and ministry of Jesus are well-known (Mt. 1:20, 28:2; Lk. 1–2, 4:11, 22:43; Jn. 20:12; Acts 1:10 f.) as are those of their activ-

ity in directing the growth of the church in the age of its infancy (Acts 5:19, 8:26, 10:3, 12:7, 27:23). In a less overt and miraculous way we may find significance in the declaration of their watching over Christ's little ones (Mt. 18:10), rejoicing over a penitent sinner (Lk. 15:10), being present in the worship of Christians (1 Cor. 11:10) perhaps bringing their prayers before God (Rev. 8:3, 4), and bearing the souls of the redeemed into Paradise (Lk. 16:22). For discussion of specific types or names of angelic beings, see **seraphim, cherubim, Michael, Gabriel.**

angling see **fishing**

Aniam (á-nī'ăm) a Manassite (1 Chr. 7:19).

Anim (ā'nĭm) a city in the mountains of Judah (Josh. 15:50), probably now Khirbet Ghuwein et-Tahta, eleven miles south of Hebron.

anise [incorrect translation in the AV of Gr. *anēthon* (RSV, dill)] a weedy umbellifer cultivated for its seeds, which are aromatic. It occurs only in Mt. 23:23, where it is stated that the Pharisees tithed its produce.

anklet referred to in Isa. 3:16, 18, 20 ("tinkling ornaments" about the feet), they consisted of glass or metal pieces fastened to the ankle bands.

Anna (ăn'á) a prophetess in Jerusalem at the time of the Lord's presentation in the temple (Lk. 2:36). She recognized and proclaimed Jesus as the Messiah.

Annas (ăn'ás) a high priest of the Jews (Lk. 3:2). At thirty-seven he was appointed by Quirinius, governor of Syria (A.D. 6), but was replaced in 14 by Ishmael, who was succeeded by Eleazar, Annas' son, followed by Simon son of Camithus, and then (ca. 25) Annas' son-in-law Joseph Caiaphas (Jn. 18:13). As head of the family (he had five sons who served as high priest) he seems to have been very influential. Jesus was taken before him first, then to Caiaphas (Jn. 18:13, 24). He is actually called high priest in Acts 4:6.

anointing the applying of oil or ointment to a person, a practice quite common in Biblical times (Deut. 28:40; Ruth 3:3; Mic. 6:15). Olive oil was the usual ingredient. Ordinarily it was for cosmetic purposes (omitted when in mourning, 2 Sam. 14:2; Mt. 6:17), for festival occasions (Ps. 23:5; Lk. 7:46), and for burial (Mk. 14:8, 16:1). Medicinal anointing is noted, but not always by oil as above (Isa. 1:6; Lk. 10:34). In religious rites inanimate objects were anointed in consecration to God (Gen. 31:13; Ex. 30:26-28). In official ceremonies anointing was the common rite of inauguration into the three typical offices of the Hebrew commonwealth: prophets (1 K. 19:16; hence

called *messiahs*, 1 Chr. 16:22; Ps. 105:15), priests (Ex. 29:29, 40:15; Num. 3:3), and kings (1 Sam. 9:16; 1 K. 1:34, 39). The king especially was called "the Lord's anointed" (1 Sam. 12:3, 5). Oil seems to have been used ceremonially, like the laying on of hands, in miraculous healing (Mk. 6:13). This is probably the use in James 5:14 where James tells the elders to anoint and pray for the recovery of the sick. The term *Christ* is the Greek equivalent of the OT *Messiah*, meaning "the anointed one." The deliverer of God's people is so designated (Ps. 2:2; Dan. 9:2 f.), with special reference to his reception of the Holy Spirit (Isa. 61:1; cf. Lk. 4:18 as well as Ps. 45:7; Heb. 1:9). Jesus of Nazareth is identified in the NT as the fulfillment of these promises (Mt. 16:16; Jn. 1:41; Acts 9:22, 17:2, 3, 18:5, 28; see also Jn. 1:32 f.; Acts 4:27, 10:38). Christians also have an unction or anointing of the Holy Spirit (1 Jn. 2:20, 27).

ant an insect mentioned twice in the OT (Prov. 6:6 and 30:25) to illustrate diligence and wisdom. Though some ants do not store up food as Solomon relates, the harvester ant which nests near fields and threshing floors do. Ants live in colonies with three outstanding types: male, female, and worker, with a single queen serving a colony of thousands.

antichrist [one "opposed" to Christ] a term used only by the apostle John on three occasions (1 Jn. 2:18, 22 and 2 Jn. 7). John obviously means one who is antagonistic to, or who denies, Christ, but the application is uncertain and much disputed. To this writer the "false Christs" (Mt. 24:5, 24) are different, as John's antichrists make no claim to *being* Christ; they rather deny (as the Docetists did) that Jesus "has come in the flesh." Two positions are generally held: (1) Some scholars claim that John does not mean a *personal* antichrist; already "there have arisen many antichrists" (1 Jn. 2:18). The evangelist says Christians had heard of antichrist's coming (from Jewish expectations), and he informs them that the truth is that anyone so denying the incarnation is antichrist. John indicates that the expectation of antichrist is fulfilled in this way. (This is the position, e.g., of Albertus Pieters, *Studies in the Revelation of St. John* [Eerdmans, 1943], pp. 178-94, who has a fine discussion.) (2) Others think John meant that such antichrists as John's "many" are forerunners of a great personal antagonist of Christ to arise at the end of the world. This figure some identify with Paul's "man of sin" (2 Thess. 2:3), Daniel's "vile person" (11:21), and the first beast of Rev. 13. (Such is the

Antioch

position of Abraham Kuyper, *The Revelation of St. John*, 1935, reprint 1963.) The arguments for a personal antichrist and the identification of the beast of Rev. 13 with him do not to this writer seem conclusive.   J.W.R.

Antioch (ăn'tĭ-ŏk) 1. In Pisidia. A city (Acts 13:14, 14:19, 21; 2 Tim. 3:11) situated on a plateau near the border of Phrygia in Asia Minor. The city was founded by Seleucus Nicator and under the Romans became a colony and was also called Caesarea. It was made a part of the Roman province of Galatia in 25 B.C. The city was a composite of Greeks, Roman colonists, native Phrygians, and a community of Jews. On his first missionary tour (Acts 13:14 ff.), Paul visited it, preached in the synagogue, and converted a great number of Gentiles, resulting in violent persecution from the Jews and wealthy women of the city, who drove Paul from the city and even followed him to Lystra (13:50 f., 14:19). Pisidian Antioch was revisited by Paul (14:21) on his return trip. He may well have visited it a third time on the second journey. Paul reminded Timothy that he knew of Paul's sufferings at Antioch (2 Tim. 3).

2. In Syria. A city founded in 301 B.C. by Seleucus Nicator, important especially in the early church as the center from which Gentile Christianity radiated to the regions of Asia Minor, Macedonia, and Achaia. It was situated on the banks of the Orontes River, some fifteen miles inland from the "Great Sea" (the Mediterranean), with Seleucia as the seaport. It was captured by the Romans in A.D. 65 and made the capital of the province of Syria. It was a large city with an estimated population of 500,000, making it the third largest city in the empire after Rome and Alexandria. Its connections with the church began early. Nicolas, one of the seven chosen in the church at Jerusalem, was a proselyte of Antioch (Acts 6:5). The Hellenistic Jews who were scattered at the death of Stephen went about preaching in various places but declaring the Gospel only to Jews. But certain men of Cyrene and Cyprus at Antioch spoke to Gentiles also, and many of them turned to the Lord (Acts 11:20 f.). Barnabas was sent to them from Jerusalem; he went to Tarsus for Saul and together they taught for a year at Antioch. Here the disciples were first called **Christians** (Acts 11:26). From Antioch messengers were sent to Jerusalem with aid when a famine was predicted (Acts 11:27 ff.). From there also Paul and various companions were sent out under divine direction on three great missionary tours (Acts 13:1 ff., 15:36 ff.,

18:18 ff.). Between the first and third of these Paul was involved with Jewish teachers at Antioch over the question of the relation of Gentile converts to the law of Moses and circumcision, a controversy which was settled by the Jerusalem council (Acts 15).   J.W.R.

Antipas (ăn'tĭ-pàs) 1. A martyr at Pergamos (Rev. 2:13).

2. A name, which does not occur in the Bible, given to Herod, the son of Herod the Great, tetrarch of Galilee and the murderer of John the Baptist (Mt. 14:1–11).

Antipatris (ăn-tĭp'à-trĭs) a town to which the soldiers conveyed Paul by night (Acts 23:31). Anciently called Caphar Saba, it was rebuilt by Herod and named in honor of his father Antipater. It is ten miles northeast of Jaffa and ten miles north of Lydda, some forty-two miles from Jerusalem.

antitype the counterpart of the word Type, by which is meant an object or picture (usually a person, institution, or event) used to represent a later reality in the redemptive scheme. In this sense Christ is an antitype of Adam (Rom. 5:14) and baptism ("which also now saves us") of the flood of Noah (1 Pet. 3:21).

Antonia (ăn-tō'nĭ-à) a fortress built by Herod at the northwest corner of the temple in Jerusalem named for his friend Antonius. It is not named but is referred to as the "castle" (AV) or "barracks" in Acts 21:34 ff., 22:24, 23:10, 16, 32.

Antothijah (ăn'tō-thī'jà) a Benjaminite, son of Jeroham (1 Chr. 8:24).

Antothite see **Anathoth**

Anub (ā'nŭb) son of Coz and descendant of Judah (1 Chr. 4:8).

anvil this instrument is suggested in Isa. 41:7.

Apelles (à-pĕl'ēz) a Christian saluted by Paul (Rom. 16:10).

apes a word which occurs in 1 K. 10:22, "once in three years came the navy of Tharshish, bringing gold and silver, ivory and apes, and peacocks" (parallel passage in 2 Chr. 9:21).

Apharsathchites or **Apharsites** (ă-fär'săth-kĭts or ă-fär'sĭts) the names of certain tribes or their officials (RSV, governors, Persians) in Samaria who protested to Darius against the rebuilding of the temple (Ezra 4:9, 5:6).

Aphek (ā'fĕk) or **Aphik** (ā'fĭk) (Judg. 1:31) the name of several sites in Palestine. 1. A royal city of the Canaanites, whose king was killed by Joshua (Josh. 12:18). It was later an important point for the Philistine forces (1 Sam. 4:1, 29:1).

2. A city at the extreme northern border of Canaan, next to the border of the Amorites

(Josh. 13:4), the site of a shrine and locale of the Astarte-Adonis cult.

3. A Canaanite city given to Asher (Josh. 19:30) but never possessed by them.

4. A city in the north of Transjordan district of Bashan on the military road from Syria to Israel (1 K. 20:26), a common spot for engagements with Syria (2 K. 13:17).

Aphekah (à-fē′kà) a city in the mountains of Judah (Josh. 15:53).

Aphiah (à-fī′à) a forefather of King Saul (1 Sam. 9:1).

Aphik see **Aphek**

Aphrah (ăf′rà) [the house of Aphrah] a site of uncertain location mentioned in Mic. 1:10.

Aphses (ăf′sēz) chief of the eighteenth of the twenty-four courses of the temple service (1 Chr. 24:15).

apocalypse (à-pŏc′á-lĭps) the word meaning "revelation," given to many books dealing with visions and concerned with the conflict of good and evil; also often concerned with the end of the world and the punishment of evil. Many of the apocryphal books are apocalypses. See **Revelation**

apocrypha (à-pŏk′rĭ-fà) a word meaning "secret, hidden," applied to the collection of books which were first canonized by the Roman Catholic Council of Trent and which formerly stood between the Old and New Testaments in many English versions. They are: 1 and 2 Esdras; Tobit; Judith; the Additions to the Book of Esther; the Wisdom of Solomon; the Wisdom of Jesus Ben Sirach or Ecclesiasticus; Baruch; the Song of the Three Children; Susanna; Bel and the Dragon; the Prayer of Manasses; 1 and 2 Maccabees. These books became accepted by the Jews of Egypt and formed a part of the LXX or Greek translation of the OT. But they were never accepted by the Jews of Palestine.

Apollonia (ăp′ŏ-lō′nĭ-à) a city of Macedonia on the route of Paul and Silas from Philippi to Thessalonica (Acts 17:1). It was some sixty-three Roman miles from Philippi and thirty-seven from Thessalonica.

Apollos (à-pŏl′ŏs) a Jew from Alexandria in Egypt, an influential person in the NT church (Acts 18:24, 19:1; 1 Cor. 1:12, 3:4 f., 16:12; Tit. 3:13). He came to Ephesus where Paul had left Aquila and Priscilla after his stay at Corinth. He was described as an eloquent man, mighty in the Scriptures. He taught accurately the way of the Lord, but knew only the baptism of John (Acts 18:25). Aquila and Priscilla taught him the Way more perfectly; and when he passed over to Corinth, he was given a letter of recommendation (Acts 18:27). At Corinth he "watered" what Paul had "planted" (1 Cor. 3:6). He was with or near Paul when he wrote 1 Corinthians (16:12). Paul had urged him to return to Corinth which he seems to have been reluctant to do probably because some had built a partisan group around him. In the letter Paul rebukes this spirit sharply. He is mentioned but once more in the NT, where Titus (3:13) is requested to send him and Zenas on their way. He has been suggested by many as a possible author of the Epistle to the Hebrews.

Apollyon (à-pŏl′yŏn) literally as in the AV margin, "a destroyer," the Greek rendering of the Heb. *Abaddon,* "the angel of the bottomless pit" (Rev. 9:11). The term is an abstraction and signifies "destruction" (Job 26:6, 28:22; Prov. 15:11). In the NT passage Apollyon is the king of the locusts who rise from the abyss at the sounding of the fifth trumpet.

apothecary a rendering in the AV of Ex. 30:25; 2 Chr. 16:14, etc. The later versions more accurately render it as "perfumer," applying it to the making of perfumes, rather than to a selling of drugs.

Appaim (ăp′ā-ĭm) son of Nadab, descended from Jerahmeel, the founder of an important family of Judah (1 Chr. 2:30 f.).

appeal a seeking of reconsideration of a judgment of a lower court by a higher. In Ex. 18:26 Moses is said to have established a system of courts for taking more difficult cases to a higher level. Deuteronomy (17:8 ff.) provides that a lower court may seek instruction from a higher. Appeals were made to judges (Judg. 4:5) and to the king (2 Sam. 15:3). Jehoshaphat established a court for the purpose (2 Chr. 19:8) and it was re-established by Ezra (7:25). Later appeal was to the Sanhedrin. A Roman citizen had the right of appeal to the people and later this meant to the emperor. Paul, as a Roman citizen, exercised this right (Acts 25:11).

Apphia (ăf′ĭ-à or ăp′fĭ-à) [from Lat. *Appia*] 1. A Christian woman addressed with Philemon and Archippus in Philemon.

2. Probably Philemon's wife.

Appian Way (ăp′ĭ-ăn) the oldest of the Roman roads extending south toward Naples and Brundisium. Paul must have traveled the road on his way to Rome (Acts 28).

Appius, Forum of a town of the Appian Way toward Naples about forty miles from Rome where some disciples met Paul on his way to Rome (Acts 28:15).

apple, apple tree [Heb. *tappuah*] the common rendering of this word (in passages like Song of S. 2:3, 5, 7:8, 8:5; Joel 1:12; Prov. 25:11) has been strongly questioned because the apple tree did not grow well in Palestine and its fruit did not have the flavor demanded by the references to it. The quince, orange, and apricot are frequently claimed as the true fruit mentioned. There is, of course, no basis for the later idea that the fruit Adam and Eve ate in the Garden was an apple. The legend is supposed to have arisen from a mistaken idea based on the Song of S. 8:5.

apple of the eye an English idiom for the pupil of the eye, meaning something dear (cf. "give my right eye"); used to translate different Hebrew expressions, either literally or figuratively (Deut. 32:10; Lam. 2:18; Ps. 17:8; Prov. 7:2).

apples of Sodom referred to by Josephus (*War* IV.viii.4), but we have no information on meaning. See **Vine of Sodom**

Aquila (ăk'wĭ-là) a Jew whom Paul found at Corinth after leaving Athens (Acts 18:2). He was a native of Pontus in Asia Minor but had lived at Rome whence he had fled with his wife Priscilla because Claudius had commanded all Jews to leave (ca. A.D. 49–50). Their names are originally Latin, and by trade they were tent-makers. After Paul met them, they lived together and plied the same trade. Later when Paul left Corinth, they accompanied him to Ephesus where they were left and where they taught the newcomer Apollos more perfectly. They were still at Ephesus when Paul wrote 1 Corinthians (16:19). But in Rom. 16:3 ff. we learn that they had returned to Rome and a church met in their home. They had endangered their lives for Paul. In 2 Tim. 4:19, they are saluted as being with Timothy, presumably at Ephesus. Prisca, a shortened form of the wife's name, is used in some cases.

Ar (ár) one of the chief places of Moab (Isa. 15:1; Num. 21:28). It was on the north border of Moab (Num. 21:15; Deut. 2:18). At times the name seems to represent the whole nation of Moab (Deut. 2:9, 18, 29; Num. 21:15). It may have been the capital city, though on the border Ar has often been identified with Areopolis and Rabbath Moab, which is located more than ten miles south of the Arnon making the identification unlikely.

Ara (ār'à) a son of Jether, head of an Asherite family (1 Chr. 7:38).

Arab (ār'ăb) a city in the mounts of Judah, probably near Hebron (Josh. 15:52).

Arabah (ăr'à-bà) a word appearing frequently in the Hebrew OT (once in the AV) to designate the deep sunken valley or trench which extends from the slopes of Mount Hermon to the Gulf of Aqabah and includes the Sea of Galilee, the Jordan River, the Dead Sea, and

veering somewhat southwest continues on to the sea. Most of its surface lies below sea level, making it one of the most remarkable depressions on the face of the earth. The part from the Sea of Galilee to the Dead Sea is called by the Arabs el-Ghor. The word has varying meanings. In one instance, it means the part south of the Dead Sea (Deut. 2:8); in another, the part east of the river (Deut. 4:49), or that west of the Jordan (Josh. 11:16); while in yet another, it means the entire valley below the Sea of Galilee (2 Sam. 4:7). Since much of the region is desert, it is often used in the sense of an arid region (Ps. 68:4; Isa. 33:9). In Josh. 11:16 and 12:8 the Arabah takes its place with "the mountain," "the lowland plains of Philistia and Esdraelon," "the South," and "the plain" of West Jordan as one of the great natural divisions of the conquered country.

Arabia (à-rā'bǐ-à) [steppe or desert] the large peninsula of southwestern Asia, referred to in the Bible either as the East or the Land of the East (Gen. 10:30, 25:6, 29:1; Num. 23:7; Judg. 6:3, 7:12; 1 K. 4:30; Isa. 2:6, 11:14), or is equivalent to Arabia (2 Chr. 9:14; Isa. 21:13; Jer. 25:24). The term is applied to (1) the whole peninsula to the Euphrates River and including the northern deserts, (2) the great desert of Arabia, the part of Northern Arabia which lay east of Palestine, and (3) Western Arabia, also called Arabia Petrea, including Sinai, Edom, Moab, and Transjordan. The larger area is a large rectangle about 1800 miles by 600 miles, making it the largest peninsula in the world. It is often mentioned in the Bible as a source of spices, incense, precious stones, and gold (1 K. 10:2, 10, 15; 2 Chr. 9:1, 9, 14; Isa. 60:6; Jer. 6:20; Ezek. 27:22). The great desert extending east from Palestine is a great undulating plain, with few oases, and visited often by fierce sand winds called *Samoon*. Its inhabitants, descended mainly from Ishmael and Keturah, led a wandering life, finding vegetation for their flocks and camels in depressions and on the prickly shrubs which grow in the desert (Isa. 13:20; Jer. 49:31; Ezek. 38:11). They are often mentioned as robbers and predators (2 Chr. 21:16, 17, 26:7; Job 1:15; Jer. 3:2). They carried on trade by way of caravan routes along chains of oases (Ezek. 27:20–24; cf. Gen. 37:25, 28; 1 K. 10:15, 25; 2 Chr. 9:14, 24; Isa. 60:6; Jer. 6:20). Petrean Arabia, which got its name from the later city Petra (earlier Sela), was inhabited by the Horites or Horim (Gen. 14:6, 36:20–22, 29–30; Deut. 2:12, 22). It was later settled by the descendants of Esau and known as Edom or Seir. Another name is Idumaea, the origin of which is traced to a marriage of Esau with a daughter of Ishmael (Gen. 28:9, 36:3). Also we find Nabataeans, traced to Nebaioth, Esau's wife's brother (Gen. 25:13; Isa. 60:7). In the NT Arabians are mentioned as present at Pentecost (Acts 2:11), and Paul is said to have gone away to Arabia from Damascus after his conversion (Gal. 1:17). That this latter meant to Sinaitic Arabia is probably an analogy of the visits of Moses and Elijah there. There is no evidence for the identification.

Arad (ā'răd) 1. A Benjaminite (1 Chr. 8:15).

2. A Canaanite city in the Negeb (Josh. 12:14). The wilderness of Judah was "south of Arad" (Judg. 1:16). The king of Arad made a surprise attack on Israel in the wilderness (Num. 21:1 ff.); the king is listed among those conquered (Josh. 12:14). The modern city is Tell 'Arad sixteen miles south of Hebron.

Arad (ā'răd) 1. A Benjaminite (1 Chr. 8:15). Chr. 7:39).

2. A man whose sons returned with Zerubbabel (Ezra 2:5; Neh. 7:10).

Aram (ā'răm) alternate name for Syria. 1. The fifth son of Shem (Gen. 10:22 f.).

2. A son of Kemuel, descendant of Nahor (Gen. 22:21).

3. An Asherite, son of Shamer (1 Chr. 7:34).

4. AV name for the son of Esrom or Hezrom (Ram in Mt. 1:3 f. and Arni in Lk. 3:33).

5. The name by which the Hebrews designated the country lying north and east of Palestine, the same as Syria, but often including much more: In Gen. 24:10 perhaps even Mesopotamia. (For Syria see Num. 23:7; 2 Sam. 8:5; 1 K. 20:20.) It is often used in compounds to designate parts of the area, as Aram-zobah (e.g., 2 Sam. 10:6). Though conquered by Israel and made a northern border, it became an independent rival of Israel (with Damascus) and later was taken by Assyria.

Aramaic (âr-á-mā'ĭc) a general designation for a group of Semitic dialects closely related to Hebrew. Attention is called to it in Gen. 31:47 by Laban's use of an Aramaic term in contrast to the Hebrew. From early times Aramaic was used in much official or governmental correspondence. So it is not strange that parts of the OT (e.g., Jer. 10:11; Dan. 2:4–7:28; Ezra 4:8–6:18, 7:12–26) are written in Aramaic. Scattered words (e.g., talitha cumi, Mk. 5:41; Maranatha, 1 Cor. 16:22) occur in the NT. Though it has been disputed, it is generally conceded that Hebrew was the native language of Palestine after the Conquest and that Jesus

and the disciples spoke it, though it is certain that they also knew Greek.

Aramitess (âr'à-mīt'ĕs) a woman of Aram (1 Chr. 7:14), otherwise a "Syrian."

Aram-naharaim [title of Ps. 60] alternatively "Mesopotamia." David warred against Aramnaharaim (cf. 1 Chr. 19:6). See **Aram**

Aran (ā'răn) a Horite, brother of Uz (Gen. 36:28).

Ararat (âr'à-răt) a mountainous district of Armenia, lying between the Black and Caspian seas and just north of the **Fertile Crescent.** In its center lies Lake Van, which like the Dead Sea has no outlet. From Ararat flow the Tigris and Euphrates rivers. Its tableland lies about 6000 feet in elevation, and above this rise mountains towering to 17,000 feet. The region is connected in the Bible (a) with the resting of Noah's ark after the flood "upon the mountains (plural) of Ararat" (Gen. 8:4), (b) with the flight of the sons of Sennacherib after they murdered their father (2 K. 19:37; Isa. 37:38), (c) with neighboring allies Minni and Ashchenaz (Jer. 51:27) as conquerors of Babylonia. The name by which the region was known in Babylonia was Urartu, a word undoubtedly cognate with the Heb. 'ararat.

Aratus (âr'à-tŭs) a Greek poet of Cilicia (fl. 270 B.C.) quoted but not named by Paul (Acts 17:28).

Araunah (à-rô'nà) a Jebusite who sold his threshing floor on Mount Moriah to David to erect an altar. (See 2 Sam. 24:18–24; 1 Chr. 21:25.) His name is sometimes written Ornan.

Arba (är'bà) progenitor of the sons of Anak, for whom the city Kirjath-arba (Hebron) was named (Gen. 35:27).

Arbathite (är'bà-thĭt) Abi-albon the Arbathite (dweller in the Arabah or Ghor), one of David's mighty men (2 Sam. 23:31).

Arbite (är'bĭt) a native of Arab, used (2 Sam. 23:35) of Paarai, one of David's guard.

Archelaus (är-kĕ-lā'ŭs) son of Herod the Great and successor, along with his brothers Antipas and Philip, to his father's territory. Archelaus received Idumaea, Samaria, and Judea, which he ruled from 4 B.C. until deposed by the Romans and banished to Gaul because of his brutal treatment of the Jews.

archery see **arms**

Archevites (är'kĕ-vĭts) the inhabitants of the city of **Erech** in Babylonia (Ezra 4:9).

Archi see **Archite** (Josh. 16:2)

Archippus (är-kĭp'ŭs) a Christian at Colosse, one of those to whom Paul addressed the Epistle to Philemon (vs. 2). He was also addressed in Colossians (4:17), being admonished to "fulfill the ministry which you have received." For an interesting hypothesis about his relation to Philemon and the church at Colosse, see John Knox, *Philemon Among the Letters of Paul* (rev. ed., 1959).

Archite (är'kīt) a Benjaminite clan near Bethel (Josh. 16:2). One member, **Hushai**, was a friend of David, aiding him in Absalom's rebellion (1 Chr. 27:33; 2 Sam. 15:32–17:23). (KJV form is Archi in Josh. 16:2.)

Arcturus (ärk-tōōr'ŭs) designation of a group of stars according to the LXX–Vulg.–KJV rendering in Job 9:9. The same original word is rendered by the LXX in Job 38:32 as "evening star." Several constellations have been proposed of which the "Great Bear" is thought to be correct by the majority of scholars.

Ard (árd) grandson (son in Gen. 46:21) of Benjamin and son of Bela (Num. 26:40). See **Addar**

Ardites descendants of **Ard** (Num. 26:40).

Ardon (är'dŏn) son of Caleb (1 Chr. 2:18).

Areli (à-rē'lī) son of Gad (Gen. 46:16; Num. 26:17).

Areopagite (ăr'ē-ŏp'à-gīt) member of court of the Areopagus or Mars' Hill (Acts 17:34).

Areopagus (ăr'ē-ŏp'à-gŭs) Greek word translated **Mars' Hill.** In the NT could refer to the court rather than the hill so called.

Aretas (ăr'ē-tăs) common appellation of many Arabian kings or chiefs; in NT of the father-in-law of Herod Antipas (see **Herod**) (2 Cor. 11:32). Aretas sought to arrest Paul.

Argob (är'gŏb) 1. A region east of the Jordan, in Bashan, the kingdom of Og, containing sixty great and fortified cities. It was allotted to Manasseh and taken by his son Jair (Deut. 3:4, 13–14; 1 K. 4:13). The exact location is uncertain, though it is sometimes identified with Trachonitis, or modern el-Leja, a curiously bounded region of basaltic rocks and boulders some twenty-two by fourteen miles in area.

2. A man listed with Arieh (2 K. 15:25 ff.) either as an accomplice of Pekah in the murder of Pekahiah or as a victim of the latter. Some interpret as a textual gloss to vs. 29 of the text, making it refer to Argob, the region of Transjordan.

Aridai (ăr'ī-dī) a son of Haman (Est. 9:9).

Aridatha (ăr'ī-dā'thà) a son of Haman (Est. 9:8).

Arieh (ăr'ī-ĕ) ally of Argob either as murderers or victims of Pekahiah. See **Argob** 2

Ariel (är'ī-ĕl) 1. A leader under Ezra of the returning exiles (Ezra 8:16).

2. The word occurs in 2 Sam. 23:20; 1 Chr. 11:22 where it means either "two lion-like men of Moab" (KJV) or "two sons of Ariel of Moab" (ASV). The RSV merely transliterates "two Ariels of Moab."

3. A poetic name given by Isaiah to the city of Jerusalem (Isa. 29:1, 2, 7); the usual suggestion "lion of God" as the meaning is uncertain.

Arimathea (ăr'ī-mà-thē'à) the city of Joseph, the secret disciple of Jesus who buried his body (Mt. 27:57; Lk. 23:51; Jn. 19:38). It is called by Luke "a city of the Jews (Judea)." The LXX (1 Sam. 1:1, 19) names the same city as the birthplace of Samuel Ramah. The city may then be the Ramathaim-zophim or Ramah in Ephraim, where Samuel lived, ten miles northeast of Lydda.

Arioch (ăr'ī-ŏk) 1. King of Ellasar, an ally of Chedorlaomer (Gen. 14:1).

2. A captain of Nebuchadnezzar's guard (Dan. 2:14–25).

Arisai (ăr'ī-sī) son of Haman (Est. 9:9).

Aristarchus (ăr'ĭs-tär'kŭs) a Thessalonian (Acts 20:4, 27:2) who accompanied Paul on his third missionary journey (19:29) and was with him on his return to Asia (20:4) as well as the voyage to Rome (27:2). The references to an Aristarchus in Col. 4:10 and Philemon 24 are probably to the same man. One so intimately associated with Paul must have been a valued fellow worker.

Aristobulus (ăr'ĭs-tŏ'bŭ-lŭs) a resident of Rome, some of whose household are greeted in Rom. 16:10.

Ark, Noah's see **Noah**

Arkites (är'kīts) one of the families descended from Canaan (Gen. 10:17; 1 Chr. 1:15). They are associated with the town of Arqa, northwest of Tripolis in Syria.

Ark of the Covenant [Ark represents Lat. *arca*, chest] the word so translated is used of a coffin (Gen. 50:26), but elsewhere it always represents the chest overshadowed with cherubim in the most holy place of the tabernacle and temple, in which were deposited the tables of the Law, the pot of manna, and Aaron's rod that budded (Heb. 9:4). The precise descriptions of the ark, which was some four feet long by two and one-fourth feet broad and deep, are given in Exodus 25. (For details of its movement and place within the temple, see Num. 4:5, 20, 7:9, 10:21; 1 K. 8:8.) The purpose of the ark may be deduced as: first, forming a repository for the divine autograph of the Ten Commandments; secondly, to symbolize God's presence in the most holy place of the tabernacle and exclude any idol from the center of worship; and thirdly, to support the mercy seat which provided a localization of the atoning grace of God, the mercy of God's forgiveness. The ark had a varied history. In the period of the judges its abode was frequently shifted (1 Sam. 7:1; 2 Sam. 6:3, 11; 1 Chr. 13:13, 15:24, 25). Finally it was brought to Jerusalem by David (2 Sam. 6; 1 Chr. 13, 15). It was taken into the temple by the priests (1 K. 8:3–9). No one knows what happened to the ark after the destruction of Solomon's temple. Later reconstructions seem to have had nothing in the most holy place.

Armageddon (är'mă-gĕd'ŏn) a term used in Rev. 16:16 and said to be Hebrew, designating the scene of the great battle between the forces of good and evil. It is a word of uncertain meaning, being understood by some to mean "mount of Megiddo" or "city of Megiddo," with reference to the area around the plain of Esdraelon, which was scene of many important battles in OT times (Judg. 4–5, 7; 1 Sam. 31:8; 2 K. 23:29, 30); and others (J. W. Bowman, vol. I of IDB) of Jerusalem, "his fruitful mountain." The imagery suggests the decisive victory.

Armenia (är-mē'nĭ-à) is nowhere mentioned under that name in the original Hebrew, though it occurs in the KJV of Isa. 37:38 (and 2 K. 19:37) for the region Mount Ararat. This is a lofty plateau whence the rivers Euphrates, Tigris, Araxes, and Acampsis arise. The country lies north of Assyria. Many OT passages (such as Ezek. 27:14, Togarmah) may refer to this region.

armlet a band worn either on the forearm or upper arm as an ornament and used widely in Biblical times. The word occurs in many passages (such as 2 Sam. 1:10; Ex. 35:22; Isa. 3:20), though the KJV usually uses "bracelet." Some of these ornaments, especially worn by princes, were of enormous weight (Gen. 24:22).

Armoni (är-mō'nī) son of Saul (2 Sam. 21:8).

armor, arms offensive or defensive weapons and protection for use in war. Chariots and machines are treated elsewhere, so only personal tools will be treated in this article. See also **army**

A. OFFENSIVE WEAPONS in Biblical times included:

1. *The Sword* (Gen. 27:40), which was lighter and shorter than the modern sword, Ehud's being only eighteen inches long (Judg. 3:16). David used that of the giant Goliath (1 Sam. 17:51, 21:9). It was sheathed (1 Sam. 17:51), slung by a girdle (1 Sam. 25:13), resting upon the thigh (Ps. 45:3) or the hips (2 Sam. 20:8). Two edges are referred to (Judg. 3:16; Ps. 149:6), and they were whetted (Deut. 32:41; Ps. 64:3). In Biblical times flint weapons might still have been in use (Josh. 5:2–3), though from archaeology it is known that copper, hardened by hammering, was known as material for weapons from very ancient times, and bronze (copper and tin) as early as the fifteenth century B.C.

2. *The Spear*, of which there were various kinds. A heavy spear [*chonith*], with a head of stone or metal mounted on a long wooden shaft (1 Sam. 17:7; Job 39:23); a light spear or javelin, carried on the back of soldiers for hurling at an enemy (1 Sam. 17:7, 26:7); and a lance or spear for thrusting [*romach*] (Num. 25:7–8; 2 Chr. 14:8).

3. *The Bow and Arrow*—the chief missile weapon. They are met with very early in both chase (Gen. 21:20) and war (48:22). Sometimes they were made of metal (2 Sam. 22:35; Job 20:24). For details, see 1 Sam. 20:20–22, 35–40.

4. *The Sling* (Judg. 20:16) is remembered as the weapon with which David killed Goliath (1 Sam. 17:40; cf. 2 K. 3:25).

5. *The Rod*—a stick or staff cut from a tree might be used as a weapon by a shepherd (Ps. 23:4) or a soldier (Ps. 2:9).

B. DEFENSIVE WEAPONS. Among these the most important were:

1. *The Breastplate*, usually as Goliath's, literally "a breastplate of scales" (1 Sam. 17:5).

2. *The Helmet*, made either of leather or metal (2 Chr. 26:14; 1 Sam. 17:5, 38; Ezek. 23:24, 27:10).

3. *The Greave*, foot and shin guard (mentioned in 1 Sam. 17:6).

4. *Shields* (bucklers or targets) were of two types: a large shield, encompassing the entire person (Ps. 5:12), and a smaller shield used in hand-to-hand fighting (see 1 K. 10:16, 17; 2 Chr. 9:15, 16).

The Roman armor of NT times consisted of much the same items, though often differing in type or material. In the NT, Paul (Eph. 6:10 ff.) describes the "whole armor." In Old and New Testaments both offensive and defensive weapons were often used as metaphors (Judg. 7:20; Eph. 6:17).

army 1. JEWISH. In the early Israelite army every man above twenty was a soldier (Num. 1:3); each tribe had its own regiment, banner, and leader with fixed position in camp or on march (Num. 2:2, 10:14), with the whole army moving at a given signal (Num. 10:5). In event of war the different units had officers who served as musterers and who appointed captains (Deut. 20:5, 9; 2 K. 25:19). The army was divided into thousands, hundreds, and families (Num. 2:34, 31:14; 2 Chr. 25:5).

With the kings arose the custom of maintaining a bodyguard, such as Saul's 3000 select warriors (1 Sam. 13:2) or David's 600 (1 Sam. 23:13, 25:13). David added foreign mercenary troops, the **Cherethites** and **Pelethites** (2 Sam. 8:18), and the **Gittites** (15:19–22). These troops won the day for him during Absalom's rebellion. David established a national militia of twelve regiments (1 Chr. 27:1), each to be called out for one month of the year; he also appointed a commander in chief (1 Sam. 14:50). Beginning with David, experiments were made with horses and chariots (cf. Deut. 17:16; 2 Sam. 8:4; 1 K. 10:26, 28, 29; 2 K. 8:21, 18:23; Isa. 31:1). In battle Israel's army was usually divided into three groups (Judg. 7:16, 9:43; 1 Sam. 11:11; 2 Sam. 18:2). Jehoshaphat added two more (2 Chr. 17:14–18). Equipment and provisions probably were furnished (1 K. 4:27, 10:16 f.; 2 Chr. 26:14), but there is no mention of pay except to mercenaries (2 Chr. 25:6).

2. ROMAN. The Roman army was divided into legions, each under six tribuni (chief captains, Acts 21:31), who commanded in turn; each legion contained ten cohorts (band, Acts 10:1); the cohorts, three maniples; and the maniples, two centuries (of 100 men each) commanded by a centurion (Mt. 8:5, 27:54; Acts 10:1, 22). Besides the legionary cohorts, there were voluntary independent cohorts (such as the Italian band, Acts 10:1, or the Augustan band, Acts 27:1). The headquarters of the Roman forces in Judea was Caesarea.

Arnan (är'năn) in the Hebrew (MT) the sons of Arnan are mentioned in the genealogy of Zerubbabel (1 Chr. 3:21). Other versions (LXX, Vulg., Syriac) read "his son, Arnan."

Arnon (är'nŏn) the river or torrent which flows through the tableland of East Jordan and flows through a deep gorge into the Dead Sea about midway of its eastern side. It formed the border between Moab and the Amorites on the north of Moab (Num. 21:13 ff.; Judg. 11:22) and later between Moab and the tribe of Reuben (Deut. 2:24; Judg. 11:13). The modern name is Wadi Mojib.

Arod (är'ŏd) son of Gad (Gen. 46:16; Num. 26:17).

Aroer (à-rō'ẽr) the name of several towns of Eastern and Western Palestine. 1. A city "by the brink" of the torrent Arnon, the southern point of the territory of Sihon and later of Reuben (Deut. 2:36; Josh. 12:2; 2 K. 10:33). Here David began his census (2 Sam. 24:5).

2. A town built by and belonging to Gad in Eastern Palestine "facing Rabbah (of Ammon)" (Num. 32:34; Josh. 13:25).

3. A town in Judah, named (in 1 Sam. 30:28) in connection with David's sharing of spoils.

Arpad or **Arphad** (är'păd) a city or district in Syria invariably named with Hamath and seemingly dependent on Damascus (2 K. 18:34; Isa. 36:19, 37:13; Jer. 49:23). Its destruction was so complete that it was proverbial.

Arphaxad (är-făk'săd) third son of Shem and ancestor of Eber in the genealogy of the Hebrews (Gen. 10:22, 24, 11:10). He lived 438 years. The Hebrew and some English versions spell Arpachshad.

arrows see **arms**

Artaxerxes (är-tág-zûrk'sēz) a name, or perhaps a title, worn by several monarchs of Persia. 1. Artaxerxes I, son of Xerxes I, known as Longimanus (465–425 B.C.). He authorized Ezra's mission to Jerusalem, 458 B.C. (Ezra 7:8, 11–26), as well as the two undertakings of Nehemiah (Neh. 2:1 ff., 13:6).

2. Artaxerxes halted the work of rebuilding Jerusalem (Ezra 4:7–23). Some claim that this was a usurper claiming to be Smerdis, deceased son of Cyrus, who took the title Artaxerxes and reigned a short time in 522 B.C. Others take him to be same as the preceding.

Artemas (är'tě-măs) a companion of Paul (Tit. 3:12). Paul expected to send him to Crete.

Artemis (är'tě-mĭs) the Greek goddess identified with the Roman Diana. A local goddess, a form of the Asian mother goddess, was worshiped under the name of "Artemis (or KJV, Diana) of the Ephesians" (Acts 19:23). Her temple was one of the seven wonders of the world.

Aruboth (à-rŭb'ŏth) one of Solomon's commissariat districts (1 K. 4:10), probably in Manasseh, not far from Samaria.

Arumah (à-rōō'mà) a place near Shechem, home of Abimelech (Judg. 9:41).

Arvad (är'văd) a city and state in Phoenicia, on an island, now called Ruad, some two to three miles off the coast, some distance above the mouth of the river Eleutherus. Its people are mentioned with Zidon as the navigators and defenders of Tyre (Ezek. 27:8, 11), and as the descendants of Canaan (Gen. 10:18; 1 Chr. 1:16).

Arza (är'zà) prefect of the palace at Tirzah to Elah king of Israel, who was assassinated by Zimri (1 K. 16:9).

Asa (ā'să) 1. Son of Abijah, grandson of Rehoboam, and third king of Judah. He is one of the four or five rulers of the Southern Kingdom who deserve to be called good kings. His zeal against idolatry is seen in his deposing

Maachah, his grandmother, from her place of influence (1 K. 15:13) and replacing the dedicated vessels in the temple (1 K. 15:15). He carried on a successful war with Baasha king of Israel (1 K. 15:16 ff.), making an alliance with Ben-hadad king of Syria (for which he was rebuked by the prophet Hanani, 2 Chr. 16:7–10). He repelled an invasion of Zerah the Ethiopian (2 Chr. 14:9–15). In his old age he was stricken with gout. He died after a reign of forty-one years in great honor (2 Chr. 16:13–14).

2. A Levite (1 Chr. 9:16).

Asadias KJV form of **Hasadiah** (1 Chr. 3:20).

Asahel (ăs′à-hĕl) 1. Nephew of David, the youngest son of his sister Zeruiah, celebrated for his swiftness of foot. At Gibeon he pursued Abner, who warned him to desist and was obliged to kill him in self-defense.

2. A Levite, an itinerant teacher who instructed the people of Judah at the time of the revival of true worship (2 Chr. 17:8).

3. A Levite under Hezekiah who had charge of the tithes (2 Chr. 31:13).

4. A priest in the time of Ezra (10:15).

Asahiah (ăs′à-hī-à) a servant sent by Josiah to inquire of the Lord about the book of the Law found by Hilkiah (2 K. 22:12, 14). Also called Asaiah (2 Chr. 34:20).

Asaiah (à-zā′yà) 1. Same as Asahiah above (2 Chr. 34:20).

2. Prince of Simeon who drove the Hamites from Gedor (1 Chr. 4:36).

3. A Levite who helped David bring the ark to Jerusalem (1 Chr. 15:6, 11).

4. The firstborn of the "Shilonites who returned from Babylon and lived at Jerusalem" (1 Chr. 9:5). Also called **Maaseiah** (Neh. 11:5).

Asaph (ā′săf) 1. A Levite, son of Berechiah, one of the leaders of David's choir (1 Chr. 6:39) to whom a number of Psalms are attributed (50, 73–83), celebrated later as a seer and composer (2 Chr. 29:30; Neh. 12:46). He seems to have been the founder of a guild or group of poets and composers (1 Chr. 25:1; 2 Chr. 20:14; Ezra 2:41).

2. The father or ancestor of Joah, recorder of Hezekiah (2 K. 18:18, 37; Isa. 36:3, 22). He could be the same as the above.

3. Keeper of the royal forest of Artaxerxes (Neh. 2:8).

Asareel (à-săr′ĭ-ĕl) or **Asarel** (ăs′à-rĕl) son of Jehaleleel in the genealogy of Judah (1 Chr. 4:16).

Asarelah (ăs′à-rē′là) or **Asharelah** (ăsh′à-rē′là) one of the sons of Asaph (1 Chr. 25:2).

Ascalon see **Ashkelon**

ascension the ascension of the Christ was predicted by OT messianic prophecies (Ps. 68:18; cf. Eph. 4:8). Jesus himself, according to John 16:7, foretold it, saying it was necessary to the sending of the Holy Spirit (see also Jn. 20:17). The ascension was witnessed by the apostles who testified to it as an act of history (Lk. 24:50–52; Acts 1:11). His enthronement was a vital part of the early preaching of the Gospel (Acts 2:32–35).

Asenath (ăs′ĕn-ăth) daughter of Potipherah priest of On, wife of Joseph (Gen. 41:45), and mother of Manasseh and Ephraim (41:50, 46:20).

Aser form of **Asher** (Lk. 2:36; Rev. 7:6).

ash a tree occurring only once (Isa. 44:14). The Heb. *oren* is understood as a pine tree (Vulg.), while a few MSS have "cedar." It is uncertain what tree is meant.

Ashan (ā′shăn) a city in the Shephelah region of Judah, assigned to Simeon (Josh. 15:42, 19:7; 1 Chr. 4:32) and later mentioned as a priestly city (1 Chr. 6:59). Now identified with Khirbet 'Asan, one and one-half miles northwest of Beer-sheba.

Ashbea (ăsh′bē-à) a proper name of either a place or a person (1 Chr. 4:21) connected with a family of linen workers.

Ashbel (ăsh′bĕl) second son of Benjamin and father of the Ashbelites (Gen. 46:21; Num. 26:38).

Ashchenaz (1 Chr. 1:6; Jer. 51:27) see **Ashkenaz**

Ashdod (ăsh′dŏd) [NT form Azotus, Acts 8:40] one of the five confederate cities (Josh. 13:3) of the Philistines, about thirty miles from the southern frontier of Palestine, three from the Mediterranean Sea, and nearly midway between Gaza and Joppa. It was assigned to Judah (Josh. 15:46 f.) but never taken, preserving its identity to Nehemiah's time (Neh. 13:23 f.) though once taken by Uzziah king of Judah (1 Chr. 26:6). There are numerous and interesting OT references (see, for example, Judg. 1:19; 1 Sam. 5:1–7; Isa. 20:1; Jer. 25:15 ff.; Amos 1:8; Zeph. 2:4; Zech. 9:6). The city was destroyed by the Maccabees (1 Macc. 5:68, 10:84) and restored by Gabinius (55 B.C.). Philip the evangelist was found here after preaching to the Ethiopian eunuch (Acts 8:40).

Ashdoth-pisgah (ăsh′dŏth-pĭz′gà) [the slopes (AV, springs) of Pisgah (Deut. 3:17, 4:49; Josh. 12:3; 13:20)] a reference to the slopes of Mount Pisgah, overlooking the Jordan.

Asher (ăsh′ẽr) or **Aser** (ā′sẽr) [NT Asẽr] 1. The eighth son of Jacob, by Zilpah, Leah's handmaid (Gen. 30:13). He was born while

Jacob was still with Laban. He had five sons (named in Gen. 46:17). In the census at Sinai (Num. 1:32 f.), Asher was more numerous than Ephraim, Manasseh, or Benjamin. Its allotted territory was on the seashore from Mount Carmel northward, with Manasseh on the south, Zebulun and Issachar on the southeast, and Naphtali on the northeast. It thus lay next to the Phoenicians. The tribe declined in importance so that its name was omitted from the list of chief rulers (1 Chr. 27:16–22). In the NT, Asher is named after Gad (Rev. 7:6). The prophetess Anna whose service at the temple is recognized at the Lord's presentation (Lk. 2:36) was from Asher.

2. A city on the southern border of Manasseh (Josh. 17:7).

Asherah (à-shē′rà) the Hebrew name of a Phoenician and Syrian goddess and the cult objects or images by which she was worshiped. (The KJV and Vulg. wrongly translate "groves," following the LXX where the word *alsos* is probably to be interpreted as a sacred place where she was worshiped.) She was associated with Baal (Judg. 3:7; 1 K. 16:29 ff.) as consort in a fertility religion with a mythology. Israelites stooped to her worship under the influence of such persons as Jezebel (1 K. 18:19).

ashes the substance remaining after the burning of materials, often especially of sacrifices, in connection with which there were ceremonies for disposal. The ashes of a red heifer burnt entire were used in purification (Num. 19). They were often used with **dust** and **sackcloth** to indicate mourning and humiliation (Jer. 6:26; Job 2:8). Used as a metaphor, ashes may refer to man's bodily elements (Gen. 18:27), destruction (Mal. 4:3), and something worthless or unworthy (Job 13:12).

Ashima (à-shī′mà) a god whose worship was introduced into Samaria by the Hamathite colonists (2 K. 17:30).

Ashkelon, Askelon, Ascalon (ăsh′kĕ-lŏn, ăs′kĕ-lŏn) one of the five cities of the lords of the Philistines (Josh. 13:3; 1 Sam. 6:17), a seacoast town about twelve miles north of Gaza. Samson went there as if to a remote place (Judg. 14:19). Other references are found in the historical books (in Josh. 13:3; 1 Sam. 6:17). Casual mention is made of it (2 Sam. 1:20; Jer. 25:20, 47:5, 7; Amos 1:8; Zeph. 2:4, 7; and Zech. 9:5), usually by way of denunciation. The town became more prominent in the era of the Maccabees and in the time of the Crusades.

Ashkenas or **Askenaz** (ăsh′kĕ-năz) one of the three sons of Gomer, son of Japhet (Gen. 10:3), and thus one of the three great divisions of the Japhetic races. They are mentioned by Jeremiah (51:27) in connection with the kingdoms of Ararat and Minni.

Ashnah (ăsh′nà) the name of two cities, both in the lowlands of Judah (Josh. 15:33, 43).

Ashpenaz (ăsh′pĕ-năz) the master of the eunuchs of Nebuchadnezzar (Dan. 1:3).

Ashtaroth or **Astaroth** (ăsh′tà-rŏth) a city on the east of Jordan, in Bashan the kingdom of Og. Probably so called from its being the seat of worship of the goddess of the same name. It was associated with Edrei (Deut. 1:4; Josh. 12:4), was settled by Machir (Josh. 13:12, 31), and became one of the cities of refuge (Josh. 21:27; 1 Chr. 6:71).

Ashtaroth see **Ashtoreth**

Ashterathite a native of Ashtaroth (1 Chr. 11:44).

Ashteroth-karnaim (ăsh′tĕ-rŏth-kàr-nā′ĭm) a place of great antiquity, the abode of the Rephaim at the time of the invasion of Chedorlaomer (Gen. 14:5), who took it. It was according to later identification located in Galaad (2 Macc. 12:21, 26).

Ashtoreth (ăsh′tō-rĕth) the principal female deity of the Canaanites. The plural form (Judg. 10:13; 1 Sam. 7:3 f.) is **Ashtaroth,** which usually refers to the images or idols of the goddess. The name is spelled Ashtarath in the local texts; the Greek spelling is Astarte. Her Assyrian counterpart was Ishtar. She was connected with Baal in the fertility cult (Judg. 2:13; 1 K. 11:5; 2 K. 23:13). The name was at times connected with places where her worship was localized.

Ashur or **Ashhur** (ăsh′ĕr) the posthumous son of Hezron, the founder of the town of Tekoa (1 Chr. 2:24, 4:5).

Ashurites (ăsh′ĕr-īts) a name occurring only in the enumeration of those over whom Ishbosheth was made king (2 Sam. 2:9). Some versions read Geshurites (cf. Josh. 12:5). The Targum connects it with Asher. The text locates it between Gilead and Jezreel.

Ashvath (ăsh′văth) one of the sons of Japhlet, of the tribe of Asher (1 Chr. 7:33).

Asia a section of the continent of Asia which, usually in the NT (possible exceptions are Acts 2:9, 19:10), meant the Roman province at the western tip of Asia Minor which had earlier been called Lydia, Mysia, and Caria. The territory was organized as a Roman province, after being willed to Rome by King Attalus III in 133 B.C. The first capital was Pergamum and later Ephesus. It was a senatorial province governed by a proconsul and considered one of the richest provinces. Various religious cults existed such as that of Artemis (Diana) at

Ephesus, the Great Mother (at various places), and Asclepius at Pergamum. The province gained the distinction of first asking permission to worship the emperor (Augustus), the request being granted in 29 B.C. The area is interesting for NT study largely because of Paul's activity there (Acts 16:6–8, 18:19–21, 19:1–20:1, three years; cf. Acts 20:4–38) and the fact that the seven cities to which Revelation was written were located there (Rev. 1:11).

Asiarch (ā'zhǐ-ârk) [chief of Asia, Acts 19:31] officers chosen annually by the cities of the Asian League, of which Ephesus was a part, who had charge of public games and religious theatrical spectacles, the expenses of which they bore. The annual office was subject to the approval of the proconsul; it might be renewed, and the title might continue with the office holder after his term of office. The men were rich, Roman, and honorable. Luke's point in detailing their siding with Paul in Acts 19 was probably to show that Paul had such men on his side. The office is mentioned also in Strabo 14.1.42 and *Martyrdom of Polycarp* 12.2.

Asiel (ăs'ĭ-ĕl) a Simeonite and ancestor of Jehu in Hezekiah's time (1 Chr. 4:35).

Askelon see **Ashkelon**

Asnah (ăs'nà) head of a family who returned with Zerubbabel (Ezra 2:20).

Asnapper (ăs-năp'ĕr) or **Osnappar** mentioned in Ezra 4:10 as "the great and noble" Asnapper. He was in charge of settling people in Samaria. He was probably a general of the Assyrian conquerors.

asp [Heb. *pethen*] the English "asp" refers to any of a number of poisonous snakes, especially the cobra, the viper, or adder. All these terms have been used to translate the original. The Hebrew mentions the reptile in six passages (Deut. 32:33; Job 20:14, 16; Ps. 58:5, 91:13; Isa. 11:8; Rom. 3:13). It is not clear what snake is meant. It is mentioned in these passages in connection with the snake charmer and as living in holes in the wall. From this many think that the Egyptian cobra is meant. Asp is used in these passages figuratively to picture cruelty (Deut. 32:33), food becoming the "gall of asps" (Job 20:14), the venomous tongue of the wicked (Rom. 3:13). In the new age the child will play unharmed on the hole of the asp (Isa. 11:8).

Aspatha (ăs-pā'thà) third of the ten sons of the Jews' enemy Haman (Est. 9:7).

Asriel (ăs'rǐ-ĕl) or **Ashriel** 1. Son of Gilead, and great-grandson of Manasseh (Num. 26:31; Josh. 17:2), whence the Asrielites.

2. A son of Manasseh by his Syrian concubine (1 Chr. 7:14).

Asrielites see **Asriel**

ass an animal which, along with the horse and zebra, constitutes the horse family. The ass or donkey is very frequently mentioned in the Bible. Five different Hebrew words occur in OT of this genus (*Asinus*): *hamor* (the male domestic ass, though also used generically); *athon* (the common domestic she-ass, 2 K. 4:22–24); *'ayir* (the young ass as in Gen. 32:16); *pere*, (a species of wild ass of Gen. 16:12); and *'arodh* (another name for the wild ass in Job 34:5). Asses in the wild state were common in the deserts of Syria, Mesopotamia, and Northern Arabia. They were noted for their swiftness. They were domesticated very early and widely used as beasts of burden (Gen. 42:26), for plowing (Lev. 19:19), for riding (Num. 22:21). A man's wealth might be counted by the number of asses he owned (Gen. 12; Job 1:3). Food laws forbade the eating of the ass as unclean (Lev. 11:1–8). The Law regulated use of the animal (Deut. 5:14; Lk. 13:15, 14:5). God used a lowly ass to rebuke the prophet Balaam (Num. 22–24; 2 Pet. 2:16). As horses were used in war, Jesus' riding on an ass as he entered Jerusalem probably was intended to show the peaceable nature of his kingdom (Mt. 21:2).

assassins [Gr. *sikarioi*, a loan word from Lat. *sicarii*, dagger men] the term used by the Romans to designate the Jewish bands who engaged in organized murder for political purposes. Such became common in the period of intrigue before A.D. 70. They are mentioned in Acts 21:38 by the captain who thought that Paul must have been one of them to be the object of such Jewish hatred as befell him.

assembly equivalent of congregation, synagogue, or church.

Asshur (ăsh'ûr) or **Assur** (ăs'ûr) or **Assyria** 1. A son of Shem, whence the Assyrians (Gen. 10:22; 1 Chr. 1:17).

2. The principal god of the Assyrians, the name appearing in proper names such as Esarhaddon.

3. A city in Assyria and at times its capital. The city may be mentioned in Ezek. 27:23 (an alternate reading is "Aram"). In Balaam's oracle (Num. 24), the word probably refers to the nation or country.

Asshurim (ăsh'ûr-ĭm) a tribe descended from Dedan, the grandson of Abraham and Keturah (Gen. 25:3), of uncertain identification. Not the same as the Assyrians.

Assir (ăs'ĕr) 1. One of the sons of Korah (Ex. 6:24; 1 Chr. 6:22).

2. Son of Ebiasaph, a forefather of Samuel (1 Chr. 6:23, 37).

3. Son of Jeconiah (1 Chr. 3:17), unless "Jeconiah the captive" is the true reading (RSV).

Assos (ăs'ŏs) a seaport of the district of Mysia in Asia, south of Troas and connected with it by a Roman road. From Troas Paul on the third missionary tour sent his companions by boat around the point of land (Cape Lectum) while he went by land to Assos, arriving before the boat (Acts 20:13–14).

Assuppim (á-sŭp'ĭm), **House of** (1 Chr. 26:15, 17) [literally house of the gatherings, a word left untranslated in the KJV but correctly rendered as storehouse (of the temple)]. See Neh. 12:25 also.

Assur (ăs'ûr) spelling in Ezra 4:2; Ps. 83:8 for **Asshur** or **Assyria.**

Assyria, Asshur a great and powerful country lying on the Tigris River in Upper Mesopotamia and Lower Armenia. Its capital was at Asshur and later at Nineveh (Gen. 10:11). The Assyrian empire is important for OT study because it threatened conquest to the monarchies of Judah and Israel during much of the period of the Divided Kingdom and did, in fact, reduce the Northern Kingdom to captivity in 722 B.C.

First mention of the Assyrians is (in Gen. 2:14) in connection with the location of the Euphrates River (Hiddekel) as one of those flowing from Eden. The Assyrian people are derived from Asshur son of Shem (Gen. 10:22). Early history of the Assyrian region is allied with the empire of Ur III up to its collapse about the end of the third millennium B.C. Assyrians made themselves felt largely through their commercial activities to the west. Semitic conquerors (Assyrians) took over the country and created an empire (Shamshi-Adad I, ca. 1812 B.C.), but for the next several hundred years this empire took second place to that, first, of the Babylonian Hammurabi dynasty and then to the Hittites (after 1600 B.C.). Finally Assyria began to rise as a power (ca. 1100 B.C.). Threatened by the Aramean kingdom of Zobah, they were helped by David's defeat of that nation (2 Sam. 3–8). Under Shalmaneser III (859–824) Assyria threatened Palestine, and, though defeated at Karkar in Syria, he claimed victory over Damascus and her king Ben-hadad. In this battle (according to the king's Monolith Inscription) Ahab king of Israel, sent 10,000 foot soldiers and 2000 chariots (853 B.C.). Under Jehu the alliance was weakened and Israel was made to pay tribute. Nearly a century later a successor, Tiglath-

pileser III (called Pul, 2 K. 15:19–20, 29, 16:9), again was successful in exacting tribute. Shalmaneser V (727–22) besieged Samaria at the rebellion of Hosea, and his brother Sargon III completed the conquest of Israel and took many of its people into exile, populating Israel with Assyrians (2 K. 17). The Assyrian kingdom lasted still another hundred years. Another king, Sennacherib, was prevented from capturing Jerusalem by the great slaughter of his army by the angel of the Lord (2 K. 18–19; Isa. 36, 37). Nineveh and Assyria fell to Nebuchadnezzar and the Babylonians in 612 B.C.

Astaroth (Deut. 1:4) spelling for **Ashtaroth.**

Astarte (ăs-tär'tĭ) the Greek spelling of the name of the goddess **Ashtoreth.**

astrologer one who seeks to discern the future by the variations and conjunctions of the heavenly bodies. The original word is variously translated in our versions by "conjurer, necromancer," "enchanter," "soothsayer," "stargazer," or "astrologer." The activity of such people led to the pseudo-science Astrology, but it was forbidden to the people of God and ridiculed by the prophets (Isa. 47:13; Jer. 10:2; Dan. 2:27, 4:7).

Astronomy see **Star**

Asyncritus (á-sĭng'krĭ-tŭs) a Christian at Rome, saluted by Paul (Rom. 16:14).

Atad (ā'tăd), **the threshing floor of** a spot beyond (east of) the Jordan where Joseph and his brethren mourned seven days over the body of Jacob (Gen. 50:10–11). The Canaanites called it **Abel-mizraim.**

Atarah (ăt'á-rá) wife of Jerahmeel (1 Chr. 2:26).

Ataroth (ăt'á-rŏth) a place name meaning "crown." 1. A town in Gad (Num. 32:3, 34), requested for possession by Reuben and Gad, east of Jordan about ten miles from the Dead Sea. It is mentioned in the Mesha Inscription.

2. A border town of Ephraim (Josh. 16:7) east of Jordan, located by N. Glueck as Tell el-Mazar.

3. Town on the border of Benjamin and Ephraim (West). Same as **Ataroth-addar** (Josh. 16:2, 5, 18:13).

4. Town near Bethlehem: **Atroth-beth-joab** [KJV, "Atroth, the house of Joab"].

Ater (ā'têr) 1. Ancestor of an exile family who returned with Zerubbabel (Ezra 2:42). They were porters or gatekeepers.

2. The children of Ater of Hezekiah returned with Zerubbabel (Ezra 2:16; Neh. 7:21). They were among the heads of families who signed the covenant with Nehemiah (10:17).

Athach (ā'thăk) a place in Judah in the Shephelah frequented by David and his men (1 Sam. 30:30). The name may represent a scribal error in the text for Ether.

Athaiah (à-thā'yà) a descendant of Pharez, son of Judah, living at Jerusalem after the Exile (Neh. 11:4). Also called Uthai (1 Chr. 9:4).

Athaliah (ăth'à-lī'à) 1. Daughter of Ahab and Jezebel, wife of King Jehoram of Judah, and mother of Ahaziah. She usurped the throne and reigned six years over the kingdom of Judah and introduced the worship of Baal into this region. To seize the throne she killed all the members of the royal family who had escaped the sword of the northern king Jehu (2 K. 11:1) except the infant Joash, who was secluded by his aunt Jehosheba, the wife of Jehoiada (2 Chr. 22:11) the high priest (2 Chr. 24:6). Later the boy was revealed by Jehoiada and anointed king. The people rallied to the lad and Athaliah was put to death when she sought to prevent the deed (2 K. 11). Athaliah represents the only interruption of the dynasty of David in the Southern Kingdom.

2. A Benjaminite of Jerusalem (1 Chr. 8:26).

3. A returned exile, one of the sons of Elam (Ezra 8:7).

Athenians natives of **Athens** (Acts 17:21).

Athens (ăth'ĕnz) the capital and chief city of the Greek province of Attica, the chief seat of Greek learning and civilization. The city was named after the goddess Athena. Paul visited Athens on the trip from Macedonia (second missionary tour) and stayed some time (Acts 17:14-34; cf. 1 Thess. 3:1), during which he delivered his famous sermon at Mars' Hill. Before this he had disputed daily in the Agora or market place. Paul found the inhabitants very inquisitive, especially the members of the philosophical sects of the Epicureans and Stoics (an attitude confirmed by Demosthenes). Paul made note of the religious nature of the city with its many gods or idols. This, too, is attested by Pausanias, who said that Athens surpassed all other peoples in the attention paid to the gods. It is interesting that Paul adapted his sermon to the thought and beliefs of this audience. The response to Paul at Athens was slight (Acts 17:32-34). From there he went to Corinth.

Athlai (ăth'là-ī) a man in Ezra's day who divorced his foreign wife (Ezra 10:28).

Atroth (ăt'rŏth) KJV separates Atroth from Shophan (Num. 32:35), but they should probably be taken as one place.

Atroth-shophan a city built by the tribe of Gad in a region taken from Sihon (Num. 32:35).

Attai (ăt'à-ī) 1. Son of Jarha, an Egyptian slave, and Ahlai the daughter of Sheshan (1 Chr. 2:35, 36), grandfather of Zabad, David's man (1 Chr. 11:41).

2. A bold warrior captain of Gad who joined David in the wilderness (1 Chr. 12:11).

3. Son of Rehoboam by Maachah the daughter of Absalom (2 Chr. 11:20).

Attalia (ăt'à-lī'à) a coastal town of Pamphylia in Southern Asia Minor from which Paul and Barnabas sailed to return to Antioch from the first missionary journey (Acts 14:25). The city was founded by and named for Attalus II of Pergamum (159-38 B.C.).

Augustus' Band a reference to Augustus' army (Acts 27:1).

Augustus Caesar (à-gŭs'tŭs sē'zêr) the first Roman emperor, during whose reign Christ was born (Lk. 2:1-7). Born in 63 B.C., he was the son of Gaius Octavius and Atia, daughter of Julia, the sister of Julius Caesar and hence a great-nephew of Julius, who educated him and made him his heir. After the murder of Caesar (44 B.C.) he was taken into the triumvirate with Antony and Lepidus. In the civil war which followed victory came to Augustus in the battle of Actium (31 B.C.). He was then saluted as Imperator by the senate and the title Augustus was conferred on him (27 B.C.). He became a friend of Herod the Great and divided the latter's dominions at his death (4 B.C.) according to his wishes among his sons, thus affecting NT history. Augustus died at Nola in Campania in A.D. 14, but he had previously taken Tiberius as co-regent.

Ava (ā'và) a place in the empire of Assyria from which people were brought to Samaria (2 K. 17:24).

Aven (ā'vĕn) 1. A mispronunciation, perhaps intentional to show disdain, of the Egyptian city of On (the city of the Sun, as the LXX has it) in Ezek. 30:17.

2. Beth-aven is Hosea's contemptuous name for the place names of Canaanite gods. Thus instead of Bethel, Beth-aven was used (Josh. 7:2, 18:12; 1 Sam. 13:5).

3. A place possibly in Syria (Amos 1:5).

avenger (of blood) the nearest of kin to a slain man whose duty it was to enforce the law of "life for life" (Num. 35:11-34).

Avim, Avims, or **Avites** (ā'vĭm, ā'vĭmz, ā'vīts) 1. A people among the early inhabitants of Palestine who lived around Gaza on the Philistine plain. Their history is told in Deut. 2:23 (displaced by the Caphtorim). In Joshua's time they remained (Josh. 13:3).

2. A city in the tribe of Benjamin (Josh. 18:23).

Avith (ā'vĭth) the city of Hadad ben-Bedad,

one of the kings of Edom before there were kings in Israel (Gen. 36:35; 1 Chr. 1:46).

awl an instrument used to pierce the ear lobe in connection with a vow of perpetual slavery (Ex. 21:6; Deut. 15:7). Many examples are now available from excavations. They were made of wood, bone, flint, or metal.

ax the common tool used for such work as cutting wood (Deut. 20:19), hewing stones (Ex. 20:25), tunneling (2 K. 20:20), and fighting. Some seven Hebrew words in addition to the Greek are represented by the English term.

Axal an obscure term (occurring only in Zech. 14:5) and considered by the KJV as a place, the limit to which the Mount of Olives will ultimately extend. The RSV following Symmachus reads "shall touch *the side* of it."

Azaliah (ăz'á-lī'á) the father of Shaphan the scribe (2 K. 22:3; 2 Chr. 34:8).

Azaniah (ăz'á-nī'á) father of Jeshua, the Levite who signed the covenant (Neh. 10:9).

Azarael or **Azareel** (á-zā'rē-ĕl) 1. A Korahite who joined David at his retreat at Ziklag (1 Chr. 12:6).

2. A Levite musician of David's time (1 Chr. 25:18).

3. Son of Jeroham, a prince of Dan, when David numbered Israel (1 Chr. 27:22).

4. Son of Bani who put away his foreign wife (Ezra 10:41).

5. A priest of Jerusalem after the exile (Neh. 11:13).

6. A Levite musician (Neh. 12:36).

Azariah (ăz'á-rī'ă) a common Hebrew name, appearing especially in the priestly family of Eleazar, whose name means the same. 1. The tenth king of Judah, more frequently called **Uzziah** (2 K. 14:21, 15:1–27; 1 Chr. 3:12).

2. A chief officer of Solomon, son of Nathan (1 K. 4:5).

3. Son of Ethan the wise (1 Chr. 2:8).

4. Son of Jehu, a Jerahmeelite, descended from an Egyptian slave of Sheshan (1 Chr. 2:38 f.).

5. Son of Johanan, high priest probably during days of Abijah and Asa (1 Chr. 6:10).

6. Son of Hilkiah, high priest near the time of the exile (1 Chr. 6:13–14).

7. Ancestor of Samuel (1 Chr. 6:36).

8. A prophet, son of Oded, in Asa's reign (2 Chr. 15:1).

9 and 10. Two sons of Jehoshaphat king of Judah (2 Chr. 21:2).

11. Son of Jehoram, perhaps a clerical error for Ahaziah (1 Chr. 22:6 cf. vs. 1).

12. A captain of Judah (2 Chr. 23:1).

13. High priest in the reign of Uzziah, often also called Azariah (2 K. 14:21, 15:1 ff.). See the interesting event of his withstanding the king (2 Chr. 26:17–20).

14. An Ephraimite captain of Ahaz (2 Chr. 28:12).

15. Father of Joel in time of Hezekiah (2 Chr. 29:12).

16. A Levite of Hezekiah's reign (2 Chr. 29:12).

17. High priest in the time of Hezekiah (2 Chr. 31:10, 13).

18. Man who helped Nehemiah repair wall (Neh. 3:23 f.).

19. A leader returning with Zerubbabel (Neh. 7:7).

20. A Levite who helped Ezra instruct the people (Neh. 8:7).

21. A priest who sealed the covenant with Nehemiah (Neh. 10:2), probably same as 18.

22. (Jer. 43:2). See **Jezaniah**

23. Original name of Abed-nego (Dan. 1:6 ff.).

24. The successor of Zadok in Solomon's temple (1 K. 4:2; 1 Chr. 6:9 f.).

Azaz (ā'zăz) a Reubenite, father of Bela (1 Chr. 5:8).

Azaziah (ăz'á-zī'á) 1. A Levite musician who played while the ark was being moved (1 Chr. 15:21).

2. A prince of Ephraim when David numbered the people (1 Chr. 27:20).

3. A Levite in the reign of Hezekiah who supervised tithes (2 Chr. 31:13).

Azbuk (ăz'bŭk) ancestor of Nehemiah (Neh. 3:16).

Azekah (ăz'ē-káh) a town of Judah in the Shephelah, near Shochoh (1 Sam. 17:1). It was the extent of Joshua's pursuit in battle of Beth-horon (Josh. 10:10), near Philistines' camp before David killed Goliath (1 Sam. 17:1), was fortified by Rehoboam (2 Chr. 11:9), and remained until the time of Babylonia's invasion (Jer. 34:7) and the return (Neh. 11:30).

Azel (ā'zĕl) a descendant of Saul (1 Chr. 8:37).

Azem (ā'zĕm) a city (Ezem in some versions) in South Judah (Josh. 15:29, 19:3).

Azgad (ăz'găd) a man whose numerous descendants accompanied Zerubbabel from the Exile. He joined in signing the covenant (Ezra 2:12, 8:12; Neh. 10:15).

Aziel (ā'zĭ-ĕl) or **Jaaziel** a Levite harper (1 Chr. 15:20).

Aziza (á-zī'zá) a man forced to divorce his foreign wife (Ezra 10:27).

Azmaveth (ăz-mā'věth) 1. One of David's mighty men (2 Sam. 23:31).
2. A descendant of Mephibosheth (1 Chr. 8:36, 9:42).
3. The father of Jeziel and Pelet, two skilled Benjaminite warriors (1 Chr. 12:3).
4. David's treasurer (1 Chr. 27:25).
5. A place evidently in Benjamin. People from there returned from the Exile (Ezra 2:24; Neh. 12:29).
Azmon (ăz'mŏn) a town on extreme south of Judah near the river of Egypt (Num. 34:4–5; Josh. 15:4).
Aznoth-tabor (ăz'nŏth-tā'bôr) a landmark on the border of Naphtali (Josh. 19:34).
Azor (ā'zôr) an ancestor of Jesus (Mt. 1:13).
Azotus see **Ashdod**
Azriel (ăz'rĭ-ĕl) 1. Head of a house in Manasseh (West), a man of renown (1 Chr. 5:24).
2. Head of Naphtalites in David's time (1 Chr. 27:19).

3. The father of Seraiah, an officer of Jehoiakim (Jer. 36:26).
Azrikam (ăz'rĭ-kăm) 1. Descendant of Zerubbabel in the royal line of Judah (1 Chr. 3:23).
2. A descendant of Saul (1 Chr. 8:38).
3. A Levite living in Nehemiah's time (1 Chr. 9:14).
4. Governor of the palace under King Ahaz, slain by Zichri (2 Chr. 28:7).
Azubah (à-zū'bà) 1. Wife of Caleb (1 Chr. 2:18).
2. Mother of King Jehoshaphat (1 K. 22:42).
Azur or properly **Azzur**
Azzah (ăz'zăh) form of the name of city of Gaza (Deut. 2:23; 1 K. 4:24).
Azzan (ăz'ăn) a prince of Issachar representing his tribe in dividing of Canaan (Num. 34:26).
Azzur or **Azur** (ăz'êr) one of the heads of the people who signed the covenant with Nehemiah (Neh. 10:17).

B

Baal (bā'ĕl, bāl) [the god] in particular, Baal refers to the old Semitic storm or rain god, the fertility god of the Canaanite peoples, who was a chief contender with Jehovah for the worship of Israel. 1. MEANING OF THE TERM. *Baal* means "owner" or "master" and may refer to men (Ex. 21:3, 28; Hos. 2:16) or places, as well as to deities. Of the latter it probably signifies that a particular deity has become dominant in a certain locality. Different gods were called the Baal of different regions. But the Canaanite god, now known well from the excavations at Ras Shamra in Northern Syria (excavated from 1929 by the French under C. F. A. Shaeffer), is the god meant in this region and is referred to as Baal in the OT.
2. BAAL'S WORSHIP. Baal was one of a pantheon of Canaanite gods, a son of Dagon, and younger than El, who was king and father of almost every other god. In the mythology El was challenged to deliver Baal into the hands of the Sea Prince, but Baal resisted and destroyed the Sea Prince. Both El and Baal are pictured with the Bull, whose horns are worn on their helmet, as a sign of fertility. Baal's wife is Anath, and he lives with her in the open fields. Here he must contend with Mot,

the god of sterility, the cause of drouth and dry season. In regular sequence Baal is defeated and goes underground. Anath, however, attacks Mot, hacks and grinds him up and scatters him on the fields. Baal returns and enters his throne on Mount Sapan. Worship rites were orgiastic and sensual (1 K. 14:23 f.).
3. ISRAEL AND BAAL. Baal's altars were present in Israel in the time of the judges Othniel (Judg. 2:13) and Gideon (6:28–32). Ahab married Jezebel, a heathen, and under sponsorship Baal almost supplanted Jehovah in Israel climaxing in the contest on Mount Carmel (1 K. 16:32, 18:17 ff.). Jehu opposed Baal (2 K. 10:18–28), but he was revived by Athaliah (2 Chr. 17:3, etc.). At her death the god's temple was destroyed (2 K. 11:18). Josiah (2 K. 23:4 f.) countered the false god once more. At times Jehovah was referred to by the term Baal, and probably some rites and formulas out of the background of the culture were used in ascribing to him reverence recognized as belonging to the supreme being. Under the great influence of the prophets (cf. Jer. 19:4, 5), the name, etc., came to be avoided.
Baal- compounds of the god's name: 1. **Baalberith** (bāl-bĭ'rĭth) [Baal of the Covenant] one

37

who comes into covenant with his worshipers—at Shechem (Judg. 8:33, 9:4).

2. **Baalzebub** (bāl-zē′bŭb) [Baal of the Flies] worshiped at Ekron (2 K. 1:2, 3, 16); occurs also in NT as Beelzebub.

Baal *Geographical:* in place names Baal usually refers to some place either where Baal was worshiped or a place near such. It occurs often in compounds. 1. A town of Simeon (1 Chr. 4:33) probably the same as **Baalath-beer** (Josh. 19:9).

2. **Baalah** (bā′á-lä) (a) early name of **Kirjath-jearim** (Josh. 15:9, 11, 60, 18:14; cf. 2 Sam. 6:2); (b) a town in South Judah (Josh. 15:29) = **Balah** (19:3) = **Bilah** (1 Chr. 4:29).

3. **Baalath** (bā′á-läth) a town of Dan, Josephus says it was near Gezer.

4. **Baalath-beer** (bā′á-läth-bē′ĕr) a town in South Judah given to Simeon-Ramath-Negeb (Josh. 19:8).

5. **Baal-gad** (bāl-găd′) town under Mount Hermon, northern point of Joshua's conquest (Josh. 11:17, 12:7, 13:5).

6. **Baal-hamon** (bāl-hā′mŏn) a place containing Solomon's fruitful vineyard (Song of S. 8:11).

7. **Baal-hermon** or **Mount Baal-hermon** (bāl-hêr′mŏn) a Hivite city, either on Mount Hermon or near it (Judg. 3:3; 1 Chr. 5:23).

8. **Baal-meon** (bāl-mē′ŏn) a Reubenite town (Num. 32:38) in Moab, associated with Nebo (1 Chr. 5:8) and mentioned on the Moabite Stone.

9. **Baal-perazim** (bāl-pĕ-rā′zĭm) place where David defeated the Philistines (2 Sam. 5:20; 1 Chr. 14:11; cf. Isa. 28:21). It was near the valley of Rephaim.

10. **Baal-shalisha** (bāl-shăl′ĭ-shä) a place near Gilgal (2 K. 4:42, cf. vs. 38).

11. **Baal-tamar** (bāl-tā′mär) a place near Gibeah in Benjamin (Judg. 20:33).

12. **Baal-zephon** (bāl-zē′fŏn) place in Egypt near where Israel crossed the Red Sea (Ex. 14:2, 9; Num. 33:7).

Baal *Personal:* 1. Descendant of Reuben carried into exile by Assyrians (1 Chr. 5:5).

2. A Gibeonite, brother of Kish, who was Saul's father (1 Chr. 8:30, 9:36).

3. **Baal-hanan** (bāl-hā′nän), an early king of Edom (Gen. 36:38, 39).

4. One of David's officers (1 Chr. 2:5, 27:28; Josh. 15:36).

Baali (bā′á-lĭ) [my Baal, my master] since Baal, meaning "Lord" or "master," was a common word, it came to be used of Israel's God: "my Lord" = *Baali*. This practice was con-demned by Hosea because of its association with false gods (Hos. 2:16).

Baalis (bā′á-lĭs) Ammonite king at the ruin of Jerusalem by Nebuchadnezzar (Jer. 40:14).

Baalzebub (bāl-zē′bŭb) [Lord of the Flies] name of the "god of Ekron" whom Ahaziah consulted concerning his sickness and for which he was rebuked (2 K. 1:2–18). It is thought that this name is identical with **Beelzebub**, but the relationship of the names is not clear.

Baana (bā′á-ná) 1. An officer of Solomon in Jezreel (1 K. 4:12).

2. Father of Zadok (Neh. 3:4).

Baanah (bā′á-ná) 1. A Benjaminite, who with his brother Rechab murdered Ish-bosheth and who was executed by David (2 Sam. 4:2–9).

2. One of David's mighty men (2 Sam. 23:29).

3. One who returned from the Exile and sealed the covenant (Ezra 2:2; Neh. 7:7).

4. Improper spelling for **Baana** (1 K. 4:16).

Baara (bā′á-rá) a wife of the Benjaminite Shaharaim (1 Chr. 8:8).

Baaseiah (bā′á-sē′yá) a Levite ancestor of Asaph the musician (1 Chr. 6:40).

Baasha (bā′á-shá) third king of the Northern Kingdom (Israel) and founder of the second dynasty. He was the son of Ahijah of Issachar, and he conspired against Nadab the king, whose whole family he killed (1 K. 15:27). He reigned twenty-four years and was buried at Tirzah (Song of S. 6:4), his capital (1 K. 16:6).

Babel (bā′bĕl), **Tower of** a tower built by mankind just after the flood in Shinar. The story presumes that those surviving the flood had remained as a unit and declares, "they were one tongue [lip]" (Gen. 11:1–9). The tower was built of burnt brick with slime (bitumen) for mortar. The desire was for a tall tower "whose top is unto heaven" (which the earlier *Smith's* interpreted as a "hyperbole for great height" (cf. Deut. 1:28; Dan. 4:11). The motive assigned was "Let us make us a name [i.e., provide a monument to human achievement] lest we be scattered abroad upon the face of the earth." The purpose was thwarted by the confusion of languages, hence the name Babel from "mixing" or "confusion." The ancient site of the tower is unknown. Attention is often called to the ruins of many large towers called ziggurats, which are found and of which ancient descriptions exist. One such is at Birs-Nimrud. These are crowned with temples for worship. Some contend that the Genesis story was inspired by the tower of the Marduk temple at **Babylon** = Babel. It may well have been just the opposite—that the custom of building such towers by the dispersed peoples carried forward the memory of that first tower.

Babylon (băb'ĭ-lŏn) [Gr. for Heb. *Babel*] name of the city and country which played an important role in OT history and is used symbolically in the NT as the great opposite or enemy of the Heavenly Jerusalem (Rev. 17:5). 1. GEOGRAPHY. The city of Babylon was located in Central Mesopotamia on the Euphrates River, some 300 miles from the Persian Gulf, about fifty miles south of Baghdad, modern capital of Iraq. An account of the city written by Herodotus (fourth century B.C.) says that it was located on both sides of the river, encompassed by walls some fifty-six miles in circuit, thus having an area of about 200 square miles. The term Babylon applied to the country refers to the alluvial area between the Tigris and Euphrates from the Gulf up to Baghdad and at times extending north of the Tigris to the Zagros Mountains. The southern part of this territory is Chaldea.

2. HISTORY. The early settlements in Babylonia were in the southern cities such as Ur, Larsa, Eridu, and Uruk, then in a group, toward the center near Nippur, and later in Babylon, Borsippa, Kish, and Sippar further north. The earliest people are called Sumerians, later Babylonians, Hurrians, and Chaldeans, and closely related to the Assyrians. The early language is Sumerian, then the old Semitic dialect Akkadian. Semitic power was established with the rise of Sargon of Agade (ca. 2350 B.C.) and the Ur III Kingdom, which followed (to 2035 B.C.). Babylon gained ascendancy under Hammurabi the great king (ca. 1728–1686) and his successors. Next came the eclipse known as the Dark Age, when the region was under the power of the Hittites (King Mursilis I, ca. 1600 B.C.). Later conquerors were the Kassites, following which Babylon became a vassal of the Assyrians. Babylonian power began to assert itself with the victory of Nebuchadnezzar I (1146–1123) over Elam and the dynasty of Nabopolassar (626–605). The latter defeated Egypt at Carchemish (605 B.C.). At his death his great son Nebuchadnezzar II became king and carried Babylon to the height of its power, including the capture of Jerusalem and its destruction (586 B.C.), at which time thousands of Jews were carried into exile to Babylon. Nebuchadnezzar lavishingly adorned and built up the capital city. His successors were short-lived and, lacking in power, Babylon fell to the Persian king Cyrus (539 B.C.). The city continued, however, until destroyed by Alexander the Great (330 B.C.). The site of the city lies presently in ruins. The entire area of Babylon and Assyria has been subject to extensive archaeological investigation from the early nineteenth century. Sir Henry Rawlinson's discovery of the Behistun Inscription (in 1846) unlocked the secrets of the Assyrian language. The city of Babylon was excavated by the Germans beginning in 1897. The latter half of the nineteenth century yielded a staggering amount of material which has been continued up to the present.

Babylonish garment [literally robe of Shinar (Josh. 7:21)] a robe or garment for which the Babylonians were celebrated.

Baca (bā'kà), **Valley of** a valley somewhere in Palestine through which the exiled Psalmist sees the pilgrims passing in their march back to the sanctuary at Zion (Ps. 84:6). No valley of this name is known. Several have been suggested, among them Gehenna and the valley of Rephaim.

Bachrites (băk'rīts) descendants of Becher (Num. 26:35).

backsliding a term used especially by Jeremiah and Hosea describing Israel's unfaithfulness to God. It is often rendered by the English "faithless" (Jer. 3:14; Hos. 11:7; Isa. 57:17).

bag is the rendering of several words in the Old and New Testaments: 1. *Charitim*—the bags in which Naaman put the silver for Gehazi (2 K. 5:32). In Isa. 3:22 it refers to luxurious feminine "handbags" (KJV, crisping pin, hair curler).

2. *Cis*—a bag for carrying weights (Deut. 25:13) and money (Prov. 16:11; Isa. 46:6).

3. *Celi* (1 Sam. 17:40)—a word more commonly rendered "vessel" or "instrument." In Gen. 42:23 it is the sack in which the money of Joseph's brothers is hid. Other uses are mentioned (in 1 Sam. 9:7, 17:40; Ezek. 34:4; Zech. 11:15–16).

4. *Tseror*—a bag which could be tied, rendered at times by "bundle" (Gen. 42:35). (See also 1 Sam. 25:29; Prov. 7:20; Hag. 1:6; 2 K. 12:10.)

5. The Greek term is *pēra* (Mt. 10:10; Mk. 6:8; Lk. 9:3, 10:4, 22:35–36)—a traveling bag, shepherd's or beggar's bag.

Bahurim (bà-hū'rĭm) a village on the road up to Jerusalem connected mostly with the flight of King David. Here Michal bade farewell to her husband on returning to David (2 Sam. 3:16). Shimei who lived here cursed David as he fled from Absalom (2 Sam. 16:5; 1 K. 2:8). Jonathan and Ahimaaz hid in a well here to elude pursuers (2 Sam. 17:18). (See also 2 Sam. 23:31 and 1 Chr. 11:33.)

Bajith (bā'jĭth) word meaning "house" and

39

treated as a place name for a Moabite temple in KJV. Some (RSV) take it as a textual error for *bath,* "the daughter of Dibon is gone up."

Bakbakkar (băk-băk'ăr) a Levite (1 Chr. 9:15).

Bakbuk (băk'bŭk) a man whose children returned from exile with Zerubbabel (Ezra 2:51; Neh. 7:53).

Bakbukiah (băk'bŭ-kī'ȧ) 1. A Levite of Nehemiah's time (Neh. 11:17).

2. Probably the same, a Levite porter (Neh. 12:25).

Bakers' Street a street where there was a concentration of baking establishments (Jer. 37:21).

baking see **bread**

Balaam (bā'lăm) the son of Beor, a man endowed with the gift of prophecy (Num. 22:5), a Midianite (Num. 31:8, 16) who lived at Pethor a city of Mesopotamia (Deut. 23:4) or Aram (Num. 23:7) and who was summoned by the Moabite king Balak to curse Israel as they advanced into Moabite territory (Num. 22:5–24:25, 31:8, 16; Deut. 23:4–5; Josh. 13:22, 24:9–10). When Balaam was first contacted, the Lord refused to allow him to go. But when Balak sent more honorable messengers and promises of more money, he "inquired what the Lord had to say more." He was told to go but was rebuked by his ass for disobeying the Lord (Num. 22:27 ff.). Balaam was sent on by God, but, instead of cursing Israel, all his curses were turned to blessings. Later he counseled Balak that by seducing the Israelites with fornication he might cause God to curse them (Num. 25). Balaam was later slain by Israel as he fought with Midian (Num. 31:8). The prophet is also mentioned in two other passages (in Neh. 13:2 and Mic. 6:5). In the NT (2 Pet. 2:15; Jude 11; Rev. 2:14) he is held up as a type of compromising and hypocritical teacher who betrays God's people for money.

Balah (bā'lȧ) a city of Simeon in Southern Judah (Josh. 19:3); in parallel lists also called **Baalah** (Josh. 15:29) and **Bilah** (1 Chr. 4:29).

Balak (bā'lăk) son of Zippor and king of Moab who hired Balaam to curse Israel (Num. 22–24). He is mentioned also in other Biblical books (Josh. 24:9; Judg. 11:25; Mic. 6:5; Rev. 2:14). See **Balaam**

baldness it may be either natural or artificial, the result of cutting off the hair. Artificial baldness was uncommon among the Jews, being an object of derision (e.g., 2 K. 2:23; Isa. 3:24, 15:2; Jer. 47:5; Ezek. 7:18). Hence baldness disqualified a priest (Lev. 21:23 LXX). Leviticus (13:41–43) pronounced baldness clean unless the sign of leprosy accompanied it. Cutting off the hair marked the conclusion of a Naza-

rite's vow (Num. 6:9; Acts 18:18) and is mentioned as a sign of mourning (Amos 8:10; Mic. 1:16). Heathen nations shaved their head in religious rites (Jer. 9:26, 25:23), and it is thus forbidden to Israel as a peculiar people (Deut. 14:1).

balm an aromatic gum or resin widely used in Biblical times for healing. Ishmaelites brought it from Gilead on the way to Egypt (Gen. 37:25). Jacob sent it to Joseph as a present (Gen. 43:11). It is referred to in Jeremiah (8:22, 46:11, and 51:8), again in connection with Gilead, as of healing value. It was imported from Tyre (Ezek. 27:17). Jeremiah uses "balm of Gilead" as a symbol of God's healing forgiveness (8:22).

balsam the name of a tree (2 Sam. 5:23); also used as a place name (Ps. 84:6). The KJV and ASV have "mulberry."

Bamah (bȧ'mȧ) a high place (Ezek. 20:29). The Hebrew word occurs frequently with the translation "high place."

Bamoth-baal (bā'mŏth) a sanctuary of Baal in Moab (Josh. 13:17), probably the same as Bamoth where Balak took Balaam (Num. 23:1 ff.). It is also mentioned in Isa. 15:2.

band 1. Something with which one is bound or fettered. The same word is often translated **rope, cord, fetter.**

2. A group or organization of people such as robbers (Job 1:17), or a company of soldiers (2 K. 6:23).

Bani (bā'nī) 1. A Gadite hero of David (2 Sam. 23:36).

2. Levite forefather of Ethan (1 Chr. 6:46).

3. A man of Judah in the line of Pharez (1 Chr. 9:4).

4. "Children of Bani" returned from the Exile (Ezra 2:10).

5. An Israelite of Bani's sons (Ezra 10:38).

6. A Levite (Neh. 3:17).

7. A Levite (Neh. 8:9, 9:4).

8. Another Levite of the sons of Asaph (Neh. 11:22). Some of these may be the same individual.

banner a standard, ensign, or flag used much as in modern time for identification or rallying (Num. 2:2; Ps. 74:4; Isa. 5:26).

banquet a festive meal for social and religious purposes, usually held in the late evenings (Isa. 5:11; Eccl. 10:16). Meats and wine—mixed three parts water to one part wine always, according to the rabbinical sources (Prov. 9:2; Song of S. 8:2)—were served to guests sitting (OT, 1 Sam. 16:11, 20:5, 18) or reclining (NT, Jn. 12:2; Lk. 7:37). Other accompaniments mentioned include perfumed ointments, flowers, white or brilliant robes, music, dancers, riddles, and merriment (2 Sam. 19:35; Judg. 14:12; Neh. 8:10; Eccl. 10:19; Isa. 5:12, 25:6, 28:1; Amos 6:5 f.; Mt. 22:11; Lk. 15:25). Invitations (Mt. 22:2 ff.; Lk. 14:17) were sent and guests seated according to rank (1 Sam. 9:22; Lk. 14:8). Other details such as offering of thanks (1 Sam. 9:13; Lk. 22:17) and governors or rulers of the feasts (Jn. 2:8) are mentioned. Occasions for such feasts were the three solemn Jewish feasts (Deut. 16:11), sacrifices (Ex. 34:15; Judg. 16:23), marriages (Gen. 29:22; Mt. 22:2), the weaning of children (Gen. 21:8), funerals (Jer. 16:7), laying foundations of buildings (Prov. 9:1–5), harvest (Judg. 9:27), sheepshearing (1 Sam. 25:36), etc. The banquets might last seven days or longer (Gen. 29:27; Judg. 14:12). The early church included such feasts in the fellowship aspects of its life. These were continued toward the end of the first century, as the reference to love feasts and to those who "feast (banquet) with you" show (Jude 12). See **agape**

baptism 1. MEANING OF THE WORD. The Gr. *baptisma* literally means a "dipping" or "immersion"; from *baptizo*, a causal or iterative form of *bapto*, I dip, or submerge. The active form *baptismos* ("dippings") is used always of Levitical or Jewish "washings" (Mk. 7:4; Heb. 9:10). The passive form *baptisma*, which gives us our English "baptism," is a resultant noun = the institution or rite. There are no instances of the use of *baptisma* outside the NT. Baptism is properly a religious rite or ordinance practiced by John the Baptist, by Jesus and his disciples (Jn. 3:22), and since the Great Commission and Pentecost (Mt. 28:19–20; Mk. 16:15–17; Acts 2:38, 19:5–6). It is generally conceded even by those practicing sprinkling in modern times that the first-century or NT action of baptism was immersion. Some claim that Lk. 11:38 ("the Pharisee marveled that he had not first bathed himself [*ebaptisthe*]") proves that it did not always imply immersion. On this one may consider Mk. 7:4, which shows that the "washing" in question was that of washing the hands "up to the elbow" before eating.

2. USES OF BAPTISM. It was used of John's baptism (Mt. 3:7; Mk. 11:30; Lk. 7:29; Acts 1:22, 10:37, 18:25, and 19:3). This rite was described as a "baptism of repentance unto remission of sins" (Mk. 1:4; Acts 13:24, 19:4) —a baptism of repentance which brings forgiveness of sins. It has been conjectured that John's practice of baptism is to be understood in the light of Jewish proselyte baptism. There is no actual evidence of this practice in the first cen-

tury, but it may possibly be inferred. That baptism in the name of Jesus and demanding faith in Jesus as the Messiah superseded that of John is clear from Acts 18:26–27, 19:1–6, and from such scriptures as Acts 10:48, "He commanded them to be baptized in the name of Jesus Christ" (cf. Acts 2:38; 1 Cor. 1:13, 15, 6:11; Mt. 28:19–20). Jesus' baptism also demanded repentance (Lk. 24:46; Acts 2:38) and promised remission of sins (Acts 2:38, "*unto* remission of sins"; cf. Acts 22:16; 1 Pet. 3:21). The rite is properly seen as the initiatory step into the body of Christ (1 Cor. 12:13). Baptism is given a central place in the teaching concerning the Christian's commitment to Christ. Theologically Paul uses two figures to set forth its significance, that of a resurrection (Rom. 6:1 ff.; Col. 2:12) and of a regeneration or rebirth (Tit. 3:5, following John 3:3, 5). In both of these figures the concepts of a union with the death of Jesus Christ and a renewal of life in him is present. From this the response of the believer is that of a renewed life, avoiding evil and lending his members as members of righteousness (Rom. 6:13; Col. 3:1). For this purpose the help of the Holy Spirit, received in baptism (Acts 2:38), is promised.

Baptist the Greek formation of the name for John signifies agent; thus "one who baptizes."

bar (bar) a word (Aramaic) meaning "son of" and often used in the names of persons (e.g., *Bar-Jonah*, son of Jonah).

Barabbas (bår-ăb'ăs) a robber (Jn. 18:40) who had committed murder in an insurrection (Mk. 15:7; Lk. 23:19) in Jerusalem and was in prison at the time of the trial of Jesus. He was released to the Jews in lieu of Jesus Christ. His full name (by coincidence) according to some MSS was Jesus Barabbas (so Codex θ at Mt. 27:16).

Barachel (băr'à-kĕl) a Buzite, the father of the third of Job's friends (Job 32:2).

Barachias (băr'à-kī'ăs) the father of Zechariah whose death is mentioned as the last OT murder (Mt. 23:35).

Barak (băr'ăk) a man of Kedesh, a refuge city in Mount Naphtali, who was summoned by Deborah the judge to deliver Israel from the yoke of Jabin and Sisera. He went but only because Deborah would go, too. In the battle on the plain of Jezreel (Esdraelon) Israel won a mighty victory and Sisera was slain (Judg. 4–5).

barbarian strictly and commonly anyone who did not speak Greek (Rom. 1:14) and thus with Greeks meaning "the whole human race." It is often used of those who spoke another tongue (1 Cor. 14:11; Acts 28:2, 4) or belonged to other than the Greek race (Col. 3:11).

Barhumite, the see **Bahurim**

Bariah (bȧ-rī'ȧ) a descendant in David's line (1 Chr. 3:22).

Bar-Jesus a magician (Acts 13:6 ff.). See **Elymas**

Bar-Jonah see **Peter**

Barkos (bȧr'kŏs) head of a family who returned from Babylon (Ezra 2:53).

Barsabbas see **Joseph Barsabbas**, and **Judas Barsabbas**

Bartholomew (bȧr-thŏl'ŏ-mū) one of the twelve apostles of Christ (Mt. 10:3; Mk. 3:18; Lk. 6:14; Acts 1:13). It has been conjectured that he is identical with Nathanael (Jn. 1:45 ff.) on the grounds that Bartholomew is the surname, that he follows Philip in the list of apostles in the Synoptics, which never themselves mention Nathanael, while John omits Bartholomew. The arguments are not conclusive, though probable.

Bartimaeus (bȧr'tĭ-mē'ŭs) a blind beggar of Jericho who was healed as he sat by the wayside as our Lord passed out of Jericho on his last journey to Jerusalem (Mk. 10:46 ff.). From Matthew's (20:29–34) and Luke's (18:35–43) accounts there seemed to be two blind men (neither of whose names was given) healed at the time.

Baruch (bȧr'ŭk) 1. The trusted friend, attendant, and scribe of Jeremiah the prophet (Jer. 32:12, 36:4–32, 36). He was of a noble family (Jer. 51:59). He was accused of influencing Jeremiah against Babylon (Jer. 37:13, 43:3) and thrown into prison. Later he was forced to go down to Egypt (Jer. 43:6). Of his death nothing is known.

2. A man who helped Nehemiah rebuild the wall of Jerusalem (Neh. 3:20).

3. A priest who signed the covenant with Nehemiah (Neh. 10:6).

4. A descendant of Pharez, son of Judah (Neh. 11:5).

Barzillai (bȧr-zĭl'ā-ī) 1. A wealthy Gileadite who showed hospitality to David when he fled from Absalom (2 Sam. 17:27), but who later declined the king's offer of ending his days at court (2 Sam. 19:32–33). His descendants could not later prove their genealogy (Ezra 2:61; Neh. 7:63).

2. A Meholathite, whose son married Michal, Saul's daughter (2 Sam. 21:8).

Bashan (bā'shăn) a district on the east of Jordan, comprising generally the northern part of the eastern tableland. It was taken by Israel after the capture of Sihon: "they turned from their road over Jordan and went up by the way

of Bashan to Edrei on the western edge of the Lejah" where they met and defeated Og king of Bashan (Num. 21:33–35; Deut. 3:1–3). This land was later given to the half-tribe of Manasseh together with half of Gilead (Josh. 13:29–31). Its only later OT references are in the list of Solomon's commissariat districts (1 K. 4:13) and its devastation of Hazael in the reign of Jehu (2 K. 10:33). In later times Bashan is generally divided into four provinces: Baulanitis, Auranitis, Trachonitis, and Batanaea.

Bashan-havoth-jair a name (KJV) given to Argob after its conquest by Jair (Deut. 3:14).

Bashemath (băsh'ē-măth) or **Basemath** 1. Hittite wife of Esau (Gen. 26:34).

2. Daughter of Ishmael, wife of Esau (Gen. 36:3–4, 10, 13, 17) from whose son Reuel four tribes of the Edomites were descended. Probably same as 1 above. She is also called Mahalath (Gen. 38:9). The Samaritan (Hebrew) text reads Mahalath instead of Bashemath in the genealogy. The name may be wrongly assigned in one text.

3. Solomon's daughter (1 K. 4:15).

bastard strictly an illegitimate child, one born of incest (Deut. 23:2) or out of wedlock (Heb. 12:8). Heathen people such as Ammon and Moab were described thus because of their incestuous origin (Gen. 19:30 ff.). The Jewish rabbinic writings generally use the term for all issue born of relations within the degrees prohibited by the Law. Bastards were not permitted to enter the assembly.

bat a flying mammal which generally hides in caves by day and emerges at night (Isa. 2:20). Numerous in Bible lands and included in the list of unclean "fowl" (Lev. 11:19; Deut. 14:18). That bats lit on heads of idols was used by Jeremiah (ch. 22) to demonstrate their lifelessness.

bath (băth) a liquid measure equal to an ephah (Ezek. 45:11, 14). The estimate is about five and one-half gallons.

bath the washing of the body for cleanliness, either ritualistic or physical. In the Bible, bathing of the body is largely religious. It was basically a ritual for removing uncleanness (Lev. 13:6, 15, 16:4, 24, 28, 22:6; Num. 19:7, 19; 2 Sam. 11:24; 2 K. 5:10). In the NT the Jews made much of ceremonial washings (Mk. 7:3 f.). Some sects bathed daily in ritual. Public baths were unknown until the coming of the Greeks; then some of the pools were so used (Jn. 5:2, 9:7). When bathing was done, anointing usually followed (Est. 2:12; Judg. 10:3). Dusty roads made foot-washing necessary and frequent (Gen. 18:4, 19:2; Jn. 13:10; 1 Tim. 5:10).

Bath-rabbim (băth′răb′ĭm), **the Gate of** a gate of the ancient city Heshbon (Song of S. 7:4 [5]), near which there were fish pools.

Bath-sheba (băth-shē′bȧ) or **Bath-shua** (-shū′a) wife of Uriah the Hittite, with whom David committed adultery, and whom he took as wife after he had Uriah killed in battle (2 Sam. 11). The child of the union died, but later Bath-sheba bore David four sons, including his successor Solomon (for other stories see 1 K. 1 and 2:21–25).

battle see **army, war**

Bavvai (băv′ī) ruler of Keilah who helped Nehemiah rebuild walls (Neh. 3:18).

bay tree a native shrub (*laurus nobilis*) which sprouts shoots around its parent stem, noted for its aromatic leaves. It is sometimes thought to be mentioned [Heb. *'zrah*] in Ps. 37:35 or Isa. 44:14; others doubt a specific tree is mentioned.

bazaar section of street used for market (e.g., 1 K. 20:34).

Bazlith (băz′lĭth) ancestor of a postexilic family (Ezra 2:52).

bdellium (dĕl′ĭ-ŭm) a substance of uncertain identification, either a precious gum or resin, or a stone or pearl. It is mentioned (Gen. 2:12) with the gold and onyx of Havilah and the color of the manna is compared to it (Num. 11:7).

Bealiah (bē′ȧ-lī′ȧ) a companion of David (1 Chr. 12:5).

Bealoth (bē′ȧ-lŏth) a town in South Judah (Josh. 15:24). See also 1 K. 4:16.

beam a bar of wood or metal used in building (1 K. 6:36), in weaving (1 Sam. 17:7, etc.), and used by Jesus (Mt. 7:3–5; Lk. 6:41–42) of a large object in the eye. Various original words are represented.

beans the beans of various (lentils, kidney-bean, vetches, etc.) leguminous plants grown for food (2 Sam. 17:28; Ezek. 4:9).

bear a large carnivorous animal known almost throughout the world and extant in Northern Palestine as late as the twentieth century. Among the many Biblical references are the following: the story of David's slaughter of one (1 Sam. 17:34, 36–37) and the slaughter of the children laughing at Elisha (2 K. 2). The bear's fierceness and dangerousness are often used as similes (Prov. 17:12; Isa. 59:11; Lam. 3:10; Hos. 13:8; Amos 5:19). It was used as an apocalyptic symbol (Dan. 7:5; Rev. 13:2).

beard people of Western Asia cherished the full beard as a badge of the dignity of manhood; Egyptians and Romans usually shaved their hair and beard. Hebrews were forbidden to trim the beard in imitation of heathen neighbors (Lev. 19:27, 21:5), except for a leper (Lev. 14:9). Shaving, plucking, or cutting the beard was a sign of mourning or disaster (Ezra 9:3; Isa. 50:6; Jer. 41:5).

beast a word usually distinguishing a wild from a domesticated animal, though at times merely differentiating mammals from fish and fowl (Gen. 1:29 f., 6:7; Ex. 9:25). It is thus for animals such as cattle or horses (1 K. 18:5). Many incidents in the OT concern them and domestic animals as property were regulated by many laws. The term "wild beast" is the translation of a different word (*thērion*).

Bebai (bē′bā-ī) head of an exile family (Neh. 7:16; Ezek. 2:11, 8:11).

Becher (bē′kêr) 1. Second son of Benjamin (according to Gen. 46:21 and 1 Chr. 7:6, but omitted in 1 Chr. 8:1). There is probably a confusion in the text between the Hebrew for Becher and *becor*, "firstborn," so that either (1) firstborn (in 1 Chr. 7:6) should read Becher, making it agree with the other passages, or (2) Becher should be *becor*, "firstborn" in the other passages, there being no such person as Becher.

2. Son of Ephraim (1 Chr. 7:20).

Bechorath (bē-kōr′ăth) grandson of Becher and ancestor of Saul (1 Sam. 9:1; 1 Chr. 7:8).

bed a place (usually an article of furniture) for lying down either in rest, sickness, or sleep. Often, especially with the poor, the bed was merely the floor or a ledge along the wall, and the cover was the outer garment worn by day (hence the law that the poor man's coat could not be taken, except it was returned every night–Deut. 24:13). Beds of wooden frames or litters are mentioned (1 Sam. 19:15; Mt. 9:2; Lk. 5:18), as are the more ornate ones of ivory (Amos 6:4), or iron (Deut. 3:13), or even gold or silver (Est. 1:6). Perfumed coverings and metal pillars are also mentioned (Song of S. 3:10; Prov. 7:16–17). In some houses special chambers for beds are mentioned (2 K. 11:2). Use of beds might be proverbial of death (Ps. 139:8) or discomfort (Isa. 28:20).

Bedad (bē′dăd) Hadad's father (Gen. 36:35).

Bedan (bē′dăn) 1. A judge (mentioned in 1 Sam. 12:11) near the time of Gideon and Japhthah but omitted in the book of Judges. Some suggest a misreading of the Hebrew for Abdon; the LXX and others have Barak.

2. Grandson of Gilead (1 Chr. 7:17).

Bedeiah (bē-dē′yȧ) a man who had taken a foreign wife (Ezra 10:35).

bee an insect living in colonies and producing honey. From its abundance Palestine was termed "a land flowing with milk and honey" (Ex. 3:8). A swarm was lodged in Samson's lion (Judg. 14:8). Several references are to their sting and temper (Deut. 1:44; Ps. 118:12; Isa. 7:18).

Beeliada (bē-ĕ-lī'à-dà) a son of David (1 Chr. 14:7); also called **Eliada.**

Beelzebub see **Baalzebub**

Beelzebul see **Baalzebul**

Beer (bē'êr) 1. One of the last camps of Israel beyond the Arnon (Num. 21:16–18). The word means "a well," possibly also named in Isa. 15:8, as **Beer-elim.**

2. A place whence Jotham fled from Abimelech (Judg. 9:21).

Beera (bē-ê'rà) an Asherite (1 Chr. 7:37).

Beerah (bē-ê'rà) a Reubenite exiled by Tiglath-pileser (1 Chr. 5:6).

Beer-elim see **Beer 1**

Beeri (bē-ê'rī) 1. Hittite father of Esau's wife Judith (Gen. 26:34).

2. Hosea's father (Hos. 1:1).

Beer-lahai-roi (bē'êr-là-hī'roi) [well of the living one who appeared to me, according to Gen. 16:7–14] here God appeared to Hagar and reassured her. Isaac dwelt by this well (Gen. 24:62, 25:11).

Beeroth (bē-ê'rŏth) one of four Hittite cities, located in later tribe of Benjamin (Josh. 18:25), who with Gibeon as leader tricked Joshua into a treaty of peace (Josh. 9:17). It is mentioned several times later (2 Sam. 4:2; Ezra 2:25; Neh. 7:29), together with one of its inhabitants (2 Sam. 23:37; 1 Chr. 11:39).

Beeroth-Bene-jaakan [wells of Jaakan's sons] a station on Israel's wilderness wanderings (Deut. 10:6).

Beer-sheba (bǐr-shē'bà) very ancient city, the most southernly in Palestine and hence frequently occurring in phrases like "from Dan to Beer-sheba" (Judg. 20:1; 2 Sam. 24:2) or the reverse (1 Chr. 21:2) of the northern and southern limits of the country or "from Geba to Beer-sheba" (2 K. 23:8) of the limits of Judah. The name arose from the oath made by Abraham and Abimelech at the digging of the well (Gen. 21:31) or from the "seven" lambs used in the compact [the Hebrew for "seven" and "oath" being very similar], or from a later incident much the same between Abimelech and Isaac (Gen. 26:31–33). Beer-sheba is mentioned on several occasions in OT history, being connected with Jacob (46:1), Samuel's sons (1 Sam. 8:2), and Elijah (1 K. 19:3). From Amos it is clear that it was a center of idol worship (Amos 8:14). It was reinhabited after the Captivity (Neh. 11:30). Its modern name is Bir es-Saba, twenty-eight miles southwest of Hebron.

Beeshterah (bē-ĕsh'têr-à) or **Ashtaroth** a city in Manasseh beyond Jordan given to sons of Gershom (Josh. 21:27).

beetle see **locust**

beheading see **punishment**

Behemoth (bē-hē'mŏth) name given an animal which dwells among the reeds and the "willows of the brook" and who does not tremble even "if a river overflow" (Job 40:15–24). In the opinion of most scholars the hippopotamus is meant, though some have argued for the elephant. In apocalyptic literature the word has reference to a mythical beast.

bekah see **weights and measures**

Bela (bē'là) 1. One of the five cities of the plain which was spared at the intercession of Lot and received the name of Zoar (Gen. 13:10, 14:2, 19:22; Isa. 15:5; Jer. 48:34). It lay on the southern extremity of the Dead Sea.

2. Son of Beor, who reigned over Edom in the city of Dinhabah about the time of the Exodus (Gen. 36:31–39; 1 Chr. 1:43–51).

3. Eldest son of Benjamin, head of Belaites (Gen. 46:21; Num. 26:38, 40; 1 Chr. 7:6, 8:1).

4. Son of Ahaz, a Reubenite (1 Chr. 5:8).

Belah same as **Bela 3**

Belaites (Num. 26:38) see **Bela 3**

Belial (bē'lǐ-ăl) sometimes by confusion Beliar, a word of contempt meaning worthless, reckless, or lawless, often used as an expression of contempt (1 Sam. 25:25), frequently with the expression "son of" or "man of" (Deut. 13:3; 1 Sam. 20:1; cf. also Deut. 15:9; Prov. 19:29). In some passages (like Nah. 1:15 H 2:1) the word is taken by some to mean a demonic or Satanic power; hence Paul seems to use it of Satan (2 Cor. 6:15). The term was widely used in Jewish apocalyptic literature of a lawless opponent of the Messiah (Testament of Levi 3:3; Sibylline Oracles III.71–73).

bellows devices usually made of skins of animals and emptied alternatively by mashing the air out with the feet, used to fan the flames of a fire (Ezek. 22:20–21; Job 20:26, 41:21; Jer. 6:29; Isa. 54:16).

bells sounding devices attached to the robe of the priest's garments "that his sound might be heard when he went in unto the holy place" (Ex. 28:34; Eccl. 45:9). Some such ornaments were also used on horses, etc. (Zech. 14:20).

Belshazzar (bĕl-shăz'êr) son and co-regent of Nabonidus and the last king of Babylon. He is called son of Nebuchadnezzar (Dan. 5:2), which means only ancestor. According to the story in Daniel he was slain in the capture of

Babylon by the Medes and Persians following a feast in which that fall had been foretold by the handwriting on the wall. Xenophon confirms that Babylon was taken by the Medes and Persians while the people feasted and that the king was killed. Archaeological tablets confirm the co-regency of Belshazzar and his father and clear up the accounts of ancient historians who mention his father as the last king of Babylon.

Belteshazzar another name for **Daniel**

Benaiah (bē-nā′yà) 1. One of David's most valiant and trusted leaders and later commander in chief under Solomon. He was the son of Jehoiada the chief priest (1 Chr. 17:5) and a native of Kabzeel (2 Sam. 23:20) in South Judah. He became chief of David's bodyguards (2 Sam. 8:18). Three principal exploits are summarized about him: the killing of two Moab warriors, that of a lion in a pit, and the defeat of an Egyptian warrior with his own spear (2 Sam. 23:20 ff.). He remained faithful to Solomon during Adonijah's rebellion (1 K. 1:8 ff.) and was made commander of the whole army (1 K. 2:35, 4:4).

2. Benaiah the **Pirathonite,** one of David's mighty men (2 Sam. 23:30; 1 Chr. 11:31, 27:14).

3. A psaltery player of David (1 Chr. 15:18).

4. A priest in the time of David (1 Chr. 15:24).

5. A Levite of the sons of Asaph (2 Chr. 20:14).

6. A Levite in the time of Hezekiah (2 Chr. 31:13).

7. A prince of the families of Simeon (1 Chr. 4:36).

8. Various men of Ezra's time who had taken strange wives (Ezra 10:25, 30, 35, 43).

9. A prince of the people in the time of Ezekiel (11:1, 13).

Ben-ammi (běn-ăm′ī) son of Lot's younger daughter and progenitor of the Ammonites (Gen. 19:38).

Bene-berak (běn′ĕ-bîr′ăk) a city of the tribe of Dan (mentioned only in Josh. 19:45), now identified with Banai Baraq, a suburb of Tel Aviv.

Bene-jaakan (běn′ĕ-jā′à-kăn) a place probably named from a tribal ancestor Jaakan, grandson of Seir the Horite (1 Chr. 1:42), where Israel camped near the border of Edom (Num. 33:31 f.).

Bene-kedem [children of the East] (Gen. 19:1; Judg. 6:3 in KJV).

Ben-hadad (běn-hā′dăd) the title of either two or three kings of Syria or Damascus [= son of **Hadad,** the old Semitic-Canaanite storm-god]

1. Ben-hadad I was grandson of Hezion king of Damascus (1 K. 15:18). He appeared in the scriptural account in the days of Asa of Judah and Baasha of Israel (1 K. 15:16–22). After Baasha won some initial advantage in the war, Asa won an alliance with Ben-hadad by gifts of treasure from the Lord's house, for which he was rebuked by the prophet (2 Chr. 16:7 ff.).

2. Ben-hadad II was a contemporary of Omri and Ahab, kings of Israel. He besieged Samaria (1 K. 20:1 ff.; 2 K. 6:8 ff., 24–25). The story of his sickness and death is recorded in 2 K. 8:7–15. Some think he is identical with the former.

3. Ben-hadad III was son of the usurper Hazael. Under him Israel regained their territory, and Syria's power was diminished (2 K. 13).

Ben-hail (běn′hāl) a prince sent by King Jehoshaphat to teach Judah's cities (2 Chr. 17:7).

Ben-hanan (běn-hā′năn) son of Shimon in the line of Judah (1 Chr. 4:20).

Beninu (bǐ-nī′nū) a Levite who sealed the covenant with Nehemiah (Neh. 10:13–14).

Benjamin (běn′jă-měn) the youngest of the sons of Jacob and progenitor of the tribe of the same name. He was the son of the beloved Rachel, who died at his birth. She named him Ben-oni [son of my sorrow], but Jacob changed the name to "son of my right hand" (Gen. 35:16–18). He was born on the road between Bethel and Bethlehem, the only one of the twelve to be born in Palestine. With his elder (full) brother Joseph he seemed to share his father's special favor, doubtless due to Jacob's love for their mother and her untimely death. Little is heard of him until Jacob's descent to Egypt. The story of Joseph's use of Benjamin to learn the feelings of his brothers is well known (Gen. 42–44). Judah's eloquent appeal for him moved Joseph as it does the modern reader (44:26–34). Ten sons are ascribed to him (Gen. 46:21). From this point on his history is lost in that of his tribe. His territory lay south of Ephraim and next to Judah. Though Benjamin was peaceable, his tribe was warlike and skilled in weapons of war (Judg. 3:15, 20:16; 1 Sam. 20:20, 36; 2 Sam. 1:29; 1 Chr. 8:40, 12:2; 2 Chr. 17:17). The tribe was almost wiped out in the terrible tragedy of Judges 19 but recovered later. Saul was of Benjamin, and after his death there was bitterness between Judah and Benjamin. However, through the wisdom of Abner the difficulties were overcome and a covenant made (2 Chr. 15:9; cf. 2 Chr. 17:17). Later Benjamin merged with the kingdom of David in Judah.

Benjamin, High Gate of a gate of Jerusalem (Jer. 20:2, 37:18, 38:7; Zech. 14:10), perhaps the same as Jeremiah's **Sheep Gate.**

Beno (bē'nō) a Levite of the sons of Merari (1 Chr. 24:26 f.); some old versions did not consider it a proper name, but render "his son."

Ben-oni (běn-ō'nī) name given to Benjamin by his dying mother, Rachel (Gen. 35:18).

Ben-zoheth (běn-zō'hěth) a descendant of Judah (1 Chr. 4:20).

Beon (bē'ŏn) place east of Jordan (Num. 32:3, 18) same as **Baal-meon.**

Beor (bē'ôr) 1. Father of Bela and early Edomite king (Gen. 36:32; 1 Chr. 1:43).

2. Balaam's father (Num. 22:5). Also called **Bosor.**

Bera (bĭr'à) king of Sodom (Gen. 14:2, 17, 21).

Berachah (běr'à-kà) friend of David at Ziklag (1 Chr. 12:3).

Berachah, Valley of [Valley of Blessing] valley where Jehoshaphat and his people assembled to bless God after a victory (2 Chr. 20:26).

Berachiah (KJV form of **Berechiah**, 1 Chr. 6:39).

Beraiah (bē-rā'yà) a Benjaminite (1 Chr. 8:21).

Berea (bêr-ē'à) a city of Southwestern Macedonia to which Paul retired with Silas and Timothy when persecuted at Thessalonica (Acts 17:10) and from which he fled when Jews from Thessalonica followed him. The Bereans are distinguished as more noble or wellbred than those of the former city because of their open-mindedness and readiness to search the Scriptures.

Berechiah (běr'ē-kī'à) 1. Son of Zerubbabel in the line of Judah (1 Chr. 3:20).

2. A man who helped rebuild the walls (Neh. 3:4).

3. A Levite (1 Chr. 9:16).

4. A doorkeeper of the ark (1 Chr. 15:23).

5. An Ephraimite prince of Ahaz's time (2 Chr. 28:12).

6. Father of Asaph (1 Chr. 15:17).

7. Father of Zechariah the prophet (Zech. 1:1).

Bered (běr'ěd) 1. A place in South Palestine near the well Lahai-roi (Gen. 16:14).

2. A son or descendant of Ephraim (1 Chr. 7:20), possibly a spelling for Becher (Num. 26:35).

Berenice see **Bernice**

Beri (běr'ī) son of Zophah, of Asher (1 Chr. 7:36).

Beriah (bē-rī'à) 1. Son of Asher (Gen. 46:17), from whom came the Beriites (Num. 26:44).

2. A son of Ephraim (1 Chr. 7:20–23), so called because "it went evil with his house," referring to a raid by men of Gath, the son being a "gift" to offset the loss.

3. A Benjaminite, expelled by the men of Gath (1 Chr. 8:13, 16).

4. A Levite (1 Chr. 23:10).

Berites (bē'rīts) a tribe of people visited by Joab while pursuing Sheba (2 Sam. 20:14).

Berith, the god see **Baal-berith**

berith the Hebrew word for "covenant."

Bernice (bêr-nī'sē) or **Berenice** the oldest daughter of Herod Agrippa I (Acts 12:1). Mention is made of her in Acts 25:13, 23, 26:30, as visiting the governor Festus with her own brother Agrippa II in the time of Paul, with whom she was suspected of living as wife. She had first married a certain Marcus, then her uncle Herod, and later married Polemo king of Cilicia, whom she left to return to Philip, later becoming mistress to Vespasian and his son Titus. The historian Josephus relates many details of her life.

Berodach-baladan see **Merodach-baladan** (2 K. 20:12).

Berothah, Berothai (bē-rō'thà, bē-rō'thī) a town located between Hamath and Damascus in Syria, mentioned with these cities in Ezek. 47:16 and 2 Sam. 8:8, probably modern Bereitan, seven miles south of Baalbek.

Berothite, the (1 Chr. 11:39) see **Beeroth**

beryl (běr'īl) a precious stone spoken of in the OT often and in the NT once only (Rev. 21:20). It is akin to but an inferior type of stone to the emerald. In the OT the originals are *tarsis* (the stone in the breastplate, Ex. 28:20, 39:13; Song of S. 5:14; Ezek. 1:16, 10:9, 28:13; Dan. 10:6). The RSV renders *soham* (KJV, onyx; LXX, chrysolite) by "beryl" (Ezek. 28:13).

Besai (bē'sī) ancestor of a family of returning exiles (Neh. 7:52; Ezra 2:49).

Besodeiah (běz'ō-dē'yà) father of Meshullam (Neh. 3:6).

Besor (bē'sôr), **the brook** an unidentified wadi or brook in extreme south of Judah crossed by David in a campaign from Ziklag against Amalek (1 Sam. 30:9–10, 21).

Betah (bē'tà) a town (2 Sam. 8:8) probably the same as Tebach in Gen. 22:24.

Beten (bē'těn) a city on border of Asher (Josh. 19:25).

beth (běth) second letter of Hebrew alphabet. In Ps. 119 it heads the second section of the Acrostic Psalm.

Beth (běth) common word for "house" in Hebrew and a frequent combining word, especially in place names (e.g., Beth-el = house of

God). It has special meaning of a temple or house of worship.

Beth-abara (bĕth-ăb′á-rà) a place of uncertain location east of Jordan where John was baptizing (Jn. 1:28) and where he baptized Jesus (vss. 29, 35). The better MSS, however, have Bethany (a place not to be confused with Bethany near Jerusalem).

Beth-anath (bĕth-á′năth) a city in Naphtali from which the Canaanites were not driven (Josh. 19:38; Judg. 1:33).

Beth-anoth (bĕth-á′nŏth) a town of Judah (Josh. 15:59) near Halhul.

Bethany (bĕth′á-nē) 1. A village situated on the Mount of Olives (Mk. 11:1; Lk. 19:29) about 1⅝ miles from Jerusalem (Jn. 11:18) on the road from Jericho to Jerusalem (Lk. 19:29, cf. vs. 1; Mk. 11:1, cf. 10:46) and intimately associated with the life of Jesus. It was the place of lodging during last week (Mt. 21:17, etc.), the scene of the supper at Simon the Leper's house (Mk. 14:3), family scene of Mary, Martha, and Lazarus (Jn. 11), and the place from which Jesus ascended (Lk. 24:50–51). It was near Bethphage and is identified today with el-'Aziriyeh.

2. Place beyond Jordan where John baptized. See **Beth-abara** (Jn. 1:28).

Beth-arabah (bĕth-ăr′á-bà) one of six cities of Judah situated in the Arabah, the depression extending beyond the Dead Sea (Josh. 15:61).

Beth-aram (bĕth-á′răm) a town of Gad east of the Jordan (Josh. 13:27), more correctly given as **Beth-haram** (Num. 32:36).

Beth-arbel (bĕth-àr′bĕl) a town sacked by Shalman (Hos. 10:14). Its modern location is disputed.

Beth-aven (bĕth-á′vĕn) a place on the mountains of Benjamin, between Bethel (Josh. 7:2) and Michmash (1 Sam. 13:5, 14:23). Hosea (4:15, 5:8, 10:5) uses the term to scorn Bethel [House of God], which has become Beth-aven [House of wickedness] by the mention of the "calves of Beth-aven."

Beth-azmaveth (bĕth-ăz′mä-vĕth) a name in Neh. 7:28; elsewhere simply called **Azmaveth** (2 Sam. 23:31).

Beth-baal-meon (bĕth′bāl-mē′ŏn) a place belonging to Reuben on the plains east of Jordan (Josh. 13:17), sometimes called **Baal-meon** (Num. 32:38) or simply **Beon** (32:3). Later it belonged to Moab (Jer. 48:23; Ezek. 25:9).

Beth-barah (bĕth-bâr′á) a place south of Gideon's victory over Midian (Judg. 7:24). Probably it is not the same as the **Beth-abara** which some MSS have in Jn. 1:28.

Beth-birei (bĕth-bĭr′ī) an unidentified place in Simeon (Southern Judah) (1 Chr. 4:31).

Beth-car (bĕth-kàr′) a place west of Mizpah to which Israel pursued the Philistines (1 Sam. 7:11).

Beth-dagon (bĕth-dā′gŏn) 1. A city in the Shephelah (Southern Judah), not far from Philistia [Dagon was a Philistine god] (Josh. 15:41).

2. A town on the border of Asher (Josh. 19:27).

Beth-diblathaim (bĕth′dĭb-lä-thā′ĭm) a town of Moab (Jer. 48:22); also called **Almon-diblathaim**.

Bethel (bĕth′ĕl) [house of God] 1. A well-known city and holy place, at or near a city anciently called Luz (Gen. 28:19), twelve miles north of Jerusalem near the spot where Ephraim and Benjamin join. The place was an ancient Canaanite town and was connected with the early patriarchs. Abraham camped near it on first entering Canaan (Gen. 12:8) and later built an altar there (13:4 f.). The name was given the spot by Jacob after the experience of his wrestling with the angel as he said, "This is none other than the house of God" (Gen. 28:17 ff.). Jacob returned there after his sojourn with Laban (Gen. 35:1–9). The area was in Benjamin's allotment (Josh. 18:21 f.), and it was captured by the sons of Joseph (Judg. 1:22–26). Here the ark of God rested (Judg. 20:26–28) for a time, and here Samuel went to judge Israel (1 Sam. 7:16, 10:3). Jeroboam set up one of his two golden calves at Bethel (1 K. 12:26–30). Because of its place as a center of idols it was denounced by the prophets (Hos. 4:15; Amos 3:14, 4:4 ff.). Priests lived here who taught those remaining after Israel's exile to fear the Lord (2 K. 17:27 f.). And people from it are listed among the returning exiles (Neh. 7:32; Ezra 2:28). Thus its history stretches from early to late OT times with more mention than any other OT place except Jerusalem. The modern site is called Beitin.

2. An unidentified city in Southern Judah (1 Sam. 30:27), also called Bethul (Josh. 19:4) and Bethuel (1 Chr. 4:30).

Beth-emek (bĕth-ē′mĕk) a border town of Asher, south of the ravine of Jiphthahel (Josh. 19:27).

Bether (bē′thêr) 1. An unknown mountain mentioned in the Song of S. 2:17. Some would translate "rugged mountains" (RSV) as though no proper name were intended.

2. A town in the Bethlehem district of Judah (Josh. 15:59, LXX; probably omitted from the Hebrew text by scribal error). It is usually identified with the capital of Bar Cocheba—a man who claimed to be a messiah (A.D. 132), led

47

a revolt against the Romans which was crushed when the capital, the last Jewish stronghold, fell (A.D. 135)—and with modern Bittir, seven miles southwest of Jerusalem.

Bethesda (bĕ-thĕs'dá) [some MSS have Beth-zatha or Bezetha] a pool at Jerusalem with five porches, located near the sheep-gate (Jn. 5:1-16). Here Jesus healed a lame man waiting with a crowd for the "troubling of the waters" in the belief that the waters healed them. Verse 4, which speaks of the angel troubling the water, is a second-century addition to the story. A reservoir near the modern Church of St. Anne in northeast Jerusalem (fifty-five by twelve feet) is thought to be the site.

Beth-ezel (bĕth-e'zĕl) a place in South Judah (Mic. 1:1).

Beth-gader (bĕth-gā'dêr) a place probably in North Judah (1 Chr. 2:51).

Beth-gamul (bĕth-gā'mŭl) a town near Dibon in the land of Moab (Jer. 48:23).

Beth-haccerem (bĕth'hă-kē'rĕm) a town in Judah near Tekoa, used as a beacon station (Neh. 3:14).

Beth-haran (bĕth-hā'răn) a Gadite fenced city east of the Jordan (Num. 32:36), same as Beth-aram (Josh. 13:27).

Beth-hoglah (bĕth-hŏg'là) a place between the border of Judah and Benjamin (Josh. 15:6, 18:19) belonging to the latter (18:21).

Beth-horon (bĕth-hō'rŏn) twin towns, an "upper" and a "lower" (Josh. 16:3, 5; 1 Chr. 7:24) on the road from Gibeon to Azekah (Josh. 10:10 f.). They lay on the border between Benjamin and Ephraim (Josh. 16:3, 5) and belonged to the Kohathites within Benjamin (Josh. 21:22; 1 Chr. 7:24). Joshua's ancestress was the builder of both cities (1 Chr. 7:24). Here during Joshua's battle with the five kings God rained hailstones on the enemy (Josh. 10:10-11). During Saul's reign it was raided (1 Sam. 13:18), but it was rebuilt by Solomon (1 K. 9:17). It was an important town down to Maccabean times. The sites are identified by modern Beit 'Ur el-Foqa and Beit 'Ur et-Tahta.

Beth-jeshimoth or **-jesimoth** (bĕth-jĕsh'ĭ-mŏth, or -jĕs'ĭ-mŏth) a town on the plains of Moab (in the Jordan valley, East), one of last camps before crossing the Jordan (Num. 33:49); given to Reuben (Josh. 12:3) but later possessed by Moab (Ex. 25:9).

Beth-lebaoth (bĕth'lē-bā'ŏth) or **Lebaoth** (Josh. 15:32) a Simeonite town (Josh. 19:6) in Southern Judah.

Bethlehem (bĕth'lē-hĕm) 1. A town in Judah (Judg. 17:7), six miles south-southwest of Jerusalem, the home of David (2 Sam. 23:15)

and the birthplace of Jesus (Mt. 2:1-16; Lk. 2:4-15; Jn. 7:42) as prophesied by Micah (5:2, in Heb. 5:1). Its earliest name was **Ephrath** or **Ephrathah** (Gen. 35:16, 19, 48:7; Josh. 15:59, LXX), a name which was to linger (Ruth 1:2; Ps. 132:6). It existed as early as Jacob's return to Palestine and after the Conquest assumed its new home (1 Sam. 17:12). Many incidents are associated with it or its inhabitants (e.g., Judg. 17:7, 19:1-9; Ruth; 1 Sam. 16:1-13; 2 Chr. 11:6; Ezra 2:21; Neh. 7:26; Jer. 41:17). The tradition that Jesus was born in a cave near the city where his parents had settled when unable to find a room dates from the time of Justin Martyr (middle of second century). Church buildings at the site of the cave have existed since Constantine (A.D. 325). The present building dates from the time of Justinian (527-65).

2. A town in Zebulun (Josh. 19:15), home and burial place of the judge Ibzan (Judg. 12:8, 10).

Beth-maachah (bĕth-mā'à-ká) a town to which Sheba was pursued by Joab (2 Sam. 20:14-15).

Beth-marcaboth (bĕth-mår'ká-bŏth) [place of chariots] a city of Simeon near Ziklag (Josh. 19:5; 1 Chr. 4:31); probably the same as **Madmannah** (Josh. 15:30 f.).

Beth-meon (bĕth-mē'ŏn) contracted name of Beth-baal-meon (Jer. 48:23).

Beth-nimrah (bĕth-nĭm'rá) a fenced city of Gad east of the Jordan (Num. 32:36) on the plains of Moab; also called simply **Nimrah** (Num. 32:3).

Beth-palet (bĕth-pā'lĕt) a town in the extreme south of Judah (Josh. 15:27; Neh. 11:26).

Beth-pazzez (bĕth-pắz'ĕz) a town of Issachar (Josh. 19:21).

Beth-peor (bĕth-pē'ôr) one of Israel's last campsites (Deut. 3:29, 4:26), burial place of Moses (Deut. 34:6) later given to Reuben (Josh. 13:20).

Bethphage (bĕth'fà-jē) a place on the Mount of Olives not far from Jerusalem and near Bethany (Mt. 21:1; Mk. 11:1; Lk. 19:29), lying on road from Jericho. It is mentioned only in the story of the triumphal entry.

Beth-rapha (bĕth-rā'fá) man in Judah's genealogy (1 Chr. 4:12).

Beth-rehob (bĕth-rē'hŏb) town on northern limits of Palestine near Laish, or Dan (Num. 13:21; Judg. 18:28), later an Aramean stronghold aiding Ammon (2 Sam. 10:6).

Beth-saida (bĕth-sā'ĭ-dà) 1. A city probably on the west side of the Sea of Galilee (Mk. 6:45; Jn. 7:21) in land of Gennesareth, near Capernaum and Chorazin (Mt. 11:21; Lk.

10:13). It was the native city of Andrew, Peter, and Philip (Jn. 1:44, 12:21).

2. Another place on the east side of the Sea of Galilee (cf. Mk. 6:31–53 and Lk. 9:10–17), where Jesus fed the 5000, and probably where he healed a blind man (Mk. 8:22). It is believed to be the place which Philip made his capital and named Julias in honor of Augustus' daughter Julia. Many scholars question the existence of the former place and think the two cities the same.

Bethshan (1 Sam. 31:10, 12) same as **Beth-shean.**

Beth-shean (bĕth-shē'ăn) a city of Western Manasseh (1 Chr. 7:29), though lying within Issachar (Josh. 17:11), from which the Canaanites were not driven out (Judg. 1:27). Its site was some fourteen miles south of Sea of Galilee near the plain of Esdraelon but within the depression of Jordan. Here the Philistines fastened the corpses of Saul and his sons (1 Sam. 31:10–12). Modern excavations have revealed the city as having a long history from 3500 B.C. to Christian times. The name was well-known in Hebrew, Egyptian, and Akkadian texts from fifteenth century onward. Its exploration had aided much in an understanding of the prehistory of Palestine.

Beth-shemesh (bĕth-shē'mĭsh) 1. A town on the north border of Judah (Josh. 15:10). It was near Kirjath-jearim and thus near the low country of Philistia. It was assigned to Dan (Josh. 19:41) but became a Levitical city (21:16). It is named in one of Solomon's administrative districts (1 K. 4:9). Here occurred the battle between Amaziah of Judah and Jehoash of Israel in which Amaziah fell (2 K. 14:11 ff.).

2. A city on the border of Issachar (Josh. 19:22).

3. A fenced city of Naphtali (Josh. 19:38; Judg. 1:33) never taken.

4. A temple or place of Egypt (Jer. 43:13), probably On or Heliopolis.

Beth-shittah (bĕth-shĭt'á) a place to which the Midianites fled after their defeat by Gideon (Judg. 7:22), west of the Jordan.

Beth-tappuah (bĕth-tăp'ū-á) a town of Judah (Josh. 15:53; 1 Chr. 2:43), now modern Taffuh, five miles west of Hebron.

Bethuel (bĕ-thū'ĕl) 1. The son of Nahor by Milcah, nephew of Abraham, and father of Rebekah (Gen. 22:22 f., 24:15, 24, 47, 28:2). He is often called the "Syrian" (25:20). From the fact that he plays a secondary role in the narratives, some have inferred that he was not a responsible person.

2. Also written **Bethul** (bĕth'ŭl) a town in the southern extremity of Judah (1 Chr. 4:30), given originally to Simeon (Josh. 19:4). In 1 Chr. 4:29, a probable scribal error, gives it as **Chesil.**

Beth-zatha see **Bethesda**

Bethzur (bĕth'zûr) a town in the mountains of Judah (Josh. 15:58). Its people helped Nehemiah rebuild the walls (Neh. 3:16; see also 2 Chr. 11:7). It was an important town in later Maccabean times. It is identified with Khirbet et-Tubeiqah, the highest city of Palestine, about four and one-half miles from Hebron.

Betonim (bĕt'ō-nĭm) a Gadite (West border city (Josh. 13:26).

betrothing see **marriage**

Beulah (bū'lá) a name meaning "bride" or "married," symbolic of the future blessedness of Jerusalem and Israel (Isa. 62:4, cf. 54:1–8). For the thought (cf. Jer. 2:2; Hos. 2:14–20) anticipating the NT figure of the church as the bride of Christ (Eph. 5:23 ff.; Rev. 21:2, 9 ff.).

Bezai (bē'zā-ī) children of this man (323 of them) returned with Zerubbabel (Ezra 2:17; Neh. 7:23); probably another of the group is mentioned later (Neh. 10:18).

Bezaleel (bē-zăl'ē-ĕl) 1. A man of Judah of great skill in working metal, wood, and stone, and chosen to construct the tabernacle (Ex. 31:1–6).

2. A man who had taken a foreign wife (Ezra 10:30).

Bezek (bē'zĕk) 1. The city whose king Adoni-bezek was defeated by Judah and Simeon with his Canaanite peoples (Judg. 1:4–5). The king fled but was taken and mutilated.

2. A place where Saul numbered his forces (1 Sam. 11:8).

Bezer (bē'zêr) 1. One of the cities of refuge (Deut. 4:43; Josh. 20:8, 21:36; 1 Chr. 6:78). It lay in the wilderness east of Jordan in the tribe of Reuben.

2. A son of Sophah of Asher (1 Chr. 7:37).

Bible the name applied to the collection of books of the Old and New Testaments comprising one complete volume. The name is derived from the Greek word for papyrus, the plant from which writing materials were derived in the first century A.D. The plural form, *ta biblia*, denotes the OT scriptures (Dan. 9:2) and apocryphal sources (e.g., 1 Macc. 1:56). The term was used by the Greek writers of the fifth century to designate the entire group of canonical books (Old and New Testaments) contrasted with the apocryphal books of the heretics. Though in meaning the term might apply to other books, it is not so used in any early Anglo-Saxon literature. The NT uses other terms such as Scripture (Acts 8:32), the Scriptures (Lk. 24:32), the Holy Scriptures (Rom. 1:2), Sacred Writings (2 Tim. 3:15), the Living Oracles (Acts 7:38), and the designations which call attention to the different books in their Hebrew arrangement: the Law, the Prophets, and the Psalms (Lk. 24:44). The NT writers clearly claim an authority fully as high, nay, even higher than the Old, things not even revealed to the prophets of the Old having been given by the Holy Spirit to those of the New (Eph. 3:5; 1 Cor. 2:9–12). The apostles write as having the Spirit of Christ (1 Cor. 7:40), as teaching and being taught by "revelation of Jesus Christ" (Gal. 1:12). Those who thus spoke by inspiration were considered (as evidenced by the earliest records of the church) to have also written by the same power. Thus early writers clearly indicate the apostolic writings were used in worship as scripture, alongside the OT (see further, **Canon**). The terms which have been used from the end of the second century to designate the dual collections are *Old* and *New Testaments,* a word used to translate Gr. *diathēkē* [Lat. *testamentum*], a term which in contemporary Greek meant a will but from its LXX and Hebrew backgrounds may clearly be seen to derive its meaning from the Heb. *berith,* meaning "covenant," "contract," or "agreement." Thus the terms refer to the writings which record and give the contents of the Old and New Covenants which God has made with his people.

Its Forms. We may speak of the Bible according to the arrangements and languages under which it has been known. I. THE HEBREW BIBLE. The OT as collected by the Jews contained the same material as our thirty-nine books, but they were arranged in only twenty-two books under three major divisions. This arrangement is mentioned in the Prologue to Ecclesiasticus as "the law and the prophets" but occurs fully in Lk. 24:44 as "the Law, the Prophets, and the Psalms." A. Under *the Law* (*torah*) are included the five books of the Pentateuch in their present order, the Hebrew titles being the first word or words of each treatise. B. Under *Prophets* are found what are now commonly called the historical books of Joshua, Judges, Samuel (not divided), and Kings (not divided), comprising the *Early Prophets*; and Isaiah, Jeremiah, Ezekiel, and the twelve minor prophets (all considered one) making up the *Later Prophets*. In the first of these designations "prophet" has its more original meaning of "one who speaks for another, i.e., a teacher"; and emphasis was here placed upon the chronicles and annals of Is-

rael's history for their didactic purpose. C. Under *Psalms* (often referred to as Sacred Writings) were included, in the following order: (1) Psalms, Proverbs, Job; (2) The Song of Solomon, Ruth, Lamentations, Ecclesiastes, and Esther (the five "rolls," read at the five feasts of the Jews), and (3) Daniel, Ezra, Nehemiah, and Chronicles. The original language of the OT was Hebrew except for small sections (such as Ezra 4:8–6:18, 7:12–26; Dan. 2:4b–7:28; Jer. 10:11) originally written in Aramaic.

II. THE GREEK BIBLE. The Greek Bible of the early church was formed in the following manner: The **Septuagint,** a Greek translation made in Egypt, was begun about 285 B.C. and completed at least by 135 B.C. (as proved by the reference in the Prologue to Ecclesiasticus). This contained the thirty-nine books of the English OT together with several additions which the Greek-speaking Jews of Alexandria accepted but which were rejected as apocryphal by Josephus and the Palestinian Jews. Several sections of the canonical books are arranged differently. As we now know from the Dead Sea Scrolls, some of this translation(s) was made from a Hebrew text different from our traditional Hebrew MSS (the Massoretic—MT). With this Greek OT the early church combined the twenty-seven books of the New Covenant to form the Greek Bible. Such is evidenced by the great uncial MSS of the fourth and fifth centuries (e.g., codices B and Aleph). Some of these Bibles have books such as the Epistle of Barnabas bound in them partly for convenience of reference and partly because, until the canon was fixed, some confusion existed as to which books should be considered Scripture. Previous to these entire collections of the Greek scriptures, smaller groupings (such as the gospels or the epistles of Paul) were put together in smaller codices as witnessed by the Chester Beatty Papyri.

III. THE LATIN BIBLE. When and by whom the Bible was translated and collected into the Latin version is unknown. The earlier version(s), known as the Old Latin, was revised by Jerome (ca. A.D. 400). Not until the Council of Trent (sixteenth century) were the OT apocryphal books officially recognized as a part of the Latin Bible by the Roman Catholic Church, a decision rejected by the Protestant tradition, on the basis of evidence from the history of the canon.

IV. THE ENGLISH BIBLE. Though parts of the Bible were translated into English from A.D. 700 (Aldhelm) and at various times (e.g., Venerable Bede, King Alfred, Aelfric, Ormin), the first person to make the Bible available in its entirety was John Wycliffe (NT 1380, OT 1382; from Latin text). The major English versions to follow were those of William Tyndale (first printed English NT 1525, translated from Erasmus' 1516 Greek Testament), Miles Coverdale (first complete printed English Bible, 1535), Thomas Matthews (1537), the Great Bible (1539), the Geneva Bible (1560), the Bishops' Bible (1568), the King James (1611), the English Revised (1881, 1885), the American Standard Edition of the Revised (1901), followed by many twentieth-century translations of either Testament or of the whole.

Chapter and Verse Divisions. The Bible in its original form had no punctuation, not to speak of divisions into chapters and verses. The Jewish scriptures even in NT times probably were marked in some way to indicate a cycle of lessons (as indicated by Lk. 4:17; Acts 13:15, 15:21; 2 Cor. 3:14). The Talmud presents a system of division somewhat like our chapter and verse divisions (e.g., the Law was divided into fifty-four sections, called *parshioth*, one for each sabbath of the Jewish intercalary year). The present chapter divisions were devised by Hugh de St. Cher and used first in the Vulg., being transferred to the English Bible by Coverdale. The present verse division was done by the French printer Robert Stephanus in his 1551 edition of the Greek Testament, adopted for the Vulg. in 1559, and for the Geneva Bible in 1560.

Bichri (bĭk'rī) father of the insurrectionist Sheba (2 Sam. 20:1).

Bidkar (bĭd'kàr) the fellow officer captain of Jehu (2 K. 9:25), who threw Joram's body into Naboth's vineyard.

Bigtha (bĭg'thà) a eunuch of Ahasuerus (Est. 1:10).

Bigthan or **Bigthana** (bĭg'thăn or bĭg'thā'nà) a eunuch of Ahasuerus (Xerxes) who plotted the king's death, a plot discovered and averted by Mordecai (Est. 2:21–23, 6:2).

Bigvai (bĭg'vā-ī) a name occurring in Ezra and Nehemiah and identifying: 1. The ancestor of a large group which returned from the Exile (Ezra 2:14; Neh. 7:19) and of a smaller group later (Ezra 8:14).

2. A leader of the same name (Ezra 2:2; Neh. 7:7, 10:16).

Bildad (bĭl'dăd) the second of Job's three friends, called a "Shuhite" (from Shuah, Abraham's son by Keturah—Gen. 25:2). His three speeches occur in Job 8, 18, 25.

Bileam (bĭl'ē-ăm) a town of West Manasseh given to the Kohathites (1 Chr. 6:70). Par-

alleled by Ibleam in Joshua's lists (17:11; Judg. 1:27).

Bilgah (bĭl'gà) 1. Head of fifteenth course of the priests in time of David (1 Chr. 24:14).

2. Priest in time of Nehemiah (Neh. 12:5, 18); same as Bilgai (?) (Neh. 10:8).

Bilgai (Neh. 10:8) see **Bilgah 2**

Bilhah (bĭl'hà) 1. Handmaid of Rachel (Gen. 29:29) and concubine of Jacob to whom Dan and Naphtali were born (Gen. 30:3–8, 35:25, 46:25; 1 Chr. 7:13; see also Gen. 35:22).

2. A town of Simeon (1 Chr. 4:29).

Bilhan (bĭl'hàn) 1. Grandson of Seir the Horite of Edom (Gen. 36:27; 1 Chr. 1:42).

2. A Benjaminite (1 Chr. 7:10).

Bilshan (bĭl'shăn) companion of Zerubbabel on the return from exile (Ezra 2:2; Neh. 7:7).

Bimhal (bĭm'hăl) an Asherite (1 Chr. 7:33).

Binea (bĭn'ī-à) descendant of Saul (1 Chr. 8:37).

binding and loosing figurative expression of the exercise of power or privilege. Peter is promised the "keys of the kingdom" (Mt. 16:18), and all the apostles were promised this power (Mt. 18:18). Peter's "keys" represented his first giving of the terms of entrance into the kingdom at Pentecost (Acts 2:38) and at Cornelius' house (Acts 10:48). The apostles were inspired revealers of God's plan of salvation. Peter and the keys of heaven is medieval fiction.

Binnui (bĭn'ū-ī) 1. A Levite in Ezra's time (Ezra 8:33).

2. A man who had taken a foreign wife (Ezra 10:30).

3. A son of Bani guilty of same deed (Ezra 10:38).

4. Alternate spelling for Bani (Neh. 7:15).

5. A Levite who helped rebuild the walls (Neh. 3:24).

Birazvith or **Birzaith** a name, apparently a place, in the genealogy of Asher (1 Chr. 7:31).

birds see **fowls**

Birsha (bĭr'shà) king of Gomorrah (Gen. 14:2, 10).

birthdays the Bible has several references and observances in honor of the day of one's birth (Gen. 40:20; Jer. 20:15). The expression "his day" (Job 1:4; Hos. 7:5; cf. Mt. 14:6) is thought to refer to the custom.

birthright the advantages belonging to the first-born of a family. From early times these advantages meant special honor, authority, and inheritance. The law of Moses allotted (Deut. 21:15–17) a "double" (or "two-thirds"; see Paul Watson, *Restoration Quarterly* 8 [1965], 70–75). Compare Elisha's request (2 K. 2:9). The firstborn was the king's successor (2 Chr.

21:3). The Jews attached the title ("firstborn") to the Messiah as one of honor (Rom. 8:29; Heb. 1:6). In the OT several lost or despised the birthright; so Esau (Gen. 25:29–34) and Reuben (Gen. 49:4; 1 Chr. 5:1).

bishop [word is derived from the Gr. *episkopos*, overseer, guardian]. The word was in use both as a general description and as a designation of office. It was especially used of the gods as watchers over human affairs. Cynic philosophers so designated themselves. A ship captain was spoken of as the guardian of the cargo, and a tutor was a guardian of children. Among the officials receiving this title were building inspectors, municipal officials at Rhodes, overseers of slaves, and officers in clubs. There is no evidence of any accepted technical significance for the word, and it had no religious connotation (although it could be used of religious officials, as it is of a temple officer of Apollo). The Greek translation of the OT shows the same usage: of God (Job 20:29); of any kind of oversight (Num. 4:16); of various officials (Num. 31:14; Judg. 9:28; 2 Chr. 34:12). Hence, an *episkopos* could perform any kind of general oversight and administration. Some have seen in the Jewish "ruler of the synagogue," who presided over the synagogue service, a partial parallel to the bishop in the church. There was in first-century Judaism, among the Essenes, an official who bears a fuller resemblance to the later bishop. From the Dead Sea Scrolls and related documents we learn of the *mebaqqer* [inspector, supervisor] who as "superintendent of the general assembly" administered funds and discipline, had to "examine every new adherent to the community," was to "enlighten the masses about the work of God," and should "bring back all of them that stray as does a shepherd his flock." But Greek writers use *epimeletes* and not *episkopos* for this functionary. In the NT *episkopos* is used of Christ (1 Pet. 2:25); of the apostles (in applying an OT quotation— Acts 1:20); and of officers in the church. In regard to the latter, bishop appears as equivalent to elder (Acts 20:17, 28, and Tit. 1:5, 7). The work of elders is that of oversight (according to some MSS of 1 Pet. 5:2). The same interchangeable usage appears in post-apostolic writings: 1 Clement 42–44 declares the apostolic institution of the office of bishops in each town and refers to these as elders; the Didache instructs the appointment of bishops and deacons with no reference to elders; and the Letter of Polycarp to the Philippians speaks of presbyters and deacons with no reference to a

bishop. It may be that the one term (elder) was more natural in a Jewish context (Acts 11:30, 14:23, 15:6) and the other (bishop) in a Gentile background (Phil. 1:1). This latter passage as well as the ones cited above from the NT and post-apostolic writers, indicates a plurality of bishops in each community. The "bishop" (1 Tim. 3:2 and Tit. 1:7) means the bishop as a type and does not refer to the number in a church. However, the work of oversight is by its nature singular (the overseer of a particular work was the bishop of that activity); whereas, elder by its Jewish background had a corporate association. Hence, *episkopos* was the natural word for use when a single head of the college of presbyters emerged in the second century (first seen in the Ignatian epistles). The prestige of James the brother of the Lord in the Jerusalem church (Acts 21:17) may have served as a prototype for the development of the single bishop. Timothy and Titus were not bishops. In the Pastoral epistles they are presented as evangelists (2 Tim. 4:5) and are distinguished from the bishops whose qualifications are given as quite a distinct office (1 Tim. 3:1 ff., 4:6 ff.; Tit. 1:5 ff., 2:1 ff.). The qualifications (laid down in 1 Tim. 3 and Tit. 1) indicate the type of man looked for and correspond to the duties of the office. As a leader and representative of the community a bishop is to be a man of blameless life and reputation, both within and without the church, and not a recent convert. As spiritual guardian he must have a fitness for teaching, both positive and negative. As administrator of the church's charity he must be honest, hospitable, and not greedy. As shepherd he must have his temper under control, a model marital relationship ("a one-woman kind of man"), and the experience of family life in the rearing of children. To these supervisors fell the leadership of the churches as the apostles, prophets, and evangelists withdrew their personal direction. Their selection and appointment is not described in detail in the NT. The scriptures indicate that there were instances of designations made by inspired prophets (Acts 20:28), appointment by apostles or evangelists (Acts 14:23; Tit. 1:5), and choice by the whole community (cf. Acts 6:1–6). The instances of appointment to a work in the church of which we have record indicate a worship service, including prayer and the laying on of hands (Acts 6:1–6, 13:1–3; 1 Tim. 4:16), and this may be inferred for bishops.   E.F.

Bithiah (bĭ-thī'á) daughter of Pharaoh and wife of Mered of Judah (1 Chr. 4:18); some have conjectured that she was a captive or a convert to Judaism.

Bithron (bĭth'rŏn) a district in the Arabah or Jordan Valley (mentioned only in 2 Sam. 2:29). RSV interprets as meaning "forenoon" and not a place.

Bithynia (bĭ-thĭn'ĭ-à) a province in Northern Asia Minor bordering on the Black Sea. It was a Roman province. Paul desired to go there to preach but was forbidden (Acts 16:7). Peter addressed Christians there (1 Pet. 1:1).

blasphemy any of a species of abusive, reviling, or cursing speech against a person (1 K. 21:10; Acts 18:6; Jude 9). But more specifically the reviling or speaking evil against God (Ps. 74:18; Isa. 52:5; Rom. 2:24). It was specifically condemned in the third commandment (Ex. 20:7) and in Lev. 24:10–16 as a sin punishable by stoning to death (cf. Lev. 24:11). The Jews considered it blasphemy to pronounce the sacred name of God (YHWH, probably "Yahweh"), and put the vowels of the word for "Lord" with it, leading to the composite "Jehovah" (KJV; RSV LORD). The blasphemy of the Holy Spirit (Mt. 12:32) is interpreted in Mark (3:28 ff.) as attributing the power by which Jesus cast out demons to the Devil.

Blastus (blăs'tŭs) the man in charge of the royal bedchambers of Herod Agrippa and who made a mediation between him and the people of Tyre and Sidon (Acts 12:20).

bless, blessing, blessedness in the OT the word translated "bless" actually means to "worship" or "adore," and the adjective "blessed" properly means "worshiped" or "adored." However, the same verb describes God's "blessing" men by bestowing his grace and kindness upon them (Gen. 1:28, 24:1; Ps. 33:12). Similarly, men may bless others when they invoke God's favor upon them (Gen. 14:19; Mt. 5:44; 1 Pet. 3:9). The adjective "blessed" (as in the Beatitudes) refers to the happiness or fortune of men who are assured of his favor because their attitudes are right before the Lord.

blindness the loss of eyesight, a common occurrence in Bible lands, for which there were many causes (ophthalmia, trachoma, gonorrheal or septic infection, and degenerative defects such as glaucoma, cataract, or optic atrophy). Blind beggars are repeatedly mentioned (Mt. 12:22), and healing of them is predicted of the Christ (Isa. 29:18). The Jews were charged to treat the blind with compassion (Lev. 19:14). Penal, miraculous, and politically motivated blindness are mentioned (Gen. 19:11; 1 Sam. 11:2; 2 K. 6:18–22; Jer. 39:7; Acts 9:9). Blindness is often used

metaphorically for spiritual hardness of heart.

blood the Scriptures ascribe blood a sacredness because of its connection with life. In giving man dominion God reserved the blood to himself. Thus blood acquired a special power: (1) that of sacrificial atonement; and (2) that of becoming a curse when wantonly shed, unless expiated (Gen. 9:4; Lev. 7:26). As to (1), the blood of sacrifices was caught by the priest, then sprinkled seven times (in case of birds squeezed at once on the altar, that of the Passover lamb put on the lintel and doorpost (Ex. 12; Lev. 4:5 ff., 16:14 ff.). As to (2), the animal's blood was buried or poured upon the ground; the blood of human life shed was associated with a curse upon the land upon which it fell; it must be avenged (Gen. 4:10, 9:4 ff.; Num. 35:33; Ps. 106:38).

blood, issue of the menstrous discharge or the *flux uteri* (Lev. 15:19–30; Mt. 9:20; Mk. 5:25; Lk. 8:43).

blood, the avenger of the law of Moses was very precise in its direction on the subject of retaliation. 1. The willful murderer was to be put to death without compensation. The nearest relative of the deceased became the authorized avenger of blood (*goel*, Num. 35:19) and was bound to execute retaliation himself if it lay in his power (the penalty seemingly was modified later by the kings). The shedder of blood was thus regarded as polluted (e.g., Num. 35:16 ff.; Deut. 19:11; 2 Sam. 14:7).·

2. The Law did not extend beyond the immediate offender (Deut. 24:16; 2 K. 14:6).

3. The involuntary killer was permitted to flee to one of six Levitical cities especially appointed as cities of refuge, three on each side of the Jordan (Num. 35:22 f.; Deut. 19:4 ff.).

Boanerges (bō'à-nûr'jēz) [sons of thunder] name given by Jesus to the two sons of Zebedee, James and John, probably because of their zeal (Mk. 9:38; Lk. 9:54; cf. Mt. 20:20).

Boaz (bō'ăz) 1. A Bethlehemite kinsman of Elimelech the husband of Naomi, who found that the nearest kinsman of Ruth the widow would not perform the duty of husband under the "Levirate law" and who performed the deed and redeemed the estates of her dead husband (Ruth 4:1 ff.). Their happy union was blessed by the birth of Obed, from whom our Lord descended (Mt. 1:5).

2. The name of one of Solomon's brazen pillars in the temple porch (1 K. 7:15, 21; 2 Chr. 3:15).

Bocheru (bō'kĕ-rōō) descendant of Saul (1 Chr. 8:38).

Bochim (bō'kĭm) [the weepers] a place so

called because of tears of rebuke—west of Jordan (Judg. 2:1, 5).

Bohan (bō'hăn) a Reubenite after whom a stone was named, set up on the border of Judah and Benjamin (Josh. 15:6).

boil see **medicine**

bolster see **pillow**

bondage see **slavery**

bonnet see **headdress**

book see **writing**

booth see **succoth; tabernacles, feast of**

booty captives of both sexes, cattle, and whatever a captured city might contain, especially money or metal. No Canaanite captives could be made (Deut. 20:14–18); otherwise the men might be put to death or made captive. (On the division of booty between warriors and others, see Num. 31:26–47; 1 Sam. 30:24 f.)

Booz alternate spelling (Mt. 1:5; Lk. 3:32) for **Boaz.**

borrowing see **loan**

Boscath (2 K. 22:1) see **Bozkath**

Bosor (bō'sôr) Aramaic pronunciation of Beor, father of **Balaam** (2 Pet. 2:15).

bottles words so translated refer either to: 1. Bottles made of whole goatskins removed without cutting except for the neck and leg openings which are tied up (Ps. 119:83; Mt. 9:17). 2. Bottles made of metal, clay, or glass. Jeremiah spoke of a "potter's earthen bottle" (Jer. 19:1). Sherds of broken bottles and vessels have been studied minutely by modern archaeologists and form one of the most important items of dating and revealing the nature of ancient civilization.

bow see **arms**

bowl bowl and "basin" were often used somewhat interchangeably and uncertainty exists as to differences. Bowls were used for liquids at meals (2 K. 4:40).

box tree the Heb. *te'ashshur* is so translated mostly on medieval authority. RSV renders "pine." (The word occurs in Isa. 41:19, 60:13; Ezek. 27:6.)

Bozez (bō'zĕz) one "tooth" or twin peak between which Jonathan entered to surprise the Philistines (1 Sam. 14:4 f.).

Bozkath (bŏz'kăth) a village in the hills of Judah (Josh. 15:39; 2 K. 22:1).

Bozrah (bŏz'rà) 1. The Edomite fortress city of Jobab (Gen. 36:33; 1 Chr. 1:44), twenty miles southeast of the Dead Sea, modern Buseira. It was often mentioned by the prophets as a symbol of Edom's strength (Isa. 34:6, 63:1; Jer. 49:13; Amos 1:12; Mic. 2:12).

2. A Moabite city in the plain east of the Dead Sea, perhaps same as **Bezer** (Jer. 48:24).

bracelet ornament worn around the wrist commonly used by both men and women (Song of S. 5:14). Archaeological remains are common.

bramble a tangled shrub with sharp spines used as illustration in a fable by Jotham (Judg. 9:8–15) and in a parable by Jesus (Lk. 6:44).

branch a secondary shoot or stem of a tree or other plant. Many different original words are so translated. In OT times kings or princes were often referred to as a shoot or branch, and so the metaphor is applied to the Messiah to come (Isa. 11:1; Jer. 23:5, 33:15; Zech. 3:8, 6:12).

brass passages so rendered in KJV should mostly be rendered **bronze** (copper-tin), inasmuch as the copper-zinc compound was unknown to OT times. (For references to such metals, see Gen. 4:22; Deut. 8:9, 33:25; Job 28:2.)

brazen serpent see **serpent**

bread a food made from flour or meal mixed with liquid, shortening, yeast or leavening, worked into a mass (kneaded), permitted to rise, and baked. The word also is sometimes a more general word meaning "food" (Gen. 3:19; Mt. 6:11). Wheat flour (Judg. 6:19) made the best bread, but other grains such as barley might be used (Judg. 7:13; 2 K. 4:42), and other ingredients might be used to "stretch" the quantity (Ezek. 4:9). Flour was mixed with water; sometimes unleavened loaves were baked; or a small portion of the previous day's batch might furnish leaven (Mt. 13:33). Baking was on hot stones (1 K. 19:6), on a pan or griddle (1 Chr. 23:29), or an oven, which was usually a large earthen jar turned upside down. In many places there were fixed ovens to which people might bring their loaves for cooking. Thus streets or sections were often called **"Bakers' Street"** (Jer. 37:21; Neh. 3:11, 12:38). Bread taken on a trip was probably a kind of biscuit. See the whole description of bread-making in Ezek. 4:9–17. With bread being such an important item, it is natural that it should furnish many illustrations and metaphorical references. Joshua called the Canaanites "our bread" (Num. 14:9); God sends his erring people "the bread of adversity" (Isa. 30:20). Jesus himself is "the bread of life" which if one eats he will never hunger (Jn. 6:35, 48–51).

breastplate see **arms**

brethren of Jesus see **James**

brick building blocks molded from clay and either dried in the sun or burnt in kilns (2 Sam. 12:31; Jer. 43:9). Mortar was mud itself or bitumen (Gen. 11:3). Straw was usually mixed with the clay or laid with the rows to give greater strength (cf. Ex. 5, where Israel was compelled to find their own straw for their quota). Though hewn rock was plentiful in Palestine, brick was the most common building material.

bride, bridegroom see **marriage**

bridge the English Bible makes no mention of bridges. Rivers were usually crossed by fords or by floating across (e.g., Xenophon's famous crossing of the Euphrates). The Romans developed the bridge extensively.

brier see **thorns**

brigandine KJV translation of "coat of mail" (Jer. 46:4).

brimstone properly speaking, **sulphur**, though applied from its etymology (from a resinous wood, gopher) to other inflammable substances. It is generally applied to divine judgment either natural (Gen. 19:24; Isa. 34:9) or the eternal lake of fire (Rev. 20:10, 21:8).

brother the Hebrew word is used not only of a male kinsman having the same parents (either one, Gen. 28:2; Judg. 8:19; or two, Gen. 28:2), but also of various other relationships: a nephew (Gen. 14:6), husband (Song of S. 4:9), a fellow tribesman (2 Sam. 19:13), or one of the same people (Ex. 2:11; Num. 20:14), an ally (Amos 1:9) or even a friend (Job 5:15), partner in office (1 K. 9:13), and at last a fellowman (Lev. 19:17). The Greek word is similarly elastic, being used for disciple (Mt. 25:40) and quite widely for a fellow Christian (1 Cor. 5:11; Lk. 10:29 f.). For "brothers of the Lord," see **James.**

Bukki (bŭk′ī) 1. High priest, fifth in the line from Aaron (1 Chr. 5:31, 6:36), called **Boccas** in Ezra 7:4.

2. Danite prince who helped divide the land (Num. 34:22).

Bukkiah (bŭ-kī′à) a Levite musician (1 Chr. 15:4, 13).

bul see **months**

bull, bullock terms used synonymously with ox, oxen, in the KJV representing several Hebrew words, sometimes for horned cattle generically or of either cow, ox, or bullock (Gen. 12:16; Isa. 65:25; Ezek. 4:15). Some later versions avoid "bullock" because its strict meaning is a "young" bull. Most general statements with reference to **cattle** apply here. "Bulls" is often used in metaphorical language (Ps. 22:12, 68:30; Isa. 10:13). Special significance was found in the bull as a sacrifice. Such sacrifices were often to be of a specific age (Lev. 22:27; 1 Sam. 1:24), though not usually (Lev. 1–5). They were to be uncastrated and without blemish (Lev. 1:3, 22:24). Sacrifices on special occasions were often individual (Judg. 6:25; 1 Sam. 1:24; Job 1:5) and were frequent in such

special services as dedications (Ex. 29:1 ff.; Num. 7) at the great feasts (e.g., Num. 28:16 ff.). The bull played an important part in the worship ritual of Near Eastern countries. He was a symbol of fertility, a basic motif in many such religions. For example, El the father god was called "The Bull," while Hadad the Baal is pictured in statues with the horns of a bull on his helmet. Such influences may have had a part in the choice of Jeroboam's calves which he set up at Dan and Bethel (1 K. 12:28).

Bunah (bū′nà) a descendant of Judah (1 Chr. 2:25).

Bunni (bŭn′ī) the name of two Levites in Nehemiah's time, referred to, one in Neh. 9:4, the other, in Neh. 11:15.

burial, sepulchres, tombs the Jews disposed of the corpses of their dead by putting them in tombs or (if these were not available) burying them in the earth. This respect was paid even to the enemy or the malefactor (1 K. 11:15; Deut. 21:23). This contrasted with many peoples who exposed or burned their dead on a funeral pyre. Burning was practiced only as a dishonor or vengeance or for punishment (Lev. 20:14, 21:9; Josh. 7:25; 1 Sam. 31:12; Amos 6:10). As to places for burial, pre-Biblical people often buried in urns beneath the floor, but later either natural or artificial cones outside the limits of the cities were niched to provide places for the dead. Coffins were not common except in Egypt, where they were shaped like the human figure (Joseph's body was put in one, Gen. 50:26). Single graves were evidently not common; the graveyard at Qumran (in open field) contained over a thousand graves. The Hebrews did not usually embalm, as was the custom in Egypt. Burial usually followed quickly upon death (Gen. 23:4; Deut. 21:23). Bodies were prepared for burial by washing and anointing (2 Chr. 16:14; Mk. 16:1–2; Acts 9:37). Graves were marked and "whited" lest passersby should defile themselves. Grave clothes are mentioned, and probably over these the corpse was swathed and fastened with bandages. Some of the famous burial places in Palestine were the cave of Machpelah, where Abraham, Sarah, Isaac, Rebekah, Leah, and Jacob were buried (Gen. 23:19, 25:9, 49:31, 50:13), and the Tombs of the Kings (2 K. 9:28; 2 Chr. 16:14).

burnt offering an offering or sacrifice wholly consumed by fire on the altar. Since at least part of each sacrifice was dedicated to God and burnt, all offerings were "burnt offerings" in some sense of the word, but the term is usually applied to *whole* burnt offerings. They are mentioned from Gen. 8:20 on (e.g., 15:9,

17, 22:2, 7, 8, 13). Later they became one regular class of sacrifice. The burnt offering was dedicatory, signifying the offering of the person of the worshiper to God, and it typified Christ's offering of himself (Heb. 5:1, 3, 7, 8). They were accompanied by drink and meal—flour and oil (see e.g., Lev. 8:18, 9:16, 14:20). Details are given mostly in Leviticus. They included: (1) daily (Ex. 29:38 ff.), (2) sabbath (Num. 28:9 f.), (3) festival occasions such as New Moon, Atonement, and the three great feasts (Num. 28:11–29:39), and (4) private burnt offerings appointed for dedication and purification (Lev. 8:18, 9:12, 12:6–8, 14:19, 15:15, 30; Num. 6). Freewill burnt offerings might be made at any time (cf. Num. 7 and 1 K. 8:64).

bush the Heb. *seneh* is used of the burning bush in which God appeared to Moses (Ex. 3:2–4; Deut. 33:16; LXX Gr. *batos*, and in Lk. 20:37; Acts 7:35; Lk. 6:44 KJV, bramble).

bushel see **measures**

Buz (bŭz) 1. Second son of Milcah and Nahor, hence nephew of Abraham (Gen. 22:21).

2. A Gadite (1 Chr. 5:14).

Buzi (bū′zī) father of Ezekiel (Ezek. 1:3).

Buzite a descendant of **Buz** or one from their territory (Arabian Desert), as for example, Elihu the Buzite (Job 32:2).

C

cab see **measures**

Cabbon (kăb′ŏn) a town in Judah (Josh. 15:40).

Cabul (kā′bŭl) 1. A border city of Asher (Josh. 19:27) in northeastern Galilee, modern Kabul, nine miles from Acre.

2. A district ceded by Solomon to Hiram of Tyre (1 K. 9:13; 2 Chr. 8:2).

Caesar (sē′zẽr) the family name of Julius Caesar adopted by Augustus and his successors, thus becoming the title of the Roman emperors (Jn. 19:12, 15; Acts 17:7).

Caesarea (sĕs′à-rē′à) an important city on the coast of Palestine, twenty-three miles south of Mount Carmel, and seventy miles from Jerusalem. The NT city was begun by Herod the Great about 25 B.C., finished in 13 B.C. and named for Caesar Augustus. It became the official capital of Palestine under Herod the Great and the Roman governors such as Felix and Festus. NT references are: Acts 8:40, 9:30, 10:1, 24, 11:11, 12:19, 18:22, 21:8, 16, 23:23, 33, 25:1, 4, 6, 13.

Caesarea Philippi (sĕs′à-rē′à fĭ-lĭp′ī) city built on a limestone terrace in valley at the base of Mount Hermon near a large spring forming one of the two main sources of the Jordan; mentioned in Scriptures only in Mt. 16:13; Mk. 8:27. It is probably the Baal-gad of the OT (Josh. 11:17 ff.; Judg. 3:3; 1 Chr. 5:23). In NT times it was called Paneion, its region Paneas, until remodeled by Herod Philip and named for Tiberius Caesar. Here Jesus asked his disciples the question of his identity and received Peter's confession that he was Christ, the Son of God. Its modern name is Banias.

cage an enclosure made of bars for keeping birds and animals (Ezek. 19:9, Eccl. 11:30) but also a prison structure (2 K. 24:12–15, 25:27–30; Rev. 18:2).

Caiaphas (kā′à-făs) high priest of Jews (A.D. 18–36) and hence during Jesus' ministry and trial (Mt. 26:3, 57; Jn. 11:49, 18:13, 14, 24, 28; Acts 4:6). Annas, his father-in-law, was high priest A.D. 7–14, and the mention of both Caiaphas and Annas in Jesus' trials is to be explained presumably by his being accorded honor after being put out of office.

Cain (kān) eldest son of Adam and Eve, a farmer, who, angered by the rejection of his sacrifice to God, slew his brother Abel (Gen. 4). He was exiled to land of Nod, where he built a city named for his son Enoch. NT references (Heb. 11:4; 1 Jn. 3:12; Jude 11) are to Cain's unrighteousness and to his "way" as that of hate and murder. Two frequent questions are (1) What was his mark? (2) Where did he get his wife? (1) The mark was probably a "sign" like that given to others (Gen. 9:3; Ex. 3:2, 17; 1 K. 19:11; Isa. 38:7, 8). (2) The narrative implies a considerable population in Cain's time (4:14).

Cain (kān) a city of Judah (Josh. 15:57).

Cainan (kā-ī′năn) (ASV, **Kenan**) 1. Son of Enos, the fourth from Adam in Christ's line (Gen. 5:9–14).

2. Son of Arphaxad, according to Lk. 3:36 found in LXX of Gen. 10:24, and 11:12 (not in Hebrew) from which Luke quoted.

cakes see **bread**

Calah (kā′lȧ) an ancient city of Assyria, founded by Nimrod (Gen. 10:11) (not Asshur as in KJV). Now called Nimrud, on Tigris just below Nineveh.

Calamus (kăl′ȧ-mŭs) a manufactured product made from an aromatic reed (Ex. 30:23; Song of S. 4:14; Ezek. 27:19). See **reed**

Calcol (kăl′kŏl) a Judahite (1 Chr. 2:6).

caldron a vessel (either metal or earthenware) for boiling flesh (1 Sam. 2:14; 2 Chr. 35:13; Mic. 3:3; Job 41:20).

Caleb (kā′lĕb) 1. One of the two faithful spies sent out by Moses (Num. 13–14). While the other spies spoke discouragingly of taking the land, Caleb and Joshua believed God would be with Israel. The refusal to believe this was taken as rebellion, and the whole generation was rejected from entering the promised land (Num. 14:23). Caleb was the son of Jephunneh and belonged to the family of Kenaz, from which he is called "the Kenezite" (Num. 13:6, 32:12; Josh. 14:6, 14). Later Caleb claimed Hebron as his possession (Josh. 14) from which he drove the sons of Anak. He offered his daughter Achsah to the one who would take Kirjath-Sepher. His younger brother Othniel thus claimed the prize. Because of various statements in the genealogies, it is conjectured that Caleb may have been a foreigner (see 1 Chr. 2; Josh. 14:14, 15:13).

2. The grandfather of Caleb the spy, according to 1 Chr. 2:9, 18, 19, 42, 50.

Caleb-Ephratah (ĕf′rá-tȧ) place where Hezron died, according to Hebrew text of 1 Chr. 2:24. Jerome says his text, which the LXX follows, reads "Caleb came in unto Ephratah, the wife of Hezron." It is thus not a place.

calf the young of the bovine. They were used for food and sacrifice. They are mentioned in various aspects (1 Sam. 6:7, 10; Isa. 27:10; Job 21:10). The wealthy enjoyed veal as a delicacy (Gen. 18:7 f.; 1 Sam. 28:24, 15:23–30; Amos 6:4). They were, like bulls, specified for some sacrifices (Lev. 9:2 f.; Mic. 6:6). Jeroboam set up worship of calves at Dan and Bethel (1 K. 12:28). Those making covenants used calves ritually in the passing among dismembered parts of a calf (Gen. 15:9 ff.; Jer. 34:18). See **cattle**

Calneh or **Calno** (căl′nĕ, căl′nō) one of four cities founded by Nimrod (Gen. 10:10), in Shinar or South Mesopotamia. Modern Nippur or Kulunu has been claimed as the site. Also called Calno (Isa. 10:9).

Calvary [Latin word used in Lk. 23:33 (fr. *calvaria*, in the Vulg.) for translating the Gr. *kranion*, which equals the Heb. *Golgotha*, skull, the place of the crucifixion] that this was on a hill (thus "Mount Calvary") is a popular idea derived from the shape of a skull. Nothing in the text so indicates. The place is disputed, the place either of the Church of the Holy Sepulchre or Gordon's Calvary being generally accepted as correct.

camel one of two large cud-chewing mammals utilized as pack and riding animals in the desert areas of Africa and Asia. The Arabian (dromedary) camel has only one large hump, while the Bactrian camel has two. The latter was the slower burden-bearing animal (Gen. 37:25); the **dromedary** was swifter (1 Sam. 30:17). Camel bones have been found datable near 2000 B.C.; and, though inscriptional evidence for early domestication is slight, the Biblical documentation for patriarchal use need not be suspected. Abraham had camels in Egypt (Gen. 12:16) and later (20:10), as did Jacob (30:43, 31:17, 32:15). The desert tribes used them in raids against Israel (Judg. 6:5). Their use by caravan traders is mentioned (e.g., when Joseph was sold, Gen. 37:25). References to large numbers and herds are too numerous to detail (1 Chr. 5:21; Job 1:3, 42:2). The camel is well adapted to the desert. Its flat foot enables it to walk on the sand. It eats the desert plants and can go as long as twenty days in cool weather without water. (See Gen. 24 for details about the care of camels.) Their wool and hide were used for clothing, their milk and sometimes their flesh (though unclean for a Jew, Lev. 11:4) were used for food. Jesus' comparison of the difficulty of the rich entering the kingdom of heaven to a camel going through the eye of a needle should not be interpreted as referring to a small gate, but as a hyperbole for the impossible—in this case, even the impossible is "possible with God" (Mt. 19:24).

Camon (kā′mŏn) burial place of Judge Jair in Gilead (Judg. 10:5).

camp see **encampment**

Camphire (kăm′fīr) whence our word camphor. The KJV translation of the Heb. *kopher* in Song of S. 1:14, 4:13. The true identification (ASV) is the henna flower, a thorny bush with white fragrant flowers which grows in clusters four to six feet tall throughout much of the Middle East.

Cana of Galilee (kā′nȧ) a village or town not far from Capernaum, where Christ turned water to wine (Jn. 2:1–11, 4:46) and where later he healed the nobleman's son from Capernaum.

It was also Nathanael's home (Jn. 21:2). Modern geographers tend to identify it with Qana el-Jelil nine miles north of Nazareth, rather than at Kefr Kenna, where Greek and Roman churches celebrate the deeds.

Canaan (kā'năn) 1. The fourth son of Ham (Gen. 10:6; 1 Chr. 1:8), whose descendants occupied the lands of Phoenicia and much of Palestine (Gen. 9:18, 22, 10:13; 1 Chr. 1:13).

2. The land inhabited in early Bible times by the Canaanites, being mostly Palestine between the Jordan and the Mediterranean and Syria or Phoenicia (cf. Ex. 15:15; Isa. 19:18; Zeph. 2:5).

Canaan, Land of [literally lowland] the country between the Jordan and the Dead Sea and the Mediterranean as opposed to the high tableland of Gilead, east of Jordan. The principal regions are (1) the maritime plain along the coast, (2) the Shephelah, or foothills, (3) the central mountain district running from Galilee through Judah, leveling off to the Negeb and "South" region toward the wilderness of Sinai, and (4) the remarkable valley of "Ghor" of the Jordan River with the (5) eastern tableland in the background. The entire area was about 12,000 square miles, comparable to the area of the state of Massachusetts.

Canaanites (kā'năn-īts) descendants of Noah and the people who came from him (Gen. 10:15-19; 1 Chr. 1:8, 13-16). Canaan was a grandson of Noah, the son of Ham (Gen. 9:18, 10:6; 1 Chr. 1:8). In Gen. 9:22 Ham is mentioned as father of Canaan; the mention of Canaan in vs. 24 as the "younger son of Noah" should be understood as "offspring." The Canaanites were the tribes which inhabited much of Palestine at the time of Joshua's invasion. They were a Semitic people. The name itself is of uncertain meaning. It is thought to be of Hurrian origin and may connect with the idea of "merchants" (Ezek. 17:4; Hos. 12:8; Zeph. 1:11; Zech. 11:7, 11). The name is applied to the area of the Phoenician coast in Egyptian inscriptions (1800 B.C.) and in the Amarna Letters (1400 B.C.). They were not confined to any one section of Palestine (Judg. 1:9-10), and in some texts the word may refer to the whole people of the land west of the Jordan (Gen. 12:6, 50:11; Josh. 7:9), though, more specifically, the people were concentrated in the plains and lowlands of the Jordan valley (Num. 13:29, 14:25; Josh. 11:3). The name may even be used of the Phoenicians (Isa. 23:11; Obad. 20). The Canaanite language belongs to the northwestern group of Semitic languages. It has many affinities with Hebrew. A script much like Egyptian hieroglyphics was used, though at other places (Ras Shamra) cuneiform was used. For the religious life, see **Baal.**

Canaanite, Simon the, or **Cananean,** [literally from Aram. jealous one, zealot] the designation of one Simon, a disciple of Jesus. In Lk. 6:15; Acts 1:13, the Greek for zealot is used. He evidently had belonged to the party of the Zealots.

Candace (kăn'dà-sē) a queen of **Ethiopia** (**Meroe**) whose treasurer Philip baptized (Acts 8:27). The term was not a proper name but a title (somewhat like "queen") worn by rulers of that land.

candle KJV translation of word for **lamp.** Candles were not used in Biblical times.

candlestick [*menorah*] the lampstand constructed at God's direction, which stood on the left or south side as the priest entered the tabernacle (Ex. 25:31-40). In the temple of Solomon the lampstands were before the most holy place (2 Chr. 4:7; 1 K. 7:49). The lamps were not "candles," which were not used in Biblical times, but olive lamps. The lampstand was constructed of seven branches.

cane an aromatic **reed** from which an oil was extracted.

cankerworm see **locust**

Canneh alternate form of **Calneh** (Ezek. 27:23).

Canon of the Scriptures the collection of books which form the original and authoritative written rule of the faith and practice of the church. The word "canon" is properly a reed or straight rod for measuring and later "rule," as in the "rule of the church" or "of truth." "Canonical" was first given to writings in the sense of "admitted by the rule" rather than (as later) *"forming part of* and *giving the rule."* It eventually came to mean as here "the index of constituent books of the Old and New Testaments." Books outside the canon are called "apocryphal" or "pseudepigraphical." The exact date and process by which the canon of the Old and New Testaments was fixed are complicated and disputed. The following is a bare summary.

1. OT CANON. Popular belief assigned to Ezra and the "great synagogue" the task of collecting and promulgating the Scriptures as part of their work in organizing the Jewish church. This tradition is now frequently doubted, but that there was some systematizing process can hardly be doubted. The thirty-nine books of our English Bible are divided into three groups known as Law, Prophets, and Psalms (or Writings = the Hagiographa). These thirty-nine are an expansion of an original twenty-two (several books like Samuel, Kings, Chronicles,

being divided and the twelve prophets counted as one book). That this arrangement of books was completed and fixed among the Palestinian Jews before NT times appears certain from the fact that the threefold division is mentioned by Jesus Ben Sirach (Prologue to Ecclesiasticus) in 139 B.C. by Josephus' statement that the Jews have only the "twenty-two" books and by the use in the NT of "the Law, the Prophets, and the Psalms" (Lk. 24:44). In Egypt where the OT had been translated into Greek, other Jewish books were collected with these and the line of separation between them and the fourteen apocryphal and the larger number of pseudepigraphical books became obscured. NT books at times either quote and/or make reference to the latter books with the result that some early Christians conjectured that they might be Scripture. Gradually as more information became available, the church settled on the thirty-nine/twenty-two canon of Palestinian Jews and Lk. 24:44 as constituting the OT Scriptures.

2. NT CANON. The process of copying and distributing the recognized books of apostles and men considered inspired is already seen in NT times, as when Paul directs copies of his letters to Colossae and Laodicea to be exchanged (Col. 4:16). Revelation was obviously sent initially to all seven churches of Asia. The NT implies the beginning of collections of books (cf. mention of "all of Paul's epistles," 2 Pet. 3:16). At the close of the NT period or the period of inspiration the church was struggling with false doctrine and false teachers as evidenced by the Pastorals, 1, 2, 3 John, Jude, and 2 Peter. In such struggles the authentic or "sound" doctrine of the apostles and prophets was pointed to as the arbiter (2 Pet. 3:2; Jude 3, 1 Tim. 6:3; 2 Tim. 3:16). As this struggle was continued in the second century, orthodox writers continued to appeal to the acknowledged apostles and prophets of Jesus Christ. When the Docetists and Gnostics began to multiply books which they claimed as genuine, Christian apologists (e.g., Irenaeus) contended that only such books should be accepted as (1) were one in doctrine with the acknowledged NT books, (2) were written by inspired apostles or their co-workers, and (3) had a history by which the lineage back to their known writers could be traced. Eventually this led to lists or canons being drawn up (e.g., Muratorian Canon, from the church at Rome, about A.D. 170). Some books were less well known than others and had a harder time winning universal recognition. The completed canon of the NT, as commonly received at

present, was ratified at the Third Council of Carthage A.D. 397.

Canticles see **Song of Songs**

Capernaum (ka-pûr'nā-ŭm) a town on the northwestern shore of the Sea of Galilee, the scene of many acts and incidents in the life of Christ (Mt. 4:13; Mk. 2:1). Though not mentioned in the OT, the passage in Isa. 9:1 (Heb. 8:23) is applied to it by Matthew. In Jesus' day it was of sufficient size to be called a city (Mt. 9:1; Mk. 1:33). It had a synagogue (Mk. 1:21; Lk. 4:33, 38; Jn. 6:59) which had been built by a Roman centurion (Mt. 8:8; Lk. 7:1, 8). It was a tax-gathering station (Mt. 9:9, 17:24; Mk. 2:14; Lk. 5:27). Capernaum was chosen as Jesus' "own city" after he had left Nazareth early in his ministry. It was the scene of much activity such as the calling of Matthew or Levi (Mt. 9:9), the miracles of the "memorable day at Capernaum" (Mk. 1:21-34), including the demoniac, Peter's mother-in-law, and many sick. Here the discourse on the bread of life (Jn. 6) was given. Jesus did not fail to condemn Capernaum for its unbelief in the midst of his miracles (Mt. 11:23 f.; Lk. 10:15). Modern Tell Hum is most certainly the site of Capernaum. Here exists an excavated Jewish synagogue which dates from the third century A.D., but which may well be the site of that of Jesus' day.

Caphtor (kăf'tôr) the primitive seat of the Philistines (Deut. 2:23; Amos 9:7), who are called the Caphtorim (Deut. 2:23) and allied with Philistines in among the Mizraites in Gen. 10:14; 1 Chr. 1:12. This "island" (Jer. 47:4) is generally held to be Crete. Except for the Bible tradition, there is no evidence otherwise for the migration of the Philistines from Crete. It must have been early as they were settled in Philistia in Abraham's time (Gen. 21:32-34). Ezekiel 25:16; Zeph. 2:5 render Cherethites "Cretans," a name identified with the Philistines. One theory is that the term Caphtor may have been a broad designation for the Aegean area narrowed to the Philistines.

capital the crown head, or ornament at the top of a pillar, variously translated.

Cappadocia (kăp'a-dō'sha) a large Roman province in NT times comprising the eastern district of Asia Minor. It is mentioned because its inhabitants were among the listeners to Peter's first sermon (Acts 2:9) and its Christian residents among the readers of his first epistle (1 Pet. 1:1). It was a wild mountainous land with few cities. The Jewish community there is mentioned in second century B.C. in a letter to Ariarthes, its king (1 Macc. 15:22). Christianity flourished there after the NT era.

captain a term used to translate a wide variety of original Hebrew and Greek words (some seventeen in all) most of which have reference to a military title designating a leader or officer. The most numerous references translate the Heb. *sar* (126 of 419 occurrences), the Hebrew counterpart of tribune. It is even used of a Jewish officer guarding the temple (Acts 4:1). In Heb. 2:10 the reference to Christ as *archegos* literally refers to a founder or leader (RSV, **pioneer**).

captivities of the Jews see **exile**

carbuncle a red stone as a ruby or garnet, used four times in KJV as a rendering of three different Hebrew words for a "sparkling" precious gem. The words are otherwise considered to mean emerald or ruby.

Carcas (kär'kăs) a eunuch of Ahasuerus (Est. 1:10).

Carchemish (kär'kĕ-mĭsh) an ancient Hittite capital city on the Euphrates, recently identified through excavations as modern Jerablus. It fell to the Assyrians (Isa. 10:9) and was captured by Pharaoh Neco after the battle of Megiddo, in which Josiah was killed (2 Chr. 35:20). It was retaken by Nebuchadnezzar shortly after (Jer. 46:2).

Careah or **Kareah** friend of Gedaliah (Jer. 40:8–43:7).

Carmel (kär'mĕl) a mountain in northwestern Palestine which borders the plain of Esdraelon on the south and juts out into the Mediterranean Sea, forming the one indentation or bay on the coast. It has interesting connections with OT history, especially with Elijah and Elisha. The mountain is about 1600 feet above the sea at the coast, from which it runs about twelve miles south-southeast and terminates abruptly in a bluff some 600 feet in height. It thus serves as a wall in the maritime plain of Sharon on the south and Esdraelon above it. In Biblical times it was covered with "wood," used frequently as an illustration by the prophets (Isa. 33:9; Mic. 7:14). The mountain belonged to Asher (Josh. 19:26), and its king fell before Joshua (Josh. 12:22). Its most famous incidents are in connection with Elijah's contest with the prophets of Baal and his calling fire down from heaven to consume the guards of Ahaziah (1 K. 1:9–16). Here Elisha received the visit of the bereaved mother whose son he was soon to restore to life (2 K. 4:25). Elisha returned to the mount after the ascension of Elijah (2 K. 2:25).

Carmi (kär'mē) 1. Son of Reuben (Gen. 46:9).

2. Father of Achan (Josh. 7:1, 18; 1 Chr. 2:7, 4:1).

carpenter see **handicraft**

Carpus (kär'pŭs) a Christian at Troas with whom Paul left a cloak (2 Tim. 4:13).

carriage the words so translated generally mean the baggage or burdens connected with travel of groups rather than vehicles (cf. 1 Sam. 17:22; Judg. 18:21).

Carshena (kär-shē'nà) a Persian prince (Est. 1:14).

cart or **wagon** usually a two-wheeled vehicle drawn by oxen as opposed to horsedrawn chariots (Gen. 45:19; Num. 7:3; 2 Sam. 6:6). They could be open or covered (Num. 7:3) and could convey persons (Gen. 45:19), burdens (1 Sam. 6:7, 8), or produce (Amos 2:13).

carving the arts of carving and engraving are mentioned mostly in connection with the building of the tabernacle and the temple (Ex. 31:5, 35:33; 1 K. 6:18, 35; Ps. 74:6) and with ornaments of priestly dress (Ex. 28:9–36). Most other references are ironical references to heathen idols (e.g., Isa. 40:18–20).

Casiphia (kà-sĭf'ĭ-à) an unknown site between Babylon and Jerusalem whence Levites were secured for the temple services (Ezra 8:17; Isa. 22:18).

Casluhim (kăs'lŭ-hĭm) a people descended from Mizraim (Gen. 10:13 f.; 1 Chr. 1:11–12), whence the Philistines came.

cassia (kăsh'à) a tree producing an aromatic bark resembling cinnamon (so translated KJV, Ecclus. 24:15); mentioned as an ingredient of the holy oil of anointing (Ex. 30:24) and as a trade produce with Tyre (Ezek. 27:19).

Castor and Pollux the Dioscuri of Acts 28:11 mentioned as the sign under which Paul's ship sailed. The reference is to the twin sons of Zeus and Leda in Greek mythology represented in the constellation *Gemini*. They were regarded as the tutelary divinities of sailors. The static electricity display on ships known as St. Elmo's fire was credited to them.

catacombs artificially dug tunnels for burials used by early Christians and Jews especially at Rome.

caterpillar strictly the larva of butterflies, moths, etc., though most authorities take the passages where the translation occurs to refer to the nymph stage of the destructive locust (1 K. 8:37; 2 Chr. 6:28; Ps. 78:46; Isa. 23:4; Joel 1:4). See **locust**

Catholic (or "General") **Epistles** the designation in many MSS of the group of epistles between Paul's and the Apocalypse (James, 1 and 2 Peter, 1, 2, and 3 John, and Jude), so-called because they were written to Christians over a large area, rather than to one individual or local church.

cattle ruminant animals with cloven hoofs much used in ancient times for their flesh as food and for their milk and its by-products. They were also important in all Near Eastern religions as animals of sacrifice. See **bull** and **calf**. The term "cattle" as used in the Bible sometimes designates other animals, such as sheep, goats, or camels (Gen. 47:16 f.; 1 Chr. 5:21) but more frequently it applies to domesticated bovines. The Jews ordinarily pastured their cattle (Deut. 11:15; Ps. 104:14), though some (2 Chr. 32:28) were kept in stalls. In OT times especially, the possession of many cattle was an indication of wealth and power.

Cauda (kō'dà) a small island off the south coast of Crete near which the ship on which Paul was being carried to Rome was driven (Acts 27:16).

cave a hole or fissure in the earth, whether natural or carved. Palestine with its limestone rocks abounded with them. The most remarkable caves mentioned in the Scriptures are (1) Lot's cave (Gen. 19:30), (2) the Cave of Machpelah (23:17), where Abraham was buried, (3) the Cave of Makkedah (Josh. 10:16), (4) the Cave of Adullam (1 Sam. 22:1), (5) the Cave of En-gedi (1 Sam. 24:3), (6) Obadiah's cave (1 K. 18:4), (7) Elijah's cave in Horeb (1 K. 19:9), (8) Lazarus' cave (Jn. 11:38), (9) the Tomb of Jesus (Mt. 27:60). In modern times the caves of Khirbet Qumran have yielded the famous Dead Sea Scrolls illustrating the custom of using caves as depositories.

cedar Heb. *'erez* represents both the juniper used for sacrificial purposes (Num. 19:6) and the giant cedar of Lebanon imported by Solomon for his building program (1 K. 5–7; 1 Chr. 14:1). Both grew on the mountains of Lebanon north of Palestine.

Cedron alternate form of **Kidron**, a brook near Jerusalem (Jn. 18:1).

ceiling descriptions of the ornate ceilings of Solomon's temple (1 K. 6:9, 15, 7:3; 2 Chr. 3:5, 9; Jer. 22:14; Hag. 1:4).

Cenchreae (sĕn'krē-à) the harbor of Corinth, seven miles east on the Saronic Gulf. Here Paul shaved his head because of a vow at the end of his stay in Corinth (Acts 18:18). On writing Romans Paul commended a servant (deaconess?) of the church there (Rom. 16:1).

censer any instrument, such as a shovel or ladle, for carrying burning coals (Ex. 25:38, 37:23) about the tabernacle or (more properly) a small portable vessel of metal fitted to receive burning coals from the altar and on which incense was sprinkled (2 Chr. 26:18; Lk. 1:9 cf. instructions in Num. 4:14 and Lev. 16:12).

census the numbering or recording of people according to their family and lineage (Num. 1:2, 3; Lk. 2:4). Three accounts of such are given in OT: (1) at Sinai (Ex. 38:26; Num. 1:2, 3); (2) at Shittim, thirty-eight years later before entering Canaan (Num. 26:2, 51); (3) by David (1 Chr. 21:6, 27:24), completed by Solomon including foreigners (1 K. 5:15, 9:20, 21; 2 Chr. 2:17 f.). In the NT the census ordered by Caesar Augustus became the occasion of Jesus' being born in Bethlehem, to which his parents had gone to be enrolled (Lk. 2:1 ff.).

centurion see **army**

Cephas see **Peter**

chaff properly speaking the husk or refuse of the grain separated by winnowing, though the word is also used to translate words which mean hay, stubble, or straw. Biblical uses are generally figurative, describing what is about to be destroyed for its uselessness or evil (e.g., Ps. 1:4; Isa. 17:13; Mt. 3:12).

chain this word, usually meaning a metal device for tying or fastening things, translates a variety of original words referring to badges of office, ornament, or confining prisoners: a manacle (Jer. 40:1), a fetter (Isa. 45:14), decorative chains (Ex. 28:14; 1 K. 7:17; 2 Chr. 3:5; Isa. 40:19), necklaces (Gen. 41:42; Dan. 5:29), prisoner's chain (Mk. 5:3–4; Acts 28:20; Rev. 20:1), and any kind of rope or tie (Acts 26:29; Heb. 11:36).

chalcedony a precious stone, mentioned only in Rev. 21:19; in modern times applied to **agate** (so RSV). The precise stone intended is uncertain.

Chalcol see **Calcol**

Chaldaea or **Chaldea** (kăl-dē'à) the southern part of Babylonia, also called Shinar, a vast alluvial plain formed by the deposits of the Euphrates and Tigris rivers and measuring some 400 miles in length and 100 miles in width. In antiquity its inhabitants, who spoke Akkadian, were tribal and generally kept aloof from the city-dwelling Babylonians. The country is marked with canals. After being dominated by the Assyrians, the Chaldeans threw off the yoke and established a mighty empire extending to Egypt and Asia Minor. During this period Palestine was conquered and the Jews exiled to Chaldea. At the fall of Babylonia the land passed to the Medes and Persians, later to the Greeks and Alexander. The words occur in the KJV actually only in Jer. 50:10, 51:24, 35; Ezek. 11:24, 16:29, 23:15 f., but see also, e.g., Dan. 5:30, 9:1.

Chaldeans (kăl-dē'ăns) the people of Chaldea or Shinar (Dan. 5:30, 9:1), also the dynasty of kings. Established by Nabopolassar and including Nebuchadnezzar, conqueror of Jerusalem. In the book of Daniel the term begins to take on a new sense and appears where the word denotes magicians and astronomers, who seemingly form a sort of priestly class and who have a peculiar "tongue" and "learning" (1:4). According to Strabo they had great seats of learning and were advanced especially in astronomical science. This later degenerated into fortune-telling, etc., in which role they acquired fame in Hellenistic Egypt and in Greece and Rome.

chamberlain two meanings are involved in this word. In the OT (2 K. 23:11; Est. 1:10) and in Acts 12:20 the meaning is one who had charge of a king or nobleman's private quarters or bedchambers, usually **eunuchs.** In Rom. 16:23 the KJV "chamberlain" translates a word meaning administrator and here apparently referring to city treasurer.

chameleon a small lizardlike animal capable of changing its skin to fit the color of its surroundings. Its appearance in Lev. 11:29–30 is questionable, as the Hebrew word is not presently identified.

chamois a small, goatlike animal. It is, however, unknown to the Biblical region, and mountain sheep is probably a better translation of Deut. 14:5.

chapiter the ornament at the top of a building pillar. See **capital**

Charashim (kär'ă-shĭm) [RSV following Heb. **Ge-harashim,** valley of the craftsmen] a place mentioned in 1 Chr. 4:14 and Neh. 11:35.

Charchemish see **Carchemish** (KJV, 2 Chr. 35:20).

charger a shallow metal serving dish; a platter (Num. 7:79; Mt. 14:8).

chariot a vehicle with dual wheels drawn by two horses, most commonly used in war, though having peaceable uses also (Gen. 41:43, 46:29; 1 K. 18:44; 2 K. 5:9; Acts 8:28). Archaeological evidence shows chariot models from very early historical times among Sumerian and other Near Eastern groups. It was the use of the horsedrawn chariot which enabled the Hyksos to conquer Syria and Egypt (ca. 1800 B.C.). Power based on its use led to later kingdoms such as the Hittite and Assyrian empires. In the Scriptures chariots are first mentioned in Egypt, where Pharaoh gave Joseph distinction by placing his chariot second in line (Gen. 41:43 cf. 46:29). But the next mention is Pharaoh's pursuit of Israel with "six hundred chosen chariots" (Ex. 14:6), thus indicating the power of an army by the number of its chariots (cf. Josh. 17:8; Judg. 1:19, 4:3; 1 Sam. 13:5; 2 Sam. 8:4; 1 Chr. 19:7). Due to the proscription of the Law concerning multiplying horses, Israel was a long time adopting chariots for its army. But the prohibition was broken by David and then Solomon (2 Sam. 8:4; 1 K. 10:25–29), and they henceforth became a part of the regular army (1 K. 22:34; 2 K. 9:16; Isa. 31:1).

charismata (că-rĭs'mà-tà) transliteration of a Greek word meaning a free gift, often used of the miraculous or spiritual gifts of NT times (e.g., 1 Cor. 12:1).

Charran NT spelling of **Haran** (Acts 7:2, 4).

chase see **hunting**

Chebar (kē'bär) a river in Chaldea on the banks of which Ezekiel saw his earlier visions among his brethren (e.g., 1:1, 3, 3:15, 23).

Chedorlaomer (kĕd'ŏr-lā-ō'mĕr) a king of **Elam,** in the time of Abraham, who with allies made war on the five kings of the valley and conquered them (Gen. 14:17). He was in turn overcome by Abraham and his allies (vss. 13–17). The meaning or significance of the name is uncertain.

cheese a form of milk solid, made from curds. It is mentioned three times in the Bible (1 Sam. 17:18; 2 Sam. 17:29; Job 10:10), but with a different word each time. The exact methods of preparation are uncertain.

Chelal (kē'lăl) man with a foreign wife (Ezra 10:30).

Chelluh (kĕl'lū) man with a foreign wife (Ezra 10:35).

Chelub (kē'lŭb) 1. A descendant of Judah (1 Chr. 4:11).

2. Father of Ezri (1 Chr. 27:26).

Chelubai probably a form of the name **Caleb** (1 Chr. 2:9).

chemarim (kĕm'ă-rĭm) KJV transliteration of words meaning "idolatrous priests" (Zeph. 1:4); see the translation in 2 K. 23:5 and Hos. 10:5.

Chemosh (kē'mŏsh) the national deity of the Moabites, "the people of Chemosh" (Num. 21:29; Jer. 48:7, 13, 46). In Judg. 11:24 he also appears as god of the Ammonites. Solomon introduced his worship, and Josiah abolished it (1 K. 11:7; 2 K. 23:13); probably an astral deity.

Chenaanah (kē-nā'ă-nà) 1. A Benjaminite (1 Chr. 7:10).

2. Father of Zedekiah the false prophet (1 K. 22:11, 24; 2 Chr. 18:10, 23).

Chenani (kē-nā'nĭ) a Levite (Neh. 9:4).

Chenaniah (kĕn'ă-nī'à) chief of Levites at removal of ark to Jerusalem (1 Chr. 15:22).

Chephar-haammonai (kĕ'fàr-hă-ăm'ō-nī) a place in Benjamin (Josh. 18:24).

Chephirah (kē-fī'rà) a Gibeonite town (Josh. 9:17) later belonging to Benjamin (18:26). See also Ezra 2:25; Neh. 7:29.

Cheran (kĕ'răn) son of the Horite Dishon (Gen. 36:26).

Cherethim (kĕr'ē-thĭm) Cherethites (Ezek. 25:16).

Cherethites and Pelethites David's lifeguards (2 Sam. 8:18, 15:18, 20:7, 23; 1 K. 1:38, 44), serving as executioners (2 K. 11:4) and couriers (1 K. 14:27); since they are a "nation" and coast dwellers, it is possible they were foreigners (2 Sam. 15:21, 30:14).

Cherith (chĕr'ĭth) the brook [wadi] in which Elijah hid himself during the early part of the three years' drought (1 K. 17:2-7). It was east of Jordan in a region of many brooks and caves, so has never been identified.

Cherub (kĕr'ŭb) 1. An unidentified Babylonian town from which some Jews of uncertain ancestry returned (Ezra 2:59; Neh. 7:61).
2. A leader of the exiles (Ezra 2:59; Neh. 7:61).

cherub (chĕr'ŭb), plural cherubim (chĕr'ŭbĭm) heavenly beings whose forms were composites of such creatures as men, eagles, lions, and oxen. They are represented in direct statements such as being placed as guardians of Eden when Adam and Eve were expelled (Gen. 3:24) and in visions of heaven (Ezek. 1:5; Rev. 4:7). They are usually interpreted as those forms "in which every imaginative people has sought to embody its notions either of Divine essence, or of the vast powers of nature which transcend that of man" (Smith's Bible Dictionary). Imagery drawn from such creatures played a large part in the symbolism of the tabernacle and temple (Ex. 26:1; Num. 7:89; Isa. 37:16; 1 K. 6:23-28).

Chesalon (kĕs'à-lŏn) a place on Mount Jearim (Josh. 15:10) on border of Judah, now Kesla, some nine miles west of Jerusalem.

Chesed (kĕ'sĕd) son of Nahor (Gen. 22:22).

Chesil (kĕ'sĭl) a town in Southern Judah (Josh. 15:30) evidently also called Bethel (Josh. 19:4) or Bethuel (1 Chr. 4:30).

chest a box or receptacle, used of (1) the ark of the covenant, the "coffin" of Joseph (Gen. 50:26), and the chest in which alms for repair of the temple were placed (2 K. 12:9, 10); (2) a merchandise of Tyre (Ezek. 27:24).

chestnut KJV translation in Gen. 30:37 and Ex. 31:8, more probably plane tree, rather than the common chestnut.

Chesulloth (kē-sŭl'ŏth) a town in Issachar (Josh. 19:18).

Chezib (kĕ'zĭb) a place = Achzib (Gen. 38:5).

Chidon (kī'dŏn) place where Uzzah touched the ark and was killed (1 Chr. 13:9); also called "threshing floor of Nacon" (2 Sam. 6:6).

children or offspring a blessing (especially male children) which was highly valued and whose absence was considered a punishment (Gen. 16:2; Deut. 7:14; 1 Sam. 1:6; 2 Sam. 6:23; 2 K. 4:14; Ps. 127:3, 5; Isa. 47:9; Jer. 20:15). Childbirth was usually without difficulty and with little assistance (Gen. 35:17, 38:29; Ex. 1:19; 1 Sam. 4:19, 20). The child was circumcised on the eighth day (Gen. 17), was nursed up to three years (Isa. 49:15), by a nurse if necessary (Ex. 2:9; Gen. 24:59, 35:8; 2 Sam. 4:4), and the weaning might be celebrated (Gen. 21:8). Children were usually under care of women (Prov. 31:1), or tutors or governors (Num. 11:12; 2 K. 10:1, 5; Isa. 49:23; Gal. 3:24); the girls remained in women's apartments or in household work (Lev. 21:9; Num. 12:14; 1 Sam. 9:11; Prov. 31:19). Parental authority and discipline were strict (Prov. 22:15, 23:13, 29:15). "Child" is often used as an address of affection, especially by John. But characteristics of children may be either rebuked in Christians (1 Cor. 13:11, 14:20) or commended ("in malice be children").

Chileab (kĭl'ē-ăb) son of David by Abigail (2 Sam. 3:3), also called Daniel (1 Chr. 3:1).

Chilion (kĭl'ĭ-ŏn) husband of Orpah (Ruth 1:2-5, 4:9).

Chilmad (kĭl'măd) a place mentioned with Sheba and Asshur as trading with Tyre (Ezek. 27:23).

Chimham (kĭm'hăm) a follower of David (2 Sam. 19:37-40). A house bearing his name remained years later at Bethlehem (Jer. 41:17).

Chinnereth, Chinneroth (kĭn'ē-rĕth, -rŏth) 1. A fortified city in the tribe of Naphtali (Josh. 19:35), now Tell el-'Oreimeh lying on a hill on the northwest of the Sea of Galilee.
2. A region in Naphtali (1 K. 15:20).
3. The inland sea which is most familiarly known as the Lake of Gennesareth or Sea of Galilee (Num. 34:11; Josh. 13:27).

Chios (kī'ŏs) an island five miles off the coast of Asia Minor (opposite Smyrna), past which Paul sailed on the return voyage from Troas to Caesarea (Acts 20:14-15). The island measured some eighteen by thirty-two miles.

chisleu see months

Chislon (kĭz'lŏn) a prince of Benjamin who

helped divide Canaan among the tribes (Num. 34:21).

Chisloth-tabor (kĭs′lŏth-tā′bêr) a border city of Zebulun and Issachar, now Iksal, three miles southeast of Nazareth. Same place as Chesulloth (Josh. 19:12).

Chittim KJV spelling of **Kittim**

Chronicles, Books of two books standing last in the Hebrew canon but arranged after 1 and 2 Kings in the LXX and in modern versions, serving with Ezra and Nehemiah as a supplement to Kings. 1. TITLE. The Hebrew title is "things of the days" meaning "events of the (former) days." In the LXX the title is *paraleipomena*, "things omitted" = "a supplement." The two books formerly stood as one but were separated in the Greek because the Greek text consumed so much more space. 2. CONTENTS. The Chronicles give a history of God's people from Adam to the time of Cyrus king of Persia. The bare outline is as follows: (a) 1 Chr. 1–9, from Adam to David; (b) chs. 10–29, the reign of David; (c) 2 Chr. 1–9, the reign of Solomon; (d) chs. 10–36, the kings of Judah ending with Cyrus. The writer drew his information from the Pentateuch and from the historical books (Joshua, Samuel, and Kings), often omitting (especially most narratives of the Northern Kingdom) or summarizing (cf. 2 K. 9 and 2 Chr. 22:7–9). Also quoted are certain books (e.g., "Books of the Kings of Israel and Judah," 1 Chr. 9:1). 3. AUTHORSHIP AND DATE. Of date and compiler there are no hints. The book ends with the decree of Cyrus in 536 B.C. However, there are similarities between it and the book of Ezra, which may signify common authorship with this book. W. F. Albright (JBL 59 [1940], 104 ff.) suggests that both tradition and internal evidence support the common authorship of Ezra for the two books. 4. PURPOSE. The aim of the writing seems to be to glorify the past history of Judah, its worship, its priestly traditions in order to effect a revival of religious interests. The book has been called "the first apology for Judaism," and it uses the same arguments as a later apologist, Josephus: the "antiquity of Judaism" and "the marvelous achievements of the Jews" (R. H. Pfeiffer, IDB). The book is a testimony to the faith of its writer in the providence of the Lord as the God of the Jews.

chronology of Bible times the science of ascertaining the dates according to our method of reckoning time (B.C.–A.D.) of the events of the Old and New Testaments. The subject is beset with many difficulties because of the lack of data and different methods of reckoning or recording dates and time. Many conclusions are tentative and approximate and should be used for comparative purposes only.

I. OLD TESTAMENT. A. *From Adam to the Call of Abraham.* The data is found in two genealogical tables in Genesis, the first from Adam to Noah (Gen. 5:3 ff.) and the second from Shem to Abram (11:10–26), and in the passages 7:6, 11, 8:13, 9:28 f., 11:32, and 12:4. But the textual sources differ greatly, the Hebrew MT giving one set, the LXX another exactly 100 years longer in each instance, and the Samaritan Pentateuch another. Compare the following table.

The chronology of Archbishop James Ussher, printed first in *Annales Veteris et Novi Testamenti* (1650–54) and later in the margins of the KJV, is obtained by taking only the MT numbers of the genealogies. With other data the creation was put at 4004 B.C., flood at 2348, and Abram's departure 1921. The MT's numbers are, however, increased to 5300–5400 B.C. by the LXX. The reason for the varying numbers is not clear. Many scholars believe the figures of the MT before the flood and the LXX after the deluge are more likely to be correct. Other scholars feel that the use of these figures to construct a chronology is entirely misguided. They feel that like the rounded number of generations (three sets of fourteens) in Mt. 1, where several are omitted which are listed in the OT genealogies, the lists are schematized (ten in each) for illustration and ease of memory. For example, the LXX text has a Cainan in Gen. 10:24 and 11:13 ("and Cainan lived a hundred and thirty years and begat Selah") after Arpachshad, and this name is contained in Lk. 3:36 in the NT genealogy. There is no proof that the writer had longer lists which he abridged in the fashion of the later writers, but it is quite possible. That the practice was common is seen, e.g., from Ruth 4:21–22 where only three generations (Boaz to David) cover a period of 365 years. From these considerations it seems that it is unwise to construct any chronology of dates for the period before Abraham or to estimate the exact date of the creation of man.

B. *From the Call of Abraham to the Exodus.* Paul stated that this period was 430 years (Gal. 3:17), the same date given in Ex. 12:40, implying that the journey of the patriarchs is included in the sojourn in Egypt. For the date of the Exodus, see **Exodus.** Two dates, 1445 (as implied by 1 K. 6:1) and somewhere in the early thirteenth century, are contended for. The

	Age of each when the next was born.			Years of each after the next was born.			Total length of the life of each.		
	Sept.	Heb.	Sam.	Sept.	Heb.	Sam.	Sept.	Heb.	Sam.
Adam	230	130		700	800		930	..	..
Seth	205	105		707	807		912	..	..
Enos	190	90		715	815		905	..	..
Cainan	170	70		740	840		910	..	..
Mahalaleel	165	65		730	830		895	..	..
Jared	162	..	62	800	..	785	962	..	847
Enoch	165	65		200	300		365	..	..
Methuselah	187 167	..	67	(782) 802	782	653	969	..	720
Lamech	188	182	53	565	595	600	753	777	653
Noah	502	..	..	448	..	..	950	..	..
Shem	100	..	..	500	..	..	600	..	..
	2264 2244	1658	1309	This was "two years after the Flood."					
Arphaxad	135	35	..	400	403	303	(535)	(438)	438
Cainan	130			330			(460)		
Salah	130	30	..	330	403	303	(460)	(433)	433
Eber	134	34	..	270	430	..	(404)	(464)	404
Peleg	130	30	..	209	..	109	(339)	(239)	239
Reu	132	32	..	207	..	107	(339)	(239)	239
Serug	130	30	..	200	..	100	(330)	(230)	230
Nahor	79 179	29	..	129	119	69	(208)	(148)	148
Terah	70	..	..	(135)	(135)	(75)	205	..	145
Abram leaves Haran	} 75	..	..						
	1145 1245	365	1015						

contention of some that non-occupation of Transjordan in the fifteenth century argues for the later date has more recently been weakened.

c. *The Conquest and the Judges.* Here the combined length of the oppressions and judgeships add up to 450 years, though some of the events and leaders, being local, were most likely concurrent.

d. *The United Kingdom.* The beginning of the Kingdom can only be conjectured. Ussher gives 1095. Full allowance for three reigns of forty years would give 120 or 975 for the end. But there are severe difficulties with this. Saul's forty years, at least, must be a rounded number.

e. *The Divided Kingdom.* Here an abundance of data exists, but it is difficult to assess. If the dates of all reigns are added up, the same totals are not obtained. Reasons for this are many: (1) Some years are given as starting in Nisan (first month in the religious calendar) and others in Tishri (first month in the civil calendar). (2) Again a difference existed in Israel and Judah and foreign kingdoms in reckoning the first year of the reign either as the year of accession or not. In the latter case the first year is counted twice as both the last of the old king and the first of the new. Ussher's date for the accession of Rehoboam in 975 is too early, scholars generally agreeing that 931 is the correct date. The Divided Kingdom era is then 931–722 B.C. The latter date is rather certain.

f. *The Southern Kingdom* alone, 722–606, from the fall of Samaria (1 K. 17) to the capture of Jerusalem by Nebuchadnezzar.

g. *The Exile.* 606–536. The first nineteen

years Jerusalem still stood, being destroyed in 586. The date 536 is that of the fall of Babylonia to Cyrus and the Medo-Persian kingdom. Events occurring after the Exile, during the intertestamental period, are not discussed here.

II. NEW TESTAMENT. The chronology of NT times is no less difficult than that of the OT. This is due to the lack of precise methods of time reckoning of both the Romans and Hebrews. Rome dated events from the founding of Rome (ab urbe condita) but usually dated events in the year of the consuls or the emperors. We have already seen the difficulty of Jewish reckoning due to a dual system of beginning the year and a lunar calendar. The following list is at best merely an approximate list of important happenings.

7/5 B.C. The Birth of Jesus. The date is uncertain being based on its preceding Herod's death, the probable date of Quirinius' census, and the age of Jesus ("about thirty years," Lk. 3:23) at his baptism.

4 B.C. The Death of Herod the Great, fixed somewhat securely by Josephus' statement that he died thirty-seven years after he was made king.

A.D. 26. The Beginning of John the Baptist's Ministry, dated in the fifteenth year of Tiberius' reign (Lk. 3:1) but allowing two years for his co-regency with Augustus.

A.D. 26/27. The Baptism of Jesus, depending upon the date of his birth and his age at baptism (Lk. 3:23).

A.D. 27. Jesus' First Passover, occurring "forty and six years" after Herod began the temple in 20 B.C.

A.D. 30. The Crucifixion of Jesus. This allows for the three Passovers mentioned by John (2:23, 6:4, 11:55) and, as seems required by the length of the Great Galilean Ministry, assumes that the feast of John 5:1 is a Passover or that there is an unnamed Passover. This makes the length of Jesus' ministry some three and one-half years.

33–35. The Conversion of Saul, conjectural.

44. The Death of Herod the King (Herod Agrippa I), Acts 12:23, mentioned by Josephus. This fixes the date of the famine in Acts 11:28 and the death of the apostle James.

48–49. Paul's First Missionary Tour (Acts 13–14).

49/50. The Jerusalem Council (Acts 15).

50–52. Paul's Second Missionary Tour, the stay at Corinth.

51/52. The Proconsulship of Gallio at Corinth, fixed by an inscription. It coincided with part of Paul's stay of eighteen months at Corinth (Acts 18:11–12).

53–57. The Third Missionary Tour, including the three-year stay at Ephesus (Acts 20:31) and the three months in Greece (Acts 20:3).

57/58–59/60. Paul's Two-Year Imprisonment at Caesarea by Felix (Acts 24–27).

59/60. The Governorship of Festus, replacing Felix. The evidence is not certain but points to this date.

59/60. Paul's Voyage to Rome, shipwreck.

59/60–61/62. Paul's Two-Year Imprisonment at Rome (Acts 28:30).

62–66. Paul's Later Journeys and Letters (1, 2 Tim., and Tit.). This date assumes the genuineness of the Pastorals.

64. The Burning of Rome, resulting in the Christians' being accused and persecuted as related by Tacitus (Annals IV.44). This was probably the persecution of 1 Peter.

66–67. The Deaths of Peter and Paul at Rome, occurring before the death of Nero in August of A.D. 68.

70. The Destruction of Jerusalem by Titus.

96. The Banishment of John to Patmos, imposed by the Emperor Domitian before his death in A.D. 96.

church [an English word derived from the Gr. kuriake, the Lord's (assembly)]. The English word "church" was used in the NT (113 times) for the Gr. ekklesia, the proper meaning of which is "congregation" or "assembly" with various implications. The derivation of ekklesia (which will be the subject of this article) from the verb ek-kaleo (I call out) is now seriously questioned. Even if it is correct, the idea of a "summoned" assembly is not historical, the called assembly at Athens was described by a different term. The general meaning is that of an "assembly" which, as in the NT, might be a chance meeting (even a mob, Acts 19:41) or more properly the city assembly = the body politic of the city (Acts 19:39).

I. IN THE GOSPELS. The word ekklesia occurs only twice in the gospels, both times in Matthew: once after Peter's confession, "Upon this rock I will build my church" (16:18) and again in 18:17, "tell it to the church." It formerly was held by liberals (especially under A. Schweitzer's eschatological view of Jesus' mission) that these passages are spurious and that Jesus did not contemplate building a church. This view has now been largely abandoned (see R. N. Flew, Jesus And His Church, 1938). There is no reason to question Jesus' use of a term equal to it. Ecclesia had been used in the LXX to translate the Heb. qahal, the assembly of Israel (Deut. 4:10; 2 Chr. 30:13). Similarly the Aramaic of Jesus' native region had a word for such a meeting. Jesus' choosing of the

Twelve, his teaching in parables, etc., presume the establishing of a people to bear his name. However, in the gospels the more frequent designation is the term "kingdom of God (or Heaven)." It is not that *ekklesia* and "kingdom" are synonymous. "Kingdom" (*basileia*) properly means the "act of ruling," "the sovereignty" of the king. But in Jesus' speech this rule is to be exercised in this world in a people or "little flock" to whom he would "give the kingdom" (Lk. 12:32).

II. IN ACTS AND THE EPISTLES. The proper viewpoint for the religious meaning of *ekklesia* in Acts and the epistles is that of a constituted assembly or religious community. Compare the uses to designate a local group such as "the *church* of the Thessalonians in God our Father" (2 Thess. 1:1), where the phrase "in God" is a modifier to describe the *kind* of assembly in question. These single communities were described as meeting in a house (Philemon 2; Rom. 16:5; Col. 4:15), in a city (1 Cor. 1:2), in a province, e.g., Galatia (Gal. 1:2), and generally as "churches" (i.e., churches of Christ, Rom. 16:16). The *ekklesia* also may refer to the occasion of the community's gathering for worship (1 Cor. 14:4-5, cf. vs. 23; Acts 11:26, 12:5; 1 Cor. 11:18; Col. 4:16). But the term is also used in a more universal sense as Christ used it in Mt. 16:18. Here the church is seen as the spiritual body of Christ wherever located (Eph. 1:23, "the church which is his body"). The people brought into spiritual relation with him make up a unit—one worldwide fellowship or community which is realized in a local situation when a community exists. In this sense the church fulfills the expectations of the OT people of God and is the people of the "last time" (Heb. 1:1-3) in which God's Spirit dwells (1 Cor. 3:16) and which anticipates the ultimate victory and blessing of God (Eph. 1:23 ff., 3:8-12, 4:4-12; Col. 1:21 ff.; Heb. 12:22 ff.). The *ekklesia* of Christ is viewed in many aspects in the NT, a series of terms being employed which is almost inexhaustible: the saints (1 Cor. 1:2), the elect (2 Tim. 2:10), disciples (Acts 11:26), believers or "faithful" (Acts 5:14; Col. 1:1), servants or slaves (1 Pet. 2:16), kingdom (Col. 1:13), priesthood (1 Pet. 2:9; Rev. 1:6, 5:10), a holy city (Heb. 12; Rev. 21-22), a holy nation and people (1 Pet. 2:9-10), a family or household (1 Tim. 3:15), a field (1 Cor. 3:5-9) and the body (Col. 1:23). Such a variety of figures help the believer to understand various aspects of his relationship within the family or community.

III. THE UNITY OF THE CHURCH. It is diffi-

cult for modern church people to realize that the church situation of the first century was not denominationalized. The oneness of the church as the body of Christ is explicitly affirmed (Eph. 4:4); Christ prayed for its unity (Jn. 17:20-21); and divisions into sects (*haireseis*) or parties is specifically condemned as a sin, a work of the flesh (Gal. 5:19-20). If there was a time when "no differing denominations existed," who is responsible that such a situation does not now exist? Christian people should ask themselves what can be done with this situation. Some excuse denominationalism; others work for a union of all bodies, each keeping its sectarian character, into a super church; still others believe in a primitivism whereby each local church could be structured according to the NT pattern and a unity of all believers achieved through a restoration of congregations to that pattern. Since the NT condemns disunity, such questions deserve serious study. The student of the Bible and church history must reckon with departures in organization, worship, and doctrine from what is seen in the NT. This is often seen as mere development under the providence of God and the guidance of the Spirit, but others see it as deviation and apostasy necessitating continual reform and restoration as God's Word stands in judgment over the human situation.

IV. THE IDENTITY OF NEW TESTAMENT CHURCHES. To describe the NT church situation so as to clarify its essential nature is not easy. As to *initiation* or entrance, the essentials of church membership (implied in the Great Commission, Mt. 28:19-20; Mk. 16:16; Lk. 24:46; see **Commission, Great**) are set forth in Acts 2:38 to believers "repent and be baptized . . . for the remission of sins . . . and they who gladly received his word were baptized and there were added together about 3000 souls" (cf. Acts 22:16; Rom. 6:1 ff.; 1 Cor. 12:13; 1 Pet. 3:21). As to its *worship*, the early church "continued steadfastly in the apostles' doctrine and fellowship, in the breaking of bread (the Lord's Supper, Acts 20:7; 1 Cor. 10:16), and in prayers" (Acts 2:41 ff.). This continuity of worship is implied also in Acts 20:7 ("the disciples came together on the first day of the week to break bread") and 1 Cor. 16:1-2 ("upon the first day of every week let each lay by in store," cf. Heb. 10:25). The epistles contain many examples or references to speaking or preaching in the assemblies (1 Cor. 14; Acts 20:7), to praying (1 Cor. 14:15; 1 Tim. 2:8), and to singing (Eph. 5:19; Col. 3:16). But Jewish forms such as animal sacrifices, incense, and instrumental music were avoided. Women were not allowed to speak to the assembly (1 Tim. 2:12; cf. 1 Cor. 14:34). Under the influence of the charismatic gifts (1 Cor. 12–14), early meetings were at times attended by miraculous manifestations but they were rigidly controlled (1 Cor. 14:27 ff.) and their value, except as signs were for confirmation of the work prior to the full revelation of the knowledge of revelation (Mk. 16:20; Acts 14:3; Heb. 2:1–4). They were to pass away (1 Cor. 13:8–10). Congregational fellowship in community feasts (love feasts) (Acts 2:44–46; 1 Cor. 11:17 ff.; 2 Pet. 2:13; Jude 12) frequently accompanied assemblies, and charity for the poor was a regular feature (Acts 6:1 ff.; 1 Tim. 5:3–16), though the community of goods which characterized the Jerusalem church was voluntary (Acts 5:4) and not continued in other churches. As to organization and ministry, the following seems to be a fair summary. It is the usual interpretation to see two types of ministries in the NT, the special or extraordinary (the apostles, prophets = inspired teachers, charismatic workers) and the ordinary (elders, deacons, teachers, preachers, etc.). Since the apostles were personal witnesses of Christ with no successors, they like the other miraculously endowed and inspired workers were temporary, serving until the permanent organization was set up. Though there was apostolic oversight both directly (2 Cor. 11:28) and through representatives such as Timothy (1 Tim. 1:3), there is no evidence of the development of a hierarchy or ruling group larger than the local congregation. Each church had a group of overseers or **bishops,** also called **elders** or **pastors** (Acts 11:30, 14:23, 20:17, 28; Phil. 1:1; 1 Tim. 3:1–7; Tit. 1:5–8). The terms were used interchangeably, and they are always spoken of in the plural in respect to the local church (1 Tim. 3:1 f., "the bishop" is generic). The separation of elder and bishop and the elevation of the latter over a church or group of churches (the monarchical bishopric) was a later development. Along with these there was a class of workers called deacons or "servants" possessing special qualifications and appointment (Phil. 1:1; 1 Tim. 3:8–13, and probably Acts 6:1 ff.). Also one finds preachers or evangelists and teachers (Eph. 4:11) which along with the elders formed the teaching corps of the churches. The NT does not reveal any system of distinction between clergy and laity with the "priesthood" associated with the former, as under the Law. Though our modern word "priest" is derived linguistically from "presbyter" or "elder," the thing signified by "priest" is specifically expressed by another word *hiereus,* and all saints or Christians are so designated (1 Pet. 2:9; Rev. 1:6, 5:10).

v. ITS ATTRIBUTES AND FUTURE. The historical creeds of Christendom, worked out in combat with error to preserve the early faith, emphasize the *unity* of the church (Eph. 4:4–15), its *holiness* (Eph. 4:24; 1 Pet. 1:15 f.), its *catholicity* or universality (which consists of its rejection of the narrowness of Judaism and its application to men of all races and nations and in its enduring to the end of time, (Mt. 28:18–20; Mk. 16:15; Lk. 24:46), and its *apostolicity* consisting in its standing on the foundation of the apostles and prophets (Eph. 2:20) and continuing in their doctrine (Acts 2:42). The church is destined for the glory which God wills for it (Eph. 5:21–27), and that destiny is set forth in the picture of the marriage feast of the Lamb and the New Jerusalem of Rev. 21–22.

cities of the plain the five cities (**Sodom, Gomorrah, Adman, Zeboiim,** and **Zoar**) near the southern tip of the Dead Sea which were destroyed when Lot fled, with only Zoar being saved. It is believed that the Dead Sea now covers their site.

Clauda see **Cauda**

Claudia (klô'dĭ-à) a Christian woman of Rome who sent salutations to Timothy (2 Tim. 4:21).

Claudius (klô'dĭ-ŭs) the fourth Roman emperor (A.D. 41–54). He was the son of Nero Drusus, born in 10 B.C. and lived the private life until acclaimed by the praetorian guard following the murder of Caligula. He is mentioned in Acts 11:28 (mention of the edict for the Jews to leave Rome) and is probably referred to in Acts 17:7. He had a speech impediment and, though seemingly well-intentioned, did not have a successful rule. He was murdered by his second wife, the infamous Agrippina, mother of Nero. He rejected divine honors, though some provinces acclaimed him, as did the Roman Senate at his death.

Claudius Lysias see **Lysias**

clay as the sediment of water remaining in pits or streets, clay is frequently used in the OT (Ps. 18:42; Isa. 57:20; Jer. 38:6). In Jn. 9:6 Jesus used it in healing the blind man. Several different OT words are used for both wet and dry native clay, for potter's clay (Isa. 41:25; Ex. 1:14; Job 4:19) and for fired clay. Besides its use for making pottery, clay was used for such things as brick sealing and grave doors or jars.

Clement (klĕm'ĕnt) a fellow worker of Paul at Philippi (Phil. 4:3).

Cleopas (klē'ŏ-păs) one of two disciples to

whom Christ appeared on the day of the resurrection as they went to Emmaus (Lk. 24:18). Probably not the same as Cleophas in Jn. 19:25.

Clopas (klō'păs) husband (or father or son) of Mary, a woman at Jesus' cross. The names Cleopas and Clopas are different and are not to be assumed as identical. Also efforts to identify this man with Alpheus and to connect these children with the brothers of Jesus assume (a) that this Mary is the same as Mary the mother of James and Joses (Mk. 15:40 = Mt. 27:56; Lk. 23:49, 24:10), (b) that this James is the same as James son of Alpheus (Mk. 3:18 = Mt. 10:3; Lk. 6:15; Acts 1:3), and, (c) that there are only three women mentioned in Jn. 19:25. There are too many possibilities against so many assumptions.

clothing see **dress**

cloud the natural barrenness of clouds in Palestine except in the rainy seasons when such clouds bring rain gives them a more defined character than in most climates. There are not many references to literal clouds, but frequent use of this characteristic as a figure, as a man with a promise but no performance is like a cloud without rain (Prov. 16:5; Isa. 18:4; Jude 12). (For other uses see Job 30:15; Lam. 2:1; Hos. 6:4.) Divine appearances often are accompanied by a cloud (Isa. 19:1). God's presence was also signified by a cloud (Ex. 29:42; 1 K. 8:10; 2 Chr. 5:14; Ezek. 43:4).

cloud, pillar of the symbolical glory-cloud, signifying God's presence to lead his chosen people or to inquire and visit offenses during the forty years of wilderness wanderings (Ex. 13:21 f.). It became a pillar of fire by night and rested near the tabernacle when Israel was to rest (Ex. 29:42 f., 33:9 f., 40:34 ff.).

Cnidus (nī'dŭs) an important city at the extreme southwest of Asia Minor on a peninsula between the islands of Cos and Rhodes past which Paul sailed on the voyage to Rome (Acts 27:7).

coal true mineral coal was not present in Palestine. Frequent Biblical references thus refer either to charcoal, to live fire coals, or to stones heated to coal-likeness. Charcoal was used for heating and cooking and in blacksmith work. The metaphor in Rom. 12:20 expresses the burning shame and confusion which men must feel when their evil is requited by good.

coat see **dress**

cock the male of fowl. There is no clearcut reference to the domestic cock in OT. The NT references are to the cockcrow (third watch, 12:00–3:00 A.M.) and to the cock's crowing at Peter's denial (Mt. 26:34).

cockatrice see **adder**

cockle KJV name for a weed occurring in Job 31:40.

codex earliest book form, so called from practice of fastening wooden boards together for writing.

Coele-Syria (sē'lĭ-sĭr'ĭ-à) [hollow Syria] name given to the region lying between the Lebanon and Anti-Lebanon mountains. The name was used later of all Palestine and Syria, even extending to Egypt. Under the Seleucids and Ptolemies all these regions were under one government. Though frequently mentioned in the Apocrypha, it is not mentioned in the OT except probably in the "plain of Aven" in Amos 1:5.

coffer KJV box in 1 Sam. 6:8, 11, 15.

coffin see **burial**

Cola or **Kola** (kō'là) a place (Judg. 15:4). See **Kola**

Col-hozeh (kŏl-hō'zà) a man of Judah (Neh. 3:15; 11:5).

collar word standing for different kinds of decorative ornaments (Prov. 1:9; Song of S. 4:9); or for pillory (Jer. 29:26), etc., in various versions.

collection offering for the saints in Rom. 15; 1 Cor. 16:1 f.; 2 Cor. 8–9.

college where Huldah lived in Jerusalem (2 K. 22:14; 2 Chr. 34:22). The margin has "in the second part" (of the city); ASV has "second quarter" (cf. Zeph. 1:10).

colony a designation of Philippi in Acts 16:12. Reference is to the location of Roman citizens in conquered territory. Such colonies had Roman legal status, including the use of magistrates (praetors) as in the case of Paul and Silas' imprisonment in Acts 16:12–40.

Colossae or **Colosse** (kŏ-lŏs'ē) a city of Phrygia in Asia Minor, close by Laodicea and Hierapolis (Col. 2:1, 4:13, 15, 16; see Rev. 1:11, 3:14). A church existed here to whom Paul addressed the Epistle to the Colossians. It was probably established during Paul's three-year stay at Ephesus (Acts 18:23, 19:10), though Col. 2:1 is generally thought to mean that the Colossians had never seen Paul face to face. Epaphras is perhaps the founder (Col. 1:7, 12, 13). It is clear from Philemon that Paul knew Philemon and Onesimus at Colosse and planned a visit on his release from Roman imprisonment (Philemon 22).

Colossians, Epistle to the (kŏ-lŏsh'ănz) the seventh in the arrangement of the epistles of the apostle Paul. It is usually surmised that the book was written at the same time as Ephesians and Philemon (cf. the common messenger Tychicus, 4:7–8 and Eph. 6:21, and also that

Onesimus, Philemon's slave, accompanied him, Col. 4:9) from Rome during Paul's imprisonment there (A.D. 60–62). Some have contended for Caesarea (Acts 24:27) or Ephesus as the place of writing, but they have found few followers. It is generally thought that Col. 2:1 implies that Paul had not himself preached at Colosse, the church being probably established by Epaphras (Col. 4:12, 1:7). The letter is concerned with the rise of false teachers who taught a human philosophy (Col. 2:8). The false teachers have usually been identified as incipient Jewish Gnostics. From Paul's refutation we infer that they taught circumcision (2:11, 3:11), the keeping of the ordinances of the Law (2:14), drink, sabbaths, and feast keeping (2:16). With this there seems to have been a dualistic denial of the work of Christ in creation (1:16 ff.) and a demand for asceticism (2:23). The book may be divided into: (1) Salutation and Expression of Thanks, 1:1–8; (2) The Pre-eminence of Christ, 1:9–2:5; (3) The Practical Application (denunciation of false teachers and ethical conduct for different classes of Christians), 2:6–4:6; and (4) Salutations: instructions for exchanging letters with the church at Laodicea.

The striking resemblance between Colossians and Ephesians raises the question of priority and genuineness. The resolution is usually that Ephesians is an expansion of Colossians. Thus those who reject the Pauline authorship of the former may still consider Colossians genuine.

J.W.R.

colt see **ass**

Comforter, the a word used to translate the Greek word *paraclete* referring to the **Holy Spirit** (Jn. 14:16 ff.).

Commission, the Great the commission or "marching orders" which Jesus repeatedly emphasized to the disciples in the appearances following the resurrection (Jn. 20:21–23; Mt. 28:18–20; Mk. 16:15–16; Lk. 24:46=47; Acts 1:8). This commission authorized the preaching of forgiveness in Jesus' name and upon the terms of pardon he laid down (faith, repentance, and baptism). It is called "the great" commission in contrast to the earlier "limited commission" (Mt. 10), which was preparatory and limited in scope and in application. It is given for all time: "Lo, I am with you always, even unto the end of the world." Some critics have attacked the commission.

Conaniah (kŏn′ȧ-nī′ȧ) a chief of the Levites in Josiah's time (2 Chr. 35:9); also a ruler of tithes and offerings in Hezekiah's time (2 Chr. 31:12 f.).

concision a mutilation. Paul so characterized

circumcision as performed by Jews who rejected the Gospel (Phil. 3:2).

concubine a woman lawfully wed to a head of a family in a position below that of a regular wife. Such a relationship was assumed and provided for by the law of Moses and no moral stigma was attached to it. The concubine might be a foreign slave bought or a captive, a Hebrew girl bought or taken in payment of a debt, or a Canaanitish woman bond or free. In the OT concubines bore supplementary family to the head of the family, sometimes at the barren wife's suggestion. Her children might become co-heirs, and many achieved distinction (Gen. 21:10, 22:24, 30:3, 31:31; Ex. 21:7, 10, 23:12).

concupiscence a word occurring in the KJV with the meaning of lust or evil desire, especially for money (Rom. 7:8; Col. 3:5) and sex (1 Thess. 4:5).

conduit a channel or tunnel for conveying water for storage or use. One of the longest in Palestine was built by Solomon bringing water from the pools of Solomon beyond Bethlehem (thirteen and one-half miles) to Jerusalem. Hezekiah built one to furnish water in Jerusalem. (2 K. 20:20), in anticipation of Sennacherib's invasion.

coney a rabbit-like animal (with short ears and legs and no tail) occurring from Africa north to Asia. It lives in caves and clefts of rocks, is about the size of a common domestic cat. It is declared unclean because it has four toes rather than two (Lev. 11:5; Deut. 14:7). RSV has rock badger.

confirmation the attempt to see the medieval and modern rite of confirmation in the laying on of hands in Acts 8:14–17, and 19:1=7 is mistaken. The bestowal of the Holy Spirit in both cases seems to be to enable some in the church to work miracles for confirmation of the preached word in the age of miracles before the Scriptures were written and recognized (see Mk. 16:20; Acts 14:3; Heb. 2:1–4). It was not merely a confirmation of their incorporation into the church. The bestowal of the indwelling Spirit (Acts 2:38; Rom. 8:9) at baptism is different from the bestowal of the Spirit for such a purpose.

congregation [Heb. *'edhah* and *qahal*; Gr. *ekklesia* or *sunagogē*] a word used to describe the Hebrew people as a whole in its peculiar aspect as a holy community, held together by religious rather than political bonds. The concept of an assembled group is usual, whether of a special assembly called for some purpose (1 K. 8:65) or gathered for one of the great feasts (Deut. 23:1), though there are some passages where the ideal concept of Israel wherever it might exist is possible (Ex. 12:19; Num. 15:15). In the wilderness the whole body of the people assembled at the door of the tabernacle *of the congregation* (Num. 10:3). Every circumcised male was a member of the congregation from the time when he could bear arms. Still Hebrew thought dealt more with the family and house or tribe, and collective representation was possible. So elders might represent the whole in assessing punishment (Num. 15:2), declaring war or peace (Josh. 9:15), with decisions binding on all (Josh. 9:18).

Coniah see **Jeconiah**

Cononiah see **Conaniah**

conscience an inner moral sense within man which condemns or approves his conduct. The word is a Greek word and the concept does not appear in the OT (though there is a sense of guilt expressed, Gen. 3:8, 42:21). Paul is the principal NT user (elsewhere only in Paul's speeches in Acts, 1 Peter and Hebrews). Rom. 2:14 f. and 1 Cor. 8–10 are typical passages in Paul.

consecration see **priest**

conversation now means "speech," but it formerly (KJV) meant "manner of life," or conduct.

conversion a word meaning "to turn" or "return." It may have a literal physical meaning (Judg. 8:13; Lk. 2:38), but most frequently in a religious sense it refers to a concrete change from one way of life to another (Jer. 3:14; Isa. 44:22, 55:7; Acts 9:35, 15:19). In the NT the act of turning to God is an active response to God's grace in Christ associated with humility (Mt. 18:3), belief (Acts 11:21), repentance (Acts 3:19, 26:20), and at times is virtually equated with baptism as the initiatory act by which the penitent sinner is pardoned and incorporated into Christ's body (cf. Acts 3:19 with Acts 2:38).

convocation [a holy summons] a word referring to Israel's solemn assemblies on the occasions of the sabbath (Lev. 23:1–3), Pentecost (Lev. 23:15–21), Passover (Ex. 12:16; Lev. 23:6, 7) or the Day of Atonement (Lev. 23:24–28).

Coos (Acts 21:1) see **Cos**

copper this elastic metal was one of the first metals used by civilized man in the Near East, since it was abundant (2 Chr. 4:18) and could be given a cutting edge by hammering it cold. Later it was mixed with tin to form **bronze** (the translation "brass" is erroneous, since the combination with zinc was unknown in Biblical times). Copper was used for numerous articles and tools: e.g., chains (Judg. 16:21),

pillars (1 K. 7:15–21), lavers (2 K. 25:13), and arms (1 Sam. 17:5 f., 38). "Coppersmith" in 2 Tim. 4:14 is a word which meant a worker in bronze, then it became a general term for metal worker.

coral [Heb. *ramoth*, rendered coral in Job 28:18; Ezek. 27:16] the ancient versions are uncertain about its meaning, but there seems to be no reason to doubt that the red coral of the Mediterranean area, which was known and valued in ancient times, was meant.

Corban (kôr'băn) in the OT an "offering" to God (Lev. 1:2, 3; Num. 7:12), especially one made in fulfillment of a vow (Lev. 27:9). Jesus spoke of it in Mk. 7:11 in referring to Jewish avoidance of duty to parents by saying that the blessings by which parents might be prospered was "corban," i.e., "an offering to God." In this way the tradition absolved one from the obligation to support his parents. Jesus condemned such setting aside of God's law as hypocrisy.

cord (rope) cord made from fibers such as flax (Est. 1:6), silver or gold (Ex. 28:24 f.; Eccl. 12:6), as well as grass (Jn. 2:15; Acts 27:32), papyrus, wood, and camel's hair, was common and used for a wide variety of purposes: tent ropes (Ex. 35:18), halters (Hos. 11:4), drawing water (Josh. 2:15), or binding prisoners (Judg. 15:13).

Core (Jude 11) see **Korah**

coriander (kō'rĭ-ăn'dēr) a plant used somewhat as caraway or poppy seeds are in modern times. It is mentioned in Ex. 16:31 and Num. 11:7 as a means of describing **manna.**

Corinth (kôr'ĭnth) a city of Greece located near the south end of the isthmus which joins the Peloponnesus to the mainland of Greece. The city lies about two miles south of the port of Lechaeum and roughly the same distance from Cenchreae, the port on the Saronic gulf. This location enabled Corinth to control traffic and to collect customs duties from sea traffic across the isthmus and from land traffic to and from the Peloponnesus. The mountain of Acrocorinth loomed about 1500 feet over the city at its southwest corner and served as part of its defenses, especially in case of siege. A pagan temple for the worship of the goddess Aphrodite, served at times by one thousand harlots, was located on the top of Acrocorinth.

Corinth was apparently occupied as early as 3000 B.C., although there is little definite history of her before ca. 900 B.C., at which time she was conquered by the Dorians. In the eighth and seventh centuries B.C., Corinth founded the colonies of Corcyra and Syracuse and owned a powerful navy. In the seventh century, under the rule of Kypselos and his son Periander, the city rose to prosperity and prominence through commerce and the manufacturing of Corinthian pottery and the famous Corinthian bronze. In later centuries the city had her ups and downs but in the main was prosperous. In the second century B.C., she was a leading member in the Achaian League, thus probably incurring Rome's disfavor. At any rate, in 146 B.C., the Roman consul L. Mummius captured, burned, and razed the city, slaying the men and selling the women and children as slaves. The site lay desolate for one hundred years, being rebuilt in 44 B.C. by Julius Caesar, who populated it largely with Roman freedmen and dispossessed Greeks. Jews and other foreigners came later. It was rebuilt as a Roman city, and coins and other artifacts enable the Roman stratum to be clearly discernible to modern archaeologists. Commerce again rose rapidly and the city was made the capital of Achaia and the seat of its proconsul. An earthquake damaged the city during the reign of Vespasian, but it was rebuilt and beautified under Hadrian, and before A.D. 200 it was probably the finest and most modern city of Greece. It has had a checkered history since and has been controlled by Byzantines, Normans, Franks, Turks, and Venetians, as well as Greeks. Since the earthquake of A.D. 1858, the new city has been situated about three miles away from the old, so that the old city is now accessible to excavations. Archaeologists have done much excavating, and with the aid of early descriptions left by Pausanias and others, most of the ancient buildings, streets, markets, temples, fountains, baths, etc., have been found and identified, through several levels of occupation.

Not much has been located that has to do with NT times in a specific way. A lintel stone from a Hebrew synagogue which may have stood in Paul's day has been found, and perhaps a portion of the judgment seat in the Agora, before which Paul was arraigned, may also have been located. A great deal of information about the life of the city in Paul's day has been learned, and this is of interest to the NT student. This large city, a cosmopolis, would easily furnish opportunity for the cultivation of sin and vice for which Corinth is well-known. The cult of Aphrodite and various other pagan religions were also represented, to furnish the strongest possible challenge to budding Christianity. True spiritual faith would have to be at its best to win followers from among the heathen who were accustomed to idolatry, animal sacrifices, vice, lust, pride, and the other common weaknesses of men.

The recovering and recounting of the several facets of life—business, recreation, health, worship—of the ancient Corinthians is no doubt quite a tedious chore to the scholar, but the ability finally to "step into the shoes" of the ancient Corinthian and feel the pulse and throb of the ancient city's life more than repays the effort.   J.D.T.

Corinthians (kô-rĭn'thĭ-ăns) two letters written by the apostle Paul to the church at **Corinth** and placed in our NT immediately after Romans as the seventh and eighth books. Their authenticity has been generally admitted, though serious questions have been raised about the unity of the second letter. Since together they form the longest single section of NT material and bear directly on a large variety of problems, they form one of the most interesting and important correspondences in the entire NT.

1. *First Corinthians.* This first letter was written from Ephesus on Paul's third missionary tour (1 Cor. 16:8, 17–19; Acts 19:1–20:1). His stay as Ephesus included a period of about three years (Acts 19:8, 10, 20:31), A.D. 54–57, though some would place it a year earlier. Since Paul's departure from Ephesus came while Titus traveled to Corinth with this letter (2 Cor. 1:15, 23, 2:12–13, 7:6, 13–16), it must have been written shortly before he left Ephesus in A.D. 57. The Corinthian church had been established on Paul's second tour. After leaving Athens Paul came to Corinth (Acts 18:1), where he waited for Timothy (1 Thess. 3:1) and Silas (Acts 18:5). He joined Aquila and Priscilla at the trade of tentmaking, while reasoning in the Jewish synagogue (Acts 18:1–3). He had success, baptizing Crispus, the ruler of the synagogue, along with many others (Acts 18:8; 1 Cor. 1:11–14). Paul remained there eighteen months (Acts 18:11). The letter was called forth by news brought by Chloe (1:11) and others (16:17) that there were party divisions (1:11 ff.), as well as other disorders at Corinth. The gravity of such disorders, including a case of incest (5:1), disturbances over the Lord's Supper (11:20 ff.), lawsuits (1:1 ff.), and denial of the resurrection (ch. 15), had already prompted sending Timothy (4:17) and now called forth this letter. On their part, the Corinthians themselves had written inquiries about several things including marriage (7:1), things sacrificed to idols (8:1), spiritual gifts (12:1 ff.), and the collection being taken up to be sent to Jeru-

salem (16:1). These things were all treated in the letter and together form a kind of skeleton outline of the epistle. Very serious also was the presence of a group of Gnosticizing Jewish teachers, apparently supplied with letters from the church at Jerusalem (2 Cor. 3:1 ff.), who taught the Gospel in such a way as to appeal to the inclination of some converts to compromise with the pagan practices of their Greek contemporaries (6:9–19, 10:6–33) and in doing so attacked Paul personally, claiming, with a show of worldly wisdom and philosophy (knowledge = gnosis), that Paul was not an apostle (9:1 ff.). Paul may have written a letter to Corinth prior to this letter (see 5:9), though the reference "I wrote" has often been interpreted as epistolary and to refer to 1 Corinthians.

2. *Second Corinthians.* The second letter was written a few months after the first, in the same year. This would put it in A.D. 56 or 57. It was written from Macedonia after Paul had left Ephesus on his way to meet Titus, who had borne the previous letter to Corinth (2:12 f., 5:8, 8:1, 9:2) and before the trip to Corinth or Achaia, where he spent three months (Acts 20:3). The exact place of writing is unknown. Undoubtedly the news brought back by Titus provided the occasion of this letter. The majority of the church had returned in their allegiance to Paul (1:13 f., 7:9, 15 f.), but the false teachers had seemingly become more hardened and opposed to him (1:10, 3:1 ff., 11–13). They had to be dealt with, and this Paul did in some of the most direct and straightforward language in the NT (see especially chs. 11–13). Corinth had also been lax in getting up its promised contribution, and Paul sent Titus and a companion ahead with instructions about this (chs. 8–9). Thus the letter as it stands divides itself into three sections: The personal matters (chs. 1–7); the collection (chs. 8–9); and the defense of Paul's apostolic authority (chs. 10–13). The question of the chronology of Paul's trips to Corinth (he seems to have made a trip from Ephesus to Corinth, 12:14, 13:1–2) and the unity of the second epistle are quite controversial. Some understand the references to the trip as being statements of intention rather than actuality. The authenticity of 2 Corinthians is generally admitted. But some scholars contend that our present epistle is a composite of at least two letters put together after Paul's death. Those who contend for the unity of the letter see the one who had "committed wrong" as the fornicator of 1 Cor. 5:1. Others think this was an influential member who lent himself to the revolt against Paul and think that part of this letter represents a "tearful letter" written by Paul against him (mainly chs. 10–13), while 6:14–7:1 is a part of the "former letter" mentioned as being written before 1 Corinthians (see 1 Cor. 5:9–11). These considerations do not deny Pauline authorship of the whole epistle, but they seriously undermine confidence in the way the book was preserved. The arguments supporting them are quite subjective. Many fine scholars such as P. E. Hughes (*Paul's Second Epistle to the Corinthians,* The New International Commentary, 1962) continue to defend the unity of the epistle.

cormorant a bird which catches fish from the sea. The word is used to translate a bird in the list of unclean birds (Lev. 11:17; Deut. 14:17) where the etymology suggests a diving bird. Another bird so rendered is probably a **pelican** (Isa. 34:11; Zeph. 2:14).

corn a term used in the KJV for different grains such as wheat, barley, spelt (Ex. 9:32) and rye (Isa. 28:25). Palestine produced these grains in abundance. They were a principal source for food and from Solomon's day were exported (Ezek. 27:17; Amos 8:5).

Cornelius (kôr-nēl'yŭs) a Roman centurion of the Italian cohort stationed at Caesarea, probably already attracted to the Jewish religion (cf. Acts 10:30 he kept the Jewish hour of prayer), who was converted by Peter at God's direct instruction. He and his family became the first Gentile converts and received (as at Pentecost "at the beginning," Acts 11:15) the baptism of the Holy Spirit to demonstrate that the Gentiles were proper subjects of the Gospel (Acts 10:45–47, 11:17, 15:8–9).

cornerstone a term referring either to the large stone placed at the foundation of a building to bind the walls together or to a capstone. Any important person might be figuratively compared to a cornerstone, and hence there arose a number of passages where the Messiah is so described as interpreted both by Jewish rabbinical sources and the NT: Ps. 118:22 = Mt. 21:42; Mk. 12:10; Lk. 20:17; 1 Pet. 2:7; Acts 4:11 and Isa. 28:16 = 1 Pet. 2:6; cf. also Eph. 2:20 with Isa. 28:16.

cornet [Heb. *shophar*] a loud-sounding instrument made of the horn of a ram or a chamois or an ox and used by the ancient Hebrews for such signals as announcing the Jubilee (Lev. 25:9), or the New Year, as a summons to war (Jer. 4:5, 19; cf. Job 39:25), and as a warning by a sentinel on the watchtower (Ezek. 28:4, 5).

Cos or **Coos** (kôs or kō'ŏs) a small island off

the coast of Asia Minor, home of a large Jewish settlement, but noticed in the Bible only because the apostle Paul passed the night there after sailing from **Miletus.**

Cosam (kō'săm) ancestor of Joseph (Lk. 3:28).

cosmetics beauty preparations for the skin and hair. Included were ointments, paint for the eyes (Ezek. 23:40; cf. Jer. 4:30), and perfume (Song of S. 1:12–14; Est. 2:12–14). The dryness of the Eastern climate makes some treatment desirable for comfort and only mourning or self-humiliation usually caused it to be left off (Dan. 10:3). However, too great use of cosmetics or their use for evil purposes are noted and condemned (Prov. 7:17).

cotton a plant from whose fruit a fiber is woven into cloth; known and used in the region of Palestine from early times. Esther 1:6 refers to cotton hanging in the palace at Susa; Isa. 19:9 makes mention of the cotton weavers of Egypt.

couch an article of furniture for reclining or sleeping. See **bed**

council a governing or advisory body having to do with religious or legal and civic affairs. The Biblical usage includes the heavenly council of God (Ps. 89:7; cf. Job 15:8), that of the tribes (Ps. 68:27; Jer. 18:18). Council sometimes refers to the courts (Mt. 10:17) and after the Exile the great Jewish court, the **Sanhedrin.** Acts 25:12 mentions the council assisting the Roman governor.

counselor one who gives advice. Parents, elders, wise men, etc., are so referred to. The Messiah is a king who is a counselor (Isa. 9:6, 11:2), as is the Holy Spirit (Jn. 14:16).

court an area enclosed in walls of a building but without roof. Especially used of tabernacle and temple (Ex. 27:9, 40:33; 1 K. 6:36; 2 K. 23:12), but used also, e.g., of a private house (2 Sam. 17:18).

cousin the Bible has no exact word for cousin. Passages so translated generally (Lk. 1:36) mean "kinsman." Usually one reads "son of a father's brother."

covenant a solemn promise or agreement, usually made sacred by an oath and a ritual. Such covenants formed an important part of the political and religious life of Near Eastern peoples. This is true also of Israel, and hence the covenant relationship is one of the most necessary for understanding the religions of both Old and New Testaments. Archaeological materials (for example, the Hittite "suzerainty covenants") furnish interesting parallels for understanding the OT. The Hebrew word is *berith*, translated into Greek by *diathēkē* in the LXX. It is used with several verbs, but "cutting a covenant," referring to the custom of cutting

or dividing a sacrificial animal and passing between the parts in ratification is the most frequent (Gen. 15; Jer. 34:18–19). Practically equivalent or descriptive terms were the "oath," derived from the ceremony, and the "testimony," referring to the stipulations or rules to which the party swore obedience. The OT contains records of many covenants of various types. There are those between countries or cities (1 Sam. 11:1; Hos. 12:1); between individuals (Jacob and Laban, Gen. 31:44 ff.); and especially between God and individuals, such as that with Noah (Gen. 9:9–17), and with Abraham (Gen. 15 and 17). Most important is that made by God with Israel at Sinai. The story of the agreement involved is related in detail in Ex. 19:1–8, 24:1–8. The covenant was embodied in a group of laws and rituals, of which the Ten Commandments as an epitome are frequently called "the covenant" (Ex. 34:28). Such regulations were often called "the testimonies" (Ex. 32:15). It is quite proper, as is usual, to emphasize that the covenant is not a mere parity transaction of two equal parties, but is an act of grace on God's part for reconciling man to himself (Deut. 7:6–8; Ps. 89:3–4), but man's response in the relationship should not be overlooked. The term *diathēkē* in the NT era meant a legal disposition of property after death—quite a one-sided matter. Despite claims that the unilateral action of God makes this the proper term (= testament) for describing both the Mosaic and the gospel relationship, it is more likely that the word should still be translated "covenant" in all the NT passages (e.g., Heb. 9:15). Undoubtedly the LXX stance here is primary. Jesus himself emphasized the events of his death as those validating the Gospel as the "New Covenant," and the Lord's Supper has special significance thus as a covenant meal (Mt. 26:28; Mk. 14:24; Lk. 22:20; 1 Cor. 11:25). The fact is also emphasized by quotation of Jeremiah's prophetic word (Jer. 31:31 ff. = Heb. 8:8 ff.).

covetousness one of the three most disgraceful things, mentioned in numerous catalogues of vice in the papyri and extrabiblical writings, meaning literally "a desire to have more." Much Biblical teaching is directed against this spirit of materialism, and many examples of covetousness as the cause of much evil are to be found (e.g., Achan, Josh. 7:21). The prohibitions and warning in the law of Moses and all of the wisdom literature are based upon the promise that God will provide enough, and the righteous individual who is liberal with his God-given possessions always has the blessings of life. The covetous and the righteous are contrasted, the one greedy for more, the other making generous use of his material possessions (cf. Mic. 2:2; Prov. 21:26). The same emphasis occurs in the NT (Heb. 13:5; 1 Tim. 6:6–10). Jesus taught that abundance is not necessary to life, but that it is a divine blessing and favor if received and rightly used (Lk. 12:15). Paul notes even the possibility of giving in a generous spirit, as opposed to a covetous one, keeping back all one can (2 Cor. 9:5). Also in the NT covetousness is frequently associated with sins of the flesh (Mk. 7:22; 1 Cor. 5:10; Eph. 5:3, 19; Heb. 13:4–5; 2 Pet. 2:2–3, 14) and is characterized as idolatry (Col. 3:5). The connection between false teaching and covetousness is noteworthy (Tit. 1:10–11; 2 Pet. 2:3). Paul felt it necessary to defend himself against the imputation of covetousness (a charge that might frequently be made against an itinerant preacher) with reference to his whole conduct and teaching (Acts 20:33; 2 Cor. 2:17, 4:2, 7:2; 1 Thess. 2:5), denying a mere pretence arising from covetousness or some pretence which covered avaricious aims.

R.L.R.

cow see **bull**

Coz (kōz) a Judahite (1 Chr. 4:8).

Cozbi (kŏz′bī) a Midianite woman who plagued Israel and was slain (Num. 25:15–18).

crane a long-necked wading bird, frequent in Palestine especially in periods of migration. The birds so named in the English translation, however (Isa. 38:14; Jer. 8:7), are generally taken to mean swallows.

creation the Biblical affirmation concerning the origin of the world, including man, is that "in the beginning God created the heavens and the earth" (Gen. 1:1). The NT further affirms that by the Christ as the divine word "were all things made that hath been made" (Jn. 1:3). The creation record of Gen. 1 is, then, accepted as a *revelation* of origins. "By faith we understand that the worlds have been formed by the word of God, so that what is seen hath not been made out of things which appear" (Heb. 1:3).

Several questions are raised concerning this understanding. The Bible places no date on either the creation of the world or of man. See **chronology.** Various attempts have been made to explain the meaning of the seven days of Gen. 1 as they relate to time: (1) literal twenty-four-hour days; (2) pictorial days—God revealed the process to Moses over a seven-day period; (3) The Gap Theory—that God created the cosmos, then it "became" waste and void, and the seven days are reconstruction; (4) Day

Age—that the day is to be interpreted as a long period of time (2 Pet. 3:8) or that there were long periods intervening between each of the days; (5) "As is," that God created the world to look as if it were already mature (as presumably was Adam). There is no indication in the Bible as to which of these meanings was intended by the author, and it is for this reason that the statement is made that there is no data given for constructing a chronology for the age of the world. For the possible age of man, see also the article on **chronology.** The theory of organic evolution (which, as admitted by its most avowed advocates, is still a mere hypothesis or theory) that everything in existence came into being through natural causes from a single origin cannot be harmonized with belief in Gen. 1–2; Heb. 11:3. It is clearly taught that man did not exist as an animal before evolving into man and that woman's creation was separate from man's. Stress has been laid on the differences in the two creation accounts (Gen. 1–2); but, if the second is taken as a retelling of the story from a different viewpoint, no contradiction need be seen. Surely the potential for creative and spiritual development demonstrated by the human race is a strong argument for the divine origin of man. The creation story of God's revelation is consonant with all that modern science and learning have demonstrated concerning him.

J.W.R.

creditor see **loans**

Crescens (krĕs′ĕnz) a companion of Paul at Rome who had left for Galatia (2 Tim. 4:10).

Crete (krēt) an island some 140 miles in length in the Mediterranean to the southeast of Greece. In early times it was the seat of a Greek civilization known to history as Minoan. The island was mountainous, famous for its 100 cities. It had a large Jewish population to which reference is frequently made (1 Macc. 15:23). Cretan Jews were present at Pentecost (Acts 2:11). Paul sailed by it on his way to Rome (Acts 27:7–21, where mention is made of its cities Fair Havens, Lasaea, and Phoenix). Paul had preached there (evidently after release from his first Roman imprisonment), had left Titus on the island to set the churches in order, and to him and the Christians there wrote the Letter to **Titus.**

Cretes (KJV, Acts 2:11), **Cretans** people of Crete.

Crispus (krĭs′pŭs) a ruler of a Jewish synagogue at Corinth converted by Paul (Acts 18:7; 1 Cor. 1:14).

cross an upright stake or pole to which most frequently a crosspiece was affixed, forming a letter T, on which condemned men were placed for punishment till death. The prisoner was usually forced to carry the cross (only the crosspiece, however) to the place of execution, where he was tied or nailed to it and elevated. This death was agonizing, slow, often hastened by breaking of the legs. The special emphasis placed by some modern groups on the simple stake (without the crossbar) is refuted by contemporary first-century references (cf. Barnabas 9:18: the cross is a T). In the faith of the Gospel death on the cross signified the saving power of Christ's atoning death and, while offensive to Jews (to whom what was hung was offensive) and foolish to the worldly wise Greek, it was to the believer the power of God for salvation (1 Cor. 1:17–21; Eph. 2:16; Col. 2:14) and thus his hope (Col. 1:20).

crown a headdress worn to indicate royal rank or special achievement. The OT speaks of the top of the head as a "crown" (Deut. 28:35), of the crown of the priest (Ex. 28:37), of the king's crown (1 Chr. 20:2), and even of the common tiara or turban as such (Job 29:14; Isa. 3:23). Paul alludes to the crown made of leaves (laurel, pine, or parsley) given to victors in the Olympic games (1 Cor. 9:25; 2 Tim. 2:5). The Gr. *stephanos* is generally used of such crowns (Rev. 2:10), while the *diadēma* is the symbol of ruling power. Symbolically one may be said to be crowned with glory, honor, or riches. Such is the meaning of the Christian's "crown of life," i.e., eternal life as the fitting reward (James 1:12; cf. Prov. 1:9, 4:9).

crown of thorns (Mt. 27:29) reference to the mockery of the Roman soldiers in plaiting a crown of thorns and placing it upon Christ's head. Since there were many kinds of thorny plants in Palestine, it is not possible to identify the kind of thorn from the general word.

crucifixion see **cross**

cruse a small flask or jug used to hold olive oil (1 K. 17:12–16). Elsewhere the term is used for the translation of "canteen" (1 Sam. 26:11–26) or where "bowl" or "dish" would be more accurate (2 K. 2:20).

crystal quartz, either clear or tinged. Ancients believed rock crystal to be ice formed by intense cold. Thus the words for crystal may also be translated "ice" (Job 28:17; Rev. 4:6, 21:11, 22:1).

cubit a measure of about eighteen inches from elbow to tip of middle finger. See **weights and measures**

cuckoo an insect-eating bird, known to visit Palestine, but evidently wrongly translated in passages like Lev. 11 and Deut. 14 where a meat-eating bird is listed as unclean (RSV, sea gull; others, owl).

cucumber the common vegetable or fruit by this name was grown in Palestine and Egypt, hence the reference (Num. 11:5) to the Israelites longing for the cucumbers of Egypt. Reference also occurs to cucumber fields (Isa. 1:8).

cummin one of the cultivated plants of Palestine (Isa. 28:25; Mt. 23:23), an herb belonging to the carrot family with seeds like caraway seeds and used for seasoning (Isa. 28:23–29). Even the Mishna of the Jews mentions tithing of such (*Ma'as*IV.5). Cf. Mt. 23:23; and Deut. 14:22–23.

cup a vessel for dipping or drinking, occurring in forms like our cups (with or without handles) and like a bowl or dish (more like modern cereal bowls). Cups were in common use and became a figure or metaphor of what one receives or suffers (Ps. 23:5, 116:13; Rev. 14:10). At the last supper Jesus used the third cup of the Passover supper (cup of blessing) as the occasion of instituting the Lord's Supper. Here, as was the custom, evidently individual cups were used ("divide this among yourselves," Lk. 22:16), though "cup" in the context is a metonymy for the contents: the fruit of the vine.

cupbearer an official who is in the confidence of the king and serves his wine (Gen. 40:1, 21, 41:9; 1 K. 10:5; Neh. 1:11).

curse the expression of a wish for harm or damnation to another person or thing. Though there are instances in the Bible of such (Gen. 9:25; Mt. 26:74), the Bible teaches that, since Christians are not God and judgment is not theirs, they must not curse their fellows (Lk. 6:28; James 3:10; cf. James 4:11).

curtain the normal use is of tent material (Ex. 26: 1–13; Song of S. 1:5; Isa. 54:2); it may also refer to the veil or separating pieces (Num. 3:26; Isa. 40:22). So NT uses it for veil between the holy and the most holy places.

Cush (kŭsh') 1. Son of Ham and grandson of Noah (Gen. 10:6–8; 1 Chr. 1:8–10). Among his "sons" were Seba and his brothers and Nimrod (probably meaning here "offspring").

2. The Hebrew word for the African country better known as **Ethiopia.**

3. A supposed enemy of David of the tribe of Benjamin as appears from Psalm 7.

Cushan (kŭsh'ăn) possibly the same as Cushan-rishathaim (Hab. 3:7; cf. Judg. 3:8–10).

Cushi (kŭsh'ī) 1. The Cushite, a member of the family of Cush (2 Sam. 18:21–32).

2. A prince in Jehoiakim's court (Jer. 36:4).

3. Zephaniah's father (Zeph. 1:1).

custom a tax (Mt. 9:9) or a conventional way of acting either by law (Gen. 31:35) or religious usage (Acts 6:14).

Cuth or **Cuthah** (cŭth′ or cū′thà) country to which Shalmaneser carried Israelite colonists (2 K. 17:24, 30).

cuttings (of the flesh) a practice of heathen worshipers in mourning for the dead, which was forbidden to the Jews (Lev. 21:5; Deut. 14:1; 1 K. 18:28).

cypress a tree of unknown identity in antiquity, often considered a species of pine or box tree and at times even considered to be the "gopher" tree used in shipbuilding. The identification of it with the modern cypress is questionable.

Cyprus an island in the Mediterranean some forty miles off the coast of Syria opposite Antioch. It is about one hundred and fifty by forty miles. In the OT it is identified with Kittim. It was known in antiquity as the supposed birthplace of the god Zeus and for its rich copper deposits (cypress = copper). It had a large Jewish population. Barnabas was a native of the island (Acts 4:36), and it was one of the first places evangelized by the Jews from Jerusalem (Acts 11:19), as well as later by Paul and Barnabas (Acts 13:4–12) and then by Barnabas and John Mark (Acts 13:11).

Cyrene (sī-rē′nĭ) the principal city of the part of Northern Africa called in ancient times Cyrenaica. The territory corresponds to modern Tripoli, and it is separated from Carthage on one hand and Egypt on the other by the desert. It was celebrated for its climate and fertility. Jews were settled there in large number. Simon, who bore the Savior's cross, was from there (Mt. 27:32); sojourners from the country were dwelling in Jerusalem at Pentecost (Acts 2:10) and gave their name to one of the synagogues in which Stephen disputed (Acts 6:9). Other NT references are to the fact that converts from this region contributed to the formation of the first Gentile church at Antioch (Acts 11:20) and that one of the teachers at Antioch, one named Lucian, was also a native of the city (Acts 13:1).

Cyrenius (sī-rē′nĭ-ŭs) KJV form of the name of the Syrian governor Quirinius (Lk. 2:2).

Cyrus (sī′rŭs) founder of the Persian empire (see Dan. 6:28, 10:1; 2 Chr. 36:22–23). He was the son of Cambyses, a Persian king. His empire was one of the great Oriental realms. He captured Babylonia in 539 B.C., and his descendants ruled the land until the defeat of Persia by Alexander the Great in the battle of Issus in 332 B.C. His special significance for Biblical studies is the liberal policy which he pursued toward the Jews in decreeing the return of the captives to Palestine and the rebuilding of the temple (2 Chr. 36:22 f.; Ezra 1:1–6). This sponsorship of the Jewish return, in fact, laid the foundations of Judaism.

D

Dabareh (dăb′à-rĕ) (Josh. 21:28) KJV spelling for **Daberath.**

Dabbasheth (dăb′à-shĕth) a border town of Zebulun (Josh. 19:11).

Daberath (dab′à-räth) a town lying between Zebulun and Issachar (Josh. 19:12, 21:28; 1 Chr. 6:72).

Dagon (dā′gŏn) the national deity of Philistia with local sites at Gaza (Judg. 16:21–30) and Ashdod (1 Sam. 5:2–7; 1 Chr. 10:10), the latter of which was destroyed in the Maccabean wars (1 Macc. 10:83 f.). Archaeology has shown that he was a major deity in Canaanite religion in general, with an established cult at Ras Shamra. In the cult texts there Baal is described as the son of Dagon. The association of Dagon with a fish motif rests upon a passage where the text is uncertain (1 Sam. 5:4) and is questioned by most scholars.

Dalmatia (dăl-mā′shà) a mountainous district of Greece next to the Adriatic Sea, where both Paul (Rom. 15:19) and Titus (2 Tim. 4:10) preached the Gospel, then a part of Illyricum.

Dalphon (dăl′fŏn) son of Haman (Est. 9:7).

Damaris (dăm′à-ris) woman converted by Paul in his visit to Athens (Acts 17:34).

Damascus (dà-măs′kŭs) a city of Syria and perhaps the oldest city in continuous habitation in the world. It is situated on the eastern slope of the Anti-Lebanon Mountain, on the Nahr-Barada (river Abana) and just north of the Nahr el-A'waj (river Pharpar). Mount Hermon

Dan

lies not far away to the southwest. These two rivers fed from the rains and snows of the mountains turn the semiarid desert into an oasis. The city is situated where the most important trade routes cross, making it a place of prominence. Josephus says that the city was founded by Uz, a grandson of Shem. It is first mentioned in Scripture in connection with Abraham (Gen. 14:15, 15:2). It is next mentioned in David's time when "the Syrians of Damascus come to succor Hadadezer king of Zobah," who fought David (2 Sam. 8:5; 1 Chr. 18:5). The name is found in Egyptian records in the sixteenth century B.C. In the Amarna period it was the center of an Amorite nation rebelling against Egypt (1300 B.C.). Later (ca. 1000 B.C.) it was able to rival Assyria as a growing power and during the periods of the kingdoms of Judah and Israel a rival of them. The kings who bore the title Ben-hadad (1 K. 15:18 ff., 20:1–43; 2 K. 6:24 ff., 8:7) are major factors in the history of monarchies. Damascus later became the capital of the Nabataean kingdom with the ruler Aretas III. It was captured by the Romans in 65 B.C., who retained it during the NT period. Aretas IV ruled when Paul escaped from it (Acts 9:2–25). The Jewish population was evidently large (Acts 9:2, 22:5–6, 26:12). From the Dead Sea Scrolls it is known that an Essene community like that at Qumran lived there also.

Dan (dăn) fifth son of Jacob by Bilhah, Rachel's maid (Gen. 30:6) and progenitor of one of the twelve tribes of Israel. The name means "judge" (Gen. 49:16). The records of the family are meager. Only one son is mentioned (Gen. 46:23), but at the census his people numbered 67,000 for the largest number of able-bodied men. (See Num. 10:25; Deut. 27:13; Josh. 19:48 for other references to the early period.) Dan received a territory just north of Judah toward the Philistine country and was never able to conquer it (Judg. 1:34, 18:1). Hence later the tribe requested permission for the removal to the northern region (Judg. 18:7, 10). Later references to Dan are slight (1 Chr. 12:35, 27:22). In 1 Chr. 2–12, Dan's name is omitted from the genealogies as it is from the list of tribes sealed in Rev. 7:2–7. The northern city became the northern outpost of Palestine, giving rise to the term "from Dan to Beer-sheba."

dance a musical instrument [Heb. *machol*], probably a percussion, made with a metal ring on a handle, to which bells were attached. David mentioned praising God on these along with other instruments (Ps. 110).

Daniel (dăn'yĕl) 1. The fourth of the "greater prophets" from the viewpoint of the English Bible, but in the Hebrew arrangement (where he is called a "seer" rather than a "prophet") the author of one of the more substantial of the works of the "Writings," the third division of the OT canon. Daniel appears to have been of royal descent (Dan. 1:3), with considerable personal endowments (1:4). With other Hebrews he was taken to Babylon in 604 B.C. and trained for the king's service. He refused to defile himself with improper food and won his way (1:6–18). He became an interpreter and adviser of the king (1:17, 2:14 ff.) and was made "ruler of the whole province." His interpretation of the king's visions forms a major part of the story (4:8–27, 5:10–28). His rivalry with other powers led him and his companions into conflict and trials in the lions' den (6:10–23) and fire. He lived even to the third year of Cyrus, when he saw his last vision (534 B.C., cf. 10:1, 4).

2. The second son of David by Abigail (1 Chr. 3:1), also called Chileab (2 Sam. 3:3).

3. A returning exile (Ezra 8:2).

4. A priest who sealed the covenant of Nehemiah (Neh. 10:6).

Daniel, Book of a book of the OT placed in the Hebrew canon between Esther and Ezra, or immediately before Esther, rather than among the prophets as in the English Bible. In certain sections it contains some of the earliest apocalyptic material of the same style and forming a background for the Revelation of John in the NT. 1. *Title.* The book receives its name from the principal character, Daniel, who as a lad with other Hebrews was carried to Babylon during the Exile and became a seer and counselor in the court of Babylon, where he lived to the time of Cyrus.

2. *Contents.* The book is generally divided into two parts: (a) chs. 1–6, containing chiefly historical events; and (b) chs. 7–12, containing Daniel's apocalyptic visions. But there is a difference in language at ch. 8. From 2:4b to 7:28 the work is in Aramaic; 8:1 resumes the original Hebrew. Hence it has been suggested that ch. 1 be taken as introduction, chs. 2–7 as a progressive history of the powers of the world and principles of divine government as seen in the life of Daniel, and chs. 8–12, which trace the fortunes of the people of God, as typical of the fortunes of the church in all ages.

3. *Genuineness.* The book nowhere assigns the writing to Daniel, but this is implied by the use of the first person in the latter portion, especially in 12:9, where "Daniel," who has been speaking, is assured of the secret nature

of the book's contents for the wicked. This, with the admitted unity of the work, argues that Daniel is the intended author. The book was doubted by the early antagonist Porphyry in the third century of our era. Modern liberal critical scholarship has overwhelmingly rejected it as a product of Daniel's pen. The arguments have included such things as the claim for the use of late linguistic terms; but, since all such data are capable of being interpreted both ways, the rejection actually turns on the historicity of Daniel's inspired predictions of political events which were to come to pass. Liberal presuppositions of the impossibility of such miracles make it necessary to put the prophecy down past the time of the rise of Greece and the oppression of Antiochus Epiphanes, whose deeds are unmistakably pictured in 8:9–14, 23–26. E. B. Pusey, the great defender of the book, in his *Lectures on Daniel the Prophet* (1883), counters by showing the difficulty of interpreting the fourth empire of the visions as anything other than the Roman empire and pointing out that the prediction of its future is no less a miracle than that of predicting the same things of Greece and Syria. The book receives testimony from the Dead Sea community of Qumran, where copies exist which place it back near the time when its critics say it was composed). Too, the Sibylline Oracles (III.381 ff.), a Jewish treatise from near 150 B.C., uses the work. W. F. Albright has said that after Qumran there is no reason to doubt the existence of any canonical book of the OT for a substantial time prior to the founding of the Essene community "except Daniel." It may well be asked Why "except Daniel"? since the same attestation exists for it. For a fuller discussion of the problems, see Edward J. Young, *An Introduction to the Old Testament*, 1958, and *The Prophecy of Daniel*, 1952.

Danites (dăn'ītz) descendants of Dan (Judg. 13:2; 1 Chr. 12:35).

Dan-jaan (dăn'jā'ăn) place mentioned only in 2 Sam. 24:6.

Dannah (dăn'ă) a city in mountain region of Judah (Josh. 15:49).

Dara (1 Chr. 2:6) see **Darda**

Darda (där'dà) a man famed for wisdom, but surpassed by Solomon (1 K. 4:31), probably same as Darda in 1 Chr. 2:6, since three of four names (but with different name for the father) are the same.

daric (där'ĭc) a gold coin of Persian origin, worth about $5, used in Palestine (Ex. 2:69, 8:27; 1 Chr. 26:7; Neh. 7:72 ff.).

Darius (dà-rī'ŭs) a name common to several rulers of Medo-Persia. The name is frequently mentioned in records of that area. Those mentioned in the Bible are: 1. Darius the Mede (Dan. 9:1), son of Ahasuerus. He was made ruler when Belshazzar was slain at the famous feast (Dan. 5), being appointed by Cyrus at the age of sixty-two (Dan. 5:30). Under his rule occurred many of the well-known incidents connected with Daniel (6:1–3, 4–9, 10–23).

2. Darius Hystaspes. When Cambyses, the son of Cyrus, committed suicide a magician named Smerdes usurped the throne. Darius formed an alliance with other princes, overthrew the pretender, and won the throne. As king he favored the Jews and allowed work which had been discontinued to be resumed (Ezra 4:1–6, 6:1–15). He invaded Greece and was defeated in the battle of Marathon 490 B.C. He died 486 B.C.

3. Darius the Persian, probably Darius Codomannus (Neh. 12:22), the last king of Persia, defeated by Alexander the Great in the battle of Arbela 330 B.C.

Darkon (där'kŏn) man whose children were among the "children of Solomon" in the returning exiles (Neh. 7:58; Ezek. 2:56).

dates the fruit of the **palm tree** (2 Chr. 31:5, margin for date = honey). Song of S. 7:7 refers to the clusters of dates. The absence of direct reference to this well-known fruit is coincidental.

Dathan (dā'thăn) a Reubenite ally of Korah (Num. 16:1; Deut. 11:6).

daughter the female offspring of a parent; also used for other close relationships (just as "son" is) e.g., Gen. 24:48, 31:43. It often means merely the female inhabitants of a place, e.g., "daughters of Jerusalem" (Lk. 23:28), of cities (Isa. 10:32), and of towns dependent on them (Num. 21:35). Also it is used figuratively to denote age ("daughter of ninety years," Gen. 17:17), and with reference to the physical organs of speech (Eccl. 12:4).

daughter-in-law one meaning of Heb. *kallah* and Gk. *nymphē* which may also mean "bride" (her status during engagement and early marriage).

David (dā'vĭd) the second and probably the best known of the kings of Israel. The sources for his life are extensive, consisting of the historical records (1 Sam. 16–1 K. 2; 1 Chr. 11–29) plus a large number of the Psalms (seventy-three of the 150 have Davidic titles). The events of his life can only be sketched. They are commonly divided into three parts.

1. *His Youth before His Introduction at Saul's Court.* David's father was Jesse, a de-

scendant of Boaz and Ruth of the tribe of Judah. There seem to have been ten children (eight sons), and David was the youngest and the son of Jesse's old age (1 Sam. 17:12, 22:3). He was born and reared at Bethlehem (cf. 1 Chr. 11:17; Lk. 2:4). From later references it is known that he spent much of his youth as a shepherd (1 Sam. 16:12, 17:34–36). His first appearance in history was at the visit of Samuel to a sacrificial feast (1 Sam. 16:1 ff., 20:6) to anoint a king from among the sons of Jesse. After all the other sons had passed by and none had been pointed out, Samuel learned that there was a younger lad tending the sheep. Here the future king of Israel was anointed. He was described as "ruddy, and withal of a beautiful countenance, and goodly to look upon" (16:12). His attire as a shepherd included the shepherd's staff and bag (17:40). His skill at music, afterwards consecrated in the Psalms, became known when he was suggested by one of Saul's men as a person "skillful in playing, and a mighty man of valor, and a man of war, and prudent in speech, and a comely person; and Jehovah is with him" (16:18). Just when this reputation as a man of war was earned is not known. His impulse for battle seconded his father's urging to go to the aid of his brothers in war with the Philistines (or so his brother guessed, 1 Sam. 17:28). Here his valor was proved by the familiar incident of his slaughter of the giant Philistine Goliath (17:31 ff.).

2. *His Relations with Saul.* The victory over Goliath was a turning point in David's life. Saul inquired of his parentage and took him to court where he became a fast friend of Jonathan. The song of praise by the Israelitish women laid the foundation for Saul's jealousy and hatred which were to poison his whole future relations with David. David's prudence and forbearance were displayed not only in the pursuit of Saul but throughout David's life. A series of narrow escapes undoubtedly helped David to a sense of a divine providence so prominent in his later hymns. During this period he first lived at Saul's court (1 Sam. 18:2–19:18), where he was armor-bearer (16:21), then captain of a thousand (18:13); he was married to Michal, second daughter of Saul. Here he was close to Abner and Jonathan and, with them, was Saul's table companion (20:25). Finally he had to flee from Saul for his life, abetted by his friends. Next was the period of escape (1 Sam. 19:18–21:15): first to Samuel at Ramah, then in refuge at Nob (1 Sam. 22:9), and at Achish, where he escaped by feigning madness (21:13). The next stage was as an independent outlaw (1 Sam. 22:1–26:25). During this period he hid in the cave of Adullam near Bethlehem, where he was joined by his family, then to the fortress later called Masada near En-gedi in the Judean wilderness (1 Sam. 22:4 f.; 1 Chr. 12:16), taking his parent to Moab. Here he was joined by the small band of Gadites (1 Chr. 12:8) and the men of Judah and Benjamin led by Amasai his nephew (1 Chr. 12:16–18). Finally, Saul became intense in his search for David. David dismissed his army and fled. At the wilderness of Ziph the natives betrayed him to Saul and David was sore pressed. Twice the rivals sighted each other (23:25–29 and 24:1–22, 26). During this period also occurred the incident with Nabal and his marriage with Abigail. At last David led his band, which had once more been gathered (600 of them), along with their families, to Achish, where he was given Ziklag (27:8). Now in swift order the Philistine nobles would not trust him in battle; the Amalekites burnt Ziklag in his absence and carried off wives and families; David pursued and recovered the spoils (1 Sam. 30); and news came of the death of Saul at Gilboa (2 Sam. 1:1–27).

3. *David's Reign.* David became king at Hebron (2 Sam. 2:11), where he reigned 7½ years (2 Sam. 2:1–5:5). He was formally anointed king, with his power mostly limited to Judah. This power began to broaden with the skirmishes over Ish-bosheth, followed by the murders (without his consent) of Abner and Ish-bosheth (2 Sam. 3:30, 4:5) and full occupation of the throne of Israel. A solemn league was ratified (5:3), and his band swelled into a "mighty host, like the host of God" (1 Chr. 12:22), command of which was given to Joab (2:28). The rule of David over all Israel covered thirty-three years (2 Sam. 5:5–1 K. 2:11). The highlights of this reign were the capture and establishment of the kingdom at Jerusalem (2 Sam. 5:9; 1 Chr. 11:7); his defeat of the Philistines (2 Sam. 5:17 ff.; 1 Chr. 14:12); the partnership with Hiram of Tyre (2 Sam. 5:11, 7:2); the removal of the ark to Jerusalem (2 Sam. 6); his plan to build a temple (2 Sam. 7), which was not accepted but which became the occasion for the covenant with God, through the prophet Nathan, that his son would build it and that his seed would be established forever (1 Sam. 7:12 ff.); his great victories over all enemies surrounding him (2 Sam. 10:19); his sin in connection with Uriah and Bath-sheba (2 Sam. 11); Absalom's revenge of Tamar and his pardon (chs. 13–14); Absalom's revolt and death (chs. 14–18);

and David's numbering of the people (ch. 24). In David's old age his son Adonijah attempted to secure the throne from Solomon, who had been designated heir. At the insistence of Bath-sheba and Nathan Solomon was crowned (1 K. 1). After sparing Adonijah and charging Solomon, David died. His life ended with a promise of the establishment of his throne forever (1 K. 2:45). Of central significance in David's life is the key role he played in the development of the promise of the Davidic Messiah. He understood that the promise for the perpetuity of his throne included a royal descendant who would mediate salvation to the people of Israel. One of his greatest contributions was the fostering of that faith which was to play such a part in the history of salvation (Ps. 2, 16, 22, 68, 85, 110).   J.W.R.

David, City of see **Jerusalem**

deacon [a transliteration of the Gr. word *diakonos*, servant, minister, in places where the context shows the word to be a technical term for an official of a local church] in Phil. 1:1, deacons are mentioned with "overseers" or "bishops" over against "saints," and in 1 Tim. 3:8-10, 12-13, a definite set of qualifications are given amid instructions concerning selection of bishops. The functionaries are also usually inferred from the references to the Seven in Acts 6:1-8, where the same word [serve] is used that Paul uses in 1 Tim. 3:10, "let them serve as deacons." That some of the Seven were later evangelists is really no argument against this, as the office has often been a training place for more advanced service. It has often been conjectured (see earlier Smith's *Bible Dictionary*) that the servants or attendants of the synagogues served as the analogy for the institution of the diaconate (cf. Lk. 4:20). Of the work of deacons the Bible says little. Early church references assign them such work as looking after the poor, preparing the place of meeting, or baptizing new converts. Perhaps such tasks were typical. It may well be that because they are "servants," ordained to be in readiness for whatever they may be needed to do, no more specific mention is made of their tasks.

deaconess a woman belonging to an order of servants of the churches and exercising functions toward their sex analogous to those of **deacons.** Though the order is documented for the immediate post-biblical period (Pliny, *Epistle* X.97), its existence in the NT period is not conclusive. The Gr. *diakonos* is common gender and its use in Rom. 16:1 of a woman could refer to such an official. The order of "enrolled" widows "pledged" to the church for some purpose (1 Tim. 5:9-16) has also been thought to refer to them. Compare also the rules given for conduct of women (1 Tim. 3:11), making up a third group within the context of church "officials." The arguments have great weight but are not conclusive.

Dead Sea the remarkable salt lake lying 1292 feet below sea level into which the Jordan River empties. In the Bible it is called the "Salt Sea" (Gen. 14:3; Deut. 3:17), "Sea of the Arabah (or KJV, Plain)" (Deut. 3:17; Josh. 3:16), or the "Eastern Sea" (Ezek. 47:18; Zech. 14:8; Joel 2:20), and sometimes simply "the Sea" as opposed to the "Great Sea," i.e., the Mediterranean (Ezek. 47:10). The sea lies sixteen miles east of Jerusalem and is the deepest part of the great chasm or rift-valley which begins in Syria, extends through Palestine as the Jordan Valley with the Sea of Galilee, and on beyond the Dead Sea through the Arabah to the Gulf of Aqabah, the eastern arm of the Gulf of Suez. It is about ten miles wide and fairly even east and west except for a peninsula on the eastern side some two-thirds down called El-Lisan ("the tongue"). Its area is thus some 300 square miles. Near the northeast corner its depth is 1300 feet, though in many parts its depth is only ten to fifteen feet. Sheer mountain walls rise from the water at many points. Its water is extremely salty (25%, five times that of the ocean) with no marine life, due not only to the sea's having no outlet, but also to the nature of the land around it. Mountains, like Jebel Usdum at the southern end, have enormous salt slabs, and there are numerous deposits of sulphur and mineral springs around it. Numerous streams, such as the Arnon on the east, empty into it, often through gorges or waterfalls. The water line varies somewhat, though the lake has been expanding over all, at least until modern irrigation dams built upstream begin to affect it. The sea is mentioned frequently as a landmark forming one of the boundaries of the whole land of Palestine (Num. 34:12; 2 K. 14:25). The plains near the sea called "valley of Siddom" in Abraham's day were of great fertility and attracted Lot (Gen. 13:10). On these plains King Chedorlaomer and his allies defeated the kings of Sodom and Gomorrah (Gen. 14:3-8). Nearby were slime or bitumen pits. This valley has been located at both the northern and southern ends of the sea. Sodom and the cities of the plain were destroyed by God's judgment (Gen. 18-19). Some have thought that the localities of these cities are now submerged by the waters of the southern portion of the sea. This has not yet been proved. (1) Credibility has been given to the idea, however, by recently uncovered evidence of the expanding nature of the water level. There was mention of a Roman ford at Lisan (no longer existing), and submerged trees along the eastern edge up to one mile in the water have been observed. (2) At En-gedi midway on the western shore a spring forms an oasis. Here David hid from Saul (1 Sam. 23: 29; cf. Song of S. 1:14). In NT times an Essene community established itself at Khirbet Qumran on the northeastern shore by a second western spring now known as 'Ain Feshkha, near which caves have yielded the famous **Dead Sea Scrolls.** There were NT settlements at Callirhoe, at the hot springs above the Arnon, where Herod the Great tried to regain his failing health, and at Machaerus nearby where Herod Antipas imprisoned John the Baptist (Mk. 1:14; 6:17). On the western shore across from Lisan the fortress of Masada served as the final holdout for the Jews against the Romans in the outbreak (A.D. 73). Ezekiel poetically pictures the revival of the region as an image depicting the coming age (47:8–12).

dearth see **famine**

Debir (dē'bêr) (*place*) the name of three places in Palestine. 1. A town in the mountains of Judah, formerly Kirjath-sepher (Josh. 15:15; Judg. 1:11), a city taken by Joshua (Josh. 11:21) which became a Levitical city. It is now generally identified with Tell Beit Mirsim, eleven miles southwest of Hebron (Josh. 15: 49).

2. A place on the northern border of Judah (Josh. 15:7).

3. A city of Gad in Eastern Gilead (2 Sam. 9:4–13, 17:27).

Debir (dē'bîr) (*person*) king of Eglon, one of five hanged by Joshua (Josh. 10:3, 23).

Deborah (dĕb'ō-rā) 1. The companion and nurse of Rebekah, who accompanied her from Bethuel's house (Gen. 24:59, 35:8).

2. A prophetess and fourth judge of Israel (Judg. 4–5). She lived under a palm tree between Ramah and Bethel in Mount Ephraim. The Canaanite king Jabin oppressed Israel. When Deborah urged Barak to fight, he refused unless she would go. Deborah's prediction of victory was fulfilled and the foreign general perished in the tent of Jael, the wife of a Kenite (Judg. 4:22, 5:24). Deborah's song of triumph (Judg. 5) is an early example of Hebrew poetry and religious sentiment.

debtor see **loan**

Decalogue (dĕk'á-lŏg) the basic ten laws given by God to Moses on Mount Sinai (Ex. 20; Deut. 5). See **covenant**

Decapolis (dē-kăp'ô-lĭs) [Gr. for "ten cities," Mt. 4:25; Mk. 5:20, 7:31] a confederation of Greek cities, the first of which were evidently built by veterans of Alexander's army. Later ones were added under the Seleucids and Ptolemies. When Pompey conquered Palestine, he reorganized the cities and restored them to their own citizens as free cities. They were thus centers of Greek culture within Jewish Palestine. Pliny enumerated them as Scythopolis, Hippos, Gadara, Pella, Philadelphia, Gerasa, Dion, Canatha, Damascus, and Raphana (*Nat. Hist.* V.xvi.74). Ptolemy (5:17) makes Capitolias one of the ten. An inscription mentions Abila. Josephus seems to omit Damascus. The cities lay mostly in the region of Gilead, in the territory east of Jordan, belonging to Manasseh. The gospel references are to Jesus' preaching in the region and to the report of one whom he had healed.

Decision, Valley of Joel's name for the gathering of the enemies of God's people for the great battle (3:14). It is the same as the valley of Jehoshaphat (Joel 3:2, 12). Some connect it (without apparent reason) with the **Kidron** Valley.

Dedan (dē'dăn) 1. The grandson of Cush (Gen. 10:6–7; 1 Chr. 1:9).

2. The grandson of Abraham by Keturah (Gen. 25:3). Since in both instances Sheba is given as a brother, the Dedan tribes are considered by some to be the result of intermarrying between descendants of the two Dedans. They were an important people often mentioned in the prophets (Isa. 21:13; Ezek. 25:13, 27:20, 38:13; Jer. 49:8).

Dedanim (Isa. 21:13) see **Dedan**

Dedication, Feast of the festival (of eight days' duration) instituted to commemorate the rededication of the temple after Judas Maccabeus had driven out the Syrians, 164 B.C. Its institution is recorded in 1 Macc. 4:52–59. An incident in the life of Jesus is recorded as taking place during this feast in "the winter" (twenty-fifth of Chislev, near the winter solstice), Jn. 10:22 ff.

deer see **fallow deer**

Degrees, Song of a title given to Ps. 120–134 in KJV (ASV, RSV translate "Ascents"). Jewish authorities (Mishnah *Middoth* 2.5) apply them to fifteen steps leading from the court of women to that of the men in the temple area saying that one was chanted for each step during ritual services. Others think they were composed for returning exiles, and still others that they were sung by pilgrims going up to the yearly feasts. One (Ps. 132) is attributed to

Solomon, four to David; others have no given authors.

Dehavites (dĭ-hà'vīts) KJV translation of Ezek. 4:9, which interprets the meaning as a group who protested rebuilding the walls of Jerusalem. The LXX and RSV point the word differently and read "men of Susa, the **Elamites.**"

Dekar or **Deker** (dē'kàr) father of one of Solomon's commissariat officers (1 K. 4:9).

Delaiah (dē-lā'yà) 1. A priest in David's time (1 Chr. 24:18).

2. A prince in Jehoiakim's court (Jer. 36:12).

3. Father of a family of returning exiles who could not prove their genealogy (Ezra 2:60; Neh. 7:62).

4. Father of a friend of Nehemiah (Neh. 6:10).

5. A descendant of David (1 Chr. 3:24).

Delilah (dē-lī'là) a woman of the Sorek valley (probably a Philistine), whom Samson loved and who was bribed by large sums of money from the lords of the Philistines to learn that the secret of his strength lay in his hair; afterwards she betrayed him to them (Judg. 16:4–18).

deluge see **flood, Noah**

Demas (dē'màs) a fellow helper of Paul during his imprisonment (Col. 4:14; Philemon 24) who later "forsook" him and "departed for Thessalonica, having loved this present world." **Demetrius** (dĕ-mē'trĭ-ŭs) 1. A disciple commended by John to Gaius (3 Jn. 12).

2. A silversmith at Ephesus who stirred up a mob against Paul at Ephesus because Paul's preaching was hurting the business of making shrines to Artemis (Diana).

demon in the Scriptures (e.g., James 2:19; Rev. 16:14), generally, spiritual beings at enmity with God who have power to afflict man with disease and to enter and possess him bringing spiritual pollution as well. In this sense the demon is usually described as an "unclean spirit" (Mt. 10:1; Mk. 1:27; Acts 8:7). The term demon in Greek has not always had this meaning. In Homer it is used interchangeably with "gods" (so Paul in 1 Cor. 10:20), later (Hesiod) of the messenger of the gods to men. In the LXX, the general use is to render words denoting the idols of heathen worship. Josephus uses the term for "evil spirit." In the gospels such evil spirits are represented as having recognition of Jesus and his divine power (Mt. 8:29; Lk. 4:41; Acts 19:15; cf. James 2:19).

demon possession, demoniacs these words in the NT apply to the phenomena of possession of people by unclean spirits and to the people

so possessed. Those so afflicted generally showed the effects of bodily disease or mental derangement. It is often claimed that the whole matter is mythical, that it is a mere externalizing of man's experiences and feelings, or that Jesus and the apostles spoke accommodatingly in line with the general belief of the contemporary world, without intending to endorse the reality of the possession. As proof of this it is pointed out that disease is usually attributed to demons (Mt. 9:32, 12:22; Mk. 9:17–27). But demoniacs are frequently distinguished from the sick (see Mk. 1:32, 16:17 f.; Lk. 6:17 f.). Jesus' words and actions imply his intention to assert their existence and power (Mt. 12:25–30; Mk. 5:10–14; Lk. 10:17 f.). Hence we conclude that there are evil spirits, subjects of the Evil One, who in the days of the Lord and his apostles were permitted by God to exercise a direct influence over the souls and bodies of certain men.

denarius (dē-nâr'ĭ-ŭs) a Roman silver coin, in wide use in NT times. It is mentioned more often than any other coin (e.g., Mt. 18:28; Mk. 6:37; Lk. 7:41; Jn. 6:7; Rev. 6:6). Translated "penny" in the KJV, the money was worth some eighteen to twenty cents in weight; but, since it represented a day's wage (Mt. 20:2, 4, 7, 9 f., 13), its buying power was much more. In Jn. 12:5 "three hundred pence" (*denarii*) would represent that many days' wages for Mary.

deposit a quantity of money or goods left with another for safekeeping. The law of Moses regulated such (Ex. 20:7, 13; cf. Lev. 6:2–4). So the Gospel is a deposit to Christians (1 Tim. 6:20; 2 Tim. 1:12, 14).

deputy a person set apart to act for another (1 K. 22:48; Jer. 51:28; Est. 8:9, 9:3; Acts 13:7, 19:38). The NT word so translated by the KJV refers to Roman governors or proconsuls.

Derbe (dûr'bē) a town in the south central portion of Asia Minor in the district of Lycaonia, near Iconium and Lystra. These three cities were visited by Paul on both the first missionary tour (Acts 14:6, 20) and the second. Gaius of Derbe accompanied Paul on the trip to Jerusalem with the contribution (Acts 20:4).

desert ordinarily a vast, burning sandy plain, destitute of trees and water. Its use in the Bible includes (1) the Arabah (Dead Sea and valley below) (2 Sam. 2:29), (2) a word meaning "pasture" (Num. 33:15–16; Jer. 25:24), (3) a word meaning a waste, desolate place (Isa. 48:21). The Gr. *erēmos* answers to 2 (Mt. 3:1; Mk. 1:13) and means unin-

desert

83

habited. So the strict meaning of the term does not occur in the Scriptures.

Deuel (dōō'ĕl) a captain of tribe of Gad (Num. 1:14, 7:47, 10:20). Cf. **Reuel** in Num. 2:14.

Deuteronomy (dōō'tĕ-rŏn'ō-mĭ) the name, derived from the LXX meaning "second law," of the fifth book of Moses. The Hebrew title is simply "these words," which is really the first expression of the original text. The book is a combination of narrative reminiscences, exhortations, and commands consisting mainly of four orations of Moses delivered to Israel just before his death "beyond the Jordan in the wilderness in the Arabah" (Deut. 1:1). The speeches are: (1) 1:1–4:40, A Review of Israel's Wilderness Experiences; (2) 5:1–26:19, Repetition of the Laws Given at Sinai; (3) 27:1–30:20, A Prophetic Address Commanding a Memorial of the Law, enlarging upon its blessings and curses, and recalling Israel anew into covenant relations with God; and (4) 31:1–34:12, Closing Incidents of Moses' Life.

The book of Deuteronomy has been under most severe attack by critics of traditional authorship and dating. It has been generally held by the supporters of the documentary hypothesis that it is a late composition, being substantially the same as the book found in the temple by the priests during the reign of Josiah (621 B.C., 2 K. 22). On the other hand, the Mosaic authorship has had strong defenders in conservative scholars who point especially to the endorsement of Jesus himself (Mt. 19:8 = Deut. 6:4–9; Jn. 5:46 = Deut. 18:15, 18) as well as the appeal to the book and its authority by Stephen (Acts 7:37) and the apostles (Acts 3:22, Rom. 12:19, Gal. 3:10).

devil one of the chief titles of Satan, meaning "slanderer" and illustrating his work of accusing man to God (Jn. 1:6–12) and God to man (cf. its use in Mt. 4:1 ff.; Jn. 13:2; Acts 10:38; Eph. 6:11; 1 Pet. 5:8). The term may be applied to one under the power of or doing the devil's work (Jn. 6:70, 8:44; 1 Jn. 3:8). The devil is described as ruler of this world, but his power was destroyed by Christ (Mt. 25:31; Rev. 2:10, 20:2, 10).

dew water condensed by the contact of cooling air with objects which have lost their heat. Dew is copious in Palestine and in the absence of abundant rainfall is important to agriculture (Ecclus. 18:16, 43:22; Gen. 27:28; Deut. 33:13; Zech. 8:12).

diadem a crown anciently made with a fillet of cloth some two inches wide bound around the head and tied behind it (2 Sam. 1:10; Zech. 9:16; Rev. 9:7). Kings usually wore on it an erect triangular piece. The diadem is thus the royal crown as opposed to *stephanos*, which was given for special achievement or merit (cf. 1 Cor. 9:25; 2 Tim. 4:8; James 1:12), though they are used loosely at times.

dial a device for telling the time of day by calculating the position of the sun's shadow. A dial is ascribed to Ahaz and used by Isaiah to give a sign to Hezekiah (2 K. 20:9–11; Isa. 38:8), the sun going back ten "degrees" or "steps."

diamond a precious stone—crystallized native carbon (Ex. 28:18, 39:11). Probably some other stone is meant by the Hebrew word. Cut diamonds probably were unknown in Bible days.

Diana (dī-ăn'à) [Gr. *Artemis*] the Roman goddess of the moon, a daughter of Jupiter and sister of Apollo. She was widely worshiped as the virgin huntress. The local "Diana of the Ephesians" (Acts 19:24–35, also called in Greek Artemis) was quite different. She was a "many-breasted" fertility goddess, a form of the Asian mother-goddess. The legend was that her image "fell from heaven." Her temple at Ephesus was one of the seven wonders of the ancient world. Paul's preaching incurred the wrath of a guild of silversmiths who made images of the idol (Acts 19).

Diblaim (dĭb'lĭ-ĭm) father of Hosea's wife Gomer (Hos. 1:3).

Diblath (dĭb'lăth) reading in Ezek. 6:14, a place in the extreme north of Israel. Probably a scribal error (interchange of Hebrew letters "r" and "d") for **Riblah.**

Dibon (dī'bŏn) 1. A city east of Jordan in Moab, thirteen miles east of Dead Sea, three miles north of the Arnon. It was alloted to Gad (Num. 32:3, 34), thus called Dibon-gad. Its possession passed back and forth from Moab (Isa. 15:2; Jer. 48:18, 22, 24) to Israel (2 K. 3:4). It has been identified with modern Dhiban, excavated by the American School of Oriental Research.

2. A town in South Judah (Neh. 11:25).

Dibon-gad (Num. 33:45 f.) see **Dibon** above

Dibri (dĭb'rī) a Danite (Lev. 24:11).

Didache (dĭd'à-kĭ) [teaching] the name applied to an early church document entitled "Teaching of the Twelve Apostles." It probably dates from A.D. 120. It contains ethical instruction under the title "The Two Ways" and instructions on church rites and problems.

didrachmon see **money, shekel**

Didymus (dĭd'ĭ-mŭs) i.e., "twin," surname of Thomas (Jn. 11:16, 20:24).

Diklah (dĭk'là) a son of Joktan (Gen. 10:27;

1 Chr. 1:21), whose settlement (an oasis?) was probably in Arabia.

Dilean (dĭl′ē-ản) a village in Shephelah of Judah (Josh. 15:38).

Dimnah (dĭm′nả) a Levitical city of Zebulun (Josh. 21:35).

Dimon (dī′mŏn), **the Waters of** streams on east of Jordan (Isa. 15:9); some consider same as **Dibon.**

Dimonah (dī-mō′nả) town probably same as **Dibon** 2 in South Judah (Josh. 15:21–32).

Dinah (dī′nả) the daughter of Jacob by Leah (Gen. 30:21; 34). As a young girl Dinah was violated by Shechem the son of Hamon the Hittite, for which her brothers Levi and Simeon destroyed the city after a stratagem. For this trickery they were later reproved by Jacob (Gen. 46:5–7).

Dinaites (dī′nả-īts) Assyrian colonists of Samaria (2 K. 17:27; Ezra 4:7–10).

Dinhabah (dĭn′hả-bả) city of Bela king of Edom (Gen. 36:32; 1 Chr. 1:43).

Dionysius the Areopagite (dī-ŏ-nĭsh′ĭ-ŭs the ăr′ē-ŏp′ả-gīt) member of the court of the Areopagus, converted by Paul at Athens (Acts 17:34).

Dioscuri (dī-ŏs′kŭ-rī) see **Castor and Pollux.**

Diotrephes (dī-ŏt′rē-fēz) a Christian described as loving the pre-eminence (3 Jn. 9).

disciple a "learner" or "pupil," implying acceptance by a pupil of his teacher's program. See **education, schools**

disease see **medicine**

dish a metal or earthen container for eating. Guests in ancient times ate from a central dish using the fingers and a piece of bread to convey the food to the mouth. To dip in the sop and hand to a friend was a gesture of esteem.

Dishan (dī′shăn) youngest son of Seir (Gen. 36:21 ff.; 1 Chr. 1:38, 42).

Dishon (dī′shŏn) 1. Fifth son of Seir (Gen. 36:21; 1 Chr. 1:38).

2. Grandson of Seir (Gen. 36:25; 1 Chr. 1:38).

Dispersion, the (of the Jews) the general title given to the Jews living outside Palestine and carrying on their worship and customs among the Gentiles (1 Pet. 1:1). The Dispersion dates largely from the Babylonian exile and was concentrated especially in Babylonia, Syria, and Egypt but in fact extended over the whole Mediterranean Area. Seleucus Nicator transplanted Babylonian Jews into Western Asia Minor. Alexandria in Egypt was a major Jewish center, and from there the Jews spread along the coast of North Africa. By NT times the Dispersion must have greatly outnumbered the Palestinian Jews. Their adoption of Greek

as a tongue, the rise of Synagogue worship, and the attraction of the ethical content of their faith to the Gentiles served to prepare the way for the spread of the Gospel in the first century. In fact, the influence of the Dispersion on the spread of Christianity can scarcely be overrated. Notice the large number of places represented in the Jewish audience at Pentecost when the church began (Acts 2:9–11).

Dives (dī′vĕs) [rich] name traditionally given the rich man in the story of Lk. 16, from the Latin for "a certain man was rich (*dives*)."

divination the effort to obtain knowledge of divine matters by the use of inspiration, fortune telling, interpretation of omens, etc. (Ezek. 13:7; Isa. 47:9; Acts 16:16). The practice in a multitude of forms was highly developed, especially among the Babylonians, Egyptians, Greeks, and Romans. The NT hints and modern archaeology confirms by the discovery of magical texts that the arts were widely practiced by the Jews (Acts 13:6, 19:13–14). This was true despite strict condemnation of such by the OT (Deut. 18:10 f.).

divorce the putting away of husband or wife, thus severing the marriage relationship. The OT law is found in Deut. 24:1–4, 19, 29. The woman does not seem generally to have had the privilege of divorce (concubines excepted, Ex. 21:11). At the sending away a "bill of divorcement" was given (Isa. 50:1; Jer. 3:8; Mt. 19:7; Mk. 10:4). The Jews of Christ's day differed as to the legal ground: the school of Shammai interpreted the law as referring to unfaithfulness, but that of Hillel extended it to petty grievances. Jesus affirmed that the permission of the Law was a concession to Jewish hardness of heart and not intended "from the beginning" (Mt. 19:4–8). Jesus affirmed that the only scriptural ground for divorce and remarriage is unfaithfulness, and remarriage on any other basis is adultery (Mt. 5:32, 19:9).

Dizahab (dī′zả-hăb) place in the desert where Moses gave his farewell address (Deut. 1:1).

docetism (dōs′ē-tĭz′ĕm) a doctrine prevalent in the early church which denied the reality of Jesus' being God in human flesh and claimed that he only "seemed" (*dokei*) to have come in the flesh (1 Jn. 3:2).

Doctor or **Teacher of the Law** title of distinction given to those expert in the Law (Lk. 5:17; Acts 5:34); used somewhat ironically of false teachers (probably Jewish Gnostics) in 1 Tim. 1:3.

Dodai (dō′dī) one of David's captains (1 Chr. 27:4).

Dodo (dō′dō) 1. A Bethlehemite father of one of David's captains (2 Sam. 23:24).

2. Father of Eleazar, second of David's three mighty men (2 Sam. 23:9).

3. Forefather of the judge **Tola** (Judg. 10:1).

Doeg (dō'ĭg) Edomite herdsman of Saul who reported to Saul that Ahimelech had helped David, leading the slaughter of Ahimelech's entire house (1 Sam. 21:1–9, 22:9–23; Ps. 52).

dog domesticated animal common in Biblical times, used for watching houses (Isa. 56:10) and herds (Job 30:1). Then also, as now, troops of hungry scavenger dogs roamed fields, streets, and dumps; they were considered vicious and unclean.

Dorcas see **Tabitha**

Dothan (dō'thăn) city mentioned as place where Joseph was sold (Gen. 37:17) and where Elisha lived (2 K. 6:13). Its modern name is Tell Dotha, some twelve miles north of Samaria. The site has been excavated by Wheaton College (Joseph E. Free) with interesting and rewarding results.

dove name loosely applied to several types of pigeon or dove. That most often referred to in the Bible being probably the rock dove or pigeon. Such birds were evidently common and are frequently mentioned, being referred to literally in the flood story (Gen. 8:8–12) and used as an illustration of swiftness (Ps. 55:6), beauty (Ps. 68:13), mournfulness (Isa. 38:14), harmlessness (Mt. 10:16), simplicity (Hos. 7:11), loving nature (Song of S. 1:15, 2:14). At Jesus' baptism the Holy Spirit descended upon him as a dove (Mt. 3:16).

dove's dung the obscure reference in 2 K. 6:25 that during the siege of Samaria "the fourth part of a cob of dove's dung" would sell for five pieces of silver has been variously interpreted. Some maintain it refers to a plant whose seed was used for food. Others note that Josephus, as well as classical writers, mentions the use of dung as food in dire circumstances. It may well be an extreme hyperbole depicting unusual scarcity of food.

dowry the property a wife brings to a marriage. See **marriage**

doxology (dŏks-ŏl'ō-jĭ) an expression (usually spontaneous) of praise to God, found e.g., in Rom. 9:5; Rev. 5:13; Jude 24.

drachma (drăk'mà) a Greek coin somewhat equivalent to the Hebrew shekel, varying in weight according to the talent, or monetary system it was based on (whether Greek, Phoenician, or Egyptian). Generally speaking it almost had the value of the Roman denarius, equal to a day's wage. It was the "silver coin" of Lk. 15:8–9.

dragon the Heb. word *tan* translated "dragon" (Job 30:29; Ps. 44:19) refers to a desert animal and probably means "jackal." The word *taunin* refers to any great monster, quite often of the reptile or serpent kind, but not exclusively. "Sea monster" or "whale" is the correct translation in passages like Gen. 1:21; but "serpents" seems correct of the land animals in Deut. 32:33; Ps. 91:13. Satan is represented as a dragon in Rev. 12:9, 20:2.

dram see **daric**

drink the principal liquids drunk in Bible lands were water, milk, and wine. Water came from wells (usually community) and cisterns. Milk came from cattle and goats and was usually kept in skins. Strong drink (*shekbar*), which apparently once meant a beer made from barley, was made from a number of grains and fruit (Lev. 10:9; Num. 6:3). Wine was drunk either as new wine or fermented. At the table and feasts it was diluted with three parts water. Vinegar, made from pouring water over skins and stalks of grapes and left to ferment, was also drunk and used as a condiment or drug. One of the chief ethical concerns of the Scriptures is for God's people to be self-controlled in their eating and drinking (Isa. 5:11; Prov. 20:1, 31:4, 6).

dromedary a word which refers to the Arabian camel with one hump, which was noted for its swiftness (Isa. 66:20). In some passages in the KJV the Hebrew word so translated rather refers to mules or mares (Est. 8:10, 14).

Drusilla (droo-sĭl'à) youngest (with **Bernice** and **Mariamne**) daughter of Herod Agrippa I. She was married to Azizus, king of Emesa, but was seduced by Felix, procurator of Judea, through a sorcerer, Simon. She accompanied Felix when Paul preached to him (Acts 24:24–25).

dualism a term used to describe some religions claiming that there are two deities, one good and one evil, and that the created world is evil because it was created by the evil god. The term is also used of the tension noted by philosophers of the antithesis of flesh and spirit in man. The early church found itself in controversy over such theories in the **docetic** and **gnostic** struggles.

duke a tribal chief or clan leader (Gen. 36:15 ff.; Ex. 15:15; Josh. 13:21).

dulcimer = bagpipe erroneous translation of word *sumphonia* in Dan. 3:5, 10, 15, where it seems rather to refer to the chorus of all instruments used in an ensemble.

Dumah (dū'mà) 1. Son of Ishmael, founder of a tribe, from which the term is given to the region of their location (Gen. 25:14; 1 Chr. 1:30).

2. A city in the hill district of Judah near Hebron (Josh. 15:52).

dung excrement of animals, birds, or humans. When it was used as manure, it was usually collected, mixed with straw, and allowed to rot (Isa. 25:10; cf. Lk. 13:8). In case of sacrifices the dung was burned outside the camp (Ex. 29:14). In the scarcity of fuel dung was dried and used for fuel, just as "buffalo chips" were on the American frontier (Ezek. 4:12, 15).

dungeon see **prison**

Dura (dū′rà) a valley in Babylon where Nebuchadnezzar set up the golden image (Dan. 3:1). It should not be confused with Dura on the Euphrates, 270 miles upstream from Babylon.

dust see **mourning**

E

eagle a large bird of prey, largest bird in the region of Palestine, where the golden and the imperial eagles were common. It is mentioned frequently (Lev. 11:13; Deut. 28:49; Prov. 23:5; Rev. 12:14). The word is also used for vulture (Mic. 1:16; Mt. 24:28).

earnest [KJV translation of Gr. *arrabon* (RSV, guarantee)] a sum of money paid as a pledge or down payment (Gen. 38:17-18). It is used figuratively of the Spirit given to the Christian as a pledge of his inheritance (2 Cor. 1:22, 5:5; Eph. 1:14).

earrings translates several words for ornaments (usually made of gold) worn in the ears (Gen. 35:4; Ex. 32:2; Num. 31:50; Job 42:11).

earth the translation at different times of the Heb. *'adhamah* (usually the ground) and *'erets* (usually the planet as opposed to the sky) and of the Gr. *gē* (earth), *kosmos* (the orderly universe), and *oikoumenē* (the inhabited earth). Often the words shade into the meanings and usage of each other. *'Adhamah* is used of the soil or ground, being that from which man's body was taken (Gen. 2:7). *'Erets* is applied to the whole world (Gen. 1:1), to land as opposed to sea (Gen. 1:10), to a country (Gen. 21:32), a plot of ground (Gen. 23:15), and the ground on which one stands (Gen. 33:3). Likewise in the NT *gē* may mean soil (Mt. 13:5), ground (Lk. 6:49), the land (as opposed to the sea, Mk. 4:1), the earth (as contrasted with the heavens Mt. 5:18), and as the inhabited globe (Lk. 21:35). *Kosmos* is ordinarily concerned with the inhabitants of "the world" rather than with the planet. *Oikoumenē* can mean the world in the sense of the inhabited earth (Lk. 4:5) or the inhabitants themselves (Acts 17:31) but is frequently used as a technical term for the Roman empire as equal to the whole world (Acts 17:6,

24:5). Extended discussion of the views of the universe in a cosmological sense, and the world in a geographical sense, are beyond the scope of this work. Often the Biblical writers show usages involved in the ancient worldview of their times. It is perhaps debatable to what extent this is a reflection of set phrases traditional with their culture (Semitic and Near Eastern background) and not strictly in accord with their religious beliefs (see Milton's use of Roman and Greek mythological language) such as is still true of modern man even in an age of science. There may be some actual evidence of pre-science in the Bible, though arguments made for such claims are often not exegetically sound. The most that can be asked is that no specific declaration of fact contradicts later discovery. This the conservative holds to be true. In geographical details, especially, the modern archaeologist and explorer wonder at the "remarkable memory of the Bible."

earthquake literally a quaking or shaking due to volcanic action or structural shifting of the earth. Occurrences mentioned in the Bible are in 1 K. 19:11; Amos 1:1; Zech. 14:5; Mt. 28:2; and Acts 16:26. Isaiah sees earthquakes as a form of the judgment of God upon the world. So they seem to be used in Revelation (8:5, 11:13, 19, 16:18).

east one Hebrew word meant "before" or "in front of" (from custom of facing east when describing the four directions); the other, along with the Gr. word *analtoe*, refers to the place of sunrising. Special significance seemed attached to the facing of the tabernacle eastward (Ex. 38:13, 14). The East refers to lands in that direction from Palestine (the Arabian desert, Chaldea, etc.).

Easter [KJV translation of Gr. for Passover in Acts 12:4] the inconsistency is corrected in all

east wind

later versions. There is no yearly NT celebration of the resurrection. Rather, it provides the basis of weekly worship on the first day of the week.

east wind the sirocco, hot wind from the desert (Jer. 4:11; Hos. 13:15). See **winds**

Ebal (ē'băl) 1. Grandson of Seir (Gen. 36:23).

2. A returnee from Babylon (Ezek. 8:6).

Ebal, Mount a mountain in Palestine in the NT province of Samaria. With Mount Gerizim it forms twin peaks separated by a pass. Ebal is 3077 feet high. Nearby was Shechem, and here Jacob's well was located (Jn. 4:20). Here the Israelites were to confirm God's covenant by the ceremony of "blessing and cursing" (Deut. 11:29, 27:1–27). The Law was to be recorded in a monument on Ebal (Deut. 27:4–8). The Samaritan Pentateuch reads "Gerizim" (27:4), but there is no real support for their claim that Gerizim was the place of the temple because of the recording of the Law there rather than on Ebal.

Ebed (ē'bĕd) 1. Father of Gaal (Judg. 9:26).

2. A returnee from Babylon (Ezra 8:6).

Ebed-melech (ē'bĕd-mēl'ĭk) a title [*ebed* = servant] from David's time for a class of court officers (usually foreign mercenaries). A man so named, an Ethiopian eunuch, helped Jeremiah escape from a cistern (Jer. 38:7 ff., 39:15 ff.).

Eben-ezer (ĕb-ĕ-nē'zẽr) [stone of help] a monument commemorating the Lord's help in the defeat of the Philistines, near Mizpah (1 Sam. 4:1–11, 5:1).

Eber (ē'bẽr) 1. The ancestor from whom the Hebrews were named (meaning "from beyond," i.e., the river Euphrates). He was great-grandson of Shem (Gen. 10:24; 1 Chr. 1:19).

2. A man of God (1 Chr. 5:13).

3. A Benjaminite (1 Chr. 8:12).

4. Another Benjaminite (1 Chr. 8:22).

5. A priest who returned from exile (Neh. 12:20).

Ebiasaph (ē-bī'ȧ-săph) a Kohathite Levite of Korah's family (Ex. 6:24; 1 Chr. 6:23).

ebony a wood prized for making furniture imported from India and Ceylon (Ezek. 27:15).

Ebronah see **Abronah**

Ecbatana (ĕk-băt'ȧ-nȧ) capital of Media and a favorite summer residence of Persian kings. It is given in the margin of ASV as the equivalent of **Achmetha**, where Cyrus' decree was found (Ezra 6:2).

Ecclesiastes (ĕ-klē'zĭ-ăs'tēz) a book belonging to the third section of the OT canon ("the Writings") and purporting to be a product, like Proverbs, of Solomon. It belongs to wisdom literature as a literary type. 1. *Title.* The title is from the LXX and means "one who officiates or speaks in the assembly." The Heb. is *koheleth*, the preacher.

2. *Author.* The book claims to have been written by (or at least in the name of) one who was "son of David" (1:1) and who was "king over Israel in Jerusalem" (1:12), one who possessed great wisdom (1:16, 2:9), and a writer and collector of proverbs (12:9). All these appear to point directly to Solomon so that it is plain that if the book is not genuine it is pseudonymous (written later and attributed to him). The writer has given what seems reasonable description of contemporary Jerusalem and Palestine (where Solomon is known to have had various gardens, springs, etc.) (2:4–9) and to specific details of Solomon's life (4:13). The likeness between it and the book of Proverbs is obvious. Many conservatives still defend the likelihood of its Solomonic authorship, citing its reception (though not without Jewish opposition) into the Jewish canon from the earliest time and the fact that there is no real linguistic or historical reason to make the claim implausible. The older argument of late Aramaic elements can no longer be pressed.

3. *Contents.* The book is the confession of a man of wide experience looking back on past life and out on the disorders and calamities which surround him. It contains the utterances which grew out of his struggles after truth, his glimpses of it, and a final recognition of it. The book pictures the wise man as applying his heart "to seek and search out by wisdom concerning all that is done under heaven" (1:12 f.) so that he might see what is good for man to do. The preacher relates how he tried pleasure (2:1), houses and vineyards (2:4), and silver and gold (2:8, 5:13) and came to see that everything was vanity and vexation (2:11, 17, 4:8). He concludes with seeming pessimism that "there is nothing better for a man than that he should eat and drink, and make his soul enjoy good in his labor" (2:24). These themes are repeated through the book. This negative and pessimistic spirit has caused many to regard the book as unworthy of a place in the Scriptures. Still it has often been pointed out that this outlook is said in the book to be experimental. This despair is from the worldly point of view. If these things are the sum of life, all is vanity. But the writer rejects this and concludes that in view of the judgment (11:9) the "whole of man is to fear God and keep his commandments." Man's responsibility grows out of his nature as a creature of God

with a spirit which returns to its maker at death (12:7). These conclusions, it has been said, are not "far from the kingdom."

Ecclesiasticus Latin title of an apocryphal book, Wisdom of Jesus, Ben Sirach.

ed [witness] inserted in some versions on basis of Syriac as the name of an altar (Josh. 22:34).

Edar, tower of (form of **Eder**) place where Jacob halted (Gen. 35:21).

Eden 1. A Levite in Hezekiah's day (2 Chr. 29:12).

2. Another Levite, probably same as preceding (2 Chr. 31:15).

3. Children of Eden in Telassar conquered by Assyria (2 K. 19:12; Isa. 27:12), site unknown.

4. Beth-eden (Amos 1:5), summer place of kings of Damascus.

Eden, Garden of the first residence of man, the district in which God planted a garden for Adam and Eve to live in. The LXX derived the Hebrew word from the root "pleasure" or "delight" and so translated the term. Scriptural data (Gen. 2:8–17) include the facts that the garden lay eastward in the area of Eden, that all kinds of trees grew there including the "tree of life" and of the "knowledge of good and evil." From the land of Eden a river flowed out to water the garden and then divided into four streams, the Pishon, Gihon, Hiddekel, and Euphrates. Information is also given concerning the lands associated with each river (e.g., the Hiddekel flowed toward the east of Assyria). Here the first parents were placed until they sinned and were driven out (Gen. 2, 3). In keeping with the idea of original happiness later writers associate Eden with happiness and delight, especially the association with God (Isa. 51:3; Ezek. 28:13, 31:9, 16, 18, 36:35; Joel 2:3). Ideas as to how this material is to be interpreted vary widely. The Jew Philo interpreted the whole as allegory. Many modern liberal scholars think the story is legendary or mythological. It seems certain that the writer of Genesis intended his story to be taken literally, and his geographical allusions seem to be an attempt at location. But we are completely at a loss now as to that location. Hiddekel equals Tigris, and Euphrates is well-known, but they do not have a single source. Pishon and Gihon are uncertain; Havilah is unknown; and even Cush is uncertain since in the OT it can mean Ethiopia or other regions (Isa. 11:11; Ezek. 38:5; 2 Chr. 14:9). Efforts to use these indications to locate the garden are unsuccessful. Two areas—the country of Armenia and

the Lower Mesopotamian valley—are generally favored, but exact details do not coincide.

Eder (ē'dẽr) 1. Site in South Judah, probably same as **Adar** (Josh. 15:21).

2. Levite of David's time (1 Chr. 23:23, 24:30).

Edom, Edomites (ē'dŭm, ē'dŭm-īts) a nation and people, as well as the territory inhabited by them, descended from Esau the brother of Jacob. Edom is the name given Esau (Gen. 25:30) because of the "red" pottage in the story of his selling his birthright. The chiefs of the tribe are given in Gen. 36:15–19. They occupied the land astride the Arabah to the south of the Dead Sea, in a land also called "Mount Seir." The territory was an oblong rectangle some one hundred by forty miles. The Horites dwelt in Seir in Abraham's day and they were smitten by Chedorlaomer. There is an archaeological gap in the Horite occupation of the land for several hundred years following this. Esau married a daughter of an Edomite chief (Gen. 36:2, 25), and his sons became chiefs, gradually absorbing the Horite people (Deut. 2:12, 22). The kingdom of Edom had eight kings before there was a king in Israel (Gen. 36:31–39). This people refused passage way to Joshua's forces (Num. 20:14–21). Resentment against Israel was deep-seated with Edom, and there was continuous conflict. Saul and David both warred against them (1 Sam. 14:47; 2 Sam. 8:14; 1 K. 11:15 f.). Solomon used Edomite seaports for his navy (2 Chr. 8:17–18). Edom revolted against Jehoram of Judah (2 K. 8:20) but was brought under control again by Amaziah (2 K. 14:7). At the devastation of Palestine and Jerusalem by Nebuchadnezzar of Babylon, Edom rejoiced and even abetted the work by grasping territory in Southern Palestine. For this they became the object of severe denunciations by Israel's prophets (Ps. 137; Obad. 10–14; Amos 1:11; Ezek. 25:12 ff.). Later governments to hold the territory were the **Nabataeans** and the **Idumaeans.** The Jews conquered Idumaea and forced Judaism upon its people. Antipater king of Idumaea was granted Palestine by the Romans for help in warding off the Parthians. His son Herod the Great links Edomite history with that of Palestine.

Edrei (ĕd'rē-ī) 1. One of chief cities of Og king of Bashan (Num. 21:33; Deut. 1:4, 3:10; Josh. 12:4). Here Israel defeated Og and gained the region which was allotted to Manasseh (Josh. 13:12, 31). It is modern Der'a on the Yarmuk river sixty miles south of Damascus.

2. A city in Naphtali (Josh. 19:37).

Eglah

Eglah (ĕg′làh) one of David's wives, mother of his sixth son, Ithream (2 Sam. 3:5).

Eglaim (ĕg′lā-ĭm) a place in Southern Moab (Isa. 15:8).

Eglon (ĕg′lŏn) a king of the Moabites, who, with the Ammonites and Amalekites, smote Israel taking the city of palm trees, whom Israel served eighteen years. They were delivered by the judge Ehud (Judg. 3:12-30).

Eglon a town of Judah (Josh. 15:39), one of the confederacy of five towns which attacked Gibeon after this city made a covenant with Joshua (Josh. 10:1 ff., 12:12, 15:39).

Egypt (ē′jĭpt) a country occupying the northeastern part of Africa, where one of the earliest and most powerful civilizations of antiquity was developed. The history of this nation came into direct contact with that of the Bible.

I. NAME. The Biblical name for Egypt is "Mizraim," given in Gen. 10:6 as a son of Ham. Hence the description of the land is the "land of Ham" (Ps. 105:23, 27) or "land of Mizraim" means that the descendants of Ham through Mizraim settled the land. The Egyptians called their country "The Two Land" referring to the union of Upper (above the first cataract at Assuan) and Lower Egypt, or the "Black Land" (in contrast to the red desert). "Egypt" is of late and uncertain origin.

II. GEOGRAPHY. Egypt is the Nile river's gift. The country is a desert waste on both sides of the valley of the great river. Its waters begin 4000 miles to the south and seasonally flood the valley giving it both fertile soil and moisture. Hard stone barriers cross the valley in six places creating six cataracts. The region of the fourth cataract is the Biblical Ethiopia. Nubia is the region between the third and first, and in the strict sense Egypt is the lower part between the first cataract and the delta. Egypt was separated from foreign areas by the desert, including the bleak Sinaitic area, and hence was fairly immune to invasion except in times of weakness. The strength of the land lay in its agriculture, with the chief crops barley, wheat, emmer, flax, vegetables, and fruits. Animals such as cattle, donkeys, horses after 1700 B.C., and camels after the Persian period were numerous.

III. RACE AND LANGUAGE. The race known from many pictorial inscriptions was a short slight-built Mediterranean type. The language was Hamitic but showed many coincidences with the Semitic tongues.

IV. HISTORY. The priest Manetho divided Egyptian history into thirty-one dynasties, and this has become a customary way of looking at the history. There are some scant remains of the predynastic period. Written history drawn from lists of kings, etc., begins about 3100 B.C. and runs to Alexander the Great (332 B.C.) to be followed by the Graeco-Roman period named from Ptolemy (after 306 B.C.). The great periods may be outlined as follows:

(1) *Predynastic.* The kingdom was founded by Menes of Thinis, who joined the two lands and had his capital at Memphis about 3200 B.C.

(2) *The Old Kingdom* (Third to Sixth dynasties, 2700-2200 B.C.). This was the great period of Egypt's power and glory, especially the Fourth Dynasty (2650-2500 B.C.), the age of art and architecture, when such things as the pyramids of Gizeh were built.

(3) *The Intermediate Periods* (Seventh to Seventeenth dynasties, 2200-1700 B.C.). Periods of weakness when the Hyksos invaders from the East took over Egypt.

(4) *The New Kingdom* (Eighteenth to Twentieth dynasties, 1580-1090 B.C.). This is the period marking the height of the Egyptian conquests, the El Amarna correspondence, and the time of the Hebrew sojourn and exodus.

(5) *The Post-Empire Periods* (Twenty-first to Thirtieth dynasties, 1100-332 B.C.). Followed by the coming of Alexander.

V. ITS CONTACT WITH BIBLICAL HISTORY. Egypt is first inferred from its connection with the sons of Ham (Gen. 10:6). It was the place of refuge for Abraham in the time of famine (Gen. 12:10), as it was of the Israelites in the days of Joseph after he was sold there and became God's instrument for preserving Israel (Gen. 45:5 f.). The story of Joseph leads naturally into that of the oppression of Israel and the Exodus (Ex. 1-12). From this point Israel found little contact with Egypt until the time of Solomon. Solomon married a daughter of Pharaoh, who conquered Gezer as a dowry for his daughter (1 K. 9:16). The rebel king Jeroboam fled to Egypt, and later this ruler led the northern tribes both into political rebellion and idolatry (1 K. 12:26 ff.). The king of Egypt captured Jerusalem in the reign of Rehoboam and robbed the temple (1 K. 14:25-26; 2 Chr. 12:1-9). Egypt became involved in the political alliances of Judah, Israel, Syria, etc., against the growing power of Assyria. Josiah's attempt to keep Egypt from joining Assyria against Babylon at Megiddo led to his death (2 K. 23). Jews took refuge in Egypt at the fall of Jerusalem, and by NT times there was a concentration of them especially at Alexandria. NT references besides the flight of Jesus' family (Mt. 2:13 ff.) include its metaphorical use in

Revelation for the enemies of God's people (11:9). J.W.R.

Egypt, River of a brook or wadi (not the river Nile), the Wadi el-'Arish, which drains north from Mount Sinai through the central Sinai Peninsula and empties into the Mediterranean. It formed the southwestern border of Canaan (Num. 34:5; 1 K. 8:65; 2 K. 24:7; 2 Chr. 7:8; Isa. 27:12; Ezek. 47:19).

Ehi (ē'hī) son of Benjamin (Gen. 46:21), probably same as **Ahiram** (Num. 26:38).

Ehud (ē'hŭd) 1. Great-grandson of Benjamin (1 Chr. 7:10; 8:6).

2. Second judge of Israel, a "left-handed" hero of tribe of Benjamin who murdered **Eglon,** Israel's oppressor (Judg. 3:12–30).

Eker (ē'kêr) a postexilic Judahite (1 Chr. 2:27).

Ekrebel KJV form of Acraba.

Ekron (ĕk'rŏn) northernmost of the five principal towns of the Philistines. It was nine miles from the Mediterranean Sea at head of valley leading to Jerusalem. It was given to Judah (Josh. 15:45 f.; Judg. 1:18) or Dan before its migration (Josh. 19:43), but was mostly possessed by the Philistines (1 Sam. 5:10).

El (ĕl) principal base of the Hebrew name for "God," probably derived from the root meaning "power."

Ela (ē'lá) one of Solomon's officers (1 K. 4:18).

Eladah or **Eleadah** (ĕl'á-dàh) an Ephraimite (1 Chr. 7:20).

Elah (ē'lá) [the Hebrew word means a terebinth, i.e., a large tree, probably an oak] 1. An Edomite (Gen. 36:41).

2. A son of Caleb the son of Jephunneh (1 Chr. 4:15).

3. King of Israel, son and successor of Baasha (1 K. 16:8–10). He was killed by Zimri while drunk.

4. Father of Hoshea, the last king of Israel (2 K. 15:30; 17:1).

5. A Benjaminite (1 Chr. 9:8).

Elah, Valley of the valley where Israel was encamped when David killed Goliath (1 Sam. 17:2, 19, 21:9). It is identified with the "valley of the Acacia" some fifteen miles southwest of Bethlehem.

Elam (ē'lăm) 1. Son of Shem (Gen. 10:22; 1 Chr. 1:17), the ancestor from which the Elamites were named. See **Elam** (country).

2. A Korahite of David's time (1 Chr. 26:3).

3. A Benjaminite chief (1 Chr. 8:24).

4. A priest at the dedication of Jerusalem's new walls (Neh. 12:42).

5. Children of two families descended from an Elam returned from exile (Ezra 2:7; Neh. 7:12; and Ezra 2:31; Neh. 7:34: "the other Elam"). Both had the same number of descendants.

Elam (country) the eastern country lying south of Assyria and east of Persia, of which the capital was Susa (Gen. 14:1, 9; Isa. 11:11, 21:2; Jer. 25:25, 49:34–39; Ezek. 32:24; Dan. 8:2). Its people are listed as descended from Shem (Gen. 10:22) and allied with Asshur and Aram. The language, different from Sumerian, Indo-European, or Semitic, is known from tablets discovered at Susa but not yet fully deciphered. The Elamites had a long history both as an independent people, and as allies of Assyria or Babylonia, or vassal to them. Elamites were among those brought to Samaria by Assyria (Ezra 4:9 f.). According to Acts 2:9, Jews from Elam were present at Pentecost.

Elasah (ĕl'á-sàh) 1. Priest with a foreign wife (Ezra 10:22).

2. Jeremiah's messenger to exiles in Babylon (Jer. 29:3).

Elath or **Eloth** (ē'lăth or ē'lŏth) a city of Edom located at the head of the Gulf of Aqabah, probably (as N. Glueck believes) the same as Ezion-geber. Israel touched it in the wanderings (Deut. 2:8). David took it (2 Sam. 8:14), and Solomon's navy used it (1 K. 9:26; cf. 2 Chr. 8:17). Later it rebelled (2 K. 8:20, 14:22). According to 2 K. 16:6 it was held by Syria.

El-bethel (ĕl'bĕth'ĕl) [the God of the house of God] name given to Luz by Jacob after God appeared to him there (Gen. 28:19).

Eldaah (ĕl-dā'ăh) son of Midian (Gen. 25:4).

Eldad (ĕl'dăd) a man who with a companion Medad prophesied much to Joshua's vexation, leading Moses to wish that all God's people were prophets (Num. 11:24–29).

elder the term "elder," or "old man," as the Hebrew literally imports, was one of extensive use as an official title among the Hebrews and surrounding nations. It had reference to various offices (Gen. 24:2, 50:7; 2 Sam. 12:17; Ezek. 27:9). As a reference to political office, it applied not only to the Hebrews, but also to the Egyptians (Gen. 50:7), the Moabites, and Midianites (Num. 22:7). Wherever a patriarchal system is in force, the office of the "elder" will be found as the keystone of the social and political fabric; it is so in the present day among the Arabs, where the Sheik (= old man) is the highest authority in the tribe. The earliest notice of the elders acting in concert as a political body is at the time of the Exodus. They were the representatives of the people, so much so that elders and people are occasionally used as equivalent terms (cf. 1 Sam. 8:4 with vss. 7, 10, 19). Their authority was undefined and extended to all matters concerning public weal. When the tribes settled down, the elders were distinguished by different titles according as they were acting as national representatives, as district governors over several tribes (Deut. 31:28; 2 Sam. 19:11), or as local magistrates in the provincial towns, whose duty it was to sit in the gate and administer justice (Deut. 19:12; Ruth 4:9, 11; 1 K. 21:8). Their considerable number and influence may be inferred from 1 Sam. 30:26 ff. They retained their position under all political changes which the Jews underwent: under the judges (Judg. 2:7; 1 Sam. 4:3); under the kings (2 Sam. 17:4); during the Captivity (Jer. 29:1; Ezek. 8:1); subsequently to the return (Ezra 5:5, 6:7, 14, 10:8, 14); under the Maccabees, when they were described sometimes as the "senate" (1 Macc. 12:6; 2 Macc. 1:10, 4:44, 11:27), sometimes by their ordinary title (1 Macc. 7:33, 11:23, 12:35); and lastly, at the commencement of the Christian era, when each Jewish community had a council of elders and the Jerusalem council of seventy-one, the Sanhedrin, was the high court of all Jewry. Luke describes the order by the collective term *presbuterion* (Lk. 22:66; Acts 22:5). The elders enjoyed seats of honor in the synagogues, and from their number seem to have been selected the rulers of the synagogue. The appointment of elders in the local churches seems to follow the order existing in the synagogues, and the term *presbuteros* as used with reference to the church is probably more closely related to the elders of the synagogue than to any other community governmental arrangement such as the one at Qumran. Each local congregation had a plurality of elders (cf. Acts 11:30, 14:23, 15:2, 4, 6, 22–23, 16:4, 20:17, 21:18; Tit. 1:5–7), the same being also designated "bishops" or "overseers" (Acts 20:17, 28; Tit. 1:5–7). See **bishop.** The term "pastors" is also by inference applied to the same order of men (Acts 20:28, *poimainein*, to pastor, shepherd—NEB; also 1 Pet. 5:1–4, where derivatives of all three terms are used. The terms elders and bishops as references to local church leaders are interchangeably used in 1 Clement 42–44; while the Didache makes exclusive use of bishop as the Epistle of Polycarp to the Philippians does of "presbyters." Each term could well be the most natural for the setting of each writing, one Jewish (presbyter) and the other Gentile (bishop). No distinction between elders and bishops occurs until after the close of the first century. R.L.R.

Elead (ĕl′ĭ-ăd) an Ephraimite (1 Chr. 7:21).

Elealah (ē′lĕ-ā′là) a city east of Jordan rebuilt by Reuben (Num. 32:3, 37), later belonging to Moab (Isa. 15:4; Jer. 48:34), now el-'Al two miles from Heshbon.

Eleasah (ĕl′ĭ-ā′sá) 1. A clan in tribe of Judah (1 Chr. 2:39 f.).

2. A descendant of Saul (1 Chr. 8:37, 9:43).

Eleazar (ĕ-lē-ā′zár) 1. Third son of Aaron, by Elisheba, daughter of Amminadab. After the death of Nadab and Abihu without children (Lev. 10:1 f.; Num. 3:4), Eleazar was appointed chief over the principal Levites (Num. 3:32). With his brother Ithamar he ministered as a priest during their father's lifetime and immediately before his death was invested on Mount Hor with the sacred garments, as the successor of Aaron in the office of high priest (Num. 20:28). With Moses he superintended the census of the people (Num. 26:3). After the conquest of Canaan he took part in the distribution of the land (Josh. 14:1). The time of his death is not mentioned in Scripture.

2. The son of Abinadab, of the hill of Kirjath-jearim (1 Sam. 7:1).

3. The son of Dodo the Ahohite, i.e., possibly a descendant of Ahoah of the tribe of Benjamin (1 Chr. 8:4); one of the three principal mighty men of David's army (2 Sam. 23:9, 10; 1 Chr. 11:12 f.).

4. A Merarite Levite, son of Mahli, and grandson of Merari (1 Chr. 23:21, 22, 24:28).

5. A priest who took part in the feast of dedication under Nehemiah (Neh. 12:42).

6. One of the sons of Parosh; an Israelite (i.e., a layman) who had married a foreign wife and had to put her away (Ezra 10:25).

7. Son of Phinehas, a Levite (Ezra 8:33).

8. The son of Eliud, in the genealogy of Jesus Christ (Mt. 1:15). R.L.R.

elect, election [the chosen or selected ones] a term used in OT of God's selection of individuals: Moses (Ps. 106:23), Saul (2 Sam. 21:6), David (Ps. 89:3), the Messiah (Isa. 42:1), and Israel (Ps. 105:6, 43; Isa. 43:20). In the NT it is used of Jesus (Lk. 9:35, 23:35), of angels (1 Tim. 5:21), and of Christians frequently.

El-elohe-Israel (ĕl′ĕl′ō-hē-ĭz′rĭ-ĕl) [God, the God of Israel] altar erected by Jacob near Shechem (Gen. 32:24).

elements an important NT term (Gr. *stoicheia*) meaning "alphabet," a series, or row of things, then "principles" or rudiments (Heb.

5:12; Col. 2:8, 20), heathen gods or rites (Gal. 4:3, 9); cosmic elements (2 Pet. 3:10–12).

Eleph (ē'lĕf) a Benjaminite town (Josh. 18:28).

elephant mentioned in OT only in margin of some versions of Job 40:15 for "Behemoth" and "elephant's teeth" for ivory (1 K. 10:22; 2 Chr. 9:41).

Eleven, the the twelve apostles minus Judas, who had died (Mt. 28:16; Mk. 16:14; Lk. 24:9, 33).

Elhanan (ĕl-hā'nàn) 1. An OT hero who slew the brother of Goliath (2 Sam. 21:19; 1 Chr. 20:5).

2. One of David's thirty guardsmen (2 Sam. 23:24; 1 Chr. 11:26).

Eli (ē'lī) priest of the family of Ithamar and one of the judges of Israel. His home was at Shiloh near the tabernacle (1 Sam. 1–4, 14:13; 1 K. 2:27). To him Samuel was brought according to his mother's vow (1 Sam. 1:1–2:11). His story concerns mostly the irreverent attitude of his two sons, Phineas and Hophni, who profaned the sacrifices. He died from a fall at the news of his sons' deaths and the capture of the ark.

Eli, Eli, lama sabachthani (ē'lī, ē'lī, lä'mà, sà-băk'thà-nī) the cry of Jesus on the Cross, translating Ps. 22:1; its meaning is given by the evangelists as "My God, my God, why hast thou forsaken me?" (Mt. 27:46; Mk. 15:34).

Eliab (ē-lī'ăb) 1. A leader of tribe of Zebulun at the census (Num. 1:9).

2. A Reubenite (Num. 26:8 f.; 16:1, 12).

3. Eldest brother of David (1 Chr. 2:13; 1 Sam. 16:6, 17:13, 28).

4. A Levite of David's time (1 Chr. 15:18, 20, 16:5).

5. A Gadite follower of David (1 Chr. 12:9).

6. An ancestor of Samuel (1 Chr. 6:27).

Eliada (ĭ-lī'à-dà) 1. One of David's sons (2 Sam. 5:16; 1 Chr. 3:8).

2. A Benjaminite warrior who led 200,000 tribesmen to Jehoshaphat's army (2 Chr. 17:17).

Eliada(h) (ĭ-lī'à-dà) father of Rezon, one of Solomon's enemies (1 K. 11:23).

Eliah (ĭ-lī'à) 1. A chieftain of Benjamin (1 Chr. 8:27).

2. Man of Ezra's time with a foreign wife (Ezra 10:26).

Eliahba (ĭ-lī'à-bà) one of David's guards (the thirty), (2 Sam. 23:32).

Eliakim (ĭ-lī'à-kĭm) 1. Son of Hilkiah; master of Hezekiah's household (Isa. 36:3; 2 K. 18:18, 26, 37), who succeeded Shebna in office (Isa. 22:15–21). At the invasion of Sennacherib king of Assyria, he headed the delegation which at-

tempted to negotiate with him and later headed the group seeking the help of the prophet Isaiah (2 K. 19:2; Isa. 37:2).

2. King Jehoiakim, king of Judah's original name (2 K. 23:34).

3. A priest at the dedication of the new wall (Neh. 12:41).

4. An ancestor of Jesus (Mt. 1:13).

5. Another and earlier ancestor of Jesus (Lk. 3:30 f.).

Eliam (ĭ-lī'ăm) 1. Father of Bath-sheba the wife of David (2 Sam. 11:3).

2. One of David's thirty warriors (2 Sam. 23:34).

Elias (ē-lī'ăs) the Greek form of the Heb.

Elijah, occurring in the KJV (e.g., Mt. 11:14). Later versions follow the practice of making the spelling of the name uniform in Old and New Testaments.

Eliasaph (ē-lī'à-săf) two men, a Danite (Num. 1:14, 2:14, 7:42, 47, 10:20) and a Levite of the house of the Gershonite (Num. 3:24) at the census in the wilderness.

Eliashib (ē-lī'à-shĭb) 1. Priest of David's time from whom the eleventh course was named (1 Chr. 24:12).

2. Descendant of royal family of Judah (1 Chr. 3:24).

3. High priest at rebuilding of the wall (Neh. 3:1, 20 f.).

4. A singer who had married a foreign wife (Ezra 10:24).

5. Son of Zattu, who had a foreign wife (Ezra 10:27).

6. Son of Bani who, with his father, had taken a foreign woman (Ezra 10:36).

Eliathah (ē-lī'à-thà) a musician of David's time (1 Chr. 25:4) over the twentieth division of the temple service (25:27).

Elidad (ē-lī'dăd) a Benjaminite prince who helped divide the land (Num. 34:21).

Eliel (ē-lī'ĕl) 1. One of the heads of Manasseh east of Jordan (1 Chr. 5:24).

2. A forefather of Samuel (1 Chr. 6:34).

3. A Benjaminite (1 Chr. 8:20).

4. Another Benjaminite (1 Chr. 3:22).

5. One of David's heroes (1 Chr. 11:46).

6. Another of David's guards (11:47).

7. A Gadite follower of David (1 Chr. 12:11).

8. A Kohath Levite when the ark was brought to Jerusalem (1 Chr. 15:9, 11).

9. A Levite temple overseer in time of Hezekiah (2 Chr. 31:13).

Elienai (ĕl-ĭ-ē'nī) a Benjaminite (1 Chr. 8:20).

Eliezer (ĕl'ĭ-ē'zêr) 1. Abraham's chief servant usually called "of Damascus," who until Abraham had a son, was his heir (Gen. 15:2).

2. Second son of Moses so called [God is my help] because of gratitude (Ex. 18:4; 1 Chr. 23:15, 17).

3. Grandson of Benjamin (1 Chr. 7:8).

4. A priest (1 Chr. 15:24).

5. A Reubenite chief (1 Chr. 27:16).

6. A prophet who rebuked Jehoshaphat for helping Ahaziah the king of Israel (2 Chr. 20:37).

7. A prudent Israelite sent by Ezra to secure people to accompany him to Jerusalem (Ezra 8:16).

8, 9, 10. Three men who had taken foreign wives (Ezra 10:18, 23, 31).

11. An ancestor of Jesus (Lk. 2:29).

Elihoenai (ĕl'ĭ-hō-ē'nī) a leader of 200 men returning from exile (Ezra 8:4).

Elihoreph (ĕl'ĭ-hō'rĕf) Solomon's scribe (1 K. 4:3).

Elihu (ē-lī'hū) 1. One of the interlocutors of the book of Job. He was a Buzite (i.e., an Aramean) (Job 32:2-6, 34:1, 35:1, 36:1).

2. An ancestor of Samuel (1 Sam. 1:1).

3. A brother of David, a ruler of Judah (1 Chr. 27:18).

4. A man of Manasseh who joined David at Ziklag (1 Chr. 12:20).

5. A Levite doorkeeper of David's time (1 Chr. 26:7).

Elijah (ē-lī'jà) the Tishbite, the great prophet and opponent of Baal worship in the time of Ahab and Jezebel. The only personal information given is that he was from Gilead, the highland country of West Jordan. When he stood before Ahab, he wore the characteristic Bedouin garb of his native region, with long hair, leathern girdle (1 K. 18:46; 2 K. 1:8), and a mantle or cape of sheepskin with which he "wrapped his face" (1 K. 19:13). The king Ahab had introduced the worship of the Phoenician god of his wife Jezebel. Against this Elijah cried out, announcing that there would be no rain "but by my word" (1 K. 17:1 ff.), a period according to NT which lasted three and one-half years (Lk. 4:25; James 5:17). During the drouth and fleeing from the wrath of the queen, he was directed to the brook Cherith (1 K. 17:5), then to Zarephath (17:8-24). Then he was to meet Ahab (18:1 f.), who was told that he and not Elijah was the "troubler of Israel." The great contest on Mount Carmel followed (18:19-40), and the drouth ended (18:41-46). Elijah fled from the anger of Jezebel to Horeb (19:1 ff.) by way of Beer-sheba. Here occurred the incident of Elijah's despondency and God's assurance that there were seven thousand who had not bowed the knee to Baal (1 K. 19:15-18).

He was given tasks: to find Elisha, who was to be his successor; anoint Hazael king of Syria and Jehu king of Israel—thus foreshadowing Ahab's downfall. Elijah appeared once more to rebuke Ahab for the theft of Naboth's vineyard and his murder and predict the dread death of the king (1 K. 21:19-25; 2 K. 9:26, 36, 37). The next incident was his interception of the messengers of the sick king Ahaziah, who sought advice from a strange oracle (1 K. 22:51; 2 K. 1:1 ff.). Finally there was the rebuking letter to Jehoram king of Judah (2 Chr. 21:12-15). The concluding story is that of his departure from Elisha and the request of the latter for a double portion of his spirit (1 K. 2:1-14). That Elijah did not die but was taken to heaven by a chariot of fire made a deep impression upon Israel.

A later prophecy of the one who was to return in his spirit and power (Mal. 4:5) led to the expectation of his literal return, a prediction which the NT sees fulfilled in the work of Jesus' forerunner, John the Baptist (Mt. 17:10-13; Lk. 1:17). Elijah has been called "the grandest and most romantic character that Israel ever produced." He was a fitting forerunner of that one who prepared the way of the Lord. He it was whose spirit returned with that of Moses on the Mount of Transfiguration to prepare Jesus for his ordeal (Lk. 9:30). Here the lesson was impressed upon Jesus' disciples that a greater glory even than that of Elijah rested upon the Lord Jesus. Elijah and Moses were not to be put on a par with Jesus. When Moses and Elijah were gone, the voice said of Christ, "Hear ye him."

Elika (ē-lī'kà) David's hero (2 Sam. 23:25).

Elim (ē'lĭm) second camping station of Israelites after crossing the Red Sea. It had twelve wells of water and seventy palm trees. Identified as Wadi Gharandel, sixty-three miles from Suez.

Elimelech (ē-lĭm'ē-lĕk) a Judahite who accompanied his wife, Naomi, and his sons to Moab, where he died. See the story of Ruth (Ruth 1-3).

Elioenai (ĕl'ĭ-ō-ē'nī) 1. Son of Neariah (1 Chr. 3:23 f.).

2. A Simeonite (1 Chr. 4:36).

3. Head of a family descended from Beecher, son of Benjamin (1 Chr. 7:8).

4. A doorkeeper of the temple (1 Chr. 26:3).

5, 6. Two men who had foreign wives (Ezra 10:22; Neh. 12:41); could be the same man.

7. Another Israelite with a foreign wife (Ezra 10:27).

Eliphal (ē-lī'făl) one of David's guards (1 Chr. 11:35).

Eliphalet (ē-lĭf'ă-lĕt) last of David's sons born at Jerusalem (2 Sam. 5:16; 1 Chr. 14:7).

Eliphaz (ĕl'ĭ-făz) 1. Son of Esau (Gen. 36:4; 1 Chr. 1:35, 36).

2. Chief of Job's three friends, called the Temanite. He argued that the world is perfect and that suffering must be the result of previous sin (Job 4, 5, 15, 22). He emphasized the unapproachable majesty and purity of God (4:12–21, 15:12–16).

Elipheleh (ē-lĭf'ē-lĕh) one of David's gatekeepers, a harper at the removal of the ark (1 Chr. 15:18, 21).

Eliphelet (ē-lĭf'ē-lĕt) 1. David's son. See **Eliphalet.**

2. Another of David's sons born at Jerusalem (1 Chr. 3:8).

3. One of David's guards (2 Sam. 23:34).

4. A descendant of Saul through Jonathan (1 Chr. 8:39).

5. Leader of a group of returning exiles (Ezra 8:13).

6. Man who had a foreign wife (Ezra 10:33).

Elisabeth see **Elizabeth**

Elisha (ē-lī'shà) the great prophet, disciple, and successor of Elijah, and the one who completed Elijah's work of eliminating Baal worship and destroying the house of the wicked Ahab and Jezebel. His designation as Elijah's successor was revealed to the prophet at Horeb (1 K. 19:16 f.). The story of his call and Elijah throwing his mantle over the young man's shoulders is told in 1 K. 19:19–21. After a brief farewell he followed Elijah, receiving a double portion of the prophet's spirit by seeing his ascension. Elisha's ministry extended some sixty years through the reigns of the Northern kings Jehoram, Jehu, Jehoahaz, and Joash. The vivid narratives which relate this long activity are filled with miracles. Among these may be mentioned the multiplying of the widow of Shunem's oil (2 K. 4:7), the raising of her son from the dead (2 K. 4:32–37), multiplying the bread of the prophets at Gilgal (4:38–44), cure of Naaman's leprosy (5:1–14), floating the servant's ax (6:1–7), smiting the Syrians with blindness (6:18), and even the reviving of the man who touched his dead bones (13:20–21). Such miracles probably represent a display of the "double spirit of Elijah" and should be viewed in the light of the display of God's power in the life and death struggle with the false religion of Baal. In addition to his prophetic ministry Elisha played a leading role as statesman-adviser of the kings of his time in their political struggles. Instances of his wisdom are seen in his advising clemency to the captured Syrians (2 K. 6:21–23) and his object lesson with the arrows to Joash the king of Israel. Elisha presents several parallels to the Lord Jesus Christ, not merely because he healed a leper, raised a dead man, and increased the loaves, but also because his loving, gentle temper and kindness of disposition—characteristic of him, above all the saints of the OT—ever ready to soothe, to heal, and to conciliate attracted to him women and simple people and made him the universal friend and father to kings, generals, widows, and poor prophets alike.

Elishah (ē-lī'shà) one of the sons of Japheth in the table of nations (Gen. 10:4; 1 Chr. 1:7). The land of his later descendants is described as "the isles of Elishah" from which Tyre received its purple and blue dyes. The exact land is unknown.

Elishama (ē-lĭsh'à-mà) 1. A prince of Ephraim at Sinai (Num. 1:10, 2:18, 7:48, 10:22). He was Joshua's grandfather (1 Chr. 7:26).

2. A son of David born at Jerusalem (2 Sam. 5:16; 1 Chr. 3:8).

3. Another son of David, also called **Elishua.**

4. A Judahite (1 Chr. 2:41).

5. Grandfather of Ishmael (2 K. 25:25).

6. Scribe to King Jehoiakim (Jer. 36:12, 20).

A priest in time of Jehoshaphat (2 Chr. 17:8).

Elishaphat (ē-lĭsh'à-făt) a captain who helped in the rebellion against Athaliah (2 Chr. 23:1).

Elisheba (ē-lĭsh'ē-bà) wife of Aaron (Ex. 6:23).

Elishua (ĕl'ĭ-shōō-à) a son of David (2 Sam. 5:15; 1 Chr. 14:15), also called **Elishama** (1 Chr. 3:6) probably by a scribal error.

Eliud (ē-lī'ŭd) an ancestor of Christ (Mt. 1:14, 15).

Elizabeth (ē-lĭz'à-bĕth) the wife of Zechariah and the mother of John the Baptist. She was herself of the priestly family and a relation (Lk. 1:36) of the mother of Jesus.

Elizaphan (ĕl'ĭ-zā'făn) 1. A Levite chief of the Kohathites at the census (Num. 3:30). He helped remove the bodies of Nadab and Abihu (Lev. 10:4; cf. 1 Chr. 15:8).

2. A leader of Zebulun at division of the land (Num. 34:25).

Elizur (ē-lī'zēr) a prince of tribe of Reuben (Num. 1:5, 2:10).

Elkanah (ĕl-kā'nà) 1. Son or descendant of Korah (Ex. 6:24).

2. A later descendant of the above by the same name (1 Chr. 6:26, 35).

3. Samuel the prophet's father, a priest (1 Chr. 6:27, 34).

4. A Levite (1 Chr. 9:16).

5. An ally of David at Ziklag (1 Chr. 12:6).

6. Ahaz's officer slain during Pekah's invasion (2 Chr. 28:7).

Elkosh (ĕl'kŏsh) the birthplace of Nahum the prophet (Nah. 1:1). Several traditions claim sites as the true one, but no identification has been made.

Ellasar (ĕl-ā'sàr) the country of King Arioch, otherwise unknown (Gen. 14).

elm (Hos. 4:13) see **oak.** No oak in Palestine.

Elmodam (ĕl-mō'dăm) or **Elmadam** (ASV, RSV) name in Jesus' genealogy (Lk. 3:28).

Elnaam (ĕl-nā'ăm) father of 2 of David's guards (1 Chr. 11:46).

Elnathan (ĕl-nā'thăn) 1. "East of Jerusalem," the maternal grandfather of Jehoiachin (2 K. 24:8).

2. Name of three Levites of Ezra's time (Ezra 8:16).

Elohim (ĕ-lō'hĭm) Heb. word for "gods"; in plural (of majesty) for "God."

Elon (ē'lŏn) 1. Esau's father-in-law (Gen. 26:34, 36:2).

2. Zebulun's son (Gen. 46:14; Num. 26: 26).

3. One of the judges of Israel (Judg. 12: 11 f.).

Elon-beth-hanan (ē'lŏn-bĕth-hā'nän) an administrative district of Solomon in Dan (1 K. 4:9).

Eloth alternate form of **Elath** (1 K. 9:26).

Elpaal (ĕl-pā'ál) a Benjaminite (1 Chr. 8:11).

Elpalet KJV form of **Elpelet,** one of David's sons (1 Chr. 14:5).

El-paran (ĕl-pā'răn) southernmost point of Chedorlaomer's raid, probably **Elath** (Gen. 14:6).

El Shaddai (ĕl shăd'à-ī) one of the names of God = "the Almighty" (Gen. 17:1; Ex. 6:3).

Eltekeh (ĕl'tĕ-kĕ) a border town of Dan (Josh. 19:44) allotted to Levites (21:23).

Eltekon (ĕl-tĕ-kŏn) unidentified town in Judah (Josh. 15:59).

Eltolad (ĕl'tŏ'lăd) a Negeb city of Judah (Josh. 15:30) allotted to Simeon (19:4; 1 Chr. 4:29).

Elul see **months**

Eluzai (ē-lū'zà-ī) ally of David at Ziklag (1 Chr. 12:5).

Elymas (ĕl'ĭ-măs) a sorcerer (also called Bar-Jesus) who tried to turn aside Sergius Paulus proconsul of Cyprus, and was smitten blind (Acts 13:4–13).

Elzabad (ĕl-zā'băd) 1. A Gadite ally of David (1 Chr. 12:12).

2. A Levite (1 Chr. 26:7).

Elzaphan see **Elizaphan**

embalming the preparation of a corpse with ointments and spices in order to preserve it. The only instances in the OT are of Jacob (Gen. 50:2, 3) and Joseph (Gen. 50:26). The art was practiced by Egyptians (evidently in view of a belief in a future life). The process is described by Herodotus (*Hist.* II.86–89). It consisted in removing the organs of the body through small openings and replacing them with ointments and spices. The body was wrapped in linens and placed in wooden coffins resembling the human shape. The entire process took some forty to seventy days (cf. Gen. 50:2–3). Biblical references make it plain that the Jews did not practice embalming.

embroidery specifically in the OT, the weaving of materials into pictures or patterns. There are numerous references of such skill, especially in connection with the construction of the tabernacle. Oholiab, of the tribe of Dan, who was skilled in this art, was called to the work (Ex. 35:35, 38:18). For later references, see Judg. 5:30; Ps. 45:14; Ezek. 27:16, 24. Pliny (*Nat. Hist.* VIII.48) makes embroidery with needle an invention of the Phrygians. But evidence seems to prove that adorning cloth with needle figures was widespread in the ancient Near East.

emerald a word used to translate a precious stone, e.g., first in second row on the breastplate of the high priest (Ex. 28:18) or one of the foundations of the New Jerusalem (Rev. 21:19). Several different original words of varying meaning are so translated.

emerods (Deut. 28:27; 1 Sam. 5:6 ff., 6:4 ff.) [RSV, **tumors**] KJV rendering for the disease hemorrhoids.

Emim, the (ē'mĭm) [the terrible ones] ancient inhabitants of eastern tableland of Palestine, displaced by the Moabites (Deut. 2:11).

Emmanuel (ē-măn'ū-ĕl) (Mt. 1:23) or **Immanuel** name given by Isaiah of the child of Isa. 7:14 = "God with us."

Emmaus (ĕ-mā'ŭs) the village to which two disciples were going when Jesus appeared to them on the resurrection day (Lk. 24:13). Luke's calculations place it seven miles from Jerusalem. No identification has been definitely made.

Emmor (ĕm'êr) father of Sychem (Acts 7:16), also called **Hamor.**

Enam (ē'năm) unidentified place in Shephelah of Judah (Josh. 15:34).

Enan (ē'năn) father of Ahira, a prince of Naphtali at the census (Num. 1:15).

encampment the resting place of an army or company of travelers at night (Ex. 16:13). It was applied to the army or caravan when on its march (Ex. 14:19; Josh. 10:5, 11:5). The encampment of Israel on the march from Egypt was the subject of specific direction from God, and details are given at length in Num. 2–3. For various other details of this and later practices, see Ex. 32:17; Lev. 24:14; Num. 10: 2–8; Deut. 23:14; Josh. 7:24 (cf. Heb. 13:12; Jn. 19:17, 20); 1 Sam. 17:20–22; 2 K. 7:10; 1 Chr. 9:18, 24; Zech. 14:15.

enchantment several words with this translation refer to a magician or sorcerer and to his devices such as casting of spells (2 K. 9:22), charming serpents (Jer. 8:17; cf. Ps. 58:5; Eccl. 10:11), omens and magic (Isa. 47:9, 12). All such methods of imposture were strictly forbidden in Scripture (Lev. 19:26; Isa. 47:9; but see 2 K. 17:17; 2 Chr. 33:6; Acts 8:9, 11, 13:6, 8; Gal. 5:20; Rev. 9:21).

Endor (ĕn'dôr) place in Manasseh (Josh. 17:11) celebrated as the place of Deborah's victory over Sisera and Jabin (Ps. 83:10) and the residence of the witch consulted by Saul (1 Sam. 28:7), near Mount Tabor.

En-eglaim (ĕn-ĕg'lā-ĭm) an unidentified locality on the Dead Sea (Ezek. 47:10).

En-gannim (ĕn-găn'ĭm) 1. A city in low country of Judah (Josh. 15:34).

2. A city on the border of Issachar (Josh. 19:21) allotted to the Levites (21:29).

En-gedi (ĕn-gē'dī) a town midway on the western shore of the Dead Sea (Josh. 15:62; Ezek. 47:10). It is located on a rich plain, one-half mile square, and is fed by a fountain issuing 400 feet up the cliff. Its early name was Hazazon-tamar. It was attacked by the federation of kings in Abraham's day (Gen. 14:7). David hid here from Saul (1 Sam. 23:29), and near here he cut off Saul's shirt (1 Sam. 24).

engine the word so translated means a device or invention and is used of military weapons such as battering ram or catapult (2 Chr. 26:15; Ezek. 26:9).

engraver one whose business was cutting names or devices on rings or seals (Ex. 28:11, 21, 36).

En-haddah (ĕn-hăd'à) city on border of Issachar (Josh. 19:21).

En-hakkore (ĕn-hăk'ō-rē) the spring at Lechi which sprang up at the cry of Samson after his exploit with the jawbone (Judg. 15:19).

En-hazor (ĕn-hā'zôr) fortified city of Naphtali, probably Khirbet Hasireh in North Galilee (Josh. 19:37).

Enoch (ē'nŭk) 1. Eldest son of Cain, who called the city he built by his own name (Gen. 4:17 f.).

2. Son of Jared and father of Methuselah (Gen. 5:21 ff.; Lk. 3:28). He is said to have "walked with God" so that God "took" or translated him (Gen. 5:24, 6:9). The author of Hebrews sees faith as the key (Heb. 11:5 f.). He is mentioned by Jude (vs. 24) along with a quoted testimony of warning as to the Lord's coming in judgment.

Enosh (ē'nōsh) or **Enos** (ē'nōs) son of Seth (Gen. 4:26, 5:6 f.; 1 Chr. 1:1; Lk. 3:38).

En-rimmon (ĕn-rĭm'ŏn) a place south of Jerusalem resettled by Judah after the Exile (Zech. 14:10; Neh. 11:29; cf. Josh. 15:32; 1 Chr. 4:32).

En-rogel (ĕn-rō'gĕl) a spring on the border between Judah and Benjamin (Josh. 15:7, 18: 16). Here Jonathan and Ahimaaz hid for news for David from within the walls (2 Sam. 17:17). See also 1 K. 1:9. Today a well exists there called Job's well.

En-shemesh (en-shĕm'ĭsh) a spring on border between Judah and Benjamin (Josh. 15:7, 18: 17), just east of Bethany. Now called "Spring of the Apostles."

ensign or **standard** not a flag but one of various symbols elevated on poles and used as a signal or symbolizing the army's cause (Isa. 13:2, 18:3; Num. 1:52; 2:2 ff.).

En-tappuah see **Tappuah**

Epaenetus (ĕp-ē'nē-tŭs) a Christian at Rome, "beloved" and "firstfruits of Achaia," greeted by Paul (Rom. 16:5).

Epaphras (ĕp'à-frăs) [short for Epaphroditus but not the same NT character] a fellow worker of Paul mentioned in Col. 1:7 f. as a teacher in the church there and Paul's informant. He joined Paul in greetings (4:12).

Epaphroditus (ē-păf-rō-dī'tŭs) a messenger [Gr. apostle = missionary] of the church at Philippi to Paul's need (Phil. 2:25–30, 4:18). He became sick and recovered and was sent back by Paul with the Epistle to the Philippians.

Ephah (ē'fà) 1. Son of Midian (Gen. 25:4; cf. Isa. 60:6).

2. Concubine of Caleb (1 Chr. 2:46).

3. A Judahite (1 Chr. 2:47).

ephah see **measures**

Ephai (ē'fī) father of a group left in Judah at deportation of Jews (Jer. 40:8).

Epher (ē'fēr) 1. Son of Midian (Gen. 25:4).

2. Son of Ezra (1 Chr. 4:17).

3. A Manassehite (1 Chr. 5:24).

Ephes-dammim (ē'fĕs-dăm'mĭm) place where Philistines camped before Goliath was killed (1 Sam. 17:1).

Ephesians, Epistle to the written by the apostle Paul during his first captivity at Rome (Acts 28:16), apparently immediately after he had written the Epistle to the Colossians and during that period (perhaps the early part of A.D. 62) when his imprisonment had not assumed the severer character which seems to have marked its close. This sublime epistle was addressed to the church at the ancient and famous city of Ephesus, that church which the apostle had himself founded (Acts 19:1 ff., cf. 18:19), with which he abode so long (Acts 20:31), and from whose elders he parted with such a warmhearted and affectionate farewell (Acts 20:17-35). The contents of this epistle easily admit of being divided into two portions, the first mainly *doctrinal* (chs. 1-3), the second *hortatory* and *practical* (chs. 4-6). With regard to the *authenticity* and *genuineness* of this epistle, despite much modern criticism, it is not too much to say that there are no just grounds for doubt. The testimonies of antiquity are unusually strong. Even if we do not press the supposed allusions in Ignatius and Polycarp, we can confidently adduce Irenaeus, Clement, Origen, Tertullian, and after them the constant and persistent tradition of the ancient church. Even Marcion did not deny that the epistle was written by Paul, nor did heretics refuse occasionally to cite it as confessedly due to him.

In more recent times, however, its genuineness has been somewhat vehemently called in question. De Wette labored to prove that it is a mere spiritless expansion of the Epistle to the Colossians, though compiled in the apostolic age; Schwegler, F. C. Baur, and others advance a step further and reject both epistles as of no higher antiquity than the age of Montanism and early Gnosticism. Reply to these earlier arguments may be found in H. A. W. Meyer, *Critical and Exegetical Handbook* (1884) and Dean Alford's *Greek Testament* (*Prolegomena,* Vol. III, pp. 6-26). Recent attacks on the epistle center in the contention of E. J. Goodspeed (*The Meaning of Ephesians,* 1933, and *The Key to Ephesians,* 1956) that the letter is by a Paulinist of ca. A.D. 85-90 who wrote it as a summary cover letter at the time of the collection and publication of the corpus of Paul's letters. For criticism of this thesis see E. F. Scott's *Commentary on Ephesians,* 1935, and G. Johnson, *The Doctrine of the Church in the New Testament.*

Two special points require brief notice: (1) The designation of the readers by *in Epheso,* "in Ephesus" (1:1) is lacking in Chester Beatty papyrus, the uncials Aleph and B, 67 (twelfth century), Basil, and possibly Tertullian. There is also an absence of Paul's usual personal salutations. These facts are offset by (a) evidence for the inclusion of the phrase, in the MSS A, D, G, *Koine,* (b) all the versions, (c) the universal designation of the epistle in all the early church, (d) the difficulty of construing the participle ("the saints being—") if no place is written. (2) The question of priority of composition between this epistle and that of Colossians is a very difficult one to adjust. On the whole, both internal and external considerations seem somewhat in favor of the priority of the Epistle to the Colossians.

R.L.R.

Ephesus an illustrious city in the district of Ionia, nearly opposite the island of Samos and about the middle of the western coast of the peninsula commonly called Asia Minor. Of the Roman province of Asia, Ephesus was the capital.

1. *Geographical Relations.* All the cities of Ionia were remarkably well situated for the growth of commercial prosperity, and none more so than Ephesus. In the time of Augustus it was the great emporium (in a way) of all the regions of Asia within the Taurus; its harbor (Panormus) at the mouth of the Cayster was elaborately constructed. Paul's life alone furnishes illustrations of its mercantile relations with Achaia on the West, Macedonia on the North, and Syria on the East. The relations of Ephesus to the inland regions of the continent are also prominently brought before us in the apostle's travels. The "upper coasts" (Acts 19:1) through which he passed when about to take up his residence in the city were the Phrygian tablelands of the interior. Two great roads at least, in Roman times, led eastward from Ephesus; one through the passes of Tmolus to Sardis (Rev. 3:1) and thence to Galatia and the Northeast, the other round the extremity of Pactyas to Magnesia and so up the valley of the Maeander to Iconium, whence the communication was direct to the Euphrates and to Syrian Antioch. There seem to have been Sardian and Magnesian gates on the east side of Ephesus corresponding to these roads. There were also coast roads leading northward to Smyrna and southward to Miletus. By the latter of these it is probable that the Ephesian elders traveled when summoned to meet Paul at Miletus (Acts 20:17, 18).

2. *Temple and Worship of Diana.* Conspicuous at the head of the harbor of Ephesus was the great temple of Diana or Artemis, the tutelary divinity of the city, the Anatolian deity having been adopted under this name. The

temple was raised on immense substructions in consequence of the swampy nature of the ground. The earlier temple, which had been begun before the Persian war, was burned in the night when Alexander the Great was born; and another structure, raised by the enthusiastic co-operation of all the inhabitants of "Asia," had taken its place. The magnificence of this sanctuary was a proverb throughout the civilized world. In consequence of this devotion the city of Ephesus was called *neokoros* (Acts 19:35) or "warden" of Diana. Another consequence of the celebrity of Diana's worship at Ephesus was that a large manufactory grew up there of portable shrines, purchased by strangers and carried on journeys or set up in their houses by devotees. Perhaps Alexander the "coppersmith" (2 Tim. 4:14) was such a manufacturer. The case of Demetrius the "silversmith" is explicit. Shrines and images were made of meteoric stone pretended to be Diana's image "fallen from heaven."

3. *Study and Practice of Magic.* Magical arts were remarkably prevalent at Ephesus. In illustration of the magical books which were publicly burned (Acts 19:19) under the influence of Paul's preaching, it is enough here to refer to the *Ephesia grammata* (mentioned by Plutarch and others), which were regarded as charms when pronounced, and when written down were carried about as amulets.

4. *Provincial and Municipal Government.* It is well-known that Asia was a proconsular province, and in harmony with this fact we find proconsuls specially mentioned (Acts 19:38). Again we learn from Pliny (V.31) that Ephesus was an assize-town; and in Luke's account the court days are alluded to as actually being held ("the courts are open") during the uproar. Ephesus itself was a "free city" and had its own assemblies and its own magistrates. The senate is mentioned by Josephus; and Luke, in the narrative before us, speaks of the *demos* (vss. 30, 33, "the people") and of its customary assemblies (vs. 39, "the regular assembly"). We even find conspicuous mention made of one of the most important municipal officers of Ephesus, the "town clerk" or keeper of the records, whom we know from other sources to have been a person of great influence and responsibility. It is remarkable to see how all these political and religious characteristics of Ephesus which appear in the NT are illustrated by inscriptions and coins full of allusions to the worship of Diana. That Jews were established there in considerable numbers is known from Josephus and might be inferred from its mercantile eminence; but it is also evident from

Acts 2:9, 6:9. It is here, and here only, that we find disciples of John the baptist explicitly mentioned after the ascension of Christ (Acts 18:25, 19:3). The case of Apollos (18:24) shows the intercourse between this place and Alexandria. The first seeds of Christian truth were possibly sown at Ephesus immediately after Pentecost (Acts 2). Paul's stay here was of more than two years in length (19:8, 9, 20:31), consuming the most important part of his third journey, during which he labored, first in the synagogue (19:8), then in the school of Tyrannus (vs. 9), and also in private (20:20), and during which he wrote the First Epistle to the Corinthians. Here we have the chief period of the evangelization of this shore of the Aegean (Acts 19:10). The address at Miletus shows that the church at Ephesus was thoroughly organized under its presbyters. At a later period Timothy was evangelist there, as we learn from the two epistles addressed to him (1 Tim. 1:3). Among Paul's other companions, Trophimus and Tychicus were natives of Asia (20:4), and the latter probably (2 Tim. 4:12), the former certainly (Acts 21:29), natives of Ephesus. In the same connection are mentioned Onesiphorus (2 Tim. 1:16–18) and his household (4:19). On the other hand must be noticed certain Ephesian antagonists of the apostle, the sons of Sceva and his party (Acts 19:14), Hymenaeus and Alexander (1 Tim. 1:20; 2 Tim. 4:14), and Phygellus and Hermogenes (2 Tim. 1:15). The site of ancient Ephesus is now desolate except for the village of Ayassoluk near the site of the Artemision. There have been excavations of other important sites such as the stadium, the theater, and the Agora.   R.L.R.

Ephlal (ĕf'lăl) descendant of Judah (1 Chr. 2:37).

ephod (ĕf'ŏd) a sacred vestment originally for the high priest (Ex. 28:4) but later worn by ordinary priests (1 Sam. 2:28, 14:3, 22:18; Hos. 3:4). For description see **high priest.** For a misuse in idolatry, see Judg. 8:27, 17:5.

Ephod a Manassehite (Num. 34:23).

Ephraim (ē'frĭ-ĕm) the younger son of Joseph and Asenath (Gen. 41:50–52), the Israelite tribe descending from him (one of the twelve), and in the prophets (especially Hosea) a designation of the Northern Kingdom, Israel (Hos. 4:17; Isa. 17:3). Though he was the younger son, Ephraim was blessed over his brother Manasseh by Jacob (Gen. 48). At the census (Num. 1:32–33) Ephraim numbered 40,500, but forty years later it had decreased to 32,500. Joshua belonged to Ephraim, and this must have given the tribe prominence. The tribe's boundaries are given in Josh. 16:1–10. Its territory lay in the central part of West Jordan, with Dan and Benjamin separating it from Judah on the south and the half tribe of Manasseh (West) lying to the north. Ephraim occupied a hill-country with rich valleys and more than usual rainfall (Deut. 33:13–16). Shiloh in Ephraim's confines was for many years the center of religious life as the site of the tabernacle (Josh. 18:1, 22:12; 1 Sam. 1:3 ff., 2:14). Samuel also was from Ephraim. After the establishment of the monarchy under David a sort of smothering resentment seemed to have existed (2 Sam. 2:8; 1 K. 12:16), which leaped into flames with the revolt of the Ephraimite Jeroboam (1 K. 11:26). Henceforth Ephraim became the leader of the Northern Kingdom to such an extent that its name became synonymous with that kingdom.

Ephraim, City of mentioned in 2 Sam. 13:23 as the sheep farm of Absalom, where the murder of Amnon took place. It is unidentified. Perhaps it is the same place as the Ephraim of Jn. 11:54.

Ephraim (place) 1. Place where Absalom's sheep farm was located and where Amnon was killed (2 Sam. 13:23).

2. A city near the wilderness where Jesus retired (Jn. 11:54), location unknown.

3. A gate of Jerusalem (2 K. 14:13; 2 Chr. 25:23; Neh. 8:16, 12:39). It was 400 cubits east of the corner gate in the first rampart.

4. The wood east of Jordan in Gilead where the battle between David and Absalom's forces was fought (2 Sam. 18:6).

Ephrain (ē′frȧ-ĭn) or **Ephron** city captured by Jeroboam (2 Chr. 13:19).

Ephrath (ĕf′răth) short form of **Ephratah,** the place where Rachel was buried (Gen. 35:16) and the ancient name of Bethlehem-Judah (Gen. 35:16, 19, 48:7). The Messiah was to be born there (Mic. 5:2).

Ephrath second wife of Caleb, mother of Hur (1 Chr. 2:19 f.).

Ephron (ē′frŏn) a Hittite from whom Abraham bought a field and the Cave of Machpelah (Gen. 23:8 f.).

Ephron (place) 1. Mountain on north border of Judah (Josh. 15:9).

2. City taken by Ahijah from Jeroboam (2 Chr. 13:19).

Epicureans (ĕp-ĭ-kū-rē′ăns) a group of philosophers who derived their name from Epicurus (341–271 B.C.), of Attic descent, whose "Garden" at Athens rivaled in popularity the "Porch" and the "Academy." The doctrines of Epicurus found wide acceptance in Asia Minor

and Alexandria, and they gained a brilliant advocate at Rome in Lucretius (95–50 B.C.). The object of Epicurus was to find in philosophy a practical guide to happiness. True pleasure and not absolute truth was the end at which he aimed; experience and not reason the test on which he relied. It is obvious that a system thus framed would degenerate by a natural descent into mere materialism; and in this form Epicureanism was the popular philosophy at the beginning of the Christian era (cf. Diogenes Laertius X.5,9). When Paul addressed "Epicureans and Stoics" (Acts 17:18) at Athens, the philosophy of life was practically reduced to the teaching of those two antagonistic schools. The Epicureans would naturally mock at the doctrine of the resurrection.

R.L.R.

epistle the epistle as a means of communication is first mentioned in OT history in connection with David's writing to Joab (2 Sam. 11:14) concerning Uriah, by whom the letter was sent and which must obviously have been sealed with the king's seal. The material used for the impression of the seal was probably the "clay" of Job 38:14. Written communications became more frequent in later history. The king of Syria sent a letter to the king of Israel (2 K. 5:5, 6). Elijah the prophet sent a writing to Jehoram (2 Chr. 21:12). The books of Ezra and Nehemiah contain or refer to many such documents (Ezra 4:6, 7, 11, 5:6, 7:11; Neh. 2:7, 9, 6:5). The epistles of the NT in their outward form are such as to reproduce with some accuracy the customary Greek and Roman style (the term "epistle," as opposed to "letter," being almost a technical one for the form employed. Among NT documents perhaps Philemon should be considered a letter as opposed to the more formal epistle). They begin (the Epistle to the Hebrews and 1 John excepted) with the name of the writer and of those to whom the epistle is addressed. Then follows the formula of salutation. Then the letter itself begins, in the first person, the singular and plural being used indiscriminately. When the substance of the letter has been completed, the individual messages follow, the former being in Paul's case dictated to an amanuensis (cf. Rom. 16:22; 1 Cor. 16:21). The scribe having done his work, Paul takes up the pen or reed and adds, in his own large characters (Gal. 6:11), the authenticating autograph (cf. 2 Thess. 3:17).

R.L.R.

Er (ûr) 1. Firstborn of Judah, slain by God for his wickedness (Gen. 38:3–7; Num. 26:19).

2. A Judahite (1 Chr. 4:21).

3. An ancestor of Jesus (Lk. 3:28).

Eran (ē'răn) grandson of Ephraim (Num. 26:36); from him come the Eranites (Num. 26:36).

Erastus (ē-răs'tŭs) name occurring three times of companions of Paul: (1) a helper of Paul sent with Timothy from Asia to Macedonia (Acts 19:22), (2) another (probably the same), 2 Tim. 4:20, (3) treasurer of Corinth who saluted Roman Christians (Rom. 16:23).

Erech (ē'rĕk) city founded by Nimrod (Gen. 10:10), an early important Sumerian, and later Babylonian city, excavated by the Germans in 1912, 1928, 1954–59; it is now called Warka near the Euphrates, 160 miles south of Baghdad.

Eri (ē'rī) son of Gad (Gen. 46:16).

Esaias NT (KJV) form of **Isaiah**.

Esarhaddon (ē'sēr-hăd'ŏn) one of the greatest kings of Assyria. Son of Sennacherib and father of Ashurbanipal (2 K. 19:37; Isa. 37:38), 681–69 B.C. Little is known of him up to the obscure circumstances of his father's death and his accession to the throne. Much of his reign was consumed in a conquest of Egypt. He spread his power far by diplomacy and was one of the great builders of Babylon. He died while on his way to put down a rebellion in Egypt.

Esau (ē'saw) the eldest son of Isaac and twin brother of Jacob. The singular appearance of the child at birth originated the name "hairy" (Gen. 25:25). Remarkable also is the struggling together of the twins even in the womb (25:22). Esau's robust frame and "rough" aspect were the types of a wild and daring nature. The peculiarities of his character soon began to develop; being a "son of the desert," he delighted to roam free and was impatient of the restraints of civilized or settled life. His old father, by a caprice of affection not uncommon, loved his willful, vagrant boy; and, his keen relish for savory food being gratified by Esau's venison, he liked him all the better for his skill in hunting (25:28). An event occurred which exhibited the reckless, profane character of Esau on the one hand and the selfish, grasping nature of his brother on the other. There is something revolting in this whole transaction. Jacob took advantage of his brother's distress to rob him of that which was dear as life itself to an Eastern patriarch. Esau married at the age of forty, and contrary to the wish of his parents. His wives were both Canaanites; and they "were bitterness of spirit unto Isaac and Rebekah" (Gen. 26:34–35). Another episode is still more painful. Jacob, through the craftiness of his mother, is again successful and se-

cures irrevocably the covenant blessing. Esau vowed vengeance. But he knew not a mother's watchful care. By a characteristic piece of domestic policy Rebekah succeeded both in exciting Isaac's anger against Esau and obtaining his consent to Jacob's departure. When Esau heard that his father had commanded Jacob to take a wife of the daughters of his kinsman Laban, he also resolved to try whether by a new alliance he could propitiate his parents. He accordingly married his cousin Mahalath, the daughter of Ishmael (28:8, 9). This marriage appeared to have brought him into connection with the Ishmaelitish tribes beyond the valley of Arabah. He soon afterward established himself in Mount Seir, still retaining, however, some interest in his father's property in Southern Palestine. He was residing in Mount Seir when Jacob returned from Padan-aram and had then become so rich and powerful that the impressions of his brother's early offenses seem to have been almost completely effaced. The forgiveness of Jacob by Esau seems apparent from Gen. 33:1–16. It does not appear that the brothers met again until the death of their father about twenty years later. They united in burying Isaac's body in the Cave of Machpelah. Of Esau's subsequent history nothing is known; for that of his descendants, see **Edom** and **Edomites**.   R.L.R.

Esdraelon (ĕs'drā-ē'lŏn) the great plain extending across Central Palestine from the Mediterranean to the Jordan, separating the mountain ranges of Carmel and Samaria from those of Galilee. This name is merely the Greek form of the Hebrew word **Jezreel**. It occurs in this exact form only twice in the Apocrypha. In the OT the plain is called the "valley of Jezreel"; by Josephus and the Apocrypha "the great plain." The name is derived from the old royal city of Jezreel, which occupied a commanding site near the eastern extremity of the plain on a spur of Mount Gilboa. The western section of Esdraelon is properly the plain of Accho, or 'Akka. The main body of the plain is a triangle. Its base on the east extends from Jenin (the ancient En-gannim) to the foot of the hills below Nazareth and is about fifteen miles long; the north side, formed by the hills of Galilee, is about twelve miles long; and the south side, formed by the Samaria range, is about eighteen miles. The apex on the west is a narrow pass opening into the plain of 'Akka. From the base of this triangular plain three branches stretch out eastward, like fingers from a hand, divided by two bleak, gray ridges—one bearing the familiar name of Mount Gilboa; the other called by natives Jebel ed-Duhy. The central

Esek

branch is the richest and most celebrated, as it is the valley of Jezreel proper—the battlefield on which Gideon triumphed and Saul and Jonathan were overthrown (Judg. 7:1 ff.; 1 Sam. 29-31). For other references, see 2 Chr. 35: 20-24; Zech. 12:11; where Megiddo is a reference to a city overlooking the same plain.

R.L.R.

Esek (ē'sĕk) Isaac's well in valley of Gerar (Gen. 26:20).

Eshan (ē'shăn) city near Hebron in Judah (Josh. 15:52).

Esh-baal (ĕsh'bā'ăl) Saul's fourth son, same as Ishbosheth (1 Chr. 8:33, 9:36; 2 Sam. 2:8, 10, 12).

Eshban (ĕsh'băn) a Horite descendant of Seir (Gen. 36:26; 1 Chr. 1:41).

Eshcol (ĕsh'kŏl) 1. An Amorite companion of Abram in rescue of Lot (Gen. 14:13, 24).

2. Valley near Hebron where spies found large cluster of grapes (Num. 13:23 f.).

Eshean (ĕsh'ē-ăn) KJV form of **Eshan** (Josh. 15:52).

Eshek (ē'shĕk) a descendant of Saul (1 Chr. 8:38 ff.).

Eshtaol (ĕsh'tā-ŏl) town in Shephelah of Judah (Josh. 15:33), given to Dan (Josh. 19:41). It was the boyhood home and burial place of Samson (Judg. 13:25, 16:31, 18:2-12).

Eshtemoa (ĕsh'tē-mō-à) or **Eshtemoh** a town in mountains of Judah (Josh. 15:50) given to the priests (21:14; 1 Chr. 6:57) and frequented by David (1 Sam. 30:28). Now es-Semu'a seven miles south of Hebron.

Eshtemoa 1. A descendant of Caleb (1 Chr. 4:17).

2. A Maacathite (1 Chr. 4:19).

Eshton (ĕsh'tŏn) a Judahite (1 Chr. 4:11 f.).

Esli (ĕs'lī) an ancestor of Jesus (Lk. 3:25).

Esrom (Mt. 1:3) see **Hezrom**

Essenes (ĕs'ēns) a sect of the Jews in the time of Christ, comparable to the Pharisees and the Sadducees. They are not mentioned in the NT by name. Before the discovery of the Dead Sea Scrolls our main sources for a study of the Essenes were descriptions by Josephus (*War* II.viii.2-13), the elder Pliny (*Nat. Hist.* V.xv.73), Philo (*Hypothetica* 11.1-18 and *Good Men Are Free* 12-13), and Hippolytus (*Philosophumena* 9.4). Though the Scrolls do not mention the Essenes by name, the comparable literature seems to prove that the community at 'Ain Feshkha and Khirbet Qumran near the north end of the Dead Sea were Essenes. The Essenes were separatists who lived in isolated community groups, avoiding the temple service, and were mostly unmarried, filling their number by initiates (after a three-year

probation period) and adoption of children. They were close students of the Scriptures, as evidenced by numerous copies of OT MSS and other literature left behind. Since the discovery of these sources in the 1940s there has been much discussion of the relationship between this group and the early church at Jerusalem. It has been conjectured that John the Baptist may have been reared by such a group. Generally it is admitted that, while there are some likenesses between Qumran and Jerusalem, there were just as many serious differences, and the likelihood of direct borrowings is remote.

Esther (ĕs'tẽr) the Persian name of Hadassah, daughter of Abihail the son of Shimei, the son of Kish, a Benjaminite (Est. 2:5-7). Esther was a beautiful Jewish maiden, whose ancestor Kish had been among the captives led away from Jerusalem by Nebuchadnezzer when Jehoiachin was taken captive. She was an orphan and had been brought up by her cousin Mordecai, who had an office in the household of Ahasuerus king of Persia and dwelt at "Shushan the palace." When Vashti was dismissed from being queen and all the fairest virgins of the kingdom had been assembled at Shushan for the king to make choice of her successor from among them, the choice fell upon Esther. The king was not aware, however, of her race and parentage; and so, on the representation of Haman the Agagite that the Jews scattered through his empire were a pernicious race, he gave him full power and authority to kill them all, young and old, women and children, and take possession of all their property. The means taken by Esther to avert this great calamity from her people and her kindred are fully related in the book of Esther. History is wholly silent both about Vashti and Esther. Herodotus happens to mention one of Xerxes' wives; Scripture mentions only two, if indeed either of them was a wife at all. It seems natural to conclude that Esther, a captive and one of the harem, was not of the highest rank of wives, but that a special honor with the name of queen may have been given to her, as to Vashti before her, as the favorite concubine or inferior wife. Offspring of neither, however, would have succeeded to the Persian throne. R.L.R.

Esther, Book of one of the latest of the canonical books of Scripture, having been written late in the reign of Xerxes or early in that of his son Artaxerxes Longimanus. The author is not known but may very probably have been Mordecai himself. Those who ascribe it to Ezra or the men of the Great Synagogue may have merely meant that Ezra edited and added it to the canon of Scripture, which he probably did.

102

The book of Esther and translations from it appear in a form different in the LXX from that in the Hebrew Bible. The canonical Esther is placed among the Hagiographa by the Jews and in that first portion called "the five rolls." It is sometimes emphatically called *Megillah* ("roll"), without other distinction, and it is read through by the Jews in their synagogues at the feast of Purim. A peculiarity of this book is that the name of God does not occur in it. It was always reckoned in the Jewish canon and is named or implied in almost every enumeration of the books composing it, from Josephus' time. Jerome mentions it by name, as do Augustine, Origen, and many others. The style of writing is remarkably chaste and simple. It does not in the least savor of romance. The Hebrew is very like that of Ezra and parts of the Chronicles: generally pure, but mixed with some words of Persian origin and some of Chaldaic affinity. In short, it is just what one would expect to find in a work of the age to which the book of Esther professes to belong. As regards the LXX version of the book, it consists of the canonical Esther with various interpolations prefixed, interspersed, and added at the close. Though the interpolations of the Greek copy are thus manifest, they make a consistent and intelligible story. But the apocryphal additions as they are inserted in some editions of the Latin Vulg., and in the English Bible, are incomprehensible. The first extrabiblical reference to Mordecai, a recently found cuneiform text, supports the claim to historicity.   R.L.R.

Etam (ē'tăm) 1. A village of unknown location in Simeon in the Negeb (1 Chr. 4:32; cf. Josh. 19:7).

2. A city of Judah in hill country of Bethlehem, named in LXX of Josh. 15:59a and also probably in 1 Chr. 4:3. It was fortified by Rehoboam (2 Chr. 11:6); according to later legend Solomon had a retreat here. Modern Khirbet el-Khokh overlooking 'Ain 'Atan (springs: "Pools of Solomon") is the site.

Etam, the Rock a cliff or crag in the story of Samson (Judg. 15:8, 11; cf. Judg. 15:9, 14, 17, 19; 2 Chr. 11:6).

Etham (ē'thăm) first stopping place after Succoth for Exodus (Ex. 13:20; Num. 33:6–8). See **Exodus**

Ethan (ē'thăn) 1. Grandson of Judah (1 Chr. 2:6, 8).

2. Ethan the Ezrahite, a man of great wisdom in Solomon's time (1 K. 4:31; in title of Ps. 89).

3. A Levite, ancestor of Asaph the singer (1 Chr. 6:42).

4. Son of Kish (1 Chr. 6:44).

Ethanim see **months**

Ethbaal (ĕth'bā'ăl) king of Sidon and father of Jezebel (1 K. 16:31).

Ether (ē'thĕr) 1. A town in the Shephelah of Simeon (Josh. 19:7).

2. A town of the Shephelah of Judah (Josh. 15:42).

Ethiopia (ē'thĭ-ō'pĭ-à) [Heb. *kush* > "Cush"] a country lying to the south of Egypt and including in its most extensive sense the modern Nubia, the Sudan, and at least the northern part of modern Ethiopia or Abyssinia. Cush was a son of Ham (Gen. 10:6–8; 1 Chr. 1:8–10). Proverbially the Ethiopian was dark-skinned (Jer. 13:23), and the Gr. *aithiops* means "dark-faced." However, the monuments show Semitic and Caucasian types among them. Numerous references to its commerce and contacts with Israel occur in the OT (Num. 12:1; 2 K. 19:9; 2 Chr. 12:3, 14:9–13, 16:7–9, 21:16; Job 28:19; Isa. 37:9). Because of its opposing Israel its doom was predicted (Isa. 11:11, 18:1 ff.; Jer. 46:9; Ezek. 29:10; Nah. 3:9). In the NT a eunuch, perhaps a proselyte, from Ethiopia in the service of its queen **Candace** came to Jerusalem to worship and on the return trip was converted by the preaching of the evangelist Philip (Acts 8:26–40).

Ethiopian properly "Cushite" (Jer. 13:23) of Zerah (2 Chr. 14:9) and Ebed-melech (Jer. 38:7).

Ethiopian eunuch Queen Candace's treasurer (probably a proselyte, and cf. Deut. 23:1) who had been to Jerusalem worshiping and was converted by the evangelist Philip (Acts 8:26–39).

Ethiopian woman a wife of Moses (Num. 12:1).

Ethnan (ĕth'năn) son of Helah, wife of Asher (1 Chr. 4:7).

Ethni (ĕth'nī) a Gershonite Levite (1 Chr. 6:41).

Eubulus (ū-bū'lŭs) a Christian at Rome (2 Tim. 4:21).

Eunice (ū'nĭs, ū-nī'sē) mother of Timothy; a Jewess who had married a Greek (Acts 16:1; 2 Tim. 1:5).

eunuch (ū'nŭk) sometimes rendered "officer," "captain," or "chamberlain" (from the Greek word for "emasculate"), usually a castrated male human, used as attendant for women's quarters in palaces. The practice of mutilating captives (Herodotus 3:49, 6:32) seems to have been common, and such people put in places of trust often became influential (2 K. 8:6, 9:32, 23:11, 25:19; Isa. 56:3 f.; Jer. 29:2, 34:19, 38:7, 41:16, 52:25). The law of Moses indicated God's displeasure with such practices by forbidding such a person to come into the sanctuary. The passage in Mt. 19:12 about those "who made themselves eunuchs for the kingdom's sake" probably refers to sublimation rather than being physical.

Euodias (ū-ō′dĭ-ås), properly **Euodia** a Christian woman at Philippi (Phil. 4:2).

Euphrates (ū-frā′tēz) the largest, the longest, and most important river of Western Asia. It is mentioned as the first of the four rivers running out of the Garden of Eden (Gen. 2:14). It rises from two sources in the Armenian mountains. These join forming a stream 120 yards wide above Malatiya. It flows south past Northern Syria and then continues south to join the Tigris before flowing into the Persian Gulf. Its entire course is some 1780 miles of which more than two-thirds is navigable. The river overflows its banks in May from the snows in the mountains. Called "the Great River," it was given as the northern boundary of covenant territory promised to Abraham and realized during the reigns of David and Solomon (Gen. 15:18; Deut. 1:7; Josh. 1:4; 1 Chr. 18:3; 2 Sam. 8:3–8; 1 K. 4:21).

Euroclydon (ū-rŏk′lĭ-dŏn) the fierce northeastern wind which struck Paul's ship south of Crete and blew it off course (Acts 27:14). RSV Euraquilo.

Eutychus (ū′tĭ-kŭs) a youth at Troas (Acts 20:9) who fell asleep and fell down from a third story window while Paul preached.

evangelist by derivation a noun formed by the agent suffix added to the verb root for "tell the good news." Thus it is the equivalent of "preacher" or "minister" of the word (1 Thess. 3:2). It is rare in classical Greek but has uses such as of the one who announced the oracles at Rhodes (CIG 12.1.675). It occurs in the NT only of Philip (Acts 21:8), of Timothy at Ephesus (2 Tim. 4:5), and of the Christian ministers (along with apostles, prophets, pastors, and teachers) who were miraculously endowed for edifying the church (Eph. 4:11). The verb form of the root is, of course, quite common. The question as to whether the word describes an "official" or is merely indicative of an activity is difficult. There is some indication in Timothy's case of formal ordination probably following a divine (prophetic) call (1 Tim. 1:18), which consisted of a setting apart through the laying on of hands (1 Tim. 4:14; 2 Tim. 1:6; cf. Acts 13:3). Meetings were probably informal with anyone permitted to speak according to his ability and impulse (cf. the situation in 1 Cor. 14). Thus the difference between the use of evangelist as a functional term and its use as an official as in Eph. 4:11 was that of a public declaration and setting

apart with the intention of making the work a full-time work to which one would give himself "wholly" (1 Tim. 4:15). Notice should be taken that an evangelist such as Timothy working at Ephesus is to be distinguished from the overseeing class of church officials called **elders, bishops,** or **pastors.** The elders or bishops (Acts 20:17, 28) were pastors or shepherds of the flocks. In no passage of their qualifications and work are elders said to be evangelists and to preach the Gospel as such. The modern practice of considering elders or bishops (as in 1 Tim. 3:1 ff.) as the NT equivalent of the modern local preacher or pastor is not correct. There is also no evidence for the frequent assertion that evangelist implied a traveling rather than a "located" preacher. In the early church the term "missionary" (Acts 14:14; Rom. 16:7) designated that group.　　　　　J.W.R.

Eve (ēv) the first woman, formed by God from Adam's side (Gen. 2:21–23), designated "woman" [fem. of *ish* = man] because she was taken out of man (vs. 23).

Evi (ē′vī) one of five kings of Midian slain by Israelites (Num. 31:8; Josh. 13:21).

Evil-merodach (ē′vĭl-mē-rō′dăk) king of Babylon, son and successor of Nebuchadnezzar, 562–60 B.C. (2 K. 25:27).

evil spirits see **demons**

excommunication the exclusion of a member of a religious group as punishment for immoral life or doctrinal error. The term is a late Latin term and does not occur in the Bible. "Cut off from" (Ex. 12:15, 19; Lev. 17:4, 9; Num. 19:20) was the common OT expression for it, while in the NT "withdraw yourselves from" (2 Thess. 3:6), "refuse" (Tit. 3:10), or "deliver to Satan" (1 Tim. 1:20) is usual. The later Jewish rabbinical practices developed an elaborate system of punishments not mentioned in the Law, but they appealed to the precedent of the Law as the basis of it (Ezra 7:26, 10:8; Neh. 13:25). For a NT reference, compare the threat to put out of the synagogue (Jn. 9:22). Jesus himself laid the basis for such discipline in the church in Mt. 18:15, 18. Paul claimed disciplinary right over his converts (2 Cor. 1:23, 13:10) and commanded excommunication in certain cases (1 Cor. 5:11; Tit. 3:10). Other pertinent references will be found in Rom. 16:17; 2 Tim. 3:1–5; 2 Jn. 10; 3 Jn. 10; Rev. 2:20; and (as some think) Gal. 1:8, 9 and 1 Cor. 16:22 ("Let him be anathema"). It is emphasized that the action is for the good of the offender in the hope that it will bring repentance (1 Cor. 5:5) and for the good of the church to protect its influence and avoid contamination (1 Cor. 5:6). Repentance, of course, brings restitution, an instance of which is found in 2 Cor. 2.

executioner the Hebrew word describes both one who inflicts the sentence of capital punishment and the more general sense of bodyguard of a monarch (Gen. 37:36; 1 K. 2:25, 34). The word in Mk. 6:27 is a Latin loanword for spy or scout but used of bodyguard.

exile see **captivity**

Exodus (ĕks'ō-dŭs) [Gr. = a going out] the event which marked the end of the Israelite sojourn in Egypt and the birth of Israel as a nation.

1. *Pre-Exodus Events.* The location of the children of Israel in Egypt came about voluntarily as a result of Jacob and his sons going to Egypt for food and to be reunited with Joseph, who had been sold and carried there. They had been favored by the friendly pharaoh and placed in Goshen, a region in the Nile delta. Later another pharaoh arose "who knew not Joseph," and he, fearing the growing number of Israel, oppressed them and sought to limit their number by destroying the male children. Among those saved was the child Moses, who was rescued and adopted by the daughter of Pharaoh, being reared in the faith of his people by his mother as a nurse. Later Moses cast his lot with his people and was commissioned by God to lead them out of Egypt. When Pharaoh resisted, he was judged by a series of ten plagues, following which Israel went out of the land and Pharaoh, who pursued them, perished with his host in the sea.

2. *Date of the Exodus.* First Kings 6:1 states that Solomon began to build the temple in the 480th year "after the children of Israel were come out of the land of Egypt." Taken literally this would date the Exodus about 1441 B.C. Support for this early date is also seen by some scholars in inscriptional data of Semites engaged in building in the reigns of the pharaohs contemporary with that date (Thutmose III) and from the Amarna Letters (about 1400 B.C.), where Canaanite rulers appeal for Pharaoh's help against the Habiru. There are, however, opposing factors. The main one is that N. Glueck's investigations in Transjordan indicate that there was a gap covering 1900–1300 B.C. in the occupation of the Transjordan cities which would conflict with the Biblical account of the opposition of Og and Sihon (Num. 21:21 ff.). Also according to some archaeologists of West Jordan (against J. B. E. Garstang) evidence of destruction of such cities as Jericho and Hazor indicates a thirteenth- rather than a fifteenth-century date. Glueck's conclusions have been tempered somewhat in more recent reports. The date in 1 K. 6:1 may have been textually altered (since there are varying dates in some sources), or the number may be taken as a round number for twelve generations, each of which was counted as forty years when in actuality many were less. At present the question seems an open one.

3. *The Journey.* The journey of Israel was led by God himself with a cloud by day and a pillar of fire by night. The route lay from Rameses in Goshen to Succoth, to Etham, whence they turned back and camped before Pi-hahiroth, and then to the Red Sea. They crossed on dry land by the dividing of the waters. From the Red Sea the journey was toward Mount Sinai, passing Marah, Elim, and Rephidim. God had directed them through this wilderness rather than the more direct route to Palestine along the coast. After Sinai and a journey to Kadesh-barnea the people were turned back into the wilderness as punishment for the faint heart at the report of the spies (Num. 13–14). The Exodus was to be completed after a total of forty years in the wilderness by the conquest under Joshua.

Exodus, Book of second book of the OT named (= "going out") from the events which make up its main content. The book is naturally divided into three parts: (1) the Egyptian Period (1:1–12:36), relating the development of the oppression, the birth and mission of Moses, the plagues, and the Exodus; (2) the Approach to Sinai (12:37–19:1), relating the Song of Moses and Miriam, the trip by Marah, where Moses sweetened the waters, the supply of quails and manna, and the attack of Amalek; (3) the Stay at Sinai (19:2–40:38), giving the transmission of the Law, directions for building the tabernacle and its furniture, with the story of its being made and set up. Sundry laws and directions, some more fully given in Leviticus, Numbers, and Deuteronomy, are related.

exorcist (ĕk'sôr-cĭst) one who expells demons through magic or incantations. It was practiced widely among the heathens, and as evidenced by both Acts 19:13 and modern discoveries was common among Jews. If actually accomplished, it was probably done by the help of Satan (cf. Mt. 12:27). Jesus cast out demons and bestowed this power upon the apostles (Mt. 10:8) and the Seventy (Lk. 10:17–19), and it was exercised by some believers (Mk. 16:17), though never called "exorcism."

expiation see **sacrifice**

Ezbai (ĕz'bā-ī) one of David's heroes (1 Chr. 11:37).

Ezbon (ĕz'bŏn) 1. A Gadite (Gen. 46:16).

2. A Benjaminite (1 Chr. 7:7).

Ezekiel (ē-zēk'yĕl) the great Hebrew prophet of the Jewish exile to Babylon, as well as the book which bears his name. With Ezra, Ezekiel certainly ranks as one of the two leaders who shaped the Judaism of later times. *Ezekiel's Life.* Little is known personally of the prophet. He was the son of a priest, Buzi, and was reared and educated to be a priest in the shadow of the temple itself. When Nebuchadnezzar captured Jehoiachin (598 B.C.), Ezekiel was among those carried into exile on the banks of the river Chebar, a stream of Babylon. Here he saw a great vision and received a call to the prophetic office (Ezek. 1:1–3:15). It is known that he was married (24:18) and had a house (8:1), but he lost his wife by a tragic stroke. He lived in high esteem by the exiles and their leaders (8:1, 11:25, 14:1, 20:1). There is no record that he returned to Jerusalem, but his ministry was directed to that community until the news of the fall of the city in 586 B.C. (to ch. 33). The last date mentioned is the twenty-seventh year of the Captivity so that the twenty-two years of his ministry covered the period when Daniel was becoming famous (Ezek. 14:14, 28:3). After the destruction of Jerusalem, his message became one of hope and promise of the future restoration and glory of the land where God was. *The Book of Ezekiel* is divided into two great parts: (1) chs. 1–24, before the destruction of Jerusalem, combined with a sevenfold parenthetical denunciation of foreign nations contained in chs. 25–33, and (2) the prophecies after the destruction of Jerusalem (chs. 34–48).

Ezel (ē'zĕl) stone near Saul's house where David and Jonathan parted (1 Sam. 20:19).

Ezem (ē'zĕm) a town of Simeon (1 Chr. 4:29).

Ezer (ē'zêr) 1. Son of Seir the Horite (Gen. 36:21).

2. Son of Ephraim slain by Gathites while on a cattle raid (1 Chr. 7:21).

3. A Judahite, son of Hur (1 Chr. 4:4).

4. An ally of David at Ziklag (1 Chr. 12:9).

5. Worker on walls of Jerusalem under Nehemiah (Neh. 3:19).

6. A singer who also worked on the walls (Neh. 12:42).

Ezion-geber or **gaber** (ē'zǐ-ŏn-gē'bêr) a port and foundry city located near Elath on Gulf of Aqaba. It was the last station of the Israelites before the wilderness of Zin (Num. 33:35 f.; Deut. 2:8). Solomon and Jehoshaphat had navies based there (1 K. 9:26, 22:48; 2 Chr. 8:17). Nelson Glueck's excavations have revealed extensive foundry and smelter ruins at the city (*The Other Side of the Jordan* [1940], pp. 89 ff.).

Eznite, the (ĕz'nīt) title given to **Adino** (2 Sam. 23:8) in KSV.

Ezra (ĕz'rà) 1. A returning priestly exile (Neh. 12:1).

2. A man of Judah in the obscure genealogy of 1 Chr. 4:17.

3. The famous scribe and priest, one of the principal actors in the return of the Jews from exile, whose memoirs (cf. Ezra 7:1, 8:15) are related in the book of Ezra and (as some think) of Nehemiah. He is also generally credited with authorship of the books of Chronicles. Ezra's genealogy is given in Ezra 7:1–5. He received permission from Artaxerxes (presumably Artaxerxes Longimanus, king of Persia) in 458 B.C. and led an expedition from Babylon (Ezra 7:1–10), armed with a decree of the king (7:12–26). The temple was rebuilt and the Passover reinstituted (3:1–6:22), though the work was hindered by adversaries. Ezra heard that many Jews had married foreign wives, contrary to the Law, and took decisive steps to correct this (chs. 9–10). The Law was read to the people (Neh. 8), and there followed pledges of dedication to the Lord and to the observance of his laws (9:38–10:39). In Jewish tradition Ezra is reckoned as a monumental figure, second only to Moses. He is credited almost personally with the revival of Judaism, with the institution of the "Great Synagogue," with which he worked to settle the Jewish canon and correct and re-edit the entire OT, changing the Hebrew script, and spread abroad the later synagogue worship. For all of this there is no documentation, but we cannot doubt that his work and influence must have been great to have made so deep an impression on later generations of his people.

Ezra, Book of a book so-called from the principal character mentioned and especially from the autobiographical character of chs. 7–10. It is generally thought that Ezra is a continuation of Chronicles and that Chronicles-Ezra-Nehemiah may have formed one great work. For the theory that this sequence of narrative is interconnected with the book of Daniel and that 2 Chr. 25–26 and Ezra 1 were written by Daniel and supplement parts of the book of Daniel, see the article on Ezra in the earlier Smith's *Bible Dictionary*. The book is divided into two parts: (1) chs. 1–6, the story of Zerubbabel's expedition to Jerusalem and the rebuilding of the temple; and (2) chs. 7–10, Ezra's expedition and the institution of extensive reforms, especially in the area of mixed marriages. The period covered by the book is eighty years from the first of Cyrus' reign (536 B.C.) to the eighth of Artaxerxes' reign (456 B.C.), though the actual events recorded are at long intervals one from the other. The text in places has suffered from faulty transcription. A large section (4:8–6:18) and the letter of the king in 7:12–26 are written in Aramaic.

Ezrahite (ĕz'rà-hīt) title of Ethan (1 K. 4:31; Ps. 89, title) and Heman (Ps. 88, title). 1 Chr. 2:6 says they were sons of Zerah, of which Ezrahite may be a gentilic form.

Ezri (ĕz'rī) David's overseer of lands (1 Chr. 27:26).

F

fable according to Neander's definition a fable is a story in which "qualities or acts of a higher class of beings may be attributed to a lower (e.g., those of men to brutes)." The Bible contains two examples: (1) the fable of the trees choosing a bramble as king (Judg. 9:8–15) (2) the cedars of Lebanon and the thistle (2 K. 14:9). "Fable" as the translation of *muthos* ("myth") in 1 and 2 Timothy, Titus, and 2 Peter is not the same. Their nature is unknown.

Fair Havens a harbor on the south side of the island of Crete, where Paul's ship touched on her way to Rome (Acts 27:8–12). The captain decided to try for Phoenix, hoping for a better place to winter.

fairs word in KJV in Ezek. 27:12, 14, 16, 19, 27, rendered more accurately as "wares" in other translations.

faith in the Biblical or religious sense means belief in the reality of the supernatural world —God in particular—and trust in that ultimate reality and his revelation for salvation. The word is frequently used in the Scriptures of trust or belief of people in each other. "Faith," so the author of Hebrews says, "is the substance (substantiation) of things hoped for, the evidence (proof or demonstration) of things not seen" (Heb. 11:1). Faith goes beyond to accept things unknown by sight, for where sight is, faith no longer exists (1 Pet. 1:8; Jn. 20:29). There is some difference in the emphasis of the Hebrew and Greek originals for faith. The Heb. *amun* has a root meaning of stability or steadfastness and hence yields the concept of holding firm or passing every test in confidence of the ultimate reward of God, that is, faithfulness. This aspect is illustrated in the context of Heb. 10:32–12:13. The Gr. *pistis*, on the other hand, more properly signifies subjective trust or confidence.

The place of faith in the scheme of redemp-

tion may be briefly summarized: God justifies men, that is, declares them righteous (Rom. 8:33). The spirit of that justification is the death of Christ (Isa. 53:11; Rom. 5:19). Yet on man's part faith is "imputed for righteousness" and is thus the means or instrument (rather than human works or righteousness) of salvation (Rom. 5:1). In this composite sense salvation is by "faith only" ("There is none other name given under heaven in which we must be saved," Acts 4:12). But when the process of salvation is viewed analytically and we inquire what faith in Jesus demands, faith is only one of the requirements: "We are not justified by faith only but by works" (James 2:24). So Jesus said, "He that believeth and is baptized shall be saved" (Mk. 16:16). Faith is used both subjectively (trust) and objectively (the faith, i.e., what is believed). So Gal. 1:23; 2 Tim. 4:7.

fallow deer one of three types of deer found in Palestine in Biblical times (with red and roe), generally thought to be referred to in Deut. 14:5 and 1 K. 4:23. RSV, though, has **roebuck.**

famine a condition of scarcity of food or provisions in varying degrees. Rainfall in Palestine is heavy in November and December and marginal at other times. If the heavy rains fail, the sustenance of the people is cut off in the parching drought of harvest-time when the country is almost devoid of moisture (Hag. 1:10–11). There were numerous springs but not enough for extensive irrigation. In Egypt where fertility is dependent on the annual overflow of the Nile, famine came when that flow failed to occur. But famines came not only through drought but also were due to swarms of locusts (Amos 4:9; Joel 1:4 ff.) or warfare (Isa. 1:7, 3:1). Among the well-known famines might be mentioned those of Abram's time (Gen.

farthing

12:10), of Joseph (Gen. 41:27, 54), of Ruth (1:1), of David (2 Sam. 21:1), of Elijah (1 K. 18), of the Emperor Claudius (Acts 11:28).

farthing the KJV rendering of two money coins: (1) the *quadrans* (Mt. 5:26; Mk. 12:42) = two mites or one fourth a Roman *as*, roughly worth about two cents, and (2) the *assarion* (Mt. 10:29; Lk. 12:6), which also in NT was the equivalent of the Roman *as*.

fasting eating sparingly or abstaining from some foods for a period of time. The Hebrews used the expression "to afflict the soul" as a description of fasting (Lev. 16:29 ff., 23:27; Num. 30:13; Ps. 35:13). 1. *The Law.* Only one fast was appointed by the Law—that on the Day of Atonement (Lev. 16:29, 31; Jer. 36:6). There are, however, numerous instances of individual abstinence for various reasons such as penitence or mourning (2 Sam. 12:16–23), impending doom (1 K. 21:27), or in the hope of receiving revelations (Ex. 34:28; 1 Sam. 28:20; 1 K. 19:8). Fasting seems in such instances to be spontaneous and corresponds somewhat to natural loss of appetite under such circumstances. Public fasts were proclaimed for the people, for example, by the king (2 Chr. 20:3). Fasts might be of different lengths (1 Sam. 31:13).

2. *After the Exile.* Zech. 7:1–7 and 8:19 indicate that Jews after the Exile observed four annual fasts: in the fourth month (commemorating the breaking of the tables of the covenant by Moses, Ex. 32); of the fifth month (the return of the spies, temple burnt by Nebuchadnezzar); of the seventh month (sack of Jerusalem by Nebuchadnezzar), and of the tenth month (anniversary of Ezekiel and the Jews' receiving the news of the destruction of Jerusalem).

3. *In the NT.* References to fasting in the NT are to "the fast," that is, that of the Day of Atonement (Acts 27:9, indicating the time of the year), and to the weekly fasts of the Jews (Lk. 5:33, 18:12). We find in some of the teachings of Jesus (1) that fasting must not be for worldly show (Mt. 6:16–18), and (2) that in answer to a question as to why his disciples did not fast like John's, since such would have been an act of sorrow for his absence, it was out of place while he was present (Mt. 9:14–15; Mk. 2:18–20). In the early church fasting is mentioned as a religious act in connection with appointment of workers in the congregation (Acts 13:2–3, 14:23). Set fasts and ascetic practices which became a part of early Christian life are unauthorized and are even condemned in principle in Scripture (Col. 2:20–23; 1 Tim. 4:1–5). There is nothing to

indicate that fasting on serious occasions under voluntary agreement would not be acceptable. It certainly is in the spirit of the long history of the practice as seen in the Scriptures.

fat the pure fat around the organs as distinguished from that mixed with the lean meat in an animal to be sacrificed (Neh. 8:10), was forbidden as food, and was stored for burning as a sweet savor (Lev. 3:3, 9, 17, 7:3; Ex. 23:18). The ground of the prohibition was that it was the richest part of the animal and belonged to God (Lev. 3:16).

fat [i.e., vat, used in KJV (Joel 2:24, 3:13)] "wine-*fat*" for the vats, either upper or lower receptacle where the grape juice was trodden or into which it ran down and was collected.

father literally the male progenitor of a family. Besides this, the term has many uses. It is often used of ancestors (Dan. 5:2; Mt. 23:30), heads of tribes (Ex. 6:14), of "old men" or "seniors" (Acts 7:2, 22:1; 1 Jn. 2:13), of those responsible for a vocation (Gen. 4:20, "father of those who dwell in tents"), a title of respect (2 K. 2:12, 6:21), of those whose spiritual lineage is recognized, as of Abraham (Rom. 4:11), or of the Devil (Jn. 8:44). By a Hebraism "father of strength" equals "a very strong man." The term is a very frequent name for God. Under the Hebrew patriarchal system the father has great power, honor, and dignity (Gen. 9:25, 27:27 ff.; Ex. 20:12, 21:15–17).

fathom [arm stretch] a measure about six feet. See **weights and measures**

feasts see **festivals**

Felix, Antonius (fē'līks, ăn-tō'nĭ-ŭs) Roman procurator or governor of Judea, (A.D. 52–60), a freedman of Emperor Claudius, who appointed him procurator. He ruled ruthlessly, using the murdering Sicarii [dagger men], e.g., in the murder of Jonathan the high priest. Paul appeared before him and was kept for ransom two years (Acts 24:26, 27). He was replaced by Festus and was accused by the Jews but saved from the death sentence by his brother Pallas. His wife was Drusilla, daughter of Agrippa I, the former wife of Azizus king of Emesa.

fenced city a walled "city" as opposed to an unwalled "village." Due to frequent invasions most towns and cities were enclosed in walls, with additional towers or parapets (2 Chr. 32:5; Deut. 3:5; Jer. 31:38).

ferret a small animal of the weasel family. In Lev. 11:30 such an animal (considered unclean) may be meant, though some think a reptile such as a lizard is meant. RSV has gecko (weasel family), Syriac lizard.

fertile crescent modern name (coined by J. H.

Breasted, d. 1935) for the quarter-moon shape of land of the Middle East stretching from Egypt through Palestine, Syria, and down the Euphrates valley to Babylonia. The area in which most Biblical history occurred.

festivals religious occasions of gathering and feasting established by the Law. They were of several kinds: (1) those connected with the sabbath: the weekly sabbath (after the Captivity the people met in the synagogue), the feast of the seventh new moon or the Feast of the Trumpets (first day of seventh month, beginning of Jewish civil year), and the sabbatical year; (2) the three great historical festivals: Passover; the Feast of Pentecost, also called Feast of Weeks, of Wheat-Harvest, or of First-fruits; and the Feast of Tabernacles or Ingathering); and (3) the Day of Atonement. The three great historical feasts were holy convocations on which all work was to cease (Ex. 12:16; Lev. 16:29, 23:21, 24, 25, 36), and all males were to appear at the tabernacle or temple and make a freewill offering (Ex. 23:14–15; Neh. 8:9–12). After the Captivity the Feast of Purim (Est. 9:20–28) and the Feast of Dedication (1 Macc. 4:56; cf. Jn. 10:22) were added. See articles on individual feasts.

Festus, Porcius (fĕs'tŭs, pōr'sĭ-ŭs) successor of Felix as procurator or governor of Judea (Acts 24:27 [A.D. 60–62]). He was the occasion of Paul's appeal to Caesar by asking him to return to Jerusalem for inquiry. When Agrippa II sat with him to hear Paul's defense, he thought Paul mad. He died in Palestine and was replaced by Albinus.

fetters word translating several original words referring to chains or shackles made of brass or iron for retaining prisoners and usually put on the feet (Judg. 16:21; 2 Sam. 3:34; Ps. 105:18; Isa. 45:14; Mk. 5:4).

fever a rise in body temperature, symptomatic of various diseases. Various original words both Hebrew and Greek are so translated. Diseases which were prevalent and are indicated by the terms include undulant (Malta) fever, erysipelas, malaria, dysentery, and a consumptive "wasting" disease (Deut. 28:22; Lk. 4:38; Acts 28:8).

field any cultivated ground whether enclosed or simply marked off with a stone as a landmark (Deut. 19:14, 27:17; Job 24:2; Prov. 22:28), often remote from a house (Gen. 4:8, 24:63; Deut. 22:25). The absence of fences made the watching of fields necessary to prevent damage from straying cattle, fire, etc. (Ex. 22:5 f.; 2 Sam. 14:30).

fig, fig tree [Lat. *ficus caricus*] a well-known tree or the fruit from it found extensively in Palestine (Gen. 3:7; Deut. 8:8; Mt. 7:16). The fruit ripens in June. It was very important to the economy of Palestine. Jesus cursed a fig tree which gave promise of having fruit out of season but was barren (Mk. 11:13–14, 20–21; Mt. 21:18–21).

fir the true fir tree grows in Lebanon. The two Hebrew words so translated (Isa. 41:19, 60:13; and Ps. 104:17; Ezek. 27:5, 31:8) are thought by some, however, to refer to "cypress" or even "plane" tree.

fire fire had many uses both domestic and religious. In *domestic* uses it was for warmth (Jer. 36:22; Mk. 14:54) as well as cooking, and so houses were built with chimneys. No fire for cooking could be lit on the sabbath (Ex. 35:3). In *fields* fires were to be watched, and anyone carelessly damaging a neighbor was to make restitution (Ex. 22:6; cf. Judg. 15:4 f.). In *religious rites* fire was necessary for sacrifices (Gen. 8:20). It was kept burning continually on the altar after it was kindled from heaven (Lev. 6:9, 13, 9:24) and rekindled at the dedication of Solomon's temple (2 Chr. 7:1–3). In some ways fire seems to have been symbolic of God's presence and power (Ex. 3:2, 14:19). This was exhibited in his leading Israel by a pillar of fire at night (Ex. 13:21 f.; 14:24). It was also used in purification rites (Num. 31:23; Ps. 66:12; Isa. 43:2). Finally, punishment of fire was inflicted for some crimes (Lev. 20:14, 21:9), and in some cases bodies of executed persons were burned (Josh. 7:25; 2 K. 23:16).

firepan [also rendered "snuffdish" and "censer"] a bronze or gold vessel of the temple used for raking out and carrying coals from the altar (Ex. 27:3, 38:3; 1 K. 7:50). It is rendered snuffdish because it was used as a snuffer for carrying trimmed portions of lamp wicks (Ex. 25:38).

firkin (fûr'kĭn) liquid measure of about ten gallons (Jn. 2:6).

firmament (fĩr'mà-mĕnt) [Heb. *raqia*] the expanse of sky stretched above the earth dividing the waters above from those below (Gen. 1:6). The Hebrew word means to expand by beating; e.g., it is used of metals so expanded (Ex. 39:3; Num. 16:39; Jer. 10:9). The idea expressed is that of a solid substance such as a "floor" (Ex. 24:10; Ezek. 1:22–26) into which the stars might be said to be fixed or set (Gen. 1:14; cf. Isa. 34:4). In such cosmological statements Bible writers undoubtedly were describing things as they appeared to people of the day, very much as people often do today even in a scientific age (for example, "the sun sets").

firstborn the first child or offspring in a family or of an animal. Because God had spared the firstborn son of Israel in the Exodus, the eldest son was regarded as devoted to the Lord and was to be redeemed by an offering within a month of birth (Ex. 13:12–15, 22:29; Num. 8:17, 18:15 f.; Lev. 27:6). The right of primogeniture seems from early time to secure the priesthood within the family, as well as the fatherly blessing (Gen. 27:1–4, 48:8–22) and a special portion of the father's goods (Deut. 21:17). The firstborn male animal also belonged to the Lord and had to be redeemed or destroyed (Ex. 13:2, 12 f., 22:29 f., 34:19 f.).

firstfruits the first produce of grain or fruit belonged to the Lord and was to be offered in God's house (Ex. 22:29, 23:19, 34:26). In addition, at the Passover (Lev. 23:5 f.), Pentecost (Ex. 34:22; Lev. 23:15, 17), and Tabernacles (Ex. 23:16; Lev. 23:39) wave and loaf offerings of firstfruits were made as tokens of thanksgiving. Individual offerings of the same type were also established (Num. 15:19, 21; Deut. 26:2–11). In the NT different things are compared to firstfruits, especially in the sense of an initial product, promising a fuller harvest, e.g., Christ, firstfruit of the dead (1 Cor. 15:23), Christians of Achaia (1 Cor. 16:15). In James 1:18 the idea is probably that of spiritual dedication.

fish cold-blooded animals living in water and receiving their oxygen through gills. They were recognized as a great division of the living things created by God (Gen. 1:21, 28, cf. 9:2; Ex. 20:4; Deut. 4:18; 1 K. 4:33). The Mosaic law made fish devoid of fins and scales unclean (Lev. 11:9 f.). The Bible does not mention species by name, but those present in the Jordan and Sea of Galilee include the catfish, types of bream, carp, and chub. In the sea are found eels, sharks, rays, and lampreys. One NT word for fish really means a preserved or cooked fish (Jn. 21:9 f.).

flag vegetation growing about lakes or marshy places such as rushes or reeds (Gen. 41:2, 18; Job 8:11).

flagon a large vessel or bottle for wine originally a skin but later of pottery also (Isa. 22:24). The word is also mistakenly used to translate a word really meaning a cake of pressed raisins (2 Sam. 6:19).

flax a cultivated plant, the fibers from which are used for cloth. The plant itself is mentioned only twice (Ex. 9:31, destruction by the plague of hail, and Josh. 2:6, spies hid in flax stalks). Elsewhere the reference is to the spun fiber or finished cloth, linen (Judg. 15:14; Prov. 31:13; Isa. 19:9, 42:3; Jer. 13:1; Ezek. 40:3, 44:17–18; Hos. 2:5–9).

flea a small insect frequent in Palestine, used by David (1 Sam. 24:14, 26:20) of his insignificance.

flesh see **food**

flint a variety of quartz used by primitive man for instruments. It is employed as metaphor for hardness (Ps. 114:8; Isa. 50:7) and mentioned as the instrument of circumcision (Ex. 4:25; Josh. 5:2–3).

flood see **Noah**

floor see **pavement**

flour see **bread**

flowers see **Palestine, botany of**

flute or **pipe** musical instrument made of hollow reeds, wood, metal, or bones, generally avoided by the Hebrews because of its association with orgiastic rites. It occurs in Daniel (3:5, 7, 10, 15) of idolatrous worship.

flux KJV form for "dysentery" (Acts 28:8).

fly translation of two Hebrew words: (1) the *zebhubh* probably the common housefly (Eccl. 10:1; Isa. 7:18); (2) the *arieba*, which again may be the housefly or one of the species of stinging flies which irritated men and beasts (Ex. 8:21–31; Ps. 78:45, 105:31—the fourth plague). The larva of the fly, **worm,** is often mentioned (Isa. 14:11; Job 7:5). In some sections the god of flies, **Baalzebub,** was worshiped to ward off the insects.

food the diet of Biblical times was simpler than ours. It differed in the smaller amount of animal food included, substitution of milk for other liquids, the use of a variety of items in the same dish, and the variety of articles used with bread. Large amounts of bread were consumed, leading to the description of bread as the "staff" of life (Lev. 26:26; Ps. 105:16). "Corn" refers to grains such as wheat or barley, eaten at times in natural state (Lev. 23:14; Mt. 12:1), parched (Lev. 2:14), beaten and mixed with oil (Lev. 2:15), or made into soft cake or dough (Num. 15:20), which might be dipped into sour wine (Ruth 2:14) or eaten with meat and gravy (Judg. 6:19). Milk products were used abundantly, either fresh (Gen. 18:8) or sour (AV, butter, Gen. 18:8; Judg. 5:25). Fruits such as figs and grapes were common. Vegetables mentioned include lentils (Gen. 25:34), beans (2 Sam. 17:28), leeks, onion, and garlic (Num. 11:5). To these should be added spices, honey (1 Sam. 14:25), eggs (Isa. 10:14; Lk. 11:12), and oil used sparingly. Ritual prohibitions governed the use of blood (Gen. 9:4), fat (Lev. 3:9), and certain unclean fish, birds, and animals (Lev. 11:1 ff.). Locusts were at times consumed (Lev. 11:22). In addition to milk and wine water was drunk most frequently, and the Hebrews knew and used various intoxicating drinks.

footman a foot soldier in the army, as opposed to the infantry or charioteers and also a runner or bodyguard of the king (1 K. 14:27; 2 Chr. 12:10 f.).

footwashing an act of hospitality (Gen. 18:4, 19:2; Judg. 19:21) performed for guests, usually by servants or by wife of the host (Lk. 7:44; 1 Tim. 5:10). Christ washed the disciples' feet as an object lesson in humility (Jn. 13:4 ff.). Footwashing never had significance as a religious rite until so used in Augustine's time (A.D. 400, *Letters* LV.33).

forehead used literally as place of the woman's veil (Jer. 3:3; cf. Gen. 24:65; Rev. 17:5) or of Aaron's turban plate (Ex. 28:38). The "hard forehead" was a symbol of audacity or stubbornness (Ezek. 3:7–9). The foreheads of those spared punishment were marked (Ezek. 9:4; cf. Rev. 9:4).

forests areas of land covered with trees, a wood (1 Sam. 23:15 ff.; 2 Chr. 27:4); sometimes even an orchard (Eccl. 2:5; Song of S. 4:13). Palestine, though never extensively forested, had many wooded areas such as that of Ephraim (Josh. 17:15 ff.), of Bethel (2 K. 2:23 f.), of Hereth (1 Sam. 22:5), of Ziph (1 Sam. 23:15 ff.), etc.

fornication [Gr. *porneia*] the general word for sexual immorality or harlotry, including not only on the part of the unmarried (Gen. 38:24; Deut. 22:20–21), but also of the married (Hos. 2:2–4, LXX). **Adultery** is a more specific word for unfaithfulness to the marriage vow. Jesus set fornication as the only grounds of divorce and remarriage (cf. Mt. 5:32, 19:9). For strict condemnation of fornication, see Gal. 5:19; Eph. 5:3–4; Rev. 21:8. See also R. H. Charles, *The Teaching of the New Testament on Divorce*, 1921.

fortification see **fenced cities**

Fortunatus (fôr-tū-nā'tŭs) one of three persons who had just come from Corinth to Ephesus with news of the Corinthians for Paul (1 Cor. 16:17).

fountain a spring of water from the earth. Such springs were strikingly abundant in Palestine and made it attractive to the migrating Hebrews. The springs often dry up in summer, but even in arid regions produce many beautiful and fertile spots (Deut. 8:7), often determining location of towns. The Heb. "*En*" in a place name means fountain, e.g., **En-gedi**. Many fountains are connected with OT incidents (Gen. 24:16; Judg. 7:1 ff.; 2 K. 2:21). The word is often used metaphorically of the source of anything (Lev. 20:18). God is called the fountain of living waters (Jer. 17:13; cf. Rev. 21:6).

fowl a bird or flying animal but usually restricted to domestic poultry. The OT in our versions (e.g., Gen. 1:20; Lev. 1:14) uses the term in the looser sense. Poultry came from India and was introduced into Palestine before NT times when the crow of the cock is noted (Mt. 23:37, 26:34).

fowler since those who caught birds used traps or snares, the term is often a metaphorical one for the subtlety of evil (Ps. 124:7; Jer. 5:26 f.).

fox a common wild animal belonging to the dog family, noted for its slyness as well as used as something of insignificance. The Hebrew word was also used of jackals, and Samson's 300 may have been such (Judg. 15:4). See Neh. 4:3; Song of S. 2:15; Ps. 63:10; Ezek. 13:4. Jesus' reference to Herod Antipas as "that fox" may have been to his craftiness or to his insignificance (Lk. 13:32).

frankincense a resin gum obtained from balsam trees by notching the bark and gathering the substance which was exuded after it had hardened. It was used as a perfume when burned, being an ingredient in the incense offered in sacrifices (Ex. 30:34 ff.). For specifications about its use see Lev. 2:1 f., 14–16, 6:14–18, 24:7; Isa. 43:23, 66:3; Jer. 17:26, 41:5. It was forbidden in a sin offering (Lev. 5:11) or a cereal (for jealousy) (Num. 5:15) offering. The principal source of frankincense was Arabia (Isa. 60:6; Jer. 6:20). It was costly and was included as a part of the gifts from the wise men to the infant Jesus (Mt. 2:11, 15).

freedmen [KJV, Libertines] a synagogue at Jerusalem (Acts 6:9), composed of former Greek-speaking Hebrew captive slaves who had won their freedom and had returned to Jerusalem.

frog a tailless amphibian, coming under the description of an unclean animal for the Jews (Lev. 11:10, 41) and mentioned mostly in connection with the second Egyptian plague (Ex. 8:2–13; Ps. 78:45, 105:30). Its use in Rev. 16:13 is likely due to the modeling of the plagues there after those of the Egypt experience.

frontlet an object worn on the forehead at the time of prayer. Included were **phylacteries**, which were small cubical leather cases in which written passages of Scripture like Ex. 13:1–10, 11–16; Deut. 6:4–9, 11:13–21 were kept.

fuller one who conditions newly woven cloth by cleaning and shrinking it. Probably dying and recleaning were also a part of his work. The basic cleaning was by "treading" (Ex. 19:10; 2 Sam. 19:24) and using water (Isa. 36:2) and borith (Mal. 3:2, "soap"), and then spreading the cloth to dry (2 K. 18:17 "the fuller's field"), see Mk. 9:3.

fuller's field a field used to spread a fuller's garments for drying. One such field lay near a road passing by the Upper Pool near Jerusalem; the scene of the interview of Isaiah and Ahaz (Isa. 7:3) and the meeting of Hezekiah's men with Sennacherib's commander (Isa. 18:17, 36:2).

funeral there is no Bible use of this word. See **burial, embalming**

furlong a measure of distance (220 yards) used in the KJV to translate *stadion*, which is strictly speaking 215 yards. (See Lk. 24:13; Jn. 6:19, 11:18; Rev. 14:20, 21:16.) It is sometimes erroneously rendered "mile."

furnace a firebox or oven made of brick or stone. It contained the firebox as a place for fuel with a flue for a draft, an open place above the fire for the material to be refined, with some opening or door for access. Furnaces were used mostly for refining ore and heating it for casting, for firing brick and ceramic or pottery objects (Gen. 19:28; Ex. 9:8; Deut. 4:20; Dan. 3:6 ff.).

G

Gaal (gā'ăl) son of Ebed of Judg. 9, a free lance who led a rebellion of discontented She-chemites against Gideon's son Abimelech king of Israel, who murdered his seventy half brothers, and being warned by his officer Zebul, defeated and drove out Gaal, and wreaked fearful vengeance on the city.

Gaash (gā'ăsh) a mountain of Ephraim on whose north side was a city given to Joshua (24:30; Judg. 2:9). Its brooks were noted (2 Sam. 23:30; 1 Chr. 11:32).

Gaba (gā'bä) see **Geba**

Gabbai (găb'bā-ī) reputedly head of a family in Jerusalem, of Benjamin (Neh. 11:8).

gabbatha (găb'bā-thä) [meaning uncertain; possibly "height"; equated to Greek word for pavement] it seems that upon it, Pilate placed his judgment seat from which he condemned Christ.

Gabriel (gā'brĭ-ĕl) [man of God] used as a proper name for one of the seven archangels in the first rank of the numberless hosts of the heavenly order (Dan. 8:16, 9:21). In both Old and New Testaments he is the announcer of comforting news—to Zechariah (Lk. 1:11–20) regarding his son to be born (John the Baptist); to the Virgin Mary concerning her son Jesus Christ (1:26–38).

Gad (găd) Jacob's seventh son, firstborn of Zilpah, Leah's maid, full brother to Asher (Gen. 30:11–13, 49:19). In the first passage, the Hebrew text has: "And Leah said 'In fortune' "; but the ancient tradition renders: "A troop cometh." The text adds further: "And she called his name 'Gad,' " which could mean "good fortune," or "a troop." In the blessing of Jacob (the second reference) a play on the word, makes it "troop," a "piratical band." Little is known of Gad. At the descent into Egypt, seven sons are noted (Gen. 46:16), each of whom—Ezbon possibly excepted—seems to have founded a tribal family (the names have plural terminations). 1. The tribe Gad (Num. 1:14, 26:15; 1 Chr. 12:8; Ezek. 48:27). On the tribal march to the Promised Land, Gad was on the south side of the tabernacle (Num. 2:14). Only Gad and Reuben came with unchanged occupation to the Palestine left by their forebears 500 years previously, they being allied in cattle-herding. Before the march over Jordan they asked for settlement on the east of the river because Gilead was a place for cattle; and after taking their part in the Conquest, they returned to boundaries of Heshbon on the south, Mahanaim on the north, Aroer on the east (now Amman), and Jordan on the west. Later the limits were extended (1 Chr. 5:11–16), to all Gilead and Bashan, to Salcah, north and east of the original bounds, the Manassites being pushed to Mount Hermon (1 Chr. 5:23). Although the tribe was fierce and warlike (1 Chr. 12:8), the chivalry of Jephthah, despite his iron hand in dispelling desert plunderers (Judg. 11), and the loyal generosity of Barzillai (2 Sam. 19:32–39), give high rating to their tribal spirit. It seems that the notable Elijah the Tishbite, was of Gad. Despite such commendable qualities, Gad contributed little to the confederacy of Israel. In Gad's territory the long and strenuous struggles between Syria and Israel were staged; and its agricultural and pastoral aspects suffered much therefrom (2 K. 10:33). The tribe became captive to Tiglath-pileser of Assyria (1 Chr. 5:26); and in Jeremiah's time its cities were presumably occupied by the Ammonites.

2. The "seer" or "the King's [David's] seer" (2 Sam. 24:11–19; 1 Chr. 21:9–13, 29:29; 2 Chr. 29:25). A prophet who appears to have joined David when in the hold (1 Sam. 22:4–5). Gad reappears at the time of the punishment touching the numbering of the people (2 Sam. 24:11–19; 1 Chr. 21:9–19). He wrote a book of the acts of David (1 Chr. 19:29), and assisted in the musical arrangements for the "house of God" (2 Chr. 29:25).

3. Properly, "the Gad," an appellative; later a proper name, as in Isa. 65:11, where the margin shows him one of two idols worshiped by the Hebrews in Babylon. Gad is generally conceded to be the god of fortune, identified with the planet Jupiter (some, Venus), the star of good fortune for astrologers. Traces of Gad worship are found in such names as Baal-gad, etc. (e.g. Josh. 11:17).

Gadara (găd′ā-rä) presumably a place inhabited by Gadarenes (Lk. 8:26). A once strong city of the **Decapolis** whose ruins are now Um Keis, capital of Perea (so, Josephus), with a large district attached, six miles southeast of the Sea of Galilee from both Scythopolis and Tiberias; famous for hot baths whose springs still exist. The first event recorded of it is its capture by Antiochus the Great, along with Pella and other places (218 B.C.). The territory of Gadara, as also of Hippos, was later added to the kingdom of Herod the Great. The deep interest in this connection lies in Jesus' healing the demoniac (Mt. 8:28–34; Mk. 5:1–21; Lk. 8:26–40) which occurred in "the country of the Gergesenes" (Mt. 8:28), or Gadarenes (Mk. 5:1; Lk. 8:26), and is rather referable to some now unknown place actually on Galilee's eastern shore (MSS readings vary; the city Gadara is not mentioned). The features of the country illustrate the narrative, the most interesting being the tombs dotting the cliffs around. Gadara was captured by Vespasian at the outbreak of the war with the Jews, all the inhabitants massacred, and villages nearby reduced to ashes.

Gadites (găd′ītes) descendants of Gad and members of his tribe.

Gaddi (găd′dī) son of Susi, the Manassite spy sent by Moses to explore Canaan (Num. 13:11).

Gaddiel (găd′dĭ-ĕl) a Zebulonite, one of the twelve spies (Num. 13:10).

Gadi (gā′dī) father of Israel's king Menahem (2 K. 15:14, 17).

Gaham (gā′hăm) son of Abraham's brother Nahor by his concubine Reumah (Gen. 22:24).

Gahar (gā′här) father of a Nethinim family which returned from captivity with Zerubbabel (Ezra 2:47; Neh. 7:49).

Gaius (gā′yŭs) a name mentioned several times in the NT: 1. The apostle Paul's host at Corinth, the convert he baptized (Rom. 16:23; 1 Cor. 1:14).

2 and 3. Perhaps the same as the Gaius of Derbe; dweller in Corinth who went with the apostle from Greece to Asia (Acts 20:4).

4. A Macedonian companion of Paul seized in the Ephesus riot (Acts 19:29).

5 and 6. The man (men) of 2 and 3 Jn.

Galal (gá′lăl) 1. A Levite, son of Asaph (1 Chr. 9:15).

2. Another Levite, of Elkanah's family (1 Chr. 9:16).

3. A third Levite, son of Jeduthun (Neh. 11:17).

Galatia (gà-lā′shà) a Greek word akin to Gauls (South) that invaded Asia Minor about 278 B.C.; called "Greek Gauls" in contrast to the Gauls of France and Northern Italy. They were a Celtic torrent, ravaging Greece and neighboring lands, invited by Nicomedes I king of Bithynia to aid him in civil war. Galatia then is the region in Northeastern Phrygia where these Greek Gauls settled, but whose territorial limits seem to have been subject to much change. The word Galatia occurs four times in the NT: 1 Cor. 16:1; Gal. 1:2; 2 Tim. 4:10; 1 Pet. 1:1. About A.D. 160 the Gauls acquired part of Lycaonia and Pisidia including Antioch, Iconium, Lystra, and Derbe, conspicuous in the story of Paul's travels. The characteristic part of Galatia lay northward of these, the people preserving much of their ancient traits and something of their language. The Phrygians made impress on their religion and customs. The prevailing speech was Greek. Around 26 B.C., Augustus made Galatia a province of the Roman empire. There is difficulty in determining the sense of the word Galatia as used by NT writers, and if always in the same sense. In Acts Paul's journeys through this district are noted in very general terms. The writer, Luke, seems to have used it as relating to race and not to the Roman province. Paul regularly uses the geographical significance. In Acts 18:23 the "Galatian region" includes Lystra and Derbe; and Phrygia takes in Iconium and Pisidian Antioch. Some (Böttger) limit the

Galatia of the epistle to its extreme southern frontier (between Derbe and Colosse).

Galatians (gà-lā'shăns), **the Epistle to the** the unanimous testimony of the early church, and references to and citations of, this epistle by such early writers as Polycarp, Justin Martyr in the first half of the second century, and by Mileto in the third quarter, and by Irenaeus, Clement of Alexandria, and Tertullian in the last quarter, clearly show Pauline authorship despite some (untenable) objections. 1. *Occasion and Purpose of the Letter.* Apparently after Paul's second visit, an influential individual persuaded the Galatians that circumcision was necessary, advertising that Paul was inconsistent, and also that he was of lesser authority than the twelve apostles. The letter was written as a sword-thrust to correct the errors embraced. The churches addressed and the date depend on the meaning attached to the term Galatia, whether South Galatia, the Roman province organized about 23 B.C., or Galatia proper (North Galatia) which was the original territory occupied by the invading Gauls. The passages in Acts bear directly on the problem involved: according to Acts 16:6, Paul, Silas, and Timothy went "through Phrygia and the region of Galatia"; while according to Acts 18:23, the apostle goes from Antioch, "over all the country of Galatia and Phrygia in order." In each case reference seems to be to the northern district, which most commentators hold is the territory generally meant in Acts. The two visits are noted in Gal. 4:13. It is argued that the missionaries were headed for Bithynia which is beyond, i.e., north of the original Gallic district. On the other hand, "No possible route to Bithynia from North Gaul could be said to bring a traveler to a point "over against Mysia" (Sir William Ramsay). Such scholars as J. B. Lightfoot, Geo. Salmon, P. N. Schmiedel advocate North Galatia, while Ramsay, William Sanday, A. Zahn and Otto Pfleiderer argue for South Galatia. Differences arise both in connection with geography and with the incidents of Gal. 2:1–10 and Acts 11:28, and 15. The problems are complicated. (For full discussion see the commentaries). The advocates of the North Galatian theory hold that it was in the second missionary journey that the Galatians were evangelized, the reference being to Gauls by blood; for to call the four cities (Antioch of Pisidia, Iconium, Lystra, and Derbe) "Galatians," would be unnatural. On the other hand South Galatians advocates cite the fact that Acts tells fully about the churches in the locality, including Antioch and Iconium; therefore a detour into North

Galatia is excluded. Acts 18:23 tells of two different regions (as required by the grammar): the Galactic, that part of old Lycaonia which was in the province of Galatia around Derbe and Lystra; and the Phrygian region of Galatia (see 16:6) around Antioch and Iconium. Also the incidental note about Barnabas as a well-known champion of the Gentiles (2:13) fits the South Galatians theory; for Barnabas was not present in the second journey when, on the North Galatians theory, the Gauls were evangelized.

II. *Scope and Contents.* (1) Apologetic (chs. 1, 2)—answers to Judaizers' "disparagement of the apostle's office and message"; and polemical (chs. 3, 4), in which is found a doctrinal exposition of gospel freedom vs. Judaistic legalism. (2) Hortatory and practical (chs. 5, 6), in which the positions and demonstrations of the previous chs. are used with great power and persuasiveness.

III. *Place and Date.* For the North Galatians theory, Ephesus is the place of writing, early in the apostle's long stay there, A.D. 57 (Acts 19:8–10). Lightfoot holds to a later date, from Macedonia (Acts 20:1–3), and rather earlier than Romans, and after 2 Corinthians. On the South Galatians theory, written from Antioch at end of second journey (Ramsay), A.D. 53 (Acts 18:22).

galbanum (găl'bà-nŭm) a perfume used in sacred incense (Ex. 30:34). The commercial galbanum comes mainly from India and the Levant. A resinous gum of brownish-yellow color, with a strong disagreeable smell, occurring in mass or in yellowish tearlike drops. Its plant source has not been determined, whether *ferula ferulago* of North Africa, Crete, Asia Minor, or *bubon galbanum*, of Cape Good Hope (so Linnaeus), or *opoidia galbanifera* (so, the Dublin College).

Galeed (găl'ê-ĕd) the name Jacob gave to the stone-heap which he and Laban made on Mount Gilead to witness their mutual covenant (Gen. 31:47, 48; cf. vss. 23, 25).

Galilee (găl'ĭ-lē) (circle or district) originally a circuit of country in Naphtali (2 K. 15:29) including Kadesh (Josh. 20:7; 1 K. 9:11), in which were twenty towns given by Solomon to Hiram king of Tyre in payment for conveying timber from Lebanon to Jerusalem. In these, many Canaanites remained (Judg. 1:30–33). Isaiah speaks of "Galilee of the Gentiles" (9:1). During the Captivity they increased and expanded—Galilee became one of the largest provinces of Palestine. In the Maccabean period only a few Jews lived there, but in Roman times it became quite Jewish. It formed part of the domain of Herod the Great, passing to the authority of Herod the tetrarch, taking in the whole northern part of the country, the territories of Issachar, Zebulun, Asher, and Naphtali. On the south it was bordered by the Carmel range and the southern border of the plain of Esdraelon, and eastward, by Beth-shan (Scythopolis, Beisan) to the Jordan River. On the east was the river Jordan and the western banks of the lakes of Galilee and Merom, while on the north and northwest were Syria and Phoenicia. It touched the Mediterranean Sea only at, and shortly northward of, the bay of Acco. It extended (maximum) about sixty miles north and south, and thirty east and west. Lower Galilee included the great plain of Esdraelon down to the Jordan and Lake Tiberias, and the hill country north to the foot of the mountain range. It was one of the richest and most beautiful sections of Palestine, being densely populous. The chief towns were Tiberias and Taricheae at the southern end of the Sea of Galilee, and Sepphoris, the largest city. Grain was grown; the highest peaks reach around 1800 feet. Celebrated in NT history are Nazareth, Cana, and Tiberias (Lk. 1:26; Jn. 2:1, 6:1). Upper Galilee, the "Galilee of the Gentiles," embraced the mountainous land between Upper Jordan and Phoenicia, the southern boundary being a line due west from the northern end of the lake to Acre. Capernaum was in Upper Galilee. The scene of the greater part of our Lord's private life and public acts was Galilee; Nazareth saw his early years; and when he entered upon his work, Capernaum was his home (Mt. 4:13, 9:1). It is notable that the first three gospels relate to our Lord's ministry in this province; the Gospel of John relates more to Judea. His parables and illustrations were influenced by features and products of this country. The apostles were of Galilee (Judas apparently being the exception). The mixture of races produced the Galilean accent (Mk. 14:70; cf. Acts 2:7). After the destruction of Jerusalem, Galilee became the chief seat of Jewish schools of learning and the residence of the most celebrated Rabbis. The Galileans were frowned upon (Jn. 1:46, 7:52). Yet it was the home of Deborah, Barak, Ibzan, Tola, Elon, and of the prophets Jonah, Elisha, and probably of Hosea.

Galilee, Sea of see **Gennesaret**

Galilee, Mountain of after our Lord's resurrection the disciples (eleven) went "into Galilee, unto the mountain where Jesus had appointed them" (Mt. 28:16). There is no hint to indicate what mountain is meant.

gall 1. [*mererah* or *meroah*, what is bitter,

(as in Job 13:26)]. Applied to bile or gall because of acute bitterness (Job 16:13, 20:25). Serpents' poison was alleged to be in their gall (Job 20:14).

2. [*rosh*, a very bitter plant (Deut. 29:18; Lam. 3:19; cf. Hos. 10:4)]. Various species of gall sprang up quickly in cornfields. Gesenius (Hebrew dict.) understands it as "poppies," perhaps a steeped solution of which is the "water of gall" (Jer. 9:15). In Hos. 10:4, "hemlock"; in Deut. 32:33 and Job 20:14, "the venom of serpents." The gall of Mt. 27:34 (cf. Ps. 69:21) and the myrrh of Mk. 15:23 are the same, according to some, whether narcotic, administered by the women, in accord with Prov. 31:6, or the ordinary beverage of the Romans, offered by the soldiers. John's note seems to refer to a different potion (Jn. 19:29).

gallery an architectural term regarding porticoes not uncommon in Eastern homes; but it is doubtful that Hebrew words thus translated are so referable. 1. In Song of S. 1:17 the same word [*rachet*] is translated "paneling," "fretted work," which in 7:6 is applied to the hair, for the carefully arranged flowing locks are compared to running streams in Palestinian pastures.

2. A different word [*attik*] in Ezek. 41:15, 42:3 seems to mean the pillar-support of a floor.

galley see **ship**

Gallim (găl'ĭm) [heaps or springs] noted only twice. 1. The native place, unknown, of the man to whom Michal, David's wife, was given (1 Sam. 25:44).

2. One of the places terrified by Sennacherib's approach (Isa. 10:34), perhaps a short distance north from Jerusalem, not known in modern times.

Gallio (găl'ĭ-ō) Junius Gallio Annaeus was Roman proconsul of Achaia under the Emperor Claudius when the apostle Paul was at Corinth, A.D. 53. Brother of Seneca, the philosopher; said to have been executed by Nero; but Jerome, in the *Chronicle of Eusebius*, says that he committed suicide in A.D. 65.

gallows see **punishment**

Gamaliel (gȧ-mā'lĭ-ĕl) 1. Son of Pedahzur, a prince, captain of the tribe of Manasseh in the census at Sinai (Num. 1:10, 2:20, 7:54, 59), and at the time of march through the wilderness (10:23).

2. A Pharisee, celebrated doctor of the Law who gave wise advice in the Sanhedrin regarding the treatment of the followers of the Lord (Acts 5:34-39). He was the preceptor of the apostle Paul (Acts 22:3), son of Rabbi Sim-

eon, grandson of the famous Hillel, and he was president of the Sanhedrin in the time of Tiberius, Caligula, and Claudius. He is thought to have died eighteen years before the destruction of Jerusalem.

games apparently not so popular among the serious-minded Hebrews. There are some juvenile games noted: Zech. 8:5 tells of children playing in the streets. Keeping tame birds (Job 41:5) and mimicry (Mt. 11:16) are mentioned. Among adults, conversation (Ps. 78:2; Prov. 1:6) and joking, riddle-guessing (Judg. 14:12–14) afforded amusement (Jer. 15:17; Prov. 20:19). Music was associated with sacred song. Dancing on occasion apparently gave healthy social entertainment (Ex. 32:6, 19; 2 Sam. 6:14; Ps. 150:4; Jer. 31:4; Eccl. 3:4). There was training in the use of sling and bow (1 Sam. 20:20). It appears that friendly tournaments were not unknown (2 Sam. 2:13, but see vs. 16!). Public games and theatrical exhibitions, so popular among the Greeks, were foreign to the Hebrew spirit which found pleasurable excitement in the great annual national festivals. Paul evidently witnessed games and contests, as those at Ephesus of local character in honor of Diana (1 Cor. 15:32), or at Corinth honoring Poseidon (1 Tim. 6:12; 2 Tim. 4:7). Crowds came to the four great Panhellenic festivals at Elis, Corinth, Delphi, and Nemea. The Olympian (at Elis) was chief, held every four years. The Pauline epistles abound with allusions to these Greek contests. The Pancratium included boxing and wrestling (1 Cor. 9:24); the Pentathlon, leaping and running, quoiting, spear-throwing, and wrestling (Eph. 6:12). Long training and strict diet were required for competitors (1 Cor. 9:25; 1 Tim. 4:8; 2 Tim. 2:5). A herald proclaimed the opening, and announced the name and country of each contestant. The judge, standing at the goal and seen through the length of the stadium (Phil. 3:14), possessed spotless integrity (2 Tim. 4:8). He decided disputes and gave the prize, a crown of leaves, whether of olive, pine, ivy, or parsley, respectively at the Olympian, the Isthmian, the Delphian, the Nemean. The palm branch tokened victory. Privileges and immunities, a triumphal procession, were accorded the victor, and the victory was often celebrated in verse. Paul uses the atmosphere of the games to illustrate most appropriately to the Corinthians (1 Cor. 9:24, 27) the glory of the Christian contest, alluding to several of the events. In 2 Tim. 4:7 in contrast to Phil. 3:12–16, we have compelling allusions. One important reference to athletic contests is in Heb. 12:1, 2; and

Rom. 7:9 echoes the Ephesian games, pertinent of the people addressed.

Gammadims (găm'mā-dĭms) found only in Ezek. 27:11. Apparently a proper name; possibly "guards."

Gamul (gā'mŭl) [weaned] Levitical leader of the twenty-second course in the sanctuary services (1 Chr. 24:17).

garden enclosure on the outskirts of a town, planted with various trees and shrubs, e.g., herbs (Deut. 11:10; 1 K. 21:2), fruits (Jer. 29:5; Amos 4:9); or a parklike pleasure ground (2 K. 25:4). Flowers were grown (Song of S. 6:2); and likely grain or vegetables between the trees. Biblical allusions show surrounding hedges of thorn (Isa. 5:2), or walls of stone (Prov. 24:31), having lodges or watchtowers (Isa. 1:8; Mk. 12:1), with watchers to protect against wild beasts and robbers. Kitchen gardens (of herbs) are noted (1 K. 21:2). The rose garden of Jerusalem, west (?) of the temple mount was one of the few which from the time of the prophets, was within the city walls. The orange, lemon, and mulberry groves of Joppa and Sidon are famous; orchards at Damascus amplify that "earthly paradise." The garden was a favorite place for devotion and resort, especially in the evening (Est. 7:7; Song of S. 4:16). Nights of the summer were spent in gardens. The most sacred and attractive one is Gethsemane, on Olivet's slopes (Jn. 18:1, 26). Water was all-important for the garden; a "well-watered" garden stood for luxuriance, fertility, material prosperity (Isa. 58:11; Jer. 31:12). To "water with the foot" seems to refer to an irrigation device (Deut. 11:10). Gardens surrounded the country houses of notables (1 K. 21:1; 2 K. 9:27); were occasionally used for burial (Jn. 19:41; 2 K. 21:18, 26); in degenerate times were centers of idolatry (Isa. 1:29, 65:3, 66:17). Little is known of the art of gardening among the Hebrews; there were gardeners (Job 27:18; Jn. 20:15); and grafting (Rom. 11:17, 24). The first garden or park was Eden (Gen. 2:8, 3:24; Ezek. 28:13, 31:8–9).

Gareb (gā'rĕb) 1. One of David's "thirty" (2 Sam. 23:38; 1 Chr. 11:40).

2. A hill near Jerusalem (Jer. 31:39), location uncertain.

garland those of Acts 14:13 were supposedly for the heads of sacrificial victims. Used to honor victors in the **games.**

garlic [Lat. *Allium sativum* (Linnaeus)] a favorite especially among Hebrews (Num. 11:5). Abounds in Egypt.

Garmite (gär'mĭt) Keilah the Garmite, supposedly descendant of Gerem, of the tribe of Judah (1 Chr. 4:19).

garner a place for storing grain (Ps. 144:13; Joel 1:17; Mt. 3:12).

garnish to adorn (2 Chr. 3:6; Job 26:13; Mt. 12:44, 23:29; Rev. 22:19).

garrison from the same Hebrew root come several words: a military post (1 Sam. 14:1, 15; 2 Cor. 11:32); a column as token of conquest especially by Egyptian and Assyrian kings, apparently by Israel in 1 Sam. 7:12; a pillar in Gen. 19:26; an officer in 1 K. 4:19. Because a different word (same root) is commonly used in the book of Samuel for garrison, it seems better to translate as "officer" the word found in 1 Sam. 10:5, 13:3; 2 Sam. 8:6, 14. S. R. Driver uses "pillar" in 1 Sam. 13:3, citing Amos 9:1. A slightly different word in Ezek. 26:11 is "pillars"; but the KJV has "garrisons."

Gashmu (găsh'mū) a variation of **Geshem.**

Gatam (gā'tăm) fourth son of Eliphaz, son of Esau (Gen. 36:11; 1 Chr. 1:36), one of the "dukes" of Eliphaz (Gen. 36:16).

gate those of ancient Eastern cities held importance both in defense and in public economy. Sometimes they represent the city itself (Gen. 22:17; Deut. 12:12; Ruth 4:10; Ps. 87:2). Used for public resort (Gen. 19:1); for deliberation, for ministering justice, for audience of important persons (Deut. 16:18; Josh. 20:4); as public markets (2 K. 7:1); in association with sacrifice (Acts 14:13; cf. 2 K. 23:8). Some contained chambers over the gateway (2 Sam. 18:24). They were carefully guarded and closed at nightfall (Deut. 3:5; Josh. 2:5; Judg. 9:40, 44). Doors of larger gates were two-leaved, plated with metal, closed with locks, fastened with metal bars (Deut. 3:5; Ps. 107:16; Isa. 45:1, 2). Gates of royalty were often ornamented richly. Sentences from the Law were inscribed on and above them (Deut. 6:9; Isa. 54:12; Rev. 21:21). Those of Solomon's temple were massive, being overlaid with gold and carvings (1 K. 6:34, 35). Those of the holy place were of olive, two-leaved, and overlaid with gold; those of the temple were fir (1 K. 6:31; Ezek. 41:23, 24, in his vision). There are figurative gates of pearl and precious stones (Isa. 54:12; Rev. 21:21). Assyrian and Egyptian gates were elaborate and ornamented. In the temple, in the houses of the wealthy, and in palaces, special keepers were set (Jer. 35:4; 2 K. 12:9).

Gath (găth) [wine press] site long unknown; supposedly Tell es-Safiyeh at the mouth of the vale of Elah. One of the five great Philistine cities (Josh. 13:3; 1 Sam. 6:17). It occupied strong position (2 Chr. 11:8) on the border of Judah and Philistia (1 Sam. 21:10; 1 Chr. 18:1). The scene of frequent struggles, often captured and recaptured (2 Chr. 26:6; Amos 6:2). Residence of remnant of the tall Anakim (Josh. 11:22), to whom Goliath and other giants belonged (1 Sam. 17:4; 2 Sam. 21:15–22; 1 Chr. 20:4–8). Captured by David (1 Chr. 18:1); previously in his outlawry, he took refuge with its king Achish (1 Sam. 21:10). David had a bodyguard of Gittites under Ittai (2 Sam. 15:18). Fortified by Rehoboam (2 Chr. 11:8), lost to Philistines, captured by Hazael (2 K. 12:17). Uzziah broke down its wall (2 Chr. 26:6). Amos (6:2) and Micah (1:10) mention it; but it is not referred to by later prophets.

Gath-hepher (găth-hê-fēr) [or Gittah-hepher, wine-press of the well] on the border of Zebulun; home of Jonah (2 K. 14:25). Likely el-Meshed, three miles northeast of Nazareth.

Gath-rimmon (găth-rĭm'mŏn) [pomegranate press] a town of Dan (Josh. 19:45) assigned to the Kohath Levites (Josh. 21:24), in the Philistine plain, not far from Joppa (19:45), apparently. Another place, same name, was assigned to the Kohath Levites (Josh. 21:25); it was west of the Jordan in Manasseh, probably Bileam. The LXX reading shows that "Gath-rimmon" is an error in copying (see Josh. 21:24).

Gauls see **Galatia**

Gaza (gā'zä) [literally, 'azzah] the meaning, "strong," fits the place—one of the five Philistine cities, the last town in the southwest of Palestine on the frontier toward Egypt, apparently the capital; of very early (Gen. 10:19) and continuous existence; besieged by Alexander the Great for five months (332 B.C.). It gave great trouble to Joshua (11:22); it was taken and lost by Judah (15:47; Judg. 1:18, 6:4). Samson carried away its gate doors (Judg. 16:1–3); his eyes put out, he was made to grind in its prison house (16:20, 21). Here also, renewed in strength, after being betrayed by Delilah his wife, he destroyed himself and a multitude of his enemies by pulling down the pillars of the temple of Dagon (23–31). Gaza continued to be a Philistine city through the times of Samuel, Saul, David (1 Sam. 6:17, 14:52; 1 K. 4:21). About 96 B.C. it was razed by the Maccabees (Alexander Jannaeus), according to Josephus. Gabinius, the Roman governor, rebuilt it on a new site, A.D. 57, the old site being known as "old," or "desert" Gaza (Acts 8:26). About A.D. 65 the Jews destroyed it but it was rebuilt. It was successively in the hands of the Greeks, Byzantine Christians (A.D.

402), Mohammedans (635), and Crusaders. Some most important Crusader campaigns took place near Gaza. It was finally lost by the Franks in 1244 (R. A. S. Macalister). A Crusaders' church, now a mosque, is there, the place being called Ghuzzeh. Deep wells of good water, fine olive groves, and soap-making are features of the town of about 16,000 inhabitants.

Gazara (gă-zā'rä or găz'ā-rä) [a place cut off] see **Gezer**

Gazathite (gā'zăth-īt) same as Gazite, inhabitant of Gaza (Josh. 13:3; Judg. 16:2).

Gazer (gā'zēr) same as **Gezer.**

Gazez (gā'zěz) [shearer] a son, and apparently also a grandson, of the elder Caleb (1 Chr. 2:46).

Gazzam (găz'zăm) [devourer] a family of Nethinim who returned from captivity with Zerubbabel (Ezra 2:48; Neh. 7:51).

Geba (gē'bä) [hill] sometimes written Gaba, as Josh. 18:24. A city of Benjamin on the northeast frontier (Josh. 21:17; 2 K. 23:8), assigned to the Levites. The scene of Jonathan's famous Philistine exploit (1 Sam. 13:3), it was fortified by Asa (1 K. 15:22). Probably not the same as Isaiah's Geba (10:29). Occupied after the Exile (Neh. 11:31). Apparently confused with the neighboring Gibeah (Judg. 20:10, 33, and elsewhere). Likely the same as the modern Jeba.

Gebal (gē'băl) [mountain] probably a maritime town of Phoenicia (Ezek. 27:9; cf. Josh. 13:9), affording builders for Solomon (1 K. 5:18, where the name Giblites is translated rather than transcribed); also ship-caulkers (Ezek. 27:9). Psalm 83:7 seems to refer to another Geba in league with Edom, Moab, and others against Israel, on an unknown occasion, its location being south of the Dead Sea.

Geber (gē'bēr) [man, hero] Solomon's purveyor for southern Gilead (1 K. 4:19), and perhaps the father of the purveyor for northern Gilead, who lived in Ramoth-gilead (vs. 13).

Gebim (gē'bĭm) [cisterns, locusts] a village north of Jerusalem (Isa. 10:31), site unknown.

Gedaliah (gĕd-ā-lī'ä) [Jehovah is great] 1. Son of Ahikam, Jeremiah's protector (Jer. 26:24), grandson of Shaphan (2 K. 22), made governor of Judah over "the poor of the land" by Nebuchadnezzar following the destruction of the temple (Jer. 40:5, 52:16). Jeremiah joined him at Mizpah, along with other Jews (40:6, 11). The anniversary of his murder by Ishmael at the seed royal (Jer. 41:18), is one of the four Jewish fasts (Zech. 8:19) observed on the third day of the seventh month Tishri.

2. A Levite harper, son of Jeduthun (1 Chr. 25:3, 9).

3. A priest in Ezra's time (Ezra 10:18).

4. Son of Pashur (Jer. 38:1).

5. Ancestor of Zephaniah (1:1).

Gedeon (gĕd'ē-on) Greek form of **Gideon.**

Geder (gē'dēr) [wall] an unidentified South Judean town (Josh. 12:13). Perhaps same as in 1 Chr. 4:39.

Gederah (gĕ-dē'räh) [wall, sheepfold] 1. A town apparently in East Judah (Josh. 15:36).

2. A village of Benjamin, as 1 Chr. 12:4 seems to suggest.

Gederite (gĕd'e-rīt) also Gederathite. See 1 Chr. 12:4 and 12:4).

Gederoth (gĕ-dē'rŏth) [sheepfolds] a town in the low country of Judah (Josh. 15:41. See 2 Chr. 28:18).

Gederothaim (gĕd-ē-rŏth-ā'ĭm) [two sheepfolds] a town in the territory of Judah (Josh. 15:36). The towns are reckoned as fourteen, but this name would make fifteen; so this could be a common noun, or the word translated "and" could equally be "or," and so this town could be a variant for the preceding one.

Gedor (gē'dôr) [wall, fortress] 1. A town in the hill-country of Judah shortly north of Hebron (Josh. 15:58).

2. Possibly a town in Simeon's territory (1 Chr. 4:39).

3. A son of Jehiel, whose brother was Ner (1 Chr. 8:30).

4. Perhaps also a village in Benjamin (1 Chr. 12:7).

Gehazi (gĕ-hā'zī) [valley of vision] Elisha's servant, sent on two occasions to the good Shunammite (2 K. 4); fraudulently obtained money and garments from Naaman; was smitten with leprosy and dismissed from service (2 K. 5). Later he or a successor of the same name, reported to King Joram the great doings of the prophet (2 K. 8).

Gehenna (gĕ-hĕn'nä) the "valley of Hinnom" was a deep, narrow glen to the south of Jerusalem, where after Ahaz' introduction of fire-gods' worship, the idolatrous Jews offered children to Molech (2 Chr. 28:3, 33:6; Jer. 7:31, 19:2-6). Later it became the image of the place of everlasting punishment.

Geliloth (gĕl'ĭ-lōth) [regions, circles] apparently the same as Gilgal, at the southern boundary of Benjamin (Josh. 15:7, 18:17).

Gemalli (gĕ-măl'lī) [camel rider?] father of the Danite spy Ammiel (Num. 13:12).

Gemariah (gĕm-ā-rī'ä) [Jehovah perfects] 1. Son of Shaphan the scribe and father of Micaiah. A noble of Judah occupying a chamber in the temple, where his plea to King Jehoiakim not to burn the scroll of Jeremiah's alarming prophecy, was overridden (Jer. 36:10–12, 25).

2. Son of Hilkiah and one of two messengers sent by Zedekiah to Nebuchadnezzar, who bore also a letter from Jeremiah to the captives in Babylon (Jer. 29:1–3).

genealogy the Hebrew term is "the book of the generations," often extended to history. Earliest Greek histories were also genealogies. The science of genealogy seems to have been of more importance among the Hebrews than for other peoples, as seen in such vital matters as the promise of the land of Canaan to the seed of Abraham, Isaac, and Jacob, and the separation of Israel from the Gentile world, the expectation of the Messiah from Judah, the exclusively hereditary priesthood of Aaron, the succession of kings of David's line, the whole division and occupation of the land on genealogical principles by tribes, families, and houses of fathers. Definite records are traceable from the beginning of national organization (Num. 1:2, 18; 1 Chr. 5:7, 17). But even before the national founder Jacob, we see stress upon genealogies. Note "generations" in Genesis, meaning here, "historical outcome." (e.g., Gen. 2:4, 5:1). The gap between Adam and Noah calls for ten generations (Gen. 5); and we have the genealogical tree regarding Noah's sons (Gen. 10). Note the Aramean line (Gen. 22:20), and the North Arabian (25:12). In Gen. 35:22–26 is the account of the sons of Jacob; also Ex. 1:1–5. In ch. 45 is the house of Israel at the descent into Egypt. In the wilderness of Sinai, by divine command, is the reckoning according to which they pitched camp, marched, made offerings, chose spies, the whole land being parceled among them. Although birth was not the sole ground of incorporation into the tribes, it continued throughout the national life to be the foundation of organization, the reigns of the more prominent kings being marked with genealogical data. Levi seems to be the only tribe without admixture of foreign blood. For the temple services, David divided the priests and Levites into courses and companies, each under the family chief—this arrangement continued until the time of Christ. On his reopening the temple and on the restoration of its services, Hezekiah reckoned the whole nation by genealogies. One of the first moves of Zerubbabel at the return was to take a census of all according to their genealogies. Proof of the continuance of the genealogical economy is seen in Augustus' empire census, which took each to his own city, and so brought about Christ's birth in Bethlehem. Again, we have the Lord's gene-alogy in Matthew and in Luke. The same idea occurs in the note about Zecharias as "of the course of Abia," of Elizabeth as "of the daughters of Aaron," and of Anna as "of the tribe of Aser." We may be sure then that the records were kept until the destruction of Jerusalem, when all were lost. A right interpretation of Scripture hangs in certain connections on a proper view of Jewish genealogical lists. Such records have respect to political and territorial divisions, as also to strictly genealogical descent. Thus, not all who are "sons," are necessarily actual children of a certain patriarch or chief father. If one house became extinct, another would succeed, and thus the "father" differed. One such account, a census drawn up later than an original, would show different divisions. The interpretation of a genealogy must observe this principle. In abbreviation of pedigrees, the generations would indicate from what chief father descent was derived. Only when it is certain that the genealogy is complete, can such be used for measuring time. Also the same names, or modifications of them, may occur in the same family, e.g., Tobias and Tobit. At times symmetry seems to be preferred to unbroken descent; links were omitted, enumerations sometimes incomplete. In Mt. 1:17 there are three sets of fourteen names. Marginal references show differences from the record in Chronicles. We simply have to accept the Hebrew custom, rather than condemn that which differs from our ideas. A genealogy appears, in instances, to be tribal rather than personal. "Son" may refer to an inhabitant (Gen. 10:2–4, 6); to a people, or a tribe (vss. 4, 13, 16–18), the ending "im" indicating gentile adjectives in the plural. Again, vs. 15 points to a town; vss. 8–10 to an individual. The words "bear" and "beget" have corresponding breadth of meaning: a grandchild (2 K. 9:20, see vs. 2); also a great-grandchild (vs. 12, and probably vss. 21, 22); and apparently a grandchild's grandchild (Mt. 1:9). Genealogies may be ascending or descending (1 Chr. 6:33–43; Ruth 4:18–22). Females are named in extraordinary cases, or in transmission of property rights (Ex. 6:23; Num. 26:33). (Some of above data is from J. D. Davis, *Dictionary of the Bible*).

Genealogy of Jesus Christ here two are given: Mt. 1:1–16 shows the direct line; Lk. 3:23–28 shows the reverse order. The former gives the genealogy of Joseph to exhibit Christ's legal title to the throne of David, according to the covenant with Abraham, while the latter, beginning with the second Adam and ascending to the first Adam, the son of God by creation, presents the Lord's physical descent on the human side, the actual son of David. Apparently as a mnemonic, Matthew has three fourteens of generations, necessitating a number of omissions. The same principle, viz., that one evangelist gives the successive heirs to David's throne, while the other shows the paternal stem of him who was the Heir, explains most of the anomalies of the two pedigrees, their agreements as well as their discrepancies, and the circumstances of there being two at all. It will be helpful to note that only Luke begins with Adam; and at Abraham, Matthew begins to parallel Luke; but at David they diverge, one line being traced through Solomon, the other through Nathan his brother. They converge again briefly at Salathiel, where Neri, of Luke's list, apparently married the daughter of Jechoniah, of Matthew's list, to beget Salathiel by her. There are difficulties which have not been solved satisfactorily. The genealogies follow.

From Matthew	From Luke
David	David
Solomon	Nathan
	Mattatha
Rehoboam	
	Menna
Abijah	
	Melea
Asa	
	Eliakim
Jehoshaphat	
	Jonam
Joram	
	Joseph
Uzziah	Judas
Jotham	Symeon
Ahaz	Levi
Hezekiah	Matthat
Manasseh	Jorim
Amon	Eliezer
Josiah	Jose (Jesus)
Jechoniah	Er
	Elmodam
Shealtiel (Salathiel)	
	Cosam
Zerubbabel	
	Addi
Abiud	Melchi
	Neri
Eliakim	
	Shealtiel (Salathiel)
Azor	Zerubbabel
	Rhesa
Zadok	
	Joanan

Achim	Juda
Eliud	Joseph
Eleazar	Semein
Matthan	Mattathias
Jacob	Maath
Joseph, husband of Mary	Naggai
	Esli
	Nahum
	Amos
	Mattathias
	Joseph
	Jannai
	Melchi
	Levi
	Matthat
	Heli
	Joseph, husband of Mary

generation definite or indefinite time, from Hebrew word for revolution (revolving). In abstract sense (Lk. 1:50; in concrete sense (Mt. 11:16). Referring to the ordinary period of human life, in the patriarchal age apparently 100 years (Gen. 15:16; see vs. 15 and Ex. 12:40). Ordinarily thirty to forty years (Job 42:16). Regarding the indefinite past (Deut. 32:7); the future (Ps. 45:17). It may refer to men of an age (or time) or to a class: to contemporaries (Gen. 6:9), to ancestors (Ps. 49:19), to posterity (Lev. 3:17).

Genesis this is the first book of the Law, with an interest and importance attaching to no other book. It is certainly the oldest alphabetical book in the world with any claim to trustworthiness. All save the first eleven chapters deals with the Hebrews as the chosen people of God. Its peculiar nature is revealed in its purpose—to show that the God of creation (Elohim) is the God of the covenant (Jehovah), who has entered into compact with one man who is to become the channel of blessing to all mankind. The name of the book comes from the LXX, and is designated by its initial word in Hebrew, meaning "In beginning." Sections are easily seen: (1) Historical data on the universe, showing God's relation to it, and introducing human history (1:1–2:3); (2) A sketch of human history before Abraham, showing God's relation to the human race, and introducing the history of the chosen people (2:4–11:26); (3) History of the covenant people to the descent into Egypt. Chapter one is the general introduction to all. Thereafter the narrative embraces ten sections, each with the caption: "These are the generations of," which is equivalent to the "historical outcome."

Through all, the chosen line is traced, after the rejected line is noted, the main stream including the notables, Abraham, Isaac, Jacob, and Joseph. Organically, the whole book may be divided into two unequal sections: (1) Creation (1:1–2:3); (2) Covenant (2:4–50:26): (a) the Covenant of works with Adam for mankind (2:4–3:24); (b) the Covenant of faith: i. with Adam and sons (4:1–8:22), ii. with mankind through Noah (chs. 9–11), iii. with one line for all the race (chs. 12–50). Whereas there is nothing heretical in a theoretical number of documents contributory to the book's make-up, the reasons for the documents, advanced by the radical, destructive, critics (J. Wellhausen, A. Kuenen, M. Noth, G. von Rad, C. Kuhl, B. W. Anderson et al) are by no means conclusive or convincing, despite wide acceptance of their views. Arguments based on style are confessedly precarious, that based on the two major divine names (Jehovah and Elohim) being now held of minor significance, for they are inconsistently used in the alleged documents; and the critics are forced to invoke, as many as necessary, editors and redactors on whom to lay the blame for the confusion of their theories. Contradictions, mistakes, repetitions (where apparent), so far from indicating different documents, are in most cases readily explainable. The prize exhibit of a duplicate and contradictory account, allegedly pointing to documents, is Gen. 1 and 2. It is fatuous: the two accounts are different in subject, object, and purpose, and are entirely complementary. Historical and theological arguments for documents and multiple contributors, are all nullified when one seeks harmony and utilizes readily afforded explanations. This does not deny difficulties, some without solution as yet. Grant the supernatural origin of the book, and problems pale. Traditionally and allegedly, Moses is responsible for Genesis. There is not one chance in ten million that any mortal could have written chapter one without divine guidance, so graphically presenting the great factors lying at the basis of all existence (time, space, matter, motion, force), while contradicting no known truth of science. The great fact in the creation account, is God—thirty-two times in thirty-one verses. And in vss. 1, 21, 27 occurs the Hebrew word *bara'*, equivalent in usage to creation *ex nihilo*. And in the face of the data noted, science stands incompetent to dogmatize—in these three instances: matter, life, the human. In each case, a higher force alone suffices. It is not necessary to explain completely the great facts of the record, from the Fall to the Exo-

dus: we do well in accepting them, proceeding on the basis of their truth. (For full and satisfactory explanation of the problems of Genesis, see W. H. Green's *Unity of the Book of Genesis* [1895], and *The Higher Criticism of the Pentateuch* [1902].) See also **Pentateuch.**

Gennesaret (jĕn-nĕs′ȧ-rĕt) [garden of Hazor?] 1. Called by Arabs el-Guweir; a fertile plain (nuts, palms, figs, grapes, olives), on the western shore of the lake, north of Magdala (Mt. 14:34; Mk. 6:54), about three by one miles in size.

2. The lake, or sea, is called in OT "the Sea of Chinnereth" (Num. 34:11), named for the town (Josh. 19:35). Called in NT "Sea of Galilee" from province Galilee, on west (Mt. 4:18); also "Sea of Tiberias" (see Jn. 6:1). It is about thirteen by six miles, being indeed but a lower section of the Jordan valley. The climate of the shores is almost tropical, summer heat being intense. The water is sweet, transparent, and sparkling; the beach, pebbly; fish are abundant now as of old. Our Lord spent most of his public life in the environs of Gennesaret, the region being then the most densely populated of all Palestine.

Gentiles the Heb. *goyim* means "nations," foreigners as opposed to Israel (Neh. 5:8), whom the Hebrews unjustly contemned (Gen. 10:5; Isa. 9:1). In the NT, the singular *ethos* refers to any nation (Mt. 24:7; Lk. 7:5); in plural only, regarding heathen, Gentiles. Sometimes the word for "Greeks" (Acts 14:1) is translated "Gentiles" (1 Cor. 10:32).

Genubath (gĕ-nū′băth) [theft] son of Hadad, an Edomite prince, by the Egyptian queen's (Tahpenes') sister, in the time of David (1 K. 11:20).

Gera (gē′rä) [grain] descendant of Benjamin (Gen. 46:21). The various Geras (Judg. 3:15; 2 Sam. 16:5; 1 Chr. 8:3) seem to be the same, son of Bela.

gerah (gē′rä) see **weights and measures**

Gerar (gē′rär) [waterpot, or perhaps a circle] ancient city on south border of Palestine near Gaza (Gen. 10:19), early occupied by the Philistines (26:1). Its subject land extended toward Kadesh and Shur (20:1; cf. 26:6, 17). It is commonly identified with the ruins of Umm Jerrar, six miles south of Gaza.

Gerasenes (gĕr′ȧ-sēns) the people of Gerasa (Mt. 8:28). MSS vary between Gerasenes, Gadarenes, Gergesenes. Gerasa is probably still echoed in Kersa, a ruin on the eastern shore of Galilee, opposite Magdala, five miles from the Jordan's entrance into the lake. Decapolis, known as Gersa, now Gerash, seems not to qualify; but south of Kersa is a place where steep hills come down close to the water (Lk. 8:33).

Gerizim (gēr'ĭ-zĭm = plural of Gerizzi, Gerizites, cf. Girzite). A mountain south of the valley in which is Nablus, ancient Shechem, designated by Moses along with Ebal, on the north, as the scene of the great ceremony upon entrance into the Promised Land. Mount Gerizim is 700 feet above the town. The Law was delivered from Mount Sinai; the blessings and the curses, affixed to performance or neglect, were to be pronounced respectively upon Gerizim and Ebal (Deut. 27; Josh. 8:33–35). For location, see Deut. 11:30. According to some, Gerizim is the hill upon which Abraham's faith "was made perfect" (Gen. 22). Probably nearby is Jacob's altar and where he tented (Gen. 33:18–20). According to Josephus, the Jewish historian about the time of Christ, the forbidden marriage (Ezra 9:2; Neh. 13:23) of Manasseh, brother to the then high priest Jadua, to the daughter of Sanballat the Cuthean (2 K. 17:24), caused such a stir among the Jews, that the father-in-law got leave from Alexander the Great to build a temple on Mount Gerizim, to give Manasseh a rival priesthood and allow him to keep his wife. H. Prideaux, who wrote concerning the time between the Testaments, tells that "thenceforth Samaria became the common refuge of the refractory Jews." Gerizim is still to the Samaritans what Jerusalem is to the Jews. It was near this mountain that the Lord talked with the woman of Samaria, Jacob's well being at its foot.

Gershom (gēr'shōm) [stranger there (Ex. 2:22, 18:3), although it seems rather to mean expulsion, there being a play upon the sound] 1. The firstborn son of Moses and Zipporah, whose circumcision is apparently noted in 4:25. Reckoned, in his line, to be among the Levites, not the priests (1 Chr. 23:14–16).

2. Eldest son of Levi (**Gershon**), according to 1 Chr. 6:16–17, 20, 43, 62, 71, 15:7.

3. Representative of the priestly line of Phinehas, of Ezra's time (8:2).

Gershon [banishment] Levi's son, founder of the Gershonite family (Gen. 46:11; Ex. 6:16; Num. 3:17), sometimes called Gershom. Though firstborn, his families were outstripped by the younger Kohath, ancestor of Moses and priestly line of Aaron. His sons gave rise to two subdivisions (Ex. 6:17; Num. 3:18; 1 Chr. 6:17).

Gershonites (see above, and Num. 3:21–26, 4:24–27, 26:57; Josh. 21:33; 1 Chr. 23:7; 2 Chr. 29:12.) Encamped on west side of the tabernacle; in charge of the tabernacle itself,

being furnished with two wagons and four oxen (Num. 3:23–26, 4:21–28, 7:7). Two families: Libnites and Shimeites, at the first census having 7500 males (Num. 3:21, 22). Their thirteen cities were: two in Manasseh, beyond Jordan; four in Issachar; four in Asher; and three in Naphtali.

Gesham (gĕ'shăm) [firm] the 1611 Bible has "Geshan." A man of Judah, a son of Jahdi (1 Chr. 2:47).

Geshem and **Gashmu** (gĕ'shĕm) [latter, Arabic; former, Hebrew; corporealness] an opponent and falsifier regarding the rebuilding Jews (Neh. 2:19, 6:1, 2, 6).

Geshur (gĕsh'ûr) [bridge] a district in northeast Bashan, adjoining Argob and Syria (Deut. 3:14; Josh. 12:5, 13:11; 2 Sam. 15:8), where David got a wife and Absalom, refuge (2 Sam. 3:3, 13:37).

Geshuri (gĕ'shû-rĭ) 1. People of Geshur (Deut. 3:14; Josh. 12:5, 13:11, 13).

2. An ancient tribe south of Philistia, toward Egypt (Josh. 13:2; 1 Sam. 27:8).

Gether (gĕ'thĕr) an Aramean family, unknown (Gen. 10:23).

Gethsemane (gĕth-sĕm'à-nē) [oil press] a "place" (Mt. 26:36; Mk. 14:32) across Kidron (Jn. 18:1), presumably at the foot of Olivet (Lk. 22:39), where, from the olives, oil was squeezed by a press; to which place the Lord often repaired (Lk. 22:39; Jn. 18:2), and in which he suffered agony, betrayal, and arrest (Mt. 26:36–56; Mk. 14:32–52; Lk. 22:39–53; Jn. 18:1–12). Only traditional is the site east of the bridge, by which the road from St. Stephen's Gate crosses the brook. Wm. M. Thomson thinks it several hundred yards northeast. Venerable olive trees seem to be later plantings: Josephus tells that in Titus' siege, all trees were cut down.

Geuel (gĕ-ū'ĕl) [majesty of God] spy representing Gad in Canaan's exploration (Num. 13:15).

Gezer (gĕ'zēr) [place cut off] ancient town of Canaan, not far from Lachish (Josh. 10:33), on the boundary line of Ephraim (16:3), assigned with suburbs to Kohathite Levites (Josh. 21:21; 1 Chr. 6:67). Original folk were not driven out (Judg. 1:29; see 1 K. 9:16). David fought battles near the place (2 Sam. 5:25; 1 Chr. 14:16, 20:4). A Pharaoh took it from repossessing Canaanites, and gave its ruins as dowry to his daughter marrying the Hebrew king. It seems to be Tell el-Jezer, eighteen miles northwest of Jerusalem.

Giah (gī'à) [breaking out as a spring] a place (village?) between Gibeon in Benjamin and the ford of Jordan near Jabbok (2 Sam. 2:24).

giants the Nephilim of Gen. 6:4 [wonderfuls, fellers]; see Num. 13:32, 33. The offspring of the "sons of God" and the daughters of men, were mighty men (gibborim), the simplest and best explanation being that the former represented the godly line and the latter, the ungodly line. The old view that angels cohabited with women, gave rise to the spurious book of Enoch. There are the Rephaim (Gen. 14:5), indicated also in 2 Sam. 21:18–22, who may have held territory west of Jordan in ancient time (see Josh. 15:8, 18:16). Interestingly, they are called "the dead" in certain passages (Ps. 88:10; Prov. 2:18; Isa. 26:14, 19), from the notion that Sheol contained "fallen spirits or buried ghosts." Branches of this unknown folk, it appears, were Emim, Anakim, Zuzim (Gen. 14:5 and Deut. 2:10; Num. 13:28). Instances of abnormally large stature are known. Of such must have been men like Og of Bashan (Deut. 3:11), and Goliath of Gath (1 Sam. 17:4), and Benaiah's kill (1 Chr. 11:23). When Hebron was taken, the escaped Anakim took refuge in the Philistine towns: of these were Goliath and others (1 Sam. 17:4; 2 Sam. 21:15–22).

Gibbar (gĭb′bär) [hero] his children returned with Zerubbabel (Ezra 2:20).

Gibbethon (gĭb′bē-thŏn) [conical height?] a Danite town (Josh. 19:44), allotted to Kohathite Levites (21:20–23); taken by the Philistines; besieged by Nadab, who was assassinated (1 K. 15:27); besieged by Omri (1 K. 16:15, 17).

Gibea (gĭb′ē-á) [hill] likely a village (1 Chr. 2:49).

Gibeah (as above) 1. A village in Judea's hill country, southeast of Hebron (Josh. 15:57).

2. A town of Benjamin near Ramah (Judg. 19:13, 14); called also Geba (masc. form). Called "Gibeah of Benjamin" and "Gibeah of the children of Benjamin" (1 Sam. 13:2; 2 Sam. 23:29); and seems same as Gibeah of Saul (1 Sam. 11:4; 2 Sam. 21:6; Isa. 10:29; see Judg. 19, 20). This was Saul's residence when called to be king (1 Sam. 10:26); it remained his home and capital (15:34, 22:6, 23:19). It is distinguished from Geba (Hos. 9:9, 10:9). It was on the road from Jerusalem to Ramah (Judg. 19:13), being commonly identified with Tell el-Ful.

3. Gibeah-in-the-field (Judg. 20:31), seems to be the place to which a highway led from Gibeah of Benjamin.

4. A place in the hill country of Ephraim, belonging to Phinehas, where Aaron's son, Eleazer, was buried (Josh. 24:33).

5. Gibeah, or "hill of God" (1 Sam. 10:5), seems identical with Gibeah of Saul (vss. 11, 14).

Gibeath (gĭb′ē-äth) a Benjaminite town in connection with Jerusalem, a variant of Gibeah (Josh. 18:28).

Gibeathite, the native of Gibeah (1 Chr. 12:3).

Gibeon (gĭb′ē-ŏn) [pertaining to a hill] chief city of the Hivites of Canaan, included in the general designation Amorite (2 Sam. 21:2), who made league with Joshua (9:3–15). In Benjaminite territory (Josh. 18:25), allotted with suburbs to priests (21:17). When Saul violated the Gibeonite treaty, his seven sons were slain to satisfy justice (2 Sam. 21:1–9). For data, see 2 Sam. 2:8–17, 3:30, 20:8; 1 Chr. 8:29, 9:35, 14:16. Before the temple was built, the tabernacle and brazen altar were there; there Solomon sacrificed and received divine message (1 K. 3:4–15; 1 Chr. 16:39, 21:29; 2 Chr. 1:3, 6, 13). Its citizens returned from exile to help in wall-building (Neh. 3:7, 7:25). It is the modern el-Jib, about six miles northwest of Jerusalem. The pool of Gibeon (2 Sam. 2:13; Jer. 41:12) is southeast of the village; the wilderness of Gibeon, the uncultivated plateau between Gibeon and Ramah (2 Sam. 2:24).

Gibeonites, the inhabitants of Gibeon, and possibly of its three dependent towns (2 Sam. 21:1–4, 9; Josh. 9:17).

Giblites, the the people of the town and kingdom of Gebal. See Josh. 13:5.

Giddalti (gĭd-dăl′tĭ) [I have magnified] singer son of Heman, the king's seer (1 Chr. 25:4, 29).

Giddel (gĭd′dĕl) [he magnifies] 1. Head of a Nethinim family (Ezra 2:47; Neh. 7:49).

2. Head of a Solomon's servants' family (Ezra 2:56; Neh. 7:58).

Gideon (gĭd′ē-ŏn) [cutting off] a Manassite, son of Joash, of Ophra, probably on west of Jordan (Judg. 6:15); fifth recorded judge; called to deliver Israel from Midianite invaders (see Judg. 6:11, 8:20). While threshing wheat to hide it from the Midianites, an angel gave him commission. He threw down Baal's altars (Judg. 6), receiving a new name, Jerubbaal [Let Baal plead, vs. 32]. Then there occurred a second notable act: clothed by the Spirit of God (6:34; cf. 1 Chr. 12:18; Lk. 24:49), and joined at trumpet call by Zebulun, Naphtali, and even reluctant Asher, and strengthened by a double sign of the fleece, reducing his army of 32,000 (Deut. 20:8), by a second move (Judg. 7), to 300, his midnight attack brought rout and slaughter to the enemy, the memory of the exploit being preserved in national tradition (1 Sam. 12:11; Ps. 83:11; Isa. 9:4, 10:26; Heb. 11:32). A forty years' peace saw him, princely in mien, settled peacefully with honors (Judg. 8:22, 29, 31). He refused the crown, but unwisely made a costly ephod out of Midianite jewelry, which became a snare to him and a means of seduction for Israel, although it seems to have been intended for worship of Jehovah. His numerous progeny are noted in 8:28–31.

Gideoni (gĭd-ē-ō'nī) [a cutting off] a Benjaminite, father of Abidan (Num. 1:11, 2:22, 7:60, 10:24).

Gidom (gī'dŏm) a village of Benjamin (?), between Gibeah and the cliff, Rimmon (Judg. 20:45). See above.

gier eagle an unclean bird of Lev. 11:18; Deut. 14:7. Gier means "vulture," (which doubtless it was), being about two feet in length, common in Palestine during its northern migration.

gift frequent, formal, and popular in the East, the Hebrew language having fifteen words for the idea, with varying significances according to their purposes: from fathers to sons (Gen. 25:6); dowry to daughters (34:12); by people at weddings (Ps. 45:12); by fellowmen expressing good will (Est. 9:22), or to gain favor (Prov. 18:16); forbidden as bribery (Ex. 23:8; Deut. 16:19; Prov. 29:4); by monarchs as service reward (Dan. 2:48); or as favor unto public rejoicing (Est. 2:18); by subjects as tribute (2 Chr. 26:8; Ps. 45:12; Mt. 2:11); required for expenses in public worship (Mt. 5:23, 24, 8:4; Lk. 21:5). Refusal was indignity; and it was insult not to bring it when position required it (1 Sam. 10:27). We have the gift of God, eternal life (Jn. 4:10; Rom. 6:23); the gift of the Holy Spirit (Jn. 14:16, 16:7; Acts 2:38), and the manifestations of the Spirit in believers (Acts 5:31; Eph. 2:8; Rom. 5:5; Gal. 5:22). All Christian virtues are gifts (graces), bestowed variously upon men, and qualifying them severally for forms of service (Rom. 12:6; 1 Cor. 7:12, 12:4, 9; Eph. 4:7–16).

Gihon (gī'hŏn) [bursting forth, as a river] 1. Second river of paradise (Gen. 2:13).

2. A spring outside Jerusalem, as partial water supply (2 Chr. 32:30, 33:14). See **Jerusalem**

3. The scene of the anointing and proclamation as king of Solomon (1 K. 1:33, 38, 45).

Gilalai (gĭl'à-lī) [weighty?] a priest's son at the Jerusalem wall consecration (Neh. 12:36).

Gilboa (gĭl-bō'à) [bubbling fountain] a mountain range east of Esdraelon, above Jezreel, where the Philistines defeated and killed Saul and Jonathan (1 Sam. 28:4, 31:1, 8; 2 Sam.

1:6, 21, 21:12; 1 Chr. 10:1, 8). The village, Jelbon, preserves the memory.

Gilead (gĭl'ē-ăd) [rugged] 1. A mountain range east of Jordan, between Bashan and Moab and Ammon (Gen. 31:21; Deut. 3:12–17), called at times "Mount Gilead," "land of Gilead," "Gilead" (Gen. 31:25; Num. 32:1; Ps. 60:7; Gen. 37:25). It extended from the parallel of the south end of Sea of Galilee, to that of the north end of the Dead Sea, 60 by 20 miles, with an elevation of about 2000 to 3000 feet. It was divided by Jabbok into two parts–the southern was Gad's, the northern included half-Manasseh (Josh. 12:2; Deut. 3:12, 13; Josh. 13:24–31). By slight change in pronunciation, Gilead became "heap of stones," built by the separating Laban and Jacob (Gen. 31:21). It appealed to Reuben and Gad, with large flocks, as a suitable dwelling place (1 Chr. 5:9, 10; Num. 32:1–42; Josh. 13:8–11). Here was famous balm (Jer. 8:22; cf. Gen. 37:25). In general, Gilead included all of East Jordan (Deut. 34:1; Josh. 22:9; Judg. 20:1; 2 Sam. 2:9).

2. Possibly a mountain abutting on the valley of Jezreel (Judg. 7:3). Many think that the true reading is Gilboa; but since Gilead was part of Naphtali (2 K. 15:29), and which in the main was across Jordan eastward, it may be that there was a Gilead, a rugged district of Naphtali, west of the river, confirming the correctness of Judg. 7:3.

3. Son of Machir, grandson of Manasseh, and founder of a tribal family (Num. 26:29, 30; Josh. 17:1).

4. Father of Jephthah (Judg. 11:1).

5. A Gadite (1 Chr. 5:14).

6. A city in neighborhood of Gilead (Hos. 6:8; cf. 12:11).

Gileadites, the a branch of Manasseh, long feuding with Ephraim (Judg. 10:3, 12:4, 5; Num. 26:29).

Gilgal (gĭl'găl) [wheel, circle] 1. Israel's first camp west of Jordan (Josh. 4:19, 20; vs. 3); site of first Passover in Canaan (vs. 10). There reproach was "rolled away" for a long-neglected ordinance (5:7–9). Joshua 15:7 and Judg. 3:19 are taken by some to mean another Gilgal, at the foot of mountains. Nor is the Gilgal of Samuel's circuit (1 Sam. 7:16), and of Saul's crowning (11:15), identified. At the Gilgal in the Jordan valley, was the muster of forces, in view of the Philistines, where Saul disobeyed (13:4, 7–8, 13–14), and where his second rebuke was received (15:12, 21, 33; cf. 34). Here too, tribal representatives welcomed David back after Absalom's death (2 Sam. 19:15, 40). Idolatry, under kings later than Jeroboam, was there denounced by prophets (Hos. 4:15, 9:15, 12:11; Amos 4:4, 5:5). This is probably the place noted, after the Captivity (Neh. 12:29), called the house of Gilgal, or Beth-gilgal, its ruin being two miles east of Jericho. The text has no certain indications.

2. A village from which Elijah and Elisha went down to Bethel (Deut. 11:30; 2 K. 2:1–4), probably Jiljulieh, seven miles northwest of Bethel.

3. A town associated with Dor and Tirzah (Josh. 12:23).

4. Possibly another Gilgal, in the Samaritan mountains (2 K. 4:38).

5. Joshua 15:7 speaks of another, possibly same as 1 above. That of Deut. 11:30 is perhaps same as that of Josh. 9:6 and 10:6, but not same as in Josh. 4:19. Who knows?

Giloh (gī′lō) [exile] village in hill country of Judah, and home of Ahithophel (Josh. 15:51; 2 Sam. 15:12). Gilonite, a native of above (2 Sam. 23:34).

Gimzo (gĭm′zō) [having sycamores] a town and its villages, in Judah, taken by Philistines in Ahab's time (2 Chr. 28:18), identified with Jimzu, several miles from Lydda.

gin trap for birds, beasts, or men (Job 18:9), with a net (Isa. 8:14), and a stick (Amos 3:5). Pronounced with hard g.

Ginath (gī′năth) [protection] father of Tibni (1 K. 16:21–22).

Ginnetho (gĭn′nē-thō) [gardener] a chief of the priests returning with Zerubbabel (Neh. 12:4, 7).

Ginnethon (as above) in Neh. 10:6, likely same as above; and in 12:16, there is a Ginnethon, in the time of Joiachim, the high priest.

girdle an essential article of dress of men and women. The common girdle was of leather (2 K. 1:9; Mt. 3:4). A finer one was of linen (Jer. 13:1; Ezra 16:10), embroidered with silk and gold or silver thread (Dan. 10:5; Rev. 1:13, 15:6), sometimes having gold and precious stones. Women made them (Prov. 31:24). A clasp or knot allowed ends to hang down in front. Women wore looser girdles (Prov. 31:17). "Girding up the loins" indicated preparation for work or battle, sword or dagger being stuck in the girdle. Sackcloth was for mourning or humiliation (Isa. 3:24; 22:12). They were used as pockets and purses, one end being folded back (Mt. 10:9; Mk. 6:8).

Girgashites, the a tribe of Canaan (Gen. 10:15–16, 15:21; Deut. 7:1; Josh. 3:10, 24:11; 1 Chr. 1:14; Neh. 9:8). The Girgasite of Gen. 10:16 is same.

Gispa (gĭs′pà) [blandishment] an overseer of the Nethinim in Nehemiah's time (11:21).

Gittaim (gĭt′tā-ĭm) [two wine presses] a village of Benjamin (Neh. 11:31, 33; 2 Sam. 4:3). Site unknown.

Gittath-hepher (Josh. 19:13, as **Gath-hepher**)

Gittites the 600 who followed David from Gath, under Ittai (2 Sam. 15:18–19). Inhabitants of Gath (2 Sam. 6:10–11).

Gittith (Gittite) attached to Ps. 8, 81, 84–a so-called title, said to be either a musical instrument or a vintage song, etc. But comparing with the psalm of Hab. 3, we note that this kind of title belongs to the end of the preceding psalm, in each case of the three psalms, which sound the note of enjoyment of divine protection and full reliance on God's care (cf. Lev. 23:33), the word relating to wine presses (in general "fruits"). These psalms were sung, it appears, in connection with the autumn Festival of Tabernacles, signalizing Jehovah as Keeper, even as the Passover psalms (44, 68), with the title of "lilies" are consonant with the Spring Festival (Passover), signalizing Jehovah as Redeemer, the two festivals with their appropriate psalms and pertinent titles, covering the whole ground of Israel's life, in very general sense.

Gizonite, the "the sons of Hashem the Gizonite" are among David's warriors (1 Chr. 11:34). Because Gizo, neither man nor place, is found in Scripture, it is suggested that here is a corruption of Gunite (see Num. 26:48), which may be true.

glass the only allusion to glass (Job 28:17), has been disputed; but in view the ancient knowledge of it, as in Egypt before the Exodus, the Hebrews must have been acquainted with glass. In the NT it is a symbol of brightness (Rev. 4:6, 15:2, 21:18). The mirror as a polished surface was known (Ex. 38:8; Job 37:18; 1 Cor. 13:12).

gleaning gathering grain or grapes after harvest (Judg. 8:2; Ruth 2:2, 7, 9, 16; Isa. 17:6). For the poor, fatherless, and widow, the Law made provision (Lev. 19:9–10, 23:22; Deut. 24:19).

glede (glēd) [glider] common kite, only in Deut. 14:13; an unclean bird.

gnat small insect abounding in marshes, with vexatious bite; only in the proverbial expression (concern for minors and neglect of majors), in Mt. 23:24.

goad a rod, eight feet or so, pointed, and sometimes with iron head, for urging cattle on (1 Sam. 13:21); used as a weapon (Judg. 3:31); figuratively, for an incentive (Eccl. 12:11); metaphorically, of an animal injuring itself (Acts 9:5), "pricks" relating to the goad.

goat the most common Hebrew word relates to male or female; most others refer to he-goats, of which there are varieties, tended with sheep by same shepherd, but in separate companies (Gen. 27:9, 30:32; Mt. 25:32). The hair made cloth (Ex. 25:4, 35:26); flesh and milk afforded food (Lev. 7:23; Deut. 14:4; Prov. 27:27); skin, at times, for clothing (Heb. 11:37). They meant wealth (Gen. 30:33, 43); were for burnt offering and sin offering (Gen. 15:9; Ex. 12:5; Lev. 1:10, 4:24). Sheep prefer grass: goats, brush and leaves. The goat flock had its leader (Jer. 50:8). For scapegoat, see **Day of Atonement.**

Goath [lowing] a place near Jerusalem (Jer. 31:39).

Gob (gŏb) [pit, locust] place where David's men met the Philistines twice (2 Sam. 21:18–19).

goblet circular vessel for wine, etc.

God in English, from root "call," object of worship; in Greek, the object of this worship, as Spirit; in Hebrew, the primary meaning is power. From nature, men may learn what God is and what he does; by revelation, we learn what his love will do for recovery of sinners and for communion with him, as also the mode of his existence, with the various phases of his work, where the ineffable mystery of the Trinity is disclosed. God's nature is revealed in three stages, corresponding to the three planes of revelation: God, the Infinite Spirit, whose "theistic proofs" are recognized in Scripture, and who is revealed to be all which is comprehended under the good, the beautiful, and the true; the Redeemer of sinners, who delivers from sin because of pity for the sinner, abhorrence of sin and righteous retribution regarding it, and by a mode in which he is just while at the same time justifying the ungodly; the Trinity (God the Father, Son, and Holy Spirit), as seen in the baptismal formula and the benediction, whereby God the Father plans, God the Son executes, and God the Spirit applies, what Infinite and Ineluctable Love conceives regarding mankind. In the prosecution of his work, there is a relative subordination, but the three Persons are alike God over all, the subordination being functional (as above), rather than with difference in nature (scheme from B. B. Warfield).

Gog [high?] 1. A Reubenite (1 Chr. 5:4).

2. The prince of Meshech and Tubal (Ezek. 38:2), described as defeated with great slaughter when invading Israel in the last times (Ezek. 38, 39). Here is a type of heathenism against God's people. The name is said to be a loan-word, from Gyges, famous in Lydian exploits.

3. A vague personification, akin to Ezekiel's Gog, who is to appear shortly before the end of the age (Rev. 20:8–15).

Golan [exile] city of Bashan (Deut. 4:43), given to the Levites from the half-tribe of Manasseh (Josh. 21:27), and one of the refuge-cities east of Jordan (20:8). It became the head of a large province, between Hermon and the Yarmuk, and from near Jordan eastward, the name being Gaulanitis, of which the greater part is flat and fertile tableland, and is probably the region called, "the plain" (1 K. 20:23, 25).

gold the most valuable of metals (Gen. 2:11–12; 1 K. 10:2, 22:48; Ps. 72:15; Job 22:24); emblem of purity and of nobility (Job 23:10; Lam. 4:1); used for ornament (Gen. 24:22); lavishly employed in connection with the tabernacle and the temple (Ex. 25:18; 1 K. 6:22, 28). It was used for idols, crowns, chains, rings, earrings (Ex. 20:23; Ps. 21:3; Gen. 41:42; Song of S. 5:14; Judg. 8:26). The ARV of Ezra 2:69 indicates early coinage.

Golgotha (gŏl'gō-thà) [skull] the place where the Lord was crucified (Mt. 27:33; Mk. 15:22; Jn. 19:17); probably a mound skull-like in appearance (or an execution spot, where skulls abounded).

Goliath (gō-lī'ăth) [exile] giant of Gath slain by David (1 Sam. 17, 21:9–10, 22:10), ten and one-half feet in height (taking the cubit as twenty-one inches). In 2 Sam. 21:19, is another Goliath.

Gomer (gō'mĕr) [perfection] 1. Eldest son of Japheth and father of Ashkenaz, Riphath, and Togarmah (Gen. 10:2–3; 1 Chr. 1:5–6; Ezek. 38:6). Probably the classical Cimmerians, coming into Asia from beyond the Caucasus, settling in Cappadocia, threatening the Assyrian empire, overrunning part of Asia Minor; afterwards driven out of Asia. Generally they are thought to be the Cimbri of Roman times, and the Cymry of Wales. "Cambria" and perhaps "Cumberland," preserve their memory.

2. Daughter of Diblaim, wife of Hosea (Hos. 1:3).

Gomorrah (gō-mŏr'rà) [accumulation, submersion] one of the five cities of the plain, or "vale of Siddim," whose kings joined battle with Chedorlaomer and allies, Abraham to the rescue (Gen. 14:2–8). Four of the five were afterward destroyed of the Lord (Gen. 19:23–29), Bela (Zoar) being spared at Lot's request. See also Gen. 18:20; Deut. 29:23; Isa. 1:9, 13:19; Jer. 23:14, 49:18; Amos 4:11; Zeph. 2:9; Mt. 10:15. For location, see **Sodom.**

gopher wood the ark's wood, perhaps of the pine family, from kinship to the word "pitch"; or cypress, as some say (Gen. 6:14).

gospel [from the Anglo-Saxon *godspel*, "good tidings"; later, "God-story." Through the Greek and Latin, we have "evangel"] the word gospel is applied to a single one, and also to all of the first four books of the NT, regarding the life and teachings of the Lord Jesus Christ, referring equally to the message (only so in the NT) and to the books. There are various designations of the Gospel, as "the Gospel of God" (Rom. 1:1), "the Gospel of Christ" (Mk. 1:1), "the Gospel of the grace of God" (Acts 20:24), "the Gospel of peace" (Eph. 6:15), "the glorious Gospel" (2 Cor. 4:4). All four were composed during the latter half of the first century A.D., Matthew and Mark, some years before the destruction of Jerusalem, Luke near that event, while John came at the end of the century.

I. AUTHENTICITY. Historical evidence from earliest times shows Matthew, Mark, Luke, and John to be the writers of the respective books, and from the beginning of the post-apostolic age, were received by the church as authoritative and true. That before the end of the second century, the four books were one collection, generally accepted and used, is shown by the testimony of Irenaeus, Papias, Tertullian, Origen, Theophilus, and Tatian. Also early writers cite the four: Barnabas, Clement of Rome, Polycarp. Justin Martyr (99–165) has much verbatim quotation from Matthew, Luke, and John, and apparently from Mark. Combined with the witnesses, other writers and other references give certification of the gospel collection at this early time. In addition, heretical sects certify the gospels, even in dissensions and hostilities; had the gospels become known later, such heretics as Gnostics and Marcionites would not have recognized them. It is safely concluded that before the end of the second century, the gospels were not only well-known but used as authoritative. As a matter of literary history nothing can be better established than the genuineness of these four books. Further the NT epistles show these gospels describing the Lord as the same kind of person, doing the same kind of works, and having the same history as according to the apostles. They may therefore be taken as trustworthy reports.

II. DIFFERENCES AND CONTENTS. The first three gospels are called synoptics ("seeing together") and are quite different from the fourth. They have as their chief theme the ministry in Galilee; the fourth, in Judea, largely. But the Lord's betrayal, arrest, and trial, his crucifixion, and resurrection are narrated by all. Aside from the passion, John has but three facts in common with the others: the feeding the five thousand (Mt. 14:21), the storm in Galilee (ch. 6), and the anointing by Mary (ch. 12). But for John, we would not know that the Lord went to Jerusalem at the prescribed feasts. It appears that John, the last witness, purposely refrained from unnecessary duplication: he also writes from a different viewpoint. The Synoptics say comparatively little about the deity of Christ: John records especially his self-testimony to it. They present mainly Christ's teachings regarding the kingdom of God, his parables, and his instruction of the people; John records his teaching about himself, usually in the form of extended discourses. But the fourth gospel implies and assumes the other three, while they are intelligible often only in the light of the facts of the fourth. Compare Jn. 1:15 with Mt. 3:11; Jn. 3:1–4 with Mt. 4:12; Jn. 6:2, 15 with the synoptic story of the Galilean ministry. His reception in Galilee and the readiness of the four apostles to follow him are explained by the events of Jn. 1 and 2; ch. 5 throws light on the sabbath controversy of Mk. 2:23.

III. THE ADDRESS OF THE GOSPELS. But the synoptics have their individual characteristics as set by their purposes and the readers to whom they addressed themselves. Thus Matthew, writing from the Jewish viewpoint, sets Christ forth as the royal Messiah (king and kingdom), citing OT proofs, and stressing the true kingdom of God in contrast to false views of Judaism. Mark, with the Gentiles in mind, the Romans in particular, represents Christ's power as shown in the miracles. Luke, long a companion of Paul, presents the Lord as the gracious Savior, Son of man, with favor to the poor, outcast, and fallen. John holds up the Lord as Son of God incarnate, the divine Word revealing the Father. No one of the gospels is intended as a complete biography. The relation of the first three to each other has occasioned much argument regarding the "Synoptic Problem."

IV. THE SYNOPTIC PROBLEM. Matthew and John were apostles, and so had personal knowledge of events recorded, or were able to secure it from those who had it. Mark was companion to Paul and Peter, and by early tradition is said to have embodied the preaching of Peter. Luke's knowledge came from eyewitnesses (Lk. 1:1–4); and he had made himself well acquainted with the facts. Thus the gospels give the testimony of the apostles. Allowing their historical data to be divided into sections: in 42 sections, all agree; 12 are given only by Matthew and Luke; 5 by only Mark and Luke;

14 by Matthew and Luke. In addition, 5 are peculiar to Matthew, 2 to Mark, and 9 to Luke. The language of all three is Greek, with Hebrew idioms, the Hebraisms being most abundant in Mark, and least so in Luke. Except for 24 verses, Mark has no major facts not found in Luke and Matthew; he often supplies details omitted by them, such as seem to come from an eyewitness. There are no instances in which Matthew and Luke harmonize exactly, where Mark does not also agree. Sometimes Mark's words have common factors with the others, forming a connecting link between them. Examples of verbal agreement between Mark and Luke are neither so long nor numerous as those between Matthew and Luke, and Matthew and Mark; but in arrangement of events, Mark and Luke often agree, where Matthew differs. These are leading particulars regarding a phenomenon which has long engaged attention: whence humanly speaking, did the writers get their materials; and does any copy from another? In the ancient church, it was held that Mark abbreviated Matthew and Luke. Some have thought that Matthew and Luke drew from Mark, the historical narrative, another source of it being an alleged early collection of sayings of the Lord purporting to come from Matthew. On the other hand it seems probable that all three were independent, employing liberally the language of the gospel story which had become current, being free to use their own words when well acquainted with the facts. Each pursues his own purpose, as noted above. Regarding this matter we should keep in mind the recorded promise of Christ to the apostles, and including any others who might be employed: "But the Comforter, even the Holy Spirit, whom the Father will send in my name, he shall teach you all things and bring to your remembrance, whatsoever I have said unto you" (Jn. 14:26). And as "all Scripture is given by inspiration of God" (2 Tim. 3:16), such matters as these are rather of academic interest, which in no sense require solution before the reader can derive blessing from the gospels as integral parts of the Word of God written.

gourd this is the rendering of the Hebrew word (Jonah 4:6-10) for the plant which grew up in a night, sheltering the prophet from the hot sun, decaying as rapidly as it grew. The LXX makes it of the pumpkin type. The Hebrew word is much like the Graeco-Egyptian word for castor-oil plant which grows very rapidly to a height of eight to ten feet. If this was the "vine," its growth was supernatural.

gourd, wild the Hebrew word here means "bursters" (2 K. 4:39), being the fruit of a wild vine of Palestine growing even in drought. There was "death in the pot" when porridge was made with this fruit. It was probably the colocynth, emerald green when other vegetation has withered, looking and smelling like cucumber when cut open, but fire-hot when touched to the lips.

governor this word represents ten Hebrew and four Greek words! One who governs a land under a supreme ruler. There is the "man of authority," as Joseph (Gen. 42:6), and Daniel (5:29). There is the "elevated person" (Gen. 17:20, 23:6); an "appointed one" (Gen. 41:34; Neh. 11-14); a "chief" (Gen. 21:22, 40:2, 47:6); one having "power" as over property and person (Josh. 12:2; 2 Chr. 23:20); two words for a "lawgiver" (Gen. 49:10; Judg. 5:9, 14); "prince of a 1000" (Judg. 6:15, mg.); same as the "dukes" (Gen. 34); an Assyrian word (likely) (1 K. 10:15, 20:24; Ezra 6:8; Neh. 3:7, 5:18); a "prominent person" (2 Sam. 5:2; 2 Chr. 28:7); a representative officer of rank (2 Cor. 11:32); the procurator (Mt. 27:2); a steward (Gal. 4:2); governor of a feast (Jn. 2:9).

Gozan (gō'zăn) [food] a town and district of Mesopotamia to which the captive Israelites were taken by the Assyrian kings (2 K. 17:6). Apparently a river (1 Chr. 5:26), perhaps here confusion. Probably the same as Gausanitis of Ptolemy and the Mygdonia of Strabo, on the Khabour River, affluent of the Euphrates.

grace denotes the love of God as displayed in free favor toward men as sinners and destitute of all claim upon him (1 Tim. 1:2). Hence the NT, which reveals the plan by which this grace is bestowed, is called "the gospel of the grace of God" (Acts 20:24). The apostolic epistles begin with the salutation, "Grace and peace be with you" (P. Schaff, D.B., 1885).

grape see **vine**

grass represented by several Hebrew and one Greek words, relating to ordinary endogenous plants of the field, to which fleeting fortune and life's brevity are likened (Job 8:12; Isa. 40:6-7). Herbs and cereals for food, and fodder for cattle, are included (Gen. 1:30; Deut. 11:15).

grasshopper see **locust**

grave see **burial**

greaves a piece of defensive armor protecting the shin, is the ordinary use; but in 1 Sam. 17:6, the only place where the word is used, it appears to be a kind of boot.

Greece, Greek, Grecians a small celebrated country in southeastern Europe, where, the Mediterranean being the highway of civilization, it possessed decided advantages. Previous to the first written records, the first Olympiad of 776 B.C., the heroic age mingled history and legend inextricably. Through four tribes, the Greeks were traced back to a common ancestor, Helen. In the heroic age, the Aeolians and the Achaeans were prominent; Homer at times calls the Greeks, Achaeans. Dorians and Ionians, in historical times, stood out, Athenians and Spartans respectively descending, from them. The early historical period of around 200 years, up to 500 B.C., saw individual growth of theoretically independent states held together by language, literature, games, and general national development. Here the foundations of architecture, art, literature, and philosophy were laid. Greece was early known by the Hebrews as Javan, i.e., Ionia (Gen. 10:4; also Joel 3:6; Dan. 8:21; Isa. 66:19; Ezek. 27:13; the Joel and Daniel references have "Grecians" and "Grecia"). Greeks and Hebrews seem to have met for the first time in Tyrian slave-markets. The name of the country Greece, occurs once in the NT (Acts 20:2). Around 500 B.C. the Greek cities of Asia fell to Persia; but toward the end of the century, Marathon, Salamis, and Plataea, saw victories which defeated Persia. Athens was supreme for seventy years, then Sparta, then Thebes; then all Greece fell under the power of Philip of Macedon. Under his son Alexander the Great, Greece came first into contact with Judea in the fourth century B.C. Following Alexander's death (332 B.C.), Palestine was ruled by Armenia, Syria, Greece, and finally Rome. But the Greek language was spoken throughout the civilized world. Christianity was preached in Greek; the NT books were written in Greek (save possibly Matthew); and evidences seem to show that the church's language was Greek until the middle of the second century A.D. Our Lord surely knew Greek, though he used Aramaic commonly. Paul ordinarily spoke Greek (see Acts 21:40). A Greek was "one of Greek descent" (Acts 16:1); but the word meant foreigner in general, when contrasted with the Jew (Rom. 1:14). After Alexander's time, those who spoke the language and enjoyed Greek privileges were "Greeks" (Jn. 12:20), including Jews (Acts 9:29).

greyhound the Hebrew original of this word implies "girt about the loins" (Prov. 30:31). "Comely in going" may refer, as the margin, to a horse. Other possibilities are: leopard, eagle, man, zebra; but "a wrestler," girded for contest, has been suggested.

grinder some say that the "grinders" of Eccl.

12:3 are women at the mill; but in Job 29:17, certainly "teeth."

grinding see **mill**

ground two Hebrew words so translated and not always distinguished (Jer. 22:29). They have wide range of meaning, some common, some peculiar to each. Both are used to describe soil, the whole earth, land or country. Earth ('eretz) is opposed to heaven (Gen. 1:1), or dry land as opposed to sea (1:20); 'adamah especially is earth as a specific substance (Gen. 2:7), and the surface of the ground (Gen. 7:4). In the NT, gē is used in the variety of meanings of the Hebrew words above; while oikoumene denotes especially the whole inhabited earth, and once in even wider sense (Heb. 2:6).

grove in two places the Hebrew word seems to mean a tree (Gen. 21:33 and 1 Sam. 22:6). Elsewhere this mysterious word apparently refers to an idol or image of some kind, there being probable connection between this thing and the sacred symbolic tree (see Ex. 34:13). From earliest times groves are mentioned in connection with worship (Gen. 12:6; Deut. 11:30). Pliny says that trees were the first temples: it was thought wrong to shut up the gods within walls! Groves were connected with temples. And in harmony with this, there were memorable trees in Israel (Josh. 24:26; Gen. 35:8). This word is used in both genders in the plural: 'asherim, 'asheroth. Connected is the Canaanitish goddess Asherah.

guard oriental kings needed defense: the guard was a most responsible and therefore honorable position. Members of bodyguards of Pharaoh and of Nebuchadnezzar (Gen. 27:36; 2 K. 25:8) were originally "cooks" who were butchers of animals, and later, executioners. Bodyguards for the Hebrew kings were "runners," going in front of the royal chariot (2 Sam. 15:1; 2 K. 10:25). "Watchers" were at times, on guard (Neh. 4:9; Job 7:12). David had foreign mercenaries, the Cherethites and Pelethites, bodyguards, over whom was Benaiah (2 Sam. 20:23). According to Mk. 6:27, the "spy" was a member of a Roman division, the bodyguard of the general.

Gudgodah (gŭd'gō-dä) Deut. 10:7—see **Horhagidgad**

guest see **hospitality**

gulf in Lk. 16:26 is the only occurrence; likely no argument for the rabbinical belief in separate compartments in the nether world, but rather pertinent to the great moral separation between two fundamentally different characters.

Guni (gū'nī) [perhaps, painted with colors] a

son of Naphtali (Gen. 46:24), founder of the family of Gunites.

Gunites, the (gû'nīts) descendants of Guni, son of Naphtali (Num. 26:48).

Gur, the going up to (gûr) probably a steep ascent on the road from the plain of Esdraelon to Ibleam. There Ahaziah, who was fleeing from Jehu after the latter had slain Jehoram, was killed (2 K. 9:27).

Gurbaal (gûr-bā'ăl) a place inhabited by Arabians. It is probably in the desert country south of Beer-sheba near Edom. Uzziah's campaigns against these Arabians were to consolidate his control of trade routes (2 Chr. 26:7).

H

Haahashtari (hā-à-hăsh'tà-rî) a Judahite descended from Ashur, the father of Tekoa by his second wife, Naarah (1 Chr. 4:6).

Habaiah (hâ-bā'yăh) children of Habaiah were among the sons of the priests who returned with Zerubbabel from Babylon. Because their names were not found in the register, they were put out of the priesthood (Ezra 2:61; Neh. 7:63).

Habakkuk (hâ-băk'kŭk) a prophet of the last days of Israel before Babylon overran Judah in 587 B.C. A later date has been argued on the ground that the "Chaldeans" of Hab. 1:6 should read "Greeks," and that the enemy referred to was Alexander the Great. A Dead Sea Scroll commentary confirms the Chaldean reading, and the earlier date is generally accepted.

Habakkuk questioned God's providence because wrongdoers seemed to go unpunished. He was assured that God would punish his people through the Chaldeans, who themselves would be judged.

Habakkuk's expression "the just shall live by his faith" (Hab. 2:4), was used by Paul in his discussions of faith (Rom. 1:17; Gal. 3:11), and is also alluded to in Hebrews (10:37-38).

The third chapter is a magnificent poem of the Lord's coming to deliver. The Lord came to do battle first with the forces of chaos (Hab. 3:3); and then he scattered the nations, and went forth for the salvation of his people. The Dead Sea Scroll commentary neither contains nor alludes to Hab. 3. This seems to support the view that it is not from the hand of Habakkuk. Nevertheless, its lofty faith in the Lord's deliverance commends it to the Bible reader as inspired.

Habaziniah (hăb-à-zĭ-nî'ä) the head of one of the families of the Rechabites, whose descendant, Jaazaniah, lived during Jeremiah's time (Jer. 35:3).

habergeon (hă-bēr'gē-ŏn) originally, a coat of mail covering the neck and chest. It was later developed to cover the thighs and lower legs.

Habor (hā'bôr) the river of Gozan, an affluent of the Euphrates, to which some of the Israelites were deported by Shalmaneser the king of Assyria after the fall of Samaria (2 K. 17:6, 18:11; 1 Chr. 5:26).

Hachaliah (hăk-à-lī'ä) the father of Nehemiah (Neh. 1:1, 10:1).

Hachilah, the Hill of (hăk'ï-lä) in southern Judah in the wilderness of Ziph. David was there hiding when the inhabitants reported his whereabouts to Saul at Gibeah (1 Sam. 23:19). The exact location is unknown.

Hachmoni, son of (hăk-mō'nî) Jehiel, a companion of David's sons (1 Chr. 27:32).

Hachmonite, the (hăk'mō-nīt) one of David's mighty men, Jashobeam (1 Chr. 11:11).

Hadad (hā'dăd) the ancient Semitic storm god. His name occurs in Syrian proper names. It is found occasionally in the altered form, Hadar (Gen. 25:15, 36:39; cf. 1 Chr. 1:30, 50). 1. A son of Ishmael and grandson of Abraham (Gen. 25:15; 1 Chr. 1:30).

2. A king of Edom who gained an important victory over Moab (Gen. 36:35-36; 1 Chr. 1:46-47).

3. A king of Edom, whose capital was Pai (1 Chr. 1:50).

4. A member of the royal household in Edom, contemporary with David and Solomon. To escape David and Joab's slaughter of all males in Edom, Hadad fled to Egypt, where he was well received by the pharaoh. After the death of David, Hadad returned to Edom and became an adversary of Solomon (1 K. 11:14-22), being able to wrest some of the more inaccessible portions of Edom from Solomon.

Hadadezer (hăd-ăd-ē'zēr) same as **Hadarezer**

Hadadrimmon (hā-dăd-rĭm'mŏn) a deity for

which mourning was made at Megiddo. The mourning referred to in Zech. 12:11 is probably a rite, mourning the death of the god, similar to the mourning for the dead Baal by his sister Anat.

Hadar (hā'där) same as **Hadad**

Hadarezer (hăd-är-ē'zēr) the king of Zobah in Syria, an ally of the Ammonites whom David soundly defeated (1 Chr. 18:3–4, 19:16–19), giving David control of Transjordan trade routes and the copper mined in Hadarezer's realm.

Hadashah (hăd-ā'shä) a town of uncertain location near Gath in the lowland of Judah (Josh. 15:37).

Hadassah (hă-dăs'sä) another name for Esther (Est. 2:7).

Hadattah (hă-dăt'tä) read with preceding word in Josh. 15:25, as Hazor-hadattah. In the Negeb district of Beersheba; the exact location is unknown.

Hadid (hā'dĭd) a town of Benjamin which with Lod and Ono (Ezra 2:33; Neh. 7:37, 11:34) formed a triangle and was located a few miles inland from Joppa.

Hadlai (hăd'lī) the father of a chief of Ephraim in the time of Pekah (2 Chr. 28:12).

Hadoram (hå-dō'răm) 1. A son of Joktan of the family of Shem (Gen. 10:27; 1 Chr. 1:21).

2. A son of Tou king of Hamath (1 Chr. 18:10), sent to congratulate David on a victory over King **Hadarezer.**

3. An officer over David's, Solomon's, and Rehoboam's, tax levy and forced labor (2 Chr. 10:18). The name also appears as Adoniram (1 K. 4:6).

Hadrach (hăd'răk) a district of Syria, north of Hamath, mentioned by Zechariah (9:1) in connection with Damascus and Hamath.

Hagab (hā'găb) the sons of Hagab were among the temple servants who returned to Jerusalem with Zerubbabel (Ezra 2:46).

Hagaba (hăg'à-bä) the sons of Hagaba were among the temple servants who returned to Jerusalem with Zerubbabel (Neh. 7:48). In a parallel list in Ezra (2:45) the name appears as Hagabah.

Hagar (hā'gär) [wandering] the Egyptian handmaid of Sarah, who because of Sarah's barrenness, was given to Abraham as a concubine, and bore Ishmael. On two occasions Sarah's jealousy led her to banish Hagar and both times an angel appeared to her: the first time (Gen. 16:1–16) the angel bade her return to Sarah and prophesied that her offspring would be numerous. The second time (Gen. 21:9–21) the angel saved Hagar and Ishmael from perishing of thirst in the wilderness and

promised that God would make of Ishmael a great nation.

Paul makes an allegorical interpretation of Hagar, characterizing her as a type of the old covenant and the slavery of the Law (Gal. 4:22–25).

Hagarenes, Hagarites (hā'gär-ēnes, hā'gär-ītes) a nomadic people dwelling east of Gilead. The sons of Reuben made war against them taking their territory and confiscating their livestock (1 Chr. 5:10, 19–20). The Hagarenes are mentioned among the enemies of God's people in Ps. 83:6.

Haggai (hăg'gī) [festal] one of the minor prophets contemporary of Zechariah, who prophesied in 520 B.C. (the second year of Darius Hystaspes, Hag. 1:1). Jewish tradition says that he was known as a prophet during the Exile.

Haggai was mainly concerned to motivate the returned exiles to complete the rebuilding of the temple (Hag. 1:1–11), and he attributed the people's hardships to their neglect of the temple. The prophet also urged cutting off all contacts with religious syncretists. He argued that the pure would not purify the unclean, but rather the impure would contaminate the holy. When the people began to rebuild the temple, Haggai saw in that fact assurance that God would bless and prosper them (Hag. 2:15–19). He hailed Zerubbabel as the signet ring to be preserved by the Lord.

Haggeri (hăg'gē-rī) according to 1 Chr. 11:38, the father of Mibhar, one of David's valiant men. The parallel passage (2 Sam. 23:36) reads "Bani the Gadite" which is probably correct.

Haggi (hăg'gī) the second son of Gad (Gen. 46:16; Num. 26:15).

Haggiah (hăg-gī'ä) a descendant of Merari, a son of Levi (1 Chr. 6:30).

Haggites, the (hăg'gītes) a Gadite family descended from Haggi (Num. 26:15).

Haggith (hăg'gĭth) one of David's wives, the mother of Adonijah (2 Sam. 3:4; 1 K. 1:5, 11, 2:13; 1 Chr. 3:2).

Hai (hā'ī) same as **Ai**

hair care and styling of the hair was a matter of custom in the Bible, and it also had religious significance. It was sometimes dressed with aromatic ointments (Ruth 3:3; Ps. 23:5; Eccl. 9:8; Mt. 6:17, 26:7; Lk. 7:46). Cutting and tearing the hair were signs of grief (Isa. 3:24, 15:2; Jer. 7:29) in a time of war or national calamity. But Israelites were forbidden to trim around the temples (Lev. 19:27) or to cut the hair when a relative died (Deut. 14:1) because of the association of these practices with pagan rites. The hair was associated with strength (Judg. 13:4–7, 16:17) and purity; and not cutting the hair was considered a sign of consecration to God by the Nazarites (Num. 6:5).

Hakkatan (hăk′kă-tăn) the father of Johanan, the chief of the sons of Azgad, who returned from Babylon with Ezra (Ezra 8:12).

Hakkoz (hăk′kŏz) this name also appears as Koz. 1. A descendant of Aaron, chosen by lot to be in the seventh of the twenty-four courses into which David divided the priesthood (1 Chr. 24:1, 6, 10).

2. A man named in a list of Judahites (1 Chr. 4:8), whose family was unable to document its claim to priestly rank, and so were excluded from the priesthood after the Exile.

Hakupha (hă-kū′fä) the sons of Hakupha were among the temple servants who returned from Babylon with Zerubbabel (Ezra 2:51; Neh. 7:53).

Halah (hā′lä) a place in Assyria to which captives were carried (2 K. 17:6, 18:11; 1 Chr. 5:26). Its exact location is uncertain.

Halak the Mount (hā′lăk) a mountain on the southern limit of Joshua's conquest (Josh. 11:7, 12:7), on the way to Seir, east of the Arabah.

Halhul (hăl′hŭl) a hill country town of Judah (Josh. 15:58), four miles from Hebron toward Jerusalem.

Hali (hā′lī) a border town of Asher (Josh. 19:25); its exact location is unknown.

hall an enclosed courtyard. The AV translation of *aule* and of *praetorion*, referring to official residences of the governor. It was used to refer to Pilate's (Mk. 15:16) and Herod's quarters (Acts 23:35), where it is called "judgment hall" (cf. Mt. 27:27; Jn. 18:28, 33, 19:9).

Hallelujah (hăl-lē-lū′yä) [praise ye Jehovah] see **Alleluia**

Hallohesh (hăl-lō′hĕsh) one of those who helped repair the walls of Jerusalem under Nehemiah, and who sealed the covenant (Neh. 3:12, 10:24).

Ham (hăm) [swarthy, dark-colored] 1. One of Noah's sons (Gen. 5:32, 6:10; 1 Chr. 1:4). The sons of Ham are listed (Gen. 10:6) as part of the table of the nations. This system of classifying peoples was apparently ethnic and geographical. The Biblical Hamites ranged from Phoenicia through Palestine, and into Africa. They included the Cushites (south of the Red Sea), the Egyptians, the Canaanites, and Put (Libya?). Modern scholars use a somewhat different system, classifying peoples according to languages. They divide the peoples of the an-

cient Near East into two broad families, the Semito-Hamitic family, and the Indo-European family; and peoples listed as Hamites in the table of the nations are included in both families. The Semito-Hamitic family includes the Canaanites, the Egyptians, and the Cushites. The Indo-European family includes the Philistines.

2. A city east of the Jordan. A modern village by that name is located four miles south of Irbit (Gen. 14:5).

3. In an account (1 Chr. 4:40) of the migration of the Simeonites to the valley of Gedar, the inhabitants of Gedar are listed as being of Ham.

4. In the Psalms (78:51, 105:23, 27, 106:22), Ham is used as a synonym for Egypt, one of the Hamite nations.

Haman (hā′măn) the prime minister of King Ahasuerus of Persia who figures in the book of Esther. Because Mordecai refused to bow down to him, Haman attempted to destroy all the Jews. His plan miscarried when Queen Esther intervened, and he was hanged (7:10).

Hamath (hā′măth) a city of Upper Syria on the Orontes River. It was the center of an independent kingdom sometimes sharing a frontier with Israel (Num. 13:21; Josh. 13:5; Judg. 3:3; 2 Sam. 8:9–10; 2 K. 14:25). In David's conquest of Hadarezer of Zobah, he perhaps had the collaboration of Toi of Hamath.

Hamath-zobah (hā-măth-zō′bä) presumed not to be the same as **Hamath** since David was allied with Toi of Hamath while Hadarezer of Hamath-zobah was allied with Damascus (2 Sam. 8:3–12). Solomon conquered Hamath-zobah (2 Chr. 8:3).

Hamathite, the (hā′măth-īt) a member of one of the families descended from Canaan (Gen. 10:18; 1 Chr. 1:16).

Hammath (hăm′măth) a fortified town of Naphtali (Josh. 19:35) just south of Tiberias on the west shore of the Sea of Galilee. It is the same as the Levitical town called Hammon (1 Chr. 6:76) and Hammoth-dor (Josh. 21:32).

Hammedatha (hăm-ĕd′ä-thä) the father of Haman (Est. 3:1, 10, 8:5, 9:24).

Hammelech (hăm′mĕ-lĕk) [the king] unnecessarily transliterated in the AV as a proper name (Jer. 36:26, 38:6).

hammer a smooth or shaped stone, held in the hand. In the Bronze Age these sometimes had holes in them for a better grip or to accommodate a handle. Mallets of stone or wood were in common use, but hammers with metal heads were rare in ancient Palestine. The Hebrew has three words translated hammer: *halmuth* (Judg. 5:26), *maqqabah* (1 K. 6:7; Isa. 44:12;

Jer. 10:4; Judg. 4:21 where it is written *maqqe-beth*), and *pattish* (Isa. 41:7; Jer. 23:29, 50:23). From their use it is not clear that these words differ.

Hammoleketh (hăm-mŏl'ĕ-kĕth) the daughter of Machir and sister of Gilead (1 Chr. 7:17–18).

Hammon (hăm'mŏn) 1. A frontier city of Asher (Josh. 19:28), perhaps near the coast five miles northeast of Ras en-Naqurah.

2. Hammon (1 Chr. 6:76) see **Hammath**

Hammoth-dor (hăm'mōth-dôr') see **Hammath**

Hamonah (hăm-ō'nä) a city named in Ezekiel (39:16), near which Gog is to be defeated.

Hamon-gog, the Valley of (hā'mōn-gŏg) the name by which a particular valley will be known (Ezek. 39:11, 15) because Gog will be buried there.

Hamor (hā'mōr) the father of Shechem, killed with him in revenge by Simeon and Levi (Gen. 33:19, 34:2 ff.).

Hamuel (hā-mū'ĕl) a man of the family or clan of Simeon (1 Chr. 4:26).

Hamul (hā'mŭl) the son of Pharez, grandson of Judah (Gen. 46:12; 1 Chr. 2:5).

Hamulites, the (hā'mŭl-ītes) the family of Hamul (Num. 26:21).

Hamutal (hā-mū'tăl) the daughter of Jeremiah of Libnah, a wife of King Josiah and mother of Jehoahaz and Zedekiah (2 K. 23:31, 24:18; Jer. 52:1).

Hanameel (hā-năm'ē-ĕl) the son of Shallum and cousin of Jeremiah. From him Jeremiah purchased a field during the siege of Jerusalem (Jer. 32:7, 9, 12 and compare vs. 44).

Hanan (hā'năn) [gracious] 1. A descendant of Benjamin (1 Chr. 8:23).

2. A Benjaminite descendant of Saul (1 Chr. 8:38, 9:44).

3. One of David's mighty men (1 Chr. 11:43).

4. The head of a family of temple servants who returned to Palestine with Zerubbabel (Ezra 2:46; Neh. 7:49).

5. A Levite who helped Ezra interpret the Law (Neh. 8:7) and also sealed the covenant (Neh. 10:10).

6. Another man who sealed the covenant (Neh. 10:22).

7. Still another who sealed the covenant (Neh. 10:26).

8. An assistant to the temple treasurer appointed by Nehemiah (Neh. 13:13).

9. The head of a group of prophets at the temple (Jer. 35:4).

Hananeel, the Tower of (hā-năn'ē-ĕl) a tower on the north wall of Jerusalem (Neh. 3:1, 12:39; Jer. 31:38; Zech. 14:10).

Hanani (hā-nā'nī) 1. A son of Heman, leader of a course of Levitical singers (1 Chr. 25:4, 25).

2. The father of Jehu, the prophet (1 K. 16:1, 7; 2 Chr. 19:2, 20:34); probably the same as Hanani of 2 Chr. 16:7.

3. A priest with a foreign wife, divorced in the time of Ezra (Ezra 10:20).

4. A brother of Nehemiah (Neh. 1:2), later made governor of Jerusalem (Neh. 7:2).

5. A musician at the dedication of the walls of Jerusalem (Neh. 12:36).

Hananiah (hăn-ă-nī'ä) [Jehovah is gracious] 1. A son of Heman, a temple singer (1 Chr. 25:4, 23).

2. An officer in Uzziah's army (2 Chr. 26:11).

3. The father of Zedekiah (Jer. 36:12).

4. A Gibeonite, the false prophet in the reign of Zedekiah who predicted an early return of the exiles from Babylon (Jer. 28:1, 5, 10–17).

5. The grandfather of Irijah, a sentry who arrested Jeremiah for allegedly deserting to the Chaldeans (Jer. 37:13).

6. The head of a Benjaminite house (1 Chr. 8:24).

7. The Hebrew name of Shadrach (Dan. 1:6–7, 11, 19, 2:17).

8. A descendant of David, a son of Zerubbabel (1 Chr. 3:19, 21).

9. A son of Bebai listed among those who put away their foreign wives under Ezra (Ezra 10:28).

10. The son of an apothecary who helped restore the walls of Jerusalem (Neh. 3:8).

11. The son of Shelemiah who helped restore the walls of Jerusalem (Neh. 3:30).

12. A priest trumpeter at the dedication of the wall of Jerusalem (Neh. 12:41).

13. The head of the priestly course of Jeremiah under Joiakim (Neh. 12:12).

14. Governor of Jerusalem under Nehemiah (Neh. 7:2, 3).

15. One who signed the pledge of reform (Neh. 10:23).

handicraft the crafts, both domestic arts and manufacturing, were frequently practiced at home in families by both men and women. Contacts with the settled cultures of Canaan increased the practice of the crafts by specialists. After the Exile, there were guilds of craftsmen. People of a particular craft sometimes lived in a special quarter of the town.

The most significant crafts of Bible times were metalworking, building and cloth manufacturing. Metals known and used were gold—

the earliest metal to be worked—silver, copper, lead, tin, and iron.

Copper was the most influential metal for handicrafts, because its manufacture into tools increased man's ability to work other materials. The Hebrews learned copper-making from the people east of the Jordan. By Solomon's time, Israel had a significant copper industry with an elaborate smelter in the south of the Arabah.

Ironworking was discovered by the Hittites in the middle of the second millennium B.C. The Bible credits Tubal-cain (Gen. 4:22) with originating it. By Joshua's time the Canaanites possessed iron (Josh. 6:24; Judg. 1:19). In their conflicts with the Philistines, the Hebrews were at a disadvantage because they did not have ironsmiths of their own.

The building crafts were mostly practiced by persons building their own homes. Only in times of prosperity were they practiced in public works. Sometimes foreign specialists were imported, as in the building of Solomon's temple (1 K. 7:13–14).

Common building materials were mud and reeds. Mud was used for sun-dried bricks or with rubble, as mortar. By the early Bronze Age bricks were made in wooden molds. Reeds were sometimes used, especially in roof construction where they were bound together and covered with mud. Stone was also used, skilled masons sometimes being able to match stones so skillfully that no mortar was necessary.

The only available roof supports were beams until the Persian period, when vaults were used. After Alexander the Great, Greek motifs were introduced, bringing such features as marble columns with ornate capitals.

The making of cloth is an ancient craft. Cotton and flax have been spun from earliest times; wool-spinning began in the Bronze Age. It was more common after iron shears were developed. In early Biblical times cotton and flax were mostly uncolored, though in some linen found in the Qumran caves, there are blue threads. Wool dye was commonly purple, scarlet, or blue, but since the wool itself was of a variety of shades, varying from white to brown, many colors were produced. Cloth of wool, linen, and cotton, was used for garments and wall-hangings, for decorative and religious use. Sometimes gold thread was woven into a fabric for the decorative effect. Goat's hair was woven into a fabric for making tents.

handkerchief, napkin, apron [the word translating the Gr. *soudarion*, which is from a Latin word meaning "sweat"] it may mean a cloth, like our handkerchiefs, or it may refer to a cloth headdress of the Arabs. In Lk. 19:20, the word

designates the wrapping of the buried pound. In Jn. 11:44 and 20:7 it refers to a cloth covering the head of the dead.

Hanes (hā′nēz) the capital of the Upper Egyptian Heptanomis (Isa. 30:4).

hanging, hangings a curtain to close an entrance, used in various places in the tabernacle (Ex. 26:36–37, 27:16, 38:18, 39:38; Num. 4:26). The hangings were used to cover the walls of the court of the tabernacle (Ex. 27:9, 35:17, 38:9; Num. 3:26, 4:26). In 2 K. 23:7, the hangings which the women wove were probably cultic garments.

Haniel (hăn′ĭ-ĕl) one of the sons of Ulla, of the tribe of Asher (1 Chr. 7:39).

Hannah (hăn′nä) [grace] wife of Elkanah and mother of Samuel (1 Sam. 1:1–2). Long barren, she vowed that if she were given a son she would dedicate him to God (1 Sam. 1:11). She bore Samuel and dedicated him to God's service (1 Sam. 1:28).

Hannathon (hăn′nā-thŏn) a border town of Zebulun (Josh. 19:14). It may be identified with a place six miles north of Nazareth, or it may be identified with el-Harbaj at the south end of the plain of Acco.

Hanniel (hăn′nĭ-ĕl) [grace of God] 1. A prince of Manasseh, on the committee to divide the land, looking to Canaan (Num. 34:23).

2. An Asherite, son of Ullah (1 Chr. 7:39).

Hanoch (hăn′ŏk) [initiated, dedicated] 1. Third in order of the children of Midian (Gen. 25:4), descendant of Abraham by Keturah (also see 1 Chr. 1:33).

2. Eldest son of Reuben (Gen. 46:9; Ex. 6:14; Num. 26:5; 1 Chr. 5:3); founder of family of Hanochites (Num. 26:5).

Hanun (hā′nŭn) [enjoying favor] 1. A king in Ammon, son and successor to David's friend, Nahash, who mistaking the purpose of an embassy (both to condole and to felicitate), ill-treated the ambassadors, shaving off half of their beards and cutting their clothing off at the waist, and prepared for war, but was defeated despite alliance with Syria (2 Sam. 10:1–11:1; 1 Chr. 19:1–20:3).

2 and 3. Two who helped repair the walls (Neh. 3:13, 30).

Hapharaim (hăf-ā-rā′ĭm) [two pits] frontier town of Issachar, thought to be represented in Khirbet el-Farriyeh, six miles northeast of Lejun (Josh. 19:19).

Hara (hā′rä) [mountainous] an unidentified Assyrian location to which captives from the ten tribes were taken (1 Chr. 5:26).

Haradah (hăr′á-dä) [terror] unidentified encampment of Israel in the wilderness (Num. 33:24-25).

Haran (hā'răn) [strong, enlightened?] 1. Third son of Terah, and so, youngest brother to Abraham (Gen. 11:26). He died at early age, leaving Lot and two daughters, Iscah and Milcah (vss. 27, 29, 31).

2. A Gershonite Levite, family of Shimei, in David's time (1 Chr. 23:9).

Haran [road, or business] 1. Mesopotamian city whither Abraham migrated with his family, 280 miles northeast of Damascus. Here Terah died (Gen. 11:31-32, 12:4-5); here Nahor settled; here Jacob lived for a time (24:24, 28:10, 29:5)—Padan-aram (25:20). Assyrians captured it (2 K. 19:12). In later times, it became a small Arab village, same name.

2. A son of Caleb by concubine Ephah.

Hararite (hā'rä-rīt) [inhabitant of a mountain] probably an inhabitant of Harar; but the designation of three of David's guard: Agee, Shammah, Sharar (2 Sam. 23:11, 33). A variant of the last in 1 Chr. 11:35.

Harbona (här-bō'nà) [ass-driver?—Persian word] a chamberlain of King Ahasuerus (Est. 1:10). In 7:9, spelled Harbonah.

hare an animal prohibited to Hebrews (Lev. 11:6; Deut. 14:7), erroneously thought, anciently, to chew the cud, based on peculiar movement of the mouth.

Harel (hā'rĕl) [mount of God] apparently part of the altar (Ezek. 43:15); perhaps the hearth of the altar of burnt offering, covered by network on which sacrifices were laid for burning.

harem see **house**

Hareph (hā'rĕf) [plucking] a son of Caleb, and ancestor of the folk of Beth-gader (1 Chr. 2:51).

Hareth, the Forest of [thicket] refuge for David after quitting the cave of Adullam (or Mizpeh of Moab? 1 Sam. 22:5).

Harhaiah (här-hā'yä) [Jehovah protects?] father of Uzziel (Neh. 3:8).

Harhas (här'hăs) [glitter] ancestor of Shallum, the husband of Huldah (2 K. 22:14).

Harhur (här'hûr) [fever] his sons were among the Nethinim, returning with Zerubbabel (Ezra 2:51; Neh. 7:53).

Harim (här'im) [snub-nosed] 1. A priest who had charge of the third division in the house of God (1 Chr. 24:8). Later notation of this line in Ezra 2:39, 10:21; Neh. 7:42, 10:5, 12:15; in Neh. 12:3, it is Rehum.

2. Founder of a non-priestly family, 320 coming from Captivity with Zerubbabel in same caravan (Ezra 2:32, 10:31; Neh. 7:35, 10:27).

Hariph (hā'rĭf) [autumnal rain] apparently

founder of a family, 112 of whom came back with Zerubbabel (Neh. 7:24), a prince of this line seems to have sealed the covenant as representative of the family (10:19). Same as Jorah (Ezra 2:18).

harlot from earliest times, prostitutes existed (Gen. 38:15; Lev. 21:7; Deut. 23:18; Josh. 2:1; Judg. 16:1). To "go a-whoring after" is used figuratively of forsaking Jehovah for false gods (Jer. 2:20, 3:1; Ezek. 16:15-16, 23:5). These unfortunates were classed with publicans, as under the ban of society (Mt. 21:32). Their children were held in contempt and were without privileges and inheritance (Jn. 8:41; Deut. 23:2; Judg. 11:1-2).

Harnepher (här-nē'fĕr) [panting?] an Asherite, son of Zophah (1 Chr. 7:36).

Harod, the Well of (hā'rŏd) [fear] the water source where Gideon's army camped opposite the Midianites, in the valley, by the hill, Moreh (Josh. 7:1). There is a spring and pool at 'Ain Jalud, northwest of Mount Gilboa, with which Dean Stanley identifies Harod.

Harodite (hā'rŏd-īt) two of David's guard are so designated, from association with the town (2 Sam. 23:25).

Haroeh (hā-rō'ĕ) [the seer] a name in Judah's lists, as a son of Shobal (1 Chr. 2:52).

Harorite, the (hā'rō-rīt) see **Harodite.** Title of a warrior of David (1 Chr. 11:27; cf. 2 Sam. 23:25).

Harosheth (hā-rō'shĕth) [carving] more fully called "Harosheth of the Gentiles," due to mixed races in it, where Sisera lived (Judg. 4:2, 13, 16), located by some on the north bank of the Kishon before entrance into the plain of Acre.

harp invented in the antediluvian period (Gen. 4:21), apparently the national instrument of the Hebrews, whether delta-shaped or like a guitar, played either with fingers (1 Sam. 16:23), or with plectrum; and small enough to be carried (Isa. 23:16). Laban knew it (Gen. 31:27); with it, David soothed Saul (1 Sam. 16:16); used by prophets (1 Sam. 10:5; Ps. 43:4); employed in the temple orchestra (1 Chr. 25:1, 3). See Ps. 137:2. In Egypt there were two kinds, a larger and a smaller. The Greek rendering is an instrument more like the lute.

harrow the instrument of 2 Sam. 12:31; 1 Chr. 20:3, is apparently more like the threshing machine than the real harrow, a wooden frame with teeth, for breaking clods. The breaking of clods seems expressed in Isa. 28:24; Job 39:10; Hos. 10:11. But how?

Harsha (här'shà) [artificer's work] probably

founder of a Nethinim family, returning with Zerubbabel (Ezra 2:52; Neh. 7:54).

hart a wild, edible, clean animal (Deut. 12:15, 14:5, 15:22; 1 K. 4:23; Ps. 42:1; Song of S. 8:14); a stag, with antlers, say, of five years of age—a suggestion.

Harum (hā′rŭm) [exalted] in obscure genealogy of Judah, father of Aharhel (1 Chr. 4:8).

Harumaph (hā-rû′măf) [flat of nose] father of a Jodaiah (Neh. 3:10).

Haruphite, the designation of Shephatiah, a Korhite with David at Ziklag (1 Chr. 12:5).

Haruz (hā′rŭz) [industrious] father-in-law of King Manasseh, and a man of Jotbah (2 K. 21:19).

harvest see **agriculture**

Hasadiah (hăs-â-dī′ä) [Jehovah shows kindness] descendant of Judah's royal line, probably son of Zerubbabel (1 Chr. 3:20).

Hasenuah (hăs-ē-nū′ä) [thorny?] 1. A Benjaminite (1 Chr. 9:7).

2. Parent of one Judah (Neh. 11:9), perhaps.

Hashabiah (hăsh-â-bī′ä) [Jehovah has imputed] 1. A Merarite Levite (1 Chr. 6:45).

2. Another Merarite Levite (1 Chr. 9:14; Neh. 11:15), who may be same as above.

3. A son of Jeduthun in charge of the twelfth course of musicians of David (1 Chr. 25:3, 19).

4. A Kohathite Levite, inspector of West Jordan land (1 Chr. 26:30; cf. 23:12).

5. A Levite, and son of Kemuel (1 Chr. 27:17).

6. A Levite chief in Josiah's time (2 Chr. 35:9).

7. A Merarite Levite with Ezra, intrusted with treasure for Jerusalem, it seems (Ezra 8:19, 24); probably also noted in Neh. 10: 11 and 12:24.

8. The man of Ezra 8:24, is listed by some as another of this name.

9. A ruler of half-Keilah, a repairer of the wall (Neh. 3:17).

10. A sealer of the covenant, though probably the same as above (Neh. 10:11).

11. Seems another of this name; here, the son of Bunni (Neh. 11:15).

12. And another, son of Mattaniah (11:22). Still another, a priest of the family of Hilkiah, in the time of Joiakim the high priest (Neh. 12:21).

Hashabnah (hā-shăb′nä) covenant-sealer with Nehemiah (10:25).

Hashabniah (hăsh-ăb-nī′ä) father of Hattush (Neh. 3:10).

2. A Levite exhorter at Ezra's covenant-sealing fast (9:5).

Hashbadana (hăsh-băd′â-nä) one stationed by Ezra when he addressed the returnees (Neh. 8:4).

Hashem (hā′shĕm) [lay waste] a Gizonite in the list of David's mighty men (1 Chr. 11:34).

Hashmonah (hăsh-mō′nä) [place of fertility] a station of the wilderness journey (Num. 23:29–30).

Hashub (hā′shŭb) [thoughtful] 1. A son of Pathath-Moab and a wall-repairer (Neh. 3:11).

2. Another wall-repairer (3:23).

3. A head of the covenant-sealers (Neh. 10:23)—apparently another of this name.

4. A Merarite Levite (Neh. 11:15).

Hashubah (hā-shū′bä) [esteemed] apparently a son of Zerubbabel (1 Chr. 3:20).

Hashum (hā′shŭm) [rich] likely a founder of a family which came back with Zerubbabel (Ezra 2:19, 10:33; Neh. 7:22; see Neh. 8:4, 10:18). In 8:4, could be another of same name.

Hashupha (hā-shū′fä) [made bare] seems to have been a founder of a Nethinim family, returning with the first caravan (Neh. 7:46).

Hasrah (hăs′rä) [want?] the form of Harhas in 2 Chr. 34:29; cf. 2 K. 22:14.

Hassenaah (hăs-sē-nā′ä) [the thorny?] his sons rebuilt the fish gate (Neh. 3:3).

Hasshub (hăs′shŭb) [thoughtful] 1. A Merarite Levite (1 Chr. 9:14; Neh. 11:15). Seems same as **Hashub.**

Hasupha (hā-sū′fä) [made bare] his sons were of the Nethinim, with Zerubbabel, returning from Babylon (Ezra 2:43; Neh. 7:46).

hat see **headdress**

Hatach (hā′tăch) a eunuch of Ahasuerus' court (Est. 4:5 ff.).

Hathath (hā′thăth) [terror] a son of Othniel (1 Chr. 4:13).

Hatipha (hăt′ĭ-fä) [captive] similar to **Hasupha** (Ezra 2:54; Neh. 7:56).

Hatita (hăt′ĭ-tä) [engraving] his sons were of the porters (gate-keepers) returning with Zerubbabel (Ezra 2:42; Neh. 7:45).

Hattil (hăt′tĭl) [tottering] his sons were of the "children of Solomon's slaves," from captivity with Zerubbabel (Ezra 2:57; Neh. 7:59).

Hattush (hăt′tŭsh) [congregated] 1. Descendant of the kings of Judah (1 Chr. 3:22).

2. Head of a father's house returning with Ezra (8:2).

3. Apparently another, who was a chief of the priests returning with Zerubbabel (Neh. 12:2, 7).

4. Son of Hashabniah, and repairer of the wall (Neh. 3:10).

5. Apparently another who with Nehemiah sealed the covenant (Neh. 10:4).

Hauran (haw′răn) [hollow land] a region

south of Damascus and touching Gilead (Ezek. 47:16, 18). In the Greek period, it was known as Auranitis, being one of four provinces. About 23 B.C., it was, with Trachonitis and Batanaea, bestowed on Herod the Great by Augustus. Later, these constituted the major part of Philip's tetrarchy (Lk. 3:1). It is very fertile; many towns were once there, among them the "giant cities of Bashan."

Havilah (hăv′ĭ-lä) [perhaps, sandy] 1. A son of Cush (Gen. 10:7).

2. A son of Joktan (vs. 29). These two, as in several cases, it appears, may represent a body of people. Gold and aromatics and precious stones, seem to indicate a location in the mountainous district of North Yemen; association with Hazarmaveth, points in the same direction, i.e., to Central Arabia. According to 1 Sam. 15:7 and Gen. 25:18 it is suggested that the name included territory some hundreds of miles north of the mountains; and some find indications of it as far as the coast of Africa. Gen. 2:11 relates it to the Garden of Eden.

Havoth-jair (hā′vôth-jā′ĭr) [Jair's circuit of villages] certain villages east of Jordan, in Bashan, taken by Jair, son of Manasseh, and called by his name, closely associated with Gilead (Deut. 3:4, 14), which at times, it seems used to include Bashan (1 Chr. 2:21, 23; Num. 32:40; 1 K. 4:13). The Scriptures leave the reader in some doubt as to the composition and number of these cities, some making distinction between Havoth-jair and sixty walled cities in the middle of Bashan in the Argob (Deut. 3:4–5; 1 K. 4:13). Compare 1 Chr. 2:22 and Judg. 10:4.

hawk a ceremonially unclean predatory bird, including a number of species of Falconidae (Lev. 11:16; Deut. 14:15), some of which are migratory (Job 39:26).

hay grass of any kind (Prov. 27:25; Isa. 15:6). There is a term for "dry grass" or "hay" (Isa. 5:24, 33:11), rendered "chaff"; even this is not handled like our hay, but merely cut in small quantities and then consumed.

Hazael (hā′zā-ĕl) [God hath seen] a Syrian whom Elijah was charged to anoint king over Syria (1 K. 19:15, 17). Around the middle of the ninth century B.C., he was sent by the then ruler, Ben-hadad II of Damascus, to inquire of the prophet if he would recover from his serious illness, which led to the murder of the king and accession of his ambitious servant (2 K. 8:7–15). He fought Judah and Israel for Ramoth-gilead (8:28). A short while later, the Assyrian king Shalmaneser twice warred against Hazael. Toward the close of Jehu's reign, in the latter part of the ninth century, Hazael smote the Hebrew "coasts" (2 K. 10:32; cf. 8:12). Then about the close of his reign he took Gath and mightily oppressed Israel threatening also Jerusalem, (12:17, 13:4–7); but he was deterred from attacking Jerusalem by gifts (2 Chr. 24:24; 2 K. 12:18), from Judah's king Jehoash. He died soon after (13:34), having reigned forty-six years.

Hazaiah (hā-zā′yä) [Jehovah sees] a Shilonite man of Judah (Neh. 11:5).

Hazar-addar undetermined landmark along southern boundary of Israel (Num. 34:4; Adar in Josh. 15:3).

Hazar-enan (hā′zàr-ē′năn) [village of fountains] town on north line of Palestine, near Damascus; unlocated (Num. 34:9; Ezek. 47:17, 48:1).

Hazar-gaddah (hā′zàr-găd′dä) [village of good fortune] town at far south of Judah, unlocated (Josh. 15:27).

Hazar-hatticon (hā′zàr-hăt′tĭ-cŏn) [middle village] unidentified town on Hauran's border (Ezek. 47:16).

Hazarmaveth (hā′zàr-mā′vĕth) [village of death] third of the sons of Joktan (likely a group under this name), living in South Arabia, where there is still a region called Hadramaut whence in ancient times, a great trade flourished with India and Africa.

hazel or almond tree, probably the latter (Gen. 30:37).

Hazarshual (hā′zàr-shŭ′ăl) [fox village] in far south of Judah, a town assigned to the Simeonites (Josh. 15:28, 19:3; 1 Chr. 4:28); in post-Captivity, occupied (Neh. 11:27).

Hazarsusah (hā′zàr-sū′sä) [horse village] a village of the Simeonites in south of Palestine (Josh. 19:5; 1 Chr. 4:31—here, "Susim").

Hazazon-tamar (hăz′à-zŏn-tā′màr) [pruning of a palm] later called En-gedi (Gen. 14:7; 2 Chr. 20:2), in the wilderness, on the western shore of the Dead Sea, in Judah (Josh. 15:62). See **En-gedi**

Hazelelponi (hăz′ĕ-lĕl-pō′nĭ) [protection of the face of] sister of Etam's sons, in Judah's genealogies (1 Chr. 4:3).

hazer topographically seems employed for "villages" of people of roving life, collections of dwellings of rough stone walls covered with tent-cloths. See the various "Hazars" above.

Hazerim (hā-zē′rĭm) habitations of the Avvim (Avims); "villages" as far as Gaza (Deut. 2:23).

Hazeroth (hā-zē′rôth) [encampments] a station of Israel in the desert, where Miriam and Aaron murmured against Moses (Num. 11:35, 12:16, 33:17; Deut. 1:1).

Haziel

Haziel (hā′zĭ-ĕl) [vision of God] a Gershonite Levite, son of Shimei (1 Chr. 23:9).

Hazo (hā′zō) [vision?] son of Nahor by Milcah (Gen. 22:22).

Hazor (hā′zôr) [enclosure] 1. A fortified city allotted to Naphtali (Josh. 19:36), once the capital of the Canaanite kingdom of Jabin, above the waters of Merom, between Ramah and Kadesh (12:19). On the defeat of his general, Sisera, Jabin fought on but was beaten and slain (Judg. 4:1–21; 1 Sam. 12:9). Some hold that this was another Jabin, which we reject. Fortified by Solomon (1 K. 9:15), its people were captured by Tiglath-pileser of Assyria (2 K. 15:29). It is thought same as Tell Khureibeh.

2. A town in Judah's far south (Josh. 15:23); and apparently, another (vs. 25); a third being noted, viz. "Hezron which is Hazor."

3. A place where Benjaminites lived after the Captivity, to the north of Jerusalem (Neh. 11:33).

4. "The kingdoms of Hazor" (Jer. 49:28–33) are probably collective village life, as over against nomad, in the Arabian desert, east of Palestine.

headdress seems not commonly used in the Mosaic era (but see Ex. 28:40). Later, for ornament, various items were worn by nobles (Job 29:14), by women (Isa. 3:23), by kings (Isa. 62:3; cf. 61:3; Ezek. 27:14), and at weddings (Isa. 61:10). The ordinary Bedouin headdress was a square handkerchief, red or yellow, folded so that three corners hung down over back and shoulders, bound around the head by a cord, something similar being used by Hebrews on occasion. Assyrian headdress is noted in Ezek. 23:15. Daniel 3:21, seems rather a cloak than a hat.

hearth cakes baked "on the hearth" (Gen. 18:6), likely conformed to Bedouin manner, on hot stones covered with ashes. The "hearth" of King Jehoiachim's winter palace (Jer. 36:23) was, we surmise, a pan or brazier of charcoal.

heath probably a kind of juniper (Jer. 27:6, 48:6—different words in Hebrew, both involving the idea of nakedness), having minute, narrow, rigid leaves. Some regard the second reference above as relating to a destitute person, as in Ps. 102:17.

heathen this means literally "dweller in the heath," suggesting the fact that the Gospel was originally found in towns, while the folk in the heath were idolaters. Pagan, with the idea of belonging to a village, and so, rustic, has similar vein. Before Israel's political status, *goyim* (nations, gentiles) referred to people generally, including the immediate descendants of Abraham (Gen. 18:18; cf. Gal. 3:16). But as Israel grew, and as laws and ritual, etc., made distinction from other people, the latter were termed *goyim*, being associated with false gods and foul practices (Lev. 18, 20), which were the chief marks of *goyim* (Num. 15:41; Deut. 28:10), the separation being in full force in monarchical times (2 Sam. 7:28; 1 K. 11:4–8, 14:24; Ps. 106:35). As national life progressed, the *goyim* were the surrounding nations generally, contacting Israel. The distinction became in time, an ecclesiastical one (see Mt. 18:17), also of ethnographical nature, with a moral sense (Ps. 9:5, 15, 17; Ezek. 7:21, 36:15; Jer. 10:25). There are the abominations of the heathen (2 K. 16:3; Ezek. 23:30; Ezra 6:21; Ps. 79:1, 6, 10). Note that in Ps. 79:6, the latter part of the verse interprets the former part—lest any charge God with injustice!

heaven English word may be "heaved up things" (Robt. Young's *Analytical Concordance*). The Hebrew word is plural (Gesenius, *Hebrew Lexicon*) in form, from root "be high"; some say "covering." This is the word which with the word for "earth," comprehends the universe (Gen. 1:1, 2:1, 14:19, 24:3; Jer. 23:24; cf. Mt. 5:18). The English translation of this word is principally singular. The word translated "firmament" (found seventeen times) is, in Gen. 1:8, called "heaven." Much misunderstood, it indicates something "beat out thin," "diaphanous"; and its translation has brought unmerited condemnation to the "science of the Bible." Both the Greek and the Latin translation grossly misrepresent Scripture here. In five instances, the AV translates variations of the word "cloud," as "heaven," or "heavens." There is the material idea of heaven as contrasted with the earth: it has windows (Gen. 7:11; 2 K. 17:2, 19), and doors (Ps. 78:23); it sends rain (2 Sam. 21:10; Ps. 147:8; James 5:18) and frost (Job 38:20); there are the "stars of heaven" (Neh. 3:16; Ezek. 32:7–8). At the consummation, this is to be done away (2 Pet. 3:10; Rev. 6:14), to give place to a new heaven as well as a new earth (Rev. 21:1). Then there is the realm beyond the material, which is the peculiar abode of God (Ps. 80:14), referred to as the God "of heaven" and the God "in heaven" (1 K. 8:30; Dan. 2:28; Mt. 5:45). We note Christ, "the Lord from heaven" (1 Cor. 15:47), who descended from heaven (Jn. 3:13), into which he has again ascended (Lk. 24:51; Acts 1:9; Eph. 4:8; 1 Pet. 3:22) and whence he shall come to judge (Rom. 8:33;

Heb. 6:20). There are the angels (Mt. 22:30). In it God's will is done (Mt. 6:10); there joy and peace reign (Lk. 15:7, 19:38). Here too are the "many mansions" (Jn. 14:2); into it Elijah passed (2 K. 2:1); in it believers have inheritance, with privilege of laying up treasures (1 Pet. 1:4; Mt. 6:20). It contrasts with hell, Satan's fate (Ps. 139:8; Lk. 10:18; 2 Pet. 2:4). The "third heaven" of the apostle Paul's rapt vision (2 Cor. 12:1–4), seems to signify the highest heaven: no one knows. We discount the Rabbis' "seven heavens." "Heaven of heavens" is their widest extent (Deut. 10:14; 1 K. 8:27; Ps. 115:16). The believers' heaven is not a state merely, but a world of space, as in many passages, and the expression "heavenly places" ("heavenlies") of Eph. 1:3. The bliss of heaven is beyond conception (see Jn. 14:2), as shown in many forms and figures (Heb. 4, 11; Rev. 3, 21, 22). [Ideas from Philip Schaff's *Bible Dictionary*, 1885.]

heave offering every hallowed thing levied, taken away from larger mass, set apart for God (Lev. 22:12; Num. 5:9, 18:8, 31:28–29). See Num. 18:9–19; Deut. 18:4; Neh. 10:39. Especially the tithe (21–24). Particular heave offerings were: those from the peace offerings (Lev. 7:13–24); from the ram of consecration, at priestly induction (Ex. 29:27); but in Aaron's case, burnt (22–25); from the first dough of new meal, yearly (Num. 15:20–21).

Heber (hē′bẽr) [union] 1. Grandson of Asher (Gen. 46:17; 1 Chr. 7:31; Num. 26:45).

2. Of Judah's tribe (1 Chr. 4:18).

3. A Gadite (5:13).

4. A Benjaminite (8:17).

5. Another Benjaminite (8:22).

6. Heber the Kenite, husband of Jael (Judg. 4:11–24).

7. The patriarch Eber (Lk. 3:25).

Heberites descendants of Heber, branch of Asher (Num. 26:45).

Hebrew, Hebrews [pertaining to Heber, or to the other side] the word first occurs of Abraham as the "crosser over," i.e., from the other side of the Euphrates (Gen. 14:13). Or it may relate to Eber, although from Gen. 11:10–26, it appears that he enjoyed no prominence; and the only word pertinent here, is Gen. 10:21, where Shem is "father of all the children of Eber," i.e., of nations east of the Euphrates. The historical use of the word "Hebrew" confirms the appellative derivation. A patronymic (e.g., Israelite) would naturally be employed among the people themselves, while the appellative—originally applied to them as strangers, would continue to designate them in relation to neighbors, and to be used by foreign nations.

Even after the substitution of the term Jew, following the Captivity, the word Hebrew still found place in the marked national contradistinction, the language. The Hebrews' language (2 K. 18:26, 28; Isa. 36:11, 13), called "the language of Canaan" (Isa. 19:18), belongs to the Semitic group, is read from right to left, has twenty-two consonants (cf. sections of Ps. 119). Vowel pointings were devised, around the sixth century (following) A.D., by the Tiberias-centered doctors called Massoretes. Except for parts of Daniel and Ezra, and a few verses elsewhere, which are in Aramaic, akin to Hebrew, the OT was originally written in Hebrew. From national organization to the Babylonian captivity, the golden age of the language, Hebrew was comparatively pure; but thereafter, it was corrupted by influx of Aramaic, until in the time of our Lord, Aramaic was the colloquial language and went even under the name of Hebrew (Mk. 5:41; Jn. 5:2; Rev. 9:11).

Hebrewess a woman of the Hebrews (Jer. 34:9).

Hebrews, the Epistle to the in the early church there was some doubt as to its canonical authority; but by the end of the fourth century, under the decided opinion of Jerome and Augustine, confirming the judgment of all Greek and Eastern churches, it was accepted as canonical; the third Council of Carthage (A.D. 397) and also a decretal of Pope Innocent (416) gave final approval and confirmation of what the church had declared, despite the fact that Luther regarded it along with James and Jude, as of lesser authority than the other NT books.

I. AUTHORSHIP. As to the writer, there has been much difference of opinion. The Western church held it not Pauline, as also did North Africa, Tertullian naming Barnabas. Hippolytus and Irenaeus were anti-Pauline. Origen upheld Paul as the ultimate writer. The Eastern church's opinion—Pauline—generally prevailed by the fifth century, and until the sixteenth, when the question was thrown open again. The book is anonymous. Hebrews is said to be unlike the Pauline epistles; from 2:3, one gathers that the writer was not an apostle; and it is unlike Paul to receive the Gospel from others (Gal. 1:11–24). In 13:23, the reference to Timothy appears not sufficient to indicate the writer; nor does "they of Italy" show locality, though the inference is that he was there. The doctrine has much in common with Paul though put in a different way. Critics say that the style is unlike Paul's, being smoother, often more eloquent, less impetuous. The omission of any address is un-Pauline. The LXX seems to be used exclusively, in references, whereas Paul employed the Hebrew OT as well. Luther suggested Apollos; Grotius, Luke; others, Silas; Neander, a man of the Pauline school. Priscilla is mentioned—due to 13:22! There are Pauline strains (cf. 6:10–11 with 1 Thess. 1:3). Despite the anti-Pauline arguments, "we are best satisfied with the arguments of those who ascribe the writership of this magnificent epistle, entirely to the apostle Paul, the great expounder of the Jewish system" (Ed., Smith D.B.).

II. DESTINATION AND DATE. The contents of Hebrews gives impression of its being written to Jewish Christians; three addressees are rivals: Palestine, Alexandria, Rome. It seems evidently written to a definite body of Christians who were in great danger of apostasy, Rome seeming best to qualify. A number of modern scholars say it was to Gentiles, being written in Italy outside of Rome (15:24), some time before the temple was destroyed, say A.D. 65 to 69 (13:10–14). Traditional Pauline writership puts the date around 63, toward the end of his imprisonment at Rome. The background of those to whom the letter was addressed is understood from the contents: the end of all the beauty and awfulness of Zion was approaching. What could take the place of the temple? the holy place? the Levitical sacrifices? What compensations could Christianity offer? Such thoughts were aggravated by persecutions suffered, renewing desires for the glories of their former Judaism, so soon to be doomed. To such situation the epistle comes, showing that the revelation in the Lord Jesus Christ is final for he leads men to God, the objective of all religion. He shows in sympathetic spirit that when Christianity "emerges from the hard shell of Judaism, it leaves behind no great truth, but carries everything to a higher plane and clearer light."

III. OUTLINE: A. *Doctrinal:* i. The revelation in Jesus Christ is final, for he is greater than prophets and angels (chs. 1–2). ii. He leads men to God (3:1–10:18): (a) Greater than Moses as apostle—a Son (chs. 3 and 4); (b) Greater than Aaron as high priest—a Son (5:1–10:18). B. *Practical*—an exhortation based on the foregoing (10:19–12:29): i. Draw near—10:19–31. ii. Don't draw back—10:32–12:29. c. *Epilogue*—13:1–17. D. *Conclusion:* Notices and benediction—13:18–25.

Hebron (hē′brŭn) [union] 1. Third son of Kohath who was second son of Levi, younger brother of Amram, father to Moses and Aaron (Ex. 6:18; Num. 3:19; 1 Chr. 6:2, 18, 23:12). Founder of the Hebronites (Num. 3:27, 26:58;

1 Chr. 26:23, 30–31), called Bene-hebron (1 Chr. 15:9). In 1 Chr. 2:42–43 it seems impossible to say whether places or founders.

2. A town in hill country of Judah (Josh. 15:54, 20:7), twenty miles both from Jerusalem and Beersheba. One of the most ancient cities, it was built seven years before Zoan (Num. 13:22), well-known in Abraham's day (Gen. 13:18). Originally Kirjath-arba (Judg. 1:10), Arba being progenitor of the Anakim (Josh. 21:11). The scene of striking events in patriarchal experiences: Sarah died there; Abraham bought for the family sepulcher, Machpelah, from Ephron the Hittite (Gen. 23:2–20); Isaac and Jacob sojourned there (Gen. 35:27, 37:14); visited by the spies (Num. 13:22); defeated by Joshua and captured (Josh. 10:1–27, 36–39); re-established after conquest of Canaan; claimed and retaken by Caleb (Judg. 1:10–15); was assigned to priests as a city of refuge (Josh. 20:7; 1 Chr. 6:54–57); David reigned there seven and one-half years (2 Sam. 2:1–3, 11, 32); Absalom's rebellion centered there (2 Sam. 15:7–10). Now called el-Khulil er-Rahman.

3. A town of Asher, now unknown, probably Ebdon or Abdon (Josh. 19:28).

Hebronites (hē′brŭn-īts) descendants of Hebron the Kohathite (Num. 3:27; 1 Chr. 26:23, 30–31).

hedge what surrounds or encloses, as for a vineyard or sheepfold, of thorns (Num. 22:24; Ps. 89:40), or of stone (Num. 32:16, likely); or regarding a partition of any kind (Mt. 21:33). It is distinct from the tangled hedge of thorny shrubs, abounding in Palestine (Isa. 5:5; Mic. 7:4), as an additional safeguard. See further Eccl. 10:8; Ps. 80:12; Nah. 3:17.

Hege, Hegai (hē′gē; hĕg′ā-ī) a chamberlain of King Ahasuerus (Est. 2:3, 8, 15).

heifer generally, a young cow; but the Hebrew has no word corresponding to our "heifer"; the two words employed are used also of cows that have calved (1 Sam. 6:7–12; Job 21:10; Isa. 7:21). The heifer was worked in agriculture (Judg. 14:18; Jer. 50:11; Hos. 10:11), also in religious connection (e.g., Gen. 15:9; 1 Sam. 16:2; Num. 19:21). Hosea 4:16 compares Israel to a heifer; so is Egypt (Jer. 46:20), and Chaldea (50:11).

heir inheritance was as early as Abraham (Gen. 15:3–4). Sons of only legal wives inherited (Gen. 21:10, 24:36, 25:5), the eldest generally being given larger portion, with certain duties attached. Concubine sons received gifts (Gen. 25:6; see Judg. 11:1, 2). Job's daughters received inheritance (42:15; see Gen. 31:14). Daughters' inheritance was a marriage portion.

If no sons, property went to daughters (Num. 27:8; but see 36:6–9); if no daughters, the brother of the deceased inherited; if no brother, the paternal uncle; and failing here, the next of kin (Num. 27:9–11). The case of Ruth shows provision for a widow without children (3:12–13, 4:1–13). 1 Chr. 2:34–41; Ezra 2:61, give other cases. Reference to wills in NT come from Greek and Roman usage (Heb. 9:17). Believers are, in a figure, heirs of God (Rom. 8:17).

Helah (hē′la) [scum, verdigris] one of the two wives of Ashur (1 Chr. 4:5).

Helam (hē′lăm) place east of Jordan where David defeated the Syrians (2 Sam. 10:16–17).

Helbah (hĕl′ba) [fatness] a town of Asher, near Sidon (Judg. 1:31).

Helbon (hĕl′bŏn) [fat] city of Syria celebrated for wines (Ezek. 27:18): now the Helbun, thirteen miles north of Damascus.

Heldai (hĕl′dī) [enduring] 1. A Netophathite of Othniel's line, David's captain for the twelfth month (1 Chr. 27:15; perhaps same as Heled of 11:30).

2. A returned exile (Zech. 6:10; seems called Helem in vs. 14).

Heleb (hē′lĕb) [fatness] hero of David's guard, son of Baanah (2 Sam. 23:29; same as Heled of 1 Chr. 11:30; apparently same as Heldai of 1 Chr. 27:15).

Helek (hē′lĕk) [smoothness] descendant of Manasseh and second son of Gilead (Num. 26:30). Helekites, family from foregoing.

Helem (hē′lĕm) [stroke] 1. A descendant of Asher (1 Chr. 7:35).

2. (Another word meaning "dream"?) A man of Zech. 6:14; seems same as Heldai.

Heleph (hē′lĕf) [change] frontier town of Naphtali (Josh. 19:33).

Helez (hē′lĕz) [alertness?] 1. An Ephraimite of David's guard (2 Sam. 23:26; 1 Chr. 11:27, 27:10).

2. A man of Judah, son of Azariah (1 Chr. 2:39).

Heli (hē′lī) [Gr. for Eli, elevation] father of Joseph, husband of the Virgin Mary (Lk. 3:23).

Helkai (hĕl′kī) [smooth] a priest of family Meraioth (Neh. 12:15).

Helkath (hĕl′kăth) [smoothness, field] a town on Asher's boundary (Josh. 19:25), given with suburbs to Gershonite Levites (21:31).

Helkath-hazzurim (hĕl′kăth-hăz-zŭr′ĭm) [field of sharp knives] scene near pool of Gibeon of combat between Joab's and Abner's men, twelve each, bringing death to all, and a general battle (2 Sam. 2:16).

hell place of the dead—one rendering of both Hebrew "Sheol" and Greek "Hades." Sheol may mean "to demand" or "to make hollow." Hades may mean "the unseen." The Hebrew conception seems to have been vague and undefined, the ancient Hebrews thinking of it as beneath the earth (Num. 16:30, 33; Ezek. 31:17; Amos 9:2), picturing it as having gates (Isa. 38:10), as dark, gloomy, lacking activity (2 Sam. 22:6; Ps. 6:5; Eccl. 9:10), to which all go (Gen. 37:35; Ps. 31:17; Isa. 38:10). But it was open before God (Job 26:6; Prov. 15:11); and God was present even there (Ps. 139:8), the spirits of his own, and also their condition, being ever under his watchful eye. "The doctrine of God's knowledge of His people after death, His presence with them and love for them, involved the blessedness of the righteous and the woe of the wicked, and the two places for them, after death, the righteous being with the Lord and the wicked being banished from His presence." And despite the limited and peculiar ideas entertained by the folk of old time and entered by the Holy Spirit for record, presented as a foil for the "grace and truth" which came by Jesus Christ, the Hebrew Scriptures do teach the doctrine of future glory, and even the resurrection (Job 19:25, 27; Ps. 16:8–11; 17:15, 49:14–15, 71:24; Dan. 12:2–3). If there are reserves in the OT, they serve but to make the more glorious the life and immortality brought to light by the Savior, to dispel all gloom regarding the future state (Lk. 23:43; Jn. 14:1–3; 2 Cor. 5:6–8; Phil. 1:23). It remained for the NT to present hell as the place of woe, involving torment, as in the sense of the word "Gehenna" in Mt. 5:22, 29–30, 10:28, 18:9, 23:15, 33; Mk. 9:47; Lk. 12:5; James 3:6. This place was where children were burnt to Molech—the valley of Hinnom, which due to the horrible practices, including perhaps the burning of offal there, the place became a symbol of eternal punishment (Mt. 5:22, 13:42, 18:8–9; Mk. 9:43). The "casting down to hell (Tartarus)" of 2 Pet. 2:4 reflects the Roman and Greek place of woe, with essentially the same meaning as Gehenna—each being the place of punishment of the lost.

Hellenist a non-Greek who spoke the language; used especially of Jews wherever living, who had adopted Greek tongue and practices; also used of proselytes of foreign parentage. When Alexander's conquests carried Greek everywhere, the Jews adopted the tongue, while maintaining their Hebrew inner character, making a double impress: countering Judaism as final and universal; and transforming it, to become the foundation of a spiritual religion uninhibited by any local restrictions.

helmet see **arms**

Helon (hē'lŏn) [strong?] father of Eliab, prince of Zebulun (Num. 1:9, 2:7, 7:24, 29, 10:16).

hem of garment edge, or border of a garment, to which was attached a sacredness, going back to Num. 15:38-39, giving symbolical meaning (see Mt. 23:5).

Hemam (hē'măm) [faithful] 1. Son of Zerah (1 Chr. 2:6), high in wisdom (1 K. 4:31), connected with Ps. 88.

2. Singer of David's time, son of Joel, and a Korahite Levite (1 Chr. 6:33, 15:17; see vs. 19, and 16:41-42). There seems some conflict about this man; but if Heman the Kohathite or his father, had married an heiress of the house of Zerah, so as to be reckoned of that genealogy, all the Heman notices may refer to the same person.

Hemath (he'măth) (Amos 6:14; 1 Chr. 2:55) see **Hamath** and **Hammath.** In the latter reference, we note a person or place touching the Kenites, and Rechab.

Hemdan (hĕm'dăn) [pleasant] a Horite, eldest son of Dishon (Gen. 36:26). In the parallel, 1 Chr. 1:41, is Amram, apparently an error, for Hamran, which differs from Hemdan by confounding the letter "r" with "d," the original undeterminable now.

hemlock bitter, poisonous herb (Hos. 10:4; Amos 6:12; elsewhere translated "gall"). Figurative use is seen in Deut. 29:18; Amos 5:7; Heb. 12:15. The evils of perverted judgment, parallel useless, harmful plants, in the place of good and nutritious vegetation.

hen [= grace] this common fowl, oddly enough, is found only in Mt. 23:37; Lk. 13:34. Son of Zephaniah, apparently same as Josiah, Zech. 6:10; the reading may very possibly be "for the kindness (favor) of the son of Zephaniah" (Zech. 6:14), taking *Hen* as a common noun, "kindness."

Hena (hē'nä) a city taken by Assyria (2 K. 18:34, 19:13; Isa. 37:13), identified by some as the modern Ana on Euphrates. The Jewish paraphrase (Targum) takes two words here as verb forms and reads: "he has driven away and overturned."

Henadad (hĕn'ä-dăd) head of a Levite family prominent in temple rebuilding (Ezra 3:9).

Hepher (hē'fĕr) [pit] 1. Youngest of Gilead's sons, head of a family (Num. 26:32, 27:1; Josh. 17:2).

2. A town west of Jordan (Josh. 12:17).

3. A man of Judah, son of Asher of Tekoa (1 Chr. 4:6).

4. A Mecherathite hero of David's guard (1 Chr. 11:30). Hepherites (Num. 26:32).

Hepzibah (hĕp'zĭ-bä) [my delight is in her] 1. Mother of King Manasseh (2 K. 21:1).

2. Symbolic name of restored Jerusalem (Isa. 62:4).

herald (Dan. 3:4).

herd, herdsman greatly regarded in patriarchal and Mosaic times. The herd was for sacrifices —the young preferred (Ex. 29:1; Num. 7:3; Ps. 69:31; Isa. 66:3); for food (Deut. 32:14; 2 Sam. 17:29); for agriculture (1 Chr. 12:40; Isa. 46:1). Cattle was one of the traditions of Israel (Ex. 10:26, 12:38). The herdsman was honorable (Gen. 47:6; 1 Sam. 11:5, 21:7; 1 Chr. 27:29, 28:1; Amos 1:1, 7:14).

Heres (hē'rēz) [sun] (Isa. 19:18, mg.) an eminence in the district of Ajalon (Judg. 1:35). Noting Josh. 18:41, it seems probable that this is same as Ir-shemesh, i.e., Beth-shemesh.

Heresh (hē'rĕsh) [silence] a Levite attached to the tabernacle (1 Chr. 9:15).

Hermas (hĕr'măs) name of a Christian resident of Rome whom Paul greeted (Rom. 16:14); said by Irenaeus and Tertullian to be writer of the "Shepherd," cited with great respect and held by some to have been inspired.

Hermes (hĕr'mēz) traditionally, one of the seventy disciples, afterward bishop of Dalmatia—a man noted in Rom. 16:14.

Hermogenes (hĕr-moj'ē-nēz) one who turned away from Paul according to his last epistle (2 Tim. 1:15).

Hermon a mountain on northeast border of Palestine, called "Sirion" by Sidonians and "Senir" or "Shenir" by Amorites (Deut. 3:8-9). Also called "Sion" (4:48). See also Josh. 11:17, 12:1; 1 Chr. 5:23. It was the northeast limit of Israel's conquest (Deut. 3:8-9; Josh. 2:1, 5, 11:3, 17, 13:5, 11; 1 Chr. 5:23). On the southern end of the Anti-Lebanon range, it rises to around 10,000 feet, covered with perpetual snow, the proper source of Jordan, noted in poetry and song, conspicuous and beautiful landmark. There are several summits (Ps. 42:6 RV). Baal may have been worshiped there (Judg. 3:3; 1 Chr. 5:23). It is now called Jebel esh-Sheik. Hermonites could be folk of Hermon, or "Hermons."

Herod name of several rulers in and around Palestine (one being called Agrippa) of Idumaean descent but Jewish faith; very ambitious for an independent Judaistic kingdom. 1. *Herod the Great.* Second son of Antipater (Antipas) who was appointed procurator of Judea by Julius Caesar (47 B.C.). Although only around twenty years of age, Herod received the government of Galilee and of Coele-Syria. Mark Antony (41 B.C.) appointed Herod and brother Phasael tetrarchs of Judea. Herod, as his father before him, had the knack of snatching victory out of defeat, and of riding every adverse wave to higher fortunes. After the battle of Philippi, he switched to Antony and Octavius, victors over Brutus and Cassius, his former patrons; and was made king of Judea. After the battle of Actium, when Antony lost to Octavius, Herod won the favor of the victor and returned to Palestine with Roman endorsement and over added territory to maintain a throne by slaughter and unmatched cruelty and ruthlessness, including members of his own family and even his Judean wife Mariamne, the most beautiful woman of the time. He ruled for twenty-eight years afterward, encouraging learning, adorning Jerusalem (his temple surpassing that of Solomon), studding his land with beautiful cities, but hated by his subjects. To compel mourning at his death, he summoned and shut up the chief men of the nation in the Hippodrome, charging Salome, his sister, and her husband to have them all slaughtered when breath left his body. It is not surprising that we read little of the slaughter of innocents in an obscure village, Bethlehem (Mt. 2:16–18), in view of the monstrous horrors perpetrated by this beast, when highest heads were "falling by the score and threatened by the hundreds." Shortly thereafter, the earth was rid of "the curse of his life"; he went "to his own place"; but "born is the King of Israel"! About 4 B.C., age seventy, the thirty-fourth of his reign (from the time of his actually gaining the kingdom), he died—*sic gloria transit mundi.*

2. *Herod Antipas* the tetrarch was son of the above by a Samaritan wife, Malthace. His father's final will made him tetrarch of Galilee and Perea (Mt. 14:1; Lk. 3:19, 9:7; Acts 13:1; cf. Lk. 3:1), giving his brother, Archelaus, the kingdom. He stole his half brother Philip's wife, Herodias, whereupon his father-in-law, Aretas of Petra (Nabataean kingdom), incensed at the divorce of his daughter, invaded his territory, inflicting great loss, Herod's defeat being attributed by many to the murder of John the Baptist, shortly before, under Herodias' influence (Mt. 14:3–12; Mk. 6:17–29; Lk. 3:19). Her ambition was his ruin—the fact that her brother Agrippa was made king while her husband remained only tetrarch, aroused her envy; and she persuaded him to go to Rome to ask for the crown. Instead he was exiled to Gaul, where he died (A.D. 39). Our Lord mentioned the "leaven of Herod" (Mk.

8:15), and spoke of him as a fox (Lk. 13:31–32). He was in Jerusalem at the time of the crucifixion, the Lord being sent to him by Pilate, resulting in reconciliation between the two (Lk. 23:7–12, 15; Acts 4:27). He founded the city of Tiberias and named it for the Emperor—his most conspicuous monument.

3. *Herod Philip I* (Philip of Mk. 6:17), was son of Herod the Great and Mariamne, distinguished from Philip the tetrarch. He married Herodias, sister of Agrippa I (by whom she had a daughter, Salome), who deserted him to make infamous marriage with his half brother Herod Antipas, above (Mt. 14:3; Mk. 6:17; Lk. 3:19). Deprived of inheritance, due to his mother's treachery, he retired to private station.

4. *Herod Philip II* was son of Herod the Great and Cleopatra, receiving the title of tetrarch and the government of Batanaea, Trachonitis, Auranitis (Gaulanitis), and parts of Jamnia (Lk. 3:1). He built a new city at Jordan's source, at Paneas, which he called Caesarea (Mt. 16:13; Mk. 8:27). He raised Bethsaida to city rank, under the name Julias; he died there (A.D. 34). He had married Salome, daughter of Herod Philip I and Herodias.

5. *Herod Agrippa I* is distinguished from Herod Agrippa II, before whom Paul was tried. He was son of Aristobulus and Bernice, and grandson of Herod the Great. After vicissitudinous life, he was imprisoned by Tiberius, till the accession of Caius (Caligula) in A.D. 37, who gave him the holdings of the tetrarchs Philip and Lysanius, ensigns of royalty, and other favors (Acts 12:1). In 39, the Emperor banished Herod the tetrarch, and gave his territory, Galilee, to Agrippa. For services rendered to Claudius, successor to the assassinated Caligula, Judea and Samaria were added to his possessions (A.D. 41), equaling the dominions of Herod the Great. A strict observer of the Law, he sought successfully the favor of the Jews, in which connection, probably, he put to death James the son of Zebedee and imprisoned Peter (Acts 12:1–19). In his fourth year over all Judea (A.D. 44), appearing at the games honoring the Emperor at Caesarea (Acts 12:21), saluted as a god, he was eaten of worms (Acts 12:20–23), and died after five days' agony, at age fifty-four. He left four children, three being mentioned: Agrippa, Drusilla, Bernice.

6. *Herod Agrippa II* was son of Herod Agrippa I and Cypros, grand-niece of Herod the Great, and brother of the notorious women, Bernice and Drusilla. He was at Rome when his father died (A.D. 44); but being only seventeen years old, Judea was placed under a procurator.

However, later, he was given Chalcis, on the western slope of Anti-Lebanon (ca. A.D. 50), and two years later, the former tetrarchies of Philip and Lysanius, with the title of king (Acts 25:13). In 54–55, Nero added to his rule certain cities of Galilee and Perea. Accompanied by Bernice (a scandalous liaison), he went to Caesarea to salute Festus, the new procurator of Judea. Paul in prison there was brought before the procurator, the king, and Bernice, successfully clearing himself (Acts 25:13–26:32). In the last Roman war, Agrippa took part with Rome; and following the fall of Jerusalem, retired with Bernice to Rome, where he became praetor. He died A.D. 100.

Herod, palace of a palace-fortress erected by Herod the Great, ca. 24 or 23 B.C., at the northwest corner of the upper city, forming with other structures, a stronghold which excited the admiration even of the Romans, the site being the modern citadel by the Jaffa Gate.

Herodians a Jewish party in the Lord's time, favorable to the Herod family, who held hope of preserving national existence in the face of Roman ambition, despite the fact that they were Idumaean and not Jewish. Logically they were in direct antagonism to the Pharisees, with whom however there was common cause against foreign rule, the two being united also in their opposition to the Lord (Mt. 22; Mk. 12; see Mk. 3:6, 8:15).

Herodias daughter of Aristobulus, one of the sons of Herod the Great and Mariamne, and so, sister of Agrippa I. She had married Herod Philip I, her uncle; then she eloped with Herod Antipas, her step-uncle, long married to the daughter of Aretas of Arabia. John the Baptist reproved the incestuous scandal—and lost his head, standing true, disregarding the cost (Mt. 14:8–11; Mk. 6:24–28)! On her husband's banishment, Herodias went with him into exile.

Herodion a Christian at Rome, called kinsman by Paul sending greeting (Rom. 16:11).

heron name of an unclean bird (Lev. 11:19; Deut. 14:18), presumably the generic name for a well-known class, generally of slow flight, with long bill and legs, eating principally fish and reptiles, and found along the Jordan and its lakes.

Hesed (hĕ'sĕd) [mercy] father of a purveyor of Solomon (1 K. 4:10).

Heshbon (hĕsh'bŏn) [reason] capital city of Sihon of the Amorites (Num. 21:26), apparently taken from Moab (25–30, 34). Assigned to the Reubenites, it was rebuilt by them (Num. 32:37; Josh. 13:17). Later it was in Gad's territory (Josh. 13:26) and was given to

the Levites (Josh. 31:39; 1 Chr. 6:81); held by Moab in time of Isaiah and Jeremiah (Isa. 15:4, 16:8–9; Jer. 48:2, 33–34). The site is marked by the ruins of Hesban, twenty miles east of Jordan, opposite the north end of the Dead Sea.

Heshmon (hĕsh'mŏn) [fatness] town on extreme south of Judah (Josh. 15:27).

Heth [terrible?] forefather of the Hittites, a son of Canaan (Gen. 10; 1 Chr. 1), therefore Hamitic.

Hethlon (hĕth'lŏn) [hiding place?] place on north border of Palestine, near the entering in of Hamath (Ezek. 47: 15, 48:1; cf. Num. 34:8).

Hezeki (hĕz'ē-kī) [my strength] a Benjaminite, descendant of Shaaraim (1 Chr. 8:17).

Hezekiah (hĕz-ē-kī'á) [Jehovah strengthens] 1. Twelfth king of Judah, son of Ahaz, and associated with his father in 728 B.C., after whose incapacity he became active ruler, at age twenty-five (2 Chr. 28:27, 29:1). He instituted quite an ambitious reform in his corrupted kingdom (2 Chr. 29:2–30:13). He "smote the Philistines as far as Gaza" (2 K. 18:8). According to 2 K. 18:9, it was in the fourth year of Hezekiah that Shalmaneser (724 B.C.) commenced, and his son Sargon II (722 B.C.) effected, the capture of Samaria of Northern Israel, and deported the ten tribes, demanding tribute of Hezekiah who refused and prepared for war (2 K. 18:7; 2 Chr. 32:3–5, 30). The Assyrian invasions began in 714 B.C. The best solution of the difficulty from our standpoint, concerning the dates and the kings involved, is as follows: In the fourteenth year of Hezekiah (2 K. 18:13), Sennacherib, acting for his still ruling father Sargon, came against Judah, and according to the Assyrian account, subjugated it, taking "all the fortified cities," Judah's tribute unavailing (vs. 14). Apparently at this time (714) Hezekiah fell ill (2 K. 20:1–11; Isa. 38), being granted a fifteen years' respite. At such juncture came messengers from Merodach-baladan of Babylon (at that period enjoying a measure of independence), ostensibly to felicitate the recovered king of Judah, and perhaps to investigate the "sign" of healing, but actually to foment alliance against Assyria. Then in 701, Sennacherib, king in his own right, invaded Judah and other places, an uprising having occurred following the death of his father, Sargon. He made victorious march, heading toward Egypt; but learning at Lachish of threatening alliance of Philistia and Ethiopia with Egypt, and unwilling to have foes at his rear, he demanded unconditional surrender of Jerusalem (2 K.

18:17; see vss. 21, 24). From Libnah, Sennacherib sent a second force to renew the demand, which occasioned Hezekiah's prayer and Isaiah's magnificent "word" (2 K. 19:8–34), guaranteeing the inviolability of the Holy City. After defeating Egypt, Sennacherib's purpose came to inglorious end (2 K. 19:35–37). A possible explanation of the mix-up in Isa. 36:1 and 38:1, is to understand that in the rearrangement of his prophecies the time-notes were confused in the historical chapters (36–39) and that Sennacherib came in his 701 invasion, in the fourteenth year of Hezekiah's added life. The reader will see the inversion chronologically in these four chapters: for 36 and 37, in time order, follow the next two chapters; but for logical purpose—to conclude the first part of his book, the chapters relating to Assyria are placed before those relating to Babylon, in order to allow chs. 38–39, to introduce Babylon as the future conqueror of Judah.

2. An ancestor of Zephaniah (1:1).

3. A son of Neariah of royal blood (1 Chr. 3:23).

Hezion (hĕz'ĭ-ŏn) [vision] father of Tabrimmon, and grandfather of Ben-hadad king of Syria; supposed identical with Rezon, of Solomon's time (1 K. 11:23).

Hezir (hē'zĭr) [pig] 1. A priest of David's time, leader of the seventeenth course of priests (1 Chr. 24:15).

2. A chief, sealing the covenant with Nehemiah (10:20).

Hezrai (hĕz'rī) [enclosed] a Carmelite mighty man of David (2 Sam. 23:35); same as Hezro (1 Chr. 11:37).

Hezron (hĕz'rŏn) [shut in] 1. A place on southern boundary of Judah (Josh. 15:3; perhaps same as Hazor of vs. 23).

2. A son of Reuben (Gen. 46:9; Ex. 6:14; Num. 26:6; 1 Chr. 5:3).

3. A son of Perez (Gen. 46:12; Num. 26:21; Ruth 4:18; 1 Chr. 2:5). Hezronites were of Hezron, son of Reuben (Num. 26:6), and a branch of Judah, descendants of Hezron (26:31).

Hiddai (hĭd'dī) [joyful] one of David's heroes, from the brooks of Gash (2 Sam. 23:30; called Hurai in 1 Chr. 11:32).

Hiddekel (hĭd-dē'kĕl) [rapid?] Hebrew name for the river Tigris, going forth in front of Assyria (Gen. 2:14; Dan. 10:4); still called by the Hebrew name by many near it. Its principal sources are in Central Armenia. It flows through the Kurdistan mountains, finally joining the Euphrates; originally it emptied directly into the Persian Gulf. It flows by the ruins of

Nineveh, on the left bank, opposite to and in the vicinity of Mosul on the right bank. Downstream, it cuts Baghdad in two, further passing Ctesiphon, the Parthian capital's ruins, and then those of Seleucia, its whole length being of 1146 miles, half that of the Euphrates.

Hiel (hī'ĕl) [God lives?] Bethel native who rebuilt Jericho in Ahab's time (1 K. 16:34), and in whom Joshua's curse was fulfilled (6:26).

Hierapolis (hī-ĕ-răp'ō-lĭs) [sacred city] Asia Minor city in the Lycus valley, in the Meander basin, not far from Colossae and Laodicea (Col. 4:13); seat of worship of the Syrian goddess Atargatis; celebrated for warm baths; now called Pambuk-Kalah-si.

Higgaion (hĭg-gī'ŏn) [meditation] a problematic psalm title (9:16; also in 19:15, 92:4); called a musical term by some. In the first reference, it is transliterated; in the others, translated, as also in Lam. 3:62. The root seems to be "to meditate." It is probably of editorial nature in 9:16.

high places pagans, and corrupted Israel, had shrines, generally on lofty heights (Num. 22:41; 1 K. 11:7, 14:23; 2 K. 17:9, 23:5, 8; Jer. 7:31; Ezek. 6:3). It seems to have been a Moabite specialty (Isa. 15:2, 16:12; Jer. 48:35). Even Abraham and others built altars on mountains (Gen. 12:7–8, 22:2–4, 31:54). It is true that Num. 33:52; Lev. 26:30, condemn future high places (after the conquest); but Israel continued to use them often. The warnings (vs. 55) were unheeded; and troubles came. In Samuel's time, the Hebrews worshiped at local sanctuaries (1 Sam. 1:9, 3:3, 9:12; ch. 21; 2 Sam. 15:32, 24:16 ff.). Thus from the time of the capture of the ark (1 Sam. 4), to Solomon's temple (1 K. 3:2), worship at high places was carried on. They were evidently permitted in Northern Israel where worship was rather primitive (1 K. 18: 30 ff.). There appears to have been much liberty exercized, and long-deferred judgment (1 K. 11:7, 15:14; 2 Chr. 20:33). Only later were these practices severely condemned by the (especially) eighth-century prophets, and others (Hos. 10:8; Amos 7:9; Mic. 1:5; Jer. 3:3, 7:31).

high priest the priest, differing from the prophet, represents men before God. The high priest is the supreme representative. The first note as to Aaron's importance was after the proclamation of the covenant (Ex. 24:1, 9). Aaron was appointed to office after the covenant and following the authorization of the tabernacle's erection (Ex. 27:21, 28:1–43). Succession was ordinarily according to primogeniture (but see Lev. 21:16–23), and political considerations sometimes were involved (1 K. 2:26–27, 35). The age for office was twenty, commonly. The mode of consecration is described in Ex. 29, the particular feature being anointing of the head with sacred oil (Ex. 29:7; Lev. 8:12; Ps. 133:2). Thus the high priest is the "anointed priest" (Lev. 4:3, 5, 16, 21:10; Num. 35:25). Others apparently had oil sprinkled on garments only (Ex. 29:21; Lev. 8:30), tradition making a difference in the amount of oil. The high priest's conduct was governed by particular laws (Lev. 21:1–15). His duties were oversight of the sanctuary, its service and treasure (2 K. 12:4, 22:4), attending to the day of atonement ceremonial in the holy of holies, and the divine appeal by Urim and Thummim (Lev. 8:8; Num. 27:21). He could also discharge any priestly function; and traditionally, he offered sacrifices on the sabbaths, new moons, and annual festivals. Besides the white raiment of the priesthood, he wore: (1) The breastplate, square of gold and blue, purple, scarlet, and fine-twined linen, set with four rows of three precious stones each, same being inscribed with the different tribe names. Within it were the Urim and Thummim. (2) The ephod, an embroidered garment with same materials as the breastplate, front and back parts being clasped at shoulder by onyx stones, each bearing the names of six tribes. It was bound at the waist by a girdle of the same materials as above. (3) The robe of the ephod, worn under the ephod and longer than it, blue only, sleeveless, with a hole for the head, and adorned with a fringe of alternate pomegranates and golden bells. (4) The mitre, a turban of linen, surmounted (Josephus) by another of blue, and this, by a triple crown of gold, with a gold plate inscribed "Holiness of Jehovah," and fastened to the front by a blue ribbon (Ex. 33). Other equipment, as tunic, girdle, breeches, and bonnet, were common to all priests (Lev. 16:4, 22). A manslayer might not leave a city of refuge while the existing high priest lived (Num. 35:25, 28). The high priest could not take part in ordinary funeral rites (Lev. 10:6). Originally the high priest was in office for life; but Herod and then the Romans, made and unmade the pontiffs at will. Christ is the high priest of our profession, corresponding to the Jewish dignitary (Heb. 3:1–3, 8:1–6, 9:24–28). The high priest line embraced about 1370 years, with about eighty high priests, beginning with Aaron and ending with Phannias, which are arranged naturally in three groups: before David; from David to the Captivity; from the return to the end of the line at Jerusalem's destruction. Here is the approximate succession, and the corresponding rulers:

Rulers:	Priests:
Moses	Aaron
Joshua	Eliezer
Othniel	Phinehas
Abishua	Abishua
Eli	Eli
Samuel	Ahitub
Saul	Ahijah
David	Zadoc and Abiathar
Solomon	Azariah
Abijah	Johanan
Asa	Azariah
Jehoshaphat	Amariah
Jehoram	Jehoiada
Ahaziah	Jehoiada
Jehoash	Jehoiada and Zechariah
Amaziah	?
Uzziah	Azariah
Jotham	?
Ahaz	Urijah
Hezekiah	Azariah
Manasseh	Shallum
Amon	"
Josiah	Hilkiah
Jehoiachim	Azariah (?)
Jehoiachin	"

Rulers:	Priests:
Zedekiah	Seraiah
Evil-merodach	Jehozadak
Zerubbabel (Cyrus and Darius)	Jeshua
Mordecai (?) (Xerxes)	Joiakim
Ezra and Nehemiah (Artaxerxes)	Eliashib
Darius Nothus	Joiada
Artaxerxes Mnemon	Johanan
Alexander the Great	Jaddua
Onias I (Ptolemy Soter, Antigonus)	Simon the Just
Ptolemy Philadelphus	Eleazer
" "	Manasseh
Ptolemy Euergetes	Onias II
Ptolemy Philopator	Simon II
Ptolemy Epiphanes and Antiochus	Onias III
Antiochus Epiphanes	Jason or Jaddua
" "	Onias or Menelaus
Demetrius	Jacimus or Alcimus
Alexander Balas	Jonathan, brother of Judas Maccabeus
Simon (Hasmonean, or Maccabee)	Simon (Maccabee)
John Hyrcanus (Hasmonean, or Asmonean)	John Hyrcanus (Maccabee)
Aristobulus (Asmonean)	Aristobulus (Maccabee)
Alexander Jannaeus (Asmonean)	"
Alexandra (Asmonean)	Hyrcanus II (Asmonean)
Aristobulus II (Asmonean)	"
Pompey the Great and Hyrcanus or Antipater	
Pacorus the Parthian	Antigonus (Asmonean)
	Ananelus; Aristobulus last of Asmoneans, murdered by Herod
Herod, king of Judea	Ananelus, restored
"	Jesus, son of Faneus
Herod the Great	Simon, son of Boethus
"	Mathtias, son of Theophilus
"	Jozarus, son of Simon
Archelaus, king of Judea	Eleazer
"	Jesus, son of Sie
"	Jozarus (second time)
Cyrenius, governor of Syria, second time	Ananus
Valerius Gratus, procurator of Judea	Ishmael, son of Phabi
"	Eleazer, son of Ananus
"	Simon, son of Kamith
Vitellius, governor of Syria	Caiaphas, called also Joseph
"	Jonathan, son of Ananus
"	Theophilus, brother of Jonathan
Herod Agrippa	Simon Cantheras
"	Matthias, brother of Jonathan, son of Ananus
"	Elionias, son of Cantheras
Herod, king of Chalcis	Joseph, son of Camei
"	Ananias, son of Nebedeus
"	Jonathan
"	Ismael, son of Fabi
"	Joseph, son of Simon
"	Ananus, son of Do, or Ananias
Appointed by people	Jesus, son of Gamaliel
Appointed by people	Matthias, son of Theophilus
Chosen by lot	Phannias, son of Samuel

147

Hilen (hī'lĕn) [strong place] city of Judah, allotted to priests (1 Chr. 6:58).

Hilkiah (hĭl-kī'ä) [the Lord is portion] a favorite priestly name: 1. Father of Eliakim, Hezekiah's chief of household (2 K. 18:18; Isa. 36:3).

2. A priest of Anathoth, likely of Eli's line (see 1 K. 2:27), and father to Jeremiah (1:1).

3. High priest under Josiah, who found the Book of the Law in the temple renovation, and aided the king (2 K. 22:4–14), being chief actor in the movement, presiding over the subsequent temple purification (2 K. 23).

4. A companion of Ezra in public reading of the law (Neh. 8:4).

5. A "chief of the priests," with Zerubbabel, in the return from Babylon, 536 B.C. (Neh. 12:7; see vs. 21).

6. A Merarite Levite, son of Amzi (1 Chr. 6:45–46).

7. Another Merarite Levite, son of Hosah (1 Chr. 26:11).

8. Father of Gemariah, an envoy of Zedekiah to Babylon (Jer. 29:3).

hill, hill country an isolated eminence, sometimes called a mountain; a tableland, range, or mountainous district. Usually applied to Zion (the hill of); also a central mountainous tract from the plain of Jezreel on north, to the Negeb or dry country on the south; also the Shephelah or lowlands of the southwest, and the steppes of the southeast. The best-known is the "hill country of Ephraim"; but there is the hill country of Judah (Josh. 11:21), of Naphtali (20:7), of Ammon (Deut. 2:37), of Gilead (3:12). Distinctive are Hermon, Tabor, and Carmel.

Hillel (hĭl-lĕl') [he has praised] father of Judge Abdon (Judg. 12:13, 15).

hin see **measures**

hind female of stag, emblem of activity (Gen. 49:21), of gentleness (Prov. 5:19), of modesty (Song of S. 2:7), of longing (Ps. 42:1), of maternal affection (Jer. 14:5).

hinge ancient doors were hung by pivots on upper and lower sides, in sockets (1 K. 7:50; see Prov. 26:14).

Hinnom, Valley of (hĭn'nŏm) called also "valley of son of Hinnom," or "of children of Hinnom." A deep, narrow ravine to the south and west of Jerusalem, near the Gate of Potsherds (Jer. 19:2). Earliest mention is found in Josh. 15:8, noting the boundary line between Judah and Benjamin as passing along the bed of the ravine. On the southern brow, Solomon made high places for Molech (1 K. 11:7). Ahaz and Manasseh made their children "pass through fire" here (2 K. 16:3). Infant sacrifice

continued for a long time in Tophet, the southeast extremity (Jer. 7:31; 2 K. 30:10). Josiah rendered it ceremonially unclean to stop the abominations (2 K. 23:10, 13–14); thereafter it appears to have become the city cesspool, sewage being carried off by the Kidron. Jeremiah had foretold awful judgment, so that it would be known as the valley of slaughter (7:31–34). Due to the fires, the pollution, and perhaps the burning of offal, the valley became a type of sin and woe; and the name *Gehinnom*, corrupted into *Gehenna*, became the symbol of eternal punishment.

hippotamus this is most likely the Heb. *behemoth*. It is associated with the crocodile (Job 40:15), as the particulars are more appropriate to this beast than to any other.

Hirah (hī'rä) [nobility] friend of Judah, an Adullamite (Gen. 38:1, 12; see vs. 20).

Hiram (hī'răm) [probably consecration] generally Huram in Chronicles; also Hirom (1 K. 5:10). 1. King of Tyre, who sent workers and materials for David's palace (2 Sam. 5:11), and also for Solomon's temple (1 K. 5:11–12). He was active in religious and civic developments, building a causeway to the island where there was a temple of Jupiter, and erecting temples to Hercules and Astarte. He gave one hundred and twenty talents of gold (1 K. 9:14), joined Solomon in getting gold from Ophir (1 K. 9:26–28), was offered in partial payment, but refused, twenty towns in Galilee (1 K. 9:10–12)—a rather curious episode; and Hiram did some city-swapping himself (2 Chr. 8:1–2). Details as to time notes, both in secular and sacred sources, have some unresolved confusion.

2. An artificer (1 K. 7:13 f., citing perhaps his stepmother; see 2 Chr. 2:14, where, presumably, his mother by birth). In the uncertainty of the text (2 Chr. 2:13, 4:16), it is supposed that the title "father" relates to his being a master workman who executed important features of Solomon's temple (1 K. 7:13–46; 2 Chr. 2:13 f.).

hire, hireling the former, synonymous with wages (Gen. 30:18). The latter, one hired for work at a wage agreed (Mal. 3:5; Jn. 10:12; Isa. 16:14; cf. Jer. 46:21). A rather common idea, based on Jn. 10:12–13, is not necessarily correct: the term itself conveys no imputation of dishonesty or unfaithfulness.

Hittites (hĭt'tīts) descendants of Cheth (Heth), second son of Canaan, first met in Abraham's time—he bought the cave of Machpelah for a burying place, at the death of Sarah, from Ephron the Hittite, the town being called Hebron, originally Kirjath-arba (also Mamre), as seen in Gen. 23:18, 25:9. They occupied the land somewhere between Northern Palestine and the Euphrates, Kadesh, Hamath, and Carchemish being important Hittite cities (Josh. 1:4; 1 K. 10:29). Early, they were rather commercial and non-numerous, not noticed among the "Canaanite and the Perizzite" inhabitants. In Exodus they are mentioned as of the occupants of Palestine. Quite a change comes when they unite with others against Joshua (9:1, 11:3). After Joshua's conquest, intermarriage occurred (Judg. 3:5–6). Two Hittites were attached to David, Ahimelech and Uriah (1 Sam. 26:6; 2 Sam. 23:39; and ch. 11). Solomon's harem included Hittites (1 K. 11:1). They are the Kheta of the Egyptian monuments, and the Hatti of the Assyrian inscriptions. For 500 years they warred, with intervals of peace, against the Egyptians under Thothmes III, Seti I, and Rameses II. From 1100 B.C., Tiglath-pileser I fought with them; and it was not until 717 B.C. that Sargon took Carchemish and ended the empire.

Hivites (hī'vīts) [possibly villager] one of the tribes of Palestine which the Israelites displaced (Ex. 3:8), commonly used in the singular only in Hebrew. A descendant, sixth in order, of Canaan son of Ham (Gen. 10:17). Their insignificance seems to account for omission from Gen. 15:19–21 and Num. 13:29. A body of Hivites dwelt at Shechem at Jacob's return to Canaan (Gen. 33:18; cf. 34:2), and were influential some time later (Judg. 9:28). At the first, they were warm, impetuous, credulous (Gen. 34). Later they became crafty, turning tables on the Israelites (Josh. 9:3–27). Their principal settlement seems to have been to the north of Western Palestine, "under Hermon," in the land of Mizpeh (Josh. 11:3; Judg. 3:3). As late as David they had villages there (2 Sam. 24:7). Those in Palestine proper, with other Canaanites, rendered bond service to Solomon (1 K. 9:20–22).

Hizki (hĭz'kī) [my strength] a Benjaminite, son of Elpaal (1 Chr. 8:17).

Hizkiah (hĭz-kī'ä) ancestor of Zephaniah the prophet (1:1).

Hizkijah (hĭz-kī'jä) according to KJV, a man who sealed the covenant with Nehemiah (10:17); but most likely to be taken with the one preceding, thus "Ater-Hizkijah."

Hobab (hō'băb) [lover] only in Num. 10:29 and Judg. 4:11. According to the latter's traditional vowel pointing, Moses' father-in-law; but this person was Reuel, his honorary title being, as it appears, Jethro ("His Excellency"). In the former reference, Hobab is the son of Reuel, the Hebrew text being equally well translated brother-in-law. Moses' father-in-law, Reuel or

Jethro, visited him at Rephidim, returning thereafter to his own land (Ex. 18:1, 5, 27). A year later, Hobab, as an experienced sheik of the desert, invited by Moses, accompanies the Israelites (Judg. 1:16; and above references). His family was still settled in Judah, south of Arad, in the time of Saul and David. He was a Kenite, of the family of Midianites (1 Sam. 15:6, 30:29).

Hobah (hō'bä) [lurking place] a town north of Damascus to which Abraham pursued the defeated Eastern kings who had pillaged Sodom.

Hod (hōd) [majesty] a son of Zophah, an Asherite (1 Chr. 7:37).

Hodaiah (hō-dā'yä) [Jehovah is praise] a son of Eleionai, of royal connection (1 Chr. 3:24); perhaps more properly, **Hodaviah.**

Hodaviah (hō-dä-vī'ä) 1. One of the heads of the half tribe of Manasseh, east of Jordan (1 Chr. 5:24).

2. A Benjaminite (1 Chr. 9:7).

3. A Levite, founder of a family (Ezra 2:40); called Judah (3:9), a synonymous name; see also Neh. 7:43.

Hodesh (hō'dĕsh) [new moon] a Benjaminite wife of Shaharaim (1 Chr. 8:9).

Hodevah see **Hodaviah** above

Hodiah (hō-dī'ä) [splendor of Jehovah] according to the questionable reading in the KJV, a wife of a Judahite named Ezra (1 Chr. 4:19; some say same as in vs. 18)

Hodijah (hō-dī'jä) 1. A Levite of Ezra-Nehemiah times (Neh. 8:7; also 9:5 and 10:10, as it appears).

2. Another Levite of the same period, if different from the one of Neh. 10:10.

3. A layman, a head of the people of same period (Neh. 10:18).

Hoglah (hŏg'lä) [partridge] the third of the five daughters of Zelophehad (Num. 26:33; Josh. 17:3).

Hoham (hō'hăm) the defeated and executed king of Hebron (Josh. 10:1=27).

Holon (hō'lŏn) [sandy?] 1. A hill country town of Judah, assigned to priests (Josh. 15:51, 21:15; Hilen in 1 Chr. 6:58).

2. Unidentified city of Moab (Jer. 48:21).

holy the basal meaning is bright, pure, shining (see Gesenius, *Lexicon*). By accommodation, it comes to mean separated, applied to utensils, ministers, days (Ex. 20:8; Lev. 21:7; Neh. 8:9); pertaining to what is separated from defilement or immorality (Ex. 22:31; 2 Cor. 7:1), and from false worship, or heathen practices (Lev. 20:6, 21:6). God is THE Holy One (Isa. 6:3; Rev. 4:8).

Holy Ghost (or **Holy Spirit**) *Spirit* more correctly expresses the idea here than the word *Ghost*. The name is used only three times in OT (Ps. 51:11; Isa. 63:10–11), but references to his work are numerous. According to the Hebrew, he is the divine principle of activity everywhere at work in the world. He is sent forth by the Lord (Ps. 104:29); given by him (Num. 11:29). He "wrestled" with chaos originally and is everywhere present (Gen. 1:2; Ps. 139:7); is energizingly immanent in the cosmical processes (Job 26:13; Isa. 59:19); is the source of physical, intellectual, and moral life (Gen. 6:3; Job 32:8; Ps. 104:30; Isa. 42:5); effects the supernatural (1 K. 18:12; 2 K. 2:16); abides with his people (Isa. 43:11; Hag. 2:5); empowers for kingdom work (Ex. 31:3; Num. 11:17; Judg. 3:10; 1 Sam. 11:6; Isa. 11:2; Zech. 4:6); instructs people (Neh. 9:20); inspires the prophets (Num. 24:2; Hos. 9:7; Zech. 7:12); was foretold as powerful in the Messianic period (Isa. 44:3; Ezek. 36:26; Zech. 12:10; Joel 2:28); is grieved by resisters (Isa. 63:10; cf. 106:33). He is promised by the departing Lord (Lk. 24:49; Jn. 7:37–39, 14:25–26, 15:26, 16:7–14; Acts 1:8). The Holy Spirit is by promise much more active in NT times than in the OT. His attributes in the latter are disclosed in their exercise in the former, his personality being stressed. The proving ground for the Holy Spirit is the OT, as for all the doctrines of the NT. So that even if those who discount the Holy Spirit references in the NT were successful in showing them as interpolations or spurious, the church would still have the doctrine of the Holy Spirit. The Greek word for spirit is neuter and in Hebrew, feminine; for such reason the reading in Rom. 8 has "it," which should be read "him." The masculine pronoun is used in Eph. 1:13–14; the sense certainly is masculine in, say, Jn. 16:13 and 14:26. The Holy Spirit is as certainly a person as is the Father or the Son. The personal pronoun is used of him (Acts 10:19–20, 13:2). Note the baptismal formula and the apostolic benediction (Mt. 28:19; 2 Cor. 13:14). The Holy Spirit can be grieved (Eph. 4:30; cf. Rom. 8:26). The Holy Spirit is memorable: in the miraculous conception of the Savior (Mt. 1:18–20); in the descent at his baptism (Mt. 3:16; Mk. 1:10; Jn. 1:32); in the effusion at Pentecost and the attendant gift of languages (Acts 2:4).

Homam (hō'măm) [destroyer] son of Lotan, grandson of Seir (1 Chr. 1:39). In Gen. 36:22—**Hemam.**

homer see **weights and measures**

honey a thick fluid collected by bees from flowers and fruits and deposited in cells of a comb (Judg. 14:8; Ps. 19:10), eaten as food or prepared in various ways (Gen. 43:11; Ex. 16:31; 1 Sam. 14:26); in early times apparently uncultivated, found in rocks, trees, etc. Account of fermentation, not used in offerings made by fire (Lev. 2:11). Artificial "honey" was prepared from various sources, as grapes and dates. Some sort came from trees by exudation. Canaan was a "land flowing with milk and honey" (Ex. 3:8).

hook 1. Fishing hooks (Amos 4:2; Isa. 19:8; Hab. 1:15).

2. A large hook or ring, attached by a cord to a stake, held live fish (Job 41:2).

3. Similar hook was used to lead bulls or lions (2 K. 19:28), camels, even prisoners, as in the case of Manasseh (2 Chr. 33:11), where the KJV has "in the thorns."

4. There were hooks for the pillars of the temple (Ex. 26:32, 37).

5. Vine dressers had pruning hooks (Isa. 2:4).

6. Fleshhooks were used in sacrificial worship (Ex. 27:3).

7. Probably hooks were employed for hanging up animals to flay them (Ezek. 40:43).

Hophni (hŏf'nī) [pertaining to the fist] and **Phinehas** the two sons of Eli, of scandalous conduct in sacerdotal functions at Shiloh (1 Sam. 2:12–17, 22), disgusting the people and provoking a curse on the house, by both an unknown prophet (vss. 27–36) and by Samuel (3:11–14). As custodians of the ark, sent out to battle with the Philistines, they were slain in the disastrous encounter (1 Sam. 4:10–11).

Hor (hôr) [mountain] 1. On the border of Edom, where Aaron died (Num. 20:25, 33:37); archaic form of *har*, Hebrew for mountain. The next stop after Kadesh (Num. 20:22), on the eastern side of the great valley of the Arabah, being the highest of the red sandstone mountains of Edom, west of the mysterious city of Petra, now supposedly Jebel Nebi-Harun, and is 6000 feet above the Dead Sea. The prospect from its summit—the last view of Aaron—contrasts with that from Nebo, for Moses.

2. A mountain on the northern boundary of Palestine, between the Mediterranean Sea and Hamath (Num. 34:7–8), probably a prominent peak of Lebanon, or possibly used for the whole range.

Horam (hō'răm) [elevation] a king of Gezer defeated and slain by Joshua (10:33).

Horeb (hō'rĕb) [dry] mentioned in (Ex. 3:1, 33:6; Deut. 1:2, 18:16; 1 K. 8:9; 2 Chr. 5:10; Ps. 106:19; Mal. 4:4). See **Sinai**

Horem (hō'rĕm) [enclosed, sacred] an unidentified fenced city of Naphtali (Josh. 19:38).

Hor-hagidgad (hôr-hă-gĭd′găd) [mountain of . . . , perhaps, thunder] a desert encampment of Israel (Num. 33:32), same as Gudgodah (Deut. 10:7), west of the Arabah, unidentified.

Hori (hō′rī) [cave dweller] 1. Son of Lotan, son of Seir (Gen. 36:22), and perhaps a tribe.

2. Simeonite father of Shaphat, the spy (Num. 13:5).

Horites, Horims aboriginal cave dwellers of Mount Seir (Gen. 14:6), and called children of Seir (Gen. 36:20). Defeated by Chedorlaomer (Gen. 14:6); governed by chieftains (36:29–30); destroyed by posterity of Esau (Deut. 2:12, 22).

Hormah (hôr′mä) [devoted, i.e., to destruction] formerly Zephath (Judg. 1:17), the chief town of a Canaanite king in Southern Palestine, reduced by Joshua being of the territory of Judah, but later assigned to Simeon (Josh. 15:30, 19:4), either escaped destruction at the first devastation (Num. 21:2), or rebuilt by returning fugitives. In the difficulty about the various notes on Hormah, it may be that Num. 21:3 is given more in detail by Judg. 1:17. And due to the fact that Num. 14:45 has the article prefixed to the word Hormah, signifying a region rather than a definite city, it is possible therefore that the rout of disobedient Israel by the Amalekites and Canaanites, which carried them as far as "the desolation," does not involve the city Hormah of Num. 21:2 and Judg. 1:17, relative to events thirty-eight years later. It may be that the name in Num. 14:45 was used proleptically, from the later devastation. The town was hospitable to outcast David; to friends there, he sent spoils of Ziklag (1 Sam. 30:30).

horn animal horns were used as trumpets or as containers for oil (Josh. 6:13; 1 Sam. 16:1, 13). In poetry, horns symbolized strength (Deut. 33:17), or offensive weapons (Ps. 18:2). To "exalt the horn" is to strengthen and prosper one (1 Sam. 2:1). To "lift his horn" is to be arrogant (Ps. 75:4–5). To weaken is to "break the horn" (Jer. 48:25). Horns stand for political power or for kingdom —because bulls push with their horns (Ps. 132:17; Dan. 7:8; cf. Rev. 17:12). Altar horns, asylums for fugitives (Ex. 27:2; 1 K. 1:50), were projections from the four corners, in shape of horns; also significant in worship (Ex. 29:12, 30:10; Ps. 118:27). A horn was a hill, a peak (Isa. 5:1). Horns of Hattin, traditionally, mount of Beatitudes.

hornet common in Palestine. To be used for driving out the Canaanites (Ex. 23:28; Josh.

24:12). There is a story that the Phaselites were driven from their country by hornets (Aelian); but the Scripture use seems figurative, regarding the terror from the Lord, at the approach of the irresistible Israelites. See Deut. 2:25; Josh. 2:11.

Horonaim (hō-rō-nā′ĭm) [caverns, ravines] a Moabite town not far from Zoar (Isa. 15:5). It seems to have been an eminence with a special approach (Jer. 48:5).

horse commonly used in warlike operations (but see Isa. 28:28). Egypt had horses from the Eighteenth Dynasty onward (Gen. 47:17; first mention, 49:17; Ex. 14:9); and also the Canaanites (Judg. 4:15). Two words are sometimes confused: one is for war horses of heavy build, used with chariots, the other, for riding, especially cavalry (example: in 1 K. 4:26, "forty thousand chariot horses, and twelve thousand cavalry horses"). Despite the prohibition (Deut. 17:16), David used horses (2 Sam. 8:4), so did Solomon (1 K. 4:26, 10:28); see also 1 K. 22:4; 2 K. 3:7, 9:18, 33; cf. Isa. 30:16; Ps. 20:7). Foreign kings and conquerors rode horses (Est. 6:8; Rev. 6:2); the lowly Messiah, an ass (Zech. 9:9). Bit and bridle (Ps. 32:9), bells for ornament (Zech. 14:20), are noted as equipment. Horses were, it seems, unshod (Isa. 5:28); were sometimes dedicated to the sun (2 K. 23:11).

horseleech only in Prov. 30:15, of the bloodsucking insect (annelid) common in Palestine. The figure indicates blood-thirsty propensity.

Hosah (hō′sä) [fleeing for refuge] 1. A town of Asher (Josh. 19:29), not far from Tyre.

2. A Merarite Levite porter (1 Chr. 16:38, 26:10).

hosanna (hō-săn′nä) [save now] brief prayer for deliverance (Ps. 118:25). Most of the prayers at the Feast of Tabernacles began thus. Used by the multitude at the triumphal entry of the Lord (Mt. 21:9, 15).

Hosea (hō-sē′ä) [save] same name as Oshea or Hoshea (Joshua, Num. 13:8, 16). 1. A king of Israel (2 K. 15:30).

2. Son of Beeri and first of the minor prophets; a prophet of the Northern Kingdom, contemporary with Amos, prophet to the same; earlier contemporary of Isaiah, as also of Micah of the Southern Kingdom. He began his work in the reign of Jeroboam II of Israel, perhaps for a dozen years under him, and continued for apparently more than forty years, the heading of the book (1:1) stating also "in the days of Uzziah, Jotham, Ahaz, and Hezekiah, of Judah." Hosea indicates nothing of the prophet's history; tradition says he was of Issachar. In the difficulty of dating Hosea, 760 B.C. is a

Hoshaiah

good location for his work. Scholars generally find two main divisions in the book: (1) Chs. 1–3. This division gives the key to the book whose theme is: the triumph of God's love. Sin, judgment, and love are the prominent ideas. In these first chapters, we see God's dealing with his people set forth in Hosea's attitude to his unfaithful wife. In the problems here presented, unless one can view the matter as allegory, it seems best to believe that the prophet married a woman with no taint, but who proved unfaithful. Through the agonies of a broken home, rescued by unquenchable love, God's constant love for his own is revealed; there is interplay of earthly and heavenly scenes and actions. (2) Chs. 4–14. The second division is as difficult to analyze as love is to understand: it appears to be a summary of the prophet's teaching, the gist of his public addresses, few hints of the historical background being given, but 2 K. 14–15 being particularly pertinent. J. D. Davis, in the *Dictionary of the Bible*, suggests: i. 4:1–6:3—the controversy of God, stressing sin and need for repentance; ii. 6:4–10:15—the grievous punishment necessary for heinous sin; iii. 11:1–13:16—the yearning and expostulation of God; iv. 14:1–9, exhortation to repentance and confession, and the promise of blessing.

Hoshaiah (hō-shā′yä) [Jehovah saves] 1. An assistant at the dedication of the walls rebuilt by Nehemiah (12:32).
(2 K. 15:30). Hoshea was not so sinful as his 43:2); possibly the same man as above.

Hoshama (hŏsh-ā′mä) [Jehovah heard?] one of the family of Jeconiah (Jehoiachin), next to last king of Judah (1 Chr. 3:18).

Hoshea (hŏsh′ē-ä) [save] 1. The earlier name of Joshua (Num. 13:8, 16).

2. Son of Azariah and prince of Ephraim in David's reign (1 Chr. 27:20).

3. Son of Elah, the nineteenth, last, and best king of Israel, following Pekah (2 K. 15:30), reigning about nine years, to 722 B.C. (2 K. 15:30). Hoshea was not so sinful as his predecessors (2 K. 17:2). After three years of subjection to the Assyrian Shalmaneser, he entered into alliance with So, king of Egypt, refusing further tribute to Assyria; but in vain, for Shalmaneser took him captive and bound him in prison (2 K. 17:3), light being thrown on his treatment, as it appears, in Mic. 5:1. We know nothing more of Hoshea.

hospitality a chief virtue especially among Semites. Note Lev. 19:33–34; Lev. 25; Deut. 15:7. Before the Law was given, we meet this virtue in Abraham (Gen. 18), and in Lot (19:1). In the NT it became more of a social virtue

than a necessity as in patriarchal life. We have the Good Samaritan (Lk. 10). See Mt. 25:43; Rom. 12:13; Heb. 13:2; 1 Pet. 4:9; Tit. 1:8. In the OT hospitality was shown by invitation to the meal if a stranger were in the house (see Abraham, above). The Oriental respect for the covenant of bread and salt, or salt alone, sprang from the high regard for hospitality.

host a multitude, especially organized (Gen. 21:22; Ex. 12:41; 1 K. 2:5). The "host of heaven" seems to refer to angels or to stars (1 K. 22:19; Deut. 4:19). "The Lord of hosts" seems to relate to more than the armies of Israel (1 Sam. 17:45; Isa. 31:4), being referable to the universe in spiritual and material aspects as forming a vast army with numerous divisions under the command of the Lord Almighty (Gen. 28:12; Ps. 89:6–8; Isa. 40:26; Neh. 9:6; Jer. 29:17).

Hotham (hō′thăm) [signet ring] an Asherite, son of Heber, family of Beriah (1 Chr. 7:32). Also probably the same name for a different spelling (1 Chr. 11:44), an Aroerite, father of two of David's mighty men.

Hothir (hō′thĭr) son of Heman, David's seer, a Kohathite Levite (1 Chr. 25:4).

hour probably not known to Hebrews of old. "Morning, evening, noonday" was sufficient at the first (Ps. 55:17). Early Jews seem to have divided the day into four parts (Neh. 9:3), the night into three watches (Judg. 7:19), which Mt. 20:1–5 echoes. Greeks got the twelve-hour day from Babylonians; probably the Hebrews got it from them in the Captivity. The Egyptians knew it early. There are two kinds of hours: the astronomical, the twenty-fourth part of a civil day; and the natural hour, the twelfth part of the natural day, the time between sunrise and sunset. These are meant in the NT, for Josephus and the Rabbis (Jn. 11:9). They constantly vary in length, being different at different times of the year. We may suppose that the Jews had gnomons, dials, clepsydra, long known to the Persians and others with whom they came into contact. For prayer, the old division into four parts was continued in temple worship (Acts 2:15, 10:9).

house dwelling place in general; derivatively as tabernacle, temple, heaven; or metaphorically as family. There were tents as in contrast to permanent habitations (Gen. 4:17–20; Isa. 38:12). Hebrews became city dwellers in Egypt and after the conquest of Canaan (Gen. 47:3; Ex. 12:7; see Deut. 6:10). Walls of houses were often mud or sun-dried brick, even when stone was available (Job 24:16; Ezek. 13:10–16). Roofs were tree branches, canes, palm leaves overlaid with layer of earth, rather im-

152

permanent and easily opened up (Mk. 2:1–12). Generally one-story, often only one-room, the interior being divided into two portions, one several feet higher than the other, the lower part occupied by cattle. Steps led to the family section, with sometimes a loft for guests, apartments not being walled off from each other (1 Sam. 28:24). Better-class houses are quadrangular with central courtyard and sometimes a well or fountain (2 Sam. 17:18). An upper chamber was built above the level of the roof (1 K. 17:19; Acts 9:37). Roofs often had battlements (Deut. 22:8), well adapted for storing and drying produce (Josh. 2:6), for walking and conversation, and for idolatrous worship or meditation and prayer (1 Sam. 9:25–26; 2 Sam. 11:2; 2 K. 23:12; Acts 10:9). Outside staircase led to the roof (Mt. 24:17). It is supposed that windows, projecting several feet, may have formed the latticed chamber, effecting the "chamber in the wall" (2 K. 4:10–11; also see 2 K. 1:2, and Acts 20:9). No special bedrooms; no chimneys, fire being made with charcoal in chafing-dish, or with wood in open court (Lk. 22:55). At Tabernacles Feast, booths were made on the roofs. Special sections were for summer or for winter use, in larger houses (Jer. 36:22; Amos 3:15). The house that Samson pulled down seems to have had tiers of balconies one above the other, where the crowds collected, the support being two large pillars set in the basement (Judg. 16:26).

Hukkok (hŭk'kōk) [decreed] town on Naphtali's border (Josh. 19:34). Supposedly now Yakuk, west of the upper Sea of Galilee.

Hukok a name (1 Chr. 6:75) for Helkath (Josh. 19:25).

Hul (hŭl) [circuit] second son of Aram (Gen. 10:23).

Huldah (hŭl'dä) [weasel] a prophetess, wife of Shallum, keeper of Josiah's wardrobe, consulted when Hilkiah found the Book of the Law (2 K. 22:14).

Humtah (hŭm'tä) [perhaps fortress] a town in hill country of Judah, unknown (Josh. 15:54).

hunter and **hunting** for meat (Gen. 27:3), or protection (1 K. 13:24); for amusement (Josephus). Nimrod probably hunted bigger "game" than animals (Gen. 10:9). People hunted alone or in groups, on foot, horseback, or in chariots (Jer. 16:16), with bows and arrows, spears (Isa. 7:24). Decoys were used, nets, traps, pits (Jer. 5:26–27; Job 18:10; 2 Sam. 23:20).

Hupham (hŭ'făm) [protected?] descendant of Benjamin, founder of the tribal family, Hupha-

mites (Num. 26:39). Perhaps same as Huppim (Gen. 46:21), and Huram (?1 Chr. 8:5; see 1 Chr. 7:12).

Huppah (hŭp'pä) [covering] a priest in David's time (1 Chr. 24:13).

Hur (hēr) [splendor] 1. Of Judah, family of Hezron, house of Caleb (1 Chr. 2:18–19); grandfather of Bazaleel (vs. 20); with Aaron, upheld Moses' arms in the fight with Amalek (Ex. 17:10–12). With Aaron, governed Israel while Moses was in the mount (24:14). Traditionally (Josephus) said to be husband of Moses' sister Miriam.

2. The fourth of five kings of Midian slain with Balaam (Num. 31:8; Josh. 13:21).

3. Father of Solomon's purveyor, in Mount Ephraim (1 K. 4:8).

4. Father of a certain Rephaiah, assisting Nehemiah (3:9).

Hurai (hū'rī) [perhaps linen weaver] one of David's mighty men from the brooks of Gaash (1 Chr. 11:32; called Hiddai in 2 Sam. 23:30).

Huram (hū'răm) [noble] 1. A Benjaminite, son of Bela (1 Chr. 8:5).

2. King of Tyre; called Hiram, except in Chronicles (1 Chr. 14:1; 2 Chr. 2:3).

3. A Tyrian artificer, called Huram (2 Chr. 2:13).

Huri (hū'rī) [linen weaver?] a Gadite (1 Chr. 5:14).

husband see **marriage**

Hushah (hū'shä) [emotion] seems a town of Judah (1 Chr. 4:4); but taken as a name of genealogy of tribe of Judah.

Hushai (hū'shī) [hasty] an Archite, counselor of David, faithful in Absalom's defection, and defeating the counsel of Ahithophel (2 Sam. 15:32–37, 17:5–16). See 1 Chr. 27:33. Probably father of Baana (1 K. 4:16).

Husham (hū'shăm) [haste] early king of Edom (Gen. 36:34; 1 Chr. 1:45–46).

Hushathite (hū'shăth-īt) designation of two of David's guards (2 Sam. 21:18, 23:27).

Hushim (hū'shīm) [perhaps opulent; rich (in children)] 1. Being plural in Gen. 46:28, this seems a tribe rather than an individual; but the name is Shuham in Num. 26:42 (by transposition of consonants).

2. A Benjaminite family (1 Chr. 7:12).

3. One of the three wives of the Benjaminite Shaharaim (1 Chr. 8:8, 11).

husk fruit of carob tree, pods shaped like horns, six to ten inches, and finger-breadth, eaten by swine and cattle; in famine, by people (Lk. 15:16).

Huz (hŭz) [firm] oldest son of Nahor and Milcah (Gen. 22:21).

Huzzab (hŭz'zăb) [established?] a poetic term

153

for Nineveh. The queen, according to the Targum (Nah. 2:7). It could be merely a part of the Hebrew verb for "place" or "establish," according to the margin.

hyacinth, modified form, **jacinth.** 1. A color (Rev. 9:17).

2. One of twelve jewels on the high priest's breastplate (ARV, Ex. 28:19). A precious stone in the foundation of New Jerusalem (ARV, Rev. 21:20). In modern usage, zircon.

hyena offal-eating animal, common in Palestine, living in caves and feeding after dark. The "valley of Zeboim" (1 Sam. 13:18) is "Valley of hyenas." Etymologically, the word in Jer. 12:9, could refer either to hyena or to speckled bird, the latter seems contextually better.

Hymenaeus (hĭ-mē-nē'ŭs) [pertaining to Hymen, the god of marriage] one of the earliest of the Gnostic heretics, who blasphemed, made shipwreck of his faith, noted in connection with Alexander (1 Tim. 1:20), and with Philetus (2 Tim. 2:17–18). Sentence was passed on him by Paul, whether excommunication, or perhaps better, bodily infirmity (see 1 Cor. 11:30), through Satanic power.

hymn a spiritual meditation for choric worship of God. The earliest hymnbook is that of the Psalms. Other religious odes: the Songs of Moses (Ex. 15:1–19; Deut. 32:1–43); of Deborah (Judg. 5); of Hannah (1 Sam. 2:1–10); of Mary (Lk. 1:46–55); of Zechariah (68–79), the last two being respectively, the Magnificat and the Benedictus, from the Latin initial words in each. Psalms were often sung to music (2 Chr. 29:27–28). In the NT, psalms are apparently distinguished from hymns (Eph. 5:19; Col. 3:16), hymn originally being used

in reference to religious composition among Greeks. In old Greek religion, the word had acquired a sacred and liturgical meaning, there being in the Pindaric hymns, accompanied by the lyre, a variety and a relationship to music, which likely engaged the attention of the early Christian hymn writers. In 1 Cor. 14:26, there is an allusion to improvised forms. In the Latin church, trochaic and iambic meters allowed depth of tone and grace of finish. Ambrose gave great prominence to these, as the greatest Latin hymnographer. Psalms 115–118 were the basis of song worship on the Paschal occasion, from which likely was taken the hymn sung by the Lord and his disciples on the night of the betrayal (Mt. 26:30). The early Christians sang hymns privately and in public worship, for edification and comfort, in their praise of God (Acts 16:25; Eph. 5:19). Fragments (as derived from meter in the Greek text), are found (1 Tim. 3:16; Eph. 5:14; see Rev. 15:3–4). Pliny (*Epistle* X.96) in the second century, reports Christians of Bithynia, in Trajan's reign, as singing songs to Christ as God.

hyssop difficulty in determining this plant may be due to reference to several species. Hebrews 9:19 seems to endorse the Greek plant *hyssopos*. Botanists differ on its identification. Long rabbinical tradition associates the Hebrew *ezob* with marjory. One type grew out of or near walls: note the extremes of contrast in 1 K. 4:33. At any rate, the Hebrew word indicates a plant which was used in connection with ceremonial purification (Lev. 14:4, 51; Num. 19:6, 18; Ps. 51:7). Hyssop is noted in connection with the Lord on the cross (Jn. 19:29; Mt. 27:48; Mk. 15:36).

I

Ibhar (ĭb'här) [chooses] a son of David (2 Sam. 5:15).

Ibleam (ĭb'lē-ăm) [people fail] a Manassite city, apparently in Issachar's territory (Judg. 1:27; Josh. 17:11; 2 K. 9:27).

Ibneiah (ĭb-nē'yä) [Jehovah builds] a Benjaminite, son of Jehoram (1 Chr. 9:8).

Ibnijah (ĭb-nī'jä) same as above: a Benjaminite (1 Chr. 9:8).

Ibri (ĭb'rī) [Hebrew] son of Jaaziah (1 Chr. 24:27).

Ibsam (ĭb'săm) [fragrant] a man of Issachar (1 Chr. 7:2).

Ibzan (ĭb'zăn) [active] native of Bethlehem in Zebulun, ruling over Israel or part for seven years, having thirty sons and thirty daughters, and likely plural wives (Judg. 12:8, 10)!

Ichabod (ĭk'à-bŏd) [Where is glory?] son of Phinehas and grandson of Eli, named in connection with the capture of the ark (1 Sam. 4:19–22).

Iconium (ī-cōn'ī-ŭm) a city of Asia Minor; according to Xenophon, the most easterly city of Phrygia. Under the Roman and Greek empires, considered the capital of Lycaonia—so most writers. It was well chosen for missionary operations, being on the communication line between east and west (Acts 13:51, 14:1, 3, 21, 18:23; see also 16:2; 2 Tim. 3:11).

Idalah (ĭd'á-lä) border town of Zebulun, site unknown (Josh. 19:15).

Idbash (ĭd'băsh) [perhaps honey-sweet] a man of Judah (1 Chr. 4:3).

Iddo (ĭd'dō) [happy, or loving, or adorned] 1. Father of Abinadab (1 K. 4:14).

2. Descendant of Gershom, son of Levi (1 Chr. 6:21).

3. Son of Zechariah (1 Chr. 27:21).

4. A seer (2 Chr. 9:29) who wrote a chronicle on the reign of Abijah, and a genealogical book touching Rehoboam (2 Chr. 13:22, 12:15), now lost, but perhaps basal in part to the existing books of Chronicles.

5. Grandfather of Zechariah (1:1, 7), who is elsewhere called son of Iddo (Ezra 5:1, 6:14). He returned from Babylon with Zerubbabel and Jeshua (Neh. 12:4).

6. Chief of the assembly at Casiphia for the second caravan from Babylon, a Nethinim (Ezra 8:17; cf. vs. 20).

idol a mental or material image. An image or sculpture or other representation of a person or being, intended for worship or as the embodiment of a deity (Ex. 20:4, 23; Judg. 17:3; 1 Sam. 5:3; Rom. 1:23). Represented by twenty-one Hebrew words! These words may mean "vanity," "falsehood," "horror," "shame," "impurity," "likeness," "shadow," "statue," "sun image," "device," "molten image." Made of silver, gold, wood, or other material (Ps. 115:4; Isa. 44:13–17). Fashioned by melting, or by placing metal plates over wooden or other frame. Some were small (Gen. 31:34), some, the size of a person (1 Sam. 19:16), some colossal (Dan. 3:1).

idolatry worship of deity in visible form, whether of the true God or of false divinities. First allusion is Rachel's stealing the teraphim (Gen. 31:19), consulted as oracles, without losing sight of the ancestors' God (Gen. 30:27). Abraham's ancestors worshiped other gods (Josh. 24:2). The Egyptians worshiped all manner of gods, against which the plagues were directed to their confusion (Ex. 6–12). Israel was to destroy all the Canaanitish gods (Ex. 23:24; Lev. 19:4; Num. 33:52; Deut. 7:5). The second commandment forbids idolatry, present-day images, pictures, symbols, etc., of the Lord, being apparently in direct contradiction. Israel taking color from neighbors,

first tried to worship the Lord by means of images: see Jeroboam; then they departed from him for idols representative of other divinities: see **Baal**. The council at Jerusalem (Acts 15) enjoined abstinence from flesh sacrificed to idols, to avoid all compromise, and to avoid casting a stumbling block before weak Christians (1 Cor. 8:4–13; see also 10:18–33). About A.D. 300, images were introduced in some churches for instruction and ornament only. In 736, the Eastern Emperor Leo, issued edict against them. In 780, Empress Irene brought image worship into the Eastern church; and the second council of Nicea gave ecclesiastical sanction.

Idumaea or **Idumea** (ĭ-dū-mē'ä) the country of Edom (Isa. 34:5–6; Ezek. 35:15; Mk. 3:8).

Igal (ī'găl) [he will vindicate] once, **Igeal,** in 1 Chr. 3:22). 1. One of the spies to search Canaan (Num. 13:7).

2. A mighty man of David (2 Sam. 23:36; see 1 Chr. 11:38—where seems identical with Joel, but may be different persons, nephew and uncle).

3. Son of Shemaiah, descendant of King Jechoniah (1 Chr. 3:22).

Igdaliah (ĭg-dā-lī'ä) [Great is Jehovah] a prophet, father of Hanan (Jer. 35:4).

Igeal see **Igal** 3

Iim (î-ĭm) [ruins] contract of Ije-abarim. 1. A town east of Jordan (Num. 33:45).

2. A town in extreme south of Judah, now unknown (Josh. 15:29).

Ije-abarim (ī'jē-ăb'á-rĭm) halting place of Israel (Num. 21:11), on southeastern boundary of Moab; unidentified.

Ijon (ī'jŏn [a ruin] fortified city of Naphtali, captured by Ben-hadad (1 K. 15:20; 2 Chr. 16:4); carried captive by Tiglath-pileser (2 K. 15:29). Probably the present Merj-Ayun, eight miles northwest of Banias.

Ikkesh (ĭk'kĕsh) [perverse] father of Ira the Tekoite (2 Sam. 23:26; 1 Chr. 11:28).

Ilai (ī'lī) [supreme] an Ahohite of David's guard (1 Chr. 11:29; called Zalmon in 2 Sam. 23:28).

Illyricum (ĭl-lī'rĭ-cŭm) a country along the eastern coast of the Adriatic, from Italy on the north, to Epirus on the south, inhabited by wild mountaineers, who were a plague to the Macedonians; conquered some time after 229 B.C. by the Romans; scene of Paul's preaching (Rom. 15:19). The territory is rather indefinite, including among other divisions, Bosnia, Herzegovina, Montenegro, the Roman term being broader than the ancient Illyria.

image see **idol**

Imla (ĭm'lä) progenitor of Micaiah the

Immanuel

prophet, meaning "(God) fills" (2 Chr. 18:7; 1 K. 22:8–9).

Immanuel (ĭm-măn′ū-ĕl) [God with us] early in Ahaz' reign (eighth century B.C.) Judah was threatened by the Syria-Israel combine, looking to a united front against the ever-threatening Assyria. To the king, inspecting the water supply in the face of the coming siege, Isaiah gives assurance of divine protection; and to prove it, he offers to the faithless Ahaz any sign he might desire to ask. To his mock-pious refusal of a sign, Isaiah proclaims the famous words of 7:14. In spite of difficulties, the data of this chapter, in Isaiah, combine to afford strongest kind of assurance—not all will agree that the passage is referable to the Messiah and, as according to the NT (Mt. 1:21–23), is fulfilled only and truly in the Virgin-born Lord Jesus Christ: (1) The expression "to you" is plural, not the recreant king but the "house of Israel" being addressed, there being no hope for the king, but only for the faithful in Israel. And since the previous offer to Ahaz (vs. 11) implies the extraordinary, this sign is beyond the commonplace. Note the "therefore" and the "Lord himself." (2) The word "behold" is significant, employed in its two forms fifty times in Isaiah. The longer form, as here, is regularly of future import. The climactic solemnity, exciting the messenger's astonishment, argues that he speaks better than he knew. (3) The word "sign" in Hebrew usage is peculiar, denoting often a future fact or an aspect of it (compare the sign to Moses at the burning bush, Ex. 3). Here then is a threat to the faithless; but a promise to the faithful, that through the nameless 'almah, God would give a divine Deliverer (in the light of the context), even while tribulation would be the lot of his own. The perpetuity of the House of David is guaranteed, as according to 2 Sam. 7, in a supernatural manner. Though the "Judas of the OT" fails, God's purpose cannot be thwarted. (4) The word translated "virgin" is subject to much dispute. The unquestioned text reading is a noun, feminine singular, with the article prefixed, possibly "the young woman," "the maid," "the virgin." The technical word for virginity is bethulah, not used here. It is not used consistently, and most commonly has a figurative sense, as "the virgin daughter of Zion," but being also employed for one not a virgin (Joel 1:8), while in the cases of Rebekah and Miriam, 'almah does signify virginity. Also it is not without deep significance that the versions of the Bible are wholly on the side of "virgin" as the proper translation. The LXX of the third century B.C. translates this word into the corresponding Greek term for virgin, parthenos. There is no evidence that any change was made in the words before the time our present copies of the LXX were made by Christians, even though H. M. Orlinsky (of the RSV translators) hints at such. On the other hand, Justin Martyr, two hundred years before our LXX copies came into being, and who would certainly have known of any variations, alleges that it was a Jewish scheme, to make alterations in order to silence Christians. Acquilla, Symmachus, and Theodotion, in their revisions of the LXX in the second century A.D., supplanted the Greek word for virgin with the word for young woman, so as to deprive Christians of their argument for the virgin birth as based on Isa. 7:14. (5) "THE virgin" is significant; the generic idea hardly fits here, nor would a son of Isaiah or any other man of the day, in view of all involved. (6) Gearing in with this verse comes the boy of ch. 9, and the fourfold name which falls nothing short of Deity, and the Branch from Jesse, of ch. 11, remarkable factors attending, with recurring "Immanuel." The "seed of the *woman*" of Gen. 3:15, and the baffling word of Jer. 31:22, "a *woman* shall encompass a man," with most peculiar nouns involved, give confirmation. And Isaiah's contemporary Micah (5:2), adds significantly: ". . . she who travaileth hath brought forth" touching the promise of one "whose goings forth have been from of old, from everlasting." All these at the least, certainly create expectation of something extraordinary. And Mt. 1:21–23 clinches the matter for all who accept the supernatural, and credit the Scripture with forthrightness. Of the three standard arguments against the Messianic interpretation, viz., that it would violate context and exegesis, would not benefit Ahaz, and would show Isaiah mistaken, only the last is of significance. For Ahaz had forfeited the right to a sign; and the subsequent context has possible contradictory interpretations, making it as favorable for one view as for the other. As to the third, Isaiah's word is not invalidated even though Messiah came half a millennium later, or more. The prophet was never disappointed; 8:18 contemplates extended delay; and verses following evidence long spiritual and moral night before the promise is fulfilled. The child of 9:7 and the root of Jesse of ch. 11, coinciding with Immanuel, are to come after the destruction of Assyria. Micah 5:1–2, inseparable from Isa. 7:14, indicates that the King is still not at hand a quarter of a century later. And in the year 701 (events of Isa. 32–35), the Messiah is still in the future; but nowhere is there expressed any disappointment, due to the failure of prophecy. Further as the years passed, and the prophet's other predictions were fulfilled and his counsels vindicated, he gained in favor and influence with king and people—an impossibility had his great word of 7:14 been false. Most students feel that Isaiah pictures the Child's future coincident with the Assyrian invasion; but there is nothing in the prophecy to mark the date of fulfillment—far or near; the point is the preservation of the kingdom connected with the coming Immanuel. Any confusion in the time element is not foreign to Scripture, note Mt. 24. And prophecy is rather moral and spiritual than temporal. Both Old and New Testaments leave uncertainty as to the time of the Lord's coming. More than one of the prophets spoke better than he knew: not always was a clear picture revealed to them. Further, if one objects on the score that events are described as taking place under Assyrian domination rather than, as in the Lord's time, under Roman rule, again, the Scripture has its peculiarities. Assyria appears to be the title for all succeeding world powers taking rise from it. Ezra 6:22 speaks of the Persian king as the king of Assyria. In 2 K. 23:29, the "king of Assyria" is customary designation for Babylon's ruler. For Isaiah, Assyria was *the* world power. Our Lord was born under a universal empire whose name at that time was Rome, conditions being similar to those of Ahaz' time. Whatever the difficulties, we cannot miss the point: God will raise up in supernatural manner, a supernatural seed to David. We conclude: whereas the people of Isaiah's day were thinking of their present situation, God contemplated the future; the crowd had in mind a physical leader, God, a spiritual Deliverer; they expected a human champion, God, a divine Sovereign; the people hoped for deliverance from Syria, Ephraim, and Assyria; God was looking to deliverance from sin. Isaiah then spoke prophetically; his great words here related to the far future, however limited and mysterious their general nature were to him, and still may be to us; the Spirit of God speaking through him, contemplated the virgin-born Messiah, whom the writer Matthew confirms, and whom we accept, the Lord Jesus Christ of Bethlehem, Judah, Son of man, Son of Mary, Son of God.

Immer (ĭm'mĕr) [talkative] 1. Founder of an important priestly family (1 Chr. 9:12; Neh. 11:13), in charge of, and giving name to, the sixteenth course of service (1 Chr. 24:14); likely of the returnees with Zerubbabel (Ezra 2:37). See also Ezra 10:20, and Neh. 3:29.

2. A person or place in Babylonia, whence exiled returned (Ezra 2:59).

Imna (ĭm'nä) [probably, (God) restrains] an Asherite, son of Helem (1 Chr. 7:35).

Imnah 1. Son of Asher (Num. 26:44; 1 Chr. 7:36).

2. A Levite, father of Kore (2 Chr. 31:14).

Imrah (ĭm'rä) [stubborn] an Asherite, son of Zophah (1 Chr. 7:36).

Imri (ĭm'rī) [eloquent] 1. Of Judah, descendant of Phares (1 Chr. 9:4).

2. Father of Zaccur (Neh. 3:2).

incense sweet compound (Josephus notes thirteen ingredients) in Israel's worship, for burning, prohibited for ordinary purposes (Ex. 30:34-38, 35:8). The altar of incense belonged to the oracle (1 K. 6:22), was put just outside the vail; odoriferous smoke enveloped the mercy seat. Each morning the high priest dressed the lamps and burned incense (Ex. 30:1-9; Lk. 1:10). Incense exerted a sanitary influence over the slaughter smell; but it had also a symbolic meaning, typical of the intercession of the high priest (Num. 16:46-47; Ps. 141:2). The worshipers prayed outside the temple while incense was being offered, all in silence (Rev. 8:1). In Rev. 8:3-4, incense accompanies the prayers of the saints; see Rev. 5:8. Idolatrous worship used incense (Jer. 48:35; 2 Chr. 34:25).

India the name occurs not before Esther (8:9). In Hebrew, *Hodu*, through the Persian *Hidhu*, from *Hindu*, the river Indus. A district on the Lower Indus, conquered and incorporated in the Persian empire by Darius, the eastern limit of his rule. Solomon's trade with Ophir through the Red Sea, bulked Indian articles. It is supposed that the Indians were ethnologically of Cush (Gen. 10:6).

inheritance see **heir**

ink, inkhorn see **writing**

inn an oriental inn little resembles an occidental hotel. Perhaps originally, a halting place for the night near water and pasture (Ex. 4:24; cf. Gen. 42:27). Travelers found hospitality in houses of welcome (Ex. 2:20; Judg. 19:15-21; Heb. 13:2). On more frequented routes, in the course of time, caravanserais were erected by the rich: probably a central well, with rooms, store-chambers and stalls around it, the traveler furnishing his own bedding and food and provender (Jer. 41:17). The inn of Lk. 2:7 likely differed from that of 10:34-35, the latter having a host to supply provisions and attend to wants of travelers.

inspiration used loosely. In religious sense, twice in Scripture (Job 32:8; 2 Tim. 3:16), the former showing that men are not independent of God intellectually, the latter having the more proper and specific sense as "God-breathed" as the ground on which the unique value of Scripture rests, having the fundamental quality by whose virtue they are the Word of God, and clothed with characteristics accordingly. The Bible is therefore recognized as the Word of God, and is treated as possessing all the qualities that would naturally flow from divine origin. The ancient heresy in the modern form, of the "Acts of God" as being the whole of revelation, views inspiration lightly. "Inspiration is the guarantee of revelation." The divine character of inspiration is explicitly expressed in the constant ascription of its words to God as Author (Mt. 1:22, 2:15; Acts 13:34; Rom. 1:2; 1 Cor. 6:16), or more specifically, to the Holy Spirit (Acts 1:16, 28:25; Heb. 3:7, 9:8, 10:15). Human writers are said to speak "by" or "in" the Holy Spirit (Mt. 22:43; Mk. 12:36), and are treated as merely the media through whom God the Holy Spirit speaks (Mt. 1:22, 2:15; Acts 1:16, 4:25; Rom. 1:2). Therefore the very words of Scripture are accounted authoritative and "not to be broken" (Mt. 22:43; Jn. 10:34-35; Gal. 3:16); its prophecies sure (Jn. 19:36-37, 20:9; Acts 1:16; 2 Pet. 1:20; cf. Ezra 1:1; Dan. 9:2); and its whole original contents, historical as well as doctrinal and ethical, not only entirely trustworthy, but designedly framed for the spiritual profit of all ages (cf. 2 Chr. 17:9; Neh. 8:1; Rom. 4:23, 9:17; Rom. 15:4; 1 Cor. 9:10, 10:11; Gal. 3:8, 22, 4:30; 2 Tim. 3:16; 1 Pet. 2:6). The NT is on par with the OT, sharing in divine qualities (1 Cor. 7:30, 14:37; Gal. 1:8; 2 Thess. 3:4, 14); their writers are the organs of God (1 Cor. 2:13, 16, 7:40; 1 Thess. 2:13, 4:2); all are concluded under the common sacred title of Scripture (1 Tim. 5:18; 2 Pet. 3:16). Plenary inspiration means that all is equally placed in the Bible under the direction of God, whether by new revelation or by inclusion (as genealogies, etc.). Verbal inspiration is the only possible kind—only by words do we know ideas. On this see for example, Deut. 18:18; Isa. 59:21; Jer. 1:9, 5:14, 36:4; Acts 1:16.

instant an adverb in the sense of steadfast (Lk. 7:4; 2 Tim. 4:2).

Iphedaiah (ĭ-fē-dā'yä) [Jehovah delivers] a Benjaminite, son of Shashak (1 Chr. 8:35).

Ir (same as **Iri;** ĭr) [probably, watchful] 1 Chr. 7:12.

Ira (ī'rä) [watchful] 1. A Jairite among David's great officers (2 Sam. 20:26).
2. Hero of David's guard (2 Sam. 23:26).
3. Another of the same (2 Sam. 23:38).

Irad (ī'răd) of Cain's line (Gen. 4:18).

Iram (ī'răm) [perhaps, watchful] Edomite chief (Gen. 36:43; 1 Chr. 1:54).

Irijah (ĭ-rī'jä) [Jehovah sees or provides] captain of the guard who arrested Jeremiah as a deserter (Jer. 37:13-14).

Irnahash (ĭr-nā'hăsh) [city of a serpent] undiscovered (1 Chr. 4:12).

iron 1. Tubal-cain worked in "brass (?) and iron" (Gen. 4:22). Canaan was a "land whose stones are iron" (Deut. 8:9). Job speaks of "iron taken from the dust" (Job 28:2). The ore seems to have been reduced in furnaces (Deut. 4:20), ten by three feet (breadth), with charcoal and blowers (Ezek. 22:20; cf. Jer. 6:29). As early as Moses were axes, etc., of iron (Num. 35:16; Deut. 3:11). Iron vessels (Josh. 6:19); implements of war (Josh. 17:16; 1 Sam. 17:7); farming, building, graving tools (2 Sam. 12:31; 1 K. 6:7; Job 19:24); fishing irons, gates, fetters, idols (Job 41:7; Ps. 105:18; Dan. 5:4)—all of iron. Generally wrought iron; casting may have been known.
2. A city of Naphtali [conspicuous?], (Josh. 19:38).

Irpeel (ĭr'pē-ĕl) [God heals] city of Benjamin, unknown (Josh. 18:27).

Irshemesh (ĭr-shĕ'mĕsh) [city of the sun] town of Dan, possibly same as Beth-shemesh (Josh. 19:41).

Iru (ī'rū) [watchful] son of Caleb (1 Chr. 4:15).

Isaac (ī'săc) [laughing one] divinely promised son of the aged Sarah and Abraham, born at Gerar, or more likely, Beer-sheba (Gen. 21:14, 31). On his name, see Gen. 17:17, 18:9, 21:6). The legal heir, Isaac's privileges were higher than those of Ishmael (Gen. 21:1-12). At twenty-five years (Josephus) he was the intended victim of Abraham's great act of faith in sacrifice (22:1-18). He dwelt at Beer-lahai-roi (24:62), was married at forty to Rebekah his cousin, who twenty years later bore him two sons (25:20, 26); was driven by famine to Gerar, where God renewed the Abrahamic promises; had experience similar (Gen. 20:2); acquired great wealth; pitched camp in the valley of Gerar, and opened the wells his father had dug (26:17); moved to Beer-sheba (26:17, 28:10); was blessed of God, erected an altar; treatied with Abimelech, *sheba* giving new occasion for linking memory of an oath with the name of the place (26:24-31, 33; cf. 21:31). When Isaac was much more than one hundred years old (27:1 with 25:26, 26:34), Rebekah contrived to transfer the blessing from the elder son, Esau, to Jacob, her favorite; and to save his life, had Isaac send him to Laban in Padan-aram to get a wife (27:46–28:5). Twenty years later, at Hebron, to which Jacob with a large family returned, he died at age 180 years, was buried by his two sons in the cave of Machpelah, beside his parents and his wife (Gen. 49:30–31). The NT alludes to Isaac as a child of promise (Gal. 4:22–23), and instances his tent life and his blessing of Esau and Jacob as evidences of his faith (Heb. 11:9, 20).

Isaiah (ī-sā'yä) [Jehovah saves] son of Amoz, a prophet of Judah in the reigns of Uzziah through Hezekiah (Isa. 1:1, 6:1, 7:3, 14:28, 20:1–2, 36–39). He lived and prophesied in Jerusalem, speaking of other nations whose fortunes touched those of Judah (chs. 13–23), as did also several other prophets. His call (6:1), in the year that Uzziah died, may have been a renewal of call (parallels of divine calling: Ezek. 33:21–33; Acts 10, 16:9–10), and his work seems to have extended over sixty years, death occurring in Manasseh's time, tradition citing him as sawn asunder by a wooden saw (Heb. 11:37). By 734 he was married, two sons being born: Shear-yashub ("a remnant shall return") and Mahar-shalal-hash-baz ("speed spoil, hasten prey"), being prophetic, and his wife being spoken of as the prophetess (7:3, 8:3). He spoke on international relationships, to Israel as church and as body politic, urging king and people to trust in God and avoid entangling alliances (8:12–14). In 734 when Syria and Northern Israel tried to force Judah to ally with them against the encroaching Assyrian (the Syro-Ephraimitic War), Isaiah declared its failure, urging Ahaz to rely solely on Jehovah; but the king had called Tiglath-pileser, to become his vassal, and rejected the sign Isaiah offered from God to guarantee God's word of promise (ch. 7; 2 K. 16:7–8, 10). In Hezekiah's reign, Assyria invaded the west in the king's fourteenth year (2 K. 18:13; Isa. 36:1), the year in which he fell sick, Isaiah foretelling recovery (2 K. 20:1–11; Isa. 38). There followed the embassy of Merodach-baladan (Isa. 39), and Sennacherib's expedition against Jerusalem, 701 B.C. (2 K. 18:14). During this time Isaiah's magnificent words proclaiming the inviolate Jerusalem heartened the king, and Jerusalem was saved, the Assyrian army being smitten by the angel of the Lord. Sennacherib withdrew from the west, to die twenty years later at the hands of his two sons.

There is difficulty about the time notes here. Either Sennacherib came two times, once in 714 and later in 701; or the 701 coming, when he sent messengers from his camp near Egypt, demanding capitulation of Jerusalem, occurred in the fourteenth year of Hezekiah's added life, i.e., in 701; for Hezekiah died ca. 699, after a reign of about twenty-eight years. And Babylon's king sent envoys to Hezekiah at a time when Assyria was in abeyance, evidently. It appears that chs. 38–39 (which deal with Babylon, and stand therefore logically connected with the second section of the book [40–66], which relates to the Babylonian captivity [29:1, 6–7]) have been placed out of chronological order, presumably by a later editor in arranging the book; for Hezekiah's illness was at least fourteen years before Assyria came (36:1). That is, the contents of 38–39 concern matters antecedent to Assyria's great invasion (noted in 36–37).

The book may be analyzed thus:

Subject: Through Judgment to Glory, chs. 1–39 and 40–66 being respectively pertinent to these two divisions.

A. (1) Judgment on the people of God, chs. 1–12. (2) Judgment on outside nations, chs. 13–23. (3) Judgment on the whole world, issuing in redemption, chs. 24–27. (4) The future, out of Israel's and world judgment, chs. 28–35. The historical interlude, chs. 36–39. B. Glory Prophecies, chs. 40–66: (1) Cyrus, the temporal agent of God's salvation, chs. 40–48. (2) The Servant, the spiritual agent, chs. 49–57. (3) The salvation itself in all its glory and blessedness, chs. 58–66.

Numberless attacks have been made on the integrity of the book, Isaiah's part being reduced by some critics to minimum. The last twenty-seven chs. have been particularly rejected as Isaianic, because they are set in Babylon, and the critics reject futuristic prophecy. But the hallmark of Isaiah is found about the same number of times in the second half as in the first—thirteen to twelve: "The Holy One of Israel." Some parts in the first half, credited to Isaiah of Jerusalem are no less futuristic than the latter part of the book, e.g., the "Little Apocalypse," chs. 24–27. It seems beyond possibility that the greatest of all the prophets —in the judgment of the critics generally, should be lost in anonymity. The Dead Sea Scrolls seem to make no allowance for two Isaiahs. The New Testament makes no difference in quotations. There are plenty of people who "do not know that there is ONE Isaiah yet"! And along with much else, there is the universal voice of both Jewish and Christian tradition, attesting Isaiah ben-Amoz as the writer of the book.

Iscah (ĭs'kä) [discerning] daughter of Haran, and sister of Milcah and thus sister of Lot

(Gen. 11:27, 29). Tradition says same as Sarai, but that would make her Abraham's niece, not his half-sister (Gen. 20:12).

Iscariot see **Judas** 6

Ishbah (ĭsh'bä) [praising one] a Judahite, "father of Eshtemoa" (1 Chr. 4:17).

Ishbak (ĭsh'băk) [relinquishing one?] Abrahamic Arab tribe, through Keturah (Gen. 25:2; 1 Chr. 1:32).

Ishbi-benob (ĭsh-bĭ-bē'nŏb) [My dwelling is on a height] Philistine giant whom Abishai slew, saving David (2 Sam. 21:16–17).

Ish-bosheth (ĭsh-bŏsh'ĕth) [man of shame] youngest son and legitimate heir of Saul (2 Sam. 2:8; with 1 Chr. 8:33, 9:39). If present at the battle of Gilboa he escaped; at Saul's death, David being refused by all tribes save Judah, Ish-bosheth at forty years of age became king, reigning two troubled years (2 Sam. 2:8–10), at Mahanaim, east of Jordan, but only in name. War and negotiations were carried on through Abner (2 Sam. 2:12, 3:6, 12), at whose death the king lost heart (2 Sam. 4:2). David sternly rebuked those who brought the head of assassinated Ish-bosheth, executed the murderers, and honorably buried the head in Abner's tomb at Hebron (4:5–12). Only a grandson of Saul remained (4:4).

Ishi (ĭsh'ī) 1. A man of the descendants of Judah, son of Appaim (1 Chr. 2:31); one of the great house of Hezron.

2. A man with a son, Zoheth (1 Chr. 4:20).

3. Head of a family of the tribe of Simeon (1 Chr. 4:42).

4. One of the heads of the tribe of Manasseh on the east of Jordan (1 Chr. 5:24).

Ishi (ĭsh'ī) a word which occurs in Hos. 2:16, and signifies "my man," "my husband." It is the Israelite term to be used in place of **Baali**, the Canaanite term, meaning the same thing but having other associations.

Ishiah (ĭ-shī'ä) the fifth of the five sons of Izrahiah; one of the heads of the tribe of Issachar in the time of David (1 Chr. 7:3).

Ishijah (ĭ-shī'jä) a lay Israelite of the Bene-harim, who had married a foreign wife (Ezra 10:31).

Ishma (ĭsh'mä) a name in the genealogy of Judah (1 Chr. 4:3).

Ishmael (ĭsh'mä-ĕl) 1. The son of Abraham by Hagar the Egyptian, his concubine; born when Abraham was eighty-six years old (Gen. 16:15–16). Ishmael was his firstborn, when he dwelt in the plain of Mamre. He was circumcised, when thirteen years old (17:25); God renewed his promise respecting Ishmael. He does not again appear until the weaning of Isaac. At the feast celebrating the weaning,

"Sarah saw the son of Hagar the Egyptian, which she had born unto Abraham, mocking," and urged Abraham to cast out him and his mother. The patriarch, comforted by God's renewed promise, that of Ishmael he would make a nation, sent them away, and they departed to the wilderness of Beer-sheba. They went to the "wilderness of Paran," where (next verse) he dwelt, and where "his mother took him a wife out of the land of Egypt" (Gen. 21:20–21). This wife is not elsewhere mentioned; she was, we infer, an Egyptian; she became the mother of his twelve sons, and daughter. Of the later life of Ishmael we know little. His death is recorded as having taken place at the age of a hundred and thirty-seven years (25:17–18).

2. One of the sons of Azel, a descendant of Saul through Meribbaal, or Mephibosheth (1 Chr. 8:38, 9:44).

3. A man of Judah, father of Zebadiah (2 Chr. 19:11).

4. Another man of Judah, son of Jehohanan; one of the captains of hundreds who assisted Jehoiada in restoring Joash to the throne (2 Chr. 23:1).

5. A priest, of the Bene-pashur, who was forced by Ezra to relinquish his foreign wife (Ezra 10:22).

6. The son of Nethaniah; a perfect marvel of craft and villainy, whose treachery forms one of the chief episodes of the history of the period immediately succeeding the first fall of Jerusalem. His exploits are related in Jer. 40:7–41:15, with a short summary in 2 K. 25:23–25.

Ishmaiah (ĭsh-mä'yä) son of Obadiah, the ruler of the tribe of Zebulun in the time of King David (1 Chr. 27:19).

Ishmeelite (ĭsh'mē-ĕl-īte) the term Ishmeelite occurs on three occasions: Gen. 37:25, 27–28, 39:1; Judg. 8:24; Ps. 83:6. From the context of the first two, it seems a general name for the Abrahamic peoples of the east country, the Bene-kedem—the supposed descendants of Abraham and Hagar through Ishmael. In the third instance the name is applied in its strict sense to the Ishmaelites. In Genesis and in 1 Chr. 2:17 the spelling is Ishmeelite; elsewhere Ishmaelite.

Ishmerai (ĭsh'mē-rī) a Benjaminite; one of the family of Elpaal (1 Chr. 8:18).

Ishod (ī'shŏd, ĭsh'ŏd) one of the tribe of Manasseh on the east of Jordan, son of Hammoleketh (1 Chr. 7:18).

Ishpah (ĭsh'pä) a Benjaminite, of the family of Beriah (1 Chr. 8:16).

Ish-pan (ĭsh'păn) a Benjaminite, one of the family of Shashak (1 Chr. 8:22).

Ishtob (ĭsh'tŏb) apparently one of the small kingdoms or states which formed part of the general country of Aram, named with Zobah, Rehob, and Maacah (2 Sam. 10:6, 8). It is probable that the real signification is "the men of Tob."

Ishuah (ĭsh'û-à) the second son of Asher (Gen. 46:17).

Ishuai (ĭsh'û-ī) the third son of Asher (1 Chr. 7:30), founder of a family bearing his name (Num. 26:44; AV, "Jesuites." Jeshui and Ishuai, identical).

Ishui (ĭsh'û-ī) the second son of Saul by his wife Ahinoam (1 Sam. 14:49).

isle the radical sense of the Hebrew word seems to be "habitable places," as opposed to water, and in this sense it occurs in Isa. 42:15. Hence it means secondarily any maritime district, whether belonging to a continent or to an island; thus it is used of the shore of the Mediterranean (Isa. 20:6, 23:2, 6), and of the coasts of Elishah (Ezek. 27:7), i.e., of Greece and Asia Minor. In this sense it is more particularly restricted to the shores of the Mediterranean, sometimes in the fuller expression "islands of the sea" (Isa. 11:11). Occasionally the word is specifically used of an island, as of Caphtor or Crete (Jer. 47:4). But more generally it is applied to any region separated from Palestine by water, as fully described in Jer. 25:22.

Ismachiah (ĭs-mà-kī'ä) a Levite, who was one of the overseers of offerings during the revival under King Hezekiah (2 Chr. 31:13).

Ismaiah (ĭs-mā'yä) a Gibeonite, one of the chiefs of those warriors who joined David at Ziklag (1 Chr. 12:4).

Ispah (ĭs'pä) a Benjaminite, of the family of Beriah; one of the heads of his tribe (1 Chr. 8:16).

Israel (ĭs'rä-ĕl) 1. The name given (Gen. 32:28) to Jacob after the wrestling of the Angel with him (Hos. 12:4) at Peniel. Gesenius' *Lexicon* interprets Israel as "soldier of God."

2. It became the national name of the twelve tribes collectively. They are so called in Ex. 3:16 and afterwards.

3. It is used in a narrower sense, excluding Judah, in 1 Sam. 11:8; 2 Sam. 20:1; 1 K. 12:16. Thenceforth it was assumed and accepted as the name of the Northern Kingdom.

4. After the Captivity, the returned exiles resumed the name as the designation of their nation. The name Israel is also said by some to denote laymen, as distinguished from priests, Levites, and other ministers (e.g., Ezra 6:16, 9:1, 10:25; Neh. 11:3).

Israel, Kingdom of 1. The prophet Ahijah of Shiloh, who was commissioned in the latter days of Solomon to announce the division of the kingdom, left one tribe (Judah) to the house of David (see 1 K. 12:21), and assigned ten to Jeroboam (1 K. 11:31, 35). These were probably Joseph (= Ephraim and Manasseh), Issachar, Zebulun, Asher, Naphtali, Benjamin, Dan, Simeon, Gad, and Reuben—Levi being intentionally omitted. Eventually the greater part of Benjamin, and probably the whole of Simeon and Dan, were included as if by common consent in the kingdom of Judah. With respect to the conquests of David, Moab appears to have been attached to the kingdom of Israel (2 K. 3:4); so much of Syria as remained subject to Solomon (see 1 K. 11:24 f.) would probably be claimed by his successor in the Northern Kingdom; and Ammon, though connected with Rehoboam whose mother was an Ammonitess (1 K. 14:21), and though afterwards tributary to Judah (2 Chr. 27:5), was at one time allied (2 Chr. 20:1)—we know not how closely or how early—with Moab. The seacoast between Accho and Japho remained in the possession of Israel.

2. The population of the kingdom is not expressly stated; and in drawing any inference from the numbers of fighting men, we must bear in mind that the numbers in the Hebrew text are strongly suspected to have been subjected to corruption.

3. Shechem was the first capital of the new kingdom (1 K. 12:25), venerable for its traditions, and beautiful in its situation. Subsequently Tirzah became the royal residence, if not the capital, of Jeroboam (1 K. 14:17) and of his successors (15:33, 16:8, 17, 23). Samaria, uniting in itself the qualities of beauty and fertility, and a commanding position, was chosen by Omri (1 K. 16:24), and remained the capital of the kingdom until it had given the last proof of its strength by sustaining for three years the onset of the hosts of Assyria. Jezreel was probably only a royal residence of some of the Israelitish kings.

4. The disaffection of Ephraim and the northern tribes, having grown in secret under the prosperous but burdensome reign of Solomon, broke out at the critical moment of that monarch's death. It was just then that Ephraim, the center of the movement, found in Jeroboam an instrument prepared to give expression to the rivalry of centuries (1 K. 12).

5. The kingdom of Israel developed no new power. It was but a portion of David's king-

dom deprived of many elements of strength. Its frontier was open and as widely extended as before; but it wanted a capital for the seat of organized power. Its territory was as fertile and as tempting to the spoiler, but its people were less united and patriotic. A corrupt religion poisoned the source of national life. These causes tended to increase the misfortunes, and to accelerate the early end of the kingdom of Israel. It lasted about 254 years, from around 975 to 721 B.C., about two thirds of the duration of its more compact neighbor Judah. But it may be doubted that the division into two kingdoms greatly shortened the independent existence of the Hebrew race, or interfered with the purposes which, it is thought, may be traced in the establishment of David's monarchy.

6. The detailed history of the kingdom of Israel will be found under the names of its nineteen kings.

Israelite (ĭs′rä-ĕl-īt) in 2 Sam. 17:25, Ithra, the father of Amasa, is called "an Israelite," while in 1 Chr. 2:17 he appears as "Jether the Ishmaelite." The latter is undoubtedly the true reading.

Issachar (ĭs′ă-kär) the ninth son of Jacob and the fifth of Leah (Gen. 30:17; cf. also 29:35). Of Issachar the individual we know nothing. At the descent into Egypt, four sons are ascribed to him, who founded the four chief families of the tribe (Gen. 46:13; Num. 26:23, 25; 1 Chr. 7:1).

Isshiah (ĭs-shī′ă) 1. A descendant of Moses by his younger son Eliezer (1 Chr. 24:21; cf. 23:17, 26:25).

2. A Levite of the house of Kohath and family of Uzziel (1 Chr. 24:25).

issue, running the texts Lev. 15:2-3, 22:4; Num. 5:2; and 2 Sam. 3:29, are probably to be interpreted of gonorrhea. In Lev. 15:3, a distinction is introduced, which merely means that the cessation of the actual flux does not constitute ceremonial cleanness, but that the patient must bide the legal time, seven days (vs. 13), and must perform the prescribed purifications and sacrifice (vs. 14).

Isuah (ĭs′ū-ă) second son of Asher (1 Chr. 7:30).

Isui (ĭs′ū-ī) third son of Asher (Gen. 46:17), founder of a family called after him, though in the AV appearing as the Ishvites (Num. 26:44).

Italy (ĭt′ă-lĭ) this word is used in the NT in the usual sense of the period, i.e., in its true geographical sense, as denoting the whole natural peninsula between the Alps and the Straits of Messina.

Ithai (ĭth′ā-ī) a Benjaminite, son of Ribai of Gibeah, one of the heroes of David's guard (1 Chr. 11:31).

Ithamar (ĭth′ă-mär) the youngest son of Aaron (Ex. 6:23). After the death of Nadab and Abihu (Lev. 10:1), Eleazar and Ithamar were appointed to succeed in the priestly office (Ex. 28:1, 40, 43; Num. 3:3-4; 1 Chr. 24:2). In the distribution of services belonging to the tabernacle, and its transport on the march of the Israelites, the Gershonites and the Merarites were placed under the superintendence of Ithamar (Ex. 38:21; Num. 4:21-33). The high priesthood passed into the family of Ithamar in the person of Eli, but for what reason we are not informed.

Ithiel (ĭth′ĭ-ĕl) 1. A Benjaminite, son of Jesaiah (Neh. 11:7).

2. One of two persons—Ithiel and Ucal—to whom Agur ben-jakeh delivered his discourse (Prov. 30:1).

Ithmah (ĭth′mä) a Moabite, one of the heroes of David's guard (1 Chr. 11:46).

Ithnan (ĭth′năn) one of the towns in the extreme south of Judah (Josh. 15:23). No trace has been discovered.

Ithra (ĭth′rä) an Israelite (2 Sam. 17:25) or Ishmaelite (1 Chr. 2:17), the father of Amasa by Abigail, David's sister.

Ithran (ĭth′răn) 1. A son of Dishon, a Horite (Gen. 36:26; 1 Chr. 1:41), and probably a phylarch of a tribe of the Horim (Gen. 36:30).

2. A descendant of Asher (1 Chr. 7:30-40).

Ithream (ĭth′rē-ăm) son of David, born of him in Hebron, and distinctly specified as the sixth, and as the child of Eglah, David's wife (2 Sam. 3:5; 1 Chr. 3:3).

Ithrite, the (ĭth′rīt) the designation of two of the members of David's guard, Ira and Gareb (2 Sam. 23:38; 1 Chr. 11:40).

Ittah-kazin (ĭt-ă-kā′zĭn) a place on the boundary of Zebulun (Josh. 19:13). It has not been identified.

Ittai (ĭt′ā-ī) 1. "Ittai the Gittite," i.e., the native of Gath, a Philistine in the army of King David. He appears only during the revolution of Absalom, first seen on the morning of David's flight. Last in the procession, came the 600 heroes who had formed David's band during his wanderings in Judah, and had been with him at Gath (2 Sam. 15:18; cf. 1 Sam. 23:13, 27:2, 30:9-10). Apparently commanding them, was Ittai the Gittite (2 Sam. 15:19). He caught the eye of the king, who at once besought him not to attach himself to a doubtful cause, but to return "with his brethren" and abide with the king (vss. 19-20). But Ittai is firm; he is David's slave, and wherever his master goes he will go. Accordingly he is allowed by David to proceed. When the army was numbered and organized by David at Mahanaim, Ittai again appears, now in command of a third part of the force (2 Sam. 18:2, 5, 12).

2. Son of Ribai, from Gibeah of Benjamin; one of the thirty heroes of David's guard (2 Sam. 23:29).

Ituraea (ĭt-û-rē'â) a small province on the northwestern border of Palestine, lying along the base of Mount Hermon, mentioned only in Lk. 3:1.

Ivah (ī'vâ) or **Ava** which is mentioned in Scripture twice (2 K. 18:34, 19:13) in connection with Hena and Sepharvaim, and once (2 K. 17:24) in connection with Babylon and Cuthah, must be sought in the general area of Babylonia; unidentified.

ivory the word in Hebrew literally signifies the "tooth" of an animal; more especially it denotes the substance of the projecting tusks of elephants. The Assyrians appear to have carried on a great traffic in ivory. Early conquests in India had made them familiar with it, and (according to one rendering of the passage) their artists supplied the luxurious Tyrians with carvings in ivory from the isles of Chittim (Ezek. 27:6). Among the merchandise of Babylon, enumerated in Rev. 18:12, are included "all manner of vessels of ivory." The skilled workmen of Hiram king of Tyre fashioned the great ivory throne of Solomon, and overlaid it with pure gold (1 K. 10:18; 2 Chr. 9:17). This was supplied by the caravans of Dedan (Isa. 21:13; Ezek. 17:15), or brought, with apes and peacocks, by the navy of Tarshish (1 K. 10:22). The Egyptians early made use of this material in decoration. Theirs was principally brought from Ethiopia, though their elephants were originally from Asia. The Ethiopians (Diodorus Siculus I.55), brought to Sesostris "ebony and gold, and the teeth of elephants." According to Pliny the Elder (III.-10), ivory was so plentiful on the borders of Ethiopia that the natives made doorposts of it, and even fences and stalls for their cattle. The Egyptian merchants traded for ivory and onyx stones to Bargaza, the port to which was carried down the commerce of Western India from Ozene. In the early ages of Greece, ivory was frequently employed for ornament. The "ivory house" of Ahab (1 K. 22:39) was probably a palace, the walls of which were paneled with ivory. Beds inlaid or veneered with ivory were in use among the Hebrews, Amos 6:4, as also among the Egyptians. By the luxurious Phoenicians, ivory was employed to ornament the boxwood rowing benches (or "hatches" according to some) of their galleys (Ezek. 27:6).

Izehar (ĭz'ê-här) the form in which the name Izhar is given in the AV of Num. 3:19 only.

Izeharites, the (ĭz'ê-hàr-īts) a family of Kohathite Levites, descended from Izhar the son of Kohath (Num. 3:27); called also in the AV "Izharites."

Izhar (ĭz'här) son of Kohath, grandson of Levi, uncle of Aaron and Moses, and father of Korah (Ex. 6:18, 21; Num. 3:19, 16:1; 1 Chr. 6:2, 18). Izhar was the head of the family of the Izharites or Izeharites (Num. 3:27; 1 Chr. 26:23, 29).

Izrahiah (ĭz-rà-hī'â) a man of Issachar, one of the Bene-uzzi (1 Chr. 7:3).

Izrahite, the (ĭz'rà-hīt) the designation of Shamhuth (1 Chr. 27:8). Its real force is probably Zerahite, that is from the great Judaic family of Zerah.

Izri (ĭz'rī) a Levite leader of the fourth course or ward in the service of the house of God (1 Chr. 25:11). In vs. 3 he is called Zeri.

J

Jaakan or **Jakan** (jā'ă-kān) the forefather of the Bene-jaakan (Deut. 10:6).

Jaakobah (jā-ă-kō'bă) one of the princes of the families of Simeon (1 Chr. 4:36).

Jaala (jā-ā'lâ) Bene-jaala were among the descendants of "Solomon's slaves" who returned from Babylon with Zerubbabel (Neh. 7:58).

The name also occurs as Jaalah (Ezra 2:56).

Jaalam (jā-ā'lăm) a son of Esau (Gen. 36:5, 14, 18; cf. 1 Chr. 1:35), and a phylarch (AV, duke) or head of a tribe of Edom.

Jaanai (jā-ā'nī) a chief man in the tribe of Gad (1 Chr. 5:12).

Jaare-oregim (jā-är'ê-ŏr'ê-jĭm) according to the

present text of 2 Sam. 21:19, a Bethlehemite, and the father of Elhanan who slew Goliath. In the parallel passage, 1 Chr. 20:5, besides other differences, Jair is found instead of Jaare, and Oregim is omitted. The conclusion of B. Kennicott appears to be a just one—that in the latter place it has been interpolated from the former, and that Jair or Jaor is the correct reading instead of Jaare.

Jaasau (jā'ă-sô) one of the Bene-bani who had married a foreign wife, and had put her away (Ezra 10:37).

Jaasiel (jā-ā'sĭ-ĕl) son of the great Abner (1 Chr. 27:21).

Jaazaniah (jā-ăz-ă-nī'ȧ) 1. One of the captains of the forces who accompanied Jahanan ben-kareah to pay his respects to Gedaliah at Mizpah (2 K. 25:23), and who appears afterwards to have assisted in recovering Ishmael's prey from his clutches (cf. Jer. 41:11). After that he probably went to Egypt with the rest (Jer. 43:4-5).

2. Son of Shaphan (Ezek. 8:11). It is possible that he is identical with 3.

3. Son of Azur; one of the princes of the people against whom Ezekiel was directed to prophesy (Ezek. 11:1).

4. A Rechabite, son of Jeremiah (Jer. 35:3).

Jaazer or **Jazer** (jā-ā'zēr or jā'zēr) a town on the east of Jordan, in or near Gilead (Num. 32:1, 3; 1 Chr. 26:31). We first hear of it in possession of the Amorites, and as taken by Israel after Heshbon, and on their way from thence to Bashan (Num. 21:32). Probably gave its name to a district of dependent or "daughter" towns (Num. 21:32), the "land of Jazer" (Num. 32:1). Present identification is uncertain.

Jaaziah (jā-ă-zī'ȧ) apparently a third son, or a descendant, of Merari the Levite (1 Chr. 24:26-27).

Jaaziel (jā-ā'zĭ-ĕl) one of the Levites of the second order appointed by David for musical service before the ark (1 Chr. 15:18).

Jabal (jā'băl) the son of Lamech and Adah (Gen. 4:20) and brother of Jubal. He is described as the father of such as dwell in tents and have cattle.

Jabbok (jăb'ŏk) a stream which intersects the mountain range of Gilead (cf. Josh. 12:2 and 5), and falls into the Jordan about midway between the Sea of Galilee and the Dead Sea. It was anciently the border of the children of Ammon (Num. 21:24; Deut. 2:37, 3:16). When the Ammonites were driven out by Sihon from their ancient territory, they took possession of the eastern plain, and of a considerable section of the eastern defiles of

Gilead, around the sources and upper branches of the Jabbok. It was on the south bank of the Jabbok the interview took place between Jacob and Esau (Gen. 32:22); and this river afterward became, toward its western part, the boundary between the kingdoms of Sihon and Og (Josh. 12:2, 5). Its modern name is Nahr ez-Zerka (river of blue).

Jabesh (jā'bĕsh) 1. Father of Shallum, the fifteenth king of Israel (2 K. 15:10, 13=14).

2. The short form of the name Jabesh-gilead (1 Chr. 10:12 only).

Jabesh-gilead or Jabesh in the territory of Gilead. In its widest sense, Gilead included the half tribe of Manasseh (1 Chr. 27:21) as well as the tribes of Gad and Reuben (Num. 32:1-42) east of the Jordan; of the cities of Gilead, Jabesh was the chief. It is first mentioned in Judg. 21:8-14. Being attacked subsequently by Nahash the Ammonite, it gave Saul an opportunity of displaying his prowess in its defense (1 Sam. 11:1-15). The site is not known.

Jabez (jā'bĕz) 1. A town in Judah, site not known, where some families of the scribes, descendants of Caleb, lived (1 Chr. 2:55).

2. Listed as a descendant of Judah (1 Chr. 4:9-10), noted for his honorable character. He prayed to be kept from evil and for an enlargement of his possessions; this was granted.

Jabin (jā'bĭn) 1. A Canaanite king who ruled in Hazor, near Kedesh. He was the leader of a confederacy of kings whom Joshua defeated at the waters of Merom (Josh. 11:1-14).

2. Another king in Canaan, who reigned in Hazor (Judg. 4:2). He also was the organizer of other forces against Israel; his commander in chief was Sisera, who was defeated by Barak at the river Kishon. Jabin continued the war but later was himself killed (Judg. 4:2-14). Due to similarities, some have surmised that the Jabin in each instance is the same person.

Jabneel (jăb'nē-ĕl) 1. A town on the extreme north border of Judah (Josh. 15:11), near the Mediterranean Sea, and nine miles north-northeast of Ashdod. It is the same location as the Philistine town of Jabneh, which was captured by Uzziah by breaching its walls (2 Chr. 26:6). It is the site of the present town of Yebnah.

2. A site on the border of Naphtali (Josh. 19:33); the location is unknown, though possibly to be identified with modern Khirbet Yamna, southwest of the Lake of Galilee.

Jabneh (jăb'nĕ) see **Jabneel** 1 (2 Chr. 26:6)

Jacan (jā'kăn) see **Jachan**

Jachan (jā'kăn) a Gadite, listed as one of the seven chief men of the tribe, (1 Chr. 5:13).

Jachin (jā'kĭn) 1. Fourth son of Simeon (Gen. 46:10; Ex. 6:15; Num. 26:12), probably identical with Jarib in 1 Chr. 4:24.

2. A descendant of Aaron, whose family formed the twenty-first division of the priests in the time of David (1 Chr. 24:17).

3. One of the twin pillars (the other was called Boaz) of bronze erected on opposite sides of the porch of Solomon's temple (1 K. 7:15-22), probably as a symbol of strength or for decoration, as they were free standing and served no structural purpose.

Jachinites, the (jā'kĭn-īts) see **Jachin** 1

jacinth (jā'sĭnth) 1. A reddish-orange stone, referred to as a color in Rev. 9:17.

2. The eleventh jewel in the foundation of the wall of the New Jerusalem (Rev. 21:20). See also **hyacinth**

jackal see **dragon**

jackal's well see **dragon well**

Jacob (jā'kŭb) [in popular etymology means "the heel catcher" and "the supplanter"] the second son of Isaac and Rebekah, younger twin of Esau (Gen. 25:21-26). He was the favorite of his mother, and she was the instigator of his deception of his blind father in receiving the first blessing (Gen. 27:1-29); this incident followed Jacob's scheme of trading a "mess of pottage" to Esau for the elder son's birthright (Gen. 25:29-34). Because of Esau's threat to Jacob due to this double fraud, Jacob was sent by Rebekah to her relatives in Haran, under pretext of seeking a wife from among her own people. En route he had a dream with the vision of a ladder connecting heaven and earth, upon which angels ascended and descended. In this vision God assured Jacob of the covenant blessings (Gen. 27:42-46, 28:1-22).

After a stay of probably twenty years or more with his uncle Laban in Paddan-aram, Jacob returned as a wealthy man, with two wives, two concubines, and eleven children. On the return, at the stream Jabbok "there wrestled a man with him until the breaking of the day" (Gen. 32:24). In that encounter his name was changed from Jacob to Israel. To some measure this was symbolic also of his change in character, decidedly for the better.

His latter days were spent in Egypt (Gen. 47:9), where he died at the age of 147 (Gen. 47:28). His body was brought back to Canaan and buried in the cave of Machpelah (Gen. 50:1-14).

Jacob, given the name Israel, is considered the patriarch of the Hebrew nation. The nation is often referred to in Scripture as the Children of Israel.

Jacob's well mentioned in Jn. 4:6, in connec-

tion with the encounter of Christ and the "woman of Samaria." It was near the Samaritan city of Sychar. According to the woman, this well was given by Jacob (4:12). The thrust of the account has nothing to do with the well, but rather with the transforming encounter of the sinful woman with Christ, which also was a pointed lesson to the disciples concerning their racial prejudice against the Samaritans.

Jada (jā'dà) son of Oman, of the house of Jerahmeel (1 Chr. 2:28, 32).

Jadau (jā'dô) a son of Nebo, who was persuaded by Ezra to put away his foreign wife (Ezra 10:43; spelled Iddo in the RSV).

Jaddua (jăd-dū'à) 1. A chief of the people who sealed the covenant with Nehemiah (Neh. 10:21).

2. A high priest, son of Jonathan, who returned from Babylon with Zerubbabel (Neh. 12:11, 22). He was the last high priest mentioned in the OT, holding office probably during the reign of Alexander the Great.

Jaddus (jăd'dŭs) see **Addus**

Jadon (jā'dŏn) a Meronothite who assisted in rebuilding the wall of Jerusalem after the Captivity (Neh. 3:7).

Jael (jā'ĕl) the wife of Heber the Kenite (Judg. 4:17). Sisera, the general of Jabin, fled in defeat of battle from Barak. He sought refuge in the tent of supposedly friendly Jael. But while he was asleep, exhausted from the battle, she drove a tent peg through his head. When the victorious Barak passed by, she proudly called him in to witness the result of her deed (Judg. 4:11-22).

The difficult part of the story to the modern mind is the praise of Deborah of the cruel and treacherous deed (Judg. 5:6, 24-27).

Jagur (jā'gĕr) a town in the extreme south of Judah, near the border of Edom (Josh. 15:21). Site unknown.

Jah (jä) an abbreviated form of the sacred name, Jehovah, used in poetry (Ps. 68:4).

Jahath (jā'hăth) 1. A descendant of Judah, son of Reaiah ben-shobal (1 Chr. 4:2).

2. A Levite, son of Libni, of the family of Gershom (1 Chr. 6:20, 43).

3. A Levite, family of Gershom, head of a subdivision of house of Shimei (1 Chr. 23:10).

4. A Levite of the house of Izhar (1 Chr. 24:22).

5. A Merarite Levite in the reign of Josiah (2 Chr. 34:12).

Jahaz (jā'hăz), also **Jahaza** (jà-hā'zà), **Jahazah** (jà-hā'zà), and **Jahzah** (jä'zà) on the plain of Moab, where Sihon king of the Amorites was defeated by the Israelites (Num. 21:23;

Deut. 2:32; Judg. 11:20). The location has not been identified. It was later taken by Mesha king of Moab, and was held by Moab in the time of Isaiah (Isa. 15:4).

Jahaza (jà-hā'zà) (Josh. 13:18) see **Jahaz**

Jahazah (jà-hā'zà) (Josh. 21:36; Jer. 48:21) see **Jahaz**

Jahaziah (jā-hà-zī'à) son of Tikvah; one of the few who opposed Ezra in his proposition to the Hebrews to put away their foreign wives (Ezra 10:15).

Jahaziel (jà-hā'zǐ-ĕl) 1. A Levite of the family of Kohath, of the house of Hebron (1 Chr. 23:19).

2. One of the warriors of Benjamin, the mighty men who joined David at Ziklag (1 Chr. 12:4).

3. One of the priests appointed by David to sound a trumpet in the sanctuary (1 Chr. 16:6).

4. A Levite of the Asaph family, who prophesied in the time of Jehoshaphat (2 Chr. 20:14).

5. Father of the chief of the people who returned from Babylon with Ezra (Ezra 8:5).

Jahdai (jä'dī) a descendant of Judah, listed in genealogy of Caleb (1 Chr. 2:47).

Jahdiel (jä-dī'ĕl) a chieftain of Manasseh (1 Chr. 5:24).

Jahdo (jä'dō) a Gadite, son of Buz (1 Chr. 5:14).

Jahzeel (jä'zǐ-ĕl) a son of Zebulun and father of family of Jahzeelites (Gen. 46:24; Num. 26:48).

Jahzeelites (jä-zē'ĕl-īts) see **Jahzeel**

Jahzerah (jä'zĕ-rà) a priest of house of Immer (1 Chr. 9:12), and probably the same as Akazai, among the returning exiles (Neh. 11:13).

Jahziel (jä'zǐ-ĕl) same as **Jahzeel**

Jair (jä'ĭr) 1. A descendant of Judah on his father's side and Manasseh on his mother's. At the time of the conquest under Moses, he took the tract of Argob (Deut. 3:14).

2. A Gileadite who judged Israel twenty-two years (Judg. 10:3-5). He may have belonged to the family of the earlier Jair, see 1 above.

3. The father of Mordecai (Est. 2:5).

4. The father of Elhanan, a hero of David's army (1 Chr. 20:5).

Jairite (jä'ĭr-īt) a descendant of one named Jair. Ira the Jairite was a chief ruler (priest) to David (2 Sam. 20:26).

Jairus (jà-ī'rŭs) a ruler of a synagogue, probably at Capernaum (Mk. 5:22; Lk. 8:41). He sought help from Jesus for his sick daughter, who was at the point of death. She was dead when Jesus reached the house, but he restored her to life again.

Jakan (jä'kăn) a descendant of the Horites. At the time of the Exodus, sons of Jakan occupied an area near Mount Hor, where Aaron died (Num. 20:21-23; Deut. 10:6; 1 Chr. 1:42). The same as **Jaakan**.

Jakeh (jä'kĕ) the father of Agur, whose sayings are collected in Prov. 30.

Jakim (jä'kĭm) 1. A descendant of Aaron and head of the twelfth course of priests under David (1 Chr. 24:12).

2. A Benjaminite (1 Chr. 8:19).

Jalam (jä'lăm) see **Jaalam**

Jalon (jä'lŏn) a son of Ezra (1 Chr. 4:17).

Jambres (jăm'brēz) see **Jannes and Jambres**

James (jāmz) 1. Son of Zebedee. One of the earliest chosen disciples, (Mt. 4:21-22; Mk. 1:19), and brother of the apostle John. With John and Simon Peter, he formed the "inner circle" of disciples of Christ. It was they who accompanied Christ to the body of Jairus' daughter and witnessed her restoration to life (Mk. 5:37; Lk. 8:51); these were the three whom Jesus took with him on the Mountain of Transfiguration (Mt. 17:1; Mk. 9:2; Lk. 9:28); and these were the three who were with Jesus in his hours of agony in the Garden of Gethsemane, the night of his arrest and trial (Mt. 26:37).

James and John were nicknamed "sons of thunder," its appropriateness indicated in their desire for Jesus to call down fire from heaven upon the Samaritan village which would not receive him (Lk. 9:54). Their personal ambition, and their misunderstanding of the true mission of Jesus, is revealed in the request that they be given first places of honor in the kingdom (Mk. 10:37). In Matthew's account (20:20-29), it was the mother of James and John who made the request.

The martyrdom of James is the only one of the Twelve recorded in the NT, (Acts 12:12). He probably was the first one put to death. Herod Agrippa I (A.D. 42-44) executed James as a part of a wide persecution against the church.

2. The Son of Alpheus. One of the Twelve (Mt. 10:3; Mk. 3:18; Lk. 6:15; Acts 1:13). Assuming that this James is the same as the one mentioned in Mt. 27:56; Mk. 15:40, 16:1; and Lk. 24:10, he bore the surname of "the Little," or "the Lesser"; probably this surname was given in contrast to James the Son of Zebedee, known in Christian tradition as "James the Great."

The disciple Levi is also a son of Alpheus. However, there is no Biblical evidence that the two were brothers.

3. The Lord's brother (Mt. 13:55; Mk. 6:3;

Gal. 1:19). He evidently was the acknowledged head, or pastor of the church in Jerusalem (Acts 12:17, 15:13, 21:18; Gal. 1:19, 2:9, 12). He is mentioned only twice in the gospels (Mt. 13:55, Mk. 6:3), but it is assumed that he became a disciple of Jesus near the end of Jesus' life, or after the resurrection.

There has been long disagreement within the church as to whether James was a blood brother of Jesus, or a step-brother, having been the son of Joseph by a former marriage. However, there is Biblical basis only for assuming that he was a blood brother, being the son of Joseph and Mary.

He was the presiding officer at the Council of Jerusalem (Acts 15:13), which seems to indicate his position of leadership in the Jerusalem church. In this position he represented the church (Gal. 2:12).

4. The brother of Judas, or the father of Judas (RSV) the disciple—not Iscariot. There is reference to him in Lk. 6:16 and Acts 1:13; nothing further is known of him. The AV translation is "brother," which has led to the assumption that this James is the brother of Jesus also, since Jesus had a brother named Judas. There is no basis for the belief that James, the brother of Jesus, was either the father or brother of Judas the disciple.

5. One of the sons of Mary. The mother is mentioned with regard to the crucifixion (Mt. 27:56; Mk. 15:40), and at the scene of the empty tomb (Mk. 16:1; Lk. 24:10). It is possible that this James is the same as the Son of Alpheus, 2 above.

James, the Epistle of one of the General, or Catholic Epistles of the New Testament. Its canonicity was disputed in the early centuries, but it was recognized as a part of the canon by the Council of Carthage (A.D. 397). Its place in the canon was questioned by Martin Luther at the time of the Reformation, for he felt that its apparent emphasis on "works" was contrary to the writings of the apostle Paul on justification by faith alone.

The author is not given in the letter, other than "James, a servant of God and of the Lord Jesus Christ." Traditionally the author has been accepted as James, the brother of the Lord, who was the leader of the church in Jerusalem. This traditional view dates the letter very early among NT writings (about A.D. 45). One argument for this very early dating is that no reference is made in it to the Council of Jerusalem (about A.D. 49). However, it could plausibly be argued that this James did write the letter after the council, as a sort of commentary or homily on the decisions of the

council, seeking to insure that the decisions for Christian freedom not be misused as license, or that faith not be misinterpreted as sterile intellectual assent. In this sense, the letter is complementary to, not in contradiction of, Paul's teaching on justification by faith alone.

Some scholars hold to a much later date for the letter, even as late as A.D. 125 or 150. This theory is predicated upon an alleged knowledge by the author of Paul's letters, which probably were not widely circulated in the church until about the close of the first century. In this case the author would not have been James, the brother of the Lord.

Jamin (jā′mĭn) 1. Second son of Simeon and founder of a tribal family (Gen. 46:10, Ex. 6:15; 1 Chr. 4:24).

2. A Jerahmeelite (1 Chr. 2:27).

3. A Levite who helped interpret the Law to the people under Ezra (Neh. 8:7).

Jaminites, the (jā′mĭn-īts) descendants of Jamin, see 1 above.

Jamlech (jăm′lĕk) a Simeonite leader or prince (1 Chr. 4:34).

Jamnia (jăm′nĭ-ȧ) same as **Jabneel**

Janai (jā′nī) same as **Jaanai**

Janna (jăn′ȧ) one of the ancestors of Christ (Lk. 3:24).

Jannai (jăn′ī) same as **Janna**

Jannes (jăn′ēz) **and Jambres** (jăm′brēz) the two Egyptian magicians who opposed Moses (Ex. 7:11–12, 22, 8:7, 18–19, 9:11). The only reference in which they are called by name is in 2 Tim. 3:8. The actual names either could have been from Jewish tradition with which Timothy was familiar, or in some unknown Jewish writing.

Janoah (jȧ-nō′ȧ) and **Janohah** (jȧ-nō′hȧ) 1. A town of Naphtali captured by Tiglath-pileser (2 K. 15:29); possibly modern Yanuh.

2. A town on the boundary line of Ephraim, now the town of Yanum (Josh. 16:6–7).

Janum (jā′nŭm) same as **Jamin**. A village in the mountains of Hebron (Josh. 15:53).

Japheth (jā′fĕth) one of the three, probably the second, son of Noah (Gen. 10:21; cf. 9:24). Traditionally his descendants occupied the areas of Gomer, Magog, Madai, Javan, Tubal, Meshech, and Tiros (Gen. 10:2).

Japhia (jȧ-fī′ȧ) 1. King of Lachish, defeated and killed by Joshua (Josh. 10:3–27).

2. A son of David, born in Jerusalem (2 Sam. 5:15).

3. A border town in Zebulun, identified with modern Yafa (Josh. 19:12).

Japhlet (jăf′lĕt) Asherite of Heber (1 Chr. 7:32–33).

Japhleti (jăf′lĕ-tī) also **Japhletite** (jăf′lĕ-tīt) a clan that lived to the south of Ephraim, apparently of different ancestry from Japhlet the Asherite (Josh. 16:3).

Japho (jā′fō) see **Joppa**

Jarah (jār′ă) a descendant of King Saul (1 Chr. 9:40); he is called Jehoadah in 1 Chr. 8:36.

Jareb (jā′rĕb) [contentious] Hosea 5:13, 10:6 contain this difficult word with various interpretations. Linguistically and historically, it seems not a proper name. We take it as a Hebrew word (root, "contend") and applicable either to the land of Assyria, or better, to its king under the sobriquet "Contender."

Jared (jā′rĕd) [descent?] antediluvian patriarch, son of Mahalaleel, and father of Enoch (Gen. 5:15-20; Lk. 3:37). In 1 Chr. 1:2, he is Jered.

Jaresiah (jā-rē-sī′ă) [Jehovah nourishes] a Benjaminite (1 Chr. 8:27).

Jarha (jār′hä) an Egyptian servant of the Judahite Sheshan, about Eli's time, who was given the daughter of his master to wife (1 Chr. 2:31), her name apparently being Ahli.

Jarib (jā′rīb, as above) 1. Son of Simeon (1 Chr. 4:24); perhaps same as Jachin (Gen. 46; Ex. 6; Num. 26).

2. A chief with Ezra at Ahava (Ezra 8:16).

3. A priest of Jeshua's house, whose foreign wife was put away (Ezra 10:18).

Jarmuth (jär′mūth) [a height] 1. A town in Judah's lowland (Shephelah), dealt with by Joshua (Josh. 10:3-27, 12:11, 15:35); assigned to Judah (15:35); inhabited after the Captivity (Neh. 11:29); marked by the ruins of Yarmuk, ten Roman miles from Eleutheropolis, on the road to Jerusalem.

Jaroah (jā-rō′ă) a Gadite descended through Buz (1 Chr. 5:14).

Jashen (jā′shĕn) [sleeping] the sons of Jashen are among David's heroes (2 Sam. 23:32); but in the parallel list in 1 Chr. 11:34, they are sons of Hashem, where "sons of" may have been part of the name, or repeated from the end of the preceding word.

Jasher, Book of (jā′shĕr) [upright] apparently a collection of poetic writings twice referred to (Josh. 10:13; 2 Sam. 1:18), and as it seems, well-known at early times.

Jashobeam (jăsh-ō-bē′ăm) [let the people return] could be one man; possibly two of this name: 1. A Hachmonite chief among David's mighty men (1 Chr. 11:11); and possibly same as Zabdiel (1 Chr. 27:2-3); and in 2 Sam. 23:8, with a different name.

2. A Benjaminite joining David at Ziklag, a

Korahite (1 Chr. 12:1-2, 6). Authorities vary here.

Jashub (jā′shŭb) [he returns] 1. Third son of Issachar and founder of a tribal family (Num. 26:24; 1 Chr. 7:1). Could be same as in Gen. 46:13, by scribal error, leaving out a letter (sh).

2. Layman son of Bani, and another putting away foreign wife (Ezra 10:29).

Jashubilehem (jăsh-ū-bī-lē′hĕm) [bread returns?] if this is a man, he was member of family of Shelah, tribe of Judah (1 Chr. 4:22); if a place, the inference is that it was on the west side of the tribe.

Jashubites (jăsh′ū-bīts) family founded by Jashub, son of Issachar (Num. 26:24).

Jasiel (jā′sĭ-ĕl) [God makes] last named of David's heroes in 1 Chr. 11:47.

Jason (jā′sŭn) [healing] a Thessalonian relative of Paul (Rom. 16:21), who entertaining the apostle and Silas, was mobbed by Jews (Acts 17). May be same as Secundus of Acts 20:4.

jasper a precious stone (Ex. 28:20, 39:13; Ezek. 28:13; Rev. 4:3, 21:11, 19). Our jasper does not accord with these descriptions, which in Revelation, seems more like diamond. The ancients had certainly a broader meaning for the word.

Jathniel (jăth′nĭ-ĕl) [God gives gifts] a Korhite Levite, doorkeeper (1 Chr. 26:2).

Jattir (jăt′tĭr) [excellence] a town in Judah's hill country (Josh. 15:48, 21:14; 1 Sam. 30:27; 1 Chr. 6:57).

Javan (jā′văn) 1. A son of Japheth (Gen. 10:2, 4). Etymologically parallel with Ionia (Greece). From various references (Isa. 66:19; Ezek. 27:13; Dan. 8:21, 10:20, 11:2; Zech. 9:13), it appears that Javan represents the Greek people.

2. A town in South Arabia (Yemen), where Phoenicians traded, and whence came cassia and calamus (Ezek. 27:19).

javelin see **arms**

Jazer (jā′zēr) [helpful] a city east of Jordan in Gilead (Num. 32:1, 3; 2 Sam. 24:5; 1 Chr. 26:31). Victorious Israel drove out the Amorites (Num. 21:32). It was assigned to, and rebuilt by, Gad (Josh. 13:25); and went to Merarite Levites for residence (Josh. 21:39; 1 Chr. 6:81). It went to Moabite hands (Isa. 16:8-9; Jer. 48:32). It was somewhere west of Rabbath Ammon, eight to ten miles, as a theory.

Jaziz (jā′zĭz) [he moves about] Hagarite overseer of David's animals (1 Chr. 27:31).

Jearim, Mount (jē′ă-rĭm) [forests] a mountain

on Judah's boundary (Josh. 15:10), about eight miles northeast of Beth-shemesh.

Jeaterai (jē-ăt'ē-rī) a Gershonite Levite (1 Chr. 6:21).

Jeberechiah (jē-bĕr-ē-kī'à) [Jehovah blesses] father of a Zechariah, contemporary of Isaiah (Isa. 8:2); here probably an accidental corruption of Berechiah.

Jebus (jē'bŭs) [trodden place] probably original name of Jerusalem, of the Jebusites (Josh. 15:63; Judg. 19:10; 1 Chr. 11:4–5), its citadel being the stronghold of Zion (2 Sam. 5:7; 1 Chr. 11:5). KJV, Jebusi = Jebus (Josh. 15:8, 18:16, 28).

Jebusite, Jebusites, the the third son of Canaan, apparently giving his name to a tribe (Gen. 10:16, 15:21; Ex. 3:8; 1 Chr. 1:14); a mountain tribe at date of the Exodus (Num. 13:29; Josh. 11:3). After Joshua slew its king (10:23–26), Jebus was allotted to Benjamin (18:28); taken and fired by Judah (Judg. 1:8, 15:8; see Josh. 15:63; Judg. 1:21, 19:11); finally taken and occupied by David (2 Sam. 5:6–7), the inhabitants appearing once more, cf. Araunah the Jebusite (2 Sam. 24:16, 18, 23; 2 Chr. 3:1; see 1 K. 9:20).

Jecamiah (jē-căm'ĭ-à) [Jehovah gathers] 1. A man of Judah (1 Chr. 2:41).

2. A descendant of Jeconiah (1 Chr. 3:18).

Jecholiah (jĕk-ō-lī'à) [Jehovah prevails] mother of King Uzziah (2 K. 15:2; 2 Chr. 26:3).

Jechonias (jĕk-ō-nī'ăs) [Jehovah establishes] variant of Jechoniah, which is Jehoiachin. See below.

Jecoliah (jĕk-ō-lī'à; as above) same as **Jecholiah.**

Jeconiah (jĕk-ō-nī'à, as above) altered form of Jehoiachin (1 Chr. 3:16; Jer. 24:1, 27:20, 28:4, 29:1; Est. 2:6).

Jedaiah (jē-dā'yà) [Jehovah shows] 1. A Simeonite (1 Chr. 4:37).

2. A son of Harumaph, repairer of the wall near his home (Neh. 3:10).

Jedaiah (as above) [Jehovah knows] 1. Priestly head of the second course of David's time (1 Chr. 24:1, 6–7); some members of the family returned from Babylon (Ezra 2:36; Neh. 7:39).

2 and 3. There seems to have been two others, returnees: Neh. 12:6–7, and vss. 7, 21.

4. A priest in Jeshua the high priest's time (Zech. 6:10, 14).

Jediael (jē-dī'ā-ĕl) [known of God] 1. A chief patriarch of Benjamin (1 Chr. 7:6, 10–11). Perhaps the same as Asahel of Gen. 46:21; Num. 26:38; 1 Chr. 8:1.

2. A Manassite who joined David at Ziklag (1 Chr. 12:20).

3. Son of Shimri and mighty man of David (11:45).

4. A Korahite doorkeeper of David's time (26:1, 2).

Jedidah (jē-dī'dä) [beloved] wife of Amon and mother of good Josiah (2 K. 22:1).

Jedidiah (jē-dĭ-dī'à) [beloved of Jehovah] Nathan's divinely directed name for Solomon (2 Sam. 12:25).

Jeduthun (jē-dū'thŭn) [praise] a Levite, one of three chief singers (musicians) in David's time (1 Chr. 16:41). This man seems to have been the same as Ethan of 1 Chr. 15:17, 19; see 2 Chr. 35:15. When the temple was completed, his division officiated (2 Chr. 5:12), and in Hezekiah's reform (29:14), and under Josiah (35:15). Psalms 39, 62, 77 are connected with this man, the title, in our opinion, being properly at the end of the preceding psalm in each case and, it is suggested, relating to a third choir, for thanksgiving and praise.

Jeezer (jē-ē'zēr) [father of help] a Manassite descendant (Num. 26:30), his name in parallel lists being Abiezer (Josh. 17:2; 1 Chr. 7:18). The family—Jeezerites.

Jegar-sahadutha (jē-gär-sā-hà-dū'thà) [Aramaic for heap of witness] Laban's name for the stone pile, memorializing the compact between himself and Jacob (Gen. 31:47).

Jehaleleel (jē-hà-lē'lē-ĕl) [he praises God] 1. Father of four, in Judah (1 Chr. 4:16).

2. A Merarite Levite (2 Chr. 29:12).

Jehdeiah (jē-dē'yä) [Jehovah inspires with joy] 1. A Levite, family of Korah, house of Amram (1 Chr. 24:20).

2. A Meronothite, keeper of David's donkeys (1 Chr. 27:20).

Jehezekel (jē-hĕz'ē-kĕl) [God strengthens] a priest charged with the twentieth course in the house of Jehovah (1 Chr. 24:16).

Jehiah (jē-hī'à) [Jehovah lives] ark doorkeeper for David (1 Chr. 15:24).

Jehiel (jē-hī'ĕl) [God lives] 1. A second-degree Levite, a psaltery-player (1 Chr. 15:18, 20, 16:5).

2. A Gershonite Levite, chief of the house of Laadan (1 Chr. 23:8, 29:8; see 26:21–22).

3. A Hachmonite, among David's officers (1 Chr. 27:32).

4. A son of Jehoshaphat, slain by his brother Johoram (2 Chr. 21:2, 4).

5. A Kohathite Levite, aiding Hezekiah's reformation, and perhaps assistant governor of temple revenues (2 Chr. 29:14, 31:13).

6. A temple ruler at Josiah's reformation (2 Chr. 35:8).

7. Father of Obadiah, Ezra's contemporary (Ezra 8:9).

8. A priest of the course of Harim, induced by Ezra to put away foreign wife (Ezra 10:21).

9. A son of Elam (Ezra 10:2).

10. One of same family putting away his foreign wife (Ezra 10:26).

11. One noted as father of Gibeon, and for father of King Saul (1 Chr. 9:35).

12. A son of Hotham the Aroerite and member of David's guard (1 Chr. 11:44).

Jehieli (jē-hī'ĕ-lī) see 2 above.

Jehizkiah (jē-hĭz-kī'á) [Jehovah strengthens] son of Shallum and a head of Ephraim in Ahaz' time: assisted in release of captives from Judah (2 Chr. 28:8–15).

Jehoadah (jē-hō'ād-á) [Jehovah adorns] son of Ahaz and descendant of Saul (1 Chr. 8:36; seems, in 9:42, to be Jarah).

Jehoaddan (jē-hō-ăd'ăn) [Jehovah makes pleasant] Jerusalemite mother of Amaziah and queen to Joash (2 K. 14:2; 2 Chr. 25:1).

Jehoahaz (jē-hō'á-hăz) [Jehovah lays hold]   1. Son and successor to Jehu: he reigned seventeen years over Israel, beginning in early ninth century; at first associated with his father (2 K. 10:35, 13:1–9). The penalty for apostasy (calf worship) was subjection to the Syrians (Hazael and Ben-hadad); but in humiliated extremity he besought divine aid, the deliverer being either, or both, Jehoash and Jeroboam (2 K. 13:23–25, 14:24–25).

2. The name given to Ahaziah, youngest son of Jehoram of Judah (2 Chr. 21:7).

3. Apparently the third son of Josiah, enthroned by the people after his father's death in preference to his elder brother, and reigning three months. Based on 2 Chr. 36:11, this man seems to have been third son, although 1 Chr. 3:15 makes him fourth, it is suggested, to degrade him. Necho of Egypt deposed him and took him in chains to Egypt, where he died. He is the Shallum of 1 Chr. 3:15 (Jer. 22:10–12), first of the lion's whelps (Ezek. 19:1–9).

Jehoash (jē-hō'ăsh) [Jehovah is strong] same as Joash. 1. Eighth king of Judah, son of Ahaziah (2 K. 11:21; cf. ch. 12, 14:13).

2. Twelfth king of Israel, son of Jehoahaz (2 K. 13:10, 25, 14:8–17).

Jehohanan (jē-hō-hăn'ăn) [Jehovah is gracious] 1. A Korahite Levite, of the sixth course of doorkeepers in David's reign (1 Chr. 26:3).

2. Second in honor, of Jehoshaphat's captains (2 Chr. 17:15).

3. Father of Ishmael, supporter of Jehoiada for restoring the line of Judah (2 Chr. 23:1).

4. A son of Bebai, persuaded of Ezra to put away foreign wife (Ezra 10:28).

5. A priest of the house of Amariah, in Joiakim's priesthood (Neh. 12:12–13).

6. A priest who helped at the wall dedication (Neh. 12:42).

Jehoiachin (jē-hoi'á-chĭn) [Jehovah establishes] son of Jehoiachim of Judah; he was king for three and one-third months, in which time Nebuchadnezzar took Jerusalem during his eighth year (2 K. 24:12), and carried him away captive, along with his wives, his mother, servants, captains, artisans, and principal men, the eunuchs included (Jer. 29:2; Ezek. 17:12, 19:9). After thirty-six years in prison, the next king, Evil-merodach, liberated and honored him (2 K. 25:27–30; Jer. 52:31, 34). Jeremiah prophesied during and after his reign, calling him Jeconiah or Coniah. His successor was Zedekiah, called his son (1 Chr. 3:16) and his brother (2 Chr. 36:10); really his uncle (2 K. 24:17).

Jehoiada (jē-hoi'á-dà) [Jehovah knows] 1. Father of Benaiah, David's warrior (2 Sam. 8:18, 23:22; 1 K. 1:32, 36, 38, 44, 2:25, 29, 34, 46; 1 Chr. 18:17). See 1 Chr. 27:5 and 12:27. According to 1 Chr. 27:34, he was son of Benaiah; but it seems most likely that Benaiah son of Jehoiada, is meant; others differ; so—

2. Son of Benaiah, second to Ahithophel (see above), which is entirely possible.

3. A high priest in Athaliah's time, whose wife concealed Joash, leading to death of Athaliah, and the crowning of Joash, the latter being true to Jehovah while Jehoiada, his uncle, lived (2 K. 11:1–12:16; 2 Chr. 22:10–24:14–22).

4. Second priest to Seraiah the high priest (Jer. 29:25–29; 2 K. 25:18).

5. Son of Paseach, helping repair a gate in Jerusalem (Neh. 3:6).

Jehoiakim a son of Josiah by Zebidah (2 K. 23:34, 36). At Josiah's death, the people chose Jehoahaz, third son (in age) of Josiah; but three months later, Pharaoh Necho set his elder brother, Eliakim, on the throne, changing his name to Jehoiachim, and carrying Jehoahaz in chains to Egypt. Early in the seventh century, despite Jeremiah's threat of judgment on unrepentance, the king contemptuously burned the roll of prophecy (Jer. 36); and in his fourth year, Nebuchadnezzar, conqueror of Pharaoh at Carchemish, came against Jerusalem and carried the king captive to Babylon (2 Chr. 36:6) but reinstated him (2 K. 24:1), and three years later, he rebelled (2 K. 24:1) but suffered greatly (2 K. 24:2). When Nebuchadnezzar himself came to Jerusalem, he bound the rebel to take him to Babylon (2 Chr. 36:6); and in a cage with hooks, he was brought before the Babylonian king, encamped near Jerusalem (Ezek. 19:5-9). But the Babylonian trip fell through for some unknown reason. There is uncertainty as to details; but in the eleventh year of his reign, it appears that Jehoiachim came to violent end, having been a vicious and irreligious man; and according to prediction, it is presumed that he was buried "with the burial of an ass," without pomp or lamentation (Jer. 22:19, 36:30).

Jehoiarib (jĕ-hō'yä-rĭb) [Jehovah contends] head of the first of twenty-four courses of priests under King David (1 Chr. 24:7). Some descendants returned from Babylon (1 Chr. 9:10; Neh. 11:10, 12:6, 19).

Jehonadab or **Jonadab** (jĕ-hō'nă-dăb) [Jehovah is bounteous] 1. Son of Rechab, founder of the Rechabites, apparently of the Kenites (1 Chr. 2:53), one settlement of whom, under four-fold division, settled near Jabez, in Judah, to whom belonged the above-noted men (see Jer. 35:6). When Jehu king of Israel found Jonadab sympathetic with suppression of Baal worship, he took him to Samaria where the Bedouin gave aid, looking to the massacre of the pagan worshipers (2 K. 10:15, 23).

2. Son of David's brother, Shimeah (2 Sam. 13:3).

Jehonathan (jĕ-hŏn'ä-thăn) [variant of Jonathan, Jehovah gives] 1. Son of Uzziah, appointed over David's storehouses (1 Chr. 27:25).

2. A Levite, sent by Jehoshaphat to teach the Law (2 Chr. 17:8).

3. A priest of the Shemaiah family, when Joiachim was high priest (Neh. 12:6, 18).

Jehoram (jĕ-hō'răm) [Jehovah is high] 1. Son of Ahab, Israel's king (2 K. 1:17, 3:1-27. [The next several chapters dealing with Elisha's ministry, seem largely to pertain to this king.] 2 K. 9:14-26).

2. Eldest son of Jehoshaphat of Judah, reigning eight years (2 K. 8:16-24).

3. A priest sent by Jehoshaphat to instruct the people (2 Chr. 17:8).

Jehoshabeath same as **Jehosheba** of 2 Chr. 22:11.

Jehoshaphat (jĕ-hŏsh'ä-făt) [Jehovah judges] 1. Son of Ahitub, and annalist in David's and Solomon's court (2 Sam. 8:16, 20:24; 1 K. 4:3).

2. A priest trumpet-blower before the ark carried from Obed-edom's house to Jerusalem (1 Chr. 15:24).

3. Son of Paruah and a purveyor of Solomon (1 K. 4:17).

4. Son of Nimshi, and father of King Jehu (2 K. 9:2, 14).

5. Son and successor of Asa as king of Judah. He became king at age thirty-five, and reigned twenty-five years (some say including five years associated with his father) late in the ninth century. He carried out the reforms of his father (1 K. 22:43, 46; 2 Chr. 17). His sin in making league with Ahab of Israel against Ramoth-gilead, contrary to Micaiah's counsel (2 Chr. 18) was severely censured by the prophet, Jehu (2 Chr. 19:2), nearly losing his life (2 Chr. 18:31). During a continuation of reform, he was miraculously delivered from a menacing confederacy of Ammon, Moab, and Edom (2 Chr. 20:6-12, 14-27). Later he was associated with Ahaziah of Israel; but the alliance and the venture were disastrous (2 Chr. 20:35-37). Further he allied with Jehoram, son of Ahab, and the Edomites, to invade Moab, with partial success (2 K. 3:6-20). He had seven sons, his death occurring at age sixty, leaving one, Jehoram, to succeed him (1 K. 22:50).

Jehoshaphat, Valley of mentioned by Joel only (3:2, 12), a spot where after the return from captivity, Jehovah will gather all heathen, to judge them for misdeeds to Israel, the name being chosen as symbolic of God's judgment (as illustrated in the unparalleled victory of 2 Chr. 20), its focus unspecified.

Jehosheba (jĕ-hŏsh'ē-bà) [Jehovah gives oath] according to Chronicles, Jehoshabeath (2 Chr. 22:11). Daughter of Joram of Israel and wife of Jehoiaha the high priest (2 K. 11:2). Called "daughter of Joram, sister of Ahaziah" (2 K. 11:2), she was the supposed daughter, not of Athaliah, but of Joram by another wife; but it is possible that Athaliah's name was omitted on account of detestation. Here is the only instance of royalty marrying the high priest—a providential circumstance, enabling and inducing her to rescue the infant son Joash when his brothers were massacred (2 K. 11:2; 2 Chr. 22:1).

Jehoshua (jĕ-hŏsh'ū-à) [Jehovah is salvation] the longer form of Joshua, given him by Moses (Num. 13:16): found once elsewhere in OT, with an "h" added (1 Chr. 7:27).

Jehovah (jĕ-hō'vä) [He will be] this is the personal designation of the God who revealed himself to the Hebrews. As distinguished from the other much used word for Deity, it has reference to the God of the covenant, whereas Elohim relates to the God of creation. Interestingly, the word is a hybrid, apparently owing origin to a mistaken idea of reverence, possibly traceable as far back as the incident related in

Lev. 24:11–16, its early pronunciation (perhaps "Jahveh") having been lost, certainly by the time of the Greek translation of the Hebrew Bible (the LXX) in the second century B.C. The translators substituted the word Lord, as did also the KJV, in which the word "Lord" is printed in small capitals. Around the sixth century A.D., when people generally, including Jews, were speaking Greek, and the proper pronunciation of their sacred tongue was in jeopardy, the Massoretic scholars, in dealing with this word, placed certain of their intricate system of vowel pointings touching the whole OT, on the consonants of the tetragrammaton, YHWH, there being up to that time no vowels as we know them in the Hebrew language. It had been the custom for the Hebrews to use the word "Lord" (Adonai) in the place of this word; or, when it follows the word Lord (Gen. 15:2), to pronounce "God" (Elohim) instead. Such substitution shows in the Massoretic pointing, so that our pronunciation "Jehovah" represents the consonants of the sacred Name, with the vowels of the Hebrew word for Lord; and this English pronunciation goes back to the sixteenth century. Because Hebrew thought differs from Greek, in stressing less the essential and more the phenomenal, the best explanation lies in connection with God's manifestation rather than with his essence; thus we translate: "He will be–," whatever is necessary for any present situation, whether as in Abraham's case "provider" (of the lamb instead of Isaac—Gen. 22:14), or "healer" (Ex. 15:26), or "banner" (17:15), or "righteousness" (Jer. 23:6), or finally "Savior," in the Person of the Lord Jesus (see Mt. 1:21). Thus Jn. 8:58 and the other instances where the Lord uses the expression "I am," are not essentially different from the Hebrew "Jehovah," there being no time sense in the Hebrew verb "I will be" (Ex. 3:14 and 6:3) is equally "I am." The first and third persons here are referable to the same person. With reference to the critical question about the use of the name Jehovah in Genesis, whereas the Ex. 6 passage states "not known before," the answer lies not in reliance on different documents, of conflicting nature, but in the simple fact that his significant manifestation was not made a matter of previous revelation, as now in the case of Moses at the great crisis of the Exodus. The "divine names" argument, supporting various documents, has been proved rather negligible. The simple and straightforward statements of Scripture are to be taken rather than the devious and discrediting explanations of the critics.

Jehovah-jireh (jē-hō′vä-jī′rĕ) [Jehovah will pro-

vide or see] the place, not known exactly, where Abraham was given a substitute for the sacrifice of his son (Gen. 22:14).

Jehovah-nissi (. . . nĭs′sī) [. . . my banner] name of the altar built by Moses at Rephidim memorializing victory over Amalek (Ex. 17:15–16).

Jehovah-shalom (. . . shā′lōm) [. . . is peace] Gideon's altar in Ophra regarding the visit of the angel of the Lord, calling him as deliverer. Expecting to die for seeing such sight, he was reassured (Judg. 6:23–24).

Jehozabad (jē-hŏz′ā-băd) [Jehovah endows] 1. A Korahite porter, son of Obed-edom (1 Chr. 26:4).

2. Son of a Moabitess and servant of Joash, and one of his assassins put to death for it (2 K. 12:21; 2 Chr. 24:26, 25:3).

3. A Benjaminite, high rank captain under Jehoshaphat (2 Chr. 17:18).

Jehozadak (jē-hŏz′ā-dăk) [Jehovah is just] father of Jeshua, high priest, captive to Babylon, by Nebuchadnezzar (Ezra 3:2, 8; 2 Chr. 6:15).

Jehu (jē′hū) [Jehovah is He?] 1. Prophet of Anathoth joining David at Ziklag (1 Chr. 12:3).

2. Prophet son of Hanani who spoke judgment on Baasha and house, for continuing in Jeroboam's sin (1 K. 16:1–4, 7); also reproving Jehoshaphat aiding ungodly Ahab (2 Chr. 19:2); and writing a book of the former's acts (20:34).

3. Founder of the fourth dynasty of Israel's rulers, son of Jehoshaphat, often called "son of Nimshi" (1 K. 19:16; 2 K. 9:2). A soldier in Ahab's service (2 K. 9:25), he was anointed king of Israel by Elisha's proxy (2 K. 9:1–10), after Ahab's murders and idolatries (1 K. 19:16–17), the commission having first been given to Elijah. En route to Jezreel to execute his charge to exterminate Ahab's house, "driving furiously" to find Joram, Ahab's son and king over Israel, he was met by advancing Joram along with the visiting king of Judah (Ahaziah), at Naboth's vineyard (2 K. 9). He killed Joram with an arrow, after charging him with gross iniquities (see 1 K. 21:19; 2 K. 9:25). Neither was Ahaziah spared (2 K. 9:27), son of Ahab's daughter. Riding on to Jezreel's gate, Jehu commanded that Jezebel, queen mother, evil genius of Ahab, be thrown out of the window, from which she looked and talked, fulfilling prophecy (1 K. 21:23; 2 K. 9:32–37). He literally waded through slaughter to his throne, executing his charge with such a blood bath as is scarcely paralleled (2 K. 10); but then, ambitious and tyrannical, he fell into sin, his reign extending over twenty-eight years, the

last of them seeing disaster (vs. 32); but the promise of his dynasty's four generations was fulfilled (2 K. 10:30, 15:8–12).

4. A descendant of Judah (1 Chr. 2:38).

5. A Simeonite (1 Chr. 4:35).

Jehubbah (jē-hŭb′bä) [hidden] an Asherite chief (1 Chr. 7:34).

Jehucal or **Jucal** (jē-hū′căl) [potent] son of Shelemiah and a prince of Judah, whom King Zedekiah sent with others to ask Jeremiah's prayers, but later wished for his death, on account of the discouragement of his predictions (Jer. 37:3, 38:1–6).

Jehud (jē′hŭd) [celebrated] a town in Dan's original territory (Josh. 19:45), identified with the village el-Yehudiyeh, eight miles southeast of Jaffa.

Jehudi (jē-hū′dī) [Jew] messenger sent to have Baruch fetch Jeremiah's roll of prophecies, and who read same before King Jehoiachim, who, enraged, slashed and burnt it (Jer. 36:14, 21, 23).

Jehudijah (jē-hū-dī′jä) [the Jewess] applied to wife of Mered to distinguish her from his Egyptian wife (1 Chr. 4:18).

Jehush (jē′hŭsh) [collector?] descendant of Saul (1 Chr. 8:39).

Jeiel (jē-ī′ĕl) [treasure of God] 1. A Reubenite (1 Chr. 5:7).

2. A Levite musician of second degree (1 Chr. 15:18, 21; and perhaps same man in 16:5).

3. A Levite of the sons of Asaph (2 Chr. 20:14).

4. A scribe-recorder of warriors in Uzziah's time (2 Chr. 26:11).

5. A Levite assisting in Hezekiah's reforms (2 Chr. 29:13).

6. A chief Levite in Josiah's time (2 Chr. 35:9).

7. A returnee with Ezra (8:13).

8. Husband of foreign wife (10:43).

Jekabzeel (jē-kăb′zē-ĕl) [God gathers] a place in South Judah (Neh. 11:25). Same as Kabziel (Josh. 15:21; 2 Sam. 23:20).

Jekameam (jē-kă-mē′ăm) [he gathers the people] a Levite of David's time, family of Kohath (2 Chr. 23:19, 24:23).

Jekamiah (jĕk-ă-mī′ä) [Jehovah gathers] 1. Son of Shallum (1 Chr. 2:41).

2. Descendant of Jeconiah (3:18).

Jekuthiel (jē-kū′thĭ-ĕl) [reverence for God] man of Judah and father of Zanoah's inhabitants (1 Chr. 4:18).

Jemimah (jē-mī′mä) [dove] eldest of Job's three daughters, born after his afflictions (Job 42:14).

Jemuel (jē-mū′ĕl) [desire of God] eldest son of

Simeon, founder of a tribal family (Gen. 46:10; Ex. 6:15), same as Nemuel of Num. 26:12; and 1 Chr. 4:21.

Jephthae Greek form of **Jephthah** (Heb. 11:32).

Jephthah (jĕf′thä) [he sets free] doubly a Gileadite—Gilead, his father, and Gilead his early home. He dwelt in Tob, Syria, after being expelled from home, being illegitimate, by his brothers (Judg. 11:1–3). As a kind of Robin Hood head of a marauding party, he seems to have become rather famous; but he was a man with a conscience who taught his daughter fear of God. Against the invading Ammonites he was besought to head the Gileadites (who had previously wronged him, in the persons of his brothers), which he magnanimously did with their promise he should be permanent leader. After attempts at conciliation, he vanquished the enemy and took their territory, having vowed, it appears rather rashly, that he would devote to God whatever came out to meet him returning home. This turned out to be his only daughter. She assented to the sacrifice (see 2 K. 3:27), with her father showing rigid adherence to the vow, asking for two months of lamentation with her companions. We prefer to think that instead of her actual death, redemption money was used (as in Lev. 27:1–8), perpetual maidenhood being her sad fate, commemorated by the daughters of Israel (Judg. 11:23–40). The querulous Ephraimites provoked their defeat also, stragglers being challenged at the fords of Jordan, their identity being shown by inability to pronounce the word "Shibboleth"; and Jephthah judged the Transjordan region for six years (12:1–7). Samuel gave him citation (1 Sam. 12:11), and in Heb. 11, he is signalized for his faith.

Jephunneh (jē-fŭn′nĕ) [will be prepared, regarded with favor?] 1. Father of Caleb, a Kenezite, Judah's spy (Num. 13:6; Josh. 14:14; 1 Chr. 4:15).

2. An Asherite chieftain (1 Chr. 7:38).

Jerah (jē′rä) [moon, month] Arabian tribe from Joktan, giving name to an Arabian region (Gen. 10:26; 1 Chr. 1:20).

Jerahmeel (jē-rä′mē-ĕl) [God has mercy] 1. Son of Hezron, Judah's grandson, founder of the tribe in southeast Judah (1 Chr. 2:9, 25–27, 33, 42; 1 Sam. 27:10, 30:29).

2. A Merarite Levite (1 Chr. 24:29).

3. One employed to arrest Jeremiah and Baruch (Jer. 36:26).

Jered (jē′rĕd) [descent] 1. Son of Mahalaleel (1 Chr. 1:2). See **Jared**

2. Descendant of Judah and father of Gedor's inhabitants (1 Chr. 4:18).

Jeremai (jĕr'ē-mī) [high] one who put away his foreign wife (Ezra 10:33).

Jeremiah (jĕr-ē-mī'ä) [Jehovah establishes] 1. Native of Libnah and the father of Mamutal, who was the wife of Josiah and the mother of Jehoahaz (2 K. 23:30–31, 24:18).

2, 3, and 4. A Benjaminite and two Gadites who joined David at Ziklag (1 Chr. 12:4, 10, 13).

5. Likely head of a father's house who sealed the covenant (Neh. 10:2).

6. A Rechabite and son of Habazaniah (Jer. 35:3).

7. Head of a house in east Manasseh (1 Chr. 5:24).

8. A priest chief returning from Babylon with Zerubbabel (Neh. 12:1; according to vs. 12, the next generation saw a father's house of his name).

9. The major prophet, son of Hilkiah of Anathoth, in Benjamin (1:1), living under kings from Josiah to the Captivity; called Jeremy (Mt. 2:17), and Jeremias (16:14). E. H. Plumtree cites him as the great example of prophetic life, who gives more in his book than does any other, about his work, feelings, and sufferings; taken by the early church as representative, or typical, of the Savior, prophesying both of sorrow and public calamity, and of the "new and better covenant of the heart." Called when young, by vision, he felt unequal to the task; but he was divinely encouraged and enabled for the double charge over the nations, of tearing down and of building up, although he was told of general but unavailing opposition (1:4–10). His public life extended through Josiah's last eighteen years, three months of Jehoahaz' rule, eleven years of Jehoiachim, three months of Jehoiachin, and eleven years and five months of Zedekiah—about forty-one years; and even then, he continued his work (chs. 43–44). Opposed, threatened with death, he stood faithful despite obloquy and persecution on every hand. His was the misunderstood and thankless task of denouncing the judgments of God on the sinful people and of exhorting them to surrender the city to preserve their lives, all this in the face of false prophets contradicting him and flattering the king about sure rescue. In the fourth year of King Jehoiachim, he dictated to Baruch the words which he had been uttering the preceding twenty years, directing him to read it before the people at the coming fast; but when it reached the king, he slashed the columns and threw them into the fire (36:1–26). Divinely instructed, he reproduced the roll, with additions (vss. 27–32). Imprisoned, released, falsely charged with deserting, put into the miry dungeon, an Ethiopian rescued him, to be placed in the guard's court, where he was when Jerusalem was taken (38:7–28). Nebuchadnezzar the conqueror gave express order for kindly treatment of the prophet: he was granted leave to go where he would. He chose to stay in Jerusalem, was given food-provision and a present, and placed under protection of Gedaliah, the installed governor of Judah, by Nebuchadnezzar (39:11–14, 40:1–6). On the murder of the governor, contrary to his wishes and advice, he was carried forcibly to Egypt (41:1–43:7). His last words were delivered at Tahpanhes (43:8–44:30), where, it is presumed, he died. Jeremiah is called "the weeping prophet": he is "the strong man of Israel." Maligned, mistreated, denied much of the common satisfactions of life, no domestic and social joys, persecuted, imprisoned, misunderstood, this man fell back on God, to become the prophet of individual responsibility and of heart religion and to open the way for the dispensation of the Spirit (Heb. 8:8, 13, 10:16–17). He appeals to the covenant whose first requirement is obedience (11:1–8): he carries religion into the inner life, where not sacrifice, but moral conduct is paramount (Jer. 7:21–28–a much misunderstood word by the critics!). Trusting in temple and in law is vain: God looks at the heart (7:4–7, 8:7–9, 11:20, 17:10, 20:12). He tells of the true glory of the future kingdom, the new covenant and the new heart with the Law written upon it (24:7, 31:33, 32:39–40). At the close of his ministry, it seems that there was a rearrangement, since prophecies of different periods are put together, and some of the same period, are separated: those of Josiah's reign (1–12); those of Jehoiachim's (13, 20, 22–23, 35–36, 45–48, 49:1–33); those of Zedekiah's (21, 24, 27–34, 37–39, 49:34–39, 50–51); those of Gedaliah's time (40–44). There is an introduction—the call (ch. 1); three sections of prophecy, often connected with the event that occasioned the utterance (chs. 2–51); and an historical appendix (ch. 52). The prophetic sections are: (1) Approaching judgment and restoration promised (chs. 2–33); (2) History of the judgment (chs. 34–44); (3) Foreign nations section (with address to Baruch, cf. 45 chs. 46–51). The LXX has many differences from the Hebrew text. A general theme may be thus: The certain downfall of Judah at the hands of the God of loving-kindness is in order to the establishment of the kingdom of righteousness based on the new covenant. (Some

adaptation of J. D. Davis, *Dictionary of the Bible*, 1920.

Jeremias same as Jeremiah, of Anathoth, the major prophet, above.

Jeremoth (jĕr'ē-mōth) [heights] 1. Head of a Benjaminite family (1 Chr. 8:14).

2. A Merarite Levite (1 Chr. 23:23; called Jerimoth in 24:30).

3. Heman descendant and head of the fifteenth course of musicians in David's reign (1 Chr. 25:4, 22).

4 and 5. Two descendants of Elam, who put away foreign wives (Ezra 10:26–27).

Jeremy = Jeremiah; see 9 above.

Jeriah (jē-rī'ä) [founded by Jehovah?] a Kohathite Levite, house of Hebron (1 Chr. 23:19, 24:23, 26:31—here called Jerijah).

Jeribai (jĕr'ĭ-bī) [contentious] a Davidic hero, son of Elnaam (1 Chr. 11:46).

Jericho (jĕr'ĭ-kō) [place of fragrance] an ancient, important city in the Jordan Valley (Deut. 34:1, 3), on the west, near the Dead Sea, known as city of palm trees (Judg. 3:13); first noted when Israel camped on the other side Jordan (Num. 22:1, 26:3). The ancient Jericho, near "Elijah's fountain," is said to be represented by a collection of mounds: the modern town, er-Riha, is a short distance southeast. There seem to have been Amoritic, Roman, and Byzantine towns in the neighborhood. The events from the sending of the spies to the destruction of covetous Achan, are found in Josh. 1–7. Joshua's curse on the city (6:26), was fulfilled for Hiel, five hundred years later (1 K. 16:34); but it seems to have referred to refortifying the place; for the site was assigned to Benjamin (18:21); was a boundary for Ephraim; and later was Judah's. The oppressing Eglon of Moab occupied it (Judg. 3:13); David's messengers tarried there until their beards grew (2 Sam. 10:5; 1 Chr. 19:5). A school of the prophets, visited oft by Elijah, flourished at Jericho (2 K. 2); Elijah and Elisha were connected with the place, in the incident of the former's translation (vss. 4, 15, 18). Pekah's Judean captives were freed in Jericho (2 Chr. 28:15); there too, Zedekiah and his men were taken, fleeing Jerusalem before the Babylonian conquerors (2 K. 25:5; Jer. 39:5, 52:8). Returnees from captivity occupied it (Ezra 2:34; Neh. 7:36) and helped to rebuild Jerusalem's walls (Neh. 3:2). Later, Maccabeans and Romans occupied the city, Antony presenting the district to Cleopatra, and she selling it to Herod, who embellished it, and died there. At Jericho, pilgrims assembled en route to Jerusalem: the Lord's journeys included it: here, Bartimaeus figures (Mt.

20:24–34; Mk. 10:46–52; Lk. 18:35–43), and Zacchaeus (Lk. 19:1–9), and the Good Samaritan (Lk. 10). In Jericho there was an early Christian church (fourth century). Councils were attended by bishops of Jericho. In 1810, there was a monastery of St. Stephen. It is more than 800 feet below the Mediterranean Sea, luxurious in tropical climate, though unhealthy for man. The district is the property of the Sultan.

Jeriel (jē'rĭ-ĕl) [founded of God] descendant of Tola, of the tribe Issachar (1 Chr. 7:2).

Jerijah see **Jeriah**

Jerimoth (jĕr'ĭ-mōth) [heights] 1, 2, and 3. Benjaminites (1 Chr. 7:7–8, 12:5).

4 and 5. See **Jeremoth** 2 and 3.

6. Ruler of Naphtali, in David's reign (1 Chr. 27:19).

7. Son of David, and father of Mahalath, wife of Rehoboam (2 Chr. 11:18).

8. A Levite overseer in the temple under Hezekiah (2 Chr. 31:13).

Jerioth (jē'rĭ-ōth) [curtains] one of Caleb's wives (1 Chr. 2:18).

Jeroboam (jĕr-ō-bō'ăm) [people become numerous] *Jeroboam I.* son of Nebat, who "made Israel to sin," founder of the kingdom of the ten tribes (1 K. 11). While overseer under Solomon, Ahijah the prophet, of Shiloh, graphically predicted his kingship, which incident led Solomon to try to kill him; but he escaped to Egypt. His following besought Solomon's successor Rehoboam, to lighten their burdens; but receiving an exasperating answer, he led the ten tribes in revolt: he fortified Shechem, established two centers of worship (Dan and Bethel) to prevent possible defection of his subjects by worshiping at Jerusalem, set up golden calves at each place, made priests of non-Levites, and changed the date of the harvest festival, in all of which, he seems to have desired to worship Jehovah (1 K. 11–12; 2 Chr. 11:13–15, 13:8–9). His idolatry, dividing the nation, contributed to its fall (2 K. 17:16), set the pattern for successive kings (1 K. 15:26, 34, 16:19, 31, 22:52; 2 K. 3:3, 10:29, 13:2, 11, 14:24, 15:9, 18, 24, 28), and lowered the spiritual tone of the whole kingdom. He was rebuked by prophets, but continued unrepentant (1 K. 13:1–14:18). He engaged in almost continual warfare with the house of David (1 K. 15:6; 2 Chr. 13:1–20), reigning twenty-two years (1 K. 14:20), and leaving his son Nadab, the kingdom (vs. 20).

2. *Jeroboam II.* Son and successor to Joash as king over the ten tribes, reigning forty-one years, following the former Jeroboam in idolatries. He elevated his kingdom to splendor, ex-

tending his domain widely, no Israelite king being so victorious (2 K. 14:23–29). Both Hosea and Amos tell of effeminacy, pride, oppression, injustice, idolatry, luxury prevalent in this reign; Hosea's first three chapters being of this time (and see Amos 1:1, 2:6–5:7, 7:1–9, 8:4–10). Shortly after his death, the Lord cut off his family with the sword, according to prophecy (2 K. 15:10).

Jeroham (jĕ-rō′hăm) [he finds mercy] 1. A Levite, Samuel's grandfather (1 Sam. 1:1; 1 Chr. 6:27, 34).

2. A Benjaminite, whose sons were chief men in Jerusalem (1 Chr. 8:27).

3. Another Benjaminite (9:8; perhaps the same man—and some hold that the following are one and the same person).

4. A priest, house of Malkijah (1 Chr. 9:12; and same as in Neh. 11:12).

5. A Benjaminite of Gedor and father of some Davidic warriors (1 Chr. 12:7).

6. Father of Dan's prince, of David's time (1 Chr. 27:22).

7. Father of an assistant in placing Joash on the throne of Judah (2 Chr. 23:1).

Jerubbaal (jĕ-rŭb′bā-ăl) [let Baal plead] same as Gideon (Judg. 6:32); also Jerubbesheth (2 Sam. 11:21).

Jeruel (jĕ-rū′ĕl) [founded of God] a wilderness in Judah where Jehoshaphat defeated Ammon, Moab, and allies (2 Chr. 20:16), west of the Dead Sea, near En-gedi.

Jerusalem (jĕ-rū′sā-lĕm) [possession of peace?] sacred capital of Judah, or Judea, of Palestine, of Jewry. The earliest known name is Urusalim, i.e., Jerusalem, used before the Hebrew conquest of Palestine, as early as sixteenth century B.C.; found in letters from subject prince to Amenophis IV of Egypt. Melchizedek's Salem (abbreviation) is likely Jerusalem; called Jebus in Joshua's time and later, during its occupation by the Jebusites; but David, conquering, restored the name Jerusalem, or Salem (Ps. 76:2; 2 Sam. 5), the name being modified later to make it a dual form, suggesting a double city. Situated on the tableland crest of Palestine's central ridge at one of its highest points, being isolated from the rest of the plateau save on the north; on other sides, being deep ravines. There are three principal hills, eastern, southwestern, northwestern: others say: northwestern (Accra), northeastern (Bezetha), southwestern (Zion), southeastern (Ophel), about all of which much discussion has raged. Some make Moriah the northern end of Ophel. General elevation is about 2400 feet, with same latitude as north end of the Dead Sea. Kidron Valley is on the east, Son of Hinnom on the

west, and Tyropoeon in the middle. Water is short; an intermittent spring in Kidron, cisterns and conduits are used; especially noted is the Siloam tunnel (2 K. 20:20; 2 Chr. 32:30). There were two main approaches to the city: (1) from the Jordan Valley by Jericho and the Mount of Olives (Lk. 17:11; 2 Sam. 15:16); (2) from the great maritime plain and Sharon, by the two Beth-horons and Gibeon. There appear to have been about twenty gates. The Mount of Olives was on the east, Gethsemane being at its foot. Jerusalem was besieged seventeen times; twice razed, its walls leveled; in which respects it stands without parallel, beginning in the time of the Judges (1:8), to the destruction by Titus the Roman in A.D. 70, and the plowing of the temple site at its obliteration by Hadrian in 132, following Bar-Cochba's rebellion. For two centuries thereafter, little is known of the city. In 326 Constantine, and later, others, did reconstruction, in 460, Eudocia repairing walls and building churches; but construction and destruction continued under alternate Roman and Persian rule, until Omar ousted the Romans in 637. In 1099 the capturing Crusaders wrought carnage, and the Latin kingdom of Jerusalem was established; then came Saladin's capture 1187; in 1517, Selim of Turkey took possession; and Moslem rule gave way to Christian with Allenby in 1917, in which year the Balfour Declaration promised a national home for Jews in Palestine. Problems of sites and buildings have increased for students, since the construction in the days of Solomon, Millo being one example. On the eastern hill, site of Jebusite Zion, David built the royal city; and north of this, he chose the location for the temple to be built by Solomon. Arguments go pro and con about Mount Zion, probably the best solution being that it is part of the temple hill and by synecdoche, often used for the whole, whereas the city of David denoting the municipality (2 Sam. 5:7), grew beyond the hill Zion, to embrace neighboring hills. The term "city of David" might then include or exclude the sanctuary. The name Zion became title for the city as a whole (2 Sam. 5:7–9; Ps. 48, 133:3). Across the Tyropoeon Valley from the temple hill, was the civil town—a disputed, but generally accepted view. Nehemiah rebuilt the walls in the return, but again doubts on the location are rife. It remained for Herod the Great to give a new city and a new temple, with fortifications, palace, theater and gymnasium, in 37 B.C., following. Jerusalem was the seat of government under the League of Nations mandate to Great Britain, 1922–48, many improvements being made during that time. In 1947, after much devastation in the Jewish-Arab conflict, following the partition resolution when Jerusalem became internationalized, the Old City was left in the hands of the Jordan kingdom, and the New, in Israel's, much of the Jewish quarter of the Old having been destroyed, and the "Wailing Wall" becoming inaccessible to the Jews. The armistice agreement of 1949 made a division between the State of Israel and the Hashemite Kingdom of Jordan. In 1950, Jerusalem became the seat of the Israeli government; but the city remained divided, the only connection being the Mandelbaum Gate, through which passage was restricted by both countries. Despite the ravages and reconstructions, the contrast between the ancient and the new, Jerusalem keeps the aspect of the Holy City. In Israel, industries flourish with a hundred new factories, under the Jewish Economic Corporation Ltd. In the Arabic part, the new buildings are largely hospitals. In 1956 the Jewish population was 164,000, the Arabic 46,000. The presence of synagogues, churches, mosques, monasteries witness to the universal importance of Jerusalem, where various races and creeds mix. It is the seat of ecclesiastical authority for many faiths.

Jerusha (jê-rû'shä) [possession] daughter of Zadoc and queen of Uzziah (2 K. 15:33; 2 Chr. 27:1).

Jeshaiah (jê-shā'yä) [Jehovah saves] 1. Son of Jeduthun and musician of David (1 Chr. 25:3).

2. A Levite, son of Rehabiah (26:25).

3. Hananiah's son, descendant of Zerubbabel (3:21).

4. Son of Athaliah returning with Ezra (8:7).

5. A Merarite Levite (vs. 19).

6. A Benjaminite, father of Ithiel (Neh. 11:7).

Jeshanah (jĕsh-ä'nä) [old] a city in the hill country of Ephraim, taken from Jeroboam by Abijah (2 Chr. 13:19), and believed the site of Herod the Great's defeat of Antigonus.

Jesharelah (jê-shä'rē-lä) [upright to God] son of Asaph and a Levitical musician (1 Chr. 25:14). Same as Asarelah.

Jeshebeab (jê-shĕb'ē-äb) [father's dwelling] descendant of Aaron, who served in the fourteenth course of the priesthood (1 Chr. 24:13). Same as Jehoiarib.

Jesher (jĕsh'ẽr) [probity] son of Caleb (1 Chr. 2:18).

Jeshimon (jĕsh-ī'mŏn) [waste] 1. Wilderness

at north end of Dead Sea, near Pisgah and Peor (Num. 21:20, 23:28).

2. A wilderness north of the hill Hachilah and of Maon (1 Sam. 23:19, 24, 26:1, 3). Probably not a proper name.

Jeshishai (jê-shī'shī) [pertaining to an old man] a Gadite of Buz (1 Chr. 5:14).

Jeshohaiah (jĕsh-ō-hā'yä) [Jehovah humbles?] a Simeonite prince (1 Chr. 4:36).

Jeshua (jĕsh'ū-ä) [Jehovah is salvation] a form of Joshua. 1. A military leader in the wars of Canaan (Neh. 8:17).

2. An Aaronic priest in David's time, in the ninth course of priests (1 Chr. 24:11).

3. A Levite of Hezekiah's reign, handling freewill offerings (2 Chr. 31:15).

4. A high priest returning with Zerubbabel in Cyrus' first year; leader in rebuilding the temple; in Zechariah's time, representative of returnees to whom divine aid was given (Ezra 2:2, 3:2–9; Zech. 3:1–10, 6:11–13).

5. A man or a family of Pahath-Moab, accompanying Zerubbabel (Ezra 2:6; Neh. 10:14).

6. A returnee, head of a Levitical family, who took active part under Zerubbabel, Ezra, and Nehemiah; perhaps designating a family or succession of its chiefs (Ezra 2:40; Neh. 7:43, 10:9). Could also be the wall repairer of 3:19.

7. A Levite, an aide in explaining the Law and developing heart-deep worship (Neh. 8:7, 9:4–5).

8. A village of South Judah (Neh. 11:26).

Jeshurun (jĕsh'ū-rŭn) [righteous one] Isa. 44:2, Jesurun. Symbolical name for the ideal Israel (Deut. 32:15, 33:5, 26).

Jesiah (jĕ-sī'ä) [Jehovah lends, or forgets?] 1. A Korhite with David at Ziklag (1 Chr. 12:6).

2. Second son of Uzziel, of Kohath (1 Chr. 23:20). Same as Jeshia.

Jesimiel (jê-sĭm'ĭ-ĕl) [God sets up] prince of Simeon (1 Chr. 4:36).

Jesse (jĕs'sē) [perhaps wealthy] father of David and son of Obed, of Boaz and Ruth (Ruth 4:18–22), great-grandson of Rahab (Mt. 1:5). Commonly called "the Bethlehemite"; genealogy twice given (Ruth 4:18–22; 1 Chr. 2:5–12). He had eight sons, resided at Bethlehem, joined David the refugee, with his house, at Adullam (1 Sam. 22:1), and was taken to Moab and left with the king, where he disappears from the record. For more, see **David**

Jesui (jĕs'ū-ī) [perhaps equal] son of Asher whose descendants were numbered in the plains of Moab (Num. 26:44). Elsewhere called Isui

(Gen. 46:17) and Ishuai (1 Chr. 7:30). From him, the Jesuites.

Jesus [Greek form of *Joshua*, contraction of *Jehoshua*, Jehovah is salvation, Num. 13:16].
1. Military leader in Canaan (see **Joshua**).
2. Ancestor of the Lord, 400 years after David (Lk. 3:29, where KJV has Jose).
3. A Jewish Christian, called also Justus, with Paul (Col. 4:11).
4. The name of our Lord.

Jesus Christ [Savior Anointed] the former is his name, the latter, his title, but often used as proper name (1 Chr. 16:29; Jn. 1:41; also Acts 19:4; Mt. 11:3). The life, person, and work of the Lord occupy the whole of the NT. He was named by angelic direction (Mt. 1:21; Lk. 1:31). Many intimations and specifications concerning the Messiah to come are found in the OT, all of which have centered historically in the person whom we know as the Lord Jesus Christ. For OT saints, it was the Messiah to come; for us, it is the Savior, the fulfillment of all, who has come. In such light we see: the Seed of the Woman, Gen. 3:15; the Blessing through Shem, 9:27; the Shiloh of Judah, 49:10; the Prophet like Moses, Deut. 18:18; the Star of Balaam, Num. 24:17; the Daysman of Job 9:33; the Ideal One of Ps. 1, 8, 15; the Suffering Benefactor, Ps. 22:22, 27; the Servant of Isa. 42; the Virgin-born Immanuel, Isa. 7:14; the Branch of Jer. 33:15; the New Thing of Jer. 31:22; the David Forever of Ezek. 37:25; the Ruler from Bethlehem Ephrathah of Mic. 5:2; the King Riding on an Ass, Zech. 9:9; the Sun of Righteousness of Mic. 5:2. The gospels show the lines of prophecy centering in him, as the calendar indicates the stages of history revolving around him. I. CHRONOL-OGY. Exact dates for the birth, baptism, and death of the Lord cannot be fixed, though there is fair agreement. Dionysius Exiguus, a Roman abbot of the sixth century, fixed on the year 754 of Rome, as the time of his birth, that being then A.D. 1. But Josephus says that Herod the Great died (see Mt. 2:19) several years previous to that date, thirty-seven years after being made king by the Romans, A.U.C. 714 (*ab urbe condita*, "from the founding of the city"). Josephus may have counted fraction of a year for full year; but 750 is the more probable death date, since Herod put to death some Jewish Rabbis, shortly before his demise, and at that time there was an eclipse of the moon; also Herod died not long before the Passover which began, in 750, on April 12. Calculations show that there was an eclipse in 750, March 12 or 13, but none in 751. It seems then fair to hold that Herod died about April 1, A.U.C. 750, which would be 4 B.C.; and because several months are required for the gospel-recorded events, between the birth of the Savior and the death of Herod, the close of 5 B.C., or the beginning of 4, marks his birth. The observance of December 25 arose not till the fourth century, having no authority; but the date is assumed December 25, 5 B.C. Luke 3:23 shows the Lord's public ministry, and the baptism, at about age thirty; that would make him thirty on December 25, A.D. 26. Luke's indefiniteness would allow the traditional baptismal date as January 6, called "twelfth night" by later tradition. Also Herod's temple, begun 20-19 B.C., using the forty-six years of Jn. 2:20, would point to A.D. 27. And further John the Baptist began his ministry in the fifteenth year of Tiberius (Lk. 3:1), reckoned as the time when the latter was associated with Augustus in the empire (A.D. 11-12). Thus there is coincidence with A.D. 26 again. As to the length of the Lord's ministry and the time of his death, dependence is placed on the Passovers of the Gospel of John. Anciently, as based on the synoptic gospels, one year was supposed the time of the ministry. But John has at least three Passovers (2:13, 6:4, 13:1); and Jn. 5:1 probably shows another. If then the Lord died at his fourth Passover, his first being April, A.D. 27, his death year was 30, and the Passover being April 7. If of course, Jn. 5:1 does not refer to a Passover, 29 was the date.

II. POLITICAL STATE OF THE JEWS. When the Lord was born, Herod the Great, an Idumaean professing the Jewish faith, able but cruel, was king, declared so by the Romans in 40 B.C., after remarkable changes of fortune, and following his father Antipater, who had been made governor of Judea by Julius Caesar. Herod depended much on the favor and defense of the Roman world rule. At Herod's death, his sons inherited: Archelaus, Judea and Samaria; Herod Antipas, Galilee and Perea; Herod Philip, the territory northeast of the Sea of Galilee (Lk. 3:1). In his tenth year Archelaus was deposed by Augustus, and thereafter Judea and Samaria were ruled by so-called procurators till the destruction of Jerusalem, 41-44 being an exception, when Herod Agrippa I, held sway (Acts 12:1). Most of the Lord's ministry was in Galilee and Perea, under Herod Antipas (Mt. 14:3; Mk. 6:14; Lk. 3:1, 19, 23:8-12), while Judea and Samaria were directly under the Romans through their governor, at that time Pontius Pilate. Though Rome tried to give the Jews as much self-rule as possible, their chief court, the Sanhedrin, having jurisdiction to a large degree, privileges being granted especially about religious observances, there was political ferment under the foreign domination. The aristocracy, embracing most of the Sadducees, were not unfriendly to Rome; the Pharisees, generally avoiding political complications, being strict religionists, devoted themselves to the conservation of Judaism. Herodians, favoring Jewish claims to the throne, nursed political patriots who sought to throw off the yoke of the empire. In such circumstances a Messianic claimant could easily become involved in difficulty. Our Lord, proclaiming the true, spiritual kingdom of God, carefully and successfully avoided entanglement.

III. RELIGIOUS CONDITION OF THE JEWS. Politics affected religion: the official classes practically forgot the purely religious hopes of the OT; the common folk thought of a material, rather than a spiritual, kingdom. Of the leading sects, the Pharisees had great influence religiously, but substituted theology, ceremony, and casuistry for the Word of God, religion being narrow, unspiritual, barren. On the other hand, the Sadducees were the priestly and aristocratic crowd; culture and politics were their interests, rejecting angel, resurrection, and spirit. They opposed the Lord lest he disturb existing political relations; the Pharisees opposed him for his unconventionality and appeal over tradition to Scripture. Externalism, ritualism, ceremonialism flourished, fanatical patriotism flaring up with popular hope. But some, as always, nourished true spiritual religion, especially the humble folk, whose expectation of Messiah to save from sin had not died out, and among whom the Lord found welcome.

IV. THE LIFE OF THE CHRIST. Malachi and Luke tell about the forerunner, John the Baptist, the angel announcing to Zechariah while doing temple duty, the birth of his son, likely October of 6 B.C. (Mal. 4:5–6; Lk. 1:39). Six months later annunciation was made to Mary betrothed to Joseph, a devout but humble Israelite of David's line (Mt. 1:1–16; Lk. 1:27–38). Mary went for protection and sympathy to the house of Zechariah, where the spirit of prophecy came upon both the mothers to be (see Lk. 1). The angel revealed to Joseph —who had thought to deal very gently with his espoused, that Mary's conception was supernatural and that the child was to be the Messiah, whereupon he made Mary his legal wife, whose son would have a legal father, and who herself would have the love and respectability of a faithful husband. Mary evidently made known all these things to Luke the physician, particularly. The virgin birth, according to prophecy (Isa. 7:14), is related only by Matthew and Luke, the other two gospels not dealing with the Lord's early life: two gospels are enough! Only the virgin birth accounts for the absolutely unique life and complete Saviorhood of the Lord. Luke explains how he came to be born in Bethlehem, according to prophecy (Mic. 5:2). The mother lived at Nazareth. Augustus' census was not completed till the governorship of Cyrenius (Quirinius) (Lk. 2:1–3), some undetermined time later; but it brought Joseph along with his wife, according to Jewish registry, to the place of his ancestry (Bethlehem), Palestinians, even though under Herod, being included in Augustus' decree. The birth in the manger—the inn being crowded, lacked not portentous signs. Shepherds heard "good tidings of great joy"; angelic chorus broke through the silent night: "Glory to God in the highest, and on earth peace, good will toward men" (Lk. 2:8–20). After the eighth-day circumcision according to the Law (Lk. 2:21), as also the maternal purification (Lev. 12; Num. 18:16), Simeon and Anna, enlightened of God about the realization of long desire, prophesied, the one rejoicing that his eyes had seen the salvation of God, and the other speaking of him "to all that looked for redemption in Israel" (Lk. 2:28–38). Heathen gave witness: Persian magi of the East, the "wise men," of the Zend religion with its belief in a Zoziosh or Redeemer, miraculously guided by the Star, sought out the Savior to pay him homage; and Herod, fearing a rival king and seeing that the wise did not return to tell him all details, slew all two-year olds and under, in Bethlehem. (The wise men therefore must have seen the Lord quite a bit later than the shepherds.) With the enormity of Herod's crimes, this slaughter was not noted by historians. Joseph, warned in a dream, escaped to Egypt, returning only after Herod's death, less than a year later, and going to Nazareth, again being directed divinely (Mt. 2:11–23). Nothing is told of the Lord's life until he was twelve years of age (Lk. 2:41–51), when the pious parents took him to Jerusalem, where he manifested both human and divine characteristics, discoursing with the Rabbis in the temple, and increasing in "wisdom and stature and in favor with God and man" (Lk. 2:52). Great changes occurred politically between the birth and the ministerial career of the Lord. Herod's widely extended kingdom was dismembered forever. The fifteenth year of the Emperor Tiberius, reckoning from his joint rule with Augustus, A.U.C. 765, John the Baptizer came upon the scene, the last of the OT prophets, with the dual work of enforcing repentance and the terrors of the old law, and reviving the almost forgotten Messianic hope (Mt. 3:1–10; Mk. 1:1–8; Lk. 3:1–18). With others at Jordan, the Lord received baptism of John, to give example, to justify baptism for all (Mt. 3:15), to assure John that his course as herald was complete (Jn. 1:33), and as public token that he was indeed the Anointed of God (Heb. 5:5). For him also it was a self-dedication, the assumption of his life work as sin-bearer. "This is my beloved Son, in whom I am well pleased" (Mt. 3:17), indicated full endowment with spiritual power for his ministry; but his humanity was shown by the temptation which immediately followed (Mt. 4:1–11; Mk. 1:12=13; Lk. 4:1–13). The three temptations are addressed to the three forms in which the curse of sin makes its appearance in the soul—to the solace of sense, the love of praise, to the desire for gain (1 Jn. 2:16). But there is one element common to them all: they are attempts to call up a willful and wayward spirit in contrast to a patient and self-denying one, to divert his purpose to worldly ends. None can tell the exact circumstances of the temptation: they are not after all necessary. The Lord must have told the matter to his disciples. It seems that if he had perceived the true nature of the Tempter, his humanity would have hardly been tempted. The kenosis (emptying, of Phil. 2) had put his Deity in abeyance. None can doubt the outward reality of the Tempter, nor the physical features of the scenes (Mt. 4:1–11; Lk. 4:1–12); nevertheless we should keep in mind the fact that the power of the temptations lay in the subtlety with which the world was presented to the Savior as more attractive than the life of stern obedience to God with its likely already understood fatal close. And now, the disciples are called, some from John the Baptist's following (Jn. 1:29, 36, 43–51): John, Andrew, Simon; and Philip and Nathanael on the next day; then to Galilee for the first miracle, and signs of his coming glory (2:1–11). Thus began the first year's ministry, called by J. Stalker, the year of obscurity, of so meager record. From Capernaum, he went to the Passover at Jerusalem (Jn. 2:13), there cleansing the temple with its avaricious, sacrilegious trade, a summons for followers, and the beginning of his reformative work against the religious abuses of the time. Resulting from other miracles and the excited talk, came the visit of Nicodemus, of Jn. 3, revealing the nature of the new kingdom and the terms of admission. Here the information stops; nothing is known for the next eight months. He was baptizing in Judea (Jn. 3:22–36) along with

John the Baptist, through the medium of his disciples, John giving place to him. The nation was unprepared to receive him, the leaders in Jerusalem rejected him: and so the record centers elsewhere than in Judea, stress being placed on his gathering believers as the nucleus of his church, among those less sophisticated and prideful, and with the purpose of gaining momentum for later storming the "citadel of prejudice." Thus when the Lord began to attract more followers than did John (4:1–3), he turned towards Galilee, to enter into the so-called year of public favor, not chronologically based, extending about eighteen months, during part of the year 27, and the year 28, and part of 29 (S. J. Andrews, *Life of Our Lord*, 1906). On the way to Galilee occurred the memorable visit with the woman at the well (4:4–42). His fame preceded him to Nazareth, where the prophet in his own country saw phantom popularity wither before unbelief (Lk. 4:18–24), whereupon Capernaum became headquarters for the Galilean ministry, as he and the disciples ministered in various parts of the land, including a Jerusalem visit (Jn. 5), with the sabbath question in connection with the healing of the impotent man, Jewish opposition and the declaration of his authority, along with the spiritual meaning of the OT and the discourse concerning himself. In Galilee again, miracles of healing and other wonderful works were done (Mt. 8–9, 12; Mk. 1–3; Lk. 4–6). His miracles were not only wonders but signs touching the scope and character of his ministry and his divine nature, most of them being directed to the suffering and sorrowing, proclaiming his love; some indicative of power over nature, only one being destructive (Mt. 21:19). They attested his divine mission, were the natural overflow of divine fullness, symbols of saving spiritual work (Stalker), all being of Messianic essence, making him understood, binding men to him, leading to faith. The increasing hostility of the Pharisees and the advancing public interest, opened the way for the appointment of the Twelve, and on one famous day, the Sermon of the Mount (Mk. 3:13; Mt. 5–7; Lk. 6:20–49). There follows a succession of tours, with miracles, in Lower Galilee with the disciples; and apparently out of the growing interest and also hostility, come the great parables (Mt. 13; Mk. 4), with consummate skill, the profoundest truths about the origin, progress, perils, and destiny of his spiritual kingdom. Warning complications, Herod's inquiry, the death of John the Baptist (Mt. 14), and other indications, brought the Galilean ministry to crisis. The crowds followed him to temporary retirement to the northeastern shore of Galilee, and the feeding of the 5000 (Mt. 14; Mk. 6; Lk. 9; Jn. 6), where their demand for his kingship showed their misunderstanding of his mission (Jn. 6:15). Back in Capernaum, the Lord's stress is again on his death and the meaning of discipleship (Jn. 6). The Galilean ministry is done: he goes to Gentile territory for the only time, for six months —Tyre, Sidon, the Decapolis, where many miracles were performed and the 4000 were fed (Mt. 15; Mk. 8). Then comes Caesarea Philippi, near Mount Hermon; Peter's confession; and discourses about his death. Next of the notable events is the transfiguration, and his further teaching about true service of self-sacrificial love, like to his conduct (Mt. 17; Mk. 9; Lk. 9). Now is the year of opposition (Stalker). It is Autumn of A.D. 29. It is impossible to know the exact data as it would be, if the chronological method were followed. Some put the events and discourses of Jn. 7–10, before the transfiguration (J. D. Davis, *Dictionary of the Bible*, 1920). The Seventy are sent out. We have the words about the light of the world, the good shepherd, about the true life and true God and service. He goes back and forth in Judea and Perea. There are the parables of the Good Samaritan, the Wedding Feast, the Lost Sheep, Coin, Son (Lk. 15), the Unjust Steward, the Rich Man and Lazarus, the Importunate Widow, the Pharisee and the Publican. Opposition becomes intense; Lazarus is raised (Jn. 11:1–46), increasing the determination to kill him (47–53); then comes his withdrawal, awaiting the Passover for the chosen time of his death. The Lord approaches the City through Perea, teaching, and stressing his death and resurrection (Mt. 19, 20; Mk. 10; Lk. 18:15–19:28). Next, comes Bethany and the anointing. The triumphal entry enrages the rulers; he cleanses the temple again. There are more great parables (Mt. 21–25), in the midst of which we note the special battle of wits with the Jewish leaders (Mt. 22); and the coming of the Greeks (Jn. 12:20–50). The cleansing was on Monday, Nisan 11, April 3; the parables and the Greeks, mark Tuesday, April 4. Wednesday saw retirement with his disciples. Thursday was the last Passover, Judas' dismissal, the New Commandment (Mt. 26; Mk. 14; Lk. 22; Jn. 13); the farewell discourses of Jn. 14–17; intercessory prayer, the agony in the Garden, the betrayal and arrest (Mt. 26; Mk. 14; Lk. 22; Jn. 18). (There are variations among authorities). On Friday, April 7, 1 to 5 A.M., his captors took him to Annas, father-in-law to Caiaphas, for preliminary trial while the Sanhedrin was assembling (Jn. 18:13–24). Before the latter he made explicit assertion of his Messiahship, bringing condemnation for blasphemy, his enemies subjecting him to ribald mockery. The law required daytime decisions; so the court met again, with the same formalities (Lk. 22:66–71); and then, the governor's permission being necessary for execution, they hastened with him to Pilate, likely in Herod's palace on the hill of Zion. When Pilate demanded charges, he was accused of "perverting the nation, and forbidding to give tribute to Caesar, saying that he himself is Christ, a King" (Jn. 18:29–32; Lk. 23:2). The Lord admitted his kingship, was examined in private, and declared eligible for liberty, his claims being nonpolitical. Afraid to thwart the will of the determined and vociferous leaders, Pilate resorted to weak expedients to shift responsibility: learning that the Lord was from Galilee, he sent him to Herod Antipas (Lk. 23:7–11), then in Jerusalem; but he refused to deal with the case. When Pilate hoped the people would advocate release because of the Lord's popularity, he saw them swayed by the Rabbis to ask for Barabbas instead. Afraid to act on conviction, further perturbed by a message from his wife, after vain attempts to secure a change of mind on the part of the now implacable and blood-thirsty crowd, he meekly consented to execution. Pilate's terror was further increased when, hoping to assuage their thirst for blood by the sight of the bleeding, thorn-crowned Lord who had been scourged, the mob cried more vehemently saying that he ought to die because he made himself the Son of God. Again making examination, and further seeking release (Jn. 19:1–12), Pilate finally gave in, when they appealed to his political ambition and practically accused him of abetting a rival king. There was grim satisfaction in seeing the Jews proclaim allegiance to the emperor (vs. 15). But the Lord's death was but an official murder, there being no crime and no real legal process. Fainting under the cross, even the short distance to Golgotha, the murderers lest they defile themselves, laid hold of Simon the Cyrenian to bear the burden; and placed on a tablet on the cross, Pilate's inscription: "Jesus of Nazareth, the King of the Jews" (Jn. 19:19). The reconciliation between Mark's third hour (i.e. from 6 A.M.) and John's sixth hour (i.e. from midnight—Roman custom), can be made by noting John's word "about the sixth hour" which could be rather indefinite. The consensus seems to be that the crucifixion was at the hour of 9 A.M., the death at noon. We have the seven words, the rending of the veil of the temple, the earthquake and the rising of many dead, the commission, and permission to Joseph of Arimathaea for burial in his new sepulcher (Mt. 27:57–66; Mk. 15:42–47; Lk. 23:50–56; Jn. 19:38–42). Saturday, April 8, the chief priests and Pharisees set a watch (Mt. 27:62–66). Sunday, April 9 (the sabbath ended at six on the evening of the sixteenth of Nisan): early in the morning, the resurrection took place, the exact time not mentioned, but on the seventeenth of Nisan. The prostration of bitter disappointment accounts for the wholly disconcerted and overwhelmed apostles, despite three recorded occasions of the Lord's forewarning of his death and resurrection on the third day. Since they lingered in Jerusalem instead of going to Galilee as instructed, he appeared to them in the city and its vicinity. The narratives are not intended to give complete accounts. Nor do they marshal evidences: they give simple testimony by those to whom he repeatedly appeared (1 Cor. 15:3–8). The following seems to have been the order of events: Two groups of pious women went to the sepulcher to complete the hasty embalming by Joseph and Nicodemus; the first company, Mary Magdalene, Mary the mother of James, and Salome (Mk. 16:1); then Joanna and other unnamed women (likely) in the second (Lk. 24:10 is a general statement, including the report of all the women). The first ones saw the stone rolled away; and Mary Magdalene, supposing the body stolen, hurried with the news to Peter and John (Jn. 20:1–2). The others, entering the tomb, heard angelic news of the resurrection and the message to the disciples (Mt. 28:1–7; Mk. 16:1–7). Hastening away, it seems that they met the other company; and all returned again to the tomb, receiving from two angels more emphatic assurance and direction (Lk. 24:1–8). On the way to the city the Lord met them (Mt. 28:9–10). Meantime Mary had followed Peter and John who confirmed her story (Jn. 20:3–10); and she, remaining after their departure from the Garden, was met by the risen Lord (vss. 11–18). Faith in the resurrection finds confirmation from others than the women. During the day, he appeared to Peter (Lk. 24:34; 1 Cor. 15:5), later to two on the way to Emmaus (Lk. 24:13–35), and in the evening to the apostles, Thomas being absent (vss. 36–43; Jn. 20:19–23), on which occasion he ate before them, certifying physical resurrection. Meeting a week later with his disciples, Thomas gave testimony, not so much however to the fact of the resurrection, as to the reality of all which the Lord claims to be

(Jn. 20:29). The disciples it seems returned to Galilee; and to seven he appeared as they were fishing (Jn. 21); and by appointment, on a mountain he met with and gave them the Great Commission (Mt. 28:16–20), which also may have been the occasion of the 500 (1 Cor. 15:6). Then he appeared to James (vs. 7), place unknown; and finally he brought them to Jerusalem and to the Mount of Olives, from which point Bethany was visible (Lk. 24:50–51); and from there he was taken up into heaven, a cloud receiving him out of their sight (Acts 1:9–12). Thus are ten recorded NT appearances, with the one to Paul on the Damascus road (1 Cor. 15:8). Likely there were other unrecorded appearances (Acts 1:3). The forty-day interim between his death and his ascension saw his fuller instruction about these vital matters, and the character of his kingdom, as he showed them that he was living though absent, near but invisible, as risen to new life but retaining the old nature and even the old but now glorified body which they had loved, as exalted yet still the same; so that they were made ready to proclaim him as the glorified Son of God and crowned king of Israel, but also the Man of Nazareth and the Lamb of God taking away the sin of the world (Jn. 1:29). Meanwhile the Jews insisted his disciples had stolen his body, fearing which they had secured a military watch to guard the tomb. Overcome with fright, the soldiers fled when the angel appeared. Money was given to keep the matter quiet, the report going out that the body was stolen while soldiers slept (Mt. 28:11–15)! Later when the number of believers grew rapidly, it was by force not proofs that the chief priests tried to quash the growing "sect" (Acts 4). In the gospels, "there is a gradual progressive revelation of Himself and of His message which constitutes one of the strongest evidences of the truthfulness of the accounts on which our knowledge is based. His human reality affords basis for His historical character related to a particular environment, presenting a career which moved naturally and steadily to a definite goal. But He declared Himself to be more than mere man (e.g., Mt. 11:27); and as self-revelation advanced, His divine dignity became more clear (Mt. 16:16; Jn. 20:28). Later reflection and experience, under Divine guidance, made Deity the more evident to the disciples, until the last surviving apostle, the fourth evangelist, presented in His earthly career, the incarnation of the personal Divine Word, His humanity never being obscured. It is John who writes, 'In the beginning was the Word; and the Word was with God, and the Word was God' (1:1); and it is John who concludes: 'These (things) are written that ye might believe that Jesus is the Christ, the Son of God; and that believing, ye might have life through His name' (20:31)." Davis, *Dictionary of the Bible*, p. 391.

Jether (jē'thēr) [abundance, eminence] 1. A form of Jethro, father-in-law to Moses (Ex. 4:18).

2. Firstborn of Gideon (Judg. 8:20–21).

3. Father of Amasa (1 K. 2:5; variation of Ithra of 2 Sam. 17:25; more properly in 1 Chr. 2:17).

4. Son of Jada (1 Chr. 2:32).

5. Son of Ezra; lineage not traced beyond his father (1 Chr. 4:17).

6. An Asherite (1 Chr. 7:38; same as Ithran [?] of preceding verse).

Jetheth (jē'thēth) chieftain of Edom (Gen. 36:40; 1 Chr. 1:51).

Jethlah (jĕth'lä) [lofty place] a town of Dan (Josh. 19:42).

Jethro (jĕth'rō) [his pre-eminence] priest-prince of Midian, and Moses' father-in-law, Reuel [friend of God] being his personal name, Jethro, his title. With him Moses spent forty years, a daughter Zipporah being his wife (Ex. 3:1–2; see Ex. 4:18–20, 24–26; 18:1–7). He rejoiced in Israel's deliverance from Egypt, offered sacrifices, suggested the appointment of judges to aid the tiring Moses (18:8–27). According to Num. 10:29 Hobab, sometimes thought to be same as Reuel, is Moses' brother-in-law, the Hebrew punctuation having been added to the consonantal text which simply means "in-law." The Hebrew pointing in Judg. 4:11 is evidently incorrect.

Jetur (jē'tūr) [nomad?] folk descended from Ishmael (Gen. 25:15; 1 Chr. 1:31, 5:19).

Jeuel (jū'ĕl) [treasure of God?] 1. A man of Judah (1 Chr. 9:6).

2. A Levite (2 Chr. 29:13).

3. Another in Ezra 8:13, called Jeiel.

Jeush (jē'ŭsh) [hastening?] 1. A son of Esau (Gen. 36:5, 14, 18; 1 Chr. 1:35).

2. A Benjaminite (1 Chr. 7:10–11).

3. A Gershonite Levite (1 Chr. 23:10–11).

4. A descendant of Jonathan (1 Chr. 8:39).

5. A son of Rehoboam of Judah (2 Chr. 11:18–19).

Jeuz (jē'ŭz) [counseling] a Benjaminite, genealogy obscure; apparently son of Sheharaim by third wife, Hodesh, and born in Moab (1 Chr. 8:10).

Jew [from Judah, via Latin] of Judah; a name applied to the Hebrews particularly after the return from Babylon. Found first 2 K. 16:6, 25:25; seven times in Jeremiah, e.g., 32:12. Finally includes all of that line anywhere (Est. 2:5; Mt. 2:2). John uses Jew to describe opponents of the Lord, indicative of limited and definite form of a national religion; earlier the name was contrasted with Greek as implying outward covenant with God (Rom. 1:16; Col. 3:11), correlative to Hellenist, less expressive than Israelite, which looked to the privileges and hopes of Jacob's children (2 Cor. 11:22; Jn. 1:47). The present situation seems to be the fulfillment of prophecy, as Lev. 26:33. Since the seat of the Israeli government, 1950, in Jerusalem, Zionism has found many advocates looking to the re-establishment of the Davidic kingdom and the realization of popular hopes. The language is Hebrew characterized by Aramaic forms and idioms acquired during the Captivity (2 K. 18:26; Neh. 8:24).

Jewess a woman of Judah or of the Hebrew people (1 Chr. 4:18, margin; Acts 16:1, 24:24).

Jewish of or belonging to Jews; an epithet (Tit. 1:14).

Jewry same as Judah and Judea; only once in OT (Dan. 5:13); is of frequent use in Old English, coming through the Norman-French.

Jezaniah (jĕz-ā-nī'ä) [Jehovah hearkens] in full, Jaazaniah. A captain who escaped during the last attack of the Chaldaeans (Babylonians) on Jerusalem, but who returned to Gedaliah, Nebuchadnezzar's appointee as governor, and who helped to bring the murderers of Gedaliah to justice. He appealed to Jeremiah about the remnant migrating to Egypt (2 K. 25:23; Jer. 40:7–8, 42:1, 43:2).

Jezebel (jĕz'ē-bĕl) [unmarried, chaste] 1. A Phoenician princess, daughter of Ethbaal, Zidonian king and former priest of Astarte (1 K. 16:31), stern, fierce, licentious wife of henpecked Ahab, a puppet (1 K. 21:25). Because of her, Baal worship on a grand scale was set up in Samaria, where she wined and dined 450 prophets of Baal and 400 of Astarte (1 K. 16:31–32, 18:19), while she slew all the Lord's prophets she could lay hands on (18:4–13). When Elijah, arousing the people, effected the slaughter of her ministers at Carmel, and when Ahab was terrified into submission, his queen only vowed terrible vengeance (1 K. 19). She fixed the judicial murder of Naboth, to seize his vineyard (21:16–22). She was condemned in specific terms (vs. 23) and a dozen years or so after Ahab's death, when Jehu came to execute pitiless vengeance on the royal household, she painted her eyelids and tired her head (either to impress the avenger or as a final act of regal splendor), and called to Jehu from a high latticed tower-window of the palace; but at his command was thrown down to the pavement, where the chariot was intentionally driven over her body, her blood spattering horses and wall. An hour later when Jehu, reflecting that after all she was a king's daughter, ordered burial, it was found that the scavenger dogs had left nothing but skull and feet and the palms of her hands (2 K. 9:7, 30–37).

2. A seductive and self-styled prophetess at Thyatira, likely symbolically named (Rev. 2:20–23).

Jezer (jē′zēr) [formation] third son of Napthali (Gen. 46:24; Num. 26:49; 1 Chr. 7:13). Founder of the tribal family.

Jeziah (jē-zī′ä) [deliverance?] Ezra 10:25.

Jeziel (jēz′ĭ-ĕl) [assembly of God] a Benjaminite joining David at Ziklag (1 Chr. 12:3).

Jezliah (jēz-lī′ä) [deliverance?] 1 Chr. 8:18.

Jezoar (jē-zō′är) [bright (oil)] 1. Perhaps same as Izahar, or Izhar (Ezra 6:18=19; Num. 3:19, 27; 1 Chr. 6:18, 38; see Num. 16:1).

2. Same as Zohar (1 Chr. 4:5–7).

Jezrahiah (jēz-rä-hī′ä) [Jehovah shines forth] overseer of singers with Nehemiah (Neh. 12:42).

Jezreel (jĕz′rê-ĕl) [God sows] 1. A man of Judah (1 Chr. 4:3).

2. Son of prophet Hosea (1:4=5).

3. A town of Judah, site unknown, whence David got wife Ahinoam (Josh. 15:56; 1 Sam. 25:43, 27:3).

4. Fortified town of Issachar close to Gilboa (1 K. 21:23; Josh. 19:17–18; cf. 1 Sam. 31:1–5 with 29:1 and 2 Sam. 4:2). "The blood of Jezreel," to be avenged (Hos. 1:4) relates to: Naboth, a citizen (1 K. 21:1, 13); to Jezebel (2 K. 9:10, 30–35); to Ahab's seventy sons' heads (10:1–11). Jezreel is associated with the battle of Gilboa (1 Sam. 29:1; cf. 2 Sam. 4:4), with Ish-bosheth's rule (2 Sam. 2:9), with Ahab and his son (1 K. 18:45; 2 K. 8:29). The Crusaders identified the place with what is now Zerin, in a plain, but admirable for fortification, with open view to the Jordan, there being two fountains nearby. The Valley of Jezreel is either the great plain intersecting Palestine just north of Carmel, or better that part which descends from Jezreel eastward to the Jordan (so, J. D. Davis' *Dictionary of the Bible*, 1911), notable in Gideon's day (Judg. 6:33), the whole central plain being commonly Jezreel, the ancient battlefield of the nations. Jezreelite and Jezreelitess relate to an inhabitant, and to a woman thereof (1 K. 21:1; 1 Sam. 27:3).

Jibsam (jĭb′säm) [fragrant] man of Issachar, family of Tola (1 Chr. 7:2).

Jidlaph (jĭd′lăf) [he weeps] son of Nahor and Milcah (Gen. 22:22).

Jimna or **Jimnah** (jĭm′nä) [he allots] 1. First-born of Asher (Num. 26:44).

2. A Levite, father of Kore (2 Chr. 31:14). See Gen. 46:17; 1 Chr. 7:30. Jimnites are descendants of above.

Jiphtah (jĭf′tä) [he frees] a town of Judah, in lowland (Shephelah) (Josh. 15:43).

Jiphthahel (jĭf′thä-ĕl) [God frees] a landmark valley on the boundary of Zebulun and Asher (Josh. 19:14, 27), identical with Jotopata, the modern Jefat, nine miles north by west of Nazareth.

Joab (jō′ăb) [Jehovah is father] 1. Son of Seraiah, reckoned with Judah (1 Chr. 4:13=14).

2. Second of three brothers, son of David's half-sister, Zeruiah, the other heroic warriors being Abishai and Asahel, appearing first in record at David's accession at Hebron in the war against Ish-bosheth who was crowned king after Saul's death, by Abner, Saul's captain. After a tournament at Gibeon, he was victor (2 Sam. 2:12–32), in the following general battle. Abner, pursued by swift-footed Asahel, reluctantly killed the youth, whose two brothers viewing the corpse were furious for vengeance, which was postponed when Abner called for peace (vs. 26). In Joab's absence, Abner quarreling with his chief, went over to David; but was denounced as a spy by the returning Joab, when David had sent him away in peace. With Abishai aiding, Joab murdered Abner whom he called back presumably for peaceful purpose (3:30, 39). They probably feared Abner might be made chief; they also avenged their brother's death at Abner's hands. Joab was made commander of all Israel's armies after the assault on the Jebusite stronghold of Zion: he repaired a part of the city (2 Sam. 4:8; cf. 1 Chr. 11:6, 8). Data on Joab's greatness may be found in 2 Sam. 12:26 ff., 14:30, 18:14= 16; 1 K. 11:14–17; 1 Chr. 11:6, 27:34. He conducted the great war against Ammon in person, the first campaign being against combined Syria and Ammon, after David had conquered Edom (2 Sam. 8:13–14). He held back to let David have credit for Rabbah (2 Sam. 11:1) in a second campaign, against Ammon. In the Ammonite war, Joab was involved in the shameful murder of Uriah by David's order (2 Sam. 11:1–25). He pleaded for reinstatement of Absalom, after the murder of Ammon (2 Sam. 14:1–21). Faithful but disobedient, after the final battle of Ephraim in Absalom's rebellion, he slew the latter (2 Sam. 18:2, 11–15). In the rebellion under

Sheba, with his own guard and the mighty men under Abishai, he entered the fray, and in the heat of the pursuit he encountered Amasa to whom David had transferred command, and treacherously killed him, he and Abishai putting down the rebellion (2 Sam. 20:1–22). He remonstrated against David's numbering the people and purposely made omission (2 Sam. 24:1–9; 1 Chr. 21:1–6). The faithful leader defected when Adonijah sought kingship (1 K. 1:7), but deserted when Solomon was proclaimed king (vss. 28–49), and fled to take hold of the horns of the altar at Gibeon, but was there slain by Benaiah, in harmony with David's deathbed wish that he be brought to justice for the murders of Abner and Amasa (2:5–6, 28–34).

3. Head of a family, most numerous of all who returned with Zerubbabel (Ezra 2:6, 8:9).

Joah (jō′ä) [Jehovah is brother] 1. Asaph's son, recorder under Hezekiah (2 K. 18:18, 26; Isa. 36:3, 11, 22).

2. A Gershonite Levite, perhaps the one assisting in Hezekiah's reformation (1 Chr. 6:21).

3. Third son of Obed-edom, and doorkeeper of David (1 Chr. 26:4).

4. A Gershonite (2 Chr. 29:12).

5. Son of Joahaz and annalist to Josiah (2 Chr. 34:8).

Joahaz (jō′ä-hăz) [Jehovah lays hold of] father of Josiah's recorder (2 Chr. 34:8).

Joanna (jō-ăn′nä) [Jehovah is gracious] ancestor of Christ of ca. 500 B.C. (Lk. 3:27, here Joanan). Herod's steward's wife (Lk. 8:3, 24:10).

Joash or **Jehoash** (jō′ăsh) [Jehovah is strong] 1. Father of Gideon (Judg. 5:11, 29–31).

2. Son of Ahab (1 K. 22:26; 2 Chr. 18:25).

3. Son of Ahaziah king of Judah who alone escaped the murderous hand of Athaliah, hidden for six years in temple chambers, and at age seven made king to free the land from tyranny and idolatries of Athaliah (2 K. 11:1–20; 2 Chr. 23:10–21). During the earlier years under the wise council of the high priest Jehoiada, all went very well, although there was religious corruption (2 K. 12:1–16); but after the priest's death, king and people set up idols; and when Zechariah son of Jehoiada denounced them, he was stoned to death in a riot, the king ordering it (2 Chr. 24:15–22; Mt. 23:35). Then Hazael of Syria menaced Jerusalem being bought off by the temple treasury contents. Joash sore diseased, his son Amaziah ruled; and it seems that in three years, his servants slew

him in bed for the murder of Zechariah (2 K. 12:20). Joash reigned forty years in the latter part of the ninth century B.C.

4. Israel's king, son of Jehoahaz, contemporary in part with the foregoing (2 K. 14:1; cf. 12:1, 13:10). Although his kingdom suffered devastation from Syria's kings, he continued the idolatrous worship at Dan and Bethel, but held Elisha the prophet in respect. The dying prophet rebuked the king for smiting, on the ground at his command, only three times, with arrows, symbolizing victories over the Syrians (2 K. 13:14–25). Second Chr. 25 presents the interesting story that climaxed in Joash's victory over Judah at Beth-shemesh, and his plundering Jerusalem.

5. A man of Judah, father of Shelah (1 Chr. 4:22).

6. A Benjaminite, family of Becher (1 Chr. 7:8).

7. A Benjaminite; came to David at Ziklag (1 Chr. 12:3).

8. An officer over David's oil-cellars (1 Chr. 27:28). NOTE: 6 and 8 seem to have a different meaning: "Jehovah hastens (to help)," being from another root.

Joatham same as **Jotham** (Mt. 1:9).

Job third son of Issachar (Gen. 46:13); same as Jashub, "he returns" (1 Chr. 7:1).

Job (jōb) [one persecuted, according to Gesenius; but others: one characterized by hostility; but Ewald, Hitzig, Cheyne: one ever turning to God] an OT saint of the land of Uz (1:1), location uncertain: (1) North Mesopotamia (Gen. 10:23); (2) Damascus area (Josephus); (3) Edom (Gen. 36:28; Lam. 4:21). Outside the book, Job is first noted in Ezekiel (14:14, 16, 20; also James 5:11). There is no reason to doubt that he is an historical personage, of remarkable experiences described with some poetic license, the book being either really historical, or religious fiction, or a composition based upon facts. Luther suggested a generally received theory: "I look upon the book of Job as a true history, yet I do not believe that all took place just as it is written, but that an ingenious, pious, and learned man brought it into its present form." Here then is a "poetic book with account of the sufferings of Job, of the argument carried on between him and his friends concerning the reasons for his troubles, and of the solution of the problem" (J. D. Davis, *Dictionary of the Bible*, 1911).

Writership is indeterminable. The general setting indicates the patriarchal period—manners, customs, general coloring, a time rather certainly before Moses, antecedent to the giving of the Law. And whereas there is nothing necessarily incompatible with the Mosaic age as to the time of composition, yet humanly speaking, the highly systematic development of the plot, and the philosophic tone of thought, evidence a mental cultivation hardly likely before Solomon's time; and certain grammatical constructions, say in the prologue, are thought to point to more recent revision. On this, who can say? But the book seems in general to be a unity, despite attacks on the prologue, and on ch. 27, and the last two chs. of the Almighty's address, and the speech of Elihu—all of which strictures may be safely rejected.

Themes. The opening shows Job to be very prosperous, with flocks, herds, servants, and a numerous family, blameless in life's relations, "perfect" (not sinless). In the world of spirits where the mysteries of existence are brought to light, the accusing angel, Satan, challenges: "Doth Job fear God for naught?" Here is the problem which the book is intended to discuss and solve. Can goodness exist regardless of reward? Can the fear of God be retained by one from whom "every inducement to selfishness is taken away"? The accuser is permitted to make trial. But the loss of possessions, family, and health, still leave Job's faith triumphant; and he is finally restored to more than former prosperity. Between the introduction and conclusion there are seen three main divisions, each susceptible of division into three minor parts. Part I: the first affliction—loss of property and family; the second—the attack on his person; and the third presents the three consolatory friends. Part II: the argument between Job and his friends, each speaking three times (except the third, twice), and Job replying to each. Part III: Elihu speaks; Jehovah speaks; Job speaks. Then, the epilogue.

Discussions and Results (extending with intervals over several days): (1) The first cycle (chs. 3–14): The friends' theory of divine government rests upon an exact and uniform correlation between sin and punishment (4:6–11; and throughout). Suffering is penal, leading to destruction for those who radically oppose God, unsubmissive to his treatment. Repentance, confession, return, amendment may expect peace and even prosperity (5:17–27). Suffering always points to special sin; the sufferer's attitude shows the true relation between him and God. Such principles are applied to the case of Job, the character of the three friends being clearly developed. To understand the arguments and position of Job, note that the direct object of trial is to see if he would deny God: his true integrity is asserted by God himself. He denied the horse-and-cart theory of

sin and punishment; he sees clearly one point: all is in God's hands (12:9–25), he being ignorant of underlying principles; and the friends are equally uninformed. But God is just: Job takes the one course open: supplication that God will give fair trial (13:18–28). Believing that all hope connected with this world ceases with death, he prays for the grave, to be reserved till God's trial of his cause and the revelation of himself in love (14:13, 15). (2) The second cycle (chs. 15–21): Unto the entire overthrow of Job's position, comes a more resolute, elaborate attempt to vindicate the theory of retributive justice. Eliphaz, as usual, lays down the basis, not hesitating to impute to Job the worst crimes (ch. 15). Bildad presses the ungodliness angle, charging that Job's special evils are peculiar penalties for one without God (ch. 17). Zophar accounting for Job's present calamities, pictures still greater ills (ch. 20). Then Job, recognizing the hand of God, but rejecting the ungodliness charge, insists he has never forsaken his Maker, nor ceased to pray (16:7–16; and 19:6–20). He pleads that the sufferings of the nonexempt righteous are divinely observed with view to future and perfect show of divine justice. Stung by the harsh bigotry of his friends, Job cites the plain fact that throughout life the ungodly, the atheistic—indeed those guilty of the crimes imputed to him, by conjecture—frequently enjoy abundant prosperity (ch. 21). (3) The third cycle (chs. 22–31): Eliphaz makes his last effort (ch. 22): He argues that the crimes were committed as charged against Job, because his punishment shows that he had succumbed to their temptations. Bildad merely adds reflections on the incomparable majesty of God and nothingness of man, Zophar being dumb, silenced. In his last rebuttals, Job neither budges nor adduces new thought, stating with brilliant force and eloquence, points already established (ch. 26). He describes beyond his opponents, the proper destruction pertinent to hypocrites (ch. 27), grandly describes wisdom (ch. 28), and concludes with a beautiful survey of his former life, in contrast to his present misery, presenting full vindication of his character from all charges and insinuations (chs. 29–31). (4) Part the fourth (chs. 32–37): Elihu, the young man, of a collateral branch of Abraham's line, with the philosophical view, takes up omitted points or the imperfectly developed, ending the discussion in which both parties had partially failed hitherto. He breaks his indignant silence with address to all, especially to Job. Neither has Job been convicted nor God vindicated. Job's assumption of innocence and arraignment of justice are due to neglect of one main object of all suffering: God *speaks* to man by chastisement, no charge of special guilt being involved. Further since God is the only source of justice, the very idea of it, being derived from his governance of the universe, any charge of injustice against God means contradiction in terms (34:10–17). Job being silent, Elihu shows that the Almightiness of God is not (so it seems to Job) associated with any contempt or neglect of his creatures. Then forcibly are stressed lessons from God's goodness and greatness in creation (ch. 36), a violent thunderstorm arising. Despite weighty truths and theories about the objects and uses of affliction, the mystery is not yet cleared up. Hence from the storm, the Theophany: God speaks. With grandeur of language he reproves and silences the murmurs of Job, not condescending to argue. The speculative questions are unnoticed; but God's absolute power is illustrated by his marvelously beautiful and comprehensive survey of creation's glory and all-embracing providence, by reference to phenomena of the animal kingdom. In a second address the charge of injustice implies the accuser more competent than God to rule the universe. Job's complete submission terminates the trial. In a rebuke to the opponents, Job's integrity is distinctly recognized, they being condemned for untruth, but pardoned through Job's intercession. Symbolizing the ultimate compensation for all earthly sufferings, comes the restoration of Job's external prosperity, out of God's personal manifestation. One great object of the book, distinctly intimated in the beginning and confirmed in the conclusion, is to show the effects of calamity in its worst forms upon a truly righteous spirit.

Jobab (jō'băb) [shouting, trumpet-call, a desert] 1. An Arabian tribe from Joktan (Gen. 10:29).

2. A king of Edom (Gen. 36:33).

3. A king of Madon, defeated at Merom by Joshua (Josh. 11:1, 12:19).

4 and 5. Two Benjaminites (1 Chr. 8:9, 18).

Jochebed (jŏk'ĕ-bĕd) [Jehovah is glory] a daughter of Levi, wife and aunt of Amram, and mother of Moses and Aaron (Ex. 2:1, 6:20; Num. 26:59). Some say the ancestress of the above, Hebrew genealogies not always being clear.

Jod (yōdh) tenth letter of the Hebrew alphabet. The letter "Y" represents "J" also, as in Jeconiah. See, "Not one jot (yodh) or one tittle (the least part of a letter, in Hebrew),"

in Mt. 5:18. Ps. 119, sect. 10, has this letter at the head of each verse thereof.

Joed (jō'ĕd) [Jehovah is witness] a Benjaminite (Neh. 11:7).

Joel (jō'ĕl) [Jehovah is God] 1. Eldest son of Samuel the prophet and father of Heman the singer (1 Sam. 8:2; 1 Chr. 6:33, 15:17; see 6:28).

2. A Kohathite Levite, ancestor of Samuel (1 Chr. 6:36; cf. 34. Probably not identical with Shaul of vs. 24, but of the collateral line, from Tahath. Some say Shaul is a corruption of Joel).

3. A Gershonite Levite, with 130 brethren helped bring the ark from the house of Obed-edom to the city of David; apparently son of Ladan, and treasurer-guardian (1 Chr. 15:7, 11–12, 23:8, 26:21–22).

4. A chief of Issachar (1 Chr. 7:3).

5. Valiant man of David and brother to Nathan (1 Chr. 11:38).

6. Son of Pedaiah and ruler of Western Manasseh in David's time (1 Chr. 27:20).

7. A chief of Gadites in Bashan, prior to reigns of Jotham of Judah, and Jeroboam II of Israel (1 Chr. 5:12, cf. vs. 17).

8. A Reubenite, probably with much cattle in Gilead (1 Chr. 5:4, 8–9).

9. A Kohathite Levite, aiding Hezekiah's temple cleansing (2 Chr. 29:12).

10. A Simeonite prince, seizing land in Gedor (1 Chr. 4:35–43).

11. Son of Nebo, led by Ezra to put away his foreign wife (Ezra 10:43).

12. A Benjaminite, overseer under Nehemiah (Neh. 11:9).

13. Son of Pethuel, and writer of the second of the minor prophets (Joel 1:1); history unknown. Presumably lived in Judea, the date of the book probably in Uzziah's time, certainly before Ahaz: he cites earlier prophecy (2:32), suggesting Isa. 4:2–3 (note verbal agreement with Obad. 17); the scattering of Israel and the Captivity (3:1, 2), are prophetic, as in Deut. 28; Hos. 6:11; Mic. 3:12, 4:10; Zion exists and the temple still stands (1:14, 2:1, 15, 17); no judgment against Assyria or Babylon, but only against Tyre, Philistia, Egypt, etc. (3:4, 19); no reference to Greeks as present and hostile to Judah, but as afar off (3:1–8). Joel 3:10 seems antecedent to Isa. 2:4. We rather hold Joel the earliest "prophetic quarry"; "the latest conglomerate," is the alternative. Joel gives grand outline of the terrible scene more detailed in later prophets, the scope being the whole Day of the Lord. The related proximate event was twofold: drought and locusts (1:4–12, 17–20), the latter being, as older commen-

tators, figurative of Israel's foes, or more likely actual locusts, looking like the horsehead and comparable to an army in devastation—a type of the dreadful day coming, to which the prophet looks, and which is fulfilled in judgment and in grace, for God's own and for the nations, looking to the final kingdom of the Lord Christ (see Acts 2).

Contents. (1) The present distress: mourn, repent, cry to God (1:2–14). (2) Explanation: the day is at hand, destruction (1:15, 2:1–11); even now repentance may avail (vss. 12=17). (3) Results of repentance: God, jealous for his land, is to give plenty in compensation, nor will allow Israel to be put again to shame (18:27). (4) The deliverance, the herald of the "afterward," when rain for earthly abundance, will be followed by the Spirit upon all flesh. The sun darkened (God's wrath), at the terrible day of 3:14–17; safety of all who call (2:28–32). In those days, captivity being over, enemies come to judgment, one picture presenting successive judgments, with the final one, universal, culminating in the establishment of Zion forever (3:1–21).

Joelah (jō-ē′lä) [let him help?] son of Jeroham of Gedor, joined David at Ziklag (1 Chr. 12:7).

Joezer (jō-ē′zēr) [Jehovah is help] a Korahite captain of David (1 Chr. 12:6).

Jogbehah (jŏg-bē′hä) [lofty] a town of Gad east of Jordan (Num. 32:35).

Jogli (jŏg′lī) [led into exile] a Danite chief and father of Bukki (Num. 34:22).

Joha (jō′hä) [Jehovah is living?] 1. A Benjaminite son of Beriah (1 Chr. 8:16).

2. A Tizite, mighty man of David (1 Chr. 11:45).

Johanan (jō-hăn′ăn) [Jehovah is gracious] 1. A Benjaminite with David at Ziklag (1 Chr. 12:4).

2. The eighth of the joining Gadites, a captain of David's army (1 Chr. 12:12, 14).

3. A member of the high-priestly line, of ca. 800 B.C. (1 Chr. 6:10).

4. An Ephraimite (2 Chr. 28:12).

5. The short-lived son of King Josiah (1 Chr. 3:15).

6. A captain, son of Kareah, submissive to Gedaliah, Nebuchadnezzar's appointee as governor, who when the latter heedless of Johanan's warning, was murdered, led the avenging forces (2 K. 25:22–23; Jer. 40:8–9, 11–15), and later counseled and carried out removal of the Jewish remnant to Egypt contrary to Jeremiah's advice (41:16–43:13).

7. A son of Elioenai (1 Chr. 3:24).

8. A son of Hakkatan, who with 110 males

came with Ezra from Babylon (Ezra 8:12).

9. Son of Eliashib, one of the chief Levites (Neh. 12:23; Ezek. 10:6).

10. Son-in-law of Meshullam (Neh. 6:18).

11. A high priest, possibly the grandson of Eliashib (Neh. 12:22; cf. vs. 11, where by error, it appears, Johanan occurs; but note that this man may be the same as 9 above: the text is not clear).

John (Heb. *Yohanan,* Jehovah is gracious) 1. *John the Baptist.* Forerunner of the Lord, to prepare his way; of the priestly race by both parents, Zechariah and Elizabeth being descendants of Aaron (Lk. 1:5, 36); of the Judean hill country, perhaps Hebron (vs. 39). To the father, performing official duties, the angel Gabriel appeared announcing a son, his name, training, equipment, and office (Lk. 1:8–17), Zechariah being smitten dumb for unbelief. The boy was born 5 B.C., the mother of our Lord being with Elizabeth for three months before the event, both having retired to the hill country (Lk. 1:24, 36–41). After circumcision on the eighth day (Lev. 12:3), when his mother confirmed the name John, and the father's tongue was loosed, a single verse tells all we know of the next thirty years (Lk. 1:80). His supernatural birth, his ascetic life, his reputation for sanctity, and the general expectation of a great appearance were enough to attract crowds to him from every quarter, his dress and food being contributory to the solemn effect. It was likely the sabbatical year A.D. 26, when release from labor allowed large attendance on the preaching, the sum of which was repentance, not legal but internal, heart-deep (Mt. 3:1–12; Mk. 1:1–8; Lk. 3:1–15). John's baptism spoke of cleansing from sin, symbolized by water; but he pointed his followers to One who coming after him, would baptize with the Holy Ghost and fire (Mt. 3:5–12). John denied that he was Elijah in person (Jn. 1:21); he quoted Isa. 40:3; but he came in the spirit and power of Elijah (Mal. 4:5–6; with Lk. 1:17); he was the preparing messenger (Mal. 3:1; with Mk. 1:2); and the Lord referred such words to John (Mt. 11:10–14, 17:12–13). When the Lord presented himself as a candidate for baptism, John must have known him, confirmation being given when the Holy Ghost descended (Mt. 3:13–17; but see Jn. 1:31=34). Popular as was John, his ministry was brief; toward the close of 27 or early in 28, having faithfully reproved Herod for adultery, he was imprisoned (Lk. 3:19–20), his ministry after the Lord's baptism, being to witness to the Savior and to instruct his own disciples (Jn. 3:23, 4:1; Acts 19:3; Mt. 9:14; Lk. 5:33,

11:1). In the castle of Machaerus, on the eastern shore of the Dead Sea, perplexed and impatient and feeling forgotten, John sent word to the Lord inquiring as to his Messiahship. The Lord simply pointed to his works, and then gave great praise to John (Mt. 11:2–15). Herod's rash vow to the seductive Salome, daughter of the adulteress Herodias, brought decapitation to the great John, whose body was then buried by his disciples, remembering his testimony and becoming thereafter, disciples of the Lord (Mt. 14:3–12; Mk. 6:16–29; Lk. 3:19–20).

2. Father of the apostle Peter, called commonly Jona (Mt. 16:17).

3. *John the Apostle.* Of the early life, little is known, as also of his last days. Birthdate is unknown. He was the son of Zebedee, and brother of James the martyr under Herod Agrippa I (Mt. 4:21; Acts 12:1–2). Inference is reasonable that he was younger than James, and that his mother was Salome, sister to the mother of the Lord, the two sons aiding the father, a master fisherman on Galilee (Mt. 4:21, 10:2, 17:1; but cf. Lk. 9:28; Mt. 27:56; Mk. 15:40, 16:1). The family seems to have been in fairly comfortable circumstances (Mk. 1:20; Lk. 8:3; Jn. 19:27). The ordinary fisher's life was interrupted by news of a prophet to whom all classes flocked, including Zebedee's sons and their friends. As the unnamed disciple (Jn. 1:37–40), the interview with the Lord brought a devotion that extended throughout his whole life. John, apparently, and with others, went with the new teacher to Galilee (Jn. 1:43), to Cana, Capernaum, Jerusalem, through Samaria, returning, to former occupations (Lk. 5:10). Later, John and James were "called" (Mt. 4:21–22), and then still later, were appointed apostles (Mt. 10:2). John with Peter and James were with the Lord, when no others were—in Jairus' house (Mk. 5:37), at the transfiguration (Mt. 17:1), when destruction of Jerusalem was forewarned (Mk. 13:2; Andrew being with them also, here), and in the hour of agony in Gethsemane (Mt. 26:37). John was the "beloved disciple," but not effeminate; he and his brother were called "sons of thunder" ("Boanerges", Mk. 3:17), and showed some rather unlovely traits (Lk. 9:49, 52–56); but chastened by grace, developed elements of strength and beauty in character (Mt. 20:20–24; Jn. 18:16, 19, 28, 19:26–27); and he was to be son to the mother left desolate. To John, with Peter, come the first tidings of the empty sepulcher (Jn. 20:2, 4–6). With others, he saw the risen Christ (Lk. 24:33–43; Jn. 20:19–30; 1 Cor.

15:5), and with them he went to Galilee according to instructions, and again saw the Lord (Mt. 26:32, 28:10, 16; Jn. 21:1–7). The notion got abroad that he was not to die (Jn. 21:22). Following the ascension, he and the other ten were for some time in the Upper Room in Jerusalem (Acts 1:13); and after Pentecost, he became Peter's colleague in active missionary work (3:1), both being imprisoned (4:19); both went to Samaria to aid in Philip's work—what a change from Mk. 3:17! John remained in Jerusalem when persecution shortly assailed the church, and was still a pillar of strength when Paul came, after his first journey (15:6; Gal. 2:9). Little is known of this period, to fill in the gap between the apostle of Jerusalem and the bishop of Ephesus. There is no indication that John was in Jerusalem when Paul last came (Acts 21). Five NT books are ascribed to John: the Fourth Gospel, three epistles, the book of Revelation. Tradition is rife and apparently worthless. He is supposed to have ministered in Ephesus; and the seven churches enjoyed his care (Rev. 1:11). Probably in 95, an exile in Patmos (Rev. 1:9), he penned Revelation. At the accession of Nerva, he is said to have returned to Ephesus—Polycarp, Papias, and Ignatius being his pupils; and Polycarp's disciple, Irenaeus, says that John lived in Ephesus until death under Trajan.

John, Gospel of both internal and external considerations support the universal belief of the early church that the apostle John is the writer, his name not mentioned in it, as is true of the others. Explicit statement (21:24), use of the first person (1:14), many minute data (1:37, 2:11, 17, 4:27, 54, 9:2, 11:8–16, 12:4–6, 13:23–26, 18:15, 19:26, 20:8), all go to show apostolic origin. The "disciple whom Jesus loved" (13:23, 19:26, 20:2), is said to be the writer (21:24). Hebraistic character of style in writing Greek, points to Jewish writership. More personal details than any, and intimate acquaintance with geography, history, customs (e.g., 1:21, 28, 46, 2:6, 3:23, 5:2–3, 7:40–52), combined with the other above features, give evidence hardly less impressive than explicit statement in the book, which is in fact practically noted in 21:24. External evidence, sufficient in itself, is that of Irenaeus (b. 115–125), bishop of Lyons in the latter part of the second century, a disciple of Polycarp who in turn was a disciple of John, his explicit word being that John wrote this gospel in Ephesus after the others had been issued. And a line of testimony from the close of the apostolic age confirms this. The Ignatian Epistles show this gospel to be familiar and authoritative in Asia Minor in the second century. Justin (A.D. 150) freely quotes it, classing it with the gospels written by the apostles and companions. The apocryphal Gospel of Peter shows that the Fourth Gospel with the other three, was its basis. Tatian's Diatessaron (170), a harmony of the gospels used in the churches, includes John. The Syriac Gospel MS, discovered by Mrs. Agnes Smith Lewis, proves that the Syrian church in the second century, approved our four gospels. And the earliest heretics of the same century, accepted the Fourth Gospel as authentic. The evidence points to Asia Minor as the place of origin, and in the latter quarter of the first century. Thus, abounding evidence confirms belief that the Fourth Gospel was written by John, being received by the church as authoritative from the beginning of the post-apostolic age. The date: 78–90; the place: Ephesus.

OUTLINE (R. C. McQuicklin, 1931): I. The sublime preview of the gospel: the Word made flesh, 1:1–18. II. Revelation to the world, 1:19–12:50: (1) the revelation which awakened faith—1:19–4:54; (2) the revelation facing unbelief and opposition—chs. 5–12. III. The revelation to his disciples, chs. 13–20: (1) the revelation of his love and conquering life in *word*—chs. 13–17; (2) in *deed*—chs. 18–20. IV. Epilogue, ch. 21. (Confirmation of John's authority lies in added historical facts, and the testimony of the Ephesian elders.) This gospel shows that the human Jesus is the Eternal Son of God, who by his person, teaching, and redeeming work has revealed God and secured eternal life for those who receive him (20:31).

John, the Epistles of *The First Epistle* is abundantly certified as to writership both externally and internally. No voice in antiquity opposes John; confirmatory are Polycarp, Papias, Irenaeus, Origen, Clement of Alexandria, Tertullian, Cyprian. It and the gospel were sent to the same churches, and may have gone together. The internal evidence is equally strong: readers' acquaintance with the gospel is assumed; many stylistic parallels occur; doctrine is the same. The epistle seeks to apply the truth whose historical revelation the gospel records. From Ephesus to the churches of Asia, at about the same time as the gospel, the object seems not mainly to oppose errors of the Docetae, or Gnostics, or Nicolaitans, or Cerinthians, or of the Judaizers, but to show that eternal life is fellowship with God through Jesus Christ. (1) The introduction—the purpose, 1:1–4. (2) The conditions of fellowship, 1:5–2:29. (3) The outcome of fellowship, 3:1–5:12. (4) Summary of purpose and recita-

tion of facts on which eternal life is based, 5:13–21. (Two verses seem to lack desirable manuscript authority, and are therefore held by the scholars as not genuine: 2:23 and 5:7).

The Second Epistle. Johannine writership seems well proved by remarkable coincidences in language and thought with 1 John. Eusebius puts the second and third epistles in the class of "disputed" books; but most ancient testimony ascribes the first epistle to John, Irenaeus e.g., quoting 2 Jn. 10–11, as coming from John the disciple of the Lord. The "elect lady" may refer to a church, although *kuria* is Greek for lady. "Walking in the truth" is the subject, the writer expressing joy at the Christian life displayed, and warning against false teachers.

The Third Epistle. This epistle is so markedly like the first and second in style and thought, that there is no reason to doubt that they are from the same hand. Loyalty to the truth stands out, the addressee, Gaius, perhaps a member of the church at Pergamum, being commended for loyalty to the truth and for hospitality. The letter is to endorse the exemplary Demetrius and to warn against false teaching of Diotrephes. The Epistles of James, Peter, and Jude, together with those of John (second and third being attached to the first, though addressed to particular receivers) are called "general" because addressed to large or to many communities.

Joiada (joi'ä-dä) [Jehovah hath known] a high priest, with whom Nehemiah dealt (Neh. 12:10, 13:28).

Joiakim (joi'ä-kĭm) [Jehovah establishes] a high priest (Neh. 12:10).

Joiarib (joi'ä-rĭb) [Jehovah defends] 1. A layman with Ezra (8:16).

2. A chief of the priests with Zerubbabel (Neh. 12:6, 9).

3. A man of Judah (Neh. 11:5).

Jokdeam (jŏk'dē-ăm) [possessed by people?] Judean town, site unknown (Josh. 15:56).

Jokim (jō'kĭm) [Jehovah sets up] a man of Judah, family of Shelah (1 Chr. 4:22).

Jokmeam (jŏk'mē-ăm) [people brought together] a town of Ephraim (1 Chr. 6:68) in Jordan valley, eastern border; spelled differently in 1 K. 4:12; perhaps same as Kibzeam (Josh. 21:22).

Jokneam (jŏk'nē-ăm) [allowed to possess people] a town near Mount Carmel, commanding the pass from west Esdraelon to the southerly plain (Josh. 12:22, 19:11); given to Merarite Levites (21:34).

Jokshan (jŏk'shăn) [fowler?] a son, and tribe, from Abraham by Keturah (Gen. 25:1–3).

Joktan (jŏk'tăn) [small] a person, and tribe,

from Shem through Eber, from whom thirteen tribes of Arabia sprang; according to Moslems —Kahtan (Gen. 10:25, 29; 1 Chr. 1:19, 23).

Joktheel (jŏk'thē-ĕl) [perhaps subjection to God] 1. A village of lowland Judah (Josh. 15:38).

2. Judah's king Amaziah's name for the conquered Sela, now Petra (2 K. 14:7; 2 Chr. 25:11–13).

Jona (jō'nà) [dove] father to Peter, addressed as Simon Bar-jona (Jn. 1:42; Mt. 16:17).

Jonadab (jŏn'ā-dăb) [Jehovah is bounteous] 1. Son of David's brother, who was "very subtil" (2 Sam. 13:3, 5–6; 32–33).

2. A son of Rechab (Jer. 35; cf. 1 Chr. 2:55; 2 K. 10:15, 23).

Jonah, Jona, or **Jonas** prophet, son of Amittai and citizen of Gath-hepher in Galilee, of Zebulun. He lived after Jehu's reign, when Israel's losses began (2 K. 10:32): he certainly preached toward the close of the reign of Jeroboam II (2 K. 14:25; Jonah 1:1). Date: ca. 780, the earliest save Joel. Charles Reade, novelist, says: "Jonah is the most beautiful book ever written in so small a compass—1328 English words." Called the storm center of OT criticism, the sad fact is that "the most evangelistic book in the OT is made light of by allusion to a fish." In the *Princeton Review* of Oct. 2, 1927, is the story of James Bartlett swallowed by a sperm whale, which his friends killed, and rescued him alive. Though not so long in the fish as Jonah, he lived; his skin was dead white thereafter. (Incidentally, the Bible does not speak of a "whale.")

Analysis: (1) The prophet's first commission and disobedience, ch. 1. (2) Jonah's prayer, ch. 2. (3) Second commission and obedience, ch. 3. (4) Dialogue: the prophet and Jehovah. The subject may be called: "The wideness of God's mercy." The key, 4:2, 10–11; cf. Acts 11:18, and the Great Commission, Mt. 28:19–20. The church holds to historicity: (1) Simplicity of language; written as a plain narrative. (2) The prophet is historical (2 K. 14:25). He seems to have written the book as a frank and humiliating confession. (3) The Lord's endorsement: Mt. 12:39–41, 16:4; Lk. 11:29–32. *The Purpose* is to give the selfish nation a new conception of God and of their own sin. The book is the first prophetic announcement of the fulfillment of the promise made to Abraham (Gen. 12; Acts 3:25). It has much supernatural. The signal "miracle" is not Jonah's being swallowed, but the repentance of the great Nineveh (even though transient). It may readily be supposed that the men who saw him disgorged, went with him to the city, and there vouched for the truth of his preaching, giving certification of the divine judgment and deliverance of his prophet, which could account for the wholesale repentance, in a day of superstition and fear. The transferred lessons, which may be looked upon as typical: (1) Nineveh's repentance *vs.* Israel's refusal (Mt. 12:41); (2) Jonah, an Israelite preaching to Gentiles, paralleled in our obligation to bring others to God; (3) Jonah of Israel, fleeing, but chastened and obedient—so Israel evicted, but repentant, to return in remnant to fulfil his mission to the world (Isa. 2:2–4, 42:1–4, 49:1–13); (4) Jonah into the depths but brought up alive: the representative Israelite and perfect Servant of the Lord (Mt. 12:40).

The story has been variously regarded as myth, legend, parable, history. The allegorical view which sees in every feature some deep significance (as the sea picturing the raging nations), is to be rejected: we assume the historical view to be the correct one.

Jonam or **Jonan** (jō'năm) [Jehovah is gracious] ancestor of Christ (Lk. 3:30).

Jonathan (jŏn'ā-thăn) [Jehovah gave] 1. A Levite, descendant of Gershon (Judg. 18:30), supposedly had left Bethlehem-judah, and passing through Ephraim, was hired by Micah (17:7–13). The Danites, northward bound, stole Micah's image and hired his mercenary priest with promise that he would be dignitary to a whole tribe (Judg. 18). Jonathan thus became the first of a line of priests in connection with the stolen idol while the tabernacle was at Shiloh, till Captivity (Judg. 18:3–6, 14–31). Interesting to relate, to avoid dishonor to Moses, the reading in vs. 30 is Manasseh, an elevated letter "n" being inserted in the text.

2. Eldest son of Saul (1 Sam. 14:49; cf. 20:31). He first appears some time after his father's accession (13:2). The exploit at Michmash signalizes him, though but for the people he might have lost his life (14:1–46). When David, rather unknown, won victory over Goliath, the unselfish Jonathan developed warm friendship even to the jeopardy of succession to his father (chs. 18–20), which lasted till death. After the final meeting of the two friends, during Saul's pursuit of David, we learn no more of Jonathan till his tragic end along with two brothers and his father at the battle of Gilboa (1 Sam. 23:16–18, 31:2, 8). The news occasioned the celebrated elegy of David. Second Sam. 21:12–14 tell of the final resting place.

3. The gifted counsellor and warrior (1 Chr. 27:32; 2 Sam. 21:21), uncle, or in Hebrew

usage, possibly the nephew, of David (1 Chr. 20:7).

4. Son of high priest Abiathar, informant for David in Absalom's rebellion; also messenger to the usurper Adonijah, at the coronation of Solomon (2 Sam. 15:36, 17:15-22; 1 K. 1:41-49); the last known descendant of Eli.

5. Mighty man of David (1 Chr. 11:34; cf. 2 Sam. 23:11).

6. An official under David (1 Chr. 27:25).

7. Possibly another Jonathan different from 3 above, for 2 Sam. 21:21-22 call him son of David's brother, Shimeah.

8. Son of Kereah; escaped in the final Chaldaean assault on Jerusalem, and resorted to Gedaliah at Mizpeh (Jer. 40:8). Perhaps the name accidentally dropped out of the corresponding 2 Kings (25:23) account.

9. Jeremiah was imprisoned in this scribe's house (37:15, 20).

10. A son of Jada (1 Chr. 2:32).

11. A descendant of Adin (Ezra 8:6).

12. Opponent of Ezra's foray against foreign wives (Ezra 10:15).

13. A Levite, Asaphite lineage (Neh. 12:35; cf. 11:15, 17).

14. A priest, time of high priest Joiakim (Neh. 12:14).

15. High priest, son of Joiada (Neh. 11:22).

Jonath elim rehokim (jō'năth-ē'lĭm-rē-hō'kĭm) [dove of the distant terebinths] some say a melody; others, a musical instrument; but most likely this title, which really belongs to the end of the preceding psalm (see Hab. 3, first and last vss.), was given by the precentor in commemoration of David's exile when he sojourned with Achish. It should be remembered that in the original there were no divisions between verses and between psalms; and so very easily, misinterpretations occurred. Title to Ps. 56.

Joppa (jŏp'pà) [from the Greek, *beauty*] in Josh. 19:46, Japho. A town on southwest coast of Palestine, and port for Jerusalem, assigned to Dan. Lebanon wood was floated down from Tyre for Solomon's temple (2 Chr. 2:16); again at the rebuilding of the temple (Ezra 3:7, 8). Jonah (1:3) embarked here for Tarshish to escape Jehovah. Tabitha lived here, raised from the dead by Peter (Acts 9:36-42). To Joppa Cornelius' servants came to invite Peter (ch. 10). The harbor is dangerous. After its last Christian occupation under St. Louis, in the thirteenth century, it fell to the Turks. It manufactures soap; there are beautiful fruit gardens, oranges especially being the finest. Arab "Yafa," is the British "Jaffa," i.e., Joppa.

Jorah (jō'rä) [autumnal rain] ancestor of a family, with Ezra returning from Babylon (2:18). In Neh. 7:24, Hariph.

Jorai (jō'rī) [Jehovah teaches] a Gadite in Gilead (1 Chr. 5:13).

Joram (jō'răm) [Jehovah is high] also Jehoram.

1. A son of Toi, king of Hamath (2 Sam. 8:10); called (1 Chr. 18:10) Hadoram.

2. A Levite from Eliezer's line (1 Chr. 26:25; cf. 23:15, 17).

3. Son of Ahab, king of Israel, who became king when his brother Ahaziah died, in middle of ninth century. To recover Moab from Mesha, its king, he enlisted Jehoshaphat of Judah and the Edomite ruler for aides, and conquered temporarily, by the help of Elisha, and through a ruse (2 K. 3:1-27). Likely king when Naaman was cured of his leprosy (5:1-27; see also 6:8-23, 24-31, 9:14-26). With Joram the dynasty of Omri ceased and that of Jehu began.

4. One of the priests sent by Jehoshaphat to instruct the people (2 Chr. 17:8).

5. Son of Jehoshaphat, associated with his father for several years; and in the fifth year of Jehoram of Israel, the kingship fell to him alone (2 K. 8:16; cf. 1:17, 3:1; also 2 Chr. 21:1-4; 2 K. 8:20-22; 2 Chr. 21:8-10, 16-19, 22:1; 2 K. 9:29, with 8:25-26; 2 Chr. 21:12-22:1).

Jordan (jôr'dăn) [descender] this is the world's unique river, both by nature and by history. The slope of Anti-Lebanon is alive with bursting fountains and gushing streams, which through the swamp above Lake Huleh, contribute water to the Jordan; but among the sometimes alleged four sources of the river, there are particularly two: Tell el-Kadi (supposedly Dan), with two great streams gushing out from a mount sixty feet above the plain (before the latter rises to Mount Hermon), forming the Leddan River; and Paneas (Baneas to the Arabs who do not sound the letter "p"), where from a high limestone iron-reddened cliff, there "bursts and bubbles along a line of thirty feet, a full-born river," a place impressive for worship from time immemorial. The town was later embellished by Philip the tetrarch, and called Caesarea (added "Philippi," to distinguish it from his father's Caesarea on the seacoast). It was to this place that our Lord withdrew for retreat and from which he steadfastly set his face to go to Jerusalem (Lk. 9:51). As the crow flies, the river, from Banias to the Dead Sea is 104 miles, being at Banias, 1000 feet above sea level; at Huleh, twelve miles distant, only seven feet above sea level; at Lake Galilee, ten miles more, it is 682 feet below sea level; while at the entrance of the

Dead Sea, sixty-five miles in direct line, it is 1292 feet below sea level. "In a space of sixty miles of latitude" between the latter two seas (Lieutenant Lynch of the American Navy, 1948), "and four miles of longitude, the Jordan traverses at least 200 miles . . . with twenty-seven threatening rapids and many of lesser magnitude." Tamarisk, oleander, and willow fringe the stream, lair of lions (Jer. 49:19), tropically fertile (Gen. 13:8–13), while in modern times, enormous deposits, in and around the waters, yield riches. Before Roman times, the river was forded. Below the Jabbok's entrance (Gen. 32:10, 33:18), passage is difficult save at certain seasons, the current being swift near Jericho. Close to Jabbok's mouth were the passages of Bethabara (possibly of the Gospel, Jn. 1:28), where Gideon waylaid the Midianites (Judg. 7:24, 8:4–5), where David twice crossed (or between Jericho and Jabbok, 2 Sam. 17:22, 24, 19:15–18), where the men of Gilead slew the Ephraimites (Judg. 12:6). Elijah and Elisha crossed at Jericho; to which place also the men of Jericho pursued the spies (2 K. 2:5–8, 13–15; Josh. 2:7; cf. Judg. 3:28); it was here too that Joshua went over (4:12–13); and (?) David (2 Sam. 10:17). In Jordan, Naaman the Syrian washed seven times at the prophet's command, likely in the upper reaches (2 K. 5:14). Tradition says that it was at the place where Israel crossed, that the Lord was baptized (Mt. 3:6, 13–17).

Jorim (jō'rĭm) [high] ancestor of Christ (Lk. 3:29).

Jorkoam (jôr'kō-ăm) [fear of people?, or expansion?] descendant of Caleb, or a place in Judah (1 Chr. 2:44).

Josabad (jŏs'à-băd) [Jehovah bestows] properly Jozabad, the Gederathite, warrior of Benjamin with David at Ziklag (1 Chr. 12:4).

Josaphat (jŏs'à-făt) [Jehovah judges] is Jehoshaphat king of Judah (Mt. 1:8).

Jose (jō'sě) [Jehovah saves] son of Eliezer, in genealogy of Christ (Lk. 3:29).

Joseph (jō'sěf) [Jehovah adds] the sound is the same as a verb of different etymology, "he takes away"; the writer (Gen. 30:23–24), following Hebrew custom, plays upon the sound and both etymologies, when he explains, not the root, but the reason for the name. The eleventh of Jacob's twelve sons, and elder son of Rachel, who at his birth, said: "The Lord shall add to me another son," and therefore she called his name Joseph (Gen. 30:22–24). At his birth, Jacob was ninety or ninety-one years old (vs. 25; cf. 31:41), favoring him because the son of his old age, and Rachel's

child, and making him a coat (perhaps, "of long sleeves") such as the better class wore (37:3). Age thirty when he became governor of Egypt (41:46), he was seventeen when sold by his brothers into that land (37:2), their envy being increased by his dreams of lordship (vss. 5–11). He was about thirty-nine when his father and company came into Egypt, on the dating of which, chronologies differ (1900 to 1700; Scripture is not explicit). Genesis 37, 39–40, tell the thrilling story of Joseph's sale into Egypt, by the foul deed of his brothers, and the traffic of merchantmen en route to Egypt, also of his providential preservation and rise to fortune and fame, after being in prison, for at least two years, under false accusation by the wife of Potiphar, captain of the guard. Long after he had correctly interpreted the dreams of two fellow prisoners, and when the monarch had dream problems, which reminded the spared butler of Joseph's divine power, he was not only released when he correctly gave the meaning of the sovereign's dreams, but on giving Pharaoh advice as to what to do in preparation against the coming emergency of famine, he was appointed superintendent of the royal granaries (head of the department of state), and one of the officials next in rank to the potentate (ch. 41; especially chs. 39–46). Joseph married Asenath of the priestly line, two sons, Manasseh and Ephraim being born before the predicted famine came. The famine whether affecting the known world or, as is likely, that part which was adjacent to Egypt (the granary of the neighboring lands), brought the money of the country into Pharaoh's hands (47:13–14) in about two years, and then successively, the cattle and the land. When Canaan was plagued Jacob, reserving Benjamin, sent his sons to Egypt for corn, where Joseph unrecognized, put them through some very severe tests, and ultimately brought them all with his father, Jacob, to live in Goshen, with the hearty approval of Pharaoh, who was most likely of the foreign Hyksos line, then ruling over Egypt, which folk were Semites themselves and so the more favorable to their distant kinsmen, the Israelites. In ch. 48 is a most interesting incident in the thrilling and touching story of this period, where Jacob, nearly blind, crosses his hands in blessing Joseph's two sons, in order that the younger might have the birthright—Ephraim, over Manasseh. Joseph died at 110, having left strict injunction that when the exodus should occur, his embalmed and "chested" body should be taken in that forty-year funeral procession, to be buried in Canaan, which was done (chs.

49–50; Heb. 11:22; Ex. 13:19; Josh. 24:32). Jacob's blessing was for the tribes as well as for Joseph (Gen. 49:22–26). In Ps. 80:1, Joseph is poetic for the two tribes, descended from his sons.

2. Father of the spy, of Issachar (Num. 13:7).

3. Son of Asaph, and a musician leader, reign of David (1 Chr. 25:2, 9).

4. A son of Bani who divorced his foreign wife (Ezra 10:42).

5. A priest of Shebaniah's family (Neh. 12:14).

6. Ancestor of Christ, between David and the Exile (Lk. 3:30).

7. Ancestor of Christ, after the Exile (Lk. 3:26).

8. Son of Mattathias, in ancestry of Christ (Lk. 3:24–25).

9. Husband of Mary, mother of Jesus (Mt. 1:16; Lk. 3:23). Thinking to put away without public exposure his supernaturally pregnant fiancée, but being informed by an angel of the facts, Joseph carried out the marriage contract (Mt. 1:18–25). Augustus' decree required return to Bethlehem, the ancestral home, for enrollment; and while there, the Lord Jesus was born (Lk. 2:4, 16). Joseph was present when the shepherds came, when also, at the temple, presentation according to the Law was made, at which time the prophetic utterances of Simeon and Anna were spoken (vs. 33). He witnessed the visit of the wise men "to the house," several years later (Mt. 2:1–11), and warned by angelic word to flee the wrath of Herod, took his family to Egypt (Mt. 2:13, 19); and later, Herod being dead, he brought them, not to Bethlehem, for fear of Archelaus, but to Nazareth his former home, where he resumed his carpenter's trade. When the Lord was twelve years old, he was taken with his parents to Jerusalem, according to the annual custom (Lk. 2:43); and after the return, no more is heard of the father, though presumably he was alive when the Lord left the carpenter shop to begin his work (Mt. 13:55; Mk. 6:3; for light on this, see Jn. 19:26–27).

10. A Jew of Arimathea, Sanhedrin member and honorable counsellor, who looked for the kingdom of God (Mk. 15:43; Lk. 2:25, 38, 23:50–51). Apparently afraid to commit himself publicly, he was none the less a disciple, who consented not to the Sanhedrin resolution to put the Lord to death. Yet he went boldly to beg of Pilate the crucified body, and put it in his new rock-hewn tomb (Mt. 27:57–60; Lk. 23:50–53; Jn. 19:38).

11. A Christian called Barsabbas, surnamed Justus, who followed with the disciples after the Lord's baptism, and was one of the two considered worthy to fill Judas' place (Acts 1:23). Eusebius says he was one of the Seventy.

Joses [Greek form of Joseph] 1. A brother of the Lord (Mk. 6:3).

2. Personal name of Barnabas, sometime colleague of Paul (Acts 4:36).

Joshah (jō′shä) [perhaps, uprightness] a Simeonite, time of Hezekiah (1 Chr. 4:34, 38–41).

Joshaphat (jŏsh′ȧ-făt) [Jehovah judges] a Mithnite, mighty man of David (1 Chr. 11:43).

Joshaviah (jŏsh-ȧ-vī′ȧ) [Jehovah sets upright] a Davidic guard (1 Chr. 11:46).

Joshbekasha (jŏsh-bĕk′ȧ-shä) [seat of hardness?] singer, son of Heman, and head of seventeenth course of musicians (1 Chr. 25:4, 24).

Joshedech or **Jehozadak** (jĕ-hŏ′zā-dăk) [Jehovah is righteous] son of Seraiah (Hag. 1:1, 12, 14, 2:2, 4; Zech. 6:11).

Joshua (jŏsh′ū-ȧ) [Jehovah is salvation] appears as Hoshea, Oshea, Jehoshua, Jeshua, and Jesus. 1. The son of Nun, tribe of Ephraim (1 Chr. 7:27). Born about the time that Moses fled to Midian, slave in Egypt's brick-fields, he was forty at the Exodus, and is first noted fighting the Amalekites at Rephidim (Ex. 17:1). He was with Moses in the mount when the golden calf was made (24:13, 32:17). Of the twelve spying the land, he was one of two to encourage the march, being one of the three to survive the forty years' wandering, thereafter being publicly ordained, before high priest and the congregation, as Moses' successor, and who, just before Moses' death, received at the tabernacle his charge from the Lord (Num. 13:17, 14:6, 27:18; Deut. 1:38, 31:14, 23). Allowing three days' preparation (Josh. 1:10–11), charging the two and one-half tribes about doing their part (vss. 12–18), spying out Jericho (Josh. 2:1), fortifying Gilgal, circumcising the people, keeping the Passover, Jordan having been crossed by supernatural guidance, Joshua was met and encouraged by the captain of the Lord's hosts, and thereafter, by divine direction and miraculous blessing, took Jericho (chs. 4–6). After the disgraceful rout at Ai, taken in a second attack, Joshua's military skill, in establishing the central camp, and mopping up the towns commanding its approaches, was exhibited in his great campaigns which broke the power of the Canaanites, but which stopped short of extermination (chs. 9–12). Joshua had already held the convocation at Ebal and Gerizim, where he read the law of Moses (Josh. 8:30–35); and after the six years during which six tribes and thirty-one petty chiefs were conquered, now stricken in years, the commander, aided by the high priest and a commission, superintended the allotments to the tribes of Israel, beginning the distribution while his camp was at Gilgal (14:6–17:18), and completing it and also the assignment of the cities of refuge and the Levitical towns after he had removed the tabernacle to Shiloh (chs. 18–21). He was given Timnath-sera in Mount Ephraim (19:50). After an interval of rest, Joshua convoked the assembly at Shechem, the place of Abraham's first altar in Canaan, and the locality where the tribes had invoked blessings and curses upon themselves, delivering apparently two solemn addresses, in which he reminded the people of the fulfillment of God's promises to the fathers, citing the condition upon which prosperity depended, and having them renew the covenant (Gen. 35:4; Josh. 24:32, 1–28). Joshua died at 110 years, and was buried in his own city.

2. An inhabitant of Beth-shemesh, at the stone of whose land, the cows stopped, returning with the Philistine offerings and the ark of God (1 Sam. 6:14, 18).

3. Governor of Jerusalem in Josiah's reign (2 K. 23:8).

4. High priest under Zerubbabel, governor of Judah (Hag. 1:1, 14, 2:2, 4; Zech. 3:1–9). **Joshua, Book of** this book follows the Pentateuch logically, being a continuation of history after Moses' death, and certifying possession of the land for which Abraham waited; but kept distinct from the five books because not written by Moses. It is the first of the so-called "former prophets" (written from the prophetic standpoint) of the traditional division of the OT into: the Law, the Prophets, the Writings (i.e., the books in our Bibles from Joshua through 2 Kings—save Ruth). Joshua's place in the canon of Scripture has never been disputed. It is expressly stated that "Joshua wrote these words in the book of the law of God" (24:26): also other books refer to events in it (Ps. 78:53–65; Isa. 28:21; Hab. 3:11–13; Acts 7:45; Heb. 4:8, 11:30–32; James 2:25). The supernatural day at Makkedah (10:12–18), the treatment of the conquered Canaanites, alleged differences and contradictions, have been charged against the credibility, morality, and integrity of the book; but none are of substantial character in the light of the supernatural providence of God, his ways of governing the world in his punitive justice (see Gen. 15:16), and in view of accurate understanding

and weighing of the challenged passages. It is, in the main, by one writer.

Outline. Its contents naturally fall into: (1) The conquest of Canaan, chs. 1–12: a. Preparation for crossing Jordan, and the passage, 1:1–4:18; b. Setting up camp, and celebration of Passover, 4:19–5:12; c. Capture of Jericho and Ai; covenant confirmed on Ebal, treaty with Gibeon, 5:13–9:27; d. Southern and northern campaigns, chs. 10–11; e. Summary, ch. 12. (2) Distribution of Canaan, chs. 13–22: a. Description of the land to be divided, ch. 13; b. Its allotment, cities of refuge, and Levitical towns, chs. 14–21; c. Difficulty about the altar of Jordan, not to divide the nation, ch. 22. (3) Joshua's farewell words and death, chs. 23–24.

Tradition shows the writer to be Joshua. It seems evident that 24:29–33 was written after Joshua's time. Davis, *Dictionary of the Bible*, 1920, indicates that the simplest theory is that the conquest of Hebron, Debir and Anah by Caleb occurred after Joshua's death, recorded proleptically (15:13–20); that Zephath is called Hormah in anticipation (12:14; see Judg. 1:17); that 19:47, on the Danite migration, was in the time of the judges. The final form of the book seems to have come while Ai was still in ruins (8:28), before the Solomonic reign, while the Canaanites were still in Gezer (cf. 16:10 with 1 K. 9:16), and before David's reign, when the Jebusites still held Jerusalem's stronghold (15:63). Traditional date for the greater part, is in Joshua's time (see 6:25) mid-fifteenth century B.C.

Josiah (jō-sī′ä) [Jehovah heals] 1. King of Judah, successor to Amon, beginning at eight years of age (ca. 640 B.C.), reigning for thirty-one years (2 K. 22:1–23:30; 2 Chr. 34–35; see Jer. 1–12 for background). In his eighth regnant year, under high priest Hilkiah's advice, he began enforcing for himself and the court the laws of God; and for six years beginning at his twelfth, he extended reform to destroying idolatry and false worship, in Judah and Jerusalem, and later also in Israel (2 K. 22:1–2; 2 Chr. 34:1–7, 33); and in his eighteenth year, while the temple was being renovated and adorned, the work being notable for financial scrupulousness, Hilkiah's discovery of, and Shaphan's reading before the king, the Book of the Law fired the sovereign with greater zeal, so much so that both king and people not only entered into covenant to worship God in accord with the Law, but with one accord they destroyed the vessels, homes, and high places of the false gods, and burnt the disinterred bones of idolatrous priests (see 1 K.

13:2), and slew living ones on their own altars, concluding the whole sweeping movement with a Passover observation not seen since Samuel's time (2 K. 23:1–25; 2 Chr. 34:29–35:19). Thirteen years later, when Pharaoh Necho of Egypt was marching against Assyria, Josiah feeling obligated, as we may suppose, to the eastern warlord, interposed at Megiddo, in Esdraelon's plain, and, mortally wounded, was hurried to Jerusalem to his untimely death—Judah's tragic loss (see 2 K. 22:20). Jeremiah, singers, and the populace made great lamentations. Josiah's reforms faded; the partial independence of his rule was lost (2 Chr. 35:20–27; see Zech. 12:11).

2. A son of Zephaniah, Zechariah's time (Zech. 6:10; perhaps same as Hen, vs. 14).

Josibiah (jŏs-ĭ-bī′ā) [Jehovah gives abode] a Simeonite, family of Asiel (1 Chr. 4:35).

Josiphiah (jŏs-ĭ-fī′ä) [Jehovah will increase] head of the house of Shelomith, returning with Ezra (8:10). Probably a word omitted; and so to be read: "of the sons of Bani, Shelomith, the son of Josiphiah."

jot [transliteration of the Gr. *iota*, equivalent of the Heb. *yodh*, "i"] generally the smallest letter, the point of the comparison lying either in its size, or in the thought that, since it could be either used or omitted in certain connections, as a writer pleased, it was a matter of small moment.

Jotbah [pleasantness] town of King Amon's grandfather (2 K. 21:19).

Jotbath (jŏt′băth) as above, or Jotbathah (Deut. 10:7; Num. 33:33). Israelitish wilderness station.

Jotham (jō′thăm) [Jehovah is upright] 1. Youngest son of Gideon, escaping the massacre of his seventy brothers, uttering from Gerizim, to the Shechemites below, the first parable recorded (Judg. 9:1–21).

2. Son of Uzziah, and co-regent with his father during the latter's leprosy (2 K. 15:5). First Chr. 5:17 seems to indicate the regency began while Jeroboam II was still king in Israel, which is in turn corroborated if the earthquake (Amos 1:1; Zech. 14:5) occurred while Jeroboam and Uzziah were still enthroned. Josephus says the earthquake occurred about the time that Uzziah was smitten. Jotham became sole ruler at age twenty-five about the middle of the eighth century B.C., reigning for sixteen years in Jerusalem. He made some reforms, did some construction, subjugated the Ammonites. Isaiah and Hosea prophesied in his reign (Isa. 1:1; Hos. 1:1). His history is in 2 K. 15 and 2 Chr. 27.

3. A son of Jahdai (1 Chr. 2:47).

Jozabad (jŏz′ā-băd) [Jehovah bestows] 1. A Gederathite who deserted to David at Ziklag (1 Chr. 12:4).

2 and 3. Two Manassites helping David pursue the Amalekites (1 Chr. 12:20).

4. A Levite of Hezekiah's reign.

5. A chief Levite, reign of Josiah (2 Chr. 35:9).

6. A Levite, son of Jeshua (Ezra 8:33); perhaps the man who helped teach the people the Law (Neh. 8:7), and who had oversight of the outward business of the house of the Lord (11:16), and also involved with a foreign wife (10:23).

7. A priest of sons of Pashur, also a xenophile (Ezra 10:22).

Jozacar (jŏz′ā-cär) [Jehovah remembers] an Ammonitess' son, one of two assassins of Joash (2 K. 12:21); by clerical error, called Zabad (2 Chr. 24:26).

Jozadak (jŏz′ā-dăk) [Jehovah is just] father of Jeshua, the high priest (Ezra 3:2, 8, 5:2, 10:18); captive to Babylon (1 Chr. 6:15). Longer form, Jehozadak.

Jubal (jū′băl) [stream, perhaps also music] younger son of Lamech by Adah, and inventor of string and wind instruments (Gen. 4:21).

Jubilee, the Year of (jū′bĭ-lē) [joyful shout, sound of trumpet] the year following the seven times seven years, begun with trumpet-blowing on Day of Atonement; in this year all land, alienated, returned to families according to the original allotment, and all Hebrew bondmen were liberated, according to Lev. 25:8–16, 23–55. The land rested, as under the preceding sabbatical year, chance produce being left to all comers. To prevent injustice a purchaser, who could retain land only until the first Jubilee thereafter (conforming to the principles of political economy), gave for the purchase only the worth of the temporary occupation till the Jubilee year. But a house in a walled city did not so revert; only those of unwalled villages, regarded as belonging to the field, reverted at Jubilee, as did also Levitical houses anywhere (Lev. 25:8–55, 27:17–18; Num. 36:4). If one had sanctified a field of his patrimony unto the Lord, it could be redeemed at any time before next Jubilee, with a stipulated payment (Lev. 27:19); but if not so redeemed, at Jubilee, it was devoted forever. If the purchaser of the fruits of a field, sanctified it, he could redeem it till the next Jubilee—the length of his claim; but it then returned to the original proprietor (vss. 22–24). All Israelitish bondmen were freed in Jubilee (Lev. 25:40–41, contingent upon another law in Ex. 21:2). Only Josephus holds that debts were remitted in

Jubilee; cf. Deut. 15:1=2. Jewish writers in general consider Jubilee observed till the destruction of the first temple. There is no direct historical notice of its observance on any occasion, although apparent allusion appears in such passages as Isa. 5:7=10, 61:1–3; Ezek. 7:12–13, 46:16–18).

Jucal (jū′căl) [he is able] (Jer. 38:1).

Juda (jū′dà) [object of praise] 1. Son of Joseph in genealogy of the Lord (Lk. 3:30).

2. Son of Joanna, or Hananiah (Lk. 3:26, 30), who seems same person as Abiud in Mt. 1:13.

3. One of the Lord's brethren, according to Mk. 6:3.

4. The patriarch Judah (Lk. 3:33; Heb. 7:13; Rev. 5:5, 7:5).

Judaea, Judea a Latin name through the Greek from the Heb. *Yehudah.* The first mention of the "province of Judea" is in Ezra 5:8, and is a division of the Persian empire (cf. Est. 8:9). With Archelaus' banishment, Judea was annexed to the Roman province of Syria, and governed by procurators under Rome, residing in Caesarea, immediately under the proconsul of Syria, ruling from Antioch (Lk. 3:1). The arrangement obtained while our Lord was ministering, Judea being often mentioned in the gospels (Lk. 23:5–7; Jn. 4:3, 7:3; Acts 1:8). In a wider and improper sense the term meant the whole Canaanitish country, or its inhabitants. Note also Mt. 19:1; Mk. 10:1. Strictly, Judea—a region roughly fifty-five miles square—extended from Joppa on the coast, to a point ten miles north of the Dead Sea, and at the south, from a point seven miles southwest from Gaza, through Beer-sheba, to the southern end of the Dead Sea.

Judah (jū′dà) [object of praise] 1. Jacob's and Leah's fourth son (Gen. 35:23). He had no part in the vengeance for Dinah, full sister (Gen. 34). He had three sons by Shuah, a Canaanitess of Adullam, and who, after two were slain for sins, and a third was not given in marriage to the widow of her former two husbands, begot twins by Tamar his daughter-in-law, through her trickery (Gen. 38:1–30, 46:12; Num. 26:19). Through one twin, Perez, Judah became ancestor to David and our Lord (Ruth 4:18–22; Mt. 1:3–16). It was Judah who proposed selling, instead of murdering, Joseph (Gen. 37:26–28); and Judah who deprecated Joseph's retaining Benjamin in Egypt; and it was Judah who made impassioned plea for Benjamin and offered to take his place (44:33=34), resulting in Joseph's disclosure of himself (45:1); it was Judah who was chosen to go before Jacob to Goshen (46:28), and

Judah who received Jacob's birthright blessing, his elder brothers being passed over on account of their sins (49:3–10).

2. A tribe sprung from Judah, with five tribal families (Num. 26:19–21; 1 Chr. 2:3–6). Nahshon and Caleb were princes (Num. 1:7, 13:6). The wilderness census numbered 74,600 (1:26–27): a second census just before entering Canaan showed 76,500 (26:22). With others, Judah blessed the people on Gerizim (Deut. 27:12). Avaricious Achan was a member of Judah (Josh. 7:1). Judah was first to possess his allotted territory, and with Simeon took Canaanitish towns and cleaned out the hill country (Judg. 1:1–20). With great detail Judah's territorial boundaries and contents are described, under Joshua's direction (15:20–63). From the extreme south point of the Dead Sea, to the Zin wilderness, near Kadesh-barnea, and on to the Mediterranean Sea—the southern borders, the eastern being the Dead Sea, and the western, the Mediterranean, while at the north, the line ran from the mouth of Jordan at the north end of the Dead Sea, west near Jericho to En-rogel and the Son of Hinnom valley, south of Jerusalem, then to Kirjath-jearim, and by Beth-shemesh, to the Sea, the whole being about fifty to ninety miles north and south, and forty-five east and west. The *South* (Josh. 15:21), was the undulating pastureland between the hills and the desert of the lower part of Palestine. The *Lowland*, or *Shephelah* (15:33), the broad belt between the mountain highlands and the sea, is the lower part of the maritime plain along the whole of Palestine's seaboard. The *Mountain*, or *Hill Country* of Judah, is south of Hebron and stretching east and west to the Dead Sea and the Shephelah, an elevated limestone plateau with considerable undulation. The *Wilderness*, sometimes seeming to be same as Arabah, is the sunken district next the Dead Sea.

3. A Levite (Ezra 3:9).

4. Another, with Zerubbabel (Neh. 12:8).

5. Another, induced by Ezra to put away his foreign wife (Ezra 10:23).

6. A Benjaminite, second in command over Jerusalem (Neh. 11:9).

7. An aid in dedicating the wall, perhaps a prince of Judah (Neh. 12:34).

Judah, Kingdom of shortly after Canaan's conquest, Othniel of Judah delivered the nation from foreign domination (Judg. 3:8–11). Neglect of God, tribal jealousies, failure to occupy heathen territory, combined to separate Judah, Dan, and Simeon as a group. Judah took little part in the campaigns of others against oppression: it had troubles of its own (Judg. 3:31,

10:7, 13:1). At this time Boaz and Ruth lived in Bethlehem. Association with the other tribes became closer in the matter of punishing Benjamin (20:1, 18), and when in the time of Samuel and Eli, the Philistines oppressed both Judah and Benjamin, Judah being included in the kingdom of Saul, after whose death Judah supported, and for seven years warred in behalf of, David their fellow tribesman for the throne. Jerusalem on the border of Judah and Benjamin became his capital, the promise of perpetuity being evidently contingent upon the wisdom and common sense of his successors (2 Sam. 7:13–16; 1 Chr. 17:12, 14, 23): under Rehoboam the ten tribes were lost to the house of David. Benjaminite towns, Bethel and Jericho, were included in the Northern Kingdom; part of Simeon and of Dan were reckoned with Judah (1 Sam. 27:6; cf. Josh. 19:1; 2 Chr. 11:10; cf. Josh. 19:41–42), and in the reigns of Asa and Abijah, additions were made from the territory of Ephraim (2 Chr. 13:19). Jeroboam's thwarting Jerusalem-centered worship by setting up golden calves at north and south ends of his kingdom (Dan and Bethel), brought accession of spiritual and political strength to Judah —the faithful migrated thither (1 K. 12:26–33, 13:33; 2 Chr. 10:16–17). Mutual hostility between the two kingdoms emboldened neighboring nations to intermeddle (1 K. 14:25–28; 2 Chr. 12:1–12). Internecine strife covered the first sixty years (1 K. 14:30, 15:7, 16) after which, the political and family alliance between Ahab and Jehoshaphat, served to introduce the destructive factor of Baal worship into Judah, which led to two rival parties which continued till the end. A less exposed frontier and less fertile soil, with a hardier and more united people, having a venerated center of administration and religion, under a hereditary sacerdotal aristocracy, and fewer revolutions—all these, with other lesser factors, combined to prolong the Southern Kingdom for 135 years longer than the Northern. Egypt, both enemy and ally, exerted great influence on Judah. After long religious and political prosperity, Judah under Ahaz, 734 B.C., became tributary to Assyria, invoking aid against Ephraim (North Israel) and Syria (Damascus) in the Syro-Ephraimitic War. A decade later Ephraim fell to the Assyrian war machine, Judah being exposed for a century and a quarter to their menacing greed, until Babylon took Nineveh, Assyria's capital. From 606 till 538 B.C. (when the Persian rule began), the Chaldeans (Babylonians) held sway, Jehoiachim of Judah being subjugated by Nebuchadnezzar (ca. 605); and in less than a score of years, Jerusalem was in ruins and the people deported to Babylon. The causes of the catastrophe are well worthy of note. Among them are: 1. The underlying reasons for the loss of Samaria, leaving Judah alone.

2. Failure to obey the command to exterminate the Canaanites.

3. Social and political alliances with heathen.

4. Moral weakness from apostasy and loss of ideals.

5. Rejection of prophetic appeals.

Judas [genitive *Juda*; Greek form of Hebrew proper name *Judah*] 1. The patriarch Judah (Mt. 1:2–3).

2. A man of Damascus in whose house the apostle Paul lodged following his miraculous experience (Acts 9:11).

3. Ancestor of the Lord living before the Exile (Lk. 3:30).

4. Judas surnamed Barsabas, leading member of the apostolic church in Jerusalem, with gift of prophecy (Acts 15:22, 32), chosen to go with Paul and Barnabas to Antioch to carry the decree about admitting Gentiles (vs. 7).

5. Judas of Galilee, leader of revolt in "the days of taxing" (Acts 5:37).

6. **Judas Iscariot** sometimes "son of Simon" (Jn. 6:71), more commonly (his only name according to the Synoptics) *Iscariotes* (Mt. 10:4; Mk. 3:19; Lk. 6:16). In the three lists of the Twelve, he is noted as the betrayer, distinguished (Lk. 6:16) from another Judas, by the term Iscariot since he was likely a man from Kerioth ("Ish Kerioth"), being the only non-Galilean (Acts 2:7). Another theory is that he was Judas "with the apron," from the word for leather apron, he holding the money bag for the company. Of his life before his call nothing is known: but by his character it is inferred that he joined for earthly advantage. The rules of the early days doubtless sheltered Judas from temptation (Mt. 10:9–10); but the new form of life (cf. Lk. 8:3) and the funds which the traveling body received and paid out, requiring a treasurer, made dishonesty easy, he perhaps being selected for financial ability. The incident of the alabaster box (Jn. 12:5–6), seems to have aroused resentment when the rebuke came, so that vindictiveness along with native covetousness, appears to have urged the traitor on. Judas may have thought that betrayal would be offset by a supernatural escape, as on other occasions. Those who would mistakenly relieve the betrayal of its opprobrium, hold the theory that forcing the hour of Messianic triumph would be a commendable move, which seems contrary to Scripture (Jn. 13:27; cf. vs. 21). The kiss (Mt. 26:47–49), probably the usual salutation, was the key to the ac-

companying band, in the midnight semidarkness. Judas was present at the Supper (Mt. 26:20), but likely left before the Eucharist (Jn. 13:30; Mt. 26:26–29; Mk. 14:22–25; Lk. 22:19–20). Luke seems to change the order of events to place the spirit of Christ and that of the disciples side by side in contrast (22:15–20, and vss. 21–24). The fever of crime having passed, and with the recollection of the sinless righteousness of the Lord (Mt. 27:3), Judas in revulsion at the whole despicable affair, flings the money on the temple floor, to hang himself and to go "to his own place" (Acts 1:25; Mt. 27:3–5, not contradictory of Acts 1:18). Judas was a son of perdition, not saved as were the others of the disciples, the words in Jn. 17:12, to be read: "And none of them is lost. BUT the son of perdition (is lost)." [The "but" here does not signify exception; rather contrast.]

7. One of the Twelve, brother or son of James (Lk. 6:16; Acts 1:13), called Thaddaeus (Mt. 10:3; Mk. 3:18).

8. One of the four brethren of the Lord (Mt. 13:55; Mk. 6:3, and probably writer of the Epistle of Jude.

Jude, Epistle of the James in the phrase "the brother of James, is evidently the writer of the Epistle of James, in which case, Jude is brother to the Lord, not an apostle, which inferences are borne out by the presence of a Judas in the Lord's brothers' list (Mt. 13:55; Mk. 6:3), and by the implication (Jude 17) that the writer was not an apostle. Perhaps due to brevity, there is no clear trace of this book in the earliest fathers, but in the latter part of the second century, it is in full use in Greek and Latin churches, being included in the Old Latin version and listed in the Muratorian Fragment, and quoted and referred to by Clement of Alexandria and Tertullian, and also by Origen. Early, sometimes questioned by some as to canonicity, it was never lacking in genuineness by those who knew it. "It was clearly from the beginning a part of the Christian canon" (B. B. Warfield). The time and place of writing are now indeterminable. The most natural date is around A.D. 66. (If 2 Pet. is prior, then perhaps the date is somewhat later than the death of that apostle in 68). Christians generally seem to be addressed. Its one chapter is an exhortation to contend earnestly for the faith, practically every great vital doctrine being found in it. There is a salutation (vss. 1–2), a concluding doxology (vss. 24–25); and after the purpose (vss. 3–4), come warning illustrations (vss. 5–16), and the exhortation (vss. 17–23).

judge 1. A civil magistrate (Ex. 21:22; Deut. 16:18). On the advice of his father-in-law, Moses organized a judiciary for Israel, with judges over the several numerical groupings (Ex. 18:13–26). There were already princes and elders for the tribal subdivisions, with civil and religious authority, now included in the new regime and retaining their hereditary judicial functions (Deut. 1:15–17; cf. 22:1). Moses gave instructions touching government for Canaan (16:18–20, 17:2, 15, 19:15–20; cf. Josh. 8:23, 23:2, 24:1; 1 Sam. 8:1). The king later became supreme judge in civil matters (2 Sam. 15:2; 1 K. 3:9, 28, 7:7; cf. 1 Sam. 8:5). David appointed Levites to the judicial office; and other officers (1 Chr. 23:4, 26:29). Jehoshaphat set judges in fortified cities, with a supreme court in Jerusalem, under a president high priest in religious matters, and a prince of Judah in civil matters (2 Chr. 19:5–8).

2. A leader raised up of God against foreign oppression, who was thereafter the guardian of the people's rights. There were twelve judges, omitting Abimelech, a petty king not called of God (Judg. 9): Othniel, Ehud, Shamgar, Deborah, Gideon, Tola, Jair, Jephthah, Ibzan, Elon, Abdon, Samson; Eli counted as a high priest; and Samuel rather as a prophet (1 Sam. 4:18, 7:15). The judges were sporadic not successive, in restricted districts, some contemporaneous, some overlapping, without power to order all the tribes to war. The period of the Judges has been called the Iron Age of Israel.

Judges, the Book of continues the narrative after Joshua, having three parts: (1) Introduction: departure to occupy districts allotted (see Josh. 15–21); list of towns left in Canaanitish possession (1:1=2:5); (2) History of the judges, from Joshua to Samson (2:6–16:31): introductory, summarizing events, and citing religious lesson (2:6–3:6); rather detailed account of six, and meager word on other six, Abimelech included (3:7–16:31); (3) Two appendices: Micah's image worship established among the Danites of the north (chs. 17–18); Gibeah's sin and punishment (chs. 19–21). The unity of the book is seen in the cue given in 2:16–19, the design being to enforce that view in admonition to later ages. The writer-compiler seems to have found certain sections already in definite shape: the words of the prophet (2:1–5); the song of Deborah (5); Jotham's fable (9:7–20); also 14:14, 18, 15:7, 16). The old Jewish idea is that Samuel is the writer, which depends upon the date, a matter of difficulty. All concede Deborah's song early; and the main section in general comes after the death of Samson (16:30–31). The expression in latter chapters, "In those days there was no king in Israel," sets them later than the kingdom's erection; the tabernacle was no longer in Shiloh (18:31); the writer was acquainted with regnal government (17:6, 18:1). The expression "the captivity of the land" (18:30) seems best referable not to Assyria (2 K. 15:29), nor to the conquest and enslavement of the northern Danites by Damascus, but to the Philistine troubles—change of one letter makes it "captivity of the ark," a quite possible error in the text. It seems hardly likely that the idolatry of Micah lasted until the fall of Samaria (the Assyrian capture, 721 B.C.); Judg. 1:21 shows that the Jebusites still occupied the stronghold at Jerusalem, when the introduction was written. We pass by the critical view of late origin, on account of the reflection of Deuteronomy's religious conception, to settle on the time of Samuel as the date of composition. Reckoned consecutively, the judges cover 410 years, which with Eli's forty, would equate with Acts 13:20. But Judg. 11:26 and 1 K. 6:1 cause trouble, which we leave to the exegetes: with letters, some much alike, for figures, the way is open for difficulties, which we must frankly face, in our present text of the Bible.

Judgment Hall the expression seems to mean several things: (1) the palace occupied by Pontius Pilate at Jerusalem, and where his judgment seat was erected (Jn. 18:28, 33, 19:9; Mk. 15:16); (2) Herod's palace at Caesarea, where Paul was confined (Acts 23:35), the Greek word *praetorium* being translated palace, Caesar's court, etc.; (3) the praetorium guard at Rome (Phil. 1:13).

Judith (jū′dĭth) [object of praise; also feminine of *yehudi*, a Jew, meaning then, a Jewess] a wife of Esau (Gen. 26:34), called also Oholibamah (36:2).

Julia (jū′lĭ-à) [feminine of Lat. Julius] a Christian woman at Rome, probably the wife of Philologus (Rom. 16:15).

Julius the centurion of "Augustus' band," charged with Paul as prisoner, en route from Caesarea to Rome (Acts 27:1), who discredited Paul's prediction (11), but afterward heeded his advice (31), later preserved the apostle's life (Acts 27:42–43).

Junias (jū′nĭ-ăs) possibly one of the seventy disciples (Origen), a Roman Jewish Christian, kinsman and fellow Christian of Paul (Rom. 16:7).

juniper the word rendered *juniper* is said to be a sort of broom, answering to the Arabic *rethem*, a leguminous plant, affording shade and protection from heat and storm (1 K. 19:4, 5; Ps. 120:4; Job 30:4).

Jupiter supreme god of the Romans, corresponding to Zeus of the Greeks, having a notable temple at Olympia in Elis, mentioned but once in Scripture (Acts 14:12–13). At Lystra his temple was outside the city ("Jupiter, which was before their city").

Jushab-hesed (jū-shăb-hē′sĕd) [Mercy is returned] son of Zerubbabel (1 Chr. 3:20).

justification a forensic term, antecedent to sanctification, and not to be confused with it. *Meaning:* (1) Acquittal on ground of innocence, where, a charge having been made, it is finally disproved, and the righteousness of the accused demonstrated, as in Ps. 51:4. (2) Acquittal in the sense of pardon. Under divine law Christ has done that which rendered it consistent to hold penitent sinners guiltless, treated as joint heirs with him, to be justified freely by his grace, "being justified by faith," they have "peace with God" (Rom. 5:1).

Justus [righteous] 1. Surname of Joseph (Barsabas of Acts 1:23).

2. A Christian at Corinth, with whom Paul lodged (Acts 18:7).

3. Surname of a friend of Paul (Col. 4:11).

Juttah (jŭt′tà) [extended, inclined] a town in Judah's hill country (Josh. 15:55) with suburbs, assigned to priests (21:16); now, Yuttah, ca. five miles south by west of Hebron; some say the city of Lk. 1:39, though more likely Hebron.

K

Kabbalah (kăb′bā-là) [reception, tradition] a rabbinical term for several traditional doctrines; also a mystical mode of interpreting the OT.

Kabzeel (kăb′zē-ĕl) [God brings together] a city of South Judah (Josh. 15:21; 2 Sam. 23:20; 1 Chr. 11:22). After the Exile called Jekabzeel (Neh. 11:25). Site unknown.

Kadesh, Kadesh-barnea (kā′dĕsh) [consecrated], (-bär'nē-à) [meaning not known] a fountain, city or town, and wilderness on southern frontier of Palestine (Num. 20:16; Josh. 15:3; Ps. 29:8; Ezek. 47:19); called Barnea to distinguish from other Kadeshes (Num. 13:26 with 32:8; Deut. 1:19 with vs. 46). Early, called En-mishpat (Gen. 14:7), in wilderness of Paran, including or merging with Zin (Num. 13:3, 26, 21:1, 27:14), eleven days' journey from Mount Sinai by way of Mount Seir (Deut. 1:2), in uttermost border of Edom (Num. 20:16), not far from highway from Palestine to Egypt, Hagar's well being between Kadesh and Bered, on road to Egypt (Gen. 16:7, 14; cf. 20:1), to which Hagar fled (16:7, 14), and where Abraham sojourned (20:1). Overrun by Chedorlaomer (14:7). Israel twice encamped at Kadesh: in second year of wandering, about the fifth month (Num. 13:20; cf. 10:11), refusing to advance on account of the discouraging report of the ten spies, and abiding there many days, condemned for their conduct (13:26; Deut. 1:46). At Kadesh, the second time, in the first month (Num. 20:1) of the fortieth year (33:36, 38; cf. Deut. 2:7, 14); Miriam died and was buried there (Num. 20:1); and there Moses smote the rock (20:1–13). From Kadesh word went to Edom for permission of passage (20:14, 16, 22; Judg. 11:16–17). Of the several suggested sites for this the most important place save Sinai for the meandering Israelites, one identified by J. Rowlands [1842] and confirmed by T. W. Holland [1878] and by H. Clay Trumbull [1881] seems best, i.e., 'Ain Kadis, about seventy-seven miles south of Hebron, and fifty-one from Beersheba, where is a copious spring of sweet water.

Kadmiel (käd'mĭ-ĕl) [God is of old] a Levite who, with his family, returned with Zerubbabel (Ezra 2:40; Neh. 7:43, 12:8); prominent on three occasions (Ezra 3:9; Neh. 9:4, 10:9).

Kadmonites (käd'mŏn-ītes) [people of the east] only Gen. 15:19 tells of this people, in the land promised to Abraham.

Kallai (käl'lī) [swift] a priest, time of Joiakim (Neh. 12:20).

Kanah (kā'nä) [place of reeds] 1. A brook forming part of boundary between Ephraim and Manasseh (on the south) (Josh. 16:8, 17:9).

2. A town on boundary of Asher (Josh. 19:28).

Kareah (kà-rē'ä) [bald] father of Johanan and Jonathan, supporting Gedaliah, Babylonian governor of Judah (2 K. 25:23; Jer. 40:8, 41:11).

Karkaa (kär'kä-à) [ravine] landmark on south boundary of Judah, site unknown (Josh. 15:3).

Karkor (kär'kôr) [foundation] unidentified place east of Jordan, where Gideon routed Zeba and Zalmunna (Judg. 8:10).

Kartah (kär'tä) [city] unidentified town of Zebulun, allotted to Merarite Levites (Josh. 21:34).

Kartan (kär'tăn) [perhaps, twin town] a town of Naphtali allotted to Gershonite Levites (Josh. 21:32). In 1 Chr. 6:76, "Kiriathaim, which is Kirjathaim."

Kattath (kăt'tăth) a city of Zebulun (Josh. 19:15). Could be Kitron (Judg. 1:30), or Kartah (Josh. 21:34), or perhaps Cana of Galilee.

Kedar (kē'där) [perhaps, mighty; to the Hebrew, is suggestive of the black tents] an Arabian tribe (Isa. 21:13, 16; Ezek. 27:21), between Arabia Petraea and Babylonia, descendants of Ishmael (Gen. 25:13), children of the east dwelling in black tents, possessing flocks and camels (Song of S. 1:5; Isa. 60:7; Jer. 49:28–29), skillful in archery, having villages in the wilderness (Isa. 42:11). Identified with Pliny's Cedrei, from whom Mohammed arose.

Kedemah (kē-dē'mä) [eastward] youngest son and tribe of Ishmael (Gen. 25:15; 1 Chr. 1:31).

Kedemoth (kē-dē'mŏth) [ancient places] Reuben's east-of-Jordan town, given to Merarite Levites, the term probably conferred on the wilderness of same name (Josh. 13:18, 21:37; 1 Chr. 6:79; Deut. 2:26=27).

Kedesh (kē'dĕsh) [sacred place] 1. A town in extreme south of Judah (Josh. 15:23).

2. A city in Issachar (1 Chr. 6:72) of the Gershonite Levites, apparently same as Kishion in Josh. 21:28.

3. A fortified city of Naphtali, appointed a city of refuge, and with suburbs allotted to the Gershonite Levites, located between Hazor and Edrei (Josh. 19:37, 20:7, 21:32; 1 Chr. 6:76). Residence of Barak (Judg. 4:6). Joshua 12:22 seems to apply to this town; some say to 2 above. It was taken by Tiglath-pileser (2 K. 15:29). Called also Kedesh in Galilee, and Kedesh-naphtali.

Kehelathah (kē-hē'lä-thäth) [an assembly] Israelitish encampment in wilderness, unidentified (Num. 33:22–23).

Keilah (kī'lä) [inclosed] a town in Judah's lowland (Josh. 15:44); delivered by David from the Philistines; thither Abiathar the priest took the ephod at the time of Nob's massacre (1 Sam. 23:6–7); and from thence David, warned supernaturally, fled (1 Sam. 23:7–13). It was inhabited after the Captivity (Neh. 3:17=18).

Keilah the Garmite apparently descendant of Caleb (1 Chr. 4:19).

Kelaiah (kē-lā'yä) [perhaps, contempt] same as **Kelita** (Ezra 10:23).

Kelita (kē-lī'tà) [littleness] a Levite returnee with Ezra (10:23); interpreter of the Law (Neh. 8:7); and with Nehemiah signed the covenant (10:10).

Kemuel (kĕm'ū-ĕl) [perhaps, congregation of God] 1. Son of Nahor and Milcah, and father of Aram (Gen. 22:21).

2. A prince of Ephraim, and commissioner in allotment of Canaan (Num. 34:24).

3. A Levite (1 Chr. 27:17).

Kenan (kē'năn) [one acquired] same as Cainan son of Enos (1 Chr. 1:2; see margin of Gen. 5:9).

Kenath (kē'năth) [possession] city on east of Jordan, northeast border of Israelitish territory, possessed by a certain Nobah who gave it his name (Num. 32:42), not permanently. Again passed into Gentile hands (1 Chr. 2:23).

Kenaz (kē'năz) [perhaps, hunting] 1. Son of Eliphaz, son of Esau, and a duke of Edom (Gen. 36:15, 42; 1 Chr. 1:53).

2. One of the same family, descendant of Caleb (1 Chr. 4:15, where the text seems corrupt). The difficulty in these passages may be understood if we adopt the suggestion that the Kenizzites overspread part of Edom and South Judah before the Conquest; and, continuing to abide there, part were absorbed by Edomites and part by the tribe of Judah.

Kenite (kē'nīt) [spear?] a tribe, a branch of which dwelt in or near Canaan, time of Abraham (Gen. 15:19), and another in Midian, with whom they were incorporated by Moses' time (Judg. 1:16, 4:11; cf. Num. 10:29). It is possible that the two had nothing in common: mystery here. The Midianite Kenites occupied the rocky strongholds near Amalek (Num. 24:20–22), probably before the Conquest living east and southeast of Hebron. Jethro, a priest and prince of Midian (Ex. 2:15, 4:18), was a Kenite (Judg. 1:16, 4:11). In the latter reference, Hobab is noted, he, as the most natural suggestion, being Moses' brother-in-law; and Reuel (titular name) and Jethro (personal name) were the same. In Hebrew the consonants for relationship by law comprise one word, whether brother or father. Whether Jethro went or not, no one knows; but Hobab, it seems, did, and certainly some of the family (Num. 10:29–32; Judg. 1:16). But, the wanderings being over, the Kenites betook themselves to the "wilderness of Judah" (see last reference), apparently seeking their forefathers' home. One sheik, Heber, went north (Judg. 4:11). Those of the south were on friendly relations with Israel in time of Saul and David (1 Sam. 15:6, 27:10, 30:29). The most nota-

ble line of this people were the Rechabites (1 Chr. 2:55; Jer. 35).

Kenizzite or **Kenezite** (kē'nĕz-īt; Gen. 15:19) an Edomite tribe (Num. 32:12; Josh. 14:6, 14). Due to the difficulty in accounting for this tribe so early as before Isaac's birth, this note may be taken as later addition by Moses or other. See above.

Keren-happuch (kē'rĕn-hăp'pŭk) [horn of paint] the youngest of Job's post-trial daughters (42:14).

Kerioth (kĕr'ī-ōth) [cities] 1. A town in far South Judah, Kerioth-hezron, which is Hazor, and probably birthplace of Judas Iscariot, i.e., Kerioth (Josh. 15:25).

2. A town of Moab (Jer. 48:24); supposed same as Ar, capital of Moab.

Keros (kē'rŏs) [reed of a weaver's loom] one of the Nethinim, returning with Zerubbabel (Ezra 2:44; Neh. 7:47).

kettle a vessel for cooking or sacrifice. "Basket" in Jer. 24:2; "caldron" in 2 Chr. 35:13; "pot" in Job 41:20.

Keturah (kē-tū'rä) [incense] a wife of Abraham (Gen. 25:1), likely "added and taken," during Sarah's lifetime (25:1–10), at least out of chronological sequence so as not to break the main narrative. The Hebrew writer commonly gives the subordinate line of descendants first, passing them by, for the main concern; and Keturah's sons are not ranked at par with Isaac (1 Chr. 1:32): they received gifts and were sent away while the father lived (25:6). Late Arabian lines include a Keturah tribe.

key a piece of wood with pegs fastened on it corresponding to holes in a wooden bolt within, carried in the girdle or on the shoulder (Isa. 22:22), possibly opened with sticky fingers (Song of S. 5:4–5). Symbol of authority (Mt. 16:19; Rev. 1:18, 3:7, 20:1); also necessary symbol of access (Lk. 11:52).

Keziah (kē-zī'ä) [cassia] second of Job's post-trial daughters (Job 42:14).

Keziz (kē'zĭz) [border] valley and city of Benjamin (Josh. 18:21).

Kibroth-hattaavah (kĭv'rōth-hăt-tä'à-va) [graves of lust] probably three days journey from Sinai (Num. 10:33); no change of location from Taberah (11:3); near the sea (22, 31). The place where the Egypt-lusting Israelites were buried (11:33–35; cf. 33:16–17).

Kibzaim (kĭb'zā-ĭm) [two heaps] a city of Mount Ephraim, given with suburbs to Kohathite Levites (Josh. 21:22). Same as Jokmeam (1 Chr. 6:68).

kid see **goat**

Kidron (kĭd'rŏn) [turbid] not a brook, but a torrent or valley, close to Jerusalem, between the city and the Mount of Olives, crossed by fleeing David (2 Sam. 15:23; cf. vs. 30), and by our Lord, to Gethsemane (Jn. 18:1; cf. Mk. 14:26; Lk. 22:39; also 2 Sam. 15:23). It was the eastern boundary of the city (1 K. 2:37; Jer. 31:40); but the name seems to have been applied to other ravines, for Shimei violated Solomon's charge when, seeking fugitive slaves, he went towards Gath (1 K. 2:37; and vss. 41–42). In Josiah's time it was a common cemetery (2 K. 18:6; Jer. 26:23), i.e., the part near the southern limits thereof; and godly kings on occasion, in cleansing the temple of idolatrous symbols, dumped here the ashes of such abominations (1 K. 15:13; 2 K. 23:4; 2 Chr. 29:16, 30:14). Josephus notes that Athaliah was executed in the Kidron valley to obviate temple defilement. "Valley of Jehoshaphat" is another name for this place.

Kinah (ki'nä) [lamentation] a village in extreme south of Judah (Josh. 15:22).

kine see **cow**

king head of the state-form of kingdom. Name of supreme ruler of Hebrews for about 500 years, to the fall of Jerusalem. Even though there were many kings (Nimrod of Gen. 10:10; Chedorlaomer of Elam, 14:1; Nebuchadnezzar of Babylon, 2 K. 25:1; Artaxerxes of Persia, Ezra 7:12; Dan. 2:1; kings of one town only, Gen. 20:2; Joshua's thirty-one conquered kings in Canaan, Josh. 12:7–24; and kings for centuries in lands adjacent to Palestine), it was not until the threat to Israel in the cruelty of Nahash toward Jabesh-gilead, combined with the maladministration of Samuel's sons (1 Sam. 11:1–2, 4–6, 12:12) that the people of the theocracy demanded a king (1 Sam. 8:3–5). Though by unbelief and in rebellion, it was not necessarily contradictory of Jehovah's rule. Moses had provided for the event. And fidelity to the Lord, as the anointed of Jehovah, was the basal requisite for tenure in office (1 K. 11:31–36). Kingship was by appointment on the part of one higher in authority (1 Sam. 9:16), by popular choice (1 Sam. 18:8), by usurpation (1 K. 15:27–28), by inheritance (11:36). The ceremonial ordinarily consisted of session, crowning, anointing, proclaiming (2 K. 11:12); also there was sacrifice, and a procession (1 K. 1:43–46). The king often led in battle (1 Sam. 8:20), made treaties (1 K. 15:19), enacted and executed laws (Est. 3:12–13), had the power of life and death (2 Sam. 14:1–11). The king had various officers: the chronicler, the scribe (2 Sam. 8:17), steward (Isa. 32:15), companion (1 K. 4:5), keeper of wardrobe (2 K. 10:22), captain of bodyguard (2 Sam. 20:23), and managers over the various divisions and departments of state. Royal revenues derived from: fields, vineyards, gardens, flocks (1 Sam. 21:7; 2 Chr. 26:10; 1 Chr. 27:25). There was the nominal tithe (1 Sam. 8:15, 17), tribute from cross-country merchants (1 K. 10:14), presents from subjects (1 Sam. 10:27), (in case of Solomon) trading vessels (1 K. 10:22), and perhaps commercial ventures (1 K. 9:28), spoils of war and tribute (2 Chr. 27:5), and compulsory labor (1 Sam. 8:12–13, 16).

kingdom 1. Territory or people ruled by a king (2 K. 15:19).

2. Sovereign rule of God over the universe (1 Chr. 29:11; Ps. 22:28; Mt. 6:13).

3. Daniel's predicted sovereignty to last forever, represented in a person like unto a Son of man (Dan. 7:13–14). John the Baptist and the Lord declared it at hand (Mt. 3:2, 4:17); the Lord taught to pray for its coming (6:10; see 10:7, 12:28), and illustrated it by parables. Called the Kingdom of Heaven and Kingdom of God, in Matthew, the former, and in Mark and Luke, the latter (Mt. 13:24; Mk. 4:11; Lk. 14:15). Spiritual in character, established by no carnal weapons (Jn. 18:33–37), begun on earth by Christ's ministry, it is to be consummated in the bliss of the eternal world (Mt. 25:31–40; Lk. 23:42–43). The kingdom is the whole spiritual commonwealth of God's people, the true company of the faithful represented by the visible organized church, but more comprehensive and greater than the visible church in any age or all ages. (J. D. Davis, *Dictionary of the Bible.*)

Kings, First and Second Books of one book originally, but divided in the LXX, in which also they are known as third and fourth books of the Kingdoms, the two Samuels being first and second. Written from the prophetic standpoint, they are placed, in the Hebrew canon, in the prophets; and the books from Joshua through 2 Kings, are known as the "former prophets," the whole being a continuous narrative from the death of Moses to the Exile. The books show the growth and decay of the kingdom, the causes operant, and the place of moral and religious forces in all, the narrative covering around 400 years, and drawing on previous historians. The contents cover the period from the accession of Solomon (around 1000 B.C.) to the end of the Judean kingdom. Material is taken from two previous Chronicles—those of Israel and of Judah (not our books of Chronicles) according to 1 K. 14:19 and vs. 29, which were apparently written before the destruction of Jerusalem (1 K. 8:8). Deliverance from Babylon not being mentioned, it seems that the books of Kings were completed toward the end of the Exile (2 K. 25:27). The writer is unknown; probably one close to Jeremiah. There are practical difficulties which in some cases seem insoluble. The disparity in the total years of the kings of the two kingdoms may be offset to some extent by noting the custom of making fragments of years equal to whole years, thus counting them twice, and by the allowance of interregnal years, say in times of chaos or when the government was administered by an Assyrian officer. The parallel histories of the two kingdoms touch in several points where synchronisms are precise, e.g., the accessions of Jeroboam I and Rehoboam (1 K. 12). Errors in our Bibles, as over against the original, always lurk in numbers, letters being used for them, and in the ready possibility of scribal errors in transcription. The writer is especially concerned with the Davidic monarchy; and as does the writer of Genesis, so does this writer dispose of less important matters before treating the main idea, thus recording Israel's events before taking up the parallel and contemporaneous data in Judah, sometimes the same event (2 K. 17:5-6, with 18:9). Three divisions are noted: (1) The reign of Solomon (1 K. 1–11). (2) Synchronistic account of both kingdoms until the Captivity of Israel (1 K. 12:1–2 K. 17). (3) Kingdom of Judah to the Exile.

Kir (kǐr) [wall] the land from which the Arameans migrated to Syria (Amos 9:7), and to which the captives of Damascus were removed by Tiglath-pileser (2 K. 16:9; Amos 1:5). A number of guesses, but no certainty as to identity.

Kir of Moab a fortified city of South Moab (Isa. 15:1), likely the same as Kir-haraseth, Kir-haresh, Kir-hareseth, Kir-heres (2 K. 3:25; Isa. 16:7, 11; Jer. 48:31, 36). It resisted the combined forces of Israel, Judah, and Edom (2 K. 3:25), modern name being Kerak, eleven miles east of the southern bay of the Dead Sea, and eighteen miles south of Arnon River, connected with Roman and Mohammedan times.

Kiriath (kǐr'ǐ-ǎth) [city, comparable to our burg] a town of Benjamin, sometimes associated with Kirjath-jearim (Josh. 18:28).

Kiriathaim (kǐr-ǐ-à-thā'ǐm) [twin cities] ancient Emim city (Gen. 14:5); rebuilt by Reubenites (Num. 32:37); taken by Moabites (Jer. 48:1, 23; Ezek. 25:9). Same as Kirjathaim. Same as Kartan (1 Chr. 6:76).

Kiriath-arba [city of Arba, or croucher] old name for Hebron, perhaps founded by Arba father of Anak (Gen. 23:2; Josh. 14:15; Judg. 1:10; see Neh. 11:25).

Kirjath-arim, as **Kirjath-jearim** (Ezra 2:25).
Kirjath-baal see below.
Kirjath-huzoth (kǐr'jäth-hǔ'zōth) [city of streets] associated with Balaam and Balak (Num. 22:39).
Kirjath-jearim (kǐr'jäth-jē'à-rǐm) [city of woods] important in history, it was originally Gibeon's (Josh. 9:17); on the western boundary line between Judah and Benjamin, but counted to Judah (Josh. 18:14–15; Judg. 18:12). Same as Baalah and Kirjath-baal. Perhaps its reputation for sanctity led the Beth-shemeshites to send the plague-bearing ark thither (1 Sam. 6:20–21), where it remained for twenty years (7:2), when David took it to the house of Obed-edom (1 Chr. 13:5–6; 2 Sam. 6:2). It lies nine miles from Jerusalem on the road to Lydda.
Kirjath-sannah (kǐr'jäth-săn'nä) [city of instruction?] see **Debir** (Josh. 15:49).
Kirjath-sepher (-sē'fěr) [-book] early name for Debir (Josh. 15:15–16).
Kish (kǐsh) [bow, power] 1. Father of Saul; a Benjaminite of the family of Matri (1 Sam. 10:21), of Abiel (9:1); also registered as a son of Ner and a descendant of Jeiel (1 Chr. 8:33, 9:36, 39), which seems to mean only that Kish was a descendant of Ner, allowing the insertion of Abiel and others between Kish and Ner. 1 Sam. 9:1 gives impression of other branches of the family tree.

2. Son of Jeiel and uncle to the preceding (1 Chr. 9:36).

3. A Benjaminite, great-grandfather to Mordecai (Est. 2:5).

4. A Levite of David's time, house of Mahli (1 Chr. 23:21–22).

Kishi (kǐsh'ī) a Merarite, ancestor of Ethan the minstrel (1 Chr. 6:44).

Kishion (kǐsh'ī-ŏn) [hardness] a town on the boundary of Issachar (Josh. 19:20), with suburbs, allotted to Gershonite Levites (21:28). Same as **Kishon.**

Kishon (kī'shŏn) [bending] a most significant stream of Central Palestine. Sisera's beaten soldiers fleeing north from Taanach, were swept away attempting to cross (Judg. 5:19–21; Ps. 83:9). The priests of Baal in contest with Elijah, were slain on its south bank (1 K. 18:40). West of Beth-shean begins the stream, tortuously pushing northwest through Esdraelon's plain. Although only fifteen to eighteen feet across, looking insignificant, its treacherous banks and muddy bottom did for the Turks and Arabs (whipped by the French at the battle of Tabor, April 16, 1799) the same that it did for Sisera's vanquished army. It goes through the plain of Acre, sand dunes studded with palm trees, interfering with its latter course toward the Mediterranean. In Ps. 83:9, it is misspelled *Kison*.

kiss affectionate salutation, generally on cheek or neck, customary among near relatives of both sexes, an oriental custom from patriarchal times (Gen. 29:11; Song of S. 8:1); between fathers and descendants (2 Sam. 14:33), and the reverse (1 K. 19:20); brother and sister, and brother and brother (Song of S. 8:1; Ex. 4:27); other kinsfolk (Ex. 18:7; Ruth 1:9); also comrades (1 Sam. 20:41; Acts 20:37). In our Lord's time, the invited guest was thus greeted by his host (Lk. 7:45); and thus also love and Christian brotherhood were manifested (Rom. 16:16; 1 Pet. 5:14). Herein lies the added infamy of Judas (Mt. 26:48–49). The kiss of kings (or idols, 1 K. 19:18) indicated great respect or allegiance (Ps. 2:12; Lk. 7:38, 45); sometimes the written decree was kissed, or the ground (Ps. 72:9). Throwing a kiss by the hand is Biblical (Job 31:27).

kite bird of prey of the falcon family, with pointed wings and a forked tail and keenness of vision, noted three times: Lev. 11:14; Deut. 14:13; Job 28:7 (here translated "vulture"). A different Hebrew word is translated as vulture, along with the word translated "kite" in the Leviticus reference. Some say that in Palestine were the red and the black and the Egyptian kite; impossible now to know which the Hebrew words mean.

Kithlish (kĭth′lĭsh) [separation?] an unidentified town in lowland Judah (Josh. 15:40).

Kitron (kĭt′rŏn) [smoke] a town of Zebulun from which Canaanites were not expelled (Judg. 1:30).

Kittim or **Chittim** (kĭt′ĭm) the descendants of Javan in the table of the nations (Gen. 10:4; 1 Chr. 1:7) and used in later OT sources to designate the island of Cyprus (Isa. 23:1, 12; Ezek. 27:6; Jer. 2:10). There was a city (Kition or Citium) on Cyprus, and Josephus considered that the name had spread from the city to all the island (*Ant.* I.iv.1). Balaam predicted ships from Kittim would help in the fight against Assyria (Num. 24:24). Many think that in Dan. 11:30 Roman ships are meant, and Rome fits the meaning of references to the Kittim in the Dead Sea Scrolls best also.

J.W.R.

kneading troughs see **bread**

knee, kneel Scripture puts weakness in the knees (Job 4:4; Ps. 109:24). Children on the knees of father seems to mean recognition as legitimate members of the family (Gen. 30:3, 50:23). Kneeling is a proper attitude in prayer (1 K. 18:42; Ps. 95:6; Acts 20:36); sitting has

no scriptural endorsement. See "to bow the knee" (1 K. 19:18; Rom. 14:11). Reverence and entreaty are thus shown (2 K. 1:13; Mt. 17:14).

knife in early times, generally of hard stone, and for sacred purposes, even after introduction of iron. Hebrews had several kinds of knives: for slaughtering and cutting up animals (Lev. 7:33–34; Num. 18:18; 1 Sam. 9:24); smaller ones for paring fruit (Josephus) and for sharpening pens, i.e., the stylus (Jer. 36:23); razor (Num. 6:5; Ezek. 5:1); pruning hooks (Isa. 18:5); lancets of Baal's priests (1 K. 18:28). The "sharp knives" for circumcision (Josh. 5:2) were of stone. There are four different Hebrew words translated "knife."

knop two Hebrew words so translated, have in common the fact that they refer to ornamental or architectural object, the one to a part of the tabernacle candlestick (Ex. 25:33–36), or to the capital of a column (Amos 9:1, where translated "lintel"); the other, a cedar-wood ornament associated with flowers in Solomon's temple, possibly in gourd shape (1 K. 6:18).

Koa problematical: apparently a people, and perhaps a by-form of Kutu of the Babylonian inscriptions, whose seat was northeast of Babylon.

Kohath (kō′hăth) [assembly?] also **Kohathites** a family derived from the second son of Levi, Kohath, the father of Amram, and he, of Moses and Aaron, although very likely there are gaps in the genealogy, as was Hebrew custom often (Gen. 46:11). Moses and Aaron were of this line, the latter being, through Kohath, the progenitor of all the priests, while those not priests, but still Levites (as also were the priests), were associated with the priests, and carried the sanctuary parts and its vessels after the priests had covered them, for the march. There were four families of the sons of Kohath (Ex. 6:18–22; 1 Chr. 23:12, 26:23–32). They were wealthy and prominent, filling various other offices than the tabernacle ministry (cf. the above references, also 2 Chr. 20:19). At the first census in the wilderness, the males from a month upward, was 8600 (Num. 3:28), and those from thirty to fifty, 2750 (4:34–37). In subsequent allotment of cities, the priests (i.e., Aaron's line), had shares with the other Kohathites, the former obtaining thirteen cities out of the tribes of Judah, Simeon, and Benjamin, and the latter, ten out of the tribes of Ephraim, Dan, and Manasseh (Josh. 21:4–5; 1 Chr. 6:61, 66–70). Korah's sister was Jochebed (Ex. 6:20); he lived 133 years (vs. 18).

Kolaiah (kō-lā′yä) [voice of Jehovah] 1. Father of false prophet Ahab (Jer. 29:21).

2. A Benjaminite (Neh. 11:7).

Korah (kō′rä) [ice, baldness] 1. A son of Esau and a duke of Edom, born in Canaan (Gen. 36:5, 14, 18).

2. Another duke, son of Eliphaz, son of Esau (Gen. 36:16), perhaps inserted by error, since not found in vss. 11 or 12, or 1 Chr. 1:36.

3. Son of Hebron (1 Chr. 2:43).

4. A Levite, family of Kohath, house of Izhar (Num. 16:1). In conjunction with Dathan, Abiram, and On (Reubenites), he rebelled against his cousins, Moses and Aaron, in the wilderness. His pet peeve, with his company, was their exclusion from the priesthood, the Levites being limited to inferior service in the tabernacle; and the appointment of Elizaphan as chief, may have further inflamed him (Num. 3:30). (The Reubenites' disaffection lay in the fact that the right of the firstborn to leadership, was possessed by Levi, including Moses and Aaron.) In Num. 16 is the whole sad story (complemented by Num. 26:9–11), where we learn that the haughty and ambitious Korah contended with Moses and Aaron, who after exposing the rebels and pleading with the Lord to spare the crowd, commanded all who were near to the adjacent Korahite and Reubenite locations, on the south of the tabernacle, to move away from the impending judgment on the rebels. The ground opened to swallow up, as it appears, only the tents of the Reubenites, Korah's children being preserved, Korah himself, we gather from vss. 27 and 32, being consumed in the shortly thereafter occurring cremation of the 250 who offered incense (vss. 35, 40). Korah is linked with Cain and Balaam (Jude 11).

Korahite, Korhite, Korathite Kohathites of Korah's line are often called sons of Korah, being singers in the Kohath division, Heman being one of them (1 Chr. 6:33). See 2 Chr. 20:19 also. Psalms "for the sons of Korah" are: 42 (combined with 43), 44–49, 84–85, 87–88. Other sons were doorkeepers in the temple and bakers (1 Chr. 9:19, 31–32). Samuel as well as Heman, was a Korhite (1 Chr. 6:33–38). For the various spellings, see Ex. 6:24; Num. 26:58; 1 Chr. 9:19, 31, 12:6.

Kore (kō′rē) [partridge] 1. A Levite, Korah's house (1 Chr. 9:19, 26:1).

2. In connection with porters, 1 Chr. 26:19 probably should read "the sons of the Korhite."

3. Son of Imlah, time of Hezekiah (2 Chr. 31:14).

Koz (kŏz) [thorn] Ezra 2:61; Neh. 3:4, 21. Same as Accoz, **Coz, Hakkoz.**

Kushaiah (kū-shā′yä) [bow of Jehovah] a Levite, family of Merari, house of Mushi (1 Chr. 15:17); in 6:44, Kishi; also Kish.

L

Laadah (lā-ā′dä) [order] man of Judah, and father of Mareshah's inhabitants (1 Chr. 4:21).

Laadan (lā′ā-dăn) [well-ordered] 1. An Ephraimite, ancestor of Joshua (1 Chr. 7:26).

2. Son of Gershom, called also Libni (1 Chr. 23:7–9, 26:21).

Laban (lā′băn) [white] 1. Son of Bethuel, and grandson of Nahor, Abraham's brother, also father of Leah and Rachel. He lived in Haran of Paddan-aram (Gen. 24:10, 15, 29:5), remaining there when Abraham went to Canaan; first met in connection with his part in the betrothal of his sister Rebekah to her cousin Isaac (Gen. 24). Next he is the host of his nephew Jacob, who fled from the sworn vengeance of his cheated brother, Esau (Gen. 29:13–14). The rich uncle (29:16, 24, 29, 30:30, 35, 31:1, 38), secured the valuable services of the swain for fourteen years as the price of his two daughters, and six more for his cattle, Jacob meeting his match, but coming off victor, despite the father-in-law's scurrilous bridal-chamber trick, his stern overlordship, his holding Jacob responsible for loss, and his strict regime which cost the son-in-law sleep, the endurance of heat by day and frost by night, and change of wages ten times (31:39–42). Jacob's crafty animal husbandry made him rich beyond his host, and excited enmity of both the man Laban and his sons. Suspecting trouble, he left unceremoniously while Laban was away from home; and being overtaken after three days flight, in Mount Gilead, east of Jordan, Jacob cited God's providence as his sole protection, entering into covenant of mutual guarantee against harm with his father-in-law, his wife meanwhile, with inherited traits of deception, getting away with the household gods of Paddan-aram; and the antagonists parted to meet no more. Laban combined idolatry with worship of his fathers' God, and practiced divination (24:50, 30:27; ARV, 31:30, 53, 35:4).

2. An unidentified place in the Sinaitic peninsula (Deut. 1:1). Could be same as Libnah (Num. 33:20); Syriac understands it as Lebanon.

Lachish (lā′kĭsh) [tenacious?] a fortified city in Judah's lowland, first noted in the Bible as in coalition with Jerusalem's king against the Gibeonites, but reduced by Joshua despite Gezer's assistance (Josh. 15:33, 39, 10:3–35, 12:11). Rehoboam fortified it (2 Chr. 11:9); fleeing Amaziah was there murdered (2 K. 14:19). In the reign of Hezekiah, Sennacherib of Assyria, en route to Egypt, from Lachish (apparently occupied by him), had correspondence with Judah's king (2 K. 18:14–17; cf. 19:8; Isa. 36:2, 37:8). It was one of the last cities to stand against the Babylonian king (Jer. 34:7). After the Exile, Jews reoccupied it and the surrounding fields (Neh. 11:30). Micah (1:13) denounces it as "the beginning of sin to the daughter of Zion." Major Conder identified it with Tell el-hesy, sixteen miles east by north of Gaza. Another site in the neighborhood preserves the name, Umm Lakis. The archaeologist J. L. Starkey (1835) found eighteen written documents, the Lachish Letters, and a ewer, "the most important discovery of modern times in respect to Biblical criticism," (quoted by Charles Marston, *The Bible Comes Alive* [1938], p. 277), its date being ca. 1500 B.C. These letters, contemporary with Jeremiah and the last kings of Judah, examples of personal correspondence in archaic Hebrew (Phoenician), indicate the general use of writing, and show startling data on the political, military, and religious history of the people just before the fall of Jerusalem, 586 B.C. (J. McK. Adams, *Ancient Records and the Bible* [1946], p. 102). Ten towns seem to have occupied the site of Lachish, the earliest being Amoritic. On the strategic site, walls, said to have been from eight to sixteen feet thick, protected the town, in pre-Conquest times, with guarding ravines on the south and west.

Lael (lā′ĕl) [devoted to God] a Gershonite, father of Eliasaph (Num. 3:24).

Lahad (lā′hăd) [oppressed] son of Jahath (1 Chr. 4:2).

Lahai-roi (lȧ-hī′roy) [(well) of the living (one) seeing me] in Gen. 24:62, 25:11, is this form

of the name of the famous well of Hagar's relief, where Isaac afterward resided (Gen. 25:11).

Lahmam (lä′măm) [place of heat, or of violence?] village in Judah's lowland (Josh. 15:40).

Lahmi (lä′mī) [my bread?, or perhaps, a Bethlehemite] brother of Goliath the Gittite (1 Chr. 20:5; see 2 Sam. 21:19).

Laish (lā′ish) [a lion] 1. A man of Gallim (1 Sam. 25:44; 2 Sam. 3:15).

2. A village (Isa. 10:30), apparently different from the next.

3. Canaanite city in extreme north of Palestine, taken by the Danites and named Dan (Judg. 18:7–29), evidently near Banias, and probably the same as Laishah, between Gallim and Anathoth (Isa. 10:30).

lakes see Palestine

Lakkum (lăk′kŭm) [obstruction] a landmark town on border of Naphtali (Josh. 19:33).

lamb there are at least five words rendered thus: Ezra 6:9, an Aramaic word, equivalent to the word oft used (as in Ex. 29:38; Lev. 4:32), and meaning, whether in masculine or feminine form, a lamb from first to third year; Deut. 32:14, a fat ram, or more probably, wether; Ex. 12:21, a collective term denoting a flock of small cattle, as distinct from larger cattle (Ezek. 45:15); Gen. 22:7; Ex. 12:3, an individual of the flock whether sheep or goats. The fat-tailed is the common sheep of Palestine, which tail is sometimes enormous, including the whole rump (Ex. 29:22). The flock is led by a shepherd; on a journey, two shepherds. In the open, folds of piled-up stones enclose the flock; the shepherd has a cave or hut. To kill a lamb for a stranger is one of the first acts of Bedouin hospitality; also on festive occasions (1 Sam. 25:18). See **Passover**

Lamech (lā′mĕk) [a young man] 1. Son of Methusael of Cain's line, the first bigamist, his two wives and daughter being the only women noted in antediluvian times (Gen. 4:18–24). Adah's Jabal and Jubal, and Zillah's Tubal-cain (Naamah, her daughter), are celebrated as inventors. In the remarkable preflood poem, Lamech, with his son's invention, the sword, swaggers that whereas God would avenge any threat to Cain, Lamech could do ten times better and then some. Luther considers the origin of the poem to be the deliberate murder of Cain by Lamech.

2. An antediluvian patriarch of Seth's line, the father of Noah who seems to express in the name, a better and happier life under God's blessing (Gen. 5:25–31).

Lamentations mournful speeches, elegies (2

lamp

Sam. 1:17–27). The title of this book, put in the Hagiographa (Sacred Writings), between Ruth and Ecclesiastes, is (as in the cases of the five books of Moses), taken from the first word of it, which seems to have been the common word for the beginning of a wailing song. No name is given; but the established belief of the Jews is that Jeremiah wrote the book; and the impression is that an eyewitness of the last days of Jerusalem, with vividness and intensity, must have been the writer. The LXX prefix very definitely names Jeremiah, "after Israel was led into captivity and Jerusalem was laid waste." A complicated alphabetical structure pervades most of the five different poems, each complete in itself, and each having distinct subjects, but brought into an over-all plan. Chapters 1–2, 4–5 have each twenty-two verses, and ch. 3, twenty-two times three, or sixty-six verses. There are twenty-two letters in the Hebrew alphabet; and in chs. 1, 2, and 4, the verses are alphabetically arranged, vs. 1 beginning with the first letter, vs. 2 with the second, and so on throughout. In ch. 3, the first three verses begin with the first Hebrew letter, and the next three, with the second, and on to the end similarly. The fifth chapter is not alphabetically arranged. The theme of the whole is the fate of the capital, with the defenders' dreadful suffering from sword, famine, and outrages of every kind, all brought on by the sins of the people along with prophets and priests. The opening verse strikes the keynote of the whole. The prophet had urged submission; and now the predicted sufferings surpass all prediction, all that had been imagined. The writer is swallowed up in deep overwhelming sorrow. The state at times is personified as a man bemoaning the hard fate (1:9, 12–22); again the prophet for the nation speaks in the first person (2:11, 3:1–51). The solitude of the city is prominent in the first poem; the destruction is conspicuous in the second; the third is quite a gospel for the heavy-laden—trust in the mercy and righteousness of Jehovah; in the fourth, the same features as in the first and second appear, with the contrast between the past glory and the later shame. The fifth poem seems to be of later date, some say by another hand. There is the continued suffering under the Chaldean rule, which appears to have wrought effectively: it has supplied multitudes with the fullest utterance of their sorrows in critical times. The weary exile years must have been soothed thereby. On the ninth day of the month Ab (July), Lamentations was read, year by year, with fasting and weeping to commemorate the misery out of which the people had been delivered. It enters into the Passion-week worship of the Latin church.

lamp a vessel with a wick and flammable liquid, for illumination, ordinarily of earthenware, with hole in center for putting in oil, and one at side for the wick, sometimes with a cover. The Hebrew word for lamp is translated light in 2 Sam. 21:17, but ordinarily candle (e.g., Jer. 25:10). Another word is often translated lamp (Heb. *lappid*, Judg. 7:16), but also firebrand, torch, lightning (Ex. 20:18; Judg. 15:4; Nah. 2:4). The Greek word for lamp (Mt. 25:1) is lights in Acts 20:8, and torches, in Jn. 18:3. The lamp may refer to one's family (Prov. 13:9). Gideon's soldiers carried them (Judg. 7:16; cf. 15:4); so also marriage processions (as above). Lamps were light-bearing parts of the golden candlestick, also of those of Solomon, before the Holy of Holies (Ex. 25:37; 2 Chr. 4:20; 1 K. 7:49; Zech. 4:2); lighted every evening and cleaned every morning (Ex. 30:7–8).

lancet found only in 1 K. 18:28. In original version (1611), lancers. The Hebrew word is commonly rendered javelin, light spear.

language see **tongues, confusion of**

lantern only in Jn. 18:3. In many eastern towns, law forbids any on the streets after nightfall without a lantern. Some had metal top and bottom, with bladder, transparent horn, or waxed cloth for sides.

Laodicea (lā-ŏd-ĭ-cē′á) [pertaining to Laodice] originally Diospolis, city of Zeus, enlarged and improved by the Seleucid, Antiochus II, and named for his wife. Chief city of Phrygia Pacatiana, in Asia Minor, near Colossae, on the Lycos, tributary of the Meander River. Here material from black sheep wool was manufactured; here a medical school whose physicians made powder for ophthalmia. Josephus tells that many Jews lived in Laodicea (*Ant.* XIV.10). Epaphras is said to have founded the church there (Col. 4:12–13). Paul, concerned for them (2:1), wrote a letter (4:15–16), perhaps leaving a copy there, thought by some to be Ephesians. One of the seven Asian churches, it was rebuked (Rev. 1:11, 3:14–22), with allusions to noted products and wealth. About A.D. 65, with other adjacent cities, it was destroyed by an earthquake; but it was rebuilt by the citizens without customary aid from Rome. The ruins are now called Eski Hissar, ca. fifty-six miles east-southeast of Smyrna.

Lappidoth (lăp′pĭ-dōth) [torches] husband of prophetess Deborah (Judg. 4:4).

lapwing only in Lev. 11:19 (and parallel in Deut. 14:18), forbidden as food. The LXX and Vulg., and general consent, say the hoopoe

208

is meant, about a foot long, grayish-brown above, wings and shoulders black, barred with white, and large crest.

Lasea (lȧ-sē′ȧ) seaport of Crete, near Fair Havens (Acts 27:8). In 1856, G. Brown discovered ruins supposedly marking the site, on the southern coast, five miles east of Fair Havens.

Lasha (lā′shȧ) [a fissure] in Gen. 10:19 only; southeast of the Dead Sea, said by Jerome et al. to be same as Callirrhoe, famous for hot springs, located about three miles east of the Dead Sea, into which the stream flows.

Lasharon (lȧ-shā′rŏn) [probably, to Sharon] a town whose king was slain by Joshua (12:18). The LXX seems to indicate that the original text was "the king of Aphek (which belongs) to Sharon."

latchet the sandal thong, proverbially used of something trivial (Gen. 14:23). Unfastening the sandals of the great, fell to the meanest slaves (Lk. 3:16).

Latin the language spoken by the Romans, but not adopted in Palestine although for hundreds of years under Rome; found only in Jn. 19:20 and Lk. 23:38. Various Latinisms are seen in the NT: farthing, centurion, legion.

lattice three Hebrew words are so rendered: Judg. 5:28; Prov. 7:6 (here, casement), parallel to window. Song of S. 2:9 has a later word of same significance. The third word means a network of crossed laths, covering a window (2 K. 1:2), through which Ahaziah fell to mortal injury.

laver basin for washing, as the brass or copper one in the tabernacle, where priests washed hands and feet before sacrificing; located between the altar and the tabernacle door. The priests were consecrated once for life; but daily must cleanse hands and feet which came into contact with defiling elements (here lies the significance of the Lord's word to Peter about need for washing only hands and feet as in Jn. 13:10). The laver and base were made of the mirrors donated by ministering women (Ex. 38:8), who probably came at stated intervals as did the Levites and priests (Deut. 18:6; Lk. 1:8, 23; see Ex. 15:20; Ps. 68:25). In Solomon's temple were molten sea and ten lavers (1 K. 7:23-26, 38-40, 43. Ahaz made rearrangements (2 K. 16:17).

law in general, a definite commandment from a recognized authority, human or divine, whether general or particular. When used with the article, without limiting words, it refers to the expressed will of God, and almost always, to the Mosaic law or the Pentateuch. The Heb. *torah* rather stresses moral authority regarding truth, and guidance in the right way. The Gr.

nomos speaks of constraining power, as imposed and enforced by recognized authority. In Paul the word assumes more abstract character, *nomos* when used by him still refers in general to the law of Moses; but without the article, thus embracing any manifestation of the "law," it includes all powers acting on the will of man by compulsion, or by pressure of external motives, whether in definite forms or not. Law as internal principle of action (Rom. 7:23), is not disparate. Also the term is employed loosely of the whole OT (Jn. 10:34, 15:25; 1 Cor. 14:21).

Law of Moses (the Law of God: Josh. 24:26; 2 Chr. 31:3) was given of God through Moses (Ex. 20:19-22; Jn. 1:17), and was written in a book (Josh. 1:7-8). It included the legislation in Exodus, Leviticus, Numbers, and Deuteronomy (Mk. 12:26 with Ex. 3:6; Mk. 7:10 with Ex. 20:12, 21:17; Jn. 7:22-23 with Lev. 12:2-3; Mt. 8:4 with Lev. 14:3; Mt. 19:8 and 22:24 with Deut. 24:1 and 25:5). It was the title of the Pentateuch, the first division of the canon (Lk. 24:44). The eternal and universal portion (Ex. 20:1-21), together with the so-called Book of the Covenant (chs. 21-23) relating to the "rights" of the Israelites, whether civil or social, on the human plane (21:1-23:13, touching persons, property, miscellaneous data, veracity, rest and beneficence), or of religious and theocratic relationship, on the divine plane (23:14-19); and persuasives to keep the covenant (23:20-33)—all was given at Sinai, the Ten Commandments only, being given direct from God, the other parts through Moses. After the consequent blood-covenant at Sinai, comes the revelation concerning communion of the people with their God—the tabernacle, which being erected, prepares the way for Leviticus with regulations about approaching God. Then comes the discipline of Numbers; and thirty-eight years later, Moses rehearsed the Law publicly before the new generation, with modifications on the basis of experience and in view of the prospective changes looking to Palestine (Deuteronomy). Thus the Pentateuch gives: the ancestry of the people (Genesis); the present life of the people (Exodus—emergence; Leviticus—laws; Numbers—discipline); and the future of the people (Deuteronomy)—an organically complete whole. It is evident that much in the Law is of local, temporary, and particularly Israelitish significance, whereas the remaining essential parts are of permanent nature and relate to the Christian era and for all time (Ex. 20:12 or Deut. 5:16 with Eph. 6:2-3). When therefore we read: "not under the law, but under grace" (Rom. 6:14), the sequence is not horizontal but vertical, grace intervening between the Law with its penalty for sin and the believer. For "law defines life." The ceremonial law (Heb. 8:7, apparently), decays, vanishes away (vs. 13; and see chs. 8–10). And so it was not imposed on Gentile converts (Acts 15:23–29). Its function was to point to the Great High Priest, who alone can take away sin. So the Law is our schoolmaster (chaperon!) to lead us to Christ (Gal. 3:24). The greatest fact in Scripture is the Abrahamic covenant (Gal. 3:8, 29); and the Mosaic regime was a shunt, for the sinful nation, to give to a world sodden in sin, a pattern of life, an exemplar, to lift men up again into the covenant line of life (3:17).

lawyer one versed in the law of Moses, a scribe, an interpreter (Mt. 22:35 with Mk. 12:28). The term probably stressed the religious rather than the legal angle. See Lk. 10:25, 11:45–52.

laying on of hands see **baptism**

Lazarus (lăz′ȧ-rŭs) [God helps] a form of the Hebrew Eleazar. 1. The beggar, in the parable of Lk. 16, ulcerous, licked by dogs, desiring crumbs from the sumptuous table of the rich man. Of the characters of the two, nothing is said. At death, Lazarus went to the traditional Abraham's bosom; the rich man to torment. Not, as appears, is the reward simply for poverty, and the condemnation, for affluence. The hint about the brothers' unbelief and need of repentance, shows a moral element: conduct, not position, enters in.

2. A member of the Bethany family, with Martha and Mary, a good man as shown by the love of his sisters and of the Lord (Jn. 11:1, 31, 36). It is inferred that he was the youngest (vs. 5). Some say Lazarus was the rich young ruler of Mt. 19. His death having occurred, the sisters sent to the Lord, beyond Jordan; but he delayed two days, two more being required for the journey. Met by Martha outside the village, the Lord called forth expression of her faith in the resurrection, and himself gave the inspiring words, so often employed, touching that fact. The three went to the sepulcher, a cave or hole in the rock with a stone to cover it. Here praying the Father, he called Lazarus forth, the miracle making profound effect, causing his enthusiastic reception at Jerusalem, and bringing the Sanhedrin to determine his death—better one man to die than the whole nation lost (Jn. 11:45–53, 12:9–19). Lazarus was present at Simon's supper (12:1–2; Mk. 14:3). Lazarus drops out of the record. There is baseless tradition about his living thirty years afterward, and preaching the Gospel till martyrdom at sixty years.

lead a quite common metal known to the ancients including Israel, found generally in combination with silver for whose purifying it was used by the process of cupellation (as seems suggested in Ezek. 22:20). Lead was found in the peninsula of Sinai; was imported from Tarshish (Ezek. 27:12); used for weights (Zech. 5:7); was of the spoils from Midian (Num. 31:22). Job 19:24 may refer to pouring molten lead into the cavities of carved letters.

leaf 1. Foliage of a tree (Gen. 3:7).
2. Part of the wing of a folding door (1 K. 6:34; Ezek. 41:24).
3. The page or column of a roll (Jer. 36:23; see vs. 2).

Leah (lē′ä) [wild cow] elder daughter of Laban, lacking the beauty of flashing eyes, by deceit married to Jacob, after he had served seven years for Rachel, his "hatred" of her being idiomatic way of saying less loved than Rachel (Gen. 29). In quick succession Leah bore Reuben, Simeon, Levi, Judah, then Issachar, Zebulun, and Dinah, before Rachel's motherhood (30:17–21). She died after Jacob returned to his father's neighborhood, and was buried in the family grave at Mahpelah (49:31). Possibly Leah means "mistress."

leasing falsehood (Ps. 4:2). Generally translated "lies" (40:4).

leather occurs twice in the KJV, in re girdle (2 K. 1:8; Mt. 3:4). Tanning and dyeing was known to Hebrews (Ex. 25:5; Acts 9:43). "Leather" may be the proper word where KVJ has skin, as regards clothing (Lev. 11:32), covering for tents (Ex. 26:14), shields (2 Sam. 1:21), sandals (Ezek. 16:10).

leaven various substances produced fermentation; but ordinary leaven was a lump of highly fermented dough, put in a mass for baking. Leaven was forbidden in all sacrifices made by fire (Lev. 2:11; so, Amos 4:5, ironically); but might be used in offerings to be eaten by man (Lev. 7:13, 23:17). Leaven was emblematic of corruption: of doctrine (Mt. 16:11); of the heart (1 Cor. 5:6–8). Also it symbolized moral influence generally (Mt. 13:33). During the Passover festival, Israel eschewed leaven, its absence symbolizing incorruptness of life; reminded of the haste in fleeing Egypt; and suggested the affliction of Egypt by the insipidity of bread (Ex. 12:39; Deut. 16:3; 1 Cor. 5:7).

Lebana (lĕb′ä-nȧ) [whiteness] a Nethinim (Neh. 7:48).

Lebanon (lĕb′ȧ-nŏn) [white] a snow-clad mountain range (Jer. 18:14), with lesser hills in all directions (Hos. 14:6), Hermon the loftiest peak (Song of S. 7:4, probably). In the Grecian period, Lebanon was restricted to the western range, the eastern being called "Anti-Lebanon" (Josh. 13:5). The valley between is Coele-Syria ["hollow"], or the Bekaa. The western range is separated from Galilee by the Litany River. Famous for trees and animals, it was the northwestern boundary of the Promised Land (Deut. 1:7; Josh. 1:4, 13:5; 1 K. 5:6–10; 2 K. 14:9; Ezra 3:7; Zech. 11:1). The western range, Lebanon proper, is nearly 100 miles long; but the eastern, counting Hermon as separate, is only sixty-five. The western heights are fertile and picturesque, with many streams, seaward-bound: the eastern slopes are rather barren. The Lebanon water supply makes the fertility of Galilee, in contrast to Samaria and Judea. In the early twentieth century, Lebanon rejoiced in a freer and better government than other Syrian parts; since the massacre of 1860, a Christian governor, appointed with European powers' approval, ruled in behalf of the Sultan. There are carriage roads; and the French railway runs from Beyrout to Damascus, at points around 5000 feet elevation. Lebanon is now a republic of the Middle East, bounded by Syria and Israel and the Mediterranean Sea, covering 4000 square miles, with a population of ca. 2,000,000 (1962), the language being Arabic. Religion is 50% Christian, and 34% Muslim. It is a member of the Arab League. It seeks to divert the waters of the Hasbani River but fears Israeli attack. It is generally prosperous economically.

Lebaoth (lĕb'à-ōth) [lioness] a town in the extreme south of Judah (Josh. 15:32); likely same as Beth-Lebaoth. May be same as Beth-birei (1 Chr. 4:31), by error in spelling.

Lebbaeus (lĕb'bē-ŭs) Judas; called also Thaddaeus: see Mt. 10:3; Mk. 3:18. In the former reference is Lebbaeus, the two similar sounding names coming from different words with same meaning.

Lebonah (lē-bō'nä) [incense] a town north of Shiloh (Judg. 21:19); identified with Lubban on road between Shechem and Jerusalem.

Lecah (lē'cä) [perhaps, journey] a name in the genealogies of Judah (1 Chr. 4:21), apparently descendant of Shelah son of Judah. By context, could be a village of Judah.

leech see **horseleech**

leeks Num. 11:5; but commonly denotes grass, from root "green," including a number of succulents. By context, leeks seems to be correct translation in the reference above. Botanical: *Allium porrum*.

lees has root idea of preservation, applied to dregs or sediment in standing wine or other liquor, preserving color or body. "Wine on the lees" (Isa. 25:6) is generous, full-bodied liquor.

"Well-refined" means with lees strained off. To "drink the lees" signifies endurance of extreme punishment (Ps. 75:8). See Jer. 48:11; Zeph. 1:12, for this expression, as contentment.

legion chief subdivision of Roman army, originally 3000 foot, with some cavalry. From 100 B.C., up to 6000; in NT times, 6000, cavalry not attached, each legion being divided into ten cohorts, and these each into three maniples, or bands, and these in turn into three (or two?) centuries, of 100 each. A centurion seems to have been in charge of ten centuries. In Scripture, legion seems to refer proverbially to a large number in orderly combination (Mt. 26:53; Mk. 5:9).

Lehabim (lē'hà-bĭm) [perhaps, flame-colored] a tribe sprung from Mizraim (Gen. 10:13; 1 Chr. 1:11). Same as **Lubim** (Libyans).

Lehi (lē'hī) [jawbone] an elevated place in Judah where the Philistines spread themselves to take Samson, supposedly between the cliff Etam and the Philistine country. On the origin of the name the text is not plain—whether from the famous exploit, or because of the shape of the ridges where performed (Judg. 15).

Lemuel (lĕm'ū-ĕl) [devoted to God] the kingly author of the prudential maxims taught him by his mother (Prov. 31), suggested as being Solomon, or Hezekiah.

lentils the plant was boiled as pottage (2 Sam. 23:11; Gen. 25:29, 34); and by the poor used as bread (Ezek. 4:9); wild and cultivated in Palestine, having broad, wholesome legumes. The Arabic corresponds to the Hebrew name, *'adas*.

leopard a spotted animal (Jer. 13:23), from its Hebrew name [*namer*]; swift (Hab. 1:8); fond of kids (Isa. 11:6); lurking near villages; dangerous to man (Jer. 5:6; Hos. 13:7–8), though ordinarily a mountain dweller (Song of S. 4:8). The English name is a compound of *leo* (lion) and *pardus* (panther), believed a hybrid. Under the Hebrew name is the cheetah included. In Dan. 7:6, the leopard refers to a fierce nation and king—Greece (8:21); and in Rev. 13:2, the composite of the four beasts of Daniel, typifies the united world powers, having the body of the leopard.

leper, leprosy scriptural leprosy is mainly the white variety, *Lepra Mosaica* (Ex. 4:6; Lev. 13:13; Num. 12:10; 2 K. 5:1, 27). But it seems that the disease noted in Lev. 13 and 14, means any severe affection spreading on the body surface. Generally leprosy in Scripture is different from elephantiasis, now so widespread. It excluded from fellowship, from the sanctuary, required mourning signs and a warning cry (Lev. 13:45; Lk. 17:12–13). Strangely,

Leshem

when the whole body was covered, the leper was adjudged clean (Lev. 13:6, 12–13), whether, having run its course, it was no longer considered a curse, or, only when the sufferer was completely defiled, could atonement privileges be allowed. According to Lev. 13, where the reader can examine the details, and the minute requirements for desegregation, it appears that the possibly seven types referred to were more akin to psoriasis than to elephantiasis, for the afflicted are spoken of as cleansed instead of cured, and no intimation is given regarding fatality. By Hebrew law the leper must segregate (Num. 5:1–4, 12:10; 2 K. 7:3, 15:5; 2 Chr. 26:21; Lk. 17:12); but in the case of outsiders, not so (cf. Naaman, Syrian, 2 K. 5:18). Miriam's seems to have been true leprosy (Num. 12:12), as also other cases, some certainly regarded as hereditary (2 Sam. 3:29; 2 K. 5:27), and ordinarily incurable (2 K. 5:7). It is of interest to note that the physician Luke employs the Greek word *lepra*, technical for psoriasis (Lk. 5:12–13). The leprosy in garments (Lev. 13:47–59) likely referred to fungus or mildew, that in houses, to dry rot (14:34–57). Chaulmoogra oil and sodium hydrocarpate have done much, together with corrective surgery and other means, to restore toward normal, the patient, as well as cure leprosy.

Leshem (lĕsh'ĕm) a variation of Laish, which is Dan (Josh. 19:47).

lethech (Hos. 3:2, margin) see **measures**

Letushim (lĕ-tū'shĭm) [perhaps, oppressed] a tribe descended from Dedan (Gen. 25:3).

Leummim (lĕ-ŭm'mĭm) [peoples] as above.

Levi (lē'vī) [adhesion] 1. Third son of Jacob and Leah (Gen. 29:34), the name signifying hope that her husband's affections would be drawn to her. He and his brother Simeon massacred the Shechemites, including Hamor and Shechem, the latter violating their sister Dinah (Gen. 34:3, 25 ff.). He had three sons: Gershom, Kohath, and Merari (Gen. 46:11); died in Egypt at age 137 (Ex. 6:16).

2 and 3. Two ancestors of Christ, one the son of Symeon, and the other, a son of Melchi (Lk. 3:24, 29–30).

4. Another name for Matthew (Mk. 2:14–17; Lk. 5:27–32; cf. Mt. 9:9–13).

leviathan (lē-vī'á-thăn) [spirally bound] a Hebrew word transliterated, save in Job 3:8, translated "mourning." Biblical references seem to indicate the crocodile (Ps. 104:26; Job 41; Ps. 74:14). The leviathan is the symbol of the fierce, terrible powers of the world afflicting the people of God, but to be ultimately destroyed (Isa. 27:1, where some say the reference is to a kind of great rock-snake). Job 3:8 may refer poetically to some fabulous dragon involved in enchantments, or to some sea monster, which conjurors of only the highest skill could summon to their aid (J. D. Davis, *Dictionary of the Bible*, 1911).

Levites (lē'vīts) descendants of Levi, son of Jacob, who had three sons: Gershom(n), Kohath, and Merari, heads of tribal families (Gen. 46:11; Ex. 6:16; Num. 3:17; 1 Chr. 6:16–48), Kohath being the family, of the house of Amram, from which came Moses and Aaron (Ex. 6:16, 18, 20, 26). Most frequently the Levites are distinguished from "the sons of Aaron" who constituted the priesthood (1 K. 8:4; Ezra 2:70; Jn. 1:19); but sometimes the word signified the whole tribe including the priests (Ex. 6:25; Lev. 25:32; Num. 35:2; Josh. 21:3), but at other times, it was an added epithet of the smaller part; thus we read of "the priests the Levites" (Josh. 3:3; Ezek. 44:15). In Genesis, Levi seems to exhibit zeal for purity of race (34:25); and not until after the Exodus is there any special pre-eminence, neither the officers appointed (Ex. 18:25), nor the young men who sacrificed (24:5), being referable to Levites. The signal position of this tribe grew out of the institution of the hereditary priesthood (Ex. 28:1), and the great crisis of Ex. 32, when its members recognized in their stern work, the superiority of the spiritual over the natural, being counted worthy to represent the ideal life, "Israel within Israel." Thenceforward the Levites occupied a distinct position, substituting for the earlier priesthood of the firstborn, as representatives of the holiness of the people, there being close numerical correspondence with those whom they replaced. As the presence of the Unseen King was set forth in the tabernacle, so the Levites were the royal guard waiting exclusively on him. The care and transportation of the costly tabernacle, and the preparation of materials for its elaborate service, entailed labors of a large number; and Levi was chosen, out of circumstances noted above (Ex. 32:26–29; Num. 3:9, 11–13, 40–41, 45). According to vs. 39, there were 22,000 Levites; but in the light of vss. 22, 28, 34–300 more, who being themselves firstborn could not substitute—a possible solution. Or here, we can easily understand a copyist's error. And for the 273 overplus firstborn in Israel, five shekels apiece were paid (46–51). For encamped Israel, the Levites were guardians of the sacred tent (Num. 1:51), but not sacrificing nor burning incense, not even seeing the holy things (4:15). On the march, only they could strike the tent, or carry its parts, or pitch tent again (Num. 1:51). They assisted the priests in their varied work (Num. 1:50–53, 3:6–9, 25–37, 4:1–33; 1 Sam. 6:15; 2 Sam. 15:24). The sons of Aaron could do any Levitical service. Twenty years was the starting point for military service: the Levitical age for service was thirty (Num. 4:3), twenty-five (8:24), and twenty (1 Chr. 23:24, 27), different periods explaining in part the differences in age. It is possible that a reduction in age and an extension of term was made by Moses, as is expressly stated to have been done by David (1 Chr. 23:24–27). It seems that eligibility for full service of every sort, was at thirty, and in kingdom days, also, for work of distinction calling for wisdom and discretion (Num. 4:1–33; 1 Chr. 23:3–5). And from David's time, the legal age was twenty, at which point, they began as assistants (1 Chr. 23:28–31; cf. 2 Chr. 29:34, 35:11); but probably not until they reached thirty, regarded as eligible for the higher offices (1 Chr. 23:3–5). They retired from active service at fifty, but could assist their successors (Num. 8:25–26). The various duties allotted in early times are found in Num. 3 and 4. Jehovah being their inheritance, the Levites had no territorial possession (Num. 18:20; Deut. 10:9, 18:2). Instead they were to have tithes from others from the produce of the land, from which they in turn offered a tithe to the priests (Num. 18:21, 24, 26; Neh. 10:37). The wanderings being past, and the tabernacle settled, the greater part of their labors ended; and distinctness and diffusion were secured by assignment to the whole tribe of forty-eight cities, with outlying suburbs for pasturage (Num. 35:2; Josh. 21:20–40). Towns for Levites proper were located in Judah, Simeon, and Benjamin; thirty-five for the others, were in the remaining tribes in the north and east (Josh. 21:5–7). It seems that among their other duties, to "the priests the Levites" was to belong the office of preserving, transcribing, and interpreting the Law (Deut. 17:9–12, 31:26). They shared in all festivals and occasions of rejoicing (Deut. 12:19, 14:26–27, 26:11). Following the Conquest of Palestine, the submissive Gibeonites relieved Gershon and Merari of much burdensome duty (Josh. 9:27). In the tumultuous times of the Judges, the Levites either failed in duty or were unable to enforce the truth. Samuel, being a Levite, and a priest only by special dedication as it were, brought better times (1 Sam. 1:28, 2:11, 18); and it is quite possible that a large contingent of the schools referred to him (1 Sam. 10:5, 10, 19:18 ff.) were of that tribe. The reign of David lifted the tribe from rather low level to greater honor (Judg. 17–18), a fuller organization of the Levites being effected, their position being recognized (1 Chr. 15:2, 27–28)—1 Chr. 23 is the special passage here. Under David the Levites were divided into four classes (assistants to priests in the sanctuary work, judges and scribes, gatekeepers, musicians); each—the second possibly being excepted—subdivided into twenty-four courses to serve in rotation (1 Chr. 24–26; cf. 15:16–24; 2 Chr. 19:8–11, 30:16–17; Ezra 6:18; Neh. 13:5). After the division of the kingdom, many of these left the Northern Kingdom for Judah and Jerusalem (2 Chr. 11:13–16). They became politically and ecclesiastically active, prominent against Jeroboam (2 Chr. 13:10–12), instructing and judging the people (2 Chr. 19:8–10), active in the counterrevolution of Jehoiada (2 Chr. 23), and in restoring the former stateliness of the temple (2 Chr. 24:5). They were in abeyance under Ahaz (2 Chr. 28:24), but with the accession of Hezekiah, became again prominent (2 Chr. 29:12–15). They were encouraged and made active (2 Chr. 30:22, 31:4). Alternate depression and elevation under Manasseh and Josiah (2 Chr. 34:8–13, 35:3, 15) were succeeded by unfaithfulness and the Exile as punishment for sin. The returning Levites with Zerubbabel were active, but later appear rather reluctant and unimpressive by the time that Ezra came, he having no great success in rallying them (Ezra 8:15, 20), the Nethinims apparently doing service for them. Their fortunes revived later (Neh. 9, 10:37–39, 13:22). After glimpses of their varying experiences in NT times (cf. Lk. 10:32), it is likely that they were merged with the crowd of captives scattered over the Roman world, to disappear from history's stage. Despite their descent into formalism and exclusiveness, they who witnessed to the great truths which might otherwise have perished, have claim to the respect and gratitude of mankind.

Leviticus (lē-vĭt′ĭ-cŭs) [relating to the Levites] the book—the third in the Pentateuch—is largely a manual for the priests regarding the technicalities of the ritual. The tabernacle having been erected and the priests appointed to minister, the next step was to regulate access to God. For this, we see the following: (1) Method of access—by blood, chs. 1–7. (2) Medium of access—the organized priesthood, chs. 8–10. (3) Conditions of access—holy life, chs. 11–22. (4) Benefits of access—the joy of feasts, 23:1–25:5. (5) Maintenance of access—obedience, ch. 26. (6) Appendix—regarding vows and tithes, ch. 27. The book of Hebrews is the NT correlative, showing the spiritual, internal, and eternal significance of the outward ordinances. Occasionally a law is repeated in a new connection and for a different purpose; and at times, the legislation is interrupted by the apposite narrative (Heb. 10:1–7, 12–20). Most of the book was given at Sinai, some perhaps framed afterwards, there being one sanctuary throughout and one altar and one priesthood (Lev. 1:5, 8:3, 19:21).

Libertines [Freedmen] a Jewish group which had a synagogue at Jerusalem; foes of the first martyr, Stephen (Acts 6:9); most likely captives of Pompey and Roman generals in the Syrian wars, enslaved at Rome, but freed later.

Libnah (lĭb'nä) [whiteness] 1. An encampment in the wilderness, unidentified (Num. 33:20).

2. A city in the southwest part of Judah, captured by Joshua (Josh. 10:29–31, 12:15, 15:42), later given to the priests (21:13; 1 Chr. 6:57). It revolted from Judah (2 K. 8:22); it was besieged by Sennacherib of Assyria (2 K. 19:8; Isa. 37:8); it was the native place of Hamutal (Hamital), the queen of Josiah, mother of Jehoahaz and of Zedekiah (2 K. 23:31, 24:18; Jer. 52:1). Site conjectural.

Libni (lĭb'nī) [white, pure] 1. Eldest son of Gershom (Ex. 6:17), and ancestor of the family of Libnites (Num. 26:58).

2. A Levite, family of Merari, house of Mahli (1 Chr. 6:29; probably some dislocation in the text; see vss. 20, 42).

Libya in Roman times, a large undefined tract, from the Nile valley, westward across the continent of Africa, with some small exceptions. The African littoral was divided into east and west, the latter being Libya Cyrenaica, which with Crete, was formed into a province (67 B.C.), its capital being Cyrene, from which representatives were in Jerusalem at Pentecost (Acts 2:10).

lice the rendering of Heb. *kinnim*, a small sucking or gnawing insect, noxious to man (Ex. 8:16–18; Ps. 105:31).

lieutenants the official title of the viceroys who governed Persian provinces (Est. 3:12; Ezra 8:36).

lign aloes see **aloes**

ligure (lĭg'ūr) an unidentifiable gem, first in third row of the high priest's breastplate (Ex. 28:19, 39:12).

Likhi (lĭk'hī) [characterized by knowledge] a Manassite, family of Shemida (1 Chr. 7:19).

lily some kind of the lily species, the Hebrew word *shoshan* being translated variously. It was found in pastures (Song of S. 2:16, 4:5), among thorns (2:2), in valleys (2:1), with sweet scent (5:13). It is quite possibly iden-

tical with the Gr. *krinon*, conspicuous on Gennesaret's shores (Mt. 6:28), and apparently of brilliant color (Song of S. 5:13); and of rapid and luxurious growth (Hos. 14:5). The temple columns had lily-work (1 K. 7). See also 7:26.

lime only three times in the Bible: Deut. 27:2, 4; Isa. 33:12; Amos 2:1. A material prepared by burning limestone, etc.; used for making mortar, plaster, and whitewashing.

linen cloth made from flax, that of Egypt being notable (Prov. 7:16; Ezek. 27:7). It was usual for royalty and the wealthy (Gen. 41:42; Est. 8:15; Lk. 16:19). The hangings of the tabernacle and the priests' garments were of linen (Ex. 25:4, 26:1, 28:15; 1 Sam. 2:19, 22:18; 2 Sam. 6:14; Ezek. 9:2; Dan. 10:5); also those of the Levite singers (2 Chr. 5:12). Linen is the raiment of the Lamb's wife (Rev. 19:8; cf. 18:16), and of the armies in heaven (19:14). Linen is the translation of seven Hebrew words, and of five Greek words, as in the following references: Gen. 41:42; Ex. 28:42; 1 Chr. 15:27; Prov. 7:16, 31:24; Jer. 13:1; Mk. 14:51; Lk. 16:19, 24:12; Rev. 15:6, 18:16. There is a different original word in each reference.

lintel the beam in the upper framework of a door (Ex. 12:22). The Hebrew word for ram is also translated lintel, meaning likely a (projecting) post (1 K. 6:31; and a number of times in Ezek. 41–42). And another Hebrew word, probably more likely chapiter or knop, as is the translation in Zeph. 2:14 (mg.) and Ex. 37:17, is rendered as lintel in Amos 9:1.

Linus (lī'nŭs) [flax?] a Christian at Rome (2 Tim. 4:21), and according to Irenaeus and Eusebius and many others, the first bishop of Rome, somewhat later than the middle of the first century. That no lofty pre-eminence was attached to the office is shown by the occurrence of his name between two other members of the church at Rome.

lion in scriptural times, found in Palestine, the cane-brakes on Jordan's banks being a favorite haunt (Jer. 49:19). There are six words to designate it. Likely of the Asiatic variety, with short curly mane, smaller and less daring than the African lion, but dangerous to flocks, villages, it was strong, courageous, ferocious (Isa. 31:4; 2 K. 17:25; Ezek. 19:3; Judg. 14:18; 2 Sam. 17:10; Gen. 49:9). Shepherds sometimes tackled them single-handed (1 Sam. 17:34; Amos 3:12). Ezekiel's living creatures included one with a lion's face (1:10); the first of the four seen by John was a lion (Rev. 4:7). The lion was the heraldic device of the tribe of Judah, the Lord being "the Lion of the tribe of Judah" (Rev. 5:5). Metaphorically, it was a fierce, malignant enemy (Ps. 7:2; 2 Tim. 4:17), and used of the archfiend (1 Pet. 5:8).

litter only Isa. 66:20 gives this meaning for the Hebrew word; palanquins, borne of men or of beasts.

lizard only in Lev. 11:30. Various kinds abound in Palestine, the most common being the green lizard. The gecko is common in all native houses, able to walk up walls and on ceilings, having disclike suckers on its toes. There is the *dabb*, a large lizard with a long, spiny tail. The land crocodile is sometimes five feet long. Sand lizards are found in soft, sandy soil. There are various others.

loaf a round mass of bread, or barley or wheat (2 K. 4:42; Lev. 23:17; Ex. 29:23). See **bread**

Lo-ammi (lō-ăm'mī) [not my people] figurative name of Hosea's second son by Gomer (Hos. 1:9–10), to denote the rejection of Israel by the Lord.

loan according to early Hebrew law, loans were for necessities, not for gain. Lending to the needy without interest was enjoined (Deut. 15:7–11; Ex. 22:25), as regards Hebrews, not foreigners (Deut. 23:20); for Hebrew borrowing was not to make money thereby. In making loans, certain prohibitions were set: the outer garment as a pledge was to be returned before sunset (Ex. 22:26–27): the owner slept in it. A widow's garment could not be taken (Deut. 24:17), nor the millstone (24:6). The creditor could not enter the borrower's house to reclaim the pledge (Deut. 24:10–11). In the year of release (the seventh), the debt was forgiven (15:1–11). In time, violations occurred (Jer. 15:10; Ezek. 18:13). Ignored regulations during the Exile, were inveighed against by Nehemiah (5:1–13). Roman law was in sharp contrast (Mt. 18:25, 34). In the time of the Lord on earth, banking was regular (Mt. 25:27; Lk. 19:23).

lock Eastern locks were usually of wood, with partly hollow bolt, from fourteen inches to two feet long, for external doors or gates, and from seven to nine for interior doors. The bolt passes through a groove in a piece attached to the door, into a socket in the doorpost. In the groove-piece are four to nine small iron or wooden pins which drop into corresponding holes in the bolt, and fix it in its place. When the lock is inside, a hole through the door admits the hand with the key (Song of S. 5:5).

locust there are about a dozen words to denote this insect, some perhaps referring to different stages of development of the same kind. It is two or more inches in length, winged, creeping, with four wings, six legs, the hindmost pair, as long as the body, used for springing (Lev.

11:21=22). They are exceedingly destructive to vegetation (Joel 1:4, 2:3); may obscure the sun (Jer. 46:23); give the suggestion of horses (Joel 2:4; Rev. 9:7). They were the eighth Egyptian plague, blown by the east wind into the Nile valley (Ex. 10). They were regarded as clean, and were used for food (Lev. 11:21; Mt. 3:4), sometimes ground and mixed with flour and water, sometimes roasted slightly, then dried in the sun, and salted, only the fleshy portion being eaten. Eggs are deposited in April or May in the ground; hatch in June; the wingless larva, very voracious, becomes the insect in another month.

Lod (lŏd) [strife] a town of Benjamin (1 Chr. 8:12; Ezra 2:33; Neh. 7:37). It is Ludd (Lydda, in Acts 9:32), eleven miles southeast of Joppa. The remains of St. George's Church are there, he being the Christian martyr of Nicomedia, adopted in the fourteenth century, as patron saint of England, and said to have been a native of the place.

Lo-debar (lō-dē'bär) [perhaps, without pasture] a place in Gilead (2 Sam. 9:4–5, 17:27).

lodge a shelter for the watchman in harvest (Isa. 1:8). To lodge generally means spending the night (Gen. 19:2).

loft see **house**

log see **weights and measures**

Lois (lō'ĭs) Timothy's grandmother, of unfeigned faith (2 Tim. 1:5).

looking glasses see **mirrors**

Lord printed with initial letter as a capital for Deity, this word refers to the Hebrew for master or my master (Ex. 4:10, 23:17), or the Greek master (Mt. 1:20). In small capitals, it represents the Hebrew word commonly pronounced "Jehovah," which is a hybrid, having the letters (consonants) which give the sacred name for the Hebrews' Deity as revealed to Moses at the mount (Ex. 3:14–15, 6:1), and the vowels of the name for master. The peculiarity arose out of an apparently false idea of reverence which disallowed the pronunciation of the sacred name as such (YHWH). In the above reference (Ex. 23:17), we find both, as elsewhere; and the translation is "Lord GOD," or more properly, "Lord Jehovah."

Lord's Day this is the day especially associated with the Lord Jesus Christ, occurring only in Rev. 1:10, its meaning being in doubt. 1. It is referred to the sabbath, the seventh day; but John does not use this customary term, current then (Isa. 58:13).

2. The day of Christ's birth; but that was neither known nor observed by the early church.

3. The day of judgment (2 Pet. 3:10); but the writer John does not speak thus of the Day

of the Lord, which is the common designation of the day of the second advent: he uses the adjective which meant the first day of the week when Christ arose from the dead.

4. The anniversary of the resurrection, our Easter. But this has no endorsement from the early fathers.

5. Friday, or crucifixion day; but this seems to have had no special stress by the apostles.

6. Sunday, or resurrection day. The first day of the week was devoted by the apostles for meeting to break bread, for communing and receiving instructions, for laying up offerings, for occupation in holy thought and prayer. On this day, the Lord arose, and during it, appeared to his followers on five different occasions. Also after eight days, i.e., according to ordinary reckoning, on the first day of the next week, he appeared to the Eleven. At Pentecost, which that year fell on the first day of the week, "they were all united with one accord in one place," had spiritual gifts conferred on them and, in turn, began to communicate those gifts to others. At Troas (Acts 20:7), when Christianity had assumed a rather settled form, Paul and companions, having arrived there, "abode seven days." And on the first day of the week, when they came together to break bread, Paul preached. To the Corinthians, Paul wrote (1 Cor. 16:1–2): ". . . upon the first day of the week . . . lay by . . . in store." Hebrews 10:25 seems to imply that a regular day for assembly was observed. And all these passages have remarkable confirmation in the fact that this same day is noted in similar manner, being associated with the Lord's resurrection, by extrabiblical usage; also it is never questioned, but is accepted as equally apostolic with baptism, ordination, etc.; and according to principal writers in the centuries after John's death, it existed as part and parcel of apostolic, and so of scriptural, Christianity. The majority of Christians therefore consider the Lord's day as one set apart by the example of the Lord and of his disciples for sacred purposes and standing in a certain relation to the sabbath, although distinguished from it. It was a day of solemn meeting for the Holy Eucharist, for united prayer, for almsgiving. Tertullian intimates that the character of the day was opposed to worldly business; and even Constantine insisted that all worldly negotiations should be intermitted. For Jewish Christians to continue to observe the seventh day and Jewish festivals, was a matter of liberty (Col. 2:16). The Christian "sabbath" is a touchstone of the faith. As the principles of the old sabbath are eternal, along with those of the other nine words, as distinct

from all the other parts of the Mosaic law, Christians have found, and find, that its being set apart to the Lord, for worship and the works of necessity and mercy, makes for vital Christianity and results in blessing for individual and for community.

Lord's Supper these words, describing the central act of Christian church worship, are given only by Paul (1 Cor. 11:20), regarding the commemorative ordinance instituted by the Lord on the evening preceding his crucifixion. From rabbinic writers, we learn that the Paschal feast was observed by the Jews of the Lord's time (differing in some details from Ex. 12), as follows: (1) Those gathered for this purpose met in the evening and reclined on couches (Mt. 26:20). The head of the household, or celebrant, began by a form of blessing "for the day and for the wine," pronounced over a cup, of which he and the others then drank. (2) All present then washed their hands, this having special benediction. (3) The table was set out with the paschal lamb, unleavened bread, bitter herbs, and the dish known as Charoseth (a sauce made of dates, figs, raisins, and vinegar, referring to the mortar of Egyptian bondage). (4) The celebrant first, then others, dipped a portion of the bitter herbs into the Charoseth, and ate them. (5) The dishes were removed, and a cup of wine brought. Next came an interval for questions by children or proselytes; and at the close the cup was passed around and drunk. (6) The dishes brought on again, the celebrant repeated the commemorative words opening strictly the Paschal supper, pronouncing solemn blessing, followed by Ps. 113 and 114. (7) A second handwashing, with short blessing, was followed by the celebrant's breaking one of the two loaves, or cakes of unleavened bread, and giving thanks over it. Then all took portions of the bread, dipped them with bitter herbs into the Charoseth, and ate them. (8) Next they ate the flesh of the lamb, with bread, as desired; and after another blessing, came a third cup known as "the cup of blessing," which was handed around. (9) This was followed by a fourth cup, and the recital of Ps. 115–118, followed by prayer. This was the cup of Hallel, or of the Song. (10) There might be, in conclusion, a fifth cup, provided that "the Great Hallel" was sung over it (perhaps Ps. 120–138). In the practice of the Lord and the disciples, to the above 1, 3, and perhaps 8, we may refer the first words and the first distribution of the cup (Lk. 22:17–18); to 2 or 7, the dipping of the sop (Jn. 13:26); to 7, or to an interval during or after 8, the distribution of the bread (Mt. 26:26; Mk.

216

14:22; Lk. 22:19; 1 Cor. 11:23-24); to 9 or 10 ("after supper" of Lk. 22:20), the thanksgiving and distribution of the cup, and the hymn with which the whole was ended. The gospel record indicates how strongly the apostles were impressed with the words which gave new meaning to the old, familiar acts. They leave unnoticed all the ceremonies of the Passover, except those transferred to the Christian church and perpetuated in it. The old was passing, all becoming new. For them, the elements were of old memorials of deliverance from Egypt: now, they partook "in remembrance" of their Lord. The festival was annual; now, "do this as oft as ye drink it" (1 Cor. 11:25), suggesting continual remembrance, no rule being given as to time and frequency. The words "this is my body," gave the unleavened bread a new character. They had been prepared for otherwise startling language by John's teaching (6:32-58); and they were thus taught to find in the bread that was broken, witness to and realization of the closest possible union with their Lord. The cup, "the new testament (covenant) in his blood," reminded them of the wondrous prophecy in which that new covenant had been foretold (Jer. 31:31-34). A quarter of a century after the institution of the Lord's Supper, we have note of the continued custom of fellowship among the baptized members of the church (Acts 2:42) in the "breaking of bread and in prayers," together with the commonly understood Agape or **love feast.** The practice was not limited to the apostles and Jewish Christians, but was celebrated in the Gentile congregations. In Corinth arose an evil which frustrated its object. Therefore the apostle Paul gives a rule which would make the union of Agape and the Lord's Supper possible without risk of profanation (1 Cor. 11:33-34). Here the observance was no longer daily (vss. 20, 33), the first day being suggested (Acts 20:7; 1 Cor. 16:2); and at this time occurs separation of what had been united, the Agape, through many stages, dying out; and the Lord's Supper suffering changes, Acts 20:11 showing light on the matter. Here, Paul's discourse continued till past midnight; then came teaching and prayers, and toward dawn, the Lord's Supper. It would be an easy step to transfer all to the morning hour. The table containing the bread was known as the Lord's table (1 Cor. 10:21); the cup of wine, as at the old Jewish Passover, was the "cup of blessing" (10:16) and also the "cup of the Lord" (vs. 21, 11:27).

Lo-ruhamah (lō-rû-hā′mä) [not obtained mercy] the symbolic name of Hosea's daughter, in re the hopeless condition of Israel (1:6).

Lot (lŏt) [covering, myrrh] son of Haran and Abraham's nephew; went with the latter to Canaan, and to and from Egypt (Gen. 11:31, 12:5, 13:1). Their disputing herdsmen handling the vast cattle herds, brought about a separation, Abraham generously giving Lot his choice, who made the fatal mistake of electing to go toward Sodom in the rich valley-land of the Jordan, where corruption was rife. Taken prisoner by Chedorlaomer and allies during an invasion, he was rescued by Abraham (Gen. 13-14). With the blessing of God, Lot seems to have preserved his integrity, practicing the courteous customs of his former days. But the city was ripe for destruction. Lot was saved by the warning angels, but his reluctant wife was overwhelmed. Later in drunken unconsciousness, he was participant in abhorrent incest, Moabites and Ammonites being his descendants (Gen. 19).

Lotan (lō′tăn) [covering?] eldest son of Seir the Horite (Gen. 36:20, 22, 29).

lots a very ancient and widespread method of deciding doubtful matters, was by placing stones or inscribed tablets in a jar, shaking them, and then drawing or emptying them out. Preceded by prayer, appeal was made to God, in OT times and later. Thus Canaan was divided (Josh. 14:2, 18:6). There is the case of Saul and Jonathan (1 Sam. 14:40-45). Priests' courses were settled by lot (1 Chr. 24); so also in the case of Judas' successor (Acts 1:15-26). See the general statement in Prov. 16:33. The lot ceased among the apostles following the descent of the Holy Spirit.

love feasts (2 Pet. 2:13; Jude 12) entertainment partaken of by the poor, and furnished from contributions of Christians in connection with the Eucharist (Lord's Supper); not clear whether before or after it. Chrysostom tells that after the early community of goods ceased, wealthy members brought food and drink; and after the Lord's Supper was concluded, all partook, promoting love among Christians. Because of abuses, certain councils of the church forbade them—Laodicea (320), Carthage (397), Orleans (541); but they were not altogether extinguished. They were revived by the Moravians and by John Wesley, and others.

Lubim (lū′bĭm) [root: thirst] an African people from whom Shishak of Egypt, drew forces for Palestinian invasion (2 Chr. 12:3, 16:8). Aids of No-amon: Thebes (Nah. 3:9). Allies with Cushites regarding Egypt (Dan. 11:43). Perhaps primitive Libyans.

Lucas (lū′căs) [light-giving] friend and companion of Paul; the beloved physician (Philemon 24; Col. 4:14; 2 Tim. 4:11).

Lucifer

Lucifer (lū'cĭ-fẽr) [light-bearer] likely the planet Venus, as the morning star, which appears as a morning or an evening star, according as it is west or east of the sun, returning to the same position about every eighteen months. It may thus be a harbinger of daylight. To it, the splendor of the Babylonian king is likened (Isa. 14:12, its only occurrence in Scripture). The Lord calls himself the "bright and morning star" (Rev. 22:16; cf. 2 Pet. 1:19). Since Jerome's day, it has been poetically applied to Satan, rebel hurled from heaven, on the erroneous supposition that Lk. 10:18 explains Isa. 14:12.

Lucius (lū'cĭ-ŭs) [regarding light] commonly supposed kinsman of Paul, from Cyrene, a teacher in the church at Antioch, who joined Paul in saluting Roman brethren; traditionally bishop of Cenchrea (Acts 13:1; Rom. 16:21). He may have been in the group to whom Peter preached at Pentecost (Acts 2:10), and is likely one of the men scattered abroad after Stephen's death; preached the Lord at Antioch (Acts 11:19-20).

Lud (lŭd) [meaning?] a person or tribe, or both, among the Semites (Gen. 10:22), whom Josephus thought to be Lydians.

Ludim (lū'dĭm; plural of Lud) a people related to the Egyptians (Gen. 10:13; 1 Chr. 1:11), mentioned as bowmen (Isa. 66:19; Jer. 46:9; Ezek. 27:10). The Lydians were of Asia Minor: these folk seem to have been of Northern Africa.

Luhith (lū'hĭth) [perhaps, made of planks] a Moabite town approached by an ascent (Isa. 15:5; Jer. 48:5).

Luke probably abbreviation of *Lucanus*. Each of the three references in NT likely indicate the third evangelist (Col. 4:14; 2 Tim. 4:11; Philemon 24). Drawing on tradition as well as Scripture, his life's main outlines follow: born at Antioch in Syria (according to Eusebius); learned medicine; was a skillful painter (according to Nicephorus); was one of the Seventy (according to Epiphanius); one of the two at Emmaus (according to Theophylact; Lk. 24:13); certainly was with Paul at Troas (Acts 16:10-17; note the "we," indicative of Lucan writership; cf. also 20:5-21:18, 27:1-28:16); Luke drops out at Philippi probably preaching during the seven-year interval (Acts 17:1; note third person here); but on the third (next) missionary journey, he rejoins Paul at Philippi, and on to Jerusalem (20:5, 21:18). Luke may have been the man in 2 Cor. 8:18 remaining in Palestine during Paul's two years in the Caesarean prison, he sailed with him to Rome (Acts 27:1), remaining for the first imprison-

ment (Col. 4:14; Philemon 24); and if 2 Timothy was written during the second prison term, Luke was faithful to the end (4:11). Thereafter nothing is known, although Epiphanius says he preached the Gospel at Dalmatia and Gallia; and tradition only, indicates the martyr's death for the "great physician," between A.D. 75 and 100.

Luke, Gospel of by common consent written by Luke, friend and companion of Paul, before Acts (1:1), possibly while Paul was in prison, between A.D. 58 and 60, this is the Gospel for the Gentiles. Jewish customs are explained (e.g., 22:1); Greek substitutes for Hebrew (6:15); limits OT quotations and prophetic references. The "most beautiful book in the world," was written to Theophilus, a Gentile Christian, statedly based upon careful investigation, for the purpose of giving assured knowledge of the truth in which the addressee had been instructed (see the most remarkable first four verses). *Contents:* (1) Advent and preparation for ministry of the Perfect Man, 1:5-4:13. (2) Public ministry in Galilee and Perea, 4:14-19:28. (3) Suffering and triumph, 19:29-24:53. Luke's writing "in order" refers rather to method than to chronology; much is topical. Luke is the most individualistic of the three Synoptic gospels (they look together); whereas Mark has sixty-eight verses peculiar to him, Luke has 541! He records the first Christian hymns, is the "father of Christian hymnology." Thanksgiving is prominent; prayer abounds—only Luke telling of six memorable occasions of our Lord's praying. His is the gospel of womanhood, of the infancy, for the humble, the poor, the outcasts, nine chapters (beginning with ch. 9) being devoted to Christ's ministry to the world.

lunatic insane with lucid intervals. A disease believed to be connected by the light, or periodic changes, of the moon. Evidently a malady affecting body and mind, which might or might not be the result of possession (Mt. 4:24, 17:15). Comparison with Mk. 9:17-26 has led to the opinion that epilepsy is meant.

Luz (lŭz) [curve] 1. Scripture references leave open the question as to the identity of Luz and Bethel or their separateness (Gen. 28:19, 35:6, 48:3; Josh. 18:13; Judg. 1:23). In the first and last references, the two are apparently identical, the name being changed. The citations from Joshua speak of the two as distinct. A likely solution is that Luz was the old Canaanitic city, and Bethel the pillar and altar nearby; and that following the destruction of Luz, the town of Bethel arose.

2. Luz is also the name of a second place

named for the first, built on Hittite territory, place unknown (Judg. 1:26).

Lycaonia (lỹ-cā-ō′nĭ-à) [said to mean: pertaining to King Lycaon, or abounding in werewolves] there is apparently an ethnological significance here; but the place is an inland, rugged district of Asia Minor, mainly suitable for grazing, its dialect perhaps a mixture of Greek and Syriac; sometimes, politically, in Cappadocia, sometimes, in Galatia (Acts 13:51–14:23).

Lycia (lỹ′cĭ-à) [pertaining to Lycus] a peninsular province of Asia Minor, immediately opposite the island of Rhodes, having promontories with deep inlets favorable to seafaring and piracy. Its fortunes varied under Persia, Greece, the Seleucids, and Rome. In the later Roman empire, its capital was Myra. On his last voyage to Jerusalem, Paul stopped at Patara, where he took ship for Phoenicia (Acts 21:1, 2). Romebound, he landed at Myra, and took passage on an Alexandrian vessel headed for Italy (27:5–6).

Lydda (lĭd′dà) the Heb. *Lod* (Acts 9:32, 35, 38; cf. 1 Chr. 8:12). A fairly large town nine miles from Joppa; from 153–145 B.C., connected governmentally with Samaria; then transferred to Judea. Here Peter visited; and the cure of Aeneas resulted in large increase of disciples (see above references). In the first century A.D., it was taken by Cassius, released by Antony, burnt by Cestius Gallus, its ruins seized by Vespasian. It became Diospolis under Hadrian. Around A.D. 400 it was an episcopal see. England's patron St. George lived, was martyred, and buried there, a church being built thereover, honoring him; but it was destroyed by the Saracens, in the early eighth century, to be taken by the Crusaders (1099), but

again destroyed, by Saladin (in 1191), and again rebuilt by Richard Cœur de Lion. The unattractive modern town is named Ludd.

Lydia (lĭd′ĭ-à) [from Ludos, its reputed founder] 1. A maritime province of western Asia Minor, fertile, mild, populous, its capital being Sardis, and Thyatira and Philadelphia being among its cities.

2. The first Pauline convert in Europe, and afterward his hostess when at Philippi (Acts 16:14–15, 40). A native of Thyatira (Rev. 2:18), this former Jewish proselyte was touched by the Gospel at a riverside sabbath-worship. She had connection with the famous dyeing works of Thyatira, and seems to have been rather wealthy.

Lysanias (lī-sā′nĭ-ăs) [ending sadness] a Tetrarch of Abilene in the fifteenth year of Tiberius (Lk. 3:1). Luke is accused of error here. But there was another Lysanias (d. 36 B.C.), who was king (not tetrarch) of Chalcis (not Abilene): Luke's statement is vindicated.

Lysias (lĭ′sĭ-ăs) Claudius Lysias (Acts 23:26) Roman commandant at Jerusalem; rescued Paul from Jewish mob: a Greek who had bought Roman citizenship (Acts 21–23).

Lystra (lĭs′trä) a city of Lycaonia and a Roman colony, where Paul cured a cripple, being offered worship as a god. Here too, he was stoned and left for dead (Acts 14:6–21; 2 Tim. 3:11). This also was the home, so it appears, of Timothy (Acts 16:1–2), his ancestors possibly being among the Jews established in those parts by Antiochus, three centuries before; but there seems to have been no influential Jewish folk there, for Luke alludes to its aspect as heathen (Acts 14).

M

Maacah, also **Maachah** (mā′à-cä) [oppression] 1. Mother of Absalom (1 Chr. 3:2; 2 Sam. 3:3).

2. A place in Syria (2 Sam. 10:6, 8), sometimes designated with Aram or Syria (1 Chr. 19:6–7).

3. Daughter of Nahor (Gen. 22:24).

4. Father of Solomon's contemporary, Achish of Gath (1 K. 2:39).

5. Wife of Machir (1 Chr. 7:15–16).

6. A concubine of Caleb (1 Chr. 2:48).

7. Wife of Jehiel, and ancestress of King Saul (1 Chr. 8:29, 9:35).

8. Father of Hanan, mighty man of David (1 Chr. 11:43).

9. Father of Simeonites' ruler, in David's time (1 Chr. 27:16).

10. The daughter, or granddaughter (2 Chr. 13:2) of Absalom, named for his mother, she being the third and favorite wife of Rehoboam,

and the mother of Abijah (1 K. 15:2; 2 Chr. 11:20–22), after whose death she reigned as queen mother. Her grandson Asa, deposed her because of idolatry (2 Chr. 15:16). She is called Michaiah in 2 Chr. 13:2, evidently a textual error, for in seven other places her name is Maacah.

Maachathi or **Maachathites** (mä-ä'cà-thī) folk of a small kingdom near Palestine (Deut. 3:14; Josh. 12:5, 13:11, 13; see 2 Sam. 10:6, 8; 1 Chr. 19:7). Individual citizens are mentioned (2 Sam. 23:34; Jer. 40:8; 2 K. 25:23; see also Josh. 12:5).

Maadai (mä-ä'dī) [perhaps, wavering] son of Bani, he divorced his foreign wife (Ezra 10:34).

Maadiah (mä-à-dī'ä) [ornament of Jehovah] a chief of the priests returning from Babylon (Neh. 12:5–7); elsewhere (vs. 17) called **Moadiah.**

Maai (mä-ä'ī) [Jehovah is compassionate?] a trumpet-blowing priest at the dedication of the wall of Jerusalem (Neh. 12:36).

Maaleh-acrabbim (mä-äl'ĕ-à-crăb'bĭm) [ascent of scorpions] full form of the name in Josh. 15:3; elsewhere "ascent of . . ."

Maarath (mä'à-răth) [place of bare trees] a town in the hill country of Judah, north of Hebron (Josh. 15:59).

Maaseiah (mä-à-sē'yä) [work of Jehovah] 1 to 4. Four persons who married foreign wives (Ezra 10:18, 21–22, 30).

5. A second-rank Levite who was a porter and a psalterist (1 Chr. 15:18; vs. 20).

6. A captain of hundreds, working with Jehoiadah to overthrow Athaliah, in favor of Joash (2 Chr. 23:1).

7. An officer in Uzziah's reign (2 Chr. 26:11).

8. A royal prince slain in Pekah's invasion of Judah (2 Chr. 28:7).

9. The governor of Jerusalem in Josiah's reign (34:8).

10. Ancestor of Seraiah and Baruch (Jer. 32:12, 51:59).

11. Father of false prophet Zedekiah (Jer. 29:21).

12. Priestly father of the temple official Zephaniah (Jer. 21:1, 29:25).

13. Doorkeeper of the temple, son of Shallum (Jer. 35:4; cf. 1 Chr. 9:19, 26:1).

14. Father of the Azariah who did some wall-building beside his house (Neh. 3:23).

15. A marching priest at the wall dedication (Neh. 12:42); perhaps one of the thirteen law expounders (8:7).

16. Another who marched in procession, one of six who stood by Ezra when he read the Law (12:41, 8:4).

17. A chief who signed the covenant with Nehemiah (10:25).

18. A Levite assistant when the Law was read (Neh. 8:7).

19. A son of Baruch (Neh. 11:5).

20. A Benjaminite, ancestor of Sallu (11:7).

Maasiai (mä-ăs'ī-ī) [perhaps same as above name] a prince who returned from Babylon and dwelt in Jerusalem (1 Chr. 9:12).

Maath (mä'äth) ancestor of the Christ (Lk. 3:26).

Maaz (mä'ăz) [anger] descendant of Judah through Jerahmeel (1 Chr. 2:27).

Maaziah (mä-à-zī'ä) [consolation of Jehovah] 1. A priest in David's reign, head of the twenty-fourth course (1 Chr. 24:1, 6, 18).

2. A priest who signed the covenant along with Nehemiah (Neh. 10:8).

Maccabees (măc'cà-bēz) [two suggested meanings: (1) from the title given Judas, the heroic leader: the "hammerer"; (2) from the initials of the Hebrew expression: "Who is like Thee among the gods?"]. The progenitor of this illustrious line was Mattathias (the name Asmonean [Hasmonean] derived from ancestor), an aged priest of the course of Joarib (1 Chr. 24:7), driven to desperation by the outrages of Antiochus Epiphanes. He revolted and fled to the mountains, followed by the faithful in Israel, his five sons carrying on the cause, Judas, the third son being the first military leader (166 B.C.). The Feast of the Dedication (Jn. 10:22), kept annually thereafter, was instituted when having taken Jerusalem, purified the temple, restored the daily sacrifice, Judas fell in 160; but the other brothers carried on the war; and under Simon, the last of the five, independence from Syria was granted, 142 B.C., by King Demetrius II.

The first book of Maccabees, of the Apocrypha, gives trustworthy but scant account of the War of Jewish Independence. Especially after John Hyrcanus, a second generation Maccabee (137–107 B.C.), who won a second independence from Syria, the pages of Judea's record are stained with blood, marred by family feuds, factional intrigues, infamy, unworthy of the noble line, until in 63 B.C., Pompey extinguished the Jewish church-state and inadvertently opened the path for Antipater, an Idumaean offshoot of the famous family Maccabean, who rode on to fortune, on whatever adverse tides arose, until his son Herod the Great was crowned "King of the Jews," in whose reign Christ was born.

Macedonia (măc-ē-dōn'ī-à) a country immediately north of Greece, little known prior to the sixth century B.C., and of no special interest for 200 years thereafter, or until Philip of Macedon and his even more illustrious son, Alexander the Great (336–323 B.C.), brought it to worldwide power and importance. In 142 it became a Roman province. Not the name but the empire is noted in the OT (Dan. 2:39, 7:6, 8:5–8). Paul, summoned in vision by one of Macedonia on his second journey, passed from Asia into Europe, and at Philippi, preached the Gospel on Macedonian soil—the account of his travels being found in Acts 16: 9–17:14. Departing from that region, he left Silas and Timothy to continue the work (17: 14–15, 18:5). He revisited the country (19: 21–22, 20:1–3; cf. 2 Cor. 2:13, 7:5; 1 Tim. 1:3). The Macedonian Christians were exemplary: witness the candor of the Bereans (Acts 17:11); the beloved Thessalonians (1 Thess. 2:8, 17–20, 3:10); the blameless, liberal and self-denying Philippians (4:10, 14–19; cf. 2 Cor. 9:2, 11:9; and see Rom. 15:26). **Macedonian** occurs rarely Acts 27:2; elsewhere (e.g., Acts 16:9), we have "of Macedonia."

Machbanai (măc′bâ-nī) [clothed with a cloak] a lion-faced Gadite hero who joined David at Ziklag (1 Chr. 12:13).

Machbenah (măc′bĕ-nä) [cloak?] the father of Machbenah is offspring of Maachah (1 Chr. 2:49), the town of the name, apparently having been founded by the family.

Machi (mā′kī) [root: thin] father of the spy from the tribe of Gad (Num. 13:15).

Machir (mā′kĭr) [sold] 1. Only and firstborn son of Manasseh (Gen. 50:23; Josh. 17:1; 1 Chr. 7:14). As posterity increased, Machir became one of the families of Manasseh (Num. 26:29): earlier, the Machitites were Manasseh solely. At the conquest time, the family was powerful, a large part of East Jordan being subdued by them (Num. 32:39; Deut. 3:15). Sometimes, Machir equals Manasseh (Judg. 5:14).

2. The son of Ammiel, in Lo-debar, east of Jordan; brought provisions to David during Absalom's rebellion (2 Sam. 9:4–5, 17:27). Lo-debar is not located, whether in Manasseh or in Gad.

Machnadebai (măc-nȧ-dē′bī) [gift of the noble one] son of Bani, induced by Ezra to divorce his foreign wife (Ezra 10:40).

Machpelah (măc-pē′lä) [duplication] the place, with trees and a cave, property of Ephron, a Hittite (Gen. 23:9, 17, 19), bought by Abraham for 400 shekels of silver as a burying-ground for his wife, supposedly at Hebron, "facing Mamre" (Gen. 23:17). Here too were buried Abraham, Isaac, and Rebekah (25: 9–10), Leah and Jacob (35:29, 47:28–31, 49: 29–33, 50:12–13). The cave is probably the one under the great mosque at Hebron, once a Christian church, 70 by 90 feet, in the south-eastern part of a quadrangle 181 by 93 (or larger), with massive forty foot walls, estimated as dating all the way from Solomon to Herod the Great, in the mosque being monuments to the above notables.

Madai (mā′dī) [middle?] apparently a people descended from Japheth (Gen. 10:2), commonly said to be the third son, the progenitor of the Medes. It seems that the people and not the man are noted in the above reference.

Madian (Acts 7:29) see **Midian**

Madmannah (măd-măn′nä) [dunghill] town in extreme south of Judah (Josh. 15:31; 1 Chr. 2:49). In Josh. 19:5, it is Beth-marcaboth.

Madmen (măd′mĕn) [as above] a town in Moab, now unknown (Jer. 48:2).

Madmenah (măd-mē′nä) [as above] a Benjaminite village north of Jerusalem, frightened by Sennacherib's approach; unknown (Isa. 10:31).

madness a disorder rendering devoid of right reason (Deut. 28:28), sometimes of human origin, sometimes of divine. In Jn. 10:20, it is connected with demoniacal possession, the judgment of God. Luke 6:11 refers to fury. References related are: 1 Sam. 21:13; Prov. 26:18; Jer. 25:16, 51:7; Lk. 6:11; Acts 12:15, 26:11.

Madon (mā′dŏn) [strife] a town of north Canaan, whose king Jabin joined confederates against Joshua at Merom, all being killed (Josh. 11:1, 12:19). Supposedly five miles from Tiberias.

Magbish (măg′bĭsh) [congregating] a man, or more likely a place, since the context (Ezra 2:20–34) in most cases relates to places. It seems to be in Benjamin's territory.

Magdala (măg′dā-là) [perhaps a tower] found only in Mt. 15:39; generally, Magdalan, a locality into whose borders, after crossing the Sea of Galilee, the Lord went, following feeding the five thousand. The parallel in Mark (8:10) has "parts of Dalmanutha." The Magdala (of Mary Magdalene), may have been one of the many towers in Palestine, e.g., one near Tiberias, on west shore of the lake.

Magdiel (măg′dĭ-ĕl) [honor of God] a duke of Esau's line (Gen. 36:43; 1 Chr. 1:54).

Magi (mā′jī) [wise men] Jeremiah 39:3 and Acts 8:9 come as close to this word as is found in Scripture. The Magi were a priestly caste, according to Herodotus, one of the six tribes of Media, retaining influence after Persia conquered Media, and into succeeding kingdoms. For the Greeks the name was associated with a foreign system of divination and the religion of a conquered foe, so that it became a byword for degenerate imposture, although it continued to have both good and bad significations, in various connections. The more favorable note is evidenced in Dan. 1:20, arising out of the relationship between Jews and Persians. Yet swarms of impostors with the name, were found all over the Roman empire. The baser meaning comes out in the NT (Acts 8:9, 13:8); but earlier, the older association with a respected, if undefined, religion stands out, as in the gospel account. Therefore whatever may have been the corruptions in religion among the Magi of Persian rule, there is legitimate inference from Mt. 2, that in these Magi we may recognize, with the church from a very early period, the first Gentile worshipers of the Christ. These strangers from the Far East, whether Arabia, Mesopotamia, Persia, were not idolaters, their form of worship being viewed with more tolerance and sympathy than that of other Gentiles. They were starwatchers, reading in them the destinies of the nations, whether deriving from Balaam's prophecy (Num. 24: 17), received from Dispersion Jews, or from traditions parallel to the OT, or from predictions of their own prophet Zoroaster. They came to pay homage to the King whose birth was indicated in the stars for them. They found him in "the house" (Mt. 2:11), likely two years later than when he was born in the stable; made their gifts; and "being warned of God," returned "to their own country another way," fading out of the record. Their number, three, is traditional.

magic, magicians related to Magi. It seems that most of the ancient nations practiced magic, the claim of supernatural powers obtained by study of occult science, or the practice of black art in connivance with evil spirits (Acts 19:19). In the Bible, the magician is one of a class of sacred scribes skilled in writing and possessed of vast information (Dan. 1:20), who often claimed occult knowledge, practiced magic (Ex. 7:11), and undertook to interpret dreams (Gen. 41:8; Dan. 2:10; see 2 Tim. 3:8). The Hebrews had no magic of their own. Being forbidden by law, it could have no recognized standing, although resorted to in times of apostasy, being borrowed from neighbors. Whereas, speaking in general, there is no reality in the art, nevertheless diabolical power is such that on occasions we can hardly doubt the fact of supernatural manifestations. The demoniacal possession in the NT record points to the reality of the duplication by the Devil of the Lord's incarnation. Laban's teraphim, which he

called "gods" (Gen. 31:19, 30, 32–35), represent a corrupt superstitious practice, in addition to his worship of the true God (vss. 24, 49–53). The meaning of teraphim is obscure—"givers of pleasure"? In one instance, they seem to have been man-sized (1 Sam. 19: 13–16). There are Micah's images in Judges (18:5–6) consulted for oracular answers (cf. Hos. 3:4–5; and Zech. 10:2). Also see 1 Sam. 15:23, and 2 K. 23:24, and the remarkable words of Ezek. 21:19–22. Also there is Joseph's cup (Gen. 44:5), by which he "divined," where writing in the cup is of significance. Joseph's interpretation of dreams was by divine aid (Gen. 40:8). Exodus 8:19 seems to show that the Egyptian magicians used sleight of hand, rather than actual magic. The Israelites were clearly commanded to avoid the abominations of the heathen (Deut. 18:9–14). Balaam was famous in this regard (Num. 22:7; Josh. 13:22). Saul and the woman (not "witch"!) of Endor (1 Sam. 28) illustrate the extremity of the king in violating the Law. Since all is handled through the medium, who described what Saul understood was Samuel, there is reason to believe that the whole was a hoax. The prophets consistently condemned magic (Isa. 2:6, 8:19, 19:3, 29:3–4, 47:12–13; Jer. 14:14, 23: 25, 27:9–10, 29:8–9; Ezek. 8:7–12, 13:17, 21:21; Zech. 10:2; but see 13:1–4). In the NT, there is little concerning the practice of magic (Acts 8:9–24, 13:6–12, 16:16–18). In sum, there is only illusive result to come from magic practice; no evidence that man can utilize supernatural power at will; no such thing as real magic in human employ.

Magog (mā′gŏg) [perhaps root: be high] name of both a person and a land; in Gen. 10:2, the former, a second son of Japheth, the latter, (Ezek. 38:2) being "of the north" (Ezek. 38: 2), and representing the Scythians, in the sense of the general tribes north of the Caucasus. The final struggle of heathenism with the kingdom of God is prophetically cited in the passages in Ezek. 38–39 where is the figure of the invasion of Israel by Magog's hordes, and their overthrow, the description and imagery being borrowed by John (Rev. 20:8–9).

Magor-missabib (mā′gŏr-mĭs′sá-bĭb) [terror round about] the prophetic name given by Jeremiah to Pashhur who ill-treated him for his preaching against idolatry (Jer. 20:3).

Magpiash (măg′pĭ-ăsh) [moth-slayer?, collector of stars?] leader who signed the covenant with Nehemiah (10:20). Same as Magbish (Ezra 2:30).

Mahalah (má-hā′lä) [tenderness] one of three

children of Hammoleketh, sister of Gilead (1 Chr. 7:18).

Mahalaleel (mȧ-hā′lá-lē-ĕl) [splendor of God] 1. Fourth from Adam and son of Cainan (Gen. 5:12–13, 16–17; 1 Chr. 1:2; Lk. 3:37).

2. A descendant of Perez (Pharez), son of Judah (Neh. 11:4).

Mahalath (mȧ-hā′lăth) [anxiety, sickness] 1. A word in the heading of Ps. 53 and 88 (here, with another word), which has baffled the commentators, being taken as "catchword of old hymn," "musical instrument," "melody," "first word of popular tune." It can refer to sickness, or is possibly from root "dance." In the light of the psalm (of Hab. 3), and the preceding words and the final expression of that psalm, it seems most reasonable, with S. W. Thirtle (*Titles of the Psalms*, 1904), to place this word with the preceding psalm, allowing it to be its subscript. There was no punctuation in the original to indicate to which psalm certain expressions pertained. Two of the ancient Greek revisions relate this word to dancing, which in Israel, was connected with rejoicing, being associated with occasions of religious emotion as at some victory in arms. Note the connection of Ps. 52 with 1 Sam. 18:6 (and incidents in chapters following), and see the propriety of Mahalath in connection with a psalm to be sung in honor of signal victory, the event being recalled by the great dancings which followed. In the second of these psalms, the word Leannoth is added ("shoutings"), the historical facts of 2 Sam. 6:5, 14–15 being the basis for this commemorative ode. Shouting is associated with dancing (1 Sam. 18:7, 21:1, 29:5). See the connection of Ps. 87 with the occasion which it was selected, if not written, to commemorate.

2. Daughter of Ishmael, and a wife of Esau (Gen. 28:9). Called also Bashemath.

3. Daughter of Jerimoth, and one of Rehoboam's eighteen wives (2 Chr. 11:18).

Mahali (mā′hȧ-lī) [weak] son of Merari (Ex. 6:19).

Mahanaim (mā-hȧ-nā′ĭm) [two camps] Jacob's name for an East Jordan place where angels of God met him after fleeing Laban's land and before he crossed the Jabbok (Gen. 32:2). On the border between Gad and Manasseh (Josh. 13:26, 30), it was assigned to the Merarite Levites (21:38–39), and later became a fortified city; was Ish-bosheth's capital (2 Sam. 2:8, 12, 39); David's resort from Absalom (17:24, 27, 18:24–33; 1 K. 2:8); seat of one of Solomon's purveyors (1 K. 4:14). Unidentified.

Mahaneh-dan (mā′hȧ-nĕh-dăn′) [camp of Dan] so named when Danite spies camped on the spot, west of Kirjath-jearim (Judg. 18:12), between Zorah and Eshtaol (13:25).

Maharai (mā-hă′rī) [impetuous] a Netophathite, mighty man of David (2 Sam. 23:28; 1 Chr. 11:30, 27:13).

Mahath (mā′hăth) [seizing] 1. Kohath Levite, ancestor of Samuel (1 Chr. 6:35; vs. 33).

2. Another Levite, tending offerings, in Hezekiah's reign (2 Chr. 31:13, 29:12).

Mahavite (mā′hȧ-vīt) unexplained designation of Eliel, warrior of David (1 Chr. 11:46). Some corruption here; for the word is plural in Hebrew but joined to the singular.

Mahazioth (mȧ-hā′zĭ-ŏth) [vision of significance?] a Levite, one of the fourteen sons of Heman, of the twenty-third lot of singers (1 Chr. 25:4, 30).

Maher-shalal-hash-baz (mā′hēr-shăl′ăl-hăsh′băz) [speed spoil, hasten prey] predicting the quick conquest of Damascus and Samaria by Assyria, these words were enjoined on Isaiah, for a tablet duly witnessed, and a year later, as the name of his son, to call public attention to the fact of God's purpose (Isa. 8:1–4).

Mahlah (mā′lä) [disease, mildness] 1. Eldest of Zelophehad's five daughters (Num. 27:1–11).

2. Perhaps same but likely another Manassite in 1 Chr. 7:18, where the person is a child of Hammoleketh.

Mahli (mā′lī) [mild] 1. Son of Merari, and ancestor of Mahlites (Ex. 6:19; Num. 3:20; 1 Chr. 6:19, 29, 24:26; also Num. 26:58). In the first of the Chronicles references, seems a gap, Libni and Shimei belonging to the family of Gershom (1 Chr. 6:20, 42), and Eleazer and Kish being later described as sons of Mahli (1 Chr. 23:21, 24:28).

2. A Levite, family Merari, house of Mushi (1 Chr. 6:47, 23:23, 24:30); seems nephew of 1 above.

Mahlon (mā′lŏn) [mild] elder son of Elimelech and Naomi, an Ephrathite of Bethlehem Judah, and first husband of Ruth (Ruth 1:2, 4:10; cf. 1 Sam. 17:12).

Mahol (mā′hŏl) [dancing] one of the big four, than whom Solomon was wiser (1 K. 4:31).

Makaz (mā′kăz) [end] undiscovered town whence one of Solomon's purveyors drew supplies (1 K. 4:9).

Makheloth (măk-hē′lŏth) [assemblies, for worship] an encampment in the wilderness (Num. 33:25–26).

Makkedah (măk-kē′dä) [place of shepherds?] a lowland Canaanite town taken by Joshua (Josh. 10:10–30), on a memorable day. Unknown.

Maktesh (măk'tĕsh) [trough] a location in Jerusalem, identified by some as the Kidron valley, whose inhabitants were denounced by Zephaniah (1:11).

Malachi (măl'á-kī) [my messenger] the prophet writer of the last OT book, known only from his work (1:1, 3:1). The NT endorses the book (Mk. 1:2, 9:11–12; Lk. 1:17; Rom. 9:13). The prophet has been traditionally identified with various characters: Ezra, Mordecai, Nehemiah, Zerubbabel. The date is 433–420, at a time when a governor was in charge (1:8), when temple and altar were standing, and sacrifices as of old (1:7–10): the work is then later than Haggai and Zechariah, at a time when religious life inspired by the return and rebuilding of temple and fortifications of the city, had begun to decline, priests and people being corrupt, similar to the situation under Nehemiah (Neh. 13). Malachi supported Nehemiah in the effort to restore righteousness. There are three natural divisions: Jehovah the loving Father and Ruler of his people, 1:2–2:9; the supreme God and Father of all, 2:10–16; the righteous and final Judge, 2:17–4:6. In each, is: a sentence; a skeptical question; a full refutation.

Malcham or **Malcam** (măl'căm) [rule] 1. A Benjaminite, son of Shaharaim (1 Chr. 8:9).

2. Chief deity of the Ammonites, by some, identified with the idol Molech; perhaps referable generally to an idol, invested with regal honors (Zeph. 1:5).

Malchiah (măl-kī'ä) [Jehovah is king] 1. Descendant of Gershom, and ancestor of Asaph (1 Chr. 6:40).

2. A son of Parosh, with foreign wife (Ezra 10:25).

3. A son of Harim, of Ezra's time (10:31).

4. Son of Rechab (Neh. 3:14).

5. "The goldsmith's son," assisting in wall-rebuilding (3:31).

6. A priest of those at the right hand of Ezra reading the Law (Neh. 8:4).

7. A priest, father of Pashur; same as **Malchijah** 1 (Neh. 11:12; Jer. 38:1).

8. The son of Hammelech [the King's son, in 1 K. 22:26; 2 Chr. 28:7], into whose dungeon Jeremiah was cast (Jer. 38:6). "King's son" seems to have been title of a special functionary.

Malchiel (măl'kī-ĕl) [God is king] son of Beriah, and founder of a tribal family (Gen. 46:17; Num. 26:45). In 1 Chr. 7:31, he is the founder (father) of Birzavith.

Malchijah (măl-kī'jä) [Jehovah is king] 1. A Levite of Gershom family (1 Chr. 6:40).

NOTE: This is the same name as **Malchiah**, and Melchiah.

2. A priest, father of Pashur (1 Chr. 9:12; Neh. 11:12; see 1 Chr. 24:9). (The Malchiah of Jer. 38:6, likely a different person.)

3. Man of the above reference.

4, 5. Two sons of Parosh, with foreign wives (Ezra 10:25).

6. Son of Harim; possessing foreign spouse; wall- and furnace-repairer (Neh. 3:11).

7. Son of Rechab; wall-repairer (3:14).

8. A goldsmith wall-repairer (Neh. 3:31).

9. An officiating priest at the wall dedication, and perhaps assistant in law explanation (Neh. 12:42, 8:4).

10. A priest who, it appears, in behalf of a father's house, signed the covenant (Neh. 10:3).

Malchiram (măl-kī'răm) [King is exalted] son of Jehoiachin, i.e., Jeconiah (1 Chr. 3:18).

Malchishua (măl-kī-shū'ä) [King is salvation] a son of Saul, killed at Gilboa (1 Sam. 14:49, 31:2; 1 Chr. 8:33, 9:39).

Malchus (măl'kŭs) [king] personal servant of the high priest, present at the Lord's garden arrest (Mt. 26:51; Mk. 14:47; Lk. 22:49–51; Jn. 18:10), the healing of whose ear severed by Peter's sword, is noted only by the physician Luke.

Maleleel or **Mahalaleel** (mā-lē'lĕ-ĕl) [praise of God] son of Cainan (Lk. 3:37).

Mallothi (măl'lô-thī) [I speak, i.e., Jehovah] son of Heman; drew the nineteenth course for singers (1 Chr. 25:4, 26).

mallows connected with the word for salt; hence, by some, salt wort (Job 30:4). Most likely a perennial shrub, with leaves like olive, found near the Dead Sea; edible in a pinch. This seems the best of a number of contestants.

Malluch (măl'lŭk) [reigning] 1. A Levite, family of Merari (1 Chr. 6:44).

2. A son of Bani (Ezra 10:29).

3. Descendant of Harim (Ezra 10:32).

4. A priest (Neh. 10:4).

5. Apparently a Levite (Neh. 10:27).

6. A priestly returner with Zerubbabel (Neh. 12:2; seems same as 4). He may be the same as Malluchi of 10:4.

mammon [Aramaic for: riches, wealth] a personification of riches in Mt. 6:24; Lk. 16:9, 11, 13).

Mamre (măm'rē) [fatness] an old name, either of Hebron or part thereof (Gen. 23:19, 35:27), west of Machpelah (23:17), where Abraham, several occasions, resided (13:18, 14:13, 18:1), in a grove. As late as the sixteenth century, "Abraham's oak," girth twenty-six feet at the ground, was honored, a mile northwest of

Hebron; but his terebinths [oaks] have been shown at different spots. An Amorite chieftain by this name (perhaps designated by the district over which he ruled), with his brothers, Eshcol and Aner, helped Abraham recover persons and spoils carried away by the eastern confederacy (Gen. 14:13, 24).

man of the several words rendered man, we note: *adam* [ruddy], the name of the person created in God's image (Gen. 2:15; and certified in Rom. 5:12–21). The pair, Adam and wife (1:26–27). An individual, husband (*'ish*, 2:24). Frailty (Enosh 4:26; Dan. 2:10). Mighty one (*gibbor*, 1 Chr. 12:8). Men (only masculine; root: "die"; hence "mortal"—this derivation denied by some who say: "mature men" (Deut. 2:34). *Anthropos* (Plato: "the being who looks up"; in general, a human being (2 Cor. 4:16). *Aner*, man as distinguished from woman (Rom. 1:27); in plural, for honor "gentlemen" (Acts 2:14). Three times only is the Hebrew word *bara'* used in Gen. 1:1, touching matter in general; vs. 21, regarding living things; vs. 27, relative to man. In these three instances the only possible explanation is divine creation. Science has no explanation of origins (hypotheses are advanced); and there is no word save in Scripture as to bridging the gap between nothing and matter, and between matter and life, and between life and mankind. The Bible cites God. Also "God created man in his own image, in knowledge, righteousness and holiness, with dominion over the creatures." Regarding man, the Genesis story is generation, degeneration, regeneration (G. Campbell-Morgan), in chs. 1, 2; and in ch. 3; and in the remainder, to the end of the Bible. Man is the son of God only in the very general sense of creation: the Bible recognizes divine sonship by adoption only (Jn. 1:12; cf. 8:41–44; Rom. 8:14–17). Man's divine dignity (Gen. 1:26–31), lost in sin (Gen. 3; Rom. 3:10–23), finds restoration in Christ (Rom. 5:12–21).

Manaen (măn'à-ĕn) [comforter] a prophet (unofficial) and teacher at Antioch, when Paul and Barnabas were appointed missionaries; foster-brother to Herod Antipas (Acts 13:1).

Manahath (măn'à-hăth) [rest] 1. One of the sons of Shobal, and descendant of Seir the Horite (Gen. 36:23); or perhaps a place indwelt by a branch of Shobal tribe (1 Chr. 1:40).

2. A place to which certain Benjaminites were carried (1 Chr. 8:6).

Manahethites (mà-nā'hĕth-īts) in the genealogies of Judah, half of these folk were of Shobal's line, and half of Salma's (1 Chr. 2:52,

54), a place rather than an ancestor being referred to.

Manasseh (mā-năs'sĕ) [causing to forget] 1. Elder son of Joseph by wife Asenath, the Egyptian (Gen. 41:51, 46:20). Like his great-uncle Esau, he lost his birthright to the younger brother, Ephraim, the divinely guided grandfather Jacob, at the time of their blessing, placing his hands crossed upon their heads, after Joseph had arranged for the elder to receive the special birthright-blessing; but Manasseh too received great mercy from God (Gen. 48:8–21). Manasseh's history is not traced. There were seven tribal families, one from Machir, the others from grandson Gilead (Gen. 1:23; Num. 26:28–34; Josh. 17:1–2). As to their number, see Num. 1:10, 34–35, 2:20–21, 7:54, 59, 26:34; 1 Chr. 12:31. Following the defeat of the East Jordan kings, half of Manasseh received permission to occupy that territory along with Reuben and Gad, after aiding in the subjugation of the West Jordan section (Num. 32, 34:14–15; Deut. 3:12–13, 29:8; Josh. 12:4–6, 18:7). They failed their commission, and gradually were assimilated in the old dwellers there (1 Chr. 5:19, 22, 25, 26), and were the first to be deported by Assyria. The division between east and west Manasseh is not clear. The warriors, Machir, Jair, Nobah, relished the conquest of the very inaccessible Gilead hills and the Argob (Num. 32:39; Deut. 3:13–15). The territory included part of Gilead and all Bashan, limited by Mahanaim in one direction (Josh. 13:29–33), being about seventy miles east and west, and forty north and south, a 2500 foot tableland, rich soil, and into later years, still the granary of much of Syria. At Bethshean, the most eastern city of West Jordan Manasseh, there was practical junction with the East Jordan half. The genealogies (Num. 26:28–34; Josh. 17; 1 Chr. 7:14–19) do not distinguish clearly between east and west Manassite families. So also with the land, cf. Josh. 17:14–18. East Manasseh had Ephraim for the south boundary; and on the northwest, Asher; and on the northeast, Issachar. But Ephraim had cities in the midst of Manasseh's inheritance (Josh. 16:9); and Manasseh had various towns in the territory of Issachar and Asher (17:11; cf. 1 Chr. 7:29). Manassites, Gideon and Jephthah, were notable characters. It seems that this tribe took little part in public affairs: some joined David at Ziklag, and a large number at Hebron (1 Chr. 12:19–20, 31, 37); some came to Asa when they saw that the Lord was with him (2 Chr. 15:9); some attended the great Passovers of Hezekiah's and Josiah's reigns (30:1, 10–11, 18, 31:1, 34:6,

9). Being far removed (mainly around Carmel), they seemed to have little interest relatively, in what took place.

2. The thirteenth king of Judah, longer reign than any other of David's house. Beginning about 699 at the age of twelve, he reversed the current of reform of his good father Hezekiah, who had done so much toward bringing back all Israel to the worship and faith of the fathers (2 Chr. 30:6-12). Despite the warning of prophets, he brought the kingdom to its lowest degradation (2 K. 21:1-16). Retribution came on apace: neighboring nations revolted to independence; the Babylonian alliance soured; Merodach was crushed and the Assyrian's wrath was vented on his supporters; Judea was overrun, the city taken, the king carried into captivity (2 Chr. 33:11). Manasseh's eyes were opened; he repented; he was restored to effect some reforms (33:15-16). He fortified Jerusalem (33:12-19). His death occurred after fifty-five years of reign; and Amon his son ascended the throne (2 K. 21:17; 2 Chr. 33:20).

3. In Judg. 18:30 is an intentional modification of the name Moses into Manasseh, the Hebrew word having the letter "n" inserted and elevated, the explanation being that it was to guard the honor of Moses. A grandson of Moses at so apparently late a period, is explained by the reference of the last five chapters of Judges to events earlier than the preceding chapters.

4 and 5. A son of Pahath-moab, and a son of Hashum, each having put away his foreign wife (Ezra 10:30, 33).

Manasses (mā-năs′sēz) see Mt. 1:10; Rev. 7:6. Same as **Manasseh.**

Manassites (mā-năs′sīts) members of tribe Manasseh (Deut. 4:43; Judg. 12:4; 2 K. 10:33).

mandrakes Hebrew *duda'im*, amatory plants, supposed to act as a love philter (Gen. 30:14-16). Apparently odoriferous (Song of S. 7:13). Said to be a handsome plant of the night-shade order, wavy leaves, and violet, white, or deep blue flowers, with small yellow fruit, slightly resembling the human body; found in the Jordan valley, Galilee, and Moab.

maneh see **weights and measures**

manger crib or trough for cattle-feeding (Lk. 2:7, 12, 16). In Palestine of old, the stable was attached to the house, or in it, a portion set aside for cattle. At the inn of the natal story, it is supposed that there was an open courtyard, enclosed by rough fence of stone, where cattle were shut at night, and where travelers, under necessity, could find space.

manna (măn′nà) [it is manna; some make it a question] there was an Oriental manna, with neither the qualities nor uses of the miraculous provision of forty years sojourn by Israel in the wilderness, first given in the region, Sin, in the second half of the second month, when the people murmured at lack of food. From Ex. 16; Num. 11:7-9; Deut. 8:3-16; Josh. 5:12; Neh. 9:20; Ps. 78:24, we learn that it came every morning, except sabbath; was small, round like hoarfrost; must be gathered early before melting; was prepared by grinding and baking, and tasted like fresh oil, and like wafers made with honey, agreeable to all palates; and that it suddenly ceased with the availability of new corn in the land of Canaan. An omerful (ca. 5.8 pints), the daily allowance, was preserved, kept from decay, to show future generations the food of wilderness sustenance.

Manoah (mā-nō′ä) [rest] father of Samson, a Danite, native of Zorah, hospitable, worshiper of Jehovah, and very reverent. He remonstrated with his son; but went to Timnath to the marriage (Judg. 13:1-23, 14:2-4).

manslayer various instances of crime allowed the guilty one to find shelter in a city of refuge: (1) death from stone or missile thrown at random (Num. 35:22-23); (2) by blow in sudden quarrel (vs. 22); (3) by axhead flying from handle (Deut. 19:5); (4) fall from unguarded roof—guilt of manslaughter is not clear here, but the law intended to avoid imputation of malice by seeking to prevent the occurrence (Deut. 22:8). In addition, the animal—supposedly not vicious—causing human death was killed and regarded unclean; but if known vicious, the owner was liable to fine and even death (Ex. 21:28, 31). And a thief apprised at night in the act, could lawfully be killed: if the sun had risen, the killing was held as murder (Ex. 22:2-3).

mantle here four distinct terms, in derivation and meaning, occur: (1) Judg. 4:18, likely an article of bedcovering, which Jael used over Sisera; (2) 1 Sam. 15:27, 28:14; Ezra 9:3, 5; Job 1:20, 2:12; Ps. 109:29, a coat or robe—in Samuel's case, the garment made by his mother, said to be miniature of the priestly garb, as worn by the prophet in later years; (3) Isa. 3:22, apparently exterior tunic with sleeves, part of lady's dress; (4) 1 K. 19:13, 19; 2 K. 2:8, 13, 14, probably sheepskin, the only garment of Elijah other than the strip of skin around loins—so it seems. In general, the mantle is said to be the large sleeveless outer garment, or an occasional one between the tunic and the outer garment.

Maoch (mā′ŏk) [oppression] father of Achish, of Gath (1 Sam. 27:2).

Maon (mā'ŏn) [dwelling] 1. A hill-country town of Judah, residence of Nabal (Josh. 15:55) eight and one-half miles south of Hebron, near which David and men took refuge (1 Sam. 23:24–25).

2. Son of Shammai, of Judah tribe, and ancestor of Beth-zur citizens (1 Chr. 2:45). Could be the inhabitants of the town of that name, parallel to such passages as 1 Chr. 1:8–9, 11, 13.

3. A people oppressing Israel, called **Maonites** in Judg. 10:12. Some authorities identify them with Midian.

Mara (mā'rä) [bitter] name chosen by Naomi to express her losses (Ruth 1:20).

Marah same as above. A place in the wilderness of Shur, or Etham, three days from where Israel crossed the Sea, where a spring of bitter water was sweetened by casting in a tree, shown of God, when the people murmured (Ex. 15:22–24; Num. 33:8). Several places bid for identification with Mara, either Hawarah, a few miles inland from the Red Sea, where a twenty-five foot well has bitter water, or 'Ayun Musa [Wells of Moses], seven and one-half miles southeast of Suez, some of whose springs have potable water, others bitter.

Maralah (măr'à-lä) [trembling] frontier village, landmark on Zebulun's boundary (Josh. 19:11).

Maranatha (mä-răn-ā'thä) [Aram., Our Lord cometh] used by Paul (1 Cor. 16:22).

marble probably any "shining" stone used for columns and pavements, from Lebanon, or Arabia, or Persia (1 Chr. 29:2; Est. 1:6; Song of S. 5:15). Josephus notes Herod's temple had monolithic pillars of white marble, twenty-five cubits high.

Marchesvan see **months**

Marcus (mär'cŭs) [large hammer] evangelist Mark, cousin to Barnabas (Col. 4:10), companion and fellow laborer of Paul and Peter (Philemon 24; 1 Pet. 5:13).

Mareshah (mā-rē'shä) [possession] 1. A city of Judah in the low country (Shephelah), Josh. 15:44. Hebron seems to have been colonized from here (1 Chr. 2:42). It apparently commanded a strategic spot, fortified and garrisoned by Rehoboam (2 Chr. 11:8). In the fourth century, Eusebius and Jerome described it as in the second mile from Beit-jibrin (Eleutheropolis). It is noted further in OT (2 Chr. 20:37; Mic. 1:15).

2. Father of Hebron, and apparently descendant of Caleb (1 Chr. 2:42).

3. In 1 Chr. 4:21, it is again named as deriving origin from Shelah, third son of Judah.

Mark same as John "whose surname was Mark"

(Acts 12:12, 25), the evangelist. His mother, Mary, was of comfortable circumstances, whose house in Jerusalem was a meeting place of Christians (see Acts 12). To her house Peter came, delivered from prison. Peter calls him "Marcus, my son" (1 Pet. 5:13), because probably led to the Savior by him. He was cousin to Barnabas ("sister's son," Col. 4:10). He went with Barnabas and Paul from Jerusalem to Antioch, and later, on their missionary journey (Acts 12:25, 13:5), but unaccountably turned back at Perga, so disapproved by Paul as to be refused companionship on the second journey (15:38). After his voyage with Barnabas to Cyprus for evangelization, Mark disappears from the record for about ten years, being next found at Rome with Paul (Col. 4:10; Philemon 24), indicating complete reconciliation (2 Tim. 4:11), with implication that Mark had been in the East, which agrees with 1 Pet. 5:13. He seems to have been with Timothy at Ephesus (2 Tim. 4:11). The naked young man at the time of the Lord's arrest (Mk. 14:51–52) seems to have been Mark; he alone tells of the incident as personal reminiscence. Ancient writers represent him as the interpreter of Peter: the translator of Peter's Aramaic into Greek; or more likely, the gospel writer conforming more than others to Peter's preaching. It is tradition only that he was with Peter at Rome (?) and was sent to Egypt, there founding the Alexandrian church, where he was bishop, and died a martyr's death. By his associations, he was certainly fit, humanly speaking, to write a gospel.

Mark, Gospel of the second of the four, but not necessarily in order of composition. Its brevity is usually not due to condensation—he gives details, moving rapidly forward with pictorial skill, with a succession of descriptive scenes. In addition to the many references to Mark's gospel as connected with Peter, there are certain peculiarities which point in that direction, suggesting at least that Peter had a kind of superintendence of it. It is not a mere epitome of the other two Synoptics. Paintings are more vivid, vigilant eyewitness notes occur, even when the same ground as others is covered. The humble origin of Peter is shown by Mark (1:16–20); Peter's denial (14:72); there is connection with Capernaum (1:29); *Peter* is noted as the Lord's name for Simon (3:16); from Mark comes the name of Jairus (4:22), also the word *carpenter* applied to the Lord (6:3); the nation of the "Syrophoenician" woman (7:26); Dalmanutha for Magdala (8:10); the Lord's suffering none to carry a vessel through the temple (11:16); Simon of

Cyrene, the father of Alexander and Rufus (15:21). These, differing from Matthew and Luke, show independence, it being natural to look to Peter as the source. Mark is more chronological than the others; stress is laid on the deeds of Christ, more than on formal verbal instruction. Mark's is the gospel for the Romans, for Gentiles, with Christ as the mighty Son of God, even while he is the Suffering Servant. Scant reference is made to the OT; none to the Law; the Lord's genealogy is omitted; particularly Jewish matters are left out; explanations unnecessary for Jews are given, e.g., Jordan is a "river," and Pharisees "fast" (1:5, 2:18). The date is before the destruction of Jerusalem, say 63–70. The last twelve verses are thought by many scholars to be not a part of the original; but if so, they were added very early, and they represent unquestioned truth and equal inspiration. There is no doubt of the genuineness of the gospel as a whole. There are two themes: (1) the ministry in Galilee (1:14–9:50); (2) the last week in Jerusalem (11:1–16:8 [20]). In between is a section about the training of the Twelve, in parts beyond (7:24–9:50).

Maroth (mā'rŏth) [bitterness] town of western lowland of Judah (Mic. 1:12).

marriage a divine institution, given of God before sin came, for the glory of God and the blessing of mankind. It is an ennobling and developmental relationship, powerfully contributory to complete human stature. The home is the unit in society. Monogamy is the divine ideal, a permanent relationship (Gen. 2:18–24; Mt. 19:5–6; 1 Cor. 6:16), dissolved by no legitimate act of man, but only by death (Mt. 19:4–6; Rom. 7:2–3). As regards all laws of God, given for man's benefit as for his glory; the permanence of marriage is for moral ends— the training of husband and wife in mutual obligations and responsibilities, and the discipline of children in obedience and virtue; for the home is the first school, the first state, the first church. In practice, the ideal has suffered. The one-husband, one-wife, relationship was violated early, due to sin. Lamech is the first polygamist (Gen. 4:19); and the purity of marriage was impaired by low motives in the choice of wives (6:2). God's disapproval of the ideal's violation, is shown even in the cases of such good men as Abraham and David, in the train of innumerable woes that followed plurality of wives. Men disregard Deity's wise provisions to their own hurt, and the hurt of others. Thus Moses, for the "hardness of . . . hearts . . . suffered" the putting away of wives (Mt. 19:8); but "from the beginning it was not so."

Moses discouraged polygamy: he regulated what he found in a situation which was not the ordination of the Creator. See Ex. 20:14, 17, 21:2–11; Lev. 18:18, 20:10; Deut. 17:17, 21:10–17, 22. In patriarchal times, there were consanguineal marriages, it appears, on religious grounds (Gen. 11:29, 28:2, 29:4). But the Mosaic law forbade alliance with persons related by blood, and even with those related by law (Lev. 18:6–18; an exception, Deut. 25:5). There was distinct prohibition regarding Canaanites, on account of idolatry (Ex. 34:16; Deut. 7:3–4). Legal disabilities touching Ammonites and Moabites (Deut. 23:3) virtually forbid intermarriage; but men could take Moabite wives (Mahlon with Ruth). Full citizenship permitted marriage in the case of Edomite or Egyptian (Deut. 23:7–8). It would seem that ordinarily the foreign wife became a proselyte (Ruth 1:16). In the NT, separation between believers and non-believers, would apply with equal force to marriage. There was special prohibition in the case of the high priest, who could marry only a virgin of his own people (Lev. 21:13–14), there being less restriction for the priests—prohibited only from taking prostitutes or divorced women (Lev. 21:7). Heiresses must marry in their tribes (Num. 36:5–9). The physically defective were forbidden Israelitish marriage (Deut. 23:1). In the Christian church, bishops and deacons could have each but one wife, which being ambiguous, may refer polygamy to marriage after first wife's decease, or to marriage after divorce, during the life of the first wife. The probable sense is second marriage of any kind. Candidates for the rather undefined order of widows (1 Tim. 5:9) also had limitations of marriage. The mutual relations of married couples are subject of frequent NT exhortations (Eph. 5:22–23; Col. 3:18–19). Early polygamy was divested of much of the degradation involved at later times: monogamy, in principle, was retained by distinction made between chief or original wife and secondary wives; in the thought that progeny was the objective; and in cases where adopted at the wife's request—children born to a slave were legally children of the mistress (Gen. 16:3, 30:4, 9); or at the instance of the father (Gen. 29:23, 28; Ex. 21:9–10). There seems but one instance of what may be called divorce, in patriarchal times (Gen. 21:14). Despite the Mosaic mitigation of divorce evils, they persisted; and although the record seems to indicate that monogamy was more prevalent after the return of Israel from captivity, no instance of polygamy being noted during this period in the Bible (contrarily, see

228

Mt. 18:25; Lk. 1:5; Acts 5:1), yet rampant abuses continued. Our Lord with his apostles dealt with the matter, re-establishing the sanctity of the marriage bond: confirming the original charter of marriage as the basis on which all regulations were to be framed (Mt. 19:4–5); restricting divorce to fornication, and prohibiting remarriage of persons divorced on improper grounds (Mt. 5:32, 19:9; Rom. 7:3; 1 Cor. 7:10–11); and generally enforcing morality (Heb. 13:4). Note especially the Apostolic Council's formal condemnation of what was apparently viewed as morally indifferent by some in the church (Acts 15:20). Since divorce and remarriage has become so widespread in this midtwentieth century, the following should be considered: in the NT, divorce seems plainly forbidden (Mk. 10:11; Lk. 16:18; 1 Cor. 7:10–11b, 39). Our Lord held divorce a concession to low moral standard, opposed to the ideal of marriage as inseparable union of body and soul (Gen. 2:23). In any and all cases this should be kept in mind. Now follows the scriptural teaching according to the NT: divorce under certain conditions appears allowable (Mt. 19:9; 1 Cor. 7:11a, 15a). It is remarriage which means fornication (here adultery), condemned of God (Ex. 20:14). Some interpret Mt. 9:19 as permitting both, if it permits the former. It is significant that in the Corinthians passage, we have, as it seems, only the inspired record of the apostle's words, as he himself states (7:12), and not the specific word of God, as in vss. 10–11. Also it is of interest certainly, to note that only the Matthean account, in sharp contrast to the parallel records in the other gospels, allows divorce (5:32, 19:9); also that, whereas there is no MS authority for omission of Matthew's statements, there is a well-defended view that Matthew's exception is an editorial addition, from the Judaic standpoint, or under pressure of practical necessity, the absolute rule being found too hard. We take the Scripture; but the suggestion certainly stresses the injunction against remarriage of divorcees. With no minimization of the evil of divorce, even the justifiable case, careful reading of Mt. 5:32 and 1 Cor. 7:15, we believe will show not so much the divorce, as the remarriage which is denounced. Remarriage shuts out reconciliation which on Christian principles should always be sought (cf. Hosea, Jer. 3, and 1 Cor. 7:11, 16). At any rate, the Protestant church, basing its position allegedly on Scripture, permits divorce (and remarriage) for the two reasons of marital unfaithfulness and (non-Biblical) willful desertion; and in recent times has practically foregone all standards officially,

requiring only presumably sincere repentance, and in some cases, a period of time before another alliance. The matrimonial customs among the ancients, and especially the Orientals, differ in much from ours. At least initially, the selection of a son's wife devolved on the kin, generally the father (Gen. 21:21, 38:6); but there were instances where the son expressed preference and the father made negotiations (Gen. 34:4, 8; Judg. 14:1–10). There is instance of what seems to have been extraordinary—where the son made arrangements (Gen. 29:18). Consent of the maid's father and brothers was sought, rather than hers; but we have Gen. 24:58 (Rebekah); see Gen. 24:51, 34:11. There are cases where a parent made selection for the daughter, or offered a suitable prospect (Ex. 2:21; Josh. 15:17; Ruth 3:1–2; 1 Sam. 18:27). Presents were given the parents and sometimes the maiden (Gen. 24:22, 53, 29:18, 27, 34:12; 1 Sam. 18:25). Between betrothal and marriage, communications between the two were effected through a deputed friend (Jn. 3:29), this espousal interval varying from a few days (Gen. 24:55) to a full year for virgins and a month for widows, in later times, in this interval the woman was virtually regarded as a wife. Unfaithfulness was punishable by death (Deut. 22:23–24; but see 24:1) —the husband had option of "putting her away" (Mt. 1:19). As to the wedding, there seem to have been no definite religious ceremonies: the espousal was ratified by an oath (Prov. 2:17; Ezek. 16:8; Mt. 2:14); and a blessing was in order (Gen. 24:60; Ruth 4:11–12). On the wedding day there was formal preparation (Gen. 24:65; Ps. 45:13–14; Isa. 3:24, 49:18, 61:10; Jer. 2:32; Eph. 5:26–27; Rev. 19:8, 21:2). The groom's adornment and activities are seen in the following: Gen. 31:27; Judg. 14:11; Song of S. 3:11; Isa. 61:10; Jer. 7:34; Mt. 9:15, 25:7. Having received the veiled bride from her parents with their blessing and those of friends (Gen. 24:59; Ruth 4:11), he conducted the whole party back to his own or his father's house, with song, music, and dancing (Ps. 45:15; Song of S. 3:6–11), being joined by maiden friends (Mt. 25:6). At the house, all friends and neighbors were invited to a feast (Gen. 29:22; Mt. 22:1–10; Lk. 14:8; Jn. 2:2), festivities continuing for seven or fourteen days (Judg. 14:12). A newly married man had exemptions (Deut. 24:5). The spiritual relation between God and his people is spoken of as a betrothal or marriage. Apostasy, through idolatry or other sin, was likened to conjugal infidelity (Isa. 1:21; Jer. 3:1–20; Ezek. 16, 23; Hos. 2). So in the NT,

Christ is the bridegroom (Mt. 9:15; Jn. 3:29; and the church is the bride (2 Cor. 11:2; Rev. 18:7, 21:2, 9, 22:17); the comparison thus shown, illustrates the position and mutual duties of husband and wife, the standard for their imitation (Eph. 5:23–32).

Marsena (mär-sē'nà) [worthy] one of seven princes who sat first in the kingdom (Est. 1:14).

Mars' Hill see **Areopagus**

Martha (mär'thà) [lady] a later Aramaic name, not found in the OT; sister of Mary and Lazarus of Bethany (Jn. 11:1–2), all devotedly attached to the Lord. Devout after the Jewish custom, she shared in Messianic hopes, accepting her Lord as Christ, believing in the resurrection (Jn. 11:24). She showed respect, seeking his comfort but, being "cumbered with much serving" and "careful and troubled about many things," she lacked the "one thing needful," and was reproved; yet her love, even imperfect, was true; and she learned that an inward craving for spiritual fellowship with the Lord was more essential than concern for external honor (Lk. 10:38–42). The house of cordial reception was called Martha's (Lk. 10: 38); the supper at Bethany, Lazarus being present, when Mary anointed his feet, saw Martha serving (Jn. 12:1–3): it was the house of Simon the leper (Mt. 26:6; Mk. 14:3), the inference being that Martha was his widow. She seems to have grown in patience and sympathy.

Mary a Roman Christian, greeted by Paul in Romans (16:6), as having toiled for him.

Mary of Cleopas (clē-ō'pãs) accurately, "Clopas." From comparison of certain statements (Mt. 27:56; Mk. 15:40; Jn. 19:25), it seems that this Mary was the wife of Cleopas, who is Alpheus (Mt. 10:3; Mk. 3:18; Lk. 6:15); and that they were parents of at least three daughters (unknown), and four sons: the apostle James the Less, Joses, Jude, Simon (Mt. 27:56; Mk. 15:40; Lk. 24:10). It is doubtful, but possible, that this woman was sister to Mary the Virgin: that would make his "brethren" his cousins, and two sisters with the same, or quite similar, name. Besides being at the Cross, she was at the tomb with Mary Magdalene (Mt. 27:61; Mk. 15:47); and again on the third day (Mt. 28:1; Mk. 16:1; Lk. 23:56, 24:10; see 24:23).

Mary Magdalene (măg'dà-lē'nĕ) [resident of Magdala?] her designation (Mt. 27:56, 61, 28:1; Mk. 15:40, 47, 16:1, 9; Lk. 8:2, 24:10; Jn. 19:25, 20:1, 28), seems to show her a resident of Magdala, the one possessed of devils, and a most devoted follower of the Lord, following their expulsion. Her first mention (Lk.

8:2) occurring closely after the account of the sinful woman's anointing the Savior's feet, in a Galilean city, is the source of the erroneous but persistent notion that she was of ill-fame (Lk. 7:36–50). Her affliction was out of the ordinary (Lk. 8:4; see Mt. 12:45), its cure accounting for her extraordinary devotion, beginning at the early Galilean ministry (Lk. 8:1–3). She was with those at the Cross (Mt. 27:56; see cross references); observed his burial (vs. 61); went with others on the third day to anoint his body (Mk. 16:1); reported to Peter and John the body removed (Jn. 20:1–2); returned to the garden where to her, first, the Lord appeared (Mk. 16:9; Jn. 20:11–17); and reported his resurrection to the other disciples (20:18). Nothing further is known of her.

Mary the mother of Mark evidently an early disciple, sister of Barnabas (Col. 4:10, where "sister's son" should likely be "cousin"), who (Acts 4:37; 12:12) apparently gave up her house to the church for meeting place, to which Peter, released from prison, repaired, his relation being quite close—he calls Mark his "son" (1 Pet. 5:13). She may have been of Levi (Acts 4:36).

Mary the Virgin there are multiple legends: there is concise authentic history in this case, deriving only from Scripture. Like Joseph, she was of Judah, lineage of David (Ps. 132:11; Lk. 1:32; Rom. 1:3). If Jn. 19:35 is construed as meaning three women at the Cross, then the Virgin Mary had a sister named Mary. The text is ambiguous: we favor four women. She was connected with Elizabeth, of Levi, lineage of Aaron (Lk. 1:36). She was a resident of Nazareth, betrothed to a carpenter named Joseph (Lk. 1:26–27), regarded by Jewish law and custom, as his wife, though not yet taken to his house. In this situation the angel Gabriel apprised her of motherhood of the long-expected Messiah. A kind of sign of this was the declared birth (three months future, Lk. 1:36), of a child of her cousin Elizabeth, at probably Juttah (Lk. 1:39), about twenty miles south of Jerusalem. When Mary went to see Elizabeth, the latter saluted her as the mother of her Lord, whereupon Mary embodied her feelings in the Magnificat, pointing back to Hannah's Song (1 Sam. 1:1–10). Shortly after her return home, Joseph learning the facts, contemplated a bill of divorcement, rather than yield his betrothed to the course of the Law; and then, being advised and satisfied by angelic revelation, he took Mary to his own house. Not long afterward, Augustus' decree brought them to Bethlehem for enrollment in the registers, looking to the taxing, which was completed only ten years afterward in the governorship of Quirinius. There, Mary bore the Savior of the world, placed in a manger. The poverty of the parents is shown by their making the offering of the poor, forty days afterward. The flight to Egypt and the return occur; and from about 3 B.C. to A.D. 26, Mary may be thought of as living humbly in Nazareth, Joseph having died at an unspecified date. On four occasions the veil is removed: (1) the marriage at Cana of Galilee (Jn. 2); (2) the attempt which she and the Lord's brethren made to speak with him (Mt. 12:46; Mk. 3:21, 31; Lk. 8:19); (3) the crucifixion (Jn. 19:26); (4) the days following the ascension (Acts 1:14). There are two other references to Mary (Mt. 13:54-55; Mk. 6:1-3; Lk. 11:27). Mary's youth was doubtless spent in the study of Scripture, with the godly example of holy women to guide her (note the Magnificat, Lk. 1:46). Faith and humility show in surrender to the divine will (Lk. 1:38), energy and earnestness in her journey from Nazareth to Hebron (1:39), thankfulness in the song of joy (1:48), thoughtfulness in pondering the shepherds' visit (Lk. 2:19), treasuring the Son's word, not fully understood (2:51). Neither in Bible nor creeds nor the fathers of the first five centuries, is there a word from which the worship of Mary could be inferred. The worship of the "Blessed Virgin" has two distinctly marked periods: (1) Arising out of the apocryphal legends regarding her birth and death (from the first century to the close of the fifth—during which time the Council of Ephesus [431] inadvertently magnified the mother at the expense of the son—), the worship of Mary was wholly external to the church, regarded as heretical, and confined to Gnostic and Collyridian defections. (2) In the sixth century, Mariolatry began to spread in the church; and despite the shock given it by the Reformation, it has continued to extend itself, the latest manifestation being the "Assumption of Mary," proclaimed by the Roman Catholic church, in our century, by which it is taught that she also, as in the case of the Lord, has been taken up bodily into heaven.

Maschil the title of the following thirteen Psalms: 32, 42, 44-45, 52-55, 64, 78, 88-89, 142. The mystery of the psalm titles seems to be very ancient, the LXX (in the third century B.C.) not knowing their explanation. A number of suggestions have been made for this title: a musical term denoting a melody requiring great skill in execution (H. A. Ewald); any sacred song relating to divine things, whose end is to promote wisdom and piety (Roediger); a word relative to the didactic nature of the psalm.

We take it to mean a composition for public instruction.

Mash (măsh) one of Aram's sons (Gen. 10:23), being Meshech in 1 Chr. 1:17, whose geographical location is said to have been at the northern boundary of Mesopotamia.

Mashal same as Misheal or Mishal (1 Chr. 6:74).

mason a workman skilled in handling bricks and stones for building (2 Sam. 5:11; 1 K. 7:9-10; 2 Chr. 23:14, 24:12; Ezra 3:10; Song of S. 5:15).

Masora, Masoretes, Masorites see **Old Testament**

Maspha same as Mizpeh of Benjamin.

Masrekah (măs-rē′kä) [vineyard] an Edomite city, site unknown (Gen. 36:36; 1 Chr. 1:47).

Massa (măs′sä) [burden] a son of Ishmael (Gen. 25:14; 1 Chr. 1:30; cf. Prov. 30:1); generally identified with the Masani, of the Arabian desert, near the Persian Gulf.

Massah [temptation] Moses' name for the place in Rephidim where the smitten rock yielded water, so named because Israel put Jehovah to test (Ex. 17:8; Ps. 95:8-9; Heb. 3:8). It is called also Meribah; and it seems unlikely that two events are involved. Other references: Deut. 6:16, 9:22, 33:8.

Mathusala Methuselah, son of Enoch (Lk. 3:37).

Matred (mā′trĕd) [driving forward] mother-in-law of Hadar king of Edom (Gen. 36:39; 1 Chr. 1:50).

Matri (mā′trī) [rainy] a Benjaminite family, from which came Kish and his son, Saul (1 Sam. 10:21).

Mattan (măt′tăn) [gift] 1. Priest of Baal, slain at his altars (who probably came with Athaliah from Samaria), in the revolution which put Joash on the throne of Judah (2 K. 11:18; 2 Chr. 23:17).

2. Father of Shephatiah (Jer. 38:1).

Mattanah (măt′tä-nä) [gift] a station of Israel's wandering, in or near Moabite territory (Num. 21:18-19), southeast of the Dead Sea.

Mattaniah (măt-tă-nī′ä) [gift of Jehovah] 1. Original name of Zedekiah king of Judah, changed by Nebuchadnezzar at enthronement (2 K. 24:17).

2. A Levite Asaphite singer (likely, 1 Chr. 9:15; 2 Chr. 20:14; Neh. 11:17, 22, 12:8, 25, 35, 13:13).

3. It may be that the names in the first two references above, refer to different men, the one of 2 Chr. 20:14, being a descendant of Asaph, and ancestor of Jahaziel, of Jehoshaphat's reign.

4 to 7. Four men: a son of Elam, one of

Mattatha

Zattu, one of Pathah-moab, one of Bani, all induced by Ezra to put away foreign wives (Ezra 10:26–27, 30, 37).

8. A Levite, the man of Neh. 13:13, thought by some to be another person, this man being father of Zaccur, and ancestor of Hanan, the under-treasurer.

9. One of the fourteen sons of Heman, horn-blowers (1 Chr. 25:4, 16).

10. An Asaphite Levite aiding King Heze-kiah's reformation (2 Chr. 29:13).

Mattatha (măt′tă-thä) [gift] a son of Nathan and grandson of David (Lk. 3:31).

Mattathah as above. Hashum's descendant, divorcing foreign wife (Ezra 10:33).

Mattathias (măt-tă-thī′ăs) [Greek form of Mattithiah, gift of Jehovah] name of two ancestors of the Christ, separated by five generations (Lk. 3:25–26).

Mattenai (măt-tĕ-nā′ī) [bestowment] 1 and 2. Two Hebrews, a son of Hashum, and a son of Bani, separating from foreign wives (Ezra 10:33, 37).

Matthan (măt′thăn) [gift] Eliezer's son, grandfather of "the husband of Mary" (Mt. 1:15). Similar position to Matthat of Lk. 3:24: could be identical.

Matthat (măt′thăt) same as above. Two ancestors of Christ, one near, one remote (Lk. 3:24, 29).

Matthew [via the Greek, gift of Jehovah] a publican (tax gatherer), in government service at Capernaum, called of the Lord to become apostle and evangelist (Mt. 10:3; Mk. 3:18; Lk. 6:15), being the same as Levi (Lk. 5:27–29), the son of Alpheus (Mk. 2:14; Lk. 5:27). Probably he received the name Matthew when he became a Christian. The Lord's acceptance of a publican seems to have led other "outcasts" (publicans were such to the Jews) to follow him, and increased Pharisaic opposition. Note the Lord's famous reply at the dinner party by host Matthew (Mt. 9:10–13; Mk. 2:15–17; Lk. 5:29–32). He appears with the others after the resurrection (Acts 1:13), nothing more being definitely known, though traditions are rife regarding his place of preaching, and touching his death.

Matthew, Gospel of universally ascribed to this man. Ancient tradition affirms the gospel first written in Hebrew (Papias, Irenaeus, Eusebius, Origen). There is much "about it and about" on the so-called Synoptic problem; but whatever the conclusion, it is apparent that our Gospel of Matthew in Greek is attributable to Matthew: he was competent, and he evidently knew firsthand the recorded words and deeds. The book is judged in the light of certain fea-tures to be addressed to Jews in the main, speaking of the King and his kingdom (note the many OT references, and such expressions as: "that it might be fulfilled" (e.g., 1:22, 2:15); Messianic references under the name, "Son of David." The date is suggested as from A.D. 60 to 70, the place being probably Palestine, the purpose being to convince Jews that Jesus of Nazareth is the expected Messiah, the fulfillment of the Law and the Messianic prophecies, centering in the person of our Lord.

The subject matter of Matthew is arranged rather topically than chronologically; but early in ch. 14 the true order of events seems to fall in with his object, and is carried on to the end. The contents may be summarized as follows: (1) The descent, birth, and infancy of the royal Messiah (chs. 1–2). (2) The beginning of the public ministry, related to John the Baptist's work; baptism, temptation, and settlement in Capernaum (3:1–4:17). (3) The Galilean ministry (4:18–9:34); four leading disciples called (4:18–22); his work and fame in Palestine (4:19–25); the sermon on the mount, and deeds illustrative of his teaching (5:1–9:34). (4) The appointment, mission, and instructions of the Twelve, headed by his compassion for the shepherdless (9:35–10:42). (5) The case of John Baptist; increasing opposition and conflict with the Pharisees; a collection of parables; the miracle of feeding the 5000, and walking on the water (11:1–15:20). (6) Further instructions, retirement from, and return to, Capernaum, including miracles (feeding the 4000), Peter's confession, prediction of his death, the Transfiguration, various teachings as greatness and forgiveness (15:21–18:35). (7) Closing ministry, in Peraea and Judea, with instruction, parable, and miracle—e.g., divorce, children, rich young ruler, laborers in the vineyard, prediction of death, Bartimaeus—chs. 19–20). (8) The last week: with parables, conflict with, and triumph, over enemies, last things; then betrayal, last Passover, arrest, trial, crucifixion and burial; the Galilean great commission and promise (chs. 21–28).

Matthias likely a variant of Mattathias, as above. The disciple elected in Judas' place, being qualified by constant attendance upon the Lord and by witness of the resurrection (Acts 1:26).

Mattithiah as above. 1. A Korahite Levite, in charge of baked offerings (1 Chr. 9:31).

2. A Levite, son of Jeduthun (1 Chr. 25:3, 21); a musician of the sanctuary (15:18, 21); under Asaph to minister before the ark in musical service (16:5); afterwards, head of the fourteenth course of musicians (25:3, 21).

3. Son of Nebo, led of Ezra to divorce strange wife (Ezra 10:43).

4. Apparently a priest, or a Levite, supporting Ezra regarding the Law (Neh. 8:4).

mattock apparently a single-headed instrument, for digging and dressing vineyards (Isa. 7:25), distinguished from other tools (1 Sam. 13:20–21).

maul a breaker, a war weapon (Prov. 25:18).

Mazzaroth (măz′zā-rōth) [lodgings?] a manifestation in the heavens, taken to be the "twelve signs" of the Zodiac, or perhaps better, a constellation cluster in the southern skies (Job 38:32).

meadow the rendering of an Egyptian word denoting reed grass (Gen. 41:2, 18); the same word in Job 8:11 is "flag." Also in Judg. 20:33, where one of the older versions translates "cave."

Meah (mē′ä) [hundred] a Jerusalem wall-tower (Neh. 3:1, 12:39), likely at the northeast part, between the tower of Hananeel and the sheepgate.

meals information is slight. To "dine" is to "eat" (Gen. 43:16), inference being that for Egypt, the principal meal was at noon. From Ex. 16:12, it can be held that Israel ate in the morning and the evening; but Ruth 2:14, suggests a light meal at noon for laborers. Josephus notes the chief meal in the evening; and some find indications that the Hebrews, like Bedouins, had the principal meal after sunset, with a lighter one at 9 or 10 in the morning. In the NT are two words translated "dinner" and "supper" (Lk. 14:12; Jn. 21:12), more properly, "breakfast" and "dinner." Posture at meals seems to have varied. The old Hebrews sat (Gen. 27:19; Judg. 19:6; 1 Sam. 20:5, 24; 1 K. 13:20), but not on chairs, the table being somewhat elevated. A change is indicated in Amos 6:4, to reclining, a custom among foreigners (Est. 1:6, 7:8), which practice was common in the Graeco-Roman period (Jn. 21:20), separate couches being provided for three, or perhaps as many as four, the same being arranged in the form of a square, the fourth side being open for service. The head was near the table, the feet toward the back of the couch, the body being diagonal, the left elbow on a cushion, the right arm free. The highest person had none at his back, the middle and lowest, resting on or near the one at his left (cf. Mt. 23:6). Women certainly on occasion ate with the men (Ruth 2:14; 1 Sam. 1:4; Job 1:4), but attending devolved upon them (Lk. 10:40); so that they may have had irregular and briefer repast. Without knives and forks, and because all dipped in the same dish,

the hands were washed before eating, which degenerated (Mk. 7:1–13). A blessing was in order (1 Sam. 9:13; Mt. 14:19, 15:36, 26:26; Lk. 9:16; Jn. 6:11; Acts 27:35). A piece of bread, as a spoon, was dipped into a single dish of pottage or of meat, food thus being conveyed into the mouth (Jn. 13:26). Occasionally separate portions were served to each (Ruth 2:14; 1 Sam. 1:4; Jn. 13:26). Prayer after meals arose from Deut. 8:10; and hands were washed. On state occasions there was more pretentiousness. To a sumptuous repast, invitations were sent (Est. 5:8; Mt. 22:3); and on the day of the feast, a second was issued (Est. 6:14; Prov. 9:3; Mt. 22:3). A kiss was proper, and water for the feet (Gen. 18:4, 19:2; Lk. 7:44–45); head, beard, feet, and sometimes clothes were perfumed (Ps. 23:5; Amos 6:6; Lk. 7:38; Jn. 12:3). On occasion, robes and a wreath were in order (Mt. 22:11; Isa. 28:1). Guests were placed according to rank (Gen. 43:33; 1 Sam. 9:22; Lk. 14:8), the larger share to the honor guest (Gen. 43:34; 1 Sam. 1:5, 9:24). A special officer tasted the viands and directed proceedings. The meal was enlivened by music, singing and dancing, and perhaps with riddles (Isa. 5:12; 2 Sam. 19:35; Ps. 69:12; Amos 6:4, 6; Mt. 14:6; Lk. 15:25; Judg. 14:12). Entertainments were sometimes prolonged (Est. 1:3–4).

Mearah (mē-ā′rä) [cave] a place east of Sidon, uncertainly identified with a district of caves, but presumably a town.

measures see **weights and measures**

meat the only exception in Scripture to meat as commonly designating other than animal food is Gen. 27:4 (savory meat), and 45:23. Our word "meat" is commonly "flesh." There is ambiguity in the case of the so-called **meat offering.** There are several words rendered "meat," of which the more interesting one may more properly be rendered "prey," "booty"; but in Ps. 111:5, "good success" seems to be proper. There is also a variety of words rendered "meat" in the NT.

meat offering in Lev. 2 and 6:14–23, the meat offering is dealt with, composed of fine flour and salt, mixed with oil and frankincense, without leaven, generally a wine drink offering added. A portion—all frankincense—was burnt on the altar as a memorial; the rest belonged to the priest; but these offerings made by the priests, were wholly burnt. For the meaning, see 1 Chr. 29:10–14. Thus there is involved neither of the two main ideas of sacrifice, viz., atonement for sin and self-dedication to God. They are taken for granted, the meat offering being subsidiary—introduced by the sin offering, and an appendage to the burnt offering. Bloodless offerings alone, did not properly belong to the regular meat offering, but were usually substitutes for other offerings (cf. Lev. 5:11; Num. 5:15).

Mebunnai (mė-bŭn'nī) [built] a Hushathite, of David's guard (2 Sam. 23:27), more properly Sibbechai or Sibbecai, as in 21:18, and 1 Chr. 11:29, 27:11.

Mecherathite related by birth or residence to an unknown place, Mecherah (1 Chr. 11:36). In 2 Sam. 23:34, "the Maachathite" is said to be more correct.

Medad see **Eldad and Medad**

Medan (mē'dăn) [judgment?] a son and tribe descended from Abraham and Keturah; nothing more (Gen. 25:2; 1 Chr. 1:32). Note the connection with Midian.

Medeba (mė-dē'bȧ) [water of quietness] in Num. 21:30, this town, on east of Jordan, seems to denote the limit of Heshbon's territory. It was allotted to the tribe of Reuben (Josh. 13:9, 16). At the time of the Conquest it belonged to the Amorites, apparently taken from Moab. Aramean mercenaries were hired by Ammon, to pitch before Medeba (1 Chr. 19:7). In Ahaz' day it was a sanctuary of Moab (Isa. 15:2). Through a second Amorite tenure, and its seizure by the Maccabees, it has persisted to later times, Jerome and Eusebius noting it. Its ruins are six miles south of Heshbon.

Medes, Media the greater part of Media is a tableland, along parallel mountain ranges, extending northwest to southeast, fertile and well-watered valleys lying between—an area of about 150,000 square miles, lying east of the Zagros mountains, south of the Caspian Sea, east of Armenia and Assyria, and west and northwest of Iran. There is excellent pasturage: the land was noted for horses. Moses notes the Medes (Madai) as descended from Japheth (Gen. 10:2), who supposedly conquered a non-Aryan and non-Semitic race, their known history beginning about the ninth century. Berosus' primitive Babylonian history, unsubstantiated, tells that the Medes conquered Babylon in the third millennium B.C., establishing a kingdom lasting 224 years. In the ninth century, Shalmaneser and successors, made the Medes part of Assyria; and although they ravaged the land and laid tribute at pleasure, Media was never absorbed. Deported Israelites, following Samaria's fall (722 B.C.) were settled in cities of Media (2 K. 17:6, 18:11); and various Assyrian kings lorded it over the land, until in the latter seventh century, Cyaxeres allied with Nabopolassar of Babylon, and took Nineveh the capital, thus terminating the great Assy-

rian empire. Around 550 Media fell to Cyrus, of the same Iranic race, to found the dual kingdom of Medo-Persia. The Medes were one of the nationalities to take part in Babylon's capture (Isa. 13:17–18; cf. Jer. 51:11, 28); and Elam and Media provided the conquerors of that city (Isa. 21:2, 9). Cyrus took Babylon in 539–538; and Darius the Mede received the kingdom (Dan. 5:31). (From Dan. 2:39, 7:5, 8:3–7, 20, it is concluded that Persia succeeded and surpassed the preceding Median power.) In 330 B.C., Media fell to Alexander the Great; following his death (323), it was joined with Syria, and later formed part of the Parthian empire.

Median (mē'dǐ-ăn) see Dan. 5:31, 9:1, 11:1, 31.

medicine for the Mediterranean area, Egypt was the earliest home of medical, as of other skills. Other nations sent to Egypt for physicians: Herodotus says that each disease had its practitioner (II.84). Among the Hebrews it appears that anyone might practice physic. The physician and his aide the apothecary are noted as early as the Exodus (Ex. 15:26; 2 Chr. 16:12; Prov. 17:22, 20:30; Jer. 8:22). As treatment, we have bandages, oil, wine, baths of oil (Isa. 1:6; Lk. 10:34; James 5:14; 1 Tim. 5:23; salves and poultices (2 K. 20:7; Jer. 8:22); roots and leaves (Ezek. 47:12). The "roller to bind" (Ezek. 30:21), was for a broken limb. There is the merchant of powders (Song of S. 3:6). The bath was an external remedy long used. And of course there was Luke the Beloved Physician, who must have been acquainted with the best medications of the time.

Megiddo (mė-gĭd'dō) [place of troops] Megiddon, in Zech. 12:11. An important town on the southern rim of the plain of Esdraelon, on the frontier line of Issachar and Manasseh, commanding a critical pass from the north, taken by Joshua, on entering Canaan (Josh. 12:21). It is celebrated in the Song of Deborah (Judg. 4). The Canaanitic folk were not driven out (Josh. 17:11; Judg. 1:27; 1 Chr. 7:29); it seems not firmly held until Solomon (1 K. 9:15). Its chief interest centers in Josiah's death (2 K. 23:28; 2 Chr. 35:22–24), memorializing deepest grief (Zech. 12:11), and the scene of terrible, final conflict (Rev. 16:16). It is either the modern el-Lejjun, or a site one mile north, Tell el-Mutasellim, nine miles west of Jezreel, where is a copious stream (Judg. 5:19).

Mehetabeel (mė-hĕt'ȧ-bēl) [less correct, Mehetabel, God blesses] 1. Ancestor of Shemaiah the prophet (Neh. 6:10).

2. Wife of Hadar, king of Edom (Gen. 36: 39; 1 Chr. 1:50).

Mehida (mē-hī'dà) [union] founder of a Nethinim family, returnees from Babylon with Zerubbabel (Ezra 2:52; Neh. 7:54).

Mehir (mē'hîr) [price] a Judahite (1 Chr. 4:11).

Meholathite, the only in 1 Sam. 18:19, where one, Adriel, belonged to a place called Meholah, perhaps Abel-meholath, Elisha's native town.

Mehujael (mē-hū'jà-ēl) [God combats] son of Irad, fourth of Cain's line (Gen. 4:18).

Mehuman (mē-hū'măn) [faithful] one of seven eunuchs (?), called chamberlains, of Ahasuerus' court (Est. 1:10).

Mehunim, (Ezra 2:50) **Mehunims,** or **Meunim** plural of adjective from Maon. A people twelve miles southeast of Petra, their capital being Ma'an, probably. Some of these folk, dwelling as strangers near Gedor, were exterminated by a combine of Israelites, in Hezekiah's time (1 Chr. 4:39, 41)—the KJV treats the word as a common noun, "habitations." In 2 Chr. 20, comparing vs. 1 with vs. 10, it appears that the inhabitants of Mount Seir were these folk; but in vs. 1, the Hebrew has "Ammonites," while in 26:7, the context rather requires "Ammonites" instead of "Meunites." In all these references, the LXX points to the Mineans, of Arabia, possibly a northern settlement of them. Some of the Meunim, likely captives and descendants, served in the Jerusalem temple (Ezra 2:50; Neh. 7:52).

Mejarkon (mē-jär'kŏn) [yellow waters] about four miles north of Joppa, a yellow stream flows into the sea, near which this town seems to have been situated, in Dan's territory (Josh. 19:46).

Mekonah (mĕk'ō-nä) [foundation] a post-Captivity town reinhabited by Judahites; unidentified (Neh. 11:28).

Melatiah (mē-là-tī'ä) [Jehovah sets free] a Gibeonite assistant in Jerusalem wall-rebuilding (Neh. 3:7).

Melchi (mĕl'kī) [perhaps a contraction for: Jehovah is king] a name of two ancestors of the Christ (Lk. 3:24, 28).

Melchisedek or **Melchizedek** (mĕl-kĭz'ē-dĕk) [king of righteousness] king of Salem (i.e., Jerusalem, based on several reasons; cf. especially Ps. 76:2), and priest of the Most High God (Gen. 14:18–20). We view this man as Balaam is to be viewed—a kind of "saltation," one who honoring God was honored by him, though not in the true line (see Acts 10:35). In his unaccountably unique appearance, he becomes the antitype of the undying priesthood

(see Heb. 5:10, 6:20; cf. Ezra 2:59, 62). Early ages invested Melchizedek with superstitious awe. A Hebrew tradition holds him a survivor of the flood—the patriarch Shem. Around the fourth century, he was thought to be a Power, an Influence, even the Holy Ghost. Some churchmen believed him the Son of God in human form; a Jewish opinion fancied him the Messiah. Abraham, evidently accepting him as a true priest of God, testified to sharing a kindred, if not the same, faith, paying tithes to him. The greatness of his person is stressed in Hebrews, in that through Abraham Levi virtually paid tithes, admitting inferiority; thus our Lord, "after the order of Melchizedek" (manner, likeness in official dignity, as king and priest), was superior to the Aaronic priesthood.

Melea (mē'lē-à) ancestor of Joseph in the Lord's genealogy (Lk. 3:31).

Melech (mē'lĕk) [king] second son of Micah, descendant of Saul (1 Chr. 8:35, 9:41).

Melicu (mĕl'ĭ-cū) [reigning] same as **Malluch.**

Melita (mĕl'ĭ-tà) [Malta] the island where Paul was shipwrecked (Acts 28:1), its natives being called barbarians, being neither Greeks nor Romans. It has excellent harbors, important both in peace and in war, early settled by Phoenicians, whose corrupted language was used in Paul's day.

Melkiah (măl-kī'ä) [Jehovah is king] a priest, father to Pashur (Jer. 21:1).

melons succulent plants with edible fruit, eaten by Hebrews in Egypt (Num. 11:5), where melons of all kinds, especially watermelon grew.

Melzar (mĕl'zär) [Persian for steward?] either a man set over Daniel and companions (Dan. 1:11, 16), or (as KJV) with the article and not thought a proper noun: therefore, "steward."

Memphis (mĕm'fĭs) [perhaps, Egyptian word; haven of good] an important ancient city, said to have been built by Menes (Herodotus), on the west bank of the Nile, about ten miles above the delta's apex, metropolis and capital of Lower Egypt, the third through the eighth (save sixth) dynasties being considered Memphite (Manetho). Built on land reclaimed from the Nile, it remained important even after the capital was transferred to Thebes and until Alexandria was established. The Hebrews called it Noph, its overthrow being predicted (Isa. 19:13; see Hos. 9:6; Jer. 46:19). Some Jews settled there after Jerusalem's fall and Gedaliah's death (Jer. 41:1). It never recovered from Cambyses' ravages (525 B.C.). Its judgment was threatened by Ezekiel (30:13, 16) as well as by those noted above. Memphis' materials were carried to Cairo for building. Two small Arab villages and twenty pyramids, with the celebrated Sphinx, remain.

Memucan (mē-mū'căn) one of Ahasuerus' seven princes, "wise men who knew the times," and seemed to have formed a council of state (Est. 1:14, 16, 21).

Menahem (mĕn'à-hĕm) [comforter] son of Gadi who slew the usurper Shallum, and seized the throne of Israel, reigning ten years (2 K. 15:14-22). He treated the captured town of Tiphsah, it appears, to terrorize his reluctant subjects (vs. 16). A remarkable event is the first appearance of Pul (Tiglath-pileser) of Assyria, a thousand talents of silver (ca. $2,000,-000) buying his friendship, same being raised by taxing the rich. Menahem adhered to calf worship of Jeroboam I, reigning from about 747 to 738, being succeeded by son Pekahiah (2 K. 15:17, 22).

Menan (mē'năn) one of Joseph's ancestors, in the genealogy of the Lord (Lk. 3:31).

Mene (mē'nē) [numbered] the first of the mysterious Aramaic words written on Belshazzar's palace wall, which Daniel read to the doom of the king and his dynasty (Dan. 5:25=26).

Meni (mē'nī) [fate, destiny] apparently the name of the god of destiny worshiped by idolatrous Hebrews (Isa. 65:11). Here the AV has "number"; and accordingly, some think that the reference is to the number of priests reveling at the feast, or to the stars (planets) which are numbered—this to be discounted.

Menna (mĕn'nà) ancestor of Christ, shortly after David (Lk. 3:31).

Meonenim (mē-ŏn'ĕ-nĭm) [augurs] an oak, or terebinth, near Shechem (Judg. 9:37; cf. Deut. 18:10; Mic. 5:12).

Meonothai (mē-ŏn'ō-thī) [my habitations] a man of Judah (1 Chr. 4:14).

Mephaath (mĕf'à-ăth) [beauty] a Reubenite town given to Merarite Levites (Josh. 13:8, 21:37; 1 Chr. 6:79). In Moabite hands in Jeremiah's time (48:21).

Mephibosheth (mē-fĭb'ō-shĕth) [destroying shame] 1. Son of King Saul, died at Gibeonite hands (2 Sam. 21:8-9).

2. Son of Jonathan, called Meribbaal (1 Chr. 8:34 and 9:40). Orphaned at five years, he became a cripple when his nurse in panic, dropped him in her flight (2 Sam. 4:4); called by David from his home in Lo-debar, to be given his father's estates and place at the royal table (9:1-13). Accused of disaffection during Absalom's rebellion, he lost part of his holdings, and later refused any restoration (16:1-4; 19:24-30). His son, Micha, continued Jonathan's line (9:12).

Merab (mē'răb) [increase] Saul's elder daughter, promised David as a wife, but given to another. David married her sister, Michal (1 Sam. 14:49, 18:17-19). Merab's five sons were executed by the Gibeonites, for Saul's sins (2 Sam. 21:8).

Meraiah (mē-rā'yä) [stubbornness] a priest of the days of Jehoiachim (Neh. 12:12).

Meraioth (mē-rā'yōth) [rebellions] 1. A priest when Eli's house had charge of the tabernacle (1 Chr. 6:6-7, 52).

2. A priest, son of Ahitub, and father of younger Zadok (1 Chr. 9:11; Neh. 11:11).

3. A priest, Jerusalem-bound with Zerubbabel (Neh. 12:15); called also Meremoth (Neh. 12:3).

Merari (mē-rā'rī) [bitter] son of Levi, head of a family (Gen. 46:11; Ex. 6:16; Num. 26:57; 1 Chr. 6:1, 16). **Merarites**, one of the three great families of Levites; at the wilderness census, 6200 males above one month, and 3200 between thirty and fifty (Num. 3:34, 4:44); two branches, Mahlites and Mushutes. They marched between Judah and Reuben, pitched on the north of the tabernacle, having charge of the pillars, bars, boards, etc., of the tabernacle and the surrounding court (Num. 3:33-37, 4:29-33, 7:8). Twelve cities were allotted (Josh. 21:34-40; 1 Chr. 6:63, 77-81). Reorganized by David (1 Chr. 23:6, 21-23); partook with other Levites in musical connection with the sanctuary, holding six of twenty-four offices (1 Chr. 6:31, 44, 25:3); aided in Hezekiah's reform (2 Chr. 29:12); a small company returned with Ezra from exile (Ezra 8:18-19).

Merathaim (mĕr-à-thă'ĭm) [two-fold rebellion] symbolically Babylon (Jer. 50:21).

merchants earliest commerce was by caravan. Arabia and Egypt had commerce with India. Quite a bit of trade was by water routes. Phoenician fleets passed through the Strait of Gibraltar. Merchants went from place to place buying and selling goods, the Hebrew word for merchant meaning "traveler," "voyager" (Gen. 23:16, 37:28; 1 K. 10:28; 2 Chr. 1:16; Prov. 31:14; Isa. 23:2; Ezek. 27:21, 36).

Mercurius (mĕr-cū'rĭ-ŭs) Roman deity, same as (Greek) Hermes, herald of the gods, attendant upon Jupiter. There is a story of the two wandering in Phrygia, unrecognized, which may have connection with the notion of the people of Lystra that Paul and Barnabas were these two (Acts 14:11-13).

mercy seat the covering of the ark; made of gold, two and one-half by one and a half cubits. Inwrought with it were two cherubs of gold, their wings stretched toward each other, and between which Jehovah's glory was manifested, and where he communed with his people (Ex. 25:17–22, 30:6; Num. 7:89; 1 Chr. 28:11; Ps. 80:1). Once a year, on the great Day of Atonement, the high priest sprinkled blood before and upon the mercy seat. He made atonement for himself and the people in the presence of the covenant law, the stone tablets being within the mercy seat (Lev. 16:2, 13–17; cf. Heb. 9:5; Rom. 3:25).

Mered (mĕ′rĕd) [rebellion] son of Ezrah, of Judah; married to a daughter of Pharaoh (1 Chr. 4:17).

Meremoth (mĕr′ē-mōth) [elevations] 1. A priest, son of Uriah, charged with the silver and gold brought from Babylon (Ezra 8:24–33); also wall-repairer (Neh. 3:4, 21); and could be the covenant-sealer of 10:5.

2. Husband of foreign wife; induced to put her away (Ezra 10:36).

3. A priest-chief accompanying Zerubbabel (Neh. 12:3), probably **Meraioth** 3; or a priest family (10:5).

Meres (mĕ′rēz) one of seven princes of Persia and Media, of Ahasuerus' time (Est. 1:14).

Meribah (mĕr′ĭ-bä) [strife] 1. A name used, in addition to Massah, to designate the location of the striving with Moses, when God gave drink from the rock (Ex. 17:1–7; Deut. 6:16, 9:22). It was at Horeb near Rephidim.

2. Another fountain or locality, near if not same as Kadesh, in the desert of Zin, where again Israel strove and water was brought forth miraculously, near the close of the wilderness wandering (Num. 20:1–24, 27:14; Deut. 32: 51, 33:8; Ps. 81:7; Ezek. 47:19, 48:28).

Meribbaal (mĕr′ĭb-bā′äl) 1 Chr. 8:34 see **Mephibosheth**

Merodach (mĕr′ō-dăk) [Assyrian and Baby-lonian, Marduk] patron deity of Babylon (Isa. 39:1; Jer. 50:2).

Merodach-baladan (mĕr′ō-dăk-băl′ā-dăn) [Merodach has given a son] called in 2 K. 20: 12, Berodach-baladan. King of Babylon, able, courageous, enterprising, who stepped up from a petty throne in Bit-Yakin to kingship, when the Assyrian army, besieging Samaria, lost its king. He rebelled and was recognized by Sargon in 721 B.C. Somewhat later, under pretext of felicitations to Hezekiah of Judah, on his recovery from illness, sought him as a confederate with half a dozen other kingdoms for an attack on the Assyrian empire, which was broken up by Sargon. After varying fortunes, he was suppressed by the Assyrians; but the Babylonians were destined to take leadership following the fall of Nineveh (626 B.C.).

Merom, waters of (mĕ′rŏm) [height] this is Lake Huleh on Jordan, eleven miles north of

Sea of Galilee, and ca. 700 feet higher, about four by three miles in dimensions, where Joshua crushed Jabin's confederacy (Josh. 11:5–7).

Meronothite (mĕ-rōn′ō-thīt) inhabitant of Meronoth (1 Chr. 27:30; Neh. 3:7); unidentified.

Meroz (mē′rŏz) [place of refuge?] a north Palestinian town failing to aid Barak against Sisera (Judg. 5:23), its suggested site being el-Murussus, four and one-half miles northwest of Beth-shean.

Mesech (Ps. 120:5; but Mĕ′shĕch in Ezek. 27:13, 32:26). A son of Japheth (Gen. 10:2), whose descendants supposedly settled in Armenia, or the mountains north of Assyria, having commerce with Tyre, and associated with Tubal and Gog (reference above; also Ezek. 38:2–3, 39:1).

Mesha (mē′shä) [deliverance] 1. A king of Moab, who failing to render customary tribute to Jehoram, was signally defeated by Jehoram and allies (Jehoshaphat of Judah and the Edomites); but effected relief from sore straits when besieged, by sacrificing his son to Chemosh openly on the city wall, so that the besiegers, fearing God's wrath for their having given occasion for human burnt offering, lifted the siege (2 K. 3:4–27). A remarkable corroboration of Scripture history here is found in the famous Moabite Stone, erected partly to commemorate this series of events.

2. A Judahite, son of Caleb, and ancestor of Ziph's inhabitants (1 Chr. 2:42).

3. A Benjaminite, son of Shaharaim (1 Chr. 8:8–9), his name derived perhaps from a slightly different root from the above, meaning retreat (?), which seems to be the root of the following:

mesha a place on the east border of Joktan (Gen. 10:30). Some think it the district, Mesene, at northwestern end of the Persian Gulf.

Meshach (mē′shăk) the eunuch's name for Mishael, one of the three faithful in Babylon, afterward of fiery furnace fame (Dan. 1:7, 2:49, 3:13–30).

Meshech see **Mesech**

Meshelemiah (mē-shĕl′ē-mī′à) [Jehovah recompenses] a Levite, family of Kohath, gatekeeper of the temple in David's time (1 Chr. 9:21, 26:1, 2, 9; in 26:14, called Shelemiah).

Meshezabeel (mē-shĕz′à-bēl) [God frees] 1. Father of a Berechiah, and assistant in rebuilding the wall (Neh. 3:4).

2. A sealer of the covenant (Neh. 10:21).

3. A man of Judah, family of Zerah (Neh. 11:24).

Meshillemith (mē-shĭl′lē-mĭth) [requital] a

priest of the course of Immer (1 Chr. 9:12; called Meshillemoth in Neh. 11:13).

Meshillemoth (mē-shǐl'ē-mŏth) 1. An Ephraimite; urged release of captives of Judah, by Pekah's army (2 Chr. 28:12).

2. A priest of Immer's line (Neh. 11:13). See above.

Meshobab (mē-shō'bǎb) [restored] a Simeonite prince; seized pastures near Gedor (1 Chr. 4:34–41).

Meshullam (mē-shǔl'lăm) [friend] 1. Grandfather of Shaphan, of Josiah's reign (2 K. 22:3).

2. Son of Zerubbabel (1 Chr. 3:19).

3. A leader among the Gadites, of Jotham's reign (1 Chr. 5:13).

4, 5, and 6. Three Benjaminites (1 Chr. 8: 17, 9:7–8).

7. Priest, father of high priest Hilkiah (1 Chr. 9:11; Neh. 11:11; called Shallum in 1 Chr. 6:12; Ezra 7:2).

8. A priest of Immer's course (1 Chr. 9:12).

9. A Kohathite Levite, superintendent of workmen repairing the temple, in Josiah's reign (2 Chr. 34:12).

10. An envoy of Ezra to enlist Levite recruits for Jerusalem (Ezra 8:16).

11. An assistant of Ezra in abolishing foreign espousals (Ezra 10:15).

12. A son of Bani, induced to put away foreign wife (Ezra 10:29).

13. Two assisting in wall-repairing (Neh. 3: 4, 6, 30, 6:18).

14. A priest, and chief who sealed the covenant (Neh. 10:7, 20)—two persons here.

15 and 16. Two priests of Jeoiakim's time (Neh. 12:13, 16).

17. A Levite porter (Neh. 12:25; also called Meshelemiah and Shelemiah in 1 Chr. 26:1, 14; and called Shullam in Neh. 7:45).

18. A prince in the procession, at wall dedication (Neh. 12:33).

19. One at Ezra's left when he read the Law (Neh. 8:4).

Meshullemeth (mē-shǔl'lē-mĕth) [female friend] wife of Manasseh and mother of Amon king of Judah (2 K. 21:19).

Mesobaite (mē-sō'bā-īt) a designation of Jasiel, warrior of David (1 Chr. 11:47); unexplained thus far.

Mesopotamia (mĕs-ō-pō-tā'mĭ-à) [. . . between rivers] called by the Hebrews Aram-naharaim, by the Greeks and Romans, as above; the name for the fertile territory between the Tigris and Euphrates rivers, excluding the mountainous northern part, at the rivers' origins, and also ordinarily, the low-lying Babylonian plain, in the other direction (Gen. 24:10; Deut. 23:4;

Judg. 3:8, 10; 1 Chr. 19:6; Acts 2:9, 7:2). There lived Bethuel and Laban; and from it both Isaac and Jacob got wives. After Gen. 24, no mention is made till the wanderings' end (Deut. 23:4). In Judg. 3, it is seat of a powerful monarchy; and from it, Ammon hired help against David (1 Chr. 19:6). It was inhabited early by various petty and independent tribes—possibly in the thirteenth century B.C. (Judg. 3:8–10; 2 K. 19:12–13; Isa. 37:12). After Assyria and its successors, Cyrus brought it wholly under the Persian yoke, to continue until Alexander the Great. Assyrian and Babylonian greatness is shown by many remarkable ruins.

Messiah (mě-sī'à) [an Aramaic term which is literally translated the "anointed one"; the corresponding Greek term is *Christos*] the Hebrew term "messiah" is applied to any person anointed with oil, such as the high priest (Lev. 4:3), or the king (2 Sam. 1:14). Although the title was likewise given to patriarchs and other notables, it became especially significant when the prophets began to use the term to denote the Davidic king who would deliver his people.

Although the expression "Son of man" is used in the intertestamental period to refer to the Messiah, it especially stresses the universalistic and otherworldly emphases (Enoch 37–71). Further development is seen in the term's frequent usage by Jesus when referring to himself. The NT concept of the suffering Messiah who dies vicariously is one of the doctrines unique to the person of Christ. His most intimate followers had difficulty in accepting this presentation of messiahship. Additional terms were used in the OT and intertestamental writings to refer to the Messiah. A popular reference conceived of the Messiah as prophet, priest, and/or king. In the OT the term Immanuel, God with us, is employed by Isaiah as a messianic symbol. Micah's approach has strong affinity with that of Isaiah. Jeremiah 23:5–6 speaks of the "righteous branch."

The gospels provide ample testimony and information concerning the Messiah and the messianic hope of the NT era. The Messiah was viewed as the royal son of David who would introduce victory and prosperity to the Jewish nation and would establish his throne at Jerusalem. Others thought not so much in the terms of this aspect of messiahship, but rather in the redemption of Jerusalem. The prophetic element of the intertestamental period likewise lingered in the NT concept. Furthermore, the title "Son of God" was used as a messianic title during the time of Jesus. Matthew 26:63

records its usage by the high priest in the presence of the Sanhedrin.

Jesus' claim of messiahship is written into the NT documents. He accepted the title, but he filled it with an ethical, spiritual, and universal connotation. His favorite expression for himself was the term "Son of man." He refers to the Son of man's giving his life a ransom for many (Mt. 20:28). By his crucifixion and resurrection he completed his earthly messianic work and inaugurated the heavenly reign.

The Jewish mind could not accept the thought of a suffering messiah whose death would atone for sin. As previously indicated, his most intimate followers rejected this basic concept. However, following his resurrection and ascension, these same men were led into a more mature understanding of his messiahship and the nature of his messianic kingdom. See **Jesus Christ**   V.E.G.

Metheg-ammah (mē'thĕg-ăm'à) a town taken by David from the Philistines (2 Sam. 8:1). In 1 Chr. 18:1 the reference seems to indicate Gath and its surrounding regions.

Methuselah (mē-thū'zĕ-là) the son of Enoch, descendant of Seth, and the father of Lamech (Gen. 5:25-27).

Methushael (mē-thū'shà-ĕl) the son of Mehujael (Gen. 4:18).

Meunim (mĭ-ū'nĭm) an Arab tribe whose capital was probably the city of Ma'an, some twelve miles southeast of Petra. Some of them, likely captives of war, served in the temple (Neh. 7:52).

Mezahab (mĕz'à-hăb) the father of Matred and grandfather of Mehetabel, who was the wife of Hadar, a king of Edom (Gen. 36:39; 1 Chr. 1:50). However, the term may refer to a district, of which Matred was a native.

Mezobaite (mĭ-zo'bĭ-īt) likely an adjective. The word describes Jaasiel of David's army (1 Chr. 11:47).

mezuzah (mĕ-zōō'zä) a Hebrew term which means "post" or "doorpost." The expression generally refers to a small container enclosing parchment upon which is written Deut. 6:4-9, 11:13-21. See **phylactery**

Miamin (mĭ'à-mĭn) 1. A descendant of Aaron (1 Chr. 24:1, 6, 9).

2. A priest or family of priests who returned from Babylon with Zerubbabel (Neh. 12:5, 7).

3. A son of Porash (Ezra 10:25).

Mibhar (mĭb'här) son of Hagri (1 Chr. 11:38). Chronicles includes this man among the mighty men of David.

Mibsam (mĭb'săm) 1. A son of Ishmael (Gen. 25:13; 1 Chr. 1:29).

2. A Simeonite (1 Chr. 4:25).

Mibzar (mĭb'zär) a clan chief of Edom (1 Chr. 1:53).

Mica (mī'kà) 1. A son of Mephibosheth (2 Sam. 9:12).

2. A Levite who sealed the covenant (Neh. 10:11).

3. A Levite whose ancestor was Asaph (1 Chr. 9:15; Neh. 11:17, 22).

Micah (mī'kà) 1. An Ephraimite of Judg. 17-18.

2. A descendant of Reuben (1 Chr. 5:5).

3. A son of Meribbaal (see **Mephibosheth**).

4. A Levite who lived during the latter part of David's reign (1 Chr. 23:20, 24:24-25).

5. The father of Abdon (2 Chr. 34:20).

Micah (mī'kà) a prophet of Judah, contemporary of Isaiah. His prophecy is the sixth of the minor prophets in the order of present canonical arrangement.

His name is a common OT name and means "Who is like Jehovah?" This prophet was reared in Maresheth, a town near Gath, close to the gateway to Egypt. Although this man may justifiably be described as a country minister, his ministry was characterized by an emphasis upon justice, fair dealings, and righteous living. He especially abhorred the prevalent sin of love of money.

This simple farmer heard the cries of distress which resounded from his people who were lacking in religious dedication and social morality. No prophet of the OT was more spectacular in his prediction of the future. He predicted the fall of Samaria, fulfilled in 722 B.C.; the destruction of Jerusalem, fulfilled in 586 B.C.; the Exile and return of Judah, fulfilled in 605-537 B.C.; and the birth of the messianic king in Bethlehem.

The prophecy falls into natural divisions, each introduced by the phrase "Hear ye." (1) Chapters 1-2 describe the coming of God to judge the sins and idolatries of Judah (1:2-4), the sentence upon Samaria (1:5-9), the devastating march of the Assyrian conquerors (1:8-16), and the woe sounded by the prophet (2:1-11). The bright spot in this section is the promise of restoration and return (2:12-13).

(2) The second section consists of chs. 3-5. Chapter 3 provides the backdrop in its direct address to the princes and leaders of the people. In strong terms the prophet rebukes their avarice and rapacity. However, this threatening is followed by a promise of restoration.

(3) The last section (chs. 6-7) pictures God in dialogue with his people. This dramatic form presents convincingly the reasonableness of God's demands and the justness of his conduct

toward them. A note of victory concludes the prophecy—victory in deliverance and in full acknowledgment of God's mercy and faithfulness to his promises.

Micah is quoted in Mt. 2:5–6 and is alluded to in Mt. 10:35–36; Mk. 13:12; Lk. 12:53; and Jn. 7:42.   V.E.G.

Micaiah (mī-kā′yà) a name which means "Who is like God?" Several OT characters bear this name. 1. Daughter of Uriel, wife of Rehoboam, and mother of King Abijah (2 Chr. 13:2).

2. A prince during the reign of Jehoshaphat (2 Chr. 17:7).

3. A prophet, the son of Imlah (2 Chr. 18:7–27). This man's prophecies were never acceptable to Ahab, as illustrated in his minority report concerning the defeat of Israel's army. To add credence to his prophecy, he recounted his vision of the Lord's throne with the heavenly hosts surrounding him.

4. The father of Achbar (2 K. 22:12; 2 Chr. 34:20).

5. A contemporary of Jeremiah and son of Gemariah (Jer. 36:11–13).

6. A kinsman (great-great-grandfather) of Zechariah, a priest in the time of Nehemiah (Neh. 11:17, 22, 12:35).

7. A priest who served in the time of Nehemiah (Neh. 12:41). This man was a member of the festive group which dedicated the rebuilt walls of Jerusalem.

Micha (mī′kà) see **Mica**

Michael (mī′kĕl) a name which means "Who is like God?" 1. Father of one of the men sent by Moses to spy out the Promised Land (Num. 13:13).

2. A Gadite, a descendant of Buz and head of a house in Gilead (1 Chr. 5:11, 13–14, 16).

3. An ancestor of Asaph (1 Chr. 6:40).

4. A son of Izrahiah, a member of the tribe of Issachar (1 Chr. 7:3).

5. A Benjaminite, family of Beriah (1 Chr. 8:16).

6. Another Gadite (1 Chr. 5:14).

7. A Manassite captain who joined David at Ziklag (1 Chr. 12:20).

8. Father of Omri of Issachar (1 Chr. 27:18).

9. One of the sons of King Jehoshaphat of Judah (2 Chr. 21:2).

10. The father of Zebadiah, one who returned with Ezra in the reign of King Artaxerxes (Ezra 8:8).

11. An archangel. A detailed angelology developed during the intertestamental period. In the canonical writings names are infrequently given to the angels. Michael, however, is mentioned in Dan. 10:13, 21, 12:1; Jude 9; and Rev. 12:7.

The angel Gabriel represents the ministration of angels toward men, but the angel Michael is the champion of men in their strife with Satan. In Rev. 12:7 he is pictured as fighting in heaven against Satan. Jude 9 records Michael's contention with Satan concerning the body of Moses. The Jews regarded Michael as the chief of the archangels.

Michah see **Micah 4**

Michal (mī′kăl) the younger of Saul's two daughters. The king proposed to give his older daughter Merab to David, but Michal fell in love with him, thus the father's initial plans were thwarted. He then offered the younger daughter to David, the price being one hundred dead Philistines. The king hoped that David would be killed (1 Sam. 18:20–25). David, however, was successful and received Michal as his wife.

Saul's jealousy resulted in Michal's being given to Phalti (1 Sam. 25:44; 2 Sam. 3:15). After some years, she was returned to David, whose love for his wife had not waned. However, on the day of David's greatest triumph—the bringing of the ark of God to its permanent resting place—as Michal watched the approaching procession from her windows, she was shocked by her husband's actions and despised him. The words of David's retaliation are reflected in the record, "Michal had no child unto the day of her death."

The reference to Michal in 2 Sam. 21:8 should likely be to Merab, her sister.

Michmas (mĭk′măs) probably a variation of Michmash, a later form (Ezra 2:27; Neh. 7:31).

Michmash (mĭk′măsh) a town which is significant in the Philistine war of Saul and Jonathan (1 Sam. 13–14). The site is near the mount of Bethel (1 Sam. 13:2). The pass of Michmash, known as Mukhmas, is seven and one-half miles northeast of Jerusalem.

Michmethath (mĭk′mĕ-thăth) a place near Shechem and one of the landmarks of the boundaries of Ephraim and Manasseh on the western side of Jordan (Josh. 17:7). However, Josh. 16:6 uses the same term to locate a former boundary. Two possible sites have been conjectured; one, Khirbet Makhneh el-Foqa, located five miles southeast of Shechem; a second, Khirbet Juleijil, located east of Shechem.

Michri (mĭk′rī) a descendant of Benjamin (1 Chr. 9:8).

Michtam (mĭk′tăm) KJV form of Miktam, a word of obscure meaning occurring in the titles of Pss. 16; 56–60. The etymology of the word is uncertain. Some have conjectured that Michtam denotes the musical character of the psalm. Others believe the term to mean "covering" or "expiation." Thus the psalm would then be a psalm of expiation.

Middin (mĭd'ĭn) a city of Judah (Josh. 15:61), one of the six specified as located in the district of the *midbar*, wilderness.

Midian (mĭd'ĭ-ăn) 1. A son of Abraham by Keturah (Gen. 25:2), the progenitor of the Midianites.

2. A region in the Arabian desert near the eastern shore of the Gulf of Aqabah. However, the nomadic Midianites did not restrict themselves to this one region; thus the "land of Midian" can accurately be located only by references to definite periods.

The Midianite influence upon Israel was indeed evil and generally led to disobedience on the part of Moses' subjects. The subtleness of the influence can readily be seen in the claim of kinship to Abraham.

Midianites (mĭd'ĭ-ăn-īts) a people of the desert (Gen. 25:2, 6). Genesis 25:4 reveals that five families of them are the posterity of Midian. Midianite merchants bought Joseph and carried him to Egypt (Gen. 37:25). Moses' father-in-law was a Midianite (Ex. 3:1). The Midianites joined the Moabites in hiring Balaam to curse Israel (Num. 22:4 ff.). The general history of Israel and the Midianites is one of struggle, war, and difficulty.

midwife this term describes a woman who assists in the delivery of a child. Exodus 1 is the most extensive reference to the responsibilities and functions of the midwife. Shiphrah and Puah (1:15) are identified as two Hebrew midwives who assist the Hebrew women by employing a birthstool. The Egyptian practice of employing birthstools harmonizes with the Exodus account.

Migdal-el (mĭg'dăl-ĕl) one of the fortified towns of the possession of Naphtali (Josh. 19:38). Its name is possibly derived from some ancient tower—"the tower of El, or God." The exact site is unknown, but the general context seems to require a location somewhere in Upper Galilee.

Migdal-gad (mĭg'dăl-găd') a village of Judah (Josh. 15:37) in the maritime lowland. By Eusebius and Jerome it is identified as "Magdala." The village was likely associated with the worship of the ancient deity of Gad.

Migdol (mĭg'dŏl) the term itself means "a tower" or "fortress." It is also used to refer to a shepherd's lookout. 1. An encampment of the Israelites while they were leaving Egypt

(Ex. 14:2; Num. 33:7–8). The site is near the Red Sea, before Pi-hahiroth and Baal-zephon.

2. Ezekiel (29:10, 30:6) mentions Migdol as a border town. Jeremiah 44:1 and 46:14 also refer to Migdol as one of the residences of the Jews in Egypt. It is possible that these places are identical.

Migron (mĭg'rŏn) a village of Benjamin near Gibeah (1 Sam. 14:2), where Saul sat under a pomegranate tree to watch the invading Philistines. A Migron is also mentioned in Isaiah's prophecy (10:28). The position here seems a little farther north than that indicated in the previous reference. The word itself means a "precipice" and possibly two places of the same name are intended.

Mijamin (mĭj'ă-mĭn) 1. A descendant of Aaron, his family becoming the sixth of the twenty-four courses into which David divided the priests (1 Chr. 24:9).

2. A priest who signed the covenant with Nehemiah (Neh. 10:7), probably the descendant of the preceding.

3. A chief of the priests who returned with Zerubbabel (Neh. 12:5, 7).

4. A son of Parosh; Ezra exhorted him to put away his foreign wife (Ezra 10:25).

Mikloth (mĭk'lŏth) 1. One of the sons of Jehiel, the father or prince of Gibeon, by his wife Maachah (1 Chr. 8:32, 9:37–38).

2. A military captain in David's reign. He served as chief officer of the Davidic forces in the second month (1 Chr. 27:4).

Mikneiah (mĭk-nē'yă) a Levite of the second rank, gatekeepers of the ark, who played the harp in David's reign (1 Chr. 15:18, 21).

Milalai (mĭl'ă-lī) a musician who assisted at the dedication of the walls of Jerusalem (Neh. 12:36).

Milcah (mĭl'kà) 1. A daughter of Haran, brother of Abraham, who became the wife of Nahor, to whom she bore eight children (Gen. 11:29, 22:20, 23, 24:15, 24, 47).

2. The fourth daughter of Zelophehad (Num. 26:33, 27:1, 36:11).

Milcom (mĭl'kŏm) see **Molech**

mile a Roman measure of length equivalent to 1618 English yards, approximately 12⁄43 of an English mile. The term occurs only in Mt. 5:41.

Miletus (mī-lē'tŭs) an important harbor on the western coast of Asia Minor. Acts 20:15 ff. records Paul's experiences there with the Ephesian elders whom he had summoned to meet him. The city was some thirty-six miles south of Ephesus. The city is also mentioned in 2 Tim. 4:20.

Miletus was more famous 500 years before Paul than in his day. A flourishing city of the

Ionian Greeks, it was absorbed by the Persian empire, only to be captured eventually by Alexander the Great. Although the city never fully recovered from this siege, it was an important trading town throughout the Roman period. Strabo mentions its four harbors.

milk an important article of diet, especially in the East. Its vital significance as a childhood food and its adaptability to all ages is seen in Gen. 18:8; Deut. 32:14; Judg. 5:25; and 1 Pet. 2:2.

mill the mill of Palestine was a relatively simple arrangement consisting of two round millstones. The stones were approximately eighteen to twenty-four inches in diameter, the lower stone being stationary, the upper one being moved by means of an upright handle attached near the edge. The millstone was generally operated by women, who usually faced each other. Insight into the woman's responsibility in operating the mill is contained in the words of Jesus (Mt. 24:41). Millstones were essential to daily life and could not be taken in pledge (Deut. 24:6). There seems to have been a larger stone which was operated by an animal (Mt. 18:6). This millstone would have been similar to that of the Egyptians and Romans.

millennium a term not appearing in the Biblical materials but used by many interpreters in referring to the "thousand years" of Rev. 20. The term is composed of the Lat. *mille* (a thousand) and *annus* (a year). The millennium is related to the coming of Christ. Premillennialists believe that the one-thousand-years reign follows his return, the postmillennialist that the millennium precedes the return, and the amillennialist interprets the millennium as a spiritual or symbolic figure. See **Revelation**

Millo (mĭl'ō) 1. A place in ancient Jerusalem. When David took the city from the Jebusites (2 Sam. 5:9; 1 Chr. 11:8), the place seemed to be in existence. Solomon raised his "levy" for the purpose of restoring this place. According to 2 Chr. 32:5 Millo seems to have been a part of the "City of David." Some interpreters have suggested that Millo was a mound, others an assembly place, still others a ditch or valley, and some even a trench filled with water. In all likelihood the term was incorporated into the Israelite nomenclature from an archaic term, perhaps Jebusite, and refers to the citadel. This is its consistent usage throughout the books of Maccabees as seen in the authors' references to the fortress on Mount Zion.

2. The house of Millo. (a) A family or clan (Judg. 9:6, 20). (b) The spot at which King Joash was murdered by his slaves (2 K. 12:20).

This may have well been in Jerusalem and in this case would have been connected with the ancient Millo discussed above.

mines, mining Job 28:1–11 serves as a descriptive passage for the mining operation. It is obvious that the Egyptians from a rather early period were engaged in mining. Copper was discovered in Wadi Magharah as early as the Fourth Dynasty. Turquoise mines in the Sinai peninsula were likewise worked. Miners were generally gangs of convicts and captives in chains, who were guarded day and night by soldiers. The work was supervised by an engineer, who selected the stone and defined the work for the convicts. The criminals and prisoners of war, as well as the slaves, worked under the whip of the taskmaster.

Harder rock was split by the application of fire, but the softer was broken with picks and chisels. The stone was then pounded in stone mortars until reduced to the size of a lentil. Afterward aged men and women ground it into a fine powder. This basic approach to gold mining represents the general mining activities.

Miniamin (mĭn'yà-mĭn) 1. A Levite in the reign of Hezekiah (2 Chr. 31:15).

2. A father's house among the priests in the days of Joiakim (Neh. 12:17).

3. A priest at the dedication of the wall of Jerusalem (Neh. 12:41).

minister this term describes various officials of a religious or civil character. In the OT, it is used to apply (a) to an attendant upon a person of high rank (Ex. 24:13; Josh. 1:1), (b) to those attached to a royal court (1 K. 10:5; 2 Chr. 22:8), (c) to the priests and Levites (Joel 1:9, 13; Ezra 8:17). In the NT three terms distinguish the varying characteristics of a minister: (a) a *leitourgos* is a subordinate public administrator (Rom. 13:6, 15:16; Heb. 8:2), (b) an *hupēretēs* is one who actually attends a superior, (c) a *diakonos* generally refers to one who serves in relationship to the ministry of the Gospel. The service aspect of this term is emphatically underscored. This general ideal of "ministry" is recorded in Mk. 1:31, a record of the healing of Peter's mother-in-law and her ministry to the disciples and in Mk. 10:45, a reference of Jesus' purpose in life.

Minni (mĭn'ī) a portion of Armenia. Jeremiah 51:27 indicates that the kingdoms of Ararat, Minni, and Ashchenaz were united for the destruction of Babylon.

Minnith (mĭn'ĭth) a town of the Ammonites (Judg. 11:33). The "wheat of Minnith" is mentioned in Ex. 27:17.

minstrel a musician, especially one who plays upon a stringed instrument such as the harp.

David was called to the court to act as a minstrel (1 Sam. 16:14–23). The story of Elisha's summoning a minstrel to play before him while waiting for God to speak is recorded in 2 K. 3:15. In addition, minstrels are also mentioned in the NT—Mt. 9:23 indicates that Jairus employed "flute players," who formed a part of the professional mourners.

mint an herb, the term occurring only in Mt. 23:23 and Lk. 19:42. The Jews were scrupulously exact in the tithing of this herb. Horse mint (*Mentha sylvestris*) is a most common mint in Syria and grows wild on the hills.

Miphkad (mĭf′kăd) the name of one of the gates of Jerusalem at the time of the rebuilding of the wall following the return from captivity (Neh. 3:31). The exact site was obviously in the city of David, not in the wall of Jerusalem proper.

miracle an event, either natural or supernatural, in which man sees an act and attestation of God. An illustration of a natural event might be God's sending the quails to supply the needs of Israel, while an example of the supernatural event can be easily seen in the creation of the world. 1. *Terminology.* In the OT the terms "sign" and "wonder" are most frequently used to define a miracle. Both of these terms occur in Deut. 13:1: "If a prophet arises among you, or a dreamer of dreams, and gives you a *sign* or a *wonder* . . ." The term sign means pledge or token; in Gen. 1:14 the sun and moon are signs of day, night, and seasons. In Ex. 12:13 blood is a sign of the Passover. The term circumcision is used as a sign of the covenant (Gen. 17:10). The term wonder means miracle or sign. This term denotes a special display of God's power as is seen in the experiences of Moses and Aaron in Egypt.

In the NT two additional terms, "power" and "work," are added to the previously mentioned words. The term power refers to the power of God, Jesus, or the Holy Spirit; in some places the term power means the miracle itself (Mk. 6:5). Matthew 11:2 tells of John's hearing of the *works* of Jesus, the term here identifying the miracles of our Lord.

2. *Criticisms and Denials.* B. Spinoza objected to miracles on the basis that they contradicted or violated natural law. D. Hume's famous essay "Essay on Miracles" established his skepticism concerning the miraculous. In this essay he likewise assumed that a "miracle is a violation of the laws of nature"; thus to Hume a miracle is contrary to experience. Of course, it is true that miracles are contrary to general experience, and thus this fact becomes an essential element of miracles' "signal char-acter." There is an essential difference between alleging a case in which, all the real antecedents or cases being similar to those to which one has daily opportunities to observe, a consequence is said to have issued quite differently from that which general experience finds to be uniform and joined with them, and alleging a case in which there is supposed, as indicated by all circumstance, an intervention of an antecedent, or cause, which one knows to exist, and to be adequate to the production of such results. This latter, of course, describes the scriptural miracles. When one speaks of miracles being contrary to the natural law of the universe, he should keep in mind that this is an event which happens in a manner contrary to the regularly observed processes of nature. God may well work in and through natural law in order to accomplish his purpose. At the same time, this medium of his working may not be regularly observed process.

3. *Attestation.* (a) Human witnesses. The character and not the number of human witnesses is important. (b) The purpose and occasion of the miracle. A miracle requires a logical basis and occasion. Jesus, for example, never used his miraculous power in any selfish fashion. He indicated to Simon Peter that he could have called for legions of angels to deliver him from the cross, but he did not rely upon this power in such an hour. It is generally agreed that miracles belong to the history of redemption. (c) A miracle harmonizes with the religious environment in which it is observed—2 Thess. 2:9 and Rev. 16:14 so indicate. The character of the miracle exhibits the character of God and does not contradict anything to be found within his character.

4. *Jesus' Ministry.* It is readily agreed that Jesus' ministry was characterized by miracles. Even his opponents acknowledged his ability to perform miracles. The miraculous ministry of Jesus so impressed his followers that the writers of the apocryphal gospels describe numerous events in an attempt to establish the miracle-working power of Jesus.

Jesus' miracles were performed publicly and privately, the greater number being performed in public. As noted above, Jesus never employed his miraculous power for selfish reasons, but rather employed miracles to meet the needs of humanity and at the same time to serve as an attestation to his divinity.

5. *Apostolic Age.* Acts 6:8, 8:5–7; Heb. 2:4, will serve as references for the working of miracles in the apostolic period. These references would indicate that miracles were worked by those other than the apostles.

Miriam (mĭr'ĭ-ăm) 1. The sister of Aaron and Moses (Ex. 15:20). She is likely the sister who watched over the ark which contained the infant Moses (Ex. 2:4–8). She is described as a prophetess (Ex. 15:20), her prophetic power reveals itself in poetic utterances (Ex. 15:1–19). Miriam complained against Moses because of his marriage to a Cushite (Num. 12:1–2). She died near the close of the Kadesh wanderings and was buried there (Num. 20:1).

2. A person of Judah and the house of Caleb (1 Chr. 4:17) but it is uncertain whether this person is a man or woman.

Mirmah (mûr'mà) a Benjaminite, a son of Shaharaim (1 Chr. 8:10).

mirror a highly polished object of metal intended to reflect objects, especially the countenance. The Hebrew women probably brought mirrors from Egypt and continued to use them following the Exodus. Archaeological discoveries indicate that the mirrors themselves were practically round, inserted into a handle of wood, stone, or metal, the form of which varied according to the desires of the owner. Some of the handles were decorated with figures of women, flowers, columns, birds, etc. The metal of which the mirrors were composed was likely to become tarnished or rusted, thus necessitating constant polishing. Such a mirror is probably alluded to in 1 Cor. 13:12.

Misgab (mĭs'găb) an unidentified city of Moab (Jer. 48:1). It is conjectured that this city is identified as Mizpah of Moab (1 Sam. 23:3).

Mishael (mĭsh'ā-ĕl) 1. A Levite, son of Uzziel, an uncle of Aaron and Moses (Ex. 6:22).

2. One who stood at Ezra's left hand when he read the Law to the people (Neh. 8:4).

3. One of Daniel's three companions in captivity (Dan. 1:6, 7, 11, 19).

Mishal (mī'shăl) a village of the territory of Asher (Josh. 19:26) allotted to the Gershonite Levites (Josh. 21:30).

Misham (mī'shăm) a Benjaminite, son of Elpaal (1 Chr. 8:12).

Mishma (mĭsh'mà) 1. A son of Ishmael and brother of Mibsam (Gen. 25:14; 1 Chr. 1:30).

2. A son of Simeon (1 Chr. 4:25), brother of Mibsam.

Mishmannah (mĭsh-măn'à) a Gadite who joined David at Ziklag (1 Chr. 12:10).

Mishraites (mĭsh'râ-īts) a family connected with Kirjath-jearim (1 Chr. 2:53).

Mispar (mĭs'pär) one who returned with Zerubbabel from Babylon (Ezra 2:2). The feminine form, Mispereth, is used in Neh. 7:7.

Mispereth (mĭs'pê-rĕth) see **Mispar**

Misrephoth-maim (mĭs'rê-fŏth-mā'ĭm) a place near Sidon. Certain contemporary scholars believe 'Ain Mesherfi to be the site. It was to this location that Joshua pursued the Canaanites who had been defeated at the waters of Merom (Josh. 11:8).

missions might be defined as the sending of the representative of a diety for the purpose of carrying a message or performing a task. Ancient history abounds with illustrations of wide diffusion of certain religious cults, although it is not precisely known how this diffusion occurred. Perhaps the transplanting of religions is closely connected with the diffusion of culture. Yet it is obvious that many examples of religious diffusion are to be found in the Scriptures. The Moabite king sent for the diviner Balaam (Num. 22), the king of Damascus sent Naaman to the king of Israel to be healed of leprosy (2 K. 5), and Jonah was sent on a missionary service to a foreign people. Judaism was extremely missionary and apparently enjoyed a certain success during the Hellenistic period. The Acts of the Apostles gives full evidence concerning the missionary journeys of those who had been scattered during the persecution and death of Stephen. The NT generally abounds with information concerning missionary activities.

mite (mīt) a coin current in Palestine in the time of Jesus (Mk. 12:41–44). This coin is worth less than one cent.

miter, mitre a headdress or turban, made of fine linen. The miter was distinguished by a golden plate which was inscribed with the words "Holiness to the Lord" and affixed in front by a blue lace (Ex. 28:4, 36–39).

Mithcah (mĭth'kä) the name of an unidentified desert encampment of the Israelites, meaning a "place of sweetness" (Num. 33:28–29).

Mithnite (mĭth'nīt) a designation of Joshaphat, one of David's army (1 Chr. 11:43).

Mithredath (mĭth'rê-dăth) 1. A treasurer of Cyrus, king of Persia, to whom the king gave the vessels of the temple (Ezra 1:8).

2. A Persian officer stationed at Samaria during the reign of Artaxerxes (Ezra 4:7).

Mitylene (mĭt-ĭ-lē'nê) the principal town of the Aegean island of Lesbos. Situated on the east coast of the island, it is the intermediate place where Paul stopped for the night between Assos and Chios (Acts 20:14–15). In Roman times the town itself was known for its beauty, and in Paul's day it enjoyed the privileges of a free city. Thus it continued as a favorite site of influential Romans.

mixed multitude Ex. 12:38 indicates that a mixed multitude accompanied the Israelites on the first stage of the Exodus. It is evident that the "mixed multitude" is a general term including all those who were not of pure Israelite blood.

Mizar (mī′zär) a mountain in the region of the Jordan and Hermon. The name appears in Ps. 42:6. The specific site is unidentified.

Mizpah, Mizpeh (mĭz′pä) the name of several places in ancient Palestine: 1. Mizpah of Gilead (Gen. 31:25, 48, 52). Where Jacob and Laban piled stones to serve both as a witness to the covenant between them and also as a landmark of the boundary between them.

2. A town in Gilead, east of the Jordan (Judg. 10:17, 11:11). This town was located in the territory of Gad.

3. A site at the base of Mount Hermon (Josh. 11:8).

4. A village in Judah (Josh. 15:38).

5. A town of Benjamin (Josh. 18:26). This town was located near Ramah (Josh. 18:25).

6. A place in Moab (1 Sam. 22:3).

Mizraim (mĭz′rā-ĭm) although Mizraim is mentioned as one of the sons of Ham in Gen. 10:6, 13, the term is more generally recognized as the usual Hebrew term for Egypt. Thus the term designates Egypt in her entirety, both Upper and Lower Egypt, settled by descendants of Ham.

Mizzah (mĭz′ä) the son of Reuel and grandson of Esau (Gen. 36:13, 17; 1 Chr. 1:37).

Mnason (nā′sŏn) a Christian who served as Paul's host during his final visit to Jerusalem (Acts 21:16). He was a native of Cyprus and in all probability a friend of Barnabas (Acts 4:36).

Moab (mō′ăb) 1. Lot's son by union with his own daughter (Gen. 19:37).

2. The descendants of Moab, Lot's son. These folk were closely related to the Ammonites and had become numerous before the Israelites' crossing of the Red Sea (Ex. 15:15). The Moabites were friendly toward the Israelites (Deut. 2:28–29) but refused permission for them to pass through their land (Judg. 11:17). Moses was not permitted to attack the Moabites, likely because of their kinship to the Israelites.

3. The country in which the Moabites live. Moab was the gently rolling plateau immediately east of the Dead Sea. The land was some sixty miles north to south and some twenty-five miles in width. Many flocks of sheep were kept in Moab. Machaerus, the place of John's imprisonment and subsequent martyrdom, is in the land of Moab.

Moabite stone (mō′ăb-īt) an inscribed stone discovered by F. Klein, a German employee of the Church Missionary Society, near the ruins of the Moabite town of Dibon in the year 1868. The slab of black basalt is three feet ten inches high, two feet wide, and ranges from one to two and a half inches in thickness. The stone is inscribed with thirty-four lines of writing in an unfamiliar character, the lines being approximately one and a fourth inches across. The language has been identified as Moabite, a dialect or language closely related to Hebrew. The language shares certain characteristic features with Hebrew (the "waw consecutive," for example). The inscription expresses gratitude to the god Chemosh for the Moabite victory over the Israelites. The inscription supplements the 1 K. 16 account by indicating that Omri was responsible for the conquest of Northern Moab.

Moadiah (mō′à-dī′à) a priest, or family of priests, who returned with Zerubbabel. The chief of the house at the time of Joiakim was Piltai (Neh. 12:17). See **Maadiah**

Moladah (mŏl′à-dà) a city which lay in the south of Judah, next to Edom (Josh. 15:26, 19:2). It was also inhabited after the Captivity (Neh. 11:26).

mole 1. A small insect-eating mammal which is rendered chameleon in some versions and translations (Lev. 11:30).

2. A mole rat, an animal very common in the Holy Land (Isa. 2:20). This animal resembles the mole and feeds on vegetables, whereas the mole is insectivorous. This little animal is somewhat larger than the mole, measuring at least eight inches in length.

Molech (mō′lĕk) a deity worshiped by the children of Ammon (1 K. 11:7). Second K. 23:10 indicates that human sacrifice was made to this deity, especially in the valley of Hinnom, which borders Jerusalem on the southwest. Extremely early the Mosaic law voiced disapproval of man's offering his children "through the fire to Molech" (Lev. 18:21, 20:1–5). Ahaz burned his children in Hinnom (2 Chr. 28:3) and Manasseh made at least one of his sons pass through the fire (2 K. 21:6). The OT abounds with other references to this worship.

Molid (mō′lĭd) the son of Abishur by his wife Abihail (1 Chr. 2:29).

Moloch see **Molech**

money a method of exchange, coins were probably being issued in the eighth century B.C. in Asia Minor. Herodotus indicates that the Lydians were the first to issue coins. Staters, composed of an alloy of gold and silver, were first formed in Lydia in Asia Minor and silver coins were first made at Aegina in approximately 700 B.C. Value was determined not by the stamp on the face of the coin but by the weight of the coin. For example, "shekel" did not refer to a coin with a particular stamp, but to a certain weight (see **shekel**). During the intertestamental period Simon Maccabeus in the year 140 B.C. coined money for his people and employed his own stamp. John Hyrcanus coined a small copper piece as did others of his successors.

Although the Jews actually had coined their own money during the Maccabean period, Grecian money continued to circulate in the Jewish communities. This money consisted primarily of drachmas and tetradrachmas. A silver drachma in the time of the Herods was equivalent to the Roman denarius and was worth approximately sixteen cents, while the silver stater or tetradrachma was evaluated at approximately sixty-six cents. The coin generally described as a mite (*lepton*) was worth approximately one-eighth cent. Only Jewish money could be offered in the temple and thus the mite of Mk. 12:42 must have been Jewish; it was likely a copper coin which had been issued by John Hyrcanus or another of the Maccabees. The talent which was employed in Palestine was money of account and not a coin as such. The talent was divided into minas and consisted of sixty minas or six thousand drachmas.

With the Roman conquest of Palestine, Roman money likewise came into circulation. The denarius was a silver coin and in the time of the empire bore the image of the ruler or some member of the ruling family. Its weight was approximately sixty grains and its evaluation the approximate equivalent to seventeen cents. The denarius was the coin used for tribute money and paid by the Jews to the imperial treasurer. A farthing or penny (*assarion*) was a small coin and was worth approximately one cent. The quadrans was valued at approximately one-fourth cent. In addition to the money coined by imperial Rome, the procurators of Judea likewise coined money. These moneys were copper pieces which were issued in the name of the imperial family and bore a legend in Greek letters. The gold coin which was current in Palestine during the NT period was the Roman *denarius aureus* which was equivalent to twenty-five silver denarii.

Jews again coined moneys during the First Revolt (A.D. 66–70) and also during the Second Revolt (A.D. 132–35). At the time of the suppression of the First Revolt and the capture of Jerusalem, the Romans issued coins with the image and name of Vespasian on one side and a Jewish captive on the other. On the side bearing the image of the Jewish female captive, the terms "Judea Subdued" or "Judea Captive" also were added for "decoration." During the

Second Revolt shekels and quarter shekels of silver and of copper were again issued by the Jews, and again they bore Hebrew inscriptions. The coins bore the image of the Beautiful Gate of the temple and at the side there appears the name Simon, the leader of the revolt.

V.E.G.

money-changer according to Ex. 30:13–15, an Israelite reaching the age of twenty was obligated to contribute to the sacred treasurer whenever the nation was numbered. This payment was an offering to God and was to be in the form of a half shekel. The money-changers confronted by Jesus (Mt. 21:12; Mk. 11:15; Lk. 19:45; and Jn. 2:15) were dealers in the temple who supplied the half shekels. They exacted a certain premium in the changing of the money from the coins in current usage to the Maccabean coins which were probably used for the purpose of offerings made to the temple treasury.

month the terms for "month" and "moon" have the same connection in the Hebrew language as in current usage and in the Indo-European languages generally. The most important point in connection with the Hebrew month is the length and the mode by which the month was calculated. The Israelites were acquainted with the year of twelve months of thirty days each with five additional days to produce conformity with the solar year of 365 days. This contact came while the Israelites were in Egypt. In Gen. 7:11 and 8:4 the months are calculated at thirty days. However, the Hebrews later appeared to use a lunar month. This observation is based on the fact that the observance of the day of the new moon was marked by special offerings to Jehovah (Num. 10:10; 2 Chr. 2:4) and by the coincidence of the Passover, which was always celebrated on the evening of the fourteenth day of the month Abib (called Nisan following the Captivity).

The usual number of months in the year was twelve, as implied in 1 K. 4:7 and in 1 Chr. 27:1–15. As closely as the Hebrew months coincided with the seasons, it follows as a matter of course that an additional month must have been inserted about every third year, which would bring the total months to thirteen. The usual method of designating the months was by a numerical order, e.g., "the second month" (Gen. 7:11), "the fourth month" (2 K. 25:3), etc. In the pre-Babylonian period, only the names of Hebrew months are found in the Bible narratives. These are: Abib, the first month; Civ, the second month; Ethanim, the seventh month; and Bul, the eighth month.

Subsequent to the Babylonian captivity the Hebrews used the names which were common among the Babylonians and other Semites. Of these, seven appear in the Bible: Nisan, the first (Neh. 2:1); Sivan, the third (Est. 8:9); Elul, the sixth (Neh. 6:15); Chislev, the ninth (Neh. 1:1); Tebeth, the tenth (Est. 2:16); Shebat, the eleventh (Zech. 1:7); and Adar, the twelfth (Est. 3:7). The names of the remaining five occur in the Talmud and are: Iyar (the second), Tammuz (the fourth), Ab (the fifth), Tishri (the seventh), and Marcheshvan (the eighth).

It is difficult to effect an identification of the Jewish months with current terminology. The following is a generalization:

1. Nisan (March–April)
2. Iyar (April–May)
3. Sivan (May–June)
4. Tammuz (June–July)
5. Ab (July–August)
6. Elul (August–September)
7. Tishri (September–October)
8. Bul (October–November)
9. Chislev (November–December)
10. Tebeth (December–January)
11. Shebat (January–February)
12. Adar (February–March)

moon the principal luminary of the night. The Hebrew terms employed to describe the moon signify "pale," "yellow," or "white." The moon held an important place in the world of nature as known and experienced by the Hebrews. In Gen. 1:14–16 the moon is described as appearing simultaneously with the sun and in terms which imply its independence of the sun so far as its light is concerned. It was appointed "to rule over the night" as the sun over the day. Genesis 1:16 reveals the inferiority of its light.

Moon worship was extensively practiced by the nations of the East and under a variety of conditions. In Egypt moon worship was honored under the form of Isis and this was one of the only two deities which demanded the reverence of all the Egyptians. In Syria it was represented by the worship of Ashtoreth. At a later period, the worship of the moon in its closer form of idol worship was introduced from Syria.

The advent of the new moon was calculated at an early period (1 Sam. 20:5, 18). Babylonian astrologists watched for it on the evening when it was expected. According to the Talmudic record, the Sanhedrin convened seven times a year early in the morning of the thirtieth day of the month.

The moon is frequently mentioned as prophesying events of the greatest importance through the temporary or permanent withdrawal of its light (Isa. 13:10; Joel 2:31; Mt. 24:29; Mk. 13:24).

Morashtite (mô-răsh′tīt) the native of the place Moresheth. The term occurs in Jer. 26:18 and Mic. 1:1 and each time as a description of the prophet Micah.

Morasthite (mô-răs′thīt) a native of a place called Moresheth.

Mordecai (môr′dĕ-kī) 1. A Jew who returned from Babylon with Zerubbabel (Neh. 7:7).

2. A Benjaminite of the Captivity, residing in Shushan. This man delivered the Jews from the destruction plotted against them by Haman, the chief minister of Xerxes. From the time of Esther's becoming queen, Mordecai was one of those who "sat in the king's gate." He saved the king's life by disclosing the conspiracy of two of the eunuchs to kill him. Furthermore, when the decree for the massacre of all the Jews of the empire was known, he earnestly advised and exhorted Esther to intercede with the king on behalf of the Jews. Ahasuerus Xerxes, who reigned from 486 to 464 B.C., rewarded Mordecai by promoting him to be the second man in the empire. This moving account is contained in the book of Esther.

Moreh (môr′ĕ) 1. The oak of Moreh was the first recorded stopping place of Abram after his entrance into the land of Canaan (Gen. 12:6). It may have been at this site that Abram's faith was tested in the offering of Isaac. It was likely here that Jacob buried the idols and remains of paganism which had been brought from Haran. Moreh is believed to have been the site on which Joshua erected a stone to commemorate the covenant which the people renewed here.

2. A hill of Moreh in the valley of Jezreel. This hill may well be the "Little Hermon."

Moresheth-gath (mō′rĕsh-ĕth-găth′) a site mentioned only by the prophet Micah (Mic. 1:14). Micah was a native of this place which is mentioned in connection with other towns of the lowland district of Judah.

Moriah (mō-rī′á) 1. The land of Moriah. On "one of the mountains" in this district Abraham prepared to offer Isaac (Gen. 22:2). The text does not indicate the name of the mountain but it was a conspicuous point from a great distance. Neither does the narrative ascertain its position. It is logical to take the "land of Moreh" as the same district with that in which the "oak of Moreh" was located.

2. The hill of Moriah. On this hill was established a threshing-floor of Araunah, a Jebusite. David purchased this floor and erected an altar on it, and 2 Chr. 3:1 indicates that Solomon built the temple on this point.

morning star a reference in 2 Pet. 1:19 indicates that this star heralds the dawn of a new day.

mortar 1. A vessel in which corn and other grains or spices are crushed. The simplest method of preparing grain for food was by pounding it between two stones. Convenience dictated that the lower of the stones should be hollow, thus holding the corn that had been crushed. Numbers 11:8 seems to indicate that the Israelites possessed mortars and hand mills very early. When the manna fell, they gathered it and either ground it in the mill, or pounded in the mortar until it was fit for use.

2. A compacting substance used to bind stones together. Numerous substances could be used for this purpose: bitumen, which was used in Babylonian structures; common mud or moistened clay; and a firm cement composed of sand, ashes, and lime, sometimes mixed with oil. The walls of houses were plastered with mud or mortar, which may have been mixed with straw and pebbles to give added protection against the weather (Lev. 14:42).

Moserah (mō-sĕʹrä) a site where the Israelites encamped in the wilderness near Bene-jaakan (Deut. 10:6). The plural form Moseroth appears in Num. 33:30. Its exact site is unknown, but it was likely near Mount Hor.

Moses (mōʹzĭz) a Levite of the family of Kohath, of the house of Amram (Ex. 6:18, 20). Exodus 6:20 identifies Jochebed as Moses' mother, but this expression may well be understood in some sense of Jochebed's being an ancestress. The Egyptian edict that all male children of the Hebrews be destroyed prompted Moses' mother to place him in a small boat or basket of papyrus, which was sealed against water by bitumen. Moses' sister remained to watch over the baby, who at this time was some three months old. When the Egyptian princess came to bathe in the sacred river, she saw the basket in the aquatic vegetation. The basket was soon retrieved by her attendants. The cry of a small baby moved the princess to compassion, and she determined to take the child to rear it as her own. Moses' sister was present to recommend the child's mother as a nurse and the infant was committed to her care. When he was old enough to be weaned, he was taken to the princess and was reared as her child. The pharaoh's daughter called the baby "Moses," the Hebrew form meaning "draw out."

As the adopted son of the pharaoh's daughter, Moses was reared and educated as an Egyptian. Acts 7:22 indicates that he was trained in the wisdom of the Egyptians. This training prepared him for governmental responsibility, but it was God's purpose that this young man might lead the Israelites out of Egypt. Upon seeing an Israelite suffering the bastinado from an Egyptian, Moses slew the Egyptian and buried the corpse in the sand. Having learned that this act was widely known, he fled from Egypt to the land of Midian. Thus, at the age of forty years he refused to be recognized as an Egyptian and cast his lot with God's people.

Moses' assistance of Jethro's daughters when watering their flocks introduced him to Jethro, a priest. The priest was hospitable toward the fugitive, employed him, and gave him Zipporah for wife. Acts 7:30 indicates that he remained in Midian for some forty years and continued in the shepherd life which he was later to surrender. Enjoying an extremely close fellowship with Jethro, he broadened his knowledge of religious thought and worship. As a shepherd, he learned the rules of the wilderness, its resources, its climate, and its difficulties. At the close of this period, he was attracted by a burning bush which yet remained unconsumed by the fire. Turning aside to inspect the bush more carefully, he received a revelation from God and a call to deliver his own people. Although Moses offered numerous excuses for not returning as a leader of God's captive people, each of these difficulties was removed.

Moses and Zipporah, along with their two infant sons, then returned to Egypt. One of them, likely the younger, remained uncircumcised because Zipporah rejected the rite, calling it bloody. Moses yielded to her desires and thus revealed himself unfaithful to his own people and to be unqualified for the high commission which God had given him. Moses suddenly became seriously ill and was at the point of death, yet Zipporah apparently discerned the cause of his illness and subjected her son to circumcision in an attempt to save her husband's life.

Having arrived in Egypt, Moses and Aaron repeatedly related to the pharaoh God's commands concerning the release of his people, but the result of these conversations was only to underscore the obstinacy of the king. A succession of plagues came upon Egypt, and eventually the pharaoh permitted Moses to lead the people out of the land of bondage. At Sinai, Moses was permitted to have an interview with God in which God spoke to him face to face "as a man speaketh unto his friend" (Ex. 24:9–11, 33:11, 17–23, 34:5–29). At this time God revealed his will to Moses, a will he continued to reveal at intervals. Moses also received the Ten Commandments from God and a short time later, during the forty days' sojourn upon the mountain, God gave Moses the dimensions and instructions concerning the tabernacle and its furniture. He also received the two tables of stone from God, only to find that in his absence the people had fashioned a golden calf and begun to worship the idol. Moses threw the stones upon the ground and broke them. Although Moses proceeded to punish the people whom he led, he likewise found himself acting as a mediator in their behalf. Upon being recalled to the mountain, Moses received two other tables which were inscribed like the first. Thus the name of Moses is always associated with the law which was given at Sinai and during the subsequent wanderings to the Promised Land.

After Moses returned from his second forty-day visit to Mount Sinai, the people observed that the skin of his face shone, sending forth beams, and they were afraid to come near their leader. After Moses called to them, they returned to him and heard all that God had spoken to him (Ex. 34:33–34; 2 Cor. 3:13).

Although the death of Zipporah is not recorded, Moses married a Cushite woman (Num. 12:1). The marriage occurred in the wilderness, and it is likely that the Cushite woman was one of the mixed multitude accompanying the Israelites in the flight from Egypt.

After leaving Kadesh, the rebellion, which was led by Korah and other princes against the authority of Moses and Aaron, was thwarted and the leaders were punished by God. At the time of the second encampment at Kadesh, Moses and Aaron committed the sin of disobedience which denied their entry into the Promised Land. After this occasion, Moses remained faithful to God and succeeded in leading his people to the boundary of the land which God had promised. The camp was eventually made at Shittim in the valley, and Moses then delivered a parting address to the people. Subsequently he directed Joshua, whom God had appointed to succeed Moses, before the high priest and in the presence of the congregation, Joshua was identified as Moses' successor, and the office of leadership was transferred to him. Moses later ascended Mount Nebo and was privileged to view the Promised Land from Nebo's height. He was one hundred and twenty years old when he died. Deuteronomy 34 indicates that God buried Moses in the land of Moab.   v.e.g.

Most High see **God, Names of**

Most Holy Place these words designate and describe the innermost room of the tabernacle (Ex. 26:34) and in later literature the innermost room of the temple (1 K. 6:16).

mote referred to in Mt. 7:3–5 and Lk. 6:41–

42. This is translated in the RSV by the term "speck."

moth the moth and its work are mentioned numerous times in the Biblical materials (Job 4:19; Ps. 39:11; Isa. 50:9; James 5:2). The Hebrew term seems to describe some species of clothes moth.

mother see **family**

mother-in-law see **family**

mount, mountain this term represents the translation of both Hebrew and Greek terms which may refer to a single mound, hill, or eminence, or the terms may refer to less isolated hills and mountains. Some of the more familiar OT designations are Hermon, Gilboa, Gilead, Zion, Samaria, and in the NT the Mount of Olives is unusually familiar. Mountain of the Amorites is specifically mentioned in Deut. 1:19–20.

mourning the emotions of the Jews expressed themselves quite vigorously in their mourning practices. Mourning appeared primarily in the following manifestations: (1) beating the breast or other parts of the body; (2) weeping and screaming; (3) adornment in sad-colored garments; (4) songs of lamentation; (5) funeral feasts; (6) antics of professional mourners employed by the bereaved.

Jewish mourning seemed to emphasize the public aspect rather than the private ceremonies of which current society thinks. Rending the clothes (Gen. 37:29), dressing in sackcloth (Gen. 37:34), ashes sprinkled on one's body (2 Sam. 13:19), black garments (2 Sam. 14:2), removal of ornaments (Deut. 21:12–13), shaving of the head (Lev. 10:6), fasting (2 Sam. 1:12), covering the lower part of the face (Lev. 13:45), cutting the flesh (Jer. 16:6, 7), involvement of friends or passersby who join in the lamentations of the bereaved (Judg. 11:40), and the mourning feast (Jer. 16:7, 8).

The period of mourning varied. In the case of Jacob mourning was seventy days (Gen. 50:3), of Aaron and Moses thirty days (Num. 20:29; Deut. 34:8). The mourning period for Saul was seven days (1 Sam. 31:13).

mouse occurs in Lev. 11:29; 1 Sam. 6:4–5; and Isa. 66:17. The term denotes a field-ravager and should likely be understood to describe the destructive rodent common to the area.

mouth the term may define the organ of eating (Judg. 7:6), the organ of speech (Mt. 5:2), the mouth of God (2 Sam. 22:9), or it may have such physical designations as the opening of a well or a cave (Gen. 29:2–3; Josh. 10:18).

mowing because of the excessive heat in the Holy Land, the business of haymaking would not be prominent; thus the reference in Amos

7:1 to the king's mowings may refer to the first growth of the grass paid as taxes to the king or to some royal right of early pasturage.
Moza (mō'zȧ) 1. Son of Caleb (1 Chr. 2:46).

2. Son of Zimri (1 Chr. 8:36–37).
Mozah (mō'zȧ) a city in Benjamin, named between Chephirah and Rekem (Josh. 18:26).
mulberry trees mentioned in 2 Sam. 5:23–24 and in 1 Chr. 14:14. Most scholars believe that the Lk. 17:6 reference is likewise to a similar tree. A black mulberry is very prominent in Palestine.
mule not mentioned until the time of David, just at the time when the Israelites were becoming well acquainted with horses. After this time, horses and mules are often mentioned together. The mule is the hybrid offspring of a male ass and a mare. Although horses are mentioned in the NT, the mule is not.
Muppim (mŭp'ĭm) a Benjaminite, one of the fourteen descendants of Rachel who belong to the original colony of the sons of Jacob in Egypt (Gen. 46:21).
murder the act of taking the life of a human being. According to Gen. 9:5–6 this act is to be punished even when caused by an animal. An animal, known to be vicious and which caused death, was destroyed, as well as its owner, if the owner had taken no steps to restrain it (Ex. 21:29, 31). The responsibility of executing punishment on the murderer is in the Law expressly laid on the "revenger of blood," but the question of guilt was to be previously decided by the Levitical tribunal. It was lawful to kill a burglar taken at night in the act, but unlawful to do so after sunrise (Ex. 22:2–3).
murrain a reference to an infectious disease affecting animals (Ex. 9:3).
Mushi (mū'shī) the son of Merari, the son of Kohath (Ex. 6:19; Num. 3:20).
music according to the narrative of Gen. 4, Jubal, the son of Lamech, was "the father of all such as handle the harp and the organ." The first mention of music after the Deluge is in the narrative of Laban's interview with Jacob (Gen. 31:27). On the banks of the Red Sea, Moses and the children of Israel sang their triumphal song of deliverance from the hosts of Egypt. Prior to the establishment of the schools of the prophets, there existed no systematic cultivation of music among the Hebrews. However, music was an essential part of the schools' activities, and professional musicians soon became attached to the court. Second Sam. 19:35 indicates that David gathered around him "singing men and singing women."

It was left to the temple to serve as the great school of music, but there existed a host of musicians throughout the country prior to the elaborate arrangements for the temple choir (2 Sam. 6:5).

Many instruments are mentioned in the Biblical accounts: cymbal (1 Chr. 16:5), psaltery, and harp—"players on instruments" (Ps. 87:7) —perforated wind instruments (1 K. 1:40), trumpets (1 Chr. 13:8), etc.

Music was not simply employed as a medium of worship. It was likewise characteristic of all banquets; the kings had their court musicians; musicians were employed as mourners at the time of death; bridal processions were accompanied with music and song (Jer. 7:34); triumphal processions celebrating victory were enlivened by singers (Ex. 15:1, 20); and absence of music meant cursing upon the land (Isa. 24:8–9). Music was likewise a characteristic of the funeral procession; the harvesters working in the field, the women toiling at the mills, and even harlots attracted attention with music (Isa. 23:15–16).

It is readily evident that music was a vital and integral part of the Hebrew life.
mustard a plant bearing extremely small seeds. The term occurs in Mt. 13:31; 17:20; Mk. 6:31; Lk. 13:19, 17:6. The parable of the mustard seed stresses the growth of the kingdom from small beginnings to vast proportions. The gospel accounts make it evident that the mustard seed was used proverbially to denote anything which was minute.
Muth-labben (mŭth-lăb'ĕn) the title of Ps. 9 is "to the chief musician upon Muth-labben." These words have occasioned unlimited conjecture. Two basic difficulties are involved in the interpretation: first, the determining of the true reading of the Hebrew, and then the interpretation of the text. The expression may possibly be the opening words of some well known song which was sung to the melody of this Psalm.
Myra (mī'rȧ) an important city of Lycia, where Paul on his voyage to Rome (Acts 27:5) was removed from the Adramyttian ship to the Alexandrian ship which ran aground on the coast of Malta. Its richly adorned tombs attest to the city's unusual wealth. Its enormous theater admits of its vast population in what may be called its Greek age.
myriad literally the term means ten thousand. At times this term signifies a number which is countless or numberless. The term occurs in Lk. 12:1; Acts 19:19; Jude 14; Rev. 5:11, 19:6.
myrrh a fragrant substance derived from the liquids of various plants and trees. 1. The

Hebrew term *mor* is used in Ex. 30:23 as one of the ingredients of the "oil of holy ointment," in Est. 2:12 as one of the substances used in the purification of women, in Prov. 7:17 as a perfume. Matthew 2:11 includes myrrh (the Greek term *smurnan*) among the gifts brought by the wise men to the infant Jesus, and in Mk. 15:23 wine is mingled with myrrh. Myrrh was also used for embalming.

2. *Lot* is also translated myrrh in Gen. 37:25, 43:11. These passages employ the term

lot to denote odorous resin which exudes from the branches of the *Cistus creticus*.

myrtle a tree which grew in the mountains near Jerusalem and whose branches were used to make booths during the Feasts of Tabernacles.

Mysia (mĭsh'ĭ-à) the northwestern region of Asia Minor. This region is mentioned in Acts 16:7-8 and seems to have been bounded on the west by the Aegean Sea, the Hellespont and Propontis on the north, Bithynia and Phrygia on the east, and Lydia on the south.

N

Naam (nā'ăm) a son of Caleb, the son of Jephunneh (1 Chr. 4:15).

Naamah (nā'à-mà) 1. One of the four women whose names are preserved in the records of the world before the Flood. She was a daughter of Lamech by his wife Zillah.

2. Mother of King Rehoboam (1 K. 14:21, 31).

3. A town of Judah in the Shephelah area (Josh. 15:41).

Naaman (nā'à-măn) 1. An Arab warrior, whose activities are preserved because of his connection with Elisha. The Biblical narrative is recorded in 2 K. 5. Naaman, a victim of leprosy, was an able Syrian general. During one of his soldiers' raids into the Israelite land, a young Israelite maid was captured and later became a slave to Naaman's wife. The young maiden later expressed to her mistress the wish that Naaman visit Elisha in Samaria, because she believed that Elisha would heal Naaman's leprosy. The king of Syria wrote a letter of introduction for Naaman and sent him to Elisha. Upon arriving before the prophet's door, the Syrian was met by a messenger who insisted that he should dip himself seven times in the Jordan. Naaman, of course, was offended by such an insistence and reminded the messenger that the rivers of Damascus were better than the rivers of Israel. However, his servants soothed his temper and he followed the instructions of Elisha. Naaman then renounced his idolatry and became a worshiper of God.

2. A member of Benjamin's family, the son of Bela (Gen. 46:21; Num. 26:40; 1 Chr. 8:3-4).

Naamathite (nā'à-mà-thīt) the Gentile name

of one of Job's friends, Zophar the Naamathite (Job 2:11, 11:1).

Naamites (nā'à-mīts) the family descended from Naaman the grandson of Benjamin (Num. 26:40).

Naarah (nā'à-rà) the second wife of Ashur, a descendant of Judah (1 Chr. 4:5-6).

Naarai (nā'à-rī) one of the valued men of David's armies (1 Chr. 11:37).

Naaran (nā'à-răn) a city of Ephraim (1 Chr. 7:28).

Naarath (nā'à-răth) a landmark on the southern boundary of Ephraim. It appears to have lain between Ataroth and Jericho (Josh. 16:7).

Nabal (nā'băl) a sheep master who lived in the area of Carmel in Judah. David and his men dwelt for some time in this area and protected Nabal and other shepherds from bands of robbers which raided the countryside. Upon requesting assistance from Nabal, David was met with absolute refusal. Thus David determined to punish Nabal and every other male living in the area. However, Abigail, Nabal's wife, gave a present to David, apologized for her husband's misconduct, and effected a peaceful solution. When she returned to their home, she found Nabal thoroughly intoxicated. The following morning, when once again Nabal was sober, he was told of the debacle and from the grave shock of the event he died approximately ten days later. The Scripture indicates that "the Lord smote Nabal," and he died. Abigail later became one of David's wives. The entire account is recorded in 1 Sam. 25:1-42.

Naboth (nā'bŏth) a Jezreelite, an owner of a small vineyard which was located in the area of Jezreel. King Ahab wished to buy the vineyard, but Naboth refused to sell it because he had inherited it from his ancestors. Jezebel, Ahab's wife, took the matter into her own hands and two of her men accused Naboth of having "cursed God and the king." Naboth and his children were dragged out of the city and executed. The site of execution was near a large reservoir and the blood from their wounds ran down into the waters below (1 K. 21:1–24, 22:34–38; 2 K. 9:30–37).

Nacon (nā'kŏn) the designation of the threshing floor at which the ark had arrived in its progress from Kirjath-jearim to Jerusalem, when Uzzah was struck dead in his too hasty zeal for its safety (2 Sam. 6:6).

Nadab (nā'dăb) 1. The oldest son of Aaron and Elisheba (Ex. 6:23; Num. 3:2).

2. King Jeroboam's son, who succeeded to the throne of Israel 954 B.C. and reigned two years (1 K. 15:25=31).

3. A son of Shammai (1 Chr. 2:28).

4. A son of Gibeon (1 Chr. 8:30, 9:36).

Naggai (năg'ī) one of the ancestors of Jesus (Lk. 3:25).

Nahalal (nà-hà'lăl) a city of Zebulun, given to the Merarite Levites (Josh. 21:35). It was probably located in the plain south of Acre.

Nahaliel (nà-hā'lĭ-ĕl) a camping site of Israel in their march to Canaan (Num. 21:19). This site is north of Arnon and between Mattanah and Bamoth.

Nahallal see **Nahalal**

Nahalol (nā'hà-lŏl) see **Nahal** (Judg. 1:30)

Naham (nā'hăm) brother of Hodiah's wife (1 Chr. 4:19).

Nahamani (nā'hà-mā-nī) a leader of those who returned from Babylon with Zerubbabel (Neh. 7:7).

Naharai (nā'hà-rī) Joab's armor-bearer (2 Sam. 23:37; 1 Chr. 11:39).

Nahash (nā'hăsh) 1. An Ammonite king who dictated to the inhabitants of Jabesh-gilead that every man must lose his right eye else he would not accept their surrender. This incited Saul, who in turn destroyed the Ammonite force (1 Sam. 11:1–11).

2. A person mentioned only once in stating the parentage of Amasa, the commander in chief of Absalom's army. This man was the father of Abigail and Zeruiah (2 Sam. 17:25).

Nahath (nā'hăth) 1. Eldest son of Reuel, the son of Esau (Gen. 36:13, 17).

2. A Kohathite Levite, son of Zophai (1 Chr. 6:26).

3. A Levite who had charge of the tithes and offerings during the reign of Hezekiah (2 Chr. 31:13).

Nahbi (nä'bī) one of the twelve spies, a member of the tribe of Naphtali (Num. 13:14).

Nahor (nā'hôr) 1. The grandfather of Abraham, and father of Terah (Gen. 11:22–25).

2. A son of Terah, and brother of Abraham (Gen. 11:26–27). He married Milcah, the daughter of his brother Haran.

3. The city of Nahor (Gen. 24:10).

Nahshon (nä'shŏn) a prince of the children of Judah at the time of the first numbering in the wilderness (Ex. 6:23; Num. 1:7). In the encampment, in the offerings of the princes, and in the order of march, the first place was assigned to Nahshon, the son of Amminadab, as captain of the host of Judah. According to Num. 26:64–65 he died in the wilderness.

Nahum (nā'hŭm) 1. *The Prophet.* The name "Nahum" appears nowhere else in the OT. The term is built upon a root which expresses the idea of consolation. The book itself stands seventh in order among the writings of the minor prophets in the present canonical arrangement. Nahum is called the Elkoshite. Of course, the previous title suggests that he was a native of Elkosh. There are four primary theories concerning the location of Elkosh: (1) a town located some twenty-four miles north of Nineveh; (2) Elkosh in Galilee; (3) Elkosh is identified as Capernaum; (4) Elkosh is held by most contemporary scholars to have been located in Southern Judah, near the home of Micah.

Inasmuch as little information is available concerning the person of Nahum, his ministry must be dated upon the basis of internal evidence. It seems obvious that Nahum preached prior to the destruction of Nineveh but after the destruction of Thebes. The burden of evidence places Nahum's activity in the seventh century B.C., possibly about 625 B.C.

2. *Literature of the Book.* Although the prophecy of Nahum is given an exalted place, since the turn of the century many scholars have claimed that a psalm of late origin is prefixed to the prophecies of Nahum. This question is only of academic interest. The striking thing is the significance which most OT scholars assign to Nahum. This prophecy has been described as most nearly approaching the prophecy of Isaiah in poetic form and expression.

3. *Message of the Prophecy.* The superscription, "the burden of Nineveh," automatically suggests the theme of the prophecy—the destruction of Nineveh. The three brief chapters into which the work is divided form a consecutive whole. Chapter 1 is introductory. The author begins his work with a declaration of the character of God, "a God jealous and avenging." Jehovah is declared to be a God

who moves with swift and terrible vengeance against his enemies. The message of this chapter is unusually specific, addressed first to Judah (1:12–13) and then to the monarch of Assyria (1:14). Chapter 2 is devoted to an intensely vivid description of the siege of the city and her subsequent destruction. The prophet's mind seized the burnished bronze shields of the scarlet-clad warriors of the besieging army, the flashing steel scythes of the war-chariots as they are drawn up in battle array, and the quivering cypress-shafts of their spears. Panic seizes their mighty ones, their ranks are broken, and they hurry to the wall only to see the covered battering-rams of the besiegers ready for the attack. No time is lost in showing the crisis as it approaches with unusual rapidity. The city is taken, and her maidens "moan as with the voice of doves." The flight becomes general, the wealth of the city becomes the spoil of the captors, and over the charred and blackened ruins the prophet asks in triumph, "Where is the lair of the lions, the feeding place of the young lions, where walked lion, lioness, lion's whelp, and none made (them) afraid?" Nahum 2:13 indicates that the downfall of Nineveh was certain because "I am against thee," says God. Chapter 3 discusses the cause of Nineveh's destruction. As the prophet is recalled from the scenes of the future to the realities of the present, he collects himself for one final outburst of withering denunciation against the Assyrian city. She will fall unpitied and unlamented, and with calmness the prophet pronounces her final doom (3:19).

nail 1. The fingernail (Deut. 21:12).

2. A stake, a tent peg (Isa. 33:20, 41:7).

3. A pin, primarily of metal used for holding pieces of wood or other materials together (1 Chr. 22:3).

Nain (nā'ĭn) a village of Galilee. A gate of this village was made illustrious because at this place Jesus raised the widow's son (Lk. 7:12). This small village was located some five miles southeast of Nazareth.

Naioth (nā'ŏth) a place in which Samuel and David took refuge together, after David had made his escape from Saul (1 Sam. 19:18–23).

Naomi (nā'ō-mī) the wife of Elimelech, and mother-in-law of Ruth (Ruth 1:2, 2:1, 3:1, 4:3). The name is derived from a root which means sweetness or pleasantness.

Naphish (nā'fĭsh) a son of Ishmael (Gen. 25:15), and head of the clan with which the Israelite tribes living east of the Jordan were at one time in sharp conflict (1 Chr. 5:18–22).

Naphtali (năf'tà-lī) 1. The sixth son of

Jacob and the second by Bilhah, Rachel's maiden.

2. The tribe of Naphtali. This tribe was divided into four divisions, traceable to the four sons of Naphtali (Gen. 46:24; Ex. 1:4; 1 Chr. 7:13). At the numbering on Sinai the tribe numbered some fifty-three thousand, four hundred fighting men (Num. 2:30). During the march through the wilderness, Naphtali occupied a position on the north of the tabernacle with Dan and Asher (Num. 2:25–31). The territory which was apportioned to Naphtali was enclosed on three sides by those of other tribes. Asher lay on the west, Zebulun on the south, and on the east Manasseh. On the north lay the great ravine which opened into the splendid valley which separates the two ranges of Lebanon. Naphtali was thus cut off from the plain of Esdraelon by the mountains of Nazareth. Thus it is seen that Naphtali had inherited primarily the mountainous country. This likely explains their extravagant self devotion and unusual heroism (Judg. 5:18). The Naphtalites later resigned themselves to contact with the heathen, which was the bane of the northern tribes generally. Naphtali was ravaged by Ben-hadad king of Syria, and many of its inhabitants were subsequently taken captives by Tiglath-pileser (1 K. 15:20; 2 Chr. 16:4; 2 K. 15:29). Though the history of the tribe of Naphtali culminates at this point, under the title of Galilee, the district which they had occupied was destined to become in every way far more important than it had ever been previously.

3. Mount Naphtali. The mountainous district which formed the main part of the inheritance of Naphtali (Josh. 20:7).

Naphtuhim (năf'tŭ-hĭm) an Egyptian tribe, mentioned only in the account of the descendants of Noah (Gen. 10:13; 1 Chr. 1:11).

Narcissus (när-sĭs'ŭs) a Roman, some members of whose household were known and greeted by Paul in his letter to the Roman Christians (Rom. 16:11).

nard see **spikenard**

Nathan (nā'thăn) 1. Son of Attai of the house of Jerahmeel, of the tribe of Judah (1 Chr. 2:36).

2. An eminent Hebrew prophet during the reigns of David and Solomon. Nathan first appears in the consultation with David about the building of the temple (2 Sam. 7:2–3, 17), he next appears as the reprover of David for the sin with Bathsheba, and his famous parable of the rich man and the lamb remains one of the OT's best-known accounts (2 Sam. 12:1–7).

3. A son or brother of one of the members

of David's guard (2 Sam. 23:36; 1 Chr. 11:38).

4. One of the leaders who returned from Babylon with Ezra on his second expedition (Ezra 8:16).

Nathanael (nȧ-thăn'ȧ-ĕl) a native of Cana (Jn. 21:2), a disciple of Jesus. The name Nathanael does not appear in the Synoptics, and John never introduces the name of Bartholomew, which name appears in the Synoptics. It is generally believed that these names refer to the same individual, Nathanael being the proper name, and Bartholomew the surname.

Nathan-melech (nă'thăn-mē'lĕk) a eunuch in the court of Josiah (2 K. 23:11).

Naum (nā'ŭm) son of Esli and father of Amos; he is listed in the genealogy of Christ (Lk. 3:25).

Nazarene (năz'ȧ-rēn) an inhabitant of Nazareth. This appellative is applied to Jesus in numerous passages. In Isa. 11:1 the Messiah is described as a *nēser*, a sprout of Jesse, a humble and despised descendant of the royal family.

Nazareth (năz'ȧ-rĕth) first mentioned in Mt. 2:23. The town of Galilee, this is the site where Joseph and Mary lived and where Jesus was reared. Nazareth is situated among the hills which constitute the southern ridges of the Lebanon, just before they sink into the plain of Esdraelon. Nazareth was located some twenty miles southwest of Capernaum and approximately eighty-eight miles north of Jerusalem.

The inhabitants of Galilee were looked upon contemptuously by the people of Judea because they spoke a ruder dialect, were less cultivated, and were more exposed by their position to contact with the heathen. Perhaps the inhabitants of Nazareth had a discreditable name among their neighbors for irreligion or some laxity of morals.

Nazirite (năz'ĭ-rīt) one of either sex who was bound by a vow of a peculiar kind to be set apart from others for the service of God. The obligation was either for life or for a defined time. Nazirites likely existed among the Hebrews, but there is no regulation concerning them in the Sinai law. However, the regulations for a temporary Nazirite vow are given in Num. 6:1–21. During the time of his vow, the Nazirite was to abstain from wine, grapes, intoxicating drink, and every product of the vine. He was forbidden to cut a hair of his head, or to approach any dead body, even that of his nearest relative. Having completed the term of the vow, he was brought to the door of the tabernacle and was required to offer a male lamb for a burnt offering, a ewe lamb for a sin offering, and a ram for a peace offering, with the usual accompaniments of peace offerings. He also brought a meat offering and a drink offering (Ex. 29:18; Lev. 7:12, 13; Num. 6:15). He was then to cut off the portion of hair that had grown during the period of his consecration and to place the locks in the fire at the sacrificial altar. See Lev. 7:32–34 for the priestly duties at this time.

One might also become a Nazirite for life instead of a restricted period. The individual could be dedicated as a Nazirite for life either at the time of his birth or even before his birth (Judg. 13:4; 1 Sam. 1:11, 28). Samson, Samuel, and John the Baptist are mentioned as Nazirites for life. It is likely that Paul took the Nazirite vow (Acts 21:20–26).

Neah (nē'ȧ) a place which was one of the landmarks on the boundary of Zebulun (Josh. 19:13).

Neapolis (nē-ăp'ō-lĭs) the seaport of **Philippi;** the site where Paul and his associates first landed in Europe (Acts 16:11). Neapolis was located approximately ten miles southeast of Philippi.

Neariah (nē'ȧ-rī'ȧ) 1. One of the six sons of Shemaiah in the line of the royal family of Judah after the Captivity (1 Chr. 3:22, 23).

2. A son of Ishi, and one of the captains of the five hundred Simeonites who, in the days of Hezekiah, drove out the Amalekites from Mount Seir (1 Chr. 4:42).

Nebai (nē'bī) family of the heads of the people who signed the covenant with Nehemiah (Neh. 10:19).

Nebaioth (nē-bā'yŏth) the tribe which descended from Ishmael (Gen. 25:13; 1 Chr. 1:29) and extremely wealthy (Isa. 60:7).

Neballat (nē-băl'ăt) a town of Benjamin, one which the Benjaminites reoccupied after the Captivity (Neh. 11:34).

Nebat (nē'băt) the father of Jeroboam, whose name is only preserved in connection with that of his distinguished son (1 K. 11:26, 12:2, 15).

Nebo (nē'bō) 1. The mountain from which Moses viewed the Promised Land (Deut. 32:49, 34:1). It is described as in the land of Moab, facing Jericho, the head or summit of a mountain called the Pisgah.

2. A town on the eastern side of the Jordan, situated in the pastoral country (Num. 32:3).

3. A town mentioned following Bethel and Ai (Ezra 2:29).

4. The name of a Chaldean god, a well-known deity of the Babylonians and Assyrians.

Nebuchadnezzar (nĕb'ŭ-kăd-nĕz'ẽr) or **Nebuchadrezzar** (nĕb'ŭ-kăd-rĕz'ẽr) one of the greatest and most powerful of the Babylonian kings. Nebuchadnezzar was the son and successor of Nabopolassar, the founder of the Babylonian empire. He seems to have been a mature man at the time of his father's rebellion against Assyria, 625 B.C. In 605 B.C. Nebuchadnezzar led an army against Pharaoh Necho of Egypt and defeated him at Carchemish, recovered Coele-Syria, Phoenicia, and Palestine, pressed forward to Egypt, was engaged in that country or upon its borders when he was recalled to Babylon. Nabopolassar, Nebuchadnezzar's father, had died after a reign of twenty-one years, and the throne was now vacant. In some alarm concerning the succession, Nebuchadnezzar hurried to the capital, reached Babylon before any disturbance had arisen, and entered peaceably into his kingdom in 604 B.C.

Much information concerning his reign is derived from Jeremiah and Ezekiel, Nebuchadnezzar's contemporaries. The book of Daniel is also an important document in this connection. According to 2 K. 24:1 Judah paid tribute to Nebuchadnezzar for some three years and then revolted. The eventual result of this revolt was the capture of Jerusalem, the burning of the temple, and the captivity of the people.

Nebuchadnezzar's policy was to transport the conquered people to other parts of the empire and use these as his laboring forces. Nebuchadnezzar died in 562 B.C. and was succeeded by his son Evil-merodach.

Nebushazban (nĕb'û-shăs'băn) an officer of Nebuchadnezzar at the time of the capture of Jerusalem (Jer. 39:13).

Nebuzaradan (nĕb'û-zăr-ā'dăn) an important officer in the court of Nebuchadnezzar. He apparently was present during the siege of Jerusalem, and from the time Tyre was in the hands of the Babylonians, every act was directed by Nebuzaradan.

Necho (nē'kō) see Pharaoh Necho (cf. 2 Chr. 35:20, 22, 36:4).

Nedabiah (nĕd'á-bī'á) a son of Jehoiachin king of Judah (1 Chr. 3:18).

neginah (nĕ-gē'nä) this is a general term by which all stringed instruments are described. It occurs in the titles of many of the psalms (see Job 30:9; Ps. 69:12; Lam. 3:14).

neginoth (nĕg'ĭ-nŏth) plural of **neginah.**

Nehelamite (nē-hĕl'á-mīt) the designation of a man named Shemaiah, a false prophet, who went with the captivity to Babylon (Jer. 29:24, 31-32).

Nehemiah (nē'hē-mī'á) 1. One of the leaders of the first expedition from Babylon to Jerusalem under Zerubbabel (Ezra 2:2; Neh. 7:7).

2. Son of Azbuk and ruler of one half of Beth-zur. This man assisted in the repair of the wall of Jerusalem (Neh. 3:16).

3. Son of Hachaliah, and apparently of the tribe of Judah. The available knowledge of this man is contained in the book which bears his name. The first information discloses that Nehemiah is at Shushan, the winter residence of the kings of Persia, and identifies the subject as a cupbearer of King Artaxerxes Longimanus. In 445 B.C. certain Jews, one of whom was a near kinsman of Nehemiah, arrived from Judea and described the deplorable conditions in Jerusalem. Nehemiah immediately conceived the idea of going to Jerusalem to assist his people. After three or four months, an opportunity presented itself to obtain the king's consent. Thus he was appointed governor of Judea, received a troop of cavalry, and letters from the king to different satraps through whose provinces he would pass. Nehemiah's work was to rebuild the city; the importance of his work cannot be overestimated. Rebuilding the city was the one step which could resuscitate the nation, preserve the Mosaic institutions, and lay the foundation of future independence. The walls soon seemed to emerge from heaps of rubbish and to encircle the city as in other days. The gateways were also rebuilt.

Nehemiah's leadership is observed in his success despite the attempts of Sanballat and Tobiah to prevent the construction. The work was halted temporarily by order of Artaxerxes, but Nehemiah's integrity was apparent to the king. After an extended delay, Nehemiah was permitted to return to Jerusalem and to complete his work by repairing the temple and dedicating the walls. Scholars generally believe that the work stopped immediately after the event that is recorded in Neh. 6:16-19 and that ch. 7 relates the measures adopted by Nehemiah upon returning from his royal visit.

Nehemiah's integrity is further demonstrated by his refusal to accept his financial allowance as governor of the people and by his provision for the poverty-stricken Jews. Nehemiah likewise provided for the support of the ministering priests and Levites. He insisted upon the sanctity of the temple precincts, and with no less firmness and impartiality he expelled from all sacred functions those of the high priest's family who had contracted heathen marriages, rebuking and punishing those of the common people who had likewise intermarried with foreigners. This same spirit is evidenced in his observance of the sabbath. Josephus states that Nehemiah died a very old man (Josephus Ant. XI.v.8).

Nehemiah, Book of the title assumes the authorship of the man Nehemiah, who was responsible for the rebuilding of the temple and the walls of Jerusalem. Many scholars believe that the books now described as Ezra and Nehemiah were originally one book. These two books do appear in the LXX as 1 Esdras. The material which is recorded in Ezra-Nehemiah is of inestimable value, providing the only Biblical-historical information of the period following the return from the Exile.

Nehemiah 1:1–7:73 is an excerpt from the memoirs of Nehemiah. Chapters 1–6 record Nehemiah's return to Jerusalem, the opposition he encountered, and the rebuilding of the walls. An extensive account of the revival led by Nehemiah is given in Neh. 7:1–13:3. This section records the reading of the Law, the significance of the Feast of Tabernacles, the renewal of the covenant, the provision for the Levites and for the defense of Jerusalem, the dedication of the city wall, and separation from the heathen. The last section of the book, Neh. 13:4–31, relates reforms effected by Nehemiah upon his return from Persia. The last petition of Nehemiah, "Remember me, O my God, for good," reveals the true character of the man. v.e.g.

nehiloth (nē'hĭ-lŏth) this term appears in the title of Ps. 5 and is probably derived from the root *chalal*, hence of flute or pipe. The term apparently is the general term for perforated wind instruments of all kinds. Neginoth designates various stringed instruments.

Nehum (nē'hŭm) one of those who returned from Babylon with Zerubbabel (Neh. 7:7).

Nehushta (nē-hŭsh'tà) the daughter of Elnathan of Jerusalem, wife of Jehoiakim, and mother of Jehoiachin, kings of Judah (2 K. 24:8).

Nehushtan (nē-hush'tăn) the name by which the brazen serpent was known (see Num. 21:9; 2 K. 18:4).

Neiel (nē-ī'ĕl) a place which formed one of the landmarks of the boundary of the tribe of Asher (Josh. 19:27).

Nekeb (nē'kĕb) one of the towns on the boundary of Naphtali (Josh. 19:33). This town lay between Adami and Jabneel.

Nekoda (nē-kō'dà) 1. The descendants of Nekoda returned among the Nethinim after the Captivity (Ezra 2:48; Neh. 7:50).

2. The sons of Nekoda were from those who went up after the Captivity from Tel-melah, Tel-harsa, and other places, but were unable to prove their descent from Israel (Ezra 2:60; Neh. 7:62).

Nemuel (nĕm'ū-ĕl) 1. A Reubenite, son of Eliab, and eldest brother of Dathan and Abiram (Num. 26:9).

2. The eldest son of Simeon (Num. 26:12; 1 Chr. 4:24), from whom were descended the valley of the Nemuelites.

Nemuelites (nĕm'ū-ĕ-līts) descendants of Nemuel, the firstborn of Simeon (Num. 26:12).

Nepheg (nē'fĕg) 1. A son of Izhar, the son of Kohath (Ex. 6:21).

2. A son of David, born in Jerusalem (2 Sam. 5:15; 1 Chr. 3:7).

Nephish see **Naphish**

Nephisim (nĭ-fī'sĭm) the family of the Nethinim who returned with Zerubbabel (Neh. 7:52).

Nephthalim see **Naphtali**

Nephtoah (nĕf-tō'à) the spring of the waters of Nephtoah was one of the landmarks in the boundary line which separated Judah from Benjamin (Josh. 15:9, 18:15). It lay northwest of Jerusalem, approximately two miles from the city.

Nephthalim see **Naphtali**

Nephusim (nĕ-fū'sĭm) the same as Nephishesim (Ezra 2:50).

Ner (nûr) 1. Son of Abiel (1 Sam. 14:51).

2. A Benjaminite, son of Jeiel and remotely related to King Saul (1 Chr. 8:33, 9:35–36).

Nereus (nēr'ūs) Roman Christian greeted by Paul (Rom. 16:15).

Nergal (nûr'găl) a chief Assyrian and Babylonian deity. The deity was of Babylonian origin; his monumental titles are: "the storm-ruler," "the king of battle," "the champion of the gods," "the male principle," et al. The only Biblical reference to Nergal is in 2 K. 17:30.

Nergal-sharezer (see Jer. 39:3, 13) one of Nebuchadnezzar's princes, holding the office of Rab-mag. This man appears among the persons who, by command of Nebuchadnezzar, released Jeremiah from prison, and thus he must have been a personage of great importance. Nergal-sharezer, known to the Greeks as Neriglissar, married the daughter of Nebuchadnezzar and later murdered Evil-merodach, his brother-in-law, and succeeded him, reigning from 560 to 556 B.C.

Neri (nē'rī) son of Melchi and father of Salathiel (Lk. 3:27).

Neriah (nē-rī'à) the son of Maaseiah and father of Baruch (Jer. 32:12, 36:4).

net used by the Hebrews for fishing and hunting. Egyptian nets were constructed of flax string. It is probable that the early Jews used similar nets, both in size and material. Nets were cast about the game (Job 19:6) or over the game (Ezek. 12:13). Nets were likewise used to catch the feet (Ps. 9:15; Lam. 1:13).

Nets were also used in fishing, either dragnets or casting nets (Mt. 13:47-48; Jn. 21:6).

Netaim (nḗ-tā'ĭm) site in Judah with royal plantations (1 Chr. 4:23).

Nethanel (nḗ-thăn'ĕl) 1. The son of Zuar and prince of the tribe of Issachar (Num. 1:8, 2:5, 7:18).

2. The fourth son of Jesse and brother of David (1 Chr. 2:14).

3. A priest in the reign of David (1 Chr. 15:24).

4. A Levite, father of Shemaiah (1 Chr. 24:6).

5. The fifth son of Obed-edom (1 Chr. 26:4).

6. One of the princes of Judah in the reign of Jehoshaphat (2 Chr. 17:7).

7. A chief of the Levites in the reign of Josiah (2 Chr. 35:9).

8. A priest of the family of Pashur in the time of Ezra (Ezra 10:22).

9. The representative of the priestly family of Jedaiah in the time of Joiakim (Neh. 12:21).

10. A Levite, of the sons of Asaph, who participated in the dedication of the wall of Jerusalem (Neh. 12:36).

Nethaniah (nĕth'à-nī'à) 1. The son of Elishama and the father of Ishmael who murdered Gedaliah (2 K. 25:23-25). Nethaniah was a member of the royal family of Judah.

2. One of the four sons of Asaph (1 Chr. 25:2, 12).

3. A Levite in the reign of Jehoshaphat (2 Chr. 17:8).

4. The father of Jehudi (Jer. 36:14).

Nethinim (nĕth'ĭ-nĭm) a title applied specifically to a group connected with the services of the temple. The term *Nathan* seems to indicate that these were particularly appointed to the liturgical offices. The Levites were given to Aaron and his sons, that is, to the priests as an order and were logically the first Nethinim. Initially they were only attendants, and their work must have been laborious. The first conquests, however, brought them their share of the captive slaves of the Midianites, and 320 were given to them to care for the tabernacle properties, while thirty-two they assigned especially to the priests. Thus these established the background for the Nethinim princes appointed to the service of the Levites (Ezra 8:20). From this time, the Nethinim probably lived within the precincts of the temple, doing the more laborious work, and so enabling the Levites to take a higher position as the religious representatives and instructors of the people.

Netophah (nḗ-tō'fà) a town, the name of which occurs only in the catalogue of those who returned with Zerubbabel from the Captivity (Ezra 2:22; Neh. 7:26). Evidently located near Bethlehem, Netophah was the home of two of David's fighting men (2 Sam. 23:28-29).

Netophathite (nḗ-tŏf'à-thīt) an inhabitant of Netophah (2 Sam. 23:28).

nettle 1. A plant which is found in the unweeded garden (Prov. 24:31). According to Zeph. 2:9 this plant is found whenever the cultivation of the land is neglected.

2. A second term, *kimmos*, is used in Isa. 34:13 and Hos. 9:6. This nettle seems to be found everywhere in Palestine.

new moon the first day of the lunar month was observed as a holy day. In addition to the daily sacrifice two young bullocks, a ram, and seven lambs of the first year were offered as a burnt offering, with the proper meat offerings and drink offerings, and a kid as a sin offering (Num. 28:11-15). As on a sabbath, trade and handicraft work were discontinued (Amos 8:5), and the temple was open for public worship (Ezek. 46:3). The new moon was an occasion for state banquets (1 Sam. 20:5-24). The new moons are generally mentioned to indicate that they were regarded as a peculiar class of holy days, distinguished from the solemn feasts and the sabbath (Ezek. 45:17). The seventh new moon of the religious year, that of Tishri, inaugurated the civil year and had a significance and rites of its own. On the thirtieth day of the month, watchmen were placed on commanding heights surrounding Jerusalem for the purpose of watching the sky. As soon as each of them detected the moon, he rushed to a house in the city, which was kept for the purpose, and there was examined by the president of the Sanhedrin. When the evidence of the appearance was deemed satisfactory, the president stood and formally announced, "It is consecrated." The information was immediately sent throughout the land from the Mount of Olives by beacon fires on the tops of the hills.

New Testament the second of the two segments into which the Biblical materials are naturally divided, the first being the OT. The term testament represents the Lat. *testamentum*, which is used to translate the Gr. *diathēkē*, covenant. The first covenant, according to Heb. 9:15-20, was dedicated with blood, but was in no sense a testament. The second is readily seen to be a testament inasmuch as the death of the testator was required to give it effectiveness.

I. GENERAL CONSIDERATIONS. The language of the twenty-seven books which compose the

NT is *koine* Greek, or common Greek. Koine Greek owes its significance and importance to the conquests of Alexander the Great. This language had been received into Palestine during the 300 years following the conquests of Alexander. This highly inflected language is most expressive, and perhaps partially explains Paul's reference to Christ's coming in the fullness of time (Gal. 4:4). Certain contemporary scholars, Matthew Black and others, have attempted to show that the NT documents surely have an Aramaic background. For further study, see Black's *An Aramaic Approach to the Gospels and Acts* (1946).

The writer of the NT documents, as other contemporaries, often employed the services of an amanuensis, to whom he dictated his letters, affixing the salutation "with his own hand" (1 Cor. 16:21; Col. 4:18; 2 Thess. 3:17). These secretaries wrote on papyrus, which was singularly fragile. The papyrus fragments which have remained until the twentieth century have been preserved under peculiar circumstances, as at Herculaneum or in Egyptian tombs. Parchment (2 Tim. 4:13) was also used and was more durable, but was proportionally rarer and more costly. It is only reasonable to conclude the autographs perished during the solemn pause which followed the apostolic age. In the time of the Diocletian persecution (A.D. 303), copies of the Christian scriptures were sufficiently numerous to furnish a special object for persecutors. At this time renegades who saved themselves by surrendering the sacred books were called traditores by their more courageous brethren. Thus, no MS of the NT of the first three centuries remains. Some of the oldest extant MSS were certainly copied from others which dated from within the first three centuries. Some 4000 to 5000 manuscript copies of the NT in whole or in part exist.

It is only natural to acknowledge inevitable corruptions of the text. Copyists became careless and sometimes were not articulate in the Greek language. Still other copyists attempted to improve the grammatical constructions and the stylistic forms of the MSS, to correct supposed errors in history and geography, and to adjust the OT quotations to correspond to the Greek of the LXX. There was likewise the attempt to harmonize the gospels. Thus, marginal notes made by a scribe of a previous generation naturally became incorporated into the text of the succeeding scribal generation. Variant readings multiplied. When each variant reading in every MS is totaled, the number approximates 200,000. It has been suggested that 95% of these have no authority and reliability

and only a small fraction of the remaining 5% actually affect the meaning and the interpretation of the NT. However, the existence of such variant readings substantiates the existence of a very significant field of criticism, textual criticism. The textual critic, through his tedious and tiring work, attempts to reproduce the original text.

II. TEXTUAL APPARATUS. (1) *The Manuscripts.* The many NT MSS fall into two divisions: uncial MSS, those in Greek capitals; and cursives, in small "long hand" and with divisions of words. In approximately the ninth century writing changed from the uncial method to the cursive. The fourth century A.D. marked a dramatic turning point in the history of the Greek NT. With the conversion of Constantine, persecutions ceased and copies of the Scriptures multiplied rapidly. It was also at this time that the fragile papyrus roll was replaced by the parchment codex for literary use. These uncial MSS, uncial itself meaning inch-long letters, represent letters which are formed singularly and without connection with other letters. The initial letters at the beginning of the paragraphs were rather large, actually one-inch letters. The primary uncial MSS are: (a) B (Codex Vaticanus). This MS is in the Vatican Library in Rome and apparently dates from the middle of the fourth century. B is probably the oldest of the uncials, and without question it is the best. This MS originally contained all of the Greek Bible, certain sections of the OT now being lost and the NT section lacks the Pastorals, Revelation, and Heb. 9:14 ff. (b) Aleph (Codex Sinaiticus). This MS of the fourth century, likely toward the close of that century, is in the British Museum in London. C. Tischendorf numbered it by the first letter of the Hebrew alphabet because of his unwillingness to place it at the end of the Roman alphabet. This MS ranks next to B, both in date and in value. This is the only uncial MS containing all of the NT. It was discovered by Tischendorf in 1844 at the Monastery of St. Catherine on Mount Sinai. (c) A (Codex Alexandrinus). A dates from the fifth century and is also on display in the British Museum. A, probably written in Alexandria, contains the whole NT except Mt. 1:1–25:6; Jn. 6:50–8:52; 2 Cor. 4:13–12:6. (d) C (Codex Ephraemi Rescriptus). C was obviously written in Egypt in the fifth century and is now in the National Library of Paris. It contains fragments of all the NT books except 2 Thess. and 2 Jn. C is important because it is a palimpsest, that is, the original MS, which contained the Greek text of the NT, has been erased so that a Greek translation of sermons or treatises was written over the vellum that once contained the entire Greek Bible. Chemicals can be employed to restore the scriptural text in most places. (e) D (Codex Bezae). A. Souter assigns this text to the fifth century, although many scholars assign it a sixth-century dating. D is in the Cambridge University Library and contains only the gospels and Acts. D is a bilingual MS, the Greek contained on the left page and the Latin on the right, one column on each page. (f) W (Washington Codex). Although the date of W is uncertain, it was surely not earlier than the fourth century and not later than the sixth. This MS is now in the Freer Art Gallery of the Smithsonian Institute in Washington, D.C. This codex has no chapter or section titles in the margin. It does, however, contain brief titles at the beginning and end of each gospel. The text likewise contains paragraph divisions with limited punctuation and abbreviation.

The second major division of NT MSS is the minuscules. As has already been noted, the uncial codex was replaced in the tenth century by the minuscule. The writing of the minuscule was much smaller than the uncial and some of the letters were formed differently. Some 2600 minuscule MSS are known. These MSS are designated by Arabic figures, but according to no prescribed system.

Of the more than 70 papyrus fragments of the NT which have been discovered, none are more important than the Chester Beatty (P45, P46, P47) and the Bodmer papyri (P66, P72, P74, P75). The Bodmer papyri contain elements of John's gospel, Jude, the Epistles of Peter, Acts, the Catholic Epistles, and Luke's gospel. The Chester Beatty papyri preserve portions of the gospels and Acts, Pauline epistles, and Revelation respectively. The earliest known portion of the Greek NT is a very tiny fragment of papyrus which dates from no later than A.D. 135–40 and contains a part of Jn. 18:31–33, 37. It is in the John Rylands Library in Manchester, England, and is known as the John Rylands Papyrus, or P52.

(2) *The Printed Text.* The first printed text of the NT was produced by Erasmus in 1516. This text was reprinted in 1518 and a corrected edition appeared in 1519, a third edition in 1522, a fourth in 1527, and a fifth in 1535. Cardinal Ximenes, a Roman Catholic of Spain, had for some years been involved in the preparation of a text of the NT. It was actually printed in 1514, but numerous delays prevented its availability before 1521. It was produced at Alcalá, which was called Complutum by the Romans; thus the edition was known

as the Complutensian edition. His NT text was only a part of his six-volume work known as the Complutensian Polyglot. Other editions of the Greek NT soon followed, but none gained more note than the texts of Robert Stephanus of Paris, which text appeared in 1546, 1549, 1550, 1551. Theodore Beza began work which resulted in the issuance of nine editions of the Greek NT between 1565 and 1604. These texts were based on Stephanus' third edition (1550). This text in turn had been based primarily upon Erasmus' fourth or fifth editions. The 1550 text of Stephanus is the *textus receptus* in England. The textus receptus of the continent is the first Elzevir edition, which was printed at Leyden in 1624. This text is based primarily upon the Stephanus edition of 1550, although it differs from this text in approximately 300 incidences. Beza's edition of 1598 served primarily as the text upon which the Authorized Version of the English Bible was based.

(3) *Chapter and Verse Divisions.* The present chapter divisions are credited to Stephen Langton, who later became Archbishop of Canterbury, and who died in 1228. The present verse divisions were made by Stephanus in the Greek NT which he published in 1551.

V.E.G.

New Year see **Feast of Trumpets**

Neziah (nê-zī'å) the founder of a family of Nethinim, who returned with Zerubbabel from the Babylonian captivity (Ezra 2:54; Neh. 7:56).

Nezib (nē'zĭb) a town of Judah, located in the district of the Shephelah or lowland (Josh. 15:43).

Nibhaz (nĭb'hăz) an idol of the Avvites, introduced by them into Samaria in the time of Shalmaneser (2 K. 17:31). There is little information concerning the character of this idol.

Nibshan (nĭb'shăn) one of the six cities of Judah (Josh. 15:62) which were in the district of *midbar* (wilderness).

Nicanor (nĭ-kā'nôr) one of the first deacons (Acts 6:5).

Nicodemus (nĭk'ô-dē'mŭs) a Pharisee, a ruler of the Jews, and a teacher of Israel (Jn. 3:1, 10), whose secret visit to Jesus was the occasion of a discourse recorded by John. Nicodemus was a member of the Jewish Sanhedrin and the few words which he spoke against the injustice of his colleagues (Jn. 7:50) may not disclose his faith, but his willingness to assist in the burial of Jesus (Jn. 19:39) indicates his faith and affection.

Nicolaitans (nĭk'ô-lā'ĭ-tănz) a party or sect mentioned in Rev. 2:6, 15, whose practice is severely reproved. This group followed the doctrine of Balaam and taught that Christians were free to eat things sacrificed to idols and to commit the excesses characteristic to heathenism. It is presumed that the Nicolaitans were the followers of some Nicolaus. Some have conjectured that the Nicolaitans are to be connected with the Nicolaus of Acts 6:5, but this conjecture is without substantial evidence.

A sect of the Nicolaitans existed in the third century among the Gnostics of that generation; they also postulated the freedom of the flesh.
Nicolaus (nĭk′ō-lā′ŭs) a native of Antioch, a proselyte of Judaism. Nicolaus became a convert and earned the reputation of being a man of honest report, full of the Holy Ghost and of wisdom. He was chosen as one of the first seven deacons, who were elected at the insistence of the Apostles for the purpose of supervising and caring for the interest of the Greek-speaking widows. It is to be questioned seriously whether the sect of the Nicolaitans mentioned in Rev. 2:6, 15 had any connection with Nicolaus.
Nicopolis (nĭ-kŏp′ō-lĭs) Paul was in Nicopolis at the time of the writing of the Epistle to Titus, and he indicates in Tit. 3:12 that he hoped to winter there. Nothing in the epistle indicates which Nicopolis is here intended, cities of this name existing in Asia, Africa, and Europe. The subscription appended to this epistle, which subscription, of course, has no authority, indicates that this is the Macedonian Nicopolis. In all probability the Nicopolis mentioned by Paul was the town in Epirus, a town on the peninsula on the west of the Bay of Actium.
Niger (nī′jĕr) the surname of Simeon, one of the teachers and prophets in the church at Antioch (Acts 13:1).
night the period of darkness (Gen. 1:5), opposed to "day," the period of light. The period of night was divided into three distinct periods: sunset to midnight, midnight to cockcrow, and cockcrow to sunrise (Ex. 14:24; Judg. 7:19; Lam. 2:19). The Grecian and Roman divisions consisted of four watches, cf. Mk. 6:48 and Lk. 12:38.
night hawk the etymology of the word points to some bird of prey, an unclean bird. The LXX and Vulg. identify the night hawk as an owl.
Nile (nīl) the great river of Egypt. 1. *Names of the Nile*. The Hebrew names of the Nile distinguish it from other rivers. They are "The Black," "The River," "The River of Egypt," and "The Nachal of Egypt," and "The Rivers of Cush."

2. *Description of the Nile*. The Nile is approximately 3700 miles long, but in a narrower sense as it presents those peculiarities which have contributed to its fame, it is approximately 1650 miles long. The banks are extremely steep and tall, at places 1000 feet in height. Below Cairo the river divides and several channels move toward the sea. These branches water the delta as the water pours over the valley; covering it with great sheets of water, the river deposits rich soil. The ordinary average increase of the soil in Egypt is estimated approximately four and one-half inches per century. Apart from this annual overflow of the Nile, Egypt would be nothing less than barren desert. The river begins rising slowly at the first part of June and between July 15 to 20 the increase becomes very rapid. Water ceases to rise toward the end of September and remains at the same height for approximately three weeks. In October the water rises again, attaining its greatest height, then decreasing and in January to March the fields gradually dry. Thus the soil is not only softened, but is likewise fertilized.

3. *Life Along the River*. The banks of the river are enlivened by the women who come to draw water and to bathe. The herds graze on the available grass and are likewise later driven to the water. The river abounds in fish (Num. 11:5); crocodiles are also plentiful and can be seen sunning themselves upon the bank. In Biblical times the river abounded in reeds and water plants. Many boats navigate its channels in search of commercial success, while small skiffs carry pleasure-seekers.

The Nile is constantly before the Biblical student in the history of Israel in Egypt. Into it the male children were cast; into it or rather in some canal or pool, was the ark of Moses placed, and there it was found by Pharaoh's daughter when she went down to bathe. When the plagues were sent, the sacred river—the main support of the people—and its waters everywhere were turned into blood.
Nimrah (nĭm′rà) a place mentioned by this name in Num. 32:3, among those which formed the districts of the land of "Jazer and the land of Gilead." If it is the same as Bethnimrah, it belonged to the tribe of Gath. Eusebius, however, cites Nimrah as a "city of Reuben in Gilead."
Nimrim (nĭm′rĭm) a location in the country of Moab, famous for its waters. The water is mentioned in the denunciations of that nation by Isaiah (15:6) and Jeremiah (48:34).
Nimrod (nĭm′rŏd) a son of Cush and a grandson of Ham. The events of his life are recorded

in Gen. 10:8–10. It is somewhat questionable whether the prowess of Nimrod rested on his achievements as a hunter or as a conqueror. The literal rendering of the Hebrew terms would doubtless apply to the former, but they may be recorded as a translation of a proverbial expression originally current in the land of Nimrod, where the terms significant of "hunter" and "hunting" appear to have been applied to the forays of the sovereigns against the surrounding nations. However, the context favors the special application of the term to the case of conquest. Nimrod is remembered chiefly because (1) he was a Cushite; (2) he established an empire in Shinar; and (3) he extended this empire northward along the course of the Tigris over Assyria, where he founded a second group of capitals, Nineveh, Rehoboth, Calah, and Resen.

Nimshi (nĭm'shī) the grandfather of Jehu, who is generally called "the son of Nimshi" (1 K. 19:16; 2 K. 9:2, 14, 20; 2 Chr. 22:7).

Nineveh (nĭn'ĕ-vĕ) the capital of the ancient kingdom and empire of Assyria. Nineveh is first mentioned in the OT in connection with the primitive dispersion and migration of the human race. In a limited sense, Nineveh represented the city which stood on the eastern bank of the Tigris, and pointed at the mouth of the tributary known as the Khosr, approximately twenty-seven miles above the conjunction of the Zab with the main stream. In a much broader sense, Nineveh represents the entire population about the capital city and occupied the district where the Tigris and the Upper Zab join.

Nineveh, constructed by people of Babylonian origin and background, worshiped the goddess Ishtar as the principal deity. This cult was soon carried as far as Egypt and southwest Asia Minor.

The Assyrians were ferocious warriors, and the cultural spoils of conquered nations and cities were soon brought to the capital and used for decoration and embellishment. In 650 B.C., Ashurbanipal gathered a great library, which consisted of documents inscribed on clay tablets and which related to history, astronomy, mathematics, ritual, and incantations. Much of the library's content consisted of older works which had been brought from Babylon. The prophet Nahum spoke vigorously against Nineveh and called her the bloody city (see Nah. 3:1).

When the Assyrian empire began to decline in military advantage, Nabopolassar, the governor of Babylon, declared himself and his state to be independent and some thirteen years later the capital Umman-manda, cooperating with Nabopolassar, captured and destroyed Nineveh.

The desolation was so complete that in the Graeco-Roman age Nineveh became like a myth. Although for generations, the ruins which occupied the presumed site of Nineveh seemed to consist of mere shapeless heaps of mounds of earth and rubbish, C. Rich, an Englishman who resided in Baghdad in the 1820s, became convinced that the ruins of Nineveh were concealed under these mounds of obvious rubbish. P. E. Botta, the French consul at Mosul, began to excavate in 1843. Although his interest was soon diverted to another site, in approximately 1850 A. H. Layard began excavation at Nimroud, eighteen miles south of Kouyunjik, and finally he began excavating at Kouyunjik which proved to be the site of Nineveh. George Smith continued this excavation in the middle 1870s. The walls of Nineveh have been traced and indicate a city of some three miles in length and approximately a mile and a half in width. This city contained approximately 1800 acres. However, it must be remembered that the Hebrews always included under the name of a great city the surrounding areas and cities of the immediate area.

The city of Nineveh is significant to the Biblical scholar because of the Assyrian place in Hebrew history. It was Assyrian society which influenced the Hebrews, and it was the Assyrian heel which ground the Hebrews into subjection.

Ninevites (nĭn'ĕ-vīts) the inhabitants of Nineveh (Lk. 11:30).

Nisan (nī'săn) following the Captivity, Abib, the first month of the year, was renamed Nisan. Nisan corresponds generally to March.

Nisroch (nĭs'rŏk) an idol of Nineveh, in whose temple Sennacherib was worshiping when assassinated by his sons, Adrammelech and Sharezer (2 K. 19:37; Isa. 37:38). Although scholars conjecture as to the origin of the name, no final decision has been reached.

nitre the term occurs in Prov. 25:20 and in Jer. 2:22. Some scholars insist that this is a reference to potassium nitrate, while others suggest that nitre is sodium carbonate and potassium carbonate. An alkali, the substance was used in washing clothes.

No (nō) this term also occurs in Nah. 3:8 as **Noamon** (nō'ăm'ŏn), a city of Egypt, also known as Thebes. The second portion of Noamon is the name of Amon, the chief deity of Thebes, mentioned or alluded to in connection with this place in Jeremiah, "Behold, I will punish Amon in No, and Pharaoh, and Egypt, with their gods and their kings" (46:25). After the Hyksos were driven from Egypt, Ahmose I turned his attention to the improvement of his kingdom and Thebes received significant attention. Gallus, the Roman, finally destroyed Thebes in the revolt of Upper Egypt in 30 B.C.

Noadiah (nō'à-dī'à) 1. A Levite, son of Binnui, who weighed the vessels of gold and silver belonging to the temple upon the return from Babylon (Ezra 8:33).

2. A prophetess who joined Sanballat and Tobiah in their attempt to intimidate Nehemiah (Neh. 6:14).

Noah (nō'à) the tenth in descent from Adam, and the son of Lamech, the grandson of Methuselah. Little is known of Lamech, Noah's father; Lamech did indicate that he called his son's name Noah because, "This name shall comfort us." Of Noah himself nothing is known from this point until he is 500 years old, at which time he begat three sons, Shem, Ham, and Japheth. Yet the Biblical record does afford a glimpse of the society in the antediluvian world (see Gen. 6).

The best-remembered event of Noah's life is not the fact that he lived in an antediluvian society, but that it was he whom God chose to build an ark. The Biblical records do indicate an age of almost universal apostasy, and in the midst of this society Noah prevailed as a righteous man. The ark was built by divine direction, and the flood itself did not come until Noah was 600 years of age. In 2 Pet. 2:5 Noah is referred to as a "preacher of righteousness." The ark was made of gopher wood, a kind of timber, which both for its lightness and its durability, was employed by the Phoenicians in building their vessels. After the boards of the ark were fastened, each was to be protected by a coating of pitch, which was to be placed on both the inside and outside of the ark. In effect, the ark became waterproof. The ark was to consist of a number of small compartments for the convenient distribution of the different animals and their food. These compartments were to be arranged in three tiers, one above another. God likewise instructed Noah concerning the provision of a window in the ark. Nothing is said concerning the shape of the ark, but its dimensions are given. It was 300 cubits in length, 50 in breadth, and 30 in height. Assuming twenty-one inches to be the measurement of the cubit, the ark would have been 525 feet in length, 87½ feet in breadth, and 52½ feet in height.

God likewise specified the inmates of the ark. Noah and his wife, his sons and their wives, along with a pair of each kind of animals, were to inhabit the ark. Birds, domestic animals, and creeping things are particularly mentioned.

Noah was to provide for the needs of each, stores "of every kind of food that is eaten." The pairs of animals were limited to one of unclean animals, but of clean animals and birds Noah was to take seven pairs.

When the ark was completed, God instructed Noah to enter the ark along with his family and provide for their use the clean animals which they needed for food and sacrifice. The flood came violently upon the ark. The Scripture indicates that Jehovah closed the door to the ark prior to the coming of the violent flood. When the "purpose of the Creator" had been accomplished, the waters began to abate. Upon observing the mountain tops, Noah then waited the same length of time that the storm had raged and then sent forth birds to discover whether the waters had subsided and had abated from the surface of the earth. He still tarried in the ark, waiting until God himself should give the order for disembarking. On the first day of the first month, Noah removed the covering from the ark and saw that the earth was dry, but it was an additional eight weeks before God gave the order to disembark. Upon disembarking, Noah built an altar and offered sacrifice to his God.

God then instructed Noah and his family to be fruitful and to multiply, so that the new world which had been cleansed by the flood might have a new beginning. As was inevitable, Noah gave his life to agriculture. One of the shocking experiences of the life of Noah is occasioned by his interest in agriculture. He had planted a vineyard, making wine from the fruit, and making himself drunk through drink. He was mocked by his son Ham, although the other sons attempted to protect their father. Upon regaining sobriety, Noah learned what had occurred and foretold shame and a degraded future for the posterity of Ham. With the curse on his youngest son was joined a blessing on the other two. Following this, nothing is known of Noah except the sum of his years. V.E.G.

Noah (nō'à) one of the five daughters of Zelophehad (Num. 26:33, 27:1, 36:11; Josh. 17:3).

Noamon see **No**

Nob (nōb) a sacerdotal city in the tribe of Benjamin and situated on some eminence near Jerusalem. In 1 Sam. 23:11 this was a town of the priests. After the ark was captured, the tabernacle was for a time pitched at Nob. During this time, David fled to Nob, and Ahimelech, uninformed concerning the existing problem between Saul and David, allowed David and his men to eat the showbread of the tabernacle. Upon receiving the report of this, Saul called the priests and ordered them executed.

Nobah (nō′bá) 1. An Israelite warrior, a Manassite, who during the conquest of the territory on the east of Jordan possessed himself of the town of Kenath and the villages or hamlets depending upon it (Num. 32:42).

2. The name given to Kenath and the villages dependent upon it by the Israelite warrior Nobah (Num. 32:42).

Nobai (nō′bī) a chief of the people who with Nehemiah sealed the covenant (Neh. 10:19).

Nod (nŏd) an area east of Eden to which Cain journeyed and lived (Gen. 4:16).

Nodab (nō′dăb) an Arab tribe mentioned in 1 Chr. 5:19.

Noe (nō′ê) the patriarch Noah (Mt. 24:37–38; Lk. 3:36, 17:26–27).

Nogah (nō′gà) one of the thirteen sons of David who were born to him in Jerusalem (1 Chr. 3:7).

Nohah (nō′hà) the fourth son of Benjamin (1 Chr. 8:2).

Non (nŏn) Nun, the father of Joshua (1 Chr. 7:27).

Noph (nŏf) a city of Egypt, Memphis. The Hebrew forms *Noph* and *Moph* are contracted from the ancient Egyptian common name, *Men-nufr* or *Men-nefru*. The Hebrew forms are regarded as representing the colloquial forms of the name, current with the Shemites, if not with the Egyptians also. See Isa. 19:13; Jer. 2:16; Ezek. 30:13; Hos. 9:6.

Nophah (nō′fà) a Moabite town, mentioned only in Num. 21:30.

nose jewel a ring of metal, sometimes of gold or silver, inserted into the side of the nostril for an ornament.

number scholars have not been able to find evidence that the ancient Hebrews used numbers in their written calculations. They rather used the letters of the alphabet to represent numbers.

It seems evident that at least some of the numbers mentioned in Scripture are intended to be representative rather than determinative. Certain numbers, as 7, 10, 40, 100, were regarded as giving the idea of completeness. "Sevenfold" occurs in Gen. 4:24, "seven times" in Lev. 26:24, and "seven ways" in Deut. 28:25. Ten is a preferential number as exemplified in the Ten Commandments and in the law of the tithe. "Seventy," compounded of seven times ten, appears frequently, e.g., seventyfold (Gen. 4:24; Mt. 18:22). Its definite use appears in the offering of seventy shekels (Num.

7:13, 19) and in seventy years of captivity (Jer. 25:11). "Five" appears in the table of punishments and of legal requirements (Ex. 22:1; Lev. 5:16; Num. 5:7). "Four" is used in reference to the four winds (Dan. 7:2), the four corners of the earth, the four creatures, four rivers of paradise (Gen. 2:10), and concerning the four beasts (Rev. 4:6). "Three" was regarded, both by the Jews and other nations, as an especially complete and mystic number. "Twelve," three times four, appears in twelve tribes, twelve stones in the high priest's breastplate, twelve apostles, twelve foundation stones, and twelve gates (Rev. 21:19–21). "Forty" appears in many numerations—forty days of Moses (Ex. 24:18), forty days in the wilderness (Num. 14:34), and forty days and nights of Elijah (1 K. 19:8). "One hundred" is used to describe a large number (Lev. 26:8), a length of the tabernacle court (Ex. 27:18), and a hundred stripes (Prov. 17:10). The mystic number 666 appears in Rev. 13:18.

Numbers the fourth book of the Law or Pentateuch. Its name is traceable to the double numbering or census. *Contents.* The book contains the history of the Israelites from the time of their leaving Sinai until their arrival at the borders of the Promised Land in the fortieth year of their wanderings. The principal divisions are:

1. Preparations for the departure from Sinai (1:1–10:10).

2. The journey from Sinai to the borders of Canaan (10:11–14:45).

3. Laws and events of the wilderness wanderings (15:1–19:22).

4. From Kadesh to the plains of Moab (20:1–36:13).

(a) The purpose of the encampment at Sinai has now been accomplished, and it is time to depart in order that the object may be achieved for which Israel has been sanctified. This object is the occupation of the Promised Land. Israel must, therefore, be organized. Thus the book opens with the numbering of the people, chs. 1–4. Chapters 5 and 6 contain certain laws which seemed to supplement the legislature in Leviticus. Chapters 7:1 to 10:10 record events occurring at this time and regulations in connection with these events.

(b) The march from Sinai to the borders of Canaan is described in this section. Chapter 10 (vss. 14–28) describes the order of the march, while certain sections of 10–12:15 describe various events of the journey. The sending of the spies and their reporting are described in 12:16–14:45.

(c) A record of the wanderings (15:1–19).

(d) The narrative returns abruptly to the

second encampment of the Israelites in Kadesh. Here Miriam died, the people murmured for water, and Moses and Aaron were forbidden to enter the Promised Land (20:1–13). The Edomites refused the request to journey through their country, turning out in arms to defend their border. Turning southward, the Israelites journeyed along the western borders of Idumaea, stopping at Mount Hor. At this point Aaron, Moses, and Eleazar ascended the mountain. After Aaron's death, the march continued southward. There is no information concerning the march along the eastern edge of Edom, but suddenly the Israelites are pictured on the borders of Moab. Here they successfully encountered and defeated the kings of the Amorites and of Baashan (21:10–35). The king of Moab thus became alarmed and sent for magicians to curse his enemies, hence the episode of Balaam (22:1–24:25). The Moabites likewise attempted to weaken the Israelites through the influence of the Moabitish women (25:1). The book concludes with the recapitulation of the various encampments of the Israelites in the desert (33:1–49), the command to destroy the Canaanites (33:50–56), the boundaries of the Promised Land (ch. 34), the appointment of the cities of the Levites and the cities of refuge (ch. 35), and further directions respecting heiresses.

V.E.G.

Nun (nŭn) the father of the Jewish captain Joshua (Ex. 33:11).

nurse 1. A nurse employed to suckle an infant (Ex. 2:7–9; 2 K. 11:2). Rebekah's nurse, Deborah, remained in the family as an honored servant.

2. A male or female who served as a foster parent, either of an infant or an older child (Num. 11:12; Ruth 4:16; 2 Sam. 4:4).

nuts 1. The term *botnim* is translated nuts, and obviously it is a reference to the fruit of the pistachio tree. Syria and Palestine are famous for these trees. See Gen. 43:11.

2. The Hebrew word *egoz* occurs in the Song of S. 6:11. This term likely refers to the walnut tree. It is found on the slope of Lebanon and of Hermon.

Nymphas (nĭm'făs) a wealthy and zealous Christian in Laodicea (Col. 4:15).

O

oak numerous terms, referring to various species of oak, occur in the OT. (1) *El* occurs in Gen. 14:6. Plural forms of the term also occur, perhaps signifying a grove or plantation (Isa. 1:29, 49:3; Ezek. 31:14). (2) *Elah* occurs in Isa. 6:13; Hos. 4:13, etc. (3) *Elon* occurs frequently in the OT and must designate some variety of oak. (4) *Ilan* occurs in Dan. 4 as the tree which Nebuchadnezzar saw in his dream. (5) *Allah* occurs only in Josh. 24:26 and is translated oak. Thus it can be seen that several species of oak grew in Palestine, and that some of the terms employed may not be used in the technical sense of the horticulturist.

oath an appeal to divine authority to ratify an assertion. Thus employing this principle, the oath which appealed to the highest authority has always been held most binding. The sovereign's name is sometimes used as a form of obligation (Gen. 43:15; 2 Sam. 11:11). Other forms of oaths employed items which were connected with God (Mt. 5:33, 23:16–22). The forms of adjuration mentioned in Scripture are: (1) Lifting up the hand (Gen. 14:22; Lev. 24:14; Deut. 33:40). (2) Putting the hand under the thigh of the person to whom the promise was made. (3) Oaths were sometimes taken before the altar or if the person was not in Jerusalem, in a position looking toward the temple (1 K. 8:31; 2 Chr. 6:22). (4) By dividing a victim and passing between or distributing the pieces (Gen. 15:10, 17; Jer. 34:18). The Christian practice in the matter of oaths was generally founded upon the Jewish procedures.

Oaths might be taken for one of many reasons: (1) Agreement or stipulation for performance of certain acts (Gen. 14:22). (2) Alliance to the sovereign (2 Chr. 36:13; Eccl. 8:2). (3) Promissory oath of a ruler (Josh. 6:26; 1 Sam. 14:24, 28). (4) A vow made in the form of an oath (Lev. 5:4). (5) Judicial oaths. A man might require a pledge from a neighbor and in the case of injury happening to the pledge, the man might wish to clear himself by oath of the blame of damage (Ex.

22:10–11; 1 K. 8:31). Witnesses were apparently examined under oath (Lev. 5:1; Deut. 19:16–19; Prov. 29:24). A wife suspected of incontinence was required to clear herself by oath (Num. 5:19–22).

Jesus condemned the use of oaths, indicating that any statement beyond "Yea, yea; nay, nay" was of the Evil One (Mt. 5:33–37). Herod the tetrarch serves as an excellent illustration of the evil which may arise from oath-taking; his oath prompted him against his will to murder John the Baptizer (Mt. 14:3–12).

Obadiah (ō′bá-dī′á) 1. One of the five sons of Izrahiah, a descendant of Issachar (1 Chr. 7:3).

2. One of the six sons of Azel, a descendant of Saul (1 Chr. 8:38, 9:44).

3. A Levite, son of Shemaiah (1 Chr. 9:16).

4. The second of the lion-faced Gadites, who joined David at Ziklag (1 Chr. 12:9).

5. One of the princes of Judah in the reign of Jehoshaphat (2 Chr. 17:7).

6. A son of Jehiel, of the sons of Joab, who came up in the second caravan with Ezra (Ezra 8:9).

7. The governor of Ahab's palace (1 K. 18:3–4).

8. A priest, or family of priests, who sealed the covenant with Nehemiah (Neh. 10:5).

9. The father of Ishmaiah, who was chief of the tribe of Zebulun in David's reign (1 Chr. 27:19).

10. A Merarite Levite in the reign of Josiah, and one of the overseers of the workmen in the restoration of the temple (2 Chr. 34:12).

11. A prophet of Judah (Obad. 1). Little is known of Obadiah except what may be gleaned from the short book that bears his name. The Hebrew tradition, adopted by Jerome, maintains that Obadiah is the same person as the Obadiah of Ahab's reign, but this tradition lacks foundation as does another account which makes him to have been a converted Idumaean. The question of his date must depend upon the interpretation of vs. 11 of his prophecy. In this verse he speaks of the conquest of Jerusalem and the captivity of Judah. If his reference is to the well-known captivity by Nebuchadnezzar, then Obadiah must have lived at the time of the Babylonian captivity and have prophesied subsequently to the year 558 B.C. If his prophecy against Edom found its first fulfillment in the conquest of that country by Nebuchadnezzar in 583 B.C., the date is then fixed. It would have been voiced at some time in the five years between 588 and 583.

Contents. The book of Obadiah is a sustained denunciation of the Edomites. In disclosing a vision of the future glory of Zion, the prophet likewise pictures a double repayment upon her enemies. Prior to the Captivity, the Edomites were in a relationship to the Jews similar to that of the Samaritans following the Captivity. They were not only neighbors, they were also relatives. The prophet complains that they looked upon and rejoiced in the destruction of Jerusalem, that they triumphed over her and plundered her, and that they cut off the fugitives who were probably making their way through Idumaea to Egypt. He ultimately visualizes the houses of Jacob and Joseph consuming the house of Esau as fire devours stubble (vs. 18). The inhabitants of the city of Jerusalem, now captive, will return to Jerusalem and occupy the entire southern portion of Judah. Idumaea will be overrun by the Jews who have dwelt in the south. Judah will, in turn, extend herself as far as the fields of Ephraim and Samaria, while Benjamin will take possession of Gilead. Summarily, the book may be outlined as follows: (1) The inevitableness of Edom's destruction, vss. 1–9. (2) The basis for the destruction, vss. 10–14. (3) The nearness of the day of Jehovah, vss. 16–21. Obadiah, which is the shortest writing in the OT, has been described by some as a "hymn of hate." Nowhere in the NT is it quoted directly.

Obal (ō′băl) a son of Joktan and apparently a founder of an Arab tribe (Gen. 10:28).

Obed (ō′bĕd) 1. Son of Boaz and Ruth the Moabitess (Ruth 4:17). Circumstances of his birth are given in the book of Ruth and form an interesting portrayal of the religious and social life of the Israelites in the days of Eli.

2. Father of Azariah, one of the captains of hundreds who joined with Jehoiada in the revolution by which Athaliah fell (2 Chr. 23:1).

3. One of David's mighty men (1 Chr. 11:47).

4. One of the gatekeepers of the temple, son of Shemaiah (1 Chr. 26:7).

5. A descendant of Jarhad. He was a grandson of Zabad, one of David's mighty men (1 Chr. 2:37–38).

Obed-edom (ō′bĕd-ē′dŏm) 1. A Levite, apparently of the family of Kohath. Described as a Gittite (2 Sam. 6:10–11), he is likely a native of the Levitical city of Gath-rimmon. After the death of Uzzah, the ark was taken into the house of Obed-edom, where it remained for three months.

2. A Levite who acted as a doorkeeper for the ark (1 Chr. 15:18, 21).

3. A Levite who marched in front of the ark on its removal to Jerusalem (1 Chr.

15:24). Some conjecture that he is the same as the Gittite described in 1.

Obil (ō′bĭl) an Ishmaelite who served as camel herder during the reign of David (1 Chr. 27:30).

oblation see **sacrifice**

Oboth (ō′bŏth) one of the encampments of the Israelites, east of Moab (Num. 21:10, 33:43).

Ochran (ŏk′răn) an Asherite, father of Pagiel (Num. 1:13, 2:27, 7:72, 77).

Oded (ō′dĕd) 1. The father of Azariah the prophet in the reign of Asa and Azariah (2 Chr. 15:1).

2. A prophet of Jehovah who lived in Samaria at the time of Pekah's invasion of Judah (2 Chr. 28:9). Upon meeting the army of the Northern Kingdom returning from battle, the prophet accused them because of their unbrotherly conduct and used Jehovah's name in exhorting them to send the captors of Judah home.

offerings see **sacrifice**

officer the *hupēretēs* is an inferior officer of the court of justice, a messenger or bailiff, as the Roman lictor. The *praktores* at Athens were officers responsible for the registration and collections of fines imposed by the courts of justice.

Og (ŏg) a king of the Amorites of Bashan, whose rule extended over sixty cities. This rule extended from Jabbok to Mount Hermon (Deut. 3:8, 10; Num. 21:23–24). Joshua 12:4–5 and 13:12 indicate that he had residences at Ashtaroth and Edrei. Og was an exceedingly large man and possessed an iron bedstead which was nine cubits long and four cubits broad. The Israelites defeated and slew Og at Edrei and took possession of his territory (Num. 21:32–35; Deut. 3:14).

Ohad (ō′hăd) one of the six sons of Simeon (Gen. 46:10; Ex. 6:15).

Ohel (ō′hĕl) one of the seven sons of Zerubbabel (1 Chr. 3:20).

Oholah (ō-hō′lá) the name signifies infidelity to Jehovah; Samaria and the kingdom of Israel are personified as a woman of bad character (Ezek. 23:1–49).

Oholiab (ō-ho′lĭ-ăb) a member of the tribe of Dan; one who assisted Bezalel in fashioning furniture for the tabernacle (Ex. 31:6, 35:34).

Oholibah (ō-hŏl′ĭ-bà) the kingdom of Judah and Jerusalem personified as a woman of bad character (Ezek. 21:1–49).

Oholibamah (ō-hŏl′ĭ-bā′mà) a wife of Esau (Gen. 36:2).

oil although numerous oils were used by the Hebrews, the oil used most widely was olive oil.

The fruit of the olive ripens in the autumn and is either picked or shaken off carefully with a light stick. The fruit is carefully cleansed and was usually taken immediately to the press. If it was impossible to press the fruit immediately, the fruit was placed in sloping trays to permit the first juice to flow into other receptacles beneath. In order to make the oil, the fruit was either pressed in a mortar, crushed in a press loaded with wood or stones, ground in a mill, or trodden with the feet. Both the olives and the oil from the fruit were kept in jars which had been carefully cleansed, the oil then being drawn out for use in other smaller vessels.

Usages. (1) Food. (2) Cosmetic. Oil was used by the Jews for anointing the body following the bath and for giving the skin and hair an improved appearance. (3) Funeral. The body was anointed with oil by the Greeks and Romans, and a similar custom seems to have prevailed among the Jews. (4) Medicinal. As oil is used in many cases in contemporary medicinal practices, it is not surprising to note that it was so used among the Jews. Celsus repeatedly speaks of the use of oil to combat fevers. Josephus mentions that among remedies employed to treat Herod the Great was the oil bath. (5) Household uses. Oil was used for the lamps, both in the homes and at the Feast of Tabernacles (Ex. 25:6, 27:20–21; Lev. 19:2). (6) Ritualistic. Oil was mixed with certain offerings, e.g., flour or mill. Kings, priests, and prophets were anointed with oil or ointment. Oil was included among the Jews firstfruit offerings (Ex. 22:29; Num. 18:12; Deut. 18:4). (7) Shields, if covered with hide were anointed with oil prior to use. Metal shields were sometimes rubbed with oil in order to polish them.

ointment used almost as extensively as oil. (1) Cosmetic. Oil of myrrh is mentioned in Est. 2:12. (2) Funeral. Ointments, as well as oil, were used to anoint the bodies and the clothes in which the bodies were wrapped (Mt. 26:12; Mk. 14:3, 8; Lk. 23:56). (3) Medicinal. The balm of Gilead was used extensively. See Isa. 1:6; Jn. 9:6; Jer. 8:22; Rev. 3:18. (4) Ritual. The special ointment was prepared to be used in consecration (Ex. 19:7, 30:23, 33, 37:29). This was composed of myrrh, cassia, cinnamon, calamus, and olive oil.

Old Testament the first of the two portions of the Bible into which the work is naturally divided. This section of the Biblical record consists of thirty-nine books, divided into three groups: history, poetry, and prophetical books. Although this division is not ironclad, it conveniently and succinctly classifies the writings of the OT.

1. *The Language of the OT.* Most of the OT was originally written in Hebrew, except Ezra 4:8–6:18, 7:12–26; Jer. 10:11; Dan. 2:4–7:28, which were written in Aramaic. The letters of the Hebrew and Aramaic alphabets are unusually similar. The Hebrews regularly made use only of consonants, leaving the reader to supply the necessary vowels. However, by A.D. 700 Jewish scholars, who resided chiefly in Tiberias and Palestine, had supplied vowel points which indicated the proper voweling and followed the traditional pronunciation. These vowel signs gave greater rigidity to the text. These Jewish scholars are called Masoretes, from the Hebrew *masoreth*, and the text supplied with vowels is known as the Masoretic text (abbreviated MT). These scholars also added accents to indicate the proper accentuation of the words and the manner in which they were to be related.

2. *The MSS of the OT Text.* These MSS are divided into two primary classes, synagogue rolls and MSS for private usage. Of the latter, some are written in the square letters, while others in the cursive characters. The synagogue rolls, separate from each other, contain the Pentateuch, appointed sections of the prophets, the so-called Megilloth (Song of S., Ruth, Lam., Eccl., and Est.). The text of the synagogue rolls is written without vowels or accents. The date of the MS is ordinarily given in the subscription.

The Hebrew text of the OT was passed from generation to generation practically unchanged since at least A.D. 150. From this form, existing MSS are derived. Scholars generally believe that the original MSS of the OT books were written on skins. See Ps. 40:7; Jer. 36:14, 23. The existing MSS are usually of parchment or leather.

3. *The Printed Text.* After the inventing of printing, the Psalter was published in 1477. Eleven years later, in 1488 the entire printed Hebrew Bible was issued in folio from Soncino. In 1492 there appeared a volume containing the Pentateuch, the Five Megilloth, and the Haphtaroth (selected lessons from the prophets). In 1494, a companion volume containing the Prophets and the Hagiographa (except the Megilloth), was printed. This was the text used by Luther in his translation.

Although space does not permit detailed listing of the various publications, one of the more important publications is the edition of the MT, with critical and Masoretic appendices prepared by S. Baer and F. Delitzsch. Genesis appeared in 1869; other books followed at intervals. Another milestone was reached in the

formation of a revised text with the publication of S. Davidson's *Hebrew Text of the Old Testament, Revised from Critical Sources,* 1855.

The Ginsburg text was issued in London in 1894, a second edition in four volumes by C. D. Ginsburg appeared in London in 1926. R. Kittel's edition, printed at Leipzig in 1906 has been revised in a second edition, appearing in 1909. The third edition by R. Kittel, P. Kahle, A. Alt, and O. Eissfeldt was published in 1937 at Stuttgart.

4. *Rudiments of Interpretation.* The knowledge of Hebrew words is gleaned from the context, from parallel passages, from the traditional interpretations preserved in Jewish commentaries and dictionaries, from the ancient versions, and from cognate languages. Syntax must be thoroughly investigated, with care being given to the particular type of literature and the special syntax involved. The interpreter must approach the OT, having first learned well the word of Paul (2 Tim. 3:16), "All Scripture is given by inspiration of God and is profitable for doctrine, for reproof, for correction, for instruction in righteousness . . ." The interpreter can likewise be instructed by the interpretation of Jesus especially illustrated in the Sermon on the Mount.   V.E.G.

olive no tree is more closely associated with the history and civilization of man than the olive tree. The history of the olive tree is interwoven with that of the Jewish people. Many of the scriptural associations of the olive tree are poetical. It has this remarkable interest in that its foliage is the earliest mentioned by name (Gen. 8:11). It is the emblem of prosperity and blessing (Ps. 42:8). To the later prophets the olive tree is a symbol of beauty and strength. Following the Captivity, when the Israelites kept the Feast of Tabernacles, they brought olive branches from the "mount" (Neh. 8:15). "The mount" is without question the famous Mount of Olives. In the Romans passage which deals with the Jewish problem (Rom. 9–11), the Gentiles are the "wild olive" grafted into the "good olive." Once the Jews belonged to the "good olive" and with the "good olive" they shall again be incorporated.

Olive yards are a matter of course in the descriptions of the country, just as vineyards and cornfields (Judg. 15:6; 1 Sam. 8:14). Almost every village had its own olive grove. Cultivation of the olive groves had a close connection with the domestic life of Israel, their trade, and even public and religious ceremonies. The oil was used in coronations, thus it was an emblem of sovereignty. The tree thrives best in warm and sunny conditions. It is of a moderate height, with knotty gnarled trunks and smooth ash-colored bark. It grows slowly, but it lives to an immense age. Its look is indicative of tenacious vigor. The leaves are not deciduous. See oil

Olives, Mount of although several general references to the Mount of Olives occur in the OT, only one specific reference to the "Mount of Olives" occurs (Zech. 14:4). See 2 Sam. 15:36; 1 K. 11:7; Neh. 8:15; Ezek. 11:23. In the NT the reference occurs in three forms: 1. "The Mount of Olives"; 2. "The Mount called *Elaion*" in Lk. 19:29, 21:37; 3. "The Mount called Olivet," in Acts 1:12.

1. *Site and Description.* The Mount of Olives is the well-known eminence on the east of Jerusalem, intimately and characteristically connected with some of the greatest and most significant events of the history of the OT, the NT, the intervening times, and one of the firmest links by which the two are united. The mountain itself is separated from Jerusalem by the valley of Kidron. The summit of the mount was considered a sabbath day's journey from the city (Acts 1:12). The Garden of Gethsemane was west of the mount, either at the base or a short distance up its ascent. The villages of Bethany and Bethphage were on the east side (Mt. 21:1). The Mount of Olives is described as a chain of hills rising into three or four summits, and having two lateral spurs. The westward spur starts at the bend of the Kidron, approximately a mile north of Jerusalem and reaches an elevation of some 2700 feet above sea level. The second spur is separated by the Kidron from the main ridge, but it also runs west and fronts the city on the south. The four peaks into which Olivet rises, beginning from the north and proceeding to the south are: Galilee, the highest, being some 2700 feet above sea level; the Mount of Ascension, regarded as the site from which Jesus ascended; Prophets, so named because the prophets' tombs are on its side; Mount of Offense, from the belief that Solomon built shrines at this site for his idolatrous wives.

2. *Importance.* The Mount of Olives is important to the Biblical student because Jesus often went there. He was descending the slope of the mount when the multitude welcomed him into the city. It was from his vantage point on the side of the mount that he looked across the valley toward the temple and prophesied the destruction of both the city and the temple. After the Passover, he retired to the Mount of Olives. It was in the Garden of Gethsemane

where he was arrested. From the mount he ascended. See Mt. 21:1, 24:23, 26:30; Mk. 13:3, 14:26; Lk. 19:37-38, 21:37, 22:39, 24:50; Jn. 8:1. v.e.g.

Olivet (ŏl'ĭ-vĕt) see **Olives, Mount of**

Olympas (ō-lĭm'păs) a Roman Christian greeted by Paul (Rom. 16:15).

Omar (ō'mēr) a son of Eliphaz, the firstborn of Esau (Gen. 36:11, 15; 1 Chr. 1:36).

Omega (ō-mē'gả) the last letter of the Greek alphabet, as Alpha is the first (Rev. 1:8, 11, 21:6).

omer (ō'mēr) a system of measure for dry materials, containing one tenth of an ephah (Ex. 16:36). See **weights and measures**

Omri (ŏm'rī) 1. One of the sons of Becher, the son of Benjamin (1 Chr. 7:8).

2. A descendant of Pharez, the son of Judah (1 Chr. 9:4).

3. Son of Michael and chief of the tribe of Issachar in the reign of David (1 Chr. 26:18).

4. A king of Israel, who was initially a "captain of the hosts." Serving under Elah at the time of his murder by Zimri at Tirzah, then the capital of the Northern Kingdom, Omri was engaged in the siege of Gibbethon, which had been occupied by the Philistines. As quickly as the army heard of Elah's death, they proclaimed Omri king. He then broke the siege of Gibbethon and attacked Tirzah, where Zimri was holding his court as king of Israel. The city was captured, and Zimri perished in the flames of the palace, having reigned only seven days. Omri then found it necessary to struggle against Tibni, whom "half the people" (1 K. 16:21) desired to raise to the throne. This struggle lasted some four years. Omri then reigned for six years at Tirzah, and at the end of that time he transferred his residence to the mountain Shomron (Samaria). At Samaria, Omri reigned for an additional six years. He was an unscrupulous but vigorous ruler, anxious to strengthen his dynasty by alliance with foreign states. Omri's death likely occurred in 919 B.C.

On (ŏn) 1. Son of Peleth and one of the chiefs of the tribe of Reuben (Num. 16:1).

2. A town of Lower Egypt, which is mentioned in the Scriptures under at least two names, Beth-shemesh (Jer. 43:13) and Heliopolis (see Ex. 1:11, LXX). The city was located on the east of the Nile, several miles from the river and approximately nineteen miles north of Memphis. It is possible that Isaiah likewise had this city in mind in his reference of 19:18. The city of Heliopolis was famous for the worship of the sun and a slight change

in the first letter of the name used by Isaiah would alter the reading from the "city of the sun" into the "city of destruction."

Onam (ō'năm) 1. One of the sons of Shobal, the son of Seir (Gen. 36:23; 1 Chr. 1:40).

2. A man of Judah, of the house of Jerahmeel (1 Chr. 2:26, 28).

Onan (ō'năn) the second son of Judah by the Canaanitess (Gen. 38:4; 1 Chr. 2:3). He sinned lest his brother should have an heir, but Onan himself died without a male child (Gen. 38:4–10, 46:12).

Onesimus (ō-něs'ĭ-mŭs) the slave in whose behalf Paul wrote the Epistle to Philemon. Onesimus was a native, or at least an inhabitant, of Colosse, since Paul in writing to the church there speaks of him (Col. 4:9) as "one of you." Slaves were numerous in Phrygia, as in all parts of the Roman world. Onesimus had escaped from his master and had fled to Rome, where he hoped to be concealed in Rome's vast population. During his sojourn in Rome, he embraced the Gospel, and Paul writes to Philemon to accept Onesimus as a Christian brother (Philemon 10, 19).

Onesiphorus (ŏn'ē-sĭf'ō-rŭs) a Christian who lived at Ephesus (2 Tim. 1:16–18). In this passage, Paul speaks of Onesiphorus in terms of grateful love and describes his unusual courage and generosity. In 2 Tim. 4:19 Paul indicates that the "household of Onesiphorus" is worthy of special greeting. When Onesiphorus was in Rome, he visited Paul, who was then imprisoned, and manifested great kindness toward him.

onion a plant which from time immemorable has been a favorite article of food among Egyptians. The onion has a bulbous root and is described by some as being milder in flavor and less pungent than the onions of today.

Ono (ō'nō) one of the towns of Benjamin which was built or rebuilt by Shamed. Some of Ono's inhabitants likely returned from the Babylonian exile (Ezra 2:33; Neh. 7:37).

onycha (ŏn'ĭ-kà) the Hebrew term *sheheleth* occurs only in Ex. 30:34 and there as one of the ingredients of a perfume made for the service of the tabernacle. It is believed to have been made of the operculum of a stromb, which gave a certain perfume when being burned.

onyx a precious stone which was found in the land of Havilah (Gen. 2:12). Two of these stones, each being inscribed with the names of six of the tribes, were attached to the shoulder pieces of the high priest's ephod (Ex. 28:9, 12). In 1 Chr. 29:2 it is indicated that David gathered these stones for the service of the proposed temple.

Ophel (ō'fĕl) the south part of the east hill of ancient Jerusalem. According to 2 Chr. 27:3 Jotham built much "on the wall of Ophel." Stretching from the catalogue of Nehemiah's repairs to the wall of Jerusalem, Ophel appears to have been near the "water gate" (Neh. 3:26). The Levites resided there (Neh. 11:21). At the foot of Ophel was the pool of Siloam.

Ophir (ō'fēr) 1. The eleventh in order of the sons of Joktan (Gen. 10:29; 1 Chr. 1:23). A tribe descended from Ophir, the dwelling of the sons of Joktan being delineated in Gen. 10: 29–30.

2. A region. The region of Ophir was celebrated for its gold (1 Chr. 29:4; Job 22:24). Hiram and Solomon sent a navy which returned with almug as well as gold (1 K. 10: 11). Josephus indicates that Ophir was the golden land in India, but one is not certain of the exact location.

Ophni (ŏf'nī) a town of Benjamin, mentioned only in Josh. 18:24, apparently located in the northeastern portion of the tribe.

Ophrah (ŏf'rà) 1. A town located in the land occupied by the tribe of Benjamin (Josh. 18:23). Jerome places it five miles east of Bethel.

2. A village west of the Jordan, likely in Manasseh (Judg. 6:15). In Judg. 6:11 this is indicated as the native place of Gideon and the scene of his exploits against Baal (Judg. 6:24). This was also his residence after accession to power (Judg. 9:5), and is the place of his burial in the family sepulchre (Judg. 8:32).

3. A son of Meonothai, of Judah (1 Chr. 4:14).

orator 1. Appears in Isa. 3:3 for what is literally "skillful in whisper, or incantation."

2. A title applied to Tertullus, who appeared as the advocate of the Jewish accusers of Paul before Felix (Acts 24:1).

orchard see **garden**

Oreb (ō'rĕb) 1. The "raven's craig," west of Jordan, at which the Midianite chieftain Oreb fell by the hand of the Ephraimites. See Judg. 7:25; Isa. 10:26.

2. One of the chiefs of the Midianite hosts which invaded Israel and who was defeated by Gideon. He was slain at a rock, which was later called Rock of Horeb. See Judg. 7:25, 8:3; Ps. 83:11; Isa. 10:26.

Oren (ō'rĕn) one of the sons of Jerahmeel (1 Chr. 2:25).

organ the Hebrew word *ugab*, or *uggab*, likely denotes a type of perforated wind instrument.

The term appears in Gen. 6:21 and is obviously a general term for all wind instruments.

Orion (ō-rī'ŏn) a constellation known to the Greeks by Orion but to the Hebrews by *cesil*. The mythological Orion is represented as a man of unusual strength and is celebrated as an iron worker and hunter. He was killed by the goddess Diana and was transferred to the heavens, thus becoming the constellation. See Job 9:9, 38:31; Amos 5:8.

ornaments personal ornaments, differing in number, variety, and weight, are indicative in Oriental life of contemporary and acceptable fashionableness. The monuments of ancient Egypt exhibit the hands of ladies loaded with rings, earrings of very great size, anklets, armlets, bracelets of the most varied character, richly ornamented necklaces, and chains of various kinds. Isaiah 3:18–23 records a detailed description of the articles which adorned the luxurious women of the prophet's day. Earrings were worn by Jacob's wives, apparently as charms but mentioned in connection with idols (Gen. 35:4). The patriarch Judah wore ornaments as a signet and suspended by a string around his neck (Gen. 38:18). The first historical reference to the ring occurs in reference to Joseph (Gen. 41:42). Saul wore a ring about the arm (2 Sam. 1:10).

Ornaments were placed aside in the time of mourning (Ex. 33:4–6).

Ornan (ôr'năn) the Jebusite king Araunah (1 Chr. 21:15, 18, 20–25, 28; 2 Chr. 3:1). See **Araunah**

Orpah (ôr'pä) a Moabite woman, wife of Chilion, and sister-in-law of Ruth. On the death of their husbands, Orpah accompanied her sister-in-law and her mother-in-law on the road to Bethlehem; however, at this point, Ruth 1:4–14 indicates that Orpah bade her mother-in-law goodbye and returned to her people and to her gods.

Oshea (ō'shē-à) Joshua, the son of Nun (Num. 13:8).

ospray, osprey an unclean bird, a dark brown eagle which frequents seacoasts and eats fish. See Lev. 11:13; Deut. 14:12.

ossifrage (ŏs'à-frĭj) an unclean bird. See Lev. 11:13 and Deut. 14:12. The bird is especially fond of bones, snakes, and tortoises. It is called by some "bone breaker" inasmuch as it takes its victim to a great height and then drops it upon a stone. This, of course, is especially true of its prey such as tortoises.

ostrich 1. The *bath hayaanah* is an unclean bird (Lev. 11:16; Deut. 14:15). Its loud cry seems to be referred to in Mic. 1:8.

2. The *ranan* is characterized by frightful sounds. The female deposits her eggs in the ground and abandons them. See Job 39:13.

3. The *yaen* occurs only in the plural number *yeenim* in Lam. 4:3.

The ostrich is a large bird, but is not capable of flying, its great power in running compensating for its inability to fly. The common ostrich is six to eight feet in height. An egg is laid every other day, until ten or twelve eggs have been produced. Each egg is approximately three pounds in weight. The male ostrich sits on the eggs much more devotedly than does the hen. It is likewise the male bird's responsibility to assume control of the younger birds.

Othni (ŏth'nī) son of Shemaiah, the firstborn of Obed-edom (1 Chr. 26:7).

Othniel (ŏth'nĭ-ĕl) son of Kenaz and younger brother of Caleb (Josh. 15:17; Judg. 1:13, 3:9; 1 Chr. 4:13). Caleb promised to give his daughter Achsah in marriage to any man who took the town of Debir. Othniel captured the city and received Achsah as wife (Josh. 15:15–17; Judg. 1:11–13).

oven both fixed and portable ovens were employed. The stationary oven was found only in towns, where regular bakers were employed (Hos. 7:4). The portable oven was adapted to a nomadic society. It consisted of a large jar made of clay, three feet in height and wider toward the bottom, with a hole for the extraction of ashes. Dry twigs and grass were used for fuel (Mt. 6:30), and the loaves were placed both inside and outside of the oven.

owl this term is used to translate several words which describe birds of larger species. 1. *Bath hayaanah* (ostrich).

2. *Yanshuph*. This bird was ceremonially unclean (Lev. 11:17; Deut. 14:16) and was frequently found in waste places. The LXX and Vulg. translate this term ibis, the sacred bird of Egypt.

3. *Kos*. This bird is mentioned in Lev. 11:17 and in Deut. 14:16. It also frequented waste places.

4. *Koppiz*. Mentioned in Isa. 34:15 only, the *koppiz* is identified by some as being a reptile, but others believe the context definitely indicates some species of bird.

5. *Lilith*. This bird is mentioned in Isa. 34:14 and is likely the screech or barn owl which is found so frequently in Palestinian ruins.

6. *Tinshemeth*. Occurring in Lev. 11:18, this term in the LXX is translated "water hen."

ox the term ox generally specifies any animal of the kind without respect to sex, although technically the term itself refers to the male of the species *Bos taurus*. The ox is mentioned in connection with Abraham (Gen. 12:16, 21:

27) and the Egyptians owned oxen at the time of the plagues (Ex. 9:3). Oxen were used for plowing (Deut. 22:10), for treading out corn (Deut. 25:4), for dragging carts and wagons (Num. 7:3; 1 Sam. 6:7), and as beasts of burden (1 Chr. 12:40). Oxen were also used for food and for sacrificial purposes.

The ox that threshed the corn was not to be muzzled and was to enjoy rest on the sabbath as well as his master. Many inscriptions of oxen are found on monuments of Egypt. These dependable animals made vital contributions to the domestic life of the ancients.

oxgoad see **goad**

Ozem (ō'zĕm) 1. Sixth son of Jesse (1 Chr. 2:15).

2. A son of Jerahmeel (1 Chr. 2:25).

Ozias (ō-zī'ăs) Uzziah, king of Judah (Mt. 1: 8–9). See **Uzziah**

Ozni (ŏz'nī) one of the sons of Gad (Num. 26:16) and the founder of the tribal family known as the Oznites.

P

Paarai (pā'á-rī) listed in 2 Sam. 23:35 as one of David's mighty men.

Paddan (păd'ăn), **Padan** (pā'dăn), and **Padan-aram** (pā'dăn-ā'răm) the tableland of Aram (Gen. 24:10, 48:7; Hos. 12:12). The term describes that portion of land which borders on the Euphrates, and otherwise called Aram-naharaim. Padan-aram plays an important part in the early history of the Hebrews. The family of their founder had settled there and were long looked upon as the aristocracy of the race, with whom alone the legitimate descendants of Abraham might intermarry, thus preserving the purity of their blood.

Padon (pā'dŏn) founder of a family of the Nethinim who returned with Zerubbabel (Ezra 2:44; Neh. 7:47).

Pagiel (pā'gĭ-ĕl) the son of Ocran and chief of the tribe of Asher at the time of the Exodus (Num. 1:13, 2:27, 7:72, 77).

Pahath-moab (pā'hăth-mō'ăb) head of the family of the tribe of Judah. The members of this family returned from the Babylonian captivity (Ezra 2:6, 8:4; Neh. 7:11). Some of them married heathen wives; Ezra condemned them and persuaded them to break the relationship (Ezra 10:30). Hashub, a member of this family, assisted in the rebuilding of the wall of Jerusalem (Neh. 3:11).

Pai (pā'ī) see **Pau**

paint the use of cosmetic dyes prevailed among the ancients. In both ancient Egypt and Assyria women customarily painted a bright rim around their eyes. The Hebrews obviously regarded this as a practice unbecoming to a woman of high character (2 K. 9:30; Jer. 4:30; Ezek. 23:40). Antimony was used for this purpose, having first been burnt and pulverized. The *kohl* used in Egypt is a soot produced by burning either a kind of frankincense or the shells of almonds. The dye materials are then moistened with oil and kept in small containers.

palace Solomon's palace was almost certainly in the city and on the brow opposite to the temple area, overlooking it and the whole city of David. The principal building located within the palace was the great hall of state and audience, called "The House of the Forest of Lebanon." This name is likely derived from the four rows of cedar pillars by which it was supported. Next in importance was the "Hall of Judgment," a quadrangular building supported by columns. The third edifice is merely called "Porch of Pillars." This was the ordinary place of business of the palace and the reception room where the king received ordinary visitors. On routine occasions the king sat in this porch to conduct the business of the kingdom. Behind this was the inner court, adorned with gardens and fountains, surrounded by cloisters for shade. Solomon constructed an ascent from his own house to the temple, which was a subterranean passage 250 feet and 42 feet wide.

Palal (pā'lăl) the son of Uzai. Palal assisted in restoring the walls of Jerusalem in the time of Nehemiah (Neh. 3:25).

palanquin (păl'ăn-kēn') this covered conveyance, which was arranged both for sitting and reclining, was carried by poles on the shoulders of several men or was carried as a litter between two animals. The palanquin, which Solomon provided for his bride, was ornately decorated. See Song of S. 3:9.

Palestine (păl'ĕs-tĭn) this term is a translation of a Hebrew word which is also rendered "Philistia" or "land of the Philistines." So, Palestine really means nothing but Philistia. At first the term was used only when referring to the southern seacoast portion of the land which was inhabited by the Philistines. This strip lay next to the Mediterranean, and was thus accessible by way of the sea. Moreover, it was the main trade route from Egypt to Phoenicia, and to the richer regions north of it. The Philistine Plain, therefore, became sooner known to the Western world than the sections of the country which lay farther inland. The name was gradually extended, and soon after the beginning of the Christian era it was the usual designation for that land known as the Holy Land. Though Biblically a misnomer, the name Palestine has been chosen here as the most convenient term under which to give a general description of this land. Since the history of Palestine is so fully given under its various headings, it is unnecessary to include it in a general description of the country. Discussions of cities and tribes will also be found under their separate headings.

I. SIZE AND LOCATION. Palestine, with all its great moral and historic significance, is but a strip of country. When the Biblical writers wished to refer to the entire length of the land from north to south, they used the expression "from Dan even to Beer-sheba," a distance of about 150 miles. And there are numerous places in the highlands which command a view of both the western and eastern frontiers at the same time. The geographical boundaries varied from time to time; therefore, the total area could be given as ranging from nine thousand to fourteen thousand square miles, depending upon the particular stage of history under discussion. For purposes of comparison, the modern state of Israel—which covers a large portion of the territory that was ancient Palestine—has an area of 7,992.6 square miles. That section not encompassed by Israel lies within the boundaries of the Hashemite Kingdom of Jordan. Bearing in mind the fact that there were no legally established territorial limits, one may say that ancient Palestine was that territory bounded by the Mediterranean on the west and the Arabian Desert on the east. On the north it was shut in by the high ranges of the Lebanon and Anti-Lebanon Mountains and the Leontes River. Mount Hermon, at the southern end of the Anti-Lebanons, was the apex of the country on the north. To the south were the deserts of the upper part of the Sinai Peninsula. When the Holy Land first made its appearance in history, it was located on the very western edge of the East. Because it lay on the shores of the Mediterranean, it was open to all the gradual influences of the rising communities of the West. In addition, the only road by which the two great rivals of the ancient world —Egypt and Assyria—could reach each other was along the broad flat coastal strip of Palestine. Thus, the land served not only as a main trade route, but also as a buffer state between the great powers and a convenient battlefield upon which they might contend for control of the East.

II. PHYSICAL DIVISIONS. Palestine is divided into four natural land features: (1) the Coastal Plain, (2) the Central Highlands, (3) the Jordan Valley, and (4) the Eastern Plateau. The striking difference between the highlands and lowlands is reflected continually in Hebrew literature. Habitual forms of expression are "going up" to Judah, Jerusalem, or Hebron; "going down" to Jericho, Caesarea, or Egypt.

(1) *The Coastal Plain.* This lowland extends along the western coast of Palestine, interrupted only by Mount Carmel, which is in reality a range of hills rising to almost 1800 feet. South of Carmel the lowland divides itself into two portions. The upper part, north of Joppa (Jaffa), is the plain of Sharon; the lower and broader section is the Philistine Plain. The entire coastal plain is covered with a rich fertile soil, but the sand dunes which line the coast have been encroaching gradually on the land. The modern state of Israel is giving special attention to the problem of these shifting sand dunes, and is taking measures to reclaim them so that they may be used for grazing and farming. North of Carmel the plain resumes its position by the sea—forming the plain of Accho —until it meets the northern mountains. Above this is ancient Phoenicia. Beginning at Accho, the plain turns in a southwestern direction and cuts across the country from the Mediterranean to the Jordan Valley. This is the plain of Esdraelon or valley of Jezreel, which is the only means of access from the coastal plain to the Jordan Valley. Because this fertile plain affords the only natural passage through the central highlands, Esdraelon became the great battlefield of Palestine. At the eastern end, leading down into the Jordan Valley, the plain is guarded on the north by the hill of Moreh (Little Hermon) and on the south by Mount Gilboa. It was here that Gideon routed the Midianites (Judg. 7:1–25). It was here too that Saul was defeated by the Philistines, after which he took his own life (1 Sam. 31:1–13).

(2) *The Central Highlands.* This mountain

range preserves from north to south—from the Lebanons to Sinai—a remarkably even and horizontal profile, broken only by the plain of Esdraelon. These mountains, in fact, formed the security of Israel. To the armies of Egypt and Assyria as they traced and retraced their way across the maritime plain, the long wall of heights with its difficult passes must have made the bare hills seem hardly worth the trouble of seizing. In the case of the Israelites, the ordinary conditions of conquest were reversed: it was the conquerors who took to the hills; the conquered kept the plains. It was in the plains where the horses and chariots of the Canaanites and Philistines had space to maneuver that the Israelites had difficulty in dislodging their enemies (Judg. 1:19, 4:3). To a people so exclusive as the Jews, there must have been a constant satisfaction in the elevation and inaccessibility of their mountain strongholds. This is evident in every page of their literature, which is tinged throughout with a highland color. The central highlands, which average 2000 feet in height, may be divided into three sections: those of Galilee in the north, Samaria in the center, and Judea in the south. The mountains of Judea, or hills of Judah, form the southernmost part of the central highlands. Probably no country equally cultivated is more monotonous, bare or uninviting in appearance than this section during the largest portion of the year. In the spring the ravines are filled with water and the bald gray rocks are covered with grass and flowers; the rest of the year, the landscape from Hebron up to Bethel is desolate indeed. It is obvious that in the ancient days of the nation when Judah and Benjamin possessed the teeming population indicated in the Bible, the condition and aspect of the country must have been very different. Forests appear to have stood in many parts of Judea until the repeated invasions and sieges caused their fall. In the western section is the Shephelah, a series of foothills lying between the mountains and the Philistine Plain. The southern section is the mineral-rich Negeb, around 5000 square miles of sand dunes and harsh hills. This parched wasteland is covered with a thick layer of fertile soil, and with sufficient water it could become productive. Beer-sheba, the trading center for the area, is on the northern edge of the Negeb. It was in this vicinity that Hagar and her son Ishmael were sent to wander in the wilderness (Gen. 21:14). The southern tip of the Negeb borders on the Gulf of Aqabah, the northeastern arm of the Red Sea. Eilat (the ancient Elath or Eloth) which lies on the northwest-

ern shore of the gulf, is modern Israel's southernmost port and trade outlet to East Africa and the Far East. The eastern portion, a desolate tract of land by the Dead Sea, is the Wilderness of Judea. Caverns characteristic of all limestone districts exist here in astonishing numbers, and there is perhaps hardly one of these caves which has not at some time or the other furnished a hiding place for some ancient Hebrew from the sweeping incursions of the Philistines or Amalekites. When David was fleeing from Saul, he hid in a cave near Engedi, on the western shore of the Dead Sea (1 Sam. 23:29, 24:1). It was in this section too that the writers of the Dead Sea Scrolls apparently took refuge, for the scrolls were found in caves overlooking the Dead Sea. To the north of Judea are the mountains of Samaria—the ancient Mount Ephraim—with the Jordan on the east and the plain of Sharon on the west. Samaria, like Judea, is rugged and mountainous; but here the hills are less steep, the soil more fertile, and the landscape slightly more open and pleasant in appearance. In the heart of Samaria was Shechem, mentioned so frequently in the early history of the Jews. Shechem, the present Nablus in the state of Jordan, lay in the sheltered and fertile valley between Mount Ebal on the north and Mount Gerizim, the site of the Samaritan temple, on the south. Even though Samaria is less forbidding in aspect than Judea, there is not a sufficient amount of vegetation and water south of the valley of Shechem to recall much of the scenery of the West. Above the valley, there is a distinct improvement. Some of the most fertile and valuable spots in the Holy Land lie in the northeast and northwest sections of Samaria. In the northern portion of the central highlands are the mountains of Galilee, divided into two natural land features. In the upper or northern part, the mountains average nearly 3000 feet above sea level. Mount Merom in Upper Galilee, which is the highest point in modern Israel, rises to a height of 3962 feet. The hills in Lower Galilee, which includes the plain of Esdraelon, become less steep as they slope toward the plain. Mount Tabor, which overlooks Esdraelon, reaches 1929 feet. It was here that Barak and Deborah assembled the Israelites before the defeat of Sisera's Canaanite army (Judg. 4:6–16). From the present appearance of this district with its fertile valleys and wooded hillsides, we might—with some allowances—gain an idea of what the southern portions of the central highlands were during the earlier periods of history.

(3) *The Jordan Valley.* This extraordinary

crevasse, through which the Jordan River flows, is part of the Great Rift Valley which extends southward deep into Africa. It separates the central highlands on the west from the eastern plateau, and is lined with steep cliffs on both sides. The valley, which is the Arabah of the Hebrews and the Ghor of the Arabs, varies in width from around one mile in the north to fourteen or fifteen in the vicinity of Jericho. The mountains on the western side are more irregular in height and their slopes less vertical than those on the east, which have a massive wall-like appearance. The valley begins with the river at its remotest springs of Hasbeiya on the slopes of Mount Hermon and accompanies it until the Jordan empties into the Dead Sea. In this distance of approximately 120 miles, the floor of the valley drops almost 3000 feet. The river twists and coils along the floor of the valley, but its general direction is almost due north and south. From its source, the river flows southward to Lake Hula (Huleh) in the northeastern tip of present-day Israel. This lake is actually a portion of a vast swamp which has been drained as part of Israel's land reclamation program. Hula is thought to be the ancient waters of Merom, the site of Joshua's defeat of Jabin and his confederates in the conquest of Canaan (Josh. 11:1-5). From Hula, the river flows into the Sea of Galilee—the present Lake Kinneret (also called Lake Tiberias and Lake Gennesaret). In a distance of approximately ten miles between Hula and the Sea of Galilee, the river drops around 680 feet. The valley, from the lower end of the Sea of Galilee to the upper end of the Dead Sea, is much deeper than that part to the north. From the Sea of Galilee, the river continues southward to empty into the Dead Sea, a distance of sixty-five miles. The river, because of its windings, is probably twice that in length. The Dead Sea, the lowest point on the face of the earth, is 1286 feet below sea level at the surface; the bottom is another 1300 feet lower at its deepest point. For most of its course, the Jordan is shallow and narrow. It is rarely more than ten feet in depth or one hundred feet in width, except during the spring when the melting snows of Hermon flood the valley. Though the Jordan is shallow and useless for navigation because of its rapids and whirlpools, it is still superior to other streams in the Holy Land. It is at least perennial and may be used for irrigation. For fully half the year, the other rivers or brooks are often mere dry lanes of hot stones.

(4) *The Eastern Plateau.* This section between the Jordan Valley and the Arabian Desert is a part of the modern state of Jordan. The territory is mentioned frequently in connection with the early history of the Israelites; however, it never played as important a part in Jewish life as the land which lay west of the Jordan, where the most significant events occurred. These highlands present much the same aspect as those to the west, although the mountains of the eastern plateau are in general higher and steeper. The more fertile part of this rugged plateau is that section near the Jordan Valley; the land becomes more arid as it slopes off into the desert. The plateau is divided into three fairly distinct divisions by rivers cutting across it. In the north, east of the Sea of Galilee, lay Bashan. This territory extended from Mount Hermon in the north to the Yarmuk River on the south. The Yarmuk now forms part of the boundary between Jordan and Syria. This area is around 2000 feet above sea level, and during OT times it was famous for its fine cattle and pasture lands (Deut. 32:14; Ps. 22:12; Ezek. 39:18; Amos 4:1). South of the Yarmuk was Gilead, cut in half by the Jabbok River which runs into the Jordan about midway between the Sea of Galilee and the Dead Sea. It was on the banks of this river that Jacob wrestled with the angel (Gen. 32:22-24). The mountains of Gilead are slightly higher than those of Bashan. Although they have a real elevation of between two and three thousand feet, they appear much steeper because of the deep depression of the Jordan Valley. This section was known for its medicinal balm (Jer. 8:22, 46:11). To the south of Gilead, and east of the Dead Sea, lay Moab. The white limestone walls of the mountains, which average 3000 feet above sea level, rise to over 4200 feet above the Dead Sea. There was no natural boundary between Moab and Gilead, and the territorial limits varied from time to time. Usually the Arnon River, about midway between the north and south ends of the Dead Sea, was the northern boundary of Moab. The Zered River formed the southern boundary separating it from Edom.

III. POLITICAL DIVISIONS. In NT times Palestine, which was under Roman rule, was made up of six provinces: (1) Judea, (2) Samaria, (3) Galilee, (4) Perea, (5) Decapolis, and (6) Northeastern Palestine. These provinces were formed partly because of political considerations and partly because of the physical features of the land. To the west of the Jordan were Judea, Samaria, and Galilee. To the east—or "beyond Jordan"—were Perea, Decapolis, and Northeastern Palestine.

(1) *Judea.* This was the most southern of

the provinces west of the Jordan, lying between the Dead Sea and the Mediterranean. The name is a corruption of Judah, the tribe which was once the chief possessor of this region. It was the heart of the Jewish nation, not because it was the largest province, but because Jerusalem lay within its borders. The Holy City of the Jews is located almost due west from the upper end of the Dead Sea. Bethlehem is six miles south, Bethany two miles east, and Jericho fifteen miles to the northeast of Jerusalem.

(2) *Samaria*. This province lay between Judea on the south and Galilee on the north. That part lying on the shores of the Mediterranean was the plain of Sharon; to the east was the Jordan. After the fall of the northern kingdom of Israel, the Assyrians evacuated the inhabitants and colonized the territory with non-Israelites (2 K. 17:1–24). These colonists intermarried with the remnant of Jews left in the land, producing a hybrid race with a hybrid religion. At the time of the Restoration, when the Samaritans wished to join in the rebuilding of the temple at Jerusalem, they were rejected (Ezra 4:1–3). They built their own temple at Mount Gerizim near Shechem, and it was to this spot that the Samaritan woman was referring when she told Jesus, "Our fathers worshiped in this mountain" (Jn. 4:20). The feud between the two races still persisted at the time of Jesus, and the orthodox Jews would have no dealings with the Samaritans (Jn. 4:9). At the present time there is a colony of around 150 Samaritans at Holon in Israel. At Nablus, Jordan, the seat of their high priest, there is another group of approximately the same size.

(3) *Galilee*. This province was the most northern of the three provinces in the western part of Palestine, and lay between the Upper Jordan and the Sea of Galilee on the east and Phoenicia in the west. Familiar towns in this province are Capernaum, Nazareth, and Cana. In the time of Jesus, there were many more Gentiles in this district than in Judea, and the Jewish people themselves were more liberal in their religious thinking. For this reason, Jesus was able to pursue his ministry with more freedom in Galilee than in the south where the people were more hardened in Jewish orthodoxy. By the standards of Judaism as practiced in Judea, the people of Galilee were regarded as corrupted by their contacts with Gentiles. This may explain, in part, the attitude of the Jewish religious leaders toward Jesus. With the exception of Judas Iscariot, apparently all the disciples were Galileans either by birth or residence (Acts 1:11).

(4) *Perea*. This province was on the east of the Jordan, opposite the Dead Sea and Samaria. The atmosphere in the regions east of the Jordan was quite different from that on the western side since Israel never had as firm a hold here, either religiously or politically. Although there was much Gentile influence in this region, the population was predominantly Jewish in NT times. This allowed the Jews to go from Judea to Galilee by way of Perea over relatively Jewish territory, thus avoiding the land of the despised Samaritans. Jesus was well received here, for we are told that great crowds followed after him (Mt. 19:1=2; Jn. 10:40–42).

(5) *Decapolis* (Ten Cities). This territory north of Perea and southeast of the Sea of Galilee also extended into Samaria and Galilee on the west of the Jordan. It had originally been a confederacy of ten Greek cities—thus the name. In NT times there were more than ten, but the name Decapolis was still used. The non-Jewish inhabitants, who retained their pagan customs, were looked down upon and regarded as lawless intruders by the Jews. Many from this district followed Jesus during the early phases of his ministry (Mt. 4:25).

(6) *Northeastern Palestine*. There is no more definite name for this territory which included several small districts and lay north of the Decapolis and northeast of the Sea of Galilee. There were only a few Jews in this section, and apparently most of them lived in the western part around the Sea of Galilee. The other inhabitants, wild Gentile tribes, had to be forcibly brought under control by their rulers from time to time.

IV. CLIMATE. The climate of the Holy Land is typically Mediterranean, somewhat similar to that of Southern California. There are only two seasons: the dry and the rainy. There is unbroken sunshine from May through mid-October. In the coastal region, this season is warm and humid, with a refreshing sea breeze; in the hill regions it is warm, dry and breezy, especially at night. The rainy season begins about mid-October, but the rainy days do not become frequent until December. Winter weather is a mixture of short but heavy rainy spells and days of brilliant sunshine. In the hilly regions during this season, temperatures drop toward the freezing point and brief snowfalls are not unusual. March and April are pleasantly cool, with occasional rains of short duration. The early rains are those of October and November, which break the summer drouth and make the land soft enough for plowing. The latter rains of March and April furnish the last moisture the crops receive before the dry season sets in. The temperature depends mainly on the altitude. The mean temperatures measured for the entire year are 60.8 at the highest altitude and 77.7 degrees at the lowest. The coldest month is January; the hottest is August, when the temperature may rise to 98 degrees in the hilly regions and as high as 120 degrees in the Jordan Valley and Dead Sea area. The average yearly rainfall for the country as a whole is 20 inches, but there are great local variations. In the driest area, the southern Negeb around Eilat, the average yearly rainfall is 0.8 inches. An important compensation for the little rainfall in the southern region is the large amount of dew, the equivalent of an additional eight inches of water annually. The wettest area is in the hills of Upper Galilee, where the yearly rainfall averages 42.5 inches.

V. PLANTS, ANIMALS, AND NATURAL RESOURCES.

(1) *Plants.* Because of the land reclamation and irrigation projects of Israel and Jordan, the land is becoming again what in the Bible is called "a land of wheat, and barley, and vines, and fig trees, and pomegranates; a land of oil olive, and honey" (Deut. 8:8). These are still found in the Holy Land, and many other crops have been introduced. The coastal plain is noted for its date palms, cotton plantations, and orange, grapefruit, and lemon groves. Bananas, avocados, guavas, and mangoes are found both in the coastal plain and the Jordan Valley. The land east of the Jordan is still known for its fine pasture lands and grain crops. In addition to the basic grains and vegetables, other crops such as tobacco, ground-nuts and sugar beets have been introduced on a comparatively large scale. Deciduous fruit trees grow everywhere, especially in the cool hills; from January to April the slopes of the Carmel range are ablaze with color. Native trees such as the Jerusalem pine, tamarisk, and carob have been used for the most part in the afforestation projects; in addition, eucalyptus trees have been planted throughout the country. The cactus is often seen in the more arid sections of the land, and medicinal herbs and wild flowers are found in abundance. As early as December, even in the mountains, the hyacinth, crocus, and narcissus are blooming. These are followed by anemones, tulips, cyclamen, iris, daisies, and many more.

(2) *Animals.* Because of the differences in climate and terrain of the various sections, Palestine had a wide variety of wild animals in OT times. By the time of the NT, however, wild beasts appear to have been relatively scarce. At present there are some wolves and leopards in Galilee, but the most common beasts of prey are hyenas, jackals, wild cats, lynx, otters, spotted weasels, and the mongoose. The wild boar is hunted, and the number of gazelles has increased. The shrew is plentiful, as are porcupines and hedgehogs. Camels, mentioned so frequently in the Bible, are seldom seen today other than in the Negeb and the desert regions to the east of the Jordan. The land abounds in numerous kinds of birds—about 400 species in all. There are vultures, eagles, kites, falcons, owls, storks, pelicans, and any number of smaller birds. Fish, too, are plentiful in Palestine. The main sources of fish are the Mediterranean, Lake Kinneret (the Sea of Galilee), the Red Sea, and the artificial fishponds which dot the countryside.

(3) *Natural Resources.* Most of the mineral resources are in the Negeb, where there are deposits of phosphates, manganese, feldspar, glass sand, flint clay, ball clay, kaolin, bitumen-bearing rock, granite, marble, and gypsum. The water of the Dead Sea contains about twenty-five per cent solid matter, mostly common salt. It also has large deposits of the minerals necessary for producing bromine, potash, and magnesium. There is peat in the Hula area, iron ore in the Negeb and Galilee, natural gas in the Dead Sea area, and petroleum in the southern part of the coastal plain. Copper is mined in large quantities in the Timnah region north of the Gulf of Aqabah, near the site of King Solomon's mines.

From this general description of Palestine, it becomes apparent that the land presents on a small scale the natural features of all regions: mountainous and desert, northern and tropical, maritime and inland, fertile fields and arid wasteland. This fact has made the allusions in the Scriptures so varied as to afford familiar illustrations to people of every land and every climate.   MRS. H.O.H.

Pallu (păl'û) the second son of Reuben, father of Eliab (Ex. 6:14; Num. 26:5, 8; 1 Chr. 5:3). Pallu was the founder of the family of the Palluites (Num. 26:5).

palm a tree which grew prolifically in the Biblical regions. It is described as being tall (Song of S. 7:7–8), straight (Jer. 10:5), a fruit tree (Joel 1:12), and as ornamental (1 K. 6:29, 32, 35). The leaves are unusually broad and were used as tokens of victory and peace (Jn. 12:13; Rev. 7:9). These leaves are so broad that they are often called branches. Measuring four to six feet in length, they are quite accessible inasmuch as young plants usually abound around the main trunk.

The following places may be enumerated in the Bible as having some connection with a palm tree, either in the derivation of the name, or in the mention of the tree as growing on the spot: (1) Elim (Ex. 15:27; Num. 33:9); (2) Elath (Deut. 2:8; 1 K. 9:26); (3) Jericho (Deut. 34:3; Judg. 1:16); (4) Hazezon-tamar —this place is mentioned in the history of Abraham and Jehoshaphat (Gen. 14:7; 2 Chr. 20:2); (5) Baal-tamar (Judg. 20:33); (6) Tamar (Ezek. 47:19, 48:28); (7) Tadmor; (8) Bethany, meaning "the house of dates"; palm trees likewise grew in the neighborhood of the Mount of Olives, thus the people "took branches of palm trees and went forth to meet him" (Jn. 12:13); (9) Phoenicia, which is likely derived from the Greek word meaning "palm"; (10) Phoenix in the island of Crete, the harbor which Paul's group could not reach because of the storm, has likely the same derivation (Acts 27:12).

palmer-worm an insect which fed upon vines, fig trees, olive trees, and the foliage of gardens and fields (Joel 1:4; Amos 4:9). This insect is generally described as a type of locust.

palsy the malady characterized by a partial loss of movement, or sensibility, or both. The partial loss might inevitably become a total loss (Mk. 2:3, 9–12). See **medicine**

Palti (păl'tĭ) 1. The Benjaminite spy, son of Raphu (Num. 13:9).

2. The man to whom Saul married Michal, David's wife (1 Sam. 25:44; 2 Sam. 3:15).

Paltiel (păl'tĭ-ĕl) the son of Azzan and prince of the tribe of Issachar (Num. 34:26).

Paltite (păl'tīt) Helez "the Paltite" is listed in 2 Sam. 23:26 among David's mighty men.

Pamphylia (păm-fĭl'ĭ-à) a stretch of the coastal region in the south of Asia Minor, bordered by Pisidia on the north and by the Gulf of Pamphylia on the south, Cilicia on the east, and Lycia on the west. Paul visited Perga and Attalia on his first missionary journey (Acts 13:13, 14:24–25, 15:38).

pan a shallow plate, which was used by the Bedouins and Syrians for baking their cakes of meal.

pannag (păn'ăg) an article of commerce exported from Palestine to Tyre (Ezek. 27:17). The nature of the export is not identified, but many suggest a kind of confection.

paper see **writing**, or **reed**

Paphos (pā'fŏs) a town located at the southwestern end of Cyprus, connected by a roadway with Salamis at the east of the island. Paul and Barnabas traveled this roadway on their first missionary journey (Acts 13:6).

papyrus a plant, the pith of which was cut into thin strips, then placed together, and used for writing materials. See **reed**

parable 1. *Definition*. The Hebrew *mashal* and the Greek *parabolē* are translated parable. The term *parabolē* signifies that which is placed alongside, or cast alongside. The parable may be defined as a brief story told by way of analogy to illustrate one principal truth. A very common definition, although not so precise, defines the parable as an earthly story with a heavenly meaning.

2. *Usage*. To suggest that the parable originated with Jesus is a grave mistake. The parabolic method of teaching had long been in vogue and was extremely popular with the scribes; in fact, parables likewise appeared in the OT, for example, Nathan's confrontation of David (2 Sam. 12:1–7). The parable must not be confused with the allegory, which personifies ideas or attributes and involves no genuine comparison. Neither must the parable be confused with the myth, which is unconscious realism, personifying attributes, etc. Many parables occur in the NT, Mt. 13 being a worthy example of the parabolic method. Parables may be listed as: the Sower, the Wheat and the Tares, the Mustard Seed, the Seed Cast into the Ground, the Hidden Treasure, the Pearl of Great Price, the Net, the Two Debtors, the Merciless Servant, the Good Samaritan, the Friend at Midnight, the Rich Fool, the Wedding Feast, the Fig Tree, the Great Supper, the Lost Sheep, the Lost Money, the Prodigal Son, the Unjust Steward, the Rich Man, the Unjust Judge, the Pharisee and the Publican, the Laborers, the Pounds, the Two Sons, the Vineyard, the Marriage Feast, the Virgins, the Talents, and the Sheep and the Goats. Perhaps other parabolic expressions are found in the gospels, but are not contained in the previous list.

Parabolic interpretation has been abused unmercifully throughout history. Numerous hermeneutical guidelines must be established to interpret accurately the parables of Jesus. The interpreter must keep in mind the point which Jesus is illustrating. It is equally important that the interpreter bear in mind the nature of the parable—it is told to illustrate *one* principal truth. Although it may have numerous applications, the parable is told for the primary purpose of illustrating one principal truth. To interpret correctly the parable, one must likewise observe the general context in which the parable is located. What is the general teaching of the context? What kind of language is involved in the parable? Does the teller proceed to interpret the parable? If so, the interpreter's problem is already solved. It must also be remembered that the details of the parable are not to

Paraclete

be pressed; the parable is intended to illustrate one basic truth, thus the details in the account are not to be pressed into allegory or personifications.

Paraclete (păr'a-klēt) the Greek term *paraklētos* means advocate, intercessor, one called alongside. This term is used in Jn. 14:16 by implication to refer to Jesus when the Master himself speaks, "And I shall ask the Father and another Paraclete he will give to you . . ." Thus Jesus describes himself as the one who counsels, the one who is called alongside, the one who intercedes for his disciples. In this verse Jesus employs *allon* (another of the same kind) to indicate that the coming Paraclete is to be the same kind of intercessor that he has been. Thus this reference to the Holy Spirit provides illumination into the work given to the Spirit. He teaches the believer, he guides him into truth, and he convicts of sin, righteousness, and judgment. It is he who makes intercession with groanings that cannot be uttered (Jn. 15:26, 16:14; Rom. 8:26–27).

paradise the term means literally "a park, or pleasure ground." The LXX refers to the garden of Eden as a paradise. The word occurs frequently in Xenophon to describe a wide, open park, enclosed against injury, yet with its natural beauty unspoiled, with stately forests, some bearing fruit, watered by clear streams, on whose banks roved large herds of antelope or sheep. Yet the language of the NT stands apart from the description of Xenophon inasmuch as the NT reference is to a spiritual paradise. Paradise likewise came to be used to refer to the place of the righteous dead, Gehenna the place of the unrighteous dead. See Lk. 23:43; 2 Cor. 12:4; Rev. 2:7, 22:2.

Parah (pā'rà) a village in the land allotted to Benjamin (Josh. 18:23); it is identified with the ruins of Farah, some five miles northeast of Jerusalem.

Paran (pā'răn) this wilderness region is located generally between Sinai and Canaan (Num. 10:12, 12:16). Paran is a stretch of chalky formation, the chalk being covered with a coarse gravel, mixed with black flint and drifting sand. Deuteronomy 33:2 and Hab. 3:3 refer to "Mount" Paran. This designation may have been assigned either to the northwestern portion of the Sinaitic Mountain group or to the whole Sinaitic cloister.

parbar (păr'băr) occurring in 1 Chr. 26:18, this term identifies a precinct on the west side of the temple enclosure, the same side with the causeway and the gate Shallecheth. The rabbis generally agree in translating *parbar* as "the

outside place." The plural *parvarim* in 2 K. 23:11 is translated "suburbs."

parched corn roasted grain, a fruit of the ancients (Lev. 23:14; 1 Sam. 17:17). Moist seeds were passed over a blazing fire which burned the chaff and roasted the grain.

parchment the hide of sheep or goats which has been soaked in lime to remove the hair, then shaved, washed, dried, stretched, and smoothed to prepare a writing material. Papyrus was commonly used in writing (2 Jn. 12). See **writing**

parents the fifth Mosaic commandment admonishes children to revere their parents, a promise being attached to this commandment's fulfillment (Ex. 20:12; Eph. 6:1–2). Deuteronomy 6:7 et al obligates the parents to rear the children in the fear of the Lord. The Mosaic law provides for punishment by death for the son who smote a parent or cursed him (Ex. 21:15, 17; Deut. 27:16). Parents should bring a rebellious son before the elders for trial and execution (Deut. 21:18–21).

parlor a term which denotes the king's audience chambers, so used in reference to Eglon (Judg. 3:20–25).

Parmashta (pär-măsh'tà) a son of Haman slain by the Jews in Shushan (Est. 9:9).

Parmenas (pär'mē-năs) one of the seven men elected to care for the needs of the Greek-speaking widows (Acts 6:5). These seven were described as "men of honest report, full of the Holy Ghost and wisdom."

Parnach (pär'năk) a Zebulunite, the father or ancestor of Elizaphan (Num. 34:25).

Parosh (pā'rŏsh) a founder of a family, the members of which returned from Babylon with Zerubbabel (Ezra 2:3; Neh. 7:8). Ezra 10:25 indicates that seven of this family had married foreign wives.

Parshandatha (pär'shăn-dā'thà) the oldest son of Haman who was also slain by the Jews in Shushan (Est. 9:7).

Parthians (pär'thĭ-ănz) Parthia was the region which stretched along the southern flank of the mountains separating the great Persian Desert from the Desert of Kharesm. It lay south of Hyrcania, east of Media, and north of Sagartia. Nothing is known of the Parthians until the time of Darius Hystaspis and at this time they are found in the district which so long retained their name. In the final struggle between the Greeks and Persians, the Parthians remained faithful to the Persians, serving at Arbela. The Parthians were rebellious, as is indicated by their revolt against the Grecians in 256 B.C. They became a power rivaling Rome and were not reluctant to try their strength against the great Roman empire. Parthian dominion lasted for approximately five centuries, beginning in the third century B.C. Jews from Parthia were present in Jerusalem on the day of Pentecost (Acts 2:9).

partridge the Heb. *kore* occurs in 1 Sam. 26:20 and in Jer. 17:11, referring to a wild bird which is hunted. The former verse refers to "hunting this bird upon the mountains," and Jeremiah uses the partridge, reportedly a bird which steals the eggs of other birds or even the young of others, as an illustration of one who collects ill-gotten wealth. The partridge was hunted in ancient times either by hawking, or by being driven until it became fatigued and could then be killed with clubs. The partridge is common in Palestine.

Paruah (pà-rōō′à) the father of Jehoshaphat, an officer in Solomon's service in Issachar (1 K. 4:17).

Parvaim (pär-vā′im) the source from which came the gold for the decoration of Solomon's temple (2 Chr. 3:6). The most likely identification is Arabia.

Pasach (pā′săk) son of Japhlet of the tribe of Asshur (1 Chr. 7:33).

Pas-dammim (păs′dăm′ím) see 1 Chr. 9:13 and 1 Sam. 17:11. Ruins bearing the name *Damun* or *Chirbet Damoun* lie near the road from Jerusalem to Beit Jibrin. Some identify this with Pas-dammim. See **Ephes-dammim**

Paseah (pà-sē′à) 1. The "sons of Paseah" were among the Nethinim who returned with Zerubbabel (Ezra 2:49).

2. A descendant of Judah; son of Eshton (1 Chr. 4:12).

Pashhur (păsh′hēr) 1. Name of one of the families of priests of the chief house of Malchijah (1 Chr. 9:12; Neh. 11:12; Jer. 21:1). In the time of Nehemiah this family appears to have become a chief house, its head the head of a course (Ezra 2:38; Neh. 7:41). The individual from whom the family was named was likely Pashhur, the son of Malchijah, who in the reign of Zedekiah was one of the chief princes of the court (Jer. 38:1).

2. The son of Immer and also the priest (1 Chr. 24:14; Neh. 10:3; Jer. 20:1). In the reign of Jehoiakim, Pashhur showed himself hostile to Jeremiah as his namesake the son of Malchiah did afterwards and put the prophet in stocks by the gate of Benjamin. Jeremiah in turn warned Pashhur that he and his house would be carried captives to Babylon (Jer. 20:1–6).

3. Father of Gedaliah (Jer. 38:1).

4. The head of the priestly family, members of which returned from the Babylonian captivity (Ezra 2:38; Neh. 7:41).

5. A priest who sealed the covenant by which it was agreed that intermarriage of their children with foreigners would be forbidden (Neh. 10:3).

passage the term occurs in the plural form in Jer. 22:20 and designates the mountain region of Abarim on the east of Jordan.

passion term used in translating a phrase of Acts 1:3, which refers to Jesus' suffering and death. In this sense, passion denotes the sufferings of Christ upon the Cross, but it is also used to designate the sufferings of Jesus following the Last Supper and prior to the Cross.

Passover 1. The first of the three great annual festivals of the Israelites, celebrated in the month Nisan on the fourteenth day.

(1) *Institution.* When the chosen people were about to be brought out of Egypt, God spoke to Moses and Aaron, commanding them to instruct all the congregation of Israel to prepare for their departure by solemn religious ordinance. On the tenth day of the month Abib, the head of each family was to select either a kid or a lamb, a male of the first year, without blemish. If his family was too small to eat all of the lamb, he was permitted to invite his nearest neighbor to join in the meal. On the fourteenth day of the month, he was to kill his lamb while the sun was setting. He was then to take the blood in a basin and with a twig of hyssop was to sprinkle it on the two side posts and on the lintel of the door of his home. The lamb was then roasted whole. It could not be boiled, neither could a bone be broken. Unleavened bread and bitter herbs were to be eaten with the flesh. No male who was uncircumcised was to join the group. Each one was to have his loins girt, to hold a staff in his hand, and to wear shoes. He was to eat hastily, and it was important to calculate the party as nearly as possible so that all of the lamb might be consumed. If any portion did remain, it was to be burned the following morning. Moses was likewise directed to inform the people of God's purpose to smite the firstborn of the Egyptians and to declare the Passover an ordinance forever. He was further admonished to give direction respecting the order and duration of the festival in future times, and parents were likewise exhorted to teach their children its meaning. The people followed Moses' directions and at midnight of the prescribed time the firstborn of the Egyptians were smitten. The pharaoh and his people then urged the Israelites to depart immediately. See Ex. 12:1–51, 13:3–10, 23:14–19, 34:18–26;

Lev. 23:4–14; Num. 9:1=14, 28:16–25; Deut. 16:1–6.

(2) *Observance.* On the fourteenth of Nisan, the house was to be searched methodically for leaven, and on the same day every male Israelite not laboring under bodily infirmity of ceremonial impurity was commanded to appear before the Lord with an offering in proportion to his means (Ex. 23:15; Deut. 16:16–17). Devout women sometimes attended. As the sun was setting, the lambs were slain, the fat and the blood given to the priests (2 Chr. 35:5–6). The lamb was then roasted whole, and eaten with unleavened bread and bitter herbs. No portion of the lamb was to be left until the morning. The same night, after the beginning of the fifteenth day of Nisan, the fat was burned by the priests and the blood was sprinkled on the altar. No work was to be done on the fifteenth. On this day and the six following days, an offering in addition to the daily sacrifice was made—two young bullocks, a ram, and seven lambs of the first year, with meat offerings for a burnt offering and a goat for a sin offering (Num. 23:19–23).

In later times the lamb was not selected before the fourteenth day of the month. Either the head of the family, or any other person who was not ceremonially unclean, took the lamb into the court of the temple. Only there could the paschal lamb be slain. The unleavened bread might be made of wheat, spelt, barley, oats, or rye. It appears to have been usually made of finest wheat. The bitter herbs (lettuce, etc.) were dipped into sauce. The Pentateuch does not mention wine in connection with the Passover, but the Mishnah enjoins that there should be no less than four cups of wine at the meal of the poorest Israelite. "The cup of blessing" is mentioned in 1 Cor. 10:16. The service of praise, "The Hallel," likewise characterized the Passover.

All work was suspended for some hours before the evening of the fourteenth of Nisan. One could not eat ordinary food following midday. No male was admitted to the Passover table unless he was circumcised, even if he was a seed of Israel (Ex. 12:48). Neither, according to the letter of the Law, was anyone of either sex admitted who was ceremonially unclean (Num. 9:6). The party customarily numbered no fewer than ten. The meal having been prepared, the family was placed around the table, the head of the family taking a place of honor, probably somewhat raised above the rest. The condiments were placed on the table although a specific order was followed in serving. The first cup of wine was filled, and the blessing was asked by the head of the family. The bitter herbs were then placed on the table and a portion of them eaten, either with or without the sauce. The unleavened bread was passed next, and afterward the lamb was placed on the table in front of the head of the family. Before the lamb was eaten, the second cup of wine was filled, and the son in compliance with Ex. 12:26 asked his father to explain the meaning of the feast. The first portion of the Hallel was then sung, after which the lamb was carved and eaten. The third cup of wine followed and soon afterward the fourth. The second part of the Hallel was then sung. Although the participants had stood at the first Passover, in later times they reclined. The first day, the fifteenth of Nisan, was observed as a sabbath and likewise the seventh day. On the second day of the festival, a sheaf of the first ripe barley was waved by the priest before the Lord to consecrate the opening of barley harvest. During this Feast of Unleavened Bread, the seven days following Passover, only unleavened bread was eaten. It is obvious that unleavened bread was associated with the rapidity of the flight from Egypt. See **Feast of Weeks**

(3) *Interpretation.* The deliverance from Egypt was regarded as the starting point of the Hebrew nation. The Israelites were raised from the condition of bondmen to that of free people who owed allegiance to Jehovah. The paschal lamb was the chief feature in the ceremonies of the festival. It was offered in the holy place, the blood was sprinkled on the altar, and the fat was burned. The significance of the lamb could hardly be overlooked. It is most significant that the Lord's crucifixion occurred at Passover. See Mt. 26:17; Mk. 14:12; Lk. 22:7; Jn. 18:28.

2. A term referring to the sacrificial offering at the festival of the Passover (Ex. 12:21; Deut. 16:2; 2 Chr. 30:17). Paul describes Christ as our Passover (1 Cor. 5:7).   v.e.g.

Patara (păt′à-rà) a Lycian city located on the southwestern shore of Lycia, not far from the left bank of the river Xanthus. Immediately opposite is the island of Rhodes. See Acts 21:1–2.

pastor a translation of a term occurring in Eph. 4:11. The term is often translated "shepherd."

pastoral letters a common designation of Paul's letters to Timothy and Titus. See 1 and 2 **Timothy** and **Titus**.

Pathros (păth′rŏs) a term used to designate Upper Egypt. The term *pathros* literally means "the southern land." Isaiah 11:11 locates this area between Egypt and Cush. Although scholars have debated the precise location of the *pathros*, it seems logical to identify the area as Upper Egypt. In Ezek. 29:14 identified as the land of the Egyptians.

Pathrusim (păth-rōō′sĭm) the inhabitants of Pathros (Gen. 10:14; 1 Chr. 1:12).

Patmos (păt′mŏs) a rocky island of the Aegean to which John the apostle was banished. One of the Sporades, Patmos is the site from which John saw the visions which he records in the book of Revelation (1:9). The tiny island is only ten miles in length and six miles in width.

patriarch the name applied in the NT to the founders of the Hebrew nation. In Heb. 7:4 the term is applied to Abraham; Luke uses it to refer to the twelve sons of Jacob (Acts 7:8–9) and to David (Acts 2:29). The name is applied particularly to godly men and heads of families, the lives of whom are recorded as occurring previous to the time of Moses.

Patrobas (păt′rō-bás) a Christian at Rome to whom Paul sends his greeting (Rom. 16:14).

Pau (pā′û) the capital city of Hadar king of Edom (Gen. 36:39).

Paul an apostle of Jesus to the Gentiles.

1. *His birth and youth.* The apostle's Hebrew name was Saul, and his native city was Tarsus. The Jewish name Saul was received from his Jewish parents. Paul spoke of himself as being "a Hebrew of the Hebrews," but he was born in a Gentile city. His father was of the tribe of Benjamin (Phil. 3:5) and a Pharisee (Acts 23:6). Paul was born a Roman citizen (Acts 22:28). As customary among the Jews, Saul was instructed in the Scriptures when quite young. As a citizen of a Gentile city, he must have learned the Greek language and possessed a certain freedom of speaking and writing. His father likewise instructed him in the trade of tentmaking, and later during his missionary travels he engaged in this trade (Acts 18:3). The mountains behind Tarsus abounded in goats from which mohair was clipped. It is not known whether his family had always lived in Tarsus, how they came to reside there, or how long Paul himself lived in the chief city of Cilicia.

The university in Tarsus was one of the outstanding universities of Paul's day, and whether a young man who purposed to become a rabbi enrolled in the university, one cannot say with finality. It would seem unlikely that he did, but inevitably he must have been under the influence of such a renowned institution. Stoicism was the dominant philosophy of the area.

2. *His Education.* Paul indicates that he was reared in Jerusalem (Acts 22:3). He was likely sent there while he was quite young, and it was

in Jerusalem that he was further educated in the Law. He speaks in terms of having been instructed "according to the strict matter of the law of our fathers" (Acts 22:3). Gamaliel, one of the most distinguished and revered rabbis of the day, became Paul's teacher. The famous Gamaliel was the grandson of Hillel. This Gamaliel spoke against the Sanhedrin intent to slay the apostles (Acts 5:34–39). Although Gamaliel could speak in behalf of the apostles, it is readily evident that he was famous for his rabbinical learning, and at his feet the young man from Tarsus was taught. Thus, Paul became versed not only in the OT, but also in the traditionalism of rabbinical interpretation. At the same time, he manifested zeal for the traditions of the fathers and the narrow Pharisaism which he had known throughout life continued to burn within his heart. It is quite evident from Paul's writings that he was not only prepared to occupy a place of importance among his countrymen, but he was readily looked upon as a brilliant young leader.

3. *His Persecution of Christians and Subsequent Conversion.* Acts 7:58 first introduces the reader to Paul the persecutor. This reference indicates that the witnesses who stoned Stephen laid their garments at the feet of a young man. Acts 8:1 indicates that Saul "was consenting unto his death." Stephen, the first Christian martyr, met his fate partially because of the influence of one destined to become the outstanding leader of all Christendom. Perhaps this experience only whetted the fanaticism of the young persecutor who soon found himself journeying to other areas in order to persecute followers of the Christ. He was no longer satisfied with local persecution and desired letters of the high priest to the synagogues in Damascus that there he might continue his deadly art of persecution.

It is most significant that Saul's conversion occurred while he was journeying to Damascus for the purpose of persecuting other Christians. Saul and his companions were traveling the usual road across the desert from Galilee to Damascus and had almost arrived at their destination when a sudden light from heaven, much brighter than the sun at its zenith, overcame the group. The entire group fell to the ground, but all other men were able to stand up without assistance. Saul's companions then assisted him, but he was blinded and only after three days and a visit from Ananias was Saul able to see again. See Acts 9:1–19, 22:1–16, 26:1–20; Gal. 1:1–16. Following the three days' lodging in the house of Judas in the city of Damascus, Ananias, chosen of God for this purpose came to Paul and laid his hands upon him, Saul then receiving his sight. In 1 Cor. 15:8, Paul mentions the Lord's appearance to him. He expresses that appearance in these words, "Last of all he was seen of me also." The new servant of the Lord broke his three days' fast with the appearance of Ananias, and then was received into the fellowship of the disciples.

Without further delay, he began the work to which God had called him, and to the astonishment of all his hearers he proclaimed Jesus in the synagogues, declaring him to be the Son of God. The Acts narrative at this point simply indicates that he was occupied in his work with increasing vigor and commitment. According to Gal. 1:17–18 he spent three years in Arabia following his conversion experience. Paul discloses no information concerning his visit to Arabia, neither concerning the district visited nor the purpose of the visit. The vehement hatred which Saul had directed toward the Christians was now directed toward him by his former colleagues in persecution. According to 2 Cor. 11:32, it was necessary for Paul to leave Damascus under the cover of darkness.

Upon arriving in Jerusalem, Paul attempted to join the disciples, but they "were all afraid of him and believed not that he was a disciple." Barnabas became his sponsor to the apostles and church at Jerusalem, assuring them of the facts of Saul's conversion and subsequent behavior in Damascus. It was his introduction which removed the fears of the apostles and Paul was accepted as a follower of the Christ. Paul's preaching in Jerusalem was as fearless as it had been in Damascus and was inevitably directed toward his friends of yesteryear, the Greek-speaking Jews (Acts 9:28–29). These who were the recipients of Paul's pointed and pungent preaching threatened his life, and once again Paul found it necessary to flee, this time traveling to Tarsus, his boyhood home (Acts 9:29–30; Gal. 1:21).

4. *Prior to the First Missionary Journey.* Paul remained in Tarsus for an indefinable period of time, likely some six to seven years. He was obviously engaged in proclamation of the Gospel and probably founded churches in Cilicia. During this period, still another movement was underway at Antioch of Syria. This church, apart from the Jerusalem church, was without question the most influential Christian body of early history. The preaching of the Gospel to the Gentiles first took root in Antioch, and from this site it was soon to be propagated. Some of those who had been persecuted as a result of the intense feeling against Stephen had scattered to the known corners of their world. Among those who journeyed to Antioch were men of Cyprus and Cyrene who preached effectively and were rewarded by a great number who believed.

The Jerusalem church, upon receiving the report concerning the events in Antioch, admonished Barnabas to journey to Antioch and investigate the workings of God in that city. As the work grew under his direction and many people were added unto the fellowship, Barnabas felt the need of assistance and traveled to Tarsus to seek Saul. Possibly because of some values which Barnabas had observed in Saul during the Damascus experience, he earnestly desired him for a helper in Antioch. There they labored together unremittingly for a year, preaching the Gospel and teaching many people. During this time Saul was subordinate to Barnabas.

Agabus, one of the prophets from Jerusalem who came to visit in Antioch, signified that there should be a great dearth throughout all the world. The disciples at Antioch were moved by this prophecy and determined to send contributions immediately to Jerusalem, the gift being conveyed by Barnabas and Saul. Having discharged their errand, Barnabas and Saul returned to Antioch, bringing with them another, John Mark, the son of Barnabas' sister. Resuming the work of teaching and prophesying, the Christians in Antioch became even more convinced that the message was not for Judea or Antioch alone, but it was a message intended for the entire world. Searching earnestly for God's expressed purpose, the Holy Ghost spoke to the group, saying, "Separate me Barnabas and Saul for the work whereunto I have called them." After much fasting and prayer, the brothers at Antioch laid their hands on Barnabas and Saul, and these two men departed for the first missionary journey.

5. *The First Missionary Journey.* The one thing which was clear to Barnabas and Saul as they left Antioch of Syria was their purpose in going—to speak the word of God. The primary characteristic of Paul's preaching was that he voiced a heavenly message. Luke indicates that as quickly as they reached Cyprus, Barnabas and Saul began to "announce the word of God." See Acts 13:1–14:28 for a description and account of the first missionary journey. It is likewise significant to note that at the present their message was preached only in the synagogues. However, having traveled throughout the island, from Salamis to Paphos, they were then asked to explain their doctrine to an eminent Gentile, Sergius Paulus, the proconsul. A

false prophet, a Jew named Barjesus (Elymas), had attached himself to the governor of the island and attempted to destroy the influence exercised by Paul and Barnabas. Then Paul denounced Elymas in remarkable terms, declaring against him God's sentence of temporary blindness. The blindness immediately fell upon him, and the proconsul was persuaded by the teaching of the apostle and became a believer (Acts 13:8–12).

At this point, Saul is no longer called by the Hebrew name, but is now referred to by the name Paul and begins to take precedence over Barnabas. From Paphos, Paul and his company sailed for Perga in Pamphylia. At this point, John Mark left the group and returned to Jerusalem. Perhaps he was homesick, perhaps he felt his mother needed him more than these two itinerant missionaries, or perhaps he simply objected to the place now occupied by Paul. Paul was so moved by his departure that he refused to permit John Mark to accompany him on the second missionary journey.

From Perga the group traveled to Antioch in Pisidia. In Pisidia they followed their usual approach, going into the synagogues on the sabbath and speaking as opportunity presented itself. Following the reading of the Law and the Prophets, the rulers of the synagogue invited them to speak any word of exhortation. It was customary for the rulers of the synagogue to so invite those who visited them to speak. Paul spoke (Acts 13:16–41); the discourse produced a strong impression and the hearers requested the apostles to repeat the message on the next sabbath. So much interest was evoked during the week of discussion which followed that almost the entire city came together to hear the word of God on the following sabbath. Success once again aroused Jewish envy, which in turn provoked the apostles to become extremely bold and outspoken. Thus it was necessary for the apostles to turn from the Jews to the Gentiles. This antagonism was to be reproduced in almost every preaching point. Especially the women of the higher classes, those who had influence with the authorities or the populace, used this influence to have the missionaries persecuted and driven from their places.

Paul and Barnabas then traveled to Iconium, where the occurrences at Antioch were repeated. Leaving Iconium, they traveled to the Lycaonian country, where they worked particularly in the cities of Lystra and Derbe. In Lystra a cripple was healed; the citizens were so influenced that they offered worship to the missionaries, calling them Jupiter and Mercury.

There also, Timothy was likely converted (Acts 16:1; 2 Tim. 1:2). Paul's popularity in Lystra was shortlived, for he was soon dragged out of the city, stoned, and left for dead. When he revived, the apostles departed for Derbe, where once again they witnessed concerning the Christ.

Although the apostles could have crossed the mountains into Cilicia and gone directly through Paul's home of Tarsus and back to Antioch of Syria, they chose to revisit the churches which had been founded on the initial segment of their missionary journey. Thus they returned from Derbe to Lystra, from Lystra to Iconium, from Iconium to Antioch of Pisidia, and from Antioch to Perga, in each place assisting in the organization of the church and encouraging the believers. From Perga they traveled to Attalia, then returned to Antioch in Syria.

Inquisitiveness and gratitude characterized the meeting of the believers following the return of Paul and Barnabas. The apostles recounted minutely their experiences in preaching, and the entire group rejoiced in the blessings of God.

6. *The Jerusalem Council*. See Acts 15; Gal. 2. The story of God's blessings upon the Gentiles prompted the true Jew to ask, "What is the Gentile's relationship to the law of Moses?" The Jerusalem council answered that question. While Paul and Barnabas were staying at Antioch, "certain men from Judea" went there and taught the people that it was necessary for the Gentile converts to be circumcised. The apostles vigorously opposed this doctrine inasmuch as they had witnessed the conversion of many Gentiles apart from this ritual. It was soon determined that the question should be discussed by a larger body in Jerusalem. Paul and Barnabas, with others, were selected to attend the conference to be held in the mother church. Even while traveling from Antioch to Jerusalem, this group announced to the brethren in Phoenicia and Samaria the conversion of the Gentiles, the news being received with great joy (Acts 15:4).

Much disputation characterized the meeting in Jerusalem. Arguments were used on both sides of the question, but when the persons of highest authority spoke, they appealed to what was stronger than arguments—the course of events, through which the will of God had been manifestly shown. After the facts had been stated, James, with incomparable simplicity and wisdom, bound up the testimony of recent facts with the testimony of ancient prophecy and gave a practical judgment upon the question. The judgment proved to be decisive. The injunction that the Gentiles should abstain from the pollutions of idols and from fornication explained itself. The abstinence from things strangled and from blood is desired as a concession to the custom of the Jews. Paul had established his point!

What constituted the matter under discussion must be understood. Circumcision and ordinances of the Law were witnesses of a separation of the chosen race from other nations. The Jews were obviously proud of that separation. But the Gospel proclaimed that the time had come in which the separation was to be eliminated, and God's good will manifested to all nations alike. It spoke of a union with God, through trust, which gave hope of a righteousness that the Law had been powerless to produce. Therefore, to insist upon Gentiles being circumcised would have been to deny the Gospel of Christ. If there was to be simply an enlarging of the separated nation by the receiving of individuals into it, then the other nations of the world remained as much on the outside of God's covenant as ever. Then there was no gospel for mankind; no justification given to men. The loss, in such a case, would have been as much to the Jew as to the Gentile.

Paul felt this most strongly, but Peter also saw that if the Jewish believers were thrown back on the Jewish law, and gave up the free and absolute grace of God, that law became a mere burden, just as heavy to the Jews as it would be to the Gentiles. The only hope for the Jew was in a Savior of mankind. They implied therefore no difference of belief when it was agreed that Paul and Barnabas should go to the heathen, while James, Cephas, and John undertook to be the apostles of the circumcision. The judgment of the council was immediately recorded in a letter addressed to the Gentile brethren in Antioch, Syria, and Cilicia. This remarkable letter stands as one of the classics in the journals of Christendom. It settles with finality the method of salvation for the Gentile. He is saved simply by Christ plus his faith and not by Christ, plus his faith, plus works of the Mosaic law.

7. *The Second Missionary Journey.* As previously indicated, the painful difference which existed between Paul and John Mark likewise affected his relationship to Barnabas. Silas became Paul's chief companion on the second missionary journey. See Acts 15:36–18:23 for Luke's account of this journey. Paul and Silas traveled through Syria and Cilicia, visiting the churches, and thus came to Derbe and Lystra.

Here they found Timothy, who had become a disciple on the former visit of the apostle. Paul requested Timothy to be circumcised, and when the two companions left Lystra they were joined by young Timothy. Luke moves rapidly through a considerable space of the apostle's life and labors by recording simply, "They went throughout Phrygia and the region of Galatia" (16:6).

Paul alludes to the content of his preaching in the Galatian epistle (Gal. 4:13–15). Although commentators differ concerning the interpretation of the words "through infirmity of the flesh," their grammatical sense implies that some illness was the occasion of Paul's preaching in Galatia. On the other hand, the form and order of the words are not what one should have expected if the apostle meant to indicate illness as the occasion of his preaching, and some interpret the words to mean a weakness of the flesh prompted his preaching to the Galatians. It is hopeless to attempt to determine positively what the infirmity was. Many scholars, supported by certain Biblical allusions, believe that this infirmity was poor eyesight. Others think of it as being malaria fever. Having passed through Phrygia and Galatia, Paul intended to visit the western coast, but the Holy Spirit directed them to Troas.

At Troas there appeared the vision of the man of Macedonia (Acts 16:9) who called the missionaries to "come over and help us." The vision was at once accepted as a heavenly invitation, the help wanted by the Macedonians was believed to be the preaching of the Gospel. At this point in the account, Luke the historian begins to employ "we" in his account. He says nothing of himself, but it is only logical to assume that the author now joins the party. The group immediately sailed from Troas, touched at Samothrace, then landed on the continent at Neapolis, whence they journeyed to Philippi.

Many Romans had settled in the Greek city, Philippi, and it was politically a colony. There were few Jews at Philippi, and on the sabbath, the apostolic company joined their countrymen at the place by the riverside where prayer was offered. See Acts 16:13. The first convert in Macedonia was an Asiatic woman who already worshiped the God of the Jews and upon her conversion besought the apostle and his friend to honor her by staying in her house. They could not resist her insistence, and during their stay at Philippi were the guests of Lydia (Acts 16:40). During the Philippian sojourn, Paul and his companions were beset by a young girl who was demon-possessed. Paul turned and exclaimed, "I command thee, in the name of Jesus Christ to come out of her." When the girl's masters realized that their hope of gain was now gone, Paul and Silas were dragged before the magistrates and charged with "troubling the city." Additional charge of introducing observances which were unlawful for Romans was likewise suggested. The Roman magistrates now yielded to the clamor of the citizens, causing the clothes of Paul and Silas to be torn from them; the apostles were then beaten and imprisoned. While in prison, Paul and Silas observed the wonder of God's power in the earthquake, their release and the jailer's conversion and baptism (Acts 16:26–34).

Paul and Silas now traveled through Amphipolis and Apollonia, stopping again at Thessalonica. At this important city there was a synagogue of the Jews. True to his custom, Paul went to them, and for three sabbath days proclaimed Jesus as the Christ. Again, as in Pisidia of Antioch, the envy of the Jews was aroused, a mob assaulting the house of Jason with whom Paul and Silas were staying as guests, dragging Jason himself and some other brethren before the magistrates. At this sign of extreme danger, the believers immediately sent Paul and Silas away by night.

The Epistles to the Thessalonians were likely written soon after the apostle's visit to Thessalonica and contain more particulars of his work in founding that church than is found in any other epistle. Leaving Thessalonica, Paul and Silas journeyed to Berea, where they found the Jews more noble than those of Thessalonica. Accordingly, they gained many converts, both Jews and Greeks; but the Jews of Thessalonica, hearing of this, sent emissaries to stir up the people, and it was soon thought best that Paul should himself leave the city, although Silas and Timothy remained behind. Some of the Thessalonians journeyed with Paul as far as Athens where the apostle was left alone to witness the most profuse idolatry side by side with the most pretentious philosophy. When he spoke on Mars' Hill in terms of Jesus and the resurrection, the Greeks believed him to be presenting a new pair of gods inasmuch as Jesus in the Greek is a masculine noun while resurrection is a feminine noun. Thus the contempt of the philosophers was mixed with their own curiosity.

Journeying to Corinth, which he visited immediately following his Athenian ministry, he remained there for some eighteen months and his work enjoyed unusual success. In the city of Corinth he met the famous couple, Aquila and Priscilla, and lived with them (Acts 18:1–3).

He followed his usual custom and preached in the synagogue, but later because of the extreme opposition of the Jews, he preached and taught in the house of Justus, a Gentile, who lived next door to the synagogue. The Acts account, as well as Paul's own account in 1 Cor. 2:1–5, alludes to the anxiety of mind with which the apostle approached his mission in the city of Corinth. He indicates in the Corinthians passage that he determined to know nothing except the crucified Jesus. Paul was joined in Corinth by young Timothy who had most recently come from Thessalonica. As a result of the information which Timothy conveyed to him, the apostle wrote the Thessalonian epistles to warn, exhort, encourage, and admonish the Thessalonian Christians. Eventually the hostility of the Jews again caught up with Paul, and Paul was accused before the proconsul Gallio of violating the Law. However, the proconsul decided that this matter pertained solely to the synagogue and that the apostle had broken no law of the Roman empire. Paul was thus permitted to continue his work in the city.

After approximately eighteen months, Paul turned from Corinth and sailed to Ephesus, from there to Caesarea, and eventually to Jerusalem. Having greeted the Jerusalem church, he returned to Antioch from which this mission had originated. The importance of the second missionary journey cannot be overestimated. It resulted in the establishment of Christianity on the European continent.

8. *The Third Missionary Journey.* See Acts 18:24–21:17 for Luke's report of this journey. Paul remains in Antioch of Syria for some time, beginning the third missionary journey in approximately A.D. 54. He purposed to travel through "the region of Galatia and Phrygia in order, establishing all the disciples" (Acts 18:23). Having arrived in Ephesus, he was impressed, not only by the need of this great city, but likewise by the unusual opportunity which the city afforded. Ephesus was the capital of Asia and was one of the more influential cities of the East. For some three years the apostle made Ephesus his base of operations. During this time many things occurred, of which the historian of the Acts chose two examples, the triumph over magical arts and the great disturbance raised by the silversmiths of Artemis. It was during this ministry that the first letter to the Corinthians was written. In this letter, he encourages the Corinthians to collect money for the church at Jerusalem by laying aside something on the first day of the week, as he had directed the churches in Galatia to do. He says that he shall tarry at Ephesus till Pente-

cost and then set out on a journey toward Corinth, through Macedonia, so as perhaps to spend the winter with them. He expresses his joy at the coming of Stephanus and his companions, and he likewise commends these individuals to the Corinthian fellowship.

Paul left Ephesus for Macedonia, and proceeded first to Troas (2 Cor. 2:12), where he might have preached the Gospel with a good hope of success. But a restless anxiety to obtain tidings concerning the church at Corinth urged him onward, and he advanced into Macedonia, where he met Titus, who brought him the news for which he was thirsting. Receiving this information prompted Paul to write the letter known as 2 Corinthians. From Macedonia Paul went to Corinth and spent the winter of A.D. 57–58 there. He likely addressed himself to the disciplinary problems which are discussed in 1 Corinthians, but the visit is even more significant because from the city of Corinth he wrote the Epistle to the Romans. In the Romans epistle he states that justification is by faith. The theme of the letter seems to be the "righteousness of God for unrighteous men."

Upon leaving Corinth, Paul began his last journey to the city of Jerusalem. Various friends from numerous Gentile churches accompanied him (Acts 20:4). His work among them had been opposed vigorously by certain Judaizers; hence, he purposed to carry a worthy offering from the Gentile Christians to the church in Jerusalem. Paul's return journey took him by way of Macedonia, Philippi, Troas, Assos, Mitylene, and Samos to Miletus. This city was located some thirty-five miles from Ephesus, and Paul requested the Ephesian elders to meet him there. The tender and heart-warming address is recorded in Acts 20:18–35. From Miletus, Paul sailed to Cos, Rhodes, Patara, and Tyre. The group remained there for a week, and the local disciples begged Paul not to journey to Jerusalem. However, after an emotional farewell he sailed to Ptolemais, and the next day the company arrived in Caesarea, where they stayed with Philip the evangelist. Here Agabus bound his own hands and feet with Paul's girdle and predicted that in like manner the Jews would bind Paul and deliver him to the Gentiles. Yet in spite of this prophetic warning, Paul insisted on visiting Jerusalem. A number of his disciples accompanied him to the Holy City, thus completing the tour described as the third missionary journey.

9. *Paul's Arrest.* Paul had become by this time a man of considerable note among his countrymen, being widely known as one who had taught with pre-eminent boldness that the way into God's favor was opened to the Gentiles and that this way did not open through the door of the Jewish law. Moreover, Paul had actually founded numerous and important Christian communities, composed of Jews and Gentiles alike. These actions had aroused the bitter enmity of Jewish pride which was almost as strong in some of those who had professed the faith of Jesus as in their unconverted brethren. Upon arriving in Jerusalem, he was now approaching a crisis in the long struggle. Although the believers at Jerusalem could not but glorify God for what they had heard, they had become alarmed by the prevalent feeling concerning Paul. In order to dispel this impression, they asked him to do publicly an act of homage to the Law and its observances.

There were present four men who were under the Nazarite vow (Num. 6:13–21). When this vow was completed, each participant was to present certain offerings in the temple, such offerings involving considerable expense. The Jew considered it a meritorious act to provide these offerings for the poor Nazarites. Paul was requested to put himself under the vow with these four men and to supply the cost of their offerings. He immediately accepted the proposal. The entire process undertaken by Paul required seven days to complete. Toward the end of this time, certain Jews from "Asia," who had come up for the Pentecostal feast and had a personal knowledge of Paul himself and of his companion Trophimus, a Gentile from Ephesus, saw Paul in the temple. They immediately prejudiced the people against him, crying out, "Men of Israel, help; this is the man that teacheth all men everywhere against the people and the law and this place; and further brought Greeks into the temple and hath polluted this holy place." Paul was then dragged from the temple, and the people would have killed him if the garrison commander had not been informed that "all Jerusalem was in an uproar." The commander, along with soldiers and centurions, hastened to the scene of the tumult. Paul was rescued from the violence of the multitude by the Roman officer, who in turn made him prisoner, and chained him to two soldiers. Paul was then interrogated by the garrison commander.

Acts 21:34–40 is a graphic description of Paul's obtaining the opportunity to address the people. The discourse which follows was spoken in Hebrew, the native dialect of the country, and was on that account listened to with more attention. The Jews cried so intently against Paul that the Roman commander assumed that

Paul had committed some heinous offense, and carried away from the multitude, commanded that he should be examined by scourging. Again the apostle took advantage of his Roman citizenship to protect himself from such an outrage. On the following day, the chief captain called the chief priest and the Sanhedrin and brought Paul before them. At this point Luke records the lengthy discourse of Paul's defense. In this discourse Paul claimed to have lived in all good conscience unto God, to have been a Pharisee and the son of a Pharisee, and to have believed in the resurrection of the dead. Paul's voicing of belief in the resurrection created still another tumult, the Pharisees and the Sadducees disagreeing violently concerning the idea of resurrection. The dissension became so great that Paul was carried away by the Roman soldiers. On the next day a conspiracy was formed when more than forty Jews bound themselves under an oath neither to eat nor to drink until they had killed Paul. The plot was discovered and Paul was carried away from Jerusalem. The chief captain, Claudius Lysias, determined to send him to Caesarea to appear before Felix the governor of Judea. Lysias then placed Paul in the care of a strong guard of soldiers, who took him by night as far as Antipatris. From that point a smaller detachment accompanied him to Caesarea, where they delivered their prisoner into the hands of the governor.

10. *Caesarean Imprisonment.* Thus to the end of the Acts story Paul is described as being in Roman custody. The Roman custody proved to be a protection to Paul, without which he would have doubtless fallen a victim to the animosity of the Jews. Tertullus was the counsel retained by the Jews and brought to Caesarea by Ananias and the elders. Paul denied Tertullus' charges of strife-making and of profaning the temple. Again he gave prominence to the hope of the resurrection, which he accepted as did his accusers. Paul referred to his demonstration of loyalty to the faith of his fathers as shown by his coming to Jerusalem to bring alms for his nation, offerings to his people, and the observing of purification ceremonies in the temple. He avowed that he had not violated the law of his fathers, nor had he done anything to be accused of disloyalty as an Israelite. Felix decided to leave Paul in custody, but to permit his friends to visit him.

Festus succeeded Felix as governor of Judea. The new governor visited Jerusalem, only to be requested by the Jews that Paul be brought to Jerusalem for trial. An ulterior motive of assassination prompted them to make such request.

Festus, however, would not comply with their request. He invited the Jews to Caesarea, and the trial which followed closely resembled the one held before Felix. During this trial Paul appealed to Caesar. In order for a procurator to send a man before Caesar, a list of crimes of the accused must accompany the prisoner. Festus sought assistance in this matter with the arrival of the Jewish king Agrippa and his sister Bernice. Paul was then brought before Agrippa and permitted to speak for himself. This discourse is recorded in Acts 26 and is a detailed account of his being led to God through his conversion to serve the Lord Jesus instead of persecuting the disciples of the Lord. Following Paul's defense, Festus and Agrippa conferred and concluded that Paul was guilty of nothing which deserved death or imprisonment. Agrippa's final answer to the inquiry of Festus was: "This man might have been set at liberty if he had not appealed unto Caesar."

11. *The Journey to Rome.* Julius, a centurion, was charged with the responsibility of transporting Paul and certain other prisoners to Rome. See Acts 27–28. Luke and Aristarchus accompanied Paul on this journey. Sailing from Caesarea, the group touched at Sidon and then proceeded to Myra in Lycia. The group transferred ships in Lycia, boarding for this portion of the journey an Alexandrian merchant ship. The wind was not favorable, and they were compelled to sail over against Cnidus on the coast of Caria. Then sailing south, they rounded Cape Salmone and reached Fair Havens, a port on the south shore of the island of Crete. The weather continued to threaten and hamper their activities. Upon leaving Fair Havens, a fierce northeasterly wind drove them southward; they passed south of Clauda, and having lightened the ship, they were driven for two weeks before the gale. During this time Paul maintained his faith in God and believed that no one would be lost. In an attempt to reach the nearby island of Melita, the ship was grounded upon the beach. The island of Melita lies some sixty miles south of Sicily. The inhabitants of the island graciously received the shipwrecked company, and Paul by his works gained special honor among them. It was on this island that a viper affixed himself to Paul's hand, but the fact that Paul lived convinced the natives that Paul was blessed of God. They had initially believed the viper to have been the instrument of God to destroy the man, but when no harm came to Paul they changed their opinions and decided that he was not only blessed of God, but a god. After a three months' stay on Melita, the soldiers and their prisoners

left in an Alexandrian ship for Italy. They touched at Syracuse, where they stayed three days, and at Rhegium, from which place they were carried by a fair wind to Puteoli, where they left their ship and the sea. At Puteoli they found brethren, for it was an important site, especially as a chief port for the traffic between Alexandria and Rome. These brethren requested them to remain awhile, and during the seven days which the apostolic group spent at Puteoli, news of the apostles' arrival was sent to Rome.

12. *Paul in Rome.* When the group arrived in Rome, the centurion delivered his prisoners into the proper custody. Paul was at once treated with special consideration and allowed to dwell by himself with the soldiers who guarded him. He invited chief persons among the Jews to visit and explained to them why he was brought to Rome to answer the charges made against him by the Jews in Palestine. He reasserted his loyalty to his nation and expressed the hope that they would understand that he was not hostile toward his fellow Jews. Yet, the reception of his message by the Jews was not favorable. He turned therefore again to the Gentiles; and for two years dwelt in his own rented house. These are the last words of Acts (28:30). To this period, epistles known as the imprisonment epistles belong. The letters to Philemon, Colossians, Ephesians, and Philippians were written during this period.

It seems that after a wearing imprisonment of two years or more at Rome, Paul was freed and spent some years in various journeyings eastward and westward. Toward the close of this time he wrote the First Letter to Timothy and his Letter to Titus. These letters seem to have been written at approximately the same time. Paul was soon arrested a second time, this time to be treated as a felon, not as an honorable prisoner (2 Tim. 2:9). He was, however, allowed to write the Second Letter to Timothy in which he expressed a confident expectation of speedy death, yet he hoped that Timothy might join him from Ephesus. According to Eusebius, he was beheaded in A.D. 67, but Jerome claims 68 as the date. In 64 Nero's persecution of the Christians spread, and it was doubtless followed by numerous outbreaks in the provinces (1 Pet. 4:13-19). During this persecution he was arrested and sent to Rome, either because he was accused of some crime committed in Rome, or because he appealed again to Caesar. It may be fairly well established that Felix was replaced by Festus in 60; thus, Paul left Caesarea that year, arriving in Rome in 61. He lived in Rome for two years or until 63. Following the dates of Euse-bius or Jerome, he was beheaded in 67 or 68.

One may likewise work backwards from A.D. 60. Paul was imprisoned for two years at Caesarea (Acts 24:27); therefore, he arrived in Jerusalem on his last visit by the Pentecost of 58. Before this he had spent the winter at Corinth, having gone from Ephesus to Greece (Acts 20:2-3). He left Ephesus, then, in the latter part of 57, and as he had remained three years in Ephesus, he must have gone there in 54. Prior to this journey, he had spent some time in Antioch (Acts 18:23). One can only add the time of a hasty visit to Jerusalem, the travels of the second missionary journey which included one and one-half years at Corinth, an undetermined time at Antioch, the important third visit to Jerusalem, another "long" residence at Antioch, the first missionary journey, again an indeterminate stay at Antioch (Acts 12:25), and arrive at Paul's second visit to Jerusalem, which nearly synchronizes with the death of Herod Agrippa in 44. During this interval of some ten years, the most important date to fix is that of the third visit to Jerusalem; this is generally placed at 50 or 51. Paul himself (Gal. 2:1) places this visit "fourteen years after"—after either his conversion or the first visit. If the "fourteen years after" referred to his conversion, then 37 or 38 would be the logical date for Paul's conversion experience. It must be remembered that the conversion was followed by three years in Arabia of Damascus (Gal. 1:18) and concluded with the first visit to Jerusalem; the space between the first visit and the second, 40 or 44, is filled by an indeterminate time, presumably two or three years at Tarsus (Acts 9:30) and one year at Antioch (Acts 11:26). The date of the martyrdom of Stephen can only be conjectured and is variously placed between 30 and the year of Paul's conversion. Other scholars date Paul's conversion variously, the period of 33 to 36 being the most popular.　　　　　　　　　v.e.g.

pavement see **gabbatha**

pavilion 1. *Soc*, an enclosed place, also rendered "tabernacle" and "den," only once "pavilion" (Ps. 27:5).

2. *Succah*, usually "tabernacle" and "booth."

3. *Shaphrur* and *shaphrir*, a word used once only, in Jer. 43:10, to signify glory or splendor, and hence probably to be understood of the splendid covering of the royal throne.

peacocks the Hebrew term *tucciyyim* is translated peacock. The peacock was among the natural products of the land of Tarshish which Solomon's fleet brought home to Jerusalem (1 K. 10:22; 2 Chr. 9:21).

pearl an article of trade, very precious. The pearl is mentioned frequently in the NT (Mt. 13:43; 1 Tim. 2:9; Rev. 17:4, 21:21). Pearls were sometimes used as ornaments and their value is best illustrated in Mt. 13:45 and in the Revelation passages.

Pedahel (pĕd'á-hĕl) a prince of the tribe of Naphtali and the son of Ammihud (Num. 34:28).

Pedahzur (pē-dä'zēr) father of Gamaliel, the chief of the tribe of Manasseh at the time of the wilderness experience (Num. 1:10, 2:20, 7:54, 59, 10:23).

Pedaiah (pē-dä'yà) 1. The father of Zebudah, mother of King Jehoiakim (2 K. 23:36).

2. A brother of Shealtiel, and father of Zerubbabel (1 Chr. 3:17–19).

3. A descendant of Parosh, one of the family of that name, who assisted Nehemiah in repairing the walls of Jerusalem (Neh. 3:25).

4. A priest who stood on Ezra's left when he read the Law to the people (Neh. 8:4).

5. A Benjaminite (Neh. 11:7).

6. A Levite in the time of Nehemiah (Neh. 13:13).

7. The father of Joel, prince of the half-tribe of Manasseh in the reign of David (1 Chr. 27:20).

Pekah (pē'kä) son of Remaliah, originally a captain of **Pekahiah** king of Israel. Pekah murdered his master, seized the throne, and became the eighteenth sovereign of the Northern Kingdom. His native country was probably Gilead inasmuch as fifty Gileadites joined him in the conspiracy against Pekahiah. Pekah, as ruler, steadily applied himself to the restoration of Israel's power. In achieving this purpose, he sought the support of a foreign alliance and obviously purposed to plunder the sister kingdom of Judah. Pekah led his army directly toward Judah's capital, destroying everything in his way. The Assyrian army then advanced through Galilee (2 K. 15:29) to Philistia, thus compelling Pekah to depart. Pekah, now fallen into the position of an Assyrian vassal, was compelled to abstain from further attacks on Judah. He ascended his throne in 757 B.C., began to war against Judea in 740 B.C., and was killed in 737 B.C.

Pekahiah (pĕk'à-hī'à) son and successor of Menahem. He came to Israel's throne in 759 B.C. and reigned two years. After a brief reign of two years, a conspiracy was organized against him by **Pekah,** who at head of fifty Gileadites, attacked the king and murdered him in his palace.

Pekod (pē'kŏd) occurring only in Jer. 50:21 and Ezek. 23:23, this appellative is applied to the Chaldeans. This group belongs to Nebuchadnezzar's empire in Ezekiel's time.

Pelaiah (pē-lā'yà) 1. A Levite who assisted Ezra in expounding the Law (Neh. 8:7).

2. A son of Elioenai, the royal line of Judea (1 Chr. 3:24).

Pelaliah (pĕl'à-lī'à) a priest, a contemporary of Ezra (Neh. 11:12).

Pelatiah (pĕl'à-tī'à) 1. A son of Hananiah, the son of Zerubbabel (1 Chr. 3:21).

2. A Simeonite, a captain of a marauding band. He lived in the time of Hezekiah and smote the Amalekites.

3. Son of Benaiah, and one of the princes of the people against whom Ezekiel was directed to utter the words of doom recorded in Ezek. 11:5–12.

4. A "chief" of the people, and likely the name of the family, who sealed the covenant with Nehemiah (Neh. 10:22).

Peleg (pē'lĕg) a son of Eber, and brother of Joktan (Gen. 10:25, 11:16). The name Peleg means "division," and the only incident connected with his history is the statement that "in his days was the earth divided." The reference may be to a division of the family of Eber, or it may refer to the scattering of Noah's descendants.

Pelet (pē'lĕt) 1. A son of Jahdai (1 Chr. 2:47).

2. A son of Azmaveth who was among the group joining David's forces at Ziklag (1 Chr. 12:3).

Peleth (pē'lĕth) 1. A Reubenite, and the father of On who joined Dathan and Abiram in their rebellion (Num. 16:1).

2. Son of Jonathan, and a descendant of Jerahmeel (1 Chr. 2:33).

Pelethites (pĕl'ē-thīts) this term, along with the term "Cherethites," designates David's bodyguard. These foreign mercenaries were under the command of Benaiah (2 Sam. 15:18–22, 20:7). Faithful to David during his later years, the Pelethites occupy a prominent place in the war in which Absalom's cause and life were lost.

pelican the Hebrew term *kaath* is translated pelican and was considered unclean (Lev. 11:18; Deut. 14:17). The pelican inhabited the wilderness and frequented ruins (Ps. 102:6; Isa. 34:11). A rather large bird, the pelican has a wing span of twelve or thirteen feet and stands five to six feet high.

Pelonite (pĕl'ô-nīt) Helez and Ahijah, two of David's mighty men, are called Pelonites (1 Chr. 11:27, 36). These men fought with David in his wars against the Philistines.

pen see **writing**

Peniel (pē-nī'ĕl) the name which Jacob assigned to the place where he had wrestled with God (Gen. 32:30). See **Penuel**

Peninnah (pē-nin'á) one of the two wives of Elkanah (1 Sam. 1:2).

penny the Gr. *denarion* is translated penny. It was the denarius, the chief Roman silver coin (Mt. 20:2, 22:19; Mk. 6:37, 12:15; Lk. 20:24; Jn. 6:7; Rev. 6:6). Its value is usually defined as seventeen cents and was the wage of a laborer in the time of Jesus.

Pentateuch (pĕn'tà-tūk) the first five books of the OT, frequently called the Five Books of Moses, are known as the Pentateuch. The Jews commonly referred to these books as the Law, the Law of Moses, the Law of the Lord, the Book of the Law, or the Book of Moses, the Book of the Law of the Lord, or the Book of the Lord. See Josh. 1:7–8, 8:31, 24:26; 1 K. 2:3; 2 Chr. 17:9, 25:3-4, 31:3; Ezra 7:6; Mt. 5:17; Lk. 2:22. The art of writing was practiced many years before the time of Moses. The year 4000 B.C. saw cuneiform being used by Sumerians in Babylonia and hieroglyphs by the Egyptians. The Ras Shamra cuneiform alphabet was in vogue in 1500 B.C. Moreover, the forms of literature which are represented in the Pentateuch were thoroughly familiar literary conceptions of Moses' day.

1. *Authorship.* The authorship of the Pentateuch has been sorely debated for unnumbered years. Although for centuries the Pentateuch was generally received as Mosaic, B. Spinoza in 1679 set himself boldly to controvert the Mosaic authorship. In 1753 the critical eye of Jean Astruc had noted that throughout Genesis and as far as Ex. 6, traces were to be found of two original documents, each characterized by the distinct uses of the names of God, the one by the name Elohim, and the other by the name Jehovah. Besides these two principal documents, he supposed Moses to have made use of ten others in the composition of the earlier part of his work. Yet this "documentary hypothesis" was too conservative and too rational for some critics. J. S. Vater and A. T. Hartmann maintained that the Pentateuch consisted merely of a number of fragments which had been strung loosely together without order or design. This approach has been called the "fragmentary hypothesis." Perhaps one of the better known names in OT criticism is that of J. Wellhausen. Although many additional writers have published the same theme, no one is more significant to the field of OT criticism than Wellhausen. Representing the work of many men, the documentary theory holds the writer J to be the author of document J, so

called because the writer refers to God as Jehovah, lived in Judah 950–850 B.C. E, the writer of the E document, so called because of his reference to God as Elohim, lived in Ephraim 750 B.C. Thus he represents a more advanced civilization and more refined environment than J. Following the fall of Samaria (722 B.C.), a redactor combined J and E in approximately 650 B.C., the resultant document being referred to as JE. D is assigned to 621 B.C., or some scholars would date the document fifty years earlier. The reformation led by Josiah was based upon this document. The book of Deuteronomy, as it is known today, represents the final result of editorial revisions and expansions of D. The Pentateuch grew and developed with the addition of D to JE. Leviticus 17–26 represent the Holiness Code, known as H. This work was likely compiled, according to the scholar who holds this theory, in approximately the middle of the sixth century. At some undefined date this document likewise was incorporated into the Priestly Code (P), the latest document of the Pentateuch. This last document was supposedly composed during the Babylonian exile. According to critics of this persuasion, the third main development of the Pentateuch was the joining of the P document to JED. This approach has consequently been known according to the designation of the documents, JEDP. The JEDP theory has received warm acclaim by many critics and sharp criticism by others. G. von Rad and M. Noth are contemporary scholars who advocate this hypothesis but are primarily interested in a form–critical approach. Ivan Engnell and J. Pedersen are among those who have reacted strongly to the Wellhausen theory.

The question of the Pentateuch's testimony to its authorship has been warmly debated. According to Ex. 24:3-4 "Moses came and told the words of Jehovah and all the judgments." These were written on a roll called the "book of the covenant" (vs. 7), and upon renewal of this covenant after the idolatry of the Israelites, Moses was again commanded by Jehovah to "write these words" (34:27). In Deut. 31:9–12 it is indicated that "Moses wrote this law" and delivered it to the custody of the priest. Obviously the question of authorship is bound to the interpretation of "this law." Two obvious questions must be answered. Is there evidence that parts of the work were not written by Moses? Is there evidence that parts of the work are later than his time? Is it probable that Moses wrote the words in Ex. 11:3 or those in Num. 12:3? Did Moses write the last chapter of Deuteronomy, the passage which gives an account of his death? At this point, many scholars reassert the observation that Genesis seems to be a compilation. The book has a unity of plan, a coherence of parts, a shapeliness and an order, but it bears also manifest traces of having been based upon an earlier work, and that earlier work itself seems to have imbedded in it fragments of still more ancient documents. Obviously, the history contained in Genesis could not have been narrated by Moses from personal knowledge; whether he was taught it by a medium of divine suggestion or was directed by the Holy Spirit to the use of earlier documents is immaterial in reference to the inspiration of the work. Certain differences become evident. The language of 1:1=2:3 is unlike that of 2:4–3:23. Chapter 14 is also construed by many to be an ancient manuscript simply because of its uniqueness; moreover, the name Jehovah prevails in some sections of Gen. 1:1 to Ex. 6:1, while Elohim prevails in others. In some sections both are employed indifferently. Furthermore, there is also a distinctive and characteristic phraseology in connection with the usage of these divine names. Additional evidence is presented by these scholars to indicate that the Pentateuch in its present form is later than the time of Moses. See Gen. 12:6, 13:7; Ex. 6:26–27, 33–36; Deut. 1:1, 34:5–12.

(a) *External Evidences.* Direct evidence for the authorship of the Law is found in Josh. 1:7–8, 8:31, 34, etc. The book of Judges does not speak of the Book of the Law. No direct mention of it appears in the books of Samuel. First mention of the law of Moses after the establishment of the monarchy is in David's charge to his son Solomon, on his death bed (1 K. 2:3). Allusion seems to be to parts of Deuteronomy and therefore favors the Mosaic authorship of that book. In Dan. 9:11, 13 the law of Moses is mentioned, but in the prophets and in the Psalms, although there are many allusions to the Law, there are none to its authorship.

Existence of a book similar to the present Pentateuch of the Samaritans.

A part of the proof for the early composition of the Pentateuch exists in the fact that the Samaritans had their own copies of it, not differing materially from those possessed by the Jews, except in a few passages which had probably been purposely tampered with and altered, for example, Ex. 12:40 and Deut. 27:4. History does not record the time when the Pentateuch was received by the Samaritans. The Samaritan Pentateuch is against any such supposition that copies of the Pentateuch may have been left in the Northern Kingdom after Shalmaneser's invasion or during the religious reforms of Hezekiah or Josiah. The Samaritan Pentateuch agrees remarkably with the Hebrew Pentateuch; until the return from Babylon, there is no evidence that the Samaritans regarded the Jews with any extraordinary dislike or hostility. But the manifest distrust and suspicion with which Nehemiah met their advances when he was rebuilding the walls of Jerusalem provoked their wrath. From this time forward, they were declared open enemies.

(b) *Indirect Evidence.* Many scholars have attempted to declare the priority of the Pentateuch upon the basis of its influence upon the life of the Jew, its being often quoted, etc. Yet the question is asked, If the Pentateuch existed as a well-known document, how in the reign of Josiah did its existence as a canonical book seem to have been forgotten?

But this represents only one side of the argument. Other scholars have argued with equal force that these books must be considered as the work of Moses, while the newer theory previously discussed considers them the product of the period of development which came to its final stage long after the time of Moses. The theory of Mosaic authorship came into existence long before anyone thought of applying the critical methods to the solution of the problems of origin. The titles of the books, although obviously not in the original manuscripts, can be considered as evidence only from the standpoint of ancient tradition. Throughout these books, Moses appears as the hero, rather than the author of these books. Although Moses is not mentioned in the book of Genesis, he is mentioned repeatedly in the last four books of the Pentateuch. The testimony of the NT must also be considered. Luke 24:44 et al have been taken to indicate that Jesus believed and taught that Moses was the author of these five books. These scholars take the words of Jesus, "Moses said," to be a reference to Mosaic authorship and not simply a reference to a book which had been known traditionally as a book of Moses. Additional attempts to defend Mosaic authorship are made by attempting to show that the language of the Pentateuch, and more especially the Egyptian account, is extremely similar to the language and customs of Egypt. Archaeology has defined the belief that the Mosaic age knew a type of civilization which some who question the Mosaic authorship had long doubted. Archaeology has illustrated that the

Israelites were more than a group of primitive nomads.

Perhaps the question of Mosaic authorship will long be debated, but the value of the Pentateuch in the religion of Israel and in contemporary understanding of God's dealing with his people cannot be overestimated. These values, regardless of their sources, continue as eternal verities and consequently speak to the heart who wishes to know more of the will and purpose of God in human experience.

Pentecost (pĕn'tē-kŏst) the second in chronology of the three annual festivals which every Israelite was expected to attend. "The Feast of Harvest" (Ex. 23:16), "The Feast of Weeks" (Num. 28:26; Lev. 23:17), or Pentecost was restricted to one day.

1. *Time*. Pentecost came a week of weeks after the consecration of the harvest season by the offering of the sheaf of first-ripe barley during the Passover on the second day, being the sixteenth of Nisan. See Lev. 23:11, 15–16; Deut. 16:9 for the method employed in establishing the day. The fifty days formerly included the period of grain harvest, which began with the offering of the first sheaf of the barley harvest at the Passover and concluded with the offering of the two first loaves from the wheat harvest offered at Pentecost. The offering of these two loaves was the distinguishing rite of the day of Pentecost. The loaves were to be leavened, each loaf containing one tenth of an ephah (approximately three and one-half quarts) of the finest flour of the new wheat (Lev. 23:17). In addition to the loaves, a peace offering of two of the lambs of the first year were to be waved before the Lord and given to the priest. At the same time, a special sacrifice was to be made of seven lambs of the first year, one young bullock, and two lambs, as a burnt offering (accompanied by the proper meat and drink offerings), and a kid for a sin offering (Lev. 23:18–19). It appears that an addition was made to the daily sacrifices of two bullocks, one ram, and seven lambs as a burnt offering. As at other festivals, a freewill offering was to be made by each person who came to the sanctuary (Deut. 16:10).

Hospitable liberality characterized the Feast of Pentecost because of its festive character, thus reminding the participant of the Feast of Tabernacles instead of Passover. The Levite, the stranger, the orphan, and the widow were to be brought within the influence of this occasion. During this festival the people were reminded of their bondage in Egypt and were especially admonished to keep the law (Deut. 16:12).

2. *Regulations Concerning Observance*. The flour for the loaves was sifted some twelve times with peculiar care. The loaves were made either the day before, or in the event of a sabbath preceding the day of Pentecost, two days before the occasion. The two lambs for a peace offering were to be waved by the priest before they were slaughtered and afterward the loaves were waved a second time along with the shoulders of the lambs. One loaf was given to the high priest and the other to the ordinary priest who officiated. Bread was eaten that same night in the temple, and no fragment of it was to remain until the following morning.

3. *Importance*. Pentecost served to remind the Jews of the giving of the Law on Mount Sinai and as a type of thanksgiving for the harvest season. The most significant observance of Pentecost was the first which occurred following the ascension of Christ (see Acts 2). At this time, the Holy Spirit came upon all believers regardless of sex, age, or class distinction. Although the spirit had worked previously within God's world, he now came to work in a special and personal way. v.e.g.

Penuel (pē-nū'ĕl) 1. An encampment east of the Jordan, named by Jacob because it was at this place that he had confronted God face to face (Gen. 32:30–31).

2. A Benjaminite, of the family of Shashak (1 Chr. 8:25).

3. A grandson of Judah, identified as the ancestor of the people of Gedor (1 Chr. 4:4).

Peor (pē'ôr) 1. A mountain in Moab in which the prophet Balaam was conducted by Balak for his final conjurations (Num. 23:28).

2. An abbreviation for Baal-peor, a Moabite deity worshiped in Mount Peor (Num. 25:18, 31:16; Josh. 22:17).

Perazim (pĕr'á-zĭm) a mountain, the name of which occurs in Isa. 28:21 and is likely to be identical with Baal-perazim.

Perea (pē-rē'á) the region beyond the Jordan, lying between Jabbok and the Arnon. Yet the term was used in a wider sense as evidenced by Josephus' reference to Gadara as the capital of Perea. See **Palestine**

Peresh (pē'rĕsh) the son of Machir and Maachah (1 Chr. 7:16).

Perez (pē'rĕz) a son of Judah, one of twins borne by Tamar. The family of Perez seems to have existed for centuries (1 Chr. 27:3; Neh. 11:4, 6).

Perez-uzza, Perez-uzzah (pĕr'rĕz-ŭz'á) a name given to the threshing floor where Uzzah was stricken dead because he touched the ark (2 Sam. 6:8; 1 Chr. 13:11).

perfumes perfumes were widely used by the ancients who were unusually sensitive to the offensive odors engendered by the heat of their climate. Perfumes were manufactured from spices of various kinds, such as cinnamon, frankincense, spikenard, myrrh, aloes, etc. Perfumes were used in the temple service, in private life, and in public affairs. See Ps. 45:8; Prov. 7:17; Isa. 3:20; Song of S. 1:3; Jn. 12:3.

Perga (pûr′gà) an important town of Pamphylia (Acts 13:13), located on the river Cestius, at a distance of seven miles from its mouth. The city was celebrated in Paul's time for its worship of Artemis (Diana), whose temple stood upon a hill outside the town.

Pergamos (pûr′gà-mŏs) or **Pergamum** (pûr′gà-mŭm) the leading city of Mysia, approximately three miles north of the river Caicus and some fifteen miles from the sea. At one time Pergamum was the capital of a wealthy kingdom, ruled by a dynasty of kings, several being known by the name Attalus. Attalus I came to the throne in 241 B.C. and was succeeded by Eumenes II in 197. The new king founded the library which eventually became second in significance only to that of Alexandria. The Attalic dynasty terminated in 133 B.C. when Attalus III, who succeeded Attalus II in 138 B.C., dying at an early age, made the Romans his heirs. The sumptuousness of the Attalic princes had raised Pergamos to the rank of first city of Asia. Pergamos had become a city of temples which were devoted to sensuous worship. A famous shrine of Asklepios, god of medicine, stood outside the city. People flocked to this shrine from all quarters. Parchment was first obtained at Pergamum and thus received the name. Pergamum is important in NT history because one of the seven letters to the churches in Asia is addressed to the church in Pergamum (Rev. 2:13). John indicates that Satan's throne was located in that city and that a faithful martyr, Antipas, had been put to death in that place.

Perida (pê-rī′dà) a group which returned from Babylon with Zerubbabel (Neh. 7:57), posterity of Solomon's children.

Perizzites (pĕr′ĭ-zīts) one of the nations inhabiting the land of promise before and at the time of its conquest by Israel. According to Gen. 13:7 they were in the land as early as the time of Abraham; Josh. 11:3 indicates that they lived in the mountain region, the area given to the tribes of Ephraim, Manasseh, and Judah. See Gen. 15:20; Ex. 3:8, 17, 23:23, 33:2, 34:11; Deut. 7:1, 20:17; Josh. 3:10, 9:1, 24:11; Judg. 3:5; Ezra 9:1; Neh. 9:8.

Persia (pûr′zhà) Persia was bounded on the west by Elam, on the north by Media, on the south by the Persian Gulf, and on the east by Carmania. The average breadth of this area was approximately 200 miles while its length was approximately 250 miles. The chief towns were Pasargadae, the ancient capital, and Persepolis, the later capital. The Persian empire extended at one time from India on the east to Egypt and Thrace on the west, and included, besides parts of Europe and Africa, the whole of Western Asia between the Black Sea, the Caucasus, the Caspian, and the Jaxartes on the north, the Arabian Desert, the Persian Gulf, and the Indian Ocean on the south.

Persians the name of the people who inhabited the country known as Persia proper.

1. *Character of the Nation.* The Persians were a people of lively and impressible minds, brave and impetuous in war, witty, passionate, not without some spirit of generosity, and of above-average intellectual capacity. Prior to Cyrus, they were noted for the simplicity of their habits, but from the date of the Median overthrow, this simplicity began to decline. Although they were brave warriors, their lack of discipline manifested itself in their fondness for pleasures at the table and in their common practice of polygamy.

2. *Religion.* Religion brought by the Persians into their empire was of simple character, differing little from natural religion, except from the standpoint of their dualism. The Persians worshiped one supreme god known as the "Great Giver of Life." Oromasdes (Ahuramazda) was "the chief of the gods," so that there were other gods besides him. Mithra was the highest of these. At times Mithra was invoked to protect the monarch. In addition to these gods, Arimanius (Ahriman)—"the Death Dealing"—was the source from which war, disease, frost, hail, poverty, sin, death, and all other evils had their origin. The Persians had their temples, but no images and likely no altars. They did not depend upon priests. Persians likely came into contact with Magianism, which had long been dominant over the greater portion of the region lying between Mesopotamia and India. The essence of this religion was worship of the elements, especially fire.

3. *Language.* The language of the ancient Persians was closely akin to the Sanskrit, or ancient language of India.

4. *History.* It seems impossible to determine the movements of the ancient Persians, although it is extremely probable that the Persians dwelt in the region east of the Caspian, moving down the Oxus, and then along the

southern shores of the Caspian Sea to Rhages and Media. These movements occurred prior to 880 B.C. About 700 B.C. the Persians were allies of Elam. Little is known of the circumstances surrounding the accession of Cyrus II 150 years later. Teispes, a chief of the tribe, conquered Elam and made himself king in the district of Anshan. His great-grandson, Cyrus II, became king of Anshan in approximately 558 B.C. He then united his people, conquering Media in 550, Lydia in 546, and Babylonia in 539. It was he who permitted the Hebrews to return to their land. After a reign of twenty-nine years, Cyrus was slain and was succeeded by Cambyses, his son. A conspiracy was formed against Cambyses, and a Magian priest, Gomates, professing to be Smerdis, the son of Cyrus, whom his brother Cambyses had put to death secretly, obtained quiet possession of the throne. Cambyses despaired of the recovery of his crown and ended his life by suicide after a reign of only seven years and five months. Gomates thus found himself the master of Persia. Yet his situation was one of great danger and difficulty. He reversed the policy of Cyrus with reference to the Jews, forbidding by an edict the further rebuilding of the temple (Ezra 4:17–22). Darius, the son of Hystaspes, led a revolt against Gomates and within seven months ruled the Persians. In the second year of his reign he permitted the Jews who wished to resume the construction of their temple and granted support and assistance from his own revenues.

Tranquillity of the Persian empire was disturbed during the first portion of Darius' reign. Some five or six years' struggle was required before he was firmly established as king. Darius reigned until 486 B.C., leaving his throne to Xerxes, who is likely to be identified as the Ahasuerus of Esther. The reigns of Xerxes and that of his son and successor, Artaxerxes, found Persia in continual war with the Greeks until 449 B.C. Artaxerxes reigned forty years and is known as the "Long-Handed." He was especially kind and friendly toward Ezra (Ezra 7:11–28) and Nehemiah (Neh. 2:1–9). Artaxerxes is the last of the Persian kings who had any special connection with the Jews and reigned forty years, dying in 424 B.C. His successors were Xerxes II, 424; Sogdianus, 424; Darius Nothus, 423–404; Artaxerxes II, 404–359; Artaxerxes Ochus, 359–338; Arses, 338–336; Darius III, 336–331. The last king was conquered by Alexander the Great in 331 B.C. With his surrender, the great Persian empire passed into oblivion.

5. *Persian Dualism.* Persian dualism is known as Zoroastrianism, so identified because of its founder Zarathustra (Lat. *Zoroaster*). This religion made a distinction between God and nature, between the spirit world and the material world, and was adverse to images of gods. Zoroastrianism projected two spirit realms, one presided over by Ahuramazda the all-wise lord, and one, an evil realm, presided over by Ahriman, the spiritual enemy. See **Persia**

Persis (pûr'sĭs) a Christian of Rome saluted by Paul (Rom. 16:12).

Peruda (pē-roō'dà) see **Perida**

pestilence see **plague**

Peter son of a man named Jonas (Mt. 16:17; Jn. 1:43, 21:16), and who followed his father's occupation of fishing on the Sea of Tiberias. His name is a translation of the Aram. *Cephas.* Christ renamed Simon, using this name to express his rock-like character.

1. LIFE. Peter was reared in Bethsaida (Jn. 1:44) and later lived in Capernaum (Mt. 8:14). His brother was named Andrew, who likewise engaged in the trade of his father (Mt. 4:18; Mk. 1:16).

Andrew introduced his brother Peter to Jesus, and it is highly probable that Peter was also a disciple of John the Baptizer, as was Andrew. Peter's character ideally suited him for leadership among the disciples of Jesus. Not only is he named first in the list of the apostles, but he is likewise always included among the inner circle, which was composed of three men: Peter, James, and John. In this closely-knit circle he is also named first. The Scriptures reveal that he was the spokesman of the apostolic band, the first to confess Jesus as the Christ, but likewise the last to be persuaded of the necessity for the Messiah to suffer. Acts 4:13 indicates that neither Peter nor John was trained in rabbinical schools. Yet within a few years following his call, he seems to have conversed fluently in Greek with Cornelius.

Peter was married quite early and his wife accompanied him on his apostolic journeys. Scholars disagree as to the precise date when he was called by Jesus, conjecturing that he was between thirty and forty years of age at the time of his call. Following his call, he was closely associated with Jesus and was impressed, not only by the teachings of the Lord, but likewise by his miracles. This indelible impression led Peter to indicate that he would never forsake the Master (Mk. 14:29). These multiplied experiences with Jesus prepared Peter for his responsibility of leadership in the early church, as exhibited in the first twelve chapters of Acts. His activities as recorded in these chapters justify his name "Peter," and his move to elect one to occupy the place of Judas further illustrates Peter's place of leadership. It was he who preached on the day of Pentecost, it was he who delivered the sermon following the healing of the lame man, it was his voice which rebuked Ananias and Sapphira, and it was his ministry which proved to be effective in the life of Cornelius, the Roman captain. The Scriptures give no distinct information concerning the ministry of Peter from this point until the writing of his epistles, with the exception of Paul's confrontation of Peter as recorded in Gal. 2:1-10. This reference and the Corinthian allusion to Peter are the only references which add anything specific during the interval from the Cornelius experience until the writing of the epistles.

II. LETTERS.

(1) *First Epistle of Peter.* The epistle claims to have been written by Peter (1:1), and the internal as well as external evidence warrants this assertion. The salutation indicates that the epistle is addressed to the "elect sojourners of the dispersion in Pontus, Galatia, Cappadocia, Asia, and Bithynia." Thus the recipients are the Christians who then lived in Asia Minor. For the most part, these churches had been founded by Paul and his companions; Paul had written his letters to the Galatians, Ephesians, and Colossians, to the Christians of this area. The letter is written from Babylon and was transmitted through Silvanus, who served as Peter's amanuensis, and who likely transmitted the letter to the readers. Babylon is interpreted variously by commentators, ancient and contemporary alike. Some suggest the term refers to the ancient country of Babylon, others see in it an allusion to Rome, while a spiritual interpretation is popular with some scholars. John 21:19 thus records the prophecy of Peter's martyrdom, and tradition relates that he died by crucifixion at approximately the same time of Paul's death. This epistle was probably written in A.D. 65.

The apostle purposed: to comfort and strengthen the dispersed Christians in a time of severe trial; to warn them of special temptations attached to their position; to enforce the practical and spiritual obligations involved in their calling; and to strengthen their faith. The epistle is concluded with salutations and announcements.

(2) *Second Epistle of Peter.* This epistle presents questions and problems of far greater difficulty than the former. The writings of the early fathers contain a few references to the epistle, none of which are unusually positive.

Moreover, the style differs materially from that of the first epistle, and the resemblance of this epistle to that of Jude is striking. In the early church numerous doubts of its authoritativeness were entertained, and in the time of Eusebius it was numbered among the disputed books. The epistle was formally admitted into the canon in A.D. 393 at the Council of Hippo. The difference in style between the epistles is explained by some scholars upon the basis that the second epistle reflects the diction and rugged personality of the apostle himself, while the first epistle was verbalized by Silvanus. Additional similarity is revealed in the presentation of both positive and negative aspects of an idea and a fondness for the plurals of abstract nouns. Apart from these two basic observations concerning the epistle, some critics suggest that the first and last chapters were written by Peter or under his direction, but that the second chapter is an interpolation.

The writer's purpose is to remind the readers of all that they have been taught, thereby rescuing them from the contemporary errors relating to Gnosticism, etc. Thus the epistle's contents accorded fully with the stated purpose. The epistle begins, as the customary approach of all NT epistles, with an apostolic greeting and then passes into its intense exhortations concerning development in grace and maturity of knowledge. Chapter 2 contains a severe denunciation of the false teachers, while the first portion of ch. 3 relates to the return of Christ and the end of the world, the latter portion of this chapter, the concluding section, containing an exhortation concerning the Christian life, recommendation of Paul's writings, and a concluding doxology.   V.E.G.

Pethahiah (pĕth'á-hī'á) 1. A priest, whose family became the nineteenth course during the reign of David (1 Chr. 24:16).

2. A Levite who lived in the time of Ezra, and who had married a foreign wife (Ezra 10:23).

3. A descendant of Zerah, and an official of the Persian king (Neh. 11:24).

Pethor (pē'thôr) a town of Mesopotamia where Balaam resided (Num. 22:5; Deut. 23:4).

Pethuel (pē-thū'ĕl) father of the prophet Joel (Joel 1:1).

Peullethai (pē-ŭl'ē-thī) a Levite, son of Obededom (1 Chr. 26:5).

Phalec (fā'lĕk) Peleg, the son of Eber (Lk. 3:35).

Phallu (făl'ōō) Pallu, the son of Reuben (Gen. 46:9).

Phalti (făl'tĭ) Palti, the son Laish of Gallim, to whom Saul gave Michal in marriage after his jealousy had excluded David as an outlaw (1 Sam. 25:44).

Phaltiel (făl'tĭ-ĕl) the same as **Phalti** (2 Sam. 3:15).

Phanuel (fá-nū'ĕl) the father of Anna, the prophetess of the tribe of Asher (Lk. 2:36).

pharaoh (fâr'ō) the title used to describe generally the ruler of Egypt; the term may appear with or without the personal name of the individual. Although some of the pharaohs mentioned in the Scriptures may be identified quite definitely, some of them, especially during the time of Abraham and Joseph, cannot be identified with a marked degree of certainty. By that time it is generally held that Lower Egypt was ruled by the shepherd kings, of whom the first and most powerful line was the Fifteenth Dynasty, the undoubted territory of which would be first entered by one coming from the east. The records are equally bare concerning certain identification of the pharaoh of Joseph. The chief points for the identification of this line are that he was a despot, that he ruled all of Egypt, that he did not hesitate to set aside Egyptian customs whenever he desired, that he seems to have desired to gain complete power over the Egyptians, and that he favored strangers. Some have suggested that these principles of his reign support the idea that he was an Egyptianized foreigner rather than an Egyptian. The pharaoh of the oppression for many years was identified as Rameses II, yet this identification creates numerous unsolved problems. Employing the archaeological evidence available, certain critics have established 1400 B.C. as the time of the destruction of the city of Jericho. Biblical chronology does support this date. See 1 K. 6:1 for the statement concerning the four hundred and eightieth year after the children of Israel were come out of Egypt, this being the fourth year of Solomon's reign. Scholars holding this position proceed to establish the year of the Exodus to be approximately 1450 B.C., the year in which Thutmose III died. Thus he would have been the pharaoh of the oppression, and Amenhotep II, his successor, must be identified as the pharaoh of the Exodus. However, other archaeologists maintain that Jericho fell later than 1400 B.C. and contend for a time between 1375 and 1300. Obviously the latter interpretation would place the date of the Exodus between 1415 and 1340 B.C. It is still contended by some historians that Rameses II was the pharaoh of the oppression and Merneptah was the pharaoh of the Exodus. According to Ex. 1:11 the children of Israel built store cities for the pharaoh, Pithom and Raamses. But this is inconclusive inasmuch as it has been determined that Avaris, the Hyksos capital, Rameses, the capital of the Nineteenth Dynasty, and Panis were successive phases of the same city, and not different cities as formerly believed. Thus it is seen that the evidence now possessed is inconclusive.

Numerous other pharaohs are mentioned in the Biblical materials. Pharaoh, father-in-law of Mered, is mentioned in 1 Chr. 4:18. This marriage may tend to aid in determining the age of the sojourn in Egypt. It is perhaps less probable that an Egyptian pharaoh would have given his daughter in marriage to an Israelite, than that a shepherd king would have done so, before the oppression. Pharaoh, the father-in-law of Hadad the Edomite is also mentioned. It is conjectured that Osochor is the pharaoh to whom Hadad fled. A pharaoh who is mentioned as being father-in-law of Solomon led an expedition into Egypt (1 K. 9:16). This pharaoh is identified as Shishak, who reigned from 945 to 924 B.C. The pharaoh who is mentioned as the opponent of Sennacherib (Isa. 36:6) is likely Tirhakah. Pharaoh Necho is the first ruler mentioned by his proper name with the title "Pharaoh" prefix. Necho was the second ruler of the Twenty-sixth Dynasty and reigned from 609 to 593 B.C. It was he who dethroned Jehoahaz and placed his brother Jehoiakim upon the throne (2 K. 23:29–34; 2 Chr. 35:20–36:4). The next king of Egypt mentioned in the Bible is Pharaoh Hophra, the second successor of Necho, from whom he was separated by the six-years' reign of Psammetichus II. The Bible relates that Zedekiah, the last king of Judah, was aided by a pharaoh against Nebuchadnezzar and that an army came out of Egypt, assisting Judah.

Perhaps the most important thing concerning the pharaoh is not to identify a particular ruler, but to recognize his supreme authority and power. To note the kindness of one pharaoh to the Hebrews and the unkindness of another is simply to interpret human life in its various relationships. The pharaoh's court is generally described as being replete with counselors, wise men, magicians, and subordinate officials who answer every wish of the pharaoh. The court is likewise well furnished with priests who were trained in the magical lore of answering questions, religious or otherwise.

V.E.G.

pharaoh's daughter three Egyptian princesses, daughters of pharaohs, are mentioned in the Bible. 1. The preserver of Moses (Ex. 2:5–10).

2. Bithiah, wife of Mered, an Israelite, daughter of a pharaoh of an uncertain age (1 Chr. 4:18).

3. A wife of Solomon (1 K. 3:1, 7:8, 9:24).
Phares, Pharez (fā′rēz) the son of Judah (Mt. 1:3; Lk. 3:33). Also **Perez**
Pharez (fā′rēz) 1. Twin son of Judah and Tamar his daughter-in-law. See Gen. 38.

2. Parosh (see Ezra 8:3).
Pharisees (făr′ĭ-sēz) one of the chief Jewish religious parties which existed prior to and during the time of Christ. The Pharisees existed alongside the two other religious groups, the Sadducees and Essenes. The term "Pharisee" means the "separated one." The name occurs neither in the OT nor in the Apocrypha, but it is usually accepted that the Pharisees were essentially the same as the Hasidim or the Assideans. Josephus gives extensive discussion of their beliefs and opinions. During the period of Hellenization, the Jews who resisted the adoption of Greek customs separated themselves from their society and adhered very rigidly to the Mosaic law. This group became more closely intertwined by the fierce persecution of Antiochus Epiphanes (174–163 B.C.). The first book of Maccabees gives a description of their attitudes and activities. The spirit of this group continued to exist and appeared first under the name Pharisees in the time of John Hyrcanus (135–105 B.C.).

1. *Doctrine.* The Pharisees accepted the spiritual realm, believing in the immortality of the soul, the resurrection of the body, and the existence of spirits. They likewise formulated as a part of their doctrine the concept of future reward and punishment according to man's life upon earth. However, the souls of the wicked were to be detained in a prison under the earth, while the souls of the worthy would be resurrected. God, according to the Pharisees, is uniquely interested in mankind, but at the same time, permits man's free will. It is very evident that doctrinally the Pharisees were the antithesis of the Sadducees. While Pharisaism honored not only the Mosaic law but the rabbinical law as well, the Sadducees' cry projected a return to the Mosaic law. Rabbinical interpretation and the law itself became of equal value. The application of the Law was meticulously minute, even to the extent of determining what constituted work and burden-bearing on the sabbath. The Pharisee, in all his minutiae, found acceptable definites and attempted to order his life by the application of these principles. Jesus sorely denounces the laws of the elders (Mt. 15:2–6).

2. *Practical Activities.* The Pharisee had lit-

tle or no interest in politics so long as he was permitted to worship as he desired. Although the Maccabees had correlated life and religion, the Pharisee of the NT period cared nothing for politics, and cared for life only as it was regulated religiously. The most influential (religious) group in the NT, the Pharisees exercised their authority because of their positions in the synagogues. While the Sadducees controlled the temple as an institution, the Pharisees lived among the people and controlled the local places of worship. John the Baptist refers to the Pharisees and Sadducees as a group of vipers, and Jesus' severe denunciations are to be found in Mt. 5:20, 16:6–12, 23:1–39. The Pharisees were actively involved in planning the death of Jesus (Mk. 3:6), but in a contemporary society they might well be looked upon as good men. Doubtless numbered among their group were men of perfect sincerity and highest character. Paul was not only a Pharisee, but considered himself a Pharisee of the Pharisees (Phil. 3:5). Gamaliel, his teacher, belonged to the same sect.

There is indisputable authority for the observation that proselytism prevailed among the Pharisees during the lifetime of Jesus (Mt. 23:15). Their zeal and religious fervor are beyond dispute, but their basic premise was in error.   V.E.G.

Pharosh (fā′rŏsh) see **Parosh**
Pharpar (fär′pär) the second of the two rivers of Damascus. This river is deemed less important because Naaman mentions it second. The two principal streams in the district of Damascus are the *Barada* and the *Awaj.* The *Barada* is generally identified with Abana, thus the *Awaj* being the Pharpar.
Pharzites (fär′zīts) the descendants of Pharez, the son of Judah (Num. 26:20).
Phebe see **Phoebe**
Phenice see **Phoenicia.** Phenice (Acts 22:12) is the name of a haven in Crete, located on the southern coast. The name was derived from the Greek word for the palm tree, which was indigenous in the island.
Phicol, Phichol (fī′kŏl) the chief captain of the army of Abimelech, king of the Philistines of Gerar in the days of Abraham and Isaac (Gen. 21:22, 26:26).
Philadelphia (fil′à-děl′fĭ-à) the town of Lydia, built by Attalus II, king of Pergamum. Philadelphia was located on the lower slopes of Mount Tmolus. The region about it was subject to earthquakes. In the time of Strabo the walls were rendered unsafe. One of the seven churches addressed in Rev. 2–3 was there. Al-

though the letters to the churches generally contained an element of condemnation, the church located in the city of "brotherly love" receives commendation by Jesus.

Philemon (fĭ-lē'mŏn) a Christian to whom Paul addressed his epistle in behalf of Onesimus. Philemon was likely a native of Colosse, or in all events lived in that city when the apostle wrote to him. Onesimus was a Colossian (Col. 4:9) and Archippus, whom Paul associates with Philemon at the beginning of his letter, was also a Colossian (Col. 4:17; Philemon 1–2). It is evident that Philemon was a man of property and influence since he is represented as the head of a numerous household and as one exercising unusual liberality toward his friends. He was indebted to the apostle Paul as the medium of his personal participation in the Gospel. It is not certain under what circumstances Paul and Philemon met, but it is evident that Philemon had the greatest respect for the apostle.

Philemon, the Epistle to one of the four letters which the apostle Paul wrote during his first Roman imprisonment. The other imprisonment epistles are the letters to the Ephesians, Colossians, and Philippians. Toward the close of his letter, the apostle expresses a hope of speedy liberation. If one assumes that Paul had reasons for such expectation, he may logically conclude that the letter was written by him no later than A.D. 64. The external testimony concerning Pauline authorship is unimpeachable. The Muratorian Fragment enumerates this as one of Paul's epistles. Tertullian mentions the epistle, and says that Marcion admitted it into his collection. Origen and Eusebius included it among the universally acknowledged writings of early Christian times.

Differences within the letter must become the basis for determining the occasion and object of the letter. It is obvious that Paul is intimately connected with the master Philemon and the servant Onesimus and is naturally anxious to effect a reconciliation between these two men. Paul employs his influence with Onesimus to induce the latter to return to Colosse and to place himself again at the disposal of his master. When Onesimus departs, Paul gives this letter as evidence that Onesimus was a true and acceptable disciple of Christ and that he was entitled as such to be received, not as a servant, but as a brother in the faith. The apostle intercedes for Onesimus as his own child, promises reparation if he had done any wrong, and demands for him not only a remission of all penalties, but the reception of sympathy, affection, and Christian

brotherhood. The result of this appeal cannot be doubted. It may be assumed from the character of Philemon that the apostle's intercession for Onesimus was not unavailing. No fitting response to the apostle's pleadings for Onesimus could involve less than a cessation of everything oppressive and harsh in his civil condition. This letter reveals the true heart of Paul and his graciousness in his relationships with his friends. In addition, it likewise illustrates the influence of Christian faith upon social conditions and relationships.

Philetus (fĭ-lē'tŭs) possibly a disciple of Hymenaeus who joined the latter in propagating the error found in 2 Tim. 2:17–18. These men seem to be guilty of declaring that the resurrection had already come.

Philip (fĭl'ĭp) the gospels contain little material concerning this apostle. He is identified as being a native of Bethsaida, the city of Andrew and Peter (Jn. 1:44). The general manner of John's reference to Philip seems to indicate that Philip had previously known the sons of Jonah and also the sons of Zebedee. Jesus met Philip at Bethany where John was baptizing and called him to discipleship. It was Philip who found Nathaniel and brought him to Jesus. In the Synoptic listing of the twelve apostles the name of Philip is uniformly at the head of the second group of four as the name of Peter is at that of the first (Mt. 10:3; Mk. 3:18; Lk. 6:14). Philip apparently was among the first company of disciples who were with the Lord at the beginning of his ministry, at the marriage in Cana, and on his first entry as a prophet into Jerusalem. When John was cast into prison and the work of declaring the Gospel required a new company of preachers, one may believe that Philip was involved in the proclamation of this gospel. Only John tells anything of Philip's person. Philip played an important role in the events preceding the feeding of the five thousand. At the time of the triumphal entry certain Greeks came to Philip and desired to see Jesus (Jn. 12:20–23). Shortly afterward it was Philip who said to Jesus, "Show us the Father and it sufficeth us" (Jn. 14:8). Philip is included among the company of disciples at Jerusalem after the ascension (Acts 1:13).

Philip the Evangelist first mentioned in the account of the dispute between the Hebrew and the Hellenistic disciples in Acts 6. He is one of the Seven appointed to supervise the daily distribution of food and alms, and thereby to remove all suspicion of partiality. The persecutions of which Saul was the leader either stopped or sharply curtailed the "daily ministrations" of the church. Teachers who had been most prominent were compelled to flee, and Philip was among them. The city of Samaria is the first scene of his activity (Acts 8). This successful ministry touches such characters as Simon the sorcerer, the Ethiopian eunuch, and finally the apostle Paul. Philip continued his work at Azotus and among other cities along the coastline, eventually moving to Caesarea. Although Philip apparently worked diligently for many years, the NT contains sparse reference to him. The last glimpse of him in the NT is in the account of Paul's journey to Jerusalem. It is to his house that Paul and his companions turned for shelter. Philip was then the father of four daughters, who professed the gift of prophetic utterance and who apparently gave themselves to the work of teaching (Acts 21:8-9).

Philippi (fĭ-lĭp'ĭ) a city of Macedonia, located approximately nine miles from the sea and some ten to twelve miles from its port Neapolis. Philip II of Macedon annexed the area (356 B.C.) which included the town; he afterwards enlarged its borders and called it by his own name. In 168 B.C., Philippi became the property of the Romans. It was left to Octavian to establish a Roman colony in Philippi. Paul visited Philippi and his experiences with Lydia of Thyatira and the Philippian jailer are of paramount significance in the records of the second missionary journey. Paul's letter to the Philippians was penned during his first Roman imprisonment and betrays his warmth of feeling and appreciation for the Philippians.

Philippians, Epistle to the this epistle, written from Rome during Paul's first imprisonment, is addressed to the Christians in the city of Philippi. It is a member of the so-called imprisonment epistles composed of Colossians, Philemon, Ephesians, and Philippians. Timothy is associated with Paul at the time of the writing and is mentioned in the salutation (1:1). It was Paul who had established this Christian community during the time of his second missionary journey. Particular incidents are recorded in Acts 16, especially the healing of the girl possessed with a spirit of divination, the conversion of Lydia, and the experience of the Philippian jailer. The Pauline authorship is well attested by the church fathers. The internal marks are those of Paul, and the message itself is characteristically Pauline. Scholars debate the actual site of writing, a minority insisting that the epistle was written at Caesarea (Acts 24:23), but the majority interprets such references as those to the "palace" and to "Caesar's household" as pointing to Rome, rather than

Caesarea. Assuming that the epistle was written at Rome during the first imprisonment, it must have been written between the years of A.D. 60-62; A.D. 62 is a date which best lends itself as the time of composition.

This epistle reflects a warmth of appreciation and understanding which can come only through meaningful and personal experiences. Paul wrote to the Philippians to express gratitude for a gift which had been sent to him. In Phil. 4:15 Paul indicates that he had received other gifts from them. Yet, gratitude and appreciation give way to admonition and exhortation as the apostle reveals his heart to the Philippians. No immediate crises in the Philippian church occasioned the letter, but the epistle abounds in advice for the Christian life. In the first chapter Paul expresses his gratitude and concern for the Philippians, but he likewise indicates the manner in which God has used a prisoner to further the Gospel. The first portion of ch. 2 exhorts the Philippians to those particular virtues he would rejoice to see them practicing at the present time, while 2:19-30 expresses his hope that he may hear a good report of them, either by sending Timothy or by going himself. In 3:1-21 Paul reverts to the tone of joy which runs through the preceding descriptions and exhortations as he bids them take heed that their joy be in the Lord and as he warns them against admitting itinerant Judaizing teachers. In 4:1-9 he appeals to unity, joy, and stability in the Lord, while 4:10-23 is a section expressing appreciation for the contribution sent by Epaphroditus for his support.

The warmth and spirit of this epistle is affected only by the abrupt change in Phil. 3:1-2. A sharp break occurs between these verses, and some scholars have explained this upon the basis that the letter now known is a combination of two epistles. One must remember, however, that Paul was a prisoner and likely recorded his message under less than ideal circumstances.   v.e.g.

Philistia (fĭ-lĭs'tĭ-à) this term occurs in Pss. 60:8, 87:4, and Isa. 14:29 and is the name given to the territory occupied by a group of Aegean origin occupying the south coast of Palestine. They were frequently at war with the Israelites. This land of the Philistines was primarily the portion of the maritime plain lying between Joppa and Gaza.

Philistines (fĭ-lĭs'tĭnz) first mentioned in Gen. 10:14, but their origin is nowhere expressly stated. They are described as the "Philistines from Caphtor" (Amos 9:7) and the "remnant of the maritime district of Caphtor" (Jer. 47:4). This seems to be the generally accepted explanation of their origin. Philistines inhabited the regions of Gerar and Beer-sheba in the time of Abraham (Gen. 21:32, 34). By the time of the Judges, the Philistines had attained an important position among Eastern peoples.

The territory of the Philistines, having once been occupied by the Canaanites, formed a portion of the Promised Land, and was assigned to the tribe of Judah (Josh. 15:2, 12, 45, 47). No portion of it, however, was ever conquered during the time of Joshua (Josh. 13:2), and even after his death no permanent conquest was effected (Judg. 3:3). The Philistines, in turn, inaugurated an aggressive policy against the Israelites. Samson and others partially overcame the Philistines but were never quite successful in permanently throwing off the yoke. Under Eli, there was an organized but unsuccessful resistance to the encroachments of the Philistines (1 Sam. 4:1). See 1 Sam. 13–14 for battles involving Saul and Jonathan. Still later David did battle with the Philistines, the foe being pursued to the gates of Gath and Ekron (1 Sam. 17). It was left to David, as recorded in 2 Sam. 5–8 and 1 Chr. 14 to break the ascendancy of the Philistines.

All of Philistia was included in Solomon's empire, but following his death the Philistines began again to assert themselves. The prophets often mentioned judgment against the Philistines (e.g., Isa. 11:14; Jer. 25:20, 47:1–7; Ezek. 25:15–17; Amos 1:6–8; Obad. 19).

The Philistines appear to have been deeply imbued with superstition, which manifests itself in the carrying of idols with them during their battles (2 Sam. 6:21) and in proclaiming victories in the idols' presence (1 Sam. 31:9). Dagon (Judg. 16:23), Ashtaroth (1 Sam. 31:10), and Baal-zebub (2 K. 1:2–6) were the chief gods worshiped by the Philistines. Priests and diviners (1 Sam. 6:2) were attached to the various seats of worship. The NT materials do not mention the Philistines by name. They obviously were blended into the Jewish nation.

Philologus (fi-lŏl'ō-gŭs) a Christian at Rome greeted by Paul in his letter to the Romans (Rom. 16:15).

philosophy the Greek term *philosophia* means "love of wisdom." Yet as the term is employed in Col. 2:8 and Acts 17:18, it is used in an unfavorable sense. Philosophy in the strictest sense is essentially a Western development. The Jews' search for wisdom was always connected with practice. The method of Greece was to proceed from life to God; the method

of Israel, from God to life. The philosophy of the Jews has thus been defined as a moral philosophy, resting on a definite connection with God. The Bible refers to wisdom and James insists that one is to ask of God if he lacks wisdom (1:5). The writer of the book of Proverbs (1:20–33) personified wisdom and defined it as existing from everlasting to everlasting.

The great philosophical thought is in sharp contrast to the wisdom or philosophy of the Hebrews. The pre-Socratic schools were those among the Greek colonies of Asia Minor. The great subject of inquiry was the constitution of the world in which they lived. The question revolved around the nature of the one underlying element. Was it air? Or was it one eternal being? These illustrate the nature of the inquiry, while the Socratic schools, arising two centuries later and exemplified in men like Plato and Aristotle, directed their inquiry to the ideals and essence of things. Their inquiries were not so abstract as to omit morality. Following Aristotle, Epicurus (342–270 B.C.) and Zeno (336–264 B.C.) directed the thought processes toward ethics and metaphysics. It was inevitable that Greek philosophy was introduced into Palestine. The Grecian period saw the advance of Greek culture into every area belonging to the Greeks. Some of the Jews, later to be known as the Pharisees, aligned themselves against the encroachments of this new culture, but it is only logical that many Jews would be attracted to the Hellenistic way of life. That Grecian philosophy influenced the world of the NT is beyond question; the extent to which Greek thought influenced the NT world may be debated.

V.E.G.

Phinehas (fĭn'ē-ăs) 1. Son of Eleazar and grandson of Aaron (Ex. 6:25). His mother was a daughter of Putiel. He terminated a plague brought by the contact of Hebrew men with Midianite women when he ran a spear through a Hebrew man and a Midianite woman who together came into the camp at Shittim. Phinehas appears to have been the chief of the Korahites, who guarded the entrances to the sacred tent and the whole of the sacred camp (1 Chr. 9:20).

2. Second son of Eli (1 Sam. 1:3, 2:34, 4:4). This degenerate son was killed in the battle with the Philistines in which the ark was taken.

3. Father of a certain Eleazar (Ezra 8:33). **Phlegon** (flē'gŏn) a Christian at Rome, saluted by Paul (Rom. 16:14).

Phoebe (fē'bē) a Christian of Cenchreae, commended to the Roman Christians by Paul when she moved there (Rom. 16:1–2). See **deaconess**

Phoenicia (fê-nĭsh'ĭ-à) a tract to the north of Palestine along the Mediterranean Sea, bounded by the sea on the west and the range of Lebanon on the east. Its chief cities were Tyre and Sidon. In NT times the territory defined by the term "Phoenicia" extended 120 to 130 miles in length and was unusually narrow. The coast afforded numerous and excellent harbors, and Mount Lebanon offered an almost inexhaustible supply of timber. Christians fled to Phoenicia as an aftermath of Stephen's persecution (Acts 11:19), Paul and Barnabas journeyed through the land on their trip from Antioch to Jerusalem (Acts 15:3), and of course, Jesus visited the towns of Tyre and Sidon (Mt. 15:21; Mk. 7:24, 31).

Phoenicians (fê-nĭsh'ăns) the people who in early history inhabited Phoenicia, and who were the great maritime and commercial people of the ancient world. Their language was Semitic, and their origin, according to them, was in the area of the Persian Gulf. Seemingly they migrated from Arabia. Their religion was a pantheistic personification of the forces of nature. In its popular form, it was especially the worship of the sun, moon, and planets—the most natural form of idolatry ever presented to the human race. Perhaps this partially explains the Hebrews' constant temptation to idolatry. Contact with the Phoenicians inevitably influenced the less versatile Jew. The Greeks and Romans attributed the invention of letters to the Phoenicians.

Phoenix (fê'nĭks) a harbor of Crete, navigable throughout the year (Acts 27:12).

Phrygia (frĭj'ĭ-à) the word was ethnological rather than political and denoted vaguely the western part of the central region of the Asia Minor peninsula. The Roman province known by this name did not exist prior to the establishment of Christianity in the peninsula of Asia Minor. Bithynia bordered on the north; Lycia, Isauria, and Pisidia formed the southern limit; Lycaonia and Galatia were the eastern neighbors; Lydia, Mysia, and Caria established the western boundary.

Phurah (fū'rà) also Purah. Gideon's servant, probably his armorbearer (1 Sam. 14:1), who accompanied him in his midnight visit to the camp of the Midianites (Judg. 7:10–11).

Phut (fŭt), **Put** (pŭt) the third name in the list of the sons of Ham (Gen. 10:6; 1 Chr. 1:8), elsewhere applied to an African country of people (Isa. 66:19; Jer. 46:9; Ezek. 27:10;

Nah. 3:9). Some scholars have located Phut south of Cush.

Phuvah (fū'và) also Puvah. A son of Issachar (Gen. 46:13).

Phygellus (fĭ-jĕl'ŭs) an Asian who deserted Paul during the latter years of the apostle's life (2 Tim. 1:15).

phylactery (fĭ-lăk'tēr-ĭ) a band, to which a small box containing excerpts of the Law was attached. This was worn on the forehead or inner left arm at the time of prayer. See **frontlet**

Pibeseth (pī-bē'sĕth) a town of Lower Egypt, mentioned only in Ezek. 30:17. It was located on the Bubastite branch of the Nile, about forty miles from Memphis. The ruins of a once-magnificent temple to Bast are there; scholars identify this goddess with Artemis.

picture idolatrous representations, either independent images or stones sculptured in low relief (Ezek. 23:14). The "pictures of silver" of Prov. 25:11 were likely wall surfaces or cornices with carvings.

piece a term referring to money in both the Old and New Testaments. The term might better be translated shekel, although at times this would also be inaccurate (Lk. 15:8).

piety the term appears in 1 Tim. 5:4 and refers to filial piety, but reverence might be a preferred translation.

pigeon see **dove**, or **turtledove**

Pi-hahiroth (pī'hà-hī'rŏth) the encampment of the Israelites at the close of the third march on leaving Egypt (Ex. 14:2, 9; Num. 23:7, 8).

Pilate (pī'lät) the Roman procurator of Judea in A.D. 26–36. His appointment came during the twelfth year of Tiberius; he arrived in Judea during the year of his appointment. His wife accompanied him, as is evidenced by her remark during the trials of Jesus (Mt. 27:19). One of Pilate's first acts was to move the headquarters of his army from Caesarea to Jerusalem. The soldiers carried their standards into the city, and the very sight of the emperor's image intimidated the Jews, who in great crowds converged upon Caesarea, where the procurator was then residing, to effect the removal of the standards. After five days of heated discussions, Pilate ordered some soldiers to threaten the complainers with death unless they ceased their disturbing. The objectors readily admitted that death was better than their city being unclean through the presence of the images. Pilate then yielded, and the standards were removed to Caesarea.

Josephus records Pilate's taking the Corban (sacred money given to God by the Jews) money and attempting to use it for the purpose of constructing an aqueduct to bring water from the southern uplands into the capital. Jewish rioters were attacked by soldiers who had concealed themselves among the Jews, and the riot was successfully squelched. This episode, plus the procurator's attempt to dedicate some shields, inscribed with the imperial name, created further disfavor with the Jews.

The Biblical student's primary interest in Pilate revolves around his confrontations of Jesus. According to Lk. 13:1 Pilate had executed certain Galileans, a group known by their lack of discipline on festive occasions. Procurators customarily lived in the Jerusalem palace of Herod during the Jewish festivals, so great was the threat of revolt. Jesus, condemned during the Passover on the charge of blasphemy, was brought to the palace early in the morning. The Jews refused to enter the palace lest they be unclean and unable to participate in the continuing festivities. Pilate did not accept the charge of disturbing the peace, but the Jews then restated their charge on political grounds. Having examined the prisoner, Pilate then announced his innocence to the Jews, who then revealed that Jesus' teaching had disturbed all of Galilee. The mention of Galilee offered the escape for which Pilate wished. He hurriedly sent the prisoner to Herod Antipas, who too was in Jerusalem for the Passover. Herod, however, declined to decide the matter and Pilate was forced to decide. He hoped to pacify the Sanhedrin by scourging Jesus and then releasing him. The accusers were determined to have his life, and even the prospects of releasing one condemned prisoner, a customary procedure, failed when the people chose Barabbas in preference to Jesus. Having ascended the *bema*, a portable tribunal which was carried about with the Roman magistrate to be placed wherever he might direct, he received the sad decision of the Jews. It was at the time of Pilate's being seated upon the *bema* that his wife indicated that she had "suffered many things in a dream because of him." Yet, Pilate no longer had a choice; in order to pacify the rabble, he chose Barabbas for pardon and reluctantly yielded to the crucifixion of Jesus. He washed his hands before the multitude as a sign of innocence of the crime. It was a sign of innocence, likely an imitation of the ceremony enjoined in Deut. 21. Pilate then ordered his soldiers to inflict the scourging preparatory to execution. Again Pilate seemed undecided, and the Jews asserted, "If thou let this man go, thou art not Caesar's friend." And for Pilate or any other procurator, such an accusation would have settled the issue. Thus ended Pilate's share in the greatest crime which has been committed in the history of man.

Josephus indicates that Pilate's anxiety to avoid offense to Caesar did not save him from political disaster. The Samaritans were rebellious, and Pilate led his troops against them, defeating them easily enough. The Samaritans, however, complained to Vitellius, then president of Syria, and he sent Pilate to Rome to answer their accusations before the emperor. Upon reaching Rome, he found that Tiberius had died and had been replaced by Caligula. One tradition suggests that Pilate was banished to Vienna to the south of France and there committed suicide. Another tradition explains that he sought to hide his sorrows on the mountain by the Lake of Lucerne and there, after spending years in remorse and despair, plunged into the gloomy waters in an attempt to quench his fear and trouble.   v.e.g.

Pildash (pĭl′dăsh) one of the eight sons of Nahor, Abraham's brother, by his wife a niece Milcah (Gen. 22:22).

Pileha (pĭl′ĕ-hä) the name of one of the chief of the people, probably a family, who signed the covenant with Nehemiah (Neh. 10:24). Also Pilha.

pillar 1. A shaft or isolated pile used to support a roof. Pillars form an important feature in Oriental architecture, partly perhaps as a reminiscence of the tent with its supporting poles, and partly also from the use of flat roofs, in consequence of which the chambers were even narrower, or divided into portions by columns. See 1 K. 7:2, 6.

2. The term also designates a monument. In early times this pillar might consist of nothing but a single stone or pile of stones (Gen. 28:18, 31:46). The stone Ezel (1 Sam. 20:19) was probably a terminal stone or a waymark. The "place" set by Saul (1 Sam. 15:12) is explained by some to be a trophy. Jacob also set up a pillar over Rachel's grave (35:20).

3. Plane of the pillar. This likely should be translated "oak of the pillar" and refers to a tree which stood near Shechem, and at which the men of Shechem and the house of Millo assembled to crown Abimelech, son of Gideon (Judg. 9:6).

pilled = **peeled** (Gen. 30:37–38; Isa. 18:2; Ezek. 29:18).

Piltai (pĭl′tī) the representative of the priestly house of Moadiah in the time of Joiakim (Neh. 12:17).

pine tree 1. The Hebrew *tidhbar* is believed by many scholars to be the oak, while other men interpret the term to mean elm.

2. *Shemen* (Neh. 8:15) is probably the wild olive.

pinnacle an edge or border of the temple, a great height from the ground. See Mt. 4:5 and Lk. 4:9. The Greek term *pterugion* means literally "a little wing."

Pinon (pī'nŏn) a chieftain of Edom, a head or founder of a tribe of that nation (Gen. 36:41; 1 Chr. 1:52).

pipe 1. The *chalil* so translated is derived from the root signifying "to bore, perforate," and is represented with sufficient correctness by the English "pipe" or "flute." This is one of the simplest, and likely therefore, one of the oldest of musical instruments. The pipe and tabret were used at the banquets of the Hebrews (Isa. 5:12) and in simpler religious services (1 Sam. 10:5). The sound of the pipe is apparently a solemn wailing note, which made it appropriate to be used in mourning and in funerals (Mt. 9:23).

2. The *ugab* (Gen. 4:21), a wind instrument of extremely ancient origin. Job 21:12 indicates that this instrument was used in merrymaking.

Piram (pī'răm) the Amorite king of Jarmuth at the time of Joshua's conquest at Canaan (Josh. 10:3, 27).

Pirathon (pĭr'à-thŏn) a place identified in Judg. 12:15 "in the land of Ephraim in the mount of the Amalekite."

Pirathonite (pĭr'à-thŏn-īt) a native or inhabitant of Pirathon. Abdon ben-Hillel (Judg. 12:13, 15) and Benaiah (1 Chr. 27:14) are so identified.

Pisgah (pĭz'gà) part of the Abarim mountain range, opposite Jericho. The top of Pisgah is mentioned in Num. 21:20; Deut. 3:27, etc. The springs or roots of Pisgah are mentioned in Deut. 3:17 and Josh. 12:3 among other references. The field of Zophim was situated on Pisgah and its highest point was called Mount Nebo (Num. 23:14; Deut. 3:27, 34:1-4).

Pisidia (pĭ-sĭd'ĭ-à) a district of Asia Minor which was bounded on the south by Lycia and Pamphylia, on the north by Phrygia, on the east by Lycaonia, and on the west by Caria. Pisidia stretched along the range of Taurus. Antioch, visited by Paul (Acts 13:14) was the chief town of Pisidia.

Pison (pī'sŏn), **Pishon** (pī'shŏn) one of the four heads into which the stream flowing through Edom was divided (Gen. 2:11).

Pispah (pĭs'pä) an Asherite, son of Jether (1 Chr. 7:38).

pit a deep hole in the ground, whether natural or artificial (Gen. 14:10, 37:20). The term may be used in a figurative or in a literal sense.

The *shachath* is best understood as the sinking of a pit. This hole is dug into the earth (Ps. 9:16). The *bor* is best understood as a pit dug for water, but it also came to be understood as a figurative place (Ezek. 31:14, 16; Ps. 28:1). The deep excavation became the place of burial (Ezek. 32:24).

pitch *kopher* was used to daub the ark of Noah. This substance is likely to be construed as asphalt. *Zepheth* is a liquid, and the ark of Moses was covered with it (Ex. 2:3).

pitcher used chiefly to designate the water jar with one or two handles, employed primarily by women for carrying water (Gen. 24:15-20). Vessels used for this purpose were carried on the head or the shoulder.

Pithom (pī'thŏm) one of the store cities built by the Israelites for the first oppressor, the pharaoh "which knew not Joseph" (Ex. 1:11). Archaeological finds have led to the clarification of its ruins, located on the south side of the canal running from Cairo to Suez through Wadi Tumilat.

Pithon (pī'thŏn) one of the four sons of Micah, the son of Mephibosheth (1 Chr. 8:35, 9:41).

plague best identified as some judgment of God sent as a punishment of sin. The plagues were generally personal in nature, although the person may be affected indirectly through the upheaval of some physical norm.

The ten plagues are identified with God's punishment of the Egyptians prior to the Israelites' permitted departure from Egypt. The occasion of the plagues is described in Ex. 2-3. The first plague occurred when Moses and Aaron came before Pharaoh, a miracle being required of them and thus Aaron's rod became a serpent. The rod was changed into an animal revered by all the Egyptians and this should have been a warning to Pharaoh. Although the Egyptian magicians produced what seemed to be the same wonder, Aaron's rod swallowed up the other rods (Ex. 7:3-12). The account of the first plague, the turning of water into blood, is recorded in Ex. 7:14-25. The Nile, believed by the Egyptians to be sacred, was likewise changed in substance. Seven days following the plague of blood, the second plague occurred in the coming of the frogs (Ex. 8:1-15). The third plague consisted of lice, sand flies, or fleas being produced from the dust (Ex. 8:16-19), and the fourth was likewise constituted by swarms of flies (Ex. 8:20-32). The fifth plague was in the form of murrain of beasts (Ex. 9:1-7), and the sixth in that of boils and blains on man and beast alike (Ex. 9:8-12). A destructive hail storm constituted the seventh plague (Ex. 9:13-35), while the strong east wind brought in multitudes of locusts which constituted the eighth plague (Ex. 10:1-20). A plague of darkness was the ninth manifestation of God's disapproval of Pharaoh and the Egyptians (Ex. 10:21-29), and the tenth, the death of the firstborn (Ex. 11:1=12:30), constituted the severest of the ten punishments.

The "plague" is also used for other judgments. See Ex. 32:35; Num. 11:23, 34; 2 Sam. 24:13-25; Mk. 5:29, 34.

plain the term "plain" translates seven Hebrew words appearing in the OT. 1. *Abel.* This word is similar to the word "meadow" (see Judg. 9:32).

2. *Bikah.* This word is used to refer to the plain or valley of Coele-Syria (Amos 1:5).

3. *Kikkar.* This term refers not merely to a plain known for its flatness or extent, but rather to one which is circular in nature (Gen. 13:10-12; Deut. 34:3; 2 Sam. 18:23).

4. *Ham-misor.* This term occurs in Deut. 3:10; Josh. 13:9-21; 2 Chr. 26:10, etc. Scholars do not agree concerning its precise meaning, but it is interesting to note that almost without variation it is used to refer to a district in the neighborhood of Heshbon and Dibon.

5. *Arabah.* This term was used to refer to the valley of the Jordan and to its continuation south of the Dead Sea.

6. *Shefelah.* Designation of the depressed, flat, or gently undulating region which intervened between the highlands of Judah and the Mediterranean and was commonly in possession of the Philistines.

7. *Elon.* The term is regarded by many scholars to mean "oak" or "grove of oaks" and thus seems to be used erroneously in referring to the plain of Moreh (Gen. 12:6) and plain of Mamre (Gen. 13:18), etc.

plaster see **mortar.** Plaster is mentioned in Lev. 14:42, 48; Deut. 27:2, 4; Josh. 8:32; Dan. 5:5. Plaster was generally used on walls and floors, but was likewise used for receiving basreliefs. The wall was first smoothed with plaster, the figures then drawn and the stone adjacent cut away so as to leave them in relief, a coat of lime whitewash placed upon, and the whitewash was followed by one coating of varnish after the painting of the figures was complete.

pledge see **loan**

Pleiades (plē′yȧ-dēz) a term used to designate a brilliant star or a cluster of stars. See Job 9:9, 38:31; and Amos 5:8. The Pleiades are a number of stars in the constellation known as the Bull. This group of stars appears in the animal's shoulder. Astronomers indicate that the Pleiades are actually composed of many stars, although a person of ordinary eyesight may observe six stars on a typically clear night.

plow see **agriculture.** The ancient Palestinian plow consisted of a pole or branch of a tree, a yoke being attached to one end. The share is coated with a thin blade of metal. The plow was pulled by oxen or cows (1 Sam. 13:20; Job 1:14; Isa. 2:4; Lk. 9:62).

plumb line consisting of a cord attached to a weight, its use being essential in the business enterprise to insure the verticality of a wall. See 2 K. 21:13; Isa. 28:17; Amos 7:7-8.

Pochereth-hazzebaim (pŏk′ē-rĕth-hă′zē-bā′ĭm) a group among the children of Solomon's servants who returned with Zerubbabel (Neh. 7:59; Ezra 2:47). It is likely that Pochereth is the individual's name, while zebaim names his home.

poetry poetry is often described as constituting the earliest form in which a people's literary desire begins to express itself. Hebrew poetry possesses many of the qualities and attributes common to all poetry, but the points of contrast are so numerous and the peculiarities so distinct that these two points alone require careful consideration. Hebrew poetry is illustrated in the lyric, the epic, and the gnomic. The lyric occupies the foremost place, the epic poem being less favored. Gnomic poetry is the product of a more advanced age and arises from the desire felt by the poet to express the results of cumulative experiences of life in a form of beauty and permanence.

1. *Lyrical Poetry.* The literature of the Hebrews abounds with illustrations of all forms of lyrical poetry in its most manifold and wide-embracing compass, ranging from short ejaculations as the Songs of the Two Lamechs and Ps. 15 to the longer chants of victory and thanksgiving like the Songs of Deborah and David (Judg. 15; Ps. 18). The lyrical form seemed to be the most popular. They abound in all periods of Hebrew history following the Exodus.

2. *Gnomic Poetry.* As lyric poetry is the expression of the poet's feelings and impulses, so gnomic poetry is the form in which the desire to communicate knowledge to others finds expression. This form of poetry, perhaps as no other, requires for its development a period of national tranquillity. It germinates from the proverbs which occurred in the mouths of the people and which embodied experiences of many with the wit of one.

3. *Dramatic Poetry.* Numerous scholars assert that no pure form of dramatic poetry is

found in the writings of the Hebrews, but they readily admit that the semi-dramatic form occurs in the book of Job, for example. Inasmuch as it represents an action and a process, it is a drama as truly and really as any poem can be which develops the working of passion and the alterations of faith, hope, distrust, triumphant confidence, and black despair, and the struggle which it depicts involves the human mind, while attempting to solve one of the most intricate problems it can be called upon to regard. It is a drama as life is a drama, the most powerful of all tragedies, but that it is a dramatic poem, intended to be represented upon a stage or capable of being so represented, may be confidently denied. All Hebrew poetry is intensely nationalistic and is also characterized by local coloring. The writers were Hebrews who drew their inspiration from the mountains and rivers of Palestine, from the beauty of their places of worship, from their experiences with their God, etc.

The essential characteristic of Hebrew poetry is its parallelism. This term, as applied to poetical structure, indicates that the spirit and sentiment of one line are conveyed in the next. *Synonymous* parallelism consists in parallel lines which correspond to each other by expressing the same sense in different but equivalent terms as in Ps. 20. *Synthetic* parallelism is also known by the term "constructive parallelism" and is parallel in the sense that the statement of the first line becomes the foundation upon which the statement of the second line is established. See Isa. 40:5-6. *Antithetic* parallelism consists of two lines which correspond with each other by an apposition of terms and sentiment. Synonymous, antithetic, and synthetic are the primary divisions of parallelism. However, certain ramifications of these divisions appear as is indicated in the example of progressive parallelism. Another common ramification of the primary types is *introverted parallelism* where the first line is parallel to the last, the second to the penultimate, etc. Other interpreters find numerous additional ramifications such as *progressive, climactic,* and *comparative.* For an example of each see Job 3:17; Ps. 29:5, 42:1.

Hebrew poetry does not rhyme as such, neither is there any regular occurrence of long and short syllables or feet. Parallelism, in Hebrew poetry, replaces the rhyme which is so prevalent in the works of the Western world.

poison an animal, vegetable, or mineral substance which produces nausea or death. Several terms are translated "poison" in the Biblical material. *Chemah* is from a term which means

"to be hot." This term designates animal poison. See Job 6:4. *Rosh* denotes primarily a vegetable poison and is only twice (Deut. 32:33; Job 20:16) used of the venom of a serpent. In the NT the term *ios* appears in Rom. 3:13 and is translated "poison." Often the term poison is used metaphorically in the Biblical accounts.   V.E.G.

Pollux see **Castor and Pollux**

polygamy see **marriage**

pomegranate this term designates either the pomegranate tree or its fruit. The pomegranate was doubtless cultivated early in Egypt; hence, the complaint of the Israelites in the wilderness of Zin (Num. 20:5). The tree, with its characteristic calyx-crowned fruit is easily recognized on the Egyptian sculptures. Carved figures of the pomegranate adorned the tops of the pillars in Solomon's temple (1 K. 7:18, 20) and worked representations of this fruit ornamented the hem of the robe of the ephod (Ex. 28:33-34). The tree reaches a height of twelve to fifteen feet and only occasional thorns are found. The pomegranate fruit is approximately the size of an orange, the red rind being hard and enclosing numerous seeds. Succulent pulp surrounds the tiny hard seeds.

pommels this term occurs in 2 Chr. 4:12-13 and 1 K. 7:41-42 to identify the closed gate projection of the temple pillars.

pond the ponds of Egypt (Ex. 7:19) were doubtless water left by the inundation of the Nile.

Pontius Pilate see **Pilate**

Pontus (pŏn'tŭs) a large district in the north of Asia Minor, extending along the coast of the Pontus Euxinus, from which circumstance the name was derived. It is mentioned three times in the NT (Acts 2:9-10, 18:2; 1 Pet. 1:1). This area reached from the Halys River to the southeastern limits of the Euxine Sea.

pool a hole in the earth, natural or artificial, used as a reservoir for water. These pools were the only resource for water during the dry season, and their failure involved drought and calamity (Isa. 42:15). At times the pools were supplied by springs, but at other times only by the rainfall.

poor the general kindness of the spirit of the law toward the poor is sufficiently shown by such passages as Deut. 15:7. Among the special enactments in their favor the following must be mentioned: (1) the right of gleaning (Lev. 19:9-10); (2) from the produce of the land in sabbatical years, the poor and the stranger were to have their portion (Ex. 23:11); (3) free entry upon the land in the jubilee year, with limitation as to town homes (Lev. 25:25–30); (4) prohibition of usury and of retention of pledges (Lev. 25:35-37); (5) permanent bondage forbidden and manumission of Hebrew bondsmen or bondswomen enjoined in the sabbatical and jubilee years (Deut. 15:12–15; Lev. 25:39-42); (6) portions from the tithes be shared by the poor after the Levites (Deut. 14:28); (7) the poor to partake of attainments at the Feasts of Weeks and Tabernacles (Deut. 16:11, 14; Neh. 8:10); (8) daily payment of wages (Lev. 19:13). Principles similar to those laid down by Moses are included in the NT, as Lk. 3:11; Acts 6:1; Gal. 2:10; and James 2:15.

poplar the translation of the Hebrew *libneh* applied to a tree, commentators generally believe this to be the white poplar, a tall tree with white wood and cottonlike leaves. Others believe this term to refer to the storax tree, a shrub which grows from nine to twelve feet high, with ovate leaves which are white underneath.

Poratha (pô-rā'thà) one of the ten sons of Haman slain by the Jews (Est. 9:8).

porch a covered walkway or colonnade connecting the principal rooms of the house. The expression in Judg. 3:23 is better described as a vestibule. The porch (Mt. 26:71) may have been the passage from the street into the first court of the house where the master of the house often received visitors and transacted business.

Porcius Festus (pôr'shĭ-ŭs fĕs'tŭs) see **Festus**

porter a gatekeeper, but the term does not express its modern connotation of a bearer of burdens.

possession see **demoniacs**

post A. 1. *Ayil*. The doorcase, including the lintel and sideposts.

2. *Ammah*. The post (Isa. 6:4).

3. *Saph*. A threshold.

B. *Rats*. A post, a runner, a guard (Est. 3:13).

pot this term is used to translate numerous words which refer to earthen jars of various shapes. They may be deep and narrow or wide and shallow, they may be petite vessels or bulging jars, they may or may not have handles. See Ex. 16:3; Lev. 6:28; 1 Sam. 2:14; 2 K. 4:2; Prov. 27:21; Jer. 35:5; Ezek. 4:9.

Potiphar (pŏt'ĭ-fēr) an Egyptian name, which was also written Potipherah. Potiphar is described as being the captain of Pharaoh's guard and the owner of Joseph (Gen. 39:1-20). The term itself means "belonging to the sun." Potiphera or Potipherah is the name of a priest of

On, the city of the sun. See Gen. 41:45-50, 46:20.

potsherd a piece of broken earthenware (Prov. 26:23).

potter an artisan who makes earthenware pots or similar utensils. The potter pressed the clay with his feet until it became a paste, then the material was placed upon a horizontal wheel called the "potter's wheel." While the wheel was turned before him, the potter used his hands to shape the vessel. Once the vessel had obtained its desired shape, the potter then glazed and baked the pottery in a furnace. See Isa. 41:25; Jer. 18:3-4; Rom. 9:20-25.

Potter's Field a piece of ground which, according to Mt. 27:7, was purchased by the priest with the thirty pieces of silver rejected by Judas and subsequently converted into a burial place for Jews not belonging to the city. The Gr. *Akeldama* translates the Aramaic, Field of Blood.

pound 1. A weight. See **weights and measures**

2. A money of account, mentioned in the parable of the ten pounds (Lk. 19:12-27), as the talent is in the parable of the ten talents (Mt. 25:14-20).

powder fine particles into which a substance is ground (Ex. 32:20).

praetor a chief civil ruler in a Roman colony (Acts 16:12).

praetorium the headquarters of the Roman military governor, wherever he happened to be. In a time of peace one of the better buildings of the city, which was the residence of the proconsul or praetor, was selected for this purpose. In the NT the term is used in three senses: (1) palace of Pontius Pilate at Jerusalem (Mt. 27:27; Mk. 15:16); (2) Herod's palace in Caesarea (Acts 23:35); (3) the imperial guard at Rome (Phil. 1:13).

prayer the experience of prayer is often defined as communion with God. Scripture does not give any theoretical explanation to the mystery which is attached to prayer. The difficulty of understanding its real efficacy arises chiefly from two sources: from the belief that man lives under general laws and from the opposing that he is master of his own destiny, and need pray for no external blessing. Although Scripture resolves the difficulty of the latter, it does not entirely that part of the mystery which depends upon the nature of God. It places it clearly before us and emphasizes most strongly those doctrines on which the difficulty turns. The subjective effect of prayer is asserted as well as its real objective efficacy. Thus, as usual in the case of such mysteries, the two apparently opposite truths are emphasized, because they are needful to man's conception of his relation to God. The key to this mystery lies in the fact that man's spiritual unity is with God in Christ and of the consequent gift of the Holy Spirit. So also it is said of the spiritual influence of the Holy Ghost on each individual mind, that while "we know not what we pray for," the indwelling Spirit makes intercession for the saints according to the will of God (Rom. 8:26–27).

The Mosaic law gives no specific directions concerning prayer. The duty is taken for granted, as an adjunct to sacrifice, rather than enforced or elaborated. It is hardly conceivable that public prayer did not follow public sacrifice. Such practice is alluded to in Lk. 1:10, and in one instance, the offering of the first-fruits, it was ordained in a striking form (Deut. 26:12–15). In later times, it certainly grew into a regular service, both in the temple and in the synagogue. Besides this public prayer, it was the custom of all of Jerusalem to go up to the temple, at regular hours if possible, for private prayer (Lk. 18:10; Acts 3:1); and those who were absent were wont to open their windows toward Jerusalem and pray toward the place of God's presence (1 K. 8:46–49; Ps. 5:7; Dan. 6:10). The regular hours of prayer seemed to have been three (Dan. 6:10), the evening, the hour of the evening sacrifice; the morning, the third hour; and the sixth hour, or noonday. Thanks were offered before a meal (Mt. 15:36; Acts 27:35). Most often the Jews stood when they prayed (1 Sam. 1:26; Mt. 6:5), unless the prayer was offered in special solemnity and humiliation, at which time they knelt (1 K. 8:54; Ezra 9:5; Dan. 6:10).

The only form of prayer given for use in the OT is the one in Deut. 26:5–15 and is connected with the offering of tithes and firstfruits. It contains in the simplest form the important elements of prayer—acknowledgment of God's mercy, self-dedication, and prayer for future blessing. The most remarkable prayers of the OT are those of Solomon at the dedication of the temple (1 K. 8:23–53) and of Joshua and his colleagues following the Captivity (Neh. 9:5–38). Luke 11:1 seems to indicate that the chief teachers of the day gave special forms of prayer to their disciples. The model prayer is contained in the Sermon on the Mount and Jn. 17 records the Lord's Prayer, the prayer of great intercession. Elements of praise, petition, intercession, and confession characterize the prayer of the Biblical materials.

preaching the public proclaiming of the Gospel, God's good news in Jesus Christ.

Kērusso is the Greek term usually employed in the NT to describe the proclamation of the Gospel. The term itself means to "proclaim as a herald." The *kērux* is the public messenger who proclaims the good news in Christ, while the *kērygma* is the message proclaimed. Paul indicates (Phil. 3:12) that the Christian proclaimer is one who has been apprehended of Christ. He is not one who simply expounds or declares a message because this is his business, but rather because God has called him to this vocation, and furthermore, the herald believes and accepts the message which he proclaims. Other NT terms used to designate the proclamation of the Gospel are *euaggelidzomai*, to evangelize, to preach the Gospel; *kataggello*, to proclaim; *apaggello*, to announce; etc. The term *didasko* occurs often in the NT and is distinguished from *kērusso* in that teaching, the form of, defines an instruction concerning a facet of the Christian life while the latter indicates the sharing of the Gospel, or the declaring of the Gospel, with one who has not heard.

The preaching of Jesus did not differ radically from the preaching of John the Baptist. John the Baptist was a herald who announced the coming of the kingdom and exhorted men to repent. Jesus likewise proclaimed the message of repentance while preaching the gospel of the kingdom. Paul, and other apostles, obviously underscored the concept of proclaiming the message of God in Christ. To the Corinthians the apostle was determined to know nothing except Christ crucified. The Acts of the apostles is replete with recorded sermons with examples of apostolic preaching. These men related the OT prophecies to what had happened in the coming of Jesus and declared that in the ministry, death, and resurrection of Jesus Christ God accomplished his purpose of salvation. NT preaching, of course, did not occur in the formalistic surroundings such as those of the contemporary world. At times, Jesus preached the Gospel to the multitudes, as did the apostles; at other times, the preaching seemed to involve a very small group which met at most any given site. V.E.G.

presents see **gifts**

priest this term is used more than 700 times in the OT and appears approximately 80 times in the NT materials. The term refers to a minister standing as a mediator between God and man. The term "priest" is applied to the priests of other nations or religions, to Melchizedek (Gen. 14:18), Potipherah (Gen. 41:45), Jethro (Ex. 2:16), and to those who discharged priestly functions in Israel before Aaron and his sons (Ex. 19:22). The term sometimes denotes one who serves as an adviser of the king (2 Sam. 8:18).

1. *Origin.* The idea of the priesthood automatically connects itself with the consciousness of sin. Men feel that they have broken a law. The power above them is holier than they are, and they dare not approach this power, but rather crave for the intervention of one whom they can think more acceptable than they. He then offers their prayers, thanksgivings, sacrifices, and in all things becomes man's representative to God. This same individual may likewise become God's representative to man. In the time of the patriarchs, the chief of the family acted as the priest, the office descending with the birthright. While in Egypt the Israelites came into contact with the priesthood of another kind and that contact must have been a rather intimate one. The marriage of Joseph with the daughter of the priest of On (Gen. 41:45), the special favor which he showed to the priestly caste in the years of famine (Gen. 47:26), the training of Moses in the palace of the pharaoh, probably in the colleges and temples of the priests (Acts 7:22)—all this must have impressed the constitution, the dress, the outer form of life, etc. upon the minds of the lawgiver and his contemporaries. No priestly caste existed at the time of the Exodus, but the continuance of solemn sacrifices (Ex. 5:1-3) implies a priesthood of some kind, and priests appear as an organized body before the promulgation of the Law on Sinai (Ex. 19:22).

2. *Consecration.* See **high priests** and **Levites.** The ceremonies of consecration are described in Ex. 29 and Lev. 8. This mysterious ritual was to be repeated for seven days, during which the priests remained within the tabernacle, separated from the people, and not until then was the consecration effected. The character imparted in this manner did not require renewal, but was a permanent inheritance from father to son through all the centuries that followed.

3. *Dress.* The "sons of Aaron" were to wear specified dress during their ministrations and at other times apparently wore the common dress of the day. The material was linen. Linen attire from the loins to the thighs over which was worn a close fitting cassock, which came nearly to the feet, characterized the clothing of the lower portion of the body. The light cassock was gathered about the body with a girdle of needlework, into which, as in the more gorgeous belt of the high priest, blue, purple, and scarlet were intermingled with white, and worked in the form of flowers (Ex. 28:39-40; Ezek. 44:17-19). They wore linen caps which were shaped like a cup-shaped flower. In all their acts of ministration they were to be barefoot.

4. *Regulations.* Before entering the tabernacle, the priests were to wash their hands and their feet (Ex. 30:17-21). During the time of their service, they were to drink no wine or strong drink (Lev. 10:9; Ezek. 44:21). Their function was to be more to them than the ties of friendship or blood, and except in the case of immediate relationship they were not to mourn for the dead (Ezek. 44:25). They were not to shave their heads, and dignity was to characterize their service. Marriages of the sons of Aaron were hedged with special rules. It is likely that the priestly families frequently intermarried, and it is certain that they were forbidden to marry an unchaste woman or one who had been divorced, or the widow of any but a priest (Lev. 21:7, 14; Ezek. 44:22).

5. *Functions.* The work of the priesthood was more stereotyped by the Mosaic regulations than any other element of the national life. The duties described in Exodus and Leviticus are the same as those recognized in the books of Chronicles. The priests were to tend the fire on the altar of burnt offerings (Lev. 6:12), to feed the golden lamp outside the veil (Ex. 27:20-21), to offer the morning and evening sacrifices, and to offer the meat offering and drink offering which normally accompanied the morning and evening sacrifices (Ex. 29:38-44). However, their chief function was that of being available at any time to do the priestly service for any guilty, penitent, or rejoicing Israelite, any of whom might come to the priest at any time. Priests were also to teach the children of Israel the statutes of the Lord (Lev. 10:11; Deut. 33:10). They blessed the people at every solemn meeting (Num. 6:22-27). During the journeys in the wilderness, it belonged to them to cover the ark and all of the vessels of the sanctuary with the purple or scarlet cloth before the Levites might approach them (Num. 4:5-15). As the people started on each day's march, they were to blow "an alarm" with long silver trumpets (Num. 10:1-8). The first book of Chronicles (12:23) likewise mentions the presence of priests on the field of battle. Deuteronomy 17:8-12 also indicates that they might act in difficulties involving criminal or civil cases.

6. *Maintenance.* The priest received one tenth of the tithes which the people paid to the Levites, one per cent on the whole produce of the country (Num. 18:26-28), a special

tithe every third year (Deut. 14:28), of the redemption money (Num. 18:14–19; Lev. 27), of spoils taken in war (Num. 31:25–47), of the showbread and certain offerings (Num. 18:8; Lev. 6:26, 29), of the firstfruits of the produce (Ex. 23:19; Lev. 2:14; Deut. 26:1–10), and from their settlement in Canaan they had certain flocks which grazed in the suburbs of their cities (Josh. 21:13–19).

7. *Classification.* The earliest historical record of any division of the priesthood belongs to the time of David. The Jews traditionally recognize an earlier division, even during the life of Aaron, but at the time of David it can be established that the priesthood was divided into twenty-four "courses" or orders (1 Chr. 24:1–19; Lk. 1:5). Each was to serve in rotation for one week, while the further assignment of special services during the week were determined by lot. It seems that each course began its work on the sabbath, the outgoing priests taking the morning sacrifice and leaving that of the evening to their successors (2 Chr. 23:8). If one accepts the numbers given by Jewish writers, the proportion of the priesthood to the population of Palestine must have been far greater than that of the clergy in the history of any Christian nation. In excess of those who were scattered throughout the country, there were 24,000 stationed permanently at Jerusalem and 12,000 at Jericho.

The chief priests described in the NT were the officiating high priests and the former high priests plus members of their families.

V.E.G.

prince the only special uses of the word "prince" are: (1) "princes of provinces" (1 K. 20:14), who were probably local governors or magistrates; (2) the "princes" mentioned in Dan. 6:1 (see Est. 1:1) were the predecessors of the satraps of Darius Hystaspis.

Prisca (prĭs′kȧ) and **Priscilla** (prĭ-sĭl′ȧ) the name Prisca appears in 2 Tim. 4:19 and in Rom. 16:3. Such variation in a Roman name is not unusual. The name of the wife is placed before that of the husband in Rom. 16:3; 2 Tim. 4:19; and in Acts 18:26. Only in Acts 18:2 and 1 Cor. 16:19 does Aquila appear first. One is disposed to conclude that Priscilla was the more energetic of the two. Yet it must be observed that the husband and wife are always mentioned together. See **Aquila**

prison it is clearly indicated that in Egypt special places were used as prisons and they were under the custody of a military officer (Gen. 40:3, 43:17). During the wandering in the desert confinement "in ward" (Lev. 24:12; Num. 15:34) is mentioned, but inasmuch as imprisonment was not directed by the Law, one knows nothing of this punishment until the time of the Kings, when the prison appears as an appendage to the palace, or a special part of it (1 K. 22:27). Later the prison is described distinctly as being in the king's house (Jer. 32:2, 37:21; Neh. 3:25). This was the case also at Babylon (2 K. 25:27). Private houses were sometimes used as places of confinement (Jer. 37:15). Prisons, other than these, were unknown in Judah prior to the Captivity. During the time of the Herods one reads of royal prisons attached to the palace or in royal fortresses (Lk. 3:20; Acts 12:4, 10). Antonia was used by the Romans as a prison at Jerusalem (Acts 23:10) and at Caesarea the praetorium of Herod served as a prison. One of the famous prisons was the Mamertine prison at Rome.

Prochorus (prŏk′ō-rŭs) one of the seven deacons, being the third on the list, and named next after Stephen and Philip (Acts 6:5).

proconsul the ruler of a Roman province whose affairs were administered by the senate. Among the senatorial provinces were Cyprus, Achaia, and Asia. It seems that the Roman provinces were often changed from the senatorial to the imperial category. See the following article.

procurator an officer of the Roman emperor who presided over an imperial province. Pontius Pilate (Mt. 27), Felix (Acts 23–24), and Festus (Acts 26:30) are described as procurators. The office is also mentioned in Lk. 3:1. The Roman provinces were divided into two groups, imperial and senatorial. An imperial province was ruled by a procurator. The NT presents the procurator only in his judicial capacity. Jesus was brought before Pontius Pilate as a political offender (Mt. 27:2, 11) and the accusation was heard by the procurator, who is seated on the judgment seat (Mt. 27:19). Felix heard Paul's accusation and defense from the judgment seat at Caesarea (Acts 24), and Paul calls him "judge" (Acts 24:10). The procurator was attended by a cohort which served as a bodyguard (Mt. 27:27); he apparently went up to Jerusalem at the time of the high festivals and there resided in the palace of Herod, which palace was called the praetorium, or "judgment hall."

prophet 1. *The Name. Nabi* is the ordinary Hebrew word for prophet. This term signifies a person who involuntarily speaks spiritual utterances under divine influence, or simply one who pours forth words. It is more harmonious with the etymology and usage of the term to regard it as signifying one who announces or pours forth the declarations of God. A second term used to designate a prophet is *roeh*. This term designates one who sees, as does the term *chozeh*. The latter term is rarely found except in the books of the Chronicles. The logical inference is that the same person may be designated by these three terms, although *nabi* is uniformly translated in the LXX by *prophētēs*. In classical Greek, *prophētēs* signifies one who speaks for another, and especially one who speaks for God.

2. *Prophetical Order.* The prophetical order was originally the instrument by which the members of the Jewish theocracy were taught and governed in things spiritual. Teaching by act and teaching by word were alike their task. But during the time of the Judges, the priesthood sank into a state of degeneracy, and the people were no longer affected by the acted lessons of the ceremonial service. They required less enigmatic warnings and exhortations. Under these circumstances, a new moral power was evoked—the Prophetic Order. Samuel, himself a Levite, of the family of Kohath (1 Chr. 6:28) was the personality used at once for effecting a reform in the sacerdotal order (1 Chr. 9:22). However, it is not to be supposed that Samuel created the Prophetic Order as a new thing before unknown. Certainly traces of the Order can be found in the Law as given to the Israelites by Moses (Deut. 13:1, 17:18, 18:20). Samuel took measure to make his work of restoration permanent as well as effective for the moment. For this purpose, he instituted groups or colleges of prophets. Such groups were found at Ramah (1 Sam. 19:19-20), Bethel (2 K. 2:3), Jericho (2 K. 2:5), Gilgal (2 K. 4:38), and elsewhere (2 K. 6:1).

3. *The Prophetic Gift.* Generally, the inspired prophet came from the college of the prophets and thus belonged to the Prophetic Order. The prophets whose books are accepted as canonical occupy that place of honor because they were endowed with a prophetic gift and likewise belonged to the Prophetic Order. Their characteristics are as follows: (a) they were the national poets of Judah; (b) they were annalists and historians; (c) they were preachers of patriotism; (d) they were preachers of morals and of spiritual religion; (e) they were extraordinary exponents of the law; (f) they held a pastoral or quasi-pastoral office; (g) they were a political power in the state; (h) the prophets were more than all of these, however, because they were instrumentalities by which God's will to man was revealed. Of course, false prophets also existed in the OT times. There were heathen prophets who spoke in the name of an idol (Deut. 18:20), and

there were false prophets who spoke in the name of the Lord (Jer. 23:16-32).

Prophecy involved not only the speaking for God but likewise included the prediction of events yet to come. The latter was a significant aspect of the prophet's work. At this point, the most important aspect of prophecy concerns the coming of the Messiah. The Messianic picture drawn by the prophets as a body contains at least the following traits: that salvation should come through the family of Abraham, Isaac, Jacob, Judah, David; that there should be a great prophet, typified by Moses; a king descended from David; a priest forever, after the order of Melchizedek; that there should be a righteous servant of God on whom the Lord would lay the iniquity of all men; that an everlasting kingdom should be given by God to one like the Son of man; and that there should be born into the world a child to be called the Mighty God, Eternal Father, Prince of Peace.

4. *The Prophetic State.* The Scripture indicates that the prophets received divine communication through the working of God's Spirit (Num. 9:17, 25, 29; 2 Pet. 1:21). The prophet thus occupied an intermediate position in communicating between God and man. God communicated with him by his Spirit and he, having received this communication, was "the spokesman" of God to man. However, the means by which the Spirit communicated with the human spirit and the conditions of the human spirit into which the divine communications were received, have not been clearly indicated. But it is obvious that such communication was received by direct declaration and manifestation, by vision, and by dream. Peter indicates that the prophets were holy men (2 Pet. 1:21) and that they were moved by God's Spirit. Exodus 24:18 records Moses' withdrawal for a period of forty days and nights, and in the quiet and solitude of Mount Sinai he communed with God. Young Samuel heard God speak during the quietness of the night (1 Sam. 3:2-10). These references assist in illustrating God's communication to the prophet.

5. *Interpretation of the Prophecy.* One must distinguish the form from the idea which the prophets wished to convey as well as the figure from what is presented by it. The interpreter must also consider the imagery of the prophetic visions and the character of literature which expresses the visions. He must also interpret according to the principle which may be deduced from the examples of visions explained in the OT and according to the principle which may

be deduced from the examples of prophecies as interpreted in the NT. Moreover, the interpreter must remember that prophetic visions are abstracted from relations in time.

6. *Use of Prophecy.* Predictive prophecy is a part and an evidence of revelation. Peter seems to describe predictive prophecy as revealing some knowledge or light, but a very feeble revelation as compared to what is manifested in the gospel history. After fulfillment, Peter says, "The word of prophecy" becomes "more sure" than it was before, that is, it is no longer merely a feeble light to guide, but it is the firm ground of confidence, and combines the apostolic testimony, serving as a trustworthy evidence.

7. *Prophets of the Old Testament.* The writing prophets of the OT are divided into two groups. The major prophets are Isaiah, Jeremiah, Ezekiel, and Daniel. The minor prophets are twelve in number: Hosea, Joel, Amos, Obadiah, Jonah, Micah, Nahum, Habakkuk, Zephaniah, Haggai, Zechariah, and Malachi. In addition to these writing prophets, numerous other individuals performed prophetic duties and thus are known as prophets.

8. *Prophets of the New Testament.* So far as predictive prophecy is concerned, the OT prophets find their counterpart in the writer of the Apocalypse, but in their general character as the human revealers of God's will, their counterpart will be found in John the Baptist, Agabus, and numerous other persons who were endowed with the extraordinary gifts of the Spirit in the apostolic age. See 1 Cor. 12:10, 28.   V.E.G.

prophetess 1. The wife of a prophet. See Isa. 8:3.

2. A woman who is called of God to occupy the prophetic office. Miriam, Deborah, the daughters of Philip, etc. occupied this office. See Ex. 15:20–21; Judg. 4:4; Acts 21:9.

proselyte (prŏs′ĕ-līt) the Greek term *proselutos* is the LXX translation of the Hebrew term *ger*, which identifies a person associated with a community which in actuality is not his own. The term, as employed in the NT, is used to describe a convert to Judaism. Matthew 23:15 indicates that the Pharisees were particularly zealous in proselyting. Acts 2 indicates that proselytes were present on the day of Pentecost. Nicolaus, one of the seven men chosen to care for the daily distribution, was a proselyte (Acts 6:5). Many proselytes followed Paul and Barnabas in Antioch of Pisidia (Acts 13). Proselytes were divided into two groups: the proselytes of righteousness and the proselytes of the gate. The proselytes of righteousness were circumcised, and following their recovery they were baptized. This group likewise offered sacrifice and adopted the entire ritual of Judaism. The proselytes of the gate gladly attended the synagogues and kept a portion of the Jewish laws and customs. These were "men who feared God" but they refused to be circumcised. Among these classes the Gospel made its initial headway in the Gentile world. It is likely that the former proselytes were as fanatical in Judaism as the Jews themselves. The proselytes of righteousness were also known as proselytes of the covenant.

The following suggests the methodology whereby one became a proselyte of Judaism. The individual was first catechized as to his motives. Then he was instructed concerning the divine protection of the Jewish people, after which he was circumcised. Often the proselyte took a new name. Baptism was required to complete his admission. When the wound was healed, he was stripped of all his clothes and in the presence of three witnesses who had acted as his teachers, which witnesses now became his sponsors, he was led into the tank or pool for baptism. As he stood there, the sponsors, or fathers of the proselyte, repeated the commandments of the Law. These he promised and vowed to keep, and then with an accompanying benediction he plunged under the water. Following his baptism, his offering or Corban was made.

Proverbs, the Book of the Hebrew word *mashal*, translated by the English "proverb" means "to be like," and thus the term primarily signifies a comparison, or a similitude, and may be applied to many sentences and expressions. The term is popularly and contemporarily used to refer to a "short pithy saying." The Proverbs are traditionally ascribed to Solomon, although the book itself claims three different authors and likewise it contains two sections which refer simply to the words of the wise. In addition to Solomon, Agur and Lemuel are listed as authors.

Contents. 1. Chapters 1–9 form a connected didactic poem, in which Wisdom is praised and the youth exhorted to devote himself to her.

2. Chapters 10–24 is composed of three parts: (a) 10:1–22:16, a collection of single proverbs and detached sentences concerning moral teaching and worldly prudence; (b) 22:17–24:21, a more connected didactic poem; (c) 24:23–34, a collection of unconnected maxims.

3. Chapters 25–29, a collection of Solo-

mon's proverbs consisting of single sentences. Chapter 30, the first appendix, is the words of Agur, while the second appendix, ch. 31, is divided into two parts, the words of Lemuel (vss. 1–9) and an alphabetical acrostic in praise of a virtuous woman (vss. 10–31).

The Proverbs are frequently quoted or alluded to in the NT. Paul, James, John, Peter, Matthew, and Mark primarily quote the Proverbs.

province a division of an empire. Babylonian and Persian empires were divided into provinces for the sake of administrative purposes. The Roman empire was likewise divided into provinces. Some were senatorial provinces, those ministered by the senate, and others were imperial provinces, the affairs of which were controlled directly by the emperor himself.

Psalms, the a collection of Hebrew religious poems or praises employed in Hebrew worship. The term *tehillim*, praises, occurs in the title of only one of the psalms, Ps. 45. The LXX entitled them *Psalmoi*, or Psalms. The collection contains 150 psalms and may be divided into five great divisions. These divisions exhibit a remarkable difference in their usage of the names Jehovah and Elohim to designate Almighty God. In Pss. 1–41, Jehovah prevails. In book II, Pss. 42–72, Elohim occurs more than five times as often as Jehovah. In book III, Pss. 73–89, Elohim occurs in the earlier psalms while Jehovah is employed in the latter psalms of this section. In book IV, Pss. 90–106, the name Jehovah is employed exclusively, and book V beginning with Ps. 107, employs Jehovah with the exception of two passages where Elohim is found. Each of these books is arranged in such manner as to close with a doxology. The first book is essentially Davidic; the second seems to have been compiled in the reign of King Hezekiah; the third was possibly compiled during the reign of Josiah; the fourth contains the remainder of the psalms up to the date of the Captivity; the fifth is compiled of the psalms of the Return.

Although the titles of the psalms are extremely ancient, there is an obvious connection between the psalms and Israelite history. The Psalms are psalms of strength, thanksgiving, deliverance of God's people, personal thanksgiving for the entirety of life, festival hymns, etc. A careful study of the psalms will indicate an immediate and direct connection with the history of Israel. Many of the psalms are from the hand of David, while numerous others are attributed to him. At least seventy-three psalms, judging from their titles, are attributed to David.

The Psalms, as they presently appear in the OT canon, served as the hymnbook of the Second Temple. These psalms were sung at private gatherings as well as in temple services. In addition to the large group of psalms attributed to David, there is likewise a collection used by the sons of Korah. There was a family of Korah, at least part of which, served as the official singers of the temple.

The Psalms are characterized by a universal recourse to communion with God. Connected with this is the faith by which the psalmist everywhere lives in God rather than in himself. It is of the essence of such faith that his view of the perfection of God should be true and vivid. The Psalter describes God as he is: the psalms glow with testimonies to his power and providence, his love and faithfulness, his holiness and righteousness. The psalms not only set forth the perfection of God, they proclaim also the duty of worshiping him by the acknowledgment and adoration of his perfection. They encourage all outward rites and means of worship. Among these they recognize the ordinance of sacrifice as an expression of the worshiper's consecration of himself to God's service. But, nonetheless, they do repudiate the outward rite when separated from that which it was designed to express. Similar depth is observable in the view taken by the psalmist of human sin. In regard to the Law, the psalmist feels that it cannot so effectually guide his own unassisted exertions as to preserve him from error (Ps. 19). The psalms bear repeated testimony to the duty of instructing others in the way of holiness.

A prophetic character permeates the psalms. The moral struggle between godliness and ungodliness is ever present. Several psalms evidence an interest in the person distinct from the speaker, and these may be termed as Messianic (see Pss. 2, 45, 110). These psalms are extremely difficult to interpret, and are usually recognized as Messianic, if not in their entirety, in part. Obviously God in his omniscience guided the psalmists in recording their own experiences for a purpose which they themselves did not understand.

Numerous evidences must be considered in establishing the date of a psalm. The critic considers style and grammatical construction, the conditions reflecting historical events contemporary with the writer, whether the writer is represented as speaking or is discussing some religious concept, and the religious conditions and periods depicted in the terminology of the psalms.

Some of the psalms likely constitute the better loved portions of Scripture and are perhaps the most often repeated, for example, Ps. 23.

psaltery a stringed instrument for music used in accompaniment. The term psaltery is normally used to translate Heb. *nebel* except in a few instances (e.g., Isa. 5:12, 14:11; Amos 5:23, 6:5) where it is translated viol. The ancient viol was a six-stringed guitar. The instrument resembles the guitar, but was superior in tone and larger in size. Its back was curved, somewhat like the vertical section of the gourd, or more nearly resembling that of a pear. The Gr. *psalterion*, from which the term psaltery is derived, denotes an instrument played with the fingers; but it occurs as the LXX translation of the Hebrew *nebel* in Neh. 12:27; Isa. 5:12, and generally in the Psalms, but in other places the general term *organon* is employed. This seems to indicate that at the time of the LXX there was no certain identification of the Hebrew instrument with any known to the translators.

The most reliable information, derived from a comparison of the terms and other available evidence, seems to indicate that the instrument was wooden, the strings made of gut, but the number of strings might vary, although ten would be generally the number attached to the instrument. The instrument was small enough to be portable; in fact, it could be carried while it was played. The psaltery was one of the instruments played by the company of prophets whom Saul had (1 Sam. 10:5), and a psaltery was used when David removed the ark to Jerusalem (2 Sam. 6:5). Psaltery was also included in the temple orchestra (1 Chr. 15:16, 20, 28), and it was subsequently in continual usage at times of worship. Its music could be combined with that of a harp (1 Sam. 10:5; 2 Sam. 6:5; 2 Chr. 9:11). Psaltery was also played at festive times (Amos 6:5). v.e.g.

Ptolemais (tŏl'ē-mā'ĭz) see **Accho.** The city which was called Accho in the earliest Jewish annals was named Ptolemais in the Macedonian and Roman periods. In the NT Ptolemais is a marked point in Paul's travels by land and sea. It is specifically mentioned in Acts 21:7 as containing a Christian community, visited for one day by Paul.

Pua (pū'à) also Puvvah, the son of Issachar (Num. 26:23).

Puah (pū'à) 1. The Father of Tola, a man of the tribe of Issachar, and judge of Israel after Abimelech (Judg. 10:1).

2. The son of Issachar (1 Chr. 7:1), elsewhere called Puvah (Phuvah).

3. One of the two midwives to whom Phar-

aoh gave instructions to kill the Hebrew male children at birth (Ex. 1:15). These women disobeyed the command of the pharaoh.

publican a man employed by the Roman government to collect taxes. The Roman senate had found it convenient as early as the Second Punic War to form the direct taxes and customs to capitalists who attempted to pay a given sum into the treasury (*in publicum*), thus the group received the name of *publicani*. These privileges were auctioned, and at times an individual capitalist did not have the resources to purchase the privilege, thus a joint company was formed, with one of the partners acting as the *magister* (managing director). Under this officer, who commonly resided at Rome transacting the business of the company, were the *sub-magistri*, who lived in the provinces. Working under them were the *portitores*, the actual custom-house officers, who examined each bale of goods exported or imported, assessed its value in a rather arbitrary fashion, wrote the ticket, and enforced the payment. The latter were commonly natives of the province in which they were stationed. The word *telonai* is the Greek term used of the *portitores*.

The system was a rather vicious one in which the *publicani* banded themselves together to support the interests of one another and thus defied all interference. They not only demanded severe laws, but also put these laws into action. The *portitores*, their agents, were encouraged in the most vexatious fraudulent extractions. They apparently overcharged whenever they had an opportunity (Lk. 3:13). They brought false charges of smuggling in the hope of extorting hushmoney (Lk. 19:8). They detained and opened letters on their suspicion. It was the basest of all livelihoods. All this was enough to bring the class into ill favor everywhere. In Judea and Galilee there were special circumstances of aggravation. This office brought out all the besetting vices of the Jewish character. The strong feeling of many Jews as to the absolute unlawfulness of paying tribute at all made matters worse. The scribes, who discussed the question (Mt. 22:15), for the most part answered it in the negative. In addition to their own faults, the publicans in the NT were regarded as traitors, defiled by their frequent contact with the heathen, and willing tools of the oppressor. The class thus practically excommunicated furnished some of the earliest disciples both of the Baptist and of our Lord. It is likely that Zacchaeus, a Jew, was a subcontractor for the revenues of the city of Jericho (Lk. 19:1–10). Matthew was obviously a tax collector for the revenues of Capernaum (Mt. 9:9; Mk. 2:14).   v.e.g.

Publius (pŭb'lĭ-ŭs) the chief man, in life the governor, of Melita, who received and lodged Paul and his companions on the occasion of their being shipwrecked off that island (Acts 28:7). Publius possessed property in Melita and may well have been the delegate of the Roman praetor of Sicily to whose jurisdiction Melita belonged.

Pudens (pū'dĕnz) a Christian friend of Timothy who joined Paul in sending greetings to the young minister (2 Tim. 4:21).

Puhites (pū'hīts) also Puthites. According to 1 Chr. 2:53, the Puthites belonged to the families of Kirjath-jearim.

Pul (pŭl, pōōl) 1. An Assyrian king, who made an expedition against Menahem, king of Israel, about 770 b.c. Menahem seemed to inherit the kingdom which was already included among the dependents of Assyria. Obviously Menahem neglected to be "confirmed" in his kingdom, an act which was tantamount to rebellion. He may have even been guilty of more overt and flagrant hostility. Whatever the circumstances were, Pul looked upon Menahem as a rebel. He consequently marched into Palestine for the purpose of punishing this vassal king. See 2 K. 15.

2. A country mentioned in Isa. 66:19. This is obviously an African country and is coupled with Tarshish and Lud.

pulse the term likely refers to grains or seeds of any kind, whether barley, wheat, millet, vetch, etc. See 2 Sam. 17:28; Dan. 1:12, 16.

punishment the earliest theory of punishment was that of simple retaliation, "blood for blood." The first punishment mentioned in Scripture, apart from that incurred in the fall itself, is that of Cain. Genesis 4:24 seems to indicate clearly that death was regarded as the fitting punishment for murder. In Mosaic times the penalty for murder was clearly defined in the Law, the murderer being put to death (Ex. 21:12, 14, 28, 36; Lev. 24:17, 21; Num. 35:31). Punishment may be described as the act essential to satisfying justice.

1. *Offenses Punishable by Death.* The following are mentioned in the Law as liable to the punishment of death: (a) striking or reviling a parent (Ex. 21:15, 17); (b) blasphemy (Lev. 24:14, 16, 23); (c) sabbath-breaking (Ex. 31:14; Num. 15:32-36); (d) witchcraft and false pretension to prophecy (Ex. 22:18; Lev. 20:27; Deut. 13:5); (e) adultery (Lev. 20:10; Deut. 22:22); (f) unchastity (Lev. 21:9; Deut. 22:21, 23); (g) rape (Deut. 22:25); (h) incestuous and unnatural relations (Ex. 22:19; Lev. 20:11, 14, 16); (i) kidnapping (Ex. 21:16; Deut. 24:7); (j) idolatry (Lev. 20:2; Num. 25:8; Deut. 13:6, 10, 15; Josh. 7, 22:20); (k) false witness under given circumstances (Deut. 19:16, 19).

2. *Offenses Involving "Cutting off from the People."* These offenses are basically described as breach of morals, breach of covenant, and breach of ritual. See Gen. 17:14; Ex. 4:24; Lev. 18:29, 20:9-21, 23:29-30; Num. 9:13, 15:30-31, among many others.

3. *Types of Punishment.* Punishments in themselves were twofold, capital and secondary. Capital punishment was performed by stoning, the ordinary mode of execution (Ex. 17:4; Lk. 20:6; Jn. 10:31; Acts 14:5); hanging (Num. 25:4; 2 Sam. 21:6); burning (Gen. 38:24); execution by the sword or spear (Ex. 19:13; Num. 25:7); strangling; crucifixion; drowning (a Roman practice); sawing asunder or crushing (2 Sam. 12:31; Heb. 9:37); pounding or beating to death (Prov. 27:22); precipitation (Josh. 7:25-26; 2 Sam. 18:17; Jer. 22:19). Secondary punishment among the Jews consisted of: retaliation, "eye for eye" (Ex. 21:24-25); compensation, that is payment (Ex. 21:18-36; Lev. 24:18-21; Deut. 19:21); stripes, which number is not to exceed forty (Deut. 25:3); scourging (Judg. 8:16); stocks (Jer. 20:2); fire, passing through the fire (2 Sam. 12:31); mutilation (Judg. 1:6); plucking out the hair (Isa. 50:6); and other methods.

Punites (pū'nīts) descendants of Pua, the son of Issachar (Num. 26:23).

Punon (pū'nŏn) one of the encampment sites of Israel during the last portion of the wilderness wandering (Num. 33:42-43).

purification ritualistic observances whereby Israelites were absolved from the taint of uncleanness. The essence of purification consisted in the use of water, whether by the way of ablution or aspersion, but in the case of legal uncleanness sacrifices of various kinds were added, and the ceremonies throughout bore a more expiatory character. Simple ablution of the person was required after sexual intercourse (Lev. 15:18; 2 Sam. 11:4); ablution of the clothes after touching the carcase of an unclean beast, or eating or tearing the carcase of a clean beast that had died a natural death (Lev. 11:25, 40); ablution both of the person and the defiled garments in the cases of gonorrhea (Lev. 15:16-17). A high degree of uncleanness resulted from prolonged gonorrhea in males and menstruation in women. Contact with persons in these states, or even with clothing or furniture that had been used by them while in these states, involved uncleanness in a minor degree (Lev. 15:5–11, 21–24). Following childbirth, the sacrifice was increased to a lamb of the first year with a pigeon or turtledove (Lev. 12:6). The uncleannesses previously mentioned were of a comparatively mild character. Leprosy was regarded by the Hebrews as nothing less than a living death. The ceremonies of purification for the leper are described in Lev. 14:4–32. The first stage of the ceremony occurred outside the camp and the second stage before the sanctuary. In the first stage, one bird was slaughtered, the second bird being dismissed, and its dismissal symbolized the punishment of death deserved and fully remitted. In the second stage, the use of oil symbolized the rededication of the leper to the service of God. The ceremonies observed in the purification of a house or garment infected with leprosy were identical with the first stage of the proceedings used for the leper (Lev. 14:33–53). Utensils were washed as a matter of ritualistic observance (Mk. 7:4). Washing of the hands before meals was conducted in a formal manner (Mk. 7:3), and minute regulations are prescribed in a treatise of the Mishna. What may have been the specific causes of uncleanness in those who came to purify themselves before the Passover (Jn. 11:55), or in those who had taken upon themselves the Nazarite's vow (Acts 21:24–26) are not specifically defined; in either case it may have been contact with a corpse. It should be observed in conclusion that the idea of uncleanness was not peculiar to the Jew. However, with other nations simple ablution sufficed; no sacrifices were demanded.

Purim the annual festival instituted to commemorate the preservation of the Jews from the massacre with which they were threatened by Haman (Est. 9). This festival was likely called Purim by the Jews in irony. Haman was very superstitious and gave much attention to casting lots (Est. 3:7). They gave the name Purim, or lots, to the festival because he had

thrown lots to ascertain what day would be auspicious for him to carry into effect the great decree which the king had issued at his insistence (Est. 9:24). The festival lasted two days and was regularly observed on the fourteenth and fifteenth of Adar, but if the fourteenth was a sabbath, or on the second or fourth day of the week, the beginning of the festival was deferred until the next day. As soon as the stars began to appear, when the fourteenth of the month had begun, candles were lighted in token of rejoicing, and the people assembled in the synagogue. After a short prayer of thanksgiving, the book of Esther was read. The reader translated the text and whenever he read the name of Haman the whole congregation cried, "May his name be blotted out." On the fifteenth the rejoicing was continued. The feast is also called the day of Mordecai (2 Macc. 15:36).

Purim was not one of the three Mosaic feasts—Passover, Pentecost, and Tabernacles.

purse a bag carried by the Hebrews (Gen. 42:35; Prov. 1:14; Isa. 46:6). This bag is described in the NT by the terms *balantion* and *glossokomon* (Lk. 10:4, 12:33, 22:35–36; Jn. 12:6, 13:29).

Put (po͝ot, pŭt) see **Phut**

Puteoli (pū-tē′ō-lī) the famous seaport in Italy and the harbor to which the Alexandrian cornships brought their cargoes (Acts 27:13). During the time of Paul, Puteoli was a place of unusual importance. The city had been founded in the sixth century B.C., its original name being Dicaearchia. The city was located on the north of the bay, the present Bay of Naples.

Putiel (pū′tĭ-ĕl) father-in-law of Eleazar, the son of Aaron (Ex. 6:25).

pygarg (pī′gärg) the Heb. *dishon*, a clean animal (Deut. 14:5), apparently an antelope. The Gr. *pugargos* denotes an animal which had a "white rump."

Pyrrhus (pĭr′ŭs) Acts 20:4 indicates that Pyrrhus is the father of Sopater.

Q

quail the Heb. *selav* is so rendered in Ex. 16:13 and Num. 11:31–32. The Israelites on two occasions during their travels to Sinai were

providentially provided quail for food. It was the spring of the year on each occasion. Quail is a brownish-white bird and flies rapidly, although it cannot fly for an extended period of time if the wind is against it. The flesh of the quail is white and by many is considered a delicacy.

Quartus (kwôr'tŭs) a Christian of Corinth (Rom. 16:23).

quaternion (kwȧ-tûr'nǐ-ŭn) a military term signifying the guard of four soldiers, two of whom were attached to the person of a prisoner while the other two kept watch outside the door of his cell (Acts 12:4).

queen *malcah* refers to a queen regnant, while this term and *shegal* refer to a queen consort. *Gebirah* refers to the queen mother. The latter term is expressive of authority.

quicksand a drifting sand, called quick because

it seems to "move with life." See Acts 27:17. The Syrtis is the broad and deep bight on the North African coast between Carthage and Cyrene.

Quirinius (kwī-rĭn'ĭ-ŭs) Roman governor of Syria in A.D. 6. Luke 2:1–5 indicates that an enrollment which took Joseph and Mary to Bethlehem as a requirement of a decree effected by Augustus occurred when Quirinius was the Roman governor of Syria.

quiver this term designates a container for arrows (Isa. 22:6; Jer. 5:16; Job 39:23). This was likely hung on the arm or swung over the warrior's back, but the Bible contains no information concerning its form or material.

R

Raamah (rā'ȧ-mȧ) the son of Cush, and father of the Cushites Sheba and Dedan. The tribe of Raamah became known as traders (Ezek. 27:22).

Raamiah (rā'ȧ-mī'ȧ) one of the chiefs who returned with Zerubbabel (Neh. 7:7).

Raamses (rā-ăm'sēz) see **Rameses**

Rabbah (răb'ȧ) 1. A strong place on the east of the Jordan which was the chief city of Ammonites (Deut. 3:11; 2 Sam. 12:26; Jer. 49:2; Ezek. 21:20). The site is mentioned as containing the bed of the giant Og (Deut. 3:11). David's first Ammonite campaign appears to have occurred early in his reign. The army under Abishai was sent as far as Rabbah to keep the Ammonites in check (2 Sam. 10:14), but the main force under Joab remained at Medeba (1 Chr. 19:7). The following year the Rabbanite war was resumed and Rabbah was made the main point of attack. Joab led a siege which lasted approximately two years before the Hebrews succeeded in capturing a portion of the city. However, the citadel which rose abruptly on the north side of the lower town still remained to be taken. Joab insisted that the honor of taking the citadel be reserved for the king. Shortly after David's arrival the fortress was taken. In the time of Amos, Rabbah again had a "wall" and "palace." So it remained until the day of the invasion of Nebuchadnezzar (Jer. 49:2–3).

2. This name was likely attached also in

Biblical times to the chief city of Moab. Its Biblical name is Ar, but Eusebius testifies that in the fourth century it possessed a special title of Rabbath Moab.

3. A city of Judah, named with Kirjath-jearim in Josh. 15:16 only.

rabbi the title of respect given by the Jews to their doctors and teachers, and often used to address Jesus (Mt. 23:7–8, 26:45, 49; Mk. 9:5, 11:21, 14:45; Jn. 1:39, 50). The meaning of the title is interpreted in expressed words by John and by implication in Matthew to mean "Master, Teacher" (Jn. 1:39; Mt. 23:8). Rab was the lowest grade of honor, Rabbi meant "my master," and Rabboni meant "my lord, my master," thus the highest of the three titles.

Rabbith (răb'ĭth) a town in the territory, possibly on the border, of Issachar (Josh. 19:20).

Rabboni see **rabbi**

Rab-mag (răb'măg) a title of office and respect, which title was borne by Nergal-sharezer. See Jer. 39:3, 13.

Rab-saris (răb'sȧ-rĭs) 1. An officer of the king of Assyria sent with Tartan and Rab-shakeh against Jerusalem in the time of Hezekiah (2 K. 18:17).

2. One of the princes of Nebuchadnezzar, who was present at the capture of Jerusalem, 588 B.C. (Jer. 39:3, 13). It is likely that the term refers to an office rather than an individual.

Rabshakeh (răb′shà-kĕ) an officer of the king of Assyria sent against Jerusalem in the reign of Hezekiah. Sennacherib, having taken other cities of Judah, was besieging Lachish, and Hezekiah then offered submission and tribute. It is questionable whether Rabshakeh refers to a person, and it is more likely that it refers to an officer, perhaps being the title of an officer.

raca (rà-kä′, rā′kà) an expression of reproach and contempt used by the Jews in the time of Jesus (Mt. 5:22).

race see **games**

Rachab (rā′kăb) see **Rahab**

Rachal (rā′kăl), **Racal** (rā′kăl) mentioned in 1 Sam. 30:29, this is the location in Judah to which David sent some of the spoils of Ziklag.

Rachel (rā′chĕl) the younger of the daughters of Laban, the wife of Jacob and mother of Joseph and Benjamin. The story of her life is contained in Gen. 29–33, 35. Rachel is described as a beautiful girl, and the love between Jacob and Rachel is described as being deep from their first meeting by the well of Haran, when he showed to her the simple courtesies of the desert life. It is recalled that Jacob served long and well for her, in which the seven years "seemed to him but a few days, for the love he had to her." The tragedy of her death at the very time her own long-delayed hopes were being accomplished further underscores the character of this thrilling account. However, it is to be remembered that she was discontented and impatient during the time of her childlessness (Gen. 30:1–2). The account of her stealing her father's idols and the concealment of her theft leads one to believe that she was not entirely free from the superstitions and idolatry which prevailed in the land (Josh. 24:2, 14). Genesis 35:19–21 indicates that she was buried "in the way to Ephrath."

Raddai (răd′ā-ī) a brother of David, the fifth son of Jesse (1 Chr. 2:14).

Ragau (rā′gô) ancestor of Jesus, son of Phalec (Lk. 3:35).

Raguel (rà-gū′ĕl), or **Reuel** (rōō′ĕl) a prince-priest of Midian, the father of Zipporah according to Ex. 2:21, and of Hobab according to Num. 10:29. Because Moses' father-in-law is named Jethro in Ex. 3:1 and Hobab in Judg. 4:11, some have conjectured that the terms meant one and the same.

Rahab (rā′hăb) the well-known woman of Jericho, who received the spies sent with Joshua to spy out the land, hid them in her house from the pursuit of her countrymen, was saved with all her family when the Israelites sacked the city, and became the wife of Salmon. At the time of the arrival of the Israelites in Canaan, she was a young unmarried woman, living in a house of her own, although she had a father and mother, brothers and sisters, living in Jericho. She was a "harlot," and she probably combined the trade of lodge-keeper for wayfaring men. The author of the Epistle to the Hebrews tells us that "by faith the harlot Rahab perished not with them that believed not, when she had received the spies with peace" (Heb. 9:31). James likewise employs her as an illustration of justification (James 2:25).

Rahab (rā′hăb) a poetical name of Egypt. The term signifies "fierceness, insolence, pride."

Raham (rā′hăm) in the genealogy of the descendants of Caleb, the son of Hezron (1 Chr. 2:44), Raham is described as the son of Shema and the father of Jorkoam.

Rahel (rā′hĕl) see **Rachel**

rain the expression "early rain" refers to the rains of the autumn (Deut. 11:14; Jer. 5:24) while the expression "latter rain" refers to the rain of spring (Prov. 16:15; Hos. 6:3; Zech. 10:1). The Hebrews used numerous terms to refer to rain. The early rain was expressed by *yoreh*, the latter rain by *malkosh*. The showers by *rebibim*, and the violent rainfall by the term *zerem*. In a country possessing so many varieties of elevation as Palestine, there must occur corresponding varieties of climate. For six months in the year, no rain falls and the harvests are gathered without any anxiety. During this period the whole land becomes dry, parched, and brown; the cisterns are empty, the springs and fountains fail, and the autumnal rains are eagerly anticipated to prepare the earth for the reception of seed. These rains begin the latter part of October, coming primarily from the west or southwest and continuing for two or three days at a time. The rains are heavy during November and December, and at no period during the winter season do the rains entirely cease. Rain falls at intervals during the month of March, but it is very rare in April.

rainbow the sign of the covenant which God made with Noah when he came forth from the ark that the waters should no more become a flood to destroy all flesh. The rainbow, which had been seen often prior to this time, became a symbol of God's mercy and faithfulness (Rev. 4:3).

raisin see **vine**

Rakem (rā′kĕm) a descendant of Machir, the son of Manasseh, and obviously the grandson of Manasseh (1 Chr. 7:16).

Rakkath (răk′ăth) a fortified town of Naphtali (Josh. 19:35).

Rakkon (răk′ŏn) a town in the inheritance of Dan (Josh. 19:46), and near Joppa.

Ram (răm) 1. Second son of Hezron, and father of Amminadab (1 Chr. 2:9–10).

2. The firstborn of Jerahmeel (1 Chr. 2:25, 27).

3. Elihu, the son of Barachel the Buzite (Job 32:2).

4. A male sheep, used as food or offering (Gen. 31:38; Lev. 1:10, 8:18). See **sheep, sacrifices**

5. Battering ram. An instrument of ancient siege operations and mentioned in Ezek. 4:2 and 21:22. This instrument was used to destroy gates and walls of a besieged city. Some of the battering rams were joined to moveable towers which held warriors and armed men. This formed a temporary building, the top of which was level with the walls of the besieged city. This tower was occupied by two warriors, one of whom fired his arrows against the besieged, while the second held a shield for his companion's protection.

Rama, Ramah (rä′mà) 1. A site in Benjamin where some captors of Judah were massacred before the larger group was deported to Babylon (Jer. 40:1).

2. The home of Elkanah, Samuel's father (1 Sam. 1:19, 2:11), the birthplace of Samuel himself, his home and official residence, the site of his altar (1 Sam. 7:17, 8:4, 15:34, 16:13, 19:18), and his burial place (1 Sam. 25:1, 28:3). First Samuel 1:1 seems to indicate that this site was in Mount Ephraim. However, the site of the town cannot be located precisely, and this difficulty leads others to conclude, on the basis of all that is known of the life of Samuel, that Rama must be restricted to the region of the tribe of Benjamin and to the neighborhood of Gibeah.

3. A fortified site of Naphtali (Josh. 19:36) named between Abamah and Hazor.

4. A landmark on the boundary of Asher (Josh. 19:29), apparently between Tyre and Sidon.

5. Ramoth-gilead (2 K. 8:29; 2 Chr. 22:6).

6. A place mentioned in the catalogue of those inhabited by the Benjaminites after their return from the captivity (Neh. 11:33).

7. Ramath of the south.

8. Ramath-lehi. The name given by Samson to the scene of his slaughter of the thousand Philistines (Judg. 15:17).

9. Ramath-mispeh. Mentioned in Josh. 13:26, apparently it is one of its northern landmarks.

Ramathaim-zophim (rä′mà-thä′ĭm-zō′fĭm) the full name of the town in which Elkanah, the father of Samuel, resided (1 Sam. 1:1).

Ramathite (rä′măth-ĭt) a native of Ramah. Shimei, the Ramathite, was responsible for the royal vineyards of King David (1 Chr. 27:27).

Rameses (răm′ĕ-sēz) a town in the district of Lower Egypt. Rameses is first mentioned in the narrative of the settling of Joseph of his father and brethren in Egypt (Gen. 47:11). Genesis 47:6 indicates that this is the region where Pharaoh instructed Joseph to settle his kinsmen. Exodus 12:37 indicates that Rameses was the starting point of the journey of the Israelites toward the Promised Land. This reference also identifies Rameses as the store city which the Israelites built for Pharaoh.

Ramiah (rà-mī′à) a son of Parosh, and a layman of Israel (Ezra 10:25).

Ramoth (rä′mŏth) 1. One of the four Levitical cities of Issachar (1 Chr. 6:73).

2. An Israelite, the son of Bani (Ezra 10:29).

3. A town in Gilead. See **Ramoth-gilead.** A town located to the south (1 Sam. 30:27). This village is further identified as a village in Simeon (Josh. 19:8).

Ramoth-gilead (rä′mŏth-gĭl′ê-ăd) also known as Ramoth in Gilead (Deut. 4:43; Josh. 20:8; 1 K. 22:3). A fortress located in Gilead, in the eastern area of Gad. First Kings 4:13 indicates that Ramoth-gilead commanded the regions Argob and the towns Jair. This town is likely to be identified with Ramath-mispeh (Josh. 13:26). It was the city of refuge for the tribe of Gad (Deut. 4:43; Josh. 20:8). It was the residence of one of Solomon's officers (1 K. 4:13). See also 1 K. 15:20–21; 2 K. 9:14.

ram's horns see **cornet, jubilee**

rams' skins when dyed red, rams' skins formed part of the materials that the Israelites were instructed to present as offerings for the making of the tabernacle (Ex. 25:5).

Rapha (rä′fà) son of Binea, among the descendants of Saul (1 Chr. 8:37).

Raphu (rä′fū) the father of Palti, the Benjaminite spy (Num. 13:9).

raven an unclean bird not allowed as food by the Mosaic law (Lev. 11:15). The bird is first mentioned in Gen. 8:7 as the bird which "went forth to and fro until the waters were dried up." The raven is also mentioned in connection with Elijah's sustenance at Cherith. This bird is black in color, omnivorous, feeding even on carrion.

razor an instrument, finely honed, used to remove beard or hair. The practice of the shaving the head after the completion of a vow must have created among the Jews a necessity for a special trade, which in turn required special tools, the razor being one of them (Lev. 14:8; Num. 6:9, 18; Judg. 13:5; Isa. 7:20; Acts 18:18).

Reaia (rē-ā′yȧ) a Reubenite, son of Micah, and apparently prince of his tribe (1 Chr. 5:5).

Reaiah (rē-ā′yȧ) 1. A descendant of Shubal, the son of Judah (1 Chr. 4:2).

2. A family of Nethinim who returned with Zerubbabel (Ezra 2:47; Neh. 7:50).

Reba (rē′bȧ) one of the five kings of the Midianites slain by the children of Israel in their avenging expedition at the time of Balaam's fall (Num. 31:8; Josh. 13:21).

Rebecca (rē-bĕk′ȧ), **Rebekah** (rē-bĕk′ȧ) daughter of Bethuel (Gen. 22:23) and sister of Laban, married to Isaac, her father's cousin. Rebecca was childless for nineteen years; then, after the prayers of Isaac, Esau and Jacob were born. See Gen. 24:19–28, 26:35. When Isaac was driven by a famine into the area of the Philistines, Rebecca's beauty became a source of danger to her husband. Some time later, Rebecca suggested the deceitful act practiced by Jacob on his blind father. In order to forestall the consequence of Esau's anger, she encouraged Isaac to send Jacob away to Padan-aram (Gen. 27) to her own kindred (Gen. 29:12). It is conjectured that she died during Jacob's sojourn in Padan-aram.

Recah (rē′kȧ) Beth-rapha, Paseah, and Tehinnah are called the "men of Recah." See 1 Chr. 4:12.

Rechab (rē′kăb) 1. The father or ancestor of Jehonabab (2 K. 10:15, 23; 1 Chr. 2:55; Jer. 35:6–19), identified by some scholars as Hobab.

2. One of the two "captains of bands" whom Ish-bosheth took into his service and who later conspired to murder him (2 Sam. 4:2).

3. The father of Malchijah who ruled Beth-haccherem (Neh. 3:14).

Rechabites (rĕk′ȧ-bīts) a Kenite tribe which came into Canaan with the Israelites, but retained their former nomadic habits. Jonadab was their captain. Although his people had been worshipers of God and had been circumcised, they were never considered a part of Israel and likely therefore did not consider themselves bound by the Mosaic law and ritual. The worship of Baal was as offensive to this group as to the Israelites. The luxury and license of Phoenician cities threatened the destruction of the simplicity of their nomadic life (Amos 2:7–8, 6:3–6). The Rechabites were to drink no wine, were not to build a house, sow seed, plant vineyards, or own vineyards. They were to dwell in tents all of their lifetime, remembering that they were strangers in the land (Jer. 35:6–7).

recorder an officer of respect and high rank in the Jewish state, exercising the functions of annalist, president of the private council, etc. In the court of David the recorder appeared among the high officers of the household (2 Sam. 8:16; 1 Chr. 18:15).

Red Sea the sea known to the Israelites simply as the "sea" or "the sea of reeds." The term "Red Sea" is a literal translation of the Greek words *eruthra thalassa*, terms of unknown origin. The "red" was derived either from the king Erythras, who reigned in the adjacent country, or from some natural phenomenon, such as the red appearance of the mountains on the western coast, the red color of the water, the red coral of the sea, the red sea weed, etc. In modern usage of the term, the greatest width of the sea is approximately 200 miles while its length is some 1500 miles. The Erythraean Sea was understood in ancient days to include not only the Red Sea, but also the Indian Ocean and Persian Gulf. Today the Red Sea includes only that body of water which separates Africa from Arabia and extends from the Gulf of Aden (Aqabah) to the Gulf of Suez.

The Red Sea is unusual in that there are no large rivers which empty into it. The hot climate contributes to excessive evaporation and pronounced salinity in the waters. As previously indicated, the Sea abounds in coral which is beautifully colored and variegated.

The Red Sea in which the Biblical student is interested lay east of Egypt (Ex. 10:19) and near it the Israelites encamped when not far from Sinai (Num. 33:10–11). The Red Sea was crossed by the Israelites, and its waters became the death trap of the pursuing Egyptians (Ex. 15:4, 22). If any crisis of the Exodus surpasses that of the passage of the Red Sea, it must be the passing of the death angel which was the harbinger of the Exodus. The Israelites began their journey from Rameses, traveling to Succoth (Ex. 13:17–18). At the end of the second day, they encamped at Etham "in the edge of the wilderness" (Ex. 13:20; Num. 23:6). The group eventually arrived at Pi-hahiroth, from which they crossed the sea. Pharaoh regretted that he had permitted the Israelites to depart and took "600 chosen chariots . . ." (Ex. 14:7). The Israelites were an encumbered multitude, their movement impaired with the presence of women, children, and cattle. Thus the pharaoh's army overtook the people by the sea (Ex. 14:9). The people then murmured against Moses, who encouraged them and insisted that God would save them.

Divine instructions are recorded in Ex. 14:15–16. When Moses stretched out his hand over the sea, the Scriptures indicate that God caused it to recede by a strong wind all that night and made the land dry, the waters being divided. The children of Israel went through the midst of the sea on dry ground, and the waters were a wall on both their left and right hands. When the Egyptian army was in the midst of the sea, Moses was again commanded to extend his hand and the sea returned to its normal condition. This event became one of the chief facts of Jewish history, perhaps brooked only by divine revelation in the Law.

reed one of several aquatic grasses.

1. *Agmon.* The drooping panicle of this plant answered to the "bowing down of the head" of which Isaiah speaks (Isa. 58:5).

2. *Gome.* The plant of the sedge family, which was common in some parts of Egypt. See Ex. 2:3; Job 8:11; Isa. 18:2.

3. *Aroth.* This term seems to denote the open grassy land on the banks of the Nile. It is translated paper reed in Isa. 19:7.

4. *Kenah.* The term is rendered stalk, branch, reed, or bone in the OT. The thick stem of this reed may have been used as walking canes or measuring reeds (Ex. 25:32; 2 K. 18:21; Job 31:22; Ezek. 29:6–7).

5. *Kalamos.* This is the common NT term for reed (Mt. 11:7, 27:29; Rev. 11:1).

Reelaiah (rē'ĕl-ā'yà) an outstanding leader, the man who accompanied Zerubbabel (Ezra 2:2).

refiner a metal worker who separates the dross from the pure ore by repeatedly passing the metal through the fire. The refiner worked with a crucible and bellows or blowpipe (Isa. 1:25; Jer. 6:29; Mal. 3:3).

refuge, cities of see **cities of refuge**

Regem (rē'gĕm) a son of Jahdai (1 Chr. 2:47).

Regem-melech (rē'gĕm-mē'lĕk) this name occurs in an obscure passage of Zechariah (7:2). He and Sherezer were sent on behalf of some of the Captivity to make inquiries at the temple concerning fasting.

Rehabiah (rē'hà-bī'à) the only son of Eliezer, and grandson of Moses (1 Chr. 23:17, 24:21, 26:25).

Rehob (rē'hŏb) 1. Father of Hadadezer, king of Zobah (2 Sam. 8:3, 12).

2. A Levite who sealed the covenant with Nehemiah (Neh. 10:11).

3. A town of Asher (Josh. 19:28).

4. The northern limits of the exploration of the spies (Num. 13:21).

Rehoboam (rē'hô-bō'ăm) son of Solomon by the Ammonite princess Naamah (1 K. 14:21,

31), and Solomon's successor (1 K. 11:43). Jewish history indicates that the tribes were never harmoniously confederated, and the withdrawal of Solomon's strong hand brought crises. When the people demanded a remission of the severe burdens imposed by Solomon, Rehoboam rejected the advice of his father's counselors, only to indicate that "my little finger is thicker than my father's loins. And now whereas my father led you with a heavy yoke, I will add to your yoke; my father chastised you with whips, but I will chastise you with scorpions." Immediately ten of the twelve tribes renounced allegiance to Rehoboam, who then sent Aboram to effect a reconciliation. However, the rebels stoned him to death, whereupon the king and all his attendants fled to Jerusalem. Rehoboam assembled an army of 180,000 men from the tribes of Judah and Benjamin and hoped to reconquer Israel. The prophet Shemaiah prohibited the expedition (1 K. 12:24), yet during Rehoboam's lifetime peaceful relations between Israel and Judah were never restored (2 Chr. 12:15; 1 K. 14:30). The king then strengthened his remaining territories by building a number of fortresses (2 Chr. 11:6–10). True worship of God was not maintained in Judah; the lascivious worship of Ashtoreth was permitted to exist by the side of true religion. These evils were punished by the Egyptian invasion. Following a reign of seventeen years, Rehoboam died in 915 B.C. and his son Abijah ascended the throne (1 K. 14:21, 31; 2 Chr. 12:13, 16). See 1 K. 14; 2 Chr. 11.

Rehoboth (rā'hô-bōth) 1. The third of a series of wells dug by Isaac (Gen. 26:22). The well lay in the valley of Gerar.

2. One of the four cities built by Asshur (Gen. 10:11).

3. A town "by the river," and built by a certain Saul, one of the early kings of the Edomites (Gen. 36:37; 1 Chr. 1:48). "The river" generally identifies the Euphrates. The exact site of the city of the certain king Saul (Shaul) is likely in northern Edom.

Rehum (rē'hŭm) 1. One of the "children of the province" who went up from Babylon with Zerubbabel (Ezra 2:2).

2. A subordinate officer, perhaps a chancellor, under the king of Persia, who administered the affairs of the country beyond the River (Ezra 5:6).

3. A Levite of the family of Bani, who assisted in rebuilding the walls of Jerusalem (Neh. 3:17).

4. One of the chief of the people who signed the covenant with Nehemiah (Neh. 10:25).

5. A priestly family, or the head of the priestly house, who went up with Zerubbabel (Neh. 12:3).

Rei (rē′ī) identified in 1 K. 1:8 as remaining loyal to David's cause when Adonijah rebelled.

reins the kidneys. The ancients believed the kidneys to be the seat of desire and longing, which explains their being coupled with the heart (Ps. 7:9; Jer. 11:20).

Rekem (rē′kĕm) 1. One of the five kings or chieftains of Midian slain by the Israelites (Num. 31:8; Josh. 13:21).

2. One of the four sons of Hebron, and father of Shammai (1 Chr. 2:43–44).

3. A town in Benjamin's allotment (Josh. 18:27).

Remaliah (rĕm′a-lī′a) the father of Pekah, captain of Pekahiah king of Israel, who slew his master and usurped his throne (2 K. 15:25–37; 2 Chr. 28:6; Isa. 7:1–9).

Remeth (rē′mĕth) a town of Issachar (Josh. 19:21).

Remmon (rĕm′ŏn) a town in the allotment of Simeon (Josh. 19:7).

Remmon-methoar (rĕm′ŏn-meth′ō-är) a site forming one of the landmarks of the eastern boundary of the territory of Zebulun (Josh. 19:13).

remnant a group of people usually striving to remain loyal to God. See 2 Chr. 30:6; Isa. 1:26; Jer. 23:3; Amos 9:8–15; Mic. 4:6–8; Zeph. 3:13; Zech. 13:9.

Rephael (rē′fà-ĕl) son of Shemaiah, the firstborn of Obed-edom (1 Chr. 26:7).

Rephah (rē′fà) son of Ephraim, and ancestor of Joshua (1 Chr. 7:25).

Rephaiah (rē-fā′yà) 1. The sons of Rephaiah appear among the descendants of Zerubbabel (1 Chr. 3:21).

2. A Simeonite chieftain in the reign of Hezekiah (1 Chr. 4:42).

3. Son of Tola, son of Issachar (1 Chr. 7:2).

4. Son of Binea and descendant of Saul (1 Chr. 9:43).

5. The son of Hur and ruler of the portion of Jerusalem (Neh. 3:9).

Rephaim (rĕf′à-ĭm) see **giants**

Rephaim, the Valley of the scene of some of David's most remarkable adventures, located near Jerusalem and Bethlehem. Josephus mentions it as "the valley which extends (from Jerusalem) to the city of Bethlehem." See 2 Sam. 5:18–22; 1 Chr. 11:15; Isa. 17:5.

Rephan (rē′făn) an idol worshiped by the Israelites in the wilderness, a god who has a star associated with his worship. See Acts 7:43. Rephan represents *Raiphan*, which etymology

is the translation of the *Kaimanu*, Saturn. See also Amos 5:26.

Rephidim (rĕf′ĭ-dĭm) a campsite of the Israelites in their march between the wilderness of Sin and Sinai. No water was available, and Moses was so antagonized that he went to Horeb by divine commandment and there struck a rock, from which water flowed (Ex. 17:1–6, 19:2; Num. 33:12–15). Water from this source also supplied the Israelites during their Sinai encampment. At this site Amalek was engaged in battle (Ex. 17:8–16).

Resen (rē′sĕn) mentioned only in Gen. 10:12, a city built by Asshur and which lay between Nineveh and Calah.

Resheph (rē′shĕf) a descendant of Ephraim (1 Chr. 7:25).

resurrection not the resuscitation of the old body but the deliverance of the entire personality from enslavement to death. The gospels record vividly the many evidences for Jesus' resurrection. See Mt. 28:1–20; Mk. 16:1–11; Lk. 24:1–53; Jn. 20:1–31, 21:1–25. The Acts of the Apostles describes the activity of the risen Christ. Perhaps the classic passage concerning the resurrection and its meaning for the Christian is 1 Cor. 15. Revelation 20 relates the resurrection and judgment. See **death, Jesus Christ.**

Reu (rē′ū) son of Peleg (Gen. 11:18–21; 1 Chr. 1:25; Lk. 3:35).

Reuben (rōō′bĕn) Jacob's firstborn child, the son of Leah, apparently born some lengthy time following the marriage of the parents. See Gen. 29:31–32. The Biblical materials present a favorable impression of Reuben's disposition. His anguish at the disappearance of his brother and the frustration of his kindly artifice for delivering him (Gen. 37:22), his recalling of the minute details of the painful scene many years afterwards (Gen. 42:22), his offer to assume the responsibility of the safety of the brother who had succeeded to Joseph's place in the family (Gen. 42:37), all testify to a warm nature. Genesis 35:22 alone records his adulterous connection with Bilhah. At the time of the migration into Egypt, Reuben's sons numbered four (Gen. 46:9; 1 Chr. 5:3). From them came the chief families of the tribe (Num. 26:5–11). The census at Mount Sinai (Num. 1:20–21) reveals that at the Exodus the numbers of the tribe were 46,500 men above twenty years of age and fit for warlike service. During the journey through the wilderness, the position of Reuben was on the south side of the tabernacle. In their flight from Egypt (Ex. 12:38) their cattle accompanied them. Thus it was only natural that they would desire land suited to their needs (Num. 32:7). It was only on their undertaking to fulfill their part in the conquest of the western country, the land of Canaan proper, and thus satisfying him that their proposal was grounded in no selfish desire to escape a full share of the difficulties of the conquest, that Moses consented to their proposal.

No judge, no prophet, no hero, belonged to the tribe of Reuben, so far as Biblical materials are concerned. In the dire extremity of their brethren in the north under Deborah and Barak, they contented themselves with the debating of the news amidst the streams of Mishor. The distant distress of his brethren could not move Reuben; he lingered among his sheepfolds and preferred the shepherd's pipe and the bleating of the flocks to the clamor of the trumpet and the turmoil of battle. No person or incident is recorded to place Reuben in any more distinct form than as a member of the community of "the Reubenites, the Gadites, and the half-tribe of Manasseh" (1 Chr. 12:37). Thus remote from the central seat of the national government and of the national religion, it is not to be wondered that Reuben chilled toward the faith of his God. The last historical notice records that the Reubenites and the Gadites, plus the half-tribe of Manasseh, were carried captive by Pul and Tiglath-pileser.

Reuel (rōō'ĕl) 1. A descendant of Esau (Gen. 36:4, 10, 13, 17; 1 Chr. 1:35, 37).

2. Moses' father-in-law (Ex. 2:18).

3. Father of Eliasaph, a leader of the tribe of Gad at the time of the census at Sinai (Num. 2:14).

4. A Benjaminite, ancestor of Elah (1 Chr. 9:8).

Reumah (rōō'mȧ) a concubine of Nahor, Abraham's brother (Gen. 22:24).

Revelation, John's the last book included in the NT and purported to have been written from the isle of Patmos.

1. *Authorship.* Was the apostle John the author of Revelation? Although other questions may shroud Revelation, this is a question of primary importance. Dionysius of Alexandria first modestly questioned the Johannine authorship, and others of much more recent date and of greater influence have likewise questioned the generally observed facts relating to Johannine authorship. The author identifies himself as John, without prefix or addition. He is also described as a servant of Christ, one who has borne testimony as an eye witness, is exiled to Patmos because of this testimony, a fellow sufferer of those whom he addresses, and an au-

thoritative channel of communication to the seven churches of Asia, of which churches the apostle John was spiritual guide. These evidences are likewise supported by those of: Justin Martyr, A.D. 150; Muratorian Fragment, 170; Melito of Sardis, 170; Theophilus, bishop of Antioch; Irenaeus; Apollonius; Clement of Alexandria, 200; Tertullian, 207; Hippolytus, 235; Origen, 250; and traditional witnesses. Nevertheless, strong arguments are marshaled in behalf of the mysterious and ambiguous John the presbyter.

2. *Date and Site of Writing.* Numerous critics suggest the reign of Nero as the most logical time for the writing of the Revelation, thus placing the book in the late 60s. Others believe, and perhaps a preponderance of evidence is to be found on this side, that Revelation belongs to the persecution under Domitian and thus places the book A.D. 95. Patmos is the generally accepted site of writing, although some commentators are led to believe that the message was written in Ephesus, immediately after the apostle's return from Patmos.

3. *Interpretation.* The Apocalypse belongs to the class of literature known as apocalyptic, especially prominent during the intertestamental period. These materials speak of days of sore judgment but also of vindication and relief. An *apokalypsis* literally means an "unveiling, a making known." Revelation 1:1-3 describes the book as a message concerning "things which must shortly come to pass," given to Jesus Christ, in turn given John for the purpose of communication to the churches of Asia Minor. These churches are identified as Ephesus, Smyrna, Pergamum, Thyatira, Sardis, Philadelphia, and Laodicea. The book contains an abundance of symbolism, which within itself has created numerous interpretive problems. Three basic approaches to the book are currently popular. The premillennial view, and there are many ramifications of this approach, suggests that Revelation is a volume of unfilled prophecy which tells of severe persecution, the revelation of the Antichrist, the return of Jesus, the battle of Armageddon, an earthly kingdom of a thousand years' duration ruled by Christ, the final overthrow of Satan, and the inauguration of the eternal order. The dispensational premillennialist injects a rapture prior to the seven years of severe tribulation (which follow the revelation of the Antichrist), while the historical premillennialist believes that the church endures the persecution and that the blessed hope is the return of Jesus. On the other hand, the postmillennialist believes that a thousand years of peace will precede the coming of

Christ. Christian principles will be found in every area of life, including municipal government. This view is the least popular today because the events of the past fifty years have shattered most convictions that the world is becoming a "better" place. The amillennialist views the thousand years as a symbol, perhaps the interval existing between the first and second comings of Christ, or as a symbolic way of indicating the completeness of Satan's binding. The interpreter persuaded of this approach believes good and evil exist side by side until the coming of Christ, then follows a general resurrection, the great white-throne judgment, and the initiation of the eternal order. Controversies have raged for many centuries, the book's message being debated as early as Justin Martyr.

4. *Message.* Regardless of one's millennial approach, Revelation is a message of victory for persecuted peoples: (1) Revelation 1:1–3:22 portrays the glorified Christ and his message to the seven churches of Asia Minor. (2) Revelation 4–5 envision God, who receives the adoration of all creation, but at the same time rules over the destinies of the universe. (3) Revelation 6–19 discloses the events of God's victory, ch. 20 depicting the total victory of Christ upon earth. (4) Revelation 21–22 disclose the glory of the New Jerusalem and further define God's provision for his people. The student must take heed lest he find himself enthralled by the meticulous arguments concerning the thousand-year period and miss the primary thrust of victory contained within the book.

V.E.G.

Rezeph (rē'zĕf) a place mentioned by Sennacherib as having been destroyed by his predecessor (2 K. 19:12; Isa. 37:12).

Rezia (rē-zī'ȧ) an Asshurite (1 Chr. 7:39).

Rezin (rē'zĭn) 1. A king of Damascus, contemporary with Pekah, king of Israel, and with Jotham and Ahaz of Judah. He attacked Jotham during the latter part of his reign (2 K. 15:37), but his chief conflict was with Ahaz, whose territory he invaded, in company with Pekah. He was defeated by Tiglath-pileser king of Assyria (2 K. 16:9).

2. The founder of one of the families of the Nethinim (Ezra 2:48; Neh. 7:50).

Rezon (rē'zŏn) son of Eliada, and founder of a Syrian kingdom. See 1 K. 11:23–25.

Rhegium (rē'jĭ-ŭm) an Italian town, originally a Greek colony, opposite Messina. The town is mentioned in the account of Paul's voyage from Syracuse to Puteoli (Acts 28:13).

Rhesa (rē'sȧ) a descendant of Zerubbabel (Lk. 3:27).

Rhoda (rō'dȧ) a maid who announced Peter's arrival at the door of Mary's house following his miraculous release from prison (Acts 12:13).

Rhodes (rōdz) an island opposite the Carian and Lycian headlands at the southwest extremity of the peninsula of Asia Minor. Its position has made the island important in history. Its imminence began about 400 B.C. with a founding of a city at the northeast extremity of the island. Following Alexander's death, its material prosperity and institutions obtained general esteem. At one time during the Roman period, it served as a seat of governmental affairs for certain districts on the mainland. Paul touched at Rhodes on his return voyage to Syria from the third missionary journey (Acts 21:1).

Ribai (rī'bī) father of Ittai, the Benjaminite of Gibeah (2 Sam. 23:29; 1 Chr. 11:31).

Riblah (rĭb'lȧ) 1. A landmark on the eastern boundary of the land of Israel, as specified by Moses (Num. 34:11).

2. City on the road between Palestine and Babylonia, in which the kings of Babylonia remained while directing the operations of their armies in Palestine and Phoenicia. Here Nebuchadnezzar waited while the sieges of Jerusalem and Tyre were being conducted by his lieutenants (2 K. 25:6, 20–21; Jer. 34:5–6). Similarly Pharaoh Necho, after his victory over the Babylonians at Carchemish returned to Riblah and summoned Jehoahaz from Jerusalem (2 K. 23:33).

riddle in Biblical literature any saying difficult of interpretation. It may refer to a "hard question" of the following nature: artifice (Dan. 8:23); proverb (Prov. 1:6); song (Ps. 49:4); oracle (Num. 12:8); and parable (Ezek. 17:2). The term has similar usages in both the Old and New Testaments.

Riddles were known to ancient Egyptians and were especially employed in banquets both by the Greeks and Romans. Riddles were generally proposed in verse, like the celebrated riddle of Samson, which actually was not a riddle because the Philistines did not possess a clue on which the solution could depend.

Rimmon (rĭm'ŏn) 1. A Benjaminite, the father of Rechab and Baanah, the murderers of Ish-bosheth (2 Sam. 4:2, 5, 9).

2. A deity worshiped by the Syrians of Damascus (2 K. 5:18).

3. A city of Zebulun, belonging to the Merarite Levites (1 Chr. 6:77).

4. A town in the southern portion of Judah, allotted to Simeon (Josh. 19:7; 1 Chr. 4:32).

5. Parez, a site during the wilderness march (Num. 33:19–20).

6. A cliff of natural fastness and security in which the 600 Benjaminites who escaped the slaughter of Gibeah took refuge (Judg. 20:45, 47).

ring the ring was regarded as an indispensable article of a Hebrew's attire, inasmuch as it contained his signet. Thus it was the symbol of authority, and as such was presented by Pharaoh to Joseph (Gen. 41:42) and by Ahasuerus to Haman (Est. 3:10). Rings of this nature were worn not only by men, but also by women, and were enumerated among the articles presented by men and women for the service of the tabernacle (Ex. 35:22). The signet ring was worn on the right hand (Jer. 22:24).

Rinnah (rĭn′à) a son of Shimon, a man of Judah (1 Chr. 4:20).

Riphath (rī′făth) the second son of Gomer and the head of a group of people descended from him (Gen. 10:3).

Rissah (rĭs′à) a campsite in the wilderness (Num. 33:21–22).

Rithmah (rĭth′mà) an encampment in the wilderness (Num. 33:18–19).

river a term describing a stream, whether dry or a torrent.

1. *Nahar.* This is the term used by the Hebrew for the perennial river (Gen. 2:10; Ex. 7:19; 2 Sam. 10:16).

2. *Nachal.* A dry valley which occasionally becomes the bed for a stream flowing temporarily.

3. *Yeor.* A term which applies to the Nile, the plural form applying to the Nile and its canals.

4. *Yubal.* A term signifying tumult or fullness (Jer. 17:8; Dan. 8:2–3, 6).

5. *Peleg.* A term used to describe a stream employed in irrigation.

6. *Aphik.* A torrent, a rush of water.

river of Egypt 1. *Nehar mitsraim.* The Nile (Gen. 15:18). 2. *Nachal mitsraim.* These terms designate a desert stream on the border of Egypt, the great wadi. The Wadi L'-areesh is a valley which is normally dry, but it runs fiercely after heavy rainfall.

Rizpah (rĭz′pä) a concubine to King Saul, and mother of his two sons Armoni and Mephibosheth. The account of 2 Sam. 21:8–11 has made her famous. The story relates the mother's watching over the bodies of her two sons and her five relatives following their crucifixion. The seven crosses were planted at the beginning of barley harvest and hung till the fall of the periodical rain in October. During all of this time, Rizpah remained at the foot of the crosses on which the bodies of her sons were exposed.

road occurring in 1 Sam. 27:10 the term means "raid" or "incursion."

robbery theft or plunder. Robbery has been one of the principal means of livelihood of the nomadic tribes. From the time of Ishmael, the Bedouin has been a wild man (Gen. 16:12). See Ex. 22 for the Mosaic law concerning theft.

Rodanim (rŏd′à-nĭm) descendants of Javan (1 Chr. 1:7).

roe, roebuck an antelope, some species of gazelle or deer. The animal was ceremonially clean and was eaten (Deut. 12:15, 22), was fleet (2 Sam. 2:18; 1 Chr. 7:8), was hunted (Prov. 6:5; Isa. 13:14), and was admired for its loveliness.

Rogelim (rŏ′gĕ-lĭm) a town of Gilead where Barzillai lived (2 Sam. 17:27, 19:31).

Rohgah (rŏ′gà) an Asshurite, of the sons of Shamer (1 Chr. 7:34).

roll the long sheet of parchment or papyrus containing writing, and generally kept wound around a stick, thus the descriptive name "roll."

Romamtiezer (rŏ-măm′tĭ-ē′zĕr) one of the sons of Heman (1 Chr. 25:4, 21), and a singer.

Roman empire the specific Biblical references to the Roman empire are confined to the NT period. Secular history, as well as intertestamental materials, is replete with the story of Rome. In 65 B.C. the Jews were still governed by the Hasmonean princes. Aristobulus had driven his brother Hyrcanus from the high priesthood, but was attacked by Aretas, the Arabian king and ally of Hyrcanus. Scaurus, Pompey's lieutenant, interfered in the contest in 64 B.C., and the next year Pompey himself marched into Judea and took Jerusalem. From this time on the Jews were, for all practical purposes, ruled by the Romans. Hyrcanus retained the high priesthood and a titular sovereignty, subject to the watchful control of Antipater, an active partisan of the Roman interest. Finally, Herod the Great, Antipater's son, was made king and was confirmed in the kingdom by Augustus, 30 B.C. During all of this time, the Jews were tributaries of Rome and their princes were mere Roman procurators. On the banishment of Archelaus in A.D. 6, Judea became an appendage of the province of Syria and was governed by a Roman procurator, who resided in Caesarea. Such were the relations of the Jewish people to the Roman government at the time when NT history begins.

When Augustus became sole ruler of the Roman world, in theory he was simply the first citizen of the republic, intrusted with temporary powers to settle the disorders of the state. Although the old magistracies were retained, their powers and prerogatives were conferred upon Augustus. Above everything else, he was the emperor. This term acquired a new significance when adopted as a permanent title by Julius Caesar. Although the empire was nominally elective, it was practically a right of adoption, and until Nero's time a type of hereditary right seemed to be recognized.

Cicero's description of the Greek states and colonies as a "fringe off the skirts of barbarism" has been well applied to the Roman dominions before the conquests of Pompey and Caesar. The Roman empire was still confined to a narrow strip encircling the Mediterranean Sea. Pompey added Asia Minor and Syria. Caesar added Gaul. Generals of Augustus overran the northwest portion of Spain and the country between the Alps and the Danube. Thus the boundaries of the empire were the Atlantic on the west, and the Euphrates on the east, the deserts of Africa, the cataracts of the Nile, and the Arabian deserts on the south, the English Channel, the Rhine, the Danube, and the Black Sea on the north. Still later Britain and Dacia were added by Trajan.

The country conquered by Rome could expect to become a subjected province, governed directly from Rome by officers sent for that purpose. At times, petty sovereigns were left in possession of a nominal independence on the borders, or within the natural limits, of the province. There were also differences in the political conditions of cities within the provinces. Some were called *free* cities, that is, they were governed by their own magistrates and were exempt from occupation by Roman garrisons. Other cities were *colonies*, that is, communities of Roman citizens transplanted, like garrisons of the imperial city, into a foreign land. Augustus divided the provinces into two classes: imperial and senatorial. See **province.** So many alterations were made in the initial arrangements that it is needless and futile to attempt such classifications. The NT writers designate governors of senatorial provinces as proconsuls (Acts 13:7, 18:12, 19:38). The imperial province was ruled by a governor. Provinces were heavily taxed for the benefit of Rome and her citizens. They are said to have been better governed under the empire than under the commonwealth, and history likewise indicates that the imperial provinces fared better than the senatorial provinces.

Roman citizenship, regardless of how it was obtained, was a valuable asset. Paul used his citizenship advantageously during his missionary experiences (Acts 16:21, 37–38, 22:25–27, 29).

Romans, Paul's Epistle to the this epistle is considered by most interpreters as Paul's outstanding work. Many scholars insist that Romans, as no other writing of Paul, reveals Pauline thought and conviction. The dominant theme of the epistle is "the righteousness of God for unrighteous men."

1. *Background.* Certain names in the salutation point to Corinth as the place from which the letter was sent (16:1–2). Gaius (16:23) is probably the person mentioned as one of the chief members of the Corinthian church in 1 Cor. 1:14. Erastus (16:23) is mentioned in connection with Corinth (2 Tim. 4:20). It is likely that the letter was written during Paul's Corinthian sojourn (Acts 20:3), during the winter and spring following the apostle's long residence at Ephesus. On this particular visit to Corinth, the visit of the third missionary journey as recorded in Acts, Paul remained some three months in Greece (Acts 20:3). The Pauline authorship is almost universally accepted, and the date is likely A.D. 56. The terminology, style, and argument all point to the apostle as the author.

Paul had long purposed to visit Rome, even wishing to extend his journey to Spain (1:9–13, 15:22–29). For the present, he was prevented from fulfilling his wish inasmuch as he was obligated to journey to Jerusalem with the alms of the Gentile Christians; thus, he addressed this letter to the Romans in order to supply the lack of his personal teaching. The concept of justification by faith is underscored in this epistle as in no other, with the possible exception of the Epistle to the Galatians.

The origin of the Roman church is obscured. It is possible that Christians, scattered by persecution, had taken the Gospel to Rome. Another proposal suggests that Jews and proselytes who had journeyed from Rome to Jerusalem for one of the annual festivals came in contact with the Gospel and took the message back to their home. Others have suggested that perhaps Roman soldiers, who had been stationed in Palestine, had accepted the Gospel and thus took it with them upon returning to Rome. It is likely that the Roman church at the time of Paul's writing was composed of both Jews and Gentiles, with the likelihood that the Gentiles were more numerous. A large Jewish colony had long existed in Rome, and it is probable that the Roman church was composed of both Jew and Gentile.

2. *Content.* Romans 1:1–17 is the introduction to the letter, consisting of the salutation, a section of thanksgiving, and a declaration of the theme (vss. 16–17). The first main section

of the epistle is 1:18–3:20 in which Paul reveals the Gentile's condemnation. The Gentile has rejected the authority of God's revelation, magnifying the sensual and physical, and falling into the basest forms of immorality (1:18–32). Chapter 2 reveals the Jew's condemnation. He has rejected likewise the revelation which God has given, the highest possible revelation. Thus Paul concludes that all men are guilty and all men are condemned. The atoning work of Jesus (3:21–31) is discussed as a part of Paul's over-all presentation of God's provision for man's redemption. Abraham (ch. 4) serves as an illustration of justification by faith. Paul indicates that justification by faith brings a sense of personal fellowship with God, a new security, etc. This relationship by faith leads Paul to discuss the Christian's relationship to sin (6:1–7:25). Again he concludes that man's release from sin is to be found only in Christ. Chapter 8 is a thrilling discussion of the results of fellowship with Christ. In it the blessings of salvation are delineated. Perhaps 8:28, "All things work together for good . . ." is the best known section of this chapter. Romans 9–11 is a discussion of the Jewish problem. In this section, Paul indicates that Israel's rejection of Christ is of paramount significance in his thinking. He further underscores the sovereignty of God, the freedom of man, and then in 11:1–36 harmonizes the two, concluding that no one can fully understand God's method of operation. This observation becomes an occasion of praise on the part of Paul. Romans, as all of the Pauline epistles, may be discussed under two broad headings, doctrinal and practical. The practical section of Romans begins with 12:1. In Romans 12–15 Paul discusses social relationships, civic duties, and the Christian's moral responsibilities toward weaker brothers. Romans 16:1–27 contains personal greetings and the benediction.

This epistle, always loved and often studied, continues to challenge the world's scholars as perhaps no other from the pen of Paul.

Rome the famous capital of the ancient world, situated on the Tiber, at a distance of about fifteen miles from its mouth. The "seven hills" (Rev. 17:9) which form the nucleus of the ancient city stand on the left bank of the Tiber. The city of Rome is mentioned in three books of the NT—Acts, the Epistle to the Romans, and 2 Timothy. Large Jewish colonies were settled quite early in Rome, perhaps as a result of the conquests of Pompey. Many of these Jews were made freedmen. Julius Caesar was kindly toward them, and they were also favored by Augustus. Claudius drove all the

Jews from Rome (Acts 18:2), but this banishment was not for an extended duration. At the time of Paul's visit (Acts 28:17) large numbers of Jews resided in Rome.

Paul's first imprisonment occurred between two famous epics in the history of the city, its restoration by Augustus and its destruction by Nero. Augustus boasted "that he had found the city of brick, and left it of marble." The streets were generally narrow and winding, flanked by densely crowded lodging houses of enormous height. Paul's first visit to Rome took place prior to the Neronian conflagration, but many of the ancient evils continued following it. The population of the city has been variously estimated; Gibbon estimates it at 1,200,-000. One half of the population consisted of slaves. A large part of the remainder of the population was composed of pauper citizens supported by public gratuities. A small group of wealthy nobility constituted the remainder of the population.

Numerous sites in and around the city are especially connected with Paul's life: (1) the Appian Way, by which he approached Rome (Acts 28:15); (2) the palace (Phil. 1:13); (3) the Mamertine Prison in which Paul was traditionally imprisoned; (4) the Ostian Road, where Paul supposedly met martyrdom. Other sites of lesser importance and significance are attached to the name of Paul.

The city of Rome, founded by Romulus in 753 B.C. was the city of power and governmental authority during the Christian era.

V.E.G.

roof see **house**

room 1. A spacial division of a house (Acts 1:13). See **house**

2. A place of social honor (Mt. 23:6; Mk. 12:39; Lk. 14:7–8).

rose a flower, but the exact Biblical description is debatable. Some suggest that the term refers to the narcissus, others to the crocus, still other scholars identify the term with the lily. The rose is a native of Persia and Media and grows in the mountains of Palestine. Rhoda, a rose (Acts 12:13) is mentioned as the maid who recognized the voice of Peter when he stood at the gate of Mary's home.

Rosh (rŏsh) 1. A son of Benjamin (Gen. 46:21). Rosh went to Egypt with Jacob and his sons.

2. A tribal people mentioned with Meshech and Tubal (Ezek. 38:2–3, 39:1).

rubies the Hebrew term *peninim* signifies a reddish-colored stone, very precious (Job 28:18; Prov. 3:15; Lam. 4:7).

rue occurring only in Lk. 11:42, this term

designates a scrubby plant approximately two feet high, but strong in medicinal values. The Talmud enumerates rue among ten herbs.

Rufus (rōō'fŭs) a son of Simon the Cyrenian (Mk. 15:21; Lk. 23:26), and a brother of Alexander. It is generally believed that the Rufus greeted by Paul in Rom. 16:13 is the same as the man mentioned in the gospel accounts.

Ruhamah (rōō-hà'mà) a symbolical name used by the Hebrews in greetings (Hos. 2:1).

ruler 1. An official of a synagogue (Lk. 8:41). 2. A member of the Sanhedrin (Jn. 3:1). 3. The official of a city (Acts 16:19). 4. The presiding officer of a feast (Jn. 2:8).

Rumah (rōō'mà) mentioned in 2 K. 23:36, this site is conjectured to be the same as Arumah near Shechem (Judg. 9:41) while others insist that it is to be identified with Dumah (Josh. 15:52). It is identified as the home of a kinsman of Jehoiakim.

runner a bodyguard or personal servant of a king (1 Sam. 22:17; 1 K. 14:28; 2 K. 10:25, 11:19). Perhaps these soldiers were identified as runners because they ran before the royal chariot.

rush see **papyrus**

rust a corrosive disfigurement of metal. See Mt. 6:19–20; James 5:3.

Ruth (rōōth) a Moabitish woman, the wife of Mahlon and later of Boaz. She and Boaz became the parents of Obed, the ancestor of David. Thus she is mentioned in Matthew's genealogy of Jesus. A severe famine in the land of Judah induced Elimelech, a native of Bethlehem, to journey to Moab with his wife Naomi and his two sons, Mahlon and Chilion. Some ten years later, Naomi, now a widow, heard that there was ample food in Judah and resolved to return to Bethlehem. Ruth, her daughter-in-law, returned with her. They arrived at Bethlehem at the beginning of the barley harvest, and Ruth gleaned in the field of Boaz, a wealthy man. Boaz treated her kindly and respectfully, eventually taking Ruth to be his wife. This beautiful love story is recorded in the book of Ruth.

rye see Ex. 9:32; Isa. 28:25. The Hebrew *cussemeth* is likely to be identified with spelt, which differs slightly from common wheat.

S

sabaoth (săb'à-ŏth) *sabaoth* is the Greek form of the Hebrew word *tsebaoth*, armies. The expression occurs in Rom. 9:29 and James 5:4 and is translated Lord of Hosts.

Sabbath the divinely ordained day of rest, so ordained of God following the six days of creative activity. "And God blessed the seventh day and hallowed it; because that in it he rested from all his work" (Gen. 2:1–3). In Ex. 16:23–29 one first finds incontrovertible institution of the day, as one given to be kept by the children of Israel. Shortly afterwards it was restated in the fourth commandment. Many of the rabbis date its first institution from the incident recorded in Ex. 15:25. But in a still later period, the prophet Isaiah utters solemn warning against profaning the day (Isa. 48:13–14). In the time of Jeremiah there seems to have been an habitual violation of the sabbath (Jer. 17:21–27). By the time of Ezekiel (Ezek. 20:12–24), the profanation of the sabbath was made foremost among the

Jews' sins. Nehemiah 10:31 indicates that the people entered into a covenant to renew the observance of the Law and in which they pledged themselves neither to buy nor to sell victuals on the sabbath. The Maccabean literature seems to indicate that only the Jews in open apostasy neglected the sabbath. In the NT, the sabbath observance is markedly emphasized.

1. *Traditional Prohibitions.* The Jews, especially the pharisaical and rabbinical schools, invented many prohibitions regarding the sabbath. A general law of sabbath observance must, according to their mode of thought, be interpreted in minute details and regulations. See Mt. 12:1–13; Jn. 5:10. That this general perversion of the sabbath had become quite ordinary is apparent from Jesus' reactions toward pharisaical observances, as well as the Pharisees' criticisms of his activities on the sabbath. The sabbath was interpreted to be the day particularly suited for entertainment, espe-

cially that of a festive nature. It must be remembered that Jesus declared himself to be "Lord of the sabbath."

2. *Historical Survey of Sabbath Observance.* Not only was the seventh day observed as a day of rest, but likewise the number seven itself became a keynote to a scale of sabbatical observance—the seventh month, the seventh year, and the jubilee year. As each seventh day was sacred, so was each seventh month and each seventh year. The seventh month opened with the Feast of Tabernacles. The most important observance of this period was the Feast of Tabernacles, the thanksgiving festival. The rules for the sabbatical year were very precise. As no labor was permitted on the seventh day, so the land was rested every seventh year. And as each forty-ninth year concluded seven of such weeks of years, so it was, or inaugurated the "Year of Jubilee." In Ex. 23:10–11 the sabbatical year is placed in close connection with the sabbath. It must also be observed that certain rights at these times were given to social classes which at other times had no rights. See also Lev. 25:2–7. Both the sabbath and the sabbatical year were to assist the Hebrew in remembering that he was not absolute owner of any property.

3. *Prescribed Scriptural Injunctions.* The general principle concerning sabbath observances revolves around the expression, "Remember the sabbath day to keep it holy . . . In it thou shalt not do *any work* . . ." (Ex. 20:8–11). It is significant to remember that the Israelites were forbidden to gather manna on a sabbath (Ex. 16:23). But the general statement "any work," left the particular application to the people involved. Obviously time is presented as a perfect entity, shaped into a week, modeled after the six days of creation and the following sabbath rest. Six days of work and rest on the seventh day conformed the life of man to the method of his Creator. Three applications of the general principle are contained in the Pentateuch (Ex. 16:29, 35:3; Num. 15:32–36). Jeremiah and Nehemiah speak against carrying goods for sale and also describe carrying such goods as a violation of the sabbath. In the intertestamental period (1 Macc. 2:34–38) engaging the enemy on the sabbath was considered unlawful. Although this belief proved costly to the Jews, during the time of Roman rule the Jews secured exemption from military service by appealing to this interpretation.

The Pentateuch indicates that the morning and evening sacrifices were both doubled on the sabbath and that fresh showbread was baked and substituted on the table for that of the previous week. This instantaneously leads to the observance that such negative rules as lighting of fires, etc., did not apply to religious ritual. Evidently there was no sabbath in holy things. Moreover, individual offerings were not breaches of the sabbath law, and likely from this principle the feasts of the rich were sanctioned on that day. Religious activities, including those of the prophet, were accepted as a part of sabbath observance (2 K. 4:23). Although the mind was to be lifted to high and holy things—God, his character, his revelations, his mighty works—the day was invested not with restrictions, but rather with thoughts of freedom and joy. Pleasure as such was never considered by the Jews to be a breach of the sabbath. Scholars debate the consistency with which the sabbatical year and Jubilee were observed; the same men are equally confident that the weekly sabbath was always partially, if not wholly, observed.

Much of the controversy surrounding the ministry of Jesus was occasioned by the legalistic and unyielding interpretation of the sabbath which the scribes and Pharisees purposed to impose upon him. Surrounding the fourth commandment were many rabbinical laws which dealt with the minutiae of life. The rabbis had declared that no burden could be borne on the sabbath, the burden being defined as anything equivalent to enough oil to anoint the smallest toe of a newly born baby. Although they found no contradiction in their observance of the rite of circumcision when the eighth day of life for the child came on the sabbath, Jesus indicated on occasion that they were attacking him for healing when they themselves were actually performing this rite of circumcision on the sabbath (Jn. 7:23). Jesus declared, "The sabbath was made for man, not man for the sabbath." These words declared the sabbath to be a privilege and a blessing, not a day of dread, misery, and fear. The apostles gave no rules for the observance of the sabbath, nor did Jesus apart from his own example. See Col. 2:16–17; Heb. 4:9. It is very obvious that the observance of the Lord's Day as a sabbath would have been almost impossible to the majority of Christians in the first stages of Christianity. In their secular world the Lord's Day was not a day of rest, but a day of ordinary and usual activity. Surely this was true until the time of Constantine. In the day of Jesus, the day for synagogue worship was Saturday (Mt. 12:9–10; Acts 13:14). Following his resurrection, the apostolic group worshiped on the first day of the week, which was the day of his resurrection from the dead (Acts 2:1, 20:7). However, it was left to later developments to postulate the Lord's Day as a day of sabbath observance.   v.e.g.

Sabbath day's journey a prescribed distance which one could travel on a sabbath. This expression is found in Acts 1:12, where the distance of the sabbath day's journey is designated as the distance between Jerusalem and Mount Olivet. This journey was described as being 2000 cubits, partially because of the reference in Num. 35:5, where the district adjoining a Levitical city extended 2000 cubits from the wall on every side, and partially from the interpretation of Josh. 3:4, that the camp of the Israelites was to be some 2000 cubits from the tabernacle, which distance they might travel on the sabbath. The sabbath day's journey approximates three-fifths of a mile. However, in rabbinical interpretation, one could conveniently travel farther than this simply by establishing a temporary residence prior to the sabbath. This was done by taking food for two meals to the given site, one meal to be eaten and the other buried, thus an individual had established a "home" on the sabbath. This made legally possible the traveling of 4000 instead of 2000 cubits on the sabbath.

Sabbatical Year as each seventh day and each seventh month were holy, so was each seventh year (Ex. 23:10–11). The Israelites were to sow and reap for six years but were to permit the land to rest on the seventh. Thus were they also to manage their vineyards. The enactment is also set forth in Lev. 25:2–7 and Deut. 15. Neither tillage nor cultivation of any sort was to be practiced. This singular institution has the aspect of total impracticability, which wears off when one considers that in no year was the owner allowed to reap the whole harvest (Lev. 19:9, 23:22). It is also clear that the owners of land were to store corn in previous years for their families' needs (Lev. 25:20–22). The sabbatical year was inaugurated during the sabbatical month, and the entire law was to be read during the Feast of Tabernacles. At the completion of the week of sabbatical years, the sabbatical scale received its completion in the year of jubilee.

Sabeans (sȧ-bē'ănz) the people of Sheba. See **Sheba**

Sabtah, Sabta (săb'tȧ) the third in order of the sons of Cush (1 Chr. 1:9). A tribe which descended from Sabeah.

Sabteca (săb'tē̇-kȧ) the fifth in order of the sons of Cush (Gen. 10:7; 1 Chr. 1:9), whose

settlements would likely be near the Persian Gulf.

Sacar (sā'kär)   1. A Hararite, father of Ahiam (1 Chr. 11:35).

2. The fourth son of Obed-edom (1 Chr. 26:4).

sackbut a wind instrument, described as an instrument similar to the modern trombone. See Dan. 3:5, 7, 10, 15.

sackcloth a coarse texture, of a dark color, made of goat's hair (Isa. 50:3; Rev. 6:12). It was used for: (1) making sacks (Gen. 42:25; Lev. 11:32); and (2) making the rough garments worn by mourners (1 K. 21:27; Job 16:15; Isa. 32:11).

sacrifice, an offering unto God

I. A HISTORICAL PERSPECTIVE.

A. *Origin.* The basic question concerning any discussion of sacrifice is the origin of the sacrificial system. Did it arise from man's natural instinct? Was it the subject of some primeval revelation? Sacrifice was universally prevalent, independent of and often opposed to man's natural reasonings concerning his relationship to God, and yet it was deeply rooted in the instincts of humanity. In a sense, the scriptures are silent concerning whether it is a distinct command of God. It suffices to indicate that from the earliest human history sacrifice was in vogue in man's approach to God.

B. *Ante-Mosaic Sacrifice.* Examination of the various sacrifices mentioned in scripture before the establishment of the Law reveals that such offerings were widespread but does question the exact intent of the sacrifices. Were they expiatory? The sacrifice of Cain and Abel is called *minchah*, although in the case of the latter it was a bloody sacrifice. Scholars have suggested that the sacrifices of both were thank offerings. Noah's sacrifice following the flood (Gen. 8:20) was called a burnt offering. The sacrifice is expressly connected with the institution of the covenant (Gen. 9:8–17). Jacob's sacrifice at Mizpah also marks a covenant with Laban, to which God is called to be a witness and a part. The sacrifice of Isaac (Gen. 22:1–13) stands alone. Yet in its principle it appears to have been of the same nature as the previous sacrifices.

C. *Mosaic Sacrifices.* These sacrifices were inaugurated by the offering of the Passover and the sacrifice of Ex. 24. The Passover is unique in its character, but it is clear that the idea of salvation from death by means of sacrifice is brought out in it with a distinctness before unknown. Leviticus seems to disclose varying forms of sacrifice: burnt offering—self-dedicatory; the meat and peace offering—eucharistic; the sin and trespass offerings—expiatory. To these may be added the incense offered after sacrifice in the holy place, the symbol of the intercession of the priest. In the consecration of Aaron and his sons (Lev. 8) the following order was observed: first came the sin offering, to prepare access to God; next, the burnt offering, to mark their dedication to his service; and finally, the meat offering of thanksgiving. Henceforth the sacrificial system was established in all its parts.

D. *Post-Mosaic Sacrifices.* The regular sacrifices in the temple were: burnt offerings (Ex. 29:38–42; Num. 28:9–29:39); the meat offering (Ex. 29:40–41; Lev. 23:10–14, 24:5, 9; Num. 28=29); the sin offering (Num. 23:15, 28:22, 30, 29:5, 16, 19, 22, 25, 28, 31, 34, 38); and incense (Ex. 30:7–8; Lev. 16:12).

II. INTERPRETATION OF SACRIFICE. The order of sacrifice in its perfect form (Lev. 8) indicates that the sin offering occupies the most important place, the burnt offering comes next, and the meat or peace offering last of all. The second could be offered only after the first had been accepted, and the third was only a subsidiary part of the second. Then in actual order of time, it has been seen that the patriarchal sacrifices partook much more of the nature of the peace offering and burnt offering, and that under the Law, the sin offering was for the first time explicitly set forth. Although religion was replete with sacrifices, the essential points between the paganistic sacrifice and the OT sacrificial system were to be found in the OT representation of God himself approaching man and in the fact that sacrifice is a scheme proceeding from God, ultimately connected with the one central fact of all human history. The sin offering represented the covenant between God and man as broken by man, but knit together again by God's appointment through the "shedding of blood." The shedding of blood, the symbol of life, signified that the death of the offender was deserved for sin, but that the death of the victim was accepted for his death by the ordinance of God's mercy. The main idea in the burnt offering was the giving of the entire victim to God, representing the devotion of the sacrificer unto him. The meat offerings were simply offerings to God of his own best gifts as a sign of thankful homage and as a means of maintaining his service and servants. Perhaps the best commentary on the Levitical system is the Epistle to the Hebrews. This epistle contains the key to the whole sacrificial doctrine. This work declares intrinsic nullity of mere material sacrifices, at the same time showing their typical and probationary character. V.E.G.

Sadducee (săd′û-sē) a Jewish religious party at the time of Christ, in general the antithesis of the Pharisees. The Sadducees were comparatively few in number but were extremely influential. Their stronghold was the temple, and as a result exerted unusual influence upon all Jews. The term Sadducee is derived from *tsadok*, "just," or "righteous." This has led many to believe that the Sadducees were followers of a certain Zadok, who lived in approximately 300 B.C. Inasmuch as the constituents of this party were of the high-priestly aristocracy, other scholars have been led to believe that the name refers to the high priest Zadok, who officiated in the time of David and in whose family the office of high priesthood remained until Maccabean times. It is true that the lineage of Zadok had decided pre-eminence (Acts 5:17).

The Pharisees conceived of the oral law as being on the same level with the Pentateuch, but the Sadducees constantly reminded them that they must return to the Mosaic law. They protested against the assertion that the fine points of the Law had been divinely settled by Moses, but at the same time they followed many of the traditions of the Pharisees. Furthermore, the Sadducees questioned the spiritual realm, denying the doctrine of the resurrection. In the Pentateuch they found a total absence of any claim by Moses concerning the resurrection of the dead. See Mk. 12:26–27 for Jesus' discussion with the Sadducees and Acts 23:8 for a further discussion of their denial of "angel or spirit." A further difference was in the interpretation of personality. The Sadducees laid great stress upon the freedom of will, which freedom the Pharisees denied. At this point it is quite easy to understand why the Sadducees were interested in politics, but at the same time the Pharisees had little or no interest in the political situation. So long as the Pharisee could worship as he desired, he cared little for political events. The Sadducee, on the other hand, was uniquely interested in contemporary politics.

John the Baptist addressed the Sadducees, as well as the Pharisees, as a generation of vipers (Mt. 3:7). The Sadducees joined the Pharisees in requiring from Jesus a heavenly sign (Mt. 16:1–4), and the Master warned his followers against both groups (Mt. 16:6–12). In addition to the Sadducees' interrogation of Jesus (Mt. 22:23–33), they also joined in the persecution of Peter and John (Acts 4:1–22).

Both groups were represented in the Sanhedrin before which Paul appeared, and the apostle created untold confusion in his statement concerning the resurrection (Acts 23:6-10).

Sadoc (sā'dŏk) a descendant of Zerubbabel, and an ancestor of Jesus (Mt. 1:14).

saffron a fragrant plant, the product used as a perfume. Technically it is the *Crocus sativus*. A light violet in color, the flowers have red veins.

Sala, Salah (sā'lȧ) the father of Eber (Lk. 3:35).

Salamis (săl'ȧ-mĭs) a city at the eastern end of the island of Cyprus, the first place visited by Paul and Barnabas on the first missionary journey after they left the mainland at Seleucia. Acts 13:5 indicates that there were synagogues there, thus many Jews must have lived on Cyprus.

Salathiel (sȧ-lā'thĭ-ĕl), **Shealtiel** (shē-ăl'tĭ-ĕl) son of Jechoniah, king of Judah, and father of Zerubbabel, according to Mt. 1:12, but son of Neri, and father of Zorobabel, according to Lk. 3:27. Luke's genealogy is likely to be followed.

Salecah (săl'ē-kȧ) also Salcah and Salchah. A city of Bashan (Deut. 3:10; Josh. 13:11; 1 Chr. 5:11).

Salem (sā'lĕm) the place of which Melchizedek was king (Gen. 14:18; Heb. 7:1-2). Jewish commentators insist that Salem (Shalem) is Jerusalem. This argument is based upon the reading of Ps. 76:2.

Salim (sā'lĭm) John 3:23 indicates that this is the site of John's baptisms, Salim being the well-known town and Aenon a place of fountains, or water, near it. Its exact location has not been identified, some scholars favoring a site four miles east of Shechem, others contending for a site some six miles northeast of Jerusalem.

Sallai (săl'â-ī) 1. A Benjaminite, who settled in Jerusalem following the Captivity (Neh. 11:8).

2. The head of one of the courses of priests who went up from Babylon with Zerubbabel (Neh. 12:20).

Sallu (săl'ū) the son of Meshallah, a Benjaminite (1 Chr. 9:7; Neh. 7:7). A Levitical house following the Captivity (see Neh. 12:7).

Salmon (săl'mŏn), **Salma** (săl'mȧ) 1. The father of Boaz (Ruth 4:20-21; Mt. 1:4-5; Lk. 3:32).

2. The name of a hill near Shechem on which Abimelech and his followers cut down the boughs with which they set fire to the Tower of Shechem. Its exact position is not known. See Judg. 9:48.

Salmone (săl-mō'nē) the east point of the island of Crete (Acts 27:7).

Salome (sȧ-lō'mē) 1. The wife of Zebedee. It is further conjectured that she was the sister of Mary, the mother of Jesus, to whom reference is made in Jn. 19:25. Others have suggested that this is a reference to Mary, the wife of Cleophas, who is mentioned immediately afterward. Matthew 20:20 indicates that Salome requested positions of honor in the kingdom for her sons, Mk. 15:40 that she was present at the time of the crucifixion, and Mk. 16:1 that she visited the sepulcher of Jesus.

2. The daughter of Herodias by her first husband, Herod Philip (Mt. 14:6). She was first married to Philip the tetrarch of Trachonitis, her paternal uncle, and then was married to Aristobulus the king of Chalcis.

salt a chemical serving as an appetizing condiment in the food of man and beast (Job 6:6; Isa. 30:24) and a valuable antidote to the effects of the heat of the climate on animal food, but also entering largely into the Hebrew religious services as an accompaniment to the various offerings (Lev. 2:13). An inexhaustible and available supply of salt was found on the southern shores of the Dead Sea. Salt could also be procured from the Mediterranean Sea. The Jews apparently distinguished between the rock salt, the salt obtained from pits, and the salt which was gained by evaporation.

In addition to the previously mentioned usages of salt, inferior qualities were used to quicken the decomposition of waste (Mt. 5:13; Lk. 14:35). Excessive amounts produced sterility, thus the custom of sowing with salt the foundations of a destroyed city (Judg. 9:45). As a most essential article of diet, salt symbolized hospitality; as an antiseptic, it symbolized durability, fidelity, and purity. Hence was derived the expression "covenant of salt" (Lev. 2:13; Num. 18:19; 2 Chr. 13:5; Ezra 4:14).

Salt, City of Joshua 15:62 indicates that the City of Salt was one of the cities of Judah which lay in the wilderness. It is obviously on the plain near the southern end of the Dead Sea.

Salt Sea the OT name of the Dead Sea (Gen. 14:3; Deut. 3:17; Josh. 15:2, 5).

Salt, Valley of a certain valley in which occurred two memorable victories of the Israelite armies. In this valley David defeated the Edomites (2 Sam. 8:13; 1 Chr. 18:12). It was also in this valley that Amaziah was victorious over some ten thousand Edomites (2 K. 14:7; 2 Chr. 25:11). These references do not locate the valley, but traditionally it has been identified as the broad open plain lying at the lower end of the Dead Sea. As of later date, the valley has been located east of Beer-sheba.

Salu (sā′lū) the father of Zimri, the prince of the Simeonites, who was slain by Phinehas (Num. 25:14). Also called Salom.

salutation a greeting, which expressed good wishes or blessings. The salutation may be classified under two headings: conversational and epistolary. The early Biblical records list such expressions as "God be gracious unto thee" (Gen. 43:29); "Blessed be thou of the Lord" (Ruth 3:10; 1 Sam. 15:13); "The Lord be with you," and "The Lord bless thee" (Ruth 2:4). The Hebrew term translated "bless" is generally *shalom*, "peace." The salutation at parting consisted originally of a simple blessing (Gen. 24:60; Josh. 22:6), but in later times the term *shalom* was introduced here also in the sense of "Go in peace." The epistolary salutation in the period subsequent to the OT finds the writer first identifying himself and then the person whom he salutes. "I salute" or "I greet" followed by a prayer for peace or grace was typical. "Grace and peace" constituted a typical Pauline salutation.

Samaria (sà-mâ′rĭ-à) a city of Palestine which served as the capital of the ten tribes (1 K. 16:23-24, 20:1; 2 K. 6:24–7:20). Located in the territory originally belonging to the tribe of Joseph and approximately six miles to the northwest of Shechem, there lies a wide-shaped valley, encircled with high hills, almost on the edge of the great plain which borders on the Mediterranean. In the center of this basin rises a less elevated oblong hill, with steep yet accessible sides, and a long flat top. Omri chose this hill as the site of the capital of the kingdom of Israel. From the time of his choice, Samaria retained its dignity as the capital of the ten tribes. Ahab built a temple to Baal there (1 K. 16:32-33), and that part of the city was called "the city of the house of Baal" (2 K. 10:25). The possessor of Samaria was considered king of Israel (2 K. 15:13-14), and woes denounced against the nation were directed against Samaria by name (Isa. 7:9). In 721 B.C., Samaria was taken by Shalmaneser, king of Assyria (2 K. 18:9=10), and the kingdom of the ten tribes was overthrown. In the time of Alexander the Great the city again enters history when the conqueror killed a large portion of the inhabitants, permitting the remainder to settle at Shechem. He replaced the Samaritans with a colony of Syro-Macedonians, who occupied the city until the time of John Hyrcanus. It was left to the Roman Pompey to return the city to its original inhabitants,

although Herod the Great actually rebuilt the city, calling it Sebaste-Augusta. In the NT the city of Samaria does not seem to be significant, but a portion of its district was involved in the NT account (Mt. 10:5; Jn. 4:4-5).

Samaritan Pentateuch (sà-măr′ĭ-tăn pĕn′tà-tūk) a recension of the commonly received Hebrew text of the Mosaic law used by the Samaritans. The recension—the Samaritan Pentateuch—is quoted by Eusebius, Cyril of Alexandria, Jerome, et al. Pietro della Valle, one of the first discoverers of the cuneiform inscriptions, acquired a completed codex from the Samaritans in Damascus in 1616. In 1623 it was placed in the Library of the Oratory in Paris, and in 1628 there appeared a brief description of it by J. Morinus in his preface to the Roman text of the LXX. The number of manuscripts in Europe gradually increased. The interest in the Samaritan Pentateuch likewise occasioned extensive controversy until W. Gesenius in 1815 pronounced the Samaritan text inferior to that of the Masoretes. In 1915 P. Kahle re-evaluated Gesenius' observation by reassessing the value of the Samaritan text. Yet, it is generally concluded that the MT is superior to that of the Samaritan Pentateuch.

The Samaritan Pentateuch has approximately 6000 variants from the MT, many of which are orthographic. The many textual changes largely reflect the religious proclivities of the Samaritans. In almost 2000 places the text harmonizes with the LXX against the Hebrew readings, which seems to prove that the translators of the LXX employed a text similar to that possessed by the Samaritans. Most scholars indicate that the Samaritan Pentateuch is traceable to the time when Manasseh, the grandson of Eliashib the high priest and son-in-law of Sanballat, was driven from Jerusalem (Neh. 13:23-30). He found refuge with the Samaritans and established worship in the rival temple which was built on Mount Gerizim.

Samaritans in a limited sense, a Samaritan was an inhabitant of the city of Samaria. But 2 K. 17:29 uses the term to designate those whom the king of Assyria had "placed in the cities of Samaria instead of the children of Israel." Samaria at first included all the tribes over which Jeroboam made himself king, whether east or west of the Jordan (1 K. 13:32). In other references in the historical books Samaria seems to designate exclusively the city. However, the prophets used the term in the expanded sense. Hence the word "Samaritan" must have designated everyone subject to the king of the northern capital. This is a general definition, although certain limitations may have been imposed at various times in the history of Samaria. For example, the territory of Simeon and Dan were early absorbed into the kingdom of Judah. With the capture of Samaria in 722 B.C., Sargon carried many of the Israelites away as captives, leaving many others in the land. Because of the rebellion of the remaining residents, he began to introduce colonists from Babylonia and Hamath (2 K. 17:24), who continued their practice of idolatry in their new home. The Samaritan schism developed when the Samaritans wished to assist the Jews in the rebuilding of the temple following Judah's return from Babylon. Upon being refused, the Samaritans threw off their masks and became open enemies, attempting in every conceivable way to frustrate the Jews in their building operations. The Samaritans, in turn, constructed a temple on Mount Gerizim. Thus their animosity became more intense than ever. In their own temple they sacrificed a Passover, and toward this site they directed their worship. They rejected Jewish books other than the Law. It was inevitable but that certain Jewish renegades would take refuge with the Samaritans from time to time. Hence, the Samaritans gradually claimed more Jewish blood, especially if such a claim furthered their interests. An excellent example is seen in their request to Alexander the Great to be excused from paying tribute money in the sabbatical year on the basis that as true Israelites they refrained from cultivating their land in the sabbatical year. Still another illustration of their claim to Jewish descent appears in the words of the woman of Samaria to Jesus (Jn. 4:12), "Art thou greater than our father Jacob, who gave us the well?" John Hyrcanus (approximately 130 B.C.) destroyed the temple on Mount Gerizim; yet, the Samaritans retained their identity and fanaticism.

The NT presents an intense hostility of the Jews toward the Samaritans, both in religious and social affairs. As previously indicated, the Samaritans were not of pure Hebrew blood, neither was their worship undefiled. Their theological concepts were essentially those of the Sadducees.

Samgarnebo (săm'gär-nē'bō) a prince of Babylon who commanded the victorious army at the capture of Jerusalem (Jer. 39:3).

Samlah (săm'là) a king of Edom (Gen. 36:36–37; 1 Chr. 1:47–48).

Samos (sā'mŏs) a famous Greek island off the coast of Asia Minor. Located southwest of Ephesus, it was visited by Paul on his return from his third missionary journey (Acts 20:15).

Samothrace (săm'ō-thrās) a famous island off the coast of Thrace and serving as an excellent landmark for sailors. Its thirty-square-mile area contains a mountain of some 5000 feet in height. See Acts 16:11, 20:6.

Samson (săm's'n) son of Manoah, a citizen of the town of Zorah, in the tribe of Dan, on the border of Judah (Josh. 15:33, 19:41). Circumstances surrounding his birth are recorded in Judg. 13, and the three following chapters relate his life and exploits. Samson is described as judge, an office which he occupied for twenty years (Judg. 15:20, 16:31), as a Nazarite (Judg. 13:5, 16:17), and as one endowed with supernatural power (Judg. 13:25, 14:6, 19).

His authority as a judge seems to have been limited to the district bordering the country of the Philistines. His actions as a deliverer do not seem to have extended beyond attacks upon the dominant Philistines. Judges 13:5 seems to indicate that the Israelites were already subjected to the Philistines at the time of Samson's birth, and inasmuch as Samson could not have begun to serve as judge before the time of his twentieth birthday, it follows that his judgeship must have coincided with the last twenty years of Philistine domination. The Scripture clearly indicates that Samson, as a Nazarite, practiced the law delineated in Num. 6. Moreover, Samson was endowed with supernatural power by the Spirit of the Lord. "The Spirit of the Lord came mightily upon him, and the cords that were upon his arms became as flax burnt with fire" (Judg. 15:14). The expression, "The Spirit of the Lord came upon him," is common to him with Othniel and Gideon (Judg. 3:10, 6:34). Yet the connection of supernatural power with the integrity of the Nazaritic vow are quite peculiar to Samson. His entire character and history have no precise parallel in Scripture. The only mention of Samson in the NT is in Heb. 11:32.

Samuel (săm'ŭ-ĕl) the last judge, first of the regular succession of prophets, and the founder of the monarchy. Samuel was the son of Elkanah and Hannah. The descent of Elkanah is involved in great obscurity; in 1 Sam. 1:1 he is described as an Ephraimite and in 1 Chr. 6:22–23 he is made a descendant of Korah, the Levite. Elkanah's family was rather large, Peninnah being the mother of several children and Hannah, besides Samuel, the mother of three sons and two daughters. The chief interest in the account of Samuel's birth is fixed upon his mother, who is described as a woman of high religious character (see 1 Sam. 1–2). She prayed earnestly to God for the gift of a child, for which she longed with a passionate devotion of silent prayer of which there is no other example in the OT. When the son was granted, he was named Samuel, "Asked or heard of God." Even before his birth, she vowed to dedicate him to the office of a Nazarite. When he was still relatively young, she and her husband took him to Shiloh, where he was consecrated to God. The child's special responsibility was to put in order the sacred candlestick and to open the doors at the rising of the sun. It was while sleeping there that he received his prophetic call (1 Sam. 3:1–18). From this moment the prophetic character of Samuel was established. The prophet warns the people against their idolatrous practices (1 Sam. 7:3–4). He convened an assembly at Mizpah, and at the very moment that he was offering the sacrifice, the Philistine host burst upon them. A violent thunderstorm came to the timely assistance of Israel, the Philistines fleeing. Thus a stone was set which remained as a memorial of Israel's triumph and gave to the place its name of Ebenezer, "the Stone of Help" (1 Sam. 7:12). This military achievement elevated Samuel to the office of judge, and in the capacity of ruler he visited Bethel, Gilgal, and Mizpah. His own residence was still his native city, Ramah. In Ramah he married, his two sons grew to maturity, and subsequently perverted the high office in the same fashion in which Samuel had witnessed that of the sons of Eli.

Samuel was the inaugurator of the transition from what is commonly called "the theocracy to the monarchy." Misdemeanor of his own sons precipitated the catastrophe which had been long in preparation. The people demanded a king. For the entire night, Samuel lay fasting and sleepless in the perplexity of doubt and difficulty. In the vision of that night was given the dark side of the new institution, which Samuel described on the following day (1 Sam. 8:9–18). He presents his reluctance to receive the new order of things. A final conflict of feeling and surrender of his office is given in the last assembly over which he presided and in his subsequent relations with Saul. The assembly was held at Gilgal, immediately following the victory over the Ammonites. The subsequent relationship to Saul was indeed mixed. Two institutions which they represented stood side by side. Samuel was still judge, judging Israel all the days of his life (1 Sam. 7:15). Samuel is described as "The prophet" (Acts 3:24, 13:20). In his old age he was known as "Samuel the Seer" (1 Sam. 9:11, 18–19; 1 Chr. 9:22). He was often consulted concerning the minutiae of life (1 Sam. 9:7–8).

From the time of the overthrow of Shiloh,

Samuel never appeared in the remotest connection with the priestly order. When he counseled Saul, it was not as the priest, but as the prophet. Saul's sin was that of disobedience to the prophetic voice (see 1 Sam. 10:8, 13:8). Moreover, Samuel was the first of the regular succession of prophets (Acts 3:24). Others, Moses, Deborah, et al, had been prophets before him, but only from Samuel on was the succession unbroken. His mother had been a prophetess. During his lifetime, long after he had been established as a prophet (1 Sam. 3:20), companies of disciples called "the sons of the prophets" came into existence. On at least two occasions Saul is described as having been in the company of Samuel's disciples (1 Sam. 10:10–11, 19:24). It must be remembered also that David was in this company of disciples, the first acquaintance of Samuel with David being when he privately anointed the latter at the house of Jesse. However, the connection thus begun with the shepherd boy must have been continued thereafter. Thus the prophet became the spiritual father of David. Samuel's death is described as occurring at the close of David's wanderings. It is said that "all the Israelites were gathered together," that they "lamented him" and "buried him." See 1 Sam. 25. Samuel is included in the roll call of OT heroes who were motivated by faith (Heb. 11:32). V.E.G.

Samuel, Books of two historical books of the OT, which are not separated from each other in the Hebrew MSS, the present division being made in the LXX translation and adopted in the Vulg. from the LXX. The work likely derived its name from the account of the birth and life of Samuel contained in the initial stages of the record.

1. *Authorship and Date.* These books, like all the historical books of the OT except Nehemiah, contain no mention of the name of their author. The title "Samuel" does not necessarily imply that the prophet was the author of these books as a whole, for the death of Samuel is recorded in the beginning of 1 Sam. 25. No other writer supplies the author's name, nor is there any mention of the author's name in the books of the Kings or of the Chronicles. Neither the Apocrypha nor Josephus mentions the author. The Mishnah is equally silent. The Babylonian Gemara, which is supposed to have been completed in its present form in approximately A.D. 500, asserts that "Samuel wrote his book." This statement, however, cannot be proved to have been made earlier than some sixteen centuries following the death of the

prophet. In A.D. 1508 I. Abrabanel, a learned Jew, suggested that the works of Samuel were written by Jeremiah. Yet this suggestion is highly improbable. Still other scholars have suggested Samuel as an author of part of the material, the remainder being by Nathan and Gad. Ahimaaz has been conjectured by some critics as the author of at least a part of the material.

There are certain indications which assist in the dating of the book. The earliest undeniable external evidence of the existence of the book would seem to be the Greek translation, the LXX. The second book of Maccabees (2:13) refers to Nehemiah and suggests that "He, founding a library, gathered together the acts of the kings, and the prophets, and of David, and the epistle of the kings concerning the holy gifts." It cannot be doubted that the acts of the kings also included in the books of Samuel, which books are equivalent to the two first books of Kings in the LXX. Thus there is external evidence that the book of Samuel was written before the second book of Maccabees. According to 1 Chr. 29:29 we have external proof that the book of Samuel was written before the Chronicles. The internal evidence points even to an earlier dating. The book seems to have been written in a time when the Pentateuch was not acted on as the rule of religious observance. In keeping with this observation, one may better understand why allusions in the books of Samuel even to the existence or time of Moses are so few. Furthermore, following the return from the Captivity, Moses became that great central figure in the thoughts and language of devout Jews which he could not fail to be when all the Law of the Pentateuch was observed. These omissions have led scholars to believe that the books were written by a Hebrew historian who lived prior to the reformation of Josiah.

An additional evidence for an early dating is the type of literature appearing in the books of Samuel. These books represent an excellent specimen of Hebrew prose in the golden age of Hebrew literature. In prose, they hold the same place which Joel and the undisputed prophecies of Isaiah hold in the poetical or prophetical language. At the same time, this argument on a linguistic basis for an early dating must not be advanced so far as to imply that, standing all alone, it would be conclusive; for some writings, the date of which is about the time of the Captivity, are in pure Hebrew.

2. *Question of Sources.* Are numerous sources compiled into the records which scholars now possess? Any information at this point is scanty. The only work which is actually quoted is the Book of Jasher. Several poetical compositions seem likewise to be included. Among them are: David's Lamentation over Saul and Jonathan called "The Bow"; David's Lamentation on the Death of Abner; a Song of David; a song called Last Words of David; and the Song of Hannah (1 Sam. 2:1–10; 2 Sam. 3:33–34, 22, etc.). Other scholars holding varying perspectives suggest still additional segments.

3. *Content.* First Samuel includes an account of Samuel's life and activities (chs. 1–7), the fuller section relating an account of the activities of Saul the king (chs. 8–31). Second Samuel relates the story of David's kingship.

Sanballat (săn-băl'ăt) a Samaritan, designated as "the Horonite" (Neh. 2:10, 19, 13:28). This likely means that he was a man of Beth-horon. According to Neh. 4:2 Sanballat had substantial political power in the province of Samaria during the Persian reign. As a political adversary, he vigorously opposed the rebuilding of the wall of Jerusalem. His companions in this hostility were Tobiah the Ammonite and Geshem the Arabian (Neh. 2:19, 4:7). For the details of their opposition see Neh. 6. Sanballat was allied with the high priest's family by the marriage of his daughter with one of the grandsons of Eliashib, great-grandfather of Juddua. Nehemiah expelled the young offender (Neh. 13:4). This obviously intensified the Samaritan schism.   V.E.G.

sandal an article used by the Hebrews for protecting the feet. It consisted simply of a sole attached to the foot by thongs. The Hebrew term *naal* implies such an article, its proper sense being that of confining or shutting up the foot with thongs (see Gen. 14:23; Isa. 5:27; Mk. 1:7). The materials employed in the construction of the sole were leather, felt, cloth, or wood; only occasionally was it covered with iron. Sandals were worn by all classes of society in Palestine, even by the very poor (Amos 8:6); both a sandal and a thong were common and inexpensive. They were not worn at all times, being removed from the feet while indoors and were put on only by persons about to undertake some business away from their homes. During the time of meals, the feet were undoubtedly uncovered, as implied in Lk. 7:38 and Jn. 13:5–6. To cast off the shoes when approaching a place or person of imminent sanctity was a mark of reverence (Ex. 3:5; Josh. 5:15). It was also an indication of violent emotion, or mourning, if a person appeared barefoot in public (2 Sam. 15:30; Ezek. 24:17, 23). To carry or to unloose a person's sandals was the responsibility of the lowest household servant and indicated inferiority on his part (Mt. 3:11; Mk. 1:7; Acts 13:25).

Sanhedrin (săn'hē-drĭn) the supreme council of the Jewish people in the NT period and earlier.

1. *Origin.* The Mishnah traces the origin of this assembly to the seventy elders appointed by Moses (Num. 11:16-17). The body continued to exist, according to the rabbinical accounts, down to the close of the Jewish commonwealth. However, it is generally admitted that the tribunal established by Moses was probably temporary and did not continue to exist after the Israelites entered Palestine. Although no definite historical information is available, it can be generally stated that the Greek etymology of the term seems to point to a period subsequent to the Macedonian supremacy in Palestine. The Sanhedrin seems to have consisted of chief priests, of the heads of the twenty-four classes into which the priests were divided, of elders, of men of age and experience, and of scribes learned in the Jewish law (Mt. 26:57-59; Mk. 15:1; Lk. 22:66; Acts 5:21).

2. *Number of Members.* The number is usually stated to be seventy-one, but not perfect agreement is found at this point. The president of the Sanhedrin was called *masi* and was chosen because of his eminence in worth and wisdom. Generally this pre-eminence was accorded to the high priest. The vice-president, called by the Jews "father of the house of judgment" sat at the right hand of the president. During a session, the Sanhedrin sat in a semicircle.

3. *The Place of Meeting.* According to the Talmud, the sections were generally convened in a hall called *gazzith,* supposed by many to have been situated in the southeast corner of one of the courts near the temple building. In special exigencies, however, it seems to have been in the residence of the high priest (Mt. 26:3). Forty years before the destruction of Jerusalem, and consequently while the Savior was teaching in Palestine, the sessions of the Sanhedrin were removed from the hall *gazzith* to a somewhat greater distance from the temple building, although still on Mount Moriah. After several other changes, its seat was finally established at Tiberias. As a judicial body, the Sanhedrin constituted a supreme court, to which belonged in the first instance the trial of the tribe fallen into idolatry, false prophets, and the high priest. As an administrative council, it determined many other important matters. Jesus was arraigned before this body as a false prophet (Jn. 11:47); Peter, John, Stephen, and

Paul appeared before the group as teachers of error and deceivers of the people. From Acts 11:2, it appears that the Sanhedrin exercised a degree of authority beyond the limits of Palestine. According to the Jerusalem Gemara, the power of inflicting capital punishment was taken from this tribunal forty years prior to the destruction of Jerusalem. This agrees with the answer of the Jews to Pilate (Jn. 19:31). The Talmud also mentions a lesser Sanhedrin of twenty-three members in every city in Palestine in which were not less than 120 householders.

Sansannah (săn-săn'à) a town in the south district of Judah, named in Josh. 15:31.

Saph (săf) the son of the giant slain by Sibbecai, the Hushathite (2 Sam. 21:18).

Saphir (sā'fēr) one of the villages of Judah to which the prophet Micah addressed himself (Mic. 1:11). Also Shaphir.

Sapphira (să-fī'rà) the wife of Ananias, and a participant both in his guilt and punishment (Acts 5:1-10).

sapphire a precious stone, apparently of a bright blue color (Ex. 24:10). The Hebrew *sappir* was the second stone in the second row of the high priest's breastplate (Ex. 28:18). It was a precious stone (Job 28:16), and was one of the stones that ornamented the king of Tyre (Ezek. 28:13). The sapphire is also described as adorning the foundation of the New Jerusalem (Rev. 21:19).

Sarah (sâr'à) 1. The wife of Abraham, and mother of Isaac. She is first mentioned in Gen. 11:29: "Abram and Nahor took them wives: the name of Abram's wife was Sarai . . ." In Gen. 20:12, Abraham speaks of her as "His sister, the daughter of the same father, but not the daughter of the same mother." Jewish tradition holds that Sarah is the same as Iscah, the daughter of Haran, and the sister of Lot. The change of her name from "Sarai" to "Sarah" was made at the same time that Abram's name was changed to Abraham, on the establishment of the covenant of circumcision between him and God. "Sarah" means princess. Sarah came with Abraham from Ur to Haran, from Haran to Canaan, and accompanied him in all the wanderings of his life. Her only independent action is to demand that Hagar and Ishmael should be removed from the household. She died at Hebron and was buried by Abraham in the cave of Machpelah. The NT refers to her as an example of conjugal obedience in 1 Pet. 3:6 and as an example of faith in Heb. 11:11.

2. The daughter of Asher (Num. 26:46).

Sarai (sā'rī) see **Sarah** 1

Saraph (sā'răf) a descendant of Shelah, the son of Judah (1 Chr. 4:22).

Sardis (sär'dĭs) a city located approximately two miles south of the river Hermus, at the foot of Mount Tmolus. Sardis was the ancient residence of the kings of Lydia. From ancient times the city was a commercial market of importance. The land surrounding was extremely fertile, chestnuts were produced in the neighborhood, the art of dyeing wool is said to have originated there, the Spartans procured gold there in the sixth century B.C., and the metal *electrum* was procured there. The city was captured by Alexander the Great in 334 B.C. and changed hands numerous times during the contest between the generals who fought bitterly to succeed Alexander. Its importance as a market diminished from the time of the invasion of Asia by Alexander. The ruins of a massive temple of Cybele bear witness to its wealth and to the architectural skill of the people who lived there. A large theater and stadium stood on the north of the Acropolis. Sardis is mentioned only in Rev. 3:1–6, but this reference is important because Sardis was built on a hill, and seemed to be inaccessible to the enemy. Jesus' admonition to watch would be especially meaningful to the citizens inasmuch as the military leaders of each generation had felt their fortress to be impregnable only to their surprise and dismay. In addition to the previously mentioned temple of Cybele, the city also boasted of temples to Artemis and Zeus.

Sardites (sär'dīts) descendants of Sered, the son of Zebulun (Num. 26:26).

sardius (sär'dĭ-ŭs) also **sardine** (sär'dĭn) the name of the stone which occupied the first place in the first row of the high priest's breastplate. Revelation 4:3 reveals John's declaration that the one whom he saw sitting on the heavenly throne "was to look upon like a jasper and a sardine stone." The sixth foundation of the wall of the Heavenly Jerusalem was a sardius (Rev. 21:20). A precious stone, the sardius has been a favored stone for the engraver. The stones differ in color, some being bright red and others being reddish or brownish-red in color.

sardonyx like the sard, this stone is a variety of agate and was frequently employed by engravers in the making of signet rings. It is also a variety of chalcedony. It is described as consisting of a white opaque layer, superimposed upon a red transparent stratum of the true red sard. The sardonyx is also mentioned as a part of the foundation of the walls surrounding the New Jerusalem (Rev. 21:20).

Sargon (sär'gŏn) one of the great Assyrian kings, mentioned in Scripture only in Isa. 20:1. Sargon succeeded Shalmaneser V. Samaria fell under Sargon's attack, or Sargon became king immediately after the fall of this city; at this point, the record is not clear (see 2 K. 17:1–6). Sargon's annals cover a space of fifteen years, 721–706 B.C. In these accounts he records his warlike expeditions against Babylonia and Susiana on the south, Media on the east, Armenia and Cappadocia toward the south, Syria, Palestine, Arabia, and Egypt toward the west and the southwest. Toward the west and southwest he apparently waged three wars—one for the possession of Gaza (720), another when Egypt herself was attacked (715), and the third occurred as an attack upon Ashdod (712). Sargon was famous not only for his military achievements, but also for his extensive building enterprises. He receives the credit for building one of the most magnificent of the Syrian palaces. He was murdered in 705 B.C. and was succeeded by his son, Sennacherib, destined to become a celebrated king.

Sarid (sā'rĭd) a chief landmark of the territory of Zebulun (Josh. 19:10, 12).

Saron (sā'rŏn) the district in which Lydda stood (Acts 9:35). Saron is the Sharon of the OT.

Sarsechim (sär'sê-kĭm) a general of Nebuchadnezzar's army at the capture of Jerusalem (Jer. 39:3). He apparently was the chief eunuch.

Saruch (sā'rŭk) also **Serug** the son of Reu (Lk. 3:35).

Satan (sā'tăn) the Hebrew term means "adversary" and is so used in Num. 22:22; 1 Sam. 29:4; 2 Sam. 19:22; 1 K. 5:4, etc. See also Mt. 12:24, 26; Lk. 11:18; Acts 5:3; 2 Cor. 4:4; 1 Tim. 5:14–15; Rev. 12:7, etc. The existence of Satan in the Biblical accounts is not proved, but rather the personal existence of a spirit of evil is repeatedly asserted in the Scripture. Every quality, every action, every activity which could indicate personality is attributed to him in undeniably clear language. The Biblical accounts prohibit any concept of evil as a native imperfection, arising from the nature of matter and any further tendency to trace the existence of evil to a rival creator, not subordinate to the creator of good. The Scripture asserts in the strongest terms the perfect supremacy of God, so that under his permission alone evil is allowed to exist (Prov. 16:4; Isa. 45:7; Amos 3:6). From the standpoint of history, the conquest of evil began virtually in God's economy immediately after the fall itself, but Scripture indicates that the atonement was in the mind of God prior to the foundation of the world. See 1 Pet. 1:20. To note the experiences of

Adam and Eve, Job, and Jesus is to recognize the existence of evil. Although the Apocryphal books deal extensively with the idea of demons, it is left to the NT records to declare finally a concept of Satan.

The NT speaks of Satan as a "spirit" in Eph. 2:2, as the ruler of the "demons" in Mt. 12:24-26, and as having "angels" subject to him in Mt. 25:41 and Rev. 12:7-9. The whole description of his power implies spiritual nature and spiritual influence. See also Jude 6 and 2 Pet. 2:4. The Scripture marks a sharp contrast between children of God and "children of Satan."

The powers of Satan are indeed multitudinous. He is depicted at times as capable of bringing monetary loss, illness, and bereavement (Job 1:10-20, 2:4-7; Lk. 13:16). Yet, it is only by God's permission that he is capable of pursuing his purposes (Job 1:12, 2:5-6; Lk. 22:31-32). He is pictured as one who rules a kingdom (Mt. 12:24-26; Lk. 11:18; Rev. 12:7), and as one who seduces men (2 Cor. 11:3; Rev. 12:9). The Genesis account of the fall supports the NT observation. Satan obviously controls demon possession (Mt. 12:22-29; Lk. 11:14, 23). He is called "the Tempter" in relationship to Jesus (Mt. 4:1-11). The NT refers to him as the Devil (slanderer). As the Prince of the power of evil, he tempts men (Mt. 4:1-11; Lk. 22:31; Acts 5:3; 1 Thess. 3:5). His relationship to slander is evidenced in Gen. 3:4-5 and Job 1:9-11, 2:4-5. He hinders men in their ministry (1 Thess. 2:18) and is even depicted as a primary agent involved in the activities of the man of sin (2 Thess. 2:1-12). Yet the NT clearly indicates that he will be overthrown (Rom. 16:20; Rev. 12:9, 20:1-2).   V.E.G.

satrap the puppet ruler of a small province or collection of small provinces, and appointed by the monarch. See Dan. 3:2, 6:1; Est. 3:12; Ezra 8:36.

satyr the term meaning "hairy" or "rough" and frequently applied to wild goats. However, in Isa. 13:21 and 34:14 the prophet predicts the desolation of Babylon and likely makes no allusion to any species of goats, whether wild or tame. The name was used to refer to a god of the Graeco-Roman world, the god represented as a companion of Bacchus. This god was represented as having the long ears of a goat, a similarly snubbed nose, and the tail of a goat. At still a later period, goat's legs were added to this mythical god. This god was lustful and a half brute.

Saul (sôl) 1. An early king of Edom, and successor of Samlah. Saul was from Rehoboth on the Euphrates (Gen. 36:37-38).

2. The first king of Israel. Kish, a Benjaminite, was his father. Kish was a powerful and wealthy chief, though the family to which he belonged was of little importance (1 Sam. 9:1, 21). A portion of his property consisted of a drove of asses. On occasion Kish sent Saul, accompanied by his servant who also acted as a guide and guardian of the young man, to search for the asses which had gone astray in the mountains, and on that occasion Saul met the prophet Samuel. At this time, Saul was probably a young man of thirty-five years of age. Samuel had been instructed of God to expect a Benjaminite and to anoint him king over Israel, an arrangement which the elders of Israel had begun to demand. In anticipation of some distinguished stranger, Samuel had instructed the cook to reserve a boiled shoulder, from which Saul, as the chief guest, tore the first morsel. The next morning at daybreak, Samuel roused Saul, and they went to the outskirts of the town where Samuel anointed Saul by pouring the consecrated oil on his head. A kiss of salutation announced to Saul that he was to be ruler and deliverer of the nation (1 Sam. 9:25-10:1). In that moment, Saul knew a new life. An assembly was convened by Samuel at Mizpah, and lots were cast to find the tribe of the family which was to produce the king. Saul was named, and by divine intimation, was found in the circle of baggage which surrounded the encampment (1 Sam. 10:17-24). His stature at once conciliated the public feeling, and for the first time the shout was raised, "Long live the king" (1 Sam. 10:23-24), and Saul returned to his native Gibeah. On returning to the city of Gibeah, he heard of the threat issued by Nahash, king of Ammon, against Jabesh-gilead. His shy nature vanished and he became a fierce warrior who began to guide Israel's future. An army of 300,000 from Israel and 30,000 from Judah followed him in the subsequently successful effort to rescue Jabesh. The people were instantaneously affected by this victory; Samuel had been named as ruler with Saul, the latter now becoming the acknowledged chief. In the second year of his reign, Saul began to organize an attempt to eliminate the Philistine yoke, which pressed on his country. An army of 3000 was formed, and Jonathan slew the Philistine officer who had so long been stationed in Saul's field (1 Sam. 13:2-4). The enmity of the Philistines was now revealed against Israel. In this crisis, Saul found himself in the position long before described by Samuel. At last,

on the seventh day, he could wait no longer; but just after the sacrifice was completed, Samuel arrived and pronounced the first curse on his impetuous zeal (1 Sam. 13:5–14). Jonathan's success ultimately effected the withdrawal of the Philistines to their own country and territory. Saul then began to attack the neighboring tribes of Moab, Ammon, Edom, Zobah, and finally Amalek (1 Sam. 14:47). Again Saul's disobedience to the prophetic command of Samuel is demonstrated. Saul first assumed the prerogative of the prophet in offering sacrifice (see 1 Sam. 13), and then refused to wage a war of extermination against the Amalekites, sparing the best of the cattle to sacrifice to the Lord and saving the king of the opponents. Because of this second act of disobedience by which he manifested a desire to assert his own will, he was rejected as king (1 Sam. 15:1–35). Samuel was then sent to Bethlehem to anoint a new king, David (1 Sam. 16:1–13).

Tragedy characterized the life of Saul from this moment. David joined Saul and served effectively, not only as a harper but likewise as a military leader (1 Sam. 16:14–23, 17:1–20:42). In Saul's better moments, he never lost the strong affection which he had contracted for David. But his acts of fierce, wild zeal increased. At last the monarchy itself broke under the weakness of his leadership. The Philistines re-entered the country, and with their chariots and horses they occupied the plain of Esdraelon. Their camp was located on the southern slope of the range now called Hermon. On the opposite side, on Mount Gilboa, stood the Israelite army. Saul now determined to engage one of the necromancers who had escaped his persecution. She was a woman living at Endor, on the other side of Little Hermon. Thousands of words have been written to explain this strange meeting but to no avail. The old man who is pictured in the interview between the woman and Saul (1 Sam. 28:3–19) is explained on one of several bases. One suggestion is that he was the accomplice of the woman, and when he appeared, she uttered a loud cry, pronouncing the man who had come seeking aid to be Saul. She knew that the king was in the neighborhood and she immediately recognized that her visitor was he. Others have suggested that the appearance was simply a spirit, unexpected by the woman, and this appearance prompted her to voice a loud cry because she was actually startled. Some have believed the spirit to be interpreted as the devil, while others suggest this to be Samuel. Regardless of the details of the visit, upon hearing the denunciation, Saul fell to the ground and remained motionless until the woman and his own servants forced him to eat. The battle occurred the next day, the Israelites being driven up the side of Mount Gilboa and the three sons of Saul being slain (1 Sam. 31:2). Saul himself, with his armor-bearer, was pursued by the archers and the charioteers of the enemy (1 Sam. 31:3; 2 Sam. 1:6). Saul was wounded, and his shield was cast away (2 Sam. 1:21). According to one account, he fell on his own sword (1 Sam. 31:4), according to another, an Amalekite came up at the moment of his death-wound and found him "fallen," but leaning upon his spear (2 Sam. 1:6, 10). Thus, at his own request, he was put out of his pain by the Amalekite, who took off his royal diadem and bracelet, and carried the news to David (2 Sam. 1:7–10). The body was stripped by the Philistines and decapitated. The armor was sent to the Philistine cities and finally deposited in the temple of Astarte, apparently located in the city of Beth-shan. The headless corpse, with those of Saul's sons, hung over the walls of the same city. Saul's head was deposited in the temple of Dagon (1 Chr. 10:10). Thus is concluded the unusual life of one so strangely endowed.

3. The Jewish name of the apostle Paul. The apostle's name was changed to Paul (Acts 13:9). There are two basic explanations concerning this change: (1) The name was derived from Sergius Paulus, the first of his Gentile converts; (2) Paulus was the apostle's Roman name in the city of Tarsus, naturally adopted in the common usage by his biographer when his labors among the heathen began.   V.E.G.

savior one who delivers or saves from any danger or evil. It is used of God (e.g., 2 Sam. 22:3; Ps. 106:21; Hos. 13:4). In the NT it is particularly used of Jesus, who saves his people from their sins (Mt. 1:21). He redeems them from their sinful condition, from the inevitable wrath of God, and brings them into a state of fellowship with God (Lk. 19:10; Rom. 5:8–11; Heb. 7:25).

saw a blade-like tool used to cut wood and stone. This blade-like instrument has sharp teeth which cut through the material. First Kings 7:9 refers to sawn stones which were used in the temple. Hebrews 11:37 speaks of victims being sawn asunder. The Egyptian saws were single-handed, although Jerome has been thought to allude to circular saws. Usually of bronze, the blade was either fitted into the handle or was attached to it by leather thongs.

scapegoat see **Atonement, Day of**

scepter the Hebrew word *shebet,* as its Greek equivalent *sképtron,* originally meant a rod or staff. It was thus specifically applied to the shepherd's crook (Lev. 27:32; Mic. 7:14) and to the wand or scepter of a ruler. The use of the staff as a symbol of authority was not confined to kings, but it could be used by any leader (see Judg. 5:14). The term is metaphorically used (Gen. 49:10; Num. 24:17; Amos 1:5). Esther 4:11 refers to the scepter of the Persian monarch as "golden," probably of massive gold.

Sceva (sē'vȧ) a Jew of Ephesus at the time of Paul's second visit to the city (Acts 19:14–16). He belonged to the high-priestly family, and his seven sons practiced exorcism (Acts 19:14).

school ancient Israel had no schools, but the children were instructed in the home (Gen. 18:19; Deut. 6:7; 2 Tim. 3:15). In addition to private instruction, the religious system of the Hebrews abounded in ample opportunity for instruction. For example, the Law was read publicly at the Feast of Tabernacles (Deut. 31:10–13). These religious festivals, and the songs concerning them, furnished teaching opportunities. In the Graeco-Roman period elementary schools existed in connection with the synagogues. There children were instructed in the Scriptures, as well as in reading and writing. Josephus indicates that slaves were often employed as tutors for the children of the wealthy. The scribes were important personalities in the educational systems.

schoolmaster the Gr. *paidagogos* may be translated "tutor" or "schoolmaster." The *paidagogos* was a trusted slave to whom the care of the children was committed. He accompanied them on journeys away from the home, serving both as their physical guide and "spiritual" instructor. Paul (Gal. 3:24) speaks of the Law as the schoolmaster to lead us to Christ.

science the term occurs only in Dan. 1:4 and 1 Tim. 6:20 as a translation of the Heb. *madda* and the Gr. *gnosis.* The term is not used in the sense of a modern systematic study; the Biblical usage simply refers to knowledge. Paul warns man against the false and counterfeit knowledge (1 Cor. 8:1, 7; Col. 2:8), but praises the true knowledge found in Christ and exhorts Christians to grow and develop in this knowledge (1 Cor. 12:8; Phil. 1:9).

scorpion an animal of varying size and with a stinger in its tail, by means of which it inflicts pain. The wilderness of Sinai is especially alluded to as being inhabited by scorpions at the time of the Exodus. The animals are also prevalent in certain parts of Palestine. It has been suggested that as many as five species are to be found near Mount Sinai. Scorpions are generally found in dark and dry places, under stones and in ruins, chiefly in warm climates. They are carnivorous in their habits and generally move with the tail elevated and poised. The stinger, situated at the extremity of the tail, has at its base a gland that secretes a poisonous fluid, which is discharged into the wound by two minute orifices at its extremity. In hot climates the sting often occasions much suffering and sometimes alarming symptoms. The term "scorpions" of 1 K. 12:11, 14; 2 Chr. 10:11, 14, obviously refers to some instrument of scourging, not to the animal.

scourge scourging is to punish by the lash. This punishment in ancient Egypt was usually with the stick, which was applied to the soles of the feet. Under the Roman method, however, the culprit was stripped, his wrists tied, his arms stretched with thongs, and he was beaten with the lash (see 1 K. 12:11, 14; 2 Cor. 11:25; Mt. 10:17; Acts 5:40). The Jews limited the scourging to thirty-nine stripes in order not to exceed the forty lashes permitted by the Law (Deut. 25:2–3). The Romans, however, limited scourging only by their strength and inclination. Using scourges of cords or thongs with pieces of metal or small, sharp bones contained therein, the Roman literally cut the victim's back to shreds. Roman citizens were protected from scourging, although it seems that lawless governors did not always observe this exemption. Criminals were generally scourged prior to crucifixion.

screech owl see **owl**

scribe 1. An individual serving as a secretary in a governmental or other secular capacity (2 K. 12:10; Ezra 4:8).

2. One who served as an amanuensis to record that which was dictated (Jer. 36:4, 18, 32). Ezekiel 9:2 describes this activity of the scribe.

3. The *sopherim,* or the *nomikoi,* copied the Law and other parts of the Scriptures (Jer. 8:8). Ezra was a noted scribe; as is evident in his experience; the scribe also was responsible for teaching the Law (Ezra 7:6–10). In this particular respect his work was very similar to that of the "lawyers" of the NT period. The scribes gave their time and attention to the study of the Law, to its interpretation, to historical interpretation and doctrinal issues, and to teaching. It is likely that each noted scribe gathered about him a group of disciples known as a school.

Scribes were an influential class in the NT period. Their position was greatly enhanced following the return from the Exile with the renewed emphasis upon the Law. Some of the scribes in the NT accepted the teachings of Jesus, while others of the group were included in the Sanhedrin. Matthew 21:15 indicates that they criticized his activities and later shared the responsibility for his death.

sea, molten (1 K. 7:23-44), **brazen** (2 K. 25:13) to replace the laver which stood in the doorway to the holy place in the tabernacle, Solomon caused a laver to be cast. Because of its size it was called a sea. It was made from brass, or copper, which was captured by David from Tibbath and Chun, cities of Hadarezer king of Zobah (1 K. 7:23-26; 1 Chr. 18:8). It was said to be fifteen feet in diameter and seven and one-half feet deep, and to hold 2000 to 3000 baths (16,000 to 24,000 gallons). The laver was mounted upon the backs of twelve oxen, three facing in each direction. It was mutilated by Ahaz who removed it from its oxen base and placed it upon a base of stone. It was finally broken up by the Assyrians (2 K. 16:14, 17, 25:13).

Sea, the Salt see **Dead Sea**

seal a portable instrument used to impress documents, and other instruments, and having the same value as the handwritten signature. Earliest methods of sealing in Egypt were engraved stones pierced through their length and hung by a string from the neck or arm. Later such engravings were set in rings. Inscriptions were engraved which identified the seal. A lump of clay was often impressed with the seal and then affixed to the parchment or papyrus, usually by means of a string. Wax was sometimes used. The signet ring was an ordinary part of a man's equipment (Gen. 38:18), and was in use among the Hebrews at a very early time (Ex. 28:11, 36).

Seba (sē'bà) the oldest son of Cush (Gen. 10:7; 1 Chr. 1:9). As such he was the head of the Cushite nation of Sebiam (Ps. 72:10; Isa. 43:3, 45:14). These passages indicate that Seba was a nation in Africa, bordering on or included in Cush, and in Solomon's time independent. Josephus says that Seba was the ancient name of the Ethiopian island and city of Meroe, which is reasonable since no ancient Ethiopian kingdom of importance could have excluded this island. It lay between the Astaboras, the Atabara, and the Astipus; the eastern or Blue Nile being formed at this point.

sebat (sē'băt) [a rod] the fifth month of the Jewish civil year.

Secacah (sē-kā'kà) [thicket] one of the six cities of Judah, situated in the wilderness near the Dead Sea (Josh. 15:61). Its exact location is unknown.

Sechu (sē'kū) [the watchtower] a place, noted for its great well, lying on the route between Gibeah and Mamah. Its present-day location is unknown, but thought to be either Bir Neballa or Suweikah.

sect a religious party such as the Pharisees or the Sadducees. A fragment of the whole religious community.

Secundus (sē-kŭn'dŭs) [fortunate] a Thessalonian who went with Paul from Corinth as far as Asia, on his return to Jerusalem from his third missionary journey (Acts 20:4).

seer see **prophet**

Segub (sē'gŭb) [elevated] 1. The youngest son of Hiel the Bethelite, who rebuilt Jericho (1 K. 16:34). About 910 B.C., Segub paid for the sin of his father with his life. A curse had been pronounced by Joshua on the man who would rebuild Jericho (Josh. 6:26).

2. Son of Hezron (1 Chr. 2:21-22), the grandson of Judah.

Seir (sē'ir) [hairy, shaggy] a chief of Horeb, for whom the country or land of Seir was called (Gen. 36:20). The land of Seir was a rough country called Gebala by Josephus, Eusebius, and Jerome.

Seir, Mount 1. The original name of the mountain ridge extending along the east side of the valley of Arabah, from the Dead Sea to the Elanticia Gulf. The northern section of the mount as far as Petra, is still called Jebal, the Arabic form of Gebal. In Biblical times the area extended much further south (Deut. 2:1-8), even to the Gulf of Aqabah, and its eastern border extended to the plateau of Arabia. God gave Esau this land and the Israelites were forbidden to enter it. There is a line of limestone hills or cliffs running across the great valley some eight miles south of the Dead Sea, forming the division between the Arabah proper and the deep Ghor north of it. They appear as shutting in the valley with their 2000 foot heights backed up by the great bulk of the mountain behind them.

2. An entirely different place from the foregoing, is the Mount Seir of Josh. 15:10. It was a boundary landmark on the north of Judah; it lay westward of Kirjath-jearim, and between it and Beth-shemesh. These are probably the Wadi Aly and the Wadi Ghurab of today. How the name was attached to an area so far removed from the Seirites no one knows.

Sela (sē'là) [the rock—Judg. 1:36; 2 Chr. 25:12; Obad. 3] possibly the city later known as Petra, the ruins of which are a short distance north of the top of the Gulf of Aqabah. It was in the midst of Mount Seir, in the region of Mount Hor, and therefore Edomite territory. It was in a valley surrounded by rocks and was even partially hewn from the rocks. It flourished into the Christian era, and was subjected by the Romans. Recent excavations reveal great temples and theaters, and exquisite workmanship in stone of various colors. Because it was situated in a deep ravine, surrounded by perpendicular cliffs and accessible only by a narrow ravine, the valley 800 to 1500 feet wide made an impregnable fortress. However, it was taken by Amaziah king of Judea (2 K. 14:7) and renamed Joktheel. The Arabs conquered it in about 300 B.C.; they inhabited it until the Roman conquest in A.D. 105.

selah (sē'lä) found only in the poetic books of the OT; occurs seventy-one times in the Psalms and three times in the Habakkuk. It is thought to be a musical notation designating a pause.

Seled (sē'lĕd) [exultation] one of the sons of Nadab, a descendant of Jerahmeel of the tribe of Judah (1 Chr. 2:30—after 450 B.C.).

Seleucia (sē-lū'shĭ-à) a town near the mouth of the Orontes, and seaport for Antioch, though it was sixteen miles away. Paul and Barnabas sailed from Seleucia on their first missionary journey (Acts 13:4). Founded by Seleucus as a seaport and fortress, it retained its importance into Roman times. It was a free city in Paul's day. Now called el-Kalusi.

Semachiah (sĕm-à-kī'à) [Jehovah sustains him] the last of the six sons of Shemaiah, son of Obed-edom (1 Chr. 26:7).

Semitic languages and writing I. GENERAL CONSIDERATIONS.

1. *Origin.* The name Semitic languages, or sometimes Shemitic languages, is based on Gen. 10:21-31 which gives the political and ethnogeographical groupings of the line of Shem. In the attempt at greater accuracy of designation other expressions have been suggested, such as Western Asiatic or Syro-Arabic but the older term has prevailed and is now generally accepted.

2. *Location.* The geographic area occupied by the peoples employing Semitic languages includes the territory covered by Mesopotamia, Syria, Palestine, Arabia, and south into Ethiopia.

3. *Classification.* The great variety of Semitic languages may be grouped under three broad geographic headings: (a) Northeast or Akkadian which includes Babylonian and Assyrian; (b) Northwest or Canaanite with Hebrew, Phoenician, Ugaritic, Moabite, Amorite, and Aramaic; (c) Southwest brings together the Arabic and Ethiopic dialects. A fourfold classification has also been suggested: (a) Eastern, or Akkadian; (b) Western with Hebrew, Phoenician, Moabite, Ugaritic, and Amorite; (c) Northern with Aramaic and the later Syriac; (d) Southern with Arabic and Ethiopic. Any attempt to separate and classify languages into geographic or ethnic groupings must be imprecise because of the very affinity of language to change and assimilate many and varied sources in the course of its history. However, on the whole, the above geographic divisions may correspond fairly closely to distinguishing linguistic characteristics.

4. *Subgroups.* (a) Northeast: *Akkadian* is the name given to the dialects of Assyria and Babylon and is derived from the name Akkade, the capital of the empire of Sargon the Great. The earliest witness to a Semitic language is preserved in Akkadian (dated ca. third millennium B.C.). Other later witnesses to this language include the Babylonian Code of Hammurabi, documents from Nuzu, the Amarna Letters, the Babylonian Epic of Creation and the historical records of Assyria and Babylonia.

(b) Northwest: This group is located within the history and geography of Syria and Palestine. *Hebrew* is best known as the language of the OT. It also appears in the post-Biblical period in the Dead Sea Scrolls, the rabbinic literature of the Mishna, Tosefta, and the Midrashim. The Jews of the Middle Ages produced poetic and philosophical literature and Biblical exegesis in rabbinic Hebrew. Modern Hebrew, which took its rise in the enlightenment of the eighteenth century, is a restoration of the Biblical Hebrew and has now become the spoken language of Jewish Palestine. The earliest extant witness to Hebrew is the Gezer Calendar (dated ca. 925 B.C.). Other early witnesses include the Samaritan ostraca and the Siloam inscription.

Phoenician. The Phoenicians were of non-Semitic origin but they spoke a Semitic dialect. Though not the inventors of the alphabet they were instrumental in spreading its use into the Western world. Literary remains are scarce in this language with the earliest being inscriptions dating from about 1500 B.C. found at Sinai, Gezer, Lachish, and other places. The identity of some of these inscriptions are given the more general designation of Canaanite. The best-known source, the Eshmunazer inscription, is dated from about the fourth century B.C. The name "Punic" identifies this literature in the later period.

Ugaritic. Evidences for this dialect were discovered recently in the region of Ugarit, modern Ras Shamra, from literary remains on clay tablets dated ca. 1400 B.C. Additional inscriptions were found at Mount Tabor. While the exact placing of this dialect within the Semitic language groupings is still under discussion, its valuable contribution to the understanding of the Hebrew language is generally acknowledged.

Moabite. The Moabite Stone, a stele of black basalt found at Diban (Dibon in the OT) in the Transjordan area, contains an inscription of Mesha, a Moabite king. The date for the stele is given as ca. 850 B.C. and it tells of the king's victory over the Israelites. The dialect shown is closely related to Hebrew and its writing constitutes an important source illustrating the form and development of Canaanite alphabet in the ninth century B.C.

Aramaic. The name for this dialect is derived from the general area in which it was spoken, Aram = the high or hill country. The dialects of these countries were called Chaldaic and at other times Syriac, both designations falling somewhat short of ideal definition. Aramaic may be divided into three major chronological groups: i. Old Aramaic. The earliest form is seen in inscriptions from Hama, Arpad, Samal, Assyria, and other places and may be dated as far back as the tenth century B.C. The Biblical portions are found in Dan. 2:4–7:28; Ezra 4:8–6:18, 7:12–26; Jer. 10:11. Affinities may be traced between these fragments thus indicating close chronological ties. ii. West Aramaic. This group includes the languages of the Nabataeans, Palmyrene Arabs, the Palestinian Jews during the time of Christ and the later Christian Aramaic written in Syriac. Within this dialect would fall also the Targumim of Onkelos and of Jonathan, the Galilean Midrashim and the Jerusalem Talmud. iii. East Aramaic. This group includes Syriac, the language of Edessa developed in Christian literature, the Babylonian Aramaic as found in the Babylonian Talmud and in the Mandaean language of the Gnostic sect in Mesopotamia.

(c) Southwest: Today *Arabic* is the major Semitic language but its literary history which begins about the fifth or sixth century after Christ is of relatively recent origin. The language is classified under three headings: i. South Arabic; ii. North Arabic; and iii. Ethiopic. (See below for a more extended treatment.)

II. HEBREW LANGUAGE. 1. The Hebrew language was used by the Semitic people who occupied a large portion of Southwestern Asia. In the north the dialect became in places harsher and its general character less pure and distinct.

To the south the language under different circumstances remained relatively pure.

2. According to Scripture (Gen. 11:10–32) a group of Semitic wanderers of the lineage of Arpachshad set forth on a journey from Ur of the Chaldees to the land of Canaan under the guidance of Terah. However, the trip was interrupted and suspended in the vicinity of Haran until the death of Terah. The second stage of the journey was completed by Abram leading a much smaller group from the original Terachite migration group. The significant point in the account is that the newcomers encountered little or no difficulty in communicating with the earlier settlers of Canaan whom they met. On what grounds is the similarity of the dialect of the Terachites to that of the occupants at the time of their immigration to be explained? One answer is that Abram and his group spoke a Hebrew dialect from Mesopotamia but in their new residence in Canaan adopted the Canaanite dialect. Another suggested explanation is that the immigrants entered Canaan speaking an Aramaic dialect but upon taking up residence in the new land adopted the local dialect which was modified by their earlier Aramaic and the resultant speech became known as Hebrew.

3. The designation "Hebrews" should be applied to all Semitic-speaking tribes that migrated to the south from the other side of the Euphrates and in that case might have been applied by the earlier inhabitants of Canaan. Abraham is the first person in the Bible to be called a Hebrew (Gen. 14:13). The term "Habiru" occurring in the Mari letters, the Amarna and Ugaritic texts and other sources, shows a philological affinity to "Hebrew" and thus may provide a broader framework within which to reconstruct the history of the term and its application in ancient times to various tribes and languages.

4. It is very difficult, if not impossible, to give any sort of accurate account of the Hebrew language prior to its assuming a written form. The extant remains of Hebrew literature are destitute of any important changes in language during the period from Moses to the Captivity. At first sight, and to modern judgment, much of this appears rather strange and possibly untenable. But the explanation of the difficulty is sought in the unbroken residence of the Hebrew people without removal or molestation.

5. From earliest times the Hebrews employed the old Canaanite alphabet of twenty-two consonants. There were no indications of vowels although certain consonants were employed for

this purpose at an early stage but such use being somewhat unsystematic. The LXX bears evidence to the haphazard nature of the system. The Dead Sea Scrolls also give a similar kind of witness indicating the secondary nature of the vocalization of the text. It may also be assumed that as long as the language remained a living, spoken language the vocalization of its literature would be necessary only to suggest proper pronunciation for difficult or controverted words. Modern Hebrew which appears without vowel pointings is a case in which this is demonstrated. Thus the lack or rise of vocalization of the text may be directly related to the use or non-use of the language colloquially.

6. The pointing system (vowel indications) as found in the present text of the OT was worked out by the Masoretes soon after A.D. 800. Punctuation and cantillation marks which were lacking in the earlier manuscripts were also provided by them.

7. A few remarks may not be out of place here with reference to some of the leading linguistic peculiarities in the different books of the OT. With the style of the Pentateuch that of Joshua very closely corresponds. The books of Ruth and Samuel show similar linguistic peculiarities. The books of Job and Ecclesiastes contain many asserted Aramaisms which have been pleaded in support of a late date of composition. In the case of Job it may be argued that such peculiarities are not so much poetical ornamentations but rather ordinary expressions and usages of early Hebrew. The book of Ecclesiastes may show a style of Hebrew of late period rather than an Aramaic origin. In addition to roughness of diction, so-called Aramaisms are to be found in Jonah and Hosea, and expressions closely allied in Amos. The writings of Nahum, Zephaniah, Habakkuk and other minor prophets are free of Aramaisms. In the case of Ezekiel, Jewish critics have sought to assign its peculiarities to a secondary Hebrew origin. The peculiarities of language in Daniel belong to another field of inquiry. With these exceptions few traces of dialects are discernible in the small remains still extant, for the most part composed in Judah and Jerusalem. The general style of Hebrew prose literature is plain and simple, but lively and pictorial. But the requisite elevation of poetical composition led to the introduction of many expressions which we do not find in Hebrew prose literature. For the existence of these we may look to the kindred languages, especially Aramaic. Some of these may be regarded as archaisms which poetry preserved. From the earliest period of the existence of a literature among the Hebrew

people to 600 B.C., the language continued generally free from major change. From that period the Hebrew dialect will be found to give way before the Aramaic.

III. ARAMAIC LANGUAGE. 1. The early population of Arabia consisted of a group of Semitic tribes, the leading one being of Ishmaelite descent. The study of Arabian history, literature, and geography especially in the southern part of the peninsula has made rapid progress within recent years. However, it is not yet possible to give a full account of the original inhabitants of this area. The earliest recorded contacts between the inhabitants of Arabia and the outside world was with the Egyptians.

2. South Arabic, also called Himyaritic, was the ancient language of Yemen and is closely related to North Arabic and Ethiopic.

3. Internal evidence demonstrates that the North Arabic dialect, at the time when it appears on the field of literary history, was being gradually developed in its remote and barren peninsular home. In its early stages it may have been a fusion of different dialects realized by the tribe of Koreish settled around Mecca. With the rise of Islam in the seventh century A.D., this dialect which provided the language of the Koran soon replaced all other dialects and became the ultimate standard for the inhabitants of the peninsula. That the Arabs possessed a literature in the pre-Islamic period is freely admitted but the earliest witness to such a literature is only fragmentary. Arabic shows all the characteristics of a Semitic language, which include triconsonantal roots, inflectional endings, etc., but with the added tendency toward conservatism. It is this last feature that makes the Arabic language the best surviving representative of the original Semitic language and thus becomes indispensable as a source of information for the Semitist. However, this does not grant to Arabic the position of a prototype of primitive Semitic language.

4. The affinity of the Ethiopic of Geez with the Semitic has long been recognized. In its lexical peculiarities it resembles Aramaic; in its grammatical ones, the Arabic. The alphabet is very curious, differing from Semitic alphabets in number, order, name and form, and by the direction of its writing. The language may have been introduced into Abyssinia and developed there by invaders or colonists from Southern Arabia. It survives as the religious language of Abyssinia.

IV. STRUCTURE OF THE SEMITIC LANGUAGES. 1. The question as to whether any amount of primitives in the Semitic languages may have derived from imitation of sounds (onomatopoeia) has received only a qualified affirmative.

2. The inquiry regarding the extent of affinity still discernible between Semitic and Japhetian roots remains unsolved. Special interest has been expressed in possible Hamito-Semitic relationship between Akkadian and Libyco-Berber.

3. It can hardly be doubted that the art of writing was known to the Israelites in the time of Moses. However, great differences of opinion prevail as to which of the Semitic tribes may justly claim the credit for the invention of the alphabet. The Ras Shamra Tablets (ca. 1400 B.C.) written in Ugaritic contain the earliest example of the use of an alphabet in any Semitic language. The origin of this alphabet is unknown but the order of the letters was adopted by the Phoenicians, Canaanites, Hebrews, and Greeks. The earliest extant Hebrew document is the Gezer Calendar, a small limestone tablet which was used for a writing exercise. The tablet (dated ca. 925 B.C.) shows that writing in Hebrew was commonly practiced at this time. The conclusion from this is that the Hebrews probably employed the alphabet already in use to render their own speech.

4. One of the basic characteristics of the Semitic languages is the triliteral root system. Some are of the opinion that the triliteral is a development from an earlier biliteral root system.

5. Some early inscriptions read downward as in Chinese. Generally, however, the writing is read from right to left, mirror reading, except Akkadian and Ethiopic which read from left to right. Some inscriptions (South Arabian) read *boustrophedon*, that is, alternately from right to left, left to right.

6. The decided dominance of consonants in the alphabet necessitated the later addition of certain diacritical signs and vowel points. In most cases such additions were a part of the later development of the language.

7. A comparison of the Semitic languages presents them as being unevenly developed. Much remains to be done in the study of South Arabic and Ugaritic. M.N.

senate in the deliberative function of politics the senate (Acts 5:21) seems to be not only those elders of the Sanhedrin, but a larger body, representative of the people in general.

Seneh (sē'ně) [thorn] one of two isolated rocks which stood in the passage of Michmash (1 Sam. 14:4) and climbed by Jonathan and his armor-bearer for a better examination of the Philistine camp.

Senir (sē'nĭr) [snow mountain] the Amorite name for Mount Hermon (Deut. 3:9).

Sennacherib (sĕ-năk'ĕr-ĭb) [the moon-god increases brothers] was the son and successor of Sargon king of Assyria. He ascended the throne in 705 B.C. The early years of his reign are well accounted for in a remarkable prism called the Taylor Cylinder, presently in the British Museum. Colonel Taylor discovered it in 1830. Complete translations can be found in Daniel D. Luckenbill's *Ancient Records of Assyria and Babylonia*, Vol. 2, and in James Pritchard's *Ancient Near Eastern Texts*, 1950. Of his later years little is preserved. After crushing the revolt of Babylonia, Sennacherib turned his attention westward to war against Palestine-Syria. After taking Sidon without a fight, the king having fled, the Assyrian host swept through the country capturing Sarepta, Acco, Ekdippa, and other cities without resistance. Ethobal was made king over the captured territory and tribute was levied. News of the victories spread and petty kings sent presents galore, hoping thereby to save their cities from ravage by swearing allegiance to Assyria. These included Moab and Edom. Askelon offered some resistance, but was soon conquered and the king sent to Assyria as captive. At Ekron he met the army of Egypt, which had formed an alliance with Hezekiah king of Judah (2 K. 18:14), and claimed a hollow victory. After the fall of Lachish, the king had carved on a wall in the city a relief of himself sitting upon a throne and receiving the plunder of the city. Inscribed are the words "Sennacherib, the king of the world, the king of Assyria, sat on his throne, and the spoils of the city of Lachish marched before him." When Sennacherib sent an insulting letter to King Hezekiah at Jerusalem, Hezekiah prayed, and an event occurred that sent Sennacherib scurrying home, and relieving Judah of the pressure that had conquered and devastated Israel. In one night the Assyrians lost, either by pestilence or some more awful stroke of divine power, 185,000 men. The camp immediately broke up, and Sennacherib fled, never to return to war against Judah. Sennacherib says of the campaign that he conquered forty-six walled cities of Judah and innumerable smaller ones, and that he captured 200,150 men of Judah with their women and children, and that he shut Hezekiah up like a bird in a cage in Jerusalem. However, he does not claim to have conquered Jerusalem (2 K. 18:14, 19:35). The Judean campaign was about 701 B.C. Sennacherib engaged in other wars after returning home, but never again attacked Judea.

Seorim (sĕ-ō'rĭm) [barley] the chief of the fourth of the twenty-four courses of priests (1 Chr. 24:8).

Sephar (sē'fär) [a numbering] "a mountain of the East" (Gen. 10:30) mentioned as one of the boundaries of the Joktanites in the northern portion of the peninsula of Arabia. It is generally accepted that Sephar is identical with the city of Zhafar in the province of Hadramaut, South Arabia.

Sepharad (sē-fä'răd) [separated] mentioned in Obad. 20 as the place where the captives of Jerusalem were held by the Assyrians. It is possibly Sardis in Asia Minor or a part of Southwest Media on the Caspian Sea (see 2 K. 17:6).

Sepharvaim (sĕ-fär-vä'yĭm) an Assyrian-conquered city from which people were taken to settle in Samaria, replacing Samaritans who were removed to oblivion during the reign of Sargon (2 K. 17:24). It is commonly identified with Sippar, whose ruins were located southwest of Baghdad on the Euphrates by Hormuzd Rassam. However, later scholarship has almost universally rejected this explanation, and accepts the identification with Sibraim (Ezek. 47:16), which lies in the Hamath district. Positive identification at this time is not possible.

Sephela (sĕf-ēl'äh) the low-lying region between the highlands of central Palestine and the Mediterranean, the northern portion of which was known as Sharon. It was and is one of the most productive regions of the Holy Land. It was in ancient times the cornfield of Syria, and as such the constant subject of war between Philistines and Israelites, and the refuge of the latter when harvest in the central country was ruined by drouth (2 K. 8:1–3).

Septuagint (sĕp-tū'a-jĭnt) this name is given to the earliest Greek translation of the OT, commonly abbreviated "LXX." The term "Septuagint" or "seventy" comes from the legend embodied in the *Letter of Aristeas*, which purports to have been written by a high official of Ptolemy II Philadelphus king of Egypt (285–245 B.C.) to his brother Philocrates giving the details of the translation of the Pentateuch into Greek. Accordng to this letter, the royal librarian, Demetrius of Phaleron, induces the king to address a letter to the high priest in Jerusalem requesting that seventy-two scholars be sent down to Egypt, six from each tribe, to translate the Pentateuch from Hebrew into Greek. The high priest responded by sending seventy-two elders to Alexandria, where they received a royal welcome, and produced the translation in seventy-two days. Demetrius read the translation before the Jewish population,

which approved it and allowed no changes to be made. This translation was then presented to the king to be placed in the royal library and the translators were sent home with rich gifts. Later writers added various miraculous elements to the story, such as the fact that each translator worked independently and came up with an identical translation, and that the translators were inspired in making their translation, and that it was the entire OT rather than the Pentateuch that was so translated. Scholars have pointed out various flaws in this letter, but the historical facts seem to be that at some time around 250 B.C. during the reign of Ptolemy Philadelphus, a translation of the Law was made in Egypt and that this was the original LXX. How many were involved in the translation, it is impossible to say. The remaining OT books were translated within the next century as the reference in the prologue to Ecclesiasticus makes this clear. The Apocryphal books continued to be translated and interspersed among the canonical books of the OT down to the Christian era.

It is well known that after the return from Babylonian captivity, the Jews in Palestine, having largely lost the knowledge of the ancient Hebrew, had the readings from the Law explained to them in the Aramaic language in their synagogues, in Targums or paraphrases. When later the books of the prophets were read in the synagogues, this was also done. The Jews at Alexandria had probably less knowledge of Hebrew than those of Palestine since their language was Hellenistic Greek. They would naturally follow the same practice as their brethren in Palestine. The Law first and afterward the prophets would be explained in Greek, which gave a basis for producing the entire OT in Greek.

1. *The Character of the LXX.* While the language of the LXX was the Koine, the commonly spoken Greek language of the period, it contains a number of Hebraisms and Aramaisms. In some parts the translation was more literal, while in others it was rather free. In Jeremiah some 2700 words of the Hebrew text are lacking. The Greek varies from good Koine Greek in the Pentateuch, part of Joshua and Isaiah, to indifferent Greek in Ezekiel, the minor prophets, 1 and 2 Chronicles, 1 Samuel, Psalms, and in parts of Jeremiah, 2 Samuel, and 1 Kings, and to extremely literal or unintelligible translations in parts of Jeremiah, Judges, Ruth, 2 Samuel, 1 and 2 Kings, Song of Solomon, and Lamentations. Scholars have pointed out the fact that the translators were misled by similarities in Hebrew words, and

were not consistent in their rendering of words. Anthropomorphic expressions concerning God were softened in this translation. The LXX did not follow the traditional Hebrew division of the Law, the Prophets, which included historical books, and "the Writings" but grouped the books according to major subject headings: Law, History, Poetry, and Prophecy. This arrangement had a profound effect on the history of the OT canon in the church. The LXX was often quoted in the NT instead of the ancient Hebrew text. As Christianity spread beyond Palestine it adopted the LXX and made this more and more its official version of the OT. It is natural that the Jews by the end of the first century should react against this, and three translations appeared in the second century to replace the LXX. Aquila's version (ca. A.D. 130) was a very literal translation, Symmachus (ca. A.D. 170) was done by an Ebionite Christian aimed at accuracy and good Greek style. The third and best known was Theodotion's translation around the end of the second century A.D. whose rendering of Daniel replaced the older LXX text in later copies of it.

2. *Criticism.* Critical study of the LXX dates back to Origen (A.D. 185–254), the great scholar of Alexandria and Caesarea, who studied Hebrew with the idea of comparing the copies of the Greek OT that the church used with the Hebrew text the Jews followed. His famous *Hexapla* presented in six parallel columns the OT text. Column I contained the Hebrew, column II—the Hebrew in Greek transliteration, column III—Aquila's version, column IV—Symmachus' version, column V—the LXX, column VI—Theodotion's version. In certain parts he used additional Greek translations (called Quinta, Sexta, and Septima) scarcely known to us. Where the LXX differed from the Hebrew text, he marked additions to the LXX that the Hebrew did not have with an obelus, and the deficiencies he supplied by inserting materials from the other columns, marking these with an asterisk, prefixed. This huge work was placed in the library of Caesarea, where Jerome later saw it, but it was probably never transcribed. Eusebius mentions the *Tetrapla*, containing the last four Greek columns, which seems to be an independent work. The most frequently copied column of the *Hexapla* was the LXX column, used by Pamphilus and Eusebius, in supplying Constantine with fifty copies for his use in the churches of Constantinople. This is commonly called the Hexaplaric recension. The *Hexapla* was probably destroyed by the Saracens in 653, but its influence continues in ancient MSS. Jerome mentions a recension made by Hesychius of Alexandria (martyred, A.D. 311), but little is known about this Egyptian recension. A third recension is attributed to Lucian who was also martyred in A.D. 311 and became the text that was quoted extensively in Theodoret and Chrysostom.

Paul de Lagarde (1827–91) is one of the great names in modern LXX research. He identified the various MSS around these three recensions and endeavored to work back from these toward an original text, or an approximation of this. His work was carried on by A. Rahlfs (1865–1935), who fostered the Göttingen LXX. Paul Kahle has challenged the view of Lagarde that these recensions and others are revisions of one basic original translation, and has set forth a theory based on the analogy of the Aramaic Targums that the LXX is really a variety of versions, one of which the Christians took over and made their own. However, this theory has not won widespread acceptance, and most scholars continue to follow the principles laid down by Lagarde in their critical work.

3. *Manuscripts.* MS evidence for the LXX is very extensive. Rahlfs had identified more than 1500 to which can be added a large number of quotations from the fathers and secondary translations. More recently a number of early LXX papyri have been brought to light, such as the Chester Beatty, the John Rylands fragments, the Scheide and Murabba'at papyri. The earlier uncial MSS of great importance include Codex Vaticanus (B), Codex Sinaiticus (Aleph), and Codex Alexandrinus (A).

4. *Printed Editions.* When producing editions of an ancient text, an editor may follow two policies: (1) print the text of one excellent MS and note in his apparatus all the variant readings in other MSS; (2) attempt to reconstruct a critical text through choosing the various readings that as an editor he believes to be most authentic, and offer the other variants in his apparatus. All the earlier printed editions follow the first method. The earliest printed edition was in the Complutensian Polyglot (1514–21) published under the auspices of Cardinal Ximenes of Spain. Later polyglots followed this text. The material upon which it is based has not survived. The Aldine edition produced in Venice in 1518–19 was based upon MSS housed at St. Mark's in Venice but is a late text of little value. The Sixtine edition published in Rome in 1586 at the order of Pope Sixtus V follows mainly the text of Codex Vaticanus. This edition became standard for almost all editions up to the nineteenth century, including the London Polyglot (1657),

Holmes and Parsons (1798–1827), the first edition in which a listing of textual variants was made, Tischendorf (1850–69) and the Clarendon Press edition (Oxford, 1875) which is the basis for the Hatch and Redpath Concordance. The modern British school began work on the Cambridge LXX in 1883 printing the text of Codex Vaticanus and providing a group of variant readings from selected MSS, patristic quotations, and other versions. The first edition of this was produced by H. B. Swete as a provisional text and the larger edition under the editorship of Brooke, McLean, and Thackeray, follows Swete's text with a rather complete critical apparatus, but the work is not completed.

The Göttingen LXX, edited by A. Rahlfs, followed the plan of creating a critical text of the LXX and providing a group of variant readings. No one MS was followed, but the readings that seemed to be original became the text, since this was an attempt to restore the original text. The convenient critical edition of this work is published by the Privilegierte Württembergische Bibelanstalt, and has become a most important basis for further study of the LXX text.

5. *The Value of the LXX for Bible Study.* The LXX gives evidence of the character and condition of the Hebrew MSS from which it was made. Being made from MSS far older than the Masoretic recension, the LXX indicates readings more ancient and more correct than those of our present Hebrew MSS and editions, and speaks decisively at places between the conflicting readings of the present MSS. However, care must be used in correcting the Hebrew MT by the LXX due to our inadequate knowledge of the translators' techniques and also to the uncertainty regarding the actual "original text" of the LXX. It proves valuable as a text when used in connection with other ancient versions. We do not attribute any paramount authority to the LXX on account of its superior antiquity to the extant Hebrew MSS; but we take it as an evidence of a more ancient Hebrew text. The close connection between the Old and New Testament makes the study of the LXX extremely valuable. It was the Bible the apostles and evangelists knew and quoted often for the proofs of their teaching. Its language provided the thought world and religious vocabulary in Greek drawn from the Hebrew OT, which were used in the NT writings. The LXX first enshrined the Word of God in the Greek language and colored the language in preparation for the NT. The NT vocabulary must be seen against the OT usage and meaning. Kittel's *Theological Dictionary* follows this practice. The many quotations of the LXX in the Greek fathers make it important in the study of the history of the early church.   F.P.

sepulcher see **burial**

Serah (sē'rā) the daughter of Asher (Gen. 46:17; 1 Chr. 7:30) called Sarah in Num. 26:46.

Seraiah (sē-rā'yà) 1. Secretary or scribe to King David (2 Sam. 8:17), probably the same as Sheva of 2 Sam. 20:25 and Shisha of 1 K. 4:3.

2. The son of Azariah, who served as high priest during the reign of Zedekiah (2 K. 25:18). Sent as a prisoner to Nebuchadnezzar when Jerusalem was captured in 587 B.C., and put to death at Riblah (Jer. 52:24–27).

3. The son of Tanhumeth the Netophathite, 588 B.C. (2 K. 25:23; Jer. 40:8).

4. The son of Kenaz and brother of Othniel (1 Chr. 4:13–14).

5. Ancestor of Jehu, a Simeonite chieftain (1 Chr. 4:35).

6. One of the priests who returned from the Captivity with Zerubbabel, 536 B.C. (Ezra 2:2).

7. One of the ancestors of Ezra the scribe (Ezra 7:1).

8. A priest, son of Neriah, who went with Zedekiah to Babylon in the fourth year of his reign (595 B.C.) as chamberlain. He was sent four years earlier to Babylon by Jeremiah, and commanded to take the roll on which the prophet had written the doom of Babylon, and sink it in the Euphrates as a symbol of how the city would sink, never to rise again (Jer. 51:60–64).

seraphim [burning, glowing] an order of celestial beings, whom Isaiah beheld in a vision standing above Jehovah as he sat upon his throne (Isa. 6:2). They are described as having three pairs of wings, with one of which they covered their faces (as a token of humility); with the second they covered their feet (a token of respect), and with the third they flew. They bore a general resemblance to the human figure (vs. 6), and their occupation was twofold: to celebrate the praises of Jehovah's holiness and power, and to act as communication between heaven and earth.

sergeant a rod holder, or one who bore a bundle of rods as a public lictor before the magistrates of cities and colonies signifying their office, and who acted as executioner of the sentences which they pronounced (Acts 16:35).

Sergius Paulus (sûr'jĭ-ŭs pô'lŭs) the proconsul of

Cyprus when Paul and Barnabas went through that island on their first missionary journey. Convinced of the truth they preached, he obeyed the Gospel and became a Christian (Acts 13:7–12).

serpent, brazen see **brazen serpent**

serpent, fiery while Israel wandered in the wilderness, they complained against God because of their hardships, and God sent fiery serpents among them. Literally, burning snakes, whose bite was venomous and filled the victim with fever and poison. The punishment was terrible. God provided a way out by commanding that a brazen serpent be made and put upon a pole in the camp. When Israel manifested its repentance and faith by looking upon the serpent, they were to be healed.

Serug (sē'rŭg) [branch] son of Reu, and great-grandfather of Abraham. His age is given in the Hebrew Bible as 230 years, 2180 B.C. (Gen. 11:20–23).

Seth (sĕth) [compensation] the third son of Adam, and father of Enos (Gen. 4:25). He died when 912 years old. It was through Seth that the lineage of the race was extended. About 3870 B.C.

Sethur (sē'thŭr) [hidden] the son of Michael, and representative of the tribe of Asher among the twelve spies sent out by Moses to view the land of promise, 1440 B.C. (Num. 13:13).

seven the frequent recurrence of certain numbers in the sacred literature of the Hebrews is obvious, but seven so far surpasses the rest both in frequence and importance of the objects with which it is associated, that it may fairly be termed *the* representative symbolic number. It prevailed also among Persians, Indians, Greeks, and Romans. The sabbath was the seventh day. The seventh month was begun with the Feast of the Trumpets. Seven weeks was the interval between the Passover and Pentecost. The seventh year was the Passover year, and the year following seven times seven years was the Jubilee year. Seven days was the length of the Feast of the Passover, and of Tabernacles. The ceremonies of the consecration of priests lasted seven days. Seven victims were offered on special occasions, as in Balaam's sacrifice (Num. 23:1). There were seven churches of Asia in John's Revelation, and saints are to forgive each other seventy times seven times.

Shaalbim (shā-ăl'bĭm) [house of foxes] a town in the allotment of Dan (Josh. 19:42; Judg. 1:35; 1 K. 4:9).

Shaalbonite, the (shā-ăl'bō-nīt) Eliahba the Shaalbonite was one of David's thirty-seven heroes (2 Sam. 23:32; 1 Chr. 11:33). He was a native of Sebaste.

Shaaph (shā'ăf) [balsam] 1. The son of Jahdai (1 Chr. 2:47).

2. The son of Caleb, the brother of Jerahmeel by his concubine Maachah, after 1445 B.C. (1 Chr. 2:49).

Shaaraim (shā-à-rā'ĭm) [two gates] a city allotted to Judah (Josh. 15:36). The Shaaraim of 1 Chr. 4:31 must be a different place.

Shaasgaz (shā-ăsh'găz) [servant of the beautiful] the eunuch in the palace of Xerxes who had custody of the women in the second house, about 525 B.C. (Est. 2:14).

Shabbethai (shăb'ê-thī) [sabbatical] a Levite in the days of Ezra (Ezra 10:15). It is apparently the same who with Jeshua and others instructed the people in the knowledge of the Law, 450 B.C. (Neh. 8:7).

Shadrach (shā'drăk) [royal] the Chaldee name for Hananiah the Hebrew, who was cast into the fiery furnace (Dan. 1–7). No other mention is made of him except the allusion of Heb. 11:33–34.

Shalem (shā'lĕm) [safe] a place near Jacob's well (Gen. 33:18–20).

Shalim (shā'lĕm) [land of foxes] the district through which Saul passed on his journey in quest of his father's asses (1 Sam. 9:4).

Shalisha (shà-lī'shà) one of the districts traversed by Saul in search of his father's asses. Near Mount Ephraim, and perhaps identical with Baal-shalisha of 2 K. 4:42. Fifteen miles north of Lydda.

Shallecheth, the Gate of (shăl'lĕ-chĕth) one of the gates of the temple (1 Chr. 26:16). Through it the refuse of the temple was thrown into the Tyropoeon Valley (1 Chr. 26:16).

Shallum (shăl'ŭm) [retribution] 1. The fifteenth king of Israel, son of Jabesh, conspired against Zechariah, killed him, and brought the dynasty of Jehu to a close, 770 B.C. After reigning in Samaria for one month, he was dethroned and killed by Menahem (2 K. 15:10–14).

2. The husband of Huldah the prophetess, 630 B.C. (2 K. 22:14).

3. A descendant of Shesham (1 Chr. 2:40–41).

4. Fourth son of Josiah king of Judah, known as Jehoahaz, 610 B.C. (1 Chr. 3:15; Jer. 22:11).

5. Son of Shaul (1 Chr. 4:25).

6. A high priest (1 Chr. 6:12–13).

7. A son of Naphtali (1 Chr. 7:13).

8. Chief of a family of porters at the east gate of the temple, 1050 B.C. (1 Chr. 9:17).

9. Son of Kore (1 Chr. 9:19–31).

10. Father of Jehizkiah the Ephraimite (2 Chr. 28:12).

11. A temple porter who married a foreign wife (Ezra 10:24).

12. One of the sons of Bani (Ezra 10:42).

13. Son of Halohesh and ruler of a district in Jerusalem (Neh. 3:12).

14. Uncle of Jeremiah (Jer. 32:7).

15. Father of Maaseiah (Jer. 35:4).

Shalmaneser (shăl-măn-ē′zēr) [fire worshiper] an Assyrian king who reigned probably between Tiglath-pileser and Sargon, 727–722 B.C. There were five kings by this name; this one is thought to be Shalmaneser V. He led the forces of Assyria into Palestine, where Hoshea, the last king of Israel, had revolted against his authority (2 K. 17:3). Hoshea submitted and consented to pay tribute, but soon thereafter concluded an alliance with Egypt and withheld tribute. This caused Shalmaneser to invade Israel in 723 B.C. and lay siege to Samaria. Hoshea refused to submit. The siege lasted three years, but finally the city fell. Shalmaneser died the same year; we know not whether before or after the fall of the city.

Shamgar (shăm′gàr) [sword] son of Anath, judge of Israel. When Israel was in a most desperate condition, Shamgar was raised up to be a deliverer. With no arms but an ox-goad, he made an assault upon the Philistines and slew 600 of them (Judg. 3:31; 1 Sam. 13:21).

Shammah (shăm′à) [astonished] 1. The son of Reuel, the son of Esau, about 1700 B.C. (Gen. 36:13–17).

2. The third son of Jesse, and brother of David (1 Sam. 16:9).

3. One of three greatest of David's mighties (2 Sam. 23:11–17).

4. The Harodite, one of David's mighty men (2 Sam. 23:25).

Shammai (shăm′à-ī) [desolate] 1. The son of Onam (1 Chr. 2:28, 32).

2. Son of Rekem (1 Chr. 2:44–45).

3. One of the descendants of Judah (1 Chr. 4:17).

Shammua (shă′mū-à) [renowned] 1. The Reubenite spy, son of Zaccur (Num. 13:4).

2. Son of David by Bathsheba, 1045 B.C. (1 Chr. 14:4).

3. A Levite, the father of Abda (Neh. 11:17).

4. The representative of the priestly family of Bilgah in the days of Joiakim (Neh. 12:18).

Shaphan (shā′fàn) [coney] the scribe, or secretary of King Josiah (2 K. 22:3, 14; 2 Chr. 34:8, 20). He appears on equality with the governor of the city and the royal recorder (2 K. 22:4).

Shaphat (shā′făt) [judge] 1. The Simeonite spy. Son of Hori (Num. 13:5).

2. Father of the prophet Elisha, before 900 B.C. (1 K. 19:16, 19).

3. One of the chiefs of the Gadites in Bashan (1 Chr. 5:12).

4. Son of Shemaiah in the royal line of Judah (1 Chr. 3:22).

5. Son of Adlai, who was over David's oxen (1 Chr. 27:29).

Shapher, Mount (shā′fēr) [brightness] a camp of the Israelites during their wilderness wandering.

Sharezer (shà-rē′zēr) [prince of fire] son of Sennacherib, whom, in conjunction with his brother, he murdered, after 711 B.C. (2 K. 19:37).

Sharron (shăr′ŭn) [a plain] a part of Palestine extending from Joppa to Mount Carmel and sloping to the Mediterranean. Noted throughout history for its beautiful flowers and fertility. The six to twelve-mile-wide plain was well watered in Biblical times, and is today the site of citrus farms. Caravans connecting Asia Minor, Mesopotamia and other eastern and southern regions were wont to pass through this beauty spot. Throughout history it has been a favorite dwelling place for man as is evidenced by its very ancient burial places.

Shaul (shā′ŭl) [asked] 1. Son of Simeon by a Canaanitish woman (Gen. 46:10).

2. One of the kings of Edom (1 Chr. 1:48–49).

Shaveh, Valley of (shā′vě) [plain] the valley of the king (Gen. 14:17). Site of a pillar set up by Absalom (2 Sam. 18:18).

shearing house, the a place on the road between Jezreel and Samaria, at which Jehu, on his way to the latter, encountered forty-two members of the royal family of Judah, whom he slaughtered (2 K. 10:12–14).

Sheba (shē′bà) [an oath] 1. Son of Bichri the Benjaminite (2 Sam. 20:1–22). He traveled through Palestine rousing the population upon David's return, Joab following in full pursuit to the fortress of Abel Beth-maachmah, where Sheba was beheaded (2 Sam. 20:3–22).

2. A son of Raamah, son of Cush (Gen. 10:7).

3. Son of Joktan (Gen. 10:28).

4. Son of Jokshan, son of Keturah (Gen. 25:3).

Shebam (shē′băm) [fragrance] one of the towns in the pastoral district on the east of Jordan—demanded by and finally deeded to the tribes of Reuben and Gad (Num. 32:3).

Shebaniah (shĕb-à-nī′à) [increased by Jehovah] 1. One of the priests who blew the trumpet before the ark when it was being removed from the house of Obed-edom for its trip to Jerusalem, about 986 B.C. (1 Chr. 15:24).

2. A Levite who stood upon the stairs and prayed (Neh. 9:4–5) and sealed the covenant with Nehemiah (10:10).

Shebna (shĕb'nà) [vigor] was "over the house" of Hezekiah's court. Prefect of the palace (Isa. 22:15). He was demoted to secretary (Isa. 36:3) and because he led the people to forget God, Isaiah was sent to prophesy his fall.

Shebuel (shē-bū'ĕl) [captive of God] a descendant of Moses, 1013 B.C. (1 Chr. 23:16). Ruler of the treasures of the house of God.

Shechem (shē'kĕm) [back or shoulder] one of the most ancient and most important of all the cities of Palestine. It is called Sichem in Gen. 12:6, Sychar in Jn. 4:5, and Sychem in Acts 7:16. Joshua 20:7 places the city on Mount Ephraim, and Judg. 9:6 places it under the summit of Gerizim, which is part of the Ephraim range. Vespasian destroyed the temple at Samaria and built Neapolis further up the valley. For many years it was thought that Neapolis and Shechem were at the same place, but recent archaeology has proven that Shechem was Tell Balatah which is northwest of Neapolis. Shechem was a great city between 2000 and 1800 B.C., and again 600 years later. Great Bronze Age fortifications have been unearthed, including a wall thirty feet high, dating from the sixteenth or seventeenth century B.C. Abraham on his first trip to Canaan pitched his tent at Shechem and built an altar under an oak. When Jacob came there, after his stay in Haran, the Canaanite city had fallen to the Hivites. Here Jacob bought a field from Hamor, chief of Shechem, which was to become the final resting place of Joseph (Gen. 33:19; Josh. 24:32; Jn. 4:5). Jacob dug a well there in order to be independent of his neighbors. Here it was that Dinah, Jacob's daughter, was seduced, resulting in the capture of Shechem and the killing of all the male inhabitants by Simeon and Levi, Jacob's sons. When Israel parceled out the land, Shechem fell to the tribe of Ephraim, but was later made a city of refuge (Josh. 21:20–21). Here the children of Israel were gathered to hear the curses and blessings of the Law pronounced. The blessings were pronounced from Mount Gerizim, and the curses from Mount Ebal (Deut. 27:11; Josh. 8:33–35). Joshua gathered the people here for his farewell address (Josh. 24:1–25). Abimelech, illegitimate son of Gideon, agitated the people of Shechem until they revolted and made him king (Judg. 9). He reigned three years and was driven from the

city. He completely destroyed Shechem and sowed the land with salt (Judg. 9:25–45). Later the city was rebuilt and Rehoboam, Solomon's son, was inaugurated king at Shechem. The actual split in the kingdom came here, with ten tribes rebelling against David. They selected Jeroboam as king (1 K. 12:16) and made Shechem the capital of their new kingdom. The city was conquered and its people carried away into captivity (2 K. 17:5–6). Strangers were moved in to replace the people in Shechem (2 K. 17:24). Later still others came (Ezra 4:2) and the city became a part of the Samaritan culture, holding Mount Gerizim as the holy place where men ought to worship (Jn. 4:5).

Shechi'nah or **Shechinah** (shĕk-ī'nà) [that which dwells] this term is not found in the Bible. Its usage in later Jewish writings denotes the visible majesty of the divine Presence, especially in reference to God's dwelling between the cherubim on the mercy seat in the tabernacle and the temple of Solomon (however, not in the temple of Zerubbabel where it was considered lacking). The use of the term is first found in the Targums where it is frequently used as a periphrasis for God to indicate the presence of God among his people, in an effort to avoid any indication of materialism. Onkelos, in passages such as Ex. 25:8 and 29:45–46 where God speaks of dwelling in the midst of his people, wrote that God's Shechinah dwelt in their midst. As regards the visible manifestation of the divine Presence among the Israelites, to which the term Shechinah later came to attach itself, the various Scriptures convey the idea of a most brilliant and glorious light, enveloped in a cloud, with usually only the cloud visible, but in some instances, the glory itself becoming apparent (Ex. 24:17, 40:34, 38; Num. 9:17–18, 22). The Haggadah contains the most frequent use of Shechinah, where the term seems calculated to impress the Jews with the nearness of God. In the later intertestamental period, a distinction came to be made between the Shechinah and the glory of God, with the glory referring to the visible form of the Shechinah, while the Shechinah came to refer to the substance of that glory. The allusions in the NT to the Shechinah are not infrequent. Thus in the account of the nativity, the words, "Lo, the angel of the Lord came upon them, and the glory of the Lord shone round about them" (Lk. 2:9), followed by the apparition of "the multitude of the heavenly host," recall the appearance of the divine glory on Sinai when "He shined forth from Paran, and came with ten thousands of saints" (Deut. 33:2; cf. Ps. 68:17; Ezek. 43:2; Acts 7:53; Heb. 2:2). The "God of glory" (Acts 7:2, 55), "the cherubims of glory" (Heb. 9:5), "the glory" (Rom. 9:4), and other like passages, are distinct references to the manifestations of the glory in the OT. When we read in Jn. 1:14, that "the Word was made flesh, and dwelt among us, and we beheld his glory," or in 2 Cor. 12:9, "that the power of Christ may rest upon me," or in Rev. 21:3, "Behold the tabernacle of God is with men, and he will dwell with them," we have not only references to the Shechinah, but are distinctly taught to connect it with the incarnation and future coming of the Messiah, as type with antitype.   c.m.

sheep an important part of the possessions of the ancient Hebrews and of Eastern nations generally. The first mention of sheep occurs in Gen. 4:2. They were used in the sacrificial offerings, both the adult animal (Ex. 20:24; 1 K. 8:63; 2 Chr. 29:33) and the lamb, i.e., "a male from one to three years old"; but young lambs of the first year were more generally used in the offerings (see e.g., Ex. 29:38; Lev. 9:3, 12:6; Num. 28:9). No lamb under eight days old was allowed to be killed (Lev. 22:27). A very young lamb was called *tâleh* (see 1 Sam. 7:9; Isa. 65:25). Sheep and lambs formed an important article of food (e.g., 1 Sam. 25:18; 1 K. 1:19, 4:23). The wool was used as clothing (Lev. 13:47; Deut. 22:11; Prov. 31:13; Job 31:20). "Rams' skins dyed red" were used as a covering for the tabernacle (Ex. 25:5). Sheep and lambs were sometimes paid as tribute (2 K. 3:4). Immense numbers of sheep were reared in Palestine in Biblical times. Sheepshearing is alluded to in Gen. 31:19, 38:13; Deut. 15:19; 1 Sam. 25:4; Isa. 53:7. Sheep dogs were employed in Biblical times, as is evident from Job 30:1, "the dogs of my flock." Shepherds in Palestine and the East generally go before their flocks, which they induce to follow by calling to them (cf. Jn. 10:4; Ps. 77:20, 80:1), though they also drove them (Gen. 33:13). The common sheep of Syria and Palestine are the broadtail (*Ovis laticaudata*), and a variety of the common sheep of this country (*Ovis aries*) called the Bidoween. The broad-tailed kind has long been reared in Syria. The whole passage in Gen. 30 which bears on the subject of Jacob's conduct in this matter has been severely and uncompromisingly condemned by some writers. It is altogether impossible to account for the complete success which attended his device of setting peeled rods before the ewes and she-goats as they came to drink in the watering troughs, on natural grounds. We must agree with the Greek fathers, and ascribe the production of Jacob's spotted sheep and goats to divine agency. As the sheep is an emblem of meekness, patience, and submission, it is expressly mentioned as typifying these qualities in the person of our blessed Lord (Isa. 53:7; Acts 8:32). The relation with his members is beautifully compared to that which in the East is so strikingly exhibited by the shepherds to their flocks.   d.d.

sheep gate, the one of the gates of Jerusalem as rebuilt by Nehemiah (Neh. 3:1, 32, 12:39). It stood between the Tower of Meah and the chamber of the corner (3:32, 12:39) or "prison gate." The latter seems to have been at the angle formed by the junction of the wall of the city of David with that of the city of Jerusalem proper, having the sheep gate on the north of it. The position of the sheep gate may therefore have been on or near that of the Bab el-Kattanin.   d.d.

sheep market, the (Jn. 5:2). The word "market" is an interpolation of our translators. To the words of the original should be supplied, not market, but gate, as in the LXX version of the passages in Nehemiah quoted in the foregoing article.   d.d.

shekel (shek'l, shek'el, she'kel) this word, derived from the Hebrew term *sheqel* [from *shaqal*, to weigh], was used to refer to a weight or later a coin. Scholars believe that the Israelites adopted their system of weights and measures from the Babylonians.

The Hebrew shekel was one fiftieth of a mina and weighed approximately 224 grains. As a silver coin a shekel was worth approximately 66 cents. One authority (the IDB, 1962) states that the weight of the shekel varied from 8.3 grains to 16.7 grains or about 0.3 ounce to 0.62 ounce. In the OT period the shekel seems to have averaged about 11.42 grains or 0.403 ounce.

The use of the shekel as coins among the Hebrews is generally dated no earlier than the time of Simon Maccabeus, ca. 141 B.C. Simon was given the power (according to 1 Macc. 15:5) to coin money with his own stamp, and scholars believe that either Simon or his son minted the first native Hebrew coins.

Apparently the shekel was made of gold, copper, or silver and originally weighed one shekel (hence the name given to the coin). The values have been estimated as follows: a gold shekel, $5.69; a copper shekel, about 3 cents; and a silver shekel from 54 to 66 cents. One ancient shekel has engraved on one side a pot of manna, or sacred bread, and the inscription "Shekel of Israel"; on the opposite side, a flower, possibly a representation of Aaron's rod that budded, and the words "Jerusalem the Holy" appear. No gold shekels have been found.

The so-called "shekel of the sanctuary" (Ex. 30:13), also known as the temple tax, was believed by many scholars until recent times to be a special coinage. It is now believed to have been the standard shekel weight.

Before coins were used in commerce, the precious metals were weighed (see, for example, 2 Chr. 3:9) and thus the terms shekel, mina or maneh, and talent referred originally to a weight. In the western parts of Asia the shekel was the basic weight, but uniformity was probably never attained over a wide area, for there were both heavy and light as well as common and royal weights for the shekel. The weight of the Israelitish shekel was about that of an American half dollar, that of the mina was about one pound four ounces, and that of the talent approximately seventy-five pounds.

For a discussion of the weights represented by the shekel, mina, and talent see **weights and measures.** H.O.W.

Shelemiah (shĕl-ê-mī'à) [repaid by Jehovah] 1. A porter at the east entrance to the tabernacle (1 Chr. 26:14). Also called Meshelemiah, Meshullam, and Shallum (see 9:17, 21; and Neh. 12:25).

2. The youngest son of Judah (Gen. 38:5).
3. The father of Hanahiah (Neh. 3:30).
4. The father of Jehucal (Jer. 37:3).
5. Son of Bani (Ezra 10:41).
6. Ancestor of Jehudi (Ezra 10:41).
7. Son of Abdeel, one of those who received orders from Jehoiakim to seize Baruch and Jeremiah, 586 B.C. (Jer. 36:26).

Sheleph (shĕ'lĕf) [a drawing forth] second son of Joktan (Gen. 10:26).

Shelesh (shĕ'lĕsh) [might] son of Helem (1 Chr. 7:35).

Shelomi (shē-lō'mī) [peaceful] father of Ahihud the Asherite, 1450 B.C. (Num. 34:27).

Shelomith (shĕl'ô-mĭth) [peaceful] 1. Daughter of Dibri the Danite, and mother of the man stoned for blasphemy, 1439 B.C. (Lev. 24:11).

2. The daughter of Zerubbabel, after 536 B.C. (1 Chr. 3:19).
3. Chief of the Izharites (1 Chr. 23:18).
4. Descendant of Eliezer the Levite, son of Moses, who was a treasurer under David, before 960 B.C. (1 Chr. 26:25–26).
5. A Gershonite (1 Chr. 23:9).
6. One whose sons returned from Babylon with Ezra (Ezra 8:10).

Shelumiel (shē-lū'mĭ-ĕl) [friend of God] son of Zurishaddai, and prince of the tribe of Simeon at the time of the Exodus (Num. 1:6, 2:12).

Shem (shĕm) [name] the oldest of Noah's sons, born when Noah was 500 years old, married, and childless at the time of the flood (Gen. 5:32). Entered the ark at ninety-eight, and two years after the flood he became the father of Arphazad, and later several other children. With the aid of his brother, Japheth, he covered the nakedness of his father, and for it received the first blessing (Gen. 9:25–27). He died at the age of 600 years. The portion of the earth occupied by his descendants begins at the northwestern extremity with Lydia and includes Syria, Chaldea, parts of Assyria, of Persia, and the Arabian Peninsula. Modern scholars have given the name Shemitic or Semitic to the languages spoken by his real or supposed descendants.

Shema (shē'mà) [report, rumor] 1. A Reubenite (1 Chr. 5:8).

2. Son of Elpaal (1 Chr. 8:13).
3. One of those who stood at Ezra's right hand when he read the Law to the people, 445 B.C. (Neh. 8:4).

Shemaah (shē-mā'à) [report, rumor] a Benjaminite of Gibeah, and father of Ahiezer, 1002 B.C. (1 Chr. 12:3).

Shemaiah (shē-mā'yà) [Jehovah has heard] 1. A prophet in the reign of Rehoboam (1 K. 12:22).

2. Son of Shechaniah (1 Chr. 3:22).
3. A prince of the tribe of Simeon (1 Chr. 4:27).
4. Son of Joel, a Reubenite, about 700 B.C. (1 Chr. 5:4).
5. Son of Hassbub (1 Chr. 9:14).
6. Father of Obadiah, a Levite (1 Chr. 9:16).
7. Son of Elizaphan (1 Chr. 15:8).
8. Son of Nethaneel, and also a scribe (1 Chr. 24:6).
9. Oldest son of Obed-edom (1 Chr. 26:4).
10. A descendant of Jeduthun the singer (2 Chr. 29:14).
11. One of the sons of Adonikam who returned with Ezra (Ezra 8:13).
12. One of Ezra's messengers (Ezra 8:16).
13. A priest of the family of Harim, who put away his foreign wife at Ezra's bidding, 458 B.C. (Ezra 10:21).
14. Son of another Harim who had also married a foreigner (Ezra 10:31).
15. Son of Delaiah, a prophet in the time of Nehemiah (Neh. 6:10).
16. The head of a priestly house who signed the covenant with Nehemiah (Neh. 10:8).
17. One of the princes of Judah at the time

of the dedication of the wall of Jerusalem, 446 B.C. (Neh. 12:34).

18. One of the singers on the same occasion (Neh. 12:36).

19. A priest (Neh. 12:42).

20. A false prophet in the time of Jeremiah (Jer. 29:24–32).

21. A Levite in the reign of Jehoshaphat, 909 B.C. (2 Chr. 17:8).

22. A Levite in the reign of Hezekiah, 726 B.C. (2 Chr. 31:15).

23. A Levite in the reign of Josiah, 628 B.C. (2 Chr. 35:9).

24. The father of Urijah, 608 B.C. (Jer. 26:20).

25. Father of Delaiah, 605 B.C. (Jer. 26:12).

Shemariah (shĕm-à-rī′à) [kept by Jehovah] 1. One of the Benjaminite warriors who came to David at Ziklag, 1054 B.C. (1 Chr. 12:5).

2. A member of Harim's family who put away his foreign wife in Ezra's time, 658 B.C. (Ezra 10:32).

Shemeber (shĕm-ē′bĕr) [lofty flight] king of Zeboiim, and ally to the king of Sodom when he was attacked by Chedorlaomer, 1912 B.C. (Gen. 14:2).

Shemer (shē′mēr) [preserved] owner of the hill on which the city of Samaria was built (1 K. 16:24).

Shemida (shĕ-mī′dà) [wise] son of Gilead, 1960 B.C. (Num. 26:32). Founder of the Shemidaites.

sheminith (shĕm′ĭ-nĭth) a musical term (1 Chr. 15:21), denoting a certain air, as the eighth, or a certain key in which the Psalm was to be sung.

Shemiramoth (shĕ-mĭr′à-mŏth) [name most high] 1. A Levite musician in David's choir (1 Chr. 15:18–20).

2. A Levite in the reign of Jehoshaphat, 909 B.C. (2 Chr. 17:8).

Shemri (shĕm′rī) [watchful] 1. A Simeonite, son of Shemaiah, 1450 B.C. (1 Chr. 4:37).

2. Father of Jediael, one of David's guards (1 Chr. 11:45).

3. A Kohathite Levite in Hezekiah's day (2 Chr. 29:13).

Shemrith (shĭm′rĭth) [vigilant] a Moabitess, mother of Jehozabad, one of the assassins of King Joash (2 Chr. 24:26).

Shemuel (shĕ-mū′ĕl) [heard of God] 1. A commissioner appointed from the tribe of Simeon to divide the land of Canaan, 1450 B.C. (1 Chr. 7:2).

Shenazer (shē-nă′zàr) [splendid leader] son of Salathiel, 1014 B.C. (1 Chr. 3:18).

Shepham (shē′făm) [fruitful] a place on the

eastern border of Canaan (Num. 34:10–11).

Shephatiah (shĕf-à-tī′à) [judged of Jehovah] 1. Fifth son of David, about 1050 B.C. (2 Sam. 3:4).

2. The family of Shephatiah, 372 in number, returned with Zerubbabel, 536 B.C. (Ezra 2:4).

3. Last son of Jehoshaphat (2 Chr. 21:2–3).

4. Son of Reuel, a Benjaminite chief dwelling in Jerusalem when the city fell, 536 B.C. (1 Chr. 9:8).

5. The Haruphite, who joined David in his retreat, 1002 B.C. (1 Chr. 12:5).

6. Son of Maachah, prince of the Simeonites in David's time, 960 B.C. (1 Chr. 27:16).

7. A descendant of Perez, before 536 B.C. (Neh. 11:4).

8. Son of Mattan, prince of Judah, who counseled Zedekiah to imprison Jeremiah, 589 B.C. (Jer. 28:1).

shepherd [one who tends] shepherds are common to all society from the earliest days. They tended the flocks, leading them out to pasture, going before them to protect and to guide, keeping watch over them, calling to them, searching for the lost, rescuing and caring for the wayward, and bringing them in at night. With the use of dogs at times (Job 30:1) and with a staff at all times, the shepherd kept the sheep in one flock. He counted them by passing them "under the rod" (Lev. 27:32) as they entered the sheepfold. He usually slept in the door to guard the sheep during the night. Tenderness was a requirement (Isa. 40:11). Sometimes in larger herds there were classes or grades of shepherds (Gen. 47:6), and some were called the "chief shepherds" (1 Pet. 5:4). The life of a shepherd was filled with hardship and danger, especially the life of a nomad, or roving shepherd who lived with his sheep, and drifting with the water and range. Those who tended sheep that were brought back to the same place each night had an easier task. The nomad shepherd existed off the land, eating the wild fruit, carob beans, sycamore fruit, or locusts. He encountered all the beasts of prey (1 Sam. 17:34; Isa. 31:4; Jer. 5:6), and dealt with robbers as well (Gen. 31:39). He clothed himself with the fleece of the sheep, carried a sling (1 Sam. 17:40), and a staff (Ps. 23:4), and occasionally a tent (Jer. 35:7). Shepherds built stone towers on promontories and hilltops to serve as watchtowers both against enemies and for the protection of the sheep (2 Chr. 26:10). Sometimes shepherds slept in caves, but most often, under the stars.

Shephi (shē'fī) [bareness] son of Shobal (1 Chr. 1:40).

Shephuphan (shĕ-fū'făn) [an adder] son of Bela, grandson of Benjamin (1 Chr. 8:5).

Sherah (shē'rà) [kinswoman] daughter of Ephraim (1 Chr. 7:24). Founder of the Beth-horons and a town called Uzzen-sherah.

Sherebiah (shĕr-ê-bī'à) [heat of Jehovah] a Levite in the time of Ezra (Ezra 8:18–24). He assisted Ezra in reading the Law, and signed the covenant with Nehemiah, 459 B.C. (Neh. 10:12).

Sheresh (shē'rĕsh) [root] son of Machir, before 1419 B.C. (1 Chr. 7:16).

Sheshach (shē'shăk) supposedly a symbolic name for Babylon (Jer. 25:26, 51:41).

Sheshai (shē'shī) [whitish] one of the sons of Anak of Hebron, 1445 B.C. (Num. 13:22).

Sheshan (shē'shăn) [noble] a descendant of Jerahmeel (1 Chr. 2:31).

Sheshbazzar (shĕsh-băz'ẽr) [fire worshiper] the Persian name given to Zerubbabel (Ezra 1:8, 11).

Shethar (shē'thàr) [a star] a prince of Persia and Media, 483 B.C. (Est. 1:14).

Shethar-boznai (shē'thàr-bŏz'ê-nī) a Persian officer in the reign of Darius, 320 B.C. (Ezra 5:3, 6).

Sheva (shē'và) [Jehovah contends] 1. A scribe of David (2 Sam. 20:25).

2. Son of Caleb ben-Hezron, 1445 B.C. (1 Chr. 2:49).

shibboleth (shĭb'bō-lĕth) [a stream] used as a password by the Gileadites under Jephthah at the passage of the Jordan, after a victory over the Ephraimites, to test the pronunciation of the "sh" sound by those who wished to cross. The Ephraimites evidently could not pronounce the sound, and were put to death as they attempted and failed; 42,000 of them fell (Judg. 12:6).

Shicron (shĭk'rŏn) [drunkenness] a landmark town at the western end of the north boundary of Judah (Josh. 15:11).

shield see **armor**

Shihon (shī'hŏn) [ruin] a town of Issachar (Josh. 19:19).

Shihor-libnath (shī'hŏr-lĭb'năth) [black of whiteness] one of the landmarks on the boundary of Asher (Josh. 19:26). Probably a small stream which enters the Mediterranean south of Athlit, now called Wadi en-Nebra.

Shilhi (shĭl'hī) [armed] father of Azubah, 946 B.C. (1 K. 22:42).

Shilhim (shĭl'hĭm) [fountains] a city in the southern portion of the tribe of Judah (Josh. 15:32).

Shillem (shĭl'ĕm) [requital] son of Naphtali (Gen. 46:24).

Shiloah (shī'lō) the name of a person in Gen. 49:10. The meaning of the word is "peaceful." It may refer to the expected Messiah, who in Isa. 9:6 is called the Prince of Peace.

Shiloah, the waters of a certain soft-flowing stream (Isa. 8:6), better known as the waters of Siloam, the only perennial spring in Jerusalem.

Shiloh (shī'lō) Judges 21:19 carefully locates Shiloh as "north of Bethel, on the east of the highway that goes up from Bethel to Shechem, and south of Lebonah." This ancient site was excavated by Danish expeditions in 1926, 1929, and 1932. It is identified with present-day Seilun, which is located on a moderate hill nine miles north of Bethel and three miles southeast of el-Lubban.

Shiloh's chief importance was as the location of the "tent of the meeting," the tabernacle. Joshua moved it here after the conquest of Canaan had been completed (Josh. 18:1). Here it remained during the period of the Judges and Shiloh became the principal center of worship in Israel. Many Israelites such as Elkanah made annual visits to this religious center for sacrifice and worship (1 Sam. 1:3).

Most likely Shiloh was destroyed following the devastating defeat the Philistines visited upon the Israelites during Eli's time (1 Sam. 4:1–22). Eli's corrupt sons were killed and the ark of the covenant was taken by the Philistine army. It is significant that Samuel's judgeship was centered in Ramah not Shiloh (1 Sam. 7:17). Jeremiah later cited the ruins of Shiloh as evidence of God's punishment (Jer. 7:12). Archaeological excavations have confirmed that Shiloh was destroyed about 1050 B.C. and sank into insignificance.   J.S.

Shilonites, the (shī'lō-nīts) mentioned among the descendants of Judah dwelling in Jerusalem (1 Chr. 9:5). Doubtless the members of the house of Shelah, who in the Pentateuch are more accurately designated as Shelanites.

Shilshah (shĭl'shà) [strong] son of Zophah, 1015 B.C. (1 Chr. 7:37).

Shimea (shĭm'ê-à) [fame] 1. Son of David by Bath-shua, 1045 B.C. (1 Chr. 3:5).

2. A Merarite Levite (1 Chr. 6:30).

3. A Gerhonite Levite (1 Chr. 6:39).

4. Brother of David (1 Chr. 20:7).

Shimeah (shĭm'ê-à) 1. Brother of David and father of Jonathan and Jonadab (2 Sam. 21:21).

2. A descendant of Mikloth, 536 B.C. (1 Chr. 8:32).

Shimeam (shĭm′ê-ăm) a descendant of Mikloth (1 Chr. 9:38).

Shimeath an Ammoritess, mother of the murderer of Joash (2 K. 12:21).

Shimei (shĭm′ê-ī) [renowned] 1. Son of Gershon, 1706 B.C. (Num. 3:18).

2. Son of Gera, a Benjaminite of the house of Saul, who lived at Bahurim (2 Sam. 16:5). When David, in his flight from Absalom, had come to Bahurim, Shimei met him with curses and stones. Abismai requested of David that he be allowed to "take off his head," but David would not allow it because, he said, "It may be that the Lord will look on mine affliction, and that the Lord will requite me good for his cursing this day." David and his company passed on, Shimei cursing him until he went out of sight (2 Sam. 16:5-13). Later, when David returned, triumphantly, just as he was crossing the Jordan, the first person to welcome him was Shimei, who threw himself at David's feet in abject repentance. David did not forget this scene, and on his deathbed recounted it in detail to his son Solomon. Solomon confined Shimei to the walls of Jerusalem on pain of death (1 K. 2:36-37). For three years this arrangement was kept, but at the end of it, for the purpose of capturing two slaves who had escaped to Gath, he went out on his ass, and made his journey successfully. When he returned, the king took him at his word, and he was slain by Benaiah, 1023 B.C. (1 K. 2:40, 41-46).

3. One of the adherents of Solomon at the time of Adonijah's usurpation, 1015 B.C. (1 K. 1:8).

4. Son of Pedaiah, and brother of Zerubbabel, 536 B.C. (1 Chr. 3:19).

5. Solomon's commissariat officer in Benjamin (1 K. 4:18).

6. A Simeonite, son of Zacchur (1 Chr. 4:26-27).

7. Son of Gog, a Reubenite (1 Chr. 5:4).

8. A Gershonite Levite (1 Chr. 6:42).

9. Son of Jeduthun (1 Chr. 25:17).

10. The Ramathite who was over David's vineyards (1 Chr. 27:27).

11. A Levite of the sons of Heman, who took part in the purification of the temple, 726 B.C. (2 Chr. 29:14).

12. Brother of Cononiah the Levite (2 Chr. 31:12-13).

13. A Levite in the time of Ezra who had married a foreign wife (Ezra 10:23).

14. One of the family of Hashum, who put away his foreign wife (Ezra 10:33).

15. Son of Bani who had married a foreign wife and put her away (Ezra 10:38).

16. Son of Kish, a Benjaminite and ancestor of Mordecai, 479 B.C. (Est. 2:5).

Shimeon (shĭm′ê-ŏn) [a hearing] a man of the house of Harim, who had married a foreign wife in Ezra's time (Ezra 10:31).

Shimites, the the descendants of Shimei, the son of Gershon (Num. 3:21).

Shimma (shĭm′â) third son of Jesse (1 Chr. 2:13).

Shimon (shī′mŏn) [desert] the four sons of Shimon are enumerated in an obscure genealogy of the tribe of Judah (1 Chr. 4:20).

Shimrath (shĭm′răth) [guard] a Benjaminite (1 Chr. 8:21).

Shimron (shĭm′rŏn) 1. A city of Zebulun (Josh. 11:1, 19:15).

2. The fourth son of Issachar (Gen. 46:13).

Shimron-meron (shĭm′rŏn-mêr′ŏn) [watch] the king of Shimron-meron was one of thirty-one kings vanquished by Joshua (Josh. 12:20).

Shimshai (shĭm′shī) [sunny] the scribe of Rehum who was a petty ruler of the conquered province of Judah and of the colony of Samaria, supported by the Persian court (Ezra 4:8-9, 17, 23).

Shinab (shī′năb) the king of Admah in the time of Abraham (Gen. 14:2).

Shinar (shī′när) the ancient alluvial plain through which the Tigris and Euphrates rivers flowed. Later known as Chaldea, or Babylonia. Brick had to be used for stone, and slime for mortar (Gen. 11:3). No stones were there. The word does not occur in Babylonian inscriptions, but "Sumer" occurs often and may be the same place.

ship shipbuilding is very ancient. The Egyptians were masters at it, and their huge boats plied the Nile carrying stone, while the smaller vessels transported people. Mesopotamia made ships of basketlike construction and lined them with bitumen. The Phoenicians were master shipbuilders, using cedar and oak, and often lavishly adorned them with ivory and boxwood. At least 3000 years of shipbuilding preceded the birth of Christ. Luke supplies us with more information about ships in Jesus' day than any other source. The account of Paul's journey to Rome (Acts 27-28) gives a good insight into merchant shipping. The ship in which Paul was wrecked had 276 persons on board (Acts 27:37), besides a cargo of wheat. Allowing a ton and a half per man, as modern estimates do, we can say that an ancient merchant ship might range from 500 to 1000 tons. Most ships of NT days were steered by two paddle-rudders hinged to the stern at the quarters, and operating in a rowlock or through a porthole as the vessel might be small or large. The imperfection of the workmanship, and unimproved materials resulted in a great tendency to leak and flounder. "Helps" (Acts 27:17), which were usually chains or ropes, were usually taken aboard, and in case of necessity, were passed around the frame of the ship, at right angles to its length, and made tight. The ship on which Paul sailed had four anchors and the ship anchored by the stern. The rig of an ancient ship was more simple and clumsy than in modern times. The main feature was one large mast, with one large square sail fastened to a yard of great length. This same general unit of rig was sometimes multiplied as in a two-mast or three-mast ship. The ancients had no compass, and very imperfect maps. They usually stayed within sight of land when possible, and were guided by the stars through the open seas.

Shiphi (shĭ'fī) [abounding] a Simeonite, a prince in the time of Hezekiah, 726 B.C. (1 Chr. 4:37).

Shiphrah (shĭf'rà) [beauty] one of the midwives of the Hebrews who disobeyed the command of Pharaoh to kill the male children, 1570 B.C. (Ex. 1:15).

Shiphtan (shĭf'tàn) [judicial] father of Kemuel, a prince of the tribe of Ephraim, 1450 B.C. (Num. 34:24).

Shisha (shĭ'shà) [Jehovah contends] father of Elihoreph, royal secretary under Solomon (1 K. 4:3). He is apparently the same as Shavsha, secretary under David, 960 B.C.

Shishak (shĭ'shăk) an Egyptian pharaoh (also known as Sheshonk I) who founded the Twenty-second Dynasty and ruled from ca. 940 to 915 B.C. His most notable achievement was his invasion of Palestine and his plunder of Jerusalem (1 K. 14:25–26; 2 Chr. 12:1–12).

Rising from obscure origins, Shishak took advantage of the weakness of the central government of Egypt and became a powerful local ruler at Bubastis. There he gained a standing for himself equal to that of the pharaoh at Thebes. He extended his influence still further by having his son named high priest of Amon at Thebes and by promoting his son's marriage to the daughter of the last pharaoh of the old dynasty. By these maneuvers he gradually concentrated the entire rule of Egypt in his own hands.

He is most likely not the pharaoh whose daughter married Solomon (1 K. 3:1), although some speculation has favored this view. It is highly improbable that Shishak would have provided asylum for Jeroboam when he fled to Egypt to escape Solomon's attempts to kill him, if Solomon had been Shishak's son-in-law (1 K. 11:26, 40).

In the fifth year of Rehoboam's reign (ca. 926 B.C.), Shishak led a vigorous campaign into Palestine and seized more than 150 cities. Fifty to sixty of them were in Israel and the remainder in Judah. There is no clear evidence that he took sides with either Jeroboam or Rehoboam in their dispute over the divided kingdom. On the contrary, Shishak appears to have taken advantage of the division to wage war with impartial fury against both. From Jerusalem he carried away the treasures of the temple and of Solomon's palace. He dedicated some of the loot to the temple of Amon at Thebes.

Considering this campaign against Palestine the most memorable victory of his rule, Shishak caused the erection of the triumphal Bubastite gate at the temple of Amon at Karnak. From it archaeologists have gathered a list of the cities that he conquered in Palestine. The victory inscription also bears the notation that the Egyptians had taken the "field of Abraham."

At the stone quarry at Megiddo, where material for the gate was obtained, archaeologists have found a damaged stela that records Shishak's war against Rehoboam and Jeroboam. A partially preserved statue at Gebal in Phoenicia lists the towns that were seized in the invasion.

P. Montel located Shishak's grave at Bubastis in 1938. Although his dynasty continued for two hundred years, none of his successors rose above mediocrity. H.A.W.

shittah, shittim tree (shĭt'ĭm) there is little doubt that the shittim tree was some species of acacia. The wood of this tree was more extensively employed in the construction of the tabernacle (see Ex. 25–26, 36–38). It grows to three or four feet in diameter, and is close-grained and very hard. It is orange-brown in color and well adapted to cabinet work.

Shittim (shĭt'ĭm) [the acacias] the place of Israel's encampment between the highlands and the Jordan. It was the place from which Joshua sent spies into Canaan (Num. 25:1, 33:49; Josh. 2:1–3).

Shiza (shĭ'zà) a Reubenite, father of Adina, 1043 B.C. (1 Chr. 11:42).

Shoa (shō'à) [rich] a district of Assyria in which the southern kingdom of Judah had been intimately connected, and which was arrayed against it for punishment (Ezek. 23:23).

Shobab (shō'băb) [rebellious] 1. Son of David by Bath-sheba (2 Sam. 5:14).

2. Apparently the son of Caleb, the son of Hezron (1 Chr. 2:18).

357

Shobach (shō'băk) [expansion] the general of Hadarezer, king of Syria who defeated David (2 Sam. 10:15-18).

Shobai (shō'bī) [glorious] the children of Shobai were a family of doorkeepers of the temple who returned with Zerubbabel, 526 B.C. (Ezra 2:42).

Shobal (shō'băl) [flowing] 1. Second son of Seir the Horite (Gen. 36:20).

2. Son of Caleb, the son of Hur, and founder of Kirjath-jearim, 1445 B.C. (1 Chr. 2:50-52).

Shobek (shō'běk) [free] one of the heads of the people who sealed the covenant with Nehemiah, 446 B.C. (Neh. 10:24).

Shobi (shō'bī) [glorious] son of Nahash of Rabbah, of the children of Ammon, 1023 B.C. (2 Sam. 17:27).

Shoham (shō'hăm) [onyx] a Merarite Levite, son of Jaaziah, 1043 B.C. (1 Chr. 24:27).

Shomer (shō'mēr) [keeper] 1. An Asherite (1 Chr. 7:32).

2. The father of Jehozabad, who slew King Joash (2 K. 12:21).

Shophach (shō'făk) [expansion] a general of Hadarezer (1 Chr. 19:16).

Shophan (shō'făn) [bareness] a fortified town east of Jordan which was possessed by Gad (Num. 32:35).

shoshannim (shō'shăn'ĭm) [lilies] a musical direction to the leader of the temple singers (Ps. 45, 69).

showbread (shō'brĕd) Ex. 25:30, 35:13, 39:36; literally "bread of the face" or "presence." Showbread was placed on a table which stood with the seven-branched candlesticks and altar of incense in the sanctuary. The table was of shittim wood (acacia) and was two cubits long, one cubit wide, and one and a half cubits high. It was overlaid with gold and had a golden crown a handbreadth wide for the border, probably to prevent items from falling off. On the table were also golden dishes, spoons, and bowls (Ex. 25:23-29). Philo and Clement of Alexandria believe that the four sides or legs of the table symbolized the four seasons.

Seemingly this table was in the sanctuary of all three temples. Solomon's temple had "the tables whereon the showbread was set," according to 2 Chr. 4:19. Ezekiel 41:22 includes the table in the plans which Zerubbabel followed in restoring the temple. Antiochus Epiphanes took the table from this second temple, but Judas Maccabeus replaced it when he cleansed and refurnished the temple. The bas relief on the Arch of Titus represents the table among the spoils taken from the Herodian temple. The details of the table in this sculpture correspond to the Exodus description. For instance, the breadth of the border of the table is about the same as that of the hand of one of the slaves carrying the table.

Every sabbath the priests placed twelve newly baked loaves on the table in two rows of six and sprinkled them with incense. On the following sabbath they would bring new loaves and eat the old in the sanctuary, from which they were not to be removed. The special recipe for these loaves is given in Lev. 24:5-9. No mention is made of leaven, and post-Biblical authorities (Josephus, Philo, and the Talmud) state that the bread was unleavened.

The terms referring to the showbread represent various meaningful facts about it. The most frequently used, *lechem panim*, means the "bread of the face or presence" and likely refers to it as an offering to the Presence of God or the Holy Shechinah (Ex. 25:30). "Bread of the ordering" (*lechem maareketh*) refers to the arrangement of the loaves in rows (1 Chr. 9:32). "Holy bread" (*lechem kodish*) contrasts it to common bread (1 Sam. 21:5). "Continual bread" (*lechem hattamid*) refers to its being always on the table (2 Chr. 2:4). The Greek term, *prothesis ton arton*, depicts the ritual of "setting forth of the loaves" (Heb. 9:2).

Philo and Josephus both feel that the twelve loaves represented the twelve months; obviously, however, they represented the twelve tribes (cf. Rev. 22:2). Cyril of Jerusalem treats the showbread as a type of the Eucharist. Clement of Alexandria feels that the mystical meaning of the bread concerns God's nourishing of his people and that it signifies "the communion of the saints." J.S.

Shuah (shoo'ȧ) [wealth] 1. Son of Abraham, 1820 B.C. (Gen. 25:2).

2. Father of Judah's wife (Gen. 38:2).

Shual (shoo'ăl) [jackal] son of Zophah, an Aherite (1 Chr. 7:36).

Shual, Land of a district north of Michmash. Not positively identified (1 Sam. 13:17).

Shubael (shoo'bâ-ĕl) 1. The son of Gershon (1 Chr. 24:20).

2. Son of Heman (1 Chr. 25:20).

Shuhite (shoo'hīt) frequent in the book of Job, applying only to Bildad. Nothing is known positively of the tribe, except that it was near the land of Uz (Job 2:11). Assyrian Suhu, on the west of the Euphrates near the mouth of the Balikh, is a likely identification.

Shulamite (shoo'lăm-īt) [peaceful] evidently derived from Shunam, a town near Mount Gilboa. It is the name applied to a woman in Song of S. 6:13.

Shunammite, the a native of Shunem. Applied to two persons: Abishag, the nurse of King David (1 K. 1:3), and the nameless hostess of Elisha (2 K. 4:12).

Shunem (shoo'něm) [double] one of the cities allotted to Issachar (Josh. 19:18). Eusebius says it was five miles south of Mount Tabor. This agrees with the present Solam, a village three miles north of Jezreel, and five from Gilboa.

Shuni (shoo'nī) [fortunate] son of Gad and founder of the Shunites, 1706 B.C. (Gen. 46:16).

Shuppim (shŭp'ĭm) [serpents] the great-grandson of Benjamin (1 Chr. 7:12).

Shur (shoor) [a wall] a place just outside Egypt. Mentioned in the narrative of Hagar's flight from Sarah (Gen. 16:7). Abraham later dwelt between Kadesh and Shur (Gen. 20:1). It is also called Ethami. The wilderness of Shur was entered by the Israelites after they had crossed the Red Sea (Ex. 15:22-23). It is also called the wilderness of Etham (Num. 33:8). Since there was a great wall across the northeastern boundary of Egypt, built as a defense against her enemies, it is reasonable that Shur [meaning, wall] was a passage point in that wall.

Shushan (shoo'shăn) [lily] the capital of Elam, and in the time of Daniel in the possession of the Babylonians. The conquest of Babylon by Cyrus transferred Shushan, or Susa, to the Persian rule. It soon became capital of their empire. Because of the great abundance of lilies, it must have been a beautiful place. The city has been excavated and signs of occupation reach back to 4000 B.C. It was explored by a French group in 1884-86 and its occupancy as late as A.D. 1200 was established. The Code of Hammurabi was unearthed at Shushan by another Frenchman in 1901. A winter residence of Persian kings, the city lay 150 miles up the river from the Persian Gulf. The palace of Belshazzar was there, and Daniel's visions came there. The great palace of Darius I, built of cedar from Lebanon and silver from Egypt, can be seen in the ruins of the city. Few archaeological discoveries have been more rich, or shed more light on ancient history than those at Shushan.

Shuthelah (shoo'thē-là) [noise of breaking] head of an Ephraimite family called after him (Num. 26:35).

Sia (sī'à) a man of Nethinim who returned with Zerubbabel (Neh. 7:47).

Sibbechai (sĭb'ē-kī) [a weaver] one of David's guard, and eighth captain of the eighth month of 24,000 men (1 Chr. 11:29). His single combat with the Philistine giant, in the battle at Gezer, stands out (2 Sam. 21:18; 1 Chr. 20:4).

Sibraim (sĭb'rĭm) [twofold hope] one of the landmarks on the northern boundary of the Holy Land as stated by Ezekiel (Ezek. 47:16).

Siddim, Vale of (sĭd'ĭm) scene of the battle between Chedorlaomer and the five confederate kings (Gen. 14:3). It contained bitumen pits which vitally affected the outcome of the battle. Usually accepted to be the flat promontory projecting into the east side of the Dead Sea. This area was submerged about 2000 B.C., along with the cities of Sodom, Gomorrah, Admah, Zeboim, and Bela.

Sidon (sī'dŏn) an ancient Phoenician city built on the mainland and upon a small island connected by a bridge. It was twenty miles north of Tyre. Mentioned in Gen. 10:15, it must have been one of the most ancient of cities. Its modern name is Saida. From the days of Solomon to the invasion from Babylon, the town is seldom mentioned, and seems to have been of little importance. Its trade was grain and slaves (Jer. 25:22). During the Persian domination, Sidon reached its highest point on prosperity, and excelled all other Phoenician cities. An unsuccessful revolt against Persia ended in its destruction in 351 B.C. The king proved a traitor and delivered the city to the Persians, and Persian troops were admitted within the gates. The Sidonians had burned their vessels to prevent anyone's leaving the city, and when they saw themselves surrounded by the Persian troops, they shut themselves up with their families and set fire each man to his own house. Some 40,000 persons are said to have perished in the flames.

Sidonians see **Zidonians**

Sihon (sī'hŏn) [warrior] king of the Amorites when Israel arrived on the border of Canaan, 1451 B.C. (Num. 21:21). Earlier he had dispossessed the Moabites, driving them south of Arnon. When Israel appeared, he immediately gathered his army and attacked them. This battle was his last. He and all his host were destroyed, and their district, from Arnon to Jabbok, became the possession of the Israelites.

Sihor (sī'hôr) [dark] a name applied to the Nile, indicating its black, muddy, or turpid condition (Jer. 2:18).

Silas (sī'làs) he first appears as one of the leaders of the church in Jerusalem (Acts 15:22), and possibly an inspired teacher (Acts 15:32). His name Silvanus (in Paul's epistles) indicates that he was a Hellenistic Jew, and he appears to have been a Roman citizen (Acts 16:37). He was selected by the elders at Jerusalem to accompany Paul and Barnabas on their return to Antioch with the decree of the apostles and elders (Acts 15:22–32). Having accomplished his mission, he returned to Jerusalem. He was soon in Antioch again, and chosen by Paul to accompany him on the second missionary journey (Acts 15:40, 17:10). At Berea he was left behind with Timothy while Paul proceeded to Athens (Acts 17:14). He rejoined Paul at Corinth (Acts 18:5). That he spent much time at Corinth is evidenced by these references: 2 Cor. 1:19; 1 Thess. 1:1; 2 Thess. 1:1.

silk listed among the treasures of the fallen Babylon (Rev. 18:12). No other unquestioned reference to silk is made in the Bible, but it was a valuable article of trade in the Roman world in NT times and was probably known to the Hebrews from the time of Solomon. Silk is produced by the silkworm, which feeds on mulberry leaves. The production of silk apparently originated in China and spread to Korea, Japan, and India.   L.D.F.

Siloam, pool of Siloam is one of the few undisputed localities in the whole of Palestine. It still retains its old name with Arabic modification, Silwan. The pool is a subterranean spring, reached in ancient times by "the stairs that go down from the city of David." Though it is meager in its supply of water today, Josephus describes it as sweet and abundant. It is located at the mouth of the valley of the Cheesemongers, or the Tyropoeon valley, where the old Jerusalem wall bends east. Jesus sent a blind man from the temple to wash in it (Jn. 9:7). An early engineering feat was the hewing of a conduit through seventeen hundred feet of solid rock to bring water from the Virgin's pool, or spring, to feed the pool of Siloam. This pool was the only spring of fresh water near Jerusalem, and in time of war or siege it was imperative that the enemy should be deprived of the use of its waters, and that the citizens should have them. Thus the conduit (2 Chr. 32:3–4). A natural siphon from some underground basin causes the waters of the Virgin's pool to overflow at intervals. During the wet season these overflows are more frequent; in dry seasons the intervals may be several days apart. This sudden overflow is referred to in John 9. The tunnel connecting the Virgin's pool with the pool of Siloam was begun with workmen working from each end. They were guided by the sound of the picks of the other workers, and when they broke through they were only a few feet apart. An inscription on the passage, discovered by accident in 1880, relates the building of the tunnel.

Siloam, Tower of this tower, evidently so well known to the disciples, and those who heard

the Lord, it needed no further identification, is completely unfamiliar to scholars of today. Our only reference is in Lk. 13:4 in which Jesus said it fell and slew eighteen people.

silver one of the elements which is found in nature as the free metal and has been known from earliest times. It was generally more valuable than gold until about 500 B.C. when it became more abundant. Abraham was rich in silver (Gen. 13:2) and it was used by him as a medium of exchange (Gen. 23:16). The Bible contains numerous references to the use of silver as money (Ex. 21:32; Judg. 17:10; Mt. 26:15). It was used for ornamental objects such as jewelry (Gen. 24:53) and as a precious metal in the tabernacle (Ex. 26:19) and in the temple (1 Chr. 28:15–16). It was commonly used in idol worship in both OT and NT times (Deut. 29:17; Acts 19:24). The testing of men's hearts is compared to the refining of silver (Ps. 66:10; Isa. 48:10). The intrinsic value of silver is used to emphasize the much greater value of wisdom (Prov. 3:14).   L.D.F.

Simeon (sĭm'ē-ŭn) 1. The second son of Jacob by Leah (Gen. 29:33). Leah's other three sons were Reuben, Levi, and Judah. Simeon was associated with Levi in the massacre of the Shechemites (Gen. 34:24–31) and was selected by Joseph as the hostage for the appearance of Benjamin (Gen. 42:19, 24, 36, 43:23). The chief families of the tribe of Simeon are mentioned in Gen. 46:10. In the census at Sinai the tribe numbered 59,300 fighting men (Num. 1:23), but by the second census at Shittim, the number had diminished to 22,200, the weakest of all the tribes. At the distribution of the land of Canaan the tribe of Simeon received the extreme southern portion containing some eighteen or nineteen cities, with their villages, encompassing the venerable well of Beer-sheba (Josh. 19:1–8; 1 Chr. 4:28–33). With the help of Judah, the Simeonites possessed these places (Judg. 1:3, 17) and were found here, most likely by Joab, during the reign of David (1 Chr. 4:31). The presence of Simeonites in the Northern Kingdom may be implied by 2 Chr. 15:9, 34:6, but the definite statement of 1 Chr. 4:41–43 proves that at that time there were still some remaining in the original seat of the tribe.

2. An ancestor of Jesus, in the Lucan genealogy (Lk. 3:30).

3. A devout Jew to whom the Holy Spirit revealed that he should not die until he had seen the Messiah. When Jesus was brought to the temple by his parents, Simeon took him into his arms and praised God (Lk. 2:25–35).

This canticle is often called the Nunc Dimittis.

F.D.D.

Simeon Niger (Acts 13:1) see **Niger**

Simon (sī'mŭn) 1. *Simon the Brother of Jesus.* The only undoubted notice of this Simon occurs in Mt. 13:55 and Mk. 6:3. Attempts have been made to identify this Simon with Simon the Canaanite and with Symeon, a prominent Jerusalem leader after A.D. 62, but such attempts are difficult to substantiate.

2. *Simon the Canaanite.* One of the twelve apostles (Mt. 10:4; Mk. 3:18), otherwise described as Simon Zelotes (Lk. 6:15; Acts 1:13). The latter term, which is peculiar to Luke, is the Greek equivalent for the Aramaic term preserved by Matthew and Mark [Canaanite]. Each of these equally points out Simon as belonging to the faction of the Zealots who were conspicuous for their fierce advocacy of the Mosaic ritual.

3. *Simon of Cyrene.* A Hellenistic Jew, born at Cyrene, on the north coast of Africa, who was present at Jerusalem at the time of the crucifixion of Jesus, either as an attendant at the feast (Acts 2:10), or as one of the numerous settlers at Jerusalem from that place (Acts 6:9). Meeting the procession that conducted Jesus to Golgotha, as he was returning from the country, he was pressed into the service to bear the cross (Mt. 27:32; Mk. 15:21; Lk. 23:26) when Jesus himself was unable to carry it any longer (cf. Jn. 19:17). Mark describes him as the father of Alexander and Rufus, perhaps because this was the Rufus known to the Roman Christians (Rom. 16:13) for whom he more especially wrote.

4. *Simon the Leper.* A resident of Bethany, distinguished as "the leper." It is possible that he had been miraculously cured by Jesus. It was in his house that Mary anointed Jesus preparatory to his death and burial (Mt. 26:6–13; Mk. 14:3–9; Jn. 12:1–8).

5. *Simon Magus.* A sorcerer at Samaria, with great power and influence among the citizenry (Acts 8:9–13). He believed and was baptized as a result of the preaching of Philip. Greatly impressed by the divine power demonstrated in Philip and subsequently witnessing the effect produced by the imposition of hands, as practiced by the apostles Peter and John, he offered them a sum of money to buy this power for himself. This request met with severe denunciation from Peter with the exhortation to repent and pray for forgiveness. In response Simon petitioned prayer on his behalf (Acts 8:14–24). The memory of his peculiar guilt has been perpetuated in the word "simony," as applied to all traffic in spiritual offices. There

are many legends concerning the subsequent activities of Simon which generally associate him with heresy and magical demonstrations but it is difficult to establish their validity.

6. *Simon Peter* see **Peter**

7. *Simon.* A Pharisee, in whose house a penitent woman anointed the head and feet of Jesus (Lk. 7:36–50).

8. *Simon the Tanner.* A Christian convert living at Joppa, at whose house Peter lodged (Acts 9:43, 10:6, 32).

9. *Simon the Father of Judas Iscariot* (Jn. 6:71, 13:2, 26). F.D.D.

Simri (sĭm'rī) [vigilant] son of Hosah, a Merarite Levite in the reign of David (1 Chr. 26:10).

Sin a city of Egypt (Ezek. 30:15–16). It is identified in the Vulg. with Pelusium, meaning muddy town. Herodotus relates that Sennacherib advanced against Pelusium, and that near it Cambyses defeated Psammenitus.

Sin, Wilderness of the vast wilderness reached by the Israelites after leaving the encampment by the Red Sea (Num. 33:11–12). In the wilderness of Sin, the manna was first gathered. The wilderness lay along the eastern shore of the Red Sea, and is thought to be the plain of El-Kaa today (Ex. 16:1, 17:1).

Sinai (sī'nī) nearly in the center of the peninsula which stretches between the horns of the Red Sea lies a wedge of granite, rising almost 9300 feet above the sea. Its name is Sinai. Here the children of Israel came to receive the Ten Commandments, soon after their departure from Egypt. The mountain mass is divided into two masses—that of Jebel Serbal, a 6759-foot heap of ravine cut, thorn-infested rock to the northwest, and the central group known as Sinai. Chief peaks in this group are Jebel Musa (Mount of Moses) and Jebel Katerin (Mount Catherine). Both are backed up and overshadowed by Um Shamer, a 9300-foot peak. These mountains are called Horeb, and sometimes Sinai. There is a great controversy over which of the names refers to the mountain range and which to an individual peak. There are numerous references to "in Horeb" which seem to lend weight to the claim that Horeb refers to the range (see Ex. 3:1, 17:6, 19:2, 33:6; 1 K. 8:9; 2 Chr. 5:10; Ps. 106:19; Mal. 4:4). The actual scene of the giving of the Law is unknown. It could have been any one of the peaks, or none of them. However, there are some things to be said in favor of Jebel Musa. It is a mountain mass two miles long and a mile wide. The southern peak is 7363 feet high; the northern peak is 6830 feet high. It is in full view of the plain of Ramah, where the Israelites were encamped. This plain is a natural camping ground about two miles long and half a mile wide and comprises one of the best natural amphitheaters on earth. In addition, the air is wonderfully clear. There is no other place in all these mountains so well adapted for the giving and receiving of the Law.

Sinim (sī'nĭm) a people mentioned in Isa. 49:12 as living at the extremity of the known world. Some think they are Hindu-Kush people that inhabited the southern part of China.

Sinites (sī'nīts) a tribe of Canaanites (Gen. 10:17; 1 Chr. 1:15).

sin offering the sin offering among the Jews was the sacrifice in which the ideas of propitiation and of atonement for sin were most distinctly marked. The ceremonial of the sin offering is described in Lev. 4 and 6. The trespass offering in Leviticus is closely connected with the sin offering, but at the same time clearly distinguished from it, being in some cases offered with it as a distinct part of the same sacrifice; as, for example, in the cleansing of the leper (Lev. 14). The distinction of ceremonial clearly indicates a difference in the idea of the two sacrifices. The nature of that difference is still a subject of great controversy. Sin offerings were 1. *regular:* (a) for all the people, of the New Moon, Passover, Pentecost, Feast of Trumpets, and Feast of Tabernacles (Num. 28:15–29:38); (b) for the priests and Levites at their consecration (Ex. 29:10–14, 36), besides the yearly offering for the high priest on the Day of Atonement (Lev. 16). 2. *special* for any sin of ignorance (Lev. 4–5). Many breaches of the Law were included in these sins of "ignorance." Josephus says that the sin offering was for those who fall into sin ignorantly, and that the trespass offering was for those who were conscious of their sins.

Sion see **Zion**

Siphmoth (sĭf'mŏth) [fruitful] one of the places in the south of Judea which David frequented during his freebooting life (1 Sam. 30:28).

Sippai (sĭp'ī) [threshold] Saph, one of the sons of Rephaim, or "the giants" slain by Sibbechai at Gezer, 1050 B.C. (1 Chr. 20:4).

Sirah, the Well of (sī'rà) [the turning] a well on the road north of Hebron from which Abner was recalled by Joab to his death at Hebron (2 Sam. 3:26).

Sirion (sĭr'ĭ-ŏn) one of the various names for Mount Hermon (Deut. 3:9).

Sisamai (sĭs'mī) a descendant of Shesham in the line of Jerahmeel.

Sisera (sĭs'ẽr-à) [battle array] 1. Captain of the army of Jabin, king of Canaan, who reigned in Hazor. The particulars of the rout of Megiddo and of Sisera's flight and death are drawn out under the heads of Barak, Deborah, Jael, Kishon, 1296 B.C.

2. After a long interval, the name appears in the list of the returning captives with Zerubbabel (Ezra 2:53).

Sitnah (sĭt'nà) [strife] second of two wells dug by Isaac in the valley of Gezer, the possession of which the herdsmen of the valley disputed with him (Gen. 26:21).

slave the institution of slavery was recognized, though not established by the Mosaic law, with a view to mitigate its hardships and to secure to every man his ordinary rights. Under Hebrew law one who had mortgaged his property might submit to servitude until he had accumulated enough to redeem it. The commission of a theft made one subject to servitude until he had repaid the theft under the provisions of the Law (Ex. 22:1–3). The exercise of parental authority was limited to the sale of a daughter of tender age to be a maidservant, with the ulterior view of her becoming the concubine of the purchaser (Ex. 21:2–7). The term of servitude might be resolved either by the satisfaction of the claim against the servant, the year of Jubilee (Lev. 25:40) or the expiration of six years from the beginning of his servitude (Ex. 21:2). The rabbinists added a fourth: the death of a master without leaving a son to claim the slave. If the servant did not wish to be free, then the master was to take him to the doorpost and pierce his ear with an awl (Ex. 21:6), driving it into the doorpost (Deut. 15:17). A servant thus affixed remained a slave forever (Ex. 21:6). The condition of a Hebrew servant was not bad. Masters were ordered to treat them as hired servants or as sojourners (Lev. 25:39). At his liberation the master was to give to the servant liberally of his flocks, his flour, and his winepress (Deut. 15:13–14).

Non-Hebrew slaves were purchased from slave traders (Lev. 25:44–45), or captured in war (Num. 31:26–28). These remained the chattel property of their masters, and their posterity remained slaves (Gen. 14:14, 17:12). Provision was made for the protection of his person (Ex. 21:20; Lev. 24:17–22) and a minor personal injury was recompensed by giving the slave his liberty. Religious privileges were favorable. The slave was to be circumcised (Gen. 17:12) and hence was qualified to partake of the paschal sacrifice (Ex. 12:44), as well as of the other religious feasts (Deut. 12:12, 18, 16:11).

slime the word slime (in more modern terminology, bitumen or asphalt) refers to a hydrocarbon related to, and usually found to occur with, petroleum and natural gas. It is a lustrous, black solid which burns with a smoky flame. The bitumen is easily melted and is impervious to water so it could be used as mortar in the construction of walls as in Gen. 11:3 or for waterproofing a small boat of reeds as in Ex. 2:3. The soldiers of Sodom and Gomorrah falling into slime pits in the valley of Siddim (Gen. 14:10) could be compared to animals that fell into the La Brea tar (bitumen) pits of Southern California. Bitumen is found in the cretaceous limestone on the west side of the Dead Sea. This occurrence has caused the Dead Sea to be called "the lake of asphalt."　　　　w.k.

Smyrna (smûr'nà) a city of Asia Minor situated on the Aegean Sea, forty miles north of Ephesus. It was founded by Alexander the Great, and was at one time called "the crown of Ionia—the ornament of Asia." Today it has a mixed population of about 200,000 people. The ancient city was inhabited by Christianity-hating Jews whose persecutions caused the church at Smyrna to be called the best of the "seven churches of Asia" in John's Revelation (Rev. 2:8–11). Against this church the Angel brought no word of reproach. At Smyrna, Polycarp labored, lived, and died a martyr (ca. A.D. 169).

snail the term used in Ps. 58:8 denotes either a *linax* or a *helix*, particularly noticeable for the slimy track they leave behind, or the way they waste away in the rocks during the dry season. Listed among unclean animals (Lev. 11:30).

snow during most winters snow falls a few times in Jerusalem, with a rare heavy fall, but usually it does not reach much depth and disappears quickly. The mountains of Lebanon are covered with snow most of the year and it is present on shaded slopes the entire summer. The Bible makes reference to a snowy day (2 Sam. 23:20; 1 Chr. 11:22). The whiteness of snow is used as a symbol of purity (Ps. 51:7; Isa. 1:18). The sinlessness and holiness of Christ are depicted by garments white as snow (Mt. 28:3; Rev. 1:14).　　　　L.D.F.

So (sō) a king of Egypt to whom Hoshea, the last king of Israel, sent messengers, but sent no presents. As a consequence of this act Hoshea was imprisoned, Samaria was conquered, and the ten tribes dispersed.

soap soap in the modern sense was probably relatively unknown in OT times. The Hebrew term *bôrith* designates any substance with cleansing qualities, and as rendered in Jer. 2:22 most likely refers to alkalies extracted from wood ashes or to the ashes themselves. The ashes of several Palestinian desert plants are rich in alkali carbonates. (In fact the ashes are called "el-kali," from which the English alkali is derived.) The cleansing power of the alkali carbonates could be utilized by a direct application of the ashes or by extracting them with water and combining with vegetable fats (e.g., olive oil) to form a simple soap.　　　　w.k.

Socho (sō'kō) a city in the low country of Judah (Josh. 15:35) fortified by Rehoboam after the revolt of the ten tribes (2 Chr. 11:7). Goliath was slain here by David. Also known as Sochoh, Shochoh, Shoco, and Ahocho in the OT. There was a second city of Socho in the mountains of Judah (Josh. 15:35).

Sodi (sō'dī) [intimate] father of Gaddiel, Zebulun's spy, 1440 B.C. (Num. 13:10).

Sodom (sŏ'dŏm) Sodom is the best known of five cities of the plain. The other cities were Gomorrah, Admah, Zeboiim and Zoar. The word is found thirty-six times in the Bible, in sixteen of these it is mentioned alone. Sodom was destroyed because of its wickedness and indeed long after its destruction it has been associated with wickedness and immorality. So great was the sin of Sodom and Gomorrah that God determined to destroy them. The extent of the prevailing immorality is seen in that not ten righteous persons could be found in all of Sodom (Gen. 18:20–33).

"Then the Lord rained on Sodom and Gomorrah brimstone and fire from the Lord out of heaven; and he overthrew those cities, and all the valley, and all the inhabitants of the cities, and what grew on the ground" (Gen. 19:24–25). So great was the destruction that Abraham was able to see the smoke from the cities from his position near Hebron.

There exists a difference of opinion among scholars as to the location of the city of Sodom. The former view was that Sodom was located north of the Dead Sea, where the Jordan Valley broadens into the "Circle" of the Jordan. This view held that the "Circle of Jordan" did not and indeed could not apply to the southern part of the Dead Sea. This argument being that since Gen. 13:10 refers to Sodom as a part of the plain of Jordan that it was of necessity north of the Dead Sea since the Jordan had ended at the northern end of the Dead Sea and did not exist at the southern part.

However, in light of more recent archaeological discoveries, a view now exists among many scholars that the location of Sodom was in the area now submerged under the water at the southern section of the Dead Sea. The arguments made for this site include the location of a mountain of salt called Jebel Usdum at the southern end of the western side of the Dead Sea. Other evidence includes the peculiar pillar of salt on Jebel Usdum which some think resembles a human form. Also, it is pointed out by the advocates of this view that the water at the southern section of the Dead Sea is more shallow than the remainder of the sea. This, they believe, indicates that this section was included in the sea at a later date.

This wicked city was destroyed with brimstone and fire by the Lord (Gen. 19:24). Its destruction should serve as a warning to wicked cities of any generation. Jesus often compared the cities of Sodom and Gomorrah to the cities in which he did most of his teaching (Mt. 11:23). The lesson of Sodom should convince us that the truism "Righteousness exalteth a nation, but sin is a reproach to any people" applies to cities as well.   w.j.

sodomites the term applies to those who practice homosexual acts. The term is first mentioned in Deut. 23:17. It probably originated due to the homosexual activities of the men of Sodom. They demanded that Lot surrender his two male guests to them that they might "know" them. A sodomite is one who practices sodomy, sexual relationship between males.
                                        w.j.

Solomon [Heb. "peaceful"] third king of Israel, son of **David,** ca. 969–922 B.C.

1. *Sources.* Knowledge of Solomon's life and reign is found primarily in 1 K. 1–11 and 2 Chr. 1–9. Both sources emphasize first his wisdom, then, events relating to the **Temple,** its dedication and its description. Second Chronicles omits the unpleasant features of his reign in line with its postexilic interests. First Kings is particularly concerned, however, to point up the lesson of Solomon's unfaithfulness to the covenant and the resultant division of the kingdom and eventual exile (1 K. 9:6–9, 11:1–40; Deut. 17:14–17). Writings imputed to Solomon in the OT are **Proverbs, Ecclesiastes, Song of Solomon,** and Psalms 72 and 127. Recent archaeological research such as excavations at **Megiddo, Hazor, Ezion-geber,** and **Beth-shemesh** have confirmed and supplemented much of the Biblical record.

2. *Accession to the Throne.* Solomon's rise to power was due in part to the intervention of his mother **Bath-sheba,** possibly David's favorite wife, and the prophet **Nathan** (1 K. 1:11–37). Apparently no clear line of succession to the throne had been established during the early kingdom period, so **Adonijah,** one of the sons of David, who was near death, planned to have himself proclaimed king with the help of **Joab, Abiathar,** and other sympathizers at **En-rogel** (1 K. 1:5–10). When Nathan learned of the plot, he and Bath-sheba warned David of this threat to their lives and reminded him of his earlier promise to make Solomon king. David sent Nathan, **Zadok** the priest and **Benaiah** to **Gihon** in a surprise move publicly and officially to anoint Solomon the new king. Adonijah's followers at En-rogel dispersed at the news. Solomon was co-regent until David's death. He then secured his throne by exiling Abiathar and executing Adonijah and Shimei on two obvious pretexts (1 K. 2:13–46), but in accordance with his father's dying request (2:5–9).

3. *Prayers and Visions.* The Lord appeared to Solomon twice, first at **Gibeon** (1 K. 3:10–15; 2 Chr. 1:6–13), some years later at the temple in Jerusalem after he had accomplished all "which he was pleased to do" (1 K. 9:1–9; 2 Chr. 7:12–22). Both appearances were in response to his prayers. He first prayed for wisdom to govern Israel and to "discern between good and evil." The Lord granted his prayer and more but on the condition of his continued faithfulness in worship. This Solomon tried to insure by building the temple and establishing the worship of God there (1 K. 8:28–30). God appeared to him again at the temple in a dream and promised to "put my name there forever" and to establish Solomon's throne for as long as Israel continued to obey. Most of the events related in 1 K. 1–11 are explained apparently as God's response to Solomon's prayer or covenant.

4. *A Reign of Wisdom.* Solomon's wisdom showed itself in his great learning, his shrewd judgments, his organizing abilities, his foreign policies, his economic measures, his building enterprises, even in his marriages. His greatest task in coming to the throne was to hold together the kingdom that David had established. Possibly to weaken tribal ties by fostering centralization of power in himself, he reorganized Israel into twelve new administrative districts, each under an officer who was responsible for providing the king's household needs for one month each year (1 K. 4:7, 22–23). Other officials appointed included two scribes, two priests, a chronicler, an officer over the twelve, head of the household, military chief, and chief taskmaster (1 K. 4:2–6). His foreign alliance with **Hiram** king of **Tyre** (ca. 969–936 B.C.) enabled Solomon to further his building enterprises (1 K. 5:1–12), and to maintain a fleet

of ships for trading purposes at Ezion-geber (10:26–28). He traded agricultural products and later twenty cities in Galilee for Hiram's assistance with building supplies, skilled labor, and architects. Solomon also maintained a large standing army even though the great powers of the East, Egypt, Assyria, Syria, were relatively quiescent in this period (1 K. 5:11, 9:10–14). Solomon insured Egypt's friendship by marriage with the pharaoh's daughter, an event perhaps unparalleled in Egyptian history. The pharaoh in question was probably Siamon or Pausennes II of the Twenty-first Dynasty. Solomon received Gezer as dowry and he rebuilt it (1 K. 9:16). His other marriages to women of the Moabites, Ammonites, Edomites, Sidonians, and Hittites were probably for political purposes also (1 K. 11:1). To carry on his extensive building program he had to begin a labor draft first from foreigners in the land and later from Israelites it would appear (1 K. 9:22, 5:13). Besides the temple (1 K. 9:15–26), his own palace (7:1–8) and the palace for pharaoh's daughter, he built the **Millo,** the wall of Jerusalem, in part, store cities, fortified cities for his chariotry and horsemen, such as Megiddo, Hazor, **Beth-horon, Baalath, Tamar, Gerar,** copper refineries and mining operations such as those at Ezion-geber (9:15–26). The extent of his mining operations and the advanced methods used have been uncovered by recent archaeological expeditions led by Nelson Glueck. Solomon was said to have been wiser than all men, knowing three thousand proverbs and a thousand and five songs (1 K. 4:29–34). His fame was so great that the Queen of Sheba visited him, perhaps for her political and economic advantage as well as out of a desire to see for herself his greatness (1 K. 10:1–10).

5. *Idolatry and Decline.* Solomon for all his wisdom did not foresee the people's dissatisfaction with the heavy burden of taxation and the labor draft. He did not understand the danger of tolerating the **high places** and the religious cults of his foreign wives (1 K. 11:1–8). He failed to remember also the power of the prophets to undermine the kingdom. God spoke to him a third time, perhaps through a prophet, calling him to account. The kingdom was to be divided. Three enemies were raised up: **Hadad** the Edomite, who had fled from his land in the time of David; **Rezon** the king of **Syria;** and **Jeroboam,** an Israelite who was to be king over the ten northern tribes in accordance with the prophecy of **Ahijah** (1 K. 11:9–40). Despite his weaknesses, later Jewish tradition held Solomon in high esteem (Neh. 13:26). The

NT speaks of his glory (Mt. 6:29; Lk. 12:27) and of his wisdom (Mt. 12:42; Lk. 11:31) as of only relative merit in light of the divine glory of nature and the incarnation of Wisdom in Christ of whom it was written, "A greater than Solomon is here."　　H.A.B.

Solomon's porch see **palace, temple**

Solomon's servants a list of them appears among the exiles who returned from the Captivity (Ezra 2:55–58; Neh. 7:57–60). They were descendants of the Canaanites, whom Solomon reduced to slavery and compelled to work in the king's stone quarries and in building palaces and cities (1 K. 5:13–14, 9:20–21; 2 Chr. 8:7–8). They seemed to have formed a distinct order, inheriting probably the same functions and the same skills as their forebearers.

son the term is used in Scripture to imply almost any kind of descendant. It is applied to a year, a bow, an arrow, etc. In the NT the word *Bar* is used, which means son. There is no restriction to immediate descendant as we use the term today.

Song of Solomon an OT book of love poems attributed to Solomon, king of Israel (1:1). The book stood in the third division of the Hebrew Bible (the "Writings" or "Psalms") as one of the five scrolls connected with the Jewish feasts. It was read at the Passover. The title "Song of Songs" means in our idiom "the Best of Songs."

1. *Authorship.* Solomonic authorship has been denied by liberals mainly on linguistic grounds, i.e., the presence of Aramaic, Persian, and Greek terms. These items are explainable. Aramaic may no longer be considered evidence for lateness. Loanwords in foreign objects accord with Solomon's commerce.

2. *Contents.* The material consists of love songs or poems with changes (shown by gender and number of personal pronouns and verbal endings), or shiftings, from a single male and female to a plurality of women—"the daughters of Jerusalem." Some differences exist as to whether the principals are two lovers or two lovers and a rival, with the former being the majority view. Locale also is most difficult to conjecture. This has led to a wide confusion of efforts to print or "divide" so as to show the sections by speaker and place. One such attempt divides the material into five scenes: (a) 1:2–2:7 (a scene in the king's country seat near the Shulamite's home); (b) 2:8–17 (scene in the bedroom of the maiden's mother —the lover comes in from the street); (c) 3:6–5:1 (city of Jerusalem); (d) 5:2–8:4 (the palace); (e) 8:5–14 (the Shulamite's home).

The theme is the constancy of love as is expressed in 8:6–7.

3. *Interpretations.* Many interpretations have been advocated: (a) *The Allegorical,* with either the Jewish or Christ's church as the bride. This was the rabbinical view and that of Origen and Hippolytus. But there is a difference between interpreting an allegory and an allegorical interpretation where no allegory is present. (b) *The Dramatic View.* A drama to be played in which Solomon's love is purified (F. Delitzsch). But the Hebrews were little given to drama. (c) *The Collection-of-Songs View.* It has been seen merely as collections of songs such as were customarily sung even to near-present times at weddings in the Near East. (d) *Borrowing from Pagan Religious Fertility Rites.* This is the view expressed by the liberal T. J. Meek in the *Interpreter's Bible.* (e) *Glorification of Pure Married Love.* This was the view of Theodore of Mopsuestia (sixth century A.D.). This view thinks the book is concerned with the simple fidelity of two married people. This view is growing among modern Evangelical interpreters (see E. J. Young, *Introduction to the OT*). J.W.R.

sop in eastern lands the meat with the broth is brought to the table in a bowl. Meat is taken from the bowl with the fingers, and the broth or gruel is then soaked up with a piece of bread held in the fingers. This is called a "sop." This is what was given by Jesus to Judas (Jn. 13:26). Matthew 26:23 well describes the practice: "He that dippeth his hand with me in the dish." Inasmuch as Jesus handed Judas the sop, he must have been sitting near the head of the table.

Sopater (sō'pȧ-tẽr) [savior of his father] son of Pyrrhus of Berea, a disciple who accompanied Paul on his return from Greece into Asia, A.D. 55 (Acts 20:4).

Sophereth (sô-fē'rĕth) [secretariat] children of a family who returned from Babylon with Zerubbabel among the descendants of Solomon's servants, 536 B.C. (Ezra 2:55).

sorcerer see **divination**

Sorek, the Valley of (sō'rĕk) [red] the home of Delilah (Judg. 16:4). Identified today with Wadi es-Sarar between Joppa and Jerusalem. It was the Philistine war route in the days of the Judges, and by this route was the ark was taken to Beth-shemesh (1 Sam. 6:10). It was a part of the territory of Dan. Hither Samson was taken after his capture.

Sosipater (sô-sĭp'ȧ-tẽr) a Christian who was mentioned by Paul as sending greetings (Rom. 16:21).

Sosthenes (sŏs'thē-nēz) a ruler of the Jewish synagogue at Corinth, who was seized and beaten in the presence of Gallio (Acts 18:12–17). Some have thought that he had become a Christian, and was maltreated thus by his own countrymen because he was known as a special friend of Paul. A better view is that Sosthenes was of the bigoted Jews, and that the "crowd" were Greeks, who, taking advantage of the indifference of Gallio, and ever ready to show their contempt of the Jews, turned their indignation against Sosthenes. In this case he must have been the successor of Crispus (Acts 18:8). Paul wrote the first epistle to the Corinthians jointly in his own name and that of a certain Sosthenes whom he terms "the brother" (1 Cor. 1:1). Some have held that he was identical with the Sosthenes mentioned in the Acts. If this is so, he must have been converted at a later period, and have been at Ephesus, and not at Corinth, when Paul wrote to the Corinthians. The name was a common one, so little stress should be laid on this coincidence.

Sotai (sō'tī) the children of Sotai were a family of the descendants of Solomon's servants who returned with Zerubbabel (Ezra 2:55; Neh. 7:57).

soul the most ancient and widely held view of man's nature is that he is a creature consisting of body, soul, and spirit. Such passages as 1 Thess. 5:23 clearly state this view: "The God of peace himself sanctify you wholly; and may your spirit and soul and body be preserved entire, without blame at the coming of our Lord Jesus Christ." Hebrews 4:12, speaks of "the dividing of soul and spirit." "God," says Josephus (*Ant.* I.1–2), "made man, taking dust from the ground, and placed in him a soul and a spirit." From the Jews, this idea was transmitted to the early Christians, being found in the writings of Justin Martyr, Tatian, Irenaeus, Clement of Alexandria, Origen, and others. The body is the material part of man's constitution. The soul (Heb. *nephesh,* Gr. *psyche*) is the principle of animal life, which man possesses in common with the brutes. To it belong understanding, emotion, and sensibility. This part of a man ceases to exist at death. The spirit (Heb. *ruach,* Gr. *pneuma*) is the principle of man's rational and immortal life, which involves conscience and will, and which enables man to be sensitive to the divine. It is this part of man which distinguishes him from the animals and which was "made in the image of God" (Gen. 1:27). At death the dust or body returns to the earth as it was, the human soul ceases to exist, and the spirit returns to God who gave it (Eccl. 12:7). Sometimes, the sacred writers speak of man as constituted of body and soul, or body and spirit, when this twofold distinction is adequate for their purposes. This does not nullify the fact that the spiritual side of man can be subdivided as explained above.

South Ramoth (rā'mŏth) one of the places frequented by David and his band of supporters during the latter part of Saul's life (1 Sam. 30:27). The towns mentioned with it show that Ramoth must have been on the southern confines of the country, the border of the desert.

sow see **swine**

sower, sowing the operation of sowing with the hand is one so simple as to need little description. The Egyptian paintings furnish many illustrations of the mode in which it was conducted. The sower held the vessel or basket containing the seed in his left hand, while with his right he scattered the seed broadcast. In wet soils, the seed was trodden in by the feet of animals (Isa. 32:20). The seed was required to be ceremonially clean (Lev. 11:37-38). The sowing season commenced in October, and continued to the end of February, wheat being put in before, and barley after the beginning of January. The Mosaic law prohibited the sowing of mixed seed (Lev. 19:19; Deut. 22:9).

Spain the Hebrews were acquainted with the position and the mineral wealth of Spain from the time of Solomon, whose alliance with the Phoenicians enlarged the circle of their geographic knowledge. This territory in the southwest of Europe was often designated as Tarshish. The apostle Paul desired to visit it (Rom. 15:24, 28), and likely carried out his intention, for Clement of Rome near the end of the first century A.D. says that Paul "reached the limits of the West." The Muratorian Fragment written about A.D. 170, states explicitly that he went to Spain. This visit must have occurred after his imprisonment at Rome mentioned in the book of Acts.

sparrow the Hebrew word *sippor* occurs some forty times in the OT, and is usually translated as "bird" or "fowl" but occasionally it is rendered "sparrow" (Ps. 84:3, 102:7). The Greek word *strouthion*, translated sparrow, occurs only twice in the NT (Mt. 10:29; Lk. 12:6-7). It was ceremonially clean and was sold and eaten. Palestine has a wide selection of birds, either identical with or similar to those found in Europe and North America. Some of the more familiar are the common sparrow of England and America, the tree sparrow, the starling, the linnet, the blackbird, the song thrush, the rock sparrow, and many others. There are

but two allusions to the singing of birds in the Scriptures (Ps. 104:12; Eccl. 12:4).

spear see **arms**

spearmen the word thus rendered in Acts 23:23 is very rare in Greek and of uncertain meaning. Two hundred *dexiolaboi* formed part of the escort which accompanied Paul in the night march from Jerusalem to Caesarea. The word literally means "one who grasps by the right hand." Codex Alexandrinus (fifth-century A.D. MSS of the NT) speaks of them as javelin-throwers (reading *dexioboloi* instead of *dexiolaboi*). Therefore, in all probability, light-armed troops were in mind, whether bowmen, slingers, or javelin-throwers. The use of "spearman" in Ps. 68:30 of AV is a mistranslation of the Hebrew words *hayyath qaneh*, which means literally "the beast of the reed."

spice, spices the most common Hebrew words thus rendered are *bosem* and *sammim*. "Spices" generally refer to various vegetable products highly valued in antiquity for purposes of fragrance and cosmetics, but not seemingly used in preparing food. The country of Sheba especially amassed wealth from her trade of spices across South Arabia (cf. 2 Chr. 9:9). In the time of Hezekiah, Judah had great stores of spices which were shown to the messengers of Merodach-baladan of Babylon along with the wealth of the Hebrews (2 K. 20:13; Isa. 39:2). Spices also played a role in the cult practices of the temple (Ex. 30:23; 1 Chr. 9:29=30).

In the NT spices were used in the preparation of the body of Jesus for his burial (Mk. 16:1; Lk. 23:56, 24:1; Jn. 19:40). The word *aroma* signifies a type of aromatic oil, salve, or perfume and is used especially in references to embalming the dead.

spider "spider" is mentioned only three times in AV. Twice the Heb. *accabhish* has reference to an arachnid, not an insect of which there are numerous species in Palestine (Job 8:14; Isa. 59:5). In the former passage the "house" (Heb. *beth*) of the spider is mentioned while Isaiah refers to its "web" (*qur*). Even though no distinction is made in the common English version, the two possibly should not be viewed as identical. In the AV "spider" in Prov. 30:28 stands for *semanith* which is a type of lizard known as a gecko (*Hemidactylus turicus*).

spikenard this is the rendition which the AV gives to the Heb. *nerd* (Song of S. 1:12, 4:13-14) and the Gr. *nardos* (Mk. 14:3; Jn. 12:3). The extracted perfume from the spikenard plant is an oil which was highly valued in antiquity. The woman who anointed the head of Jesus with the cruse of spikenard as he sat at meat in the house of Simon the leper in Bethany was criticized for having wasted a jar worth at least three hundred denarii, which was equal to about fifty-five or sixty dollars (Mk. 14:3–5).

spinning since spinning is so ancient, going back to the Stone Age, by the time the Israelites appear it was traditional enough not to warrant description. The mention of the distaff and spindle (Prov. 31:19) implies the use of the same instruments which have been in vogue for hand spinning down to the present day. The Israelite women brought spun linen and goat's hair for the making of the tabernacle (Ex. 35:25–26). Other textiles commonly spun were flax, cotton, and wool. See also Mt. 6:26 and Lk. 12:27.

spirit the word "spirit" almost defies definition. First of all, both the Heb. *ruach* and the Gr. *pneuma* mean both "wind" and "spirit." It is not always easy to choose the proper translation as is evident from Heb. 1:7 where the AV "spirits" probably should be rendered "winds." The statement that God is a spirit implies at least that God has no physical body. But this does not reveal the nature of spirit (Isa. 31:3). The word is also used to designate supernatural beings whether good or evil (1 Sam. 16:14; 1 K. 22:21). As the rational principle in man (1 Cor. 2:11), it is placed in contrast to the soul (see 1 Thess. 5:23; Heb. 4:12 and especially 1 Cor. 2:14–15 in the original, where the AV "natural man" is the "soul-type" man as distinguished from the "spiritual").

Spirit, Holy an allusion to the Holy Spirit as a part of the "Trinity" is to be found in the Great Commission (Mt. 28:19) and in Paul (2 Cor. 13:14). As the Father and the Son are real persons, so must the Holy Spirit be also. Jesus promises that he will send the Spirit as a Comforter (Jn. 16:7) and that the Spirit will guide the disciples into all truth (Jn. 16:13). Paul teaches that Christians are sealed with the Holy Spirit which is an earnest of their inheritance (Eph. 1:13–14; 2 Cor. 5:5).

Unfortunately it is not always easy to determine when "spirit" should be capitalized since ancient MSS make no such distinction between proper and common nouns. For this reason it is difficult to be certain whether "the Spirit" is actually intended in such passages as Rom. 8:1–8. This makes a clear understanding of the doctrine of the Holy Spirit very elusive.

sponge the word is used three times in the NT (Mt. 27:48; Mk. 15:36; Jn. 19:29) in reference to the drink of vinegar offered to Jesus as he hung on the Cross. The commercial value of the sponge was known from very early times.

spouse see **marriage**

Stachys (stā′kĭs) a Christian whom Paul sa-

lutes as "my beloved" in the letter to the Romans (16:9).

stacte the name of one of the sweet spices which composed the holy incense (Ex. 30:34). The storax and the opobalsamum are likely trees from which the spice was made.

standards see **ensigns**

star early in man's history (Gen. 22:17), the number of stars and their groupings attracted man's attention. Job referred to Orion, Pleiades, the Bear, and other constellations (Job 9:9; 38:31–32). The stars were recognized as the handiwork of God (Gen. 1:16; Ps. 8:3), and under his control (Isa. 13:10; Jer. 31:35). In the course of time some of the Israelites followed the pagans in worshiping the stars (Deut. 4:19; 2 K. 17:16; Amos 5:26); altars were erected and incense was burnt to them (2 K. 21:5, 23:5). Several stars mentioned in the NT deserve attention:

(1) The morning star (RV, Rev. 2:28, 22:16). Both phrases, "the morning star," and "the bright and morning star," are probably designations of Christ as the herald to his people of the eternal day. The figure may have been derived from the familiar apocalyptic saying that in the Messianic kingdom the righteous shall shine as the stars (Dan. 12:3).

(2) The day star (2 Pet. 1:19). This is, according to some, a figurative description of the signs which will immediately precede the second coming of Christ. Others understand it as the spirit's illumination of the believer's heart.

(3) The star of the Wise Men (Mt. 2:9). Traditionally the story of the Wise Men from the East coming to honor the birth of the Lord (Mt. 2:1–12) has included the appearance of the guiding star, a supernatural phenomenon which appeared in some country (possibly Persia) far to the east of Jerusalem, to men who were versed in the study of celestial matters, conveying to their minds a supernatural impulse to travel to Jerusalem, where they would find a newborn king. On arriving at Jerusalem, after diligent inquiry, and consultation with the priests and learned men, they were directed to proceed to Bethlehem. The star which they had seen in the east reappeared to them, and preceded them, until it took up its station over the place where the young child was. Others, however, consider this series of events a natural phenomenon providentially used to direct the Wise Men. In December 1603, the astronomer Kepler noted a conjunction of Jupiter and Saturn, joined later by Mars, and still later by a brilliant new star. He made ingenious calculations and came up with the idea that the

star of the Wise Men was likely this conjunction of planets. Others have followed Kepler's lead and modified or added to this natural explanation. It is probably wiser to leave the matter a supernatural sign than to try to explain it naturally, because such explanations are rather unrealistic. B.B.B.

stater see **money**

steel in all cases where the word steel occurs in the AV, the RV correctly substitutes brass. In Nah. 2:3 Heb. *pelādāh* (in AV, torches) apparently means brass as in RV.

Stephanas (stĕf'à-nås) a Christian convert of Corinth, whose household Paul baptized as the "firstfruits of Achaia" (1 Cor. 1:16, 16:15, 17).

Stephen (stē'vĕn) the first Christian martyr also heads the list of the seven men chosen by the Jerusalem Christians to rectify the complaints of the Hellenistic Christians that their widows were being neglected in the distribution of alms (Acts 6:1–6). Stephen is described as a man "full of faith and of the Holy Spirit" (Acts 6:5); as a preacher "full of grace and power" (Acts 6:8), and irresistible in "wisdom and spirit" (Acts 6:10). His Hellenistic name indicates a Hellenistic origin and explains why he devoted himself to teaching in the synagogues of Hellenistic Jews from North Africa, Alexandria, and Asia Minor. The charges against Stephen (Acts 6:13–14) would indicate that his preaching in the synagogues was similar to his defense oration (Acts 7:1–53). He said that all Jewish history since the promises to Abraham, the giving of the Law, and the conquest of Canaan was but preparation for the Righteous One whom they had killed as their fathers had killed the prophets that foretold his coming. Until this time the apostles and the church had continued worshiping in the temple, but Stephen challenges temple worship by saying, "the Most High dwelleth not in temples made with hands" (Acts 7:48; cf. Jn. 4:21–24). His trial before the Sanhedrin ends abruptly as the angry mob rushes upon him and drags him outside the gates of Jerusalem. There he is stoned. The witnesses were responsible for leading in the execution (Deut. 17:7; cf. Jn. 8:7). According to custom, they laid their outer garments for safety at the feet of one of the prominent leaders in the affair. By taking the clothes into his custody he signified his assent to the stoning. Saul of Tarsus was the person who officiated on this occasion. See **Paul**

stocks in the AV "stocks" is applied to two different instruments of punishment. One device was the pillory, which locked the arms and head of a person between two wooden boards.

Jeremiah seems to have been confined in such a device (Jer. 20:2), and it appears to have been a common mode of punishment in his day (Jer. 29:27) since prisons contained a chamber for the special purpose, termed "the house of the pillory" (2 Chr. 16:10; AV, prison house). The stocks, properly, consisted of a wooden frame in which the feet alone were confined. It is spoken of in Job 13:27, 33:11; Acts 16:24. The term used in Prov. 7:22 (AV, stocks) more properly means a fetter.

Stoics the Stoics and Epicureans, who are mentioned together in Acts 17:18, represent the two opposite schools of practical philosophy which survived the fall of higher speculation in Greece. When Paul appeared in Athens, Stoicism had been a school for about three and a half centuries. The name came from the Stoa or Porch where Zeno of Citium (ca. 280 B.C.) had taught in Athens. Stoicism was essentially pantheistic. Reason was exalted to the suppression of man's emotional nature. Stoic morality was rigid and cold and an act was declared good or evil in itself, with pleasure never to be made the end of an action. One should resign himself to his fate and keep all disturbing influences to a minimum by holding his feelings in rigid self-control. Its most eminent exponents were the slave Epictetus, the philosopher Seneca, and the Emperor Marcus Aurelius.

stomacher the Hebrew word so translated describes some article of female attire (Isa. 3:24), the character of which is mere conjecture.

stones besides the ordinary uses made of stones, we may mention that large stones were set up to commemorate any remarkable events (Gen. 28:18, 31:45, 35:14; Josh. 4:9; 1 Sam. 7:12). Such stones were occasionally consecrated by anointing (Gen. 28:18). A similar practice existed in heathen countries; however, the only point of resemblance between the two consists in the custom of anointing. It appears from Isa. 57:6 that the worship of stones prevailed among the heathen nations surrounding Palestine and was borrowed from them by apostate Israelites. Stones were used metaphorically to denote hardness or insensibility (1 Sam. 25:37; Ezek. 11:19, 36:26), as well as firmness of strength (Gen. 49:24). Christians are called "living stones" and help rear that living temple in which Christ, himself "a living stone" is the cornerstone (Eph. 2:20–22; 1 Pet. 2:4–8).

stones, precious because of the very primitive understanding of the ancient Greeks and Hebrews of the chemistry and crystallography of stones, their categories for stones do not correspond at all with our modern categories and names. Thus, it is very difficult to translate their terms into modern equivalents. Precious stones were used in trade by the Tyrians (Ezek. 27:16). The art of engraving on precious stones was known from the earliest times (Gen. 38:18; Ex. 28:17–21). Precious stones are used in Scripture in a figurative sense, to signify value, beauty, durability, etc., in those objects with which they are compared (Isa. 54:11–12; Lam. 4:7; Rev. 4:3, 21:19, 21).

stoning see **punishments**

stork the white stork is one of the largest and most conspicuous of land birds, standing nearly four feet high, the jet black of its wings and its bright red beak and legs contrasting finely with the pure white of its plumage (Zech. 5:9). In the neighborhood of man, it devours readily all kinds of offal and garbage. For this reason, doubtless, it is placed in the list of unclean birds by the Mosaic law (Lev. 11:19; Deut. 14:18). Both the white and the black stork have a rather wide migratory range; both are numerous in Palestine. While the black stork is never found about buildings, preferring marshy places in forests and breeding on the top of the loftiest trees, the white stork attaches itself to man, and, for the service which it renders in the destruction of reptiles and the removal of offal, has been repaid from the earliest times by protection and reverence.

strain at the AV renders Mt. 23:24, "Ye blind guides, which strain at a gnat and swallow a camel." It is recognized today that "strain at" was a typographical error in the AV (not the fault of the translators), and should read "strain out," referring to the Jewish tradition of straining insects out of their liquors. The sarcasm of Jesus' statement becomes clearer when it is realized that both gnats and camels were considered unclean, and the Pharisees, he said, strained out the insect only to swallow the large beast upon which a person could ride.

stranger at least three meanings can be attached to this word in Biblical usage. The "stranger" (*zar*, from *zur*, to turn aside, depart) of 1 K. 3:18; Isa. 1:7; Ezek. 7:21, 28:7, 10, may refer to any outsider, including the "strange woman" of Prov. 2:16, whom the Hebrews equated with a prostitute. But the "strange women" whom Solomon loved (1 K. 11:1) could more accurately be called "foreign women" (from *nokri*), and it is with such foreigners that the Hebrews were explicitly forbidden to marry (Deut. 7:1–6). It was toward the "sojourner" (*gēr*) in the land, however, that the Hebrews were commanded by law to show respect and provide protection (Num. 15:14–16; Deut. 10:19), primarily because they themselves were

once sojourners on foreign soil (Gen. 15:13; Ex. 20:10, 22:21, 23:9). In contrast to the foreigner, whose allegiance still lay with another nation, the sojourning multitudes in Palestine were composed of (1) the "mixed multitude" that accompanied the Israelites out of Egypt (Ex. 12:38); (2) Canaanites who clung tenaciously to their native soil; (3) war captives; (4) and fugitives, merchants, hired servants, etc. All of these in some degree "resided" in the land, and Hebrew law toward such groups was definitely liberal. Numerous civil laws guaranteed certain rights and privileges to the sojourner (Lev. 19:33–34, 23:22; Num. 35:15; Deut. 24:19–21; Josh. 20:9). He even shared in much of the religious life of Israel (Ex. 12:19; Lev. 16:29, 17:10, 13, 18:26), though circumcision was required if he chose to keep the Passover (Ex. 12:48).

NT usage usually denotes anyone who is an alien or who is far from home (Mt. 25:35; Lk. 17:18; Jn. 10:5; Acts 2:10; Heb. 13:2).

straw wheat and barley straw, mixed with beans and barley, was often used by ancient Hebrews as fodder for their horses, camels, cattle, and asses (Gen. 24:25; Judg. 19:19; 1 K. 4:28; Isa. 11:7, 65:25) though apparently not for litter. The Egyptians mixed this straw with clay to make bricks that did not crack. The straw that the Israelites were compelled to gather for bricks (Ex. 5:7, 12, 16) was the stubble that was left in the field after the prime straw had been cut.

stream of Egypt usually rendered as "river of Egypt," referring to a desert stream marking the boundary between Canaan and the tribe of Judah, "stream of Egypt" appears in the AV only in Isa. 27:12.

street most streets of Biblical towns were narrow, gloomy, and unplanned. Though some were broad enough for chariots (Jer. 17:25; Nah. 2:4), their crowded ranks of merchants and craftsmen made them more centers of trade than throughways for vehicles. One notable exception was the beautiful street called Straight in Damascus, which even today is an important east-west artery. The fact that streets were rarely paved made the street of pure gold in Rev. 21:21 seem all the more desirable to inhabitants of the earthly Jerusalem.

stripes see **punishments**

stumbling block the figurative use of this term which predominates in both the OT and NT (Isa. 8:14; Ezek. 3:20, 7:19; 1 Cor. 1:23; Rev. 2:14) derives from the literal commandment not to "put a stumbling block before the blind" (Lev. 19:14). Biblical writers saw many metaphorical applications of this concept, such as Paul's injunction not to eat meat lest it become a stumbling block to the weak (1 Cor. 8:9).

Suah (sū'ah) an Asherite, a son of Zophah (1 Chr. 7:36).

suburbs usually denotes "pasture lands" surrounding the Levitical cities, which were to be "their perpetual possession" (Lev. 25:34). In 2 K. 23:11, "suburbs" (Heb. *parwar*, cf. "Parbar" in 1 Chr. 26:18) refers to the "precincts," or possibly "forecourt," of the temple.

Succoth (sŭk'ŏth) 1. An ancient city of Gad (Josh. 13:27), east of the Jordan, known for its pottery and brassware (1 K. 7:46; 2 Chr. 4:17). The name is associated with Jacob, for it was here that he set up "booths" (*succoth*) for his cattle upon his return from his reconciliation with Esau at Penuel (Gen. 33:16–17). It was also here that Gideon was refused food in his pursuit of the kings of Midian, but was later avenged (Judg. 8:4–16). The valley of Succoth is mentioned in Ps. 60:6 and 108:7.

2. Site of the first encampment of the Israelites when they left Egypt (Ex. 12:37; Num. 33:5), apparently a day's journey southeast of Rameses. Identified with Tel el-Maskhutah in Goshen.

Succoth-benoth (sŭk'ŏth-bē'nŏth) an idol to a deity or deities set up in Samaria by the Babylonians after 722 B.C. (2 K. 17:30; cf. Amos 5:26). The name—apparently a corruption of Sarpanita, the consort of Marduk, the patron god of Babylon—means "booths (or tabernacles) of daughters," suggesting either places of prostitution in honor of their idol, or small tabernacles containing images of female deities.

Suchathites (sū'kăth-īt) the last named of the three families of scribes who lived in Jabez of Judah (1 Chr. 2:55).

suffer used in Mt. 19:14; Mk. 10:14; and Lk. 18:16 in the sense of "to let," "to permit."

Sukkims (sŭk'ims) allied components of the Egyptian army of Shishak when he invaded Judah (2 Chr. 12:3). Associated with the Lubim (Libyans) and the Cushim (Ethiopians), the Sukkims were probably wandering tentdwellers of Northern Africa.

Sumer see **Babylonia**

sun in the history of the creation, the sun is described as the "greater light" in contradistinction to the moon, or "lesser light," in conjunction with which it was to serve for "signs, and for seasons, and for days, and for years," while its special office was "to rule the day" (Gen. 1:14–16). The joint influence assigned to the sun and moon in deciding the seasons, both for agricultural operations and for religious festivals, and also in regulating the length and

subdivisions of the years, correctly describes the combination of the lunar and solar year, which prevailed at all events subsequently to the Mosaic period. The sun ruled the day, not only in reference to its powerful influences, but also in deciding the length of the day, and supplying the means of calculating its progress. Sunrise and sunset are the only defined points of time in the absence of artificial contrivances for telling the hour of the day. Between these two points, the Jews recognized three periods; when the sun became hot, about nine A.M. (1 Sam. 11:9; Neh. 7:3), the double light or noon (Gen. 43:16; 2 Sam. 4:5), and "the cool of the day," shortly before sunset (Gen. 3:8). The worship of the sun, as the most prominent and powerful agent in the kingdom of nature, was widely diffused throughout the countries adjacent to Palestine. The Hebrews must have been well acquainted with the idolatrous worship of the sun during the captivity in Egypt. In the metaphorical language of Scripture, the sun is emblematic of the Law of God (Ps. 19:4–7), of the presence of God (Ps. 84:11), of the person of the Savior (Mal. 4:2; Jn. 1:9), and of the glory and purity of heavenly beings (Rev. 1:16, 10:1, 12:1).

suretyship the practice of one person making himself liable for the obligations of another (Prov. 22:26–27). In the absence of commerce, the Mosaic law laid down no rules on the subject of suretyship; but it is evident that, in the time of Solomon, commercial dealings had become so multiplied that suretyship in the commercial sense was common (Prov. 6:1, 11:15, 17:18, 20:16, 22:26, 27:13). Also in older times the notion of one man becoming a surety for a service to be discharged by another was in full force (Gen. 44:32). The surety, of course, became liable for his client's debts in case of his failure.

Susa (sōō'sà) see **Shushan**

Susanchites (sōō'săn-kīts) this term is found only once (Ezra 4:9) in the Bible. There can be no doubt that it designates either the inhabitants of the city of Susa or those of the country—Susis or Susiana.

Susanna (sŭ-zăn'nà) one of the women who ministered to the Lord (Lk. 8:3).

Susi (sū'sī) the father of Gaddi, the Manassite spy (Num. 13:11).

swaddling band a cloth in which infants were wrapped (Job 38:9; Ezek. 16:4; Lk. 2:7, 12). A baby was laid crosswise on a square piece of cloth and two corners were turned over its body, one over its feet, and one under its head. The whole was then fastened by bands wound around the outside.

swallow a bird which frequented the temple at Jerusalem, and nested there (Ps. 84:3). It was known for its swiftness of flight, its nesting in the public buildings, its mournful, garrulous note, and its regular migration. Many species of swallow occur in Palestine (Isa. 38:14; Jer. 8:7).

swan this bird is listed in Lev. 11:18 and Deut. 14:16 among the group of unclean birds. It is likely to refer to the porphyrio or ibis rather than to the owl or pelican, as some have suggested.

swearing see **oath**

sweat, bloody one of the physical phenomena attending Christ's agony in the Garden of Gethsemane mentioned by Luke (Lk. 22:44) in the words, "as it were great drops of blood falling down to the ground." The genuineness of this verse and the preceding has been doubted, but is now generally acknowledged. Of this malady, known in medical science by the term *diapedesis*, there have been examples recorded both in ancient and modern times. Under extreme pressures, the human body, which commonly breaks out suddenly in perspiration under the influence of strong mental excitement, has also been known to have an oozing of the blood corpuscles through the walls of the blood vessels without rupture. This appears to be what took place during Christ's crucifixion.

swine the flesh of swine was forbidden as food by the Levitical law (Lev. 11:7; Deut. 14:8). The abhorrence which the Jews as a nation had of it may be inferred from Isa. 65:4. Although no explanation of why swine were classed as unclean is given in the Scriptures, it is probable that dietetical considerations may have influenced Moses in his prohibition of swine's flesh. It is generally believed that its use in hot countries is liable to induce cutaneous disorders. At the time of our Lord's ministry, it would appear that the Jews occasionally violated the law of Moses with respect to swine's flesh. Whether "the herd of swine" into which the demons were allowed to enter (Mt. 8:32; Mk. 5:13) were the property of the Jewish or Gentile inhabitants of Gadara, does not appear from the text.

sword see **arms**

sycamine tree (sĭk′å-mĭn) mentioned only once in the Scriptures (Lk. 17:6), it is likely that the sycamine is the mulberry tree. Both white and black mulberry trees are common in Syria and Palestine. This tree is distinct from the sycamore of Lk. 19:4.

sycamore (sĭk′å-mōr) a fig tree, abundant in the lowland of Judah (1 K. 10:27; 1 Chr.

27:28; 2 Chr. 1:15, 9:27), in the Jordan Valley (Lk. 19:4), and in Egypt (Ps. 78:47). Its timber was used, though it was less durable than cedar (Isa. 9:10). It attains the size of a walnut tree, has widespreading branches, and affords a delightful shade. On this account, it is frequently planted by the waysides. Its leaves are heart-shaped, downy on the underside, and fragrant. The fruit grows directly from the trunk itself on little sprigs and in clusters like the grape. To make it edible, each fruit, three or four days before gathering, must it is said be punctured with a sharp instrument or the fingernail. This was the original employment of the prophet Amos (Amos 7:14). So great was the value of these trees that David appointed for them in his kingdom a special overseer, as he did for the olives (1 Chr. 27:28).

Sychar (sī′kår) see **Shechem**

Sychem (sī′kĕm) see **Shechem**

Syene (sī-ē′nê) a town of Egypt on the frontier of Cush or Ethiopia, properly called Seveneh. The prophet Ezekiel speaks of the desolation of Egypt "from Migdol to Seveneh, even unto the border of Cush" (Ezek. 29:10), and of its people being slain "from Migdol to Seveneh" (Ezek. 30:6). Migdol was on the eastern border; and Seveneh is thus rightly identified with the town of Syene, which was always the last town of Egypt on the south, though at one time it was included in the name Nubia.

synagogue the word synagogue means a congregation of people. The word is used frequently in the LXX version of the OT for the Hebrew congregation. The Greek word indicates a gathering of people for religious or other purposes. No mention is made of the synagogue in the Hebrew texts of the OT.

A knowledge of the history and worship of the synagogue is of great importance since this was the characteristic institution of Judaism. Nor can the synagogue be separated from a most intimate connection with the life and ministry of Jesus since he attended and participated in the synagogue services in his youth and manhood.

The origin of the synagogue cannot be ascertained. The synagogue seems to have arisen during the Babylonian exile in abeyance of temple worship. The later synagogue services imply that the early synagogues were places of instruction for young and old, and as a place for prayer and Scripture reading. The whole context of Ezra presupposes the habit of solemn and probably periodic meetings (Ezra 8:15; Neh. 8:2, 9:1; Zech. 7:5). It appears that synagogues were organized in Palestine by the postexilic Jews after the restoration of temple worship in Jerusalem. Whenever the law of Moses was read in the temple, there were simultaneous periods of Scripture readings and prayers conducted in the several Jewish synagogues during the appointed Jewish devotions.

The widespread location of Jewish synagogues in Palestine is indicated in the NT (Mt. 4:23, 9:35; Acts 6:9, 24:12). Two Galilean synagogues receive special attention. One was Nazareth where Jesus stood up to speak (Lk. 4:16), and the Capernaum synagogue where Jesus taught on the sabbath (Lk. 4:31–33).

Synagogues were located in other parts of the Roman empire as attested by Luke in describing Paul's missionary journeys: in Damascus, Syria (Acts 9:2, 20); Salamis, Cyprus (Acts 13:5); Antioch of Pisidia (Acts 13:14); Iconium, Phrygia (Acts 14:1); Philippi, Macedonia (Acts 16:13); Thessalonica (Acts 17:1); Berea (Acts 17:10, 11); Athens (Acts 17:16–17); Corinth (Acts 18:4); Ephesus (Acts 18:19, 19:18); and others.

Structure. Little is known about the structure of the ancient synagogues nor their locations since few contemporary comments about the synagogues were made. One Jewish source placed the location at the highest point in the city. There is good reason to suppose the synagogues were built in the first century A.D., near a stream of water for ablution purposes (Acts 16:13).

The size of the Jewish synagogue varied with the congregation. Following the destruction of the temple in A.D. 70, a need was recognized to design the structure of the synagogue for worship and teaching purposes. The location of the ark was the controlling feature. The ark contained the books of Moses in the sacred position of the synagogue that faced Jerusalem. Naturally the "chief seats" of the synagogue were located here after which the Pharisees and Sadducees so eagerly sought (Mt. 23:6). Other articles of furniture were the eight-branched lamp lighted only on the greater festivals and another lamp was kept burning perpetually. Next to the ark was the *bema*, a reading desk facing the ark where the Scriptures were read and prayers recited. The *bema* rested on a raised platform where speakers addressed the audience. The congregation was divided with seats on one side for women and the other side for men. The "Court of Women" provided the reason for this arrangement.

Officers. The highest functionary of the synagogue was the Rabbi (meaning: my master). Should a village be too small to support a synagogue, the people were dependent on the services of the nearest Rabbi.

Where a fuller congregation was possible, there was a "college of elders" (Lk. 7:3), presided over by one known as the "chief of the synagogue" (Lk. 8:41, 49, 13:14; Acts 18:8, 17). This officer (*archisynagogos*) was the officiating minister and the chief reader of the Law and prayers. The *chazzan*, or "minister" of the synagogue (Lk. 4:20) had duties resembling those of a Christian deacon such as preparing the synagogue for worship, assigning functions of worship, and handing the scroll of the Law to a reader. A synagogue could function in a community provided ten men in the community attended the services.

Worship. At the beginning of the Christian era the synagogue had become a public institution for Jewish worship. The edifice was erected by the community, or sometimes by a pious Gentile (Lk. 7:5). The constant parts of the synagogue worship were prayers and reading from the Scriptures. At the end of the first century A.D., there were eighteen fixed prayers. Moses was read on sabbaths and all other Jewish holy days (Acts 13:5, 15, 15:21). Ultimately the Pentateuch was divided so all of "Moses" could be read in a definite time. In addition to the Pentateuch there were readings from the prophets. In addition to the acts of worship, the synagogues were used to instruct in the duties of revealed religion. Furthermore, quarters were provided in the synagogue for the instruction of children.

Finally, the importance of the Jewish synagogue may be summed up in the statement that here the religion of Judaism was formed and has been sustained for 2500 years.

Synagogue, the Great on the Jews' return from Babylon, a great synagogue was appointed according to rabbinic tradition, to reorganize the religious life of the people. It consisted of 120 members known as the men of the Great Synagogue, succeeded by scribes. The existence of such a body is based upon statements in Nehemiah (Neh. 8–9, 10:2–28). The absence of any historical mention of the body in Josephus, Philo, and other similar sources has led critics to assume the whole statement to be a rabbinic invention.

Syntyche (sĭn'tĭ-chē) a female member of the church at Philippi (Phil. 4:2–3).

Syracuse this was a major Greek city founded in the eighth century B.C., located in the southeastern Mediterranean and served as a convenient place for ships to touch at because of its excellent harbor. The apostle Paul spent three days here en route to Rome (Acts 28:12).

Syria Syria is the term used throughout our version for the Heb. *Aram* (Deut. 26:5) as well as the Gr. *Syria*. Most probably Syria is for *Tsyria*, the country about Tsur, or Tyre, which was the first of the Syrian towns known to the Greeks. It is difficult to fix the limits of Syria because the boundaries of the area varied with the political control by such as the Assyrians. Syria proper can be located between the confines of Amanus and Taurus on the north, by the Euphrates and the Arabian Desert on the east, by Palestine on the south. This tract is about 300 miles from north to south and from 50 to 150 miles broad. The general character of the land is mountainous. The most fertile areas are adjacent to the Lebanons. The small fertile valleys are fed by the Orontes, the Upper Euphrates, and by other streams, supporting vineyards, farming, and herding. The Syrians are especially noted for their fine wares in wool and silk, and ornamental metals.

The foremost of the Syrian cities as given prominence in the Bible are Damascus, Antioch on the Orontes, and in different periods to Tyre, Sidon, and Carchemish.

History. The first occupants of Syria appear to have been of Hamitic descent. The Canaanitish races, the Hittites, Jebusites, Amorites, etc., are connected in Scripture with Egypt and Ethiopia, Cush and Mizraim (Gen. 10:6, 15–18). These tribes occupied not only Lower Palestine, but also Lower Syria and later Upper Syria. After a while the first comers, who were still to a great extent nomads, received Semitic infusion probably from the east. The only Syrian city whose existence we can find distinctly marked at this time is Damascus (Gen. 15:2). Next to Damascus must be placed Hamath (Num. 13:21, 34:8). Syria at this time and for many centuries afterward seems to have been broken up into a number of petty kingdoms. In turn the Amorites, Hittites, and the Hyksos dominated Syria.

The relation between the Jews and Syrians was generally antagonistic. During David's reign, the king laid claim on the lands of Syria extending to the boundary of the Euphrates that God had promised to Abraham (Gen. 15:18). The conflicts of King David with the Syrians are detailed in the following Scripture passages—2 Sam. 8:3–4, 13, 10:6; 1 K. 4:21. David was successful in his enterprises against the Syrians. Solomon, however, could not completely hold the frontiers of his father's empire (1 K. 11:23–25).

On the separation of the two kingdoms, soon after the succession of Rehoboam, Syria shook off the yoke of both the kingdom of Judah and the Northern Kingdom, and became attached to the great Assyrian empire, from which it passed to the Babylonians and from there to the Persians. In 333 B.C., it submitted to Alexander without a struggle. Upon the death of Alexander, Syria became a great kingdom for the first time. On the division of the provinces among his generals (321 B.C.), Seleucus Nicanor received Mesopotamia and Syria. The country then grew rich with the wealth which flowed in from all sides.

Syria holds important places in both the Old and the New Testament. Syria passed under the control of the Romans who divided the province into three political divisions (64 B.C.) —Syria, Syria Phoenice, and Syria Palestina. The provinces followed the most extended boundaries of King David's domain.

Jesus visited only the region about Tyre and Sidon. Here he made a reference to the healing of Naaman the leper by Elisha (2 K. 5:14; Lk. 4:27). The journey of Saul of Tarsus is narrated in Acts 9. The Syrian church, partly by the exertions of the apostle Paul, grew to be one of the most flourishing (Acts 13:1, 15:23, 35, 41). It would be difficult to evaluate the importance that Syria experienced in the affairs of the Israelites, and later Christians, as long as they occupied Palestine.

Syriac versions see **Versions, Syriac**

Syrophoenician this is found only in one place in the Bible (Mk. 7:26). The coinage of the word "Syrophoenician" seems to have been the work of the Romans. The word perhaps denoted a race of mixed origins. In later times, a geographic sense of the term superseded the ethnic one. The Emperor Hadrian divided **Syria** into three parts—one being Syria Phoenice.

T

Taanach (tā'ȧ-năk) an ancient Canaanitish city, whose king is enumerated among the thirty-one conquered by Joshua (Josh. 12:21). It was nominally possessed by the half-tribe of Manasseh (Josh. 17:11, 21:25; 1 Chr. 7:29), but was bestowed on the Kohathite Levites (Josh. 21:25). The battle between Barak and Sisera was fought near Taanach (Judg. 5:19). The place was important in Solomon's time (1 K. 4:12). It is often mentioned in connection with Megiddo for both were chief towns in the rich district which formed the western portion of the great plain of Esdraelon (1 K. 4:12). Taanuk, on the site of the ancient city, was known to Eusebius and still exists, some five miles southeast of ancient Megiddo.

Taanath-shiloh (tā'ȧ-năth-shī'lô) a town named once only in the Scriptures (Josh. 16:6). It was a border city and served as one of the landmarks between the territory of Ephraim and Manasseh. Its exact location is unknown.

Tabbaoth (tă-bā'ŏth) a family of Nethinim who returned with Zerubbabel (Ezra 2:43; Neh. 7:46).

Tabbath (tăb'ăth) a place mentioned only in Judg. 7:22, in describing the flight of the Midianite host after Gideon's night attack.

Tabeal (tā'bē-ăl) the son of Tabeal was apparently an Ephraimite in the allied army of Pekah the son of Remaliah, and Rezin of Damascus. It appears that these two kings took him with them to besiege Jerusalem in the reign of Ahaz possibly intending to place him on the throne of David as their puppet king of Judah (Isa. 7:6).

Tabeel (tā'bē-ĕl) an officer of the Persian government in Samaria in the reign of Artaxerxes (Ezra 4:7).

Taberah (tăb'ê-rȧ) a place in the wilderness of Paran where the Israelites murmured and the fire of the Lord burned among them in the uttermost part of the camp (Num. 11:3; Deut. 9:22).

tabering an obsolete word used only in Nah. 2:7 (AV), signifying beating upon a musical instrument, such as the tabor, tabret, tambourine, or timbrel.

tabernacle the tabernacle was a provisional tent where the Lord met his people (Ex. 33:7-10). It was the "tent of Jehovah," called by the same name as the tent of the people, in the midst of which it stood. It was also called the "sanctuary," and the "tabernacle of the congregation." The first ordinances given to Moses, after the proclamation of the outline of the law from Sinai, related to the ordering of the tabernacle, its furniture, and its service, as the type which was to be followed when the people came to their own home, "found a place" for the abode of God. During the forty days of Moses' retirement with God on Sinai, an exact pattern of the whole was shown him, and all was made according to it (Ex. 25:9, 40, 26:30, 39:32, 42, 43; Num. 8:4; Acts 7:44; Heb. 8:5). The description of the plan is preceded by an account of the freewill offerings which the children of Israel were to be asked to make for its execution. The materials were: (a) Metals: gold, silver and brass; (b) Fabrics: blue, purple, scarlet, and fine white linen; also, a fabric of goats' hair; (c) Skins: of the ram, dyed red, and of the badger; (d) Wood: the shittim wood, of the wild acacia of the desert; (e) Oil, spices, and incense, for anointing the priests, and burning in the tabernacle; (f) Gems: onyx stones, and the precious stones for the breastplate of the high priest. The people gave jewels and plates of gold and silver and brass; wood, skins, hair, and linen; the women wove; the rulers offered precious stones, oil, spices, and incense; and the artists soon had more than they needed (Ex. 25:1-8, 35:4-29, 36:5-7). The superintendence of the work was entrusted to Bezaleel, of the tribe of Judah, and to Aholiab, of the tribe of Dan, who was skilled in "all manner of workmanship" (Ex. 31:2, 6, 35:30, 34). The tabernacle was a portable building, designed to contain the sacred ark, the special symbol of God's presence, and was surrounded by an outer court.

1. *The Court of the Tabernacle*, in which the tabernacle itself stood, was an oblong space, one hundred cubits by fifty (i.e., one hundred and fifty by seventy-five feet), having its longer axis east and west, with its front to the east.

tabernacle

It was surrounded by canvas screens five cubits in height, and supported by pillars of brass five cubits apart, to which the curtains were attached by hooks and fillets of silver (Ex. 27:10). This enclosure was only broken on the eastern side by the entrance, which was twenty cubits wide, and closed by curtains of fine twined linen wrought with needle work and of the most gorgeous colors. In the outer or eastern half of the court was placed the altar of burnt offering, and, between it and the tabernacle itself, the laver, at which the priests washed their hands and feet on entering the tabernacle.

2. *The Tabernacle.* It was itself placed toward the western end of this court. It was an oblong rectangular structure, thirty cubits in length by ten in width (forty-five by fifteen feet) and ten in height; the interior being divided into two chambers, the first or outer of twenty cubits in length, the inner of ten cubits, and consequently an exact cube. The former was the holy place (Heb. 9:12), containing the golden candlestick on one side, the table of showbread opposite, and between them, in the center, the altar of incense. The latter was the most holy place, or the Holy of Holies, containing the ark, surrounded by the cherubim, with the Two Tables inside. The two sides, and the farther or western end, were enclosed by boards of shittim wood overlaid with gold, twenty on the north and south sides, six on the west side, and the cornerboards doubled. They stood upright, edge to edge, their lower ends being made with tenons, which dropped into sockets of silver, and the cornerboards being coupled at the top with rings. They were finished with golden rings through which passed bars of shittim wood overlaid with gold, five to each side, and the middle bar passing from end to end, so as to brace the whole together. Four successive coverings of curtains looped together were placed over the open top, and fell down over the sides. The first, or inmost, was a splendid fabric of linen, embroidered with figures of cherubim, in blue, purple, and scarlet and looped together by golden fastenings. It seems probable that the ends of this set of curtains hung down within the tabernacle, forming a sumptuous tapestry. The next was a woolen covering of goats' hair; the third, of rams' skins dyed red; and the outermost, of badgers' skins (probably seal skins). Although no indication in the text of Scripture expressly indicates so, it is generally believed that these coverings were stretched over a tent ridge above the tabernacle. Otherwise the flat roof would have been a problem in time of rain. The front

of the sanctuary was closed by a hanging of fine linen, embroidered in blue, purple, and scarlet, and supported by golden hooks, on five pillars of shittim wood overlaid with gold, and standing in brass sockets; and the covering of goats' hair was so made as to fall down over this when required. A more sumptuous curtain of the same kind, embroidered with cherubim, hung on four such pillars, with silver sockets, divided the holy from the most holy place. It was called the veil, as it hid from the eyes of all but the high priest the inmost sanctuary, where Jehovah dwelt on his mercy seat, between the cherubim above the ark. Hence, "to enter within the veil" is to have the closest access to God. It was only passed by the high priest once a year, on the Day of Atonement. The holy place was entered by the priests daily, to offer incense at the time of morning and evening prayer and to renew the lights on the golden candlestick; and, on the sabbath, to remove the old showbread, and to place the new upon the table.

3. *The Sacred Furniture and Instruments of the Tabernacle.* These are described in separate articles, and therefore it is only necessary to give a list of them here. In the outer court there was the altar of burnt offering and the brazen laver. In the holy place there were three objects: the altar of incense in the center, so as to be directly in front of the ark of the covenant (Ex. 30:1-8), the table of showbread on the north side, and the golden candlestick on the south side. These objects were all considered as being placed before the presence of Jehovah, who dwelt in the holiest of all, though with the veil between. In the Holy of Holies, within the veil, and shrouded in darkness, there was but one object, the ark of the covenant, containing the two tables of stone, inscribed with the Ten Commandments.

4. *History of the Tabernacle.* The tabernacle was dedicated on the first day of the second year after the departure of the Israelites from Egypt. A cloud rested upon it by day and a pillar of fire rested upon it by night during the period of the wilderness wanderings. Each time the cloud moved the Levites took the structure to pieces and put it together again at the new camping ground (Ex. 40:34-38). During the conquest of Canaan the ark remained in the camp at Gilgal. After the settlement of the Israelites, Joshua set up the tabernacle at Shiloh, where it remained during the period of the Judges (Josh. 18:1). With the capture of the ark by the Philistines, the tabernacle lost its glory and its value (Ps. 78:60). During a large part of David's reign and until the building of

the temple in Solomon's reign, the tabernacle was at the high place of Gideon (1 Chr. 16:39, 21:29). Finally when the temple was completed, Solomon laid the tabernacle up in the temple (1 K. 8:4; 2 Chr. 5:5), which was constructed on the same model, but with dimensions twice as large.

Tabernacles, Feast of the last of the three great annual festivals of the Hebrews, which lasted from the fifteenth until the twenty-second of the seventh month, Tishri. Every able-bodied man of Israel was required to appear before the Lord at the temple in Jerusalem on each of these three occasions (Ex. 23:16–17; Lev. 23:34–36, 39–43; Num. 29:12–38; Deut. 16:13–15, 31:10–13; 1 K. 9:25, 12:32–33; 2 Chr. 8:12–13; Zech. 14:16). The time of the festival fell in autumn, when the whole of the chief fruits of the ground, the corn, the wine, and the oil, were gathered in (Ex. 23:16; Lev. 23:39; Deut. 16:13–15). Its duration was strictly only seven days (Lev. 23:34; Deut. 16:13). But it was followed by a day of holy convocation, distinguished by sacrifices of its own, which was sometimes spoken of as an eighth day (Lev. 23:36; Neh. 8:18). This latter passage contains an account of the observance of the feast of Ezra. During the seven days of the feast, the Israelites were commanded to dwell in booths or huts formed of the boughs of trees. The boughs were of the olive, palm, pine, myrtle, and other trees with thick foliage (Neh. 8:15–16). The burnt offerings of the Feast of Tabernacles were by far more numerous than those of any other festival. There were offered on each day two rams, fourteen lambs, and a kid for a sin offering. Most peculiar was the arrangement of the sacrifices of the bullocks, in all amounting to seventy (Num. 29:12–38). The eighth day was a day of holy convocation of peculiar solemnity. On the morning of this day, the Hebrews left their huts, and dismantled them, and took up their abode again in their houses. The special offerings of the day were a bullock, a ram, seven lambs, and a goat for a sin offering (Num. 29:36, 38). When the Feast of Tabernacles fell on a sabbatical year, portions of the Law were read each day in public, to men, women, children, and strangers (Deut. 31:10–13). We find Ezra reading the Law during the festival "day by day, from the first day to the last day" (Neh. 8:18). There are two particulars in the observance of the Feast of Tabernacles which appear to be referred to in the NT, but are not noticed in the OT. These were, the ceremony of pouring out some water of the pool of Siloam, and the display of some

great lights in the court of the women in the evening. Both men and women assembled in the court of the women, expressly to hold a rejoicing of the drawing of the water of Siloam. There were set upon the court two lofty stands, each supporting four great lamps. These were lighted on each night of the festival. Though all the Hebrew annual festivals were seasons of rejoicing, the Feast of Tabernacles was, in this respect, distinguished above them all. The main purposes of the Feast of Tabernacles are plainly set forth (Ex. 23:16; Lev. 23:43). It was to be at once a thanksgiving for the harvest, and a commemoration of the time when the Israelites dwelt in tents during their passage through the wilderness. Jews who were unable to attend the festivities at Jerusalem because of the distance of their homes, kept the festival at the synagogue of the town where they lived, but with certain limitations.

Tabitha (tăb′ĭ-thá) also called Dorcas, a Christian woman of Joppa who was full of good works (Acts 9:36). Tabitha died while Peter was in the neighboring town of Lydda which was close to Joppa. Two disciples were sent to urge Peter to come to Joppa. When he arrived in the upper chamber where the body of Dorcas was being kept, he discovered she had already been prepared for burial and a great many people were weeping because of her passing. They showed Peter the garments and coats which Dorcas had made. Peter asked all of them to leave the room; and after praying said, "Tabitha, arise" (Acts 9:40). She opened her eyes, sat up, and with help of the apostle, arose from her couch. This great miracle produced an extraordinary effect in Joppa and was the occasion of many believing in the Lord. Luke gives Dorcas as the Greek equivalent for Tabitha.

Tabor (tā′bēr) Tabor is mentioned in 1 Chr. 6:77 as a city of the Merarite Levites.

Tabor and **Mount Tabor** (tā′bēr) a limestone mountain in Galilee approximately six miles east of Nazareth. Its sides rise steeply from the valley of Jezreel, converging at the top to form a dome-shaped surface. Although Tabor reaches a maximum elevation of only 1843 feet, its isolation and steep sides give it a majestic appearance. Tabor does not appear in the NT but is prominent in the OT. It is first mentioned by name in connection with the division of the land among the tribes after the Conquest as a meeting place of the territories of Issachar, Naphtali, and Zebulun (Josh. 19:22). Barak, at the commandment of Deborah, assembled his forces on Tabor and went into the plain and conquered Sisera on the banks of Kishon (Judg. 4:6–15). During the oppression of Midian, it was the place where two Midianite kings, Zebah and Zalmunna, killed the brother of Gideon (Judg. 8:18). There is a tradition that Mount Tabor was the site of the transfiguration. This cannot be determined since the name of the mount is not given in the gospel narratives (Mt. 17:1–8; Mk. 9:2–8; Lk. 9:28–36).

Tabor, the plain of this is translated the Oak of Tabor in the ASV. It is mentioned in 1 Sam. 10:3 as one of the points in the return trip of Saul after his anointing. Ewald seems to consider it certain that Tabor and Deborah are merely different modes of pronouncing the same name. He accordingly identified the Oak of Tabor as the tree under which Deborah, Rachel's nurse, was buried (Gen. 35:8). This can be received only as a conjecture, even though it is ingenious.

tabret see **timbrel**

Tabrimon (tăb'rĭm-ŏn) properly Tabrimmon. The father of Ben-hadad I the king of Damascus (1 K. 15:18).

tache the word occurs in the KJV and is equivalent to clasp. It is used in describing the structure of the tabernacle and its fittings (Ex. 26:6, 11, 33, 35:11, 36:13, 39:33). It indicates the small hooks by which a curtain is suspended to the rings from which it hangs, or connected vertically, as in the case of the veil of the Holy of Holies.

Tachmonite (tăk'mŏ-nīt) "the Tachmonite that sat in the seat," chief among David's captains (2 Sam. 23:8) is in 1 Chr. 11:11 called "Jashobeam an Hachmonite," or, as the margin gives it, "son of Hacmoni." Kennicott has shown that the words translated "he that sat in the seat" are a corruption of Jashobeam and that "the Tachmonite" is a corruption of the "son of Hahmoni," which was the family or local name of Jashobeam. Therefore he concludes "Jashobeam the Hachmonite" to have been the true reading.

Tadmor (tăd'mŏr) called Tadmor in the wilderness (2 Chr. 8:4), was built by Solomon. One of the reasons for Solomon's prosperity was his ability to control the trade routes between Egypt and Arabia and also those between Asia Minor and Mesopotamia. Tadmor controlled the caravan routes between the Red Sea, the Persian Gulf, and the Mediterranean. It is generally believed that Tadmor is the same city known to the Greeks and Romans as Palmyra.

Tahan (tā'hăn) a descendant of Ephraim (Num. 26:35). In 1 Chr. 7:25, he appears as the son of Telah.

Tahanites (tā'hȧ-nīts) the descendants of the preceding (Num. 26:35).

Tahath (tā'hăth) 1. A Kohathite Levite, ancestor of Samuel and Heman (1 Chr. 6:24–37). Further described as the son of Bered and great-grandson of Ephraim (1 Chr. 7:20). 2. The name of a desert station between Makheloth and Tarah (Num. 33:26). The site has not been identified.

Tahpanhes (tä'păn-hēz), or **Tehaphnehes** (tē-hăf'nē-hēz), or **Tahapanes** (tȧ-hăp'ȧ-nēz) this was an Egyptian city of great importance during the time of the prophets Jeremiah and Ezekiel. The name is Egyptian and resembles that of the Egyptian queen Tahpenes. When Johanan and the other captains went into Egypt, they came to Tahpanhes (Jer. 43:7). The Jews in Jeremiah's time remained here (Jer. 44:1). It was an important town in Lower Egypt on the eastern border mentioned with Noph or Memphis (Jer. 2:16, 46:14). Here stood a house of Pharaoh Nophra, before which Jeremiah hid great stones (Jer. 43:8–10).

Tahpenes (tä'pē-nēz) a proper name of an Egyptian queen. She was the wife of Pharaoh who received Hadad the Edomite and who gave him her sister in marriage (1 K. 11:18–20).

Tahrea (tä'rē-ȧ) son of Micah and grandson of Mephibosheth (1 Chr. 9:41).

Tahtimhodshi, the Land of (tä'tĭm-hŏd-shī) one of the places visited by Joab during his census of the land of Israel. It is located between Gilead and Dan-jaan (2 Sam. 24:6).

talent the greatest weight of the Hebrews. See **weights and measures**

Talitha Cumi (tăl'ĭ-thȧ koo'mĕ) two Syriac words (Mk. 5:41) signifying "Damsel, arise."

Talmai (tăl'mî) 1. One of the three sons of "the Anak" who were slain by the men of Judah (Num. 13:22; Josh. 15:14; Judg. 1:10). 2. Son of Ammihud, king of Geshur (2 Sam. 3:3, 13:37; 1 Chr. 3:2). He was probably a petty chieftain dependent on David.

Talmon (tăl'mŏn) the head of a family of doorkeepers in the temple (1 Chr. 9:17; Neh. 11:19). Some of his descendants returned with Zerubbabel (Ezra 2:42; Neh. 7:45). They were employed in their hereditary office in the days of Nehemiah and Ezra (Neh. 12:25).

Tamah (tā'mȧ) the children of Tamah, or Thamah (Ezra 2:53), were among the Nethinim who returned with Zerubbabel (Neh. 7:55).

Tamar (tā'mĕr) the name of three remarkable women in the history of Israel: 1. The wife successively of two sons of Judah, Er and Onan (Gen. 38:6–30). Her importance in the Bible grows out of her importance to the lineage of

Judah. Er and Onan had died without issue. Bath-shua, Judah's wife, died leaving him one child Shelah, whom Judah was unwilling to trust to the union with Tamar. Accordingly she resorted to the dangerous expedient of entrapping the father himself into the union, which resulted in the birth of twins, Pharez and Zarah. It was through Pharez the Messianic genealogy through Judah was continued.

2. Daughter of David and Maachah the Geshurite princess, and thus sister of Absalom (2 Sam. 13:1–32; 1 Chr. 3:9). She and her brother were alike, remarkable for their extraordinary beauty. This fatal beauty inspired a frantic passion in her half brother, Amnon, the eldest son of David by Ahinoam, who misused her (2 Sam. 13:1–32). Amnon was later murdered by Absalom (2 Sam. 13:29).

3. The daughter of Absalom (2 Sam. 14:27). She ultimately, by her marriage with Uriah of Gibeah, became the mother of Maachiah, the future queen of Judah, the wife of Abijah (1 K. 15:2).

4. An undetermined place on the southeastern frontier of Judah named in Ezek. 47:19.

Tanach (tā′năk) a slight variation of the name Taanach (Josh. 21:25).

Tanhumeth (tăn-hū′mĕth) the father of Seraiah in the time of Gedaliah (2 K. 25:23; Jer. 40:8).

Taphath (tā′făth) the daughter of Solomon who was married to Ben-abinadad (1 K. 4:11).

Tappuah (tăp-pū′á) 1. A city of Judah in the district of the Shephelah, or lowland (Josh. 15:34).

2. A place on the boundary of the "children of Joseph" (Josh. 16:8, 17:8).

3. One of the sons of Hebron, of the tribe of Judah (1 Chr. 2:43).

Tappuah, the Land of a district named in the specification of the boundary between Ephraim and Manasseh (Josh. 17:8).

Tarah (tā′rá) a desert station of the Israelites between Tahath and Mithcah (Num. 33:27).

Taralah (tăr′á-là) one of the towns in the allotment of Benjamin (Josh. 18:27).

Tarea (tā′rê-á) the same as **Tahrea**, the son of Micah (1 Chr. 8:35).

tares this weed mentioned by Jesus (Mt. 13:25) was the "darnel." The darnel, before it ripens into the ear, is very similar in appearance to wheat. For this reason the tares were allowed to grow until they were distinguished from wheat. Then the tares were gathered and burned. Even though the tares spreads of itself, an enemy could scatter the seed in another's field.

Tarpelites, the (tär′pĕl-ītes) a race of colonists who were planted in the cities of Samaria after the captivity of the northern kingdom of Israel (Ezra 4:9).

Tarshish (tär′shĭsh) 1. Probably Tartessus, a city and emporium of the Phoenicians in the south of Spain. The Phoenicians developed the city because of its mineral wealth. "Tarshish" is the Phoenician word for "mine" or "smeltry." There seems to have been a special relation between Tarshish and Tyre, as there was at one time between Tartessus and the Phoenicians. In time "the ships of Tarshish," especially designed for long voyages, which sailed the Mediterranean and the Red Sea, carried gold, silver, tin, iron, and lead (Ezek. 27:12).

2. From the book of Chronicles, it may be assumed that there was a Tarshish accessible from the Red Sea, in addition to the Tarshish in the south of Spain. This with regard to the ships of Tarshish, which Jehoshaphat caused to be constructed at Ezion-geber on the Aellanitic Gulf of the Red Sea were to go to Tarshish (1 K. 22:48). It is said in the Chronicles (2 Chr. 9:21) that the ships of Solomon were to have gone to Tarshish to bring cargoes of gold, silver, ivory, apes, and peacocks. It is reasonable to assume that the "ships of Tarshish" came to signify any distant place where the ships took on cargo (1 K. 10:22). The gold could have come from Africa or Ophir in Arabia; the ivory and the apes could have been imported from Africa, but the peacocks point to the Indian Ocean.

3. Tarshish occurs in Gen. 10:4 and is represented as one of the sons of Javan.

Tarsus (tär′sŭs) the chief city and capital of Cilicia, while a "no mean city" is made illustrious because it was the birthplace and early residence of the apostle Paul (Acts 9:11, 21:39, 22:3). Even in the flourishing period of Greek history, it was a city of considerable consequence. The city flourished under Alexander the Great, and as a member of the Seleucid kingdom, though for a time it was under the rule of the Ptolemies. In the civil war of Rome, it took the side of Caesar, and Augustus made it a free city. Tarsus was a place of much commerce and great cultural importance.

Tartak (tär′tăk) one of the gods of the Avite or Avvite, colonists of Samaria (2 K. 17:31).

Tartan (tär′tăn) occurs only in 2 K. 18:17 and Isa. 20:1, has been generally regarded as a proper name with the probability that it could be a title or official designation.

Tatnai (tăt′nī) satrap of the province west of the Euphrates in the time of Darius Hystaspes (Ezra 5:3, 6, 6:6, 13).

Taverns, the Three see **Three Taverns**

taxes 1. Under the Judges the only taxes incumbent upon the people were the tithes, the firstfruits, the redemption-money of the firstborn. The payment by each Israelite of the half shekel as "atonement money," for the service of the tabernacle, on taking the census of the people (Ex. 30:13), does not appear to have the character of a recurring tax, but to have been supplementary to the freewill offering of Ex. 25:1–7, levied for the consecration of the tabernacle.

After the return from Babylon there was an annual payment for maintaining the fabric and services of the temple; this practice began as a voluntary compact to pay one-third of a shekel (Neh. 10:32). This is the *didrachama* in the time of Jesus (Mt. 27:24) which was paid by every Jew.

2. The kingdom with its centralized government and greater magnificence involved larger expenditures and heavier taxations. The chief burdens seem to have been: a tithe of the soil and livestock (1 Sam. 8:15, 17); forced military service for a month every year (1 Sam. 8:12; 1 K. 9:22); gifts to the king (1 Sam. 10:27, 16:20, 17:18); import duties (1 K. 10:15); the monopoly of certain branches of commerce (1 K. 9:28, 10:28–29, 22:48).

3. Under the Persian empire the taxes paid by the Jewish people were the same as other subject races. In Judah, as in the other provinces, the inhabitants had to provide for the maintenance of the governor's household besides money payments of forty shekels a day (Neh. 5:14–15).

4. Under the Egyptian kings, the taxes paid by the Jews became heavier. The "farming" system of taxation in its worst form was adopted. The contract sum for the taxes of Phoenicia, Judah, and Samaria has been estimated at about 8000 talents. An unscrupulous individual would bid twice the amount, and thus by force and cruelty extract an even larger sum from the people.

5. The pressure of Roman taxation, though not greater, was probably more galling, as it was more thorough and systematic, and a more distinctive mark of bondage. The taxes were systematically formed, and the publicans appeared as a new curse to the country (Mt. 27:24; Rom. 13:7). In addition to this, there was a poll tax paid by a very few and regarded as a special badge of servitude.

taxing two distinct registrations of taxings are mentioned in the NT and both of them by Luke. The first was the result of an edict of Caesar Augustus for all the Roman empire to be taxed (Lk. 2:1). The second and more important one is distinctly associated with the revolt of Judas of Galilee (Acts 5:37). In both cases, the census was taken for the purpose of taxation.

Tebah (tē'bà) eldest of the sons of Nahor, by his concubine Reumah (Gen. 22:24).

Tebaliah (tĕb-à-lī'à) third son of Hosah of the children of Merari (1 Chr. 26:11).

Tebeth (tē'bĕth) see **month**

Tehinnah (tē-hĭn'nà) the father or founder of Ir-Nahash, the city Nahash, and the son of Eshton (1 Chr. 4:12).

teil tree see **oak**

Tekoa and **Tekoah** (tē-kō'à) 1. A town in the tribe of Judah (2 Chr. 11:6), on the range of hills which rises near Hebron, and stretches eastward toward the Dead Sea. Jerome says Tekoa was six Roman miles from Bethlehem. The "wise woman" whom Joab employed to effect a reconciliation between David and Absalom was taken from this place (2 Sam. 14:2). It was one of the places which Rehoboam fortified at the beginning of his reign, as a defense against invasion from the south (2 Chr. 11:6). Some of the people from Tekoa took part in building the walls of Jerusalem after the return from captivity (Neh. 3:5, 27). But Tekoa is chiefly memorable as the birthplace of the prophet Amos (Amos 1:1).

2. A name occurring in the genealogies of Judah (1 Chr. 2:24, 4:5) as the son of Ashur.

Tekoite (tē-kō'īt) the Ira ben Ikkesh, one of David's warriors, is thus designated (2 Sam. 23:26; 1 Chr. 11:28, 27:9). The common people among the Tekoites displayed great activity in the repairs of the walls of Jerusalem under Nehemiah (Neh. 3:5, 27).

Telah (tē'là) a descendant of Ephraim, and ancestor of Joshua (1 Chr. 7:25).

Telaim (tē-lā'ĭm) the place at which Saul collected and numbered his forces before his attack on Amalek (1 Sam. 15:4).

Telassar (tē-lăs'ẽr) mentioned in 2 K. 19:12 and Isa. 37:12 as a city inhabited by the "children of Eden," which had been conquered, and was held in the time of Sennacherib by the Assyrians.

Telem (tē'lĕm) 1. One of the cities in the extreme south of Judah (Josh. 15:24). It occurs between Ziph and Bealoth, but has not been identified.

2. A porter or doorkeeper of the temple in the time of Ezra (Ezra 10:24).

Tel-harsa, or **Tel-haresha** (tĕl-här'sà) or (tĕl-här'ē-shà) one of the Babylonian towns mentioned in Ezra 2:59 and Neh. 7:61.

Tel-melah (tĕl-mē'là) joined with Tel-harsa and Cherub in the two passages mentioned above.

Tema (tē'mà) the ninth son of Ishmael (Gen. 25:15; 1 Chr. 1:30); whence the tribe named after him (mentioned in Job 6:19; Jer. 25:23); and also the land occupied by this tribe (Isa. 21:13–14). The name is identified satisfactorily with Teyma, a small town on the confines of Syria, between it and Wadi-l-kura, on the road of the Damascus pilgrim caravan.

Teman (tē'măn) 1. A son of Eliphaz, son of Esau by Adah (Gen. 36:11, 15, 42; 1 Chr. 1:36, 53).

2. A country and probably a city named after the Edomite phylarch, or from which he took his name. It is probable that Teman was a southern portion of the land of Edom. Teman is mentioned in five places by the prophets, in four of which it is connected with Edom, and in two with Dedan (Jer. 49:7–8).

Temani (tĕm'à-nī) see **Teman**

Temanite see **Teman**

Temeni (tĕm'ê-nī) son of Ashur, the father of Tekoa, by his wife Naarah (1 Chr. 4:6).

temple 1. TEMPLE OF SOLOMON. David first proposed to replace the tabernacle with a permanent structure but was forbidden to do so by the prophet Nathan (2 Sam. 7:5). The task was left for Solomon who commenced the great undertaking in the fourth year of his reign with the assistance of King Hiram of Syria, and completed it in seven years, about 1005 B.C. The arrangements of the temple were identical with the tabernacle except the dimensions (1 K. 5:1–13).

The interior of the temple was sixty cubits in length, twenty cubits in width, and thirty cubits in height. The porch of the temple was twenty cubits wide and ten cubits deep. Chambers with windows were built along the side walls of the temple. Taking all the parts together, the temple of Solomon measured eighty by forty cubits (1 K. 6:1–6).

The walls of the temple were covered with cedar and the floor with fir so there was no stone seen. The most holy place was overlaid with pure gold (1 K. 6:14–22). The enclosure of the temple was a low wall consisting of three courses of stone and a row of cedar beams (1 K. 6:36). No mention is made in the Bible of any porticoes, gateways, or any architectural ornaments in this enclosure.

Furniture. The furniture in Solomon's temple included the great brazen altar of burnt offering in the open courtyard. Another feature was the molten sea of bronze, ten cubits from rim to rim and five cubits in height (1 K. 7:23–26). It rested upon twelve bronze oxen facing to the four points of the compass. There were other bronze articles for ablution purposes and for the altar (1 K. 7:27–45).

The holy place contained the ten golden candlesticks (1 K. 7:49; 2 Chr. 4:7); the table of showbread; and the incense altar overlaid with gold (1 K. 7:48–50).

The most holy place contained two huge cherubim of olive wood overlaid with gold ten cubits high (1 K. 6:23–27). The ark of the covenant containing the tablets of the Decalogue rested under the wings of the cherubim. Passage from the holy place to the most holy place led through double doors of olive wood embellished with carvings of cherubim, palm trees, and open flowers overlaid with gold (1 K. 6:31–32). It was in this sanctuary that the invisible presence of the Lord dwelt.

2. TEMPLE OF ZERUBBABEL. We have few particulars regarding the temple the Jews built after their return from captivity and no description to let us realize its appearance. The Biblical accounts of the second temple are meager in detail. Ezra focuses attention on the decree of Cyrus (Ezra 6:3–5). Another account in Haggai stresses the urgent need to rebuild the temple (Hag. 1:1–6); and who compares the lesser glory of the second temple with that of the one of Solomon (Hag. 2:3). Zechariah predicts the rebuilding of the temple (Zech. 1:16), and the laying of the foundation.

Zerubbabel's temple exceeded the dimensions of Solomon's temple being one hundred cubits in length and sixty cubits high. The magnificence of the second temple did not compare with the splendor of the first temple judging from Ezra's reports (Ezra 3:12). The ark of the covenant was absent in the second temple since its whereabouts was never known after the Captivity.

3. TEMPLE OF EZEKIEL. The third temple described in Ezekiel existed only in the vision of the prophet which he saw while he was residing on the banks of the Chebar in Babylonia. It was not the description of a temple that would ever exist in Jerusalem (Ezek. 40–47). Messianic expectations are couched in Ezekiel's description. For example, the "brazen sea" is replaced with a stream of living water flowing from the temple site to the Dead Sea causing the desert to bloom enriching the lives of the inhabitants (Ezek. 47:1–12).

4. TEMPLE OF HEROD. For our knowledge of the last and greatest of the Jewish temples, we are indebted almost wholly to the account of Josephus. The Bible in spite of numerous references in the NT unfortunately contains nothing to assist the researchers of antiquity in this respect. The arrangements and dimensions of

the temple of Herod were similar to those of Zerubbabel. It was surrounded by an inner enclosure of great strength and magnificence measuring 180 cubits by 200 cubits, adorned by porchways and ten gateways of great splendor. Beyond this was an outer enclosure measuring 400 cubits each way.

The temple of Herod was not an alteration but a completely new and complex structure which beggars description. It is clear that the temple was surrounded by a wall on all four sides serving as fortification, with a fort, Antonia, located on the northwest corner. The broad outer court within the walls was designated as the Court of the Gentiles. Gates led through a low balustrade into the court surrounding the temple. One was known as the "Beautiful Gate" (Acts 3:2, 10). As one ascended through one of the entrances into the inner court, there was a warning for Gentiles to go no further by a death threat.

The temple proper was located in the heart of the temple enclosure. The Jew and his wife could enter into the building known as the Women's Court. Only the Jewish men could go into the Court of Israel where the great altar stood. The sanctuary faced east with first the holy place and the most holy place. Nothing can be added to describe the interior of the sanctuary since it had to follow the patterns of the tabernacle and the temple of Solomon.

In summary, it may be said Herod's temple was of incomparable beauty and splendor. From the beginning, forty-six years passed in building the temple (Jn. 2:20). The outer wall was a spacious and elegant arcade with synagogues and shops to provide for all the secular and religious needs of the Jews. The main area contained the general meeting place of the Great Sanhedrin Court.

Ten Commandments these are the basic laws of the Hebrew nation. While traditionally they have been called the "Ten Commandments," the Scriptures refer to them as the "Ten Words" (Ex. 34:28; Deut. 4:13, 10:4), the "Covenant" (Ex. 19:5; 1 K. 8:21; 2 Chr. 6:11), or very often, as the "Testimony" (Ex. 25:16, 21, 31:18). The term "commandments" had come into use by the time of Christ (Lk. 18:20). The listing of the commands appears twice in the Scriptures, the earliest being found in Ex. 20:1–17, and the later listing being found in Deut. 5:6–21. The differences between the two listings are slight, with the major one being a reference in the first statement of the command in connection with the sabbath, as connected with the fact that God rested on the seventh day in creating

the earth. The second listing does not mention this, but refers to the sabbath in connection with God's deliverance of the people from Egypt. The slight differences, of course, do not constitute contradictions. The commandments were spoken by God at Mount Sinai, and were written on two tables of stone (Ex. 31:18). The writing evidently was on both front and back of stones (Ex. 32:15). There has been some disagreement among later scholars about how the commandments should be divided, since the Bible does not number them individually. The Jews of later generations considered Ex. 20:2, "I am the Lord thy God, which have brought thee out of the land of Egypt, out of the house of bondage" as the first commandment. Most others have considered this as a preface statement to the entire group of ten, since it is not stated in the form of a commandment. Roman Catholic and Lutheran churches have accepted the division advocated by Augustine, which claims the first three commandments to have been written on one tablet, while the seven remaining were written on the second tablet. Augustine grouped the commandments against having other gods and against making graven images together as one, and then divided the last commandment concerning coveting into two parts, against a neighbor's wife, and against a neighbor's property. By far the largest group of scholars has divided the commandments into two groups, with the first four commandments being those against polytheism, idolatry, taking God's name in vain, and the keeping of the sabbath, all of which were considered to have been on the first tablet of stone. This leaves then for the second tablet of stone the remaining six commandments, with the final one being a restriction against coveting, both of a neighbor's wife and a neighbor's goods. This division is the oldest that is known. It was recognized by Josephus (*Ant.* III.5), by Philo (*Decalogue*), and by many others both in ancient and modern times. In Mk. 10:19, Jesus named the last six of the commandments as a unit in talking with the rich young ruler, thus seeming to give his acceptance to this grouping. According to it the first four commandments have to do with man's relation to God, and the last six have to do with man's relation to his fellowman. To the ten commandments which we find in the Bible, the Samaritan Pentateuch has added an eleventh, "But when the Lord thy God shall have brought thee into the land of Canaan, thou goest to possess it, thou shalt set thee up two great stones, and shalt plaster them with plaster, and shalt write upon these stones all the words of this Law. Moreover, after thou shalt have passed over Jordan, thou shalt set up those stones, which I command thee this day, on Mount Gerizim, and thou shalt build there an altar to the Lord thy God, an altar of stones; thou shalt not lift up any iron thereon. . . ." This addition has every mark of being a bold attempt to claim for the schismatic worship on Mount Gerizim the solemn sanction of the voice of God, but does not have the ring of authenticity.

tent the earliest dwellings mentioned in the Bible were movable tents, such as are used by the nomad races, by shepherds, and by armies (Gen. 4:20, 25:27; Judg. 8:11). Ordinarily these tents were made of black goats' hair cloth (Song of S. 1:5), and were fastened by ropes and stakes (Ex. 35:18; Isa. 54:2). Tents vary in size, with some of them being large enough to have as many as nine tent poles and several compartments. When pastureland is exhausted, the nomads take down their tents, pack them on camels, and remove to another place (Gen. 26:17, 22, 25; Isa. 38:12). Not until the time that the Hebrews returned from Egyptian bondage did they become inhabitants of cities with permanent dwellings.

tent of meeting Exodus 33:7–11 refers to a temporary tent where God met with his people. It seems to have been the headquarters of the camp, where judicial proceedings carried on by Moses took place (Ex. 18:13, 33:7; Deut. 19:17). This tent was cared for by Joshua (Ex. 33:11) while the regular tabernacle was cared for by Aaron (Deut. 10:6).

Terah the father of Abram, Nahor, and Haran, and through them the ancestor of the great families of the Israelites, Ishmaelites, Midianites, Moabites, and Ammonites (Gen. 11:24–32). He lived in Ur of Chaldees most of his life, where he worshiped other divinities than Jehovah (Josh. 24:2). He moved with Abraham and Lot to Haran in his old age and died there at the age of 205 years (Gen. 11:25–32).

teraphim images of household gods, which were connected with magical rites and varied in size from those that were small enough to be hidden in a saddle of a camel (Gen. 31:19, 30, 34) to one apparently large enough to resemble a man (1 Sam. 19:13). Rachel carried away the teraphim of her father Laban and sat upon them in her saddle while Michal hid one in David's bed to deceive her father's messengers. Laban regarded his teraphim as gods, and they likely also carried with them the right of ownership to property. Teraphim were used by those who brought in corrupt practices and added

them to the worship of Jehovah. Teraphim were consulted for oracular answers by the Israelites (Judg. 18:5–6; 1 Sam. 15:22–23, 19:13, 16; Zech. 10:2), and by the Babylonians, in the case of Nebuchadnezzar (Ex. 21:19–22). On every revival of true religion in Israel, the teraphim were swept away with other idols (2 K. 23:24).

Teresh one of the two eunuchs whose plot to assassinate Ahasuerus was discovered by Mordecai (Est. 2:21, 6:2). He was hanged.

Tertius (tûr'shĭ-ŭs) Paul's amanuensis, who wrote for him the Roman letter (Rom. 16:22).

Tertullus (tĕr-tŭl'ŭs) he is identified as "a certain orator" (Acts 24:1–8), and was employed by the high priest and Sanhedrin to accuse the apostle Paul at Caesarea before the Roman procurator, Antonius Felix. He evidently belonged to the class of professional orators. We may infer that he was of Roman, or, in all events, of Italian origin. The exordium of his speech is designed to conciliate the good will of the procurator, and is accordingly overcharged with flattery. The commendations of Tertullus were not altogether unfounded, as Felix had really succeeded in putting down several seditious movements.

tetrarch (tĕ'trärk) properly the sovereign or governor of the fourth part of a country. 1. Herod Antipas (Mt. 14:1; Lk. 3:1, 19, 9:7; Acts 13:1), who is commonly distinguished as "Herod the tetrarch," although the title of "king" is also assigned to him both by Matthew (14:9) and by Mark (6:14, 22).

2. Herod Philip, who is said by Luke (3:1) to have been "tetrarch of Ituraea, and of the region of Trachonitis."

3. Lysanias, who is said (Lk. 3:1) to have been "tetrarch of Abilene." The title of tetrarch was at this time probably applied to petty tributary princes without any such determinate meaning. But it appears from Josephus that the tetrarchies of Antipas and Philip were regarded as constituting each a fourth part of their father's kingdom. We conclude that in these two cases, at least, the title was used in its strict and literal sense.

Thaddeus (thă-dē'ŭs) a name in Mark's catalogue of the twelve apostles (3:18); from a comparison with the catalogue of Luke (6:15; Acts 1:13), it seems that the three names of Judas, Lebbeus, and Thaddeus were borne by one and the same person. We know nothing of his life, labors, and death. He is only mentioned among those who could only partly see the spiritual kingdom of Jesus (Jn. 14:22). Tradition claims that he died at Edessa.

Thahash (thā'hăsh) son of Nahor by his concubine Reumah (Gen. 22:24).

Thamah (thā'mȧ) ancestor of a family of Nethinim who returned with Zerubbabel (Ezra 2:53).

Thamar see **Tamar**

Thamnatha (thăm'nă-thà) a city of Judea, now called Tibneh, located halfway between Jerusalem and the Mediterranean.

thank offering or **peace offering** sacrifice. Its ceremonial is described in Lev. 3. The peace offerings, unlike other sacrifices, were not ordained to be offered in fixed and regular course. It seems to have been entirely spontaneous, offered as occasion arose, from the feeling of the sacrificer himself (Lev. 19:5). Peace offerings were made for the people on a great scale at periods of unusual solemnity or rejoicing. In two cases only (Judg. 20:26; 2 Sam. 24:25), peace offerings are mentioned as offered with burnt offerings at a time of national sorrow and fasting.

Thara (thā'rȧ) Terah, the father of Abraham (Lk. 3:34).

Tharra (thăr'rȧ) a form of Teresh (Est. 12:1).

Tharshish (thär'shĭsh) a Benjaminite, one of the family of Bilhan and the house of Jediael (1 Chr. 7:10).

theater (thē-ȧ'tẽr) for the general subject, see *Dictionary of Antiquities*, pp. 995-98. For the explanation of the Biblical allusions, two or three points only require notice. The Greek term, like the corresponding English term, denotes the place where dramatic performances are exhibited, and also the scene itself, or spectacle, which is witnessed there. It occurs in the first sense in Acts 19:29. It was in the theater at Caesarea that Herod Agrippa I gave audience to the Tyrian deputies and was himself struck with death, because he heard so gladly the impious acclamations of the people (Acts 12:21-23). The other sense of the term occurs in 1 Cor. 4:9, where the KJV renders, "God hath set forth us, the apostles, last, as it were appointed to death; for we are made a spectacle unto the world, and to angels, and to men." Instead of "spectacle" some might prefer the more energetic Saxon, "gazing stock," as in Tyndale, Cranmer, and the Geneva Bible.

Thebes (thēbz) [AV, No, the multitude of No, populous No] a chief city of ancient Egypt, long the capital of the upper country, and the seat of the Diospolitan dynasties, that ruled over all Egypt at the era of its highest splendor. It was situated on both sides of the Nile, 400 or 500 miles from its mouth. The sacred name of Thebes was P-amen, "the abode of Amon," which the Greeks reproduced in their *Diospolis*, especially with the addition, the Great. No-amon is the name of Thebes in the Hebrew Scriptures (Jer. 46:25; Nah. 3:8). The origin of the city is lost in antiquity. R. Niebuhr is of the opinion that Thebes was much older than Memphis, and that, "after the centre of Egyptian life was transferred to Lower Egypt, Memphis acquired its greatness through the ruin of Thebes." But both cities date from our earliest authentic knowledge of Egyptian history. The first allusion to Thebes in classical literature is the familiar passage of the *Iliad*: "Egyptian Thebes, where are vast treasures laid up in the houses; where are a hundred gates, and from each two hundred men go forth with horses and chariots." In the first century before Christ, Diodorus visited Thebes, and he devoted several sections of his general work to its history and appearance. Though he saw the city when it had sunk to quite secondary importance, he confirms the tradition of its early grandeur—its circuit of 140 stadia, the size of its public edifices, the magnificence of its temples, the number of its monuments, the dimensions of its private houses, some of them four or five stories high—all giving it an air of grandeur and beauty surpassing not only all other cities of Egypt, but of the world. The monuments of Thebes are the most reliable witnesses for the ancient splendor of the city. These are found in almost equal proportions upon both sides of the river. The plan of the city, as indicated by the principal monuments, was nearly quadrangular, measuring two miles from north to south and four from east to west. Its four great landmarks were, Karnak and Luxor upon the Arabian side, and Qoornah and Medeenet Haboo upon the Libyan side. There are indications that each of these temples may have been connected with those facing it upon two sides by grand *dromoi* lined with sphinxes and other colossal figures. Upon the western bank there was almost a continuous line of temples and public edifices for a distance of two miles from Qoornah to Medeenet Haboo; and Wilkinson conjectures that from a point near the latter, perhaps in the line of the colossi, the "Royal Street" ran down to the river which was crossed by a ferry terminating at Luxor, on the eastern side. Behind this long range of temples and palaces are the Libyan hills, which for a distance of five miles are excavated to the depth of several hundred feet for sepulchral chambers. Some of these in the number and variety of their chambers, the finish of their sculptures, and the beauty and freshness of their frescoes, are among the most remarkable monuments of Egyptian grandeur and skill. The eastern side of the river is distinguished by the remains of Luxor and Karnak, the latter being of itself a city of temples. The approach to Karnak from the south is marked by a series of majestic gateways and towers, which are the appendages of later times to the original structure. The temple properly faces the river, i.e., toward the northwest. The courts and propylaea connected with this structure occupy a space nearly 1800 feet square, and the buildings represent nearly every dynasty of Egypt. Ezekiel proclaims the destruction of Thebes by the arm of Babylon (30:14–16); and Jeremiah predicted the same overthrow (46:25–26). The city lies today a nest of Arab hovels amid crumbling columns and drifting sands. The Persian invader (Cambyses, 525 B.C.) completed the destruction that the Babylonians had begun.

Thebez (thē′bĕz) a town mentioned only in Judg. 9:50, in which Abimelech was fatally wounded by a millstone thrown by a woman from a tower in the city. Thebez is usually identified with the town of Tubas, which still stands about thirteen miles from Shechem.

Thelasar (thē-lā′sẽr) another form of the name examined under **Telassar** (2 K. 19:12).

Theophilus (thē-ŏf′ĭ-lŭs) person to whom Luke addresses his gospel (1:3, "most excellent Theophilus"), as well as the Acts of the Apostles (Acts 1:1). The name actually means "friend of God," but there is no other Biblical evidence as to the identity of Luke's correspondent. Some suppose that the two books were not written to a real person named Theophilus, but rather that they were dedicated to all "friends of God." It appears likely, however, that Theophilus was an actual person, since writings were usually dedicated or written to individuals, and since Luke referred to Theophilus as "most excellent." Although the works were certainly not intended for Theophilus only, it does appear that he was an authentic acquaintance of the author whom he considered worthy of the honor of the dedication.

Some go on to the supposition that Theophilus was a Roman official, judging from the use of the title "most excellent" or "most noble," as this title was used in reference to Felix (Acts 23:26) and Festus (Acts 26:25).

Thessalonians, First Epistle to the (thĕs-à-lō′nĭ-ăns) written by the apostle Paul from Corinth around the year 52 some time after he had founded the Thessalonian church (Acts 17:1–10). Timothy had just returned from Thessalonica, bringing "good news of your faith and love," and this epistle is an expression of the apostle's gratitude on receiving this news. Paul urges the young church to stand firm under persecution. Also he allays much of their concern about theoretical difficulties involved in the second coming of Christ, which they expected at any moment. It is clear that he holds the Thessalonian church in high esteem, and that this epistle was suggested mostly by personal feeling.

Thessalonians, Second Epistle to the written from Corinth shortly after the first, and seems to have been motivated by the desire to stem the Thessalonian's obsession with Christ's second coming. He closes by warning them against impurity and urging them on to hard work.

Thessalonica (thĕs-à-lô-nī′kà) the Roman city on the Macedonian shore of the Aegean Sea (named after Thessalonica, the sister of Alexander the Great), which Paul visited with Silas and Timothy, on his second missionary journey (Acts 17:1–9). It was located on the great Via Egnatia, which connected Rome with the whole region north of the Aegean Sea. Placed as it was, Thessalonica was an invaluable center for the spread of the Gospel. Strabo, in the first century, speaks of Thessalonica as the most populous city in Macedonia. The city, called Salonika today, is still a very active commercial center of modern Greece.

Theudas (thū′dàs) the name of an insurgent mentioned in Gamaliel's speech before the Jewish council (Acts 5:35–39) at the time of the arraignment of the apostles. He appeared, according to Luke's account, at the head of about four hundred men. Josephus speaks of a Theudas who played a similar part in the time of Claudius, about A.D. 44, i.e., some ten or twelve years at least later than the delivery of Gamaliel's speech; and since Luke places his Theudas, in the order of time, before Judas the Galilean, who made his appearance soon after the dethronement of Archelaus, i.e., A.D. 6 or 7, it has been charged that the writer of the Acts either fabricated the speech put into the mouth of Gamaliel, or has brought into it a transaction which took place thirty years or more after the time when it is said to have occurred. Various solutions of the difficulty have been offered. Apart from the possibility of some confusion or misunderstanding about the same Theudas, Luke and Josephus may well have been referring to different individuals, since the name Theudas was a common one.

thief anyone who appropriates what is not his own, as the petty pilferer (Jn. 12:6), the robber or highwayman (Lk. 10:30; RV, robber), the burglar (Mt. 6:20). The highwayman, like Barabbas, often rebelled against Roman rule and fomented strife (Mk. 15:7). The two thieves who were crucified with Christ were of this class. They likely belonged to lawless bands by which Palestine was at that time and afterward infested. Against these brigands every Roman procurator had to wage continual war. It was necessary to use armed police to encounter them (Lk. 22:52). Of the previous history of the two who suffered on Golgotha, we know nothing. Both reviled Jesus on the cross (Mt. 27:44), but subsequently one was touched with awe at the meekness and forgiving spirit of Jesus, and with the fear of God in his heart, confessed the sinfulness of his own past life and acknowledged the righteousness of the Lord (Lk. 23:39-43).

Thimnathat (thĭm'nȧ-thä) see **Timnah**

thistle see **thorns and thistles**

Thomas (tŏm'ȧs) one of the twelve apostles (Mt. 10:3). According to Eusebius, his real name was Judas. This may have been a mere confusion with Thaddeus, who is mentioned in the extract. But it may also be that Thomas was a surname. He was also called Didymus, a Greek name, which means, like Thomas, a twin. Out of this name has grown the tradition that he had a twin sister, Lydia, or that he was a twin brother of our Lord; which last, again, would confirm his identification with Judas (Mt. 13:55). In the listing of the apostles, he is coupled with Matthew (Mt. 10:3; Mk. 3:18; Lk. 6:15) and with Philip (Acts 1:13). Almost all that we know of him is derived from the Gospel of John, in which he is pictured as a man slow to believe, seeing all the difficulties of a case, and yet full of ardent love for his master. When Jesus was going to Jerusalem, thus facing special danger, Thomas said to his fellow disciples, "Let us also go, that we may die with him" (Jn. 11:16). During the Last Supper, Thomas said unto him, "Lord, we know not whither thou goest, and how can we know the way?" (Jn. 14:5). In reply Jesus spoke the well-known words, "I am the way, and the truth, and the life" (Jn. 14:6). Thomas was absent when Jesus appeared to the group of the apostles upon the night of his resurrection day. Upon hearing from the other apostles of Jesus' appearance, Thomas expressed doubt by saying, "Except I see in his hands the prints of the nails, and put my finger into the print of the nails, and put my hand into his side, I will not believe" (Jn. 20:25). Eight days later when Jesus appeared to the apostles, Thomas beholding him said, "My Lord and my God" (Jn. 20:28). In the NT we hear of Thomas only twice again. Once from the Sea of Galilee with the seven disciples, where he is listed next after Peter (Jn. 21:2),

and again in the assemblage of the apostles after the ascension (Acts 1:13). Early traditions, as believed in the fourth century, represent him as preaching in Parthia or Persia and as finally buried at Edessa. Later traditions carry him farther east. His martyrdom is said to have been occasioned by a lance, and is commemorated by the Latin church on December 21, by the Greek church on October 6, and by the Indians on July 1. The tradition that he preached in India is evidenced by a place near Madras known as St. Thomas' Mount.

thorns and thistles Palestine abounds with many different kinds of prickly or thorny shrubs. Among these some of the more common are the box thorn, the acanthus, the artichoke, the thorny caper, the thorny burnet, the star thistle, the sow thistle, the milk thistle, and many other varieties. Perhaps as many as a score of different words are used to refer to these spiny plants. Of greatest interest of all the thorns was that plaited by the Roman soldiers and placed on Christ's head (Mt. 27:29). However, it is not possible to identify the species which was used for this purpose. Figuratively speaking, the apostle Paul referred to some physical infirmity as a "thorn in the flesh" (2 Cor. 12:7). He described it as a messenger of Satan and, although much speculation concerning its identity has resulted, the nature of the infirmity is unknown.

Three Taverns a small station on the Appian Way, along which the apostle Paul traveled from Puteoli to Rome (Acts 28:15). The distances, reckoning southward from Rome are given as follows in the Antonine Itinerary: "To Aricia, sixteen miles; to Three Taverns, seventeen miles; to Appii Forum, ten miles." It appears that this was a frequent meeting place of travelers and it was here that a number of Roman Christians met Paul on his trip to Rome.

threshing see **agriculture**

threshold 1. See **gate**

2. Of the two Hebrew words translated by the English word threshold, one, *miphthan*, seems to mean a projecting beam or corbel (Ezek. 9:3, 10:4-18).

3. The word *asuppim*, mentioned in 1 Chr. 26:15-17, refers to the enclosure of the "house of the Lord," apparently at its southwest corner. Nehemiah 12:25 alludes to the same place. It is likely that the reference in both cases is to a storage chamber where temple goods were kept.

throne the Hebrew term *kisse* applies to any elevated seat occupied by a person in authority whether a high priest (1 Sam. 1:9), a judge (Ps. 122:5), or a military chief (Jer. 1:15). The use of a chair in a country where the usual postures were squatting and reclining was at all times regarded as a symbol of dignity (2 K. 4:10; Prov. 9:14). The characteristic feature in the royal throne was its elevation: Solomon's throne was approached by six steps (1 K. 10:19; 2 Chr. 9:18); and the Lord's throne is described as "high and lifted up" (Isa. 6:1). The materials and workmanship were costly. It was furnished with arms or "stays." The steps were also lined with pairs of lions. As to the form of the chair, we are only informed, in 1 K. 10:19, that "the top was round behind." The king sat on his throne on state occasions. At such times, he appeared in his royal robes. The throne was a symbol of supreme power and dignity (Gen. 41:40). Similarly, "to sit upon the throne" implied the exercise of regal power (Deut. 17:18; 1 K. 16:11).

Thummin see **Urim and Thummin**

thunder the noise which follows a flash of lightning is quite unusual in Palestine during the summer months. From the middle of April to the middle of September, it is seldom heard. Hence, it was selected by Samuel as a striking expression of the divine displeasure toward the Israelites (1 Sam. 12:17). Thunder was regarded by the Hebrews as the voice of Jehovah (Job 37:2, 4-5, 40:9; Ps. 18:13, 29:3-9; Isa. 30:30-31), who dwelt behind the thunder cloud (Ps. 81:7). Thunder was, to the mind of the Jew, the symbol of divine power (Ps. 29:3), and vengeance (1 Sam. 2:10; 2 Sam. 22:14).

Thyatira (thī'à-tī'rà) a city of Asia Minor, on the Lycus River, and on the road from Pergamos to Sardis. Seleucus Nicator founded the city at the beginning of the third century B.C. and called it Thyatira, though it was built upon the site of previous cities. This city became famous because of the citizens' skill in dyeing purple cloth. Lydia, a seller of purple in Philippi, was from this city (Acts 16:14). The city contained one of the seven churches of Asia (Rev. 1:11, 2:18-29). The modern town of Ak Hissar is thought to be located on the site of ancient Thyatira.

thyine wood (thy'ine wood) Revelations 18:12 contains the only mention of this wood in the Bible. Botanists today classify it as *Callitris quadrivalvis*, a large tree of the cypress family, which grows to a height of fifteen to twenty-five feet. It was much prized by the Greeks and Romans, on account of the beauty of its wood for various ornamental purposes. The resin from this tree is known as gum.

Tiberias (tī-bē'rī-ăs) a city built by Herod the tetrarch, and named by him after the reigning Roman emperor Tiberius Caesar (Josephus *Ant.* XVIII.ii.3; *War* II.9) and first mentioned in Jn. 6:23, 21:1. It is situated approximately two thirds of the way from north to south of the Sea of Galilee on the western side. Tiberias was the capital of Galilee from the time of its origin until the reign of Herod Agrippa II, who changed the seat of power back again to Sepphoris. There is no indication in the Scriptures that Jesus ever visited the city of Tiberias, even though it was situated within easy distance of his boyhood home and of much of his public ministry. Many of the inhabitants in Christ's day were Greeks and Romans, and foreign customs prevailed there to such an extent as to give offense to the stricter Jews. This city figures prominently in the wars between the Jews and Romans. Subsequent to the fall of Jerusalem, the Sanhedrin, after a temporary stay in Mania, moved to Tiberias about the middle of the second century. The Mishnah was compiled at this place by the great Judah Hakkodesh about A.D. 190. This city also figured prominently in the battles between the Crusaders and the Moslems. The modern name of the city is Tubarieh, and the population, largely Arab, numbers three to four thousand.

The Sea of Tiberias (Jn. 6:1, 21:1) is more generally called the Sea of Galilee.

Tiberius Caesar (tī-bēr'ī-ŭs sē'zēr) Tiberius Claudius Nero was the second Roman emperor and successor of Augustus. He reigned from A.D. 14 to 37. He was the son of Tiberius Claudius Nero and Livia and hence a stepson of Augustus. He was born at Rome on the sixteenth of November in 42 B.C. He became emperor in his fifty-fifth year, after having distinguished himself as a commander in various wars, and having evinced talents of a high order as an orator and as an administrator of civil affairs. Although he had gained a reputation for the possession of the sterner virtues of the Roman character, on being raised to the supreme power, his life was characterized by inactivity, sloth, and self-indulgence. He was despotic in his government, cruel, and vindictive in his disposition. He died at the age of seventy-eight after a reign of twenty-three years.

Tibhath (tĭb'hăth) a city of Habadezer king of Zobah (1 Chr. 18:8), which in 2 Sam. 8:8 is called Betah. Its exact position is unknown.

Tibni (tĭb'nī) son of Ginath (1 K. 16:15-23). After the fall of Baasha's short-lived reign, three generals of the army fought to be king of the northern kingdom of Israel—Omri, Zimri, and Tibni. Zimri, after his defeat at the hands of

Omri, took his own life in his palace. Then a civil war erupted as Omri and Tibni strove for first place. After four years of fighting, Tibni died, apparently from natural causes, and Omri ascended the throne.

Tidal (tī′dăl) an ally of Amraphel, Chedorlaomer, and Arioch in an aggressive war against Sodom and Gomorrah wherein Lot, the nephew of Abraham, and all his family and possessions were taken as spoils (Gen. 14:1–12). Tidal was one of the several Hittite kings whose name and country have never been definitely identified. He was king of Goiim, often translated "Nations of Gentiles." See articles on Amraphel, etc., named above.

Tiglath-pileser (tĭg-lăth-pī-lē′zĕr) [Lord of the Tigris] alternately written Tilgath-pilneser (1 Chr. 5:6, 26; 2 Chr. 28:20). King of Assyria (745–727 B.C.) and, under the name of Pul, king of Babylon from New Year's Day 728 to the time of his death in 727 B.C. Asshur-nirari III was his father and Shalmaneser V his son. Tiglath-pileser usurped the throne of Assyria and probably assumed the name of Tiglath-pileser I who reigned 1115–1103 B.C. He was the second Assyrian king to have contact with the Israelites. That contact began about 743 B.C. Arpad, Tyre, and Damascus, along with other cities, paid him tribute for a time but later revolted. Arpad was besieged but held out until 740 (Isa. 10:9, 36:19, 37:13). In 738 he was receiving tribute from many kings, among whom were Rezin of Damascus, Hiram of Tyre, and Menahem of Samaria (2 K. 15:19). Political conditions in that area brought Tiglath-pileser back in 734. He came to help Ahaz of Judah, by the latter's position, in warding off an attack by Pekah of Israel and Rezin of Damascus. Pekah surrendered quickly and thus saved Samaria from destruction (2 K. 15:29). Rezin, without his ally, was defeated and took refuge in his capital. Tiglath-pileser besieged Damascus, and it fell in 732. When Pekah was slain by his own people, Tiglath-pileser enthroned Hoshea in Israel and the latter, along with Ahaz in Judah and practically every other king in the west, paid tribute to the Assyrian ruler. Tiglath-pileser took away large numbers of captives from each conquered territory (1 Chr. 5:26) and replaced them with thousands of persons from other districts of his realm. That large importation gave rise to the later mottled population of Syria. It also lessened the threat of revolt in the territory placed under tribute and Assyrian rulers.

Tigris (tī′grĭs) [arrow] river of Mesopotamia, from Old Persian Tigra. A twin river to the Euphrates and, like it, it has two sources; the principal one near the southwestern side of a lake high in the Armenian mountains, the other source in the region northwest of Diarbekir. The Tigris flows first in an easterly direction for about twenty-five miles and then more or less southeasterly until its final junction with the Euphrates north of Basra. Thence they flow as one to the Persian Gulf. After flowing about 150 miles from its source, the Tigris descends rapidly through precipitous ravines and gorges until it dashes into the Mesopotamian plains just north of the site of ancient Nineveh. In ancient times it continued to the gulf in its own bed, but later merged with the Euphrates to form the Shatt-el-Arab of today. Its over-all length is 1150 miles. It is navigable from the gulf to Mosul, a city opposite the site of old Nineveh, but it is only safe for small, rugged crafts. Before World War I the Germans completely excavated Ashur, the capital of ancient Assyria. Ashur flourished when the Tigris was more navigable than it is today. It ranges in width from 100 to 250 yards. It is generally swift and turgid. Like the Euphrates, it has a flooding period from March until mid-May caused by melting snow in the mountains. After returning to normal level in midsummer, the autumnal rains cause another rise in October and November, but it is not equal to the spring rise. The Tigris receives mention in Scripture. Its Hebrew name, Hiddekel, appears in Gen. 2:14 and Daniel had one of his visions on the bank of the Tigris (Dan. 10:4).

Tikvah (tĭk′vä) 1. The father of Shallum, the husband of the prophetess Huldah (2 K. 22:14). In 2 Chr. 34:22, the name appears as Tokhath or Tikvath.

2. The father of Jahaziah (Ezra 10:15).

tile a baked clay slab or tablet. In Babylonia and other countries tiles were commonly used as writing material in earliest time (Ezek. 4:1). While the clay was soft the writing characters were impressed on the surface and then the clay was baked, making the writing indelible. Tiles were also used as roofing material in many countries (Lk. 5:19), but not commonly in Palestine. While it is quite possible that the house where Jesus healed a man let down through the roof did have a tile roof, it is also possible that in writing of it Luke, accustomed to the tiled roof of Greek houses, uses the expression "through the tiles" as an idiomatic expression, meaning simply through the roof. See also **bricks, pottery, seal**

Tilgath-pilneser (tĭl′găth-pĭl-nē′zĕr) a variation, and possibly a corruption, of the name **Tiglath-pileser** (1 Chr. 5:6, 26; 2 Chr. 28:20).

Tilon (tī′lŏn) one of the four sons of Shimon,

whose family is reckoned in the genealogies of Judah (1 Chr. 4:20).

timbrel or **tabret** (tĭm'brĕl, tăb'rĕt) a kind of drum, likely a hand-drum for tambourine. It was used in very early times by the Syrians of Padan-aram at their merrymakings (Gen. 31:27). It was played principally by women (Ex. 15:20; Judg. 11:34; 1 Sam. 18:6; Ps. 68:25) as an accompaniment to the song and dance (Judg. 11:34), and appears to have been worn by them as an ornament (Jer. 31:4). In its simplest form it appears to have been a hoop (sometimes with pieces of brass fixed in it to make a jingling), over which a piece of parchment was distended. It was beat with the fingers, and was the true tympanum of the ancients.

Timeus (tī-mē'ŭs) the father of the blind man Bartimeus, of Jericho (Mk. 10:46).

Timna (tĭm'nà) 1. A concubine of Eliphaz, son of Esau, and mother of Amalek (Gen. 36:12). It may be presumed that she was the same as Timna, sister of Lotan (Gen. 36:22; 1 Chr. 1:39).

2. A duke of Edom in the last list in Gen. 36:40–43 (1 Chr. 1:51–54). The word Timna is sometimes translated **Timnah.**

Timnah (tĭm'nà) 1. A place which formed one of the landmarks on the north boundary on the allotment of Judah (Josh. 15:10). It is probably identical with the Thimnathah of Josh. 19:43, and with the **Timnath** occupied by the Philistines in the time of Samson (Judg. 14:1, 2, 5). The site today is occupied by Tibnah, a small village approximately three miles west of Beth-shemesh, and fifteen miles southwest of Jerusalem.

2. A town in the hill country of Judah (Josh. 15:57). It may be the place referred to in Gen. 38:12–14. It is distinct from the place named above.

3. The scene of the adventure of Judah with his daughter-in-law, Tamar (Gen. 38:12–14). There is no indication of its position, so it may be identified either with one or the other of the locations mentioned above.

Timnath (tĭm'năth) see **Timnah**

Timnath-serah (tĭm'năth-sē'rà) a city in the hill country of Ephraim presented to Joshua after the partition of the country (Josh. 19:50), and in the border of which he was buried (Josh. 24:30). It is located "in Mount Ephraim, on the north side of Mount Gaash." In Judg. 2:9, the name is altered to Timnathheres. This city is likely the modern Tibnah, where Samaritan tradition locates the graves of Joshua and Caleb.

Timon (tī'mŏn) one of the Seven appointed to serve tables in the Jerusalem church (Acts 6:1–6), thus relieving the apostles for their spiritual duties.

Timothy (tĭm'ô-thĭ) a traveling companion and associate of the apostle Paul in the work of preaching the Gospel to the Gentile world. Paul speaks of him as "my beloved and faithful child in the Lord" (1 Cor. 4:17), and "my true child in the faith" (1 Tim. 1:2), indicating not only his warm feelings for his young friend, but also implying that he had been the means of Timothy's conversion. The relationship began when Paul visited Lystra in Lycaonia on his first missionary journey (2 Tim. 1:5). Evidently on this first journey Timothy's mother, Eunice, and grandmother, Lois, were converted to Christ, and there is likelihood that the young man, Timothy, was also brought into the church. His mother was a Jewess, but his father was a Greek or Gentile (Acts 16:1). Timothy had been taught from a child the sacred OT writings (2 Tim. 3:15), but he had never been circumcised (Acts 16:3). Whether converted by Paul or later through the efforts of his mother, Timothy became so active in Christian work that when Paul visited Lystra on his second journey, he found that the young man was well-reported of by the brethren both at Lystra and Iconium (Acts 16:2). Paul determined to take him with him on his journeys and the young man was set apart for the work of evangelist by the laying on of hands of both the presbytery and the apostle (1 Tim. 4:14; 2 Tim. 1:6). So that the Jews might not be offended in Timothy, Paul had him circumcised (Acts 16:3), thus conciliating the Jews on a matter that was no longer religiously significant but about which the Jews still had strong feelings. Henceforth Timothy was one of Paul's most constant companions. Together with Silvanus, and probably with Luke also, they journeyed to Philippi (Acts 16:12), and there already the young evangelist was conspicuous at once for his filial devotion and zeal (Phil. 2:22). He appears again at Berea, and remains there when Paul and Silas were obliged to leave (Acts 17:14), going on afterward to join his teacher at Athens (1 Thess. 3:2). From Athens, he was sent back to Thessalonica but later joined Paul in Corinth. His name appears with Paul's in the opening words of both the letters written from that city to the Thessalonians (1 Thess. 1:1; 2 Thess. 1:1). When we next locate him, he is being sent on in advance when the apostle was contemplating the long journey which was to include Macedonia, Achaia, Jerusalem, and Rome (Acts 19:22). It is probable that he returned by the same route, and met Paul according to a previous arrangement (1 Cor. 16:11), and was thus with him when the second letter was written to the church of Corinth (2 Cor. 1:1). He returned with Paul to Corinth and joined in the messages of greeting to the disciples he had known personally at Corinth, and who had since found their way to Rome (Rom. 16:21). He traveled with Paul on the return portion of the third missionary journey to Jerusalem (Acts 20:3–6), but there is no mention of him on Paul's journey from Jerusalem to Caesarea, and on to Rome (Acts 27–28). He must have joined Paul shortly after his arrival in Rome however, for he was present there when Paul wrote the epistles to the Philippians, the Colossians, and to Philemon (Phil. 1:1, 2:19; Col. 1:1; Philemon 1). From the two epistles addressed to him, we are able to learn a few things concerning his later life. From 1 Tim. 1:3, we learn that after Paul's release from his first imprisonment in Rome, Timothy revisited Asia with Paul. He was then left behind at Ephesus (1 Tim. 1:3) to deal with problems that had arisen there when Paul moved on into Macedonia. Paul's deep personal feelings for Timothy and his strong confidence in Timothy are apparent in the two letters that he wrote to him. The last recorded words of the apostle expressed the earnest hope, repeated yet more earnestly, that he might see him once again (2 Tim. 4:9, 21). It is generally thought that Timothy reached Paul before his death and comforted him. The only further reference to him is Heb. 13:23, which indicates that Timothy had suffered imprisonment but had been set free.

Timothy, Epistles of Paul to the first epistle was probably written in the interval between Paul's first and second imprisonments at Rome. The absence of any local reference but that in 1:3 suggests Macedonia or some neighboring district. In some MSS and versions, Laodicea is named in the inscription as the place from which it was sent. The second epistle appears to have been written soon afterwards, and in all probability at Rome. The following are the characteristic features of these epistles: (1) The ever-deepening sense in Paul's heart of the divine mercy, of which he was the object, as shown in the insertion of the word "mercy" in the salutations of both epistles, and in the "obtained mercy" of 1 Tim. 1:13. (2) The greater abruptness of the second epistle. From first to last there is no plan and no treatment of subjects carefully thought out. Paul speaks of strong overflowing emotion, memories of the past, anxieties about the future. (3) The ab-

sence, as compared with Paul's other epistles, of OT references is interesting. This may be a result of his message, or possibly explain his request for the "books and parchments" which had been left behind (2 Tim. 4:13). (4) The conspicuous position of the "faithful sayings" takes the place occupied in other epistles by the OT Scriptures. The way in which these are cited as authoritative and the variety of subjects which they cover suggest the thought that, in them, we have specimens of the prophecies of the apostolic church which had most impressed themselves on the mind of the apostle, and of the disciples generally. First Corinthians 14 shows how deep a reverence he felt for such spiritual utterances. In 1 Tim. 4:1, we have a distinct reference to them. (5) We note also the tendency of the apostle's mind to dwell more on the universality of the redemptive work of Christ (1 Tim. 2:3, 6, 4:10), and his strong desire that all the teaching of his disciples should be "sound." (6) We also see the importance attached by him to the practical details of administration. The gathered experience of a long life had taught him that the life and well-being of the church required these for its safeguard. (7) The recurrence of doxologies (1 Tim. 1:17, 6:15–16; 2 Tim. 4:18), as from one living perpetually in the presence of God, shows Paul to be one to whom the language of adoration was his natural speech.

tin among the various metals found among the spoils of the Midianites, tin is enumerated (Num. 31:22). It was known to the Hebrew metal workers as an alloy of other metals (Isa. 1:25; Ezek. 22:18, 20). The markets of Tyre were supplied with it by the ships of Tarshish (Ezek. 27:12). It was used for plummets (Zech. 4:10), and was so plentiful as to furnish the writer of Ecclus. 47:18 with a figure by which to express the wealth of Solomon. As to the country from which the Hebrews obtained tin, see **Tarshish.**

Tiphash (tĭf′sȧ) mentioned in 1 K. 4:24 as the limit of Solomon's empire toward the Euphrates, and in 2 K. 15:16 it is said to have been attacked by Menahem. It was known to the Greeks and Romans under the name of Thapsacus, and was the point where it was usual to cross the Euphrates. Thapsacus has been generally placed at the modern Deir; but the Euphrates expedition proved that there is no ford at Deir, and that the only ford in this part of the course of the Euphrates is at Suriveh, forty-five miles below Balis, and 165 above Deir. This then must have been the position of Thapsacus.

Tiras (tī′răs) the youngest son of Japheth

(Gen. 10:2), usually identified with the Thracians, as presenting the closest verbal approximation to the name.

Tirathites (tī′răth-īts) a family of scribes dwelling at Jabez who were of the Kenites (1 Chr. 2:55).

tire an ornamental headdress worn on festive occasions (Ezek. 24:17, 23).

Tirhakah (tûr′há-ká) king of Ethiopia (Cush), the opponent of Sennacherib (2 K. 19:9; Isa. 37:9). He may be identified with Tarkos or Tarakos, who was the third and last king of the Twenty-fifth Dynasty, which was of the Ethiopians. His accession was probably about 695 B.C. Possibly Tirhakah ruled other kingdoms including Ethiopia before becoming king of Egypt.

Tirhanah (tǐr′há-ná) a son of Caleb by his concubine Maachah (1 Chr. 2:48).

Tiria (tǐr′ǐ-á) a son of Jehalelel (1 Chr. 4:16).

Tirshatha (tûr-shā′thá) (always written with the article). The title of the governor of Judah under the Persians, perhaps derived from a Persian root signifying "stern," "severe," is added as a title after the name of Nehemiah (Neh. 8:9, 10:1), and occurs also in three other places. In the margin of the AV (Ezra 2:63; Neh. 7:70, 10:1), it is rendered "governor."

Tirzah (tûr′zà) youngest of the five daughters of Zelophehad (Num. 26:33, 27:1, 36:11; Josh. 17:3).

Tirzah (tûr′zà) an ancient Canaanite city, whose king is enumerated among those overthrown in the conquest of the country (Josh. 12:24). It reappears as a royal city, the residence of Jeroboam and of his successors (1 K. 14:17–18). Tirzah reappears as the seat of the conspiracy of Menahem ben-Gaddi against the wretched Shallum (2 K. 15:14, 16). Its reputation for beauty throughout the country must have been widespread. It is in this sense that it is mentioned in the Song of Solomon. Eusebius mentions it in connection with Menahem, and identifies it with a "village of Samaritans in Batanaea." Its site is Telluzah, a place in the mountains north of Nablus.

Tishbite, the (tǐsh′bīt) the well-known designation of Elijah (1 K. 17:1, 21:17, 28; 2 K. 1:3, 8, 9:36). Assuming that a town is alluded to, as Elijah's native place, it is not necessary to infer that it was itself in Gilead, as many have imagined. The commentators and lexicographers, with few exceptions, adopt the name "Tishbite" as referring to the place Thisbe in Naphtali, which is found in the LXX text of Tobit 1:2.

tithe numerous instances of the use of tithes are found both in profane and also in Biblical history, prior to or independently of the appointment of the Levitical tithes under the Law. In Biblical history, the two prominent instances are: (1) Abraham presenting the tenth of all the spoils of his victory to Melchizedek (Gen. 14:20; Heb. 7:2, 6). (2) Jacob, after his vision at Luz, devoting a tenth of all his property to God in case he should return home in safety (Gen. 28:22). The first enactment of the Law in respect of tithes is the declaration that the tenth of all produce, as well as of flocks and cattle, belongs to Jehovah, and must be offered to him. (3) That the tithe was to be paid in kind, or, if redeemed, with an addition of one fifth to its value (Lev. 27:30–33). This tenth, called *terumoth*, is ordered to be assigned to the Levites, as the reward of their service; and it is ordered further, that they are themselves to dedicate to the Lord a tenth of these receipts, which is to be devoted to the maintenance of the high priest (Num. 18:21–28). This legislation is modified or extended in the book of Deuteronomy, i.e., from thirty-eight to forty years later. Commands are given to the people: (1) To bring their tithes, together with their votive and other offerings and firstfruits, to the chosen center of worship, the metropolis, there to be eaten in festive celebration in company with their children, their servants, and the Levites (Deut. 12:15–18). (2) All of the produce of the soil was to be tithed every year, and these tithes, with the firstlings of the flock and herd, were to be eaten in the metropolis. (3) But in case of distance, permission is given to convert the produce into money, which is to be taken to the appointed place, and there laid out in the purchase of food for a festal celebration, in which the Levite is, by special command, to be included (Deut. 14:22–27). (4) Then follows the direction, that at the end of three years all of the tithes of that year are to be gathered, and laid up "within the gates," and that a festival is to be held, in which the stranger, the fatherless, and the widow, together with the Levite, are to partake (Deut. 14:28–29). (5) Lastly, it is ordered that after taking the tithe in each third year, "which is the year of tithing," an exculpatory declaration is to be made by every Israelite, that he has done his best to fulfill the divine command (Deut. 26:12–14). From all this we gather that: (a) one tenth of the whole produce of the soil was to be assigned for the maintenance of the Levites; (b) out of this the Levites were to dedicate a tenth to God, for the use of the high priest; (c) a tithe, in all probability a second tithe, was to be applied to festival purposes; (d) in every third year, either this festival tithe or a third tenth was to be eaten in company with the poor and the Levites. The question arises: Were there three tithes taken in this third year, or is the third tithe only the second under a different description? It must be allowed that the third tithe is not without support. Josephus distinctly says that one tenth was to be given to the priests and Levites, and one tenth was to be applied to feasts in the metropolis, and that a tenth besides these was every third year to be given to the poor (Tobit 1:7-8). On the other hand, Maimonides says the third and sixty years' second tithe was shared between the poor and the Levites, that is to say, that there was no third tithe. Of these opinions, that which maintains three separate and complete tithings seems improbable. It is plain that under the kings the tithe-system partook of the general neglect into which the observance of the Law declined, and that Hezekiah, among his other reforms, took effectual means to revive its use (2 Chr. 31:5, 12, 19). Similar measures were taken after the Captivity by Nehemiah (Neh. 12:44); and, in both these cases, special officers were appointed to take charge of the stores and storehouses for the purpose. Yet, notwithstanding partial evasion or omission, the system itself was continued to a late period in Jewish history (Mt. 23:23; Lk. 18:12; Heb. 7:5-8).

Titus (ti'tŭs) 1. A God-fearing man who lived in Corinth and whose house joined the synagogue (Acts 18:7, RV). His surname was Justus.

2. One of the apostle Paul's most intimate traveling companions. Although he is never mentioned in Acts, he is frequently mentioned in Paul's epistles, one of which is directed to him. He was a Gentile (Gal. 2:3), and accompanied Paul and Barnabas to Jerusalem when the issue of circumcision for Gentile Christians was considered (Acts 15:2; Gal. 2:1, 3). Paul refers to him as "my true child through a common faith" (Tit. 1:4, RV), so it is thought that he was converted by Paul. The Judaizers at Jerusalem were offended by the fact that Titus had not been circumcised, but Paul insisted on his right to freedom from this OT ceremony and was sustained by the other apostles (Gal. 2:3-5). After his stay in Ephesus, Paul sent Titus to Corinth with a reproof of certain sins practiced by the Christians there (2 Cor. 2:13, 7:6, 13, 8:6, 16, 12:18). When Paul left Ephesus, he expected to meet Titus at Troas (2 Cor. 2:12-13), and to hear from him a report of the reaction of the Corinthians. Although Titus failed to meet Paul at Troas, he did meet him in Macedonia and brought a good report from Corinth (2 Cor. 7:6, 13-14). He was immediately sent back to Corinth with the second letter to the Corinthians (2 Cor. 8:6, 18, 23). Our next mention of Titus came after Paul's release from his first Roman imprisonment. Paul's letter to Titus tells us that he had been left in Crete to complete the organization of the churches and to guide the young Christians. Later he was instructed to join Paul at Nicopolis. The final mention in the NT is in 2 Tim. 4:10, where he is mentioned as having gone to Dalmatia.

Titus, Epistle to there are no specialties in this epistle which require any very elaborate treatment distinct from the other pastoral letters of Paul. If those two are not genuine, it would be difficult confidently to maintain the genuineness of this. On the other hand, if the Epistles to Timothy are received as Paul's there is not the slightest reason for doubting the authorship of that to Titus. Nothing can well be more explicit than the quotations in Irenaeus, Clement of Alexandria, Tertullian, to say nothing of earlier allusions in Justin Martyr, Theophilus, and Clement of Rome. As to internal features, we may notice in the first place, that the epistle has all the characteristics of the other pastoral epistles. This tends to show that this letter was written about the same time and under similar circumstances with the other two. But, on the other hand, this epistle has marks in its phraseology and style which assimilate it to the general body of the epistles of Paul. As to any difficulty arising from supposed indications of advanced hierarchical arrangements, it is to be observed that in this epistle *presbuteros* and *episkopos* are used synonymously (1:5, 7), just as they are in the address at Miletus, about the year A.D. 58 (Acts 20:17, 28). At the same time, this epistle has features of its own, especially a certain tone of abruptness and severity, which probably arises, partly out of the circumstances of the Cretan population, partly out of the character of Titus himself. No very exact subdivision is either necessary or possible. As to the time and place and other circumstances of the writing of this epistle, the following scheme of filling up Paul's movements after his first imprisonment will satisfy all conditions of the case: we may suppose that (possibly after accomplishing his long-projected visit to Spain) he has gone to Ephesus, and taken voyages thence, first to Macedonia, and then to Crete; during the former he may have written the First Epistle to Timothy, and after returning from the latter to have written the Epistle to Titus, being at the time of dispatching it, on the point of starting for Nicopolis, to which place he went, taking Miletus and Corinth on the way. At Nicopolis, we may conceive him to have been finally apprehended, and taken to Rome, whence he wrote the Second Epistle to Timothy.

Tizite, the (tī′zīt) the designation of Joha, one of the heroes of David's army (1 Chr. 11:45). It occurs nowhere else, and nothing is known of the place or family which it denotes.

Toah (tō′à) a Kohathite Levite, ancestor of Samuel and Herman (1 Chr. 6:34). He is called Tohu in 1 Sam. 1:1.

Tob, the Land of (tŏb) the place in which Jephthah took refuge when expelled from home by his half brother (Judg. 11:3); and where he remained, at the head of a band of freebooters till he was brought back by the sheiks of Gilead (vs. 5). The narrative implies that the land of Tob was not far distant from Gilead: at the same time, from the nature of the case, it must have lain out toward the eastern deserts. It is undoubtedly mentioned again in 2 Sam. 10:6, 8, as Ishtob, that is, man of Tob, meaning, according to a common Hebrew idiom, the "men of Tob." No identification of this ancient district with any modern one has yet been attempted. The name Tell Dobbe, or, as it is given by the latest explorer of those regions, Tell Dibbe, attached to a ruined site at the south end of Lejah, a few miles northwest of Kenawat, and also that of ed-Dab, some twelve hours east of the mountain el-Kuleib, are both suggestive of Tob.

Tobadonijah (tŏb-ăd-ō-nī′jà) one of the Levites sent by Jehoshaphat through the cities of Judah to teach the Law to the people (2 Chr. 17:8).

Tobiah (tō-bī′à) 1. "The children of Tobiah" were a family who returned with Zerubbabel, but were unable to prove their connection with Israel (Ezra 2:60; Neh. 7:62).

2. "Tobiah the slave, the Ammonite," played a conspicuous part in the rancorous opposition made by Sanballat the Moabite and his adherents to the rebuilding of Jerusalem. The two races of Moab and Ammon found in these men fit representatives of that hereditary hatred to the Israelites which began before the entrance into Canaan, and was not extinct when the Hebrews had ceased to exist as a nation. But Tobiah, though a slave (Neh. 2:10, 19), unless this is a title of opprobrium, and an Ammonite, found means to ally himself with a priestly family, and his son Johanan married the daughter of Meshullam, the son of

Berechiah (Neh. 6:18). He himself was the son-in-law of Shechaniah the son of Arah (Neh. 6:18), and these family relations created for him a strong faction among the Jews. Ewald conjectures that Tobiah had been a page ("slave") at the Persian court, and, being in favor there, had been promoted to be satrap of the Ammonites. But it almost seems that against Tobiah there was a stronger feeling of animosity than against Sanballat, and that this animosity found expression in the epithet "the slave," which is attached to his name.

Tobias the Greek form of the name Tobiah or Tobijah. 1. The son of Tobit, and central character in the apocryphal book of that name.

2. The father of Hyrcanus, apparently a man of great wealth and reputation at Jerusalem in the time of Seleucus Philopator (ca. 187 B.C.). In the high-priestly schism which happened afterward, "the sons of Tobias" took a conspicuous part.

Tobiel the father of Tobit, and grandfather of Tobias.

Tobijah (tō-bī′jà) 1. One of the Levites sent by Jehoshaphat to teach the Law in the cities of Judah (2 Chr. 17:8).

2. One of the Captivity in the time of Zechariah, in whose presence the prophet was commended to take crowns of silver and gold, and put them on the head of Joshua the high priest (Zech. 6:10, 14). Rosenmuller conjectures that he was one of a deputation who came up to Jerusalem, from the Jews who still remained in Babylon, with contributions of gold and silver for the temple. But Maurer considers that the offerings were presented by Tobijah and his companions.

Tochen (tō′kĕn) a place mentioned (1 Chr. 4:32) among the towns of Simeon.

Togarmah (tō-gär′mà) a son of Gomer and brother of Ashkenaz and Riphath (Gen. 10:3). Togarmah, as a geographical term, is connected with Armenia; and the subsequent notices of the name (Ezek. 27:14, 38:6) accord with this view. The Armenian language presents many peculiarities which distinguish it from other branches of the Indo-European family; but in spite of this, however, no hesitation is felt by philologists in placing it among the Indo-European languages.

Tohu (tō′hù) an ancestor of Samuel the prophet, perhaps the same as Toah (1 Sam. 1:1, cf. 1 Chr. 6:34).

Toi (tō′ê) king of Hamath on the Orontes who, after the defeat of his powerful enemy, the Syrian king Hadadezer, by the army of David, sent his son Joram, or Hadoram, to congratulate the victor and do him homage with presents of gold and silver and brass (2 Sam. 8:9-10).

Tola (tō'lȧ) 1. The firstborn of Issachar, and ancestor of the Tolaites (Gen. 46:13; Num. 26:23; 1 Chr. 7:1-2).

2. Judge of Israel after Abimelech (Judg. 10:1-2). He is described as "the son of Puah, the son of Dodo, a man of Issachar." Tola judged Israel for twenty-three years at Shamir in Mount Ephraim, where he died and was buried.

Tolad (tō'lăd) one of the towns of Simeon (1 Chr. 4:29). In the list of Joshua, the name is given in the fuller form of El-Tolad.

Tolaites (tō'lȧ-īts) the descendants of Tola, the son of Issachar (Num. 26:23).

tomb unlike the Egyptians, the Hebrews usually buried their dead in caverns, or natural caves which often were extended by excavation (Gen. 23:9; Isa. 22:16; Mt. 27:60; Jn. 11:38). From the time when Abraham purchased the field of Ephron the Hittite at Hebron, in which was the cave of Machpelah, for the burial of his wife, Sarah (Gen. 23:19), to the funeral rites prepared for Dorcas (Acts 9:37), there is no mention of any sarcophagus, or even coffin, in any Jewish burial. The burial of their dead was marked with the same simplicity that characterized all their religious observances. The cliffs of Palestine, especially those about Jerusalem, are full of natural caves which became ideal sepulchers. The entrances to such a cavern, or to the various niches within the larger caverns, were closed by stones, specially cut to fit, in order to exclude animals that might prey upon the dead. From the time when Abraham established the burying place of his family at Hebron until the time when David fixed that of his family in the city of Jerusalem, the Jewish rulers had no fixed or favorite place for burial. Each was buried on his own property, or where he died, either for the sanctity or convenience of the place chosen. Of the twenty-two kings of Judah who reigned at Jerusalem from 1048 to 590 B.C., eleven or exactly one half, were buried at one location in the "city of David." Of all these, it is merely said that they were buried in "the sepulchers of their fathers" or "of the kings" in the city of David, except of two, Asa and Hezekiah (Neh. 3:16; Ezek. 43:7, 9). Repeated statements in the books of Kings and Chronicles leave no doubt that these burial places were in Jerusalem in the immediate vicinity of the temple. It has not been possible to identify the burial place of any individual, however, though the general location is known.

tongues from the fact that the word tongue refers to the organ of speech in the mouth, the word has also come to stand for speech or language (Gen. 10:5; Acts 2:8, 11). According to the Genesis record, from the beginning until some time after the flood, all men spoke one language (Gen. 11:1). Because of the presumptuous desire of man to make himself a city and build a tower into the heavens, God frustrated man's plans by producing differences of speech, which resulted in confusion and in the scattering of people abroad (Gen. 11:2-9). This occurred at the tower of Babel when the descendants of Noah began to speak several different languages and many different dialects. The Biblical record assumes a unity of the human race and a unity of language until this point in history. No explanation is given in the Scriptures as to the origin, but its exercise is evidently regarded coeval with the creation of man. Speech, being inherent in man as a reflective being, was regarded as handed down from father to son by the same process of imitation by which it is still perpetuated. The confusion of tongues and the dispersion of nations are spoken of in the Bible as contemporaneous events, after the occurrence at the tower of Babel.

Miraculous speaking in tongues was used on the day of Pentecost, when the church began some fifty days after Christ's resurrection, as a sign of God's approval of the unusual events taking place. The disciples were all together when suddenly there came from heaven a sound like that of a rushing mighty wind, and the Holy Spirit sat upon each one of the apostles (Acts 2:1-4). Immediately thereafter the apostles spoke in tongues that to them were unknown, but which were understood by the variety of nationalities then present in Jerusalem. Each man heard in his own native tongue. This miraculous demonstration was God's way of authenticating the Gospel that began to be preached in its fullness on that day. Later in the NT certain Christians were endowed with the gift of speaking in tongues. The apostle Paul contrasted speech and prayer in a foreign language, uninterpreted, with speaking and praying so as to be understood (1 Cor. 12:10, 30, 14:13-16, 27-28). Those who had the gift were instructed to use it for the purpose of edification and not to exhibit their skill before their brethren, who did not understand what they said unless an interpreter were present. Miraculous speaking in tongues was one of the signs that followed those who believed (Mk. 16:17). This was a visible gift of the Holy Spirit bestowed in connection with the preaching of the apostles, or by the apostles through the laying on of their hands (Acts 8:14–24, 10:44–46, 19:1–7). This was a phenomenon of the apostolic age and gradually disappeared thereafter.

tongues, gift of the promise of our Lord to his disciples, "They shall speak with new tongues" (Mk. 16:17), was fulfilled on the day of Pentecost, when cloven tongues like fire sat upon the disciples, and "every man heard them speak in his own language" (Acts 2:1–12). It is usually supposed that this supernatural knowledge of languages was given to the disciples for their work as evangelists; but it appears from the narrative that the "tongues" were used as an instrument, not of teaching, but of praise, and those who spoke them seemed to others to be under the influence of some strong excitement, "full of new wine." Moreover, the gift of tongues is definitely asserted to be a fulfillment of the prediction of Joel 2:28; and we are led, therefore, to look for that which answers to the gift of tongues in the other element of prophecy which is included in the OT use of the word; and this is found in the ecstatic praise, the burst of song (1 Sam. 10:5–13, 19:20–24; 1 Chr. 25:3). The First Epistle to the Corinthians supplies fuller data. The spiritual gifts are classified and compared, arranged, apparently, according to their worth. The facts which may be gathered are briefly these: (1) The phenomena of the gift of tongues were not confined to one church, or section of a church. (2) The comparison of gifts, in both lists given by Paul (1 Cor. 12:8–10, 28–30), places that of tongues, and the interpretation of tongues, lowest in the scale. (3) The main characteristic of the "tongue" is that it is unintelligible. The man "speaks mysteries," prays, blesses, gives thanks, in the tongue (1 Cor. 14:15–16), but no one understands him. (4) The "tongues," however, must be regarded as real languages. The "divers kinds of tongues" (1 Cor. 12:28), the "tongues of men" (1 Cor. 13:1), point to differences of some kind, and it is easier to conceive of these as differences of language than as belonging to utterances all equally wild and inarticulate. (5) Connected with the "tongues," there was the corresponding power of interpretation.

topaz a semiprecious stone; it is usually yellow in color but appears in other colors. There is some disagreement among scholars as to whether the topaz of the Bible is the same stone as the topaz of today, various jewel stones having been called by different terms in varying ages of civilization and in various localities. In all places in the Bible except in the book of Job where the topaz is mentioned, it is used to refer to decoration. Job 28:19 declares that the topaz of Ethiopia is of less value than wisdom.

Tophel (tō′fĕl) one of the place-limits of the general area where Moses addressed the Israelites (Deut. 1:1). It is sometimes identified with *Tufileh* on a wadi of the same name running north of Bozra toward the northwest into the Ghor and southeast to the corner of the Dead Sea.

Topheth or **Tophet** (tō′fĕth) or (tō′fĕt) the name Topheth occurs only in the OT (2 K. 23:10; Isa. 30:33; Jer. 7:31–32, 19:6, 11–14). It lay somewhere east or southeast of Jerusalem; for Jeremiah went out by the Sun gate, or east gate, to go to it (Jer. 19:2). It was in "the valley of the Son of Hinnom" (7:31), which is "by the entry of the east gate" (19:2). Thus it was not identical with Hinnom. Hinnom by old writers is always placed east of the city. The word *Tophet* has been variously translated; *latitudo*, garden, drum, place of burning or burying, abomination. The most natural seems that suggested by the occurrence of the word in two consecutive verses, in one of which it is a *tabret*, and in the other *Tophet* (Isa. 30:32–33). The Hebrew words are nearly identical; and Tophet was probably the king's "music grove" or garden, denoting originally nothing evil or hateful. Certainly there is no proof that it took its name from the drums beaten to drown the cries of the burning victims that passed through the fire to Molech (Jer. 32:35). It is associated with sacrifices to Baal. It was made the place of abomination, the very gate or pit of hell. The pious kings defiled it, and threw down its altars and high places, pouring into it all the filth of the city, till it became the "abhorrence" of Jerusalem (2 K. 23:10).

Tormah (tôr′mà) it occurs only in the margin of Judg. 9:31. By a few commentators, it has been conjectured that the word was originally the same with Arumah in vs. 41.

tortoise this word occurs only in Lev. 11:29 as the name of some unclean animal. Although several kinds of tortoises are common in the Holy Land, the reference here is probably to some kind of lizard.

Tou (tō′ōō) a king of Hamath (1 Chr. 18:9–10). An alternative form is Toi.

tower watchtowers or fortified posts in frontier or exposed situations are mentioned in Scripture, as the tower of Edar (Gen. 35:21; Isa. 21:5, 8, 11; Mic. 4:8). They were usually constructed of brick or stone and were of various sizes. Besides military structures, mention is made of towers built in vineyards as an almost necessary appendage to them (Isa. 5:2; Mt. 21:33; Mk. 12:1). Such towers are still in use in Palestine in vineyards, especially near Hebron, and are used as lodges for keepers of the vineyards.

town clerk the title ascribed to the magistrate at Ephesus who appeased the mob in the theater at the time of the tumult excited by Demetrius and his fellow craftsmen (Acts 19:35). The original service of this class of men was to record the laws and decrees of the state, and to read them to the public. Because of shifting patterns in civic administration, duties of the town clerk frequently varied from administration to administration.

Trachonitis (trăk-ō-nī′tĭs) this place is mentioned only once in the Bible (Lk. 3:1). It is mentioned as the name of the tetrarchy of Philip.

trance in the only passage (Num. 24:4, 16) in which this word occurs in the English of the OT there is no corresponding word in Hebrew. In the NT the word appears three times (Acts 10:10, 11:5, 22:17). The meaning of the Greek is obvious. The *ekstasis* is the state in which a man has passed out of the usual order of his life, beyond the usual limits of consciousness and volition. In this condition the mental powers are wholly or partly unresponsive to external impressions but are left free to contemplate mysteries not capable of understanding by usual rational processes.

trespass offering see **sin offering**

trial the subject of trials under the Jewish law is discussed under the topics of **Judges** and **Sanhedrin.** The trials of Jesus are included under the general topic **Jesus Christ.**

There are, however, some instances relative to trials discussed in the Scripture not included in the above subjects. 1. The trial of Jesus before Pilate was, in a legal sense, a trial for an offense which was punishable by death (Lk. 23:2, 38; Jn. 19:12, 15).

2. The trials of the apostles, of Stephen, and of Paul before the high priest, were conducted according to Jewish rules (Acts 4:1, 5:27, 6:12, 22:30, 23:1).

3. The trial of Paul and Silas at Philippi, was held before the praetors on the charge of innovation in religion. Such crimes were punishable by death or banishment (Acts 16:19, 22).

4. The trial before Gallio was an attempt to charge Paul of the same crime (Acts 18:12–17).

5. The trials of Paul at Caesarea were conducted according to Roman rules of judicature (Acts 25–26). The highest court of appeal was

to Caesar which Paul was able to do because of his Roman citizenship.

6. Acts 19:38–39 mentions an assembly that met in Ephesus. The town clerk asked the mob to allow a lawful assembly to decide the issues before the people. Roman law did not recognize the mob even when vented against Christianity.

tribute tribute is also discussed under the broader topic of **taxes.** The tribute was a tax imposed upon a subjugated nation or people. Such a tax is mentioned in Judg. 1:28; Ezra 4:13; Neh. 5:4; Est. 10:1; Mt. 17:25. The Roman government required the payment of tribute by the Hebrew people. In an attempt to trap Jesus, the Pharisees asked him if it were lawful to pay tribute to Caesar (Mt. 22:17). Instead of giving an answer of yes or no, he asked for a coin. Its inscription was that of Caesar. Jesus answered his querists by stating: "Render unto Caesar the things that are Caesar's and unto God the things that are God's." In this manner Jesus recognized that two realms existed—God's and Caesar's. God requires his subjects to pay taxes or tribute if required by the earthly rulers. The same conclusion was reached by Paul in Rom. 13 when he suggested that Christians should "obey the powers that be." He added, among a much longer list of duties to government, "tribute to whom tribute is due." The Christian cannot, Paul asserted, refuse to pay taxes because he might want to do so; it is a duty toward God.

The half shekel is referred to in the KJV of the Bible as tribute money (Mt. 17:24–25). However, this tax was levied by the Sanhedrin upon the Hebrews for the general expense of the temple. Such a levy was based upon Ex. 30:13 which required each male Israelite above the age of twenty to pay the tax. Later the tribute was required of every Hebrew above the age of twenty. Peter was asked if Jesus paid such a tax. Jesus paid it although he was opposed to the way it was collected. The Sanhedrin by making the temple offering a fixed annual tax, collecting it as men collected tribute for Caesar, were lowering, not raising, the religious condition of the people. Such forced tribute money was extracted from "strangers" not "sons." For this reason Jesus was opposed to the payment of tribute money for the upkeep of the temple.

tribute money see **taxes, tribute**

Tripolis the Greek name of a Phoenician city of great commercial importance which served at one time as a point of federal union for Aradus, Sidon, and Tyre. The ancient Tripolis was finally destroyed by the Sultan El Mansour in the year A.D. 1289; and the modern Tura-blous is situated some two miles distant to the east, and is no longer a port. El Myna, which is perhaps on the site of the ancient Tripolis, is a small fishing village.

Troas (trō'ăz) the city from which Paul first sailed to carry the Gospel from Asia to Europe (Acts 16:8, 11). It is mentioned on other occasions including Acts 20:5-6; 2 Cor. 2:12-13; 2 Tim. 4:13. The full name of the city was Alexandria Troas. At times it was called simply Alexandria while on other occasions Troas. The former part of the name indicates the period in which it was founded. It was first built by Antigonus and peopled with the inhabitants of various neighboring cities. Afterward it was embellished by Lysimachus and named Alexandria Troas. Its situation was on the coast of Mysia, opposite the southeastern extremity of the island of Tenedos. Under the Romans it was one of the most important towns of the province of Asia. The modern name is Eski-Stamboul. The ruins of Eski-Stamboul are considerable. The walls, which may represent the extent of the city in the apostle's time, enclose a rectangular space, extending for more than a mile from east to west, and nearly a mile from north to south. The harbor is still distinctly traceable in a basin about 400 feet long and 200 feet wide.

Trogyllium (trō-jĭl'ĭ-ŭm) a rocky extremity of Mount Mycale on the west coast of Asia Minor that juts into the sea opposite Samos. The name is mentioned once in the NT (Acts 20:15). To the east of the point there is an anchorage which is still called St. Paul's Bay. See **Samos**

troop, band these words are employed in the Bible to represent a force gathered for the object of marauding and plunder.

Trophimus see **Tychicus**

trumpet see **cornet**

Trumpets, Feast of (Lev. 23:24; Num. 29:1) it was the Feast of the New Moon which fell on the first of Tishri. It differed from the ordinary festivals of the new moon in several important ways. It was one of the seven days of the holy convocation. Instead of the mere blowing of the trumpets of the temple at the time of the offering of the sacrifices, it was "a day of blowing of trumpets." In addition to the daily sacrifices and the eleven victims offered on the first of every month, there were offered a young bullock, a ram, and seven lambs of the first year, with the accustomed meal offerings, and a kid for a sin offering (Num. 29:1-6). The regular monthly offering

was thus repeated, with the exception of the young bullock.

It has been conjectured that Ps. 81, one of the songs of Asaph, was composed expressly for the Feast of Trumpets. The psalm is used in the service for the day by the modern Jews.

Various meanings have been assigned to the Feast of Trumpets. Maimonides considered that its purpose was to awaken the people from their spiritual slumber to prepare for the solemn humiliation of the Day of Atonement, which followed it within ten days (see Joel 2:15). Some have supposed that it was intended to introduce the seventh or sabbatical month of the year. Philo and some early Christian writers regarded it as a memorial of the giving of the Law on Sinai. But there seems to be no sufficient reason to call in question the common opinion of Jews and Christians that it was the festival of the New Year's Day of the civil year, the first of Tishri, the month which commenced the sabbatical year and the year of Jubilee.

Tryphena and **Tryphosa** (trī-fē'nà and trī-fō'sà) two Christian women at Rome enumerated in the conclusion of Paul's letter to the Romans (16:12). It is possible they were sisters in the flesh, but probably were only fellow Christians in the city of Rome.

Tryphosa (trī-fō'sà) see **Tryphena**

Tubal (tū'băl) in the ancient ethnological tables of Genesis and 1 Chronicles, Tubal is reckoned with Javan and Meshech among the sons of Japheth (Gen. 10:2; 1 Chr. 1:5). The three are again associated in the enumeration of the sources of the wealth of Tyre (Ezek. 27:13). Tubal and Javan (Isa. 66:19), Meshech and Tubal (Ezek. 32:26, 38:2-3, 39:1), are nations of the north (Ezek. 38:15, 39:2). Josephus identifies the descendants of Tubal with the Iberians, that is, not the Spaniards, but the inhabitants of a tract of country, between the Caspian and Euxine seas, which nearly correspond to the modern Georgia.

Tubal-cain (tū'băl-kān') the son of Lamech the Cainite by his wife, Zillah (Gen. 4:22). He is called a furbisher of every cutting instrument of copper and iron.

turtle and **turtledove** first mentioned in Gen. 15:9, the turtledove is a species of pigeon. Because of its plaintive note and because it is gentle and harmless, the turtledove has been a symbol of a defenseless and innocent people (Ps. 74:19). First sacrificed by Abraham, the turtledove was included as a burnt offering under the Mosaic law (Lev. 1:14). It was a sin offering and was a substitute offering for purification of a woman after childbirth if she was poor (Lev. 5:7, 12:6, 8, 15:14, 29–30; Num. 6:10–11). The turtledove may have been the only domesticated fowl until the time of Solomon who introduced the peacock and possibly other birds from India. This bird is known for its habit of pairing for life, and its fidelity for its mate. It is a migratory bird, arriving in Palestine in March and leaving for the south at the approach of winter. There are several varieties, including the rock dove, the ring dove, and the palm dove.

Tychicus (tĭk′ĭ-kŭs) and **Trophimus** (trŏf′ĭ-mŭs) both were companions of Paul and are mentioned as natives of Asia. (1) In Acts 20:4, Tychicus and Trophimus are expressly said to be "of Asia," but, while Trophimus went with Paul to Jerusalem (Acts 21:29), Tychicus was left behind in Asia, probably at Miletus (Acts 20:15, 38). (2) How Tychicus was employed in the interval before Paul's first imprisonment, we cannot tell; but in that imprisonment he was with the apostle again, as we see from Col. 4:7–8. Together with Onesimus, he was doubtless the bearer both of this letter and the following as well to Philemon. (3) The language concerning Tychicus in Eph. 6:21–22, is very similar though not exactly in the same words. (4) The next references are in the Pastoral Epistles, the first in chronological order being Tit. 3:12. Here Paul (writing possibly from Ephesus) says that it is probable that he may send Tychicus to Crete, about the time when he himself goes to Nicopolis. (5) In 2 Tim. 4:12 (written at Rome during the second imprisonment), he says, "I am herewith sending Tychicus to Ephesus." From the same epistle (2 Tim. 4:20), we learn that Trophimus had been left by the apostle a little time previously, in infirm health, at Miletus. It is probable that Tychicus and Trophimus were the two brethren who were associated with Titus (2 Cor. 8:16–24), in conducting the business of the collection for the poor Christians in Judea.

Tyrannus (tī-răn′ŭs) the name of the man in whose school or place of audience Paul taught the Gospel for two years during his sojourn at Ephesus (Acts 19:9), after he had been denied access for this purpose to the Jewish synagogue. Tyrannus is presumed to have been a Greek teacher of philosophy or rhetoric.

Tyre a celebrated commercial city of antiquity, situated in Phoenicia, on the eastern coast of the Mediterranean Sea. Its Hebrew name signifies a rock, which agrees well with the site of Es-Sur, the modern town, located on a rocky peninsula, formerly an island. Even though Tyre was founded after Sidon, (Gen. 10:19; Isa. 23:12), its sister city some twenty miles away, it is a city of great antiquity (Isa. 23:7). Originally the city is thought to have stood on the mainland, but to have been transferred for the purpose of safety to the neighboring rocky island which gave its name to the general locality. Biblical writers allude to its location in the sea (Ezek. 26:17, 27:32). As early as the time of Joshua it was referred to as a strong place or fortified city (Josh. 19:29). David and Solomon received materials from Hiram king of Tyre for the erection of the temple and of their own houses (2 Sam. 5:11; 1 K. 5:1; 1 Chr. 14:1; 2 Chr. 2:3–16). The people of Tyre were more concerned with commerce than with making war. In addition to supplying timber and stone, they produced purple dyes, metal work, and glassware, trading with people at great distances (1 K. 9:26–28). Old Testament prophets spoke out against the practice of the Tyrians of buying Hebrew captives from their enemies and selling them as slaves to the Greeks and Edomites (Joel 3:4–8; Amos 1:9–10). Isaiah 23 contains a prophecy against Tyre though the city survived several sieges before being destroyed ultimately. Shalmaneser approximately 721 B.C. came against the city. Some time after 622 B.C., Nebuchadnezzar, after invading Jerusalem, also invaded Tyre. In 332 B.C., Tyre was assailed the third time by a great conqueror, Alexander the Great. He found the city situated on an island nearly half a mile from the mainland, so he constructed an enormous artificial mole from the mainland to the fortified city, thus conquering it. This land bridge still remains connecting the mainland with the former island ruins. Christ visited the coast of Tyre and Sidon (Mt. 15:21–28; Mk. 7:24–31). A Christian settlement existed there in the first century (Acts 21:3–6). The Biblical scholar Origen was buried in Tyre after his death in A.D. 254. The Moslems overran the city in A.D. 638. At the time of the Crusades, Tyre was still a flourishing city, when it surrendered to the Christians on the twenty-seventh of June, 1144. While the city is now largely in ruins, it is still occupied by a small population.

U

Ucal (ū'kăl) [I am strong] a word of uncertain meaning found in Prov. 30:1. Most interpreters regard it as the name of one of the two sons or pupils to whom Agur addressed his instructions. Some regard it as a verb and render "I am consumed" or "I am faint."

Uel (ū'ĕl) [will of God] a contemporary of Ezra who is listed as having taken a foreign wife (Ezra 10:34).

Ulai (ū'lī) [pure water] a river near Susa where Daniel (8:2, 16) saw the vision of the ram and the he-goat. It is mentioned in Assyrian inscriptions and has been identified with the Eulaeus of the classical writers.

Ulam (ū'lăm) [leader] 1. A descendant of Gilead from the tribe of Manasseh (1 Chr. 7:16–17).

2. The firstborn of Eshek, a descendant of the house of Saul. His two sons were known as "mighty men of valor" (1 Chr. 8:39–40).

Ulla (ŭl'à) a descendant of the tribe of Asher and head of a family (1 Chr. 7:39).

Ummah (ŭm'äh) one of the cities of the allotment of Asher (Josh. 19:30). It is usually identified with Acco which is the reading here in several Greek MSS.

unclean, uncleanness from the earliest of God's relation with the nation Israel, emphasis was given to the holiness of the people because God was to be in their midst and they were to be unto him "a holy nation" (Ex. 19:6): "ye shall therefore be holy, for I am holy" (Lev. 11:45). This gives rise to the clear distinction between the clean and the unclean made in the Law. The most ancient recognition between the clean and the unclean is found in the selection of the animals that were to be taken into the ark, "the clean" and "the not clean" (Gen. 7:2–8).

I. THE LAW. In the Mosaic law physical, ceremonial, and moral or ethical uncleanness are emphasized: at times these overlap. The priests were to keep this distinction clear (Lev. 10:10); but this they failed to do (Ezek. 22:26). This uncleanness may be divided as follows:

1. *Flesh to Be Eaten and Not Eaten* (Lev. 11). Beasts to be eaten, considered clean, were those with the cloven hoof and that chewed the cud (vss. 3–8); but flesh that touched an unclean thing was not to be eaten, it thus became unclean (7:9). Fishes that had no fins or scales were unclean (vss. 9–12). Birds that fed upon carrion, or birds of prey, were forbidden (vss. 13–19). Among the creeping things all were unclean, except those that leap, with legs above their feet, of the locust and grasshopper family. Also included among the unclean were animals that go upon their paws (vss. 24–27). Rodents and animals of the lizard or crocodile family were likewise unclean and forbidden (vss. 29–31). When certain of these unclean creatures were found in a vessel or dead in a house, that which had been touched by it was unclean.

Many suggestions are offered for these distinctions and for the prohibition of the eating of the "unclean." Probably the real reason is that the unclean are unfit for human food, not having been created for this purpose.

2. *Contact with Dead Bodies.* One was made unclean by touching the carcass of the body of an unclean animal (Lev. 5:2). Likewise, contact with the dead body of a person, or of a bone or grave, in the tent or on the field, made one unclean. The tent in which the man died, and the open vessels of the tent were considered unclean. The sprinkling of the water of purifying (ashes of a heifer mixed with "living" water) was the divine provision for cleansing (Num. 19).

3. *Issues and Secretions.* When a woman gave birth to a male she was unclean for forty days; when the child was a female the time was eighty days (Lev. 12). If a man had an issue in his flesh he was unclean; and the bed upon which he slept, that on which he sat, or that touched by the issue was unclean (Lev. 15:1–12). The same law held for the woman with an issue (vss. 19–30). That touched by the seed of copulation, even the woman involved, should be unclean till the evening (Lev. 15:16–18). In the camp of a holy war, a war under Jehovah, a nocturnal accident rendered one unclean, causing him to be put out of the camp for a definite period (Deut. 23:9–11).

4. *The Uncleanness of Leprosy* (see **leprosy**). There were various types of leprosy and of tests by which to determine the uncleanness or cleanness of the leper (Lev. 13:1–14:33). During the period of his uncleanness the leper was to go about as if in death, with his hair loose and his clothes rent, and having his upper lip covered, crying "Unclean, unclean" (13:45–46). In the day of his cleansing a rather elaborate ritual was observed (14:1–32). When either clothing or a house was affected by leprosy the priest should investigate and determine what should be done with either (Lev. 14:33–57). The priest who gave the tests or investigated the various cases was not considered unclean by the investigation.

5. *The Time of Uncleanness.* That which was defiled by touching the unclean, unclean animals, vessels, a clean animal that had died, the bed, chair, or clothes of the unclean, seed of copulation, the garment it touched, the woman included, a woman with an issue, or one who should go into a house considered unclean, were to be unclean until even, and were to be cleansed by bathing and washing of garments or vessels involved. Those unclean by contact with the human dead were to be unclean seven days, and to be cleansed by the water of purifying. Those unclean by issues were to be unclean so long as the period lasted. The woman unclean from giving birth to a child was unclean forty or eighty days. The leper could be unclean until death. The unclean at the time of the Passover could not eat it at the appointed time, but provision was made for his eating of it at a later date (Num. 9:10).

II. THE PROPHETS. The Exile rendered the nation unclean, but Ezekiel foretold that the returned remnant would be cleansed from its uncleanness (36:17–29). Isaiah envisioned the new spiritual Zion as being free from the unclean—these should have no part in the new; it should be for the redeemed (35:8, 52:1). Zechariah prophesied of the fountain that should be opened in Jerusalem for sin and uncleanness (13:1). He also saw the unclean spirits pass out of the land in that day (13:2).

III. THE NEW TESTAMENT. The Synoptic gospels and Acts give special emphasis to "unclean spirits" (see **spirits**). No emphasis is given to ceremonial uncleanness; when mentioned it is with reference to the Jewish ritual. The emphasis is put on moral uncleanness, viciousness, and the practice of every kind of immorality as separating one from God. These defile the individual, and are condemned. Only the blood of Christ can cleanse from this defilement.   H.H.

unclean meats beasts that parted the hoof and chewed the cud were clean under the law of Moses; all others were unclean (Lev. 11:1–8). All marine life that did not have fins and scales were unclean (Lev. 11:9–12). Birds of prey and certain others were unclean (Lev. 11:13–19). Winged creeping things going on all fours were unclean but those that in addition to the four legs and two others for hopping such as the grasshopper were clean (Lev. 11:20–23). Fat, blood, things sacrificed to idols, that which died of itself, or was torn of beasts were also unclean (Lev. 7:22–27, 17:10–16). A kid in its mother's milk was also forbidden as food (Deut. 14:21).

Under the NT, the same classification does not exist. Jesus made all foods (meats) clean (Mk. 7:19) and, therefore, it is not what enters the man that defiles him. Peter remonstrated with the Lord when he was told to kill and eat some animals that under the law of Moses were unclean (Acts 10:14). But the Lord responded by saying that no one should make common that which God had cleaned (Acts 10:15). Although the main lesson taught Peter was that the Gentiles were to share in the blessings of Christ, it is also evident that the lesson is taught that all foods are clean and that the distinction made under the Law does not exist under the NT system. Further, God created foods to be received with thanksgiving by them that know and love the truth (1 Tim. 4:3) because "every creature of God is good, and nothing is to be rejected, if it be received with thanksgiving; for it is sanctified through the word of God and prayer" (1 Tim. 4:4–5).

However, there are certain restrictions which Christians cannot ignore except on pain of sin. The Holy Spirit instructs "that ye abstain from things sacrificed to idols, and from blood, and from things strangled . . ." (Acts 15:29).
                                                                C.D.H.

unicorn [translated "wild ox," ASV; RSV] mentioned in nine passages (Num. 23:22, 24:8; Deut. 33:17; Job 39:9–10; Ps. 22:21, 29:6, 92:10; Isa. 34:7). From the side it appeared to have one horn, thus possibly the reason for the designation "unicorn" (derived from the LXX), but in reality it had two (Deut. 33:17). The animal was fierce, powerful and untamable, thus never domesticated. Many scholars identify it with the *Bos primigenius*, a kind of buffalo which roamed Syria in ancient times. See A. H. Godbey, "The Unicorn in the OT," AJSL 56 (1939), 256–96.
                                                                M.C.

unknown god while walking along the streets

of Athens Paul saw an altar having the inscription "to the unknown god" (Acts 17:23). It had probably been erected by a worshiper who did not know what god to thank for some benefit he had received. Pausanias (second century A.D.) refers to such altars along the road leading from the harbor to Athens and one such inscription has actually been found, although an exact parallel to this inscription in the singular is not known.   J.H.

Unni (ŭn'nĭ) [depressed] 1. A musician of the tribe of Levi who was appointed by Daniel to be a doorkeeper at the tabernacle in Jerusalem (1 Chr. 15:18, 20).

2. A Levite who came to Jerusalem with Zerubbabel after the Babylonian captivity (Neh. 12:9), also spelled Unno (ASV).

Uphaz (Jer. 10:9; Dan. 10:5) see **Ophir**

upper room a room frequently built on the roofs of houses to take advantage of cooling breezes and enjoy a measure of seclusion. In the OT they seem to be commonly found in the homes of the well-to-do (Judg. 3:20; Jer. 22:13). In the NT used for the Last Supper (Mk. 14:15; Lk. 22:12) and for assemblies (Acts 1:13, 20:8). Dorcas was put in one (Acts 9:37).   J.H.

Ur (ûr) [light] situated about ten miles west of the present Euphrates River and about 220 miles from Baghdad, about 160 miles from the head of the Persian Gulf, and about 140 miles southeast of ancient Babylon, the site of the ancient Ur has been excavated in recent times. It was in Lower Mesopotamia which is now Iraq. Between 1922 and 1934, extensive excavation was accomplished by a joint expedition of the British Museum and the Museum of the University of Pennsylvania under the direction of Sir C. Leonard Woolley. Although the city was rediscovered in 1854, it was not until the first half of the twentieth century that serious excavating was done.

This is probably one of the oldest cities of the world and was the first home of Abraham. Abraham, Sarah, and Lot "went forth . . . from Ur of the Chaldees, to go into the land of Canaan" (Gen. 11:31) and thus we are first introduced to the city in the Bible. Later God said to Abraham, "I am Jehovah that brought thee out of Ur of the Chaldees" (Gen. 15:7).

Ruins examined and interpreted indicate that the city was in existence before the third millennium B.C. and was characterized by an exceedingly high civilization. The city flourished with its high culture, commerce, and art until the time of Cyrus when its ziggurat and other buildings were left desolate to decay and fall

into ruin. Dated tablets found in its ruins indicate the city was inhabited until about the middle of the fifth century before Christ but from that time henceforth "there is silence."

Evidence seems to reveal that just prior to Abraham's day the city was at its period of greatest importance. A city of idolatry, it was rather large with approximately 500,000 people in this period. About 1960 B.C. it was overrun by the Elamites and it is suggested that this might be the approximate time when Abraham left the city. Nanna (the moon-god) and his consort Nin-gal were the chief deities. Apparently, the ziggurat and buildings associated with it were used for the worship of this moon-god. Shrines in homes also indicate that worship of idols was engaged in at home.

From such an idolatrous environment, Abraham was called by Jehovah to go into another land. Possibly, Joshua may have included this period, as well as the sojourn in Haran, in his charge to Israel when he said, ". . . choose you this day whom ye will serve; whether the gods which your fathers served that were beyond the River . . ." (Josh. 24:15).

Excavations reveal that the city was oblong, lying in a northwest to southeast direction. Its temples and worship areas lay primarily in the northern end with a cemetery in the southern part. Streets were narrow and often winding. Houses seem to have had flat roofs. Some have suggested that the ziggurat may have been the tower of Babel but Woolley and others feel that the tower of Babel was in Babylon to the northwest.   C.D.H.

Urbane [polite] a fellow worker of Paul who resided in Rome (Rom. 16:9), to whom he sent a personal greeting.

Uri 1. The father of Bezaleel (Ex. 31:2, 35:30, 38:22; 1 Chr. 2:20; 2 Chr. 1:5). His son was one of the craftsmen who made the ornaments for the tabernacle.

2. The father of one of the twelve men appointed by Solomon to be provision officers; his son's name was Geber (1 K. 4:19).

3. One of the porters of the temple who lived during the time of Ezra (Ezra 10:24).

Uriah, Urijah (ū·rī'à) [Jehovah is my light] 1. A Hittite, a foreigner in the army of David, enrolled in the chronicle of "the mighty men of the armies," one of the thirty (2 Sam. 23:39; 1 Chr. 11:41). Uriah lives in Biblical history as a valiant, loyal, and well-disciplined soldier, in contrast to the momentary selfish weakness of the great King David (2 Sam. 11). Under Joab he went to Rabbah, the capital of the Ammonites, to battle. In his absence David committed adultery with Bath-sheba, the beautiful Hebrew wife of Uriah. Bath-sheba became pregnant; David sought to cover his sin by having Uriah recalled from the battle, thinking Uriah would consider the baby as his own. Uriah's devotion as a soldier and his loyalty to the army would not suffer him to go down to his own house. Even when made drunken by the king he did not go. David returned him to Joab with instruction that he be put in the hottest spot of the battle. Joab complied, in which battle Uriah was killed. David took Bath-sheba to be his own wife, leading to the censure of Jehovah through Nathan the prophet (2 Sam. 12:1–15). The bitterness of David's repentance is expressed in Ps. 51. Through the descendants of Bath-sheba Jesus was born (Mt. 1:16).

2. A priest in the days of Ahaz king of Judah. Ahaz went to Damascus to meet Tiglath-pileser king of Assyria, from there he sent the pattern and instructions to the priest to build an altar after the pattern of the heathen altar (2 K. 16:19–16). The priest obeyed the king, for which it is possible that his name was omitted from the register of priests (1 Chr. 6:5–15).

3. A priest who was a faithful witness to Isaiah's prophecy (Isa. 8:2). Probably the same as 2.

4. A prophet, the son of Shemiah of Kirjath-jearim, who prophesied against Jerusalem. When threatened by King Jehoiakim he fled into Egypt. He was apprehended by the king and slain (Jer. 26:20–23).

5. A priest in the days of Ezra (Ezra 8:33; Neh. 3:4, 21).

6. A priest who stood by Ezra as he read the Law (Neh. 8:4).   H.H.

Urias same as **Uriah** the Hittite, the husband of Bath-sheba (Mt. 1:6).

Uriel (ū′rĭ-ĕl) 1. A chief of the Kohathite Levites who helped David bring the ark from the house of Obed-edom to Jerusalem (1 Chr. 6:24, 15:5, 11).

2. A man of Gibeah, the father of Maachah or Michaiah, the wife of King Rehoboam and mother of King Abijah of Judah (2 Chr. 13:2).

Urijah see **Uriah**

Urim (ū′rĭm) and **Thummin** (thŭm′ĭn) [lights and perfections] first mentioned in Ex. 28:30, there is much dispute over the meaning of the expression. Most often *Urim* is defined to mean lights, *Thummin*, perfections. Of what materials and in what form these consisted, nothing is said in Scripture. Whatever their composition or shape, they were small enough to fit into the breastplate, which was attached to the ephod worn by the high priest (Ex. 28:28, 30; Lev. 8:8). Some have suggested they were stones, others, wood, still others, metal.

Questions apparently were carefully phrased so as to be adapted to simple answers such as "yes" or "no." This seems evident from the use made of them by Joshua and Moses (Num. 27:20–22) and David (1 Sam. 23:10–13). Saul inquired but Jehovah did not answer him (1 Sam. 28:6). The manner in which the Urim and Thummin were used and in what manner the answer was given is not revealed. However, it is evident that men who used them readily understood the answer. Some have suggested the manner may have been the same as with dice. Apparently prearranged signs were decided upon before the question or inquiry was presented.

That Urim and Thummin were a significant blessing is certain from the statement of Moses' blessing from Mount Nebo when he said of Levi, "Thy Thummin and thy Urim are with thy godly one" (Deut. 33:8). Aaron—and succeeding high priests—was to wear the ephod on which was the breastplate with the Urim and Thummin "when he goeth in before Jehovah" (Ex. 28:30).

Urim and Thummin are last mentioned in Ezra 2:63 and Neh. 7:65 but it is not clear from these passages the use that was made of them in this postexilic period.   C.D.H.

usury see **loan**

Uthai (ū′thī) 1. A descendant of Judah living in Jerusalem after the Babylonian captivity (1 Chr. 9:4); probably the same as Athaiah (Neh. 11:4).

2. One of the seventy-one members of the family of Bigvai who returned from Babylon with Ezra (Ezra 8:14).

Uz (ŭz) 1. The territory where Job lived (Job 1:1; Jer. 25:20), east of Palestine in the general area of the Arabian Desert. The "daughter of Edom" dwelt there (Lam. 4:21); and bands of Sabeans and Chaldeans plundered the region (Job 1:15, 17). Although bordering the desert (Job 1:19), it was good pastureland (Job 1:3, 42:12). F. Delitzsch located it in the land of Bashan.

2. One of the sons of Aram (Gen. 10:23).

3. One of the sons of Nahor by Milcah (Gen. 22:21), otherwise called Huz (KJV).

4. One of the sons of Dishan (Gen. 36:28).
          M.C.

Uzai (ū′zī) the father of Palal, who assisted Nehemiah with the rebuilding of the Jerusalem wall (Neh. 3:25).

Uzal (ū′zăl) a son of Joktan (Gen. 10:27; 1 Chr. 1:21) and ancestor of an Arabian tribe referred to by Ezekiel (27:19). Arabic tradition gives this as the original name of San'a, the capital of Yemen.

Uzzah or **Uzza** (ŭz'à) [strength] a son of Abinadab, in whose house at Kiriath-jearim the ark of the covenant rested for twenty years. When David arranged to transport the ark to Jerusalem, Uzzah drove the oxcart. At the threshing floor of Nacon the oxen stumbled, and Uzzah, putting forth his hand to prevent the ark from falling, was struck dead. David named the place Penez-uzzah (the breaking forth on Uzzah). Uzzah's rashness was conditioned by the improper mode of transporting the ark (1 Chr. 15:13) and David recognized the punishment as a judgment on the people in general "because we sought him not after the due order" (2 Sam. 6:3–11; 1 Chr. 13:7–14).

J.H.

Uzzah, Garden of (ŭ'zà) the garden where both Manasseh and his son Amon, kings of Judah, were buried (2 K. 21:18, 26), located near Manasseh's palace.

Uzzen-sherah (ŭz'ĕn-shē'rà) a town built by Sherah, the daughter of Ephraim or of Beriah (1 Chr. 7:24), probably located in the hill country of Ephraim near Upper and Lower Beth-horon.

Uzzi (ŭz'ī) [strong] 1. The son of Bukki, and father of Zerahiah, of the family of Aaron (1 Chr. 6:5, 51; Ezra 7:4).

2. The son of Tola, one of Issachar's descendants (1 Chr. 7:2–3).

3. The son of Bela from the tribe of Benjamin (1 Chr. 7:7).

4. The son of Michri and father of Elah (1 Chr. 9:8), a Benjaminite who returned to Jerusalem after the Babylonian captivity.

5. The overseer of the Levites in Jerusalem after the Babylonian captivity (Neh. 11:22), son of Bani and a great-grandson of Mattaniah the son of Mica.

6. The head of the priestly family of Jedaiah (Neh. 12:19), who also lived after the Babylonian captivity.

Uzzia (ŭ'zī-à) [strength] one of David's guard who was from Ashtorath (1 Chr. 11:44).

Uzziah (ŭ'zī-à) [Jehovah is (my) strength], or Azariah [Jehovah has helped, or is keeper] the eleventh king in the Davidic dynasty (2 K. 15:1–7; 2 Chr. 26). He came to the throne at the age of sixteen (2 K. 15:2), seemingly by popular demand of "all the people of Judah." According to both Kings and Chronicles he reigned fifty-two years. However, the exact date is debated, the most probable being 791–740 B.C. The earlier part of his reign may have been as co-regent with his father; latter part is certainly with his son, Jehoram, as co-regent with him, probably from 750 to 740 B.C.

The greatest prosperity since Solomon was experienced during the reign of Uzziah. He was outstanding as a warrior and builder, and took an unusual interest in animal husbandry and agriculture. He conquered North and East Philistia, extending his campaigns to the south till his fame reached the entrance of Egypt. Eastward, he campaigned against the Ammonites and Arabians of Gur-baal (unknown) and the Meunim (probably Arabs who dwelt in Petra). He regained control over Elath (ancient Eziongeber), at the head of the Gulf of Aqabah. These conquests gave to Uzziah the control of trade routes in both the west and southeast. He built towers about Jerusalem, and to protect his trade routes, he built fortresses in the wilderness, probably the Negeb and east of the Dead Sea. Also he hewed cisterns and conserved water for flocks and for irrigation. These all contributed to the prosperity of his reign. His army was well equipped; and he is credited with the introduction of a stone-slinging catapult, an advance in military artillery for the time.

Assyria underwent a period of weakness between the years 781–746 B.C., during which period a plague devastated the country. This gave Uzziah added opportunity to carry on his military and economic exploits without interference from the eastern power.

The victories and prosperity of his reign "caused his heart to be lifted up." In his pride he went into the temple to burn incense, a service observed only by priests. As a result of the sacrilege Uzziah became a leper to the end of his life. He dwelt in a house apart, which left the rule of the kingdom in the hand of his son, Jehoram, who ruled as co-regent until the death of the king. Uzziah was buried in the burying place of his father.

2. A descendant of Kohath, a Levite (1 Chr. 6:24).

3. Father of Jonathan, a treasurer in the time of David (1 Chr. 27:25) after the Exile.

4. A priest who had taken a foreign wife (Ezra 10:21).

5. A descendant of Judah who dwelt in Jerusalem after the Exile (Neh. 11:4).   H.H.

Uzziel (ŭ-zī'ĕl) [God is strong] 1. Fourth son of Kohath, father of Michael, Elzaphan or Elizaphan, and Zithri, and uncle to Aaron (Ex. 6:18, 22; Lev. 10:4).

2. A Simeonite captain, son of Ishi, who had a successful expedition against the Amalekites in the days of Hezekiah (1 Chr. 4:42).

3. Son of Bela and head of a Benjaminite family (1 Chr. 7:7).

4. One of David's musicians, a son of Heman (1 Chr. 25:4) called Azarel in vs. 18.

5. A Levite, of the sons of Jeduthun, engaged in the reform carried on in the days of Hezekiah (2 Chr. 29:14–19).

6. Son of Harhaiah, a member of the guild of goldsmiths, who helped Nehemiah in re-building the walls of Jerusalem (Neh. 3:8).

J.H.

Uzzielites, the (ŭ-zī′ê-līts) the descendants of Uzziel, and one of the four great families of the Kohathites (Num. 3:27; 1 Chr. 26:23. Amminadab and 112 members of the clan assisted David in the transfer of the ark to Jerusalem (1 Chr. 15:10).

J.H.

V

Vajezatha (vȧ-jĕz′ȧ-thȧ) one of the ten sons of Haman whom the Jews slew in Shushan (Est. 9:9).

vale, valley Palestine is a land of countless hills and depressions (Deut. 8:7), the most distinctive of which is the rift valley (cf. "plains of Jordan," Gen. 13:11) through which the Jordan flows. This rift which stretches from Lebanon to Aqabah varies in elevation from 1600 feet above sea level to 1274 feet below sea level at the Dead Sea and is the lowest spot on earth. The Jordan valley divides the country into its two distinctive parts.

Five Hebrew words are rendered "valley" ("vale" is the poetic form) in the AV:

1. *'Emek*, as the "valley of Jezreel" (Judg. 6:33; Hos. 1:5) or the "valley of Aijalon" (Josh. 10:12), etc.

2. *Ge*, as "valley of the sons of Hinnom" (*Ge-ben-hinnom*, 2 K. 23:10) which encircles Jerusalem southwest and south; or "valley of the shadow of death" (Ps. 23:4), etc.

3. *Naḥal* may be a brook or river, but may also be a level area as "valley of Eshcol" (Deut. 1:24) or "valley of Sorek" (Judg. 16:4), etc.

4. *Biq'ah* is rendered "valley" in Deut. 34:3; Josh. 11:8, 17, 12:7; 2 Chr. 35:22; Zech. 12:11 (the latter two examples are rendered "plain" in the RSV).

5. *Shephelah* is the foothills between the coastal plain and the central highlands of Palestine which are, strictly speaking, not a valley. The AV translates "the vale" in Deut. 1:7; Josh. 10:40; 1 K. 10:27; 2 Chr. 1:15; Jer. 33:13; and "the valley" in Josh. 9:1, 11:2, 16, 12:8, 15:33; Judg. 1:9; and Jer. 32:44. The ASV and RSV translate these passages "lowland" and "Shephelah."

The valleys of Palestine were scenes of battles (Gen. 14:8; 1 Sam. 17:19) and were suitable for cultivation of grapes and grain (Num. 13:23; 1 Sam. 6:13) and for grazing (1 Chr. 27:29). In figurative speech, the "valley of the shadow of death" (Ps. 23:4) implies great danger, while the "valley of the sons of Hinnom" furnishes the name of the place of eternal punishment—Gehenna (Mt. 5:30, etc.).

J.P.L.

Vaniah (vä-nī′ăh) one of the sons of Bani who had married a foreign wife (Ezra 10:36).

Vashni (văsh′nī) the firstborn of Samuel as the text now stands (1 Chr. 6:28 [13]). But since in 1 Sam. 8:2 the name of his firstborn is Joel, it has been conjectured that in the Chronicles the name of Joel has dropped out and "Vashni" is a corruption of *Vesheni* "and (the) second" now made into a proper name.

Vashti (văsh′tī) the "queen" of Ahasuerus who, for refusing to show herself to the king's guests at the royal banquet when sent for by the king, was repudiated and deposed (Est. 1:9–22). Ahasuerus is now thought to be identified with Xerxes I. Herodotus (VII.61) gives Amestris as the name of his queen. We have not at our disposal material adequate to explain her relation to Vashti. Vashti is unknown outside the book of Esther.

veil 1. Veil (sometimes vail) translates seven words in the AV, some of which doubtless are really other articles of feminine clothing. Though the Middle Assyrian law #40 demands covering for the legitimate wife, veils were not universally used in the Biblical world. Faces were covered by the prospective bride in the case of Rebekah (Gen. 24:65) and by Tamar when playing the harlot to hide her identity (Gen. 38:14, 19). The face covering may also be used to protect the wearer from the heat and dust. Moses covered his face when he came from the mountain to conceal its splendor (Ex. 34:33–35; 2 Cor. 3:13–16). Paul required the woman praying or prophesying to be veiled (1 Cor. 11:4–16).

2. Veil also refers to the curtain which separated the rooms of the **tabernacle** (Ex. 26:31; Mt. 27:51).

veil of the tabernacle and temple see **tabernacle, temple**

versions, ancient, of the Old and New Testaments. (NOTE: In treating of the ancient versions that have come down to us, in whole or in part, they will be described in the alphabetical order of the languages.) It may be premised that in most of them the OT is not a version from the Hebrew, but merely a secondary translation from the LXX in some one of its early forms.

ARABIC VERSIONS. Exactly when the first Arabic translation came into being is not known. Most scholars believe that it was made some time after the spread of the Arabic language through the conquests of Islam, but others prefer a date prior to the seventh century. The oldest known copy of an Arabic version is assigned to the eighth century. The best-known early translation is the work of Saadia ha-Gaon (d. 942), who served as head of the rabbinic school at Sura in Babylonia. It is a translation made directly from the Hebrew text, and the extant portion includes the Pentateuch, Isaiah, the Minor Prophets (?), Psalms, Proverbs, Job, Song of Songs, and Daniel. Subsequently, other translations were made from the Greek, Samaritan, Syriac, Coptic, and Latin. Because of these many translations, made at different times and places and from different types of texts, the study of the Arabic versions remains a complicated problem.

ARMENIAN VERSION. Armenia, the region north of Mesopotamia and east of Asia Minor, was largely converted to Christianity by the first half of the fourth century, but it was not until the following century that the Armenians received the Scriptures in their own tongue. This was brought about by the efforts of Sahak (Isaac the Great, 390–439) and was made possible by the work of Mesrop (d. 439), a Christian teacher who devised an alphabet for the Armenian language. The book of Proverbs was translated first, and then followed the entire NT. Whether the translation was originally made from the Greek or the Syriac is still a matter of dispute; both views are supported by early traditions and are contended for by modern scholars. With the exception of the Latin Vulg., there are extant more MSS of the Ar-

menian than of any other version: more than 1200 have been enumerated, and several hundred others are known to exist in the Soviet Union. La Croze called the Armenian Version "the queen of the versions," a fit description in view of its beautiful diction and over-all accuracy.

COPTIC VERSIONS. Coptic is the latest form of the language used by the ancient Egyptians. Its alphabet is composed of Greek uncial characters, with the addition of seven letters taken from Egyptian demotic. There are extant today parts of the Bible from six Coptic dialects: (a) Sahidic, a dialect of Upper or Southern Egypt, formerly known as Thebaic; (b) Bohairic, a dialect of Lower or Northern Egypt, formerly called Memphitic; (c) Fayyumic; (d) Middle Egyptian; (e) Achmimic; and (f) Sub-Achmimic. Of these the most important are the Sahidic and the Bohairic. The Sahidic is regarded as the earliest of the Egyptian versions and was made ca. A.D. 200. A large collection of Coptic MSS is preserved at the J. Pierpont Morgan Library in New York. Included in this group of MSS is a Sahidic copy of the four gospels (Matthew, Mark and John are complete; fourteen leaves are missing from Luke), which is dated in the eighth or ninth century. Earlier MSS of the Sahidic exist, of course; but many of them, such as the papyri MSS, are fragmentary in their contents. The Bohairic Version is one of the later Coptic versions. In time Bohairic came to be the predominant dialect in Egypt, and thus the majority of Coptic MSS are in Bohairic. For students of NT textual studies, the Sahidic and Bohairic are especially significant since they generally confirm the type of text known as Alexandrian. The Coptic versions of the OT are based on the LXX.

ETHIOPIC VERSION. Near the middle of the fourth century, the king of Aksum in Abyssinia was converted to Christianity. Shortly after this a translation of the Bible from Greek was begun, although it may not have been completed until a century or so later. There are a number of MSS extant in Ethiopic, but all of them are of late dates. The earliest known MS is a thirteenth-century copy of the four gospels; most other MSS are dated from the fifteenth to the seventeenth centuries. In the epistles of Paul, the Ethiopic Version frequently agrees with one of the Chester Beatty papyri known as P^{46}.

GEORGIAN VERSION. Little is known of this early translation, but perhaps it deserves brief mention. Georgia is a mountainous region that lies between the Black and Caspian seas and is now a part of the Soviet Union. This area was Christianized in the fourth and fifth centuries; its translation of the Scriptures was made not long after that. Its oldest extant MS is of a Psalter dated ca. A.D. 700, while its earliest NT MS is dated a century later. In the NT the Georgian Version frequently stands in agreement with the so-called Caesarean text.

GOTHIC VERSION. Ulfilas (d. 383), often called the apostle to the Goths, is generally credited with making the first translation of the Bible into Gothic. Tradition says that he translated the entire Bible, but it is doubtful if he translated more than the NT portion. Ulfilas' work was a quite literal translation based on Greek MSS current around Constantinople in the middle of the fourth century. The version exists today only in fragments. The most important MS is of the fifth or sixth century and is housed in the University Library of Uppsala. It contains parts of all gospels in the so-called Western order (Matthew, John, Luke, and Mark). It is a luxury codex, written on purple vellum in large silver and gold letters, and is known as Codex Argenteus (the Silver Codex). The few other MSS that exist, with the exception of a leaf from a bilingual Gothic-Latin MS, are all palimpsests. The Pauline epistles have survived in part, but no MSS have as yet been discovered of Acts, Hebrews, General Epistles, and Revelation.

GREEK VERSIONS OF THE OLD TESTAMENT. 1. *The LXX* see **Septuagint.**

2. *Aquila.* In the second century three translations, which differed from the LXX, were made from the Hebrew OT into Greek. The first of these was made by Aquila, a proselyte born in Pontus. His translation was characterized by extreme literalness, so much so that it was often unintelligible to readers who did not know Hebrew as well as Greek. Except for certain citations from it, only fragments of Kings and Psalms have survived. Aquila's translation was completed ca. A.D. 130.

3. *Theodotion.* Another version from the second century is that of Theodotion. A convert to Judaism from Ephesus, he did his work sometime in the reign of Commodus (A.D. 180–92). Actually, he was responsible for a revision of the LXX rather than an independent translation. Two books of the OT are of special interest in the version of Theodotion. One is the book of Job, which follows the Hebrew text more closely than the LXX and contains about one sixth more material. The other, book of Daniel, has an entirely different form from the LXX. In most editions of the LXX, Theodotion's version of Daniel is followed.

4. *Symmachus.* Toward the end of the second century, Symmachus, an Ebionite, produced another Greek translation. The result of his work is the opposite of Aquila's, for his translation is remarkably free from Hebraisms. His Hebrew text, along with those of Aquila and Theodotion, was very similar to our Hebrew text today.

5. *The Fifth, Sixth, and Seventh Versions.* Besides the translations of Aquila, Symmachus, and Theodotion, the great critical work of Origen comprised three other versions. About A.D. 240, Origen produced his great work known as the *Hexapla*. It was an arrangement of the OT, six columns to each page. The first two columns were of the Hebrew text, one in Hebrew and the other in transliterated Greek characters. The third, fourth, and sixth columns were the versions of Aquila, Symmachus, and Theodotion; the fifth column presented a new text of the LXX. To the four Greek versions of his Hexapla, Origen added three other anonymous Greek versions—the Quinta, the Sexta, and the Septima (the fifth, the sixth, and the seventh). Unfortunately, Origen's monument of scholarship has not survived, except in fragments.

LATIN VERSIONS see **Vulgate**

SAMARITAN VERSIONS see **Samaritan Pentateuch**

SLAVONIC VERSION. Not long after the middle of the ninth century, two brothers, Cyril and Methodius, went as missionaries from Salonika to Great Moravia. Cyril is credited with the invention of the Slavonic alphabet; both he and Methodius were responsible in some sense for the translation of the Scriptures into Old Slavonic. Their OT was a version of the LXX, while their NT was based on typical Byzantine-type Greek MSS.

SYRIAC VERSIONS. Syriac is a Semitic language similar to the Aramaic dialect spoken by Jesus and his apostles. Some five or six forms of the Syriac version are known today, but their relations to each other are not clearly defined. 1. *The Old Syriac.* Of the many versions of the NT, the Syriac is thought to be the oldest. It dates back to the second century or even earlier. The Old Syriac is attested to primarily by two fragmentary MSS of the four gospels, the Sinaitic Syriac and the Curetonian Syriac. These MSS date back to the fourth and fifth centuries respectively, but the form of their texts goes back much earlier. Usually the Old Syriac version is in agreement with the so-called Western text. Closely related to the Old Syriac is the Diatessaron, a harmony of the four gospels made ca. A.D. 170 by Tatian, a disciple of Justin

Martyr. Information on the Diatessaron is scanty since copies of it, after Tatian was declared a heretic, were sought out and destroyed. In recent years the Diatessaron has been the focal point of much debate. It is the belief of many scholars today, however, that the Diatessaron was originally written in Syriac, and as such holds an important place in the making of early versions.

2. *The Peshitta*. The term itself means "the simple" and is used to distinguish the version from others that included marks and notes which served as critical apparatus. The Peshitta Version of the OT is quite old; it is to be dated perhaps in the first or second century A.D. It is evident that a number of persons shared in producing the version, for the quality and style of translation varies from book to book. The oldest known MS of the Peshitta is also the oldest MS of any portion of the Bible whose precise date is known; this is a MS of the Pentateuch which is dated A.D. 442. The Peshitta version of the NT goes back to the fourth century A.D. It was not a new translation, but a revision of the Old Syriac in comparison with the current form of the Greek text. When originally made, the Peshitta did not include 2 Peter, 2 and 3 John, Jude, and Revelation. These books, however, were added in the later revisions mentioned below.

3. *The Philoxenian and Harclean*. But there was some dissatisfaction with the Peshitta, and attempts were made to provide new revisions. In A.D. 508, Philoxenus of Mabbug commissioned the translation of the whole Bible from Greek. A century later the name of Thomas of Harkel, bishop of Mabbug, comes into prominence. Exactly how he added to the work of revision is not known. Either he reissued the version of Philoxenus and appended to it marginal notes as derived from two or three Greek MSS, or he made a completely new revision accompanied by significant marginal notes.

4. *The Palestinian Syriac*. Usually mentioned in this connection is the Palestinian Syriac, whose language is more properly termed Palestinian Aramaic. It has survived chiefly in lectionary copies of the gospels. It dates from about the fifth century and is based on Greek MSS of the so-called Caesarean type of text.

5. *The Syro-Hexaplar*. Another Syriac version was made in 617–18 by Paul, bishop of Tella in Mesopotamia. This was the OT counterpart of the Harclean revision of the NT. Paul's work is a translation of the LXX text in Origen's Hexapla, including marginal apparatus and readings from Aquila, Symmachus, and Theodotion. Much of the Syro-Hexaplaric text has

survived. It is especially important as a witness of the Hexaplaric text of the LXX.

TARGUMS. The term *targum* is used to refer to an Aramaic paraphrase or interpretative expansion of some part of the OT. Following the Babylonian captivity, Aramaic replaced Hebrew as the spoken tongue of the Jews. It was necessary, therefore, in order to facilitate understanding, to provide for the people a translation in Aramaic. The beginnings of this practice may be alluded to in Neh. 8:8. Here it is said that Ezra and other Jewish leaders "read from the book, from the law of God, clearly; and they gave the sense, so that the people understood the reading" (RSV). An alternative rendering for "clearly" is "with interpretation," as the RSV footnote indicates. At first and for centuries, the Targums were strictly oral. Later they were reduced to writing and subsequently became obsolete. Targums are extant today of all the OT, except the books of Ezra, Nehemiah, and Daniel. It is characteristic of the Targums to avoid any direct reference to the Name of God and to change all anthropomorphisms ascribed to God. Below are listed the main divisions of the Targums.

1. *The Pentateuch*. The official Targum of the Pentateuch is the Targum of Onkelos. It dates perhaps as early as the second or third century A.D. Although it embodies early Palestinian traditions, it shows evidence of Babylonian reworking. In contrast to others, it is regarded as a conservative Targum, not being given to extraneous stories as found in the Midrash. Its Hebrew text is the practical equivalent of the Masoretic text.

2. *The Prophets*. The official Targum of the Prophets is known as the Targum of Jonathan. It also received its final form in Babylonia. Though not as literal as Targum Onkelos, it follows the text of the Former Prophets (Joshua, Judges, 1 and 2 Samuel, 1 and 2 Kings) more closely than that of the Latter Prophets (Isaiah, Jeremiah, Ezekiel, and the twelve minor prophets).

3. *The Hagiographa*. The oldest of these Targums goes back to the fifth century, but most of them are much later. They cover various books and differ widely among themselves, ranging from paraphrases to independent commentaries. All of the Targums, however, are valuable: they supply helpful information on the OT text and preserve numerous traditional interpretations of OT passages as held by the Jews. N.R.L.

Versions, English 1. *Wycliffe*. The name of John Wycliffe is correctly associated with the first English translation of the complete Bible.

But how much of it was the work of Wycliffe is not known. Westcott believed that Wycliffe was responsible for the NT, and that he had finished this work by the year of 1380. Others disagree. At any rate, all are united in attributing the work in some sense to Wycliffe. The OT portion was completed ca. 1382. It was mostly the work of Nicholas de Hereford, who was one of Wycliffe's most zealous supporters. Extant MSS of the Wycliffe Bible show that there were two versions, an early and a later version. It is generally agreed that the later version is a revision of the earlier, and that it was executed by John Purvey ca. 1388. The chief defect of these versions is that they were based on the Latin Vulg. instead of the original Greek and Hebrew.

2. *Tyndale.* The true father of the English Bible is William Tyndale (1494–1536). Early in life Tyndale made it his ambition to give to the English people a translation of the Bible based not on Latin but on the original tongues. He once said to one of his opponents: "If God spare my life, ere many years I will cause a boy that driveth the plow shall know more of the Scripture than thou doest." In 1524, it was necessary for Tyndale to leave England in order to pursue his determined course. In the following year at Worms, after much difficulty, he was finally successful in having his English NT printed; and early in 1526, copies of it were smuggled into England. There the books were bought eagerly, and there also they were opposed as eagerly. In October of 1526, Cuthbert Tunstall, bishop of London, ordered all copies of the forbidden books to be gathered; these he publicly burned at Paul's Cross. Having translated the NT from Greek, Tyndale took up his work of translating the OT from Hebrew. By 1530, he had translated and published the Pentateuch; then followed Jonah (1531), a revised Genesis (1534), and two additional editions of his NT (1534–35). His heroic life was brought to a close in 1536. To Tyndale belongs the honor of having given the first example of a translation based on true principles. Nine tenths of the AV is due to Tyndale.

3. *Coverdale.* A complete translation of the Bible, bearing the name of Miles Coverdale, appeared in 1535. Printed probably at Zurich, it was based mainly on "the Douche [Luther's German version] and the Latyn." Because of Tyndale's controversial works and his caustic marginal notes, there was no hope of obtaining Henry VIII's sanction for anything that bore Tyndale's name. But Coverdale's gentle manner, aided by the influence of Thomas Cromwell, changed the king's attitude toward a translation in English. Of Coverdale's Bible, the king said, "In God's name let it go abroad among our people."

4. *Matthew and Taverner.* In 1537 there appeared another English version, probably printed at Antwerp. It was issued under the name of Thomas Matthew, although it was actually edited by John Rogers, a friend of Tyndale. While in prison, Tyndale had turned over his unfinished work on the OT to Rogers; and this, plus Coverdale and Tyndale's NT, constituted "Matthew's" Bible. The king's license was given to it, as well as to the 1537 edition of Coverdale. Taverner's Bible, the work of a layman named Richard Taverner, was published in 1539. A revision of Matthew's Bible, its chief virtue is the improvement of renderings that it offers in the NT.

5. *The Great Bible.* Coming from the same year as Taverner's and from the same press, there appeared an English Bible which, because of its size, is known as the Great Bible. It was edited by Coverdale and was essentially the Tyndale version minus the marginal notes. Reprinted again and again, it was, with the exception of Mary's reign, the Authorized Version of the English church until 1568.

6. *The Geneva Bible.* To escape persecution during the reign of Mary, a number of English Protestants settled in Geneva. There in 1557 the English congregation, under the leadership of William Whittingham, put out a new version of the NT. This was followed by the complete Bible in 1560, often called the "Breeches Bible" because of its translation in Gen. 3:7: "They sewed fig leaves together and made themselves breeches." Produced in legible type, in small form, with accompanying commentary and illustrations, it became the Bible for the family as the Great Bible was the Bible for the church. It was the first translation to print each verse as a paragraph and to put words in italics not represented in the original texts.

7. *The Bishops' Bible.* The Geneva Bible, however, was not acceptable to the English church officials. Its commentary presented the views of John Calvin and of the Reformation. A revision of the Great Bible was therefore begun by the English clergy, and when completed in 1568 was known as the Bishops' Bible. Four years later a second edition appeared, but the Bishops' Bible neither measured up to the scholarship nor attained to the popularity of the Geneva Bible.

8. *The Rheims-Douai Bible.* The zeal of Protestant versions and editions eventually

forced into being a Roman Catholic translation of the Bible. An edition of the NT was produced in 1582 at the English college of Rheims; and in 1609–10 the college at Douai issued a translation of the OT. The Rheims-Douai translation was thus the first Roman Catholic edition of the English Bible. It was translated, however, not from the original languages of Scripture, but on the basis of the Latin Vulg.

9. *The Authorized Version.* It remained for the Authorized Version of 1611, better known as the King James Version, to do what its many predecessors had been unable to do—provide a translation for public and private use which was satisfactory to all. King James had summoned in 1604 a meeting of representatives of diverse religious groups to discuss the question of religious toleration. At this gathering, known as the Hampton Court Conference, Dr. John Reynolds of Oxford raised the possibility of a new translation. The king welcomed the suggestion and laid down general requirements that were to be met. Briefly stated, the following were the instructions given to the translators: (a) The Bishops' Bible was to be followed, and as little altered as the original would permit. (b) The names of prophets and others were to be retained as they were commonly used. (c) The old ecclesiastical words were to be kept. (d) When a word has different meanings, the meaning is to be kept, when possible, which is most often used by the ancient fathers. (e) The division of the chapters was to be altered either not at all, or as little as possible. (f) No marginal notes were to be affixed, but only for the explanation of Hebrew and Greek words. (g) "Such quotations of places to be marginally set down as shall serve for the fit reference of one Scripture to another." (h) and (i) These state procedures to be followed by companies of translators. (j) Provides for differences of opinion between two companies by referring them to a general meeting. (k) Gives power, in cases of difficulty, to consult any scholars. (l) Invites suggestions from any quarter. (m) Names the directors of the work: Andrews, dean of Westminster; Barlow, dean of Chester; and the Regius professors of Hebrew and Greek at both universities. (n) Names translations to be followed when they agree more with the original than the Bishops' Bible: Tyndale's, Matthew's, Coverdale's, Whitchurch's (Great Bible), and Geneva. (o) Authorizes universities to appoint three or four overseers of the work. Fifty-four men were originally appointed by the king, but it seems that only forty-seven actually engaged in the work of translation. These were divided into six working companies, two at Westminster, two at Oxford, and two at Cambridge. Each company was assigned selected books to be translated; and the work of each company was sent to and reviewed by the other companies, appointed delegates of each company smoothing out the difficult spots. In this way the translation was the product of the revisers as a whole. It was in 1611, seven years after the convening of the Hampton Court Conference, when the first copies of the new version came from the press. It was dedicated to the king, and on its title page were the words "Appointed to be read in Churches." Accompanying it was an informative preface entitled "The Translators to the Reader," in which the translators sought to justify their efforts against the many voices of critics who felt that their old Bibles were good enough. The Authorized Version has passed through many editions and has been modernized considerably during the course of years. Appointed for use in public worship, it immediately displaced the Bishops' Bible in the churches; but in private use the new translation received stiff competition from the popular Geneva Bible. Within a few decades, however, it had established itself as *the* translation for English-speaking people around the world. It was inevitable, however, that there would be revisions of the Authorized Version. The best known of these are the English Revised Version (1881, 1885), the American Standard Version (1901), and the Revised Standard Version (1946, 1952). These translations, while reflecting the latest in Biblical scholarship, have consciously sought to preserve the language of the Tyndale-King James tradition. N.R.L.

villages villages in the OT were distinguished from cities in that they were smaller, usually unwalled, and less easily defended (Lev. 25:29–31; Deut. 3:5; Ezek. 38:11). In Talmudic literature a village was defined as a place which did not have a synagogue, but it is the OT's description which is used in the NT (Mk. 1:38–39; Lk. 8:1). Some villages may have been isolated (Est. 9:19), but they are more often mentioned as belonging to certain cities, perhaps even in the sense of jurisdiction (Josh. 15:32–62, 17:11; 1 Chr. 6:56; Mk. 8:27). Some may have been unwalled suburbs built up against or near the walled cities. They were usually enclosures of simple, one-room huts made of mud, stone, or perhaps even grass or palm leaves. Some camps were also called villages (Gen. 25:16, RSV). R.H.

vine although other types of vine are mentioned (Deut. 32:32; 2 K. 4:39; Num. 11:5;

Isa. 1:8), the principal vine in the Bible is the grapevine. It is first mentioned in Gen. 9:20. It was such an important part of the economy of Israel that one who planted a vineyard was not drafted into military service until it produced (Deut. 20:6).

Isaiah 5:1–6 has a description of a vineyard. Not all vineyards were enclosed (Deut. 23:24), although often they were fenced with stone or a hedge to keep out animals (Ps. 80:12; Song of S. 2:15; Mt. 21:33; Mk. 12:1). In some cases they were further protected by watchtowers (Isa. 5:2; Mt. 21:33; Mk. 12:1). Supports were used to keep the grapes off the ground. Vineyards were pruned (Lev. 25:3; Joel 3:10; Jn. 15:2).

Although seemingly forbidden by the Law (Deut. 22:9), sometimes fig trees were planted in the vineyard (Lk. 13:6).

The needy could glean the vineyard when the harvest was over (Lev. 19:10; Deut. 24:21); and passersby could partake of the vine, but they were forbidden to take grapes with them (Deut. 23:24).

At harvest time in baskets or in carts the grapes were carried to the wine press where the juices were trampled out by barefoot workers (Isa. 16:10; Jer. 25:30, 48:33; Amos 9:13). Wine was stored in goatskins (Mt. 9:17), or in pottery (Jer. 35:5). Raisin cakes were made (Isa. 16:7).

The fruit of the vine was tithed (Deut. 12:17, 14:23). Grapes were used to pay debts (2 Chr. 2:10), and taxes (1 Sam. 8:14).

The vineyard rested during the sabbatical year (Ex. 23:10–11; Lev. 25:3–5).

The fruitful vine became a symbol of peace and prosperity (Num. 13:23), and it was a golden era indeed when each one could sit under his own vine (1 K. 4:25; Mic. 4:4; Zech. 3:10; Hos. 2:15; Amos 9:13–14). On the other hand, the desolated vineyard symbolized dire judgment on a people (Isa. 16:6–14).

Jesus drew his parables from scenes of everyday life, and thus we are not surprised that several parables concerned vineyards; such as the new wine being put in new wineskins (Mt. 9:17); the laborers in the vineyard (Mt. 20:1–6); the two sons (Mt. 21:28–32); the wicked husbandmen (Mt. 21:33–43; Mk. 12:1–11; Lk. 20:9–18); and the fig tree which was in the vineyard (Lk. 13:6–9). Christ used also the fruit of the vine to symbolize his blood of the New Covenant (Mt. 26:27–29).

James emphasized that just as a vine does not yield figs, the Christian should not use his tongue to bear the opposite fruits of blessing and cursing (3:5–12; cf. Lk. 6:44).

A person might be likened to a fruitful (Gen. 49:22) and spreading vine (Ezek. 17:1–8; Ps. 128:3). Symbolically speaking, Israel was the vine God had taken out of Egypt and planted in the land (Ps. 80:8–14; Isa. 5:1–7). In at least one case the remnant was likened to a vine (Jer. 6:9). But even this choice vine through apostasy could become like a wild vine (Jer. 2:21; cf. Isa. 5:1–7; Hos. 10:1); the vine of Sodom (Deut. 32:32); and a dead vine which was consumed by fire (Ezek. 15:1–4; cf. 19:10–14; Jn. 15:6).

Christ is now the true vine in whom men must abide in order to partake of the life which flows from him and to bear fruit. Otherwise disciples are cut off and burned (Jn. 15:1–8).

The tramping out of grapes in the wine press is used as a symbol of a judgment of God on the earth (Rev. 14:17–20).   J.D.B.

vine of Sodom a figure of speech in the Song of Moses describing the vine of the wicked whose grapes are poison, whose clusters are bitter, and whose wine is compared to the poison of serpents and the venom of asps (Deut. 32:32–33). The Wisdom of Solomon (10:7) refers to a deceptive fruit in a setting of Sodom that never ripens. Josephus (*War* IV.viii.4) describes an attractive fruit which dissolves into smoke and ashes when touched, making a suitable connection with the ashes of Sodom.

The identification with known plants involves considerable conjecture. If the plant is to be identified with the "apple of Sodom (*Solanum sodomeum*)" it is a shrub which grows up to four or five feet and is covered with sharp thorns. Its bitter fruit resembles a tomato, but is full of black seeds mingled with silky hairs resembling ashes. If it is the vine *Citrullus colocynthis*, it climbs over shrubs and fences and has a fruit about the size and color of an orange which when ripe has a bitter taste and dusty powder and seeds in its rind. J.P.L.

vinegar the Heb. *ḥomeṣ*, translated "vinegar," literally means sour; the Gr. *ozos*, sharp (to the taste). Since it was derived from wine or strong drink which had turned sour, it was forbidden to Nazarites (Num. 6:3). It is described as a disagreeable beverage in the OT (Ps. 69:21; Prov. 10:26) but as a welcome seasoning (Ruth 2:14). It was vinegar, or perhaps *posca*, a mixture of egg, water, and vinegar, which the soldiers offered Jesus in his dying moments (Mt. 27:48; Mk. 15:36; Lk. 23:36; Jn. 19:29–30) as a fulfillment of Ps. 69:21.   R.H.

viol see **psaltery**

viper see **serpent**

virgin 1. (Heb. *bethulah*; Gr. *parthenos*). A young woman who has not had sexual intercourse (Gen. 24:16; 1 Cor. 7:25, 28, 34, 36 f.) as Mary (Lk. 1:27) or Tamar (2 Sam. 13:2). It is applied to men in Rev. 14:4.

In Israel if a bride proved not to be a virgin she should be stoned. The groom who falsely accused his bride of not being a virgin was fined and deprived of the later option of divorce (Deut. 22:13–20).

2. *'Almah*: a word of seven occurrences in the Hebrew Bible: Gen. 24:43; Ex. 2:8; Prov. 30:19; Ps. 68:25; Song of S. 1:3, 6:8; Isa. 7:14; also in musical notations (*Alamoth* or *Al muth*) and in the headings of certain psalms: 1 Chr. 15:20; Pss. 9:1, 46:1, 48:15 (14). The dispute over whether *parthenos* (as LXX in Gen. 24:43 and Isa. 7:14; but *neanis* in Ex. 2:8; Ps. 68:26 [25] and Song of S. 1:3, 6:8) is the proper rendering of Isa. 7:14 can be traced back at least to the time of Aquila who insisted that *neanis* (maiden) is correct. English versions like the Greek and Latin versions vacillate considerably over the rendering of *'almah*. The AV alternates between "maid" (Ex. 2:8; Prov. 30:19), "damsels" (Ps. 68:26 [25]), and "virgin" (Gen. 24:43; Song of S. 1:3, 6:8; and Isa. 7:14) and transliterates the musical notations. ASV alternates between "maiden" and "damsel" except in Isa. 7:14 and Song of S. 1:3, 6:8, the latter two of which have "maiden" as an alternate marginal rendering. The RSV alternates between "young woman," "girl," and "maiden" in all the passages with "young woman" in Isa. 7:14. The use of Isa. 7:14 in Matthew may be a case of typological interpretation.

In figurative language "virgin daughter" may frequently refer to a city as "virgin daughter of Zion" for Jerusalem (Isa. 37:22; Jer. 14:17). It is also used for Sidon (Isa. 23:12) and Babylon (Isa. 47:1). The church is likened to a chaste virgin (2 Cor. 11:2).   J.P.L.

Vophsi (vŏph′sī) father of Nahbi, the Naphtalite spy (Num. 13:14).

vows basically a vow was a voluntary pledge to God either to perform some specific deed or to refrain from a given activity. Vowing, thus, was primarily a spontaneous religious act arising out of a person's need for special help in difficult circumstances. Consequently, the OT normally never required one to take a vow, but it carefully regulated and demanded the fulfilling of a vow once it had been made (Deut. 23:21–23; Eccl. 5:4).

Conditional vows, also referred to as "positive vows," are the most common in the OT. They pledged one to a given course of action if God granted to him his wish. Examples of this form of vow can be seen in Jacob's vow

at Bethel (Gen. 28:18–22), Jephthah's promise of a sacrifice for military victory (Judg. 11:30–31), Hannah's petition for a son (1 Sam. 1:11). Aside from the specific pledges made in these cases, the number of items which might be vowed are varied, as can be seen from the list in Lev. 27. The Psalms (50:14, 56:12–13, 61:5, 8, 66:13–15, 116:14–18) are particularly rich in their descriptions of the paying of vows.

Abstinence vows normally pledged one to abstain from an enjoyable pursuit until a given purpose was accomplished (cf. Num. 30:3; 1 Sam. 14:24; Ps. 132:1–5). This practice may underlie Uriah's stubbornness in 2 Sam. 11:9–13. A special and severe form of this vow was the ban whereby the people were obligated to destroy a city and their potential booty in honor of God and the victory he gave them (Num. 21:1–3). The element of abstention is also seen in the Nazarite's refusal to cut his hair or consume strong drink (Num. 6:1–21).

Among the more important principles governing the exercise of vows were the following regulations: (a) Vows could not be fulfilled by offering less than promised (Lev. 22:17–25; Mal. 1:14), something unclean (Deut. 23:18), or by a possession which already belonged to God such as the firstlings (Lev. 27:26–27). (b) The vows of a daughter or wife were subject to the approval or disapproval of the father or husband, but not those of a widow or divorcée (Num. 30). (c) The money values to be used in redeeming devoted objects is carefully prescribed in Lev. 27.

On at least two occasions in the NT Jesus criticized abuses involved with vow-making (Mt. 15:4–6; Mk. 7:10–13). Twice in Acts Paul made a vow (Acts 18:18, 21:23–24); the latter time he joined with four others who had made a vow. In Acts 23:12–14 the Jewish conspirators seeking Paul's life vowed not to eat or drink until they had killed Paul.   G.R.

Vulgate, the in the days of the apostles and shortly thereafter the Bible was read in the Greek. Soon after, people began to put the Scriptures in their own language, such as Syriac, Coptic, and Latin. North Africa made the first translations into Latin sometime in the second century A.D. By the middle of the third century there were many Old Latin versions. As Latin became the language of the world, there arose a greater demand for the Scriptures in this language. Since the Latin versions were from Africa, those in Rome deemed them unfit for their use and so began to revise them. Consequently, there arose a need for one standard text with which to combat heresy and unify the Western church. This led Damasus, bishop of Rome, to ask Jerome to produce a version in Latin that all could accept.

Jerome, whose real name was Eusebius Hieronymus, was born in Dalmatia about 340. After some time in Antioch, he moved to Rome in 382 as Damasus' adviser. In 383 Jerome issued a revision of the Psalms called the Roman Psalter. In 392 he issued a second revision later known as the Gallican Psalter because it was first chiefly used by the churches in Gaul. He then began a careful translation of the Bible into Latin, from 390 to 405. Much of his work was done while he lived in Bethlehem. Jerome's translation was very literal; he was careful to translate from the original Hebrew and Greek (the Old Latin versions were translated from Greek translations of the Hebrew). Although he rejected the Apocrypha as inspired, he also made a translation or revision of some of those books.

This new translation was later called the Vulg. because it is written in the "vulgar" or "common" language (from the Lat. *vulgata*). Originally the word vulgar meant that used by everyone. The history of this word is a sad commentary on the way everyone talks.

At first the Vulg. was not accepted, as is true of most new translations. Many declaimed it because it did not follow the LXX, which some regarded as inspired as the original Hebrew text. Jerome's Hebrew translation of the Psalms was never accepted by the church. More used the Gallican Psalter, but some used the Roman Psalter. One of the greatest enemies of the new translation was Rufinus, a one-time friend of Jerome's.

Because of its intrinsic worth, gradually the Vulg. replaced the other Latin versions. After the seventh century the other Latin versions disappeared. On April 8, 1546, the Council of Trent declared the Vulg. as the authoritative version of the church, and even today it is accepted as such by the Roman Catholic church.

Of course, by the sixteenth century there were serious problems in reconstructing the exact text of Jerome's work. In 1590 the Sixtine edition of the Vulg. was produced; this was so called after Sixtus V, the man who was Pope when it was published. It was quickly replaced by the Clementine edition of 1592, named after Pope Clement VIII. The Clementine edition even today is the authoritative edition of the Vulg. for the Roman Catholic church. The outstanding critical edition of the Vulg. is the Oxford edition of J. Wordsworth and H. J. White, first published in 1889. N.P.

vulture used by the AV to render three Hebrew words: *da'ah* (Lev. 11:14); *dayyah* (Deut. 14:13); and *'ayyah* (Job 28:7). The specific identification of these unclean birds who live on carrion is uncertain. The RV used "falcon" and "kite" for these words and uses "vulture" for *raham*. It is now thought that *nesher* (Lev. 11:13), rather than being the "eagle" as rendered in the AV may in some instances be the griffon vulture.

W

wages our English term "wages" is found seventeen times in the Scriptures and has been translated from seven different Hebrew and Greek words, in which are to be found the shades of emphasis given the term in Scripture. In Jer. 22:13 woe is pronounced upon him who "useth his neighbor's service without wages," i.e., for gratis. In Gen. 29:15, 31:7, 41, the idea is of reward for service performed, while in Lev. 19:13 one can see the importance placed in the Mosaic law that a man's wage be paid promptly. Genesis 30:28, 31:8; Ex. 2:9; Ezek. 29:18, 29:19; Mal. 3:5; and Hag. 1:6 all exhibit the meaning found in the word meaning payment of contract for services performed. One cannot, however, say anything definite concerning whether or not payment consisted of money, food provisions, or the spoils of war. The context must decide this phase of the question. In Jn. 4:36 and 2 Pet. 2:15 the emphasis is a figurative one, while in Lk. 3:14; Rom. 6:23; and 2 Cor. 11:8 the term refers to a definite stipend or provision.   P.M.C.

wagon see **cart** and **chariot**

walls 1. Stone walls in Palestine were built around fields from stones rolled off the field to make it suitable for cultivation (Isa. 5:5). A path through the vineyards might have stone walls on either side (Num. 22:24). More recently Arabs enclosed areas with prickly-pear hedges (cf. Hos. 2:6).

2. City and house walls were often made of unhewn stones or brick set in mud or mortar. Walls might be of great height and breadth (Deut. 1:28; Josh. 2:15; Acts 9:25) and often laid on solid rock foundations (Lk. 6:48). Paneling may have been used on house interiors. It is a mark of wealth that one use hewn stones for building (Isa. 9:10; Amos 5:11). Excavations have revealed city walls that re-use hewn stones of an earlier period along with rubble. A core of rubble is often used between larger facing stones to give strength. These walls were the chief means of defense and metaphorically may express the idea of protection (Isa. 26:1).

wandering in the wilderness see **wilderness of wandering**

war there are two primary concepts of war in the Scriptures: (1) 1 Sam. 17:9; Josh. 9:2; Lk. 14:31 portray war in the sense of combat, either between individuals or armies. (2) Eph. 6:10–12; 2 Cor. 10:3; 1 Tim. 1:18–19 emphasize war in a spiritual sense between the forces of right and wrong.

In the OT it was the power of God which delivered the Hebrews from Egypt (Ex. 15:1–18; Deut. 4:34), hence before entering a war, the Hebrews sought the approval and active participation of God in their wars (Ex. 17:16; 1 Sam. 28:6, 30:8; 2 Sam. 5:19). The man who led the Hebrew forces was to be one who had the Spirit of God; otherwise he ventured into an act without the sanction of God (Judg. 6:34, 11:29, 16:20; 1 Sam. 16:14). All victory was thus attributed to the power of God (2 Sam. 22:35; Ps. 144:1; Judg. 5).

Because God fought with his people, the numerical strength of the army was not an important question (Judg. 7; 1 Sam. 14:6), however God did require that those who served be free of any financial or marital entanglements (Deut. 20:5–9). The military camps were places where God walked (Deut. 23:14), and thus were to be kept clean according to the Law (Deut. 23:12–13; 1 Sam. 21:4). Before entering upon a battle, spies were generally sent into enemy territory (Num. 13:1–17; Josh. 2:1; 1 Sam. 26:4). Before battle, a sacrifice was offered (1 Sam. 7:9); and usually a keynote address of encouragement was given either by the military leader or by a priest (2 Chr. 20:20; Deut. 20:2). Often, the ark of the covenant was carried into battle as a sign of the presence of God (1 Sam. 4:4–18). Upon entering into the battle the priests were to sound the alarm with the trumpets (Num. 10:9; 2 Chr. 13:12–16).

Combat at that time in history was largely hand to hand; however, early armies were not without strategy. Wars were generally fought in the spring following the rigors of winter (2 Sam. 11:1). The Scriptures furnish us with the following forms of strategy adopted by the Hebrew people: (a) ambush (Josh. 8:4), (b) feint (Judg. 20:20), (c) flank movement (2 Sam. 5:23), and (d) surprise attack (Josh. 11:7). The battles themselves generally took the form of rout (Judg. 7:19–23) or a siege (Ezek. 4:2). Sometimes, the battles were decided by the choosing of champions who represented their respective armies (1 Sam. 17).

Israel was not unlike her neighbors in the severe treatment administered to the conquered. The bodies of the dead were plundered (1 Sam. 31:8). The survivors were often killed (2 Sam. 12:31), or mutilated (Judg. 1:6), or taken into captivity (Num. 31:26; Deut. 20:14). Following a war, success was often marked by the erection of victory monuments (1 Sam. 7:12) and by victory songs and dances (Ex. 15; Judg. 5; 1 Sam. 18:6–8; 2 Sam. 22).

One very important feature of the word "war" in the OT is its usage by the prophets when Israel apostatizes and thus, herself, becomes the object of God's wrath (Isa. 63:10; Jer. 21:5). On occasions like this, God used the military power of foreign nations as instruments of his judgment (Isa. 10:5; Jer. 25:1–9) and withdrew his power from Israel until she turned to him in repentance (Isa. 1:16–20). Another important concept in the prophets is that much of Israel's failure is to be attributed to a failure to trust in God's power and to place trust in material representations of strength. God is concerned that his people return to a position of unwavering trust in the power of God rather than in human implements (Isa. 30:1–5; Jer. 9:23, 31:1–3; Hos. 7:12).

In the NT "war" seems to take on a more spiritual significance rather than a physical one. Jesus rebuked Peter for using the sword (Mt. 26:51–54). He placed major emphasis upon making peace (Mt. 5:9). And on more than one occasion he emphasized meeting hate and violence with love and good deeds (Mt. 5:43–44; Lk. 6:27). Likewise, the early church viewed war as an act by the state, not by the church. Thus, the Christian's war was a continual one against the evil that warred against the soul and against the passions of the flesh (1 Cor. 14:8; Eph. 6:13–17). To the faithful warrior who would not be overcome by the evil

washing the hands and feet

forces, the crown of life and the sharing in the fruits of the great final victory would be his at the end of time (2 Thess. 2:8; 2 Tim. 4:7; Rev. 17:14, 20:7-10).   P.M.C.

washing the hands and feet washing the hands began in the interest of hygienic purity, but in the Bible it is mostly mentioned in a ceremonial sense. Under the Law the unclean man was to wash his hands before touching anyone (Lev. 15:11). By NT times the Pharisees had transformed this practice into a matter of ritual observance in which the disciples of Jesus did not participate. This brought the hostility of the Jews upon them (Mt. 15:2; Mk. 7:1-3). The word *pugmē* which goes untranslated in the RSV, as "oft" in AV, and "diligently" in ASV, literally means "with the fist." It probably describes part of the meticulous ritual of the Jews. It is thought that a small amount of water was poured on the upturned fingers of one hand. Luke 11:38 indicates that the hands may have been dipped in water on some occasions. Washing the hands was practiced to indicate that one disowned responsibility for a certain action (Mt. 27:24-25). Many think this is based on a practice in Deut. 21:6-7. Hands and feet were to be washed in connection with the services of the tabernacle (Ex. 30:19, 21). Orientals wore sandals and the first act performed by a host when visitors came was to provide food for their animals, water with which they might wash their feet, and food to eat (Gen. 18:4, 19:2, 24:32, 43:24; Judg. 19:21). The washing served both a refreshing and a cleansing purpose. Washing the feet of another was an expression of humility (1 Sam. 25:41). It was often an expression of love and devotion (Lk. 7:38-44; Jn. 12:3). Jesus washed the disciples' feet (Jn. 13:1-16), teaching them that the one who served most was to be regarded as the greatest (Lk. 22:24). Such a practice was characteristic of Christian women who were devoted to good works (1 Tim. 5:10).   F.J.

watches of night the Jews, like the Greeks and Romans, divided the night into military watches instead of hours, each watch representing the period for which sentinels remained on duty. The proper Jewish reckoning recognized only three such watches: the first or "beginning of the watches" (Lam. 2:19), the middle watch (Judg. 7:19), and the morning watch (Ex. 14:24; 1 Sam. 11:11). These would last respectively from sunset to 10 P.M., from 10 P.M. to 2 A.M., and from 2 A.M. to sunrise. The Rabbis debated whether there were three or four watches. The Romans had four, and in the NT we read of four. They were described

either according to their numerical order, as in the case of the "fourth watch" (Mt. 14:25), or by the terms "evening, midnight, cockcrowing, and morning" (Mk. 13:35). These terminated respectively at 9 P.M., midnight, 3 A.M., and 6 A.M.   F.J.

water of jealousy (Num. 5:11-31). When an Israelite husband had a "spirit of jealousy," suspecting his wife of sexual unfaithfulness, he could bring her before the priest and by means of supernatural intervention determine if she was guilty or innocent. Along with his wife the man brought a cereal offering of jealousy, of remembrance. This brought the sin to remembrance. Having set the woman before the Lord the priest would put dust from the tabernacle floor into the holy water in an earthen vessel. The woman took an oath accepting the consequences. The curses were written in a book, washed off in the water of bitterness and the woman was made to drink it. If she was guilty the water caused bitter pain. Her body was to swell and her thigh to fall away. This is a difficult phrase to interpret; the swelling body may refer to pregnancy and the falling thigh to a premature birth. If she was innocent of the charge she was free to go and conceive. This is the only ordeal in the OT, but such was not uncommon in the Middle East. The Nuzi tablets provided that a woman who had committed adultery be driven out naked. A woman suspected of adultery was to throw herself into the river according to the Code of Hammurabi. The river was thought to judge as God in the case. The law prescribed by Moses was not uncertain in its effects like those of other nations; the guilty could not escape punishment, because this was a judgment of God. The use of barley, the earthen vessel, the dust, and the unbinding of the hair all serve to indicate the disgraceful nature of this sin. We do not have the concept here that water of itself was able to destroy the perjured adulteress; this was simply the medium used by Jehovah. There is no indication of this ordeal being practiced at any other time in the OT. It may have been a regulation solely for the "camp" during the wilderness wandering (Num. 5:1-4).   F.J.

water of separation see **purification**

wave offering this rite was inseparably connected with the peace offerings. At this time the fat of the animal was burned on the altar; it was the Lord's portion. The offerer and the priest cooperated to wave the breast of the animal. The act consisted of waving or swinging the breast toward the altar and back again. The movement forward represented the symbolic transference of the sacrifice to God, and the movement back the reception of it back again as a gift from God to the priests who served him. The wave breast was the portion for the high priest and his sons. The right thigh (not "shoulder" as in AV) was "heaved" or "raised." This was given to the priest who offered the sacrifice. The rest of the animal could be eaten by the offerer with certain restrictions. Scriptures relating to this offering are Ex. 29:22–28; Lev. 7:28–36, 8:22–29, 9:18–21, 10:14–15; Num. 18:11, 18. The lamb and oil of the guilt offering was to be waved at the cleansing of a leper (Lev. 14:12, 24). A sheaf of firstfruits of the harvest was waved at the Passover; a lamb and bread of the firstfruits were waved on Pentecost (Lev. 23:9–21). The cereal offering of jealousy was waved (Num. 5:25), as was the offering of the Nazarite at the time of his separation (Num. 6:20). The Levites are symbolically offered before the Lord as a wave offering of the people of Israel (Num. 8:11). F.J.

way many different Hebrew and Greek words are translated "way" in the English Bible. Besides the obvious literal sense of a road or track, the word is used to indicate a course of conduct, habit, or manner. An eagle, a serpent, a ship, and a man each have a way (Prov. 30:19). The term is used in the singular and plural of human conduct, either good (Ps. 119:1, 9; 1 Cor. 4:17; 2 Pet. 2:15) or bad (Jonah 3:8, 10; James 1:8, 5:20). The Lord's plan for man is his way (Gen. 18:19; Ps. 18:21, 25:9). His way is radically different from that of man (Isa. 55:8–9; Rom. 11:33). Man has the freedom of will to consider God's ways and turn to them (Ps. 119:59). He can avoid the evil (Ps. 119:101, 104, 128) or follow it (Isa. 53:6; 2 Pet. 2:15; Jude 11). The Dead Sea sect (Qumran) described themselves as "the Way" in the Wilderness. Jesus claimed to be the way to the Father (Jn. 14:4, 6) and opened up the "new and living way" (Heb. 10:20). The religion of Jesus Christ, which Paul at first persecuted but later espoused, was commonly called the "way" in the book of Acts (9:2, 19:9, 23, 22:4, 24:14, 22). A concordance should be consulted for the many other occurrences of this word. F.J.

weapons see **arms**

weasel an unclean quadruped (*ḥoled*) occurring only in Lev. 11:29, listed with the mouse and lizard. Precise identity cannot be established. The AV and RSV follow the LXX, Targum, and Vulg. in the rendering "weasel." Kohler, on the basis of Syriac and Arabic analogies suggests a "mole-rat" in which suggestion he is followed by the new Jewish Publication Society of America's version, *The Torah.*

weaving the art of weaving appears to be coeval with the first dawning of civilization. In what country, or by whom, it was invented we know not; but we find it practiced with great skill by the Egyptians at a very early period. The "garments of fine linen" such as Joseph wore (Gen. 41:42) were the product of Egyptian looms; and their quality, as attested by archaeological specimen, was in many cases extraordinary. The Israelites were probably acquainted with the process before their sojourn in Egypt, but likely attained great proficiency there. Certain of the tribe of Judah were filled with ability and craftsmanship to execute the curtains of the tabernacle and other artistic textures (Ex. 35:35). There seems to have been guilds of weavers among them at a later time (1 Chr. 4:21). The Egyptians were still known for their manufacture of "fine" flax and "white cotton" (RSV) (Isa. 19:9; Ezek. 27:7). The character of the loom, and the process of weaving, can only be inferred from incidental notices. The Egyptian loom was usually upright, and the weaver stood at his work. The cloth was fixed sometimes at the top, sometimes at the bottom. The Bible does not notice the loom itself, but speaks of the beam to which the warp was attached (1 Sam. 17:7; 2 Sam. 21:19); and of the pin to which the cloth was fixed and on which it was rolled (Judg. 16:13–14). It was not uncommon for one's life to be spoken of figuratively in weaving terms (Job 7:6; Isa. 38:12). The terms "warp" and "woof" are used in Lev. 13:48. The Jewish weavers produced various textures. The coarser kinds, such as tent cloth, sackcloth, and the "hairy garments" of the poor, were made of goat's hair or camel's hair (Ex. 26:7; Mt. 3:4). Bedouin tents are made of goat's hair today. Wool was extensively used for ordinary clothing (Lev. 13:47; Prov. 27:26, 31:13; Ezek. 27:18); while for finer work, flax was used, varying in quality and producing the different textures described in the Bible as "linen" and "fine linen." The mixture of wool and flax in cloth intended for a garment was forbidden by the Law (Lev. 19:19; Deut. 22:11). The tunic worn by Jesus was woven without a seam (Jn. 19:23). F.J.

wedding see **marriage**

week a period of seven days, a unit of time in ancient and modern usage. The first Bible reference is Gen. 29:27, but the idea is earlier (Gen. 2:3, 7:4, 8:10). The Hebrew term *shebu'a,* from *sheb'a,* involved the idea of seven, apparently an allusion to the creation account (Gen. 1–2). The day of the week was often stated (Gen. 1:5, 8, 13, 19, 23, 31, 2:2), but might be implied (Lev. 23:15–16). The resting of God on the seventh day became the basis for the sabbath, which marked the end of the week (Ex. 20:8–11). The NT term *sabbaton* was used of the sabbath, or seventh day (Mt. 12:8, 28:1; Mk. 2:27), and of the week as a whole (Mk. 16:9; 1 Cor. 16:2).

The relationship of the week to the year raises several difficult problems. Adequate space is not available here, nor have all questions been settled, but a general statement may be made. The non-Jewish nations used two arrangements. One involved twelve months of thirty days, with five feast days interspersed within the year. Another involved a seven-week period plus one feast day, repeated seven times, with feast days filling the remaining time in the solar year.

The Jews used the lunar month and solar year arrangement, though the means of determining the beginning and end of the cycle is not clear, and perhaps was changed through their history. The lunar month involved a difficulty presumably aided by an alternation between twenty-nine-day months and those of thirty days. This resulted in variations in the cycle of years, with the consequent intercalation of a thirteenth month about once in three years. This intercalation was arranged by the civil authorities as needed and though the custom is not described in the Bible, it is apparently implied (Num. 9:11; 1 K. 12:32–33; 2 Chr. 30:2–3).

The week held an important place in Jewish religion (Ex. 34:22; Deut. 16:9; 2 Chr. 8:13), and was involved in the prophecy of Daniel (9:24–27, 10:2–3).

The Jewish week was at first connected with the agricultural seasons (Lev. 23:15–16), but by NT times the seven-day week was used without much regard for the relationship to the season.   w.w.

weeks, feast of see **Pentecost**

weights and measures problems of communication and exchange make necessary the establishment of common units and standards of weight and measurement. The Jewish people were not only concerned with their national trade, but the exchange with other nations gave rise to problems of weight, length, and capacity. In the beginning use might be made of physical phenomena for measuring distance, grains, or eggs for capacity, the finger, palm, or elbow to fingertip for length of small objects. But, as life became more complex more exact

units had to be found. This problem was clearly seen in the OT (Lev. 19:35–36; Deut. 25:13–16; Prov. 11:1, 16:11; Hos. 12:7). In meeting this need certain areas are to be considered.

I. BALANCES. Three words are used in the OT for the balance, the most frequent being *moznayim* (Lev. 19:36; Job 31:6; Ps. 62:9; Prov. 11:1, 16:11, 20:23; Isa. 40:15; Jer. 32:10; Ezek. 5:1; Hos. 12:7; Amos 8:5; Mic. 6:11). The NT uses the term balance only once, from *zugos*, a lever of a balance, a balance, a pair of scales (Rev. 6:5).

From inscriptions the balance involved a crossbeam suspended by a pin or string from an upright beam, or perhaps with smaller balances the hand might serve for the upright member. To each end of the crossbeam hooks were attached. To these strings were tied with a bag or tray suspended from each end. A standard such as a stone could be placed in one container and the object to be weighed in the other (Deut. 25:13). An insight into the accuracy of the measure by balances is gained from the dust in the balance (Isa. 40:15).

II. WEIGHTS. The Bible tells of certain weights being used, but does not give the details of exact weight. This information must be gained from Bible statements and conclusions from archaeological research. Consequently, with gaps in many areas of importance, there is much to be desired in equating ancient weights with modern usage. In fact, with inscribed and uninscribed objects of weight now recovered, variation between these units suggests the great likelihood that over the years different weights were given to the same term, a condition which increases the problem immensely. Because of the problems and uncertainties only approximate results can be given.

1. *Old Testament Weights.*

(a) *Talent.* A Babylonian talent is estimated from 66–69 pounds in one count, and from 132–38 in another, called the royal weight. If related to the Jewish talent, this fact gives insight into the problem of variation.

From the computations of smaller units, the Jewish talent is estimated from 75–93 pounds. Though predominantly used of gold weight (Ex. 25:39, 37:24; 2 Sam. 12:30; 1 K. 9:28; 2 Chr. 3:8; Ezra 8:26), the talent was used of silver (Ex. 38:27; 1 K. 16:24; 2 K. 5:5; 1 Chr. 22:14; Est. 3:9), brass (Ex. 38:29) and iron (1 Chr. 29:7). From Ex. 38:24–31 it may be concluded that gold, silver, and brass (RSV, bronze) were weighed with a common talent.

(b) *Shekel* (from the Heb. *sheqel*, a weight). The Bible does not state how many shekels were contained in a talent, but the general estimate gives approximately 3000 (see *maneh*, below). This gives the weight of the shekel as 11.42 grams, 0.403 ounce.

The shekel was divided into the half shekel for the ransom of the soul (Ex. 30:13), termed the "shekel of the sanctuary" (Ex. 30:24, 38:24–26; Lev. 5:15, 27:3; Num. 3:50, 7:13). Also, one-third (Neh. 10:32), and one-fourth (1 Sam. 9:8) shekel is mentioned.

The shekel was used as a general term for weight (1 Sam. 17:5, 7; 2 Sam. 14:26, 21:16; Ezek. 4:10; Amos 8:5). It was used in weight of gold and silver (Gen. 20:15–16; Ex. 21:32; 2 Chr. 3:9), and possibly as a measure of value (Josh. 7:21).

The earliest reference in the Bible implies the recognition of weight and value (Gen. 23:15–16), and probably suggests the use of a single standard. But, from the Exodus there seems to have been two standards, one for ordinary business (Ex. 38:29; 2 K. 7:1; Amos 8:5), and the other for religious usage, the shekel of the sanctuary (Ex. 30:13; Lev. 5:15). Reference is also made to the shekel after the king's weight (2 Sam. 14:26). The relationship between these two, possibly three, means of evaluating the shekel is not clear. Regardless of the problem in the interim, Ezek. 45:12 seems to indicate a single shekel value was to be followed after the Captivity; accordingly shekel coins after this period have a nearly equal weight.

(c) *Beka* (from the Heb. *beqa*, split, or a fraction). From this word is derived the half shekel (Gen. 24:22; Ex. 38:26). Various weights inscribed *beqa* have been found. Though there is no exact agreement in weight, these generally equal one half of the calculated shekel weight.

(d) *Gerah* (from the Heb. *gerah*, perhaps kernel, bean, or seed). This is the smallest weight, representing one twentieth of the shekel of the sanctuary (Ex. 30:13; Lev. 27:25; Num. 3:47, 18:16; Ezek. 45:12).

(e) *Maneh* (from the Heb. *maneh*, a weight, perhaps originally a specific part of a weight). This term is translated maneh (Ezek. 45:12; RSV has mina) and pound (Ezra 2:69; Neh. 7:71–72; RSV has minas). Ezekiel 45:12 has the maneh composed of sixty shekels—20, 25, 15. This measure agrees with the Babylonian method, which reckoned a talent (see above) to include 3600 shekels. However, another method, called the Phoenician, reckoned the maneh in other passages as including fifty shekels. This latter method is generally considered more correct, and gives the talent the content of 3000 shekels. The whole area of

talent-maneh relationship awaits final solution, with consequent uncertainty at present.

Generally speaking, the shekel weighed about as much as the American half dollar, the maneh about one and one-fourth pounds, and the talent some 75–93 pounds.

2. *Other Weights.*

(a) *Dram* (from the Heb. *adarkonim* and *darkemonim*) in 1 Chr. 29:7; Ezra 2:69, 8:27; Neh. 7:70–72. In these passages the ASV and RSV render "daric." The Hebrew term implies value, and apparently weight. Accepting the translation daric, the weight may be equated with the Persian weight of the same name, about 125–30 grains Troy.

(b) In the NT two expressions are involved in the "pound." The term in Lk. 19:13, 16, 18, 20, 24, 25 was a sum of money (from the Gr. *mna*), apparently worth about $18–20. The term in Jn. 12:3, 19:39 (from the Gr. *litra*, Lat. *libra*) was a weight of about twelve ounces.

III. MEASURES OF LENGTH. The Hebrews made use of several linear measurements, whether of size or distance. The simplest measurements would involve parts of the forearm, but the resultant variation suggests the need of a fairly well accepted standard. This basic unit of measurement was the cubit. An ascending scale will indicate the various uses.

1. *The fingerbreadth* (from the Heb. *etzba*, a finger) in Jer. 52:21. This use in measurement occurs only here, though the finger is mentioned many times elsewhere. The distance equals approximately three quarters of an inch.

2. *The handbreadth* (from the Heb. *tephah* or *tophah*). This indicated the width of the four fingers pressed closely together, approximately three to four inches. The usage is very early in Israel's history, being used of the table of showbread (Ex. 25:25, 37:12). Later the measurement is used concerning the molten sea of the temple of Solomon (1 K. 7:26; 2 Chr. 4:5). The Psalmist uses the term to indicate the brevity of life (Ps. 39:5). It is used concerning a measuring reed which involved a long cubit, the handbreadth being added (Ezek. 40:5, 43:13), and of hooks (Ezek. 40:43) in the temple in Ezekiel.

3. *The span* (from the Heb. *zereth*). This referred to the distance from the end of the thumb to the end of the little finger when both were extended. This unit is also very early in Israel's history (Ex. 28:16, 39:9). It appears in the height of the Goliath (1 Sam. 17:4), and the altar (Ezek. 43:13). Isaiah refers to the heavens by the use of this term (Isa. 40:12,

48:13, though a different Hebrew term appears in the latter verse).

4. *The cubit* (from the Heb. *ammah*), apparently the forearm, and in Judg. 3:16 (from *gomed*) a short cubit, from elbow to knuckles of clenched hand. The term cubit is of frequent occurrence, more than 200 instances being noted in the OT. The NT uses the term *pechus* four times (Mt. 6:27; Lk. 12:25; Jn. 21:8; Rev. 21:17).

(a) The OT cubit. The cubit was the length of the forearm to the tip of the middle finger. But variation in the length of arms suggests the difference between different cubits. The exact length, if one length ever prevailed, is not known. The Siloam Inscription, found in 1880, tells that the length of Hezekiah's tunnel (2 K. 20:20; 2 Chr. 32:30) was 1200 cubits. The length today is nearly 1800 feet, the resulting cubit being about eighteen inches. However, the beginning of the tunnel and the end position in Hezekiah's day are not known. Also, other periods may have utilized other measurements. The conclusion must be left open, the length of eighteen inches for the cubit being tentatively adopted.

Also, one must consider two ways of referring to the cubit: i. There was a common cubit (Deut. 3:11, KJV has "after the cubit of a man"). This may suggest a second cubit in use at this time. In fact, some have argued for a third cubit from this verse. ii. Ezekiel refers to a cubit of a cubit and handbreadth length (40:5, 43:13). This would be approximately twenty to twenty-one inches.

The cubit finds expression in many interesting passages. The ark (Gen. 6:15–16), the flood (Gen. 7:20), the tabernacle with its various courts, walls, and articles (Ex. 25:10 ff.), Goliath (1 Sam. 17:4), the temple with its various dimensions (1 K. 6:2 ff.), Haman's gallows (Est. 5:14, 7:9), the temple in Ezekiel's day (Ezek. 40:5 ff.), Nebuchadnezzar's image (Dan. 3:1), and the roll of Zechariah (Zech. 5:2) involve this unit.

The term in Judg. 3:16 would suggest a long knife or sword, certainly a dangerous weapon.

(b) The NT cubit. The question in Mt. 6:27 and Lk. 12:25 involves the meaning of "stature." The Greek term *helikia* may mean length of life or bodily stature. One's view of the context must decide, the former being most likely. Accordingly the term "cubit" would seem to be inappropriate, some such idea as "one hour" being more likely. However, some learned arguments support the reference to bod-

ily stature and/or "cubit" as the correct reference in this highly disputed passage.

The measurement in Jn. 21:8 and Rev. 21:17, "two hundred cubits," would mean approximately 100 yards were involved in the distance. The highly symbolic language of Rev. 21:1–27 would urge caution in using a literal view of the cubit in vs. 7.

5. *The reed* (from the Heb. *qaneh*, stalk, reed) is used of a measuring rod in Ezek. 40:5–8, 41:8, 42:17–19. The same problems involved in the cubit above are involved here, making the exact measurement unknown. However, the computation from the above remarks would give a rod or reed approximately nine to nine and one-half feet long. Some conclude the length was nearer eleven feet.

6. *The furlong* (from the Gr. *stadion*) in Lk. 24:13; Jn. 6:19, 11:18; Rev. 14:20, 21:16. This term is a loanword from the Greek. As a term of measure of distance the term involved 600 Greek (625 Roman, about 607 English) feet. The term originated from the Greek race courses, especially at Olympia. Paul uses this sense of the term to illustrate the Christian life (1 Cor. 9:24).

7. Several indefinite measures:

(a) *The pace* (2 Sam. 6:13), also translated "step" eleven times, would be approximately thirty to thirty-six inches.

(b) *The mile* (Gr. *milion*) was a loanword from the Roman mile (Mt. 5:41). The term referred to 1000 paces in Jewish thought. As a fixed measure in Roman times the term came to indicate 4854 feet, somewhat shorter than the "mile" of today.

(c) *The day's journey* (Gen. 30:36, 31:23; Ex. 3:18, 5:3; Num. 10:33, 11:31; Deut. 1:2; 1 K. 19:4; 2 K. 3:9; Jonah 3:3; and Lk. 2:44) must have been a general term, dependent on various circumstances. Some estimates are ten, twenty, twenty-five, and thirty miles.

(d) *The sabbath day's journey* (Acts 1:12). This is given as the distance between Jerusalem and the Mount of Olives, according to Josephus nearly three fourths of a mile. In determining this distance the Jews had utilized an ancient scene, and a prohibition of work. They were not to go out of their places on the sabbath (Ex. 16:29). However, an exception was made in traveling to the tabernacle. But, how far could this be extended? Since the distance between the people and the ark had been 2000 cubits (Josh. 3:4), and the limits of the suburbs of the Levitical cities had been 2000 cubits (Num. 35:5), this distance (of 2000 cubits) was accepted as permissible for travel on the sabbath. With the cubit equaling about eighteen inches, this distance would involve some three thousand feet. In this way a fairly constant measurement of distance was possible.

(e) *The fathom* (from the Gr. *orguia*) in Acts 27:28. This nautical term measured the distance between the fingertips of the outstretched arms, about six feet.

(f) *Measurement of area*, though of a different nature from distance, may be treated here because of its relatively scarce occurrence in the Bible. The usual means of expression stated area in terms of cubits (Ezek. 40:27) or reeds (Ezek. 41:8, 42:16–19). However, the idea of a square area is found (Rev. 21:16), though the unit of measurement is the cubit. There is also the reference to square measure of area in 1 Sam. 14:14. This passage refers to half a furrow length in an acre of ground. The Hebrew text, though disputed in some parts, uses the term *semed* (couple, pair). Because of this reference to couple or pair, the term is referred to the amount of land a span of oxen could plow, evidently in a day. If true, this indefinite measurement would indicate a large area of land. Certainly the term *semed* refers to such area in Isa. 5:10. From the ASV margin the term *semed* may be understood as meaning one acre of land (1 Sam. 14:14).

IV. MEASUREMENTS OF CAPACITY.

A. The OT utilized several units of capacity, such usage being capable of division into liquid and dry measure:

1. *Liquid measurement.*

(a) *The log* (from the Heb. *log*). This term was used of oil (Lev. 14:10, 12, 15, 21, 24). According to the Talmud this term contained approximately three fourths of a pint.

(b) *The hin* (from the Heb. *hin*). This measure contained approximately one gallon. The explanations vary from less than one gallon to nearly a gallon and a fourth. The term hin is used (Ex. 30:24; Lev. 19:36; Ezek. 45:24, 46:5, 7, 11). Smaller divisions of the term are also found: the sixth of a hin (Ezek. 4:11), the fourth (Ex. 29:40; Lev. 23:13), the third (Num. 15:6–7), and the half (Num. 15:9–10) being mentioned.

(c) *The bath* (from the Heb. *bath*). This measurement equaled the ephah (Ezek. 45:11), and was one tenth of a homer (Ezek. 45:11). The exact amount is unknown, estimates varying from five and one-half to seven and one-half gallons. The contents of the laver were measured in baths (1 K. 7:26, 38), and so were the wine yields (Isa. 5:10). Ezekiel mentions the need for a just or righteous bath (45:10).

(d) *The cor* (from the Heb. *cor*). This measurement involves ten baths (Ezek. 45:14). By calculation this would contain fifty-five to seventy-five gallons.

2. *Dry measure.*

(a) *The handful,* from several Hebrew terms, is used in many verses (Lev. 2:2, 5:12; 1 K. 17:12; Ps. 72:16; Jer. 9:22). In the nature of the case this term must have remained undefined.

(b) *The cab* (from the Heb. *qab*). No exact content can be given this term (2 K. 6:25), estimates varying from one to two quarts.

(c) *The omer* (from the Heb. *omer*). This measure equaled one tenth of an ephah (Ex. 16:36). It was used concerning the gathering of the manna (Ex. 16:16, 18, 22, 33, 36). The amount was about one and one-half to two quarts.

(d) *The measure or seah* (from the Heb. *seah*). The occurrences of this term are rendered "measure" in the KJV. It is used of fine meal (Gen. 18:6), parched grain (1 Sam. 25:18), seed (1 K. 18:32), and barley (2 K. 7:1, 16, 18). Estimates vary from one half to two thirds of a peck.

(e) *The ephah* (from the Heb. *ephah*). This measure equaled one tenth of a homer (Ezek. 45:11), and was equal to the liquid measure termed a bath (Ezek. 45:11). The term is frequent in the OT, at least twenty-seven times. It was used of fine flour (Lev. 5:11), barley (Num. 5:15), and parched grain (1 Sam. 17:17). There is an admonition given concerning a just ephah (Lev. 19:36; Ezek. 45:10). The term refers to between two and a half and three pecks.

(f) *The half homer* (from the Heb. *lethek*). The term is found only in Hos. 3:2, of barley. The amount is estimated from two to more than three bushels.

(g) *The homer* (from the Heb. *homer*). This measure contained ten ephahs (Ezek. 45:11). It was used of barley seed (Lev. 27:16), of the quails (Num. 11:32), and other general measurements (Isa. 5:10; Ezek. 45:11, 14). It seems to have been the standard dry measure, other smaller measurements being given with reference to it. The estimates vary, from nearly four bushels to more than six bushels, some even giving eight or eleven bushels. *The cor* (from the Heb. *cor*) was equal to the homer (Ezek. 45:14), being apparently used of the container involved in the passage. The term *cor*, in Hebrew, is used of liquid measure in 1 K. 5:11; Ezek. 45:14, and of dry measure concerning fine flour (1 K. 4:22), meal (1 K. 4:22), wheat (1 K. 5:11; 2 Chr. 2:10), and barley (2 Chr. 2:10; Ezra 7:22). The KJV well

renders the Heb. *cor* in the above passages, except Ezek. 45:14, by the term "measure." Interestingly enough, the Greek of Lk. 16:7 renders the term *koros*, with estimates varying from ten to twelve bushels.

B. The NT utilized several terms for capacity, though not so frequently as the OT:

(1) *The firkin* (from the Gr. *metretes*) in Jn. 2:6. This liquid measure is similar in content to the Hebrew bath, and involved some nine gallons. The water pots, evidently of stone, *lithinos*, contained twenty to thirty gallons each.

(2) *The measure* (from the Gr. *choinix*) in Rev. 6:6. This measure contained nearly a quart of grain.

(3) *The measure* (from the Gr. *saton*) in Mt. 13:33; Lk. 13:21. This measure contained about a peck and a half.

(4) *The measure* (from the Gr. *koros*) in Lk. 16:7, was discussed under the Hebrew homer.

(5) *The pot* (from the Gr. *xestes*) in Mk. 7:4, 8. This term referred to a liquid measure of about a pint. Later the term came to be used of a pitcher or jug without reference to the amount contained.

(6) *The pound* (from the Gr. *litra*) in Jn. 12:3, 19:39. This term was used of both weight and capacity, equaling about twelve ounces of liquid.

V. CONCLUDING REMARKS. The several statements above concerning the uncertain results from various estimates must not be misunderstood. This uncertainty does not mean the Hebrews were unconcerned with true weights and measures since attention has been called to the numerous instances of admonition in this area (e.g., Ezek. 45:10). But, the problem is difficult when one seeks to gain equivalents in English for ancient Hebrew and Greek terms. Limited access to measures and containers of the time, the variations of the measurement through the years, and the lack of such fixed standards as modern exchange makes necessary can be invoked to explain the divergence. Because of these facts the preceding remarks concerning English equivalents must be taken at best as approximate. Further light from archaeological discovery may yet shine on this area of Bible study.   w.w.

well the lack of rainfall in Palestine makes the wells of great importance. Several terms are used in the OT and NT for the well. The most frequent term is *beer*, a spring, a well made by digging (Gen. 21:25, 30, 24:11, 29, 26:15, 18–22, 25, 32, 29:2–3, 8; Ex. 2:15; Num. 20:17, 21:17–18, 22, etc.). The term *bor*,

means a pit, a well, a cistern which one might dig (Deut. 6:11; 1 Sam. 19:22; 2 Sam. 3:26, 23:15–16; 1 Chr. 11:17–18; 2 Chr. 26:10; Neh. 9:25). The term *mayan* and its related term *ayin* refer to a spring, then a well (Josh. 18:15; 2 K. 3:19, 25; Ps. 84:6; Isa. 12:3; and Gen. 24:13, 16, 29–30, 42–43, 45, 49:22; Ex. 15:27; Neh. 2:13). The NT uses two words for well: *pēgē*, a spring, a fountain (Jn. 4:6, 14; 2 Pet. 2:17), and *phrear*, a well, a pit (Jn. 4:11–12).

The significance of the well is seen in its inclusion in certain place names, i.e., Beer (Num. 21:16; Josh. 9:21), Beer-elim (Isa. 15:8), Beer-lahai-roi (Gen. 16:14).

On occasion a well would be fitted with steps (Gen. 24:16). A covering might be placed over the well (Gen. 29:3; Ex. 21:33; 2 Sam. 17:19). Around the well a curb might be built (Jn. 4:6). The water would be carried in containers (Gen. 24:16), the water being lifted by means of a rope and waterskin attachment (Jn. 4:11).

The well would have great significance for its owner, being the occasion of at least one great dispute in Isaac's day (Gen. 26:18–23). In a time of war the besieged city would need the protection of its water supply, hence concern to prevent an adequate supply (2 K. 3:19, 25). To protect the water supply of Jerusalem Hezekiah dug a tunnel from the spring Gihon into the city (2 K. 20:20; 2 Chr. 32:30).   w.w.

whale the AV translated both Heb. *tan* or *tannim* (Gen. 1:21; Job 7:12; Ezek. 32:2) and *dag* as "whale," while the Greek term is *ketos* (Mt. 12:40). The term involving Jonah is *dag* (Gen. 9:2; Num. 11:22; 1 K. 4:33; 2 Chr. 33:14; Neh. 3:3, 12:39; Job 12:8, 41:7; Ps. 8:8; Ezek. 38:20; Hos. 4:3; Jonah 1:17, 2:10; Hab. 1:14; Zeph. 1:3, 10). One should note the translation of the term *tannim* by dragon (Deut. 32:33, etc.). Certainly the Jewish people knew of large sea "monsters" or animals, as the above verses indicate.

The meaning of the term in Jonah 1:17, 2:10, has overshadowed all other concerns about the whale or *tannim*. Neither *dag* nor *ketos* designate a specific species of fish. The term "whale" might more appropriately be translated "a huge fish" or "sea monster," avoiding the more precise "whale." However, the Mediterranean Sea knows the humpback whale, the fin whale, and various large sharks. Records of men swallowed by whales can be found in various studies of Jonah, one occurring in 1891 involving the whaling ship *Star of the East* and a James Bartley, being most interesting. With the consideration that whales

420

have been found with humans, even horses, inside them, and that the term may not refer to a whale exclusively (being more properly a large fish), the rationalistic attempts to set aside the historicity of Jonah may be dismissed. Also, the support of the incident as historical by Jesus (Mt. 12:40) suffices for the believer. w.w.

wheat *ḥiṭṭah* is one of the cereal grains (sometimes called "corn") of the Middle East which was grown in many regions from a very early time and is first mentioned in the Bible in Gen. 30:14. It is one of the crops of Palestine as described in the characterization of the Promised Land (Deut. 8:8). Bread was made of its flour (Ex. 29:2), but it was also roasted and eaten (Lev. 2:14; Ruth 2:14, 23). It was valued in payment of debts (2 Chr. 2:10) and tribute (2 Chr. 27:5). Egypt was particularly well-known for its wheat which at times was shipped to Rome (Acts 27:6, 38). A multiheaded variety grew there (Gen. 41:22) though in Palestine it is likely that the single-headed variety was grown.

Wheat was often sown in the winter broadcast and then plowed in or trampled by cattle (Isa. 32:20), but at times it seems to have been put in rows (Isa. 28:25). The harvest came from the end of April to June depending on the weather, soil, and locality. Good ground might produce a hundredfold (Mt. 13:8).

Wheat is used in Scripture in parable (Mt. 13:25 ff.) and in various figures of speech (Mt. 3:12; Jn. 12:24; 1 Cor. 15:37).

whirlwind the words *sa'ar* (Jer. 23:19), *suphah* (Prov. 1:27), *se'arah* (Job 38:1) are rendered "whirlwind" in the AV and may refer to a violent windstorm. *Galgal* (Isa. 17:13; cf. Ps. 77:18; Ezek. 10:13) though rendered "wheel" or "rolling thing" may have the same connotation. Palestine experiences winds of destructive violence. Lake Galilee is subject to sudden squalls (Lk. 8:23). A whirlwind carried off Elijah (2 K. 2:11). Dust whirlwinds comparable to those seen in western Texas may be seen in Israel during the summer in the Negeb (cf. Job 37:9). The whirlwind is also a metaphor for violent overwhelming destruction.

widow there are indications in both the Old and New Testaments that the life of a widow in ancient times was a difficult one. Frequently the widow was the object of exploitation and injustice (Job 22:9; Ps. 94:6; Isa. 1:23; Zech. 7:10; Mal. 3:5; Mk. 12:40; Lk. 18:1–8). She had no right of legal inheritance and thus was dependent on her children (Ex. 20:12; Mk. 7:11–12) and the goodwill of the community (Deut. 14:28–29; Acts 6:1). And the figure of

widowhood became a symbol of desolation and sorrow (Isa. 47:8–9; Lam. 1:1).

The OT pictures God as the special protector of the widow (Deut. 10:18; Ps. 146:9; Prov. 15:25). He specifically prohibited their mistreatment (Ex. 22:22–23) and the strong prophetic denunciation of malefactors of widows further reveals God's concern (Zech. 7:10; Mal. 3:5). Other legislation designed to help the widow includes: (a) prohibition against taking her garment as a pledge (Deut. 24:17); (b) provision for the leaving of designated grains and grapes for her at harvest time (Deut. 24:19–21). She shared in the tithe every third year (Deut. 26:12). The provision of Levirate marriage would also have aided the childless widow (Deut. 25:5 f.).

In the NT the early church almost immediately assumed the care of many widows (Acts 6:1–6) and later Paul lays down specific qualifications for the aiding of widows (1 Tim. 5:3–16). James' admonition (1:27) seems to summarize God's compassion for the widow.

G.R.

wife see **marriage**

wild beasts see **beast**

wilderness of wandering the materials from which the events of the wilderness wandering may be reconstructed are found in Ex. 13–19; Num. 10–14, 21–25; and Deut. 1–2. Another passage which is of particular importance is Num. 33 in which forty stages of the journey of the Israelites from Egypt to Canaan, excluding the encampments on the plain of Moab, are given. It is not possible, however, to trace the journeys from Num. 33 with any great certainty for several reasons: (a) The identity of some of the places mentioned is unknown; (b) Some of the encampments listed in Num. 33 do not appear elsewhere; (c) Some place names, such as Meribah, which occur in other accounts, are omitted. Yet the general direction and extent of the journey is indicated.

There is uncertainty about the place from which the wilderness wandering began. It is not possible to fix the point at which Israel emerged from the sea into the wilderness of Etham (Num. 33:6–7). It seems that the Israelites entered the Sinai Peninsula at the upper end of the Gulf of Suez in the marshy area comprising the **Red** ("Reed") **Sea.**

In Ex. 14:22 the first part of the journey after crossing the Red Sea was the wilderness of Shur, while in Num. 33:6–7 the same area is called the wilderness of Etham.

The general location of the wilderness of Shur is indicated by such passages as Gen. 25:18 and 1 Sam. 27:8 which indicate that it was east of Egypt. The name may be regarded as a general designation of the area of the Sinai Peninsula east of Lake Timsah. In this wilderness the Israelites traveled toward the south in a line parallel to the Gulf of Suez. The first stage of the journey lasted three days when they arrived at Marah, where the bitter water was sweetened by Moses (Ex. 15:22–25). The location of Marah is uncertain.

From Marah the journey was continued to the second stop at Elim where there were twelve springs and seventy palm trees. This place is sometimes identified with the Wadi Gharandel which is about forty miles southeast of Suez.

Leaving Elim the Israelites continued moving toward the southeast, entering the wilderness of Sin. This area cannot definitely be located although it has been suggested that it is the same as Pelusium, which is called Sin in Ezek. 30:15–16. Exodus 16:1 simply states that Sin lay between Elim and Sinai. The wilderness of Sin is usually identified with Dabbet er-Ramleh in the southwestern part of the Sinai Peninsula. It was in the wilderness of Sin that the people murmured against Moses and Aaron and were provided with manna (Ex. 16:16–21).

From Sin Israel moved on to Dophkah (Num. 33:12) in the area where the Egyptians obtained copper and turquoise (identified with Serabit el-Khadim). Moving on to Rephidim which lay between the wilderness of Sin and Sinai the Israelites found no water and again complained against Moses (Ex. 17:1–3). At the command of God Moses struck the rock and water came forth for the people.

While at Rephidim Israel encountered the first opposition since entering the Sinai Peninsula. The Amalekites attacked, but Israel was able to withstand the attack. It is at this time that Joshua is introduced into the Biblical narrative, establishing himself as a mighty warrior (Ex. 17:13).

In the third month after leaving Egypt the Israelites arrived at Mount Sinai. The exact location of the mountain is not certain, but Jebel Musa (the Mountain of Moses) is usually identified with the mountain where Moses received the Law. After encampment at Sinai that lasted about one year (Num. 10:11) the people followed the cloud, which symbolized the presence of God, northeastward to the wilderness of Paran (Num. 10:11–12).

The identification of the exact location of the wilderness of Paran is complicated. In Num. 33:36 Paran is not mentioned but Kadesh is identified with the wilderness of Zin. But in the LXX Paran is identified with Kadesh. Numbers 13:26 locates Kadesh in the wilderness of Paran, and the LXX of Num. 33:36 makes the same identification. These variations probably only reflect the difficulty of determining boundaries in desert areas.

In the wilderness of Paran difficulties beset the Israelites and opposition toward Moses arose. The people complained for lack of foods they had enjoyed in Egypt (Num. 11:4–6) and were supplied with quail. Then a plague broke out in the camp and many died (Num. 11:31–35). Also, Miriam and Aaron caused a crisis when they criticized Moses for marrying a Cushite woman (either Ethiopian or possibly a woman from the Kushu, a tribe associated with Midian in Hab. 3:7). As a punishment for this rebellion Miriam became a leper.

But the most significant crisis occurred at Kadesh-barnea on the northern border of the wilderness of Paran. Considering an invasion of Canaan from the south, Moses sent twelve spies who traveled as far south as Hebron, collecting grapes from the valley of Eshcol near Hebron. The report of ten of the spies was unfavorable; they spoke of the strength of the people settled in the land; however, Caleb, along with Joshua, encouraged the people to go on into the land, but this advice was rejected and some of the people began to speak of going back to Egypt (Num. 13:25–14:4). Because of the lack of trust exhibited by Israel God condemned the people to a period of wandering in the wilderness (Num. 14:34).

Kadesh-barnea became a center for Israel for thirty-eight years (Deut. 2:14). Kadesh, which is identified with 'Ain Qudeis, was well suited for this purpose because of the supply of water provided by 'Ain Qudeis, 'Ain Qoseimeh, and 'Ain Qudeirat about twelve miles to the northeast. Kadesh appears in the OT under several other names including En-mishpat (Gen. 14:7), Meribah (Num. 27:14), and Marah (Ex. 17:7).

At the close of the period of wandering in the wilderness of Zin, which is also identified with Kadesh (Num. 20:13, 33:36) Israel began a march toward the eastern side of the Dead Sea with the aim of crossing the Jordan into Canaan from the east. The way was not easy, for Edom lay between Kadesh and the King's Highway, the direct road from the Gulf of Aqabah to Syria (Num. 20:14–21). The king of Edom refused passage through his territory and Israel detoured around Edom. On this leg of the journey Aaron died and was buried at Mount Hor (Num. 20:28). Josephus (Ant. IV.iv.7) identifies Mount Hor with a mountain in the vicinity of Petra now called Jebel Harun. However, this site is disputed, for the mountain lies within the territory of Edom. A site nearer Kadesh has been suggested as a more likely location. This identification conforms better to the statement of Num. 33:37 which locates Mount Hor on the edge of Edom and to Deut. 10:6 which says Aaron died at Moserah which is listed in Num. 33:30 as an encampment on the way from Kadesh to Eziongeber.

During the journey Israel was attacked by the king of Arad near Mount Hor (Num. 21:1). The people also complained against Moses and encountered a plague of venomous serpents (Num. 21:6-9). However, they journeyed on around Edom and northward to Moab and the territory from the Arnon valley to the Jabbok River (Num. 21:21-32). Also, Israel defeated Og the king of Bashan (Num. 21:33-35), bringing the area of the Transjordan under the control of Israel.   J.K.Z.

will due to the right of the redemption of property and the return of the land to families of the original owners in the Jubilee year (Lev. 25:8-16, 23-55), the bequests with reference to lands were limited. An exception seems to have been made with reference to houses in the walled cities (Lev. 25:30). It is not certain that the case of Ahithophel (2 Sam. 17:23) and of Hezekiah (2 K. 20:1; Isa. 38:1) refer to wills.

Galatians 3:15 seems to involve the idea of a will; while Heb. 9:16-17 clearly presents the new covenant under the concept of a will which became of force after, not before, the death of the testator. See **heir, testament**   J.D.B.

willows willows are mentioned in Lev. 23:40; Job 40:22; Ps. 137:2; Isa. 15:7, 44:4; Ezek. 17:5, each referring to a tree beside water. The word (*'arabah*) can be translated as either willow or poplar, both belonging to the genus *Salicaceae*. Both grow abundantly in the Near East, especially along the banks of the Jordan. Popular fancy envisions the Israelites hanging their harps on the "weeping willows" of Babylonia (Ps. 137:2), but since this particular tree was introduced to this area from the Far East at a much later date, one of the other willows or the poplar is likely. Branches from the willow tree were used in the Feast of Booths (Lev. 23:40). The ease of rooting and the rapid growth of this tree is suggested in Ezekiel's allegory of the two eagles (17:5).   R.H.

Willows, the Brook of the a wadi mentioned by Isaiah (15:7) in his dirge over Moab. His language implies that it is one of the boundaries of the country, and is possibly identical

with the wadi mentioned by Amos (6:14) as the then recognized southern limit of the Northern Kingdom. This latter is translated as the river of the "wilderness," but the Hebrew term for this and the one for willow are all but identical. The likeliest identification for this brook is the Wadi el-Ḥesa (see **Zered**). This area is swampy and quite suitable for willows.   R.H.

wimple an old English word for hood or veil, used in the AV of Isa. 3:22. The same Hebrew word is translated "veil" in Ruth 3:15, but it signifies rather a kind of shawl or mantle as rendered by ASV in both locations.

window see **house**

winds the Hebrews recognized the existence of four prevailing winds, broadly equivalent to the four points of the compass: east, west, north, and south. This is indicated by their custom of using the term "four winds" as a synonym for the "four quarters" of the hemisphere (Jer. 49:36; Ezek. 37:9; Dan. 8:8; Zech. 2:6; Mt. 24:31). The north wind, or, as it was usually called, "the north," was the coldest of the four and, consequently, was considered good for vegetation (Song of S. 4:16). In Prov. 25:23 it is described as bringing rain, but in this case we must understand the northwest wind. The north wind prevails from June to the autumnal equinox; the northwest wind from the equinox to the beginning of November. The east wind crosses the parched Arabian Desert before reaching Palestine and was therefore termed "the wind of the wilderness" (Job 1:19; Jer. 13:24). It blows with force and can stand for any violent or destructive wind (Gen. 41:6; Job 27:21; Ps. 48:7; Ezek. 27:26; Jonah 4:8). In Palestine the east wind prevails from February to June. The south wind, which sweeps up the Arabian Peninsula, is extremely hot and dry (Job 37:17; Lk. 12:55). This wind normally occurs in the springtime. The west and southwest winds arrive in Palestine loaded with moisture gathered from the Mediterranean bringing rain (1 K. 18:43-45). Westerly winds in Palestine prevail from November to February. In addition to the four regular winds the Bible tells of local squalls which occur on the Sea of Galilee (Mk. 4:37; Lk. 8:23). In the narrative of Paul's prison voyage to Rome we meet with the term *lips*, a southwest wind (Acts 27:12); *choros*, a northwest wind (Acts 27:12); *notos*, a southerly wind (Acts 27:13, 28:13); and *euroclydon*, a violent wind coming from the northeast (Acts 27:14).   R.H.

wine the use and importance of wine in the life of the people of Palestine and the Middle East can be seen in the fact that Noah (Gen. 9:20–21) made wine, and that the fruitfulness of Canaan was exhibited to Moses by the returning spies bringing clusters of grapes so huge they had to be transported on poles (Num. 13:21–27). The wine of Palestine was almost exclusively made from grape juice although some was made from pomegranates (Song of S. 8:2).

In the OT wine is used in a number of connections: (a) as a good gift from the Lord (Gen. 27:28; Ps. 104:15); (b) bread and wine are often mentioned as food and drink (Gen. 14:18); (c) wine was used as a drink offering to the Lord (Ex. 29:40; Lev. 23:13); (d) priests were forbidden to drink wine during their service (Lev. 10:9); (e) a Nazarite was forbidden to drink wine during the period of his vow (Num. 6:3–4); (f) wine is used in a metaphorical sense to signify reconciliation with God (Isa. 55:1), offerings of wisdom (Ps. 16:5; Prov. 9:5), sign of God's wrath (Jer. 25:15), sign of the seductive enticements of foreign vices (Jer. 51:7).

The making of wine was very important to the Hebrew people. The grapes were usually harvested in August and September and spread out in the sun for a time until the vintage occurred in September. At that time, the people of a village would leave their homes and erect booths around the vineyards in which to live so they could work uninterrupted. It was a time of great rejoicing (Isa. 16:10; Jer. 25:30, 48:33). The grapes would then be placed in the wine press and the work of treading then took place. Several men would work together in this occupation and would sing and encourage one another in the activity (Isa. 16:10; Jer. 25:30, 48:33). Following the treading, the wine would be gathered into jars or new skins for storage and for further fermentation, which of course, had already begun (Jer. 13:12, 48:11; Lk. 5:38).

Wine was used in everyday life in a number of instances: (a) at banquets (Jn. 2:1); (b) as an item of trade (2 Chr. 2:8–10); and (c) as medicine (Lk. 10:34; 1 Tim. 5:23). Because of the climate of Palestine, fermentation began almost immediately after the pressing out of the juice, thus there is little reason to maintain that the wine used by Jesus and his disciples on occasions (Mt. 11:19; Lk. 22:18; Jn. 2:1) was not fermented wine. Also, it seems to be the emphasis of Scripture that to dilute wine with water was to ruin the wine (Isa. 1:22). Wine was on occasions mixed with spices (Ps. 75:8; Prov. 9:2), but this wine was, of course, highly intoxicating. It would thus seem that the Bib-lical emphasis is against the consumption of wine to excess whereby one became drunk (Isa. 5:11, 56:11; Ezek. 44:21; Lk. 21:34; Rom. 14:21; Eph. 5:18; 1 Tim. 3:3–8, 5:23; 1 Pet. 4:3), but no absolute prohibitive commandment is to be found.   P.M.C.

wine press from ancient wine presses that remain and also from pictures preserved on ancient tombs, etc., we can be reasonably sure that the wine presses used in both OT and NT times consisted of a pair of rectangular (sometimes circular) pits hewn in rock formations to a depth of two or three feet. The upper excavation, in which the grapes were trodden, was connected to the lower excavation by a pipe or channel, and thus the juice could flow naturally into the lower excavation where it would be allowed to remain for fermentation purposes or removed into jars. Generally, the upper excavation was wider and shallower than the lower excavation which consisted of less area but which was deeper. The making of wine by treading the grapes in the wine press was a common sight in both OT and NT times and thus the action of treading is cited in Lam. 1:15 where the Lord hath trodden "as in a wine press the virgin daughter of Judah." In Isa. 63:2–3, the Lord, in his anger, has trodden the wine press alone to avenge unrighteousness. A similar emphasis is found in Rev. 14:19–20 where the end is pictured as in the time of harvest when the sickle is put forth, the vintage gathered, and the wine press, which is God's wrath, is filled and is trodden (cf. also Rev. 19:15).   P.M.C.

winnowing see **agriculture**

Wise Men see **Magi**

witch, witchcrafts see **magic**

witness in the Bible a witness is one who could give firsthand testimony of any event. Among special provisions with respect to evidence are the following: (a) Two or more witnesses were required to validate any charge in both the Jewish and Christian communities (Num. 35:30; Deut. 17:6, 19:15; 1 K. 21:10; Jn. 8:17; 2 Cor. 13:1; 1 Tim. 5:19). (b) The witness who withheld the truth was under a curse (Lev. 5:1; Judg. 17:2; Prov. 29:24). (c) False witness was forbidden in the Ten Commandments (Ex. 20:16; Deut. 5:20). (d) False witnesses were to receive the punishment prescribed for the ones they accused (Deut. 19:16–19). (e) The witnesses were the first executioners (Deut. 17:7; Acts 7:58). (f) In the case of an animal left in the charge of another and torn by wild beasts, the keeper was to bring the carcass as "witness" of the fact and disproof of his criminality (Ex. 22:13; Amos 3:12). (g) According to Josephus women and slaves were not to be admitted as witnesses (Paul mentions only male witnesses to the resurrection of Jesus in 1 Cor. 15:3–8). In the NT the term witness was applied to anyone who attested to his faith in the Gospel or events in the life of Jesus (Lk. 24:48; Acts 1:8, 10:41). Because this testimony often led to personal suffering or death the special meaning of the word "martyr," the Greek word for "witness," has arisen.   R.H.

wizard see **magic**

wolf except for three instances (Isa. 11:6, 65:25; Jn. 10:12), wolf in the Bible occurs only in comparisons and in figures of speech. The *canis lupus*, a large carnivorous animal, was well-known in ancient Palestine and was a real threat to the flocks of shepherds. Isaiah's vision of peace describes the wolf dwelling with a lamb (Isa. 11:6, 65:25).

In comparisons, the tribe of Benjamin is a ravenous wolf (Gen. 49:27). The enemies of Judah (Jer. 5:6), her princes (Ezek. 22:27), her judges (Zeph. 3:3) are likened to wolves, as are also the Chaldean's horses (Hab. 1:8). In the NT false prophets (Mt. 7:15) and teachers (Acts 20:29) as well as persecutors and opponents of the church are compared to wolves (Mt. 10:16).   J.P.L.

woman woman was created to correspond to man (Gen. 2:21–24). Though the Hebrew woman was under the authority of her father and later of her husband, she enjoyed considerable freedom and was not shut up in the harem. Rebekah traveled unveiled until she came into the presence of Isaac (Gen. 24:64–65). Jacob publicly kissed Rachel (Gen. 29:11). Though women did not ordinarily inherit property, in a case of a sonless home the daughters might inherit (Num. 27). It was a man's world, but Hebrew law protected woman's person. Rape was punishable. Harlotry was forbidden.

Women gleaned in grain harvest (Ruth 2:23), kept sheep (Gen. 29:6), and brought water from the well (Gen. 24:13), in addition to cooking and doing other household tasks. Women participated in public celebrations (Ex. 15:20–21; Judg. 11:34). Deborah served as a judge (Judg. 5). Women enjoyed the gift of prophecy (Ex. 15:20; 2 K. 22:14; Neh. 6:14; Lk. 2:36; Acts 21:9). Warnings against the loose woman are frequent in Proverbs while in contrast the virtues of the capable housewife (who in some cases seems to have been almost a merchant) are sung (Prov. 11:16, 12:4, 31:10 ff.).

In the NT women are considered "joint heirs of the grace of life" (1 Pet. 3:7). There is

neither male nor female in Christ (Gal. 3:28). She is charged by Paul to be a "keeper at home" (Tit. 2:5) and to keep silence in the church (1 Cor. 14:34 ff.; 1 Tim. 2:12). Her interest in dress is frequently noticed (Isa. 3:18 ff.) and she is charged to dress modestly (1 Tim. 2:9). All varieties of women may be found among Biblical characters.   J.P.L.

wood see **forest**

wool the fleece of sheep used in the Bible for textiles (Lev. 13:47; Deut. 22:11; Job 31:20; Prov. 31:13; Ezek. 34:3; Hos. 2:5, 9). Wool was also valuable in payment of debts and tribute. Mesha, king of Moab, paid in lambs and "wool" of rams (2 K. 3:4). White wool of Damascus was valued in the markets of Tyre (Ezek. 27:18).

The priest was forbidden to wear wool in Ezekiel's temple (Ezek. 44:17).

The whiteness of wool is a symbol of purity (Isa. 1:18), and is sometimes compared with the whiteness of snow (Ps. 147:16) and with hair (Dan. 7:9; Rev. 1:14).   J.P.L.

woolen (linen and) for reasons no longer known the Israelite was forbidden to wear a garment of mixed (*sha'atnez*) wool and linen (Lev. 19:19; Deut. 22:11). Josephus (*Ant.* IV.viii.11) suggests that such a garment was reserved for the priests alone. Later laws concerning diverse kinds made by the Rabbis will be found in the Mishnah treatise *Kil'aim* 9:1 ff.

worm worm in the AV renders several Hebrew words:

(1) *Sas* is the larva of the moth (Isa. 51:8).

(2) *Rimmah* is the maggot in decayed food (Ex. 16:24) or decaying bodies (Job 7:5, 17:14, 21:26; Isa. 14:11). It is parallel to *tole'ah* in Ex. 16:24 (cf. vs. 20); Job 25:6; and Isa. 14:11.

(3) *Tole'ah, tola'at, tola'* (Gr. *skōlēx*) is a plant-eating insect (Jonah 4:7; Deut. 28:39), but is also the maggot in food (Ex. 16:20) or decaying bodies (Isa. 14:11) for which reason it appears in the punishment of the wicked (Isa. 66:24; quoted by Jesus [AV], Mk. 9:44, 46, 48). It is also a symbol of the insignificance of man (Ps. 22:6 [7]; cf. *rimmah*, Job 25:6) or of Israel (Isa. 41:14). The death of King Herod is attributed to worms (Acts 12:23; Josephus *Ant.* XIX.viii.2, without specifically mentioning worms says the death took place five days later after great pain).

(4) *Zohalim 'ereṣ* (Mic. 7:17) are crawling things which may be serpents (cf. Deut. 32:24, AV).   J.P.L.

wormwood wormwood belongs to the plant genus *artemesia*. In the Bible wormwood (*la'anah*) is used in a metaphorical sense for bitterness and sorrow. Idolatry is a "root that beareth wormwood" (Deut. 29:18). In the end a loose woman is as bitter as wormwood (Prov. 5:4). Unrighteous judges "turn justice to wormwood" (Amos 5:7). Calamity is compared to wormwood (Jer. 9:15, 23:15; Lam. 3:15, 19). The name of the star which fell upon the rivers at the sound of the third angel's trumpet is "Wormwood" (Rev. 8:11). J.P.L.

worship worship is used in the AV for homage paid to both divine and human superiors (Lk. 14:10; RSV = "honor"). The basic ideas of the Hebrew terms seem to be to serve, to bow down, or to prostrate oneself. The Greek terms used to translate these mean: to serve, to do obeisance, or to venerate.

In the OT approach to the deity required washings and ritual cleanliness—to sanctify oneself (Ex. 28:41, 30:29). Worship is to be offered to God alone (Ex. 34:14; Mt. 4:10; Acts 10:25 f.; Rev. 10:10).

Prayer was known from the patriarchal period (Gen. 24:12-14) and might be either personal (1 Sam. 1:10) or national (Amos 7:2, 5). The prayer of Solomon at the dedication of the temple (1 K. 8:23-39) and the prayer of penitence of Ezra at the time of the return (Ezra 9:6 ff.) are notable examples.

Trumpets were blown at intervals at early times (Num. 10:1-10) but the Pentateuch gives no instructions concerning music as a part of worship. Arrangements for temple music and musicians are made by David at the Lord's command (2 Chr. 29:25). Our sources are inadequate to determine with definiteness whether or not music was a part of the early synagogue service.

Earliest worship was by sacrifice. The earliest examples are those of Cain and Abel (Gen. 4:3 ff.). "Calling on the name of the Lord" is traced back to the time of Enos (Gen. 4:26). Under the Law, sacrifices were both of animals and of cereal grains ("meat offering" in AV) and oil and wine. The victim in animal sacrifice was wholly burned in the burnt offering, but in other types of offerings the worshiper and his friends and the poor consumed the offering after the priest had taken a portion (see Lev. 1-7) for various sorts of sacrifices). Human sacrifice, known to the neighbors of Israel (2 K. 3:27), though condemned by the prophets (Mic. 6:7) was engaged in in desperate crises as in the case of Jephthah's daughter (Judg. 11:30-40) or by the syncretistic kings Ahaz and Manasseh (2 K. 16:3, 21:6). The prophets have a great deal to say about sacrifice unaccompanied by the ethical religious life (1 Sam. 15:22; Amos 5:21-24; Hos. 5:6, 8:11-13; Isa.

1:11-15; Jer. 6:20). The book of Psalms should caution us against a tendency to play down the inward aspects of OT worship.

Worship by sacrifice was at first at the altar which might be erected at any suitable spot. From the time of Mount Sinai the tabernacle became a center of sacrificial worship. In Canaan the "high place" was an open air shrine with altar, stone pillar, and wooden post. Following the building of the temple by Solomon, worship centered in the temple as the place "God shall choose out of all your tribes to put his name there (Deut. 12:5 ff.). The historical books reveal considerable laxity on the matter, which affair culminated in the great reform of Josiah in 622 B.C. which abolished other shrines (2 K. 23:8).

In addition to daily sacrifices, the Feast of Passover, the Feast of Weeks, and the Feast of Tabernacles were annual seasons demanding special acts of worship.

By the NT period the synagogue had developed into a thriving institution alongside of the temple, but differing from it in that there were synagogues in every location where a multitude of Jews lived. Also sacrifice was not a function of the synagogue. Synagogue origins are clouded with obscurity. There is no certain allusion to them in the OT, but in inscriptions they can be traced to the third century B.C. At the synagogue men gathered to read the Law, to study, to hear a homily, to pray, and to listen to the priestly benediction. Its aim was to instruct the whole people in its law. After the demise of the temple in A.D. 70, the synagogue became the center of Judaism. There are Palestinian synagogue inscriptions from the first century A.D. and remains from synagogue buildings from the third century.

Jesus emphasized the spiritual aspects of worship—a worship not attached to holy places (Jn. 4:21-24). Early Christians gathered in the temple courts and went to synagogue meetings, but also held their own meetings. From 1 Cor. 14 one would judge that there was an informal type of service. Women were not allowed to speak. Reading, prayer, the Lord's Supper, the giving of money, and singing (Acts 2:42; Eph. 5:19) were engaged in. Meetings took place on the first day of the week (Acts 20:7). Reports of such worship from the early second century are to be found in the correspondence of Pliny to Trajan, the Didache, and in Justin Martyr (*Apol.* I.65–67).

worshiper in the AV worshiper occurs once as a translation of *neocoros* (Acts 19:35), but this term is more correctly rendered "temple keeper" or "temple guardian" in the ASV and more recent versions. In the emperor cult *neocoros* was applied to those cities that built temples in honor of the emperor. In rare cases it applied to other deities and is applied to Ephesus on a coin dating from the time of Nero (A.D. 54–68).

In the OT "worshiper" renders a noun form of *'abad* (2 K. 10:19, 21, 23; Ps. 97:7). In the NT it is a rendering of *theosebēs* (Jn. 9:31) and *proskunētēs* (Jn. 4:23) and of a participle from *latreuein* (Heb. 9:9, 10:2). Whereas the AV uses relative clauses to render participial phrases from these roots, the RSV uses nouns in Heb. 10:2; Rev. 14:11 and for the additional phrase *seobemenou ton theon* (Acts 16:14, 18:7). Though carrying various shades of meaning these words circulate around the concept of serving, reverencing, and prostrating oneself before God.   J.P.L.

wrestling see **games**

writing although the first mention of writing in the Bible is in Ex. 17:14, it is obvious that the practice began long before that. The earliest writing was symbolic, such as picture drawing, notched sticks, or even the arrangement of pebbles. The earliest examples of a systematic style of writing are the cuneiform tablets of the Sumerians (in Mesopotamia) and the hieroglyphs of Egypt.

The cuneiform tablets of Mesopotamia date back to the fourth millennium B.C. They were made by pressing a stick into wet clay; when the clay dried, the writing was left intact. They were called cuneiform because they were wedge-shaped characters. A stick with a triangular shaped end was used in this writing.

The hieroglyphic writing of the Egyptians was originally pictorial in nature. The word hieroglyph means "sacred writing," or the writing the priests used. From this early hieroglyphic style came two later forms of Egyptian writing, hieratic and demotic.

The invention of the alphabet is usually attributed to the Phoenicians. Originally the letters represented some concrete object, as A represented an ox, B represented a house, etc.

It is thought that the OT was for the most part written in the early Phoenician script at first. Hebrew writing dating before 600 B.C., as far as we can tell, was always in this script; for example, the Gezer Calendar (900 B.C.) and the Siloam Inscription (700 B.C.). It has been suggested that Ezra and other scribes transcribed the OT from the early script into the present Hebrew script of square characters.

The NT was first written in large capital letters called uncials; these MSS had no sentence or word division. Later the MSS were written in smaller letters resembling handwriting called minuscules.

The earliest writing material was probably stone. The Ten Commandments were written on stone; the Siloam Inscription and the Moabite Inscription of Mesha were on stone. Job 19:24 alludes to the practice of chiseling the letters out of rock and filling them in with lead. The earliest Egyptian writings were on stone, e.g., the Palermo Stone.

As mentioned earlier, clay tablets were commonly used in Mesopotamia. Thousands of these tablets have been found at places such as Nuzi and Mari. Some are still untranslated.

Very early the Egyptians began to use the papyrus plant to write on (whence comes our word paper). The process of making papyrus is described in Pliny *Nat. Hist.* XIII.11–13. The stem of the papyrus plant is cut into strips which are placed side by side to dry. Then other such strips are glued across the first ones. When this is dried and polished it makes an excellent writing surface. The side where the strips run in the same direction as one writes is preferred; this is called the *recto*. The other side, used only when there is no more room, is called the *verso*. Often writing is scraped off an old papyrus and a new message is written over it; such a papyrus is called a palimpsest. The dry Egyptian climate will preserve papyrus indefinitely. Papyri have been found dating as early as 2500 to 2350 B.C. Probably the autographs of the NT were written on papyrus.

Parchment and vellum, both made from animal skins, became popular before the days of Christ. Pergamum was the center of the parchment industry when Eumenes II (197–158 B.C.) was its ruler. According to the story, the king of Egypt stopped shipping papyrus in order to cripple the library at Pergamum. Not to be outdone, the men in Pergamum started using parchment.

Broken pieces of pottery were also used very early for writing. These were called *ostraca* (singular, *ostracon*). Ostraca were good for short messages, but impractical for longer ones.

Of course, on the stone, chisels were the writing implements. Sticks used on the clay and later on wax tablets were called *styli* (singular, *stylus*). Reeds with the end torn to serve as a quill were used on the other writing media. For ink the juice of the cuttle fish or a mixture of soot and gum were used.

The three main forms of writing were tablets, scroll, and codex. The papyrus or parchment was glued or sewed together to form scrolls, sometimes over 100 feet long. About the first century A.D. the book, or codex form, began to be used.

Since very few of the people could read or write, the production and transmission of early writing was left to a select group of men known as scribes.   N.P.

X

Xanthicus see **month**

Y

yarn linen yarn (*mikweh*) is an article of commerce in the AV (1 K. 10:28; 2 Chr. 1:16); however, the obscure term is rendered "drove" in ASV, and is now thought on the basis of Akkadian evidence to be a place name—Kue in Cilicia—whence Solomon acquired horses.
                                                                    J.P.L.
year the early Hebrews had a year of twelve lunar months (Abib, Ziv, Ethanim, and Bul are four surviving names) with the first of each month set by the appearance of the new moon. This calendar was retained for religious observances which were connected with agricultural seasons, giving a year of 354+ days. In order to adjust it to the solar calendar (a year is 365¼ days) later used, it was necessary to intercalate an extra month ("Second Adar" about March or April in the third, sixth, eighth, eleventh, seventeenth, and nineteenth years of a nineteen-year cycle (this custom is not mentioned in Scripture). There is some evidence in non-biblical sources of divergent practices on calendar matters in the Jewish sects.

The new year began with Abib or Nisan (Ex. 12:2, 23:15; Est. 3:7), but side by side with this custom was also the agricultural (or civil) year which began in autumn (Ex. 23:16, 34:22; Lev. 25:4, 9) and indicated the time of year by agricultural occupation (e.g., firstfruits, ingatherings, etc.). Later the new moon of the

seventh month was kept as New Year's Day (cf. Ezra 3:6; Neh. 8:2).

The year is divided into (a) two seasons: summer and winter (Gen. 8:22; Ps. 74:17; Zech. 14:8); (b) twelve months (1 K. 4:7; 1 Chr. 27:15); and (c) weeks. See **months, weeks**   J.P.L.
yoke the English translation of several Hebrew words and the Gr. *dzugos*. A yoke was basically a wooden frame (probably made by carpenters who also made plows) placed over the necks of two animals (usually oxen) to join them together in order to increase their efficiency. The amount of ground a pair of oxen could plow in one day (about an acre) came to be called a "yoke" in Hebrew (1 Sam. 14:14; Isa. 5:10) as well as the pair of oxen themselves (1 Sam. 11:7; Lk. 14:19). The word was eventually applied to anyone who was in servitude (Gen. 27:40; 1 K. 12:11; Isa. 9:4; 1 Tim. 6:1), and to "break the yoke" meant to secure one's freedom from that servitude (Jer. 28:12–13). It is in this sense of servitude that Jesus said "my yoke is easy" (Mt. 11:29). The person who insisted on retaining the law of Moses as a part of Christianity was "putting a yoke on the neck of disciples" (Acts 15:10) and becoming "entangled again in a yoke of bondage" (Gal. 5:1).   J.M.

Z

Zaanaim, the Plain of (zā-ā-nǎ'ǐm) in the AV Heber the Kenite was encamped on the plain of Zaanaim which is by Kedesh, i.e., Kedesh-Naphtali, when Sisera took refuge in his tent. The exact location of Zaanaim is unidentified. Kadesh is located on the high ground north of Safed and west of Lake Huleh. The ASV and RSV more correctly translate *elon* as "oak" rather than "plain." The oak [AV transliterated "allon"] in Zaanaim is also listed as a frontier marker of Naphtali (Josh. 19:33). J.P.L.

Zaanan (zā'ā-nǎn) a place named by Micah (1:11) in his address to the towns of the Shephelah. Zaanan is perhaps identical with Zenan (Josh. 15:37).

Zaavan (zā'ā-vǎn) a Horite chief, son of Ezer the son of Seir (Gen. 36:27; AV: Zavan, 1 Chr. 1:42).

Zabad (zā'bǎd) 1. Son of Nathan, descendant of Jerahmeel grandson of Perez son of Judah (1 Chr. 2:36–37).

2. Son of Tahath, an Ephraimite (1 Chr. 7:20–21).

3. Son of Ahlai, one of David's mighty men (1 Chr. 11:41).

4. Son of Shimeath, an Ammonitess who joined with Jehozabad in slaying Joash king of Judah (2 Chr. 24:26; but cf. 2 K. 12:21).

5. One of the sons of Zattu who after the Captivity had married a foreign woman (Ezra 10:27).

6. One of the sons of Hashum who had also married a foreign woman (Ezra 10:33).

7. One of the sons of Nebo who had married a foreign woman (Ezra 10:43). T.B.U.

Zabbai (zǎb-bā'ī) 1. One of the descendants of Behai, who had married a foreign wife in the days of Ezra (Ezra 10:28).

2. Father of Baruch, who assisted Nehemiah in rebuilding the city wall (Neh. 3:20), though the *Qere* here is Zaccai.

Zabbud (zǎb'bǔd) RSV, Zakkur; one of the sons of Bigvai, who returned from Babylon with Ezra (Ezra 8:14).

Zabdi (zǎb'dī) 1. Son of Zerah, the son of Judah, and ancestor of Achan (Josh. 7:1, 17–18).

2. A Benjaminite of the sons of Shimhi (1 Chr. 8:19).

3. David's officer over the produce of the vineyards for the wine cellars (1 Chr. 27:27).

4. Son of Asaph the minstrel (Neh. 11:17); called elsewhere Zaccur (Neh. 12:35) and Zichri (1 Chr. 9:15).

Zabdiel (zǎb'dǐ-ĕl) 1. Father of Jashobeam, a chief of David's guard (1 Chr. 27:2).

2. A priest, son of the great men, or as recent versions merely transliterate, "Haggedolim" (Neh. 11:14).

Zabud (zā'bǔd) the son of Nathan (1 K. 4:5), a priest (AV, "principal officer") and "king's friend" at the court of Solomon, which latter position had been occupied by Hushai the Archite during the reign of David (2 Sam. 15:37, 16:16; 1 Chr. 27:33).

Zabulon (zǎ-bū'lŏn) the Greek form of the name Zebulun (Mt. 4:13, 15; Rev. 7:8).

Zaccai (zǎc-cā'ī) the sons of Zaccai, to the number of 760, returned with Zerubbabel (Ezra 2:9; Neh. 7:14).

Zacchaeus (zǎc-kē'ŭs) [pure] a chief tax collector at Jericho whose encounter with Jesus is recorded only by Luke (19:1–10). Zacchaeus held a special office, it would seem, from the term "chief publican." His particular job was similar to our "District Director of Internal Revenue." Jericho was a center of collection of the Roman taxes from the Jews, and Zacchaeus had several collectors under him. He was a wealthy Jew, short of stature, and therefore climbed into a tree in order that he might see Jesus as his caravan passed beneath. When Jesus came to the tree, a sycamore with wide trunk and low branches, he spoke to Zacchaeus and told him he would eat at his house. Jesus spent the night with Zacchaeus, for which he received the criticism of the Jews because he stayed with a sinner. This reaction was due to the odium attached to the office by the Jews themselves. No doubt the blessing received that night by this tax collector was well worth all persecution heaped upon him. T.B.U.

Zacchur (zǎc'cŭr) 1. A Reubenite, father of one of the spies (Num. 13:4).

2. A Simeonite of the family of Mishma (1 Chr. 4:26).

3. A descendant of Levi through Merari (1 Chr. 24:27).

4. A musician in the postexilic Asaph course (1 Chr. 25:2).

5. One of the rebuilders of the walls of Jerusalem (Neh. 3:2).

6. A Levite who signed the reform pledge (Neh. 10:12).

7. Ancestor of Hanan (Neh. 13:13).

Zachariah (zăc-ă-rī'ăh) 1. The AV spelling of the name of the fourteenth king of Israel, successor to Jeroboam II (2 K. 14:29, 15:8, 11). Other versions spell the name Zechariah. After a reign of six months (ca. 746–745 B.C.) his assassination by Shallum brought an end to the house of Jehu.

2. The father of Abi, Hezekiah's mother in the AV (2 K. 18:2). See **Zechariah** 25

Zacharias 1. One of the rulers of the temple at the time of Josiah's Passover, and the same as Zechariah of 2 Chr. 35:8.

2. One of the holy singers at Josiah's Passover; the name appears in place of "Heman" in 2 Chr. 35:15.

3. One of the men of understanding with whom Ezra consulted upon discovering the absence of priests and Levites (Ezra 8:16).

4. Zacharias (Zechariah) who stood at Ezra's left hand as he read and expounded the Law (Neh. 8:4).

5. One of the sons of Babi who went up at the head of his family with Ezra (Ezra 8:11).

6. One of the sons of Elam who had taken foreign wives (Ezra 10:26).

7. Son of Barachias, whom the Lord says was slain by the Jews between the altar and the temple (Mt. 23:35; Lk. 11:51). There has been much dispute as to who this Zacharias was. Many of the Greek fathers have maintained that the father of John the Baptist is the person to whom our Lord alludes, but there can be little or no doubt that the allusion is to Zechariah, the son of Jehoida (2 Chr. 24:20–21).

8. Father of John the Baptist (Lk. 1:5 ff.). He was a priest of the course of Abijah, of blameless reputation, and still childless in his old age. On one occasion when it was the turn of the course of Abijah to minister in the temple, Zacharias was chosen by lot to burn incense. While fulfilling this duty, he was visited by the angel Gabriel, who announced to him that he would become the father of the forerunner of the Messiah. Zacharias doubted the promise and was punished by being stricken

dumb. At the birth of the child, however, Zacharias insisted that his son be named John, in keeping with the injunction of Gabriel, and his powers of speech returned unto him. According to Lk. 1:67–79, Zacharias was the author of the hymn which describes God's deliverance of Israel from sin through Christ.

C.H.

Zacher (zā'chĕr) (ASV, Zecher) one of the sons of Jehiel, the father of Gibeon, by his wife Maachah (1 Chr. 8:31).

Zadok (zā'dŏk) 1. A son of Ahitub (2 Sam. 8:17) and a descendant of Eleazar, son of Aaron, eleven generations removed from Aaron (1 Chr. 24:3). Zadok joined David at Hebron after the death of Saul (1 Chr. 12:28). Early in David's reign Zadok was jointly priest with Abiathar (2 Sam. 8:17). The two stayed in Jerusalem during Absalom's revolt (2 Sam 15:24–29) and stimulated the people to bring David back (2 Sam. 19:11). Zadok and Nathan joined to anoint Solomon king in the face of Adonijah's usurpation which Abiathar was aiding (1 K. 1:7–8). Abiathar was deposed by Solomon, while Zadok remained sole occupant of the position (1 K. 2:26–27, 35). In the vision of Ezekiel the "sons of Zadok" are the legitimate priests (Ezek. 40:46).

2. A priest and father of Shallum (1 Chr. 6:12).

3. Father of Jerusha, King Uzziah's wife and mother of Jotham (2 K. 15:33; 2 Chr. 27:1).

4. A son of Baana and a repairer of the wall of Jerusalem (Neh. 3:4), perhaps identical with the character of Neh. 10:21.

5. A priest, son of Immer, and repairer of the wall of Jerusalem opposite his house (Neh. 3:28 f.). Perhaps identical with the scribe of Neh. 13:13.

6. An ancestor of Jesus (Mt. 1:14). See **Sadoc**

Zaham (zā'hăm) son of Rehoboam by Abihail the daughter of Eliab (2 Chr. 11:19).

Zair (zā'ĭr) a place named in 2 K. 8:21 only, in the account of Joram's expedition against the Edomites. The king's effort failed and the Edomite revolt succeeded. The parallel account in Chronicles (2 Chr. 21:9) gives no place name. The location of the site is uncertain.

Zalaph (zā'lăph) father of Hanun, who assisted in rebuilding the city wall (Neh. 3:30).

Zalmon (zăl'mŏn) an Ahohite, one of David's thirty mighty men (2 Sam. 23:28).

Zalmon, Mount a wooded eminence in the immediate neighborhood of Shechem which was the source of wood used by Abimelech in burning the Tower of Shechem (Judg. 9:48).

Though sometimes conjectured to be a part of Mount Gerizim, it is an unidentified site.

Zalmonah (zăl-mō'năh) the name of a desert station of the Israelites which they reached after leaving Mount Hor and before arriving at Punon. The location is uncertain (Num. 33:41).

Zalmunna (zăl-mŭn'nă) one of the two "kings" of Midian whose capture and death by the hands of Gideon himself formed the last act of his great conflict with Midian (Judg. 8:5–21; Ps. 83:11).

Zamzummims (zăm-zŭm'mĭms) the Ammonite name for the people who by others were called Rephaim (Deut. 2:20 only). They are described as having originally been a powerful and numerous nation of giants. From a slight similarity between the two names, and from the mention of Emim in connection with each, it is usually assumed that the Zamzummim are identical with Zuzim, but at best the identification is very conjectural.

Zanoah (ză-nō'ăh) in the genealogical lists of the tribe of Judah in 1 Chr. Jekuthiel is said to have been the father of Zanoah (4:18). Zanoah is also the name of a town of Judah (Josh. 15:34).

Zanoah the name of two towns in the territory of Judah. 1. In the Shephelah (Josh. 15:34), named in the same group with Zoreah and Jarmuth. It was reinhabited after the Exile (Neh. 11:30) and its inhabitants restored the valley gate of Jerusalem (Neh. 3:13). It is likely to be identified with Khirbet Zanu' ca. three miles south-southeast of Beth-shemesh.

2. A town in the highland district associated with the mountain proper (Josh. 15:56). It has been conjectured that it may be Khirbet Beit Amra which is ca. one and one-fourth miles northwest of Yatta.

Zaphnath-paaneah (zăph'năth-pă-ă-nē'ăh) the Egyptian name assigned to Joseph (Gen. 41:45). Josephus (Ant. II.vi.1) and the Targum interpret the name as "revealer of secrets." Modern opinion is that the name may mean "the god speaks and he lives."

Zaphon (ză'phŏn) the name of a place mentioned in the enumeration of the allotment of the tribe of Gad (Josh. 13:27). Nelson Glueck conjectures that it may be Tell el-Qos.

Zara, Zarah (ză'ră) the son of Judah (Gen. 38:30; Mt. 1:3). The same as Zerah.

Zareah (ză-rē'ăh) the same as Zorah and Zoreah (Neh. 11:29).

Zareatan (zăr'ĕ-tăn) see Zarthan (Josh. 3:16).

Zareathites, the (ză-rē'ă-thīts) the inhabitants of Zareah or Zorah (1 Chr. 2:53).

Zared, the Valley of (zăr'ĕd) the name is accurately Zered (Num. 21:12).

Zarephath (zăr'ĕ-făth) a Phoenician town situated on the coast of the Mediterranean about eight miles south of Sidon and fourteen miles north of Tyre. Josephus (Ant. VIII.xiii.2) states that it was "not far from Sidon and Tyre." Jerome says (Onom. "Sarefta") that it "lay on the public road." Mentioned in a papyrus from the fourteenth century, the town was famous for its production of excellent glassware. The Akkadian name of the town indicates that Zarephath, like neighboring Tyre and Sidon, produced dye. In 1 K. 17:8–24 one may read how the prophet Elijah was ordered by God to go to Zarephath. There he met a poor widow whom he helped by miraculously refilling her jar of meal and cruse of oil. Zarephath is mentioned in Obad. 20. In Lk. 4:26 in the AV Zarephath appears as the Greek Sarepta. It is now called Sarafand. J.H.

Zareth-shahar (zăr'ĕth-shā'här) a place mentioned only in Josh. 13:19 (ASV, Zereth-shahar), in the catalogue of towns allotted to Reuben. It is named between Sibmah and Beth-peor, and is particularly specified as "in Mount ha-Emek" (AV, "in the Mount of the Valley"). The location of the site is uncertain, though some conjecture that it may be modern Zarat.

Zarhites, the (zär'hīts) (ASV, Zerahites) a branch of the tribe of Judah, descended from Zerah the son of Judah (Num. 26:13, 20; Josh. 7:17; 1 Chr. 27:11, 13).

Zartanah (zär'tă-năh) ASV, Zarethan; a place named in 1 K. 4:12 to define the position of Beth-shean. It is possibly identical with Zarthan, but nothing positive can be said on this point.

Zarthan (zär'thăn) ASV, Zarethan. 1. A place in the plain of Jordan mentioned in connection with Succoth (1 K. 7:46).

2. It is also named in the account of the passage of the Jordan by the Israelites (AV, Zaretan; Josh 3:16), as defining the position of Adam.

3. A place with the similar name of Zartanah (1 K. 4:12).

4. Further (2 Chr. 4:17) Zeredathah (ASV, Zeredan) is substituted for Zarthan. It is conjectured that it may be identical with Tell es-Sa'idiyah.

Zatthu (zăt'thû) one of the signers of the pledge of reform in the time of Ezra (Neh. 10:14). Elsewhere the name is Zattu.

Zattu (zăt'tû) the sons of Zattu were a family of laymen of Israel who returned with Zerubbabel (Ezra 2:8; Neh. 7:13). Members of this family put away foreign wives (Ezra 10:27). See **Zatthu**

431

Zavan see **Zaavan** (1 Chr. 1:42).

Zaza (zā'ză) one of the sons of Jonathan, a descendant of Jerahmeel (1 Chr. 2:33).

Zebadiah (zĕb-ă-dī'ăh) [Jehovah has given]
1. A Benjaminite of the sons of Beriah (1 Chr. 8:15).

2. A Benjaminite of the sons of Elpaal (1 Chr. 8:17).

3. One of the sons of Jeroham of Gedor who joined David at Ziklag (1 Chr. 12:7).

4. Son of Asahel the brother of Joab and an officer of David (1 Chr. 27:7).

5. Son of Michael of the sons of Shephatiah who accompanied Ezra in the return from Babylon (Ezra 8:8).

6. A priest of the sons of Immer who had married a foreign wife after the return from Babylon (Ezra 10:20).

7. Third son of Meshelemiah the Korhite and a temple doorkeeper (1 Chr. 26:2).

8. A Levite in the reign of Jehoshaphat (2 Chr. 17:8).

9. The son of Ishmael and prince of the house of Judah in the reign of Jehoshaphat (2 Chr. 19:11).   J.P.L.

Zebah (zē'bäh) one of the two Midianite kings (Zalmunna was the other) captured and slain by Gideon (Judg. 8:5–21; Ps. 83:11) which act led to Gideon's being acclaimed as ruler over Israel. Pursuing the invaders across Jordan, Gideon surprised them and their 15,000 men in Karkor. On the return journey after having wreaked vengeance upon Succoth and Penuel for slighting him, Gideon personally slew the proud kings in blood revenge for his slain brothers. Gideon then made an ephod of the gold earrings and collars seized from the Midianites and placed it in Ophrah, his city.
                                                            J.P.L.

Zebaim (zĕ-bā'ĭm) the sons of Pochereth of Zebaim (AV) are mentioned in the catalogue of families of "Solomon's slaves" who returned from the Captivity with Zerubbabel (Ezra 2:57; Neh. 7:59). The ASV and RSV combine words and transliterate to read Pochereth-hazzebaim.

Zebedee (zĕb'ĕ-dĕ) a fisherman of Galilee, the father of the apostles James and John (Mt. 4:21), and the husband of Salome (Mt. 27:56; Mk. 15:40). It has been inferred from the mention of his "hired servants" (Mk. 1:20), and from the acquaintance between the apostle John and Annas the high priest (John 18:15) that the family of Zebedee were in easy circumstances (cf. 19:27), although not above manual labor (Mt. 4:21). He appears only once in the gospel narratives (Mt. 4:21–22; Mk. 1:19–20) where he is seen in his boat with his two sons mending their nets.   J.P.L.

Zebina (zĕ-bī'nă) one of the sons of Nebo who had taken foreign wives after the return from Babylon (Ezra 10:43).

Zeboim, Zeboiim (zĕ-bŏ'ĭm) 1. One of the five cities of the plain of Jordan (sometimes mentioned with Admah) whose king was captured by Chedorlaomer (Gen. 14:2, 8), which was destroyed by fire for wickedness (Gen. 19:17–29; Deut. 29:23) and whose destruction serves as an example for later generations (Hos. 11:8). It is conjectured that it is today submerged under the south part of the Dead Sea.

2. A city near Hadid (site unknown) in Judea occupied by Jews after the return from exile (Neh. 11:34).

3. The valley of Zeboim (1 Sam. 13:18) whence the Philistines came to threaten Saul and Jonathan which may be the Wadi Abu Daba'.   J.P.L.

Zebudah (zĕ-bū'dăh) (ASV, RSV = Zebidah) daughter of Pedaiah of Rumah, wife of Josiah, and mother of King Jehoiakim (2 K. 23:36).

Zebul (zĕ'bŭl) chief man (AV, ruler) of the city of Shechem at the time of the contest between Abimelech and the native Canaanites led by Gaal (Judg. 9:28–41).

Zebulonite (zĕb'ū-lŏn-īt) a member of the tribe of Zebulun. Applied only to Elon, the one judge produced by the tribe (Judg. 12:11–12).

Zebulunites, the the members of the tribe of Zebulun (Num. 26:27 only).

Zebulun (zĕb'ū-lŭn) from the Heb. *zvd*, to present (cf. Akkadian *zabalu* which may mean "to exalt"—Gen. 30:20, "my husband will honor me") or *zvl*, to dwell (cf. Gen. 49:13, "Zebulun shall dwell . . .").

1. The sixth and last son of Leah and Jacob and the tenth son of Jacob (Gen. 29:21–30:20). It has been suggested that Zebulun was represented by his sons among the group of Jacob's sons that went to Egypt from Canaan. This assumption is erroneous because: (a) All the sons of Jacob except Reuben are listed among the migrants to Egypt, not in their own names but in the names of their sons, just as was Zebulun (Gen. 46:8–27). (b) It is clear that such a method of listing does not exclude the father of the sons because the sons of Judah are listed (46:12) and then Judah is subsequently mentioned (46:28). (c) Jacob blessed Zebulun, as well as the other sons, while in Egypt (Gen. 49:13).

2. One of the twelve tribes of Hebrews which bore the name of its founder (described above) numbering 57,400 at the time of the exodus from Egypt (Num. 1:31). The exact boundaries of the tribe when settled in Canaan are not certain but it appears not to have in-

herited the vast territory designated by Jacob in his last charge to Zebulun (Gen. 49:13). Rather than reaching the sea as Jacob had said (and as Josephus declared, *Ant.* V.i.22, from the Sea of Galilee to the Mediterranean) Zebulun was bordered on the west by Asher (Josh. 19:24-29) and on the east by Naphtali (Josh. 19:32-34), thus being isolated from the Mediterranean Sea on the west and the Sea of Chinnereth (Sea of Galilee) on the east. The reason for this failure to occupy more territory is stated in Judg. 1:30: "Zebulun did not drive out the inhabitants . . ." Through lack of faith all of Israel failed to completely drive out the inhabitants of Canaan and ultimately occupied only about one fifth of the land promised them —from the Mediterranean Sea to the Euphrates and from Syria to the Arabah (Deut. 11:24; Josh. 1:4).

The tribe is commended in the Song of Deborah (Judg. 5:1, 14) for its bravery in battle against the Canaanites and they responded to the call of Gideon against the Midianites (Judg. 6:35). The tribe was well represented among those who supported David against Saul at Hebron (1 Chr. 12:33, 40).   J.M.

Zechariah (zĕch-ă-rī'ăh) 1. Zechariah, the eleventh in the sequence of the twelve minor prophets is the son of Berechiah and the grandson of Iddo (in Ezra 5:1, 6:14, it is likely that "son of Iddo" is used in the looser sense of descendant). A priest returned from Babylon (Neh. 12:16), Zechariah began his prophetic career in the eighth month of the second year of Darius, or in November 520 B.C., which is two months later than the first oracle of Haggai. The careers of the two prophets overlap one month. Zechariah's career continued for at least two years.

The returned exiles led by Zerubbabel had laid the foundation of the temple in 536 B.C. (Ezra 3:8 ff.). Local opposition had frustrated the project and it had been at a standstill for sixteen years. Through the influence of Zechariah and Haggai the people were encouraged to resume construction and carry the project through to completion by 518 B.C. (Ezra 6:14 f.). Later legend made him and Haggai to be members of the Great Synagogue. The legendary material on the prophets knows no martyrdom for Zechariah. It is likely that the gospels refer to a different Zechariah (2 Chr. 24:20; Mt. 23:35; Lk. 11:51).

The Book of Zechariah. The book of Zechariah has three principal sections: (1) chs. 1-8; (2) chs. 9-11; (3) chs. 12-14. The first section contains a call to repentance in which God's warnings through the former

prophets and his execution of their threats in the Exile is the substance (1:1-6). There follows a series of eight night visions each of which has its interpretation showing them to be relevant to problems of rebuilding of the temple (1:7-6:15): a. The rider on the red horse followed by other horses in the valley of myrtles patrols the earth and reports that all is at rest. The shaking of the nations promised by Hag. 2:20 is not in sight, but despite the absence of such upheavals, God's pity has been stirred and Jerusalem will be rebuilt (1:7-17). b. The four horns and four smiths represent those who have scattered Judah and those who will destroy the destroyers (1:18-21). There is no longer effective opposition to the building of the Lord's house. c. The man with the measuring line is charged not to lay out the walls of the city, for it is to be inhabited as a city without walls. The Lord is to be her protector (2:1-13). d. Joshua the high priest in filthy garments after accusal by Satan is clothed with clean garments and Satan is rebuked (3:1-10). The import is that the priesthood will be qualified to serve in the new temple. e. The golden candlestick with seven lampstands and two olive trees (4:1-14). The two anointed ones seem to be Joshua and Zerubbabel, the leaders of the returned community, the latter of whom despite difficulties in the way, will complete the temple. f. The flying scroll carries a curse on all evildoers in the land (5:1-4). The land will be cleansed of evil. g. The woman sitting in a large dry measure which is carried to Shinar (5:5-11) represents wickedness and its removal from the land. h. Four chariots go from between the copper mountains to patrol the earth (6:1-8). These seem to symbolize God's providence with the earth in its control.

The import of the night visions is that all opposition to rebuilding the temple will be overcome. Three Israelites return from Babylon with gifts for Jerusalem and so Zechariah makes crowns and puts them on the head of Joshua the high priest as a sign that the Messiah will be priest and king on his throne (6:9-14).

In 518 a deputation came to the prophet to inquire whether the fast days that had been instituted during the Captivity to commemorate the calamities of Jerusalem were any longer meaningful since work on the temple had progressed so well. The prophet makes clear that it is not fasting, but obedience, justice, and kindness that is significant before God. The fasts shall henceforth be festivals (7:1-7).

A series of ten short oracles introduced by "thus saith the Lord" assures that the Lord

Zechariah

will dwell in Zion and prosperity is sure to come. Jerusalem is a city where boys and girls will play in the streets and men and women will sun themselves (8:1–23).

The second portion of Zechariah contains three sections not clearly related to the rebuilding of the temple. The third person pronoun is used rather than the first person that was in the first part of the book. Two main sections begin with "An oracle, the word of the Lord" (9:1, 12:1). The first of these sections threatens the neighboring nations whose territory lies within the greater Palestine boundaries, but it also announces the coming of the Messianic king riding upon an ass. His dominion will be from sea to sea (9:1–10). This portion of the book has a goodly percentage of symbolic language. The allegory of the good and foolish shepherds (11:1–17) furnishes us no clue as to the identity of the participants. The shepherd finally asks for his wages which prove to be thirty shekels of silver and which are cast to the potter. The stick "union" is broken to symbolize division between Judah and Israel.

Chapters 12–14 are made up of two sections, each of which deals with final events in an apocalyptic way. In the first an attack on Jerusalem results in victory for Judah through the Lord's aid. Great mourning is carried out for one pierced. A fountain for cleansing is opened and false prophets are cut off. The historical events that lie back of this section cannot be definitely traced. The second section announces the approach of the Day of the Lord with an assault on Zion, the intervention of Jehovah and men fleeing from an earthquake. The whole scene results in a transformed earth.

Though not cited by name, Zechariah has greatly influenced the NT: (1) The branch of Jesse (Zech. 3:8, 6:12) and the priestly king are a part of the Messianic hope as also are the king who reigns from sea to sea (Zech. 9:10) and the fountain for cleansing (Zech. 13:1). (2) The king riding on the donkey (Zech. 9:9; cf. Mt. 21:4 f.). (3) The thirty pieces of silver and the potter's field (Zech. 11:12 f.; cf. Mt. 26:15, 27:9 f.). (4) Looking on him whom they have pierced (Zech. 12:10; Jn. 19:37). (5) Smite the shepherd and the sheep are scattered (Zech. 13:7; cf. Mt. 26:31)—all exercise an influence.

Critical Views. Since the time of Joseph Mede (1653) the unity of Zechariah has been under challenge. Mede observed that Mt. 27:9–10 cites Zech. 11:12–13 as from Jeremiah. Others have argued that this is either an ancient scribal error in Matthew or that the statement may have been made earlier by Jeremiah. Since Mede's day it has become a commonplace in critical study to separate the books into three sections, only the first of which (chs. 1–8) is usually attributed to Zechariah. The latter two are thought of as anonymous oracles that have been attached to those of Zechariah. Efforts to date these sections both pre- and postexilic have settled into a general consensus in some circles for a postexilic date. Their apocalyptic nature is a significant item in the argument.

Opponents of the critical view argue for the unity of the book on the basis of the unanimous Jewish and Christian tradition of the early period and upon the basis that phrases like "eyes of the Lord," "the Lord of Hosts," and "pass through and return" occur in both halves of the book.

2. Son of Meshelemiah, a Kohathite, and keeper of the north gate of the tabernacle of the congregation (1 Chr. 9:21).

3. One of the sons of Jehiel (1 Chr. 9:37).

4. A Levite of the second order in the temple band as arranged by David, appointed to play "with psalteries on Alamoth" (1 Chr. 15:18, 20).

5. One of the princes of Judah in the reign of Jehoshaphat (2 Chr. 17:7).

6. Son of the high priest Jehoiada in the reign of Joash king of Judah, who was stoned with stones by the people (2 Chr. 24:20). Some identify him with the martyred prophet referred to by Jesus (Mt. 23:35).

7. A Kohathite Levite in the reign of Josiah (2 Chr. 34:12).

8. The leader of the sons of Pharaoh who returned with Ezra (Ezra 8:3).

9. Son of Bebai (Ezra 8:11).

10. One of the chiefs of the people whom Ezra summoned in council at the river Ahava (Ezra 8:16). Possibly also the man who stood at Ezra's left hand when he expounded the Law (Neh. 8:4).

11. One of the family of Elam who had married a foreign wife after the Captivity (Ezra 10:26).

12. Ancestor of Athaiah (Neh. 11:4).

13. A Shilonite descendant of Perez (Neh. 11:5).

14. A priest son of Pashur (Neh. 11:12).

15. The representative of the priestly family of Iddo in the days of Joiakim the son of Jeshua (Neh. 12:16).

16. One of the priests, son of Jonathan, who blew with the trumpets at the dedication of the city wall by Ezra and Nehemiah (Neh. 12:35, 41).

17. A chief of the Reubenites at the time of the captivity by Tiglath-pileser (1 Chr. 5:7).

434

18. One of the priests who accompanied the ark from the house of Obed-edom (1 Chr. 15:24).

19. Son of Isshiah, a Kohathite Levite descended from Uzziel (1 Chr. 24:25).

20. Fourth son of Hosah of the children of Merari (1 Chr. 26:11).

21. A descendant of Manasseh (1 Chr. 27:21).

22. The father of Jahaziel (2 Chr. 20:14).

23. Fourth of the sons of Jehoshaphat (2 Chr. 21:2).

24. A prophet in the reign of Uzziah who appears to have acted as the king's counselor (2 Chr. 26:5).

25. The father of Abijah, Hezekiah's mother (2 Chr. 29:1).

26. One of the family of Asaph in the reign of Hezekiah (2 Chr. 29:13).

27. One of the rulers of the temple in the reign of Josiah (2 Chr. 35:8).

28. The son of Jeberechiah who was taken by the prophet Isaiah as one of the witnesses to his writing Maher-shalal-hash-baz (Isa. 8:2). Some have conjectured that he is identical with 26 above. See also **Zachariah** which is the AV spelling of the name in 2 K. 14:29, 15:8, 11, 18:2.   J.P.L.

Zedad (zē'dăd) one of the landmarks on the north border of the land of Israel, as promised by Moses (Num. 34:8) and the description by Ezekiel (47:15). It is likely identical with Sadad which is north of the road leading from Palmyra to Riblah and southeast of Homs.

Zedekiah (zĕd-ē-kī'ăh) [righteousness of Jehovah] 1. A court prophet who assured Ahab victory against his enemies at Ramoth-gilead (1 K. 22:11; 2 Chr. 18:1–27). He was apparently a leader among four hundred prophets.

2. A false prophet in the time of Jeremiah, sixth century B.C. who lived in Babylon (Jer. 29:21–23).

3. A prince of Judah in the time of King Jehoiakim (Jer. 36:12).

4. The last king of the Southern Kingdom (Judah) which fell to the Babylonians in 587 B.C. Placed on the throne when he was twenty-one years of age by Nebuchadnezzar king of Babylon, he was little more than a puppet king who replaced his nephew Jehoiachin when the latter was carried into Babylonian captivity. His name was changed at that time from Mattaniah to Zedekiah, perhaps to indicate that he was a puppet king (2 K. 24:17–18) in which capacity he served for eleven years (ca. 598–587 B.C.– 2 K. 24:18).

He is viewed by Jeremiah (chs. 21–38) and Ezekiel (ch. 16) as he is described in 2 K.

24–25—a weakling who, like his brother Jehoiakim (a previous king of Judah—2 K. 24:1–7), did that which was evil in the sight of the Lord (2 K. 24:19). Although he had taken an oath of allegiance to Nebuchadnezzar (Ezek. 17:13, 16) and sworn by the name of the Lord, apparently (17:19) he broke that covenant and made an alliance with Egypt against the advice of Jeremiah the prophet who spoke with him frequently (Jer. 37:2–3, 17, 38:14) and prophesied the fall of Jerusalem (Jer. 38:17–23).

The rebellion of Zedekiah against Nebuchadnezzar led to the siege and destruction of Jerusalem (2 K. 24:20, 25:5) in which Zedekiah was captured while trying to escape. He was subsequently punished by being forced to watch his sons executed before having his own eyes put out (2 K. 25:7) and was then bound in chains and carried to Babylon.   J.M.

Zeeb see **Oreb**

Zelah (zē'lăh) a city in the allotment of Benjamin (Josh. 18:28); contained the family tomb of Kish the father of Saul (2 Sam. 21:14). The site is possibly Khirbet Salah, northwest of Jerusalem.

Zelek (zē'lĕk) an Ammonite, one of David's thirty mighty men (2 Sam. 23:37; 1 Chr. 11:39).

Zelophehad (zē-lŏph'ĕ-hăd) son of Hepher, son of Gilead, son of Machir, son of Manasseh (Josh. 17:3). He was apparently the second son of his father Hepher (1 Chr. 7:15). Zelophehad came out of Egypt with Moses, but died in the wilderness, as did the whole of that generation (Num. 14:35, 27:3). On his death without male heirs, his five daughters just after the second numbering in the wilderness, came before Moses and Eleazar to claim the inheritance of their father in the tribe of Manasseh. The claim was admitted by divine direction with the stipulation that heiresses marry within the father's tribe (Num. 26:33, 27:1–11, 36:8).

Zelotes (zē-lō'tēs) the epithet given to the apostle Simon to distinguish him from Simon Peter (Lk. 6:15; Acts 1:13. See **Canaanite, Simon 5**

Zelzah (zĕl'zăh) a place named only once (1 Sam. 10:2) as on the boundary of Benjamin, close to Rachel's sepulcher.

Zemaraim (zĕm-ă-rā'ĭm) 1. A town in the allotment of Benjamin (Josh. 18:22) perhaps identical with Ras ez-Zeimara, four miles north of Jericho.

2. Mount Zemaraim, which was "in Mount Ephraim," that is to say, within the general district of the highlands of that great tribe (2 Chr. 13:4) where Abijah delivered a speech

rebuking Jeroboam. The site of the mountain has not been located.

Zemarite, the (zĕm'ā-rīt) one of the Hamite tribes who, in the genealogical table of Gen. 10 (vs. 18) and in 1 Chr. 1 (vs. 16), are represented as "sons of Canaan." Nothing is certainly known of this ancient tribe. Their area may be that of the town called Sumra north of Lebanon between Arvad and Tripoli.

Zemira (zĕ-mī'rā) one of the sons of Becher the son of Benjamin (1 Chr. 7:8).

Zenan (zē'năn) a town in the allotment of Judah situated in the district of the Shephelah (Josh. 15:37). It is probably identical with Zaanan (Mic. 1:11). It is conjectured to be 'Araq el-Kharba.

Zenas (zē'năs) a believer, and as may be inferred from the context, a preacher of the Gospel who is mentioned in Tit. 3:13 in connection with Apollos. He is further described as "the lawyer." It is impossible to determine whether Zenas was a Roman, Jewish, or Greek lawyer.

Zephaniah (zĕph-ă-nī'äh) 1. The ninth in order of the twelve prophets. His pedigree is traced to his fourth ancestor, Hezekiah (1:1), believed to be the celebrated king of that name. In ch. 1 the utter desolation of Judea is predicted as a judgment for idolatry and neglect of the Lord, the luxury of princes, and the violence and deceit of their dependents (3–9). The prosperity, security and insolence of the people are contrasted with the horrors of the day of wrath (10–18). Chapter 2 contains a call to repentance (1–3), with predictions of the ruin of the cities of the Philistines, of the restoration of the house of Judah after the visitation (4–7). Other enemies of Judah, Moab and Ammon, are threatened with perpetual destruction (8–15). In ch. 3 the prophet addresses Jerusalem, which he reproves sharply for vice and disobedience (1–7). He then concludes with a series of promises (8–20). The chief characteristics of this book are the unity and harmony of the composition, the grace, energy, and dignity of its style, and the rapid and effective alternations of threats and promises. The general tone of the last portion is Messianic, but without any specific reference to the person of our Lord. The date of the book is given in the inscription; viz. the reign of Josiah, from ca. 640 to 609 B.C. Moreover, the prophecy was probably delivered before the eighteenth year of Josiah.

2. The son of Maaseiah (Jer. 21:1), and *sagan* or second priest in the reign of Zedekiah. He succeeded Jehoiada (Jer. 29:25–26), and was probably a ruler of the temple, whose office included the duty to punish pretenders to the gift of prophecy. In this capacity he was appealed to by Shemaiah, the Nehelamite, to punish Jeremiah (Jer. 29:29). Twice was he sent from Zedekiah to inquire of Jeremiah the issue of the siege of the city by the Chaldeans (Jer. 21:1) and to implore him to intercede for the people (Jer. 37:3). On the capture of Jerusalem he was taken and slain at Riblah (Jer. 52:24, 27; 2 K. 25:18, 21).

3. Father of Josiah (Zech. 6:10) and of Hen, according to the reading of the received text of Zech. 6:14. C.H.

Zephath see **Hormah**

Zephathah, the Valley of (zĕph'ă-thäh) the spot near Mareshah in which Asa joined battle with Zerah the Ethiopian (2 Chr. 14:10 only).

Zepho (zē'phō) son of Eliphaz son of Esau (Gen. 36:11) and one of the "dukes" (ASV, chiefs) of the Edomites (vs. 15). In 1 Chr. 1:36 he is called Zephi.

Zephon (zē'phŏn) **Ziphion** (Gen. 46:16) the son of Gad (Num. 26:15) and ancestor of the Zephonites.

Zer (zër) a fortified town in the allotment of Naphtali (Josh. 19:35 only), the location of which is uncertain.

Zerah (zē'räh) 1. A son of Reuel son of Esau (Gen. 36:13; 1 Chr. 1:37) and one of the "dukes" (ASV, chiefs) of the Edomites (Gen. 36:17).

2. Less properly, Zarah, twin son of his elder brother Phares, of Judah and Tamar (Gen. 38:30; 1 Chr. 2:6; Mt. 1:3). His descendants were called Zarhites (Num. 26:20).

3. Son of Simeon (1 Chr. 4:24) called Zohar in Gen. 46:10.

4. A Levite of the family of Gershom (1 Chr. 6:21, 41).

5. The Ethiopian or Cushite, an invader of Judah, defeated at Mareshah by Asa 913–873 B.C. See **Asa**. It is not certain that Zerah is to be identified with Osorkon, second king of the Egyptian twenty-second dynasty as some have thought or Osorkon II, his second successor (2 Chr. 14:9–15).

Zerahiah (zĕr-ă-hī'äh) 1. A priest, son of Uzzi (Ezra 7:4).

2. One of the sons of Pahath-moab (Ezra 8:4).

Zerahites, the see **Zarhites**

Zered (zē'rĕd) (Deut. 2:13–14), or **Zared** (Num. 21:12) a brook or valley running into the Dead Sea near its southeast corner which today is identified with Wadi el-Hesa. It lay between Moab and Edom and is the limit of the thirty-eight years of the Israelite's wandering (Deut. 2:14).

Zereda (zĕr'ĕ-dă) the native place of Jeroboam

(1 K. 11:26). Zereda has been supposed to be identical with Zeredathah and Zarthan or Zartanah, but the two last were in the valley of the Jordan while Zeredah was, according to the repeated statement of the LXX, on Mount Ephraim.

Zeredathah (2 Chr. 4:17) see **Zarthan**

Zererath (Judg. 7:22) see **Zarthan**

Zeresh (zē'rĕsh) the wife of Haman the Agagite (Est. 5:10, 14, 6:13).

Zereth (zē'rĕth) son of Ashur the father of Tekoa, by his wife Helah (1 Chr. 4:7).

Zeri (zē'rī) one of the sons of Jeduthun in the reign of David (1 Chr. 25:3).

Zeror (zē'rôr) a Benjaminite, ancestor of Kish the father of Saul (1 Sam. 9:1).

Zeruah (zē-rū'äh) the mother of Jeroboam the son of Nebat (1 K. 11:26).

Zerubbabel (zē-rŭb'bă-bĕl) "begotten in Babylon," Hebrew name (Gr. *Zorobabel*) of a Babylonian Jew who has been identified by some as Sheshbazzar (Ezra 1:8, 5:14, 16) and by others as his nephew (because Sheshbazzar seems to be dead at the time described in Ezra 5:6–17). He is referred to as the "son of Shealtiel" (Ezra 3:2, 8, 5:2; Neh. 12:1; Hag. 1:1, 12, 14, 2:2, 23; Mt. 1:12; Lk. 3:27) but once is called the "son of Pedaiah" who was the brother of Shealtiel (1 Chr. 3:17–18). Discounting a scribal error two possibilities of dealing with the problem present themselves as worthy of consideration: (1) By the Levirate law of marriage (Deut. 25:5–10) Zerubbabel may have been the actual son of Pedaiah and Shealtiel's widow but legally the son of Shealtiel; and (2) less likely, the name may here refer to a cousin, the son of Pedaiah, who has the same name. It was a common name in Babylon, we know, from inscriptions that have been discovered dating to the time of Darius.

Zerubbabel was prominent: (1) among Babylonians and Persians who eventually appointed him "governor of Judah" (Hag. 1:1, 14) and gave him authority to return to Jerusalem and rebuild the temple destroyed by Nebuchadnezzar in 586 B.C. He restored the courses of priests and Levites (Ezra 3:8, 6:18; Neh. 12:47), and recorded the genealogies of the Jews who returned to Jerusalem from Babylon (Neh. 7:5). He is not mentioned, however, at the time of the dedication of the temple in 515 B.C. (Ezra 6:15 ff.). (2) Among the Hebrews whose writers praised him as a coreligious leader with Joshua the high priest (Ezra 3; Zech. 6; Neh. 12:1) and list him in the Davidic line as a grandson of the exiled king of Judah Jehoiachin (1 Chr. 3:17–19), and (3) among Christians of the first century who placed him

in the ancestral line of Jesus Christ (Mt. 1:12; Lk. 3:27). J.M.

Zeruiah (zĕr-ū-ī'äh) the mother of the three leading heroes of David's army—Abishai, Joab, and Asahel—known as the "sons of Zeruiah." She and Abigail are specified in 1 Chr. 2:13–17 as "sisters of the sons of Jesse" (vs. 16). The expression is in itself enough to raise a suspicion that she was not a daughter of Jesse, a suspicion which is corroborated by the statement of 2 Sam. 17:25 that Abigail was the daughter of Nahash. It has been conjectured that the mother may have been married to Nahash prior to her marriage to Jesse. See **Nahash**. Of Zeruiah's husband there is no mention in the Bible.

Zetham (zē'thăm) the son of Laadan, a Gershonite Levite (1 Chr. 23:8).

Zethan (zē'thăn) a Benjaminite of the sons of Bilhan (1 Chr. 7:10).

Zethar (zē'thär) one of the seven eunuchs of Ahasuerus (Est. 1:10).

Zia (zī'ä) one of the Gadites who dwelt in Bashan (1 Chr. 5:13).

Ziba (zī'bă) a servant of the house of Saul made a servant to Mephibosheth by David to till his lands. Through the pretense that Mephibosheth was disloyal at the time of the revolt of Absalom, Ziba received the lands for himself from David. When the deceit came to light at the end of the revolt, in anger David restored half of them to Mephibosheth (2 Sam. 9:2–12, 16:1–4, 19:17, 29). See **Mephibosheth**

Zibia (zī'bī-ă) a Benjaminite, apparently the son of Shaharaim by his wife Hodesh (1 Chr. 8:9).

Zibiah (zī'bī-äh) a native of Beer-sheba, and mother of King Joash (2 K. 12:1; 2 Chr. 24:1).

Zibeon (zĭb'ē-ŏn) father of Anah, whose daughter Aholibamah was Esau's wife (Gen. 36:2). Although called a Hivite, he is probably the same as Zibeon the son of Seir the Horite (vss. 20, 24, 29; 1 Chr. 1:38, 40).

Zichri (zĭch'rī) 1. Son of Izhar the son of Kohath (Ex. 6:21).

2. A Benjaminite of the sons of Shimhi (1 Chr. 8:19).

3. A Benjaminite of the sons of Shashak (1 Chr. 8:23).

4. A Benjaminite of the sons of Jeroham (1 Chr. 8:27).

5. Son of Asaph (1 Chr. 9:15), likely elsewhere called Zabdi (Neh. 11:17) and Zaccur (1 Chr. 25:2, 10; Neh. 12:35).

6. A descendant of Eliezer the son of Moses and father of Shelomoth (1 Chr. 26:25).

7. The father of Eliezer, the chief of the

Reubenites in the reign of David (1 Chr. 27:16).

8. Of the tribe of Judah, father of Amasiah (2 Chr. 17:16).

9. Father of Elishaphat who with Jehoiada was one of the conspirators against Athaliah (2 Chr. 23:1).

10. An Ephraimite hero in the invading army of Pekah the son of Remaliah (2 Chr. 28:7).

11. Father or ancestor of Joel (Neh. 11:9).

12. A priest of the family of Abijah, in the days of Joiakim the son of Jeshua (Neh. 12:17).					J.P.L.

Ziddim (zĭd'dĭm) a fortified town in the allotment of Naphtali the location of which is uncertain (Josh. 19:35).

Zidon or **Sidon** (zī'dŏn) an ancient city (modern Saida, Lebanon) of a long and turbulent history located on the Phoenician coast twenty-five miles north of Tyre. The city is called Sidon (fishery) in the RSV and in the NT of AV and ASV, and its mariners and merchants were widely known (Ezek. 27:8). In Genesis Zidon is the firstborn of Canaan (Gen. 10:15) and the city marked one of the extremities of the land of the Canaanites (Gen. 10:19). In earlier times perhaps more important than Tyre as is seen when Sidonians is a generic name for the Phoenicians (Josh. 13:6; Judg. 18:7), Sidon was later eclipsed by Tyre with which it is often mentioned. Its territory extended to that of Zebulun (Gen. 29:13) and Asher (Josh. 19:28) and the Sidonians oppressed the Israelites (Judg. 10:12). Sidon's people cut wood for Solomon (1 K. 5:6) and for the returned exiles (Ezra 3:7). Solomon yielded to their cults (1 K. 11:5–7). Baal was the chief god (1 K. 16:31), but Ashtoreth was also worshiped (1 K. 11:5, 33; 2 K. 23:13). Religious conflict became most acute with the innovations of Jezebel, the daughter of Ethbaal king of Sidon (1 K. 16:31).

Sidon is threatened by the prophets: (Isa. 33:12; Jer. 27:3; Ezek. 28:20–23; Joel 3:4). Joel accuses the people of Sidon of plundering Jerusalem in the slave trade. Sidon underwent the successive domination of Assyria, Egypt, Babylon, Persia, Greece, and Rome. During the Persian period it recovered its significance to become the most important Phoenician city, but it was destroyed after a revolt in 351 B.C. Recovering again, the region (about fifty miles from Nazareth) becomes the northernmost point in the journeys of Jesus (Mt. 15:21; Mk. 7:24, 31); its people came to Galilee to hear him (Mk. 3:8); and he referred to their wickedness and lack of opportunity (Mt. 11:21). Herod was later angry with its people who depended upon

his territory (Acts 12:20). Paul landed there on his voyage to Rome and visited friends (Acts 27:3).

Zif (1 K. 6:37) ASV, RSV = Ziv. See **month**

Ziha (zī'hă) 1. The children of Ziha were a family of Nethinim who returned with Zerubbabel (Ezra 2:43).

2. Chief of the Nethinim in Ophel (Neh. 11:21).

Ziklag (zĭk'lăg) is first mentioned in the catalogue of the towns of Judah in Josh. 15:31 and occurs in the same connection among the places allotted out of the territory of Judah to Simeon (19:5). We next encounter it in the possession of the Philistines (1 Sam. 27:6) when it was, at David's request, bestowed upon him by Achish king of Gath. He resided there for a year and four months (1 Sam. 27:7, 30:14, 26; 1 Chr. 12:1, 20). It was there he received the news of Saul's death (2 Sam. 1:1, 4:10). He then relinquished it for Hebron (2:1). Ziklag is finally mentioned as being reinhabited by the people of Judah after their return from the Captivity (Neh. 11:28). It is conjectured that Ziklag is to be identified with Tell el-Khuweilfeh ca. five miles southsouthwest of Tell Beit Mirsim.

Zillah (zī'lăh) one of the wives of Lamech descendant of Cain and mother of Jubal-cain (Gen. 4:19–22).

Zilpah (zĭl'păh) a Syrian given by Laban to his daughter Leah as an attendant (Gen. 29:24), and by Leah to Jacob as a concubine. She was the mother of Gad and Asher (Gen. 30:9–13, 35:26, 37:2, 46:18).

Zilthai (zĭl'thā-ī) RSV and ASV, Zillethai. 1. A Benjaminite (1 Chr. 8:20).

2. One of the captains of thousands of Manasseh who deserted to David at Ziklag (1 Chr. 12:20).

Zimmah (zĭm'măh) 1. A Gershonite Levite, ancestor of Joah (1 Chr. 6:20; 2 Chr. 29:12).

2. Another Gershonite (1 Chr. 6:42).

Zimran (zĭm'răn) the eldest son of Keturah and Abraham (Gen. 25:2; 1 Chr. 1:32). His descendants are not mentioned, nor is any hint given that he was the founder of a tribe.

Zimri (zĭm'rī) 1. A descendant of Judah through Zerah (1 Chr. 2:6).

2. The son of Salu, a Simeonite chieftain, slain by Phinehas with the Midianitish princess Cozbi (Num. 25:14).

3. Fifth sovereign of the Northern Kingdom (Israel), who occupied the throne for the brief period of seven days ca. 876 B.C. Originally in command of half the chariots in the royal army, he gained the crown by the murder of King Elah, son of Bassha. But the army,

which at that time was besieging the Philistine town of Gibbethon, when they heard of Elah's murder, proclaimed their general Omri king. He immediately marched against Tirzah and took the city. Zimri retreated into the innermost part of the late king's palace, set it on fire, and perished in the ruins (1 K. 16:9–20).

4. A descendant of Jonathan (1 Chr. 8:36).

Zin the name of a wilderness in the Sinai Peninsula southwest of the Dead Sea through which Israel passed on their way to Canaan (Num. 20:1), possibly lying north of the wilderness of Paran. Kadesh-barnea lay on its edge, while it formed a part of the southern border of Canaan (Num. 34:3–4; Josh. 15:1, 3). From here the spies were sent out (Num. 13:21), and here murmuring took place (Num. 27:12–14). Here also the Israelites stopped after leaving Ezion-geber (Num. 33:36).

Zina or **Zizah** (zī'nă) the second son of Shimei (1 Chr. 23:10).

Zion see **Jerusalem**

Zior a town belonging to the same group with Hebron, in the mountain district of Judah (Josh. 15:54). The site is unidentified.

Ziph (zīph) the name of two towns in Judah:

1. In the south, named between Ithnan and Telem (Josh. 15:24). It does not appear again in the history, but has been conjectured to be Khirbet ez-Zeifeh.

2. In the highland district, named between Carmel and Juttah (Josh. 15:55). The place is immortalized by its connection with David (1 Sam. 23:14–15, 24, 26:2). These passages show that at that time it had near it a wilderness (i.e., a waste pasture-ground) and a wood. The latter has disappeared, but the former remains.

The name of Zif is found about three miles southeast of Hebron attached to a rounded hill of some 100 feet in height which is called Tell Zif. In the AV its inhabitants are called in one passage the Ziphims (Ps. 54), but more usually the Ziphites (1 Sam. 23:19, 26:1).

Ziphah (zī'phăh) another son of Jehaleleel of the tribe of Judah (1 Chr. 4:16).

Ziphims, the the inhabitants of Ziph. In this form the name is found in the AV only in the title of Ps. 54. In the narrative it occurs in the more usual form of Ziphites.

Ziphion (zīph'ĭ-ŏn) son of Gad (Gen. 46:16), likely to be identified with Zephon (Num. 26:15).

Ziphites, the the inhabitants of Ziph (1 Sam. 23:19, 26:1).

Ziphron (zīph'rŏn) a point in the northern boundary of the Promised Land as specified by Moses (Num. 34:9). The location is unknown.

Zippor (zĭp'pôr) father of Balak, king of Moab (Num. 22:2, 4, 10, 16, 23:18; Josh. 24:9; Judg. 11:25).

Zipporah (zĭp'pō-räh) daughter of Reuel or Jethro, the priest of Midian, wife of Moses, and mother of his two sons Gershom and Eliezer (Ex. 2:21, 4:25, 18:2; cf. 6). The only incidents recorded in her life are her marriage, the birth of her son and that of the circumcision of Gershom (Ex. 4:24–26).

Zithri (zĭth'rī) properly "Sithri." One of the sons of Uzziel, the son of Kohath (Ex. 6:22).

Ziz, the cliff of the pass by which the horde of Moabites, Ammonites, and Mehunim made their way up from the shores of the Dead Sea to the wilderness of Judah near Tekoa (2 Chr. 20:16 only; cf. 20). It was perhaps the wadi along which the road from En-gedi to Bethlehem formerly ran.

Ziza (zī'ză) 1. Son of Shiphi, a chief of the Simeonites in the reign of Hezekiah (1 Chr. 4:37).

2. Son of Rehoboam by Maachah the daughter of Absalom (2 Chr. 11:20).

Zoan (zō'ăn) an ancient city of Lower Egypt located in the Delta on the Tanite branch of the Nile. It is contended by some scholars that Zoan, Avaris, Raamses (Ex. 1:11), and Tanis are names used at successive periods for the same site which today is identified with San el-Ḥagar. Though older than the Hyksos period (ca. 1700 B.C.), Avaris was the Hyksos capital of Egypt. The location was later reconstructed by Seti I and Rameses II. If this identification is correct, the possibility of a relationship between the Hyksos and the Hebrews supplies a feasible reason for explaining that Hebron which existed in Abraham's day is seven years older than Zoan (Num. 13:22). The Lord is said to have wrought his wonders (the ten plagues) there (Ps. 78:42–43). It is the residence of the princes of Egypt (Isa. 19:13, 30:4). It is among the cities to be destroyed by Nebuchadnezzar in Ezekiel's oracle (Ezek. 30:14).

Zoar (zō'ăr) one of the five cities of the Jordan plain also called Bela and ruled by a king who was defeated by Chedorlaomer (Gen. 14:2, 8). It was in the direction of Zoar that Lot looked as he moved toward Sodom (Gen. 13:10) and to it he fled when Sodom and the other cities were overthrown (Gen. 19:22–23, 30), which would imply that it was near Sodom, perhaps east toward the Moabite region. The site is not certainly identified. Zoar was one of the limits of the view of Moses from Pisgah (Deut. 34:3). Fugitives from Moab flee there in the oracle of Isaiah (15:5). The cry of Moab goes up from Zoar in Jeremiah's oracle (Jer. 48:34).

J.P.L.

Zoba or **Zobah** (zō'bă) one of five Aramean states connected with Israel's history during the period of the Judges and the United Kingdom. (The other four are Aram-naharaim, Maacah, Geshur, and Tob.) It is located north of the Sea of Galilee in the Anti-Lebanon Mountains.

The name Zobah is derived from a word meaning "bright yellow." It could refer to the golden fields of grain there, or more probably, to the yellow brass so abundant there (see 2 Sam. 8:3).

Zobah is first mentioned in 1 Sam. 14:47 as fighting against Saul. Some forty years later we find Zobah under an outstanding king, Hadadezer. He had wars with Toi king of Hamath (2 Sam. 8:10), and held various petty Syrian princes under his yoke (2 Sam. 10:19).

David attacked Hadadezer in the early part of his reign and dealt him a sound defeat (2 Sam. 8:3–12). Some time later Zobah again came up against David. This war was provoked by the Ammonites, who had hired the services of the Syrians of Zobah. Again David's forces defeated them (2 Sam. 10:6–19).

Zobah originally included Damascus, but in the days of David Rezon rebelled against Hadadezer and set up his own kingdom in Damascus (1 K. 11:23–25). Rezon proved to be a fierce adversary of Solomon.

Solomon also probably engaged in a war with Zobah (2 Chr. 8:3). This is the last mention of Zobah in the Bible. The name, however, is found at a later date in the inscriptions of Assyria, where the kingdom of Zobah seems to intervene between Hamath and Damascus.

N.P.

Zobebah (zō-bē'băh) son of Coz, of the tribe of Judah (1 Chr. 4:8).

Zohar (zō'här) 1. Father of Ephron the Hittite (Gen. 23:8, 25:9).

2. One of the sons of Simeon (Gen. 46:10; Ex. 6:15); called Zerah in 1 Chr. 4:24.

zoheleth, the stone this stone was by En-rogel where Adonijah slew sheep and oxen (1 K. 1:9). The Targum rendered the phrase "rolling stone," but the RSV translates the term "serpent's stone." The exact location is unknown. Some have attempted to connect it with the widespread practice of representing the deity as a serpent, hence a stone consecrated to such a deity. There can be no certainty.

Zoheth (zō'hĕth) son of Ishi of the tribe of Judah (1 Chr. 4:20).

Zophah (zō'phăh) son of Helem, or Hotham, the son of Heber, an Asherite (1 Chr. 7:35–36).

Zophai (zō'phā-ī) a Kohathite Levite, son of Elkanah, and ancestor of Samuel (1 Chr. 6:26 [11]). In vs. 35 he is called Zuph.

Zophar one of the three friends of Job, called a Naamathite (Job 2:11, 11:1, 20:1, 42:9).

Zophim, the Field of (zō'phĭm) a spot on or near the top of Pisgah, from which Balaam had his second view of the encampment of Israel (Num. 23:14). It is possible that Zophim is not a proper name and that we should read "field of the watchers." The same Hebrew root lies back of Mizpah. It has been conjectured that the name may survive in Tela'at es-Safa.

Zorah (zōr'äh) a town (also AV Zoreah and Zareah) in the allotment of the tribes of Dan (Josh. 19:41) from which the Danite spies migrated to Laish (Judg. 18:2). Zorah is in the lists of towns of the Shephelah near Eshtaol (Josh. 15:33). It was the home of Samson's father (Judg. 13:2, 25), and Samson was buried near here (Judg. 16:31). Zorah was fortified by Rehoboam (2 Chr. 11:10) and was resettled after the Exile (Neh. 11:29). The site today is about fourteen miles west of Jerusalem on the north side of the valley of Sorek, and to the northwest of Beth-shemesh.

J.P.L.

Zorathites, the (zôr'ă-thīts) i.e., the people of Zorah, mentioned in 1 Chr. 4:2 as descended from Shobal.

Zoreah another form (Josh. 15:33) of the name usually given in the AV as Zorah.

Zorites, the (zôr'īts) are named in the genealogies of Judah (1 Chr. 2:54) apparently among the descendants of Salma and near connections of Joab.

Zorobabel (Mt. 1:13; Lk. 3:27). See **Zerubbabel**.

Zuar (zū'är) father of Nethaneel, the chief of the tribe of Issachar at the time of the Exodus (Num. 1:8, 2:5, 7:18, 23, 10:15).

Zuph, the Land of a district at which Saul and his servant arrived after passing through those of Shalisha, of Shalim, and of the Benjaminites to arrive at the city of Samuel (1 Sam. 9:5 only). The exact location of the area is unknown.

Zuph a Kohathite Levite, ancestor of Elkanah and Samuel (1 Sam. 1:1; 1 Chr. 6:35 [20]). In 1 Chr. 6:26 he is called **Zophai**.

Zur (zŭr) 1. Father of Cozbi (Num. 25:15) and one of the five princes of Midian who were slain by the Israelites when Balaam fell (Num. 31:8).

2. Son of Jehiel the father of Gibeon and brother of Kish, father of Saul (1 Chr. 8:30, 9:36).

Zuriel (zū'rĭ-ĕl) son of Abihail and chief of the Merarite Levites who encamped north of the tabernacle at the time of the Exodus (Num. 3:35).

Zurishaddai (zū′rĭ-shăd-dī) father of Shelumiel, the chief of the tribe of Simeon at the time of the Exodus (Num. 1:6, 2:12, 7:36, 41, 10:19).

Zuzims, the (zū′zĭms) the name of an ancient people living in Ham who, lying in the path of Chedorlaomer and his allies, were attacked and overthrown by them (Gen. 14:5 only). Nothing more is known of them. Though in the first century B.C. it was conjectured that they were identical with the Zamzummim (Genesis Apocryphon, column XXI, line 29) and though this same conjecture has been independently made by some scholars more recently, there are difficulties in the identification, one of which is that the Zamzummim seem to have lived further south.

Y20